NATIONAL
SCRABBLE
ASSOCIATION

Official Tournament and Club Word List

SECOND EDITION

NATIONAL
SCRABBLE ASSOCIATION

Official Tournament and Club Word List

SECOND EDITION

Merriam-Webster, Incorporated
Springfield, Massachusetts

PREFACE

This official tournament word list is derived from *The Official SCRABBLE® Players Dictionary, Fourth Edition*, supplemented with nine-letter words and their inflected forms taken from *Merriam-Webster's Collegiate® Dictionary, Eleventh Edition*. This list contains words only, no definitions or part-of-speech labels, and includes all inflected forms spelled out in full. A few ten-letter words appear in this list if they are inflected forms of shorter words or if they are the base forms (such as *greenlight*) of inflected forms (as *greenlit*) that are entries. This list contains some words that are excluded from *The Official SCRABBLE® Players Dictionary*, for example, trademarks, because they are usually capitalized but which are indicated in a standard dictionary as having some lowercase use. No entry in this word list, however, should be regarded as affecting the validity of any trademark or service mark. This list also includes qualified words that are considered offensive and therefore may be inappropriate for family use.

This word list has been prepared for use solely as a quick reference for all tournament play sponsored by the National SCRABBLE® Association. It is not intended to replace *The Official SCRABBLE® Players Dictionary* or any other dictionary preferred by players as a final reference, but it does represent, as of the date of the copyright, the most up-to-date revisions in *The Official SCRABBLE® Players Dictionary*.

National SCRABBLE® Association

For information on SCRABBLE® clubs, tournaments, publications, and other activities, contact:

National SCRABBLE® Association
Box 700
Greenport, NY 11944
Phone : (631) 477-0033
Fax: (631) 477-0294
info@scrabble-assoc.com
www.scrabble-assoc.com

OUR TRADEMARK • SCRABBLE® BRAND CROSSWORD GAME

Parker Brothers takes pride in offering this book to participants in tournaments and contests sponsored by the National SCRABBLE® Association. The SCRABBLE® trademark, registered in the United States Patent and Trademark Office, is one of our most valued assets as it represents our seal and reputation for excellence and quality.

As a trademark, it must be capitalized, and when describing products, be followed by a generic name of the game, such as SCRABBLE® Brand Crossword Game. The SCRABBLE® trademark means "made by" or "sponsored by" Parker Brothers, a division of Hasbro, Inc.

Your cooperation in the continued proper use of our trademark is appreciated, and we hope that this dictionary will enhance enjoyment of our products.

Hasbro, Inc.
443 Shaker Road
East Longmeadow, MA 01028

A

AA	ABASEMENTS	ABCOULOMB	ABETS	ABJURING
AAH	ABASER	ABCOULOMBS	ABETTAL	ABLATE
AAHED	ABASERS	ABDICABLE	ABETTALS	ABLATED
AAHING	ABASES	ABDICATE	ABETTED	ABLATES
AAHS	ABASH	ABDICATED	ABETTER	ABLATING
AAL	ABASHED	ABDICATES	ABETTERS	ABLATION
AALII	ABASHEDLY	ABDICATING	ABETTING	ABLATIONS
AALIIS	ABASHES	ABDICATOR	ABETTOR	ABLATIVE
AALS	ABASHING	ABDICATORS	ABETTORS	ABLATIVES
AARDVARK	ABASHMENT	ABDOMEN	ABEYANCE	ABLATOR
AARDVARKS	ABASHMENTS	ABDOMENS	ABEYANCES	ABLATORS
AARDWOLF	ABASIA	ABDOMINA	ABEYANCIES	ABLAUT
AARDWOLVES	ABASIAS	ABDOMINAL	ABEYANCY	ABLAUTS
AARGH	ABASING	ABDOMINALS	ABEYANT	ABLAZE
AARRGH	ABATABLE	ABDUCE	ABFARAD	ABLE
AARRGHH	ABATE	ABDUCED	ABFARADS	ABLED
AAS	ABATED	ABDUCENS	ABHENRIES	ABLEGATE
AASVOGEL	ABATEMENT	ABDUCENT	ABHENRY	ABLEGATES
AASVOGELS	ABATEMENTS	ABDUCENTES	ABHENRYS	ABLEISM
AB	ABATER	ABDUCES	ABHOR	ABLEISMS
ABA	ABATERS	ABDUCING	ABHORRED	ABLEIST
ABACA	ABATES	ABDUCT	ABHORRENT	ABLEISTS
ABACAS	ABATING	ABDUCTED	ABHORRER	ABLER
ABACI	ABATIS	ABDUCTEE	ABHORRERS	ABLES
ABACK	ABATISES	ABDUCTEES	ABHORRING	ABLEST
ABACUS	ABATOR	ABDUCTING	ABHORS	ABLINGS
ABACUSES	ABATORS	ABDUCTION	ABIDANCE	ABLINS
ABAFT	ABATTIS	ABDUCTIONS	ABIDANCES	ABLOOM
ABAKA	ABATTISES	ABDUCTOR	ABIDE	ABLUENT
ABAKAS	ABATTOIR	ABDUCTORES	ABIDED	ABLUENTS
ABALONE	ABATTOIRS	ABDUCTORS	ABIDER	ABLUSH
ABALONES	ABAXIAL	ABDUCTS	ABIDERS	ABLUTED
ABAMP	ABAXILE	ABEAM	ABIDES	ABLUTION
ABAMPERE	ABAYA	ABED	ABIDING	ABLUTIONS
ABAMPERES	ABAYAS	ABEGGING	ABIDINGLY	ABLY
ABAMPS	ABBA	ABELE	ABIGAIL	ABMHO
ABANDON	ABBACIES	ABELES	ABIGAILS	ABMHOS
ABANDONED	ABBACY	ABELIA	ABILITIES	ABNEGATE
ABANDONER	ABBAS	ABELIAN	ABILITY	ABNEGATED
ABANDONERS	ABBATIAL	ABELIAS	ABIOGENIC	ABNEGATES
ABANDONING	ABBE	ABELMOSK	ABIOSES	ABNEGATING
ABANDONS	ABBES	ABELMOSKS	ABIOSIS	ABNEGATOR
ABAPICAL	ABBESS	ABERRANCE	ABIOTIC	ABNEGATORS
ABAS	ABBESSES	ABERRANCES	ABJECT	ABNORMAL
ABASE	ABBEY	ABERRANCIES	ABJECTION	ABNORMALS
ABASED	ABBEYS	ABERRANCY	ABJECTIONS	ABNORMITIES
ABASEDLY	ABBOT	ABERRANT	ABJECTLY	ABNORMITY
ABASEMENT	ABBOTCIES	ABERRANTS	ABJURE	ABO
	ABBOTCY	ABERRATED	ABJURED	ABOARD
	ABBOTS	ABET	ABJURER	ABODE
	ABBOTSHIP	ABETMENT	ABJURERS	ABODED
	ABBOTSHIPS	ABETMENTS	ABJURES	ABODES

ABODING	ABOULIC	ABRUPTLY	ABSONANT	ABUNDANCES
ABOHM	ABOUND	ABS	ABSORB	ABUNDANT
ABOHMS	ABOUNDED	ABSCESS	ABSORBANT	ABUSABLE
ABOIDEAU	ABOUNDING	ABSCESSED	ABSORBANTS	ABUSE
ABOIDEAUS	ABOUNDS	ABSCESSES	ABSORBED	ABUSED
ABOIDEAUX	ABOUT	ABSCESSING	ABSORBENT	ABUSER
ABOIL	ABOVE	ABSCISE	ABSORBENTS	ABUSERS
ABOITEAU	ABOVES	ABSCISED	ABSORBER	ABUSES
ABOITEAUS	ABRACHIA	ABSCISES	ABSORBERS	ABUSING
ABOITEAUX	ABRACHIAS	ABSCISIN	ABSORBING	ABUSIVE
ABOLISH	ABRADABLE	ABSCISING	ABSORBS	ABUSIVELY
ABOLISHED	ABRADANT	ABSCISINS	ABSTAIN	ABUT
ABOLISHER	ABRADANTS	ABSCISSA	ABSTAINED	ABUTILON
ABOLISHERS	ABRADE	ABSCISSAE	ABSTAINER	ABUTILONS
ABOLISHES	ABRADED	ABSCISSAS	ABSTAINERS	ABUTMENT
ABOLISHING	ABRADER	ABSCOND	ABSTAINING	ABUTMENTS
ABOLITION	ABRADERS	ABSCONDED	ABSTAINS	ABUTS
ABOLITIONS	ABRADES	ABSCONDER	ABSTERGE	ABUTTAL
ABOLLA	ABRADING	ABSCONDERS	ABSTERGED	ABUTTALS
ABOLLAE	ABRASION	ABSCONDING	ABSTERGES	ABUTTED
ABOMA	ABRASIONS	ABSCONDS	ABSTERGING	ABUTTER
ABOMAS	ABRASIVE	ABSEIL	ABSTINENT	ABUTTERS
ABOMASA	ABRASIVES	ABSEILED	ABSTRACT	ABUTTING
ABOMASAL	ABREACT	ABSEILING	ABSTRACTED	ABUZZ
ABOMASI	ABREACTED	ABSEILS	ABSTRACTER	ABVOLT
ABOMASUM	ABREACTING	ABSENCE	ABSTRACTEST	ABVOLTS
ABOMASUS	ABREACTS	ABSENCES	ABSTRACTING	ABWATT
ABOMINATE	ABREAST	ABSENT	ABSTRACTS	ABWATTS
ABOMINATED	ABRI	ABSENTED	ABSTRICT	ABY
ABOMINATES	ABRIDGE	ABSENTEE	ABSTRICTED	ABYE
ABOMINATING	ABRIDGED	ABSENTEES	ABSTRICTING	ABYES
ABOON	ABRIDGER	ABSENTER	ABSTRICTS	ABYING
ABORAL	ABRIDGERS	ABSENTERS	ABSTRUSE	ABYS
ABORALLY	ABRIDGES	ABSENTING	ABSTRUSER	ABYSM
ABORIGINE	ABRIDGING	ABSENTLY	ABSTRUSEST	ABYSMAL
ABORIGINES	ABRIS	ABSENTS	ABSURD	ABYSMALLY
ABORNING	ABROACH	ABSINTH	ABSURDER	ABYSMS
ABORT	ABROAD	ABSINTHE	ABSURDEST	ABYSS
ABORTED	ABROGABLE	ABSINTHES	ABSURDISM	ABYSSAL
ABORTER	ABROGATE	ABSINTHS	ABSURDISMS	ABYSSES
ABORTERS	ABROGATED	ABSOLUTE	ABSURDIST	ACACIA
ABORTING	ABROGATES	ABSOLUTER	ABSURDISTS	ACACIAS
ABORTION	ABROGATING	ABSOLUTES	ABSURDITIES	ACADEME
ABORTIONS	ABROGATOR	ABSOLUTEST	ABSURDITY	ACADEMES
ABORTIVE	ABROGATORS	ABSOLVE	ABSURDLY	ACADEMIA
ABORTS	ABROSIA	ABSOLVED	ABSURDS	ACADEMIAS
ABORTUS	ABROSIAS	ABSOLVENT	ABUBBLE	ACADEMIC
ABORTUSES	ABRUPT	ABSOLVENTS	ABUILDING	ACADEMICS
ABOS	ABRUPTER	ABSOLVER	ABULIA	ACADEMIES
ABOUGHT	ABRUPTEST	ABSOLVERS	ABULIAS	ACADEMISM
ABOULIA	ABRUPTION	ABSOLVES	ABULIC	ACADEMISMS
ABOULIAS	ABRUPTIONS	ABSOLVING	ABUNDANCE	ACADEMY

ACAJOU	ACCENTORS	ACCOLADES	ACCURATE	ACETA
ACAJOUS	ACCENTS	ACCOLADING	ACCURSED	ACETABULA
ACALEPH	ACCENTUAL	ACCOMPANIED	ACCURST	ACETABULUM
ACALEPHAE	ACCEPT	ACCOMPANIES	ACCUSABLE	ACETABULUMS
ACALEPHE	ACCEPTANT	ACCOMPANY	ACCUSABLY	ACETAL
ACALEPHES	ACCEPTED	ACCOMPANYING	ACCUSAL	ACETALS
ACALEPHS	ACCEPTEE	ACCORD	ACCUSALS	ACETAMID
ACANTHA	ACCEPTEES	ACCORDANT	ACCUSANT	ACETAMIDE
ACANTHAE	ACCEPTER	ACCORDED	ACCUSANTS	ACETAMIDES
ACANTHI	ACCEPTERS	ACCORDER	ACCUSE	ACETAMIDS
ACANTHINE	ACCEPTING	ACCORDERS	ACCUSED	ACETATE
ACANTHOID	ACCEPTIVE	ACCORDING	ACCUSER	ACETATED
ACANTHOUS	ACCEPTOR	ACCORDION	ACCUSERS	ACETATES
ACANTHUS	ACCEPTORS	ACCORDIONS	ACCUSES	ACETIC
ACANTHUSES	ACCEPTS	ACCORDS	ACCUSING	ACETIFIED
ACAPNIA	ACCESS	ACCOST	ACCUSTOM	ACETIFIER
ACAPNIAS	ACCESSARIES	ACCOSTED	ACCUSTOMED	ACETIFIERS
ACARBOSE	ACCESSARY	ACCOSTING	ACCUSTOMING	ACETIFIES
ACARBOSES	ACCESSED	ACCOSTS	ACCUSTOMS	ACETIFY
ACARI	ACCESSES	ACCOUNT	ACE	ACETIFYING
ACARIASES	ACCESSING	ACCOUNTED	ACED	ACETIN
ACARIASIS	ACCESSION	ACCOUNTING	ACEDIA	ACETINS
ACARICIDE	ACCESSIONED	ACCOUNTS	ACEDIAS	ACETONE
ACARICIDES	ACCESSIONING	ACCOUTER	ACELDAMA	ACETONES
ACARID	ACCESSIONS	ACCOUTERED	ACELDAMAS	ACETONIC
ACARIDAN	ACCESSORIES	ACCOUTERING	ACELLULAR	ACETOSE
ACARIDANS	ACCESSORY	ACCOUTERS	ACENTRIC	ACETOUS
ACARIDS	ACCIDENCE	ACCOUTRE	ACEPHALIC	ACETOXYL
ACARINE	ACCIDENCES	ACCOUTRED	ACEQUIA	ACETOXYLS
ACARINES	ACCIDENT	ACCOUTRES	ACEQUIAS	ACETUM
ACAROID	ACCIDENTS	ACCOUTRING	ACERATE	ACETYL
ACAROLOGIES	ACCIDIA	ACCREDIT	ACERATED	ACETYLATE
ACAROLOGY	ACCIDIAS	ACCREDITED	ACERB	ACETYLATED
ACARPOUS	ACCIDIE	ACCREDITING	ACERBATE	ACETYLATES
ACARUS	ACCIDIES	ACCREDITS	ACERBATED	ACETYLATING
ACAUDAL	ACCIPITER	ACCRETE	ACERBATES	ACETYLENE
ACAUDATE	ACCIPITERS	ACCRETED	ACERBATING	ACETYLENES
ACAULINE	ACCLAIM	ACCRETES	ACERBER	ACETYLIC
ACAULOSE	ACCLAIMED	ACCRETING	ACERBEST	ACETYLS
ACAULOUS	ACCLAIMER	ACCRETION	ACERBIC	ACHALASIA
ACCEDE	ACCLAIMERS	ACCRETIONS	ACERBITIES	ACHALASIAS
ACCEDED	ACCLAIMING	ACCRETIVE	ACERBITY	ACHE
ACCEDENCE	ACCLAIMS	ACCRUABLE	ACEROLA	ACHED
ACCEDENCES	ACCLIMATE	ACCRUAL	ACEROLAS	ACHENE
ACCEDER	ACCLIMATED	ACCRUALS	ACEROSE	ACHENES
ACCEDERS	ACCLIMATES	ACCRUE	ACEROUS	ACHENIAL
ACCEDES	ACCLIMATING	ACCRUED	ACERVATE	ACHES
ACCEDING	ACCLIVITIES	ACCRUES	ACERVULI	ACHIER
ACCENT	ACCLIVITY	ACCRUING	ACERVULUS	ACHIEST
ACCENTED	ACCLIVOUS	ACCUMBENT	ACES	ACHIEVE
ACCENTING	ACCOLADE	ACCURACIES	ACESCENT	ACHIEVED
ACCENTOR	ACCOLADED	ACCURACY	ACESCENTS	ACHIEVER

ACHIEVERS	ACIDULATES	ACQUESTS	ACROGENS	ACTINIDES
ACHIEVES	ACIDULATING	ACQUIESCE	ACROLECT	ACTINISM
ACHIEVING	ACIDULENT	ACQUIESCED	ACROLECTS	ACTINISMS
ACHILLEA	ACIDULOUS	ACQUIESCES	ACROLEIN	ACTINIUM
ACHILLEAS	ACIDURIA	ACQUIESCING	ACROLEINS	ACTINIUMS
ACHINESS	ACIDURIAS	ACQUIRE	ACROLITH	ACTINOID
ACHINESSES	ACIDY	ACQUIRED	ACROLITHS	ACTINOIDS
ACHING	ACIERATE	ACQUIREE	ACROMIA	ACTINON
ACHINGLY	ACIERATED	ACQUIREES	ACROMIAL	ACTINONS
ACHIOTE	ACIERATES	ACQUIRER	ACROMION	ACTINS
ACHIOTES	ACIERATING	ACQUIRERS	ACRONIC	ACTION
ACHIRAL	ACIFORM	ACQUIRES	ACRONICAL	ACTIONER
ACHOLIA	ACINAR	ACQUIRING	ACRONYCAL	ACTIONERS
ACHOLIAS	ACING	ACQUIT	ACRONYM	ACTIONS
ACHOO	ACINI	ACQUITS	ACRONYMIC	ACTIVATE
ACHROMAT	ACINIC	ACQUITTAL	ACRONYMS	ACTIVATED
ACHROMATS	ACINIFORM	ACQUITTALS	ACROPETAL	ACTIVATES
ACHROMIC	ACINOSE	ACQUITTED	ACROPHOBE	ACTIVATING
ACHROMOUS	ACINOUS	ACQUITTER	ACROPHOBES	ACTIVATOR
ACHY	ACINUS	ACQUITTERS	ACROPOLIS	ACTIVATORS
ACICULA	ACKEE	ACQUITTING	ACROPOLISES	ACTIVE
ACICULAE	ACKEES	ACRASIA	ACROSOMAL	ACTIVELY
ACICULAR	ACLINIC	ACRASIAS	ACROSOME	ACTIVES
ACICULAS	ACMATIC	ACRASIN	ACROSOMES	ACTIVISM
ACICULATE	ACME	ACRASINS	ACROSPIRE	ACTIVISMS
ACICULUM	ACMES	ACRE	ACROSPIRES	ACTIVIST
ACICULUMS	ACMIC	ACREAGE	ACROSS	ACTIVISTS
ACID	ACNE	ACREAGES	ACROSTIC	ACTIVITIES
ACIDEMIA	ACNED	ACRED	ACROSTICS	ACTIVITY
ACIDEMIAS	ACNES	ACRES	ACROTIC	ACTIVIZE
ACIDHEAD	ACNODE	ACRID	ACROTISM	ACTIVIZED
ACIDHEADS	ACNODES	ACRIDER	ACROTISMS	ACTIVIZES
ACIDIC	ACOCK	ACRIDEST	ACRYLATE	ACTIVIZING
ACIDIFIED	ACOELOUS	ACRIDINE	ACRYLATES	ACTOR
ACIDIFIER	ACOLD	ACRIDINES	ACRYLIC	ACTORISH
ACIDIFIERS	ACOLYTE	ACRIDITIES	ACRYLICS	ACTORLY
ACIDIFIES	ACOLYTES	ACRIDITY	ACT	ACTORS
ACIDIFY	ACONITE	ACRIDLY	ACTA	ACTRESS
ACIDIFYING	ACONITES	ACRIDNESS	ACTABLE	ACTRESSES
ACIDITIES	ACONITIC	ACRIDNESSES	ACTED	ACTRESSY
ACIDITY	ACONITUM	ACRIMONIES	ACTIN	ACTS
ACIDLY	ACONITUMS	ACRIMONY	ACTINAL	ACTUAL
ACIDNESS	ACORN	ACRITARCH	ACTINALLY	ACTUALITIES
ACIDNESSES	ACORNED	ACRITARCHS	ACTING	ACTUALITY
ACIDOPHIL	ACORNS	ACRITICAL	ACTINGS	ACTUALIZE
ACIDOPHILS	ACOUSTIC	ACROBAT	ACTINIA	ACTUALIZED
ACIDOSES	ACOUSTICS	ACROBATIC	ACTINIAE	ACTUALIZES
ACIDOSIS	ACQUAINT	ACROBATS	ACTINIAN	ACTUALIZING
ACIDOTIC	ACQUAINTED	ACRODONT	ACTINIANS	ACTUALLY
ACIDS	ACQUAINTING	ACRODONTS	ACTINIAS	ACTUARIAL
ACIDULATE	ACQUAINTS	ACROGEN	ACTINIC	ACTUARIES
ACIDULATED	ACQUEST	ACROGENIC	ACTINIDE	ACTUARY

ACTUATE	ADAMANCIES	ADDRESSED	ADEPTEST	ADJECTIVE
ACTUATED	ADAMANCY	ADDRESSEE	ADEPTLY	ADJECTIVES
ACTUATES	ADAMANT	ADDRESSEES	ADEPTNESS	ADJOIN
ACTUATING	ADAMANTLY	ADDRESSER	ADEPTNESSES	ADJOINED
ACTUATION	ADAMANTS	ADDRESSERS	ADEPTS	ADJOINING
ACTUATIONS	ADAMSITE	ADDRESSES	ADEQUACIES	ADJOINS
ACTUATOR	ADAMSITES	ADDRESSING	ADEQUACY	ADJOINT
ACTUATORS	ADAPT	ADDRESSOR	ADEQUATE	ADJOINTS
ACUATE	ADAPTABLE	ADDRESSORS	ADHERABLE	ADJOURN
ACUITIES	ADAPTED	ADDREST	ADHERE	ADJOURNED
ACUITY	ADAPTER	ADDS	ADHERED	ADJOURNING
ACULEATE	ADAPTERS	ADDUCE	ADHERENCE	ADJOURNS
ACULEATED	ADAPTING	ADDUCED	ADHERENCES	ADJUDGE
ACULEI	ADAPTION	ADDUCENT	ADHEREND	ADJUDGED
ACULEUS	ADAPTIONS	ADDUCER	ADHERENDS	ADJUDGES
ACUMEN	ADAPTIVE	ADDUCERS	ADHERENT	ADJUDGING
ACUMENS	ADAPTOR	ADDUCES	ADHERENTS	ADJUNCT
ACUMINATE	ADAPTORS	ADDUCIBLE	ADHERER	ADJUNCTLY
ACUMINATED	ADAPTS	ADDUCING	ADHERERS	ADJUNCTS
ACUMINATES	ADAXIAL	ADDUCT	ADHERES	ADJURE
ACUMINATING	ADD	ADDUCTED	ADHERING	ADJURED
ACUMINOUS	ADDABLE	ADDUCTING	ADHESION	ADJURER
ACUTANCE	ADDAX	ADDUCTION	ADHESIONS	ADJURERS
ACUTANCES	ADDAXES	ADDUCTIONS	ADHESIVE	ADJURES
ACUTE	ADDED	ADDUCTIVE	ADHESIVES	ADJURING
ACUTELY	ADDEDLY	ADDUCTOR	ADHIBIT	ADJUROR
ACUTENESS	ADDEND	ADDUCTORS	ADHIBITED	ADJURORS
ACUTENESSES	ADDENDA	ADDUCTS	ADHIBITING	ADJUST
ACUTER	ADDENDS	ADEEM	ADHIBITS	ADJUSTED
ACUTES	ADDENDUM	ADEEMED	ADIABATIC	ADJUSTER
ACUTEST	ADDENDUMS	ADEEMING	ADIEU	ADJUSTERS
ACYCLIC	ADDER	ADEEMS	ADIEUS	ADJUSTING
ACYCLOVIR	ADDERS	ADEMPTION	ADIEUX	ADJUSTIVE
ACYCLOVIRS	ADDIBLE	ADEMPTIONS	ADIOS	ADJUSTOR
ACYL	ADDICT	ADENINE	ADIPIC	ADJUSTORS
ACYLATE	ADDICTED	ADENINES	ADIPOCERE	ADJUSTS
ACYLATED	ADDICTING	ADENITIS	ADIPOCERES	ADJUTANCIES
ACYLATES	ADDICTION	ADENITISES	ADIPOCYTE	ADJUTANCY
ACYLATING	ADDICTIONS	ADENOID	ADIPOCYTES	ADJUTANT
ACYLATION	ADDICTIVE	ADENOIDAL	ADIPOSE	ADJUTANTS
ACYLATIONS	ADDICTS	ADENOIDS	ADIPOSES	ADJUVANT
ACYLOIN	ADDING	ADENOMA	ADIPOSIS	ADJUVANTS
ACYLOINS	ADDITION	ADENOMAS	ADIPOSITIES	ADMAN
ACYLS	ADDITIONS	ADENOMATA	ADIPOSITY	ADMASS
AD	ADDITIVE	ADENOSES	ADIPOUS	ADMASSES
ADAGE	ADDITIVES	ADENOSINE	ADIT	ADMEASURE
ADAGES	ADDITORY	ADENOSINES	ADITS	ADMEASURED
ADAGIAL	ADDLE	ADENOSIS	ADJACENCE	ADMEASURES
ADAGIO	ADDLED	ADENYL	ADJACENCES	ADMEASURING
ADAGIOS	ADDLES	ADENYLS	ADJACENCIES	ADMEN
ADAMANCE	ADDLING	ADEPT	ADJACENCY	ADMIRABLE
ADAMANCES	ADDRESS	ADEPTER	ADJACENT	ADMIRABLY

ADMIRAL	ADOPTEE	ADSORBING	ADVECTS	ADVOCATED
ADMIRALS	ADOPTEES	ADSORBS	ADVENT	ADVOCATES
ADMIRALTIES	ADOPTER	ADULARIA	ADVENTIVE	ADVOCATING
ADMIRALTY	ADOPTERS	ADULARIAS	ADVENTIVES	ADVOCATOR
ADMIRE	ADOPTING	ADULATE	ADVENTS	ADVOCATORS
ADMIRED	ADOPTION	ADULATED	ADVENTURE	ADVOWSON
ADMIRER	ADOPTIONS	ADULATES	ADVENTURED	ADVOWSONS
ADMIRERS	ADOPTIVE	ADULATING	ADVENTURES	ADWOMAN
ADMIRES	ADOPTS	ADULATION	ADVENTURING	ADWOMEN
ADMIRING	ADORABLE	ADULATIONS	ADVERB	ADYNAMIA
ADMISSION	ADORABLY	ADULATOR	ADVERBIAL	ADYNAMIAS
ADMISSIONS	ADORATION	ADULATORS	ADVERBIALS	ADYNAMIC
ADMISSIVE	ADORATIONS	ADULATORY	ADVERBS	ADYTA
ADMIT	ADORE	ADULT	ADVERSARIES	ADYTUM
ADMITS	ADORED	ADULTERER	ADVERSARY	ADZ
ADMITTED	ADORER	ADULTERERS	ADVERSE	ADZE
ADMITTEE	ADORERS	ADULTERIES	ADVERSELY	ADZED
ADMITTEES	ADORES	ADULTERY	ADVERSITIES	ADZES
ADMITTER	ADORING	ADULTHOOD	ADVERSITY	ADZING
ADMITTERS	ADORINGLY	ADULTHOODS	ADVERT	ADZUKI
ADMITTING	ADORN	ADULTLIKE	ADVERTED	ADZUKIS
ADMIX	ADORNED	ADULTLY	ADVERTENT	AE
ADMIXED	ADORNER	ADULTNESS	ADVERTING	AECIA
ADMIXES	ADORNERS	ADULTNESSES	ADVERTISE	AECIAL
ADMIXING	ADORNING	ADULTRESS	ADVERTISED	AECIDIA
ADMIXT	ADORNMENT	ADULTRESSES	ADVERTISES	AECIDIAL
ADMIXTURE	ADORNMENTS	ADULTS	ADVERTISING	AECIDIUM
ADMIXTURES	ADORNS	ADUMBRAL	ADVERTIZE	AECIUM
ADMONISH	ADOS	ADUMBRATE	ADVERTIZED	AEDES
ADMONISHED	ADOWN	ADUMBRATED	ADVERTIZES	AEDILE
ADMONISHES	ADOZE	ADUMBRATES	ADVERTIZING	AEDILES
ADMONISHING	ADRENAL	ADUMBRATING	ADVERTS	AEDINE
ADMONITOR	ADRENALIN	ADUNC	ADVICE	AEGIS
ADMONITORS	ADRENALINS	ADUNCATE	ADVICES	AEGISES
ADNATE	ADRENALLY	ADUNCOUS	ADVISABLE	AENEOUS
ADNATION	ADRENALS	ADUST	ADVISABLY	AENEUS
ADNATIONS	ADRIFT	ADVANCE	ADVISE	AEOLIAN
ADNEXA	ADROIT	ADVANCED	ADVISED	AEON
ADNEXAL	ADROITER	ADVANCER	ADVISEDLY	AEONIAN
ADNOUN	ADROITEST	ADVANCERS	ADVISEE	AEONIC
ADNOUNS	ADROITLY	ADVANCES	ADVISEES	AEONS
ADO	ADS	ADVANCING	ADVISER	AEPYORNIS
ADOBE	ADSCRIPT	ADVANTAGE	ADVISERS	AEPYORNISES
ADOBELIKE	ADSCRIPTS	ADVANTAGED	ADVISES	AEQUORIN
ADOBES	ADSORB	ADVANTAGES	ADVISING	AEQUORINS
ADOBO	ADSORBATE	ADVANTAGING	ADVISOR	AERATE
ADOBOS	ADSORBATES	ADVECT	ADVISORIES	AERATED
ADONIS	ADSORBED	ADVECTED	ADVISORS	AERATES
ADONISES	ADSORBENT	ADVECTING	ADVISORY	AERATING
ADOPT	ADSORBENTS	ADVECTION	ADVOCACIES	AERATION
ADOPTABLE	ADSORBER	ADVECTIONS	ADVOCACY	AERATIONS
ADOPTED	ADSORBERS	ADVECTIVE	ADVOCATE	AERATOR

AERATORS	AEROMETERS	AFAR	AFFIX	AFFRONTED
AERIAL	AEROMETRIES	AFARS	AFFIXABLE	AFFRONTING
AERIALIST	AEROMETRY	AFEARD	AFFIXAL	AFFRONTS
AERIALISTS	AERONAUT	AFEARED	AFFIXED	AFFUSION
AERIALLY	AERONAUTS	AFEBRILE	AFFIXER	AFFUSIONS
AERIALS	AERONOMER	AFF	AFFIXERS	AFGHAN
AERIE	AERONOMERS	AFFABLE	AFFIXES	AFGHANI
AERIED	AERONOMIC	AFFABLY	AFFIXIAL	AFGHANIS
AERIER	AERONOMIES	AFFAIR	AFFIXING	AFGHANS
AERIES	AERONOMY	AFFAIRE	AFFIXMENT	AFIELD
AERIEST	AEROPAUSE	AFFAIRES	AFFIXMENTS	AFIRE
AERIFIED	AEROPAUSES	AFFAIRS	AFFIXTURE	AFLAME
AERIFIES	AEROPHOBE	AFFECT	AFFIXTURES	AFLATOXIN
AERIFORM	AEROPHOBES	AFFECTED	AFFLATUS	AFLATOXINS
AERIFY	AEROPHORE	AFFECTER	AFFLATUSES	AFLOAT
AERIFYING	AEROPHORES	AFFECTERS	AFFLICT	AFLUTTER
AERILY	AEROPHYTE	AFFECTING	AFFLICTED	AFOOT
AERO	AEROPHYTES	AFFECTION	AFFLICTER	AFORE
AEROBAT	AEROPLANE	AFFECTIONS	AFFLICTERS	AFOREHAND
AEROBATIC	AEROPLANES	AFFECTIVE	AFFLICTING	AFORESAID
AEROBATS	AEROPULSE	AFFECTS	AFFLICTS	AFORETIME
AEROBE	AEROPULSES	AFFERENT	AFFLUENCE	AFOUL
AEROBES	AEROSAT	AFFERENTS	AFFLUENCES	AFRAID
AEROBIA	AEROSATS	AFFIANCE	AFFLUENCIES	AFREET
AEROBIC	AEROSCOPE	AFFIANCED	AFFLUENCY	AFREETS
AEROBICS	AEROSCOPES	AFFIANCES	AFFLUENT	AFRESH
AEROBIUM	AEROSOL	AFFIANCING	AFFLUENTS	AFRIT
AEROBRAKE	AEROSOLS	AFFIANT	AFFLUX	AFRITS
AEROBRAKED	AEROSPACE	AFFIANTS	AFFLUXES	AFT
AEROBRAKES	AEROSPACES	AFFICHE	AFFORD	AFTER
AEROBRAKING	AEROSTAT	AFFICHES	AFFORDED	AFTERCARE
AERODROME	AEROSTATS	AFFIDAVIT	AFFORDING	AFTERCARES
AERODROMES	AERUGO	AFFIDAVITS	AFFORDS	AFTERCLAP
AERODUCT	AERUGOS	AFFILIATE	AFFOREST	AFTERCLAPS
AERODUCTS	AERY	AFFILIATED	AFFORESTED	AFTERDAMP
AERODYNE	AESTHESIA	AFFILIATES	AFFORESTING	AFTERDAMPS
AERODYNES	AESTHESIAS	AFFILIATING	AFFORESTS	AFTERDECK
AEROFOIL	AESTHETE	AFFINAL	AFFRAY	AFTERDECKS
AEROFOILS	AESTHETES	AFFINE	AFFRAYED	AFTERGLOW
AEROGEL	AESTHETIC	AFFINED	AFFRAYER	AFTERGLOWS
AEROGELS	AESTHETICS	AFFINELY	AFFRAYERS	AFTERLIFE
AEROGRAM	AESTIVAL	AFFINES	AFFRAYING	AFTERLIFES
AEROGRAMS	AESTIVATE	AFFINITIES	AFFRAYS	AFTERLIVES
AEROLITE	AESTIVATED	AFFINITY	AFFRICATE	AFTERMATH
AEROLITES	AESTIVATES	AFFIRM	AFFRICATED	AFTERMATHS
AEROLITH	AESTIVATING	AFFIRMANT	AFFRICATES	AFTERMOST
AEROLITHS	AETHER	AFFIRMANTS	AFFRICATING	AFTERNOON
AEROLITIC	AETHEREAL	AFFIRMED	AFFRIGHT	AFTERNOONS
AEROLOGIC	AETHERIC	AFFIRMER	AFFRIGHTED	AFTERPAIN
AEROLOGIES	AETHERS	AFFIRMERS	AFFRIGHTING	AFTERPAINS
AEROLOGY	AETIOLOGIES	AFFIRMING	AFFRIGHTS	AFTERS
AEROMETER	AETIOLOGY	AFFIRMS	AFFRONT	AFTERTAX

AFTERTIME	AGEDLY	AGGADIC	AGISTED	AGNOSTIC
AFTERTIMES	AGEDNESS	AGGADOT	AGISTING	AGNOSTICS
AFTERWARD	AGEDNESSES	AGGADOTH	AGISTS	AGO
AFTERWORD	AGEE	AGGER	AGITA	AGOG
AFTERWORDS	AGEING	AGGERS	AGITABLE	AGON
AFTMOST	AGEINGS	AGGIE	AGITAS	AGONAL
AFTOSA	AGEISM	AGGIES	AGITATE	AGONE
AFTOSAS	AGEISMS	AGGRADE	AGITATED	AGONES
AG	AGEIST	AGGRADED	AGITATES	AGONIC
AGA	AGEISTS	AGGRADES	AGITATING	AGONIES
AGAIN	AGELESS	AGGRADING	AGITATION	AGONISE
AGAINST	AGELESSLY	AGGRAVATE	AGITATIONS	AGONISED
AGALACTIA	AGELONG	AGGRAVATED	AGITATIVE	AGONISES
AGALACTIAS	AGEMATE	AGGRAVATES	AGITATO	AGONISING
AGALLOCH	AGEMATES	AGGRAVATING	AGITATOR	AGONIST
AGALLOCHS	AGENCIES	AGGREGATE	AGITATORS	AGONISTES
AGALWOOD	AGENCY	AGGREGATED	AGITPROP	AGONISTIC
AGALWOODS	AGENDA	AGGREGATES	AGITPROPS	AGONISTS
AGAMA	AGENDAS	AGGREGATING	AGLARE	AGONIZE
AGAMAS	AGENDUM	AGGRESS	AGLEAM	AGONIZED
AGAMETE	AGENDUMS	AGGRESSED	AGLEE	AGONIZES
AGAMETES	AGENE	AGGRESSES	AGLET	AGONIZING
AGAMIC	AGENES	AGGRESSING	AGLETS	AGONS
AGAMID	AGENESES	AGGRESSOR	AGLEY	AGONY
AGAMIDS	AGENESIA	AGGRESSORS	AGLIMMER	AGORA
AGAMOUS	AGENESIAS	AGGRIEVE	AGLITTER	AGORAE
AGAPAE	AGENESIS	AGGRIEVED	AGLOW	AGORAS
AGAPAI	AGENETIC	AGGRIEVES	AGLY	AGOROT
AGAPE	AGENIZE	AGGRIEVING	AGLYCON	AGOROTH
AGAPEIC	AGENIZED	AGGRO	AGLYCONE	AGOUTI
AGAPES	AGENIZES	AGGROS	AGLYCONES	AGOUTIES
AGAR	AGENIZING	AGHA	AGLYCONS	AGOUTIS
AGARIC	AGENT	AGHAS	AGMA	AGOUTY
AGARICS	AGENTED	AGHAST	AGMAS	AGRAFE
AGAROSE	AGENTIAL	AGILE	AGMINATE	AGRAFES
AGAROSES	AGENTING	AGILELY	AGNAIL	AGRAFFE
AGARS	AGENTINGS	AGILENESS	AGNAILS	AGRAFFES
AGAS	AGENTIVAL	AGILENESSES	AGNATE	AGRAPHA
AGATE	AGENTIVE	AGILITIES	AGNATES	AGRAPHIA
AGATES	AGENTIVES	AGILITY	AGNATIC	AGRAPHIAS
AGATEWARE	AGENTRIES	AGIN	AGNATICAL	AGRAPHIC
AGATEWARES	AGENTRY	AGING	AGNATION	AGRARIAN
AGATIZE	AGENTS	AGINGS	AGNATIONS	AGRARIANS
AGATIZED	AGER	AGINNER	AGNIZE	AGRAVIC
AGATIZES	AGERATUM	AGINNERS	AGNIZED	AGREE
AGATIZING	AGERATUMS	AGIO	AGNIZES	AGREEABLE
AGATOID	AGERS	AGIOS	AGNIZING	AGREEABLY
AGAVE	AGES	AGIOTAGE	AGNOMEN	AGREED
AGAVES	AGGADA	AGIOTAGES	AGNOMENS	AGREEING
AGAZE	AGGADAH	AGISM	AGNOMINA	AGREEMENT
AGE	AGGADAHS	AGISMS	AGNOSIA	AGREEMENTS
AGED	AGGADAS	AGIST	AGNOSIAS	AGREES

AGRESTAL	AIDING	AIRBRUSHING	AIRLIFTING	AIRSTRIKE
AGRESTIC	AIDLESS	AIRBURST	AIRLIFTS	AIRSTRIKES
AGRIA	AIDMAN	AIRBURSTS	AIRLIKE	AIRSTRIP
AGRIAS	AIDMEN	AIRBUS	AIRLINE	AIRSTRIPS
AGRIMONIES	AIDS	AIRBUSES	AIRLINER	AIRT
AGRIMONY	AIGLET	AIRBUSSES	AIRLINERS	AIRTED
AGROLOGIC	AIGLETS	AIRCHECK	AIRLINES	AIRTH
AGROLOGIES	AIGRET	AIRCHECKS	AIRMAIL	AIRTHED
AGROLOGY	AIGRETS	AIRCOACH	AIRMAILED	AIRTHING
AGRONOMIC	AIGRETTE	AIRCOACHES	AIRMAILING	AIRTHS
AGRONOMIES	AIGRETTES	AIRCRAFT	AIRMAILS	AIRTIGHT
AGRONOMY	AIGUILLE	AIRCREW	AIRMAN	AIRTIME
AGROUND	AIGUILLES	AIRCREWS	AIRMEN	AIRTIMES
AGRYPNIA	AIKIDO	AIRDATE	AIRMOBILE	AIRTING
AGRYPNIAS	AIKIDOS	AIRDATES	AIRN	AIRTS
AGS	AIL	AIRDROME	AIRNS	AIRWARD
AGUACATE	AILANTHIC	AIRDROMES	AIRPARK	AIRWAVE
AGUACATES	AILANTHUS	AIRDROP	AIRPARKS	AIRWAVES
AGUE	AILANTHUSES	AIRDROPPED	AIRPLANE	AIRWAY
AGUELIKE	AILED	AIRDROPPING	AIRPLANES	AIRWAYS
AGUES	AILERON	AIRDROPS	AIRPLAY	AIRWISE
AGUEWEED	AILERONS	AIRED	AIRPLAYS	AIRWOMAN
AGUEWEEDS	AILING	AIRER	AIRPORT	AIRWOMEN
AGUISH	AILMENT	AIRERS	AIRPORTS	AIRWORTHIER
AGUISHLY	AILMENTS	AIREST	AIRPOST	AIRWORTHIEST
AH	AILS	AIRFARE	AIRPOSTS	AIRWORTHY
AHA	AIM	AIRFARES	AIRPOWER	AIRY
AHCHOO	AIMED	AIRFIELD	AIRPOWERS	AIS
AHEAD	AIMER	AIRFIELDS	AIRPROOF	AISLE
AHED	AIMERS	AIRFLOW	AIRPROOFED	AISLED
AHEM	AIMFUL	AIRFLOWS	AIRPROOFING	AISLES
AHI	AIMFULLY	AIRFOIL	AIRPROOFS	AISLEWAY
AHIMSA	AIMING	AIRFOILS	AIRS	AISLEWAYS
AHIMSAS	AIMLESS	AIRFRAME	AIRSCAPE	AIT
AHING	AIMLESSLY	AIRFRAMES	AIRSCAPES	AITCH
AHIS	AIMS	AIRGLOW	AIRSCREW	AITCHBONE
AHISTORIC	AIN	AIRGLOWS	AIRSCREWS	AITCHBONES
AHOLD	AINS	AIRHEAD	AIRSHED	AITCHES
AHOLDS	AINSELL	AIRHEADED	AIRSHEDS	AITS
AHORSE	AINSELLS	AIRHEADS	AIRSHIP	AIVER
AHOY	AIOLI	AIRHOLE	AIRSHIPS	AIVERS
AHS	AIOLIS	AIRHOLES	AIRSHOT	AJAR
AHULL	AIR	AIRIER	AIRSHOTS	AJEE
AI	AIRBAG	AIRIEST	AIRSHOW	AJIVA
AIBLINS	AIRBAGS	AIRILY	AIRSHOWS	AJIVAS
AID	AIRBOAT	AIRINESS	AIRSICK	AJOWAN
AIDE	AIRBOATS	AIRINESSES	AIRSPACE	AJOWANS
AIDED	AIRBORNE	AIRING	AIRSPACES	AJUGA
AIDER	AIRBOUND	AIRINGS	AIRSPEED	AJUGAS
AIDERS	AIRBRUSH	AIRLESS	AIRSPEEDS	AKEE
AIDES	AIRBRUSHED	AIRLIFT	AIRSTREAM	AKEES
AIDFUL	AIRBRUSHES	AIRLIFTED	AIRSTREAMS	AKELA

AKELAS	ALARUM	ALBUMIN	ALDERMEN	ALEXIA
AKENE	ALARUMED	ALBUMINS	ALDERS	ALEXIAS
AKENES	ALARUMING	ALBUMOSE	ALDICARB	ALEXIN
AKIMBO	ALARUMS	ALBUMOSES	ALDICARBS	ALEXINE
AKIN	ALARY	ALBUMS	ALDOL	ALEXINES
AKINESIA	ALAS	ALBURNOUS	ALDOLASE	ALEXINS
AKINESIAS	ALASKA	ALBURNUM	ALDOLASES	ALFA
AKINETIC	ALASKAS	ALBURNUMS	ALDOLS	ALFAKI
AKVAVIT	ALASTOR	ALBUTEROL	ALDOSE	ALFAKIS
AKVAVITS	ALASTORS	ALBUTEROLS	ALDOSES	ALFALFA
AL	ALATE	ALCADE	ALDRIN	ALFALFAS
ALA	ALATED	ALCADES	ALDRINS	ALFAQUI
ALABASTER	ALATES	ALCAHEST	ALE	ALFAQUIN
ALABASTERS	ALATION	ALCAHESTS	ALEATORIC	ALFAQUINS
ALACHLOR	ALATIONS	ALCAIC	ALEATORY	ALFAQUIS
ALACHLORS	ALB	ALCAICS	ALEC	ALFAS
ALACK	ALBA	ALCAIDE	ALECITHAL	ALFILARIA
ALACKADAY	ALBACORE	ALCAIDES	ALECS	ALFILARIAS
ALACRITIES	ALBACORES	ALCALDE	ALEE	ALFILERIA
ALACRITY	ALBAS	ALCALDES	ALEF	ALFILERIAS
ALAE	ALBATA	ALCAYDE	ALEFS	ALFORJA
ALAMEDA	ALBATAS	ALCAYDES	ALEGAR	ALFORJAS
ALAMEDAS	ALBATROSS	ALCAZAR	ALEGARS	ALFREDO
ALAMO	ALBATROSSES	ALCAZARS	ALEHOUSE	ALFRESCO
ALAMODE	ALBEDO	ALCHEMIC	ALEHOUSES	ALGA
ALAMODES	ALBEDOES	ALCHEMIES	ALEMBIC	ALGAE
ALAMOS	ALBEDOS	ALCHEMIST	ALEMBICS	ALGAECIDE
ALAN	ALBEIT	ALCHEMISTS	ALENCON	ALGAECIDES
ALAND	ALBERTITE	ALCHEMIZE	ALENCONS	ALGAL
ALANDS	ALBERTITES	ALCHEMIZED	ALEPH	ALGAROBA
ALANE	ALBESCENT	ALCHEMIZES	ALEPHS	ALGAROBAS
ALANG	ALBICORE	ALCHEMIZING	ALERT	ALGARROBA
ALANIN	ALBICORES	ALCHEMY	ALERTED	ALGARROBAS
ALANINE	ALBINAL	ALCHYMIES	ALERTER	ALGARROBO
ALANINES	ALBINIC	ALCHYMY	ALERTEST	ALGARROBOS
ALANINS	ALBINISM	ALCID	ALERTING	ALGAS
ALANS	ALBINISMS	ALCIDINE	ALERTLY	ALGEBRA
ALANT	ALBINO	ALCIDS	ALERTNESS	ALGEBRAIC
ALANTS	ALBINOS	ALCOHOL	ALERTNESSES	ALGEBRAS
ALANYL	ALBINOTIC	ALCOHOLIC	ALERTS	ALGERINE
ALANYLS	ALBITE	ALCOHOLICS	ALES	ALGERINES
ALAR	ALBITES	ALCOHOLS	ALEURON	ALGICIDAL
ALARM	ALBITIC	ALCOVE	ALEURONE	ALGICIDE
ALARMABLE	ALBITICAL	ALCOVED	ALEURONES	ALGICIDES
ALARMED	ALBIZIA	ALCOVES	ALEURONIC	ALGID
ALARMEDLY	ALBIZIAS	ALDEHYDE	ALEURONS	ALGIDITIES
ALARMING	ALBIZZIA	ALDEHYDES	ALEVIN	ALGIDITY
ALARMISM	ALBIZZIAS	ALDEHYDIC	ALEVINS	ALGIDNESS
ALARMISMS	ALBS	ALDER	ALEWIFE	ALGIDNESSES
ALARMIST	ALBUM	ALDERFLIES	ALEWIVES	ALGIN
ALARMISTS	ALBUMEN	ALDERFLY	ALEXANDER	ALGINATE
ALARMS	ALBUMENS	ALDERMAN	ALEXANDERS	ALGINATES

ALGINS	ALIENNESS	ALIVE	ALKOXY	ALLEMANDE
ALGOID	ALIENNESSES	ALIVENESS	ALKY	ALLEMANDES
ALGOLOGIES	ALIENOR	ALIVENESSES	ALKYD	ALLERGEN
ALGOLOGY	ALIENORS	ALIYA	ALKYDS	ALLERGENS
ALGOMETER	ALIENS	ALIYAH	ALKYL	ALLERGIC
ALGOMETERS	ALIF	ALIYAHS	ALKYLATE	ALLERGIES
ALGOMETRIES	ALIFORM	ALIYAS	ALKYLATED	ALLERGIN
ALGOMETRY	ALIFS	ALIYOS	ALKYLATES	ALLERGINS
ALGOR	ALIGHT	ALIYOT	ALKYLATING	ALLERGIST
ALGORISM	ALIGHTED	ALIZARIN	ALKYLIC	ALLERGISTS
ALGORISMS	ALIGHTING	ALIZARINE	ALKYLS	ALLERGY
ALGORITHM	ALIGHTS	ALIZARINES	ALKYNE	ALLETHRIN
ALGORITHMS	ALIGN	ALIZARINS	ALKYNES	ALLETHRINS
ALGORS	ALIGNED	ALKAHEST	ALL	ALLEVIANT
ALGUM	ALIGNER	ALKAHESTS	ALLANITE	ALLEVIANTS
ALGUMS	ALIGNERS	ALKALI	ALLANITES	ALLEVIATE
ALIAS	ALIGNING	ALKALIC	ALLANTOIC	ALLEVIATED
ALIASES	ALIGNMENT	ALKALIES	ALLANTOID	ALLEVIATES
ALIASING	ALIGNMENTS	ALKALIFIED	ALLANTOIDES	ALLEVIATING
ALIASINGS	ALIGNS	ALKALIFIES	ALLANTOIDS	ALLEY
ALIBI	ALIKE	ALKALIFY	ALLANTOIN	ALLEYS
ALIBIED	ALIKENESS	ALKALIFYING	ALLANTOINS	ALLEYWAY
ALIBIES	ALIKENESSES	ALKALIN	ALLANTOIS	ALLEYWAYS
ALIBIING	ALIMENT	ALKALINE	ALLAY	ALLHEAL
ALIBIS	ALIMENTAL	ALKALIS	ALLAYED	ALLHEALS
ALIBLE	ALIMENTED	ALKALISE	ALLAYER	ALLIABLE
ALICYCLIC	ALIMENTING	ALKALISED	ALLAYERS	ALLIANCE
ALIDAD	ALIMENTS	ALKALISES	ALLAYING	ALLIANCES
ALIDADE	ALIMONIED	ALKALISING	ALLAYS	ALLICIN
ALIDADES	ALIMONIES	ALKALIZE	ALLEE	ALLICINS
ALIDADS	ALIMONY	ALKALIZED	ALLEES	ALLIED
ALIEN	ALINE	ALKALIZER	ALLEGE	ALLIES
ALIENABLE	ALINED	ALKALIZERS	ALLEGED	ALLIGATOR
ALIENAGE	ALINEMENT	ALKALIZES	ALLEGEDLY	ALLIGATORS
ALIENAGES	ALINEMENTS	ALKALIZING	ALLEGER	ALLIUM
ALIENATE	ALINER	ALKALOID	ALLEGERS	ALLIUMS
ALIENATED	ALINERS	ALKALOIDS	ALLEGES	ALLOBAR
ALIENATES	ALINES	ALKALOSES	ALLEGIANT	ALLOBARS
ALIENATING	ALINING	ALKALOSIS	ALLEGIANTS	ALLOCABLE
ALIENATOR	ALIPED	ALKALOTIC	ALLEGING	ALLOCATE
ALIENATORS	ALIPEDS	ALKANE	ALLEGORIC	ALLOCATED
ALIENED	ALIPHATIC	ALKANES	ALLEGORIES	ALLOCATES
ALIENEE	ALIQUANT	ALKANET	ALLEGORY	ALLOCATING
ALIENEES	ALIQUOT	ALKANETS	ALLEGRO	ALLOCATOR
ALIENER	ALIQUOTS	ALKENE	ALLEGROS	ALLOCATORS
ALIENERS	ALIST	ALKENES	ALLELE	ALLOD
ALIENING	ALIT	ALKIE	ALLELES	ALLODIA
ALIENISM	ALITERACIES	ALKIES	ALLELIC	ALLODIAL
ALIENISMS	ALITERACY	ALKINE	ALLELISM	ALLODIUM
ALIENIST	ALITERATE	ALKINES	ALLELISMS	ALLODS
ALIENISTS	ALITERATES	ALKOXIDE	ALLELUIA	ALLOGAMIES
ALIENLY	ALIUNDE	ALKOXIDES	ALLELUIAS	ALLOGAMY

ALLOGENIC	ALLOW	ALMAH	ALOGICAL	ALT
ALLOGRAFT	ALLOWABLE	ALMAHS	ALOHA	ALTAR
ALLOGRAFTED	ALLOWABLES	ALMANAC	ALOHAS	ALTARS
ALLOGRAFTING	ALLOWABLY	ALMANACK	ALOIN	ALTER
ALLOGRAFTS	ALLOWANCE	ALMANACKS	ALOINS	ALTERABLE
ALLOGRAPH	ALLOWANCED	ALMANACS	ALONE	ALTERABLY
ALLOGRAPHS	ALLOWANCES	ALMANDINE	ALONENESS	ALTERANT
ALLOMETRIES	ALLOWANCING	ALMANDINES	ALONENESSES	ALTERANTS
ALLOMETRY	ALLOWED	ALMANDITE	ALONG	ALTERCATE
ALLOMORPH	ALLOWEDLY	ALMANDITES	ALONGSIDE	ALTERCATED
ALLOMORPHS	ALLOWING	ALMAS	ALOOF	ALTERCATES
ALLONGE	ALLOWS	ALME	ALOOFLY	ALTERCATING
ALLONGES	ALLOXAN	ALMEH	ALOOFNESS	ALTERED
ALLONYM	ALLOXANS	ALMEHS	ALOOFNESSES	ALTERER
ALLONYMS	ALLOY	ALMEMAR	ALOPECIA	ALTERERS
ALLOPATH	ALLOYED	ALMEMARS	ALOPECIAS	ALTERING
ALLOPATHIES	ALLOYING	ALMES	ALOPECIC	ALTERITIES
ALLOPATHS	ALLOYS	ALMIGHTY	ALOUD	ALTERITY
ALLOPATHY	ALLS	ALMNER	ALOW	ALTERNANT
ALLOPATRIES	ALLSEED	ALMNERS	ALP	ALTERNANTS
ALLOPATRY	ALLSEEDS	ALMOND	ALPACA	ALTERNATE
ALLOPHANE	ALLSORTS	ALMONDS	ALPACAS	ALTERNATED
ALLOPHANES	ALLSPICE	ALMONDY	ALPENGLOW	ALTERNATES
ALLOPHONE	ALLSPICES	ALMONER	ALPENGLOWS	ALTERNATING
ALLOPHONES	ALLUDE	ALMONERS	ALPENHORN	ALTERS
ALLOPLASM	ALLUDED	ALMONRIES	ALPENHORNS	ALTHAEA
ALLOPLASMS	ALLUDES	ALMONRY	ALPHA	ALTHAEAS
ALLOSAUR	ALLUDING	ALMOST	ALPHABET	ALTHEA
ALLOSAURS	ALLURE	ALMS	ALPHABETED	ALTHEAS
ALLOSTERIES	ALLURED	ALMSGIVER	ALPHABETING	ALTHO
ALLOSTERY	ALLURER	ALMSGIVERS	ALPHABETS	ALTHORN
ALLOT	ALLURERS	ALMSHOUSE	ALPHAS	ALTHORNS
ALLOTMENT	ALLURES	ALMSHOUSES	ALPHORN	ALTHOUGH
ALLOTMENTS	ALLURING	ALMSMAN	ALPHORNS	ALTIGRAPH
ALLOTROPE	ALLUSION	ALMSMEN	ALPHOSIS	ALTIGRAPHS
ALLOTROPES	ALLUSIONS	ALMUCE	ALPHOSISES	ALTIMETER
ALLOTROPIES	ALLUSIVE	ALMUCES	ALPHYL	ALTIMETERS
ALLOTROPY	ALLUVIA	ALMUD	ALPHYLS	ALTIMETRIES
ALLOTS	ALLUVIAL	ALMUDE	ALPINE	ALTIMETRY
ALLOTTED	ALLUVIALS	ALMUDES	ALPINELY	ALTIPLANO
ALLOTTEE	ALLUVION	ALMUDS	ALPINES	ALTIPLANOS
ALLOTTEES	ALLUVIONS	ALMUG	ALPINISM	ALTITUDE
ALLOTTER	ALLUVIUM	ALMUGS	ALPINISMS	ALTITUDES
ALLOTTERS	ALLUVIUMS	ALNICO	ALPINIST	ALTO
ALLOTTING	ALLY	ALNICOS	ALPINISTS	ALTOIST
ALLOTYPE	ALLYING	ALODIA	ALPS	ALTOISTS
ALLOTYPES	ALLYL	ALODIAL	ALREADY	ALTOS
ALLOTYPIC	ALLYLIC	ALODIUM	ALRIGHT	ALTRICIAL
ALLOTYPIES	ALLYLS	ALOE	ALS	ALTRUISM
ALLOTYPY	ALMA	ALOES	ALSIKE	ALTRUISMS
ALLOVER	ALMAGEST	ALOETIC	ALSIKES	ALTRUIST
ALLOVERS	ALMAGESTS	ALOFT	ALSO	ALTRUISTS

ALTS	AMAH	AMAZONIANS	AMBLYOPIC	AMEBOCYTES
ALUDEL	AMAHS	AMAZONITE	AMBO	AMEBOID
ALUDELS	AMAIN	AMAZONITES	AMBOINA	AMEER
ALULA	AMALGAM	AMAZONS	AMBOINAS	AMEERATE
ALULAE	AMALGAMS	AMBAGE	AMBONES	AMEERATES
ALULAR	AMANDINE	AMBAGES	AMBOS	AMEERS
ALUM	AMANITA	AMBAGIOUS	AMBOYNA	AMELCORN
ALUMIN	AMANITAS	AMBARI	AMBOYNAS	AMELCORNS
ALUMINA	AMANITIN	AMBARIES	AMBRIES	AMEN
ALUMINAS	AMANITINS	AMBARIS	AMBROID	AMENABLE
ALUMINATE	AMARANTH	AMBARY	AMBROIDS	AMENABLY
ALUMINATES	AMARANTHS	AMBEER	AMBROSIA	AMEND
ALUMINE	AMARELLE	AMBEERS	AMBROSIAL	AMENDABLE
ALUMINES	AMARELLES	AMBER	AMBROSIAN	AMENDED
ALUMINIC	AMARETTI	AMBERGRIS	AMBROSIAS	AMENDER
ALUMINIUM	AMARETTO	AMBERGRISES	AMBROTYPE	AMENDERS
ALUMINIUMS	AMARETTOS	AMBERIES	AMBROTYPES	AMENDING
ALUMINIZE	AMARNA	AMBERINA	AMBRY	AMENDMENT
ALUMINIZED	AMARONE	AMBERINAS	AMBSACE	AMENDMENTS
ALUMINIZES	AMARONES	AMBERJACK	AMBSACES	AMENDS
ALUMINIZING	AMARYLLIS	AMBERJACKS	AMBULACRA	AMENITIES
ALUMINOUS	AMARYLLISES	AMBEROID	AMBULACRUM	AMENITY
ALUMINS	AMAS	AMBEROIDS	AMBULANCE	AMENS
ALUMINUM	AMASS	AMBERS	AMBULANCES	AMENT
ALUMINUMS	AMASSABLE	AMBERY	AMBULANT	AMENTIA
ALUMNA	AMASSED	AMBIANCE	AMBULATE	AMENTIAS
ALUMNAE	AMASSER	AMBIANCES	AMBULATED	AMENTS
ALUMNI	AMASSERS	AMBIENCE	AMBULATES	AMERCE
ALUMNUS	AMASSES	AMBIENCES	AMBULATING	AMERCED
ALUMROOT	AMASSING	AMBIENT	AMBULATOR	AMERCER
ALUMROOTS	AMASSMENT	AMBIENTS	AMBULATORS	AMERCERS
ALUMS	AMASSMENTS	AMBIGUITIES	AMBULETTE	AMERCES
ALUMSTONE	AMATEUR	AMBIGUITY	AMBULETTES	AMERCING
ALUMSTONES	AMATEURS	AMBIGUOUS	AMBUSCADE	AMERICIUM
ALUNITE	AMATIVE	AMBIPOLAR	AMBUSCADED	AMERICIUMS
ALUNITES	AMATIVELY	AMBIT	AMBUSCADES	AMESACE
ALVEOLAR	AMATOL	AMBITION	AMBUSCADING	AMESACES
ALVEOLARS	AMATOLS	AMBITIONED	AMBUSH	AMETHYST
ALVEOLATE	AMATORY	AMBITIONING	AMBUSHED	AMETHYSTS
ALVEOLI	AMAUROSES	AMBITIONS	AMBUSHER	AMETROPIA
ALVEOLUS	AMAUROSIS	AMBITIOUS	AMBUSHERS	AMETROPIAS
ALVINE	AMAUROTIC	AMBITS	AMBUSHES	AMETROPIC
ALWAY	AMAZE	AMBIVERT	AMBUSHING	AMI
ALWAYS	AMAZED	AMBIVERTS	AMEBA	AMIA
ALYSSUM	AMAZEDLY	AMBLE	AMEBAE	AMIABLE
ALYSSUMS	AMAZEMENT	AMBLED	AMEBAN	AMIABLY
AM	AMAZEMENTS	AMBLER	AMEBAS	AMIANTHUS
AMA	AMAZES	AMBLERS	AMEBEAN	AMIANTHUSES
AMADAVAT	AMAZING	AMBLES	AMEBIASES	AMIANTUS
AMADAVATS	AMAZINGLY	AMBLING	AMEBIASIS	AMIANTUSES
AMADOU	AMAZON	AMBLYOPIA	AMEBIC	AMIAS
AMADOUS	AMAZONIAN	AMBLYOPIAS	AMEBOCYTE	AMICABLE

AMICABLY	AMITY	AMNIOTES	AMOUNTS	AMPULE
AMICE	AMMETER	AMNIOTIC	AMOUR	AMPULES
AMICES	AMMETERS	AMOEBA	AMOURS	AMPULLA
AMICI	AMMINE	AMOEBAE	AMP	AMPULLAE
AMICUS	AMMINES	AMOEBAEAN	AMPED	AMPULLAR
AMID	AMMINO	AMOEBAN	AMPERAGE	AMPULLARY
AMIDASE	AMMO	AMOEBAS	AMPERAGES	AMPULS
AMIDASES	AMMOCETE	AMOEBEAN	AMPERE	AMPUTATE
AMIDE	AMMOCETES	AMOEBIC	AMPERES	AMPUTATED
AMIDES	AMMONAL	AMOEBOID	AMPERSAND	AMPUTATES
AMIDIC	AMMONALS	AMOK	AMPERSANDS	AMPUTATING
AMIDIN	AMMONIA	AMOKS	AMPHIBIA	AMPUTATOR
AMIDINE	AMMONIAC	AMOLE	AMPHIBIAN	AMPUTATORS
AMIDINES	AMMONIACS	AMOLES	AMPHIBIANS	AMPUTEE
AMIDINS	AMMONIAS	AMONG	AMPHIBOLE	AMPUTEES
AMIDO	AMMONIATE	AMONGST	AMPHIBOLES	AMREETA
AMIDOGEN	AMMONIATED	AMORAL	AMPHIBOLIES	AMREETAS
AMIDOGENS	AMMONIATES	AMORALISM	AMPHIBOLY	AMRITA
AMIDOL	AMMONIATING	AMORALISMS	AMPHIGORIES	AMRITAS
AMIDOLS	AMMONIC	AMORALITIES	AMPHIGORY	AMSINCKIA
AMIDONE	AMMONIFIED	AMORALITY	AMPHIOXI	AMSINCKIAS
AMIDONES	AMMONIFIES	AMORALLY	AMPHIOXUS	AMTRAC
AMIDS	AMMONIFY	AMORETTI	AMPHIOXUSES	AMTRACK
AMIDSHIP	AMMONIFYING	AMORETTO	AMPHIPOD	AMTRACKS
AMIDSHIPS	AMMONITE	AMORETTOS	AMPHIPODS	AMTRACS
AMIDST	AMMONITES	AMORINI	AMPHORA	AMU
AMIE	AMMONITIC	AMORINO	AMPHORAE	AMUCK
AMIES	AMMONIUM	AMORIST	AMPHORAL	AMUCKS
AMIGA	AMMONIUMS	AMORISTIC	AMPHORAS	AMULET
AMIGAS	AMMONO	AMORISTS	AMPING	AMULETS
AMIGO	AMMONOID	AMOROSO	AMPLE	AMUS
AMIGOS	AMMONOIDS	AMOROUS	AMPLENESS	AMUSABLE
AMIN	AMMOS	AMOROUSLY	AMPLENESSES	AMUSE
AMINE	AMNESIA	AMORPHISM	AMPLER	AMUSED
AMINES	AMNESIAC	AMORPHISMS	AMPLEST	AMUSEDLY
AMINIC	AMNESIACS	AMORPHOUS	AMPLEXUS	AMUSEMENT
AMINITIES	AMNESIAS	AMORT	AMPLEXUSES	AMUSEMENTS
AMINITY	AMNESIC	AMORTISE	AMPLIDYNE	AMUSER
AMINO	AMNESICS	AMORTISED	AMPLIDYNES	AMUSERS
AMINS	AMNESTIC	AMORTISES	AMPLIFIED	AMUSES
AMIR	AMNESTIED	AMORTISING	AMPLIFIER	AMUSIA
AMIRATE	AMNESTIES	AMORTIZE	AMPLIFIERS	AMUSIAS
AMIRATES	AMNESTY	AMORTIZED	AMPLIFIES	AMUSING
AMIRS	AMNESTYING	AMORTIZES	AMPLIFY	AMUSINGLY
AMIS	AMNIA	AMORTIZING	AMPLIFYING	AMUSIVE
AMISS	AMNIC	AMOSITE	AMPLITUDE	AMYGDALA
AMITIES	AMNIO	AMOSITES	AMPLITUDES	AMYGDALAE
AMITOSES	AMNION	AMOTION	AMPLY	AMYGDALE
AMITOSIS	AMNIONIC	AMOTIONS	AMPOULE	AMYGDALES
AMITOTIC	AMNIONS	AMOUNT	AMPOULES	AMYGDALIN
AMITROLE	AMNIOS	AMOUNTED	AMPS	AMYGDALINS
AMITROLES	AMNIOTE	AMOUNTING	AMPUL	AMYGDULE

AMYGDULES	ANAEROBIA	ANALOGUE	ANARCHIST	ANCHORMEN
AMYL	ANAEROBIC	ANALOGUES	ANARCHISTS	ANCHORS
AMYLASE	ANAEROBIUM	ANALOGY	ANARCHS	ANCHOS
AMYLASES	ANAGLYPH	ANALYSAND	ANARCHY	ANCHOVETA
AMYLENE	ANAGLYPHS	ANALYSANDS	ANARTHRIA	ANCHOVETAS
AMYLENES	ANAGOGE	ANALYSE	ANARTHRIAS	ANCHOVIES
AMYLIC	ANAGOGES	ANALYSED	ANARTHRIC	ANCHOVY
AMYLOGEN	ANAGOGIC	ANALYSER	ANAS	ANCHUSA
AMYLOGENS	ANAGOGIES	ANALYSERS	ANASARCA	ANCHUSAS
AMYLOID	ANAGOGY	ANALYSES	ANASARCAS	ANCHUSIN
AMYLOIDS	ANAGRAM	ANALYSING	ANATASE	ANCHUSINS
AMYLOPSIN	ANAGRAMMED	ANALYSIS	ANATASES	ANCHYLOSE
AMYLOPSINS	ANAGRAMMING	ANALYST	ANATHEMA	ANCHYLOSED
AMYLOSE	ANAGRAMS	ANALYSTS	ANATHEMAS	ANCHYLOSES
AMYLOSES	ANAL	ANALYTE	ANATHEMATA	ANCHYLOSING
AMYLS	ANALCIME	ANALYTES	ANATOMIC	ANCIENT
AMYLUM	ANALCIMES	ANALYTIC	ANATOMIES	ANCIENTER
AMYLUMS	ANALCIMIC	ANALYTICS	ANATOMISE	ANCIENTEST
AMYOTONIA	ANALCITE	ANALYZE	ANATOMISED	ANCIENTLY
AMYOTONIAS	ANALCITES	ANALYZED	ANATOMISES	ANCIENTRIES
AN	ANALECTA	ANALYZER	ANATOMISING	ANCIENTRY
ANA	ANALECTIC	ANALYZERS	ANATOMIST	ANCIENTS
ANABAENA	ANALECTS	ANALYZES	ANATOMISTS	ANCILLA
ANABAENAS	ANALEMMA	ANALYZING	ANATOMIZE	ANCILLAE
ANABAS	ANALEMMAS	ANAMNESES	ANATOMIZED	ANCILLARIES
ANABASES	ANALEMMATA	ANAMNESIS	ANATOMIZES	ANCILLARY
ANABASIS	ANALEPTIC	ANANKE	ANATOMIZING	ANCILLAS
ANABATIC	ANALEPTICS	ANANKES	ANATOMY	ANCIPITAL
ANABIOSES	ANALGESIA	ANAPAEST	ANATOXIN	ANCON
ANABIOSIS	ANALGESIAS	ANAPAESTS	ANATOXINS	ANCONAL
ANABIOTIC	ANALGESIC	ANAPEST	ANATTO	ANCONE
ANABLEPS	ANALGESICS	ANAPESTIC	ANATTOS	ANCONEAL
ANABLEPSES	ANALGETIC	ANAPESTICS	ANCESTOR	ANCONES
ANABOLIC	ANALGETICS	ANAPESTS	ANCESTORED	ANCONOID
ANABOLISM	ANALGIA	ANAPHASE	ANCESTORING	ANCRESS
ANABOLISMS	ANALGIAS	ANAPHASES	ANCESTORS	ANCRESSES
ANABRANCH	ANALITIES	ANAPHASIC	ANCESTRAL	AND
ANABRANCHES	ANALITY	ANAPHOR	ANCESTRIES	ANDANTE
ANACLISES	ANALLY	ANAPHORA	ANCESTRY	ANDANTES
ANACLISIS	ANALOG	ANAPHORAL	ANCHO	ANDANTINI
ANACLITIC	ANALOGIC	ANAPHORAS	ANCHOR	ANDANTINO
ANACONDA	ANALOGIES	ANAPHORIC	ANCHORAGE	ANDANTINOS
ANACONDAS	ANALOGISM	ANAPHORS	ANCHORAGES	ANDESITE
ANACRUSES	ANALOGISMS	ANAPLASIA	ANCHORED	ANDESITES
ANACRUSIS	ANALOGIST	ANAPLASIAS	ANCHORESS	ANDESITIC
ANADEM	ANALOGISTS	ANAPTYXES	ANCHORESSES	ANDESYTE
ANADEMS	ANALOGIZE	ANAPTYXIS	ANCHORET	ANDESYTES
ANAEMIA	ANALOGIZED	ANARCH	ANCHORETS	ANDIRON
ANAEMIAS	ANALOGIZES	ANARCHIC	ANCHORING	ANDIRONS
ANAEMIC	ANALOGIZING	ANARCHIES	ANCHORITE	ANDOUILLE
ANAEROBE	ANALOGOUS	ANARCHISM	ANCHORITES	ANDOUILLES
ANAEROBES	ANALOGS	ANARCHISMS	ANCHORMAN	ANDRADITE

ANDRADITES	ANES	ANGIOMA	ANGULATES	ANIMATES
ANDRO	ANESTRI	ANGIOMAS	ANGULATING	ANIMATING
ANDROECIA	ANESTROUS	ANGIOMATA	ANGULOSE	ANIMATION
ANDROECIUM	ANESTRUS	ANGLE	ANGULOUS	ANIMATIONS
ANDROGEN	ANETHOL	ANGLED	ANHEDONIA	ANIMATISM
ANDROGENS	ANETHOLE	ANGLEPOD	ANHEDONIAS	ANIMATISMS
ANDROGYNE	ANETHOLES	ANGLEPODS	ANHEDONIC	ANIMATIST
ANDROGYNES	ANETHOLS	ANGLER	ANHINGA	ANIMATISTS
ANDROGYNIES	ANEUPLOID	ANGLERS	ANHINGAS	ANIMATO
ANDROGYNY	ANEUPLOIDS	ANGLES	ANHYDRIDE	ANIMATOR
ANDROID	ANEURIN	ANGLESITE	ANHYDRIDES	ANIMATORS
ANDROIDS	ANEURINS	ANGLESITES	ANHYDRITE	ANIME
ANDROLOGIES	ANEURISM	ANGLEWORM	ANHYDRITES	ANIMES
ANDROLOGY	ANEURISMS	ANGLEWORMS	ANHYDROUS	ANIMI
ANDROMEDA	ANEURYSM	ANGLICE	ANI	ANIMIS
ANDROMEDAS	ANEURYSMS	ANGLICISE	ANIL	ANIMISM
ANDROS	ANEW	ANGLICISED	ANILE	ANIMISMS
ANDS	ANGA	ANGLICISES	ANILIN	ANIMIST
ANE	ANGAKOK	ANGLICISING	ANILINE	ANIMISTIC
ANEAR	ANGAKOKS	ANGLICISM	ANILINES	ANIMISTS
ANEARED	ANGARIA	ANGLICISMS	ANILINGUS	ANIMOSITIES
ANEARING	ANGARIAS	ANGLICIZE	ANILINGUSES	ANIMOSITY
ANEARS	ANGARIES	ANGLICIZED	ANILINS	ANIMUS
ANECDOTA	ANGARY	ANGLICIZES	ANILITIES	ANIMUSES
ANECDOTAL	ANGAS	ANGLICIZING	ANILITY	ANION
ANECDOTE	ANGEL	ANGLING	ANILS	ANIONIC
ANECDOTES	ANGELED	ANGLINGS	ANIMA	ANIONS
ANECDOTIC	ANGELFISH	ANGLO	ANIMACIES	ANIS
ANECHOIC	ANGELFISHES	ANGLOS	ANIMACY	ANISE
ANELASTIC	ANGELIC	ANGORA	ANIMAL	ANISEED
ANELE	ANGELICA	ANGORAS	ANIMALIAN	ANISEEDS
ANELED	ANGELICAL	ANGOSTURA	ANIMALIC	ANISES
ANELES	ANGELICAS	ANGOSTURAS	ANIMALIER	ANISETTE
ANELING	ANGELING	ANGRIER	ANIMALIERS	ANISETTES
ANEMIA	ANGELS	ANGRIEST	ANIMALISM	ANISIC
ANEMIAS	ANGELUS	ANGRILY	ANIMALISMS	ANISOGAMIES
ANEMIC	ANGELUSES	ANGRINESS	ANIMALIST	ANISOGAMY
ANEMOLOGIES	ANGER	ANGRINESSES	ANIMALISTS	ANISOLE
ANEMOLOGY	ANGERED	ANGRY	ANIMALITIES	ANISOLES
ANEMONE	ANGERING	ANGST	ANIMALITY	ANKERITE
ANEMONES	ANGERLESS	ANGSTROM	ANIMALIZE	ANKERITES
ANEMOSES	ANGERLY	ANGSTROMS	ANIMALIZED	ANKH
ANEMOSIS	ANGERS	ANGSTS	ANIMALIZES	ANKHS
ANENST	ANGINA	ANGUINE	ANIMALIZING	ANKLE
ANENT	ANGINAL	ANGUISH	ANIMALLY	ANKLEBONE
ANERGIA	ANGINAS	ANGUISHED	ANIMALS	ANKLEBONES
ANERGIAS	ANGINOSE	ANGUISHES	ANIMAS	ANKLED
ANERGIC	ANGINOUS	ANGUISHING	ANIMATE	ANKLES
ANERGIES	ANGIOGRAM	ANGULAR	ANIMATED	ANKLET
ANERGY	ANGIOGRAMS	ANGULARLY	ANIMATELY	ANKLETS
ANEROID	ANGIOLOGIES	ANGULATE	ANIMATER	ANKLING
ANEROIDS	ANGIOLOGY	ANGULATED	ANIMATERS	ANKUS

ANKUSES	ANNOUNCES	ANOINTED	ANOXEMIA	ANTEFIXES
ANKUSH	ANNOUNCING	ANOINTER	ANOXEMIAS	ANTEING
ANKUSHES	ANNOY	ANOINTERS	ANOXEMIC	ANTELOPE
ANKYLOSE	ANNOYANCE	ANOINTING	ANOXIA	ANTELOPES
ANKYLOSED	ANNOYANCES	ANOINTS	ANOXIAS	ANTENATAL
ANKYLOSES	ANNOYED	ANOLE	ANOXIC	ANTENNA
ANKYLOSING	ANNOYER	ANOLES	ANSA	ANTENNAE
ANKYLOSIS	ANNOYERS	ANOLYTE	ANSAE	ANTENNAL
ANKYLOTIC	ANNOYING	ANOLYTES	ANSATE	ANTENNAS
ANLACE	ANNOYS	ANOMALIES	ANSATED	ANTENNULE
ANLACES	ANNUAL	ANOMALOUS	ANSERINE	ANTENNULES
ANLAGE	ANNUALIZE	ANOMALY	ANSERINES	ANTEPAST
ANLAGEN	ANNUALIZED	ANOMIC	ANSEROUS	ANTEPASTS
ANLAGES	ANNUALIZES	ANOMIE	ANSWER	ANTERIOR
ANLAS	ANNUALIZING	ANOMIES	ANSWERED	ANTEROOM
ANLASES	ANNUALLY	ANOMY	ANSWERER	ANTEROOMS
ANNA	ANNUALS	ANON	ANSWERERS	ANTES
ANNAL	ANNUITANT	ANONYM	ANSWERING	ANTETYPE
ANNALIST	ANNUITANTS	ANONYMITIES	ANSWERS	ANTETYPES
ANNALISTS	ANNUITIES	ANONYMITY	ANT	ANTEVERT
ANNALS	ANNUITY	ANONYMOUS	ANTA	ANTEVERTED
ANNAS	ANNUL	ANONYMS	ANTACID	ANTEVERTING
ANNATES	ANNULAR	ANOOPSIA	ANTACIDS	ANTEVERTS
ANNATTO	ANNULARLY	ANOOPSIAS	ANTAE	ANTHELIA
ANNATTOS	ANNULATE	ANOPHELES	ANTALGIC	ANTHELICES
ANNEAL	ANNULATED	ANOPIA	ANTALGICS	ANTHELION
ANNEALED	ANNULET	ANOPIAS	ANTALKALI	ANTHELIONS
ANNEALER	ANNULETS	ANOPSIA	ANTALKALIES	ANTHELIX
ANNEALERS	ANNULI	ANOPSIAS	ANTALKALIS	ANTHELIXES
ANNEALING	ANNULLED	ANORAK	ANTARCTIC	ANTHEM
ANNEALS	ANNULLING	ANORAKS	ANTAS	ANTHEMED
ANNELID	ANNULMENT	ANORECTIC	ANTBEAR	ANTHEMIA
ANNELIDAN	ANNULMENTS	ANORECTICS	ANTBEARS	ANTHEMIC
ANNELIDANS	ANNULOSE	ANORETIC	ANTE	ANTHEMING
ANNELIDS	ANNULS	ANORETICS	ANTEATER	ANTHEMION
ANNEX	ANNULUS	ANOREXIA	ANTEATERS	ANTHEMS
ANNEXE	ANNULUSES	ANOREXIAS	ANTECEDE	ANTHER
ANNEXED	ANOA	ANOREXIC	ANTECEDED	ANTHERAL
ANNEXES	ANOAS	ANOREXICS	ANTECEDES	ANTHERID
ANNEXING	ANODAL	ANOREXIES	ANTECEDING	ANTHERIDS
ANNONA	ANODALLY	ANOREXY	ANTECHOIR	ANTHERS
ANNONAS	ANODE	ANORTHIC	ANTECHOIRS	ANTHESES
ANNOTATE	ANODES	ANORTHITE	ANTED	ANTHESIS
ANNOTATED	ANODIC	ANORTHITES	ANTEDATE	ANTHILL
ANNOTATES	ANODIZE	ANOSMATIC	ANTEDATED	ANTHILLS
ANNOTATING	ANODIZED	ANOSMIA	ANTEDATES	ANTHOCYAN
ANNOTATOR	ANODIZES	ANOSMIAS	ANTEDATING	ANTHOCYANS
ANNOTATORS	ANODIZING	ANOSMIC	ANTEED	ANTHODIA
ANNOUNCE	ANODYNE	ANOTHER	ANTEFIX	ANTHODIUM
ANNOUNCED	ANODYNES	ANOVULANT	ANTEFIXA	ANTHOID
ANNOUNCER	ANODYNIC	ANOVULANTS	ANTEFIXAE	ANTHOLOGIES
ANNOUNCERS	ANOINT	ANOVULAR	ANTEFIXAL	ANTHOLOGY

ANTHOZOAN	ANTICULT	ANTIMAN	ANTIPOLES	ANTISNOB
ANTHOZOANS	ANTICULTS	ANTIMASK	ANTIPOPE	ANTISNOBS
ANTHOZOIC	ANTIDORA	ANTIMASKS	ANTIPOPES	ANTISOLAR
ANTHRACES	ANTIDOTAL	ANTIMERE	ANTIPORN	ANTISPAM
ANTHRAX	ANTIDOTE	ANTIMERES	ANTIPOT	ANTISTAT
ANTHROPIC	ANTIDOTED	ANTIMERIC	ANTIPRESS	ANTISTATE
ANTHURIUM	ANTIDOTES	ANTIMINE	ANTIPYIC	ANTISTATS
ANTHURIUMS	ANTIDOTING	ANTIMONIC	ANTIPYICS	ANTISTICK
ANTI	ANTIDRAFT	ANTIMONIES	ANTIQUARIES	ANTISTORIES
ANTIABUSE	ANTIDRUG	ANTIMONY	ANTIQUARK	ANTISTORY
ANTIACNE	ANTIELITE	ANTIMONYL	ANTIQUARKS	ANTISTYLE
ANTIAGING	ANTIELITES	ANTIMONYLS	ANTIQUARY	ANTISTYLES
ANTIAIR	ANTIFAT	ANTIMUSIC	ANTIQUATE	ANTITANK
ANTIALIEN	ANTIFLU	ANTIMUSICS	ANTIQUATED	ANTITAX
ANTIAR	ANTIFOAM	ANTIMYCIN	ANTIQUATES	ANTITHEFT
ANTIARIN	ANTIFOG	ANTIMYCINS	ANTIQUATING	ANTITOXIC
ANTIARINS	ANTIFRAUD	ANTING	ANTIQUE	ANTITOXIN
ANTIARMOR	ANTIFUR	ANTINGS	ANTIQUED	ANTITOXINS
ANTIARS	ANTIGANG	ANTINODAL	ANTIQUELY	ANTITRADE
ANTIATOM	ANTIGAY	ANTINODE	ANTIQUER	ANTITRADES
ANTIATOMS	ANTIGEN	ANTINODES	ANTIQUERS	ANTITRAGI
ANTIAUXIN	ANTIGENE	ANTINOISE	ANTIQUES	ANTITRAGUS
ANTIAUXINS	ANTIGENES	ANTINOME	ANTIQUING	ANTITRUST
ANTIBIAS	ANTIGENIC	ANTINOMES	ANTIQUITIES	ANTITUMOR
ANTIBLACK	ANTIGENS	ANTINOMIC	ANTIQUITY	ANTITUMORS
ANTIBODIES	ANTIGLARE	ANTINOMIES	ANTIRADAR	ANTITYPE
ANTIBODY	ANTIGRAFT	ANTINOMY	ANTIRADARS	ANTITYPES
ANTIBOSS	ANTIGUN	ANTINOVEL	ANTIRAPE	ANTITYPIC
ANTIBUG	ANTIHELICES	ANTINOVELS	ANTIRED	ANTIULCER
ANTIBUSER	ANTIHELIX	ANTINUKE	ANTIRIOT	ANTIUNION
ANTIBUSERS	ANTIHELIXES	ANTINUKER	ANTIROCK	ANTIURBAN
ANTIC	ANTIHERO	ANTINUKERS	ANTIROLL	ANTIVENIN
ANTICALLY	ANTIHEROES	ANTINUKES	ANTIROYAL	ANTIVENINS
ANTICAR	ANTIHUMAN	ANTIPAPAL	ANTIRUST	ANTIVENOM
ANTICHLOR	ANTIJAM	ANTIPARTIES	ANTIRUSTS	ANTIVENOMS
ANTICHLORS	ANTIKING	ANTIPARTY	ANTIS	ANTIVIRAL
ANTICITY	ANTIKINGS	ANTIPASTI	ANTISAG	ANTIVIRUS
ANTICIVIC	ANTIKNOCK	ANTIPASTO	ANTISENSE	ANTIVIRUSES
ANTICK	ANTIKNOCKS	ANTIPASTOS	ANTISERA	ANTIWAR
ANTICKED	ANTILABOR	ANTIPATHIES	ANTISERUM	ANTIWEAR
ANTICKING	ANTILEAK	ANTIPATHY	ANTISERUMS	ANTIWEED
ANTICKS	ANTILEFT	ANTIPHON	ANTISEX	ANTIWHITE
ANTICLINE	ANTILIFE	ANTIPHONIES	ANTISHARK	ANTIWOMAN
ANTICLINES	ANTILIFER	ANTIPHONS	ANTISHIP	ANTLER
ANTICLING	ANTILIFERS	ANTIPHONY	ANTISHOCK	ANTLERED
ANTICLY	ANTILOCK	ANTIPILL	ANTISHOCKS	ANTLERS
ANTICODON	ANTILOG	ANTIPODAL	ANTISKID	ANTLIKE
ANTICODONS	ANTILOGIES	ANTIPODALS	ANTISLEEP	ANTLION
ANTICOLD	ANTILOGS	ANTIPODE	ANTISLIP	ANTLIONS
ANTICRACK	ANTILOGY	ANTIPODES	ANTISMOG	ANTONYM
ANTICRIME	ANTIMACHO	ANTIPOLAR	ANTISMOKE	ANTONYMIC
ANTICS	ANTIMALE	ANTIPOLE	ANTISMUT	ANTONYMIES

ANTONYMS	ANYWAYS	APERITIFS	APHORIST	APLOMBS
ANTONYMY	ANYWHERE	APERS	APHORISTS	APNEA
ANTRA	ANYWHERES	APERTURAL	APHORIZE	APNEAL
ANTRAL	ANYWISE	APERTURE	APHORIZED	APNEAS
ANTRE	AORIST	APERTURED	APHORIZER	APNEIC
ANTRES	AORISTIC	APERTURES	APHORIZERS	APNOEA
ANTRORSE	AORISTS	APERY	APHORIZES	APNOEAL
ANTRUM	AORTA	APES	APHORIZING	APNOEAS
ANTRUMS	AORTAE	APETALIES	APHOTIC	APNOEIC
ANTS	AORTAL	APETALOUS	APHRODITE	APO
ANTSIER	AORTAS	APETALY	APHRODITES	APOAPSES
ANTSIEST	AORTIC	APEX	APHTHA	APOAPSIDES
ANTSINESS	AOUDAD	APEXES	APHTHAE	APOAPSIS
ANTSINESSES	AOUDADS	APHAGIA	APHTHOUS	APOCARP
ANTSY	APACE	APHAGIAS	APHYLLIES	APOCARPIES
ANURAL	APACHE	APHANITE	APHYLLOUS	APOCARPS
ANURAN	APACHES	APHANITES	APHYLLY	APOCARPY
ANURANS	APAGOGE	APHANITIC	APIACEOUS	APOCOPATE
ANURESES	APAGOGES	APHASIA	APIAN	APOCOPATED
ANURESIS	APAGOGIC	APHASIAC	APIARIAN	APOCOPATES
ANURETIC	APANAGE	APHASIACS	APIARIANS	APOCOPATING
ANURIA	APANAGES	APHASIAS	APIARIES	APOCOPE
ANURIAS	APAREJO	APHASIC	APIARIST	APOCOPES
ANURIC	APAREJOS	APHASICS	APIARISTS	APOCOPIC
ANUROUS	APART	APHELIA	APIARY	APOCRINE
ANUS	APARTHEID	APHELIAN	APICAL	APOCRYPHA
ANUSES	APARTHEIDS	APHELION	APICALLY	APOD
ANVIL	APARTMENT	APHELIONS	APICALS	APODAL
ANVILED	APARTMENTS	APHERESES	APICES	APODICTIC
ANVILING	APARTNESS	APHERESIS	APICULATE	APODOSES
ANVILLED	APARTNESSES	APHERETIC	APICULI	APODOSIS
ANVILLING	APATETIC	APHESES	APICULUS	APODOUS
ANVILS	APATHETIC	APHESIS	APIECE	APODS
ANVILTOP	APATHIES	APHETIC	APIMANIA	APOENZYME
ANVILTOPS	APATHY	APHID	APIMANIAS	APOENZYMES
ANXIETIES	APATITE	APHIDES	APING	APOGAMIC
ANXIETY	APATITES	APHIDIAN	APIOLOGIES	APOGAMIES
ANXIOUS	APATOSAUR	APHIDIANS	APIOLOGY	APOGAMOUS
ANXIOUSLY	APATOSAURS	APHIDS	APISH	APOGAMY
ANY	APE	APHIS	APISHLY	APOGEAL
ANYBODIES	APEAK	APHOLATE	APISHNESS	APOGEAN
ANYBODY	APED	APHOLATES	APISHNESSES	APOGEE
ANYHOW	APEEK	APHONIA	APIVOROUS	APOGEES
ANYMORE	APELIKE	APHONIAS	APLANATIC	APOGEIC
ANYON	APER	APHONIC	APLASIA	APOLLO
ANYONE	APERCU	APHONICS	APLASIAS	APOLLOS
ANYONS	APERCUS	APHORISE	APLASTIC	APOLOG
ANYPLACE	APERIENT	APHORISED	APLENTY	APOLOGAL
ANYTHING	APERIENTS	APHORISES	APLITE	APOLOGIA
ANYTHINGS	APERIES	APHORISING	APLITES	APOLOGIAE
ANYTIME	APERIODIC	APHORISM	APLITIC	APOLOGIAS
ANYWAY	APERITIF	APHORISMS	APLOMB	APOLOGIES

APOLOGISE	APOSTLES	APPELLANTS	APPLETS	APPRESSED
APOLOGISED	APOSTOLIC	APPELLATE	APPLIABLE	APPRISE
APOLOGISES	APOTHECE	APPELLEE	APPLIANCE	APPRISED
APOLOGISING	APOTHECES	APPELLEES	APPLIANCES	APPRISER
APOLOGIST	APOTHECIA	APPELLOR	APPLICANT	APPRISERS
APOLOGISTS	APOTHECIUM	APPELLORS	APPLICANTS	APPRISES
APOLOGIZE	APOTHEGM	APPELS	APPLIED	APPRISING
APOLOGIZED	APOTHEGMS	APPEND	APPLIER	APPRIZE
APOLOGIZES	APOTHEM	APPENDAGE	APPLIERS	APPRIZED
APOLOGIZING	APOTHEMS	APPENDAGES	APPLIES	APPRIZER
APOLOGS	APP	APPENDANT	APPLIQUE	APPRIZERS
APOLOGUE	APPAL	APPENDANTS	APPLIQUED	APPRIZES
APOLOGUES	APPALL	APPENDED	APPLIQUEING	APPRIZING
APOLOGY	APPALLED	APPENDENT	APPLIQUES	APPROACH
APOLUNE	APPALLING	APPENDENTS	APPLY	APPROACHED
APOLUNES	APPALLS	APPENDICES	APPLYING	APPROACHES
APOMICT	APPALOOSA	APPENDING	APPOINT	APPROACHING
APOMICTIC	APPALOOSAS	APPENDIX	APPOINTED	APPROBATE
APOMICTS	APPALS	APPENDIXES	APPOINTEE	APPROBATED
APOMIXES	APPANAGE	APPENDS	APPOINTEES	APPROBATES
APOMIXIS	APPANAGES	APPERTAIN	APPOINTER	APPROBATING
APOPHASES	APPARAT	APPERTAINED	APPOINTERS	APPROVAL
APOPHASIS	APPARATS	APPERTAINING	APPOINTING	APPROVALS
APOPHONIES	APPARATUS	APPERTAINS	APPOINTOR	APPROVE
APOPHONY	APPARATUSES	APPESTAT	APPOINTORS	APPROVED
APOPHYGE	APPAREL	APPESTATS	APPOINTS	APPROVER
APOPHYGES	APPARELED	APPETENCE	APPORTION	APPROVERS
APOPHYSES	APPARELING	APPETENCES	APPORTIONED	APPROVES
APOPHYSIS	APPARELLED	APPETENCIES	APPORTIONING	APPROVING
APOPLEXIES	APPARELLING	APPETENCY	APPORTIONS	APPS
APOPLEXY	APPARELS	APPETENT	APPOSABLE	APPULSE
APOPTOSES	APPARENT	APPETISER	APPOSE	APPULSES
APOPTOSIS	APPARITOR	APPETISERS	APPOSED	APRACTIC
APOPTOTIC	APPARITORS	APPETITE	APPOSER	APRAXIA
APORIA	APPEAL	APPETITES	APPOSERS	APRAXIAS
APORIAS	APPEALED	APPETIZER	APPOSES	APRAXIC
APORT	APPEALER	APPETIZERS	APPOSING	APRES
APOS	APPEALERS	APPLAUD	APPOSITE	APRICOT
APOSPORIC	APPEALING	APPLAUDED	APPRAISAL	APRICOTS
APOSPORIES	APPEALS	APPLAUDER	APPRAISALS	APRIORITIES
APOSPORY	APPEAR	APPLAUDERS	APPRAISE	APRIORITY
APOSTACIES	APPEARED	APPLAUDING	APPRAISED	APRON
APOSTACY	APPEARING	APPLAUDS	APPRAISEE	APRONED
APOSTASIES	APPEARS	APPLAUSE	APPRAISEES	APRONING
APOSTASY	APPEASE	APPLAUSES	APPRAISER	APRONLIKE
APOSTATE	APPEASED	APPLE	APPRAISERS	APRONS
APOSTATES	APPEASER	APPLECART	APPRAISES	APROPOS
APOSTIL	APPEASERS	APPLECARTS	APPRAISING	APROTIC
APOSTILLE	APPEASES	APPLEJACK	APPREHEND	APSE
APOSTILLES	APPEASING	APPLEJACKS	APPREHENDED	APSES
APOSTILS	APPEL	APPLES	APPREHENDING	APSIDAL
APOSTLE	APPELLANT	APPLET	APPREHENDS	APSIDES

APSIS	AQUATONES	ARAPAIMAS	ARBUTEAN	ARCHEAN
APT	AQUAVIT	ARAROBA	ARBUTES	ARCHED
APTER	AQUAVITS	ARAROBAS	ARBUTUS	ARCHENEMIES
APTERAL	AQUEDUCT	ARAUCARIA	ARBUTUSES	ARCHENEMY
APTERIA	AQUEDUCTS	ARAUCARIAS	ARC	ARCHER
APTERIUM	AQUEOUS	ARB	ARCADE	ARCHERIES
APTEROUS	AQUEOUSLY	ARBALEST	ARCADED	ARCHERS
APTERYX	AQUIFER	ARBALESTS	ARCADES	ARCHERY
APTERYXES	AQUIFERS	ARBALIST	ARCADIA	ARCHES
APTEST	AQUILEGIA	ARBALISTS	ARCADIAN	ARCHETYPE
APTITUDE	AQUILEGIAS	ARBELEST	ARCADIANS	ARCHETYPES
APTITUDES	AQUILINE	ARBELESTS	ARCADIAS	ARCHFIEND
APTLY	AQUIVER	ARBITER	ARCADING	ARCHFIENDS
APTNESS	AR	ARBITERS	ARCADINGS	ARCHFOE
APTNESSES	ARABESK	ARBITRAGE	ARCANA	ARCHFOES
APYRASE	ARABESKS	ARBITRAGED	ARCANE	ARCHICARP
APYRASES	ARABESQUE	ARBITRAGES	ARCANUM	ARCHICARPS
APYRETIC	ARABESQUES	ARBITRAGING	ARCANUMS	ARCHIL
AQUA	ARABIC	ARBITRAL	ARCATURE	ARCHILS
AQUACADE	ARABICA	ARBITRARY	ARCATURES	ARCHINE
AQUACADES	ARABICAS	ARBITRATE	ARCCOSINE	ARCHINES
AQUAE	ARABICIZE	ARBITRATED	ARCCOSINES	ARCHING
AQUAFARM	ARABICIZED	ARBITRATES	ARCED	ARCHINGS
AQUAFARMED	ARABICIZES	ARBITRATING	ARCH	ARCHITECT
AQUAFARMING	ARABICIZING	ARBITRESS	ARCHAEA	ARCHITECTS
AQUAFARMS	ARABILITIES	ARBITRESSES	ARCHAEAL	ARCHIVAL
AQUALUNG	ARABILITY	ARBOR	ARCHAEAN	ARCHIVE
AQUALUNGS	ARABINOSE	ARBOREAL	ARCHAEANS	ARCHIVED
AQUANAUT	ARABINOSES	ARBORED	ARCHAEON	ARCHIVES
AQUANAUTS	ARABIZE	ARBOREOUS	ARCHAIC	ARCHIVING
AQUAPLANE	ARABIZED	ARBORES	ARCHAICAL	ARCHIVIST
AQUAPLANED	ARABIZES	ARBORETA	ARCHAISE	ARCHIVISTS
AQUAPLANES	ARABIZING	ARBORETUM	ARCHAISED	ARCHIVOLT
AQUAPLANING	ARABLE	ARBORETUMS	ARCHAISES	ARCHIVOLTS
AQUARELLE	ARABLES	ARBORIST	ARCHAISING	ARCHLY
AQUARELLES	ARACEOUS	ARBORISTS	ARCHAISM	ARCHNESS
AQUARIA	ARACHNID	ARBORIZE	ARCHAISMS	ARCHNESSES
AQUARIAL	ARACHNIDS	ARBORIZED	ARCHAIST	ARCHON
AQUARIAN	ARACHNOID	ARBORIZES	ARCHAISTS	ARCHONS
AQUARIANS	ARACHNOIDS	ARBORIZING	ARCHAIZE	ARCHOSAUR
AQUARIST	ARAGONITE	ARBOROUS	ARCHAIZED	ARCHOSAURS
AQUARISTS	ARAGONITES	ARBORETA	ARCHAIZER	ARCHRIVAL
AQUARIUM	ARAK	ARBORS	ARCHAIZERS	ARCHRIVALS
AQUARIUMS	ARAKS	ARBOUR	ARCHAIZES	ARCHWAY
AQUAS	ARAME	ARBOURED	ARCHAIZING	ARCHWAYS
AQUATIC	ARAMES	ARBOURS	ARCHANGEL	ARCIFORM
AQUATICS	ARAMID	ARBOVIRAL	ARCHANGELS	ARCING
AQUATINT	ARAMIDS	ARBOVIRUS	ARCHDUCAL	ARCKED
AQUATINTED	ARANEID	ARBOVIRUSES	ARCHDUCHIES	ARCKING
AQUATINTING	ARANEIDAN	ARBS	ARCHDUCHY	ARCO
AQUATINTS	ARANEIDS	ARBUSCLE	ARCHDUKE	ARCS
AQUATONE	ARAPAIMA	ARBUSCLES	ARCHDUKES	ARCSINE
		ARBUTE		

ARCSINES	AREOLOGY	ARGUE	ARIOSI	ARMILLAE
ARCTIC	AREPA	ARGUED	ARIOSO	ARMILLARY
ARCTICS	AREPAS	ARGUER	ARIOSOS	ARMILLAS
ARCUATE	ARES	ARGUERS	ARISE	ARMING
ARCUATED	ARETE	ARGUES	ARISEN	ARMINGS
ARCUATELY	ARETES	ARGUFIED	ARISES	ARMISTICE
ARCUATION	ARETHUSA	ARGUFIER	ARISING	ARMISTICES
ARCUATIONS	ARETHUSAS	ARGUFIERS	ARISTA	ARMLESS
ARCUS	ARF	ARGUFIES	ARISTAE	ARMLET
ARCUSES	ARFS	ARGUFY	ARISTAS	ARMLETS
ARDEB	ARGAL	ARGUFYING	ARISTATE	ARMLIKE
ARDEBS	ARGALA	ARGUING	ARISTO	ARMLOAD
ARDENCIES	ARGALAS	ARGUMENT	ARISTOS	ARMLOADS
ARDENCY	ARGALI	ARGUMENTA	ARK	ARMLOCK
ARDENT	ARGALIS	ARGUMENTS	ARKOSE	ARMLOCKS
ARDENTLY	ARGALS	ARGUMENTUM	ARKOSES	ARMOIRE
ARDOR	ARGENT	ARGUS	ARKOSIC	ARMOIRES
ARDORS	ARGENTAL	ARGUSES	ARKS	ARMONICA
ARDOUR	ARGENTIC	ARGYLE	ARLES	ARMONICAS
ARDOURS	ARGENTINE	ARGYLES	ARM	ARMOR
ARDUOUS	ARGENTINES	ARGYLL	ARMADA	ARMORED
ARDUOUSLY	ARGENTITE	ARGYLLS	ARMADAS	ARMORER
ARE	ARGENTITES	ARHAT	ARMADILLO	ARMORERS
AREA	ARGENTOUS	ARHATS	ARMADILLOS	ARMORIAL
AREAE	ARGENTS	ARHATSHIP	ARMAGNAC	ARMORIALS
AREAL	ARGENTUM	ARHATSHIPS	ARMAGNACS	ARMORIES
AREALLY	ARGENTUMS	ARIA	ARMAMENT	ARMORING
AREAS	ARGIL	ARIARY	ARMAMENTS	ARMORLESS
AREAWAY	ARGILLITE	ARIAS	ARMATURE	ARMORS
AREAWAYS	ARGILLITES	ARID	ARMATURED	ARMORY
ARECA	ARGILS	ARIDER	ARMATURES	ARMOUR
ARECAS	ARGINASE	ARIDEST	ARMATURING	ARMOURED
ARECOLINE	ARGINASES	ARIDITIES	ARMBAND	ARMOURER
ARECOLINES	ARGININE	ARIDITY	ARMBANDS	ARMOURERS
AREIC	ARGININES	ARIDLY	ARMCHAIR	ARMOURIES
ARENA	ARGLE	ARIDNESS	ARMCHAIRS	ARMOURING
ARENAS	ARGLED	ARIDNESSES	ARMED	ARMOURS
ARENE	ARGLES	ARIEL	ARMER	ARMOURY
ARENES	ARGLING	ARIELS	ARMERS	ARMPIT
ARENITE	ARGOL	ARIETTA	ARMET	ARMPITS
ARENITES	ARGOLS	ARIETTAS	ARMETS	ARMREST
ARENOSE	ARGON	ARIETTE	ARMFUL	ARMRESTS
ARENOUS	ARGONAUT	ARIETTES	ARMFULS	ARMS
AREOLA	ARGONAUTS	ARIGHT	ARMHOLE	ARMSFUL
AREOLAE	ARGONS	ARIL	ARMHOLES	ARMURE
AREOLAR	ARGOSIES	ARILED	ARMIES	ARMURES
AREOLAS	ARGOSY	ARILLATE	ARMIGER	ARMY
AREOLATE	ARGOT	ARILLODE	ARMIGERAL	ARMYWORM
AREOLATED	ARGOTIC	ARILLODES	ARMIGERO	ARMYWORMS
AREOLE	ARGOTS	ARILLOID	ARMIGEROS	ARNATTO
AREOLES	ARGUABLE	ARILS	ARMIGERS	ARNATTOS
AREOLOGIES	ARGUABLY	ARIOSE	ARMILLA	ARNICA

ARNICAS	ARRANGER	ARROGANCIES	ARSONISTS	ARTIST
ARNOTTO	ARRANGERS	ARROGANCY	ARSONOUS	ARTISTE
ARNOTTOS	ARRANGES	ARROGANT	ARSONS	ARTISTES
AROID	ARRANGING	ARROGATE	ART	ARTISTIC
AROIDS	ARRANT	ARROGATED	ARTAL	ARTISTRIES
AROINT	ARRANTLY	ARROGATES	ARTEFACT	ARTISTRY
AROINTED	ARRAS	ARROGATING	ARTEFACTS	ARTISTS
AROINTING	ARRASED	ARROGATOR	ARTEL	ARTLESS
AROINTS	ARRASES	ARROGATORS	ARTELS	ARTLESSLY
AROMA	ARRAY	ARROW	ARTEMISIA	ARTS
AROMAS	ARRAYAL	ARROWED	ARTEMISIAS	ARTSIER
AROMATASE	ARRAYALS	ARROWHEAD	ARTERIAL	ARTSIEST
AROMATASES	ARRAYED	ARROWHEADS	ARTERIALS	ARTSINESS
AROMATIC	ARRAYER	ARROWING	ARTERIES	ARTSINESSES
AROMATICS	ARRAYERS	ARROWLESS	ARTERIOLE	ARTSY
AROMATIZE	ARRAYING	ARROWLIKE	ARTERIOLES	ARTWORK
AROMATIZED	ARRAYS	ARROWROOT	ARTERITIDES	ARTWORKS
AROMATIZES	ARREAR	ARROWROOTS	ARTERITIS	ARTY
AROMATIZING	ARREARAGE	ARROWS	ARTERY	ARUGOLA
AROSE	ARREARAGES	ARROWWOOD	ARTFUL	ARUGOLAS
AROUND	ARREARS	ARROWWOODS	ARTFULLY	ARUGULA
AROUSABLE	ARREST	ARROWWORM	ARTHRITIC	ARUGULAS
AROUSAL	ARRESTANT	ARROWWORMS	ARTHRITICS	ARUM
AROUSALS	ARRESTANTS	ARROWY	ARTHRITIDES	ARUMS
AROUSE	ARRESTED	ARROYO	ARTHRITIS	ARUSPEX
AROUSED	ARRESTEE	ARROYOS	ARTHROPOD	ARUSPICES
AROUSER	ARRESTEES	ARS	ARTHROPODS	ARVAL
AROUSERS	ARRESTER	ARSE	ARTHROSES	ARVO
AROUSES	ARRESTERS	ARSENAL	ARTHROSIS	ARVOS
AROUSING	ARRESTING	ARSENALS	ARTICHOKE	ARYL
AROYNT	ARRESTIVE	ARSENATE	ARTICHOKES	ARYLS
AROYNTED	ARRESTOR	ARSENATES	ARTICLE	ARYTENOID
AROYNTING	ARRESTORS	ARSENIC	ARTICLED	ARYTENOIDS
AROYNTS	ARRESTS	ARSENICAL	ARTICLES	ARYTHMIA
ARPEGGIO	ARRHIZAL	ARSENICALS	ARTICLING	ARYTHMIAS
ARPEGGIOS	ARRIBA	ARSENICS	ARTICULAR	ARYTHMIC
ARPEN	ARRIS	ARSENIDE	ARTIER	AS
ARPENS	ARRISES	ARSENIDES	ARTIEST	ASAFETIDA
ARPENT	ARRIVAL	ARSENIOUS	ARTIFACT	ASAFETIDAS
ARPENTS	ARRIVALS	ARSENITE	ARTIFACTS	ASANA
ARQUEBUS	ARRIVE	ARSENITES	ARTIFICE	ASANAS
ARQUEBUSES	ARRIVED	ARSENO	ARTIFICER	ASARUM
ARRACK	ARRIVER	ARSENOUS	ARTIFICERS	ASARUMS
ARRACKS	ARRIVERS	ARSES	ARTIFICES	ASBESTIC
ARRAIGN	ARRIVES	ARSHIN	ARTILLERIES	ASBESTINE
ARRAIGNED	ARRIVING	ARSHINS	ARTILLERY	ASBESTOS
ARRAIGNER	ARRIVISTE	ARSINE	ARTILY	ASBESTOSES
ARRAIGNERS	ARRIVISTES	ARSINES	ARTINESS	ASBESTOUS
ARRAIGNING	ARROBA	ARSINO	ARTINESSES	ASBESTUS
ARRAIGNS	ARROBAS	ARSIS	ARTISAN	ASBESTUSES
ARRANGE	ARROGANCE	ARSON	ARTISANAL	ASCARED
ARRANGED	ARROGANCES	ARSONIST	ARTISANS	ASCARID

ASCARIDES	ASCUS	ASKANCE	ASPERSIONS	ASSAIL
ASCARIDS	ASDIC	ASKANT	ASPERSIVE	ASSAILANT
ASCARIS	ASDICS	ASKED	ASPERSOR	ASSAILANTS
ASCEND	ASEA	ASKER	ASPERSORS	ASSAILED
ASCENDANT	ASEPSES	ASKERS	ASPHALT	ASSAILER
ASCENDANTS	ASEPSIS	ASKESES	ASPHALTED	ASSAILERS
ASCENDED	ASEPTIC	ASKESIS	ASPHALTIC	ASSAILING
ASCENDENT	ASEXUAL	ASKEW	ASPHALTING	ASSAILS
ASCENDENTS	ASEXUALLY	ASKEWNESS	ASPHALTS	ASSAIS
ASCENDER	ASH	ASKEWNESSES	ASPHALTUM	ASSASSIN
ASCENDERS	ASHAMED	ASKING	ASPHALTUMS	ASSASSINS
ASCENDING	ASHAMEDLY	ASKINGS	ASPHERIC	ASSAULT
ASCENDS	ASHCAKE	ASKOI	ASPHODEL	ASSAULTED
ASCENSION	ASHCAKES	ASKOS	ASPHODELS	ASSAULTER
ASCENSIONS	ASHCAN	ASKS	ASPHYXIA	ASSAULTERS
ASCENSIVE	ASHCANS	ASLANT	ASPHYXIAL	ASSAULTING
ASCENT	ASHED	ASLEEP	ASPHYXIAS	ASSAULTS
ASCENTS	ASHEN	ASLOPE	ASPHYXIES	ASSAY
ASCERTAIN	ASHES	ASLOSH	ASPHYXY	ASSAYABLE
ASCERTAINED	ASHFALL	ASOCIAL	ASPIC	ASSAYED
ASCERTAINING	ASHFALLS	ASOCIALS	ASPICS	ASSAYER
ASCERTAINS	ASHIER	ASP	ASPIRANT	ASSAYERS
ASCESES	ASHIEST	ASPARAGUS	ASPIRANTS	ASSAYING
ASCESIS	ASHINESS	ASPARAGUSES	ASPIRATA	ASSAYS
ASCETIC	ASHINESSES	ASPARKLE	ASPIRATAE	ASSEGAI
ASCETICAL	ASHING	ASPARTAME	ASPIRATE	ASSEGAIED
ASCETICS	ASHLAR	ASPARTAMES	ASPIRATED	ASSEGAIING
ASCI	ASHLARED	ASPARTATE	ASPIRATES	ASSEGAIS
ASCIDIA	ASHLARING	ASPARTATES	ASPIRATING	ASSEMBLE
ASCIDIAN	ASHLARS	ASPECT	ASPIRATOR	ASSEMBLED
ASCIDIANS	ASHLER	ASPECTS	ASPIRATORS	ASSEMBLER
ASCIDIATE	ASHLERED	ASPECTUAL	ASPIRE	ASSEMBLERS
ASCIDIUM	ASHLERING	ASPEN	ASPIRED	ASSEMBLES
ASCITES	ASHLERS	ASPENS	ASPIRER	ASSEMBLIES
ASCITIC	ASHLESS	ASPER	ASPIRERS	ASSEMBLING
ASCLEPIAD	ASHMAN	ASPERATE	ASPIRES	ASSEMBLY
ASCLEPIADS	ASHMEN	ASPERATED	ASPIRIN	ASSENT
ASCOCARP	ASHORE	ASPERATES	ASPIRING	ASSENTED
ASCOCARPS	ASHPLANT	ASPERATING	ASPIRINS	ASSENTER
ASCOGONIA	ASHPLANTS	ASPERGES	ASPIS	ASSENTERS
ASCOGONIUM	ASHRAM	ASPERGILL	ASPISES	ASSENTING
ASCORBATE	ASHRAMS	ASPERGILLS	ASPISH	ASSENTIVE
ASCORBATES	ASHTRAY	ASPERITIES	ASPS	ASSENTOR
ASCORBIC	ASHTRAYS	ASPERITY	ASQUINT	ASSENTORS
ASCOSPORE	ASHY	ASPERS	ASRAMA	ASSENTS
ASCOSPORES	ASIDE	ASPERSE	ASRAMAS	ASSERT
ASCOT	ASIDES	ASPERSED	ASS	ASSERTED
ASCOTS	ASININE	ASPERSER	ASSAGAI	ASSERTER
ASCRIBE	ASININELY	ASPERSERS	ASSAGAIED	ASSERTERS
ASCRIBED	ASININITIES	ASPERSES	ASSAGAIING	ASSERTING
ASCRIBES	ASININITY	ASPERSING	ASSAGAIS	ASSERTION
ASCRIBING	ASK	ASPERSION	ASSAI	ASSERTIONS

ASSERTIVE	ASSOILS	ASTER	ASTRAL	ATAGHAN
ASSERTOR	ASSONANCE	ASTERIA	ASTRALLY	ATAGHANS
ASSERTORS	ASSONANCES	ASTERIAS	ASTRALS	ATALAYA
ASSERTS	ASSONANT	ASTERISK	ASTRAY	ATALAYAS
ASSES	ASSONANTS	ASTERISKED	ASTRICT	ATAMAN
ASSESS	ASSORT	ASTERISKING	ASTRICTED	ATAMANS
ASSESSED	ASSORTED	ASTERISKS	ASTRICTING	ATAMASCO
ASSESSES	ASSORTER	ASTERISM	ASTRICTS	ATAMASCOS
ASSESSING	ASSORTERS	ASTERISMS	ASTRIDE	ATAP
ASSESSOR	ASSORTING	ASTERN	ASTRINGE	ATAPS
ASSESSORS	ASSORTS	ASTERNAL	ASTRINGED	ATARACTIC
ASSET	ASSUAGE	ASTEROID	ASTRINGES	ATARACTICS
ASSETLESS	ASSUAGED	ASTEROIDS	ASTRINGING	ATARAXIA
ASSETS	ASSUAGER	ASTERS	ASTROCYTE	ATARAXIAS
ASSHOLE	ASSUAGERS	ASTHENIA	ASTROCYTES	ATARAXIC
ASSHOLES	ASSUAGES	ASTHENIAS	ASTRODOME	ATARAXICS
ASSIDUITIES	ASSUAGING	ASTHENIC	ASTRODOMES	ATARAXIES
ASSIDUITY	ASSUASIVE	ASTHENICS	ASTROLABE	ATARAXY
ASSIDUOUS	ASSUMABLE	ASTHENIES	ASTROLABES	ATAVIC
ASSIGN	ASSUMABLY	ASTHENY	ASTROLOGIES	ATAVISM
ASSIGNAT	ASSUME	ASTHMA	ASTROLOGY	ATAVISMS
ASSIGNATS	ASSUMED	ASTHMAS	ASTRONAUT	ATAVIST
ASSIGNED	ASSUMEDLY	ASTHMATIC	ASTRONAUTS	ATAVISTIC
ASSIGNEE	ASSUMER	ASTHMATICS	ASTRONOMIES	ATAVISTS
ASSIGNEES	ASSUMERS	ASTIGMIA	ASTRONOMY	ATAXIA
ASSIGNER	ASSUMES	ASTIGMIAS	ASTUTE	ATAXIAS
ASSIGNERS	ASSUMING	ASTILBE	ASTUTELY	ATAXIC
ASSIGNING	ASSUMPSIT	ASTILBES	ASTYLAR	ATAXICS
ASSIGNOR	ASSUMPSITS	ASTIR	ASUNDER	ATAXIES
ASSIGNORS	ASSURABLE	ASTOMATAL	ASWARM	ATAXY
ASSIGNS	ASSURANCE	ASTOMOUS	ASWIRL	ATE
ASSIST	ASSURANCES	ASTONIED	ASWOON	ATECHNIC
ASSISTANT	ASSURE	ASTONIES	ASYLA	ATELIC
ASSISTANTS	ASSURED	ASTONISH	ASYLLABIC	ATELIER
ASSISTED	ASSUREDLY	ASTONISHED	ASYLUM	ATELIERS
ASSISTER	ASSUREDS	ASTONISHES	ASYLUMS	ATEMOYA
ASSISTERS	ASSURER	ASTONISHING	ASYMMETRIES	ATEMOYAS
ASSISTING	ASSURERS	ASTONY	ASYMMETRY	ATEMPORAL
ASSISTIVE	ASSURES	ASTONYING	ASYMPTOTE	ATENOLOL
ASSISTOR	ASSURGENT	ASTOUND	ASYMPTOTES	ATENOLOLS
ASSISTORS	ASSURING	ASTOUNDED	ASYNAPSES	ATES
ASSISTS	ASSUROR	ASTOUNDING	ASYNAPSIS	ATHANASIES
ASSIZE	ASSURORS	ASTOUNDS	ASYNDETA	ATHANASY
ASSIZES	ASSWAGE	ASTRACHAN	ASYNDETIC	ATHEISM
ASSLIKE	ASSWAGED	ASTRACHANS	ASYNDETON	ATHEISMS
ASSOCIATE	ASSWAGES	ASTRADDLE	ASYNDETONS	ATHEIST
ASSOCIATED	ASSWAGING	ASTRAGAL	AT	ATHEISTIC
ASSOCIATES	ASTASIA	ASTRAGALI	ATABAL	ATHEISTS
ASSOCIATING	ASTASIAS	ASTRAGALS	ATABALS	ATHELING
ASSOIL	ASTATIC	ASTRAGALUS	ATABRINE	ATHELINGS
ASSOILED	ASTATINE	ASTRAKHAN	ATABRINES	ATHENAEUM
ASSOILING	ASTATINES	ASTRAKHANS	ATACTIC	ATHENAEUMS

ATHENEUM	ATOMIZE	ATROCITIES	ATTEMPTED	ATTORNEY
ATHENEUMS	ATOMIZED	ATROCITY	ATTEMPTER	ATTORNEYS
ATHEROMA	ATOMIZER	ATROPHIA	ATTEMPTERS	ATTORNING
ATHEROMAS	ATOMIZERS	ATROPHIAS	ATTEMPTING	ATTORNS
ATHEROMATA	ATOMIZES	ATROPHIC	ATTEMPTS	ATTRACT
ATHETOID	ATOMIZING	ATROPHIED	ATTEND	ATTRACTED
ATHETOSES	ATOMS	ATROPHIES	ATTENDANT	ATTRACTER
ATHETOSIS	ATOMY	ATROPHY	ATTENDANTS	ATTRACTERS
ATHETOTIC	ATONABLE	ATROPHYING	ATTENDED	ATTRACTING
ATHIRST	ATONAL	ATROPIN	ATTENDEE	ATTRACTOR
ATHLETE	ATONALISM	ATROPINE	ATTENDEES	ATTRACTORS
ATHLETES	ATONALISMS	ATROPINES	ATTENDER	ATTRACTS
ATHLETIC	ATONALIST	ATROPINS	ATTENDERS	ATTRIBUTE
ATHLETICS	ATONALISTS	ATROPISM	ATTENDING	ATTRIBUTED
ATHODYD	ATONALITIES	ATROPISMS	ATTENDINGS	ATTRIBUTES
ATHODYDS	ATONALITY	ATT	ATTENDS	ATTRIBUTING
ATHROCYTE	ATONALLY	ATTABOY	ATTENT	ATTRIT
ATHROCYTES	ATONE	ATTACH	ATTENTION	ATTRITE
ATHWART	ATONEABLE	ATTACHE	ATTENTIONS	ATTRITED
ATILT	ATONED	ATTACHED	ATTENTIVE	ATTRITES
ATINGLE	ATONEMENT	ATTACHER	ATTENUATE	ATTRITING
ATLANTES	ATONEMENTS	ATTACHERS	ATTENUATED	ATTRITION
ATLAS	ATONER	ATTACHES	ATTENUATES	ATTRITIONS
ATLASES	ATONERS	ATTACHING	ATTENUATING	ATTRITIVE
ATLATL	ATONES	ATTACK	ATTEST	ATTRITS
ATLATLS	ATONIA	ATTACKED	ATTESTANT	ATTRITTED
ATMA	ATONIAS	ATTACKER	ATTESTANTS	ATTRITTING
ATMAN	ATONIC	ATTACKERS	ATTESTED	ATTUNE
ATMANS	ATONICITIES	ATTACKING	ATTESTER	ATTUNED
ATMAS	ATONICITY	ATTACKMAN	ATTESTERS	ATTUNES
ATMOMETER	ATONICS	ATTACKMEN	ATTESTING	ATTUNING
ATMOMETERS	ATONIES	ATTACKS	ATTESTOR	ATWAIN
ATOLL	ATONING	ATTAGIRL	ATTESTORS	ATWEEN
ATOLLS	ATONINGLY	ATTAIN	ATTESTS	ATWITTER
ATOM	ATONY	ATTAINDER	ATTIC	ATYPIC
ATOMIC	ATOP	ATTAINDERS	ATTICISM	ATYPICAL
ATOMICAL	ATOPIC	ATTAINED	ATTICISMS	AUBADE
ATOMICITIES	ATOPIES	ATTAINER	ATTICIST	AUBADES
ATOMICITY	ATOPY	ATTAINERS	ATTICISTS	AUBERGE
ATOMICS	ATRAZINE	ATTAINING	ATTICIZE	AUBERGES
ATOMIES	ATRAZINES	ATTAINS	ATTICIZED	AUBERGINE
ATOMISE	ATREMBLE	ATTAINT	ATTICIZES	AUBERGINES
ATOMISED	ATRESIA	ATTAINTED	ATTICIZING	AUBRETIA
ATOMISER	ATRESIAS	ATTAINTING	ATTICS	AUBRETIAS
ATOMISERS	ATRESIC	ATTAINTS	ATTIRE	AUBRIETA
ATOMISES	ATRETIC	ATTAR	ATTIRED	AUBRIETAS
ATOMISING	ATRIA	ATTARS	ATTIRES	AUBRIETIA
ATOMISM	ATRIAL	ATTEMPER	ATTIRING	AUBRIETIAS
ATOMISMS	ATRIP	ATTEMPERED	ATTITUDE	AUBURN
ATOMIST	ATRIUM	ATTEMPERING	ATTITUDES	AUBURNS
ATOMISTIC	ATRIUMS	ATTEMPERS	ATTORN	AUCTION
ATOMISTS	ATROCIOUS	ATTEMPT	ATTORNED	AUCTIONED

AUCTIONING	AUDITORIES	AUNTLY	AUSFORMS	AUTHORISED
AUCTIONS	AUDITORIUM	AUNTS	AUSLANDER	AUTHORISES
AUCTORIAL	AUDITORIUMS	AUNTY	AUSLANDERS	AUTHORISING
AUCUBA	AUDITORS	AURA	AUSPEX	AUTHORITIES
AUCUBAS	AUDITORY	AURAE	AUSPICATE	AUTHORITY
AUDACIOUS	AUDITS	AURAL	AUSPICATED	AUTHORIZE
AUDACITIES	AUGEND	AURALITIES	AUSPICATES	AUTHORIZED
AUDACITY	AUGENDS	AURALITY	AUSPICATING	AUTHORIZES
AUDAD	AUGER	AURALLY	AUSPICE	AUTHORIZING
AUDADS	AUGERS	AURAR	AUSPICES	AUTHORS
AUDIAL	AUGHT	AURAS	AUSTENITE	AUTISM
AUDIBLE	AUGHTS	AURATE	AUSTENITES	AUTISMS
AUDIBLED	AUGITE	AURATED	AUSTERE	AUTIST
AUDIBLES	AUGITES	AUREATE	AUSTERELY	AUTISTIC
AUDIBLING	AUGITIC	AUREATELY	AUSTERER	AUTISTICS
AUDIBLY	AUGMENT	AUREI	AUSTEREST	AUTISTS
AUDIENCE	AUGMENTED	AUREOLA	AUSTERITIES	AUTO
AUDIENCES	AUGMENTER	AUREOLAE	AUSTERITY	AUTOBAHN
AUDIENT	AUGMENTERS	AUREOLAS	AUSTRAL	AUTOBAHNEN
AUDIENTS	AUGMENTING	AUREOLE	AUSTRALES	AUTOBAHNS
AUDILE	AUGMENTOR	AUREOLED	AUSTRALS	AUTOBUS
AUDILES	AUGMENTORS	AUREOLES	AUSUBO	AUTOBUSES
AUDING	AUGMENTS	AUREOLING	AUSUBOS	AUTOBUSSES
AUDINGS	AUGUR	AURES	AUTACOID	AUTOCADE
AUDIO	AUGURAL	AUREUS	AUTACOIDS	AUTOCADES
AUDIOBOOK	AUGURED	AURIC	AUTARCH	AUTOCLAVE
AUDIOBOOKS	AUGURER	AURICLE	AUTARCHIC	AUTOCLAVED
AUDIOGRAM	AUGURERS	AURICLED	AUTARCHIES	AUTOCLAVES
AUDIOGRAMS	AUGURIES	AURICLES	AUTARCHS	AUTOCLAVING
AUDIOLOGIES	AUGURING	AURICULA	AUTARCHY	AUTOCOID
AUDIOLOGY	AUGURS	AURICULAE	AUTARKIC	AUTOCOIDS
AUDIOS	AUGURY	AURICULAR	AUTARKIES	AUTOCRACIES
AUDIOTAPE	AUGUST	AURICULARS	AUTARKIST	AUTOCRACY
AUDIOTAPED	AUGUSTER	AURICULAS	AUTARKISTS	AUTOCRAT
AUDIOTAPES	AUGUSTEST	AURIFORM	AUTARKY	AUTOCRATS
AUDIOTAPING	AUGUSTLY	AURIS	AUTECIOUS	AUTOCRINE
AUDIPHONE	AUK	AURIST	AUTECISM	AUTOCROSS
AUDIPHONES	AUKLET	AURISTS	AUTECISMS	AUTOCROSSES
AUDIT	AUKLETS	AUROCHS	AUTEUR	AUTODYNE
AUDITABLE	AUKS	AUROCHSES	AUTEURISM	AUTODYNES
AUDITED	AULD	AURORA	AUTEURISMS	AUTOECISM
AUDITEE	AULDER	AURORAE	AUTEURIST	AUTOECISMS
AUDITEES	AULDEST	AURORAL	AUTEURISTS	AUTOED
AUDITING	AULIC	AURORALLY	AUTEURS	AUTOFOCUS
AUDITION	AUNT	AURORAS	AUTHENTIC	AUTOFOCUSES
AUDITIONED	AUNTHOOD	AUROREAN	AUTHOR	AUTOGAMIC
AUDITIONING	AUNTHOODS	AUROUS	AUTHORED	AUTOGAMIES
AUDITIONS	AUNTIE	AURUM	AUTHORESS	AUTOGAMY
AUDITIVE	AUNTIES	AURUMS	AUTHORESSES	AUTOGENIC
AUDITIVES	AUNTLIER	AUSFORM	AUTHORIAL	AUTOGENIES
AUDITOR	AUNTLIEST	AUSFORMED	AUTHORING	AUTOGENY
AUDITORIA	AUNTLIKE	AUSFORMING	AUTHORISE	AUTOGIRO

AUTOGIROS	AUTOPILOT	AVAILS	AVERTER	AVIONS
AUTOGRAFT	AUTOPILOTS	AVALANCHE	AVERTERS	AVIRULENT
AUTOGRAFTED	AUTOPSIC	AVALANCHED	AVERTIBLE	AVISO
AUTOGRAFTING	AUTOPSIED	AVALANCHES	AVERTING	AVISOS
AUTOGRAFTS	AUTOPSIES	AVALANCHING	AVERTS	AVO
AUTOGRAPH	AUTOPSIST	AVANT	AVES	AVOCADO
AUTOGRAPHED	AUTOPSISTS	AVARICE	AVGAS	AVOCADOES
AUTOGRAPHING	AUTOPSY	AVARICES	AVGASES	AVOCADOS
AUTOGRAPHS	AUTOPSYING	AVASCULAR	AVGASSES	AVOCATION
AUTOGYRO	AUTOROUTE	AVAST	AVIAN	AVOCATIONS
AUTOGYROS	AUTOROUTES	AVATAR	AVIANIZE	AVOCET
AUTOHARP	AUTOS	AVATARS	AVIANIZED	AVOCETS
AUTOHARPS	AUTOSOMAL	AVAUNT	AVIANIZES	AVODIRE
AUTOING	AUTOSOME	AVE	AVIANIZING	AVODIRES
AUTOLYSE	AUTOSOMES	AVELLAN	AVIANS	AVOID
AUTOLYSED	AUTOTELIC	AVELLANE	AVIARIES	AVOIDABLE
AUTOLYSES	AUTOTOMIC	AVENGE	AVIARIST	AVOIDABLY
AUTOLYSIN	AUTOTOMIES	AVENGED	AVIARISTS	AVOIDANCE
AUTOLYSING	AUTOTOMY	AVENGEFUL	AVIARY	AVOIDANCES
AUTOLYSINS	AUTOTOXIC	AVENGER	AVIATE	AVOIDED
AUTOLYSIS	AUTOTOXIN	AVENGERS	AVIATED	AVOIDER
AUTOLYTIC	AUTOTOXINS	AVENGES	AVIATES	AVOIDERS
AUTOLYZE	AUTOTROPH	AVENGING	AVIATIC	AVOIDING
AUTOLYZED	AUTOTROPHS	AVENS	AVIATING	AVOIDS
AUTOLYZES	AUTOTYPE	AVENSES	AVIATION	AVOS
AUTOLYZING	AUTOTYPES	AVENTAIL	AVIATIONS	AVOSET
AUTOMAKER	AUTOTYPIES	AVENTAILS	AVIATOR	AVOSETS
AUTOMAKERS	AUTOTYPY	AVENTURIN	AVIATORS	AVOUCH
AUTOMAN	AUTUMN	AVENTURINS	AVIATRESS	AVOUCHED
AUTOMAT	AUTUMNAL	AVENUE	AVIATRESSES	AVOUCHER
AUTOMATA	AUTUMNS	AVENUES	AVIATRICE	AVOUCHERS
AUTOMATE	AUTUNITE	AVER	AVIATRICES	AVOUCHES
AUTOMATED	AUTUNITES	AVERAGE	AVIATRIX	AVOUCHING
AUTOMATES	AUXESES	AVERAGED	AVIATRIXES	AVOW
AUTOMATIC	AUXESIS	AVERAGELY	AVICULAR	AVOWABLE
AUTOMATICS	AUXETIC	AVERAGES	AVID	AVOWABLY
AUTOMATING	AUXETICS	AVERAGING	AVIDIN	AVOWAL
AUTOMATON	AUXILIARIES	AVERMENT	AVIDINS	AVOWALS
AUTOMATONS	AUXILIARY	AVERMENTS	AVIDITIES	AVOWED
AUTOMATS	AUXIN	AVERRABLE	AVIDITY	AVOWEDLY
AUTOMEN	AUXINIC	AVERRED	AVIDLY	AVOWER
AUTONOMIC	AUXINS	AVERRING	AVIDNESS	AVOWERS
AUTONOMIES	AUXOTROPH	AVERS	AVIDNESSES	AVOWING
AUTONOMY	AUXOTROPHS	AVERSE	AVIFAUNA	AVOWS
AUTONYM	AVA	AVERSELY	AVIFAUNAE	AVULSE
AUTONYMS	AVADAVAT	AVERSION	AVIFAUNAL	AVULSED
AUTOPEN	AVADAVATS	AVERSIONS	AVIFAUNAS	AVULSES
AUTOPENS	AVAIL	AVERSIVE	AVIGATOR	AVULSING
AUTOPHAGIES	AVAILABLE	AVERSIVES	AVIGATORS	AVULSION
AUTOPHAGY	AVAILABLY	AVERT	AVION	AVULSIONS
AUTOPHYTE	AVAILED	AVERTABLE	AVIONIC	AVUNCULAR
AUTOPHYTES	AVAILING	AVERTED	AVIONICS	AW

AWA	AWHILE	AXIOLOGY	AZAN	AZURITES
AWAIT	AWHIRL	AXIOM	AZANS	AZYGOS
AWAITED	AWING	AXIOMATIC	AZEDARACH	AZYGOSES
AWAITER	AWKWARD	AXIOMS	AZEDARACHS	AZYGOUS
AWAITERS	AWKWARDER	AXION	AZEOTROPE	
AWAITING	AWKWARDEST	AXIONS	AZEOTROPES	
AWAITS	AWKWARDLY	AXIS	AZEOTROPIES	B
AWAKE	AWL	AXISED	AZEOTROPY	
AWAKED	AWLESS	AXISES	AZIDE	
AWAKEN	AWLS	AXITE	AZIDES	BA
AWAKENED	AWLWORT	AXITES	AZIDO	BAA
AWAKENER	AWLWORTS	AXLE	AZIMUTH	BAAED
AWAKENERS	AWMOUS	AXLED	AZIMUTHAL	BAAING
AWAKENING	AWN	AXLES	AZIMUTHS	BAAL
AWAKENINGS	AWNED	AXLETREE	AZINE	BAALIM
AWAKENS	AWNING	AXLETREES	AZINES	BAALISM
AWAKES	AWNINGED	AXLIKE	AZLON	BAALISMS
AWAKING	AWNINGS	AXMAN	AZLONS	BAALS
AWARD	AWNLESS	AXMEN	AZO	BAAS
AWARDABLE	AWNS	AXOLOTL	AZOIC	BAASES
AWARDED	AWNY	AXOLOTLS	AZOLE	BAASKAAP
AWARDEE	AWOKE	AXON	AZOLES	BAASKAAPS
AWARDEES	AWOKEN	AXONAL	AZON	BAASKAP
AWARDER	AWOL	AXONE	AZONAL	BAASKAPS
AWARDERS	AWOLS	AXONEMAL	AZONIC	BAASSKAP
AWARDING	AWRY	AXONEME	AZONS	BAASSKAPS
AWARDS	AX	AXONEMES	AZOTE	BABA
AWARE	AXAL	AXONES	AZOTED	BABAS
AWARENESS	AXE	AXONIC	AZOTEMIA	BABASSU
AWARENESSES	AXED	AXONS	AZOTEMIAS	BABASSUS
AWASH	AXEL	AXOPLASM	AZOTEMIC	BABBITRIES
AWAY	AXELS	AXOPLASMS	AZOTES	BABBITRY
AWAYNESS	AXEMAN	AXSEED	AZOTH	BABBITT
AWAYNESSES	AXEMEN	AXSEEDS	AZOTHS	BABBITTED
AWE	AXENIC	AY	AZOTIC	BABBITTING
AWEARY	AXES	AYAH	AZOTISE	BABBITTRIES
AWEATHER	AXIAL	AYAHS	AZOTISED	BABBITTRY
AWED	AXIALITIES	AYAHUASCA	AZOTISES	BABBITTS
AWEE	AXIALITY	AYAHUASCAS	AZOTISING	BABBLE
AWEIGH	AXIALLY	AYATOLLAH	AZOTIZE	BABBLED
AWEING	AXIL	AYATOLLAHS	AZOTIZED	BABBLER
AWELESS	AXILE	AYE	AZOTIZES	BABBLERS
AWES	AXILLA	AYES	AZOTIZING	BABBLES
AWESOME	AXILLAE	AYIN	AZOTURIA	BABBLING
AWESOMELY	AXILLAR	AYINS	AZOTURIAS	BABBLINGS
AWESTRUCK	AXILLARIES	AYS	AZUKI	BABE
AWFUL	AXILLARS	AYURVEDA	AZUKIS	BABEL
AWFULLER	AXILLARY	AYURVEDAS	AZULEJO	BABELS
AWFULLEST	AXILLAS	AYURVEDIC	AZULEJOS	BABES
AWFULLY	AXILS	AYURVEDICS	AZURE	BABESIA
AWFULNESS	AXING	AZALEA	AZURES	BABESIAS
AWFULNESSES	AXIOLOGIES	AZALEAS	AZURITE	BABICHE

BABICHES	BACCHANAL	BACKCLOTHS	BACKHOEING	BACKSEAT
BABIED	BACCHANALS	BACKCOURT	BACKHOES	BACKSEATS
BABIER	BACCHANT	BACKCOURTS	BACKHOUSE	BACKSET
BABIES	BACCHANTE	BACKCROSS	BACKHOUSES	BACKSETS
BABIEST	BACCHANTES	BACKCROSSED	BACKING	BACKSHORE
BABIRUSA	BACCHANTS	BACKCROSSES	BACKINGS	BACKSHORES
BABIRUSAS	BACCHIC	BACKCROSSING	BACKLAND	BACKSIDE
BABIRUSSA	BACCHII	BACKDATE	BACKLANDS	BACKSIDES
BABIRUSSAS	BACCHIUS	BACKDATED	BACKLASH	BACKSLAP
BABKA	BACCIFORM	BACKDATES	BACKLASHED	BACKSLAPPED
BABKAS	BACH	BACKDATING	BACKLASHES	BACKSLAPPING
BABOO	BACHED	BACKDOOR	BACKLASHING	BACKSLAPS
BABOOL	BACHELOR	BACKDRAFT	BACKLESS	BACKSLASH
BABOOLS	BACHELORS	BACKDRAFTS	BACKLIGHT	BACKSLASHES
BABOON	BACHES	BACKDROP	BACKLIGHTED	BACKSLID
BABOONERIES	BACHING	BACKDROPPED	BACKLIGHTING	BACKSLIDDEN
BABOONERY	BACILLAR	BACKDROPPING	BACKLIGHTS	BACKSLIDE
BABOONISH	BACILLARY	BACKDROPS	BACKLIST	BACKSLIDES
BABOONS	BACILLI	BACKDROPT	BACKLISTED	BACKSLIDING
BABOOS	BACILLUS	BACKED	BACKLISTING	BACKSPACE
BABU	BACK	BACKER	BACKLISTS	BACKSPACED
BABUL	BACKACHE	BACKERS	BACKLIT	BACKSPACES
BABULS	BACKACHES	BACKFIELD	BACKLOAD	BACKSPACING
BABUS	BACKBEAT	BACKFIELDS	BACKLOADED	BACKSPIN
BABUSHKA	BACKBEATS	BACKFILL	BACKLOADING	BACKSPINS
BABUSHKAS	BACKBENCH	BACKFILLED	BACKLOADS	BACKSTAB
BABY	BACKBENCHES	BACKFILLING	BACKLOG	BACKSTABBED
BABYDOLL	BACKBEND	BACKFILLS	BACKLOGGED	BACKSTABBING
BABYDOLLS	BACKBENDS	BACKFIRE	BACKLOGGING	BACKSTABS
BABYHOOD	BACKBIT	BACKFIRED	BACKLOGS	BACKSTAGE
BABYHOODS	BACKBITE	BACKFIRES	BACKMOST	BACKSTAGES
BABYING	BACKBITER	BACKFIRING	BACKOUT	BACKSTAIR
BABYISH	BACKBITERS	BACKFIT	BACKOUTS	BACKSTAMP
BABYISHLY	BACKBITES	BACKFITS	BACKPACK	BACKSTAMPED
BABYPROOF	BACKBITING	BACKFITTED	BACKPACKED	BACKSTAMPING
BABYPROOFED	BACKBITTEN	BACKFITTING	BACKPACKING	BACKSTAMPS
BABYPROOFING	BACKBLOCK	BACKFLIP	BACKPACKS	BACKSTAY
BABYPROOFS	BACKBLOCKS	BACKFLIPPED	BACKPEDAL	BACKSTAYS
BABYSAT	BACKBOARD	BACKFLIPPING	BACKPEDALED	BACKSTOP
BABYSIT	BACKBOARDS	BACKFLIPS	BACKPEDALING	BACKSTOPPED
BABYSITS	BACKBONE	BACKFLOW	BACKPEDALLED	BACKSTOPPING
BABYSITTING	BACKBONED	BACKFLOWS	BACKPEDALLING	BACKSTOPS
BACALAO	BACKBONES	BACKHAND	BACKPEDALS	BACKSTORIES
BACALAOS	BACKCAST	BACKHANDED	BACKREST	BACKSTORY
BACCA	BACKCASTS	BACKHANDING	BACKRESTS	BACKSWEPT
BACCAE	BACKCHAT	BACKHANDS	BACKROOM	BACKSWING
BACCARA	BACKCHATS	BACKHAUL	BACKROOMS	BACKSWINGS
BACCARAS	BACKCHECK	BACKHAULED	BACKRUSH	BACKSWORD
BACCARAT	BACKCHECKED	BACKHAULING	BACKRUSHES	BACKSWORDS
BACCARATS	BACKCHECKING	BACKHAULS	BACKS	BACKTRACK
BACCATE	BACKCHECKS	BACKHOE	BACKSAW	BACKTRACKED
BACCATED	BACKCLOTH	BACKHOED	BACKSAWS	BACKTRACKING

BACKTRACKS	BADGERED	BAGGERS	BAILIE	BAKEWARE
BACKUP	BADGERING	BAGGIE	BAILIES	BAKEWARES
BACKUPS	BADGERLY	BAGGIER	BAILIFF	BAKING
BACKWARD	BADGERS	BAGGIES	BAILIFFS	BAKINGS
BACKWARDS	BADGES	BAGGIEST	BAILING	BAKLAVA
BACKWASH	BADGING	BAGGILY	BAILIWICK	BAKLAVAS
BACKWASHED	BADINAGE	BAGGINESS	BAILIWICKS	BAKLAWA
BACKWASHES	BADINAGED	BAGGINESSES	BAILMENT	BAKLAWAS
BACKWASHING	BADINAGES	BAGGING	BAILMENTS	BAKSHEESH
BACKWATER	BADINAGING	BAGGINGS	BAILOR	BAKSHEESHES
BACKWATERS	BADLAND	BAGGY	BAILORS	BAKSHISH
BACKWOOD	BADLANDS	BAGHOUSE	BAILOUT	BAKSHISHED
BACKWOODS	BADLY	BAGHOUSES	BAILOUTS	BAKSHISHES
BACKWRAP	BADMAN	BAGLIKE	BAILS	BAKSHISHING
BACKWRAPS	BADMEN	BAGMAN	BAILSMAN	BAL
BACKYARD	BADMINTON	BAGMEN	BAILSMEN	BALACLAVA
BACKYARDS	BADMINTONS	BAGNIO	BAIRN	BALACLAVAS
BACLOFEN	BADMOUTH	BAGNIOS	BAIRNISH	BALALAIKA
BACLOFENS	BADMOUTHED	BAGPIPE	BAIRNLIER	BALALAIKAS
BACON	BADMOUTHING	BAGPIPED	BAIRNLIEST	BALANCE
BACONS	BADMOUTHS	BAGPIPER	BAIRNLY	BALANCED
BACTERIA	BADNESS	BAGPIPERS	BAIRNS	BALANCER
BACTERIAL	BADNESSES	BAGPIPES	BAIT	BALANCERS
BACTERIALS	BADS	BAGPIPING	BAITED	BALANCES
BACTERIAS	BAFF	BAGS	BAITER	BALANCING
BACTERIN	BAFFED	BAGSFUL	BAITERS	BALAS
BACTERINS	BAFFIES	BAGUET	BAITFISH	BALASES
BACTERIUM	BAFFING	BAGUETS	BAITFISHES	BALATA
BACTERIZE	BAFFLE	BAGUETTE	BAITH	BALATAS
BACTERIZED	BAFFLED	BAGUETTES	BAITING	BALBOA
BACTERIZES	BAFFLEGAB	BAGWIG	BAITS	BALBOAS
BACTERIZING	BAFFLEGABS	BAGWIGS	BAIZA	BALCONIED
BACTEROID	BAFFLER	BAGWORM	BAIZAS	BALCONIES
BACTEROIDS	BAFFLERS	BAGWORMS	BAIZE	BALCONY
BACULA	BAFFLES	BAH	BAIZES	BALD
BACULINE	BAFFLING	BAHADUR	BAKE	BALDACHIN
BACULUM	BAFFS	BAHADURS	BAKEAPPLE	BALDACHINS
BACULUMS	BAFFY	BAHT	BAKEAPPLES	BALDAQUIN
BAD	BAG	BAHTS	BAKED	BALDAQUINS
BADASS	BAGASS	BAHUVRIHI	BAKEHOUSE	BALDED
BADASSED	BAGASSE	BAHUVRIHIS	BAKEHOUSES	BALDER
BADASSES	BAGASSES	BAIDARKA	BAKELITE	BALDEST
BADDER	BAGATELLE	BAIDARKAS	BAKELITES	BALDFACED
BADDEST	BAGATELLES	BAIL	BAKEMEAT	BALDHEAD
BADDIE	BAGEL	BAILABLE	BAKEMEATS	BALDHEADS
BADDIES	BAGELS	BAILED	BAKER	BALDIES
BADDY	BAGFUL	BAILEE	BAKERIES	BALDING
BADE	BAGFULS	BAILEES	BAKERS	BALDISH
BADGE	BAGGAGE	BAILER	BAKERY	BALDLY
BADGED	BAGGAGES	BAILERS	BAKES	BALDNESS
BADGELESS	BAGGED	BAILEY	BAKESHOP	BALDNESSES
BADGER	BAGGER	BAILEYS	BAKESHOPS	BALDPATE

BALDPATED	BALLAST	BALLYARD	BANALITY	BANDMATES
BALDPATES	BALLASTED	BALLYARDS	BANALIZE	BANDOG
BALDRIC	BALLASTER	BALLYHOO	BANALIZED	BANDOGS
BALDRICK	BALLASTERS	BALLYHOOED	BANALIZES	BANDOLEER
BALDRICKS	BALLASTING	BALLYHOOING	BANALIZING	BANDOLEERS
BALDRICS	BALLASTS	BALLYHOOS	BANALLY	BANDOLIER
BALDS	BALLED	BALLYRAG	BANANA	BANDOLIERS
BALDY	BALLER	BALLYRAGGED	BANANAS	BANDONEON
BALE	BALLERINA	BALLYRAGGING	BANAUSIC	BANDONEONS
BALED	BALLERINAS	BALLYRAGS	BANCO	BANDORA
BALEEN	BALLERS	BALM	BANCOS	BANDORAS
BALEENS	BALLET	BALMACAAN	BAND	BANDORE
BALEFIRE	BALLETIC	BALMACAANS	BANDA	BANDORES
BALEFIRES	BALLETS	BALMIER	BANDAGE	BANDS
BALEFUL	BALLGAME	BALMIEST	BANDAGED	BANDSAW
BALEFULLY	BALLGAMES	BALMILY	BANDAGER	BANDSAWS
BALER	BALLHAWK	BALMINESS	BANDAGERS	BANDSHELL
BALERS	BALLHAWKS	BALMINESSES	BANDAGES	BANDSHELLS
BALES	BALLIES	BALMLIKE	BANDAGING	BANDSMAN
BALING	BALLING	BALMORAL	BANDAID	BANDSMEN
BALISAUR	BALLISTA	BALMORALS	BANDANA	BANDSTAND
BALISAURS	BALLISTAE	BALMS	BANDANAS	BANDSTANDS
BALK	BALLISTIC	BALMY	BANDANNA	BANDWAGON
BALKANIZE	BALLON	BALNEAL	BANDANNAS	BANDWAGONS
BALKANIZED	BALLONET	BALONEY	BANDAS	BANDWIDTH
BALKANIZES	BALLONETS	BALONEYS	BANDBOX	BANDWIDTHS
BALKANIZING	BALLONNE	BALS	BANDBOXES	BANDY
BALKED	BALLONNES	BALSA	BANDEAU	BANDYING
BALKER	BALLONS	BALSAM	BANDEAUS	BANE
BALKERS	BALLOON	BALSAMED	BANDEAUX	BANEBERRIES
BALKIER	BALLOONED	BALSAMIC	BANDED	BANEBERRY
BALKIEST	BALLOONING	BALSAMING	BANDER	BANED
BALKILY	BALLOONS	BALSAMS	BANDEROL	BANEFUL
BALKINESS	BALLOT	BALSAS	BANDEROLE	BANEFULLY
BALKINESSES	BALLOTED	BALUSTER	BANDEROLES	BANES
BALKING	BALLOTER	BALUSTERS	BANDEROLS	BANG
BALKLINE	BALLOTERS	BAM	BANDERS	BANGED
BALKLINES	BALLOTING	BAMBINI	BANDICOOT	BANGER
BALKS	BALLOTS	BAMBINO	BANDICOOTS	BANGERS
BALKY	BALLPARK	BAMBINOS	BANDIED	BANGING
BALL	BALLPARKS	BAMBOO	BANDIES	BANGKOK
BALLAD	BALLPOINT	BAMBOOS	BANDINESS	BANGKOKS
BALLADE	BALLPOINTS	BAMBOOZLE	BANDINESSES	BANGLE
BALLADEER	BALLROOM	BAMBOOZLED	BANDING	BANGLES
BALLADEERS	BALLROOMS	BAMBOOZLES	BANDIT	BANGS
BALLADES	BALLS	BAMBOOZLING	BANDITO	BANGTAIL
BALLADIC	BALLSIER	BAMMED	BANDITOS	BANGTAILS
BALLADIST	BALLSIEST	BAMMING	BANDITRIES	BANI
BALLADISTS	BALLSY	BAMS	BANDITRY	BANIAN
BALLADRIES	BALLUTE	BAN	BANDITS	BANIANS
BALLADRY	BALLUTES	BANAL	BANDITTI	BANING
BALLADS	BALLY	BANALITIES	BANDMATE	BANISH

BANISHED	BANNEROL	BAPTISM	BARBERING	BAREHAND
BANISHER	BANNEROLS	BAPTISMAL	BARBERRIES	BAREHANDED
BANISHERS	BANNERS	BAPTISMS	BARBERRY	BAREHANDING
BANISHES	BANNET	BAPTIST	BARBERS	BAREHANDS
BANISHING	BANNETS	BAPTISTRIES	BARBES	BAREHEAD
BANISTER	BANNING	BAPTISTRY	BARBET	BARELY
BANISTERS	BANNISTER	BAPTISTS	BARBETS	BARENESS
BANJAX	BANNISTERS	BAPTIZE	BARBETTE	BARENESSES
BANJAXED	BANNOCK	BAPTIZED	BARBETTES	BARER
BANJAXES	BANNOCKS	BAPTIZER	BARBICAN	BARES
BANJAXING	BANNS	BAPTIZERS	BARBICANS	BARESARK
BANJO	BANQUET	BAPTIZES	BARBICEL	BARESARKS
BANJOES	BANQUETED	BAPTIZING	BARBICELS	BAREST
BANJOIST	BANQUETER	BAR	BARBIE	BARF
BANJOISTS	BANQUETERS	BARATHEA	BARBIES	BARFED
BANJOS	BANQUETING	BARATHEAS	BARBING	BARFING
BANK	BANQUETS	BARB	BARBITAL	BARFLIES
BANKABLE	BANQUETTE	BARBAL	BARBITALS	BARFLY
BANKBOOK	BANQUETTES	BARBARIAN	BARBITONE	BARFS
BANKBOOKS	BANS	BARBARIANS	BARBITONES	BARGAIN
BANKCARD	BANSHEE	BARBARIC	BARBLESS	BARGAINED
BANKCARDS	BANSHEES	BARBARISM	BARBS	BARGAINER
BANKED	BANSHIE	BARBARISMS	BARBULE	BARGAINERS
BANKER	BANSHIES	BARBARITIES	BARBULES	BARGAINING
BANKERLY	BANTAM	BARBARITY	BARBUT	BARGAINS
BANKERS	BANTAMS	BARBARIZE	BARBUTS	BARGE
BANKING	BANTENG	BARBARIZED	BARBWIRE	BARGED
BANKINGS	BANTENGS	BARBARIZES	BARBWIRES	BARGEE
BANKIT	BANTER	BARBARIZING	BARCA	BARGEES
BANKITS	BANTERED	BARBAROUS	BARCAROLE	BARGELLO
BANKNOTE	BANTERER	BARBASCO	BARCAROLES	BARGELLOS
BANKNOTES	BANTERERS	BARBASCOES	BARCAS	BARGEMAN
BANKROLL	BANTERING	BARBASCOS	BARCHAN	BARGEMEN
BANKROLLED	BANTERS	BARBATE	BARCHANS	BARGES
BANKROLLING	BANTIES	BARBE	BARD	BARGHEST
BANKROLLS	BANTLING	BARBECUE	BARDE	BARGHESTS
BANKRUPT	BANTLINGS	BARBECUED	BARDED	BARGING
BANKRUPTED	BANTY	BARBECUER	BARDES	BARGUEST
BANKRUPTING	BANYAN	BARBECUERS	BARDIC	BARGUESTS
BANKRUPTS	BANYANS	BARBECUES	BARDING	BARHOP
BANKS	BANZAI	BARBECUING	BARDS	BARHOPPED
BANKSIA	BANZAIS	BARBED	BARE	BARHOPPING
BANKSIAS	BAOBAB	BARBEL	BAREBACK	BARHOPS
BANKSIDE	BAOBABS	BARBELL	BAREBOAT	BARIATRIC
BANKSIDES	BAP	BARBELLS	BAREBOATS	BARIC
BANNABLE	BAPS	BARBELS	BAREBONED	BARILLA
BANNED	BAPTISE	BARBEQUE	BARED	BARILLAS
BANNER	BAPTISED	BARBEQUED	BAREFACED	BARING
BANNERED	BAPTISES	BARBEQUES	BAREFIT	BARISTA
BANNERET	BAPTISIA	BARBEQUING	BAREFOOT	BARISTAS
BANNERETS	BAPTISIAS	BARBER	BAREGE	BARITE
BANNERING	BAPTISING	BARBERED	BAREGES	BARITES

BARITONAL	BARNY	BARRAGE	BARRING	BASCULE
BARITONE	BARNYARD	BARRAGED	BARRIO	BASCULES
BARITONES	BARNYARDS	BARRAGES	BARRIOS	BASE
BARIUM	BAROGRAM	BARRAGING	BARRISTER	BASEBALL
BARIUMS	BAROGRAMS	BARRANCA	BARRISTERS	BASEBALLS
BARK	BAROGRAPH	BARRANCAS	BARROOM	BASEBOARD
BARKED	BAROGRAPHS	BARRANCO	BARROOMS	BASEBOARDS
BARKEEP	BAROMETER	BARRANCOS	BARROW	BASEBORN
BARKEEPER	BAROMETERS	BARRATER	BARROWS	BASED
BARKEEPERS	BAROMETRIES	BARRATERS	BARS	BASELESS
BARKEEPS	BAROMETRY	BARRATOR	BARSTOOL	BASELINE
BARKER	BARON	BARRATORS	BARSTOOLS	BASELINER
BARKERS	BARONAGE	BARRATRIES	BARTEND	BASELINERS
BARKIER	BARONAGES	BARRATRY	BARTENDED	BASELINES
BARKIEST	BARONESS	BARRE	BARTENDER	BASELY
BARKING	BARONESSES	BARRED	BARTENDERS	BASEMAN
BARKLESS	BARONET	BARREL	BARTENDING	BASEMEN
BARKS	BARONETCIES	BARRELAGE	BARTENDS	BASEMENT
BARKY	BARONETCY	BARRELAGES	BARTER	BASEMENTS
BARLEDUC	BARONETS	BARRELED	BARTERED	BASENESS
BARLEDUCS	BARONG	BARRELFUL	BARTERER	BASENESSES
BARLESS	BARONGS	BARRELFULS	BARTERERS	BASENJI
BARLEY	BARONIAL	BARRELING	BARTERING	BASENJIS
BARLEYS	BARONIES	BARRELLED	BARTERS	BASEPLATE
BARLOW	BARONNE	BARRELLING	BARTISAN	BASEPLATES
BARLOWS	BARONNES	BARRELS	BARTISANS	BASER
BARM	BARONS	BARRELSFUL	BARTIZAN	BASES
BARMAID	BARONY	BARREN	BARTIZANS	BASEST
BARMAIDS	BAROQUE	BARRENER	BARWARE	BASH
BARMAN	BAROQUELY	BARRENEST	BARWARES	BASHAW
BARMEN	BAROQUES	BARRENLY	BARYE	BASHAWS
BARMIE	BAROSAUR	BARRENS	BARYES	BASHED
BARMIER	BAROSAURS	BARRES	BARYON	BASHER
BARMIEST	BAROSCOPE	BARRET	BARYONIC	BASHERS
BARMS	BAROSCOPES	BARRETOR	BARYONS	BASHES
BARMY	BAROUCHE	BARRETORS	BARYTA	BASHFUL
BARN	BAROUCHES	BARRETRIES	BARYTAS	BASHFULLY
BARNACLE	BARQUE	BARRETRY	BARYTE	BASHING
BARNACLED	BARQUES	BARRETS	BARYTES	BASHINGS
BARNACLES	BARQUETTE	BARRETTE	BARYTIC	BASHLYK
BARNED	BARQUETTES	BARRETTES	BARYTON	BASHLYKS
BARNEY	BARRABLE	BARRICADE	BARYTONE	BASIC
BARNEYS	BARRACK	BARRICADED	BARYTONES	BASICALLY
BARNIER	BARRACKED	BARRICADES	BARYTONS	BASICITIES
BARNIEST	BARRACKER	BARRICADING	BAS	BASICITY
BARNING	BARRACKERS	BARRICADO	BASAL	BASICS
BARNLIKE	BARRACKING	BARRICADOED	BASALLY	BASIDIA
BARNS	BARRACKS	BARRICADOES	BASALT	BASIDIAL
BARNSTORM	BARRACOON	BARRICADOING	BASALTES	BASIDIUM
BARNSTORMED	BARRACOONS	BARRICADOS	BASALTIC	BASIFIED
BARNSTORMING	BARRACUDA	BARRIER	BASALTINE	BASIFIER
BARNSTORMS	BARRACUDAS	BARRIERS	BASALTS	BASIFIERS

BASIFIES	BASSES	BASTS	BATIK	BATTLES
BASIFIXED	BASSET	BAT	BATIKED	BATTLING
BASIFY	BASSETED	BATBOY	BATIKING	BATTS
BASIFYING	BASSETING	BATBOYS	BATIKS	BATTU
BASIL	BASSETS	BATCH	BATING	BATTUE
BASILAR	BASSETT	BATCHED	BATISTE	BATTUES
BASILARY	BASSETTED	BATCHER	BATISTES	BATTY
BASILECT	BASSETTING	BATCHERS	BATLIKE	BATWING
BASILECTS	BASSETTS	BATCHES	BATMAN	BAUBEE
BASILIC	BASSI	BATCHING	BATMEN	BAUBEES
BASILICA	BASSINET	BATE	BATON	BAUBLE
BASILICAE	BASSINETS	BATEAU	BATONS	BAUBLES
BASILICAL	BASSIST	BATEAUX	BATS	BAUD
BASILICAN	BASSISTS	BATED	BATSMAN	BAUDEKIN
BASILICAS	BASSLY	BATES	BATSMEN	BAUDEKINS
BASILISK	BASSNESS	BATFISH	BATT	BAUDRONS
BASILISKS	BASSNESSES	BATFISHES	BATTALIA	BAUDRONSES
BASILS	BASSO	BATFOWL	BATTALIAS	BAUDS
BASIN	BASSOON	BATFOWLED	BATTALION	BAUHINIA
BASINAL	BASSOONS	BATFOWLER	BATTALIONS	BAUHINIAS
BASINED	BASSOS	BATFOWLERS	BATTEAU	BAULK
BASINET	BASSWOOD	BATFOWLING	BATTEAUX	BAULKED
BASINETS	BASSWOODS	BATFOWLS	BATTED	BAULKIER
BASINFUL	BASSY	BATGIRL	BATTEMENT	BAULKIEST
BASINFULS	BAST	BATGIRLS	BATTEMENTS	BAULKING
BASING	BASTARD	BATH	BATTEN	BAULKS
BASINLIKE	BASTARDIES	BATHE	BATTENED	BAULKY
BASINS	BASTARDLY	BATHED	BATTENER	BAUSOND
BASION	BASTARDS	BATHER	BATTENERS	BAUXITE
BASIONS	BASTARDY	BATHERS	BATTENING	BAUXITES
BASIPETAL	BASTE	BATHES	BATTENS	BAUXITIC
BASIS	BASTED	BATHETIC	BATTER	BAWBEE
BASK	BASTER	BATHHOUSE	BATTERED	BAWBEES
BASKED	BASTERS	BATHHOUSES	BATTERER	BAWCOCK
BASKET	BASTES	BATHING	BATTERERS	BAWCOCKS
BASKETFUL	BASTILE	BATHLESS	BATTERIE	BAWD
BASKETFULS	BASTILES	BATHMAT	BATTERIES	BAWDIER
BASKETRIES	BASTILLE	BATHMATS	BATTERING	BAWDIES
BASKETRY	BASTILLES	BATHOLITH	BATTERS	BAWDIEST
BASKETS	BASTINADE	BATHOLITHS	BATTERY	BAWDILY
BASKETSFUL	BASTINADED	BATHOS	BATTIER	BAWDINESS
BASKING	BASTINADES	BATHOSES	BATTIEST	BAWDINESSES
BASKS	BASTINADING	BATHROBE	BATTIK	BAWDRIC
BASMATI	BASTINADO	BATHROBES	BATTIKS	BAWDRICS
BASMATIS	BASTINADOED	BATHROOM	BATTINESS	BAWDRIES
BASOPHIL	BASTINADOES	BATHROOMS	BATTINESSES	BAWDRY
BASOPHILE	BASTINADOING	BATHS	BATTING	BAWDS
BASOPHILES	BASTING	BATHTUB	BATTINGS	BAWDY
BASOPHILS	BASTINGS	BATHTUBS	BATTLE	BAWL
BASQUE	BASTION	BATHWATER	BATTLED	BAWLED
BASQUES	BASTIONED	BATHWATERS	BATTLER	BAWLER
BASS	BASTIONS	BATHYAL	BATTLERS	BAWLERS

BAWLING	BEACHCOMBED	BEAKERS	BEARERS	BEAUTIFULLER
BAWLS	BEACHCOMBING	BEAKIER	BEARGRASS	BEAUTIFULLEST
BAWSUNT	BEACHCOMBS	BEAKIEST	BEARGRASSES	BEAUTIFY
BAWTIE	BEACHED	BEAKLESS	BEARHUG	BEAUTIFYING
BAWTIES	BEACHES	BEAKLIKE	BEARHUGS	BEAUTS
BAWTY	BEACHGOER	BEAKS	BEARING	BEAUTY
BAY	BEACHGOERS	BEAKY	BEARINGS	BEAUX
BAYADEER	BEACHHEAD	BEAM	BEARISH	BEAVER
BAYADEERS	BEACHHEADS	BEAMED	BEARISHLY	BEAVERED
BAYADERE	BEACHIER	BEAMIER	BEARLIKE	BEAVERING
BAYADERES	BEACHIEST	BEAMIEST	BEARS	BEAVERS
BAYAMO	BEACHING	BEAMILY	BEARSKIN	BEBEERINE
BAYAMOS	BEACHSIDE	BEAMING	BEARSKINS	BEBEERINES
BAYARD	BEACHWEAR	BEAMINGLY	BEARWOOD	BEBEERU
BAYARDS	BEACHY	BEAMISH	BEARWOODS	BEBEERUS
BAYBERRIES	BEACON	BEAMISHLY	BEAST	BEBLOOD
BAYBERRY	BEACONED	BEAMLESS	BEASTIE	BEBLOODED
BAYED	BEACONING	BEAMLIKE	BEASTIES	BEBLOODING
BAYING	BEACONS	BEAMS	BEASTINGS	BEBLOODS
BAYMAN	BEAD	BEAMY	BEASTLIER	BEBOP
BAYMEN	BEADED	BEAN	BEASTLIEST	BEBOPPER
BAYONET	BEADER	BEANBAG	BEASTLY	BEBOPPERS
BAYONETED	BEADERS	BEANBAGS	BEASTS	BEBOPS
BAYONETING	BEADHOUSE	BEANBALL	BEAT	BECALM
BAYONETS	BEADHOUSES	BEANBALLS	BEATABLE	BECALMED
BAYONETTED	BEADIER	BEANED	BEATEN	BECALMING
BAYONETTING	BEADIEST	BEANERIES	BEATER	BECALMS
BAYOU	BEADILY	BEANERY	BEATERS	BECAME
BAYOUS	BEADINESS	BEANIE	BEATIFIC	BECAP
BAYS	BEADINESSES	BEANIES	BEATIFIED	BECAPPED
BAYWOOD	BEADING	BEANING	BEATIFIES	BECAPPING
BAYWOODS	BEADINGS	BEANLIKE	BEATIFY	BECAPS
BAZAAR	BEADLE	BEANO	BEATIFYING	BECARPET
BAZAARS	BEADLEDOM	BEANOS	BEATING	BECARPETED
BAZAR	BEADLEDOMS	BEANPOLE	BEATINGS	BECARPETING
BAZARS	BEADLES	BEANPOLES	BEATITUDE	BECARPETS
BAZILLION	BEADLIKE	BEANS	BEATITUDES	BECAUSE
BAZILLIONS	BEADMAN	BEANSTALK	BEATLESS	BECCAFICO
BAZOO	BEADMEN	BEANSTALKS	BEATNIK	BECCAFICOS
BAZOOKA	BEADROLL	BEAR	BEATNIKS	BECHALK
BAZOOKAS	BEADROLLS	BEARABLE	BEATS	BECHALKED
BAZOOMS	BEADS	BEARABLY	BEAU	BECHALKING
BAZOOS	BEADSMAN	BEARBERRIES	BEAUCOUP	BECHALKS
BDELLIUM	BEADSMEN	BEARBERRY	BEAUCOUPS	BECHAMEL
BDELLIUMS	BEADWORK	BEARCAT	BEAUISH	BECHAMELS
BE	BEADWORKS	BEARCATS	BEAUS	BECHANCE
BEACH	BEADY	BEARD	BEAUT	BECHANCED
BEACHBALL	BEAGLE	BEARDED	BEAUTEOUS	BECHANCES
BEACHBALLS	BEAGLES	BEARDING	BEAUTIES	BECHANCING
BEACHBOY	BEAK	BEARDLESS	BEAUTIFIED	BECHARM
BEACHBOYS	BEAKED	BEARDS	BEAUTIFIES	BECHARMED
BEACHCOMB	BEAKER	BEARER	BEAUTIFUL	BECHARMING

BECHARMS	BECRAWLED	BEDCHAIRS	BEDIM	BEDRENCHING
BECK	BECRAWLING	BEDCOVER	BEDIMMED	BEDRID
BECKED	BECRAWLS	BEDCOVERS	BEDIMMING	BEDRIDDEN
BECKET	BECRIME	BEDDABLE	BEDIMPLE	BEDRIVEL
BECKETS	BECRIMED	BEDDED	BEDIMPLED	BEDRIVELED
BECKING	BECRIMES	BEDDER	BEDIMPLES	BEDRIVELING
BECKON	BECRIMING	BEDDERS	BEDIMPLING	BEDRIVELLED
BECKONED	BECROWD	BEDDING	BEDIMS	BEDRIVELLING
BECKONER	BECROWDED	BEDDINGS	BEDIRTIED	BEDRIVELS
BECKONERS	BECROWDING	BEDEAFEN	BEDIRTIES	BEDROCK
BECKONING	BECROWDS	BEDEAFENED	BEDIRTY	BEDROCKS
BECKONS	BECRUST	BEDEAFENING	BEDIRTYING	BEDROLL
BECKS	BECRUSTED	BEDEAFENS	BEDIZEN	BEDROLLS
BECLAMOR	BECRUSTING	BEDECK	BEDIZENED	BEDROOM
BECLAMORED	BECRUSTS	BEDECKED	BEDIZENING	BEDROOMED
BECLAMORING	BECUDGEL	BEDECKING	BEDIZENS	BEDROOMS
BECLAMORS	BECUDGELED	BEDECKS	BEDLAM	BEDRUG
BECLASP	BECUDGELING	BEDEHOUSE	BEDLAMITE	BEDRUGGED
BECLASPED	BECUDGELLED	BEDEHOUSES	BEDLAMITES	BEDRUGGING
BECLASPING	BECUDGELLING	BEDEL	BEDLAMP	BEDRUGS
BECLASPS	BECUDGELS	BEDELL	BEDLAMPS	BEDS
BECLOAK	BECURSE	BEDELLS	BEDLAMS	BEDSHEET
BECLOAKED	BECURSED	BEDELS	BEDLESS	BEDSHEETS
BECLOAKING	BECURSES	BEDEMAN	BEDLIKE	BEDSIDE
BECLOAKS	BECURSING	BEDEMEN	BEDMAKER	BEDSIDES
BECLOG	BECURST	BEDESMAN	BEDMAKERS	BEDSIT
BECLOGGED	BED	BEDESMEN	BEDMATE	BEDSITS
BECLOGGING	BEDABBLE	BEDEVIL	BEDMATES	BEDSONIA
BECLOGS	BEDABBLED	BEDEVILED	BEDOTTED	BEDSONIAS
BECLOTHE	BEDABBLES	BEDEVILING	BEDOUIN	BEDSORE
BECLOTHED	BEDABBLING	BEDEVILLED	BEDOUINS	BEDSORES
BECLOTHES	BEDAMN	BEDEVILLING	BEDPAN	BEDSPREAD
BECLOTHING	BEDAMNED	BEDEVILS	BEDPANS	BEDSPREADS
BECLOUD	BEDAMNING	BEDEW	BEDPLATE	BEDSPRING
BECLOUDED	BEDAMNS	BEDEWED	BEDPLATES	BEDSPRINGS
BECLOUDING	BEDARKEN	BEDEWING	BEDPOST	BEDSTAND
BECLOUDS	BEDARKENED	BEDEWS	BEDPOSTS	BEDSTANDS
BECLOWN	BEDARKENING	BEDFAST	BEDQUILT	BEDSTEAD
BECLOWNED	BEDARKENS	BEDFELLOW	BEDQUILTS	BEDSTEADS
BECLOWNING	BEDAUB	BEDFELLOWS	BEDRAGGLE	BEDSTRAW
BECLOWNS	BEDAUBED	BEDFRAME	BEDRAGGLED	BEDSTRAWS
BECOME	BEDAUBING	BEDFRAMES	BEDRAGGLES	BEDTICK
BECOMES	BEDAUBS	BEDGOWN	BEDRAGGLING	BEDTICKS
BECOMING	BEDAZZLE	BEDGOWNS	BEDRAIL	BEDTIME
BECOMINGS	BEDAZZLED	BEDIAPER	BEDRAILS	BEDTIMES
BECOWARD	BEDAZZLES	BEDIAPERED	BEDRAPE	BEDU
BECOWARDED	BEDAZZLING	BEDIAPERING	BEDRAPED	BEDUIN
BECOWARDING	BEDBOARD	BEDIAPERS	BEDRAPES	BEDUINS
BECOWARDS	BEDBOARDS	BEDIGHT	BEDRAPING	BEDUMB
BECQUEREL	BEDBUG	BEDIGHTED	BEDRENCH	BEDUMBED
BECQUERELS	BEDBUGS	BEDIGHTING	BEDRENCHED	BEDUMBING
BECRAWL	BEDCHAIR	BEDIGHTS	BEDRENCHES	BEDUMBS

BEDUNCE	BEEFWOOD	BEFINGER	BEFUDDLED	BEGLAMORS
BEDUNCED	BEEFWOODS	BEFINGERED	BEFUDDLES	BEGLAMOUR
BEDUNCES	BEEFY	BEFINGERING	BEFUDDLING	BEGLAMOURED
BEDUNCING	BEEHIVE	BEFINGERS	BEG	BEGLAMOURING
BEDWARD	BEEHIVES	BEFIT	BEGALL	BEGLAMOURS
BEDWARDS	BEEKEEPER	BEFITS	BEGALLED	BEGLOOM
BEDWARF	BEEKEEPERS	BEFITTED	BEGALLING	BEGLOOMED
BEDWARFED	BEELIKE	BEFITTING	BEGALLS	BEGLOOMING
BEDWARFING	BEELINE	BEFLAG	BEGAN	BEGLOOMS
BEDWARFS	BEELINED	BEFLAGGED	BEGAT	BEGOGGLED
BEDWARMER	BEELINES	BEFLAGGING	BEGAZE	BEGONE
BEDWARMERS	BEELINING	BEFLAGS	BEGAZED	BEGONIA
BEDWETTER	BEEN	BEFLEA	BEGAZES	BEGONIAS
BEDWETTERS	BEEP	BEFLEAED	BEGAZING	BEGORAH
BEE	BEEPED	BEFLEAING	BEGET	BEGORRA
BEEBEE	BEEPER	BEFLEAS	BEGETS	BEGORRAH
BEEBEES	BEEPERS	BEFLECK	BEGETTER	BEGOT
BEEBREAD	BEEPING	BEFLECKED	BEGETTERS	BEGOTTEN
BEEBREADS	BEEPS	BEFLECKING	BEGETTING	BEGRIM
BEECH	BEER	BEFLECKS	BEGGAR	BEGRIME
BEECHEN	BEERIER	BEFLOWER	BEGGARDOM	BEGRIMED
BEECHES	BEERIEST	BEFLOWERED	BEGGARDOMS	BEGRIMES
BEECHIER	BEERINESS	BEFLOWERING	BEGGARED	BEGRIMING
BEECHIEST	BEERINESSES	BEFLOWERS	BEGGARIES	BEGRIMMED
BEECHMAST	BEERS	BEFOG	BEGGARING	BEGRIMMING
BEECHMASTS	BEERY	BEFOGGED	BEGGARLY	BEGRIMS
BEECHNUT	BEES	BEFOGGING	BEGGARS	BEGROAN
BEECHNUTS	BEESTINGS	BEFOGS	BEGGARY	BEGROANED
BEECHWOOD	BEESWAX	BEFOOL	BEGGED	BEGROANING
BEECHWOODS	BEESWAXES	BEFOOLED	BEGGING	BEGROANS
BEECHY	BEESWING	BEFOOLING	BEGIN	BEGRUDGE
BEEDI	BEESWINGS	BEFOOLS	BEGINNER	BEGRUDGED
BEEDIES	BEET	BEFORE	BEGINNERS	BEGRUDGER
BEEF	BEETLE	BEFOUL	BEGINNING	BEGRUDGERS
BEEFALO	BEETLED	BEFOULED	BEGINNINGS	BEGRUDGES
BEEFALOES	BEETLER	BEFOULER	BEGINS	BEGRUDGING
BEEFALOS	BEETLERS	BEFOULERS	BEGIRD	BEGS
BEEFCAKE	BEETLES	BEFOULING	BEGIRDED	BEGUILE
BEEFCAKES	BEETLING	BEFOULS	BEGIRDING	BEGUILED
BEEFEATER	BEETROOT	BEFRET	BEGIRDLE	BEGUILER
BEEFEATERS	BEETROOTS	BEFRETS	BEGIRDLED	BEGUILERS
BEEFED	BEETS	BEFRETTED	BEGIRDLES	BEGUILES
BEEFIER	BEEVES	BEFRETTING	BEGIRDLING	BEGUILING
BEEFIEST	BEEYARD	BEFRIEND	BEGIRDS	BEGUINE
BEEFILY	BEEYARDS	BEFRIENDED	BEGIRT	BEGUINES
BEEFINESS	BEEZER	BEFRIENDING	BEGLAD	BEGULF
BEEFINESSES	BEEZERS	BEFRIENDS	BEGLADDED	BEGULFED
BEEFING	BEFALL	BEFRINGE	BEGLADDING	BEGULFING
BEEFLESS	BEFALLEN	BEFRINGED	BEGLADS	BEGULFS
BEEFS	BEFALLING	BEFRINGES	BEGLAMOR	BEGUM
BEEFSTEAK	BEFALLS	BEFRINGING	BEGLAMORED	BEGUMS
BEEFSTEAKS	BEFELL	BEFUDDLE	BEGLAMORING	BEGUN

BEHALF	BEIGY	BELAYER	BELITTLES	BELOVEDS
BEHALVES	BEING	BELAYERS	BELITTLING	BELOW
BEHAVE	BEINGS	BELAYING	BELIVE	BELOWS
BEHAVED	BEJABBERS	BELAYS	BELL	BELS
BEHAVER	BEJABERS	BELCH	BELLBIRD	BELT
BEHAVERS	BEJEEBERS	BELCHED	BELLBIRDS	BELTED
BEHAVES	BEJEEZUS	BELCHER	BELLBOY	BELTER
BEHAVING	BEJESUS	BELCHERS	BELLBOYS	BELTERS
BEHAVIOR	BEJEWEL	BELCHES	BELLE	BELTING
BEHAVIORS	BEJEWELED	BELCHING	BELLED	BELTINGS
BEHAVIOUR	BEJEWELING	BELDAM	BELLEEK	BELTLESS
BEHAVIOURS	BEJEWELLED	BELDAME	BELLEEKS	BELTLINE
BEHEAD	BEJEWELLING	BELDAMES	BELLES	BELTLINES
BEHEADAL	BEJEWELS	BELDAMS	BELLHOP	BELTS
BEHEADALS	BEJUMBLE	BELEAGUER	BELLHOPS	BELTWAY
BEHEADED	BEJUMBLED	BELEAGUERED	BELLICOSE	BELTWAYS
BEHEADER	BEJUMBLES	BELEAGUERING	BELLIED	BELUGA
BEHEADERS	BEJUMBLING	BELEAGUERS	BELLIES	BELUGAS
BEHEADING	BEKISS	BELEAP	BELLING	BELVEDERE
BEHEADS	BEKISSED	BELEAPED	BELLINGS	BELVEDERES
BEHELD	BEKISSES	BELEAPING	BELLMAN	BELYING
BEHEMOTH	BEKISSING	BELEAPS	BELLMEN	BEMA
BEHEMOTHS	BEKNIGHT	BELEAPT	BELLOW	BEMADAM
BEHEST	BEKNIGHTED	BELEMNITE	BELLOWED	BEMADAMED
BEHESTS	BEKNIGHTING	BELEMNITES	BELLOWER	BEMADAMING
BEHIND	BEKNIGHTS	BELFRIED	BELLOWERS	BEMADAMS
BEHINDS	BEKNOT	BELFRIES	BELLOWING	BEMADDEN
BEHOLD	BEKNOTS	BELFRY	BELLOWS	BEMADDENED
BEHOLDEN	BEKNOTTED	BELGA	BELLPULL	BEMADDENING
BEHOLDER	BEKNOTTING	BELGAS	BELLPULLS	BEMADDENS
BEHOLDERS	BEL	BELIE	BELLS	BEMAS
BEHOLDING	BELABOR	BELIED	BELLWORT	BEMATA
BEHOLDS	BELABORED	BELIEF	BELLWORTS	BEMEAN
BEHOOF	BELABORING	BELIEFS	BELLY	BEMEANED
BEHOOVE	BELABORS	BELIER	BELLYACHE	BEMEANING
BEHOOVED	BELABOUR	BELIERS	BELLYACHED	BEMEANS
BEHOOVES	BELABOURED	BELIES	BELLYACHES	BEMEDALED
BEHOOVING	BELABOURING	BELIEVE	BELLYACHING	BEMINGLE
BEHOVE	BELABOURS	BELIEVED	BELLYBAND	BEMINGLED
BEHOVED	BELACED	BELIEVER	BELLYBANDS	BEMINGLES
BEHOVES	BELADIED	BELIEVERS	BELLYFUL	BEMINGLING
BEHOVING	BELADIES	BELIEVES	BELLYFULS	BEMIRE
BEHOWL	BELADY	BELIEVING	BELLYING	BEMIRED
BEHOWLED	BELADYING	BELIKE	BELLYLIKE	BEMIRES
BEHOWLING	BELATED	BELIQUOR	BELON	BEMIRING
BEHOWLS	BELATEDLY	BELIQUORED	BELONG	BEMIST
BEIGE	BELAUD	BELIQUORING	BELONGED	BEMISTED
BEIGES	BELAUDED	BELIQUORS	BELONGING	BEMISTING
BEIGNE	BELAUDING	BELITTLE	BELONGINGS	BEMISTS
BEIGNES	BELAUDS	BELITTLED	BELONGS	BEMIX
BEIGNET	BELAY	BELITTLER	BELONS	BEMIXED
BEIGNETS	BELAYED	BELITTLERS	BELOVED	BEMIXES

BEMIXING	BENDAYING	BENNETS	BENZOYLS	BERGAMOT
BEMIXT	BENDAYS	BENNI	BENZYL	BERGAMOTS
BEMOAN	BENDED	BENNIES	BENZYLIC	BERGERE
BEMOANED	BENDEE	BENNIS	BENZYLS	BERGERES
BEMOANING	BENDEES	BENNY	BEPAINT	BERGS
BEMOANS	BENDER	BENOMYL	BEPAINTED	BERHYME
BEMOCK	BENDERS	BENOMYLS	BEPAINTING	BERHYMED
BEMOCKED	BENDIER	BENS	BEPAINTS	BERHYMES
BEMOCKING	BENDIEST	BENT	BEPIMPLE	BERHYMING
BEMOCKS	BENDING	BENTGRASS	BEPIMPLED	BERIBERI
BEMUDDLE	BENDS	BENTGRASSES	BEPIMPLES	BERIBERIS
BEMUDDLED	BENDWAYS	BENTHAL	BEPIMPLING	BERIMBAU
BEMUDDLES	BENDWISE	BENTHIC	BEQUEATH	BERIMBAUS
BEMUDDLING	BENDY	BENTHON	BEQUEATHED	BERIME
BEMURMUR	BENDYS	BENTHONIC	BEQUEATHING	BERIMED
BEMURMURED	BENE	BENTHONS	BEQUEATHS	BERIMES
BEMURMURING	BENEATH	BENTHOS	BEQUEST	BERIMING
BEMURMURS	BENEDICK	BENTHOSES	BEQUESTS	BERINGED
BEMUSE	BENEDICKS	BENTO	BERAKE	BERK
BEMUSED	BENEDICT	BENTONITE	BERAKED	BERKELIUM
BEMUSEDLY	BENEDICTS	BENTONITES	BERAKES	BERKELIUMS
BEMUSES	BENEFIC	BENTOS	BERAKING	BERKS
BEMUSING	BENEFICE	BENTS	BERASCAL	BERLIN
BEMUZZLE	BENEFICED	BENTWOOD	BERASCALED	BERLINE
BEMUZZLED	BENEFICES	BENTWOODS	BERASCALING	BERLINES
BEMUZZLES	BENEFICING	BENUMB	BERASCALS	BERLINS
BEMUZZLING	BENEFIT	BENUMBED	BERATE	BERM
BEN	BENEFITED	BENUMBING	BERATED	BERME
BENADRYL	BENEFITER	BENUMBS	BERATES	BERMED
BENADRYLS	BENEFITERS	BENZAL	BERATING	BERMES
BENAME	BENEFITING	BENZENE	BERBERIN	BERMING
BENAMED	BENEFITS	BENZENES	BERBERINE	BERMS
BENAMES	BENEFITTED	BENZENOID	BERBERINES	BERMUDAS
BENAMING	BENEFITTING	BENZENOIDS	BERBERINS	BERNICLE
BENCH	BENEMPT	BENZIDIN	BERBERIS	BERNICLES
BENCHED	BENEMPTED	BENZIDINE	BERBERISES	BEROBED
BENCHER	BENES	BENZIDINES	BERCEUSE	BEROUGED
BENCHERS	BENGALINE	BENZIDINS	BERCEUSES	BERRETTA
BENCHES	BENGALINES	BENZIN	BERDACHE	BERRETTAS
BENCHING	BENIGHTED	BENZINE	BERDACHES	BERRIED
BENCHLAND	BENIGN	BENZINES	BEREAVE	BERRIES
BENCHLANDS	BENIGNANT	BENZINS	BEREAVED	BERRY
BENCHLESS	BENIGNITIES	BENZOATE	BEREAVER	BERRYING
BENCHMARK	BENIGNITY	BENZOATES	BEREAVERS	BERRYLESS
BENCHMARKED	BENIGNLY	BENZOIC	BEREAVES	BERRYLIKE
BENCHMARKING	BENISON	BENZOIN	BEREAVING	BERSEEM
BENCHMARKS	BENISONS	BENZOINS	BEREFT	BERSEEMS
BENCHTOP	BENJAMIN	BENZOL	BERET	BERSERK
BEND	BENJAMINS	BENZOLE	BERETS	BERSERKER
BENDABLE	BENNE	BENZOLES	BERETTA	BERSERKERS
BENDAY	BENNES	BENZOLS	BERETTAS	BERSERKLY
BENDAYED	BENNET	BENZOYL	BERG	BERSERKS

BERTH	BESHIVERING	BESMUDGING	BESTING	BETATTERS
BERTHA	BESHIVERS	BESMUT	BESTIR	BETAXED
BERTHAS	BESHOUT	BESMUTS	BESTIRRED	BETEL
BERTHED	BESHOUTED	BESMUTTED	BESTIRRING	BETELNUT
BERTHING	BESHOUTING	BESMUTTING	BESTIRS	BETELNUTS
BERTHS	BESHOUTS	BESNOW	BESTOW	BETELS
BERYL	BESHREW	BESNOWED	BESTOWAL	BETH
BERYLINE	BESHREWED	BESNOWING	BESTOWALS	BETHANK
BERYLLIUM	BESHREWING	BESNOWS	BESTOWED	BETHANKED
BERYLLIUMS	BESHREWS	BESOM	BESTOWER	BETHANKING
BERYLS	BESHROUD	BESOMS	BESTOWERS	BETHANKS
BES	BESHROUDED	BESOOTHE	BESTOWING	BETHEL
BESCORCH	BESHROUDING	BESOOTHED	BESTOWS	BETHELS
BESCORCHED	BESHROUDS	BESOOTHES	BESTREW	BETHESDA
BESCORCHES	BESIDE	BESOOTHING	BESTREWED	BETHESDAS
BESCORCHING	BESIDES	BESOT	BESTREWING	BETHINK
BESCOUR	BESIEGE	BESOTS	BESTREWN	BETHINKING
BESCOURED	BESIEGED	BESOTTED	BESTREWS	BETHINKS
BESCOURING	BESIEGER	BESOTTING	BESTRID	BETHORN
BESCOURS	BESIEGERS	BESOUGHT	BESTRIDDEN	BETHORNED
BESCREEN	BESIEGES	BESPAKE	BESTRIDE	BETHORNING
BESCREENED	BESIEGING	BESPANGLE	BESTRIDES	BETHORNS
BESCREENING	BESLAVED	BESPANGLED	BESTRIDING	BETHOUGHT
BESCREENS	BESLIME	BESPANGLES	BESTRODE	BETHS
BESEECH	BESLIMED	BESPANGLING	BESTROW	BETHUMP
BESEECHED	BESLIMES	BESPATTER	BESTROWED	BETHUMPED
BESEECHER	BESLIMING	BESPATTERED	BESTROWING	BETHUMPING
BESEECHERS	BESMEAR	BESPATTERING	BESTROWN	BETHUMPS
BESEECHES	BESMEARED	BESPATTERS	BESTROWS	BETIDE
BESEECHING	BESMEARER	BESPEAK	BESTS	BETIDED
BESEEM	BESMEARERS	BESPEAKING	BESTUD	BETIDES
BESEEMED	BESMEARING	BESPEAKS	BESTUDDED	BETIDING
BESEEMING	BESMEARS	BESPOKE	BESTUDDING	BETIME
BESEEMS	BESMILE	BESPOKEN	BESTUDS	BETIMES
BESES	BESMILED	BESPOUSE	BESWARM	BETISE
BESET	BESMILES	BESPOUSED	BESWARMED	BETISES
BESETMENT	BESMILING	BESPOUSES	BESWARMING	BETOKEN
BESETMENTS	BESMIRCH	BESPOUSING	BESWARMS	BETOKENED
BESETS	BESMIRCHED	BESPREAD	BET	BETOKENING
BESETTER	BESMIRCHES	BESPREADING	BETA	BETOKENS
BESETTERS	BESMIRCHING	BESPREADS	BETAINE	BETON
BESETTING	BESMOKE	BESPRENT	BETAINES	BETONIES
BESHADOW	BESMOKED	BEST	BETAKE	BETONS
BESHADOWED	BESMOKES	BESTEAD	BETAKEN	BETONY
BESHADOWING	BESMOKING	BESTEADED	BETAKES	BETOOK
BESHADOWS	BESMOOTH	BESTEADING	BETAKING	BETRAY
BESHAME	BESMOOTHED	BESTEADS	BETAS	BETRAYAL
BESHAMED	BESMOOTHING	BESTED	BETATRON	BETRAYALS
BESHAMES	BESMOOTHS	BESTIAL	BETATRONS	BETRAYED
BESHAMING	BESMUDGE	BESTIALLY	BETATTER	BETRAYER
BESHIVER	BESMUDGED	BESTIARIES	BETATTERED	BETRAYERS
BESHIVERED	BESMUDGES	BESTIARY	BETATTERING	BETRAYING

BETRAYS	BEWARES	BEZANT	BIASSING	BICKERING
BETROTH	BEWARING	BEZANTS	BIATHLETE	BICKERS
BETROTHAL	BEWEARIED	BEZAZZ	BIATHLETES	BICOASTAL
BETROTHALS	BEWEARIES	BEZAZZES	BIATHLON	BICOLOR
BETROTHED	BEWEARY	BEZEL	BIATHLONS	BICOLORED
BETROTHEDS	BEWEARYING	BEZELS	BIAXAL	BICOLORS
BETROTHING	BEWEEP	BEZIL	BIAXIAL	BICOLOUR
BETROTHS	BEWEEPING	BEZILS	BIAXIALLY	BICOLOURS
BETS	BEWEEPS	BEZIQUE	BIB	BICONCAVE
BETTA	BEWEPT	BEZIQUES	BIBASIC	BICONVEX
BETTAS	BEWIG	BEZOAR	BIBB	BICORN
BETTED	BEWIGGED	BEZOARS	BIBBED	BICORNE
BETTER	BEWIGGING	BEZZANT	BIBBER	BICORNES
BETTERED	BEWIGS	BEZZANTS	BIBBERIES	BICORNS
BETTERING	BEWILDER	BHAKTA	BIBBERS	BICRON
BETTERS	BEWILDERED	BHAKTAS	BIBBERY	BICRONS
BETTING	BEWILDERING	BHAKTI	BIBBING	BICUSPID
BETTOR	BEWILDERS	BHAKTIS	BIBBS	BICUSPIDS
BETTORS	BEWINGED	BHANG	BIBCOCK	BICYCLE
BETWEEN	BEWITCH	BHANGRA	BIBCOCKS	BICYCLED
BETWIXT	BEWITCHED	BHANGRAS	BIBELOT	BICYCLER
BEUNCLED	BEWITCHER	BHANGS	BIBELOTS	BICYCLERS
BEVATRON	BEWITCHERS	BHARAL	BIBLE	BICYCLES
BEVATRONS	BEWITCHES	BHARALS	BIBLES	BICYCLIC
BEVEL	BEWITCHING	BHEESTIE	BIBLESS	BICYCLING
BEVELED	BEWORM	BHEESTIES	BIBLICAL	BICYCLIST
BEVELER	BEWORMED	BHEESTY	BIBLICISM	BICYCLISTS
BEVELERS	BEWORMING	BHISTIE	BIBLICISMS	BID
BEVELING	BEWORMS	BHISTIES	BIBLICIST	BIDARKA
BEVELLED	BEWORRIED	BHOOT	BIBLICISTS	BIDARKAS
BEVELLER	BEWORRIES	BHOOTS	BIBLIKE	BIDARKEE
BEVELLERS	BEWORRY	BHUT	BIBLIOTIC	BIDARKEES
BEVELLING	BEWORRYING	BHUTS	BIBLIST	BIDDABLE
BEVELS	BEWRAP	BI	BIBLISTS	BIDDABLY
BEVERAGE	BEWRAPPED	BIACETYL	BIBS	BIDDEN
BEVERAGES	BEWRAPPING	BIACETYLS	BIBULOUS	BIDDER
BEVIES	BEWRAPS	BIALI	BICAMERAL	BIDDERS
BEVOMIT	BEWRAPT	BIALIES	BICARB	BIDDIES
BEVOMITED	BEWRAY	BIALIS	BICARBS	BIDDING
BEVOMITING	BEWRAYED	BIALY	BICAUDAL	BIDDINGS
BEVOMITS	BEWRAYER	BIALYS	BICE	BIDDY
BEVOR	BEWRAYERS	BIANNUAL	BICENTRIC	BIDE
BEVORS	BEWRAYING	BIAS	BICEP	BIDED
BEVY	BEWRAYS	BIASED	BICEPS	BIDENTAL
BEWAIL	BEY	BIASEDLY	BICEPSES	BIDENTATE
BEWAILED	BEYLIC	BIASES	BICES	BIDER
BEWAILER	BEYLICS	BIASING	BICHROME	BIDERS
BEWAILERS	BEYLIK	BIASNESS	BICIPITAL	BIDES
BEWAILING	BEYLIKS	BIASNESSES	BICKER	BIDET
BEWAILS	BEYOND	BIASSED	BICKERED	BIDETS
BEWARE	BEYONDS	BIASSEDLY	BICKERER	BIDI
BEWARED	BEYS	BIASSES	BICKERERS	BIDING

BIDIS	BIGAMOUS	BIGOTRIES	BILEVELS	BILLIARDS
BIDS	BIGAMY	BIGOTRY	BILGE	BILLIE
BIELD	BIGARADE	BIGOTS	BILGED	BILLIES
BIELDED	BIGARADES	BIGS	BILGES	BILLING
BIELDING	BIGAROON	BIGSTICK	BILGIER	BILLINGS
BIELDS	BIGAROONS	BIGTIME	BILGIEST	BILLION
BIENNALE	BIGARREAU	BIGWIG	BILGING	BILLIONS
BIENNALES	BIGARREAUS	BIGWIGS	BILGY	BILLIONTH
BIENNIA	BIGEMINAL	BIHOURLY	BILHARZIA	BILLIONTHS
BIENNIAL	BIGEMINIES	BIJECTION	BILHARZIAS	BILLON
BIENNIALS	BIGEMINY	BIJECTIONS	BILIARY	BILLONS
BIENNIUM	BIGENERIC	BIJECTIVE	BILINEAR	BILLOW
BIENNIUMS	BIGEYE	BIJOU	BILINGUAL	BILLOWED
BIER	BIGEYES	BIJOUS	BILINGUALS	BILLOWIER
BIERS	BIGFEET	BIJOUX	BILIOUS	BILLOWIEST
BIESTINGS	BIGFOOT	BIJUGATE	BILIOUSLY	BILLOWING
BIFACE	BIGFOOTED	BIJUGOUS	BILIRUBIN	BILLOWS
BIFACES	BIGFOOTING	BIKE	BILIRUBINS	BILLOWY
BIFACIAL	BIGFOOTS	BIKED	BILK	BILLS
BIFARIOUS	BIGGER	BIKER	BILKED	BILLY
BIFF	BIGGEST	BIKERS	BILKER	BILLYCAN
BIFFED	BIGGETY	BIKES	BILKERS	BILLYCANS
BIFFIES	BIGGIE	BIKEWAY	BILKING	BILLYCOCK
BIFFIN	BIGGIES	BIKEWAYS	BILKS	BILLYCOCKS
BIFFING	BIGGIN	BIKIE	BILL	BILOBATE
BIFFINS	BIGGING	BIKIES	BILLABLE	BILOBATED
BIFFS	BIGGINGS	BIKING	BILLABONG	BILOBED
BIFFY	BIGGINS	BIKINI	BILLABONGS	BILOBULAR
BIFID	BIGGISH	BIKINIED	BILLBOARD	BILOCULAR
BIFIDITIES	BIGGITY	BIKINIS	BILLBOARDED	BILSTED
BIFIDITY	BIGGY	BILABIAL	BILLBOARDING	BILSTEDS
BIFIDLY	BIGHEAD	BILABIALS	BILLBOARDS	BILTONG
BIFILAR	BIGHEADED	BILABIATE	BILLBUG	BILTONGS
BIFILARLY	BIGHEADS	BILANDER	BILLBUGS	BIMA
BIFLEX	BIGHORN	BILANDERS	BILLED	BIMAH
BIFOCAL	BIGHORNS	BILATERAL	BILLER	BIMAHS
BIFOCALED	BIGHT	BILAYER	BILLERS	BIMANOUS
BIFOCALS	BIGHTED	BILAYERS	BILLET	BIMANUAL
BIFOLD	BIGHTING	BILBERRIES	BILLETED	BIMAS
BIFOLIATE	BIGHTS	BILBERRY	BILLETER	BIMBETTE
BIFORATE	BIGLY	BILBIES	BILLETERS	BIMBETTES
BIFORKED	BIGMOUTH	BILBO	BILLETING	BIMBO
BIFORM	BIGMOUTHS	BILBOA	BILLETS	BIMBOES
BIFORMED	BIGNESS	BILBOAS	BILLFISH	BIMBOS
BIFURCATE	BIGNESSES	BILBOES	BILLFISHES	BIMENSAL
BIFURCATED	BIGNONIA	BILBOS	BILLFOLD	BIMESTER
BIFURCATES	BIGNONIAS	BILBY	BILLFOLDS	BIMESTERS
BIFURCATING	BIGOS	BILE	BILLHEAD	BIMETAL
BIG	BIGOSES	BILECTION	BILLHEADS	BIMETALS
BIGAMIES	BIGOT	BILECTIONS	BILLHOOK	BIMETHYL
BIGAMIST	BIGOTED	BILES	BILLHOOKS	BIMETHYLS
BIGAMISTS	BIGOTEDLY	BILEVEL	BILLIARD	BIMODAL

BIMONTHLIES	BINOCULAR	BIOHERMS	BIOREGION	BIPARTY
BIMONTHLY	BINOCULARS	BIOLOGIC	BIOREGIONS	BIPED
BIMORPH	BINOMIAL	BIOLOGICS	BIORHYTHM	BIPEDAL
BIMORPHS	BINOMIALS	BIOLOGIES	BIORHYTHMS	BIPEDALLY
BIN	BINS	BIOLOGISM	BIOS	BIPEDS
BINAL	BINT	BIOLOGISMS	BIOSAFETIES	BIPHASIC
BINARIES	BINTS	BIOLOGIST	BIOSAFETY	BIPHENYL
BINARISM	BINTURONG	BIOLOGISTS	BIOSCOPE	BIPHENYLS
BINARISMS	BINTURONGS	BIOLOGY	BIOSCOPES	BIPINNATE
BINARY	BINUCLEAR	BIOLYSES	BIOSCOPIES	BIPLANE
BINATE	BIO	BIOLYSIS	BIOSCOPY	BIPLANES
BINATELY	BIOACTIVE	BIOLYTIC	BIOSENSOR	BIPOD
BINAURAL	BIOASSAY	BIOMARKER	BIOSENSORS	BIPODS
BIND	BIOASSAYED	BIOMARKERS	BIOSOCIAL	BIPOLAR
BINDABLE	BIOASSAYING	BIOMASS	BIOSOLID	BIPYRAMID
BINDER	BIOASSAYS	BIOMASSES	BIOSOLIDS	BIPYRAMIDS
BINDERIES	BIOCENOSE	BIOME	BIOSPHERE	BIRACIAL
BINDERS	BIOCENOSES	BIOMES	BIOSPHERES	BIRADIAL
BINDERY	BIOCHEMIC	BIOMETER	BIOSTROME	BIRADICAL
BINDI	BIOCHIP	BIOMETERS	BIOSTROMES	BIRADICALS
BINDING	BIOCHIPS	BIOMETRIC	BIOTA	BIRAMOSE
BINDINGLY	BIOCIDAL	BIOMETRIES	BIOTAS	BIRAMOUS
BINDINGS	BIOCIDE	BIOMETRY	BIOTECH	BIRCH
BINDIS	BIOCIDES	BIOMORPH	BIOTECHS	BIRCHED
BINDLE	BIOCLEAN	BIOMORPHS	BIOTERROR	BIRCHEN
BINDLES	BIOCYCLE	BIONIC	BIOTERRORS	BIRCHES
BINDS	BIOCYCLES	BIONICS	BIOTIC	BIRCHING
BINDWEED	BIOETHIC	BIONOMIC	BIOTICAL	BIRD
BINDWEEDS	BIOETHICS	BIONOMICS	BIOTICS	BIRDBATH
BINE	BIOFILM	BIONOMIES	BIOTIN	BIRDBATHS
BINER	BIOFILMS	BIONOMIST	BIOTINS	BIRDBRAIN
BINERS	BIOFOULER	BIONOMISTS	BIOTITE	BIRDBRAINS
BINES	BIOFOULERS	BIONOMY	BIOTITES	BIRDCAGE
BINGE	BIOFUEL	BIONT	BIOTITIC	BIRDCAGES
BINGED	BIOFUELED	BIONTIC	BIOTOPE	BIRDCALL
BINGEING	BIOFUELS	BIONTS	BIOTOPES	BIRDCALLS
BINGER	BIOG	BIOPHILIA	BIOTOXIN	BIRDDOG
BINGERS	BIOGAS	BIOPHILIAS	BIOTOXINS	BIRDDOGGED
BINGES	BIOGASES	BIOPIC	BIOTRON	BIRDDOGGING
BINGING	BIOGASSES	BIOPICS	BIOTRONS	BIRDDOGS
BINGO	BIOGEN	BIOPIRACIES	BIOTURBED	BIRDED
BINGOES	BIOGENIC	BIOPIRACY	BIOTYPE	BIRDER
BINGOS	BIOGENIES	BIOPIRATE	BIOTYPES	BIRDERS
BINIT	BIOGENOUS	BIOPIRATES	BIOTYPIC	BIRDFARM
BINITS	BIOGENS	BIOPLASM	BIOVULAR	BIRDFARMS
BINNACLE	BIOGENY	BIOPLASMS	BIOWEAPON	BIRDFEED
BINNACLES	BIOGRAPHIES	BIOPSIC	BIOWEAPONS	BIRDFEEDS
BINNED	BIOGRAPHY	BIOPSIED	BIPACK	BIRDHOUSE
BINNING	BIOGS	BIOPSIES	BIPACKS	BIRDHOUSES
BINOCLE	BIOHAZARD	BIOPSY	BIPAROUS	BIRDIE
BINOCLES	BIOHAZARDS	BIOPSYING	BIPARTED	BIRDIED
BINOCS	BIOHERM	BIOPTIC	BIPARTITE	BIRDIEING

BIRDIES	BIRSES	BISMUTHIC	BITING	BIVINYLS
BIRDING	BIRTH	BISMUTHS	BITINGLY	BIVOUAC
BIRDINGS	BIRTHDAY	BISNAGA	BITMAP	BIVOUACKED
BIRDLIFE	BIRTHDAYS	BISNAGAS	BITMAPPED	BIVOUACKING
BIRDLIKE	BIRTHED	BISON	BITMAPS	BIVOUACKS
BIRDLIME	BIRTHING	BISONS	BITS	BIVOUACS
BIRDLIMED	BIRTHINGS	BISONTINE	BITSIER	BIWEEKLIES
BIRDLIMES	BIRTHMARK	BISQUE	BITSIEST	BIWEEKLY
BIRDLIMING	BIRTHMARKS	BISQUES	BITSTOCK	BIYEARLY
BIRDMAN	BIRTHNAME	BISTATE	BITSTOCKS	BIZ
BIRDMEN	BIRTHNAMES	BISTER	BITSTREAM	BIZARRE
BIRDS	BIRTHRATE	BISTERED	BITSTREAMS	BIZARRELY
BIRDSEED	BIRTHRATES	BISTERS	BITSY	BIZARRES
BIRDSEEDS	BIRTHROOT	BISTORT	BITT	BIZARRO
BIRDSEYE	BIRTHROOTS	BISTORTS	BITTED	BIZARROS
BIRDSEYES	BIRTHS	BISTOURIES	BITTEN	BIZE
BIRDSHOT	BIRTHWORT	BISTOURY	BITTER	BIZES
BIRDSONG	BIRTHWORTS	BISTRE	BITTERED	BIZNAGA
BIRDSONGS	BIRYANI	BISTRED	BITTERER	BIZNAGAS
BIRDWATCH	BIRYANIS	BISTRES	BITTEREST	BIZONAL
BIRDWATCHED	BIS	BISTRO	BITTERING	BIZONE
BIRDWATCHES	BISCOTTI	BISTROIC	BITTERISH	BIZONES
BIRDWATCHING	BISCOTTO	BISTROS	BITTERLY	BIZZES
BIREME	BISCUIT	BISULCATE	BITTERN	BLAB
BIREMES	BISCUITS	BISULFATE	BITTERNS	BLABBED
BIRETTA	BISCUITY	BISULFATES	BITTERNUT	BLABBER
BIRETTAS	BISE	BISULFIDE	BITTERNUTS	BLABBERED
BIRIANI	BISECT	BISULFIDES	BITTERS	BLABBERING
BIRIANIS	BISECTED	BISULFITE	BITTIER	BLABBERS
BIRK	BISECTING	BISULFITES	BITTIEST	BLABBING
BIRKIE	BISECTION	BIT	BITTINESS	BLABBY
BIRKIES	BISECTIONS	BITABLE	BITTINESSES	BLABS
BIRKS	BISECTOR	BITCH	BITTING	BLACK
BIRL	BISECTORS	BITCHED	BITTINGS	BLACKBALL
BIRLE	BISECTRICES	BITCHEN	BITTOCK	BLACKBALLED
BIRLED	BISECTRIX	BITCHERIES	BITTOCKS	BLACKBALLING
BIRLER	BISECTS	BITCHERY	BITTS	BLACKBALLS
BIRLERS	BISERIATE	BITCHES	BITTY	BLACKBIRD
BIRLES	BISERRATE	BITCHIER	BITUMEN	BLACKBIRDED
BIRLING	BISES	BITCHIEST	BITUMENS	BLACKBIRDING
BIRLINGS	BISEXUAL	BITCHILY	BIUNIQUE	BLACKBIRDS
BIRLS	BISEXUALS	BITCHING	BIVALENCE	BLACKBODIES
BIRO	BISHOP	BITCHY	BIVALENCES	BLACKBODY
BIROS	BISHOPED	BITE	BIVALENCIES	BLACKBOY
BIRR	BISHOPING	BITEABLE	BIVALENCY	BLACKBOYS
BIRRED	BISHOPRIC	BITEPLATE	BIVALENT	BLACKBUCK
BIRRETTA	BISHOPRICS	BITEPLATES	BIVALENTS	BLACKBUCKS
BIRRETTAS	BISHOPS	BITER	BIVALVE	BLACKCAP
BIRRING	BISK	BITERS	BIVALVED	BLACKCAPS
BIRROTCH	BISKS	BITES	BIVALVES	BLACKCOCK
BIRRS	BISMUTH	BITEWING	BIVARIATE	BLACKCOCKS
BIRSE	BISMUTHAL	BITEWINGS	BIVINYL	BLACKDAMP

BLACKDAMPS	BLACKTAILS	BLANDISH	BLASTOFF	BLAZONRY
BLACKED	BLACKTOP	BLANDISHED	BLASTOFFS	BLAZONS
BLACKEN	BLACKTOPPED	BLANDISHES	BLASTOMA	BLEACH
BLACKENED	BLACKTOPPING	BLANDISHING	BLASTOMAS	BLEACHED
BLACKENER	BLACKTOPS	BLANDLY	BLASTOMATA	BLEACHER
BLACKENERS	BLACKWOOD	BLANDNESS	BLASTS	BLEACHERS
BLACKENING	BLACKWOODS	BLANDNESSES	BLASTULA	BLEACHES
BLACKENS	BLADDER	BLANK	BLASTULAE	BLEACHING
BLACKER	BLADDERS	BLANKED	BLASTULAR	BLEAK
BLACKEST	BLADDERY	BLANKER	BLASTULAS	BLEAKER
BLACKFACE	BLADE	BLANKEST	BLASTY	BLEAKEST
BLACKFACES	BLADED	BLANKET	BLAT	BLEAKISH
BLACKFIN	BLADELESS	BLANKETED	BLATANCIES	BLEAKLY
BLACKFINS	BLADELIKE	BLANKETING	BLATANCY	BLEAKNESS
BLACKFISH	BLADER	BLANKETS	BLATANT	BLEAKNESSES
BLACKFISHES	BLADERS	BLANKING	BLATANTLY	BLEAKS
BLACKFLIES	BLADES	BLANKLY	BLATE	BLEAR
BLACKFLY	BLADING	BLANKNESS	BLATHER	BLEARED
BLACKGUM	BLADINGS	BLANKNESSES	BLATHERED	BLEAREYED
BLACKGUMS	BLAE	BLANKS	BLATHERER	BLEARIER
BLACKHEAD	BLAEBERRIES	BLARE	BLATHERERS	BLEARIEST
BLACKHEADS	BLAEBERRY	BLARED	BLATHERING	BLEARILY
BLACKING	BLAFF	BLARES	BLATHERS	BLEARING
BLACKINGS	BLAFFS	BLARING	BLATS	BLEARS
BLACKISH	BLAGGING	BLARNEY	BLATTED	BLEARY
BLACKJACK	BLAGGINGS	BLARNEYED	BLATTER	BLEAT
BLACKJACKED	BLAH	BLARNEYING	BLATTERED	BLEATED
BLACKJACKING	BLAHS	BLARNEYS	BLATTERING	BLEATER
BLACKJACKS	BLAIN	BLASE	BLATTERS	BLEATERS
BLACKLAND	BLAINS	BLASPHEME	BLATTING	BLEATING
BLACKLANDS	BLAM	BLASPHEMED	BLAUBOK	BLEATS
BLACKLEAD	BLAMABLE	BLASPHEMES	BLAUBOKS	BLEB
BLACKLEADS	BLAMABLY	BLASPHEMIES	BLAW	BLEBBING
BLACKLEG	BLAME	BLASPHEMING	BLAWED	BLEBBINGS
BLACKLEGS	BLAMEABLE	BLASPHEMY	BLAWING	BLEBBY
BLACKLIST	BLAMED	BLAST	BLAWN	BLEBS
BLACKLISTED	BLAMEFUL	BLASTED	BLAWS	BLED
BLACKLISTING	BLAMELESS	BLASTEMA	BLAZE	BLEED
BLACKLISTS	BLAMER	BLASTEMAL	BLAZED	BLEEDER
BLACKLY	BLAMERS	BLASTEMAS	BLAZER	BLEEDERS
BLACKMAIL	BLAMES	BLASTEMATA	BLAZERED	BLEEDING
BLACKMAILED	BLAMING	BLASTEMIC	BLAZERS	BLEEDINGS
BLACKMAILING	BLAMS	BLASTER	BLAZES	BLEEDS
BLACKMAILS	BLANCH	BLASTERS	BLAZING	BLEEP
BLACKNESS	BLANCHED	BLASTIE	BLAZINGLY	BLEEPED
BLACKNESSES	BLANCHER	BLASTIER	BLAZON	BLEEPER
BLACKOUT	BLANCHERS	BLASTIES	BLAZONED	BLEEPERS
BLACKOUTS	BLANCHES	BLASTIEST	BLAZONER	BLEEPING
BLACKPOLL	BLANCHING	BLASTING	BLAZONERS	BLEEPS
BLACKPOLLS	BLAND	BLASTINGS	BLAZONING	BLELLUM
BLACKS	BLANDER	BLASTMENT	BLAZONINGS	BLELLUMS
BLACKTAIL	BLANDEST	BLASTMENTS	BLAZONRIES	BLEMISH

BLEMISHED	BLIGHTY	BLISS	BLOCKAGES	BLOODLIKE
BLEMISHER	BLIMEY	BLISSED	BLOCKBUST	BLOODLINE
BLEMISHERS	BLIMP	BLISSES	BLOCKBUSTED	BLOODLINES
BLEMISHES	BLIMPISH	BLISSFUL	BLOCKBUSTING	BLOODLUST
BLEMISHING	BLIMPS	BLISSING	BLOCKBUSTS	BLOODLUSTS
BLENCH	BLIMY	BLISSLESS	BLOCKED	BLOODRED
BLENCHED	BLIN	BLISTER	BLOCKER	BLOODROOT
BLENCHER	BLIND	BLISTERED	BLOCKERS	BLOODROOTS
BLENCHERS	BLINDAGE	BLISTERING	BLOCKHEAD	BLOODS
BLENCHES	BLINDAGES	BLISTERS	BLOCKHEADS	BLOODSHED
BLENCHING	BLINDED	BLISTERY	BLOCKIER	BLOODSHEDS
BLEND	BLINDER	BLITE	BLOCKIEST	BLOODSHOT
BLENDE	BLINDERS	BLITES	BLOCKING	BLOODWORM
BLENDED	BLINDEST	BLITHE	BLOCKISH	BLOODWORMS
BLENDER	BLINDFISH	BLITHEFUL	BLOCKS	BLOODWORT
BLENDERS	BLINDFISHES	BLITHELY	BLOCKY	BLOODWORTS
BLENDES	BLINDFOLD	BLITHER	BLOCS	BLOODY
BLENDING	BLINDFOLDED	BLITHERED	BLOG	BLOODYING
BLENDS	BLINDFOLDING	BLITHERING	BLOGGER	BLOOEY
BLENNIES	BLINDFOLDS	BLITHERS	BLOGGERS	BLOOIE
BLENNIOID	BLINDGUT	BLITHEST	BLOGGING	BLOOM
BLENNY	BLINDGUTS	BLITZ	BLOGGINGS	BLOOMED
BLENT	BLINDING	BLITZED	BLOGS	BLOOMER
BLESBOK	BLINDLY	BLITZER	BLOKE	BLOOMERIES
BLESBOKS	BLINDNESS	BLITZERS	BLOKES	BLOOMERS
BLESBUCK	BLINDNESSES	BLITZES	BLOND	BLOOMERY
BLESBUCKS	BLINDS	BLITZING	BLONDE	BLOOMIER
BLESS	BLINDSIDE	BLIZZARD	BLONDER	BLOOMIEST
BLESSED	BLINDSIDED	BLIZZARDS	BLONDES	BLOOMING
BLESSEDER	BLINDSIDES	BLIZZARDY	BLONDEST	BLOOMLESS
BLESSEDEST	BLINDSIDING	BLOAT	BLONDINE	BLOOMS
BLESSEDLY	BLINDWORM	BLOATED	BLONDINED	BLOOMY
BLESSER	BLINDWORMS	BLOATER	BLONDINES	BLOOP
BLESSERS	BLINI	BLOATERS	BLONDINING	BLOOPED
BLESSES	BLINIS	BLOATING	BLONDISH	BLOOPER
BLESSING	BLINK	BLOATS	BLONDNESS	BLOOPERS
BLESSINGS	BLINKARD	BLOATWARE	BLONDNESSES	BLOOPING
BLEST	BLINKARDS	BLOATWARES	BLONDS	BLOOPS
BLET	BLINKED	BLOB	BLOOD	BLOSSOM
BLETHER	BLINKER	BLOBBED	BLOODBATH	BLOSSOMED
BLETHERED	BLINKERED	BLOBBING	BLOODBATHS	BLOSSOMING
BLETHERING	BLINKERING	BLOBS	BLOODED	BLOSSOMS
BLETHERS	BLINKERS	BLOC	BLOODFIN	BLOSSOMY
BLETS	BLINKING	BLOCK	BLOODFINS	BLOT
BLEW	BLINKS	BLOCKABLE	BLOODIED	BLOTCH
BLIGHT	BLINTZ	BLOCKADE	BLOODIER	BLOTCHED
BLIGHTED	BLINTZE	BLOCKADED	BLOODIES	BLOTCHES
BLIGHTER	BLINTZES	BLOCKADER	BLOODIEST	BLOTCHIER
BLIGHTERS	BLIP	BLOCKADERS	BLOODILY	BLOTCHIEST
BLIGHTIES	BLIPPED	BLOCKADES	BLOODING	BLOTCHILY
BLIGHTING	BLIPPING	BLOCKADING	BLOODINGS	BLOTCHING
BLIGHTS	BLIPS	BLOCKAGE	BLOODLESS	BLOTCHY

BLOTLESS	BLOWJOBS	BLUEBALL	BLUENOSED	BLUNDERER
BLOTS	BLOWN	BLUEBALLS	BLUENOSES	BLUNDERERS
BLOTTED	BLOWOFF	BLUEBEARD	BLUEPOINT	BLUNDERING
BLOTTER	BLOWOFFS	BLUEBEARDS	BLUEPOINTS	BLUNDERS
BLOTTERS	BLOWOUT	BLUEBEAT	BLUEPRINT	BLUNGE
BLOTTIER	BLOWOUTS	BLUEBEATS	BLUEPRINTED	BLUNGED
BLOTTIEST	BLOWPIPE	BLUEBELL	BLUEPRINTING	BLUNGER
BLOTTING	BLOWPIPES	BLUEBELLS	BLUEPRINTS	BLUNGERS
BLOTTO	BLOWS	BLUEBERRIES	BLUER	BLUNGES
BLOTTY	BLOWSED	BLUEBERRY	BLUES	BLUNGING
BLOUSE	BLOWSIER	BLUEBILL	BLUESHIFT	BLUNT
BLOUSED	BLOWSIEST	BLUEBILLS	BLUESHIFTS	BLUNTED
BLOUSES	BLOWSILY	BLUEBIRD	BLUESIER	BLUNTER
BLOUSIER	BLOWSY	BLUEBIRDS	BLUESIEST	BLUNTEST
BLOUSIEST	BLOWTORCH	BLUEBLOOD	BLUESMAN	BLUNTING
BLOUSILY	BLOWTORCHED	BLUEBLOODS	BLUESMEN	BLUNTLY
BLOUSING	BLOWTORCHES	BLUEBOOK	BLUEST	BLUNTNESS
BLOUSON	BLOWTORCHING	BLUEBOOKS	BLUESTEM	BLUNTNESSES
BLOUSONS	BLOWTUBE	BLUECAP	BLUESTEMS	BLUNTS
BLOUSY	BLOWTUBES	BLUECAPS	BLUESTONE	BLUR
BLOVIATE	BLOWUP	BLUECOAT	BLUESTONES	BLURB
BLOVIATED	BLOWUPS	BLUECOATS	BLUESY	BLURBED
BLOVIATES	BLOWY	BLUECURLS	BLUET	BLURBING
BLOVIATING	BLOWZED	BLUED	BLUETICK	BLURBIST
BLOW	BLOWZIER	BLUEFIN	BLUETICKS	BLURBISTS
BLOWBACK	BLOWZIEST	BLUEFINS	BLUETS	BLURBS
BLOWBACKS	BLOWZILY	BLUEFISH	BLUEWEED	BLURRED
BLOWBALL	BLOWZY	BLUEFISHES	BLUEWEEDS	BLURREDLY
BLOWBALLS	BLUB	BLUEGILL	BLUEWOOD	BLURRIER
BLOWBY	BLUBBED	BLUEGILLS	BLUEWOODS	BLURRIEST
BLOWBYS	BLUBBER	BLUEGRASS	BLUEY	BLURRILY
BLOWDOWN	BLUBBERED	BLUEGRASSES	BLUEYS	BLURRING
BLOWDOWNS	BLUBBERER	BLUEGUM	BLUFF	BLURRY
BLOWED	BLUBBERERS	BLUEGUMS	BLUFFABLE	BLURS
BLOWER	BLUBBERING	BLUEHEAD	BLUFFED	BLURT
BLOWERS	BLUBBERS	BLUEHEADS	BLUFFER	BLURTED
BLOWFISH	BLUBBERY	BLUEING	BLUFFERS	BLURTER
BLOWFISHES	BLUBBING	BLUEINGS	BLUFFEST	BLURTERS
BLOWFLIES	BLUBS	BLUEISH	BLUFFING	BLURTING
BLOWFLY	BLUCHER	BLUEJACK	BLUFFLY	BLURTS
BLOWGUN	BLUCHERS	BLUEJACKS	BLUFFNESS	BLUSH
BLOWGUNS	BLUDGE	BLUEJAY	BLUFFNESSES	BLUSHED
BLOWHARD	BLUDGED	BLUEJAYS	BLUFFS	BLUSHER
BLOWHARDS	BLUDGEON	BLUEJEANS	BLUING	BLUSHERS
BLOWHOLE	BLUDGEONED	BLUELINE	BLUINGS	BLUSHES
BLOWHOLES	BLUDGEONING	BLUELINER	BLUISH	BLUSHFUL
BLOWIER	BLUDGEONS	BLUELINERS	BLUME	BLUSHING
BLOWIEST	BLUDGER	BLUELINES	BLUMED	BLUSTER
BLOWINESS	BLUDGERS	BLUELY	BLUMES	BLUSTERED
BLOWINESSES	BLUDGES	BLUENESS	BLUMING	BLUSTERER
BLOWING	BLUDGING	BLUENESSES	BLUNDER	BLUSTERERS
BLOWJOB	BLUE	BLUENOSE	BLUNDERED	BLUSTERING

BLUSTERS	BOATHOUSES	BOBSTAY	BODYCHECKING	BOGGLERS
BLUSTERY	BOATING	BOBSTAYS	BODYCHECKS	BOGGLES
BLYPE	BOATINGS	BOBTAIL	BODYGUARD	BOGGLING
BLYPES	BOATLIFT	BOBTAILED	BODYGUARDED	BOGGY
BO	BOATLIFTED	BOBTAILING	BODYGUARDING	BOGIE
BOA	BOATLIFTING	BOBTAILS	BODYGUARDS	BOGIES
BOAR	BOATLIFTS	BOBWHITE	BODYING	BOGLE
BOARD	BOATLIKE	BOBWHITES	BODYSUIT	BOGLES
BOARDABLE	BOATLOAD	BOCACCIO	BODYSUITS	BOGS
BOARDED	BOATLOADS	BOCACCIOS	BODYSURF	BOGUS
BOARDER	BOATMAN	BOCCE	BODYSURFED	BOGUSLY
BOARDERS	BOATMEN	BOCCES	BODYSURFING	BOGUSNESS
BOARDING	BOATNECK	BOCCI	BODYSURFS	BOGUSNESSES
BOARDINGS	BOATNECKS	BOCCIA	BODYWORK	BOGWOOD
BOARDLIKE	BOATS	BOCCIAS	BODYWORKS	BOGWOODS
BOARDMAN	BOATSMAN	BOCCIE	BOEHMITE	BOGY
BOARDMEN	BOATSMEN	BOCCIES	BOEHMITES	BOGYISM
BOARDROOM	BOATSWAIN	BOCCIS	BOFF	BOGYISMS
BOARDROOMS	BOATSWAINS	BOCHE	BOFFED	BOGYMAN
BOARDS	BOATYARD	BOCHES	BOFFIN	BOGYMEN
BOARDWALK	BOATYARDS	BOCK	BOFFING	BOHEA
BOARDWALKS	BOB	BOCKS	BOFFINS	BOHEAS
BOARFISH	BOBBED	BOD	BOFFO	BOHEMIA
BOARFISHES	BOBBER	BODACIOUS	BOFFOLA	BOHEMIAN
BOARHOUND	BOBBERIES	BODE	BOFFOLAS	BOHEMIANS
BOARHOUNDS	BOBBERS	BODED	BOFFOS	BOHEMIAS
BOARISH	BOBBERY	BODEGA	BOFFS	BOHO
BOARS	BOBBIES	BODEGAS	BOG	BOHOS
BOART	BOBBIN	BODEMENT	BOGAN	BOHRIUM
BOARTS	BOBBINET	BODEMENTS	BOGANS	BOHRIUMS
BOAS	BOBBINETS	BODES	BOGART	BOHUNK
BOAST	BOBBING	BODHRAN	BOGARTED	BOHUNKS
BOASTED	BOBBINS	BODHRANS	BOGARTING	BOIL
BOASTER	BOBBLE	BODICE	BOGARTS	BOILABLE
BOASTERS	BOBBLED	BODICES	BOGBEAN	BOILED
BOASTFUL	BOBBLES	BODIED	BOGBEANS	BOILER
BOASTING	BOBBLING	BODIES	BOGEY	BOILERS
BOASTS	BOBBY	BODILESS	BOGEYED	BOILING
BOAT	BOBBYSOX	BODILY	BOGEYING	BOILINGLY
BOATABLE	BOBCAT	BODING	BOGEYMAN	BOILOFF
BOATBILL	BOBCATS	BODINGLY	BOGEYMEN	BOILOFFS
BOATBILLS	BOBECHE	BODINGS	BOGEYS	BOILOVER
BOATED	BOBECHES	BODKIN	BOGGED	BOILOVERS
BOATEL	BOBOLINK	BODKINS	BOGGIER	BOILS
BOATELS	BOBOLINKS	BODS	BOGGIEST	BOING
BOATER	BOBS	BODY	BOGGINESS	BOINGS
BOATERS	BOBSLED	BODYBOARD	BOGGINESSES	BOINK
BOATFUL	BOBSLEDDED	BODYBOARDED	BOGGING	BOINKED
BOATFULS	BOBSLEDDING	BODYBOARDING	BOGGISH	BOINKING
BOATHOOK	BOBSLEDS	BODYBOARDS	BOGGLE	BOINKS
BOATHOOKS	BOBSLEIGH	BODYCHECK	BOGGLED	BOISERIE
BOATHOUSE	BOBSLEIGHS	BODYCHECKED	BOGGLER	BOISERIES

BOITE	BOLLWORM	BOMBARDONS	BONDER	BONHOMOUS
BOITES	BOLLWORMS	BOMBARDS	BONDERS	BONIATO
BOLA	BOLO	BOMBAST	BONDING	BONIATOS
BOLAR	BOLOGNA	BOMBASTER	BONDINGS	BONIER
BOLAS	BOLOGNAS	BOMBASTERS	BONDLESS	BONIEST
BOLASES	BOLOGRAPH	BOMBASTIC	BONDMAID	BONIFACE
BOLD	BOLOGRAPHS	BOMBASTS	BONDMAIDS	BONIFACES
BOLDER	BOLOMETER	BOMBAX	BONDMAN	BONINESS
BOLDEST	BOLOMETERS	BOMBAZINE	BONDMEN	BONINESSES
BOLDFACE	BOLONEY	BOMBAZINES	BONDS	BONING
BOLDFACED	BOLONEYS	BOMBE	BONDSMAN	BONITA
BOLDFACES	BOLOS	BOMBED	BONDSMEN	BONITAS
BOLDFACING	BOLSHEVIK	BOMBER	BONDSTONE	BONITO
BOLDLY	BOLSHEVIKI	BOMBERS	BONDSTONES	BONITOES
BOLDNESS	BOLSHEVIKS	BOMBES	BONDUC	BONITOS
BOLDNESSES	BOLSHIE	BOMBESIN	BONDUCS	BONK
BOLDS	BOLSHIES	BOMBESINS	BONDWOMAN	BONKED
BOLE	BOLSHY	BOMBINATE	BONDWOMEN	BONKERS
BOLECTION	BOLSON	BOMBINATED	BONE	BONKING
BOLECTIONS	BOLSONS	BOMBINATES	BONEBLACK	BONKS
BOLERO	BOLSTER	BOMBINATING	BONEBLACKS	BONNE
BOLEROS	BOLSTERED	BOMBING	BONED	BONNES
BOLES	BOLSTERER	BOMBINGS	BONEFISH	BONNET
BOLETE	BOLSTERERS	BOMBLET	BONEFISHES	BONNETED
BOLETES	BOLSTERING	BOMBLETS	BONEHEAD	BONNETING
BOLETI	BOLSTERS	BOMBLOAD	BONEHEADS	BONNETS
BOLETUS	BOLT	BOMBLOADS	BONELESS	BONNIE
BOLETUSES	BOLTED	BOMBPROOF	BONEMEAL	BONNIER
BOLIDE	BOLTER	BOMBPROOFED	BONEMEALS	BONNIEST
BOLIDES	BOLTERS	BOMBPROOFING	BONER	BONNILY
BOLIVAR	BOLTHEAD	BOMBPROOFS	BONERS	BONNINESS
BOLIVARES	BOLTHEADS	BOMBS	BONES	BONNINESSES
BOLIVARS	BOLTHOLE	BOMBSHELL	BONESET	BONNOCK
BOLIVIA	BOLTHOLES	BOMBSHELLS	BONESETS	BONNOCKS
BOLIVIANO	BOLTING	BOMBSIGHT	BONEY	BONNY
BOLIVIANOS	BOLTLESS	BOMBSIGHTS	BONEYARD	BONOBO
BOLIVIAS	BOLTLIKE	BOMBYCID	BONEYARDS	BONOBOS
BOLL	BOLTONIA	BOMBYCIDS	BONEYER	BONSAI
BOLLARD	BOLTONIAS	BOMBYCOID	BONEYEST	BONSPELL
BOLLARDS	BOLTROPE	BOMBYX	BONFIRE	BONSPELLS
BOLLED	BOLTROPES	BOMBYXES	BONFIRES	BONSPIEL
BOLLING	BOLTS	BONACI	BONG	BONSPIELS
BOLLIX	BOLUS	BONACIS	BONGED	BONTEBOK
BOLLIXED	BOLUSES	BONANZA	BONGING	BONTEBOKS
BOLLIXES	BOMB	BONANZAS	BONGO	BONUS
BOLLIXING	BOMBABLE	BONBON	BONGOES	BONUSES
BOLLOCKS	BOMBARD	BONBONS	BONGOIST	BONY
BOLLOX	BOMBARDED	BOND	BONGOISTS	BONZE
BOLLOXED	BOMBARDER	BONDABLE	BONGOS	BONZER
BOLLOXES	BOMBARDERS	BONDAGE	BONGS	BONZES
BOLLOXING	BOMBARDING	BONDAGES	BONHOMIE	BOO
BOLLS	BOMBARDON	BONDED	BONHOMIES	BOOB

BOOBED	BOOKABLE	BOOMBOX	BOOTJACK	BORATED
BOOBIE	BOOKCASE	BOOMBOXES	BOOTJACKS	BORATES
BOOBIES	BOOKCASES	BOOMED	BOOTLACE	BORATING
BOOBING	BOOKED	BOOMER	BOOTLACES	BORAX
BOOBIRD	BOOKEND	BOOMERANG	BOOTLEG	BORAXES
BOOBIRDS	BOOKENDS	BOOMERANGED	BOOTLEGGED	BORDEAUX
BOOBISH	BOOKER	BOOMERANGING	BOOTLEGGING	BORDEL
BOOBOISIE	BOOKERS	BOOMERANGS	BOOTLEGS	BORDELLO
BOOBOISIES	BOOKFUL	BOOMERS	BOOTLESS	BORDELLOS
BOOBOO	BOOKFULS	BOOMIER	BOOTLICK	BORDELS
BOOBOOS	BOOKIE	BOOMIEST	BOOTLICKED	BORDER
BOOBS	BOOKIES	BOOMING	BOOTLICKING	BORDEREAU
BOOBY	BOOKING	BOOMINGLY	BOOTLICKS	BORDEREAUX
BOOCOO	BOOKINGS	BOOMKIN	BOOTS	BORDERED
BOOCOOS	BOOKISH	BOOMKINS	BOOTSTRAP	BORDERER
BOODIES	BOOKISHLY	BOOMLET	BOOTSTRAPPED	BORDERERS
BOODLE	BOOKLET	BOOMLETS	BOOTSTRAPPING	BORDERING
BOODLED	BOOKLETS	BOOMS	BOOTSTRAPS	BORDERS
BOODLER	BOOKLICE	BOOMTOWN	BOOTY	BORDURE
BOODLERS	BOOKLORE	BOOMTOWNS	BOOZE	BORDURES
BOODLES	BOOKLORES	BOOMY	BOOZED	BORE
BOODLING	BOOKLOUSE	BOON	BOOZER	BOREAL
BOODY	BOOKMAKER	BOONDOCK	BOOZERS	BOREAS
BOOED	BOOKMAKERS	BOONDOCKS	BOOZES	BOREASES
BOOGER	BOOKMAN	BOONIES	BOOZIER	BORECOLE
BOOGERMAN	BOOKMARK	BOONLESS	BOOZIEST	BORECOLES
BOOGERMEN	BOOKMARKED	BOONS	BOOZILY	BORED
BOOGERS	BOOKMARKING	BOOR	BOOZINESS	BOREDOM
BOOGEY	BOOKMARKS	BOORISH	BOOZINESSES	BOREDOMS
BOOGEYED	BOOKMEN	BOORISHLY	BOOZING	BOREEN
BOOGEYING	BOOKOO	BOORS	BOOZY	BOREENS
BOOGEYMAN	BOOKOOS	BOOS	BOP	BOREHOLE
BOOGEYMEN	BOOKPLATE	BOOST	BOPEEP	BOREHOLES
BOOGEYS	BOOKPLATES	BOOSTED	BOPEEPS	BORER
BOOGIE	BOOKRACK	BOOSTER	BOPPED	BORERS
BOOGIED	BOOKRACKS	BOOSTERS	BOPPER	BORES
BOOGIEING	BOOKREST	BOOSTING	BOPPERS	BORESCOPE
BOOGIEMAN	BOOKRESTS	BOOSTS	BOPPING	BORESCOPES
BOOGIEMEN	BOOKS	BOOT	BOPS	BORESOME
BOOGIES	BOOKSHELF	BOOTABLE	BORA	BORIC
BOOGY	BOOKSHELVES	BOOTBLACK	BORACES	BORIDE
BOOGYING	BOOKSHOP	BOOTBLACKS	BORACIC	BORIDES
BOOGYMAN	BOOKSHOPS	BOOTED	BORACITE	BORING
BOOGYMEN	BOOKSTALL	BOOTEE	BORACITES	BORINGLY
BOOHOO	BOOKSTALLS	BOOTEES	BORAGE	BORINGS
BOOHOOED	BOOKSTAND	BOOTERIES	BORAGES	BORK
BOOHOOING	BOOKSTANDS	BOOTERY	BORAL	BORKED
BOOHOOS	BOOKSTORE	BOOTH	BORALS	BORKING
BOOING	BOOKSTORES	BOOTHS	BORANE	BORKS
BOOJUM	BOOKWORM	BOOTIE	BORANES	BORN
BOOJUMS	BOOKWORMS	BOOTIES	BORAS	BORNE
BOOK	BOOM	BOOTING	BORATE	BORNEOL

BORNEOLS	BOSKIER	BOTANIZED	BOTTOMED	BOULEVARD
BORNITE	BOSKIEST	BOTANIZER	BOTTOMER	BOULEVARDS
BORNITES	BOSKINESS	BOTANIZERS	BOTTOMERS	BOULLE
BORNITIC	BOSKINESSES	BOTANIZES	BOTTOMING	BOULLES
BORON	BOSKS	BOTANIZING	BOTTOMRIES	BOUNCE
BORONIC	BOSKY	BOTANY	BOTTOMRY	BOUNCED
BORONS	BOSOM	BOTAS	BOTTOMS	BOUNCER
BOROUGH	BOSOMED	BOTCH	BOTTS	BOUNCERS
BOROUGHS	BOSOMING	BOTCHED	BOTULIN	BOUNCES
BORRELIA	BOSOMS	BOTCHEDLY	BOTULINAL	BOUNCIER
BORRELIAS	BOSOMY	BOTCHER	BOTULINS	BOUNCIEST
BORROW	BOSON	BOTCHERIES	BOTULINUM	BOUNCILY
BORROWED	BOSONIC	BOTCHERS	BOTULINUMS	BOUNCING
BORROWER	BOSONS	BOTCHERY	BOTULINUS	BOUNCY
BORROWERS	BOSQUE	BOTCHES	BOTULINUSES	BOUND
BORROWING	BOSQUES	BOTCHIER	BOTULISM	BOUNDABLE
BORROWINGS	BOSQUET	BOTCHIEST	BOTULISMS	BOUNDARIES
BORROWS	BOSQUETS	BOTCHILY	BOUBOU	BOUNDARY
BORSCH	BOSS	BOTCHING	BOUBOUS	BOUNDED
BORSCHES	BOSSDOM	BOTCHY	BOUCHEE	BOUNDEN
BORSCHT	BOSSDOMS	BOTEL	BOUCHEES	BOUNDER
BORSCHTS	BOSSED	BOTELS	BOUCLE	BOUNDERS
BORSHT	BOSSES	BOTFLIES	BOUCLES	BOUNDING
BORSHTS	BOSSIER	BOTFLY	BOUDIN	BOUNDLESS
BORSTAL	BOSSIES	BOTH	BOUDINS	BOUNDNESS
BORSTALS	BOSSIEST	BOTHER	BOUDOIR	BOUNDNESSES
BORT	BOSSILY	BOTHERED	BOUDOIRS	BOUNDS
BORTS	BOSSINESS	BOTHERING	BOUFFANT	BOUNTEOUS
BORTY	BOSSINESSES	BOTHERS	BOUFFANTS	BOUNTIED
BORTZ	BOSSING	BOTHIES	BOUFFE	BOUNTIES
BORTZES	BOSSISM	BOTHRIA	BOUFFES	BOUNTIFUL
BORZOI	BOSSISMS	BOTHRIUM	BOUGH	BOUNTY
BORZOIS	BOSSY	BOTHRIUMS	BOUGHED	BOUQUET
BOS	BOSTON	BOTHY	BOUGHLESS	BOUQUETS
BOSCAGE	BOSTONS	BOTONEE	BOUGHPOT	BOURBON
BOSCAGES	BOSUN	BOTONNEE	BOUGHPOTS	BOURBONS
BOSCHBOK	BOSUNS	BOTRYOID	BOUGHS	BOURDON
BOSCHBOKS	BOT	BOTRYOSE	BOUGHT	BOURDONS
BOSCHVARK	BOTA	BOTRYTIS	BOUGHTEN	BOURG
BOSCHVARKS	BOTANIC	BOTRYTISES	BOUGIE	BOURGEOIS
BOSH	BOTANICA	BOTS	BOUGIES	BOURGEON
BOSHBOK	BOTANICAL	BOTT	BOUILLON	BOURGEONED
BOSHBOKS	BOTANICALS	BOTTLE	BOUILLONS	BOURGEONING
BOSHES	BOTANICAS	BOTTLED	BOULDER	BOURGEONS
BOSHVARK	BOTANIES	BOTTLEFUL	BOULDERED	BOURGS
BOSHVARKS	BOTANISE	BOTTLEFULS	BOULDERER	BOURN
BOSK	BOTANISED	BOTTLER	BOULDERERS	BOURNE
BOSKAGE	BOTANISES	BOTTLERS	BOULDERING	BOURNES
BOSKAGES	BOTANISING	BOTTLES	BOULDERS	BOURNS
BOSKER	BOTANIST	BOTTLING	BOULDERY	BOURREE
BOSKET	BOTANISTS	BOTTLINGS	BOULE	BOURREES
BOSKETS	BOTANIZE	BOTTOM	BOULES	BOURRIDE

BOURRIDES	BOWERY	BOWWOWING	BOYCOTTERS	BRACKEN
BOURSE	BOWFIN	BOWWOWS	BOYCOTTING	BRACKENS
BOURSES	BOWFINS	BOWYER	BOYCOTTS	BRACKET
BOURSIN	BOWFRONT	BOWYERS	BOYFRIEND	BRACKETED
BOURSINS	BOWHEAD	BOX	BOYFRIENDS	BRACKETING
BOURTREE	BOWHEADS	BOXBALL	BOYHOOD	BRACKETS
BOURTREES	BOWHUNTER	BOXBALLS	BOYHOODS	BRACKISH
BOUSE	BOWHUNTERS	BOXBERRIES	BOYISH	BRACONID
BOUSED	BOWING	BOXBERRY	BOYISHLY	BRACONIDS
BOUSES	BOWINGLY	BOXBOARD	BOYLA	BRACT
BOUSING	BOWINGS	BOXBOARDS	BOYLAS	BRACTEAL
BOUSOUKI	BOWKNOT	BOXCAR	BOYO	BRACTEATE
BOUSOUKIA	BOWKNOTS	BOXCARS	BOYOS	BRACTED
BOUSOUKIS	BOWL	BOXED	BOYS	BRACTEOLE
BOUSY	BOWLDER	BOXER	BOZO	BRACTEOLES
BOUT	BOWLDERS	BOXERS	BOZOS	BRACTLESS
BOUTIQUE	BOWLED	BOXES	BRA	BRACTLET
BOUTIQUES	BOWLEG	BOXFISH	BRABBLE	BRACTLETS
BOUTIQUEY	BOWLEGGED	BOXFISHES	BRABBLED	BRACTS
BOUTON	BOWLEGS	BOXFUL	BRABBLER	BRAD
BOUTONS	BOWLER	BOXFULS	BRABBLERS	BRADAWL
BOUTS	BOWLERS	BOXHAUL	BRABBLES	BRADAWLS
BOUVARDIA	BOWLESS	BOXHAULED	BRABBLING	BRADDED
BOUVARDIAS	BOWLFUL	BOXHAULING	BRACE	BRADDING
BOUVIER	BOWLFULS	BOXHAULS	BRACED	BRADOON
BOUVIERS	BOWLIKE	BOXIER	BRACELET	BRADOONS
BOUZOUKI	BOWLINE	BOXIEST	BRACELETS	BRADS
BOUZOUKIA	BOWLINES	BOXILY	BRACER	BRAE
BOUZOUKIS	BOWLING	BOXINESS	BRACERO	BRAES
BOVID	BOWLINGS	BOXINESSES	BRACEROS	BRAG
BOVIDS	BOWLLIKE	BOXING	BRACERS	BRAGGART
BOVINE	BOWLS	BOXINGS	BRACES	BRAGGARTS
BOVINELY	BOWMAN	BOXLIKE	BRACH	BRAGGED
BOVINES	BOWMEN	BOXTHORN	BRACHES	BRAGGER
BOVINITIES	BOWPOT	BOXTHORNS	BRACHET	BRAGGERS
BOVINITY	BOWPOTS	BOXWOOD	BRACHETS	BRAGGEST
BOW	BOWS	BOXWOODS	BRACHIA	BRAGGIER
BOWED	BOWSE	BOXY	BRACHIAL	BRAGGIEST
BOWEL	BOWSED	BOY	BRACHIALS	BRAGGING
BOWELED	BOWSES	BOYAR	BRACHIATE	BRAGGY
BOWELING	BOWSHOT	BOYARD	BRACHIATED	BRAGS
BOWELLED	BOWSHOTS	BOYARDS	BRACHIATES	BRAHMA
BOWELLESS	BOWSING	BOYARISM	BRACHIATING	BRAHMAS
BOWELLING	BOWSPRIT	BOYARISMS	BRACHIUM	BRAID
BOWELS	BOWSPRITS	BOYARS	BRACHS	BRAIDED
BOWER	BOWSTRING	BOYCHICK	BRACING	BRAIDER
BOWERBIRD	BOWSTRINGED	BOYCHICKS	BRACINGLY	BRAIDERS
BOWERBIRDS	BOWSTRINGING	BOYCHIK	BRACINGS	BRAIDING
BOWERED	BOWSTRINGS	BOYCHIKS	BRACIOLA	BRAIDINGS
BOWERIES	BOWSTRUNG	BOYCOTT	BRACIOLAS	BRAIDS
BOWERING	BOWWOW	BOYCOTTED	BRACIOLE	BRAIL
BOWERS	BOWWOWED	BOYCOTTER	BRACIOLES	BRAILED

BRAILING	BRAMBLE	BRANTAIL	BRATTICING	BRAWN
BRAILLE	BRAMBLED	BRANTAILS	BRATTIER	BRAWNIER
BRAILLED	BRAMBLES	BRANTS	BRATTIEST	BRAWNIEST
BRAILLER	BRAMBLIER	BRAS	BRATTISH	BRAWNILY
BRAILLERS	BRAMBLIEST	BRASH	BRATTLE	BRAWNS
BRAILLES	BRAMBLING	BRASHER	BRATTLED	BRAWNY
BRAILLING	BRAMBLINGS	BRASHES	BRATTLES	BRAWS
BRAILLIST	BRAMBLY	BRASHEST	BRATTLING	BRAXIES
BRAILLISTS	BRAN	BRASHIER	BRATTY	BRAXY
BRAILS	BRANCH	BRASHIEST	BRATWURST	BRAY
BRAIN	BRANCHED	BRASHLY	BRATWURSTS	BRAYED
BRAINCASE	BRANCHES	BRASHNESS	BRAUNITE	BRAYER
BRAINCASES	BRANCHIA	BRASHNESSES	BRAUNITES	BRAYERS
BRAINED	BRANCHIAE	BRASHY	BRAVA	BRAYING
BRAINIAC	BRANCHIAL	BRASIER	BRAVADO	BRAYS
BRAINIACS	BRANCHIER	BRASIERS	BRAVADOES	BRAZA
BRAINIER	BRANCHIEST	BRASIL	BRAVADOS	BRAZAS
BRAINIEST	BRANCHING	BRASILEIN	BRAVAS	BRAZE
BRAINILY	BRANCHLET	BRASILEINS	BRAVE	BRAZED
BRAINING	BRANCHLETS	BRASILIN	BRAVED	BRAZEN
BRAINISH	BRANCHY	BRASILINS	BRAVELY	BRAZENED
BRAINLESS	BRAND	BRASILS	BRAVENESS	BRAZENING
BRAINPAN	BRANDED	BRASS	BRAVENESSES	BRAZENLY
BRAINPANS	BRANDER	BRASSAGE	BRAVER	BRAZENS
BRAINS	BRANDERS	BRASSAGES	BRAVERIES	BRAZER
BRAINSICK	BRANDIED	BRASSARD	BRAVERS	BRAZERS
BRAINSTEM	BRANDIES	BRASSARDS	BRAVERY	BRAZES
BRAINSTEMS	BRANDING	BRASSART	BRAVES	BRAZIER
BRAINWASH	BRANDINGS	BRASSARTS	BRAVEST	BRAZIERS
BRAINWASHED	BRANDISH	BRASSED	BRAVI	BRAZIL
BRAINWASHES	BRANDISHED	BRASSERIE	BRAVING	BRAZILEIN
BRAINWASHING	BRANDISHES	BRASSERIES	BRAVO	BRAZILEINS
BRAINY	BRANDISHING	BRASSES	BRAVOED	BRAZILIN
BRAISE	BRANDLESS	BRASSICA	BRAVOES	BRAZILINS
BRAISED	BRANDLING	BRASSICAS	BRAVOING	BRAZILS
BRAISES	BRANDLINGS	BRASSIE	BRAVOS	BRAZING
BRAISING	BRANDS	BRASSIER	BRAVURA	BREACH
BRAIZE	BRANDY	BRASSIERE	BRAVURAS	BREACHED
BRAIZES	BRANDYING	BRASSIERES	BRAVURE	BREACHER
BRAKE	BRANK	BRASSIES	BRAW	BREACHERS
BRAKEAGE	BRANKS	BRASSIEST	BRAWER	BREACHES
BRAKEAGES	BRANNED	BRASSILY	BRAWEST	BREACHING
BRAKED	BRANNER	BRASSING	BRAWL	BREAD
BRAKELESS	BRANNERS	BRASSISH	BRAWLED	BREADBOX
BRAKEMAN	BRANNIER	BRASSWARE	BRAWLER	BREADBOXES
BRAKEMEN	BRANNIEST	BRASSWARES	BRAWLERS	BREADED
BRAKES	BRANNIGAN	BRASSY	BRAWLIE	BREADING
BRAKIER	BRANNIGANS	BRAT	BRAWLIER	BREADLESS
BRAKIEST	BRANNING	BRATS	BRAWLIEST	BREADLINE
BRAKING	BRANNY	BRATTICE	BRAWLING	BREADLINES
BRAKY	BRANS	BRATTICED	BRAWLS	BREADNUT
BRALESS	BRANT	BRATTICES	BRAWLY	BREADNUTS

BREADROOT
BREADROOTS
BREADS
BREADTH
BREADTHS
BREADY
BREAK
BREAKABLE
BREAKABLES
BREAKAGE
BREAKAGES
BREAKAWAY
BREAKAWAYS
BREAKDOWN
BREAKDOWNS
BREAKER
BREAKERS
BREAKEVEN
BREAKEVENS
BREAKFAST
BREAKFASTED
BREAKFASTING
BREAKFASTS
BREAKING
BREAKINGS
BREAKNECK
BREAKOUT
BREAKOUTS
BREAKS
BREAKUP
BREAKUPS
BREAKWALL
BREAKWALLS
BREAM
BREAMED
BREAMING
BREAMS
BREAST
BREASTED
BREASTFED
BREASTFEED
BREASTFEEDING
BREASTFEEDS
BREASTING
BREASTPIN
BREASTPINS
BREASTS
BREATH
BREATHE
BREATHED
BREATHER
BREATHERS

BREATHES
BREATHIER
BREATHIEST
BREATHILY
BREATHING
BREATHINGS
BREATHS
BREATHY
BRECCIA
BRECCIAL
BRECCIAS
BRECCIATE
BRECCIATED
BRECCIATES
BRECCIATING
BRECHAM
BRECHAMS
BRECHAN
BRECHANS
BRED
BREDE
BREDES
BREE
BREECH
BREECHED
BREECHES
BREECHING
BREECHINGS
BREED
BREEDER
BREEDERS
BREEDING
BREEDINGS
BREEDS
BREEKS
BREES
BREEZE
BREEZED
BREEZES
BREEZEWAY
BREEZEWAYS
BREEZIER
BREEZIEST
BREEZILY
BREEZING
BREEZY
BREGMA
BREGMATA
BREGMATE
BREGMATIC
BREN
BRENS

BRENT
BRENTS
BRETHREN
BREVE
BREVES
BREVET
BREVETCIES
BREVETCY
BREVETED
BREVETING
BREVETS
BREVETTED
BREVETTING
BREVIARIES
BREVIARY
BREVIER
BREVIERS
BREVITIES
BREVITY
BREW
BREWAGE
BREWAGES
BREWED
BREWER
BREWERIES
BREWERS
BREWERY
BREWING
BREWINGS
BREWIS
BREWISES
BREWPUB
BREWPUBS
BREWS
BREWSKI
BREWSKIES
BREWSKIS
BRIAR
BRIARD
BRIARDS
BRIARROOT
BRIARROOTS
BRIARS
BRIARWOOD
BRIARWOODS
BRIARY
BRIBABLE
BRIBE
BRIBED
BRIBEE
BRIBEES
BRIBER

BRIBERIES
BRIBERS
BRIBERY
BRIBES
BRIBING
BRICK
BRICKBAT
BRICKBATS
BRICKED
BRICKIER
BRICKIEST
BRICKING
BRICKKILN
BRICKKILNS
BRICKLE
BRICKLES
BRICKLIKE
BRICKS
BRICKWORK
BRICKWORKS
BRICKY
BRICKYARD
BRICKYARDS
BRICOLAGE
BRICOLAGES
BRICOLE
BRICOLES
BRIDAL
BRIDALLY
BRIDALS
BRIDE
BRIDES
BRIDEWELL
BRIDEWELLS
BRIDGE
BRIDGED
BRIDGES
BRIDGING
BRIDGINGS
BRIDLE
BRIDLED
BRIDLER
BRIDLERS
BRIDLES
BRIDLING
BRIDOON
BRIDOONS
BRIE
BRIEF
BRIEFCASE
BRIEFCASES
BRIEFED

BRIEFER
BRIEFERS
BRIEFEST
BRIEFING
BRIEFINGS
BRIEFLESS
BRIEFLY
BRIEFNESS
BRIEFNESSES
BRIEFS
BRIER
BRIERROOT
BRIERROOTS
BRIERS
BRIERWOOD
BRIERWOODS
BRIERY
BRIES
BRIG
BRIGADE
BRIGADED
BRIGADES
BRIGADIER
BRIGADIERS
BRIGADING
BRIGAND
BRIGANDS
BRIGHT
BRIGHTEN
BRIGHTENED
BRIGHTENING
BRIGHTENS
BRIGHTER
BRIGHTEST
BRIGHTISH
BRIGHTLY
BRIGHTS
BRIGS
BRILL
BRILLIANT
BRILLIANTS
BRILLO
BRILLOS
BRILLS
BRIM
BRIMFUL
BRIMFULL
BRIMFULLY
BRIMLESS
BRIMMED
BRIMMER
BRIMMERS

BRIMMING	BRISES	BROACHED	BROCHETTES	BROMATES
BRIMS	BRISK	BROACHER	BROCHURE	BROMATING
BRIMSTONE	BRISKED	BROACHERS	BROCHURES	BROME
BRIMSTONES	BRISKER	BROACHES	BROCK	BROMELAIN
BRIMSTONY	BRISKEST	BROACHING	BROCKAGE	BROMELAINS
BRIN	BRISKET	BROAD	BROCKAGES	BROMELIAD
BRINDED	BRISKETS	BROADAX	BROCKET	BROMELIADS
BRINDLE	BRISKING	BROADAXE	BROCKETS	BROMELIN
BRINDLED	BRISKLY	BROADAXES	BROCKS	BROMELINS
BRINDLES	BRISKNESS	BROADBAND	BROCOLI	BROMES
BRINE	BRISKNESSES	BROADBANDS	BROCOLIS	BROMIC
BRINED	BRISKS	BROADBEAN	BROGAN	BROMID
BRINELESS	BRISLING	BROADBEANS	BROGANS	BROMIDE
BRINER	BRISLINGS	BROADBILL	BROGUE	BROMIDES
BRINERS	BRISS	BROADBILLS	BROGUERIES	BROMIDIC
BRINES	BRISSES	BROADCAST	BROGUERY	BROMIDS
BRING	BRISTLE	BROADCASTED	BROGUES	BROMIN
BRINGDOWN	BRISTLED	BROADCASTING	BROGUISH	BROMINATE
BRINGDOWNS	BRISTLES	BROADCASTS	BROIDER	BROMINATED
BRINGER	BRISTLIER	BROADEN	BROIDERED	BROMINATES
BRINGERS	BRISTLIEST	BROADENED	BROIDERER	BROMINATING
BRINGING	BRISTLING	BROADENER	BROIDERERS	BROMINE
BRINGS	BRISTLY	BROADENERS	BROIDERIES	BROMINES
BRINIER	BRISTOL	BROADENING	BROIDERING	BROMINISM
BRINIES	BRISTOLS	BROADENS	BROIDERS	BROMINISMS
BRINIEST	BRIT	BROADER	BROIDERY	BROMINS
BRININESS	BRITANNIA	BROADEST	BROIL	BROMISM
BRININESSES	BRITANNIAS	BROADISH	BROILED	BROMISMS
BRINING	BRITCHES	BROADLEAF	BROILER	BROMIZE
BRINISH	BRITH	BROADLEAVES	BROILERS	BROMIZED
BRINK	BRITHS	BROADLOOM	BROILING	BROMIZES
BRINKS	BRITS	BROADLOOMS	BROILS	BROMIZING
BRINS	BRITSKA	BROADLY	BROKAGE	BROMO
BRINY	BRITSKAS	BROADNESS	BROKAGES	BROMOS
BRIO	BRITT	BROADNESSES	BROKE	BRONC
BRIOCHE	BRITTANIA	BROADS	BROKEN	BRONCHI
BRIOCHES	BRITTANIAS	BROADSIDE	BROKENLY	BRONCHIA
BRIOLETTE	BRITTLE	BROADSIDED	BROKER	BRONCHIAL
BRIOLETTES	BRITTLED	BROADSIDES	BROKERAGE	BRONCHIUM
BRIONIES	BRITTLELY	BROADSIDING	BROKERAGES	BRONCHO
BRIONY	BRITTLER	BROADTAIL	BROKERED	BRONCHOS
BRIOS	BRITTLES	BROADTAILS	BROKERING	BRONCHUS
BRIQUET	BRITTLEST	BROCADE	BROKERINGS	BRONCO
BRIQUETS	BRITTLING	BROCADED	BROKERS	BRONCOS
BRIQUETTE	BRITTLY	BROCADES	BROKING	BRONCS
BRIQUETTED	BRITTS	BROCADING	BROKINGS	BRONZE
BRIQUETTES	BRITZKA	BROCATEL	BROLLIES	BRONZED
BRIQUETTING	BRITZKAS	BROCATELS	BROLLY	BRONZER
BRIS	BRITZSKA	BROCCOLI	BROMAL	BRONZERS
BRISANCE	BRITZSKAS	BROCCOLIS	BROMALS	BRONZES
BRISANCES	BRO	BROCHE	BROMATE	BRONZIER
BRISANT	BROACH	BROCHETTE	BROMATED	BRONZIEST

BRONZING	BROTHELS	BROWSERS	BRUNG	BRUTES
BRONZINGS	BROTHER	BROWSES	BRUNIZEM	BRUTIFIED
BRONZY	BROTHERED	BROWSING	BRUNIZEMS	BRUTIFIES
BROO	BROTHERING	BRR	BRUNT	BRUTIFY
BROOCH	BROTHERLY	BRRR	BRUNTS	BRUTIFYING
BROOCHES	BROTHERS	BRUCELLA	BRUSH	BRUTING
BROOD	BROTHS	BRUCELLAE	BRUSHBACK	BRUTISH
BROODED	BROTHY	BRUCELLAS	BRUSHBACKS	BRUTISHLY
BROODER	BROUGHAM	BRUCIN	BRUSHED	BRUTISM
BROODERS	BROUGHAMS	BRUCINE	BRUSHER	BRUTISMS
BROODIER	BROUGHT	BRUCINES	BRUSHERS	BRUTS
BROODIEST	BROUHAHA	BRUCINS	BRUSHES	BRUX
BROODILY	BROUHAHAS	BRUGH	BRUSHFIRE	BRUXED
BROODING	BROW	BRUGHS	BRUSHFIRES	BRUXES
BROODLESS	BROWALLIA	BRUIN	BRUSHIER	BRUXING
BROODMARE	BROWALLIAS	BRUINS	BRUSHIEST	BRUXISM
BROODMARES	BROWBAND	BRUISE	BRUSHING	BRUXISMS
BROODS	BROWBANDS	BRUISED	BRUSHLAND	BRYOLOGIES
BROODY	BROWBEAT	BRUISER	BRUSHLANDS	BRYOLOGY
BROOK	BROWBEATEN	BRUISERS	BRUSHLESS	BRYONIES
BROOKED	BROWBEATING	BRUISES	BRUSHOFF	BRYONY
BROOKIE	BROWBEATS	BRUISING	BRUSHOFFS	BRYOPHYTE
BROOKIES	BROWED	BRUIT	BRUSHUP	BRYOPHYTES
BROOKING	BROWLESS	BRUITED	BRUSHUPS	BRYOZOAN
BROOKITE	BROWN	BRUITER	BRUSHWOOD	BRYOZOANS
BROOKITES	BROWNED	BRUITERS	BRUSHWOODS	BUB
BROOKLET	BROWNER	BRUITING	BRUSHWORK	BUBAL
BROOKLETS	BROWNEST	BRUITS	BRUSHWORKS	BUBALE
BROOKLIKE	BROWNIE	BRULOT	BRUSHY	BUBALES
BROOKLIME	BROWNIER	BRULOTS	BRUSK	BUBALINE
BROOKLIMES	BROWNIES	BRULYIE	BRUSKER	BUBALIS
BROOKS	BROWNIEST	BRULYIES	BRUSKEST	BUBALISES
BROOM	BROWNING	BRULZIE	BRUSQUE	BUBALS
BROOMBALL	BROWNISH	BRULZIES	BRUSQUELY	BUBBA
BROOMBALLS	BROWNNESS	BRUMAL	BRUSQUER	BUBBAS
BROOMCORN	BROWNNESSES	BRUMBIES	BRUSQUEST	BUBBIES
BROOMCORNS	BROWNNOSE	BRUMBY	BRUT	BUBBLE
BROOMED	BROWNNOSED	BRUME	BRUTAL	BUBBLED
BROOMIER	BROWNNOSES	BRUMES	BRUTALISE	BUBBLEGUM
BROOMIEST	BROWNNOSING	BRUMMAGEM	BRUTALISED	BUBBLEGUMS
BROOMING	BROWNOUT	BRUMMAGEMS	BRUTALISES	BUBBLER
BROOMRAPE	BROWNOUTS	BRUMOUS	BRUTALISING	BUBBLERS
BROOMRAPES	BROWNS	BRUNCH	BRUTALITIES	BUBBLES
BROOMS	BROWNY	BRUNCHED	BRUTALITY	BUBBLIER
BROOMY	BROWRIDGE	BRUNCHER	BRUTALIZE	BUBBLIES
BROOS	BROWRIDGES	BRUNCHERS	BRUTALIZED	BUBBLIEST
BROS	BROWS	BRUNCHES	BRUTALIZES	BUBBLING
BROSE	BROWSABLE	BRUNCHING	BRUTALIZING	BUBBLY
BROSES	BROWSABLES	BRUNET	BRUTALLY	BUBBY
BROSY	BROWSE	BRUNETS	BRUTE	BUBINGA
BROTH	BROWSED	BRUNETTE	BRUTED	BUBINGAS
BROTHEL	BROWSER	BRUNETTES	BRUTELY	BUBKES

BUBO	BUCKO	BUDGET	BUGBEARS	BUILDINGS
BUBOED	BUCKOES	BUDGETARY	BUGEYE	BUILDS
BUBOES	BUCKOS	BUDGETED	BUGEYES	BUILDUP
BUBONIC	BUCKRA	BUDGETEER	BUGGED	BUILDUPS
BUBS	BUCKRAM	BUDGETEERS	BUGGER	BUILT
BUBU	BUCKRAMED	BUDGETER	BUGGERED	BUIRDLY
BUBUS	BUCKRAMING	BUDGETERS	BUGGERIES	BULB
BUCCAL	BUCKRAMS	BUDGETING	BUGGERING	BULBAR
BUCCALLY	BUCKRAS	BUDGETS	BUGGERS	BULBED
BUCCANEER	BUCKS	BUDGIE	BUGGERY	BULBEL
BUCCANEERED	BUCKSAW	BUDGIES	BUGGIER	BULBELS
BUCCANEERING	BUCKSAWS	BUDGING	BUGGIES	BULBIL
BUCCANEERS	BUCKSHEE	BUDLESS	BUGGIEST	BULBILS
BUCK	BUCKSHEES	BUDLIKE	BUGGINESS	BULBLET
BUCKAROO	BUCKSHOT	BUDS	BUGGINESSES	BULBLETS
BUCKAROOS	BUCKSKIN	BUDWORM	BUGGING	BULBOUS
BUCKAYRO	BUCKSKINS	BUDWORMS	BUGGY	BULBOUSLY
BUCKAYROS	BUCKTAIL	BUFF	BUGHOUSE	BULBS
BUCKBEAN	BUCKTAILS	BUFFABLE	BUGHOUSES	BULBUL
BUCKBEANS	BUCKTEETH	BUFFALO	BUGLE	BULBULS
BUCKBOARD	BUCKTHORN	BUFFALOED	BUGLED	BULGE
BUCKBOARDS	BUCKTHORNS	BUFFALOES	BUGLER	BULGED
BUCKBRUSH	BUCKTOOTH	BUFFALOING	BUGLERS	BULGER
BUCKBRUSHES	BUCKWHEAT	BUFFALOS	BUGLES	BULGERS
BUCKED	BUCKWHEATS	BUFFED	BUGLEWEED	BULGES
BUCKEEN	BUCKYBALL	BUFFER	BUGLEWEEDS	BULGHUR
BUCKEENS	BUCKYBALLS	BUFFERED	BUGLING	BULGHURS
BUCKER	BUCKYTUBE	BUFFERING	BUGLOSS	BULGIER
BUCKEROO	BUCKYTUBES	BUFFERS	BUGLOSSES	BULGIEST
BUCKEROOS	BUCOLIC	BUFFEST	BUGOUT	BULGINESS
BUCKERS	BUCOLICS	BUFFET	BUGOUTS	BULGINESSES
BUCKET	BUD	BUFFETED	BUGS	BULGING
BUCKETED	BUDDED	BUFFETER	BUGSEED	BULGINGLY
BUCKETFUL	BUDDER	BUFFETERS	BUGSEEDS	BULGUR
BUCKETFULS	BUDDERS	BUFFETING	BUGSHA	BULGURS
BUCKETING	BUDDHA	BUFFETS	BUGSHAS	BULGY
BUCKETS	BUDDHAS	BUFFI	BUHL	BULIMIA
BUCKETSFUL	BUDDIED	BUFFIER	BUHLS	BULIMIAC
BUCKEYE	BUDDIES	BUFFIEST	BUHLWORK	BULIMIAS
BUCKEYES	BUDDING	BUFFING	BUHLWORKS	BULIMIC
BUCKHOUND	BUDDINGS	BUFFO	BUHR	BULIMICS
BUCKHOUNDS	BUDDLE	BUFFOON	BUHRS	BULK
BUCKING	BUDDLEIA	BUFFOONS	BUHRSTONE	BULKAGE
BUCKISH	BUDDLEIAS	BUFFOS	BUHRSTONES	BULKAGES
BUCKLE	BUDDLES	BUFFS	BUILD	BULKED
BUCKLED	BUDDY	BUFFY	BUILDABLE	BULKHEAD
BUCKLER	BUDDYING	BUG	BUILDDOWN	BULKHEADS
BUCKLERED	BUDGE	BUGABOO	BUILDDOWNS	BULKIER
BUCKLERING	BUDGED	BUGABOOS	BUILDED	BULKIEST
BUCKLERS	BUDGER	BUGBANE	BUILDER	BULKILY
BUCKLES	BUDGERS	BUGBANES	BUILDERS	BULKINESS
BUCKLING	BUDGES	BUGBEAR	BUILDING	BULKINESSES

BULKING	BULLISHLY	BUMBLER	BUNCHIEST	BUNKMATES
BULKS	BULLNECK	BUMBLERS	BUNCHILY	BUNKO
BULKY	BULLNECKS	BUMBLES	BUNCHING	BUNKOED
BULL	BULLNOSE	BUMBLING	BUNCHY	BUNKOING
BULLA	BULLNOSES	BUMBLINGS	BUNCO	BUNKOS
BULLACE	BULLOCK	BUMBOAT	BUNCOED	BUNKS
BULLACES	BULLOCKS	BUMBOATS	BUNCOING	BUNKUM
BULLAE	BULLOCKY	BUMELIA	BUNCOMBE	BUNKUMS
BULLATE	BULLOUS	BUMELIAS	BUNCOMBES	BUNN
BULLBAT	BULLPEN	BUMF	BUNCOS	BUNNIES
BULLBATS	BULLPENS	BUMFS	BUND	BUNNS
BULLBRIER	BULLPOUT	BUMFUZZLE	BUNDIST	BUNNY
BULLBRIERS	BULLPOUTS	BUMFUZZLED	BUNDISTS	BUNRAKU
BULLDOG	BULLRING	BUMFUZZLES	BUNDLE	BUNRAKUS
BULLDOGGED	BULLRINGS	BUMFUZZLING	BUNDLED	BUNS
BULLDOGGING	BULLRUSH	BUMKIN	BUNDLER	BUNT
BULLDOGS	BULLRUSHES	BUMKINS	BUNDLERS	BUNTED
BULLDOZE	BULLS	BUMMALO	BUNDLES	BUNTER
BULLDOZED	BULLSHAT	BUMMALOS	BUNDLING	BUNTERS
BULLDOZER	BULLSHIT	BUMMED	BUNDLINGS	BUNTING
BULLDOZERS	BULLSHITS	BUMMER	BUNDS	BUNTINGS
BULLDOZES	BULLSHITTED	BUMMERS	BUNDT	BUNTLINE
BULLDOZING	BULLSHITTING	BUMMEST	BUNDTS	BUNTLINES
BULLDYKE	BULLSHOT	BUMMING	BUNG	BUNTS
BULLDYKES	BULLSHOTS	BUMP	BUNGALOW	BUNYA
BULLED	BULLSNAKE	BUMPED	BUNGALOWS	BUNYAS
BULLET	BULLSNAKES	BUMPER	BUNGED	BUOY
BULLETED	BULLWEED	BUMPERED	BUNGEE	BUOYAGE
BULLETIN	BULLWEEDS	BUMPERING	BUNGEES	BUOYAGES
BULLETINED	BULLWHIP	BUMPERS	BUNGHOLE	BUOYANCE
BULLETING	BULLWHIPPED	BUMPH	BUNGHOLES	BUOYANCES
BULLETINING	BULLWHIPPING	BUMPHS	BUNGING	BUOYANCIES
BULLETINS	BULLWHIPS	BUMPIER	BUNGLE	BUOYANCY
BULLETS	BULLY	BUMPIEST	BUNGLED	BUOYANT
BULLFIGHT	BULLYBOY	BUMPILY	BUNGLER	BUOYANTLY
BULLFIGHTS	BULLYBOYS	BUMPINESS	BUNGLERS	BUOYED
BULLFINCH	BULLYING	BUMPINESSES	BUNGLES	BUOYING
BULLFINCHES	BULLYRAG	BUMPING	BUNGLING	BUOYS
BULLFROG	BULLYRAGGED	BUMPKIN	BUNGLINGS	BUPKES
BULLFROGS	BULLYRAGGING	BUMPKINLY	BUNGS	BUPKUS
BULLHEAD	BULLYRAGS	BUMPKINS	BUNION	BUPPIE
BULLHEADS	BULRUSH	BUMPS	BUNIONS	BUPPIES
BULLHORN	BULRUSHES	BUMPTIOUS	BUNK	BUPPY
BULLHORNS	BULWARK	BUMPY	BUNKED	BUPRESTID
BULLIED	BULWARKED	BUMS	BUNKER	BUPRESTIDS
BULLIER	BULWARKING	BUN	BUNKERED	BUQSHA
BULLIES	BULWARKS	BUNA	BUNKERING	BUQSHAS
BULLIEST	BUM	BUNAS	BUNKERS	BUR
BULLING	BUMBLE	BUNCH	BUNKHOUSE	BURA
BULLION	BUMBLEBEE	BUNCHED	BUNKHOUSES	BURAN
BULLIONS	BUMBLEBEES	BUNCHES	BUNKING	BURANS
BULLISH	BUMBLED	BUNCHIER	BUNKMATE	BURAS

BURB	BURGLARS	BURLIEST	BURROS	BUSBOY
BURBLE	BURGLARY	BURLILY	BURROW	BUSBOYS
BURBLED	BURGLE	BURLINESS	BURROWED	BUSBY
BURBLER	BURGLED	BURLINESSES	BURROWER	BUSED
BURBLERS	BURGLES	BURLING	BURROWERS	BUSES
BURBLES	BURGLING	BURLS	BURROWING	BUSGIRL
BURBLIER	BURGONET	BURLY	BURROWS	BUSGIRLS
BURBLIEST	BURGONETS	BURN	BURRS	BUSH
BURBLING	BURGOO	BURNABLE	BURRSTONE	BUSHBUCK
BURBLY	BURGOOS	BURNABLES	BURRSTONES	BUSHBUCKS
BURBOT	BURGOUT	BURNED	BURRY	BUSHED
BURBOTS	BURGOUTS	BURNER	BURS	BUSHEL
BURBS	BURGRAVE	BURNERS	BURSA	BUSHELED
BURD	BURGRAVES	BURNET	BURSAE	BUSHELER
BURDEN	BURGS	BURNETS	BURSAL	BUSHELERS
BURDENED	BURGUNDIES	BURNIE	BURSAR	BUSHELING
BURDENER	BURGUNDY	BURNIES	BURSARIAL	BUSHELLED
BURDENERS	BURIAL	BURNING	BURSARIES	BUSHELLER
BURDENING	BURIALS	BURNINGLY	BURSARS	BUSHELLERS
BURDENS	BURIED	BURNINGS	BURSARY	BUSHELLING
BURDIE	BURIER	BURNISH	BURSAS	BUSHELMAN
BURDIES	BURIERS	BURNISHED	BURSATE	BUSHELMEN
BURDOCK	BURIES	BURNISHER	BURSE	BUSHELS
BURDOCKS	BURIN	BURNISHERS	BURSEED	BUSHER
BURDS	BURINS	BURNISHES	BURSEEDS	BUSHERS
BUREAU	BURKA	BURNISHING	BURSERA	BUSHES
BUREAUS	BURKAS	BURNOOSE	BURSES	BUSHFIRE
BUREAUX	BURKE	BURNOOSED	BURSIFORM	BUSHFIRES
BURET	BURKED	BURNOOSES	BURSITIS	BUSHGOAT
BURETS	BURKER	BURNOUS	BURSITISES	BUSHGOATS
BURETTE	BURKERS	BURNOUSES	BURST	BUSHIDO
BURETTES	BURKES	BURNOUT	BURSTED	BUSHIDOS
BURG	BURKING	BURNOUTS	BURSTER	BUSHIER
BURGAGE	BURKITE	BURNS	BURSTERS	BUSHIEST
BURGAGES	BURKITES	BURNSIDES	BURSTING	BUSHILY
BURGEE	BURL	BURNT	BURSTONE	BUSHINESS
BURGEES	BURLADERO	BURP	BURSTONES	BUSHINESSES
BURGEON	BURLADEROS	BURPED	BURSTS	BUSHING
BURGEONED	BURLAP	BURPING	BURTHEN	BUSHINGS
BURGEONING	BURLAPS	BURPS	BURTHENED	BUSHLAND
BURGEONS	BURLED	BURQA	BURTHENING	BUSHLANDS
BURGER	BURLER	BURQAS	BURTHENS	BUSHLESS
BURGERS	BURLERS	BURR	BURTON	BUSHLIKE
BURGESS	BURLESK	BURRED	BURTONS	BUSHMAN
BURGESSES	BURLESKS	BURRER	BURWEED	BUSHMEN
BURGH	BURLESQUE	BURRERS	BURWEEDS	BUSHPIG
BURGHAL	BURLESQUED	BURRIER	BURY	BUSHPIGS
BURGHER	BURLESQUES	BURRIEST	BURYING	BUSHTIT
BURGHERS	BURLESQUING	BURRING	BUS	BUSHTITS
BURGHS	BURLEY	BURRITO	BUSBAR	BUSHVELD
BURGLAR	BURLEYS	BURRITOS	BUSBARS	BUSHVELDS
BURGLARIES	BURLIER	BURRO	BUSBIES	BUSHWA

BUSHWAH	BUSTING	BUTLED	BUTTRESSES	BUZZED
BUSHWAHS	BUSTLE	BUTLER	BUTTRESSING	BUZZER
BUSHWAS	BUSTLED	BUTLERIES	BUTTS	BUZZERS
BUSHWHACK	BUSTLER	BUTLERS	BUTTSTOCK	BUZZES
BUSHWHACKED	BUSTLERS	BUTLERY	BUTTSTOCKS	BUZZING
BUSHWHACKING	BUSTLES	BUTLES	BUTTY	BUZZINGLY
BUSHWHACKS	BUSTLINE	BUTLING	BUTUT	BUZZWIG
BUSHY	BUSTLINES	BUTS	BUTUTS	BUZZWIGS
BUSIED	BUSTLING	BUTT	BUTYL	BUZZWORD
BUSIER	BUSTS	BUTTALS	BUTYLATE	BUZZWORDS
BUSIES	BUSTY	BUTTE	BUTYLATED	BWANA
BUSIEST	BUSULFAN	BUTTED	BUTYLATES	BWANAS
BUSILY	BUSULFANS	BUTTER	BUTYLATING	BY
BUSINESS	BUSY	BUTTERBUR	BUTYLENE	BYCATCH
BUSINESSES	BUSYBODIES	BUTTERBURS	BUTYLENES	BYCATCHES
BUSING	BUSYBODY	BUTTERCUP	BUTYLS	BYE
BUSINGS	BUSYING	BUTTERCUPS	BUTYRAL	BYELAW
BUSK	BUSYNESS	BUTTERED	BUTYRALS	BYELAWS
BUSKED	BUSYNESSES	BUTTERFAT	BUTYRATE	BYES
BUSKER	BUSYWORK	BUTTERFATS	BUTYRATES	BYGONE
BUSKERS	BUSYWORKS	BUTTERFLIED	BUTYRIC	BYGONES
BUSKIN	BUT	BUTTERFLIES	BUTYRIN	BYLAW
BUSKINED	BUTADIENE	BUTTERFLY	BUTYRINS	BYLAWS
BUSKING	BUTADIENES	BUTTERFLYING	BUTYROUS	BYLINE
BUSKINS	BUTANE	BUTTERIER	BUTYRYL	BYLINED
BUSKS	BUTANES	BUTTERIES	BUTYRYLS	BYLINER
BUSLOAD	BUTANOL	BUTTERIEST	BUXOM	BYLINERS
BUSLOADS	BUTANOLS	BUTTERING	BUXOMER	BYLINES
BUSMAN	BUTANONE	BUTTERNUT	BUXOMEST	BYLINING
BUSMEN	BUTANONES	BUTTERNUTS	BUXOMLY	BYNAME
BUSS	BUTCH	BUTTERS	BUXOMNESS	BYNAMES
BUSSED	BUTCHER	BUTTERY	BUXOMNESSES	BYPASS
BUSSES	BUTCHERED	BUTTES	BUY	BYPASSED
BUSSING	BUTCHERER	BUTTHEAD	BUYABLE	BYPASSES
BUSSINGS	BUTCHERERS	BUTTHEADS	BUYBACK	BYPASSING
BUST	BUTCHERIES	BUTTIES	BUYBACKS	BYPAST
BUSTARD	BUTCHERING	BUTTING	BUYER	BYPATH
BUSTARDS	BUTCHERLY	BUTTINSKI	BUYERS	BYPATHS
BUSTED	BUTCHERS	BUTTINSKIES	BUYING	BYPLAY
BUSTER	BUTCHERY	BUTTINSKIS	BUYOFF	BYPLAYS
BUSTERS	BUTCHES	BUTTINSKY	BUYOFFS	BYPRODUCT
BUSTIC	BUTCHNESS	BUTTOCK	BUYOUT	BYPRODUCTS
BUSTICATE	BUTCHNESSES	BUTTOCKS	BUYOUTS	BYRE
BUSTICATED	BUTE	BUTTON	BUYS	BYRES
BUSTICATES	BUTENE	BUTTONED	BUZUKI	BYRL
BUSTICATING	BUTENES	BUTTONER	BUZUKIA	BYRLED
BUSTICS	BUTEO	BUTTONERS	BUZUKIS	BYRLING
BUSTIER	BUTEONINE	BUTTONING	BUZZ	BYRLS
BUSTIERS	BUTEONINES	BUTTONS	BUZZARD	BYRNIE
BUSTIEST	BUTEOS	BUTTONY	BUZZARDS	BYRNIES
BUSTINESS	BUTES	BUTTRESS	BUZZCUT	BYROAD
BUSTINESSES	BUTLE	BUTTRESSED	BUZZCUTS	BYROADS

BYS	CABBAGY	CABLEWAYS	CACHEXIES	CADDIES
BYSSAL	CABBALA	CABLING	CACHEXY	CADDIS
BYSSI	CABBALAH	CABMAN	CACHING	CADDISED
BYSSUS	CABBALAHS	CABMEN	CACHOU	CADDISES
BYSSUSES	CABBALAS	CABOB	CACHOUS	CADDISFLIES
BYSTANDER	CABBALISM	CABOBS	CACHUCHA	CADDISFLY
BYSTANDERS	CABBALISMS	CABOCHED	CACHUCHAS	CADDISH
BYSTREET	CABBALIST	CABOCHON	CACIQUE	CADDISHLY
BYSTREETS	CABBALISTS	CABOCHONS	CACIQUES	CADDY
BYTALK	CABBED	CABOMBA	CACIQUISM	CADDYING
BYTALKS	CABBIE	CABOMBAS	CACIQUISMS	CADE
BYTE	CABBIES	CABOODLE	CACKLE	CADELLE
BYTES	CABBING	CABOODLES	CACKLED	CADELLES
BYWAY	CABBY	CABOOSE	CACKLER	CADENCE
BYWAYS	CABDRIVER	CABOOSES	CACKLERS	CADENCED
BYWORD	CABDRIVERS	CABOSHED	CACKLES	CADENCES
BYWORDS	CABER	CABOTAGE	CACKLING	CADENCIES
BYWORK	CABERNET	CABOTAGES	CACODEMON	CADENCING
BYWORKS	CABERNETS	CABRESTA	CACODEMONS	CADENCY
BYZANT	CABERS	CABRESTAS	CACODYL	CADENT
BYZANTINE	CABESTRO	CABRESTO	CACODYLIC	CADENTIAL
BYZANTS	CABESTROS	CABRESTOS	CACODYLS	CADENZA
	CABEZON	CABRETTA	CACOETHES	CADENZAS
C	CABEZONE	CABRETTAS	CACOMIXL	CADES
	CABEZONES	CABRILLA	CACOMIXLE	CADET
	CABEZONS	CABRILLAS	CACOMIXLES	CADETS
	CABILDO	CABRIOLE	CACOMIXLS	CADETSHIP
CAB	CABILDOS	CABRIOLES	CACONYM	CADETSHIPS
CABAL	CABIN	CABRIOLET	CACONYMIES	CADGE
CABALA	CABINED	CABRIOLETS	CACONYMS	CADGED
CABALAS	CABINET	CABS	CACONYMY	CADGER
CABALETTA	CABINETRIES	CABSTAND	CACOPHONIES	CADGERS
CABALETTAS	CABINETRY	CABSTANDS	CACOPHONY	CADGES
CABALETTE	CABINETS	CACA	CACTI	CADGING
CABALISM	CABINING	CACAO	CACTOID	CADGY
CABALISMS	CABINMATE	CACAOS	CACTUS	CADI
CABALIST	CABINMATES	CACAS	CACTUSES	CADIS
CABALISTS	CABINS	CACHALOT	CACUMINAL	CADMIC
CABALLED	CABLE	CACHALOTS	CACUMINALS	CADMIUM
CABALLERO	CABLECAST	CACHE	CAD	CADMIUMS
CABALLEROS	CABLECASTED	CACHECTIC	CADASTER	CADRE
CABALLING	CABLECASTING	CACHED	CADASTERS	CADRES
CABALS	CABLECASTS	CACHEPOT	CADASTRAL	CADS
CABANA	CABLED	CACHEPOTS	CADASTRE	CADUCEAN
CABANAS	CABLEGRAM	CACHES	CADASTRES	CADUCEI
CABARET	CABLEGRAMS	CACHET	CADAVER	CADUCEUS
CABARETS	CABLER	CACHETED	CADAVERIC	CADUCITIES
CABBAGE	CABLERS	CACHETING	CADAVERS	CADUCITY
CABBAGED	CABLES	CACHETS	CADDICE	CADUCOUS
CABBAGES	CABLET	CACHEXIA	CADDICES	CAECA
CABBAGEY	CABLETS	CACHEXIAS	CADDIE	CAECAL
CABBAGING	CABLEWAY	CACHEXIC	CADDIED	CAECALLY

CAECILIAN	CAGIER	CAKEWALK	CALCANEUS	CALECHE
CAECILIANS	CAGIEST	CAKEWALKED	CALCAR	CALECHES
CAECUM	CAGILY	CAKEWALKING	CALCARATE	CALENDAL
CAEOMA	CAGINESS	CAKEWALKS	CALCARIA	CALENDAR
CAEOMAS	CAGINESSES	CAKEY	CALCARS	CALENDARED
CAESAR	CAGING	CAKIER	CALCEATE	CALENDARING
CAESAREAN	CAGY	CAKIEST	CALCEDONIES	CALENDARS
CAESAREANS	CAHIER	CAKINESS	CALCEDONY	CALENDER
CAESARIAN	CAHIERS	CAKINESSES	CALCES	CALENDERED
CAESARIANS	CAHOOT	CAKING	CALCIC	CALENDERING
CAESARISM	CAHOOTS	CAKY	CALCICOLE	CALENDERS
CAESARISMS	CAHOW	CALABASH	CALCICOLES	CALENDRIC
CAESARS	CAHOWS	CALABASHES	CALCIFIC	CALENDS
CAESIUM	CAID	CALABAZA	CALCIFIED	CALENDULA
CAESIUMS	CAIDS	CALABAZAS	CALCIFIES	CALENDULAS
CAESTUS	CAIMAN	CALABOOSE	CALCIFUGE	CALENTURE
CAESTUSES	CAIMANS	CALABOOSES	CALCIFUGES	CALENTURES
CAESURA	CAIN	CALADIUM	CALCIFY	CALESA
CAESURAE	CAINS	CALADIUMS	CALCIFYING	CALESAS
CAESURAL	CAIQUE	CALAMANCO	CALCIMINE	CALESCENT
CAESURAS	CAIQUES	CALAMANCOES	CALCIMINED	CALF
CAESURIC	CAIRD	CALAMANCOS	CALCIMINES	CALFLIKE
CAFE	CAIRDS	CALAMAR	CALCIMINING	CALFS
CAFES	CAIRN	CALAMARI	CALCINE	CALFSKIN
CAFETERIA	CAIRNED	CALAMARIES	CALCINED	CALFSKINS
CAFETERIAS	CAIRNGORM	CALAMARIS	CALCINES	CALIBER
CAFETORIA	CAIRNGORMS	CALAMARS	CALCINING	CALIBERS
CAFETORIUM	CAIRNS	CALAMARY	CALCITE	CALIBRATE
CAFETORIUMS	CAIRNY	CALAMATA	CALCITES	CALIBRATED
CAFF	CAISSON	CALAMATAS	CALCITIC	CALIBRATES
CAFFEIN	CAISSONS	CALAMI	CALCIUM	CALIBRATING
CAFFEINE	CAITIFF	CALAMINE	CALCIUMS	CALIBRE
CAFFEINES	CAITIFFS	CALAMINED	CALCSPAR	CALIBRED
CAFFEINIC	CAJAPUT	CALAMINES	CALCSPARS	CALIBRES
CAFFEINS	CAJAPUTS	CALAMINING	CALCTUFA	CALICES
CAFFS	CAJEPUT	CALAMINT	CALCTUFAS	CALICHE
CAFTAN	CAJEPUTS	CALAMINTS	CALCTUFF	CALICHES
CAFTANED	CAJOLE	CALAMITE	CALCTUFFS	CALICLE
CAFTANS	CAJOLED	CALAMITES	CALCULATE	CALICLES
CAGE	CAJOLER	CALAMITIES	CALCULATED	CALICO
CAGED	CAJOLERIES	CALAMITY	CALCULATES	CALICOES
CAGEFUL	CAJOLERS	CALAMUS	CALCULATING	CALICOS
CAGEFULS	CAJOLERY	CALANDO	CALCULI	CALIF
CAGELIKE	CAJOLES	CALASH	CALCULOUS	CALIFATE
CAGELING	CAJOLING	CALASHES	CALCULUS	CALIFATES
CAGELINGS	CAJON	CALATHI	CALCULUSES	CALIFS
CAGER	CAJONES	CALATHOS	CALDARIA	CALIPASH
CAGERS	CAJUPUT	CALATHUS	CALDARIUM	CALIPASHES
CAGES	CAJUPUTS	CALCANEA	CALDERA	CALIPEE
CAGEY	CAKE	CALCANEAL	CALDERAS	CALIPEES
CAGEYNESS	CAKED	CALCANEI	CALDRON	CALIPER
CAGEYNESSES	CAKES	CALCANEUM	CALDRONS	CALIPERED

CALIPERING	CALLOSE	CALPACS	CALYPTRAS	CAMEOS
CALIPERS	CALLOSES	CALPAIN	CALYX	CAMERA
CALIPH	CALLOSITIES	CALPAINS	CALYXES	CAMERAE
CALIPHAL	CALLOSITY	CALQUE	CALZONE	CAMERAL
CALIPHATE	CALLOUS	CALQUED	CALZONES	CAMERAMAN
CALIPHATES	CALLOUSED	CALQUES	CAM	CAMERAMEN
CALIPHS	CALLOUSES	CALQUING	CAMAIL	CAMERAS
CALISAYA	CALLOUSING	CALTHROP	CAMAILED	CAMES
CALISAYAS	CALLOUSLY	CALTHROPS	CAMAILS	CAMION
CALIX	CALLOW	CALTRAP	CAMARILLA	CAMIONS
CALK	CALLOWER	CALTRAPS	CAMARILLAS	CAMISA
CALKED	CALLOWEST	CALTROP	CAMAS	CAMISADE
CALKER	CALLS	CALTROPS	CAMASES	CAMISADES
CALKERS	CALLUS	CALUMET	CAMASS	CAMISADO
CALKIN	CALLUSED	CALUMETS	CAMASSES	CAMISADOES
CALKING	CALLUSES	CALUMNIES	CAMBER	CAMISADOS
CALKINGS	CALLUSING	CALUMNY	CAMBERED	CAMISAS
CALKINS	CALM	CALUTRON	CAMBERING	CAMISE
CALKS	CALMATIVE	CALUTRONS	CAMBERS	CAMISES
CALL	CALMATIVES	CALVADOS	CAMBIA	CAMISIA
CALLA	CALMED	CALVADOSES	CAMBIAL	CAMISIAS
CALLABLE	CALMER	CALVARIA	CAMBISM	CAMISOLE
CALLALOO	CALMEST	CALVARIAL	CAMBISMS	CAMISOLES
CALLALOOS	CALMING	CALVARIAN	CAMBIST	CAMLET
CALLAN	CALMINGLY	CALVARIAS	CAMBISTS	CAMLETS
CALLANS	CALMLY	CALVARIES	CAMBIUM	CAMMIE
CALLANT	CALMNESS	CALVARIUM	CAMBIUMS	CAMMIES
CALLANTS	CALMNESSES	CALVARIUMS	CAMBOGIA	CAMO
CALLAS	CALMS	CALVARY	CAMBOGIAS	CAMOMILE
CALLBACK	CALO	CALVE	CAMBRIC	CAMOMILES
CALLBACKS	CALOMEL	CALVED	CAMBRICS	CAMORRA
CALLBOARD	CALOMELS	CALVES	CAMCORDER	CAMORRAS
CALLBOARDS	CALORIC	CALVING	CAMCORDERS	CAMORRIST
CALLBOY	CALORICS	CALVITIES	CAME	CAMORRISTS
CALLBOYS	CALORIE	CALX	CAMEL	CAMOS
CALLED	CALORIES	CALXES	CAMELBACK	CAMP
CALLEE	CALORIFIC	CALYCATE	CAMELBACKS	CAMPAGNA
CALLEES	CALORIZE	CALYCEAL	CAMELEER	CAMPAGNE
CALLER	CALORIZED	CALYCES	CAMELEERS	CAMPAIGN
CALLERS	CALORIZES	CALYCINAL	CAMELHAIR	CAMPAIGNED
CALLET	CALORIZING	CALYCINE	CAMELHAIRS	CAMPAIGNING
CALLETS	CALORY	CALYCLE	CAMELIA	CAMPAIGNS
CALLING	CALOS	CALYCLES	CAMELIAS	CAMPANILE
CALLINGS	CALOTTE	CALYCULAR	CAMELID	CAMPANILES
CALLIOPE	CALOTTES	CALYCULI	CAMELIDS	CAMPANILI
CALLIOPES	CALOTYPE	CALYCULUS	CAMELLIA	CAMPANULA
CALLIPEE	CALOTYPES	CALYPSO	CAMELLIAS	CAMPANULAS
CALLIPEES	CALOYER	CALYPSOES	CAMELLIKE	CAMPCRAFT
CALLIPER	CALOYERS	CALYPSOS	CAMELS	CAMPCRAFTS
CALLIPERED	CALPAC	CALYPTER	CAMEO	CAMPED
CALLIPERING	CALPACK	CALYPTERS	CAMEOED	CAMPER
CALLIPERS	CALPACKS	CALYPTRA	CAMEOING	CAMPERS

CAMPESINO	CANAKINS	CANDIDACIES	CANGUES	CANNOLIS
CAMPESINOS	CANAL	CANDIDACY	CANICULAR	CANNON
CAMPFIRE	CANALBOAT	CANDIDAL	CANID	CANNONADE
CAMPFIRES	CANALBOATS	CANDIDAS	CANIDS	CANNONADED
CAMPHENE	CANALED	CANDIDATE	CANIKIN	CANNONADES
CAMPHENES	CANALING	CANDIDATES	CANIKINS	CANNONADING
CAMPHINE	CANALISE	CANDIDER	CANINE	CANNONED
CAMPHINES	CANALISED	CANDIDEST	CANINES	CANNONEER
CAMPHIRE	CANALISES	CANDIDLY	CANING	CANNONEERS
CAMPHIRES	CANALISING	CANDIDS	CANINITIES	CANNONING
CAMPHOL	CANALIZE	CANDIED	CANINITY	CANNONRIES
CAMPHOLS	CANALIZED	CANDIES	CANISTEL	CANNONRY
CAMPHOR	CANALIZES	CANDLE	CANISTELS	CANNONS
CAMPHORIC	CANALIZING	CANDLED	CANISTER	CANNOT
CAMPHORS	CANALLED	CANDLELIT	CANISTERS	CANNULA
CAMPI	CANALLER	CANDLENUT	CANITIES	CANNULAE
CAMPIER	CANALLERS	CANDLENUTS	CANKER	CANNULAR
CAMPIEST	CANALLING	CANDLEPIN	CANKERED	CANNULAS
CAMPILY	CANALS	CANDLEPINS	CANKERING	CANNULATE
CAMPINESS	CANAPE	CANDLER	CANKEROUS	CANNULATED
CAMPINESSES	CANAPES	CANDLERS	CANKERS	CANNULATES
CAMPING	CANARD	CANDLES	CANNA	CANNULATING
CAMPINGS	CANARDS	CANDLING	CANNABIC	CANNY
CAMPION	CANARIES	CANDOR	CANNABIN	CANOE
CAMPIONS	CANARY	CANDORS	CANNABINS	CANOEABLE
CAMPO	CANASTA	CANDOUR	CANNABIS	CANOED
CAMPONG	CANASTAS	CANDOURS	CANNABISES	CANOEING
CAMPONGS	CANCAN	CANDY	CANNAS	CANOEIST
CAMPOREE	CANCANS	CANDYGRAM	CANNED	CANOEISTS
CAMPOREES	CANCEL	CANDYGRAMS	CANNEL	CANOER
CAMPOS	CANCELED	CANDYING	CANNELON	CANOERS
CAMPOUT	CANCELER	CANDYTUFT	CANNELONS	CANOES
CAMPOUTS	CANCELERS	CANDYTUFTS	CANNELS	CANOLA
CAMPS	CANCELING	CANE	CANNER	CANOLAS
CAMPSHIRT	CANCELLED	CANEBRAKE	CANNERIES	CANON
CAMPSHIRTS	CANCELLER	CANEBRAKES	CANNERS	CANONESS
CAMPSITE	CANCELLERS	CANED	CANNERY	CANONESSES
CAMPSITES	CANCELLING	CANELLA	CANNIBAL	CANONIC
CAMPSTOOL	CANCELS	CANELLAS	CANNIBALS	CANONICAL
CAMPSTOOLS	CANCER	CANEPHOR	CANNIE	CANONICALS
CAMPUS	CANCERED	CANEPHORS	CANNIER	CANONISE
CAMPUSED	CANCEROUS	CANER	CANNIEST	CANONISED
CAMPUSES	CANCERS	CANERS	CANNIKIN	CANONISES
CAMPUSING	CANCHA	CANES	CANNIKINS	CANONISING
CAMPY	CANCHAS	CANESCENT	CANNILY	CANONIST
CAMS	CANCROID	CANEWARE	CANNINESS	CANONISTS
CAMSHAFT	CANCROIDS	CANEWARES	CANNINESSES	CANONIZE
CAMSHAFTS	CANDELA	CANFIELD	CANNING	CANONIZED
CAN	CANDELAS	CANFIELDS	CANNINGS	CANONIZER
CANAILLE	CANDENT	CANFUL	CANNISTER	CANONIZERS
CANAILLES	CANDID	CANFULS	CANNISTERS	CANONIZES
CANAKIN	CANDIDA	CANGUE	CANNOLI	CANONIZING

CANONRIES	CANTING	CANZONET	CAPITELLUM	CAPRIOLING
CANONRY	CANTLE	CANZONETS	CAPITOL	CAPRIS
CANONS	CANTLES	CANZONI	CAPITOLS	CAPROCK
CANOODLE	CANTO	CAP	CAPITULA	CAPROCKS
CANOODLED	CANTON	CAPABLE	CAPITULAR	CAPS
CANOODLES	CANTONAL	CAPABLER	CAPITULUM	CAPSAICIN
CANOODLING	CANTONED	CAPABLEST	CAPIZ	CAPSAICINS
CANOPIC	CANTONING	CAPABLY	CAPIZES	CAPSICIN
CANOPIED	CANTONS	CAPACIOUS	CAPLESS	CAPSICINS
CANOPIES	CANTOR	CAPACITIES	CAPLET	CAPSICUM
CANOPY	CANTORIAL	CAPACITOR	CAPLETS	CAPSICUMS
CANOPYING	CANTORS	CAPACITORS	CAPLIN	CAPSID
CANOROUS	CANTOS	CAPACITY	CAPLINS	CAPSIDAL
CANS	CANTRAIP	CAPARISON	CAPMAKER	CAPSIDS
CANSFUL	CANTRAIPS	CAPARISONED	CAPMAKERS	CAPSIZE
CANSO	CANTRAP	CAPARISONING	CAPO	CAPSIZED
CANSOS	CANTRAPS	CAPARISONS	CAPOEIRA	CAPSIZES
CANST	CANTRIP	CAPE	CAPOEIRAS	CAPSIZING
CANT	CANTRIPS	CAPED	CAPON	CAPSOMER
CANTABILE	CANTS	CAPELAN	CAPONATA	CAPSOMERE
CANTABILES	CANTUS	CAPELANS	CAPONATAS	CAPSOMERES
CANTAL	CANTY	CAPELET	CAPONIER	CAPSOMERS
CANTALA	CANULA	CAPELETS	CAPONIERS	CAPSTAN
CANTALAS	CANULAE	CAPELIN	CAPONIZE	CAPSTANS
CANTALOUP	CANULAR	CAPELINS	CAPONIZED	CAPSTONE
CANTALOUPS	CANULAS	CAPELLINI	CAPONIZES	CAPSTONES
CANTALS	CANULATE	CAPER	CAPONIZING	CAPSULAR
CANTATA	CANULATED	CAPERED	CAPONS	CAPSULATE
CANTATAS	CANULATES	CAPERER	CAPORAL	CAPSULE
CANTDOG	CANULATING	CAPERERS	CAPORALS	CAPSULED
CANTDOGS	CANVAS	CAPERING	CAPOS	CAPSULES
CANTED	CANVASED	CAPERS	CAPOTE	CAPSULING
CANTEEN	CANVASER	CAPES	CAPOTES	CAPSULIZE
CANTEENS	CANVASERS	CAPESKIN	CAPOUCH	CAPSULIZED
CANTER	CANVASES	CAPESKINS	CAPOUCHES	CAPSULIZES
CANTERED	CANVASING	CAPEWORK	CAPPED	CAPSULIZING
CANTERING	CANVASS	CAPEWORKS	CAPPER	CAPTAIN
CANTERS	CANVASSED	CAPFUL	CAPPERS	CAPTAINCIES
CANTHAL	CANVASSER	CAPFULS	CAPPING	CAPTAINCY
CANTHARIDES	CANVASSERS	CAPH	CAPPINGS	CAPTAINED
CANTHARIS	CANVASSES	CAPHS	CAPRIC	CAPTAINING
CANTHI	CANVASSING	CAPIAS	CAPRICCI	CAPTAINS
CANTHITIS	CANYON	CAPIASES	CAPRICCIO	CAPTAN
CANTHITISES	CANYONEER	CAPILLARIES	CAPRICCIOS	CAPTANS
CANTHUS	CANYONEERS	CAPILLARY	CAPRICE	CAPTION
CANTIC	CANYONING	CAPITA	CAPRICES	CAPTIONED
CANTICLE	CANYONINGS	CAPITAL	CAPRIFIG	CAPTIONING
CANTICLES	CANYONS	CAPITALLY	CAPRIFIGS	CAPTIONS
CANTILENA	CANZONA	CAPITALS	CAPRINE	CAPTIOUS
CANTILENAS	CANZONAS	CAPITATE	CAPRIOLE	CAPTIVATE
CANTINA	CANZONE	CAPITATED	CAPRIOLED	CAPTIVATED
CANTINAS	CANZONES	CAPITELLA	CAPRIOLES	CAPTIVATES

CAPTIVATING	CARAFE	CARBANION	CARBOXYLS	CARDIAC
CAPTIVE	CARAFES	CARBANIONS	CARBOY	CARDIACS
CAPTIVES	CARAGANA	CARBARN	CARBOYED	CARDIAE
CAPTIVITIES	CARAGANAS	CARBARNS	CARBOYS	CARDIAS
CAPTIVITY	CARAGEEN	CARBARYL	CARBS	CARDIGAN
CAPTOPRIL	CARAGEENS	CARBARYLS	CARBUNCLE	CARDIGANS
CAPTOPRILS	CARAMBA	CARBAZOLE	CARBUNCLES	CARDINAL
CAPTOR	CARAMBOLA	CARBAZOLES	CARBURET	CARDINALS
CAPTORS	CARAMBOLAS	CARBIDE	CARBURETED	CARDING
CAPTURE	CARAMEL	CARBIDES	CARBURETING	CARDINGS
CAPTURED	CARAMELS	CARBINE	CARBURETS	CARDIO
CAPTURER	CARANGID	CARBINEER	CARBURETTED	CARDIOID
CAPTURERS	CARANGIDS	CARBINEERS	CARBURETTING	CARDIOIDS
CAPTURES	CARANGOID	CARBINES	CARBURISE	CARDITIC
CAPTURING	CARAPACE	CARBINOL	CARBURISED	CARDITIS
CAPUCHE	CARAPACED	CARBINOLS	CARBURISES	CARDITISES
CAPUCHED	CARAPACES	CARBO	CARBURISING	CARDON
CAPUCHES	CARAPAX	CARBOLIC	CARBURIZE	CARDONS
CAPUCHIN	CARAPAXES	CARBOLICS	CARBURIZED	CARDOON
CAPUCHINS	CARASSOW	CARBOLIZE	CARBURIZES	CARDOONS
CAPUT	CARASSOWS	CARBOLIZED	CARBURIZING	CARDS
CAPYBARA	CARAT	CARBOLIZES	CARCAJOU	CARDSHARP
CAPYBARAS	CARATE	CARBOLIZING	CARCAJOUS	CARDSHARPS
CAR	CARATES	CARBON	CARCANET	CARE
CARABAO	CARATS	CARBONADE	CARCANETS	CARED
CARABAOS	CARAVAN	CARBONADES	CARCASE	CAREEN
CARABID	CARAVANED	CARBONADO	CARCASES	CAREENED
CARABIDS	CARAVANER	CARBONADOED	CARCASS	CAREENER
CARABIN	CARAVANERS	CARBONADOES	CARCASSES	CAREENERS
CARABINE	CARAVANING	CARBONADOING	CARCEL	CAREENING
CARABINER	CARAVANNED	CARBONADOS	CARCELS	CAREENS
CARABINERS	CARAVANNING	CARBONARA	CARCERAL	CAREER
CARABINES	CARAVANS	CARBONARAS	CARCINOID	CAREERED
CARABINS	CARAVEL	CARBONATE	CARCINOIDS	CAREERER
CARACAL	CARAVELLE	CARBONATED	CARCINOMA	CAREERERS
CARACALS	CARAVELLES	CARBONATES	CARCINOMAS	CAREERING
CARACARA	CARAVELS	CARBONATING	CARCINOMATA	CAREERISM
CARACARAS	CARAWAY	CARBONIC	CARD	CAREERISMS
CARACK	CARAWAYS	CARBONIUM	CARDAMOM	CAREERIST
CARACKS	CARB	CARBONIUMS	CARDAMOMS	CAREERISTS
CARACOL	CARBACHOL	CARBONIZE	CARDAMON	CAREERS
CARACOLE	CARBACHOLS	CARBONIZED	CARDAMONS	CAREFREE
CARACOLED	CARBAMATE	CARBONIZES	CARDAMUM	CAREFUL
CARACOLER	CARBAMATES	CARBONIZING	CARDAMUMS	CAREFULLER
CARACOLERS	CARBAMIC	CARBONOUS	CARDBOARD	CAREFULLEST
CARACOLES	CARBAMIDE	CARBONS	CARDBOARDS	CAREFULLY
CARACOLING	CARBAMIDES	CARBONYL	CARDCASE	CAREGIVER
CARACOLLED	CARBAMINO	CARBONYLS	CARDCASES	CAREGIVERS
CARACOLLING	CARBAMOYL	CARBORA	CARDED	CARELESS
CARACOLS	CARBAMOYLS	CARBORAS	CARDER	CARER
CARACUL	CARBAMYL	CARBOS	CARDERS	CARERS
CARACULS	CARBAMYLS	CARBOXYL	CARDIA	CARES

CARESS	CARIOSITY	CARNIES	CAROUSALS	CARR
CARESSED	CARIOUS	CARNIFIED	CAROUSE	CARRACK
CARESSER	CARITAS	CARNIFIES	CAROUSED	CARRACKS
CARESSERS	CARITASES	CARNIFY	CAROUSEL	CARRAGEEN
CARESSES	CARJACK	CARNIFYING	CAROUSELS	CARRAGEENS
CARESSING	CARJACKED	CARNITINE	CAROUSER	CARREFOUR
CARESSIVE	CARJACKER	CARNITINES	CAROUSERS	CARREFOURS
CARET	CARJACKERS	CARNIVAL	CAROUSES	CARREL
CARETAKE	CARJACKING	CARNIVALS	CAROUSING	CARRELL
CARETAKEN	CARJACKS	CARNIVORA	CARP	CARRELLS
CARETAKER	CARK	CARNIVORE	CARPACCIO	CARRELS
CARETAKERS	CARKED	CARNIVORES	CARPACCIOS	CARRIAGE
CARETAKES	CARKING	CARNIVORIES	CARPAL	CARRIAGES
CARETAKING	CARKS	CARNIVORY	CARPALE	CARRIED
CARETOOK	CARL	CARNOSAUR	CARPALIA	CARRIER
CARETS	CARLE	CARNOSAURS	CARPALS	CARRIERS
CAREWORN	CARLES	CARNOTITE	CARPED	CARRIES
CAREX	CARLESS	CARNOTITES	CARPEL	CARRIOLE
CARFARE	CARLIN	CARNS	CARPELS	CARRIOLES
CARFARES	CARLINE	CARNY	CARPENTER	CARRION
CARFUL	CARLINES	CAROACH	CARPENTERED	CARRIONS
CARFULS	CARLING	CAROACHES	CARPENTERING	CARRITCH
CARGO	CARLINGS	CAROB	CARPENTERS	CARRITCHES
CARGOES	CARLINS	CAROBS	CARPENTRIES	CARROCH
CARGOS	CARLISH	CAROCH	CARPENTRY	CARROCHES
CARHOP	CARLOAD	CAROCHE	CARPER	CARROM
CARHOPPED	CARLOADS	CAROCHES	CARPERS	CARROMED
CARHOPPING	CARLS	CAROL	CARPET	CARROMING
CARHOPS	CARMAKER	CAROLED	CARPETBAG	CARROMS
CARIBE	CARMAKERS	CAROLER	CARPETBAGGED	CARRONADE
CARIBES	CARMAN	CAROLERS	CARPETBAGGING	CARRONADES
CARIBOU	CARMEN	CAROLI	CARPETBAGS	CARROT
CARIBOUS	CARMINE	CAROLING	CARPETED	CARROTIER
CARICES	CARMINES	CAROLLED	CARPETING	CARROTIEST
CARIED	CARN	CAROLLER	CARPETINGS	CARROTIN
CARIES	CARNAGE	CAROLLERS	CARPETS	CARROTINS
CARILLON	CARNAGES	CAROLLING	CARPI	CARROTS
CARILLONNED	CARNAL	CAROLS	CARPING	CARROTTOP
CARILLONNING	CARNALITIES	CAROLUS	CARPINGLY	CARROTTOPS
CARILLONS	CARNALITY	CAROLUSES	CARPINGS	CARROTY
CARINA	CARNALLY	CAROM	CARPOLOGIES	CARROUSEL
CARINAE	CARNATION	CAROMED	CARPOLOGY	CARROUSELS
CARINAL	CARNATIONS	CAROMING	CARPOOL	CARRS
CARINAS	CARNAUBA	CAROMS	CARPOOLED	CARRY
CARINATE	CARNAUBAS	CAROTENE	CARPOOLER	CARRYALL
CARINATED	CARNELIAN	CAROTENES	CARPOOLERS	CARRYALLS
CARING	CARNELIANS	CAROTID	CARPOOLING	CARRYBACK
CARIOCA	CARNET	CAROTIDAL	CARPOOLS	CARRYBACKS
CARIOCAS	CARNETS	CAROTIDS	CARPORT	CARRYING
CARIOLE	CARNEY	CAROTIN	CARPORTS	CARRYON
CARIOLES	CARNEYS	CAROTINS	CARPS	CARRYONS
CARIOSITIES	CARNIE	CAROUSAL	CARPUS	CARRYOUT

CARRYOUTS	CARTS	CASEASES	CASHIER	CASSIAS
CARRYOVER	CARTULARIES	CASEATE	CASHIERED	CASSIMERE
CARRYOVERS	CARTULARY	CASEATED	CASHIERING	CASSIMERES
CARS	CARTWHEEL	CASEATES	CASHIERS	CASSINA
CARSE	CARTWHEELED	CASEATING	CASHING	CASSINAS
CARSES	CARTWHEELING	CASEATION	CASHLESS	CASSINE
CARSICK	CARTWHEELS	CASEATIONS	CASHMERE	CASSINES
CART	CARUNCLE	CASEBOOK	CASHMERES	CASSINGLE
CARTABLE	CARUNCLES	CASEBOOKS	CASHOO	CASSINGLES
CARTAGE	CARVACROL	CASED	CASHOOS	CASSINO
CARTAGES	CARVACROLS	CASEFIED	CASHPOINT	CASSINOS
CARTE	CARVE	CASEFIES	CASHPOINTS	CASSIS
CARTED	CARVED	CASEFY	CASIMERE	CASSISES
CARTEL	CARVEL	CASEFYING	CASIMERES	CASSOCK
CARTELISE	CARVELS	CASEIC	CASIMIRE	CASSOCKS
CARTELISED	CARVEN	CASEIN	CASIMIRES	CASSOULET
CARTELISES	CARVER	CASEINATE	CASING	CASSOULETS
CARTELISING	CARVERS	CASEINATES	CASINGS	CASSOWARIES
CARTELIZE	CARVES	CASEINS	CASINI	CASSOWARY
CARTELIZED	CARVING	CASELOAD	CASINO	CAST
CARTELIZES	CARVINGS	CASELOADS	CASINOS	CASTABLE
CARTELIZING	CARWASH	CASEMATE	CASITA	CASTANET
CARTELS	CARWASHES	CASEMATED	CASITAS	CASTANETS
CARTER	CARYATIC	CASEMATES	CASK	CASTAWAY
CARTERS	CARYATID	CASEMENT	CASKED	CASTAWAYS
CARTES	CARYATIDES	CASEMENTS	CASKET	CASTE
CARTHORSE	CARYATIDS	CASEOSE	CASKETED	CASTEISM
CARTHORSES	CARYOPSES	CASEOSES	CASKETING	CASTEISMS
CARTILAGE	CARYOPSIDES	CASEOUS	CASKETS	CASTELLAN
CARTILAGES	CARYOPSIS	CASERN	CASKING	CASTELLANS
CARTING	CARYOTIN	CASERNE	CASKS	CASTER
CARTLOAD	CARYOTINS	CASERNES	CASKY	CASTERS
CARTLOADS	CASA	CASERNS	CASQUE	CASTES
CARTOGRAM	CASABA	CASES	CASQUED	CASTIGATE
CARTOGRAMS	CASABAS	CASETTE	CASQUES	CASTIGATED
CARTON	CASAS	CASETTES	CASSABA	CASTIGATES
CARTONED	CASAVA	CASEWORK	CASSABAS	CASTIGATING
CARTONING	CASAVAS	CASEWORKS	CASSATA	CASTING
CARTONS	CASBAH	CASEWORM	CASSATAS	CASTINGS
CARTOON	CASBAHS	CASEWORMS	CASSATION	CASTLE
CARTOONED	CASCABEL	CASH	CASSATIONS	CASTLED
CARTOONING	CASCABELS	CASHABLE	CASSAVA	CASTLES
CARTOONS	CASCABLE	CASHAW	CASSAVAS	CASTLING
CARTOONY	CASCABLES	CASHAWS	CASSENA	CASTOFF
CARTOP	CASCADE	CASHBOOK	CASSENAS	CASTOFFS
CARTOPPER	CASCADED	CASHBOOKS	CASSENE	CASTOR
CARTOPPERS	CASCADES	CASHBOX	CASSENES	CASTOREUM
CARTOUCH	CASCADING	CASHBOXES	CASSEROLE	CASTOREUMS
CARTOUCHE	CASCARA	CASHED	CASSEROLES	CASTORS
CARTOUCHES	CASCARAS	CASHES	CASSETTE	CASTRATE
CARTRIDGE	CASE	CASHEW	CASSETTES	CASTRATED
CARTRIDGES	CASEASE	CASHEWS	CASSIA	CASTRATER

CASTRATERS	CATALYSIS	CATCH	CATENATE	CATHETER
CASTRATES	CATALYST	CATCHABLE	CATENATED	CATHETERS
CASTRATI	CATALYSTS	CATCHALL	CATENATES	CATHEXES
CASTRATING	CATALYTIC	CATCHALLS	CATENATING	CATHEXIS
CASTRATO	CATALYZE	CATCHER	CATENOID	CATHODAL
CASTRATOR	CATALYZED	CATCHERS	CATENOIDS	CATHODE
CASTRATORS	CATALYZER	CATCHES	CATER	CATHODES
CASTRATOS	CATALYZERS	CATCHFLIES	CATERAN	CATHODIC
CASTS	CATALYZES	CATCHFLY	CATERANS	CATHOLIC
CASUAL	CATALYZING	CATCHIER	CATERED	CATHOLICS
CASUALLY	CATAMARAN	CATCHIEST	CATERER	CATHOUSE
CASUALS	CATAMARANS	CATCHING	CATERERS	CATHOUSES
CASUALTIES	CATAMENIA	CATCHMENT	CATERESS	CATION
CASUALTY	CATAMITE	CATCHMENTS	CATERESSES	CATIONIC
CASUARINA	CATAMITES	CATCHPOLE	CATERING	CATIONS
CASUARINAS	CATAMOUNT	CATCHPOLES	CATERS	CATJANG
CASUIST	CATAMOUNTS	CATCHPOLL	CATERWAUL	CATJANGS
CASUISTIC	CATAPHORA	CATCHPOLLS	CATERWAULED	CATKIN
CASUISTRIES	CATAPHORAS	CATCHUP	CATERWAULING	CATKINATE
CASUISTRY	CATAPHYLL	CATCHUPS	CATERWAULS	CATKINS
CASUISTS	CATAPHYLLS	CATCHWORD	CATES	CATLIKE
CASUS	CATAPLASM	CATCHWORDS	CATFACE	CATLIN
CAT	CATAPLASMS	CATCHY	CATFACES	CATLING
CATABOLIC	CATAPLEXIES	CATCLAW	CATFACING	CATLINGS
CATACLYSM	CATAPLEXY	CATCLAWS	CATFACINGS	CATLINS
CATACLYSMS	CATAPULT	CATE	CATFALL	CATMINT
CATACOMB	CATAPULTED	CATECHIN	CATFALLS	CATMINTS
CATACOMBS	CATAPULTING	CATECHINS	CATFIGHT	CATNAP
CATALASE	CATAPULTS	CATECHISE	CATFIGHTS	CATNAPER
CATALASES	CATARACT	CATECHISED	CATFISH	CATNAPERS
CATALATIC	CATARACTS	CATECHISES	CATFISHES	CATNAPPED
CATALEPSIES	CATARRH	CATECHISING	CATGUT	CATNAPPER
CATALEPSY	CATARRHAL	CATECHISM	CATGUTS	CATNAPPERS
CATALEXES	CATARRHS	CATECHISMS	CATHARSES	CATNAPPING
CATALEXIS	CATATONIA	CATECHIST	CATHARSIS	CATNAPS
CATALO	CATATONIAS	CATECHISTS	CATHARTIC	CATNIP
CATALOES	CATATONIC	CATECHIZE	CATHARTICS	CATNIPS
CATALOG	CATATONICS	CATECHIZED	CATHEAD	CATOPTRIC
CATALOGED	CATAWBA	CATECHIZES	CATHEADS	CATRIGGED
CATALOGER	CATAWBAS	CATECHIZING	CATHECT	CATS
CATALOGERS	CATBIRD	CATECHOL	CATHECTED	CATSPAW
CATALOGIC	CATBIRDS	CATECHOLS	CATHECTIC	CATSPAWS
CATALOGING	CATBOAT	CATECHU	CATHECTING	CATSUIT
CATALOGS	CATBOATS	CATECHUS	CATHECTS	CATSUITS
CATALOGUE	CATBRIER	CATEGORIC	CATHEDRA	CATSUP
CATALOGUED	CATBRIERS	CATEGORIES	CATHEDRAE	CATSUPS
CATALOGUES	CATCALL	CATEGORY	CATHEDRAL	CATTAIL
CATALOGUING	CATCALLED	CATENA	CATHEDRALS	CATTAILS
CATALOS	CATCALLER	CATENAE	CATHEDRAS	CATTALO
CATALPA	CATCALLERS	CATENARIES	CATHEPSIN	CATTALOES
CATALPAS	CATCALLING	CATENARY	CATHEPSINS	CATTALOS
CATALYSES	CATCALLS	CATENAS	CATHEPTIC	CATTED

CATTERIES	CAULIS	CAUTIONS	CAVIES	CEBID
CATTERY	CAULK	CAUTIOUS	CAVIL	CEBIDS
CATTIE	CAULKED	CAVALCADE	CAVILED	CEBOID
CATTIER	CAULKER	CAVALCADES	CAVILER	CEBOIDS
CATTIES	CAULKERS	CAVALERO	CAVILERS	CECA
CATTIEST	CAULKING	CAVALEROS	CAVILING	CECAL
CATTILY	CAULKINGS	CAVALETTI	CAVILLED	CECALLY
CATTINESS	CAULKS	CAVALIER	CAVILLER	CECITIES
CATTINESSES	CAULS	CAVALIERED	CAVILLERS	CECITY
CATTING	CAUSABLE	CAVALIERING	CAVILLING	CECROPIA
CATTISH	CAUSAL	CAVALIERS	CAVILS	CECROPIAS
CATTISHLY	CAUSALGIA	CAVALLA	CAVING	CECUM
CATTLE	CAUSALGIAS	CAVALLAS	CAVINGS	CEDAR
CATTLEMAN	CAUSALGIC	CAVALLIES	CAVITARY	CEDARBIRD
CATTLEMEN	CAUSALITIES	CAVALLY	CAVITATE	CEDARBIRDS
CATTLEYA	CAUSALITY	CAVALRIES	CAVITATED	CEDARN
CATTLEYAS	CAUSALLY	CAVALRY	CAVITATES	CEDARS
CATTY	CAUSALS	CAVATINA	CAVITATING	CEDARWOOD
CATWALK	CAUSATION	CAVATINAS	CAVITIED	CEDARWOODS
CATWALKS	CAUSATIONS	CAVATINE	CAVITIES	CEDARY
CAUCUS	CAUSATIVE	CAVE	CAVITY	CEDE
CAUCUSED	CAUSATIVES	CAVEAT	CAVORT	CEDED
CAUCUSES	CAUSE	CAVEATED	CAVORTED	CEDER
CAUCUSING	CAUSED	CAVEATING	CAVORTER	CEDERS
CAUCUSSED	CAUSELESS	CAVEATOR	CAVORTERS	CEDES
CAUCUSSES	CAUSER	CAVEATORS	CAVORTING	CEDI
CAUCUSSING	CAUSERIE	CAVEATS	CAVORTS	CEDILLA
CAUDAD	CAUSERIES	CAVED	CAVY	CEDILLAS
CAUDAL	CAUSERS	CAVEFISH	CAW	CEDING
CAUDALLY	CAUSES	CAVEFISHES	CAWED	CEDIS
CAUDATE	CAUSEWAY	CAVELIKE	CAWING	CEDULA
CAUDATED	CAUSEWAYED	CAVEMAN	CAWS	CEDULAS
CAUDATES	CAUSEWAYING	CAVEMEN	CAY	CEE
CAUDATION	CAUSEWAYS	CAVENDISH	CAYENNE	CEES
CAUDATIONS	CAUSEY	CAVENDISHES	CAYENNED	CEIBA
CAUDEX	CAUSEYS	CAVER	CAYENNES	CEIBAS
CAUDEXES	CAUSING	CAVERN	CAYMAN	CEIL
CAUDICES	CAUSTIC	CAVERNED	CAYMANS	CEILED
CAUDILLO	CAUSTICS	CAVERNING	CAYS	CEILER
CAUDILLOS	CAUTERANT	CAVERNOUS	CAYUSE	CEILERS
CAUDLE	CAUTERANTS	CAVERNS	CAYUSES	CEILI
CAUDLES	CAUTERIES	CAVERS	CAZIQUE	CEILIDH
CAUGHT	CAUTERIZE	CAVES	CAZIQUES	CEILIDHS
CAUL	CAUTERIZED	CAVETTI	CEANOTHUS	CEILING
CAULD	CAUTERIZES	CAVETTO	CEANOTHUSES	CEILINGED
CAULDRON	CAUTERIZING	CAVETTOS	CEASE	CEILINGS
CAULDRONS	CAUTERY	CAVIAR	CEASED	CEILIS
CAULDS	CAUTION	CAVIARE	CEASEFIRE	CEILS
CAULES	CAUTIONED	CAVIARES	CEASEFIRES	CEINTURE
CAULICLE	CAUTIONER	CAVIARS	CEASELESS	CEINTURES
CAULICLES	CAUTIONERS	CAVICORN	CEASES	CEL
CAULINE	CAUTIONING	CAVIE	CEASING	CELADON

CELADONS	CELLBLOCKS	CEMENTUM	CENTENARIES	CENTS
CELANDINE	CELLED	CEMENTUMS	CENTENARY	CENTU
CELANDINES	CELLI	CEMETERIES	CENTER	CENTUM
CELEB	CELLING	CEMETERY	CENTERED	CENTUMS
CELEBRANT	CELLIST	CENACLE	CENTERING	CENTUPLE
CELEBRANTS	CELLISTS	CENACLES	CENTERINGS	CENTUPLED
CELEBRATE	CELLMATE	CENOBITE	CENTERS	CENTUPLES
CELEBRATED	CELLMATES	CENOBITES	CENTESES	CENTUPLING
CELEBRATES	CELLO	CENOBITIC	CENTESIMI	CENTURIAL
CELEBRATING	CELLOIDIN	CENOTAPH	CENTESIMO	CENTURIES
CELEBRITIES	CELLOIDINS	CENOTAPHS	CENTESIMOS	CENTURION
CELEBRITY	CELLOS	CENOTE	CENTESIS	CENTURIONS
CELEBS	CELLPHONE	CENOTES	CENTIARE	CENTURY
CELERIAC	CELLPHONES	CENOZOIC	CENTIARES	CEORL
CELERIACS	CELLS	CENSE	CENTIGRAM	CEORLISH
CELERIES	CELLULAR	CENSED	CENTIGRAMS	CEORLS
CELERITIES	CELLULARS	CENSER	CENTILE	CEP
CELERITY	CELLULASE	CENSERS	CENTILES	CEPE
CELERY	CELLULASES	CENSES	CENTIME	CEPES
CELESTA	CELLULE	CENSING	CENTIMES	CEPHALAD
CELESTAS	CELLULES	CENSOR	CENTIMO	CEPHALIC
CELESTE	CELLULITE	CENSORED	CENTIMOS	CEPHALIN
CELESTES	CELLULITES	CENSORIAL	CENTIPEDE	CEPHALINS
CELESTIAL	CELLULOID	CENSORING	CENTIPEDES	CEPHALOUS
CELESTIALS	CELLULOIDS	CENSORS	CENTNER	CEPHEID
CELESTINE	CELLULOSE	CENSUAL	CENTNERS	CEPHEIDS
CELESTINES	CELLULOSES	CENSURE	CENTO	CEPS
CELESTITE	CELLULOUS	CENSURED	CENTONES	CERACEOUS
CELESTITES	CELOM	CENSURER	CENTOS	CERAMAL
CELIAC	CELOMATA	CENSURERS	CENTRA	CERAMALS
CELIACS	CELOMS	CENSURES	CENTRAL	CERAMIC
CELIBACIES	CELOSIA	CENSURING	CENTRALER	CERAMICS
CELIBACY	CELOSIAS	CENSUS	CENTRALEST	CERAMIDE
CELIBATE	CELOTEX	CENSUSED	CENTRALLY	CERAMIDES
CELIBATES	CELOTEXES	CENSUSES	CENTRALS	CERAMIST
CELIBATIC	CELS	CENSUSING	CENTRE	CERAMISTS
CELL	CELT	CENT	CENTRED	CERASTES
CELLA	CELTS	CENTAI	CENTRES	CERATE
CELLAE	CEMBALI	CENTAL	CENTRIC	CERATED
CELLAR	CEMBALIST	CENTALS	CENTRICAL	CERATES
CELLARAGE	CEMBALISTS	CENTARE	CENTRING	CERATIN
CELLARAGES	CEMBALO	CENTARES	CENTRINGS	CERATINS
CELLARED	CEMBALOS	CENTAS	CENTRIOLE	CERATODUS
CELLARER	CEMENT	CENTAUR	CENTRIOLES	CERATODUSES
CELLARERS	CEMENTA	CENTAUREA	CENTRISM	CERATOID
CELLARET	CEMENTED	CENTAUREAS	CENTRISMS	CERCAL
CELLARETS	CEMENTER	CENTAURIC	CENTRIST	CERCARIA
CELLARING	CEMENTERS	CENTAURIES	CENTRISTS	CERCARIAE
CELLARS	CEMENTING	CENTAURS	CENTROID	CERCARIAL
CELLARWAY	CEMENTITE	CENTAURY	CENTROIDS	CERCARIAN
CELLARWAYS	CEMENTITES	CENTAVO	CENTRUM	CERCARIANS
CELLBLOCK	CEMENTS	CENTAVOS	CENTRUMS	CERCARIAS

CERCI	CERTAINER	CESSPITS	CHAETA	CHAIRMAN
CERCIS	CERTAINEST	CESSPOOL	CHAETAE	CHAIRMANED
CERCISES	CERTAINLY	CESSPOOLS	CHAETAL	CHAIRMANING
CERCUS	CERTAINTIES	CESTA	CHAETOPOD	CHAIRMANNED
CERE	CERTAINTY	CESTAS	CHAETOPODS	CHAIRMANNING
CEREAL	CERTES	CESTI	CHAFE	CHAIRMANS
CEREALS	CERTIFIED	CESTODE	CHAFED	CHAIRMEN
CEREBELLA	CERTIFIER	CESTODES	CHAFER	CHAIRS
CEREBELLUM	CERTIFIERS	CESTOI	CHAFERS	CHAIS
CEREBELLUMS	CERTIFIES	CESTOID	CHAFES	CHAISE
CEREBRA	CERTIFY	CESTOIDS	CHAFF	CHAISES
CEREBRAL	CERTIFYING	CESTOS	CHAFFED	CHAKRA
CEREBRALS	CERTITUDE	CESTUS	CHAFFER	CHAKRAS
CEREBRATE	CERTITUDES	CESTUSES	CHAFFERED	CHALAH
CEREBRATED	CERULEAN	CESURA	CHAFFERER	CHALAHS
CEREBRATES	CERULEANS	CESURAE	CHAFFERERS	CHALAZA
CEREBRATING	CERUMEN	CESURAS	CHAFFERING	CHALAZAE
CEREBRIC	CERUMENS	CETACEAN	CHAFFERS	CHALAZAL
CEREBRUM	CERUSE	CETACEANS	CHAFFIER	CHALAZAS
CEREBRUMS	CERUSES	CETACEOUS	CHAFFIEST	CHALAZIA
CERECLOTH	CERUSITE	CETANE	CHAFFINCH	CHALAZION
CERECLOTHS	CERUSITES	CETANES	CHAFFINCHES	CHALAZIONS
CERED	CERUSSITE	CETE	CHAFFING	CHALCID
CEREMENT	CERUSSITES	CETES	CHAFFS	CHALCIDS
CEREMENTS	CERVELAS	CETOLOGIES	CHAFFY	CHALCOGEN
CEREMONIES	CERVELASES	CETOLOGY	CHAFING	CHALCOGENS
CEREMONY	CERVELAT	CEVICHE	CHAGRIN	CHALDRON
CERES	CERVELATS	CEVICHES	CHAGRINED	CHALDRONS
CEREUS	CERVEZA	CHABAZITE	CHAGRINING	CHALEH
CEREUSES	CERVEZAS	CHABAZITES	CHAGRINNED	CHALEHS
CERIA	CERVICAL	CHABLIS	CHAGRINNING	CHALET
CERIAS	CERVICES	CHABOUK	CHAGRINS	CHALETS
CERIC	CERVID	CHABOUKS	CHAI	CHALICE
CERING	CERVINE	CHABUK	CHAIN	CHALICED
CERIPH	CERVIX	CHABUKS	CHAINE	CHALICES
CERIPHS	CERVIXES	CHACHKA	CHAINED	CHALK
CERISE	CESAREAN	CHACHKAS	CHAINES	CHALKED
CERISES	CESAREANS	CHACMA	CHAINFALL	CHALKIER
CERITE	CESARIAN	CHACMAS	CHAINFALLS	CHALKIEST
CERITES	CESARIANS	CHACONNE	CHAINING	CHALKING
CERIUM	CESIUM	CHACONNES	CHAINMAN	CHALKS
CERIUMS	CESIUMS	CHAD	CHAINMEN	CHALKY
CERMET	CESPITOSE	CHADAR	CHAINS	CHALLA
CERMETS	CESS	CHADARIM	CHAINSAW	CHALLAH
CERNUOUS	CESSATION	CHADARS	CHAINSAWED	CHALLAHS
CERO	CESSATIONS	CHADLESS	CHAINSAWING	CHALLAS
CEROS	CESSED	CHADOR	CHAINSAWS	CHALLENGE
CEROTIC	CESSES	CHADORS	CHAIR	CHALLENGED
CEROTYPE	CESSING	CHADRI	CHAIRED	CHALLENGES
CEROTYPES	CESSION	CHADS	CHAIRING	CHALLENGING
CEROUS	CESSIONS	CHAEBOL	CHAIRLIFT	CHALLIE
CERTAIN	CESSPIT	CHAEBOLS	CHAIRLIFTS	CHALLIES

CHALLIS	CHAMOMILES	CHANDLERIES	CHAPARRAL	CHARACTER
CHALLISES	CHAMP	CHANDLERS	CHAPARRALS	CHARACTERED
CHALLOT	CHAMPAC	CHANDLERY	CHAPATI	CHARACTERING
CHALLOTH	CHAMPACA	CHANFRON	CHAPATIS	CHARACTERS
CHALLY	CHAMPACAS	CHANFRONS	CHAPATTI	CHARADE
CHALONE	CHAMPACS	CHANG	CHAPATTIS	CHARADES
CHALONES	CHAMPAGNE	CHANGE	CHAPBOOK	CHARAS
CHALOT	CHAMPAGNES	CHANGED	CHAPBOOKS	CHARASES
CHALOTH	CHAMPAIGN	CHANGEFUL	CHAPE	CHARBROIL
CHALUMEAU	CHAMPAIGNS	CHANGER	CHAPEAU	CHARBROILED
CHALUMEAUS	CHAMPAK	CHANGERS	CHAPEAUS	CHARBROILING
CHALUPA	CHAMPAKS	CHANGES	CHAPEAUX	CHARBROILS
CHALUPAS	CHAMPED	CHANGEUP	CHAPEL	CHARCOAL
CHALUTZ	CHAMPER	CHANGEUPS	CHAPELS	CHARCOALED
CHALUTZIM	CHAMPERS	CHANGING	CHAPERON	CHARCOALING
CHAM	CHAMPERTIES	CHANGS	CHAPERONE	CHARCOALS
CHAMADE	CHAMPERTY	CHANNEL	CHAPERONED	CHARCOALY
CHAMADES	CHAMPING	CHANNELED	CHAPERONES	CHARD
CHAMBER	CHAMPION	CHANNELER	CHAPERONING	CHARDS
CHAMBERED	CHAMPIONED	CHANNELERS	CHAPERONS	CHARE
CHAMBERING	CHAMPIONING	CHANNELING	CHAPES	CHARED
CHAMBERS	CHAMPIONS	CHANNELLED	CHAPITER	CHARES
CHAMBRAY	CHAMPLEVE	CHANNELLING	CHAPITERS	CHARGE
CHAMBRAYS	CHAMPLEVES	CHANNELS	CHAPLAIN	CHARGED
CHAMELEON	CHAMPS	CHANOYU	CHAPLAINS	CHARGER
CHAMELEONS	CHAMPY	CHANOYUS	CHAPLET	CHARGERS
CHAMFER	CHAMS	CHANSON	CHAPLETED	CHARGES
CHAMFERED	CHANCE	CHANSONS	CHAPLETS	CHARGING
CHAMFERER	CHANCED	CHANT	CHAPMAN	CHARGRILL
CHAMFERERS	CHANCEFUL	CHANTABLE	CHAPMEN	CHARGRILLED
CHAMFERING	CHANCEL	CHANTAGE	CHAPPATI	CHARGRILLING
CHAMFERS	CHANCELS	CHANTAGES	CHAPPATIS	CHARGRILLS
CHAMFRAIN	CHANCER	CHANTED	CHAPPED	CHARIER
CHAMFRAINS	CHANCERIES	CHANTER	CHAPPIE	CHARIEST
CHAMFRON	CHANCERS	CHANTERS	CHAPPIES	CHARILY
CHAMFRONS	CHANCERY	CHANTEUSE	CHAPPING	CHARINESS
CHAMISA	CHANCES	CHANTEUSES	CHAPS	CHARINESSES
CHAMISAS	CHANCIER	CHANTEY	CHAPT	CHARING
CHAMISE	CHANCIEST	CHANTEYS	CHAPTER	CHARIOT
CHAMISES	CHANCILY	CHANTIES	CHAPTERAL	CHARIOTED
CHAMISO	CHANCING	CHANTING	CHAPTERED	CHARIOTING
CHAMISOS	CHANCRE	CHANTOR	CHAPTERING	CHARIOTS
CHAMMIED	CHANCRES	CHANTORS	CHAPTERS	CHARISM
CHAMMIES	CHANCROID	CHANTRIES	CHAQUETA	CHARISMA
CHAMMY	CHANCROIDS	CHANTRY	CHAQUETAS	CHARISMAS
CHAMMYING	CHANCROUS	CHANTS	CHAR	CHARISMATA
CHAMOIS	CHANCY	CHANTY	CHARABANC	CHARISMS
CHAMOISED	CHANDELLE	CHAO	CHARABANCS	CHARITIES
CHAMOISES	CHANDELLED	CHAOS	CHARACID	CHARITY
CHAMOISING	CHANDELLES	CHAOSES	CHARACIDS	CHARIVARI
CHAMOIX	CHANDELLING	CHAOTIC	CHARACIN	CHARIVARIED
CHAMOMILE	CHANDLER	CHAP	CHARACINS	CHARIVARIING

CHARIVARIS	CHARTABLE	CHASTISERS	CHAUSSURE	CHECHAKO
CHARK	CHARTED	CHASTISES	CHAUSSURES	CHECHAKOS
CHARKA	CHARTER	CHASTISING	CHAW	CHECK
CHARKAS	CHARTERED	CHASTITIES	CHAWBACON	CHECKABLE
CHARKED	CHARTERER	CHASTITY	CHAWBACONS	CHECKBOOK
CHARKHA	CHARTERERS	CHASUBLE	CHAWED	CHECKBOOKS
CHARKHAS	CHARTERING	CHASUBLES	CHAWER	CHECKED
CHARKING	CHARTERS	CHAT	CHAWERS	CHECKER
CHARKS	CHARTING	CHATCHKA	CHAWING	CHECKERED
CHARLADIES	CHARTIST	CHATCHKAS	CHAWS	CHECKERING
CHARLADY	CHARTISTS	CHATCHKE	CHAY	CHECKERS
CHARLATAN	CHARTLESS	CHATCHKES	CHAYOTE	CHECKING
CHARLATANS	CHARTS	CHATEAU	CHAYOTES	CHECKLESS
CHARLEY	CHARWOMAN	CHATEAUS	CHAYS	CHECKLIST
CHARLEYS	CHARWOMEN	CHATEAUX	CHAZAN	CHECKLISTED
CHARLIE	CHARY	CHATELAIN	CHAZANIM	CHECKLISTING
CHARLIES	CHASE	CHATELAINS	CHAZANS	CHECKLISTS
CHARLOCK	CHASEABLE	CHATOYANT	CHAZZAN	CHECKMARK
CHARLOCKS	CHASED	CHATOYANTS	CHAZZANIM	CHECKMARKED
CHARLOTTE	CHASER	CHATROOM	CHAZZANS	CHECKMARKING
CHARLOTTES	CHASERS	CHATROOMS	CHAZZEN	CHECKMARKS
CHARM	CHASES	CHATS	CHAZZENIM	CHECKMATE
CHARMED	CHASING	CHATTED	CHAZZENS	CHECKMATED
CHARMER	CHASINGS	CHATTEL	CHEAP	CHECKMATES
CHARMERS	CHASM	CHATTELS	CHEAPEN	CHECKMATING
CHARMEUSE	CHASMAL	CHATTER	CHEAPENED	CHECKOFF
CHARMEUSES	CHASMED	CHATTERED	CHEAPENER	CHECKOFFS
CHARMING	CHASMIC	CHATTERER	CHEAPENERS	CHECKOUT
CHARMINGER	CHASMS	CHATTERERS	CHEAPENING	CHECKOUTS
CHARMINGEST	CHASMY	CHATTERING	CHEAPENS	CHECKREIN
CHARMLESS	CHASSE	CHATTERS	CHEAPER	CHECKREINS
CHARMS	CHASSED	CHATTERY	CHEAPEST	CHECKROOM
CHARNEL	CHASSEING	CHATTIER	CHEAPIE	CHECKROOMS
CHARNELS	CHASSEPOT	CHATTIEST	CHEAPIES	CHECKROW
CHARPAI	CHASSEPOTS	CHATTILY	CHEAPISH	CHECKROWED
CHARPAIS	CHASSES	CHATTING	CHEAPJACK	CHECKROWING
CHARPOY	CHASSEUR	CHATTY	CHEAPJACKS	CHECKROWS
CHARPOYS	CHASSEURS	CHAUFER	CHEAPLY	CHECKS
CHARQUI	CHASSIS	CHAUFERS	CHEAPNESS	CHECKSUM
CHARQUID	CHASTE	CHAUFFER	CHEAPNESSES	CHECKSUMS
CHARQUIS	CHASTELY	CHAUFFERS	CHEAPO	CHECKUP
CHARR	CHASTEN	CHAUFFEUR	CHEAPOS	CHECKUPS
CHARRED	CHASTENED	CHAUFFEURED	CHEAPS	CHEDDAR
CHARRIER	CHASTENER	CHAUFFEURING	CHEAT	CHEDDARS
CHARRIEST	CHASTENERS	CHAUFFEURS	CHEATABLE	CHEDDARY
CHARRING	CHASTENING	CHAUNT	CHEATED	CHEDDITE
CHARRO	CHASTENS	CHAUNTED	CHEATER	CHEDDITES
CHARROS	CHASTER	CHAUNTER	CHEATERS	CHEDER
CHARRS	CHASTEST	CHAUNTERS	CHEATING	CHEDERS
CHARRY	CHASTISE	CHAUNTING	CHEATS	CHEDITE
CHARS	CHASTISED	CHAUNTS	CHEBEC	CHEDITES
CHART	CHASTISER	CHAUSSES	CHEBECS	CHEECHAKO

CHEECHAKOS	CHEETAHS	CHEMOS	CHESSMAN	CHEWY
CHEEK	CHEF	CHEMOSORB	CHESSMEN	CHEZ
CHEEKBONE	CHEFDOM	CHEMOSORBED	CHEST	CHI
CHEEKBONES	CHEFDOMS	CHEMOSORBING	CHESTED	CHIA
CHEEKED	CHEFED	CHEMOSORBS	CHESTFUL	CHIANTI
CHEEKFUL	CHEFFED	CHEMOSTAT	CHESTFULS	CHIANTIS
CHEEKFULS	CHEFFING	CHEMOSTATS	CHESTIER	CHIAO
CHEEKIER	CHEFING	CHEMURGIC	CHESTIEST	CHIAS
CHEEKIEST	CHEFS	CHEMURGIES	CHESTILY	CHIASM
CHEEKILY	CHEGOE	CHEMURGY	CHESTNUT	CHIASMA
CHEEKING	CHEGOES	CHENILLE	CHESTNUTS	CHIASMAL
CHEEKLESS	CHELA	CHENILLES	CHESTS	CHIASMAS
CHEEKS	CHELAE	CHENOPOD	CHESTY	CHIASMATA
CHEEKY	CHELAS	CHENOPODS	CHETAH	CHIASMI
CHEEP	CHELASHIP	CHEONGSAM	CHETAHS	CHIASMIC
CHEEPED	CHELASHIPS	CHEONGSAMS	CHETH	CHIASMS
CHEEPER	CHELATE	CHEQUE	CHETHS	CHIASMUS
CHEEPERS	CHELATED	CHEQUER	CHETRUM	CHIASTIC
CHEEPING	CHELATES	CHEQUERED	CHETRUMS	CHIAUS
CHEEPS	CHELATING	CHEQUERING	CHEVALET	CHIAUSES
CHEER	CHELATION	CHEQUERS	CHEVALETS	CHIBOUK
CHEERED	CHELATIONS	CHEQUES	CHEVALIER	CHIBOUKS
CHEERER	CHELATOR	CHERIMOYA	CHEVALIERS	CHIBOUQUE
CHEERERS	CHELATORS	CHERIMOYAS	CHEVELURE	CHIBOUQUES
CHEERFUL	CHELICERA	CHERISH	CHEVELURES	CHIC
CHEERFULLER	CHELICERAE	CHERISHED	CHEVERON	CHICA
CHEERFULLEST	CHELIFORM	CHERISHER	CHEVERONS	CHICALOTE
CHEERIER	CHELIPED	CHERISHERS	CHEVIED	CHICALOTES
CHEERIEST	CHELIPEDS	CHERISHES	CHEVIES	CHICANE
CHEERILY	CHELOID	CHERISHING	CHEVIOT	CHICANED
CHEERING	CHELOIDS	CHERNOZEM	CHEVIOTS	CHICANER
CHEERIO	CHELONIAN	CHERNOZEMS	CHEVRE	CHICANERIES
CHEERIOS	CHELONIANS	CHEROOT	CHEVRES	CHICANERS
CHEERLEAD	CHEMIC	CHEROOTS	CHEVRET	CHICANERY
CHEERLEADING	CHEMICAL	CHERRIES	CHEVRETS	CHICANES
CHEERLEADS	CHEMICALS	CHERRY	CHEVRON	CHICANING
CHEERLED	CHEMICS	CHERT	CHEVRONS	CHICANO
CHEERLESS	CHEMISE	CHERTIER	CHEVY	CHICANOS
CHEERLY	CHEMISES	CHERTIEST	CHEVYING	CHICAS
CHEERO	CHEMISM	CHERTS	CHEW	CHICCORIES
CHEEROS	CHEMISMS	CHERTY	CHEWABLE	CHICCORY
CHEERS	CHEMISORB	CHERUB	CHEWED	CHICER
CHEERY	CHEMISORBED	CHERUBIC	CHEWER	CHICEST
CHEESE	CHEMISORBING	CHERUBIM	CHEWERS	CHICHI
CHEESED	CHEMISORBS	CHERUBIMS	CHEWIER	CHICHIER
CHEESES	CHEMIST	CHERUBS	CHEWIEST	CHICHIEST
CHEESIER	CHEMISTRIES	CHERVIL	CHEWINESS	CHICHIS
CHEESIEST	CHEMISTRY	CHERVILS	CHEWINESSES	CHICK
CHEESILY	CHEMISTS	CHESHIRE	CHEWING	CHICKADEE
CHEESING	CHEMO	CHESHIRES	CHEWINK	CHICKADEES
CHEESY	CHEMOKINE	CHESS	CHEWINKS	CHICKAREE
CHEETAH	CHEMOKINES	CHESSES	CHEWS	CHICKAREES

CHICKEE	CHIGGERS	CHILLING	CHINCAPINS	CHIPPED
CHICKEES	CHIGNON	CHILLIS	CHINCH	CHIPPER
CHICKEN	CHIGNONED	CHILLNESS	CHINCHES	CHIPPERED
CHICKENED	CHIGNONS	CHILLNESSES	CHINCHIER	CHIPPERING
CHICKENING	CHIGOE	CHILLS	CHINCHIEST	CHIPPERS
CHICKENS	CHIGOES	CHILLUM	CHINCHY	CHIPPIE
CHICKORIES	CHILBLAIN	CHILLUMS	CHINE	CHIPPIER
CHICKORY	CHILBLAINS	CHILLY	CHINED	CHIPPIES
CHICKPEA	CHILD	CHILOPOD	CHINES	CHIPPIEST
CHICKPEAS	CHILDBED	CHILOPODS	CHINING	CHIPPING
CHICKS	CHILDBEDS	CHILTEPIN	CHINK	CHIPPY
CHICKWEED	CHILDCARE	CHILTEPINS	CHINKAPIN	CHIPS
CHICKWEEDS	CHILDCARES	CHIMAERA	CHINKAPINS	CHIRAL
CHICLE	CHILDE	CHIMAERAS	CHINKED	CHIRALITIES
CHICLES	CHILDES	CHIMAERIC	CHINKIER	CHIRALITY
CHICLY	CHILDHOOD	CHIMAR	CHINKIEST	CHIRIMOYA
CHICNESS	CHILDHOODS	CHIMARS	CHINKING	CHIRIMOYAS
CHICNESSES	CHILDING	CHIMB	CHINKS	CHIRK
CHICO	CHILDISH	CHIMBLEY	CHINKY	CHIRKED
CHICORIES	CHILDLESS	CHIMBLEYS	CHINLESS	CHIRKER
CHICORY	CHILDLIER	CHIMBLIES	CHINNED	CHIRKEST
CHICOS	CHILDLIEST	CHIMBLY	CHINNING	CHIRKING
CHICS	CHILDLIKE	CHIMBS	CHINO	CHIRKS
CHID	CHILDLY	CHIME	CHINONE	CHIRM
CHIDDEN	CHILDREN	CHIMED	CHINONES	CHIRMED
CHIDE	CHILE	CHIMER	CHINOOK	CHIRMING
CHIDED	CHILES	CHIMERA	CHINOOKS	CHIRMS
CHIDER	CHILI	CHIMERAS	CHINOS	CHIRO
CHIDERS	CHILIAD	CHIMERE	CHINS	CHIROPODIES
CHIDES	CHILIADAL	CHIMERES	CHINSTRAP	CHIROPODY
CHIDING	CHILIADIC	CHIMERIC	CHINSTRAPS	CHIROPTER
CHIDINGLY	CHILIADS	CHIMERISM	CHINTS	CHIROPTERS
CHIEF	CHILIARCH	CHIMERISMS	CHINTSES	CHIROS
CHIEFDOM	CHILIARCHS	CHIMERS	CHINTZ	CHIRP
CHIEFDOMS	CHILIASM	CHIMES	CHINTZES	CHIRPED
CHIEFER	CHILIASMS	CHIMING	CHINTZIER	CHIRPER
CHIEFEST	CHILIAST	CHIMLA	CHINTZIEST	CHIRPERS
CHIEFLY	CHILIASTS	CHIMLAS	CHINTZY	CHIRPIER
CHIEFS	CHILIDOG	CHIMLEY	CHINWAG	CHIRPIEST
CHIEFSHIP	CHILIDOGS	CHIMLEYS	CHINWAGGED	CHIRPILY
CHIEFSHIPS	CHILIES	CHIMNEY	CHINWAGGING	CHIRPING
CHIEFTAIN	CHILIS	CHIMNEYS	CHINWAGS	CHIRPS
CHIEFTAINS	CHILL	CHIMP	CHIP	CHIRPY
CHIEL	CHILLED	CHIMPS	CHIPBOARD	CHIRR
CHIELD	CHILLER	CHIN	CHIPBOARDS	CHIRRE
CHIELDS	CHILLERS	CHINA	CHIPMUCK	CHIRRED
CHIELS	CHILLEST	CHINAS	CHIPMUCKS	CHIRREN
CHIFFON	CHILLI	CHINAWARE	CHIPMUNK	CHIRRES
CHIFFONS	CHILLIER	CHINAWARES	CHIPMUNKS	CHIRRING
CHIGETAI	CHILLIES	CHINBONE	CHIPOTLE	CHIRRS
CHIGETAIS	CHILLIEST	CHINBONES	CHIPOTLES	CHIRRUP
CHIGGER	CHILLILY	CHINCAPIN	CHIPPABLE	CHIRRUPED

CHIRRUPING	CHIVE	CHOCKFULL	CHOLINE	CHOPSOCKY
CHIRRUPS	CHIVES	CHOCKING	CHOLINES	CHOPSTICK
CHIRRUPY	CHIVIED	CHOCKS	CHOLLA	CHOPSTICKS
CHIRU	CHIVIES	CHOCOLATE	CHOLLAS	CHORAGI
CHIRUS	CHIVVIED	CHOCOLATES	CHOLO	CHORAGIC
CHIS	CHIVVIES	CHOCOLATY	CHOLOS	CHORAGUS
CHISEL	CHIVVY	CHOICE	CHOMP	CHORAGUSES
CHISELED	CHIVVYING	CHOICELY	CHOMPED	CHORAL
CHISELER	CHIVY	CHOICER	CHOMPER	CHORALE
CHISELERS	CHIVYING	CHOICES	CHOMPERS	CHORALES
CHISELING	CHLAMYDES	CHOICEST	CHOMPING	CHORALLY
CHISELLED	CHLAMYDIA	CHOIR	CHOMPS	CHORALS
CHISELLER	CHLAMYDIAE	CHOIRBOY	CHON	CHORD
CHISELLERS	CHLAMYS	CHOIRBOYS	CHONDRITE	CHORDAL
CHISELLING	CHLAMYSES	CHOIRED	CHONDRITES	CHORDATE
CHISELS	CHLOASMA	CHOIRGIRL	CHONDROMA	CHORDATES
CHIT	CHLOASMAS	CHOIRGIRLS	CHONDROMAS	CHORDED
CHITAL	CHLOASMATA	CHOIRING	CHONDROMATA	CHORDING
CHITCHAT	CHLORACNE	CHOIRS	CHONDRULE	CHORDS
CHITCHATS	CHLORACNES	CHOKE	CHONDRULES	CHORE
CHITCHATTED	CHLORAL	CHOKEABLE	CHOOK	CHOREA
CHITCHATTING	CHLORALS	CHOKEBORE	CHOOKS	CHOREAL
CHITIN	CHLORATE	CHOKEBORES	CHOOSE	CHOREAS
CHITINOID	CHLORATES	CHOKED	CHOOSER	CHOREATIC
CHITINOUS	CHLORDAN	CHOKEDAMP	CHOOSERS	CHORED
CHITINS	CHLORDANE	CHOKEDAMPS	CHOOSES	CHOREGI
CHITLIN	CHLORDANES	CHOKEHOLD	CHOOSEY	CHOREGUS
CHITLING	CHLORDANS	CHOKEHOLDS	CHOOSIER	CHOREGUSES
CHITLINGS	CHLORELLA	CHOKER	CHOOSIEST	CHOREIC
CHITLINS	CHLORELLAS	CHOKERS	CHOOSING	CHOREMAN
CHITON	CHLORIC	CHOKES	CHOOSY	CHOREMEN
CHITONS	CHLORID	CHOKEY	CHOP	CHOREOID
CHITOSAN	CHLORIDE	CHOKIER	CHOPHOUSE	CHORES
CHITOSANS	CHLORIDES	CHOKIEST	CHOPHOUSES	CHORIAL
CHITS	CHLORIDIC	CHOKING	CHOPIN	CHORIAMB
CHITTER	CHLORIDS	CHOKINGLY	CHOPINE	CHORIAMBS
CHITTERED	CHLORIN	CHOKY	CHOPINES	CHORIC
CHITTERING	CHLORINE	CHOLA	CHOPINS	CHORINE
CHITTERS	CHLORINES	CHOLAS	CHOPLOGIC	CHORINES
CHITTIES	CHLORINS	CHOLATE	CHOPLOGICS	CHORING
CHITTY	CHLORITE	CHOLATES	CHOPPED	CHORIOID
CHIVALRIC	CHLORITES	CHOLECYST	CHOPPER	CHORIOIDS
CHIVALRIES	CHLORITIC	CHOLECYSTS	CHOPPERED	CHORION
CHIVALRY	CHLOROSES	CHOLENT	CHOPPERING	CHORIONIC
CHIVAREE	CHLOROSIS	CHOLENTS	CHOPPERS	CHORIONS
CHIVAREED	CHLOROTIC	CHOLER	CHOPPIER	CHORISTER
CHIVAREEING	CHLOROUS	CHOLERA	CHOPPIEST	CHORISTERS
CHIVAREES	CHOANA	CHOLERAIC	CHOPPILY	CHORIZO
CHIVARI	CHOANAE	CHOLERAS	CHOPPING	CHORIZOS
CHIVARIED	CHOCK	CHOLERIC	CHOPPY	CHOROID
CHIVARIES	CHOCKED	CHOLEROID	CHOPS	CHOROIDAL
CHIVARIING	CHOCKFUL	CHOLERS	CHOPSOCKIES	CHOROIDS

CHORTEN	CHRISMAL	CHRONIC	CHUFFS	CHURCH
CHORTENS	CHRISMON	CHRONICLE	CHUFFY	CHURCHED
CHORTLE	CHRISMONS	CHRONICLED	CHUG	CHURCHES
CHORTLED	CHRISMS	CHRONICLES	CHUGALUG	CHURCHIER
CHORTLER	CHRISOM	CHRONICLING	CHUGALUGGED	CHURCHIEST
CHORTLERS	CHRISOMS	CHRONICS	CHUGALUGGING	CHURCHING
CHORTLES	CHRISTEN	CHRONON	CHUGALUGS	CHURCHINGS
CHORTLING	CHRISTENED	CHRONONS	CHUGGED	CHURCHLIER
CHORUS	CHRISTENING	CHRYSALID	CHUGGER	CHURCHLIEST
CHORUSED	CHRISTENS	CHRYSALIDES	CHUGGERS	CHURCHLY
CHORUSES	CHRISTIE	CHRYSALIDS	CHUGGING	CHURCHMAN
CHORUSING	CHRISTIES	CHRYSALIS	CHUGS	CHURCHMEN
CHORUSSED	CHRISTY	CHRYSALISES	CHUKAR	CHURCHY
CHORUSSES	CHROMA	CHTHONIAN	CHUKARS	CHURL
CHORUSSING	CHROMAS	CHTHONIC	CHUKKA	CHURLISH
CHOSE	CHROMATE	CHUB	CHUKKAR	CHURLS
CHOSEN	CHROMATES	CHUBASCO	CHUKKARS	CHURN
CHOSES	CHROMATIC	CHUBASCOS	CHUKKAS	CHURNED
CHOTT	CHROMATICS	CHUBBIER	CHUKKER	CHURNER
CHOTTS	CHROMATID	CHUBBIEST	CHUKKERS	CHURNERS
CHOUGH	CHROMATIDS	CHUBBILY	CHUM	CHURNING
CHOUGHS	CHROMATIN	CHUBBY	CHUMMED	CHURNINGS
CHOUSE	CHROMATINS	CHUBS	CHUMMIER	CHURNS
CHOUSED	CHROME	CHUCK	CHUMMIEST	CHURR
CHOUSER	CHROMED	CHUCKED	CHUMMILY	CHURRED
CHOUSERS	CHROMES	CHUCKHOLE	CHUMMING	CHURRING
CHOUSES	CHROMIC	CHUCKHOLES	CHUMMY	CHURRO
CHOUSH	CHROMIDE	CHUCKIES	CHUMP	CHURROS
CHOUSHES	CHROMIDES	CHUCKING	CHUMPED	CHURRS
CHOUSING	CHROMIER	CHUCKLE	CHUMPING	CHUTE
CHOW	CHROMIEST	CHUCKLED	CHUMPS	CHUTED
CHOWCHOW	CHROMING	CHUCKLER	CHUMS	CHUTES
CHOWCHOWS	CHROMINGS	CHUCKLERS	CHUMSHIP	CHUTING
CHOWDER	CHROMITE	CHUCKLES	CHUMSHIPS	CHUTIST
CHOWDERED	CHROMITES	CHUCKLING	CHUNK	CHUTISTS
CHOWDERING	CHROMIUM	CHUCKS	CHUNKED	CHUTNEE
CHOWDERS	CHROMIUMS	CHUCKY	CHUNKIER	CHUTNEES
CHOWED	CHROMIZE	CHUDDAH	CHUNKIEST	CHUTNEY
CHOWHOUND	CHROMIZED	CHUDDAHS	CHUNKILY	CHUTNEYS
CHOWHOUNDS	CHROMIZES	CHUDDAR	CHUNKING	CHUTZPA
CHOWING	CHROMIZING	CHUDDARS	CHUNKS	CHUTZPAH
CHOWS	CHROMO	CHUDDER	CHUNKY	CHUTZPAHS
CHOWSE	CHROMOGEN	CHUDDERS	CHUNNEL	CHUTZPAS
CHOWSED	CHROMOGENS	CHUFA	CHUNNELS	CHYLE
CHOWSES	CHROMOS	CHUFAS	CHUNTER	CHYLES
CHOWSING	CHROMOUS	CHUFF	CHUNTERED	CHYLOUS
CHOWTIME	CHROMY	CHUFFED	CHUNTERING	CHYME
CHOWTIMES	CHROMYL	CHUFFER	CHUNTERS	CHYMES
CHRESARD	CHROMYLS	CHUFFEST	CHUPPA	CHYMIC
CHRESARDS	CHRONAXIE	CHUFFIER	CHUPPAH	CHYMICS
CHRISM	CHRONAXIES	CHUFFIEST	CHUPPAHS	CHYMIST
CHRISMA	CHRONAXY	CHUFFING	CHUPPAS	CHYMISTS

CHYMOSIN	CIGARS	CINEPHILES	CIRCUIT	CISTERN
CHYMOSINS	CIGS	CINERARIA	CIRCUITAL	CISTERNA
CHYMOUS	CIGUATERA	CINERARIAS	CIRCUITED	CISTERNAE
CHYTRID	CIGUATERAS	CINERARIUM	CIRCUITIES	CISTERNAL
CHYTRIDS	CILANTRO	CINERARY	CIRCUITING	CISTERNS
CIAO	CILANTROS	CINEREOUS	CIRCUITRIES	CISTRON
CIBOL	CILIA	CINERIN	CIRCUITRY	CISTRONIC
CIBOLS	CILIARY	CINERINS	CIRCUITS	CISTRONS
CIBORIA	CILIATE	CINES	CIRCUITY	CISTS
CIBORIUM	CILIATED	CINGULA	CIRCULAR	CISTUS
CIBOULE	CILIATELY	CINGULAR	CIRCULARS	CISTUSES
CIBOULES	CILIATES	CINGULATE	CIRCULATE	CITABLE
CICADA	CILIATION	CINGULUM	CIRCULATED	CITADEL
CICADAE	CILIATIONS	CINNABAR	CIRCULATES	CITADELS
CICADAS	CILICE	CINNABARS	CIRCULATING	CITATION
CICALA	CILICES	CINNAMIC	CIRCUS	CITATIONS
CICALAS	CILIOLATE	CINNAMON	CIRCUSES	CITATOR
CICALE	CILIUM	CINNAMONS	CIRCUSY	CITATORS
CICATRICE	CIMBALOM	CINNAMONY	CIRE	CITATORY
CICATRICES	CIMBALOMS	CINNAMYL	CIRES	CITE
CICATRIX	CIMEX	CINNAMYLS	CIRQUE	CITEABLE
CICATRIXES	CIMICES	CINQUAIN	CIRQUES	CITED
CICATRIZE	CINCH	CINQUAINS	CIRRATE	CITER
CICATRIZED	CINCHED	CINQUE	CIRRHOSED	CITERS
CICATRIZES	CINCHES	CINQUES	CIRRHOSES	CITES
CICATRIZING	CINCHING	CION	CIRRHOSIS	CITHARA
CICELIES	CINCHONA	CIONS	CIRRHOTIC	CITHARAS
CICELY	CINCHONAS	CIOPPINO	CIRRHOTICS	CITHER
CICERO	CINCHONIC	CIOPPINOS	CIRRI	CITHERN
CICERONE	CINCTURE	CIPHER	CIRRIFORM	CITHERNS
CICERONES	CINCTURED	CIPHERED	CIRRIPED	CITHERS
CICERONI	CINCTURES	CIPHERER	CIRRIPEDE	CITHREN
CICEROS	CINCTURING	CIPHERERS	CIRRIPEDES	CITHRENS
CICHLID	CINDER	CIPHERING	CIRRIPEDS	CITIED
CICHLIDAE	CINDERED	CIPHERS	CIRROSE	CITIES
CICHLIDS	CINDERING	CIPHONIES	CIRROUS	CITIFIED
CICISBEI	CINDEROUS	CIPHONY	CIRRUS	CITIFIES
CICISBEO	CINDERS	CIPOLIN	CIRSOID	CITIFY
CICISBEOS	CINDERY	CIPOLINS	CIS	CITIFYING
CICOREE	CINE	CIPOLLINO	CISALPINE	CITING
CICOREES	CINEAST	CIPOLLINOS	CISCO	CITIZEN
CIDER	CINEASTE	CIRCA	CISCOES	CITIZENLY
CIDERS	CINEASTES	CIRCADIAN	CISCOS	CITIZENRIES
CIG	CINEASTS	CIRCINATE	CISLUNAR	CITIZENRY
CIGAR	CINEMA	CIRCLE	CISPLATIN	CITIZENS
CIGARET	CINEMAS	CIRCLED	CISPLATINS	CITOLA
CIGARETS	CINEMATIC	CIRCLER	CISSIES	CITOLAS
CIGARETTE	CINEOL	CIRCLERS	CISSOID	CITOLE
CIGARETTES	CINEOLE	CIRCLES	CISSOIDS	CITOLES
CIGARILLO	CINEOLES	CIRCLET	CISSY	CITRAL
CIGARILLOS	CINEOLS	CIRCLETS	CIST	CITRALS
CIGARLIKE	CINEPHILE	CIRCLING	CISTED	CITRATE

CITRATED	CIVISM	CLAM	CLANGORING	CLARIONET
CITRATES	CIVISMS	CLAMANT	CLANGORS	CLARIONETS
CITREOUS	CIVVIES	CLAMANTLY	CLANGOUR	CLARIONING
CITRIC	CIVVY	CLAMBAKE	CLANGOURED	CLARIONS
CITRIN	CLABBER	CLAMBAKES	CLANGOURING	CLARITIES
CITRINE	CLABBERED	CLAMBER	CLANGOURS	CLARITY
CITRINES	CLABBERING	CLAMBERED	CLANGS	CLARKIA
CITRININ	CLABBERS	CLAMBERER	CLANK	CLARKIAS
CITRININS	CLACH	CLAMBERERS	CLANKED	CLARO
CITRINS	CLACHAN	CLAMBERING	CLANKIER	CLAROES
CITRON	CLACHANS	CLAMBERS	CLANKIEST	CLAROS
CITRONS	CLACHS	CLAMLIKE	CLANKING	CLARY
CITROUS	CLACK	CLAMMED	CLANKS	CLASH
CITRUS	CLACKED	CLAMMER	CLANKY	CLASHED
CITRUSES	CLACKER	CLAMMERS	CLANNISH	CLASHER
CITRUSY	CLACKERS	CLAMMIER	CLANS	CLASHERS
CITTERN	CLACKING	CLAMMIEST	CLANSMAN	CLASHES
CITTERNS	CLACKS	CLAMMILY	CLANSMEN	CLASHING
CITY	CLAD	CLAMMING	CLAP	CLASP
CITYFIED	CLADDAGH	CLAMMY	CLAPBOARD	CLASPED
CITYSCAPE	CLADDAGHS	CLAMOR	CLAPBOARDED	CLASPER
CITYSCAPES	CLADDED	CLAMORED	CLAPBOARDING	CLASPERS
CITYWARD	CLADDING	CLAMORER	CLAPBOARDS	CLASPING
CITYWIDE	CLADDINGS	CLAMORERS	CLAPPED	CLASPS
CIVET	CLADE	CLAMORING	CLAPPER	CLASPT
CIVETLIKE	CLADES	CLAMOROUS	CLAPPERS	CLASS
CIVETS	CLADISM	CLAMORS	CLAPPING	CLASSABLE
CIVIC	CLADISMS	CLAMOUR	CLAPS	CLASSED
CIVICALLY	CLADIST	CLAMOURED	CLAPT	CLASSER
CIVICISM	CLADISTIC	CLAMOURING	CLAPTRAP	CLASSERS
CIVICISMS	CLADISTS	CLAMOURS	CLAPTRAPS	CLASSES
CIVICS	CLADODE	CLAMP	CLAQUE	CLASSIC
CIVIE	CLADODES	CLAMPDOWN	CLAQUER	CLASSICAL
CIVIES	CLADODIAL	CLAMPDOWNS	CLAQUERS	CLASSICALS
CIVIL	CLADOGRAM	CLAMPED	CLAQUES	CLASSICO
CIVILIAN	CLADOGRAMS	CLAMPER	CLAQUEUR	CLASSICS
CIVILIANS	CLADS	CLAMPERS	CLAQUEURS	CLASSIER
CIVILISE	CLAFOUTI	CLAMPING	CLARENCE	CLASSIEST
CIVILISED	CLAFOUTIS	CLAMPS	CLARENCES	CLASSIFIED
CIVILISES	CLAG	CLAMS	CLARET	CLASSIFIES
CIVILISING	CLAGGED	CLAMSHELL	CLARETS	CLASSIFY
CIVILITIES	CLAGGING	CLAMSHELLS	CLARIES	CLASSIFYING
CIVILITY	CLAGS	CLAMWORM	CLARIFIED	CLASSILY
CIVILIZE	CLAIM	CLAMWORMS	CLARIFIER	CLASSING
CIVILIZED	CLAIMABLE	CLAN	CLARIFIERS	CLASSIS
CIVILIZER	CLAIMANT	CLANG	CLARIFIES	CLASSISM
CIVILIZERS	CLAIMANTS	CLANGED	CLARIFY	CLASSISMS
CIVILIZES	CLAIMED	CLANGER	CLARIFYING	CLASSIST
CIVILIZING	CLAIMER	CLANGERS	CLARINET	CLASSISTS
CIVILLY	CLAIMERS	CLANGING	CLARINETS	CLASSLESS
CIVILNESS	CLAIMING	CLANGOR	CLARION	CLASSMATE
CIVILNESSES	CLAIMS	CLANGORED	CLARIONED	CLASSMATES

CLASSON	CLAWED	CLEARABLE	CLENCHED	CLEWING
CLASSONS	CLAWER	CLEARANCE	CLENCHER	CLEWS
CLASSROOM	CLAWERS	CLEARANCES	CLENCHERS	CLICHE
CLASSROOMS	CLAWING	CLEARCUT	CLENCHES	CLICHED
CLASSWORK	CLAWLESS	CLEARCUTS	CLENCHING	CLICHES
CLASSWORKS	CLAWLIKE	CLEARCUTTING	CLEOME	CLICK
CLASSY	CLAWS	CLEARED	CLEOMES	CLICKABLE
CLAST	CLAXON	CLEARER	CLEPE	CLICKED
CLASTIC	CLAXONS	CLEARERS	CLEPED	CLICKER
CLASTICS	CLAY	CLEAREST	CLEPES	CLICKERS
CLASTS	CLAYBANK	CLEAREYED	CLEPING	CLICKING
CLATHRATE	CLAYBANKS	CLEARING	CLEPSYDRA	CLICKLESS
CLATHRATES	CLAYED	CLEARINGS	CLEPSYDRAE	CLICKS
CLATTER	CLAYEY	CLEARLY	CLEPSYDRAS	CLICKWRAP
CLATTERED	CLAYIER	CLEARNESS	CLEPT	CLIENT
CLATTERER	CLAYIEST	CLEARNESSES	CLERGIES	CLIENTAGE
CLATTERERS	CLAYING	CLEARS	CLERGY	CLIENTAGES
CLATTERING	CLAYISH	CLEARWEED	CLERGYMAN	CLIENTAL
CLATTERS	CLAYLIKE	CLEARWEEDS	CLERGYMEN	CLIENTELE
CLATTERY	CLAYMORE	CLEARWING	CLERIC	CLIENTELES
CLAUCHT	CLAYMORES	CLEARWINGS	CLERICAL	CLIENTS
CLAUGHT	CLAYPAN	CLEAT	CLERICALS	CLIFF
CLAUGHTED	CLAYPANS	CLEATED	CLERICS	CLIFFIER
CLAUGHTING	CLAYS	CLEATING	CLERID	CLIFFIEST
CLAUGHTS	CLAYSTONE	CLEATS	CLERIDS	CLIFFLIKE
CLAUSAL	CLAYSTONES	CLEAVABLE	CLERIHEW	CLIFFS
CLAUSE	CLAYTONIA	CLEAVAGE	CLERIHEWS	CLIFFY
CLAUSES	CLAYTONIAS	CLEAVAGES	CLERISIES	CLIFT
CLAUSTRA	CLAYWARE	CLEAVE	CLERISY	CLIFTS
CLAUSTRAL	CLAYWARES	CLEAVED	CLERK	CLIMACTIC
CLAUSTRUM	CLEAN	CLEAVER	CLERKDOM	CLIMATAL
CLAVATE	CLEANABLE	CLEAVERS	CLERKDOMS	CLIMATE
CLAVATELY	CLEANED	CLEAVES	CLERKED	CLIMATES
CLAVATION	CLEANER	CLEAVING	CLERKING	CLIMATIC
CLAVATIONS	CLEANERS	CLEEK	CLERKISH	CLIMATIZE
CLAVE	CLEANEST	CLEEKED	CLERKLIER	CLIMATIZED
CLAVER	CLEANING	CLEEKING	CLERKLIEST	CLIMATIZES
CLAVERED	CLEANLIER	CLEEKS	CLERKLY	CLIMATIZING
CLAVERING	CLEANLIEST	CLEF	CLERKS	CLIMAX
CLAVERS	CLEANLY	CLEFS	CLERKSHIP	CLIMAXED
CLAVES	CLEANNESS	CLEFT	CLERKSHIPS	CLIMAXES
CLAVI	CLEANNESSES	CLEFTED	CLEVEITE	CLIMAXING
CLAVICLE	CLEANS	CLEFTING	CLEVEITES	CLIMB
CLAVICLES	CLEANSE	CLEFTS	CLEVER	CLIMBABLE
CLAVICORN	CLEANSED	CLEIDOIC	CLEVERER	CLIMBDOWN
CLAVIER	CLEANSER	CLEMATIS	CLEVEREST	CLIMBDOWNS
CLAVIERS	CLEANSERS	CLEMATISES	CLEVERISH	CLIMBED
CLAVIFORM	CLEANSES	CLEMENCIES	CLEVERLY	CLIMBER
CLAVUS	CLEANSING	CLEMENCY	CLEVIS	CLIMBERS
CLAW	CLEANUP	CLEMENT	CLEVISES	CLIMBING
CLAWBACK	CLEANUPS	CLEMENTLY	CLEW	CLIMBS
CLAWBACKS	CLEAR	CLENCH	CLEWED	CLIME

CLIMES	CLIQUE	CLOCKWORKS	CLONK	CLOTHINGS
CLINAL	CLIQUED	CLOD	CLONKED	CLOTHLIKE
CLINALLY	CLIQUES	CLODDIER	CLONKING	CLOTHS
CLINCH	CLIQUEY	CLODDIEST	CLONKS	CLOTS
CLINCHED	CLIQUIER	CLODDISH	CLONS	CLOTTED
CLINCHER	CLIQUIEST	CLODDY	CLONUS	CLOTTING
CLINCHERS	CLIQUING	CLODPATE	CLONUSES	CLOTTY
CLINCHES	CLIQUISH	CLODPATES	CLOOT	CLOTURE
CLINCHING	CLIQUY	CLODPOLE	CLOOTS	CLOTURED
CLINE	CLITELLA	CLODPOLES	CLOP	CLOTURES
CLINES	CLITELLUM	CLODPOLL	CLOPPED	CLOTURING
CLING	CLITIC	CLODPOLLS	CLOPPING	CLOUD
CLINGED	CLITICIZE	CLODS	CLOPS	CLOUDED
CLINGER	CLITICIZED	CLOG	CLOQUE	CLOUDIER
CLINGERS	CLITICIZES	CLOGGED	CLOQUES	CLOUDIEST
CLINGFISH	CLITICIZING	CLOGGER	CLOSABLE	CLOUDILY
CLINGFISHES	CLITICS	CLOGGERS	CLOSE	CLOUDING
CLINGIER	CLITORAL	CLOGGIER	CLOSEABLE	CLOUDLAND
CLINGIEST	CLITORIC	CLOGGIEST	CLOSED	CLOUDLANDS
CLINGING	CLITORIDES	CLOGGILY	CLOSEDOWN	CLOUDLESS
CLINGS	CLITORIS	CLOGGING	CLOSEDOWNS	CLOUDLET
CLINGY	CLITORISES	CLOGGY	CLOSELY	CLOUDLETS
CLINIC	CLIVERS	CLOGS	CLOSENESS	CLOUDLIKE
CLINICAL	CLIVIA	CLOISONNE	CLOSENESSES	CLOUDS
CLINICIAN	CLIVIAS	CLOISONNES	CLOSEOUT	CLOUDY
CLINICIANS	CLOACA	CLOISTER	CLOSEOUTS	CLOUGH
CLINICS	CLOACAE	CLOISTERED	CLOSER	CLOUGHS
CLINK	CLOACAL	CLOISTERING	CLOSERS	CLOUR
CLINKED	CLOACAS	CLOISTERS	CLOSES	CLOURED
CLINKER	CLOAK	CLOISTRAL	CLOSEST	CLOURING
CLINKERED	CLOAKED	CLOMB	CLOSET	CLOURS
CLINKERING	CLOAKING	CLOMP	CLOSETED	CLOUT
CLINKERS	CLOAKROOM	CLOMPED	CLOSETFUL	CLOUTED
CLINKING	CLOAKROOMS	CLOMPING	CLOSETFULS	CLOUTER
CLINKS	CLOAKS	CLOMPS	CLOSETING	CLOUTERS
CLINQUANT	CLOBBER	CLON	CLOSETS	CLOUTING
CLINQUANTS	CLOBBERED	CLONAL	CLOSEUP	CLOUTS
CLINTONIA	CLOBBERING	CLONALLY	CLOSEUPS	CLOVE
CLINTONIAS	CLOBBERS	CLONE	CLOSING	CLOVEN
CLIP	CLOCHARD	CLONED	CLOSINGS	CLOVER
CLIPBOARD	CLOCHARDS	CLONER	CLOSURE	CLOVERED
CLIPBOARDS	CLOCHE	CLONERS	CLOSURED	CLOVERS
CLIPPABLE	CLOCHES	CLONES	CLOSURES	CLOVERY
CLIPPED	CLOCK	CLONIC	CLOSURING	CLOVES
CLIPPER	CLOCKED	CLONICITIES	CLOT	CLOWDER
CLIPPERS	CLOCKER	CLONICITY	CLOTH	CLOWDERS
CLIPPING	CLOCKERS	CLONIDINE	CLOTHE	CLOWN
CLIPPINGS	CLOCKING	CLONIDINES	CLOTHED	CLOWNED
CLIPS	CLOCKLIKE	CLONING	CLOTHES	CLOWNERIES
CLIPSHEET	CLOCKS	CLONINGS	CLOTHIER	CLOWNERY
CLIPSHEETS	CLOCKWISE	CLONISM	CLOTHIERS	CLOWNING
CLIPT	CLOCKWORK	CLONISMS	CLOTHING	CLOWNISH

CLOWNS	CLUES	CNIDA	COAGULUMS	COAPPEARED
CLOY	CLUING	CNIDAE	COAL	COAPPEARING
CLOYED	CLUMBER	CNIDARIAN	COALA	COAPPEARS
CLOYING	CLUMBERS	CNIDARIANS	COALAS	COAPT
CLOYINGLY	CLUMP	COACH	COALBIN	COAPTED
CLOYS	CLUMPED	COACHABLE	COALBINS	COAPTING
CLOZAPINE	CLUMPIER	COACHED	COALBOX	COAPTS
CLOZAPINES	CLUMPIEST	COACHER	COALBOXES	COARCTATE
CLOZE	CLUMPING	COACHERS	COALED	COARSE
CLOZES	CLUMPISH	COACHES	COALER	COARSELY
CLUB	CLUMPLIKE	COACHING	COALERS	COARSEN
CLUBABLE	CLUMPS	COACHMAN	COALESCE	COARSENED
CLUBBABLE	CLUMPY	COACHMEN	COALESCED	COARSENING
CLUBBED	CLUMSIER	COACHWORK	COALESCES	COARSENS
CLUBBER	CLUMSIEST	COACHWORKS	COALESCING	COARSER
CLUBBERS	CLUMSILY	COACT	COALFIELD	COARSEST
CLUBBIER	CLUMSY	COACTED	COALFIELDS	COASSIST
CLUBBIEST	CLUNG	COACTING	COALFISH	COASSISTED
CLUBBING	CLUNK	COACTION	COALFISHES	COASSISTING
CLUBBISH	CLUNKED	COACTIONS	COALHOLE	COASSISTS
CLUBBY	CLUNKER	COACTIVE	COALHOLES	COASSUME
CLUBFACE	CLUNKERS	COACTOR	COALIER	COASSUMED
CLUBFACES	CLUNKIER	COACTORS	COALIEST	COASSUMES
CLUBFEET	CLUNKIEST	COACTS	COALIFIED	COASSUMING
CLUBFOOT	CLUNKING	COADAPTED	COALIFIES	COAST
CLUBHAND	CLUNKS	COADJUTOR	COALIFY	COASTAL
CLUBHANDS	CLUNKY	COADJUTORS	COALIFYING	COASTALLY
CLUBHAUL	CLUPEID	COADMIRE	COALING	COASTED
CLUBHAULED	CLUPEIDS	COADMIRED	COALITION	COASTER
CLUBHAULING	CLUPEOID	COADMIRES	COALITIONS	COASTERS
CLUBHAULS	CLUPEOIDS	COADMIRING	COALLESS	COASTING
CLUBHEAD	CLUSTER	COADMIT	COALPIT	COASTINGS
CLUBHEADS	CLUSTERED	COADMITS	COALPITS	COASTLAND
CLUBHOUSE	CLUSTERING	COADMITTED	COALS	COASTLANDS
CLUBHOUSES	CLUSTERS	COADMITTING	COALSACK	COASTLINE
CLUBMAN	CLUSTERY	COADUNATE	COALSACKS	COASTLINES
CLUBMEN	CLUTCH	COAEVAL	COALSHED	COASTS
CLUBROOM	CLUTCHED	COAEVALS	COALSHEDS	COASTWARD
CLUBROOMS	CLUTCHES	COAGENCIES	COALY	COASTWISE
CLUBROOT	CLUTCHING	COAGENCY	COALYARD	COAT
CLUBROOTS	CLUTCHY	COAGENT	COALYARDS	COATDRESS
CLUBS	CLUTTER	COAGENTS	COAMING	COATDRESSES
CLUBWOMAN	CLUTTERED	COAGULA	COAMINGS	COATED
CLUBWOMEN	CLUTTERING	COAGULANT	COANCHOR	COATEE
CLUCK	CLUTTERS	COAGULANTS	COANCHORED	COATEES
CLUCKED	CLUTTERY	COAGULASE	COANCHORING	COATER
CLUCKING	CLYPEAL	COAGULASES	COANCHORS	COATERS
CLUCKS	CLYPEATE	COAGULATE	COANNEX	COATI
CLUE	CLYPEI	COAGULATED	COANNEXED	COATING
CLUED	CLYPEUS	COAGULATES	COANNEXES	COATINGS
CLUEING	CLYSTER	COAGULATING	COANNEXING	COATIS
CLUELESS	CLYSTERS	COAGULUM	COAPPEAR	COATLESS

COATRACK	COBBY	COCHAIRED	COCKINESS	COCOBOLOS
COATRACKS	COBIA	COCHAIRING	COCKINESSES	COCOMAT
COATROOM	COBIAS	COCHAIRS	COCKING	COCOMATS
COATROOMS	COBLE	COCHIN	COCKISH	COCONUT
COATS	COBLES	COCHINEAL	COCKLE	COCONUTS
COATTAIL	COBNUT	COCHINEALS	COCKLEBUR	COCOON
COATTAILS	COBNUTS	COCHINS	COCKLEBURS	COCOONED
COATTEND	COBRA	COCHLEA	COCKLED	COCOONING
COATTENDED	COBRAS	COCHLEAE	COCKLES	COCOONINGS
COATTENDING	COBS	COCHLEAR	COCKLIKE	COCOONS
COATTENDS	COBWEB	COCHLEAS	COCKLING	COCOPLUM
COATTEST	COBWEBBED	COCHLEATE	COCKLOFT	COCOPLUMS
COATTESTED	COBWEBBIER	COCINERA	COCKLOFTS	COCOS
COATTESTING	COBWEBBIEST	COCINERAS	COCKNEY	COCOTTE
COATTESTS	COBWEBBING	COCK	COCKNEYFIED	COCOTTES
COAUTHOR	COBWEBBY	COCKADE	COCKNEYFIES	COCOUNSEL
COAUTHORED	COBWEBS	COCKADED	COCKNEYFY	COCOUNSELED
COAUTHORING	COCA	COCKADES	COCKNEYFYING	COCOUNSELING
COAUTHORS	COCAIN	COCKAMAMY	COCKNEYS	COCOUNSELLED
COAX	COCAINE	COCKAPOO	COCKPIT	COCOUNSELLING
COAXAL	COCAINES	COCKAPOOS	COCKPITS	COCOUNSELS
COAXED	COCAINISM	COCKATEEL	COCKROACH	COCOYAM
COAXER	COCAINISMS	COCKATEELS	COCKROACHES	COCOYAMS
COAXERS	COCAINIZE	COCKATIEL	COCKS	COCOZELLE
COAXES	COCAINIZED	COCKATIELS	COCKSCOMB	COCOZELLES
COAXIAL	COCAINIZES	COCKATOO	COCKSCOMBS	COCREATE
COAXIALLY	COCAINIZING	COCKATOOS	COCKSFOOT	COCREATED
COAXING	COCAINS	COCKBILL	COCKSFOOTS	COCREATES
COAXINGLY	COCAPTAIN	COCKBILLED	COCKSHIES	COCREATING
COB	COCAPTAINED	COCKBILLING	COCKSHUT	COCREATOR
COBALAMIN	COCAPTAINING	COCKBILLS	COCKSHUTS	COCREATORS
COBALAMINS	COCAPTAINS	COCKBOAT	COCKSHY	COCULTURE
COBALT	COCAS	COCKBOATS	COCKSPUR	COCULTURED
COBALTIC	COCCAL	COCKCROW	COCKSPURS	COCULTURES
COBALTINE	COCCI	COCKCROWS	COCKSURE	COCULTURING
COBALTINES	COCCIC	COCKED	COCKSWAIN	COCURATOR
COBALTITE	COCCID	COCKER	COCKSWAINS	COCURATORS
COBALTITES	COCCIDIA	COCKERED	COCKTAIL	COD
COBALTOUS	COCCIDIUM	COCKEREL	COCKTAILED	CODA
COBALTS	COCCIDS	COCKERELS	COCKTAILING	CODABLE
COBB	COCCOID	COCKERING	COCKTAILS	CODAS
COBBER	COCCOIDAL	COCKERS	COCKUP	CODDED
COBBERS	COCCOIDS	COCKEYE	COCKUPS	CODDER
COBBIER	COCCOLITH	COCKEYED	COCKY	CODDERS
COBBIEST	COCCOLITHS	COCKEYES	COCO	CODDING
COBBLE	COCCOUS	COCKFIGHT	COCOA	CODDLE
COBBLED	COCCUS	COCKFIGHTS	COCOANUT	CODDLED
COBBLER	COCCYGEAL	COCKHORSE	COCOANUTS	CODDLER
COBBLERS	COCCYGES	COCKHORSES	COCOAS	CODDLERS
COBBLES	COCCYX	COCKIER	COCOBOLA	CODDLES
COBBLING	COCCYXES	COCKIEST	COCOBOLAS	CODDLING
COBBS	COCHAIR	COCKILY	COCOBOLO	CODE

CODEBOOK	CODLIN	COENACTS	COEVOLVED	COFOUNDING
CODEBOOKS	CODLING	COENAMOR	COEVOLVES	COFOUNDS
CODEBTOR	CODLINGS	COENAMORED	COEVOLVING	COFT
CODEBTORS	CODLINS	COENAMORING	COEXERT	COG
CODEC	CODON	COENAMORS	COEXERTED	COGENCIES
CODECS	CODONS	COENDURE	COEXERTING	COGENCY
CODED	CODPIECE	COENDURED	COEXERTS	COGENT
CODEIA	CODPIECES	COENDURES	COEXIST	COGENTLY
CODEIAS	CODRIVE	COENDURING	COEXISTED	COGGED
CODEIN	CODRIVEN	COENOBITE	COEXISTING	COGGING
CODEINA	CODRIVER	COENOBITES	COEXISTS	COGITABLE
CODEINAS	CODRIVERS	COENOCYTE	COEXTEND	COGITATE
CODEINE	CODRIVES	COENOCYTES	COEXTENDED	COGITATED
CODEINES	CODRIVING	COENOSARC	COEXTENDING	COGITATES
CODEINS	CODROVE	COENOSARCS	COEXTENDS	COGITATING
CODELESS	CODS	COENURE	COFACTOR	COGITATOR
CODEN	COED	COENURES	COFACTORS	COGITATORS
CODENS	COEDIT	COENURI	COFEATURE	COGITO
CODER	COEDITED	COENURUS	COFEATURED	COGITOS
CODERIVE	COEDITING	COENZYME	COFEATURES	COGNAC
CODERIVED	COEDITOR	COENZYMES	COFEATURING	COGNACS
CODERIVES	COEDITORS	COEQUAL	COFF	COGNATE
CODERIVING	COEDITS	COEQUALLY	COFFEE	COGNATELY
CODERS	COEDS	COEQUALS	COFFEEPOT	COGNATES
CODES	COEFFECT	COEQUATE	COFFEEPOTS	COGNATION
CODESIGN	COEFFECTS	COEQUATED	COFFEES	COGNATIONS
CODESIGNED	COELIAC	COEQUATES	COFFER	COGNISE
CODESIGNING	COELOM	COEQUATING	COFFERDAM	COGNISED
CODESIGNS	COELOMATA	COERCE	COFFERDAMS	COGNISES
CODEVELOP	COELOMATE	COERCED	COFFERED	COGNISING
CODEVELOPED	COELOMATES	COERCER	COFFERING	COGNITION
CODEVELOPING	COELOME	COERCERS	COFFERS	COGNITIONS
CODEVELOPS	COELOMES	COERCES	COFFIN	COGNITIVE
CODEX	COELOMIC	COERCIBLE	COFFINED	COGNIZANT
CODFISH	COELOMS	COERCIBLY	COFFING	COGNIZE
CODFISHES	COELOSTAT	COERCING	COFFINING	COGNIZED
CODGER	COELOSTATS	COERCION	COFFINS	COGNIZER
CODGERS	COEMBODIED	COERCIONS	COFFLE	COGNIZERS
CODICES	COEMBODIES	COERCIVE	COFFLED	COGNIZES
CODICIL	COEMBODY	COERECT	COFFLES	COGNIZING
CODICILS	COEMBODYING	COERECTED	COFFLING	COGNOMEN
CODIFIED	COEMPLOY	COERECTING	COFFRET	COGNOMENS
CODIFIER	COEMPLOYED	COERECTS	COFFRETS	COGNOMINA
CODIFIERS	COEMPLOYING	COESITE	COFFS	COGNOVIT
CODIFIES	COEMPLOYS	COESITES	COFINANCE	COGNOVITS
CODIFY	COEMPT	COETERNAL	COFINANCED	COGON
CODIFYING	COEMPTED	COEVAL	COFINANCES	COGONS
CODING	COEMPTING	COEVALITIES	COFINANCING	COGS
CODIRECT	COEMPTS	COEVALITY	COFOUND	COGWAY
CODIRECTED	COENACT	COEVALLY	COFOUNDED	COGWAYS
CODIRECTING	COENACTED	COEVALS	COFOUNDER	COGWHEEL
CODIRECTS	COENACTING	COEVOLVE	COFOUNDERS	COGWHEELS

COHABIT	COHUNE	COINHERING	COLBY	COLICROOTS
COHABITED	COHUNES	COINING	COLBYS	COLICS
COHABITER	COIF	COINMATE	COLCANNON	COLICWEED
COHABITERS	COIFED	COINMATES	COLCANNONS	COLICWEEDS
COHABITING	COIFFE	COINS	COLCHICUM	COLIES
COHABITS	COIFFED	COINSURE	COLCHICUMS	COLIFORM
COHEAD	COIFFES	COINSURED	COLCOTHAR	COLIFORMS
COHEADED	COIFFEUR	COINSURER	COLCOTHARS	COLIN
COHEADING	COIFFEURS	COINSURERS	COLD	COLINEAR
COHEADS	COIFFEUSE	COINSURES	COLDBLOOD	COLINS
COHEIR	COIFFEUSES	COINSURING	COLDCOCK	COLIPHAGE
COHEIRESS	COIFFING	COINTER	COLDCOCKED	COLIPHAGES
COHEIRESSES	COIFFURE	COINTERRED	COLDCOCKING	COLISEUM
COHEIRS	COIFFURED	COINTERRING	COLDCOCKS	COLISEUMS
COHERE	COIFFURES	COINTERS	COLDER	COLISTIN
COHERED	COIFFURING	COINTREAU	COLDEST	COLISTINS
COHERENCE	COIFING	COINTREAUS	COLDISH	COLITIC
COHERENCES	COIFS	COINVENT	COLDLY	COLITIS
COHERENCIES	COIGN	COINVENTED	COLDNESS	COLITISES
COHERENCY	COIGNE	COINVENTING	COLDNESSES	COLLAGE
COHERENT	COIGNED	COINVENTS	COLDS	COLLAGED
COHERER	COIGNES	COIR	COLE	COLLAGEN
COHERERS	COIGNING	COIRS	COLEAD	COLLAGENS
COHERES	COIGNS	COISTREL	COLEADER	COLLAGES
COHERING	COIL	COISTRELS	COLEADERS	COLLAGING
COHESION	COILED	COISTRIL	COLEADING	COLLAGIST
COHESIONS	COILER	COISTRILS	COLEADS	COLLAGISTS
COHESIVE	COILERS	COITAL	COLECTOMIES	COLLAPSE
COHO	COILING	COITALLY	COLECTOMY	COLLAPSED
COHOBATE	COILS	COITION	COLED	COLLAPSES
COHOBATED	COIN	COITIONAL	COLES	COLLAPSING
COHOBATES	COINABLE	COITIONS	COLESEED	COLLAR
COHOBATING	COINAGE	COITUS	COLESEEDS	COLLARD
COHOG	COINAGES	COITUSES	COLESLAW	COLLARDS
COHOGS	COINCIDE	COJOIN	COLESLAWS	COLLARED
COHOLDER	COINCIDED	COJOINED	COLESSEE	COLLARET
COHOLDERS	COINCIDES	COJOINING	COLESSEES	COLLARETS
COHORT	COINCIDING	COJOINS	COLESSOR	COLLARING
COHORTS	COINED	COJONES	COLESSORS	COLLARS
COHOS	COINER	COKE	COLEUS	COLLATE
COHOSH	COINERS	COKED	COLEUSES	COLLATED
COHOSHES	COINFECT	COKEHEAD	COLEWORT	COLLATES
COHOST	COINFECTED	COKEHEADS	COLEWORTS	COLLATING
COHOSTED	COINFECTING	COKELIKE	COLIC	COLLATION
COHOSTESS	COINFECTS	COKES	COLICIN	COLLATIONS
COHOSTESSED	COINFER	COKING	COLICINE	COLLATOR
COHOSTESSES	COINFERRED	COKY	COLICINES	COLLATORS
COHOSTESSING	COINFERRING	COL	COLICINS	COLLEAGUE
COHOSTING	COINFERS	COLA	COLICKIER	COLLEAGUES
COHOSTS	COINHERE	COLANDER	COLICKIEST	COLLECT
COHOUSING	COINHERED	COLANDERS	COLICKY	COLLECTED
COHOUSINGS	COINHERES	COLAS	COLICROOT	COLLECTING

COLLECTOR
COLLECTORS
COLLECTS
COLLEEN
COLLEENS
COLLEGE
COLLEGER
COLLEGERS
COLLEGES
COLLEGIA
COLLEGIAL
COLLEGIAN
COLLEGIANS
COLLEGIUM
COLLEGIUMS
COLLET
COLLETED
COLLETING
COLLETS
COLLIDE
COLLIDED
COLLIDER
COLLIDERS
COLLIDES
COLLIDING
COLLIE
COLLIED
COLLIER
COLLIERIES
COLLIERS
COLLIERY
COLLIES
COLLIGATE
COLLIGATED
COLLIGATES
COLLIGATING
COLLIMATE
COLLIMATED
COLLIMATES
COLLIMATING
COLLINEAR
COLLINS
COLLINSES
COLLINSIA
COLLINSIAS
COLLISION
COLLISIONS
COLLOCATE
COLLOCATED
COLLOCATES
COLLOCATING
COLLODION

COLLODIONS
COLLOGUE
COLLOGUED
COLLOGUES
COLLOGUING
COLLOID
COLLOIDAL
COLLOIDS
COLLOP
COLLOPS
COLLOQUIA
COLLOQUIES
COLLOQUIUM
COLLOQUIUMS
COLLOQUY
COLLOTYPE
COLLOTYPES
COLLOTYPIES
COLLOTYPY
COLLUDE
COLLUDED
COLLUDER
COLLUDERS
COLLUDES
COLLUDING
COLLUSION
COLLUSIONS
COLLUSIVE
COLLUVIA
COLLUVIAL
COLLUVIUM
COLLUVIUMS
COLLY
COLLYING
COLLYRIA
COLLYRIUM
COLLYRIUMS
COLOBI
COLOBOMA
COLOBOMATA
COLOBUS
COLOBUSES
COLOCATE
COLOCATED
COLOCATES
COLOCATING
COLOCYNTH
COLOCYNTHS
COLOG
COLOGNE
COLOGNED
COLOGNES

COLOGS
COLOMBARD
COLOMBARDS
COLON
COLONE
COLONEL
COLONELCIES
COLONELCY
COLONELS
COLONES
COLONI
COLONIAL
COLONIALS
COLONIC
COLONICS
COLONIES
COLONISE
COLONISED
COLONISES
COLONISING
COLONIST
COLONISTS
COLONITIS
COLONITISES
COLONIZE
COLONIZED
COLONIZER
COLONIZERS
COLONIZES
COLONIZING
COLONNADE
COLONNADES
COLONS
COLONUS
COLONY
COLOPHON
COLOPHONIES
COLOPHONS
COLOPHONY
COLOR
COLORABLE
COLORABLY
COLORADO
COLORANT
COLORANTS
COLORBRED
COLORBREED
COLORBREEDING
COLORBREEDS
COLORCAST
COLORCASTED
COLORCASTING

COLORCASTS
COLORED
COLOREDS
COLORER
COLORERS
COLORFAST
COLORFUL
COLORIFIC
COLORING
COLORINGS
COLORISM
COLORISMS
COLORIST
COLORISTS
COLORIZE
COLORIZED
COLORIZER
COLORIZERS
COLORIZES
COLORIZING
COLORLESS
COLORMAN
COLORMEN
COLORS
COLORWAY
COLORWAYS
COLOSSAL
COLOSSEUM
COLOSSEUMS
COLOSSI
COLOSSUS
COLOSSUSES
COLOSTOMIES
COLOSTOMY
COLOSTRAL
COLOSTRUM
COLOSTRUMS
COLOTOMIES
COLOTOMY
COLOUR
COLOURED
COLOURER
COLOURERS
COLOURING
COLOURS
COLPITIS
COLPITISES
COLS
COLT
COLTER
COLTERS
COLTISH

COLTISHLY
COLTS
COLTSFOOT
COLTSFOOTS
COLUBRID
COLUBRIDS
COLUBRINE
COLUGO
COLUGOS
COLUMBARIES
COLUMBARY
COLUMBIC
COLUMBINE
COLUMBINES
COLUMBITE
COLUMBITES
COLUMBIUM
COLUMBIUMS
COLUMEL
COLUMELLA
COLUMELLAE
COLUMELS
COLUMN
COLUMNAL
COLUMNAR
COLUMNEA
COLUMNEAS
COLUMNED
COLUMNIST
COLUMNISTS
COLUMNS
COLURE
COLURES
COLY
COLZA
COLZAS
COMA
COMADE
COMAE
COMAKE
COMAKER
COMAKERS
COMAKES
COMAKING
COMAL
COMANAGE
COMANAGED
COMANAGER
COMANAGERS
COMANAGES
COMANAGING
COMAS

COMATE	COMEDIES	COMIX	COMMITS	COMMUNISMS
COMATES	COMEDO	COMMA	COMMITTAL	COMMUNIST
COMATIC	COMEDONES	COMMAND	COMMITTALS	COMMUNISTS
COMATIK	COMEDOS	COMMANDED	COMMITTED	COMMUNITIES
COMATIKS	COMEDOWN	COMMANDER	COMMITTEE	COMMUNITY
COMATOSE	COMEDOWNS	COMMANDERS	COMMITTEES	COMMUNIZE
COMATULA	COMEDY	COMMANDING	COMMITTING	COMMUNIZED
COMATULAE	COMELIER	COMMANDO	COMMIX	COMMUNIZES
COMATULID	COMELIEST	COMMANDOES	COMMIXED	COMMUNIZING
COMATULIDS	COMELILY	COMMANDOS	COMMIXES	COMMUTATE
COMB	COMELY	COMMANDS	COMMIXING	COMMUTATED
COMBAT	COMEMBER	COMMAS	COMMIXT	COMMUTATES
COMBATANT	COMEMBERS	COMMATA	COMMODE	COMMUTATING
COMBATANTS	COMER	COMMENCE	COMMODES	COMMUTE
COMBATED	COMERS	COMMENCED	COMMODIFIED	COMMUTED
COMBATER	COMES	COMMENCER	COMMODIFIES	COMMUTER
COMBATERS	COMET	COMMENCERS	COMMODIFY	COMMUTERS
COMBATING	COMETARY	COMMENCES	COMMODIFYING	COMMUTES
COMBATIVE	COMETH	COMMENCING	COMMODITIES	COMMUTING
COMBATS	COMETHER	COMMEND	COMMODITY	COMMY
COMBATTED	COMETHERS	COMMENDAM	COMMODORE	COMONOMER
COMBATTING	COMETIC	COMMENDAMS	COMMODORES	COMONOMERS
COMBE	COMETS	COMMENDED	COMMON	COMORBID
COMBED	COMFIER	COMMENDER	COMMONAGE	COMOSE
COMBER	COMFIEST	COMMENDERS	COMMONAGES	COMOUS
COMBERS	COMFINESS	COMMENDING	COMMONER	COMP
COMBES	COMFINESSES	COMMENDS	COMMONERS	COMPACT
COMBINE	COMFIT	COMMENSAL	COMMONEST	COMPACTED
COMBINED	COMFITS	COMMENSALS	COMMONLY	COMPACTER
COMBINEDS	COMFORT	COMMENT	COMMONS	COMPACTERS
COMBINER	COMFORTED	COMMENTED	COMMOTION	COMPACTEST
COMBINERS	COMFORTER	COMMENTER	COMMOTIONS	COMPACTING
COMBINES	COMFORTERS	COMMENTERS	COMMOVE	COMPACTLY
COMBING	COMFORTING	COMMENTING	COMMOVED	COMPACTOR
COMBINGS	COMFORTS	COMMENTS	COMMOVES	COMPACTORS
COMBINING	COMFREY	COMMERCE	COMMOVING	COMPACTS
COMBLIKE	COMFREYS	COMMERCED	COMMUNAL	COMPADRE
COMBO	COMFY	COMMERCES	COMMUNARD	COMPADRES
COMBOS	COMIC	COMMERCING	COMMUNARDS	COMPANIED
COMBS	COMICAL	COMMIE	COMMUNE	COMPANIES
COMBUST	COMICALLY	COMMIES	COMMUNED	COMPANION
COMBUSTED	COMICS	COMMINGLE	COMMUNER	COMPANIONED
COMBUSTING	COMING	COMMINGLED	COMMUNERS	COMPANIONING
COMBUSTOR	COMINGLE	COMMINGLES	COMMUNES	COMPANIONS
COMBUSTORS	COMINGLED	COMMINGLING	COMMUNING	COMPANY
COMBUSTS	COMINGLES	COMMINUTE	COMMUNION	COMPANYING
COME	COMINGLING	COMMINUTED	COMMUNIONS	COMPARE
COMEBACK	COMINGS	COMMINUTES	COMMUNISE	COMPARED
COMEBACKS	COMITIA	COMMINUTING	COMMUNISED	COMPARER
COMEDIAN	COMITIAL	COMMISSAR	COMMUNISES	COMPARERS
COMEDIANS	COMITIES	COMMISSARS	COMMUNISING	COMPARES
COMEDIC	COMITY	COMMIT	COMMUNISM	COMPARING

COMPART	COMPLETE	COMPOST	CON	CONCERTING
COMPARTED	COMPLETED	COMPOSTED	CONATION	CONCERTO
COMPARTING	COMPLETER	COMPOSTER	CONATIONS	CONCERTOS
COMPARTS	COMPLETERS	COMPOSTERS	CONATIVE	CONCERTS
COMPAS	COMPLETES	COMPOSTING	CONATUS	CONCH
COMPASS	COMPLETEST	COMPOSTS	CONCAVE	CONCHA
COMPASSED	COMPLETING	COMPOSURE	CONCAVED	CONCHAE
COMPASSES	COMPLEX	COMPOSURES	CONCAVELY	CONCHAL
COMPASSING	COMPLEXED	COMPOTE	CONCAVES	CONCHAS
COMPED	COMPLEXER	COMPOTES	CONCAVING	CONCHES
COMPEER	COMPLEXES	COMPOUND	CONCAVITIES	CONCHIE
COMPEERED	COMPLEXEST	COMPOUNDED	CONCAVITY	CONCHIES
COMPEERING	COMPLEXING	COMPOUNDING	CONCEAL	CONCHO
COMPEERS	COMPLEXLY	COMPOUNDS	CONCEALED	CONCHOID
COMPEL	COMPLIANT	COMPRADOR	CONCEALER	CONCHOIDS
COMPELLED	COMPLICE	COMPRADORS	CONCEALERS	CONCHOS
COMPELLER	COMPLICES	COMPRESS	CONCEALING	CONCHS
COMPELLERS	COMPLICIT	COMPRESSED	CONCEALS	CONCHY
COMPELLING	COMPLIED	COMPRESSES	CONCEDE	CONCIERGE
COMPELS	COMPLIER	COMPRESSING	CONCEDED	CONCIERGES
COMPEND	COMPLIERS	COMPRISAL	CONCEDER	CONCILIAR
COMPENDIA	COMPLIES	COMPRISALS	CONCEDERS	CONCISE
COMPENDIUM	COMPLIN	COMPRISE	CONCEDES	CONCISELY
COMPENDIUMS	COMPLINE	COMPRISED	CONCEDING	CONCISER
COMPENDS	COMPLINES	COMPRISES	CONCEIT	CONCISEST
COMPERE	COMPLINS	COMPRISING	CONCEITED	CONCISION
COMPERED	COMPLOT	COMPRIZE	CONCEITING	CONCISIONS
COMPERES	COMPLOTS	COMPRIZED	CONCEITS	CONCLAVE
COMPERING	COMPLOTTED	COMPRIZES	CONCEIVE	CONCLAVES
COMPETE	COMPLOTTING	COMPRIZING	CONCEIVED	CONCLUDE
COMPETED	COMPLY	COMPS	CONCEIVER	CONCLUDED
COMPETENT	COMPLYING	COMPT	CONCEIVERS	CONCLUDER
COMPETES	COMPO	COMPTED	CONCEIVES	CONCLUDERS
COMPETING	COMPONE	COMPTING	CONCEIVING	CONCLUDES
COMPILE	COMPONENT	COMPTS	CONCENT	CONCLUDING
COMPILED	COMPONENTS	COMPUTE	CONCENTER	CONCOCT
COMPILER	COMPONY	COMPUTED	CONCENTERED	CONCOCTED
COMPILERS	COMPORT	COMPUTER	CONCENTERING	CONCOCTER
COMPILES	COMPORTED	COMPUTERS	CONCENTERS	CONCOCTERS
COMPILING	COMPORTING	COMPUTES	CONCENTS	CONCOCTING
COMPING	COMPORTS	COMPUTING	CONCEPT	CONCOCTOR
COMPLAIN	COMPOS	COMPUTIST	CONCEPTI	CONCOCTORS
COMPLAINED	COMPOSE	COMPUTISTS	CONCEPTS	CONCOCTS
COMPLAINING	COMPOSED	COMRADE	CONCEPTUS	CONCORD
COMPLAINS	COMPOSER	COMRADELY	CONCEPTUSES	CONCORDAL
COMPLAINT	COMPOSERS	COMRADERIES	CONCERN	CONCORDAT
COMPLAINTS	COMPOSES	COMRADERY	CONCERNED	CONCORDATS
COMPLEAT	COMPOSING	COMRADES	CONCERNING	CONCORDS
COMPLECT	COMPOSITE	COMSYMP	CONCERNS	CONCOURS
COMPLECTED	COMPOSITED	COMSYMPS	CONCERT	CONCOURSE
COMPLECTING	COMPOSITES	COMTE	CONCERTED	CONCOURSES
COMPLECTS	COMPOSITING	COMTES	CONCERTI	CONCRETE

CONCRETED	CONDOR	CONFERRED	CONFLATES	CONGEED
CONCRETES	CONDORES	CONFERREE	CONFLATING	CONGEEING
CONCRETING	CONDORS	CONFERREES	CONFLICT	CONGEES
CONCUBINE	CONDOS	CONFERRER	CONFLICTED	CONGENER
CONCUBINES	CONDUCE	CONFERRERS	CONFLICTING	CONGENERS
CONCUR	CONDUCED	CONFERRING	CONFLICTS	CONGENIAL
CONCURRED	CONDUCER	CONFERS	CONFLUENT	CONGER
CONCURRING	CONDUCERS	CONFERVA	CONFLUENTS	CONGERIES
CONCURS	CONDUCES	CONFERVAE	CONFLUX	CONGERS
CONCUSS	CONDUCING	CONFERVAL	CONFLUXES	CONGES
CONCUSSED	CONDUCIVE	CONFERVAS	CONFOCAL	CONGEST
CONCUSSES	CONDUCT	CONFESS	CONFORM	CONGESTED
CONCUSSING	CONDUCTED	CONFESSED	CONFORMAL	CONGESTING
CONDEMN	CONDUCTING	CONFESSES	CONFORMED	CONGESTS
CONDEMNED	CONDUCTOR	CONFESSING	CONFORMER	CONGII
CONDEMNER	CONDUCTORS	CONFESSOR	CONFORMERS	CONGIUS
CONDEMNERS	CONDUCTS	CONFESSORS	CONFORMING	CONGLOBE
CONDEMNING	CONDUIT	CONFETTI	CONFORMS	CONGLOBED
CONDEMNOR	CONDUITS	CONFETTO	CONFOUND	CONGLOBES
CONDEMNORS	CONDYLAR	CONFIDANT	CONFOUNDED	CONGLOBING
CONDEMNS	CONDYLE	CONFIDANTS	CONFOUNDING	CONGO
CONDENSE	CONDYLES	CONFIDE	CONFOUNDS	CONGOES
CONDENSED	CONDYLOID	CONFIDED	CONFRERE	CONGOS
CONDENSER	CONDYLOMA	CONFIDENT	CONFRERES	CONGOU
CONDENSERS	CONDYLOMAS	CONFIDER	CONFRONT	CONGOUS
CONDENSES	CONDYLOMATA	CONFIDERS	CONFRONTED	CONGRATS
CONDENSING	CONE	CONFIDES	CONFRONTING	CONGRESS
CONDIGN	CONED	CONFIDING	CONFRONTS	CONGRESSED
CONDIGNLY	CONELRAD	CONFIGURE	CONFUSE	CONGRESSES
CONDIMENT	CONELRADS	CONFIGURED	CONFUSED	CONGRESSING
CONDIMENTS	CONENOSE	CONFIGURES	CONFUSES	CONGRUENT
CONDITION	CONENOSES	CONFIGURING	CONFUSING	CONGRUITIES
CONDITIONED	CONEPATE	CONFINE	CONFUSION	CONGRUITY
CONDITIONING	CONEPATES	CONFINED	CONFUSIONS	CONGRUOUS
CONDITIONS	CONEPATL	CONFINER	CONFUTE	CONI
CONDO	CONEPATLS	CONFINERS	CONFUTED	CONIC
CONDOES	CONES	CONFINES	CONFUTER	CONICAL
CONDOLE	CONEY	CONFINING	CONFUTERS	CONICALLY
CONDOLED	CONEYS	CONFIRM	CONFUTES	CONICITIES
CONDOLENT	CONFAB	CONFIRMED	CONFUTING	CONICITY
CONDOLER	CONFABBED	CONFIRMER	CONGA	CONICS
CONDOLERS	CONFABBING	CONFIRMERS	CONGAED	CONIDIA
CONDOLES	CONFABS	CONFIRMING	CONGAING	CONIDIAL
CONDOLING	CONFECT	CONFIRMS	CONGAS	CONIDIAN
CONDOM	CONFECTED	CONFIT	CONGE	CONIDIUM
CONDOMS	CONFECTING	CONFITEOR	CONGEAL	CONIES
CONDONE	CONFECTS	CONFITEORS	CONGEALED	CONIFER
CONDONED	CONFER	CONFITS	CONGEALER	CONIFERS
CONDONER	CONFEREE	CONFITURE	CONGEALERS	CONIINE
CONDONERS	CONFEREES	CONFITURES	CONGEALING	CONIINES
CONDONES	CONFERRAL	CONFLATE	CONGEALS	CONIN
CONDONING	CONFERRALS	CONFLATED	CONGEE	CONINE

CONINES
CONING
CONINS
CONIOSES
CONIOSIS
CONIUM
CONIUMS
CONJOIN
CONJOINED
CONJOINER
CONJOINERS
CONJOINING
CONJOINS
CONJOINT
CONJUGAL
CONJUGANT
CONJUGANTS
CONJUGATE
CONJUGATED
CONJUGATES
CONJUGATING
CONJUNCT
CONJUNCTS
CONJUNTO
CONJUNTOS
CONJURE
CONJURED
CONJURER
CONJURERS
CONJURES
CONJURING
CONJUROR
CONJURORS
CONK
CONKED
CONKER
CONKERS
CONKING
CONKS
CONKY
CONN
CONNATE
CONNATELY
CONNATION
CONNATIONS
CONNECT
CONNECTED
CONNECTER
CONNECTERS
CONNECTING
CONNECTOR
CONNECTORS

CONNECTS
CONNED
CONNER
CONNERS
CONNEXION
CONNEXIONS
CONNING
CONNIVE
CONNIVED
CONNIVENT
CONNIVER
CONNIVERIES
CONNIVERS
CONNIVERY
CONNIVES
CONNIVING
CONNOTE
CONNOTED
CONNOTES
CONNOTING
CONNS
CONNUBIAL
CONODONT
CONODONTS
CONOID
CONOIDAL
CONOIDS
CONOMINEE
CONOMINEES
CONQUER
CONQUERED
CONQUERER
CONQUERERS
CONQUERING
CONQUEROR
CONQUERORS
CONQUERS
CONQUEST
CONQUESTS
CONQUIAN
CONQUIANS
CONS
CONSCIOUS
CONSCIOUSES
CONSCRIBE
CONSCRIBED
CONSCRIBES
CONSCRIBING
CONSCRIPT
CONSCRIPTED
CONSCRIPTING
CONSCRIPTS

CONSENSUS
CONSENSUSES
CONSENT
CONSENTED
CONSENTER
CONSENTERS
CONSENTING
CONSENTS
CONSERVE
CONSERVED
CONSERVER
CONSERVERS
CONSERVES
CONSERVING
CONSIDER
CONSIDERED
CONSIDERING
CONSIDERS
CONSIGN
CONSIGNED
CONSIGNEE
CONSIGNEES
CONSIGNER
CONSIGNERS
CONSIGNING
CONSIGNOR
CONSIGNORS
CONSIGNS
CONSIST
CONSISTED
CONSISTING
CONSISTS
CONSOL
CONSOLE
CONSOLED
CONSOLER
CONSOLERS
CONSOLES
CONSOLING
CONSOLS
CONSOMME
CONSOMMES
CONSONANT
CONSONANTS
CONSORT
CONSORTED
CONSORTIA
CONSORTING
CONSORTIUM
CONSORTIUMS
CONSORTS
CONSPIRE

CONSPIRED
CONSPIRER
CONSPIRERS
CONSPIRES
CONSPIRING
CONSTABLE
CONSTABLES
CONSTANCIES
CONSTANCY
CONSTANT
CONSTANTS
CONSTRAIN
CONSTRAINED
CONSTRAINING
CONSTRAINS
CONSTRICT
CONSTRICTED
CONSTRICTING
CONSTRICTS
CONSTRUAL
CONSTRUALS
CONSTRUCT
CONSTRUCTED
CONSTRUCTING
CONSTRUCTS
CONSTRUE
CONSTRUED
CONSTRUER
CONSTRUERS
CONSTRUES
CONSTRUING
CONSUL
CONSULAR
CONSULATE
CONSULATES
CONSULS
CONSULT
CONSULTED
CONSULTER
CONSULTERS
CONSULTING
CONSULTOR
CONSULTORS
CONSULTS
CONSUME
CONSUMED
CONSUMER
CONSUMERS
CONSUMES
CONSUMING
CONTACT
CONTACTED

CONTACTEE
CONTACTEES
CONTACTING
CONTACTOR
CONTACTORS
CONTACTS
CONTAGIA
CONTAGION
CONTAGIONS
CONTAGIUM
CONTAIN
CONTAINED
CONTAINER
CONTAINERS
CONTAINING
CONTAINS
CONTE
CONTEMN
CONTEMNED
CONTEMNER
CONTEMNERS
CONTEMNING
CONTEMNOR
CONTEMNORS
CONTEMNS
CONTEMPO
CONTEMPT
CONTEMPTS
CONTEND
CONTENDED
CONTENDER
CONTENDERS
CONTENDING
CONTENDS
CONTENT
CONTENTED
CONTENTING
CONTENTS
CONTES
CONTESSA
CONTESSAS
CONTEST
CONTESTED
CONTESTER
CONTESTERS
CONTESTING
CONTESTS
CONTEXT
CONTEXTS
CONTINENT
CONTINENTS
CONTINUA

CONTINUAL	CONTUMELIES	CONVEXITIES	COOEEING	COOLER
CONTINUE	CONTUMELY	CONVEXITY	COOEES	COOLERS
CONTINUED	CONTUSE	CONVEXLY	COOER	COOLEST
CONTINUER	CONTUSED	CONVEY	COOERS	COOLIE
CONTINUERS	CONTUSES	CONVEYED	COOEY	COOLIES
CONTINUES	CONTUSING	CONVEYER	COOEYED	COOLING
CONTINUING	CONTUSION	CONVEYERS	COOEYING	COOLISH
CONTINUO	CONTUSIONS	CONVEYING	COOEYS	COOLLY
CONTINUOS	CONTUSIVE	CONVEYOR	COOF	COOLNESS
CONTINUUM	CONUNDRUM	CONVEYORS	COOFS	COOLNESSES
CONTINUUMS	CONUNDRUMS	CONVEYS	COOING	COOLS
CONTO	CONUS	CONVICT	COOINGLY	COOLTH
CONTORT	CONVECT	CONVICTED	COOK	COOLTHS
CONTORTED	CONVECTED	CONVICTING	COOKABLE	COOLY
CONTORTING	CONVECTING	CONVICTS	COOKBOOK	COOMB
CONTORTS	CONVECTOR	CONVINCE	COOKBOOKS	COOMBE
CONTOS	CONVECTORS	CONVINCED	COOKED	COOMBES
CONTOUR	CONVECTS	CONVINCER	COOKER	COOMBS
CONTOURED	CONVENE	CONVINCERS	COOKERIES	COON
CONTOURING	CONVENED	CONVINCES	COOKERS	COONCAN
CONTOURS	CONVENER	CONVINCING	COOKERY	COONCANS
CONTRA	CONVENERS	CONVIVIAL	COOKEY	COONHOUND
CONTRACT	CONVENES	CONVOKE	COOKEYS	COONHOUNDS
CONTRACTED	CONVENING	CONVOKED	COOKHOUSE	COONS
CONTRACTING	CONVENOR	CONVOKER	COOKHOUSES	COONSKIN
CONTRACTS	CONVENORS	CONVOKERS	COOKIE	COONSKINS
CONTRAIL	CONVENT	CONVOKES	COOKIES	COONTIE
CONTRAILS	CONVENTED	CONVOKING	COOKING	COONTIES
CONTRALTI	CONVENTING	CONVOLUTE	COOKINGS	COOP
CONTRALTO	CONVENTS	CONVOLUTED	COOKLESS	COOPED
CONTRALTOS	CONVERGE	CONVOLUTES	COOKOFF	COOPER
CONTRARIES	CONVERGED	CONVOLUTING	COOKOFFS	COOPERAGE
CONTRARY	CONVERGES	CONVOLVE	COOKOUT	COOPERAGES
CONTRAS	CONVERGING	CONVOLVED	COOKOUTS	COOPERATE
CONTRAST	CONVERSE	CONVOLVES	COOKS	COOPERATED
CONTRASTED	CONVERSED	CONVOLVING	COOKSHACK	COOPERATES
CONTRASTING	CONVERSER	CONVOY	COOKSHACKS	COOPERATING
CONTRASTS	CONVERSERS	CONVOYED	COOKSHOP	COOPERED
CONTRASTY	CONVERSES	CONVOYING	COOKSHOPS	COOPERIES
CONTRITE	CONVERSING	CONVOYS	COOKSTOVE	COOPERING
CONTRIVE	CONVERSO	CONVULSE	COOKSTOVES	COOPERS
CONTRIVED	CONVERSOS	CONVULSED	COOKTOP	COOPERY
CONTRIVER	CONVERT	CONVULSES	COOKTOPS	COOPING
CONTRIVERS	CONVERTED	CONVULSING	COOKWARE	COOPS
CONTRIVES	CONVERTER	CONY	COOKWARES	COOPT
CONTRIVING	CONVERTERS	COO	COOKY	COOPTED
CONTROL	CONVERTING	COOCH	COOL	COOPTING
CONTROLLED	CONVERTOR	COOCHES	COOLANT	COOPTION
CONTROLLING	CONVERTORS	COOCOO	COOLANTS	COOPTIONS
CONTROLS	CONVERTS	COOED	COOLDOWN	COOPTS
CONTUMACIES	CONVEX	COOEE	COOLDOWNS	COOS
CONTUMACY	CONVEXES	COOEED	COOLED	COOT

COOTER	COPILOT	COPROLITES	COPYRIGHT	CORBY
COOTERS	COPILOTS	COPROLOGIES	COPYRIGHTED	CORD
COOTIE	COPING	COPROLOGY	COPYRIGHTING	CORDAGE
COOTIES	COPINGS	COPS	COPYRIGHTS	CORDAGES
COOTS	COPIOUS	COPSE	COQUET	CORDATE
COP	COPIOUSLY	COPSES	COQUETRIES	CORDATELY
COPACETIC	COPLANAR	COPTER	COQUETRY	CORDED
COPAIBA	COPLOT	COPTERS	COQUETS	CORDELLE
COPAIBAS	COPLOTS	COPUBLISH	COQUETTE	CORDELLED
COPAL	COPLOTTED	COPUBLISHED	COQUETTED	CORDELLES
COPALM	COPLOTTING	COPUBLISHES	COQUETTES	CORDELLING
COPALMS	COPOLYMER	COPUBLISHING	COQUETTING	CORDER
COPALS	COPOLYMERS	COPULA	COQUILLE	CORDERS
COPARENT	COPOUT	COPULAE	COQUILLES	CORDGRASS
COPARENTED	COPOUTS	COPULAR	COQUINA	CORDGRASSES
COPARENTING	COPPED	COPULAS	COQUINAS	CORDIAL
COPARENTS	COPPER	COPULATE	COQUITO	CORDIALLY
COPARTNER	COPPERAH	COPULATED	COQUITOS	CORDIALS
COPARTNERED	COPPERAHS	COPULATES	COR	CORDIFORM
COPARTNERING	COPPERAS	COPULATING	CORACLE	CORDING
COPARTNERS	COPPERASES	COPURIFIED	CORACLES	CORDINGS
COPASETIC	COPPERED	COPURIFIES	CORACOID	CORDITE
COPASTOR	COPPERING	COPURIFY	CORACOIDS	CORDITES
COPASTORS	COPPERS	COPURIFYING	CORAL	CORDLESS
COPATRON	COPPERY	COPY	CORALLINE	CORDLESSES
COPATRONS	COPPICE	COPYABLE	CORALLINES	CORDLIKE
COPAY	COPPICED	COPYBOOK	CORALLOID	CORDOBA
COPAYMENT	COPPICES	COPYBOOKS	CORALROOT	CORDOBAS
COPAYMENTS	COPPICING	COPYBOY	CORALROOTS	CORDON
COPAYS	COPPING	COPYBOYS	CORALS	CORDONED
COPE	COPPRA	COPYCAT	CORANTO	CORDONING
COPECK	COPPRAS	COPYCATS	CORANTOES	CORDONNET
COPECKS	COPRA	COPYCATTED	CORANTOS	CORDONNETS
COPED	COPRAH	COPYCATTING	CORBAN	CORDONS
COPEMATE	COPRAHS	COPYDESK	CORBANS	CORDOVAN
COPEMATES	COPRAS	COPYDESKS	CORBEIL	CORDOVANS
COPEN	COPREMIA	COPYEDIT	CORBEILLE	CORDS
COPENS	COPREMIAS	COPYEDITED	CORBEILLES	CORDUROY
COPEPOD	COPREMIC	COPYEDITING	CORBEILS	CORDUROYED
COPEPODS	COPRESENT	COPYEDITS	CORBEL	CORDUROYING
COPER	COPRESENTED	COPYGIRL	CORBELED	CORDUROYS
COPERS	COPRESENTING	COPYGIRLS	CORBELING	CORDWAIN
COPES	COPRESENTS	COPYHOLD	CORBELINGS	CORDWAINS
COPESETIC	COPRINCE	COPYHOLDS	CORBELLED	CORDWOOD
COPESTONE	COPRINCES	COPYING	CORBELLING	CORDWOODS
COPESTONES	COPRODUCE	COPYIST	CORBELS	CORE
COPIED	COPRODUCED	COPYISTS	CORBICULA	CORED
COPIER	COPRODUCES	COPYLEFT	CORBICULAE	COREDEEM
COPIERS	COPRODUCING	COPYLEFTS	CORBIE	COREDEEMED
COPIES	COPRODUCT	COPYREAD	CORBIES	COREDEEMING
COPIHUE	COPRODUCTS	COPYREADING	CORBINA	COREDEEMS
COPIHUES	COPROLITE	COPYREADS	CORBINAS	COREIGN

COREIGNS	CORNBALL	CORNICLE	CORONATES	CORRELATE
CORELATE	CORNBALLS	CORNICLES	CORONATING	CORRELATED
CORELATED	CORNBRAID	CORNIER	CORONEL	CORRELATES
CORELATES	CORNBRAIDED	CORNIEST	CORONELS	CORRELATING
CORELATING	CORNBRAIDING	CORNIFIED	CORONER	CORRIDA
CORELESS	CORNBRAIDS	CORNIFIES	CORONERS	CORRIDAS
COREMIA	CORNBREAD	CORNIFY	CORONET	CORRIDOR
COREMIUM	CORNBREADS	CORNIFYING	CORONETED	CORRIDORS
COREOPSIS	CORNCAKE	CORNILY	CORONETS	CORRIE
CORER	CORNCAKES	CORNINESS	CORONOID	CORRIES
CORERS	CORNCOB	CORNINESSES	COROTATE	CORRIVAL
CORES	CORNCOBS	CORNING	COROTATED	CORRIVALS
CORF	CORNCRAKE	CORNMEAL	COROTATES	CORRODE
CORGI	CORNCRAKES	CORNMEALS	COROTATING	CORRODED
CORGIS	CORNCRIB	CORNPONE	CORPORA	CORRODES
CORIA	CORNCRIBS	CORNPONES	CORPORAL	CORRODIES
CORIANDER	CORNEA	CORNROW	CORPORALS	CORRODING
CORIANDERS	CORNEAL	CORNROWED	CORPORATE	CORRODY
CORING	CORNEAS	CORNROWING	CORPORATES	CORROSION
CORIUM	CORNED	CORNROWS	CORPOREAL	CORROSIONS
CORK	CORNEITIS	CORNS	CORPOSANT	CORROSIVE
CORKAGE	CORNEITISES	CORNSTALK	CORPOSANTS	CORROSIVES
CORKAGES	CORNEL	CORNSTALKS	CORPS	CORRUGATE
CORKBOARD	CORNELIAN	CORNU	CORPSE	CORRUGATED
CORKBOARDS	CORNELIANS	CORNUA	CORPSES	CORRUGATES
CORKED	CORNELS	CORNUAL	CORPSMAN	CORRUGATING
CORKER	CORNEOUS	CORNUS	CORPSMEN	CORRUPT
CORKERS	CORNER	CORNUSES	CORPULENT	CORRUPTED
CORKIER	CORNERED	CORNUTE	CORPUS	CORRUPTER
CORKIEST	CORNERING	CORNUTED	CORPUSCLE	CORRUPTERS
CORKINESS	CORNERMAN	CORNUTO	CORPUSCLES	CORRUPTEST
CORKINESSES	CORNERMEN	CORNUTOS	CORPUSES	CORRUPTING
CORKING	CORNERS	CORNY	CORRADE	CORRUPTLY
CORKLIKE	CORNET	CORODIES	CORRADED	CORRUPTOR
CORKS	CORNETCIES	CORODY	CORRADES	CORRUPTORS
CORKSCREW	CORNETCY	COROLLA	CORRADING	CORRUPTS
CORKSCREWED	CORNETIST	COROLLARIES	CORRAL	CORS
CORKSCREWING	CORNETISTS	COROLLARY	CORRALLED	CORSAC
CORKSCREWS	CORNETS	COROLLAS	CORRALLING	CORSACS
CORKWOOD	CORNFED	COROLLATE	CORRALS	CORSAGE
CORKWOODS	CORNFIELD	CORONA	CORRASION	CORSAGES
CORKY	CORNFIELDS	CORONACH	CORRASIONS	CORSAIR
CORM	CORNHUSK	CORONACHS	CORRASIVE	CORSAIRS
CORMEL	CORNHUSKS	CORONAE	CORRECT	CORSE
CORMELS	CORNICE	CORONAL	CORRECTED	CORSELET
CORMLIKE	CORNICED	CORONALLY	CORRECTER	CORSELETS
CORMOID	CORNICES	CORONALS	CORRECTEST	CORSES
CORMORANT	CORNICHE	CORONARIES	CORRECTING	CORSET
CORMORANTS	CORNICHES	CORONARY	CORRECTLY	CORSETED
CORMOUS	CORNICHON	CORONAS	CORRECTOR	CORSETING
CORMS	CORNICHONS	CORONATE	CORRECTORS	CORSETRIES
CORN	CORNICING	CORONATED	CORRECTS	CORSETRY

CORSETS	CORYMBS	COSMIC	COSTLIER	COTQUEAN
CORSLET	CORYPHAEI	COSMICAL	COSTLIEST	COTQUEANS
CORSLETS	CORYPHAEUS	COSMID	COSTLY	COTRUSTEE
CORTEGE	CORYPHEE	COSMIDS	COSTMARIES	COTRUSTEES
CORTEGES	CORYPHEES	COSMISM	COSTMARY	COTS
CORTEX	CORYZA	COSMISMS	COSTREL	COTTA
CORTEXES	CORYZAL	COSMIST	COSTRELS	COTTAE
CORTICAL	CORYZAS	COSMISTS	COSTS	COTTAGE
CORTICATE	COS	COSMOGONIES	COSTUME	COTTAGER
CORTICES	COSCRIPT	COSMOGONY	COSTUMED	COTTAGERS
CORTICOID	COSCRIPTED	COSMOLINE	COSTUMER	COTTAGES
CORTICOIDS	COSCRIPTING	COSMOLINED	COSTUMERIES	COTTAGEY
CORTICOSE	COSCRIPTS	COSMOLINES	COSTUMERS	COTTAR
CORTIN	COSEC	COSMOLINING	COSTUMERY	COTTARS
CORTINA	COSECANT	COSMOLOGIES	COSTUMES	COTTAS
CORTINAS	COSECANTS	COSMOLOGY	COSTUMEY	COTTER
CORTINS	COSECS	COSMONAUT	COSTUMIER	COTTERED
CORTISOL	COSEISMAL	COSMONAUTS	COSTUMIERS	COTTERS
CORTISOLS	COSEISMALS	COSMOS	COSTUMING	COTTIER
CORTISONE	COSEISMIC	COSMOSES	COSY	COTTIERS
CORTISONES	COSEISMICS	COSMOTRON	COSYING	COTTON
CORULER	COSES	COSMOTRONS	COT	COTTONED
CORULERS	COSET	COSPONSOR	COTAN	COTTONING
CORUNDUM	COSETS	COSPONSORED	COTANGENT	COTTONS
CORUNDUMS	COSEY	COSPONSORING	COTANGENTS	COTTONY
CORUSCANT	COSEYS	COSPONSORS	COTANS	COTURNIX
CORUSCATE	COSH	COSS	COTE	COTURNIXES
CORUSCATED	COSHED	COSSACK	COTEAU	COTYLEDON
CORUSCATES	COSHER	COSSACKS	COTEAUX	COTYLEDONS
CORUSCATING	COSHERED	COSSET	COTED	COTYLOID
CORVEE	COSHERING	COSSETED	COTENANCIES	COTYPE
CORVEES	COSHERS	COSSETING	COTENANCY	COTYPES
CORVES	COSHES	COSSETS	COTENANT	COUCH
CORVET	COSHING	COST	COTENANTS	COUCHANT
CORVETS	COSIE	COSTA	COTERIE	COUCHED
CORVETTE	COSIED	COSTAE	COTERIES	COUCHER
CORVETTES	COSIER	COSTAL	COTES	COUCHERS
CORVID	COSIES	COSTALLY	COTHURN	COUCHES
CORVIDS	COSIEST	COSTAR	COTHURNAL	COUCHETTE
CORVINA	COSIGN	COSTARD	COTHURNI	COUCHETTES
CORVINAS	COSIGNED	COSTARDS	COTHURNS	COUCHING
CORVINE	COSIGNER	COSTARRED	COTHURNUS	COUCHINGS
CORY	COSIGNERS	COSTARRING	COTIDAL	COUDE
CORYBANT	COSIGNING	COSTARS	COTILLION	COUGAR
CORYBANTES	COSIGNS	COSTATE	COTILLIONS	COUGARS
CORYBANTS	COSILY	COSTED	COTILLON	COUGH
CORYDALIS	COSINE	COSTER	COTILLONS	COUGHED
CORYDALISES	COSINES	COSTERS	COTING	COUGHER
CORYMB	COSINESS	COSTING	COTINGA	COUGHERS
CORYMBED	COSINESSES	COSTIVE	COTINGAS	COUGHING
CORYMBOSE	COSMETIC	COSTIVELY	COTININE	COUGHS
CORYMBOUS	COSMETICS	COSTLESS	COTININES	COULD

COULDEST
COULDST
COULEE
COULEES
COULIBIAC
COULIBIACS
COULIS
COULISSE
COULISSES
COULOIR
COULOIRS
COULOMB
COULOMBIC
COULOMBS
COULTER
COULTERS
COUMARIC
COUMARIN
COUMARINS
COUMARONE
COUMARONES
COUMAROU
COUMAROUS
COUNCIL
COUNCILOR
COUNCILORS
COUNCILS
COUNSEL
COUNSELED
COUNSELEE
COUNSELEES
COUNSELING
COUNSELLED
COUNSELLING
COUNSELOR
COUNSELORS
COUNSELS
COUNT
COUNTABLE
COUNTABLY
COUNTDOWN
COUNTDOWNS
COUNTED
COUNTER
COUNTERED
COUNTERING
COUNTERS
COUNTESS
COUNTESSES
COUNTIAN
COUNTIANS
COUNTIES

COUNTING
COUNTLESS
COUNTRIES
COUNTRY
COUNTS
COUNTY
COUP
COUPE
COUPED
COUPES
COUPING
COUPLE
COUPLED
COUPLEDOM
COUPLEDOMS
COUPLER
COUPLERS
COUPLES
COUPLET
COUPLETS
COUPLING
COUPLINGS
COUPON
COUPONING
COUPONINGS
COUPONS
COUPS
COURAGE
COURAGES
COURANT
COURANTE
COURANTES
COURANTO
COURANTOES
COURANTOS
COURANTS
COURGETTE
COURGETTES
COURIER
COURIERS
COURLAN
COURLANS
COURSE
COURSED
COURSER
COURSERS
COURSES
COURSING
COURSINGS
COURT
COURTED
COURTEOUS

COURTER
COURTERS
COURTESAN
COURTESANS
COURTESIED
COURTESIES
COURTESY
COURTESYING
COURTEZAN
COURTEZANS
COURTIER
COURTIERS
COURTING
COURTLIER
COURTLIEST
COURTLY
COURTROOM
COURTROOMS
COURTS
COURTSHIP
COURTSHIPS
COURTSIDE
COURTSIDES
COURTYARD
COURTYARDS
COUSCOUS
COUSCOUSES
COUSIN
COUSINAGE
COUSINAGES
COUSINLY
COUSINRIES
COUSINRY
COUSINS
COUTEAU
COUTEAUX
COUTER
COUTERS
COUTH
COUTHER
COUTHEST
COUTHIE
COUTHIER
COUTHIEST
COUTHS
COUTURE
COUTURES
COUTURIER
COUTURIERS
COUVADE
COUVADES
COVALENCE

COVALENCES
COVALENCIES
COVALENCY
COVALENT
COVARIANT
COVARIATE
COVARIATES
COVARIED
COVARIES
COVARY
COVARYING
COVE
COVED
COVELLINE
COVELLINES
COVELLITE
COVELLITES
COVEN
COVENANT
COVENANTED
COVENANTING
COVENANTS
COVENS
COVER
COVERABLE
COVERAGE
COVERAGES
COVERALL
COVERALLS
COVERED
COVERER
COVERERS
COVERING
COVERINGS
COVERLESS
COVERLET
COVERLETS
COVERLID
COVERLIDS
COVERS
COVERSINE
COVERSINES
COVERSLIP
COVERSLIPS
COVERT
COVERTLY
COVERTS
COVERTURE
COVERTURES
COVERUP
COVERUPS
COVES

COVET
COVETABLE
COVETED
COVETER
COVETERS
COVETING
COVETOUS
COVETS
COVEY
COVEYS
COVIN
COVING
COVINGS
COVINS
COW
COWAGE
COWAGES
COWARD
COWARDICE
COWARDICES
COWARDLY
COWARDS
COWBANE
COWBANES
COWBELL
COWBELLS
COWBERRIES
COWBERRY
COWBIND
COWBINDS
COWBIRD
COWBIRDS
COWBOY
COWBOYED
COWBOYING
COWBOYS
COWED
COWEDLY
COWER
COWERED
COWERING
COWERS
COWFISH
COWFISHES
COWFLAP
COWFLAPS
COWFLOP
COWFLOPS
COWGIRL
COWGIRLS
COWHAGE
COWHAGES

COWHAND	COWSHED	COZEN	CRACKDOWN	CRAGGY
COWHANDS	COWSHEDS	COZENAGE	CRACKDOWNS	CRAGS
COWHERB	COWSKIN	COZENAGES	CRACKED	CRAGSMAN
COWHERBS	COWSKINS	COZENED	CRACKER	CRAGSMEN
COWHERD	COWSLIP	COZENER	CRACKERS	CRAKE
COWHERDS	COWSLIPS	COZENERS	CRACKHEAD	CRAKES
COWHIDE	COWY	COZENING	CRACKHEADS	CRAM
COWHIDED	COX	COZENS	CRACKING	CRAMBE
COWHIDES	COXA	COZES	CRACKINGS	CRAMBES
COWHIDING	COXAE	COZEY	CRACKLE	CRAMBO
COWIER	COXAL	COZEYS	CRACKLED	CRAMBOES
COWIEST	COXALGIA	COZIE	CRACKLES	CRAMBOS
COWING	COXALGIAS	COZIED	CRACKLIER	CRAMMED
COWINNER	COXALGIC	COZIER	CRACKLIEST	CRAMMER
COWINNERS	COXALGIES	COZIES	CRACKLING	CRAMMERS
COWL	COXALGY	COZIEST	CRACKLINGS	CRAMMING
COWLED	COXCOMB	COZILY	CRACKLY	CRAMOISIE
COWLICK	COXCOMBIC	COZINESS	CRACKNEL	CRAMOISIES
COWLICKS	COXCOMBRIES	COZINESSES	CRACKNELS	CRAMOISY
COWLING	COXCOMBRY	COZY	CRACKPOT	CRAMP
COWLINGS	COXCOMBS	COZYING	CRACKPOTS	CRAMPED
COWLS	COXED	COZZES	CRACKS	CRAMPFISH
COWLSTAFF	COXES	CRAAL	CRACKSMAN	CRAMPFISHES
COWLSTAFFS	COXING	CRAALED	CRACKSMEN	CRAMPIER
COWLSTAVES	COXITIDES	CRAALING	CRACKUP	CRAMPIEST
COWMAN	COXITIS	CRAALS	CRACKUPS	CRAMPING
COWMEN	COXLESS	CRAB	CRACKY	CRAMPIT
COWORKER	COXSWAIN	CRABABBLE	CRADLE	CRAMPITS
COWORKERS	COXSWAINED	CRABABBLES	CRADLED	CRAMPON
COWPAT	COXSWAINING	CRABBED	CRADLER	CRAMPONS
COWPATS	COXSWAINS	CRABBEDLY	CRADLERS	CRAMPOON
COWPEA	COY	CRABBER	CRADLES	CRAMPOONS
COWPEAS	COYDOG	CRABBERS	CRADLING	CRAMPS
COWPIE	COYDOGS	CRABBIER	CRAFT	CRAMPY
COWPIES	COYED	CRABBIEST	CRAFTED	CRAMS
COWPLOP	COYER	CRABBILY	CRAFTER	CRANBERRIES
COWPLOPS	COYEST	CRABBING	CRAFTERS	CRANBERRY
COWPOKE	COYING	CRABBY	CRAFTIER	CRANCH
COWPOKES	COYISH	CRABEATER	CRAFTIEST	CRANCHED
COWPOX	COYLY	CRABEATERS	CRAFTILY	CRANCHES
COWPOXES	COYNESS	CRABGRASS	CRAFTING	CRANCHING
COWRIE	COYNESSES	CRABGRASSES	CRAFTS	CRANE
COWRIES	COYOTE	CRABLIKE	CRAFTSMAN	CRANED
COWRITE	COYOTES	CRABMEAT	CRAFTSMEN	CRANES
COWRITER	COYOTILLO	CRABMEATS	CRAFTWORK	CRANIA
COWRITERS	COYOTILLOS	CRABS	CRAFTWORKS	CRANIAL
COWRITES	COYPOU	CRABSTICK	CRAFTY	CRANIALLY
COWRITING	COYPOUS	CRABSTICKS	CRAG	CRANIATE
COWRITTEN	COYPU	CRABWISE	CRAGGED	CRANIATES
COWROTE	COYPUS	CRACK	CRAGGIER	CRANING
COWRY	COYS	CRACKBACK	CRAGGIEST	CRANIUM
COWS	COZ	CRACKBACKS	CRAGGILY	CRANIUMS

CRANK	CRASES	CRAWDADS	CREAMERIES	CREDIBLY
CRANKCASE	CRASH	CRAWFISH	CREAMERS	CREDIT
CRANKCASES	CRASHED	CRAWFISHED	CREAMERY	CREDITED
CRANKED	CRASHER	CRAWFISHES	CREAMIER	CREDITING
CRANKER	CRASHERS	CRAWFISHING	CREAMIEST	CREDITOR
CRANKEST	CRASHES	CRAWL	CREAMILY	CREDITORS
CRANKIER	CRASHING	CRAWLED	CREAMING	CREDITS
CRANKIEST	CRASIS	CRAWLER	CREAMPUFF	CREDO
CRANKILY	CRASS	CRAWLERS	CREAMPUFFS	CREDOS
CRANKING	CRASSER	CRAWLIER	CREAMS	CREDS
CRANKISH	CRASSEST	CRAWLIEST	CREAMWARE	CREDULITIES
CRANKLE	CRASSLY	CRAWLING	CREAMWARES	CREDULITY
CRANKLED	CRASSNESS	CRAWLS	CREAMY	CREDULOUS
CRANKLES	CRASSNESSES	CRAWLWAY	CREASE	CREED
CRANKLING	CRATCH	CRAWLWAYS	CREASED	CREEDAL
CRANKLY	CRATCHES	CRAWLY	CREASER	CREEDS
CRANKOUS	CRATE	CRAWS	CREASERS	CREEK
CRANKPIN	CRATED	CRAYFISH	CREASES	CREEKS
CRANKPINS	CRATER	CRAYFISHES	CREASIER	CREEL
CRANKS	CRATERED	CRAYON	CREASIEST	CREELED
CRANKY	CRATERING	CRAYONED	CREASING	CREELING
CRANNIED	CRATERINGS	CRAYONER	CREASY	CREELS
CRANNIES	CRATERLET	CRAYONERS	CREATABLE	CREEP
CRANNOG	CRATERLETS	CRAYONING	CREATE	CREEPAGE
CRANNOGE	CRATERS	CRAYONIST	CREATED	CREEPAGES
CRANNOGES	CRATES	CRAYONISTS	CREATES	CREEPED
CRANNOGS	CRATING	CRAYONS	CREATIN	CREEPER
CRANNY	CRATON	CRAZE	CREATINE	CREEPERS
CRANREUCH	CRATONIC	CRAZED	CREATINES	CREEPIE
CRANREUCHS	CRATONS	CRAZES	CREATING	CREEPIER
CRAP	CRAUNCH	CRAZIER	CREATINS	CREEPIES
CRAPE	CRAUNCHED	CRAZIES	CREATION	CREEPIEST
CRAPED	CRAUNCHES	CRAZIEST	CREATIONS	CREEPILY
CRAPELIKE	CRAUNCHING	CRAZILY	CREATIVE	CREEPING
CRAPES	CRAVAT	CRAZINESS	CREATIVES	CREEPS
CRAPING	CRAVATS	CRAZINESSES	CREATOR	CREEPY
CRAPOLA	CRAVE	CRAZING	CREATORS	CREESE
CRAPOLAS	CRAVED	CRAZY	CREATURAL	CREESES
CRAPPED	CRAVEN	CRAZYWEED	CREATURE	CREESH
CRAPPER	CRAVENED	CRAZYWEEDS	CREATURES	CREESHED
CRAPPERS	CRAVENING	CREAK	CRECHE	CREESHES
CRAPPIE	CRAVENLY	CREAKED	CRECHES	CREESHING
CRAPPIER	CRAVENS	CREAKIER	CRED	CREMAINS
CRAPPIES	CRAVER	CREAKIEST	CREDAL	CREMATE
CRAPPIEST	CRAVERS	CREAKILY	CREDENCE	CREMATED
CRAPPING	CRAVES	CREAKING	CREDENCES	CREMATES
CRAPPY	CRAVING	CREAKS	CREDENDA	CREMATING
CRAPS	CRAVINGS	CREAKY	CREDENDUM	CREMATION
CRAPSHOOT	CRAW	CREAM	CREDENT	CREMATIONS
CRAPSHOOTS	CRAWDAD	CREAMCUPS	CREDENZA	CREMATOR
CRAPULENT	CRAWDADDIES	CREAMED	CREDENZAS	CREMATORIES
CRAPULOUS	CRAWDADDY	CREAMER	CREDIBLE	CREMATORS

CREMATORY	CREPING	CREVASSES	CRIKEY	CRINOIDAL
CREME	CREPITANT	CREVASSING	CRIME	CRINOIDS
CREMES	CREPITATE	CREVICE	CRIMELESS	CRINOLINE
CREMINI	CREPITATED	CREVICED	CRIMES	CRINOLINES
CREMINIS	CREPITATES	CREVICES	CRIMINAL	CRINUM
CRENATE	CREPITATING	CREW	CRIMINALS	CRINUMS
CRENATED	CREPON	CREWCUT	CRIMINATE	CRIOLLO
CRENATELY	CREPONS	CREWCUTS	CRIMINATED	CRIOLLOS
CRENATION	CREPT	CREWED	CRIMINATES	CRIPE
CRENATIONS	CREPUSCLE	CREWEL	CRIMINATING	CRIPES
CRENATURE	CREPUSCLES	CREWELS	CRIMINE	CRIPPLE
CRENATURES	CREPY	CREWING	CRIMINI	CRIPPLED
CRENEL	CRESCENDI	CREWLESS	CRIMINIS	CRIPPLER
CRENELATE	CRESCENDO	CREWMAN	CRIMINOUS	CRIPPLERS
CRENELATED	CRESCENDOED	CREWMATE	CRIMINY	CRIPPLES
CRENELATES	CRESCENDOES	CREWMATES	CRIMMER	CRIPPLING
CRENELATING	CRESCENDOING	CREWMEN	CRIMMERS	CRIS
CRENELED	CRESCENDOS	CREWNECK	CRIMP	CRISES
CRENELING	CRESCENT	CREWNECKS	CRIMPED	CRISIC
CRENELLE	CRESCENTS	CREWS	CRIMPER	CRISIS
CRENELLED	CRESCIVE	CRIB	CRIMPERS	CRISP
CRENELLES	CRESOL	CRIBBAGE	CRIMPIER	CRISPATE
CRENELLING	CRESOLS	CRIBBAGES	CRIMPIEST	CRISPATED
CRENELS	CRESS	CRIBBED	CRIMPING	CRISPED
CRENSHAW	CRESSES	CRIBBER	CRIMPLE	CRISPEN
CRENSHAWS	CRESSET	CRIBBERS	CRIMPLED	CRISPENED
CRENULATE	CRESSETS	CRIBBING	CRIMPLES	CRISPENING
CREODONT	CRESSY	CRIBBINGS	CRIMPLING	CRISPENS
CREODONTS	CREST	CRIBBLED	CRIMPS	CRISPER
CREOLE	CRESTAL	CRIBROUS	CRIMPY	CRISPERS
CREOLES	CRESTED	CRIBS	CRIMSON	CRISPEST
CREOLISE	CRESTING	CRIBWORK	CRIMSONED	CRISPHEAD
CREOLISED	CRESTINGS	CRIBWORKS	CRIMSONING	CRISPHEADS
CREOLISES	CRESTLESS	CRICETID	CRIMSONS	CRISPIER
CREOLISING	CRESTS	CRICETIDS	CRINGE	CRISPIEST
CREOLIZE	CRESYL	CRICK	CRINGED	CRISPILY
CREOLIZED	CRESYLIC	CRICKED	CRINGER	CRISPING
CREOLIZES	CRESYLS	CRICKET	CRINGERS	CRISPLY
CREOLIZING	CRETIC	CRICKETED	CRINGES	CRISPNESS
CREOSOL	CRETICS	CRICKETER	CRINGING	CRISPNESSES
CREOSOLS	CRETIN	CRICKETERS	CRINGLE	CRISPS
CREOSOTE	CRETINISM	CRICKETING	CRINGLES	CRISPY
CREOSOTED	CRETINISMS	CRICKETS	CRINITE	CRISSA
CREOSOTES	CRETINOID	CRICKEY	CRINITES	CRISSAL
CREOSOTIC	CRETINOUS	CRICKING	CRINKLE	CRISSUM
CREOSOTING	CRETINS	CRICKS	CRINKLED	CRISTA
CREPE	CRETONNE	CRICOID	CRINKLES	CRISTAE
CREPED	CRETONNES	CRICOIDS	CRINKLIER	CRISTATE
CREPES	CREVALLE	CRIED	CRINKLIEST	CRISTATED
CREPEY	CREVALLES	CRIER	CRINKLING	CRIT
CREPIER	CREVASSE	CRIERS	CRINKLY	CRITERIA
CREPIEST	CREVASSED	CRIES	CRINOID	CRITERIAL

CRITERION
CRITERIONS
CRITERIUM
CRITERIUMS
CRITIC
CRITICAL
CRITICISE
CRITICISED
CRITICISES
CRITICISING
CRITICISM
CRITICISMS
CRITICIZE
CRITICIZED
CRITICIZES
CRITICIZING
CRITICS
CRITIQUE
CRITIQUED
CRITIQUES
CRITIQUING
CRITS
CRITTER
CRITTERS
CRITTUR
CRITTURS
CROAK
CROAKED
CROAKER
CROAKERS
CROAKIER
CROAKIEST
CROAKILY
CROAKING
CROAKS
CROAKY
CROC
CROCEIN
CROCEINE
CROCEINES
CROCEINS
CROCHET
CROCHETED
CROCHETER
CROCHETERS
CROCHETING
CROCHETS
CROCI
CROCINE
CROCK
CROCKED
CROCKERIES

CROCKERY
CROCKET
CROCKETED
CROCKETS
CROCKING
CROCKPOT
CROCKPOTS
CROCKS
CROCODILE
CROCODILES
CROCOITE
CROCOITES
CROCS
CROCUS
CROCUSES
CROFT
CROFTER
CROFTERS
CROFTS
CROISSANT
CROISSANTS
CROJIK
CROJIKS
CROMLECH
CROMLECHS
CRONE
CRONES
CRONIES
CRONISH
CRONY
CRONYISM
CRONYISMS
CROOK
CROOKBACK
CROOKBACKS
CROOKED
CROOKEDER
CROOKEDEST
CROOKEDLY
CROOKER
CROOKERIES
CROOKERY
CROOKEST
CROOKING
CROOKNECK
CROOKNECKS
CROOKS
CROON
CROONED
CROONER
CROONERS
CROONING

CROONS
CROP
CROPLAND
CROPLANDS
CROPLESS
CROPPED
CROPPER
CROPPERS
CROPPIE
CROPPIES
CROPPING
CROPS
CROQUET
CROQUETED
CROQUETING
CROQUETS
CROQUETTE
CROQUETTES
CROQUIS
CRORE
CRORES
CROSIER
CROSIERS
CROSS
CROSSABLE
CROSSARM
CROSSARMS
CROSSBAR
CROSSBARRED
CROSSBARRING
CROSSBARS
CROSSBEAM
CROSSBEAMS
CROSSBILL
CROSSBILLS
CROSSBOW
CROSSBOWS
CROSSBRED
CROSSBREDS
CROSSBREED
CROSSBREEDING
CROSSBREEDS
CROSSBUCK
CROSSBUCKS
CROSSCUT
CROSSCUTS
CROSSCUTTING
CROSSE
CROSSED
CROSSER
CROSSERS
CROSSES

CROSSEST
CROSSFIRE
CROSSFIRES
CROSSHAIR
CROSSHAIRS
CROSSHEAD
CROSSHEADS
CROSSING
CROSSINGS
CROSSJACK
CROSSJACKS
CROSSLET
CROSSLETS
CROSSLY
CROSSNESS
CROSSNESSES
CROSSOVER
CROSSOVERS
CROSSROAD
CROSSROADS
CROSSRUFF
CROSSRUFFED
CROSSRUFFING
CROSSRUFFS
CROSSTALK
CROSSTALKS
CROSSTIE
CROSSTIED
CROSSTIES
CROSSTOWN
CROSSTREE
CROSSTREES
CROSSWALK
CROSSWALKS
CROSSWAY
CROSSWAYS
CROSSWIND
CROSSWINDS
CROSSWISE
CROSSWORD
CROSSWORDS
CROSTINI
CROSTINO
CROTCH
CROTCHED
CROTCHES
CROTCHET
CROTCHETS
CROTCHETY
CROTON
CROTONBUG
CROTONBUGS

CROTONS
CROUCH
CROUCHED
CROUCHES
CROUCHING
CROUP
CROUPE
CROUPES
CROUPIER
CROUPIERS
CROUPIEST
CROUPILY
CROUPOUS
CROUPS
CROUPY
CROUSE
CROUSELY
CROUSTADE
CROUSTADES
CROUTE
CROUTES
CROUTON
CROUTONS
CROW
CROWBAR
CROWBARRED
CROWBARRING
CROWBARS
CROWBERRIES
CROWBERRY
CROWD
CROWDED
CROWDEDLY
CROWDER
CROWDERS
CROWDIE
CROWDIES
CROWDING
CROWDS
CROWDY
CROWED
CROWER
CROWERS
CROWFEET
CROWFOOT
CROWFOOTS
CROWING
CROWN
CROWNED
CROWNER
CROWNERS
CROWNET

CROWNETS	CRUDITIES	CRUMPETS	CRUSTACEA	CRYOSTATS
CROWNING	CRUDITY	CRUMPING	CRUSTAL	CRYOTRON
CROWNLESS	CRUDS	CRUMPLE	CRUSTED	CRYOTRONS
CROWNS	CRUEL	CRUMPLED	CRUSTIER	CRYPT
CROWS	CRUELER	CRUMPLES	CRUSTIEST	CRYPTAL
CROWSFEET	CRUELEST	CRUMPLIER	CRUSTILY	CRYPTIC
CROWSFOOT	CRUELLER	CRUMPLIEST	CRUSTING	CRYPTICAL
CROWSTEP	CRUELLEST	CRUMPLING	CRUSTLESS	CRYPTO
CROWSTEPS	CRUELLY	CRUMPLY	CRUSTOSE	CRYPTOGAM
CROZE	CRUELNESS	CRUMPS	CRUSTS	CRYPTOGAMS
CROZER	CRUELNESSES	CRUNCH	CRUSTY	CRYPTONYM
CROZERS	CRUELTIES	CRUNCHED	CRUTCH	CRYPTONYMS
CROZES	CRUELTY	CRUNCHER	CRUTCHED	CRYPTOS
CROZIER	CRUET	CRUNCHERS	CRUTCHES	CRYPTS
CROZIERS	CRUETS	CRUNCHES	CRUTCHING	CRYSTAL
CRU	CRUISE	CRUNCHIER	CRUX	CRYSTALS
CRUCES	CRUISED	CRUNCHIEST	CRUXES	CTENIDIA
CRUCIAL	CRUISER	CRUNCHILY	CRUZADO	CTENIDIUM
CRUCIALLY	CRUISERS	CRUNCHING	CRUZADOES	CTENOID
CRUCIAN	CRUISES	CRUNCHY	CRUZADOS	CUADRILLA
CRUCIANS	CRUISING	CRUNODAL	CRUZEIRO	CUADRILLAS
CRUCIATE	CRUISINGS	CRUNODE	CRUZEIROS	CUATRO
CRUCIBLE	CRULLER	CRUNODES	CRWTH	CUATROS
CRUCIBLES	CRULLERS	CRUOR	CRWTHS	CUB
CRUCIFER	CRUMB	CRUORS	CRY	CUBAGE
CRUCIFERS	CRUMBED	CRUPPER	CRYBABIES	CUBAGES
CRUCIFIED	CRUMBER	CRUPPERS	CRYBABY	CUBANELLE
CRUCIFIER	CRUMBERS	CRURA	CRYING	CUBANELLES
CRUCIFIERS	CRUMBIER	CRURAL	CRYINGLY	CUBATURE
CRUCIFIES	CRUMBIEST	CRUS	CRYOBANK	CUBATURES
CRUCIFIX	CRUMBING	CRUSADE	CRYOBANKS	CUBBIES
CRUCIFIXES	CRUMBLE	CRUSADED	CRYOGEN	CUBBISH
CRUCIFORM	CRUMBLED	CRUSADER	CRYOGENIC	CUBBY
CRUCIFORMS	CRUMBLES	CRUSADERS	CRYOGENICS	CUBBYHOLE
CRUCIFY	CRUMBLIER	CRUSADES	CRYOGENIES	CUBBYHOLES
CRUCIFYING	CRUMBLIEST	CRUSADING	CRYOGENS	CUBE
CRUCK	CRUMBLING	CRUSADO	CRYOGENY	CUBEB
CRUCKS	CRUMBLY	CRUSADOES	CRYOLITE	CUBEBS
CRUD	CRUMBS	CRUSADOS	CRYOLITES	CUBED
CRUDDED	CRUMBUM	CRUSE	CRYOMETER	CUBER
CRUDDIER	CRUMBUMS	CRUSES	CRYOMETERS	CUBERS
CRUDDIEST	CRUMBY	CRUSET	CRYONIC	CUBES
CRUDDING	CRUMHORN	CRUSETS	CRYONICS	CUBIC
CRUDDY	CRUMHORNS	CRUSH	CRYOPHYTE	CUBICAL
CRUDE	CRUMMIE	CRUSHABLE	CRYOPHYTES	CUBICALLY
CRUDELY	CRUMMIER	CRUSHED	CRYOPROBE	CUBICITIES
CRUDENESS	CRUMMIES	CRUSHER	CRYOPROBES	CUBICITY
CRUDENESSES	CRUMMIEST	CRUSHERS	CRYOSCOPE	CUBICLE
CRUDER	CRUMMY	CRUSHES	CRYOSCOPES	CUBICLES
CRUDES	CRUMP	CRUSHING	CRYOSCOPIES	CUBICLY
CRUDEST	CRUMPED	CRUSILY	CRYOSCOPY	CUBICS
CRUDITES	CRUMPET	CRUST	CRYOSTAT	CUBICULA

CUBICULUM	CUDGELLED	CULL	CULTIVATE	CUMULI
CUBIFORM	CUDGELLING	CULLAY	CULTIVATED	CUMULOUS
CUBING	CUDGELS	CULLAYS	CULTIVATES	CUMULUS
CUBISM	CUDS	CULLED	CULTIVATING	CUNCTATOR
CUBISMS	CUDWEED	CULLENDER	CULTLIKE	CUNCTATORS
CUBIST	CUDWEEDS	CULLENDERS	CULTRATE	CUNDUM
CUBISTIC	CUE	CULLER	CULTRATED	CUNDUMS
CUBISTS	CUED	CULLERS	CULTS	CUNEAL
CUBIT	CUEING	CULLET	CULTURAL	CUNEATE
CUBITAL	CUES	CULLETS	CULTURATI	CUNEATED
CUBITI	CUESTA	CULLIED	CULTURE	CUNEATELY
CUBITS	CUESTAS	CULLIES	CULTURED	CUNEATIC
CUBITUS	CUFF	CULLING	CULTURES	CUNEIFORM
CUBOID	CUFFED	CULLION	CULTURING	CUNEIFORMS
CUBOIDAL	CUFFING	CULLIONS	CULTURIST	CUNIFORM
CUBOIDS	CUFFLESS	CULLIS	CULTURISTS	CUNIFORMS
CUBS	CUFFLINK	CULLISES	CULTUS	CUNNER
CUCKOLD	CUFFLINKS	CULLS	CULTUSES	CUNNERS
CUCKOLDED	CUFFS	CULLY	CULVER	CUNNING
CUCKOLDING	CUIF	CULLYING	CULVERIN	CUNNINGER
CUCKOLDRIES	CUIFS	CULM	CULVERINS	CUNNINGEST
CUCKOLDRY	CUING	CULMED	CULVERS	CUNNINGLY
CUCKOLDS	CUIRASS	CULMINANT	CULVERT	CUNNINGS
CUCKOO	CUIRASSED	CULMINATE	CULVERTS	CUNT
CUCKOOED	CUIRASSES	CULMINATED	CUM	CUNTS
CUCKOOING	CUIRASSING	CULMINATES	CUMARIN	CUP
CUCKOOS	CUISH	CULMINATING	CUMARINS	CUPBEARER
CUCULLATE	CUISHES	CULMING	CUMBER	CUPBEARERS
CUCUMBER	CUISINART	CULMS	CUMBERED	CUPBOARD
CUCUMBERS	CUISINARTS	CULOTTE	CUMBERER	CUPBOARDS
CUCURBIT	CUISINE	CULOTTES	CUMBERERS	CUPCAKE
CUCURBITS	CUISINES	CULPA	CUMBERING	CUPCAKES
CUD	CUISSE	CULPABLE	CUMBERS	CUPEL
CUDBEAR	CUISSES	CULPABLY	CUMBIA	CUPELED
CUDBEARS	CUITTLE	CULPAE	CUMBIAS	CUPELER
CUDDIE	CUITTLED	CULPRIT	CUMBRANCE	CUPELERS
CUDDIES	CUITTLES	CULPRITS	CUMBRANCES	CUPELING
CUDDLE	CUITTLING	CULT	CUMBROUS	CUPELLED
CUDDLED	CUKE	CULTCH	CUMIN	CUPELLER
CUDDLER	CUKES	CULTCHES	CUMINS	CUPELLERS
CUDDLERS	CULCH	CULTI	CUMMER	CUPELLING
CUDDLES	CULCHES	CULTIC	CUMMERS	CUPELS
CUDDLIER	CULET	CULTIGEN	CUMMIN	CUPFERRON
CUDDLIEST	CULETS	CULTIGENS	CUMMINS	CUPFERRONS
CUDDLING	CULEX	CULTISH	CUMQUAT	CUPFUL
CUDDLY	CULEXES	CULTISHLY	CUMQUATS	CUPFULS
CUDDY	CULICES	CULTISM	CUMSHAW	CUPID
CUDGEL	CULICID	CULTISMS	CUMSHAWS	CUPIDITIES
CUDGELED	CULICIDS	CULTIST	CUMULATE	CUPIDITY
CUDGELER	CULICINE	CULTISTS	CUMULATED	CUPIDS
CUDGELERS	CULICINES	CULTIVAR	CUMULATES	CUPLIKE
CUDGELING	CULINARY	CULTIVARS	CUMULATING	CUPOLA

CUPOLAED	CURARIZED	CURETTAGE	CURN	CURSERS
CUPOLAING	CURARIZES	CURETTAGES	CURNS	CURSES
CUPOLAS	CURARIZING	CURETTE	CURR	CURSING
CUPPA	CURASSOW	CURETTED	CURRACH	CURSIVE
CUPPAS	CURASSOWS	CURETTES	CURRACHS	CURSIVELY
CUPPED	CURATE	CURETTING	CURRAGH	CURSIVES
CUPPER	CURATED	CURF	CURRAGHS	CURSOR
CUPPERS	CURATES	CURFEW	CURRAJONG	CURSORIAL
CUPPIER	CURATING	CURFEWS	CURRAJONGS	CURSORILY
CUPPIEST	CURATIVE	CURFS	CURRAN	CURSORS
CUPPING	CURATIVES	CURIA	CURRANS	CURSORY
CUPPINGS	CURATOR	CURIAE	CURRANT	CURST
CUPPY	CURATORS	CURIAL	CURRANTS	CURT
CUPREOUS	CURB	CURIE	CURRED	CURTAIL
CUPRIC	CURBABLE	CURIES	CURREJONG	CURTAILED
CUPRITE	CURBED	CURING	CURREJONGS	CURTAILER
CUPRITES	CURBER	CURIO	CURRENCIES	CURTAILERS
CUPROUS	CURBERS	CURIOS	CURRENCY	CURTAILING
CUPRUM	CURBING	CURIOSA	CURRENT	CURTAILS
CUPRUMS	CURBINGS	CURIOSITIES	CURRENTLY	CURTAIN
CUPS	CURBS	CURIOSITY	CURRENTS	CURTAINED
CUPSFUL	CURBSIDE	CURIOUS	CURRICLE	CURTAINING
CUPULA	CURBSIDES	CURIOUSER	CURRICLES	CURTAINS
CUPULAE	CURBSTONE	CURIOUSEST	CURRICULA	CURTAL
CUPULAR	CURBSTONES	CURIOUSLY	CURRICULUM	CURTALAX
CUPULATE	CURCH	CURITE	CURRICULUMS	CURTALAXES
CUPULE	CURCHES	CURITES	CURRIE	CURTALS
CUPULES	CURCULIO	CURIUM	CURRIED	CURTATE
CUR	CURCULIOS	CURIUMS	CURRIER	CURTER
CURABLE	CURCUMA	CURL	CURRIERIES	CURTESIES
CURABLY	CURCUMAS	CURLED	CURRIERS	CURTEST
CURACAO	CURD	CURLER	CURRIERY	CURTESY
CURACAOS	CURDED	CURLERS	CURRIES	CURTILAGE
CURACIES	CURDIER	CURLEW	CURRIJONG	CURTILAGES
CURACOA	CURDIEST	CURLEWS	CURRIJONGS	CURTLY
CURACOAS	CURDING	CURLICUE	CURRING	CURTNESS
CURACY	CURDLE	CURLICUED	CURRISH	CURTNESSES
CURAGH	CURDLED	CURLICUES	CURRISHLY	CURTSEY
CURAGHS	CURDLER	CURLICUING	CURRS	CURTSEYED
CURANDERA	CURDLERS	CURLIER	CURRY	CURTSEYING
CURANDERAS	CURDLES	CURLIEST	CURRYCOMB	CURTSEYS
CURANDERO	CURDLING	CURLILY	CURRYCOMBED	CURTSIED
CURANDEROS	CURDS	CURLINESS	CURRYCOMBING	CURTSIES
CURARA	CURDY	CURLINESSES	CURRYCOMBS	CURTSY
CURARAS	CURE	CURLING	CURRYING	CURTSYING
CURARE	CURED	CURLINGS	CURS	CURULE
CURARES	CURELESS	CURLPAPER	CURSE	CURVATURE
CURARI	CURER	CURLPAPERS	CURSED	CURVATURES
CURARINE	CURERS	CURLS	CURSEDER	CURVE
CURARINES	CURES	CURLY	CURSEDEST	CURVEBALL
CURARIS	CURET	CURLYCUE	CURSEDLY	CURVEBALLED
CURARIZE	CURETS	CURLYCUES	CURSER	CURVEBALLING

CURVEBALLS	CUSSEDLY	CUTENESSES	CUTTABLE	CYANOGEN
CURVED	CUSSER	CUTER	CUTTAGE	CYANOGENS
CURVEDLY	CUSSERS	CUTES	CUTTAGES	CYANOSED
CURVES	CUSSES	CUTESIE	CUTTER	CYANOSES
CURVET	CUSSING	CUTESIER	CUTTERS	CYANOSIS
CURVETED	CUSSO	CUTESIEST	CUTTHROAT	CYANOTIC
CURVETING	CUSSOS	CUTEST	CUTTHROATS	CYANOTYPE
CURVETS	CUSSWORD	CUTESY	CUTTIES	CYANOTYPES
CURVETTED	CUSSWORDS	CUTEY	CUTTING	CYANS
CURVETTING	CUSTARD	CUTEYS	CUTTINGLY	CYANURATE
CURVEY	CUSTARDS	CUTGRASS	CUTTINGS	CYANURATES
CURVIER	CUSTARDY	CUTGRASSES	CUTTLE	CYBER
CURVIEST	CUSTODES	CUTICLE	CUTTLED	CYBERCAFE
CURVING	CUSTODIAL	CUTICLES	CUTTLES	CYBERCAFES
CURVY	CUSTODIAN	CUTICULA	CUTTLING	CYBERCAST
CUSCUS	CUSTODIANS	CUTICULAE	CUTTY	CYBERCASTS
CUSCUSES	CUSTODIES	CUTICULAR	CUTUP	CYBERNATE
CUSEC	CUSTODY	CUTIE	CUTUPS	CYBERNATED
CUSECS	CUSTOM	CUTIES	CUTWATER	CYBERNATES
CUSHAT	CUSTOMARIES	CUTIN	CUTWATERS	CYBERNATING
CUSHATS	CUSTOMARY	CUTINISE	CUTWORK	CYBERNAUT
CUSHAW	CUSTOMER	CUTINISED	CUTWORKS	CYBERNAUTS
CUSHAWS	CUSTOMERS	CUTINISES	CUTWORM	CYBERPORN
CUSHIER	CUSTOMISE	CUTINISING	CUTWORMS	CYBERPORNS
CUSHIEST	CUSTOMISED	CUTINIZE	CUVEE	CYBERPUNK
CUSHILY	CUSTOMISES	CUTINIZED	CUVEES	CYBERPUNKS
CUSHINESS	CUSTOMISING	CUTINIZES	CUVETTE	CYBERSEX
CUSHINESSES	CUSTOMIZE	CUTINIZING	CUVETTES	CYBERSEXES
CUSHION	CUSTOMIZED	CUTINS	CWM	CYBORG
CUSHIONED	CUSTOMIZES	CUTIS	CWMS	CYBORGS
CUSHIONING	CUSTOMIZING	CUTISES	CYAN	CYBRARIAN
CUSHIONS	CUSTOMS	CUTLAS	CYANAMID	CYBRARIANS
CUSHIONY	CUSTOS	CUTLASES	CYANAMIDE	CYCAD
CUSHY	CUSTUMAL	CUTLASS	CYANAMIDES	CYCADEOID
CUSK	CUSTUMALS	CUTLASSES	CYANAMIDS	CYCADEOIDS
CUSKS	CUT	CUTLER	CYANATE	CYCADS
CUSP	CUTANEOUS	CUTLERIES	CYANATES	CYCAS
CUSPAL	CUTAWAY	CUTLERS	CYANIC	CYCASES
CUSPATE	CUTAWAYS	CUTLERY	CYANID	CYCASIN
CUSPATED	CUTBACK	CUTLET	CYANIDE	CYCASINS
CUSPED	CUTBACKS	CUTLETS	CYANIDED	CYCLAMATE
CUSPID	CUTBANK	CUTLINE	CYANIDES	CYCLAMATES
CUSPIDAL	CUTBANKS	CUTLINES	CYANIDING	CYCLAMEN
CUSPIDATE	CUTCH	CUTOFF	CYANIDS	CYCLAMENS
CUSPIDES	CUTCHERIES	CUTOFFS	CYANIN	CYCLASE
CUSPIDOR	CUTCHERY	CUTOUT	CYANINE	CYCLASES
CUSPIDORS	CUTCHES	CUTOUTS	CYANINES	CYCLE
CUSPIDS	CUTDOWN	CUTOVER	CYANINS	CYCLECAR
CUSPIS	CUTDOWNS	CUTOVERS	CYANITE	CYCLECARS
CUSPS	CUTE	CUTPURSE	CYANITES	CYCLED
CUSS	CUTELY	CUTPURSES	CYANITIC	CYCLER
CUSSED	CUTENESS	CUTS	CYANO	CYCLERIES

CYCLERS	CYLINDER	CYNICISMS	CYTOKINES	DABBLED
CYCLERY	CYLINDERED	CYNICS	CYTOKININ	DABBLER
CYCLES	CYLINDERING	CYNOSURAL	CYTOKININS	DABBLERS
CYCLEWAY	CYLINDERS	CYNOSURE	CYTOLOGIC	DABBLES
CYCLEWAYS	CYLINDRIC	CYNOSURES	CYTOLOGIES	DABBLING
CYCLIC	CYLIX	CYPHER	CYTOLOGY	DABBLINGS
CYCLICAL	CYMA	CYPHERED	CYTOLYSES	DABCHICK
CYCLICALS	CYMAE	CYPHERING	CYTOLYSIN	DABCHICKS
CYCLICITIES	CYMAR	CYPHERS	CYTOLYSINS	DABS
CYCLICITY	CYMARS	CYPRES	CYTOLYSIS	DABSTER
CYCLICLY	CYMAS	CYPRESES	CYTOLYTIC	DABSTERS
CYCLIN	CYMATIA	CYPRESS	CYTON	DACE
CYCLING	CYMATIUM	CYPRESSES	CYTONS	DACES
CYCLINGS	CYMBAL	CYPRIAN	CYTOPLASM	DACHA
CYCLINS	CYMBALEER	CYPRIANS	CYTOPLASMS	DACHAS
CYCLIST	CYMBALEERS	CYPRINID	CYTOPLAST	DACHSHUND
CYCLISTS	CYMBALER	CYPRINIDS	CYTOPLASTS	DACHSHUNDS
CYCLITOL	CYMBALERS	CYPRINOID	CYTOSINE	DACITE
CYCLITOLS	CYMBALIST	CYPRINOIDS	CYTOSINES	DACITES
CYCLIZE	CYMBALISTS	CYPRUS	CYTOSOL	DACKER
CYCLIZED	CYMBALOM	CYPRUSES	CYTOSOLIC	DACKERED
CYCLIZES	CYMBALOMS	CYPSELA	CYTOSOLS	DACKERING
CYCLIZINE	CYMBALS	CYPSELAE	CYTOTOXIC	DACKERS
CYCLIZINES	CYMBIDIA	CYST	CYTOTOXIN	DACOIT
CYCLIZING	CYMBIDIUM	CYSTEIN	CYTOTOXINS	DACOITIES
CYCLO	CYMBIDIUMS	CYSTEINE	CZAR	DACOITS
CYCLOID	CYMBLING	CYSTEINES	CZARDAS	DACOITY
CYCLOIDAL	CYMBLINGS	CYSTEINIC	CZARDASES	DACQUOISE
CYCLOIDS	CYME	CYSTEINS	CZARDOM	DACQUOISES
CYCLONAL	CYMENE	CYSTIC	CZARDOMS	DACRON
CYCLONE	CYMENES	CYSTINE	CZAREVNA	DACRONS
CYCLONES	CYMES	CYSTINES	CZAREVNAS	DACTYL
CYCLONIC	CYMLIN	CYSTITIDES	CZARINA	DACTYLI
CYCLONITE	CYMLING	CYSTITIS	CZARINAS	DACTYLIC
CYCLONITES	CYMLINGS	CYSTOCARP	CZARISM	DACTYLICS
CYCLOPEAN	CYMLINS	CYSTOCARPS	CZARISMS	DACTYLS
CYCLOPES	CYMOGENE	CYSTOCELE	CZARIST	DACTYLUS
CYCLOPS	CYMOGENES	CYSTOCELES	CZARISTS	DAD
CYCLORAMA	CYMOGRAPH	CYSTOID	CZARITZA	DADA
CYCLORAMAS	CYMOGRAPHS	CYSTOIDS	CZARITZAS	DADAISM
CYCLOS	CYMOID	CYSTOLITH	CZARS	DADAISMS
CYCLOSES	CYMOL	CYSTOLITHS		DADAIST
CYCLOSIS	CYMOLS	CYSTOTOMIES		DADAISTIC
CYCLOTRON	CYMOPHANE	CYSTOTOMY	D	DADAISTS
CYCLOTRONS	CYMOPHANES	CYSTS		DADAS
CYDER	CYMOSE	CYTASTER		DADDIES
CYDERS	CYMOSELY	CYTASTERS	DAB	DADDLE
CYESES	CYMOUS	CYTIDINE	DABBED	DADDLED
CYESIS	CYNIC	CYTIDINES	DABBER	DADDLES
CYGNET	CYNICAL	CYTOGENIES	DABBERS	DADDLING
CYGNETS	CYNICALLY	CYTOGENY	DABBING	DADDY
CYLICES	CYNICISM	CYTOKINE	DABBLE	DADGUM

DADO	DAH	DAIRYMAN	DAMAGED	DAMNING
DADOED	DAHABEAH	DAIRYMEN	DAMAGER	DAMNINGLY
DADOES	DAHABEAHS	DAIS	DAMAGERS	DAMNS
DADOING	DAHABIAH	DAISES	DAMAGES	DAMOSEL
DADOS	DAHABIAHS	DAISHIKI	DAMAGING	DAMOSELS
DADS	DAHABIEH	DAISHIKIS	DAMAN	DAMOZEL
DAEDAL	DAHABIEHS	DAISIED	DAMANS	DAMOZELS
DAEDALEAN	DAHABIYA	DAISIES	DAMAR	DAMP
DAEDALIAN	DAHABIYAS	DAISY	DAMARS	DAMPED
DAEMON	DAHL	DAK	DAMASCENE	DAMPEN
DAEMONES	DAHLIA	DAKERHEN	DAMASCENED	DAMPENED
DAEMONIC	DAHLIAS	DAKERHENS	DAMASCENES	DAMPENER
DAEMONS	DAHLS	DAKOIT	DAMASCENING	DAMPENERS
DAFF	DAHOON	DAKOITIES	DAMASK	DAMPENING
DAFFED	DAHOONS	DAKOITS	DAMASKED	DAMPENS
DAFFIER	DAHS	DAKOITY	DAMASKEEN	DAMPER
DAFFIEST	DAIDZEIN	DAKS	DAMASKEENED	DAMPERS
DAFFILY	DAIDZEINS	DAL	DAMASKEENING	DAMPEST
DAFFINESS	DAIKER	DALAPON	DAMASKEENS	DAMPING
DAFFINESSES	DAIKERED	DALAPONS	DAMASKING	DAMPINGS
DAFFING	DAIKERING	DALASI	DAMASKS	DAMPISH
DAFFODIL	DAIKERS	DALASIS	DAME	DAMPLY
DAFFODILS	DAIKON	DALE	DAMES	DAMPNESS
DAFFS	DAIKONS	DALEDH	DAMEWORT	DAMPNESSES
DAFFY	DAILIES	DALEDHS	DAMEWORTS	DAMPS
DAFT	DAILINESS	DALES	DAMIANA	DAMS
DAFTER	DAILINESSES	DALESMAN	DAMIANAS	DAMSEL
DAFTEST	DAILY	DALESMEN	DAMMAR	DAMSELFLIES
DAFTLY	DAILYNESS	DALETH	DAMMARS	DAMSELFLY
DAFTNESS	DAILYNESSES	DALETHS	DAMMED	DAMSELS
DAFTNESSES	DAIMEN	DALLES	DAMMER	DAMSON
DAG	DAIMIO	DALLIANCE	DAMMERS	DAMSONS
DAGGA	DAIMIOS	DALLIANCES	DAMMING	DAN
DAGGAS	DAIMON	DALLIED	DAMMIT	DANAZOL
DAGGER	DAIMONES	DALLIER	DAMN	DANAZOLS
DAGGERED	DAIMONIC	DALLIERS	DAMNABLE	DANCE
DAGGERING	DAIMONS	DALLIES	DAMNABLY	DANCEABLE
DAGGERS	DAIMYO	DALLY	DAMNATION	DANCED
DAGGLE	DAIMYOS	DALLYING	DAMNATIONS	DANCER
DAGGLED	DAINTIER	DALMATIAN	DAMNATORY	DANCERS
DAGGLES	DAINTIES	DALMATIANS	DAMNDEST	DANCES
DAGGLING	DAINTIEST	DALMATIC	DAMNDESTS	DANCING
DAGLOCK	DAINTILY	DALMATICS	DAMNED	DANDELION
DAGLOCKS	DAINTY	DALS	DAMNEDER	DANDELIONS
DAGO	DAIQUIRI	DALTON	DAMNEDEST	DANDER
DAGOBA	DAIQUIRIS	DALTONIAN	DAMNEDESTS	DANDERED
DAGOBAS	DAIRIES	DALTONIC	DAMNER	DANDERING
DAGOES	DAIRY	DALTONISM	DAMNERS	DANDERS
DAGOS	DAIRYING	DALTONISMS	DAMNIFIED	DANDIACAL
DAGS	DAIRYINGS	DALTONS	DAMNIFIES	DANDIER
DAGWOOD	DAIRYMAID	DAM	DAMNIFY	DANDIES
DAGWOODS	DAIRYMAIDS	DAMAGE	DAMNIFYING	DANDIEST

DANDIFIED	DANKEST	DARKENER	DARTER	DATEBOOK
DANDIFIES	DANKLY	DARKENERS	DARTERS	DATEBOOKS
DANDIFY	DANKNESS	DARKENING	DARTING	DATED
DANDIFYING	DANKNESSES	DARKENS	DARTINGLY	DATEDLY
DANDILY	DANS	DARKER	DARTLE	DATEDNESS
DANDLE	DANSEUR	DARKEST	DARTLED	DATEDNESSES
DANDLED	DANSEURS	DARKEY	DARTLES	DATELESS
DANDLER	DANSEUSE	DARKEYS	DARTLING	DATELINE
DANDLERS	DANSEUSES	DARKIE	DARTS	DATELINED
DANDLES	DAP	DARKIES	DASH	DATELINES
DANDLING	DAPHNE	DARKING	DASHBOARD	DATELINING
DANDRIFF	DAPHNES	DARKISH	DASHBOARDS	DATER
DANDRIFFS	DAPHNIA	DARKLE	DASHED	DATERS
DANDRUFF	DAPHNIAS	DARKLED	DASHEEN	DATES
DANDRUFFS	DAPPED	DARKLES	DASHEENS	DATING
DANDRUFFY	DAPPER	DARKLIER	DASHER	DATIVAL
DANDY	DAPPERER	DARKLIEST	DASHERS	DATIVE
DANDYISH	DAPPEREST	DARKLING	DASHES	DATIVELY
DANDYISM	DAPPERLY	DARKLINGS	DASHI	DATIVES
DANDYISMS	DAPPING	DARKLY	DASHIER	DATO
DANEGELD	DAPPLE	DARKNESS	DASHIEST	DATOS
DANEGELDS	DAPPLED	DARKNESSES	DASHIKI	DATTO
DANEGELT	DAPPLES	DARKROOM	DASHIKIS	DATTOS
DANEGELTS	DAPPLING	DARKROOMS	DASHING	DATUM
DANEWEED	DAPS	DARKS	DASHINGLY	DATUMS
DANEWEEDS	DAPSONE	DARKSOME	DASHIS	DATURA
DANEWORT	DAPSONES	DARKY	DASHPOT	DATURAS
DANEWORTS	DARB	DARLING	DASHPOTS	DATURIC
DANG	DARBAR	DARLINGLY	DASHY	DAUB
DANGED	DARBARS	DARLINGS	DASSIE	DAUBE
DANGER	DARBIES	DARN	DASSIES	DAUBED
DANGERED	DARBS	DARNATION	DASTARD	DAUBER
DANGERING	DARE	DARNATIONS	DASTARDLY	DAUBERIES
DANGEROUS	DARED	DARNDEST	DASTARDS	DAUBERS
DANGERS	DAREDEVIL	DARNDESTS	DASYMETER	DAUBERY
DANGING	DAREDEVILS	DARNED	DASYMETERS	DAUBES
DANGLE	DAREFUL	DARNEDER	DASYURE	DAUBIER
DANGLED	DARER	DARNEDEST	DASYURES	DAUBIEST
DANGLER	DARERS	DARNEDESTS	DATA	DAUBING
DANGLERS	DARES	DARNEL	DATABANK	DAUBINGLY
DANGLES	DARESAY	DARNELS	DATABANKS	DAUBRIES
DANGLIER	DARIC	DARNER	DATABASE	DAUBRY
DANGLIEST	DARICS	DARNERS	DATABASED	DAUBS
DANGLING	DARING	DARNING	DATABASES	DAUBY
DANGLY	DARINGLY	DARNINGS	DATABASING	DAUGHTER
DANGS	DARINGS	DARNS	DATABLE	DAUGHTERS
DANIO	DARIOLE	DARSHAN	DATARIES	DAUNDER
DANIOS	DARIOLES	DARSHANS	DATARY	DAUNDERED
DANISH	DARK	DART	DATCHA	DAUNDERING
DANISHES	DARKED	DARTBOARD	DATCHAS	DAUNDERS
DANK	DARKEN	DARTBOARDS	DATE	DAUNT
DANKER	DARKENED	DARTED	DATEABLE	DAUNTED

DAUNTER	DAYBED	DAZES	DEADLINED	DEALINGS
DAUNTERS	DAYBEDS	DAZING	DEADLINES	DEALS
DAUNTING	DAYBOOK	DAZZLE	DEADLINING	DEALT
DAUNTLESS	DAYBOOKS	DAZZLED	DEADLOCK	DEAMINASE
DAUNTS	DAYBREAK	DAZZLER	DEADLOCKED	DEAMINASES
DAUPHIN	DAYBREAKS	DAZZLERS	DEADLOCKING	DEAMINATE
DAUPHINE	DAYCARE	DAZZLES	DEADLOCKS	DEAMINATED
DAUPHINES	DAYCARES	DAZZLING	DEADLY	DEAMINATES
DAUPHINS	DAYDREAM	DE	DEADMAN	DEAMINATING
DAUT	DAYDREAMED	DEACIDIFIED	DEADMEN	DEAMINIZE
DAUTED	DAYDREAMING	DEACIDIFIES	DEADNESS	DEAMINIZED
DAUTIE	DAYDREAMS	DEACIDIFY	DEADNESSES	DEAMINIZES
DAUTIES	DAYDREAMT	DEACIDIFYING	DEADPAN	DEAMINIZING
DAUTING	DAYDREAMY	DEACON	DEADPANNED	DEAN
DAUTS	DAYFLIES	DEACONED	DEADPANNING	DEANED
DAVEN	DAYFLOWER	DEACONESS	DEADPANS	DEANERIES
DAVENED	DAYFLOWERS	DEACONESSES	DEADS	DEANERY
DAVENING	DAYFLY	DEACONING	DEADWOOD	DEANING
DAVENPORT	DAYGLOW	DEACONRIES	DEADWOODS	DEANS
DAVENPORTS	DAYGLOWS	DEACONRY	DEAERATE	DEANSHIP
DAVENS	DAYLIGHT	DEACONS	DEAERATED	DEANSHIPS
DAVIES	DAYLIGHTED	DEAD	DEAERATES	DEAR
DAVIT	DAYLIGHTING	DEADBEAT	DEAERATING	DEARER
DAVITS	DAYLIGHTS	DEADBEATS	DEAERATOR	DEAREST
DAVY	DAYLILIES	DEADBOLT	DEAERATORS	DEARIE
DAW	DAYLILY	DEADBOLTS	DEAF	DEARIES
DAWDLE	DAYLIT	DEADEN	DEAFEN	DEARLY
DAWDLED	DAYLONG	DEADENED	DEAFENED	DEARNESS
DAWDLER	DAYMARE	DEADENER	DEAFENING	DEARNESSES
DAWDLERS	DAYMARES	DEADENERS	DEAFENINGS	DEARS
DAWDLES	DAYROOM	DEADENING	DEAFENS	DEARTH
DAWDLING	DAYROOMS	DEADENINGS	DEAFER	DEARTHS
DAWED	DAYS	DEADENS	DEAFEST	DEARY
DAWEN	DAYSIDE	DEADER	DEAFISH	DEASH
DAWING	DAYSIDES	DEADEST	DEAFLY	DEASHED
DAWK	DAYSMAN	DEADEYE	DEAFNESS	DEASHES
DAWKS	DAYSMEN	DEADEYES	DEAFNESSES	DEASHING
DAWN	DAYSPRING	DEADFALL	DEAIR	DEASIL
DAWNED	DAYSPRINGS	DEADFALLS	DEAIRED	DEATH
DAWNING	DAYSTAR	DEADHEAD	DEAIRING	DEATHBED
DAWNLIKE	DAYSTARS	DEADHEADED	DEAIRS	DEATHBEDS
DAWNS	DAYTIME	DEADHEADING	DEAL	DEATHBLOW
DAWS	DAYTIMES	DEADHEADS	DEALATE	DEATHBLOWS
DAWSONITE	DAYWORK	DEADLIER	DEALATED	DEATHCUP
DAWSONITES	DAYWORKER	DEADLIEST	DEALATES	DEATHCUPS
DAWT	DAYWORKERS	DEADLIFT	DEALATION	DEATHFUL
DAWTED	DAYWORKS	DEADLIFTED	DEALATIONS	DEATHLESS
DAWTIE	DAZE	DEADLIFTING	DEALER	DEATHLIKE
DAWTIES	DAZED	DEADLIFTS	DEALERS	DEATHLY
DAWTING	DAZEDLY	DEADLIGHT	DEALFISH	DEATHS
DAWTS	DAZEDNESS	DEADLIGHTS	DEALFISHES	DEATHSMAN
DAY	DAZEDNESSES	DEADLINE	DEALING	DEATHSMEN

DEATHTRAP	DEBEARD	DEBUNK	DECAMPS	DECENNARY
DEATHTRAPS	DEBEARDED	DEBUNKED	DECANAL	DECENNIA
DEATHY	DEBEARDING	DEBUNKER	DECANE	DECENNIAL
DEAVE	DEBEARDS	DEBUNKERS	DECANES	DECENNIALS
DEAVED	DEBENTURE	DEBUNKING	DECANT	DECENNIUM
DEAVES	DEBENTURES	DEBUNKS	DECANTED	DECENNIUMS
DEAVING	DEBILITIES	DEBUT	DECANTER	DECENT
DEB	DEBILITY	DEBUTANT	DECANTERS	DECENTER
DEBACLE	DEBIT	DEBUTANTE	DECANTING	DECENTERED
DEBACLES	DEBITED	DEBUTANTES	DECANTS	DECENTERING
DEBAG	DEBITING	DEBUTANTS	DECAPOD	DECENTERS
DEBAGGED	DEBITS	DEBUTED	DECAPODAL	DECENTEST
DEBAGGING	DEBONAIR	DEBUTING	DECAPODAN	DECENTLY
DEBAGS	DEBONAIRE	DEBUTS	DECAPODANS	DECENTRE
DEBAR	DEBONE	DEBYE	DECAPODS	DECENTRED
DEBARK	DEBONED	DEBYES	DECARE	DECENTRES
DEBARKED	DEBONER	DECADAL	DECARES	DECENTRING
DEBARKER	DEBONERS	DECADE	DECATHLON	DECEPTION
DEBARKERS	DEBONES	DECADENCE	DECATHLONS	DECEPTIONS
DEBARKING	DEBONING	DECADENCES	DECAY	DECEPTIVE
DEBARKS	DEBOUCH	DECADENCIES	DECAYABLE	DECERN
DEBARMENT	DEBOUCHE	DECADENCY	DECAYED	DECERNED
DEBARMENTS	DEBOUCHED	DECADENT	DECAYER	DECERNING
DEBARRED	DEBOUCHES	DECADENTS	DECAYERS	DECERNS
DEBARRING	DEBOUCHING	DECADES	DECAYING	DECERTIFIED
DEBARS	DEBRIDE	DECAF	DECAYLESS	DECERTIFIES
DEBASE	DEBRIDED	DECAFS	DECAYS	DECERTIFY
DEBASED	DEBRIDES	DECAGON	DECEASE	DECERTIFYING
DEBASER	DEBRIDING	DECAGONAL	DECEASED	DECIARE
DEBASERS	DEBRIEF	DECAGONS	DECEASES	DECIARES
DEBASES	DEBRIEFED	DECAGRAM	DECEASING	DECIBEL
DEBASING	DEBRIEFER	DECAGRAMS	DECEDENT	DECIBELS
DEBATABLE	DEBRIEFERS	DECAHEDRA	DECEDENTS	DECIDABLE
DEBATABLY	DEBRIEFING	DECAHEDRON	DECEIT	DECIDE
DEBATE	DEBRIEFS	DECAHEDRONS	DECEITFUL	DECIDED
DEBATED	DEBRIS	DECAL	DECEITS	DECIDEDLY
DEBATER	DEBRUISE	DECALCIFIED	DECEIVE	DECIDER
DEBATERS	DEBRUISED	DECALCIFIES	DECEIVED	DECIDERS
DEBATES	DEBRUISES	DECALCIFY	DECEIVER	DECIDES
DEBATING	DEBRUISING	DECALCIFYING	DECEIVERS	DECIDING
DEBAUCH	DEBS	DECALITER	DECEIVES	DECIDUA
DEBAUCHED	DEBT	DECALITERS	DECEIVING	DECIDUAE
DEBAUCHEE	DEBTLESS	DECALOG	DECELERON	DECIDUAL
DEBAUCHEES	DEBTOR	DECALOGS	DECELERONS	DECIDUAS
DEBAUCHER	DEBTORS	DECALOGUE	DECEMVIR	DECIDUATE
DEBAUCHERS	DEBTS	DECALOGUES	DECEMVIRI	DECIDUOUS
DEBAUCHES	DEBUG	DECALS	DECEMVIRS	DECIGRAM
DEBAUCHING	DEBUGGED	DECAMETER	DECENARIES	DECIGRAMS
DEBEAK	DEBUGGER	DECAMETERS	DECENARY	DECILE
DEBEAKED	DEBUGGERS	DECAMP	DECENCIES	DECILES
DEBEAKING	DEBUGGING	DECAMPED	DECENCY	DECILITER
DEBEAKS	DEBUGS	DECAMPING	DECENNARIES	DECILITERS

DECILITRE	DECLARERS	DECOMPOSES	DECRETALS	DEDUCIBLY
DECILITRES	DECLARES	DECOMPOSING	DECRETIVE	DEDUCING
DECILLION	DECLARING	DECONGEST	DECRETORY	DEDUCT
DECILLIONS	DECLASS	DECONGESTED	DECRIAL	DEDUCTED
DECIMAL	DECLASSE	DECONGESTING	DECRIALS	DEDUCTING
DECIMALLY	DECLASSED	DECONGESTS	DECRIED	DEDUCTION
DECIMALS	DECLASSES	DECONTROL	DECRIER	DEDUCTIONS
DECIMATE	DECLASSING	DECONTROLLED	DECRIERS	DEDUCTIVE
DECIMATED	DECLAW	DECONTROLLING	DECRIES	DEDUCTS
DECIMATES	DECLAWED	DECONTROLS	DECROWN	DEE
DECIMATING	DECLAWING	DECOR	DECROWNED	DEED
DECIMATOR	DECLAWS	DECORATE	DECROWNING	DEEDED
DECIMATORS	DECLINE	DECORATED	DECROWNS	DEEDIER
DECIMETER	DECLINED	DECORATES	DECRY	DEEDIEST
DECIMETERS	DECLINER	DECORATING	DECRYING	DEEDING
DECIMETRE	DECLINERS	DECORATOR	DECRYPT	DEEDLESS
DECIMETRES	DECLINES	DECORATORS	DECRYPTED	DEEDS
DECIPHER	DECLINING	DECOROUS	DECRYPTING	DEEDY
DECIPHERED	DECLINIST	DECORS	DECRYPTS	DEEJAY
DECIPHERING	DECLINISTS	DECORUM	DECUMAN	DEEJAYED
DECIPHERS	DECLIVITIES	DECORUMS	DECUMBENT	DEEJAYING
DECISION	DECLIVITY	DECOS	DECUPLE	DEEJAYS
DECISIONED	DECO	DECOUPAGE	DECUPLED	DEEM
DECISIONING	DECOCT	DECOUPAGED	DECUPLES	DEEMED
DECISIONS	DECOCTED	DECOUPAGES	DECUPLING	DEEMING
DECISIVE	DECOCTING	DECOUPAGING	DECURIES	DEEMS
DECK	DECOCTION	DECOUPLE	DECURION	DEEMSTER
DECKED	DECOCTIONS	DECOUPLED	DECURIONS	DEEMSTERS
DECKEL	DECOCTIVE	DECOUPLER	DECURRENT	DEEP
DECKELS	DECOCTS	DECOUPLERS	DECURVE	DEEPEN
DECKER	DECODE	DECOUPLES	DECURVED	DEEPENED
DECKERS	DECODED	DECOUPLING	DECURVES	DEEPENER
DECKHAND	DECODER	DECOY	DECURVING	DEEPENERS
DECKHANDS	DECODERS	DECOYED	DECURY	DEEPENING
DECKHOUSE	DECODES	DECOYER	DECUSSATE	DEEPENS
DECKHOUSES	DECODING	DECOYERS	DECUSSATED	DEEPER
DECKING	DECOLLATE	DECOYING	DECUSSATES	DEEPEST
DECKINGS	DECOLLATED	DECOYS	DECUSSATING	DEEPFREEZE
DECKLE	DECOLLATES	DECREASE	DEDAL	DEEPFREEZES
DECKLES	DECOLLATING	DECREASED	DEDANS	DEEPFREEZING
DECKS	DECOLLETE	DECREASES	DEDICATE	DEEPFROZE
DECLAIM	DECOLLETES	DECREASING	DEDICATED	DEEPFROZEN
DECLAIMED	DECOLOR	DECREE	DEDICATEE	DEEPLY
DECLAIMER	DECOLORED	DECREED	DEDICATEES	DEEPNESS
DECLAIMERS	DECOLORING	DECREEING	DEDICATES	DEEPNESSES
DECLAIMING	DECOLORS	DECREER	DEDICATING	DEEPS
DECLAIMS	DECOLOUR	DECREERS	DEDICATOR	DEEPWATER
DECLARANT	DECOLOURED	DECREES	DEDICATORS	DEER
DECLARANTS	DECOLOURING	DECREMENT	DEDUCE	DEERBERRIES
DECLARE	DECOLOURS	DECREMENTS	DEDUCED	DEERBERRY
DECLARED	DECOMPOSE	DECREPIT	DEDUCES	DEERFLIES
DECLARER	DECOMPOSED	DECRETAL	DEDUCIBLE	DEERFLY

DEERHOUND
DEERHOUNDS
DEERLIKE
DEERS
DEERSKIN
DEERSKINS
DEERWEED
DEERWEEDS
DEERYARD
DEERYARDS
DEES
DEET
DEETS
DEEWAN
DEEWANS
DEF
DEFACE
DEFACED
DEFACER
DEFACERS
DEFACES
DEFACING
DEFALCATE
DEFALCATED
DEFALCATES
DEFALCATING
DEFAME
DEFAMED
DEFAMER
DEFAMERS
DEFAMES
DEFAMING
DEFANG
DEFANGED
DEFANGING
DEFANGS
DEFAT
DEFATS
DEFATTED
DEFATTING
DEFAULT
DEFAULTED
DEFAULTER
DEFAULTERS
DEFAULTING
DEFAULTS
DEFEAT
DEFEATED
DEFEATER
DEFEATERS
DEFEATING
DEFEATISM

DEFEATISMS
DEFEATIST
DEFEATISTS
DEFEATS
DEFEATURE
DEFEATURES
DEFECATE
DEFECATED
DEFECATES
DEFECATING
DEFECATOR
DEFECATORS
DEFECT
DEFECTED
DEFECTING
DEFECTION
DEFECTIONS
DEFECTIVE
DEFECTIVES
DEFECTOR
DEFECTORS
DEFECTS
DEFENCE
DEFENCED
DEFENCES
DEFENCING
DEFEND
DEFENDANT
DEFENDANTS
DEFENDED
DEFENDER
DEFENDERS
DEFENDING
DEFENDS
DEFENSE
DEFENSED
DEFENSES
DEFENSING
DEFENSIVE
DEFENSIVES
DEFER
DEFERENCE
DEFERENCES
DEFERENT
DEFERENTS
DEFERMENT
DEFERMENTS
DEFERRAL
DEFERRALS
DEFERRED
DEFERRER
DEFERRERS

DEFERRING
DEFERS
DEFFER
DEFFEST
DEFI
DEFIANCE
DEFIANCES
DEFIANT
DEFIANTLY
DEFICIENT
DEFICIENTS
DEFICIT
DEFICITS
DEFIED
DEFIER
DEFIERS
DEFIES
DEFILADE
DEFILADED
DEFILADES
DEFILADING
DEFILE
DEFILED
DEFILER
DEFILERS
DEFILES
DEFILING
DEFINABLE
DEFINABLY
DEFINE
DEFINED
DEFINER
DEFINERS
DEFINES
DEFINIENS
DEFINIENTIA
DEFINING
DEFINITE
DEFIS
DEFLATE
DEFLATED
DEFLATER
DEFLATERS
DEFLATES
DEFLATING
DEFLATION
DEFLATIONS
DEFLATOR
DEFLATORS
DEFLEA
DEFLEAED
DEFLEAING

DEFLEAS
DEFLECT
DEFLECTED
DEFLECTING
DEFLECTOR
DEFLECTORS
DEFLECTS
DEFLEXED
DEFLEXION
DEFLEXIONS
DEFLOWER
DEFLOWERED
DEFLOWERING
DEFLOWERS
DEFOAM
DEFOAMED
DEFOAMER
DEFOAMERS
DEFOAMING
DEFOAMS
DEFOCUS
DEFOCUSED
DEFOCUSES
DEFOCUSING
DEFOCUSSED
DEFOCUSSES
DEFOCUSSING
DEFOG
DEFOGGED
DEFOGGER
DEFOGGERS
DEFOGGING
DEFOGS
DEFOLIANT
DEFOLIANTS
DEFOLIATE
DEFOLIATED
DEFOLIATES
DEFOLIATING
DEFORCE
DEFORCED
DEFORCER
DEFORCERS
DEFORCES
DEFORCING
DEFOREST
DEFORESTED
DEFORESTING
DEFORESTS
DEFORM
DEFORMED
DEFORMER

DEFORMERS
DEFORMING
DEFORMITIES
DEFORMITY
DEFORMS
DEFRAG
DEFRAGGED
DEFRAGGER
DEFRAGGERS
DEFRAGGING
DEFRAGS
DEFRAUD
DEFRAUDED
DEFRAUDER
DEFRAUDERS
DEFRAUDING
DEFRAUDS
DEFRAY
DEFRAYAL
DEFRAYALS
DEFRAYED
DEFRAYER
DEFRAYERS
DEFRAYING
DEFRAYS
DEFROCK
DEFROCKED
DEFROCKING
DEFROCKS
DEFROST
DEFROSTED
DEFROSTER
DEFROSTERS
DEFROSTING
DEFROSTS
DEFT
DEFTER
DEFTEST
DEFTLY
DEFTNESS
DEFTNESSES
DEFUEL
DEFUELED
DEFUELING
DEFUELLED
DEFUELLING
DEFUELS
DEFUNCT
DEFUND
DEFUNDED
DEFUNDING
DEFUNDS

DEFUSE	DEGREASES	DEIGN	DELAINES	DELFT
DEFUSED	DEGREASING	DEIGNED	DELATE	DELFTS
DEFUSER	DEGREE	DEIGNING	DELATED	DELFTWARE
DEFUSERS	DEGREED	DEIGNS	DELATES	DELFTWARES
DEFUSES	DEGREES	DEIL	DELATING	DELI
DEFUSING	DEGUM	DEILS	DELATION	DELICACIES
DEFUZE	DEGUMMED	DEIONIZE	DELATIONS	DELICACY
DEFUZED	DEGUMMING	DEIONIZED	DELATOR	DELICATE
DEFUZES	DEGUMS	DEIONIZER	DELATORS	DELICATES
DEFUZING	DEGUST	DEIONIZERS	DELAY	DELICIOUS
DEFY	DEGUSTED	DEIONIZES	DELAYABLE	DELICT
DEFYING	DEGUSTING	DEIONIZING	DELAYED	DELICTS
DEGAGE	DEGUSTS	DEISM	DELAYER	DELIGHT
DEGAME	DEHISCE	DEISMS	DELAYERS	DELIGHTED
DEGAMES	DEHISCED	DEIST	DELAYING	DELIGHTER
DEGAMI	DEHISCENT	DEISTIC	DELAYS	DELIGHTERS
DEGAMIS	DEHISCES	DEISTICAL	DELE	DELIGHTING
DEGAS	DEHISCING	DEISTS	DELEAD	DELIGHTS
DEGASES	DEHORN	DEITIES	DELEADED	DELIME
DEGASSED	DEHORNED	DEITY	DELEADING	DELIMED
DEGASSER	DEHORNER	DEIXIS	DELEADS	DELIMES
DEGASSERS	DEHORNERS	DEIXISES	DELEAVE	DELIMING
DEGASSES	DEHORNING	DEJECT	DELEAVED	DELIMIT
DEGASSING	DEHORNS	DEJECTA	DELEAVES	DELIMITED
DEGAUSS	DEHORT	DEJECTED	DELEAVING	DELIMITER
DEGAUSSED	DEHORTED	DEJECTING	DELECTATE	DELIMITERS
DEGAUSSER	DEHORTING	DEJECTION	DELECTATED	DELIMITING
DEGAUSSERS	DEHORTS	DEJECTIONS	DELECTATES	DELIMITS
DEGAUSSES	DEHYDRATE	DEJECTS	DELECTATING	DELINEATE
DEGAUSSING	DEHYDRATED	DEJEUNER	DELED	DELINEATED
DEGENDER	DEHYDRATES	DEJEUNERS	DELEGABLE	DELINEATES
DEGENDERED	DEHYDRATING	DEKAGRAM	DELEGACIES	DELINEATING
DEGENDERING	DEICE	DEKAGRAMS	DELEGACY	DELIRIA
DEGENDERS	DEICED	DEKALITER	DELEGATE	DELIRIOUS
DEGERM	DEICER	DEKALITERS	DELEGATED	DELIRIUM
DEGERMED	DEICERS	DEKALITRE	DELEGATEE	DELIRIUMS
DEGERMING	DEICES	DEKALITRES	DELEGATEES	DELIS
DEGERMS	DEICIDAL	DEKAMETER	DELEGATES	DELISH
DEGLAZE	DEICIDE	DEKAMETERS	DELEGATING	DELIST
DEGLAZED	DEICIDES	DEKAMETRE	DELEGATOR	DELISTED
DEGLAZES	DEICING	DEKAMETRES	DELEGATORS	DELISTING
DEGLAZING	DEICTIC	DEKARE	DELEING	DELISTS
DEGRADE	DEICTICS	DEKARES	DELES	DELIVER
DEGRADED	DEIFIC	DEKE	DELETABLE	DELIVERED
DEGRADER	DEIFICAL	DEKED	DELETE	DELIVERER
DEGRADERS	DEIFIED	DEKEING	DELETED	DELIVERERS
DEGRADES	DEIFIER	DEKES	DELETES	DELIVERIES
DEGRADING	DEIFIERS	DEKING	DELETING	DELIVERING
DEGREASE	DEIFIES	DEKKO	DELETION	DELIVERS
DEGREASED	DEIFORM	DEKKOS	DELETIONS	DELIVERY
DEGREASER	DEIFY	DEL	DELF	DELL
DEGREASERS	DEIFYING	DELAINE	DELFS	DELLIES

DELLS	DEMAGOGING	DEMERGER	DEMO	DEMOUNTING
DELLY	DEMAGOGS	DEMERGERED	DEMOB	DEMOUNTS
DELOUSE	DEMAGOGUE	DEMERGERING	DEMOBBED	DEMPSTER
DELOUSED	DEMAGOGUED	DEMERGERS	DEMOBBING	DEMPSTERS
DELOUSER	DEMAGOGUES	DEMERGES	DEMOBS	DEMULCENT
DELOUSERS	DEMAGOGUING	DEMERGING	DEMOCRACIES	DEMULCENTS
DELOUSES	DEMAGOGY	DEMERIT	DEMOCRACY	DEMULSIFIED
DELOUSING	DEMAND	DEMERITED	DEMOCRAT	DEMULSIFIES
DELPHIC	DEMANDANT	DEMERITING	DEMOCRATS	DEMULSIFY
DELPHINIA	DEMANDANTS	DEMERITS	DEMODE	DEMULSIFYING
DELPHINIUM	DEMANDED	DEMERSAL	DEMODED	DEMUR
DELPHINIUMS	DEMANDER	DEMES	DEMOED	DEMURE
DELS	DEMANDERS	DEMESNE	DEMOING	DEMURELY
DELT	DEMANDING	DEMESNES	DEMOLISH	DEMURER
DELTA	DEMANDS	DEMETON	DEMOLISHED	DEMUREST
DELTAIC	DEMANTOID	DEMETONS	DEMOLISHES	DEMURRAGE
DELTAS	DEMANTOIDS	DEMIC	DEMOLISHING	DEMURRAGES
DELTIC	DEMARCATE	DEMIES	DEMON	DEMURRAL
DELTOID	DEMARCATED	DEMIGOD	DEMONESS	DEMURRALS
DELTOIDEI	DEMARCATES	DEMIGODS	DEMONESSES	DEMURRED
DELTOIDEUS	DEMARCATING	DEMIJOHN	DEMONIAC	DEMURRER
DELTOIDS	DEMARCHE	DEMIJOHNS	DEMONIACS	DEMURRERS
DELTS	DEMARCHES	DEMILUNE	DEMONIAN	DEMURRING
DELUDE	DEMARK	DEMILUNES	DEMONIC	DEMURS
DELUDED	DEMARKED	DEMIMONDE	DEMONICAL	DEMY
DELUDER	DEMARKING	DEMIMONDES	DEMONISE	DEMYSTIFIED
DELUDERS	DEMARKS	DEMIREP	DEMONISED	DEMYSTIFIES
DELUDES	DEMAST	DEMIREPS	DEMONISES	DEMYSTIFY
DELUDING	DEMASTED	DEMISABLE	DEMONISING	DEMYSTIFYING
DELUGE	DEMASTING	DEMISE	DEMONISM	DEN
DELUGED	DEMASTS	DEMISED	DEMONISMS	DENAR
DELUGES	DEME	DEMISES	DEMONIST	DENARI
DELUGING	DEMEAN	DEMISING	DEMONISTS	DENARII
DELUSION	DEMEANED	DEMISSION	DEMONIZE	DENARIUS
DELUSIONS	DEMEANING	DEMISSIONS	DEMONIZED	DENARS
DELUSIVE	DEMEANOR	DEMISTER	DEMONIZES	DENARY
DELUSORY	DEMEANORS	DEMISTERS	DEMONIZING	DENATURE
DELUSTER	DEMEANOUR	DEMIT	DEMONS	DENATURED
DELUSTERED	DEMEANOURS	DEMITASSE	DEMOS	DENATURES
DELUSTERING	DEMEANS	DEMITASSES	DEMOSES	DENATURING
DELUSTERS	DEMENT	DEMITS	DEMOTE	DENAZIFIED
DELUXE	DEMENTED	DEMITTED	DEMOTED	DENAZIFIES
DELVE	DEMENTIA	DEMITTING	DEMOTES	DENAZIFY
DELVED	DEMENTIAL	DEMIURGE	DEMOTIC	DENAZIFYING
DELVER	DEMENTIAS	DEMIURGES	DEMOTICS	DENDRIMER
DELVERS	DEMENTING	DEMIURGIC	DEMOTING	DENDRIMERS
DELVES	DEMENTS	DEMIVOLT	DEMOTION	DENDRITE
DELVING	DEMERARA	DEMIVOLTE	DEMOTIONS	DENDRITES
DEMAGOG	DEMERARAN	DEMIVOLTES	DEMOTIST	DENDRITIC
DEMAGOGED	DEMERARAS	DEMIVOLTS	DEMOTISTS	DENDROID
DEMAGOGIC	DEMERGE	DEMIWORLD	DEMOUNT	DENDRON
DEMAGOGIES	DEMERGED	DEMIWORLDS	DEMOUNTED	DENDRONS

DENE	DENSE	DENTURISTS	DEPENDENT	DEPLOYS
DENERVATE	DENSELY	DENUDATE	DEPENDENTS	DEPLUME
DENERVATED	DENSENESS	DENUDATED	DEPENDING	DEPLUMED
DENERVATES	DENSENESSES	DENUDATES	DEPENDS	DEPLUMES
DENERVATING	DENSER	DENUDATING	DEPEOPLE	DEPLUMING
DENES	DENSEST	DENUDE	DEPEOPLED	DEPOLISH
DENGUE	DENSIFIED	DENUDED	DEPEOPLES	DEPOLISHED
DENGUES	DENSIFIES	DENUDER	DEPEOPLING	DEPOLISHES
DENI	DENSIFY	DENUDERS	DEPERM	DEPOLISHING
DENIABLE	DENSIFYING	DENUDES	DEPERMED	DEPONE
DENIABLY	DENSITIES	DENUDING	DEPERMING	DEPONED
DENIAL	DENSITY	DENY	DEPERMS	DEPONENT
DENIALS	DENT	DENYING	DEPICT	DEPONENTS
DENIED	DENTAL	DENYINGLY	DEPICTED	DEPONES
DENIER	DENTALIA	DEODAND	DEPICTER	DEPONING
DENIERS	DENTALITIES	DEODANDS	DEPICTERS	DEPORT
DENIES	DENTALITY	DEODAR	DEPICTING	DEPORTED
DENIGRATE	DENTALIUM	DEODARA	DEPICTION	DEPORTEE
DENIGRATED	DENTALIUMS	DEODARAS	DEPICTIONS	DEPORTEES
DENIGRATES	DENTALLY	DEODARS	DEPICTOR	DEPORTER
DENIGRATING	DENTALS	DEODORANT	DEPICTORS	DEPORTERS
DENIM	DENTATE	DEODORANTS	DEPICTS	DEPORTING
DENIMED	DENTATED	DEODORIZE	DEPILATE	DEPORTS
DENIMS	DENTATELY	DEODORIZED	DEPILATED	DEPOSABLE
DENITRATE	DENTATION	DEODORIZES	DEPILATES	DEPOSAL
DENITRATED	DENTATIONS	DEODORIZING	DEPILATING	DEPOSALS
DENITRATES	DENTED	DEONTIC	DEPILATOR	DEPOSE
DENITRATING	DENTICLE	DEORBIT	DEPILATORS	DEPOSED
DENITRIFIED	DENTICLES	DEORBITED	DEPLANE	DEPOSER
DENITRIFIES	DENTIFORM	DEORBITING	DEPLANED	DEPOSERS
DENITRIFY	DENTIL	DEORBITS	DEPLANES	DEPOSES
DENITRIFYING	DENTILED	DEOXIDIZE	DEPLANING	DEPOSING
DENIZEN	DENTILS	DEOXIDIZED	DEPLETE	DEPOSIT
DENIZENED	DENTIN	DEOXIDIZES	DEPLETED	DEPOSITED
DENIZENING	DENTINAL	DEOXIDIZING	DEPLETER	DEPOSITING
DENIZENS	DENTINE	DEOXY	DEPLETERS	DEPOSITOR
DENNED	DENTINES	DEPAINT	DEPLETES	DEPOSITORS
DENNING	DENTING	DEPAINTED	DEPLETING	DEPOSITS
DENOMINAL	DENTINS	DEPAINTING	DEPLETION	DEPOT
DENOTABLE	DENTIST	DEPAINTS	DEPLETIONS	DEPOTS
DENOTE	DENTISTRIES	DEPART	DEPLETIVE	DEPRAVE
DENOTED	DENTISTRY	DEPARTED	DEPLORE	DEPRAVED
DENOTES	DENTISTS	DEPARTEE	DEPLORED	DEPRAVER
DENOTING	DENTITION	DEPARTEES	DEPLORER	DEPRAVERS
DENOTIVE	DENTITIONS	DEPARTING	DEPLORERS	DEPRAVES
DENOUNCE	DENTOID	DEPARTS	DEPLORES	DEPRAVING
DENOUNCED	DENTS	DEPARTURE	DEPLORING	DEPRAVITIES
DENOUNCER	DENTULOUS	DEPARTURES	DEPLOY	DEPRAVITY
DENOUNCERS	DENTURAL	DEPEND	DEPLOYED	DEPRECATE
DENOUNCES	DENTURE	DEPENDANT	DEPLOYER	DEPRECATED
DENOUNCING	DENTURES	DEPENDANTS	DEPLOYERS	DEPRECATES
DENS	DENTURIST	DEPENDED	DEPLOYING	DEPRECATING

DEPREDATE	DERAIL	DERMA	DESCENDS	DESICCATING
DEPREDATED	DERAILED	DERMAL	DESCENT	DESIGN
DEPREDATES	DERAILING	DERMAS	DESCENTS	DESIGNATE
DEPREDATING	DERAILS	DERMATOID	DESCRIBE	DESIGNATED
DEPRENYL	DERANGE	DERMATOME	DESCRIBED	DESIGNATES
DEPRENYLS	DERANGED	DERMATOMES	DESCRIBER	DESIGNATING
DEPRESS	DERANGER	DERMESTID	DESCRIBERS	DESIGNED
DEPRESSED	DERANGERS	DERMESTIDS	DESCRIBES	DESIGNEE
DEPRESSES	DERANGES	DERMIC	DESCRIBING	DESIGNEES
DEPRESSING	DERANGING	DERMIS	DESCRIED	DESIGNER
DEPRESSOR	DERAT	DERMISES	DESCRIER	DESIGNERS
DEPRESSORS	DERATE	DERMOID	DESCRIERS	DESIGNING
DEPRIVAL	DERATED	DERMOIDS	DESCRIES	DESIGNINGS
DEPRIVALS	DERATES	DERMS	DESCRY	DESIGNS
DEPRIVE	DERATING	DERNIER	DESCRYING	DESILVER
DEPRIVED	DERATS	DEROGATE	DESECRATE	DESILVERED
DEPRIVER	DERATTED	DEROGATED	DESECRATED	DESILVERING
DEPRIVERS	DERATTING	DEROGATES	DESECRATES	DESILVERS
DEPRIVES	DERAY	DEROGATING	DESECRATING	DESINENCE
DEPRIVING	DERAYS	DERRICK	DESELECT	DESINENCES
DEPROGRAM	DERBIES	DERRICKS	DESELECTED	DESINENT
DEPROGRAMED	DERBY	DERRIERE	DESELECTING	DESIRABLE
DEPROGRAMING	DERE	DERRIERES	DESELECTS	DESIRABLES
DEPROGRAMMED	DERELICT	DERRIES	DESERT	DESIRABLY
DEPROGRAMMING	DERELICTS	DERRINGER	DESERTED	DESIRE
DEPROGRAMS	DEREPRESS	DERRINGERS	DESERTER	DESIRED
DEPSIDE	DEREPRESSED	DERRIS	DESERTERS	DESIRER
DEPSIDES	DEREPRESSES	DERRISES	DESERTIC	DESIRERS
DEPTH	DEREPRESSING	DERRY	DESERTIFIED	DESIRES
DEPTHLESS	DERIDE	DERVISH	DESERTIFIES	DESIRING
DEPTHS	DERIDED	DERVISHES	DESERTIFY	DESIROUS
DEPURATE	DERIDER	DESALT	DESERTIFYING	DESIST
DEPURATED	DERIDERS	DESALTED	DESERTING	DESISTED
DEPURATES	DERIDES	DESALTER	DESERTION	DESISTING
DEPURATING	DERIDING	DESALTERS	DESERTIONS	DESISTS
DEPURATOR	DERINGER	DESALTING	DESERTS	DESK
DEPURATORS	DERINGERS	DESALTS	DESERVE	DESKBOUND
DEPUTABLE	DERISIBLE	DESAND	DESERVED	DESKMAN
DEPUTE	DERISION	DESANDED	DESERVER	DESKMEN
DEPUTED	DERISIONS	DESANDING	DESERVERS	DESKS
DEPUTES	DERISIVE	DESANDS	DESERVES	DESKTOP
DEPUTIES	DERISORY	DESCANT	DESERVING	DESKTOPS
DEPUTING	DERIVABLE	DESCANTED	DESERVINGS	DESMAN
DEPUTIZE	DERIVATE	DESCANTER	DESEX	DESMANS
DEPUTIZED	DERIVATES	DESCANTERS	DESEXED	DESMID
DEPUTIZES	DERIVE	DESCANTING	DESEXES	DESMIDIAN
DEPUTIZING	DERIVED	DESCANTS	DESEXING	DESMIDS
DEPUTY	DERIVER	DESCEND	DESICCANT	DESMOID
DERAIGN	DERIVERS	DESCENDED	DESICCANTS	DESMOIDS
DERAIGNED	DERIVES	DESCENDER	DESICCATE	DESMOSOME
DERAIGNING	DERIVING	DESCENDERS	DESICCATED	DESMOSOMES
DERAIGNS	DERM	DESCENDING	DESICCATES	DESOLATE

DESOLATED	DESPOTS	DETAILER	DETERMINES	DETOXIFYING
DESOLATER	DESPUMATE	DETAILERS	DETERMINING	DETOXING
DESOLATERS	DESPUMATED	DETAILING	DETERRED	DETRACT
DESOLATES	DESPUMATES	DETAILINGS	DETERRENT	DETRACTED
DESOLATING	DESPUMATING	DETAILS	DETERRENTS	DETRACTING
DESOLATOR	DESSERT	DETAIN	DETERRER	DETRACTOR
DESOLATORS	DESSERTS	DETAINED	DETERRERS	DETRACTORS
DESORB	DESTAIN	DETAINEE	DETERRING	DETRACTS
DESORBED	DESTAINED	DETAINEES	DETERS	DETRAIN
DESORBING	DESTAINING	DETAINER	DETERSIVE	DETRAINED
DESORBS	DESTAINS	DETAINERS	DETERSIVES	DETRAINING
DESOXY	DESTINE	DETAINING	DETEST	DETRAINS
DESPAIR	DESTINED	DETAINS	DETESTED	DETRIMENT
DESPAIRED	DESTINES	DETASSEL	DETESTER	DETRIMENTS
DESPAIRER	DESTINIES	DETASSELED	DETESTERS	DETRITAL
DESPAIRERS	DESTINING	DETASSELING	DETESTING	DETRITION
DESPAIRING	DESTINY	DETASSELLED	DETESTS	DETRITIONS
DESPAIRS	DESTITUTE	DETASSELLING	DETHATCH	DETRITUS
DESPATCH	DESTITUTED	DETASSELS	DETHATCHED	DETRUDE
DESPATCHED	DESTITUTES	DETECT	DETHATCHES	DETRUDED
DESPATCHES	DESTITUTING	DETECTED	DETHATCHING	DETRUDES
DESPATCHING	DESTRIER	DETECTER	DETHRONE	DETRUDING
DESPERADO	DESTRIERS	DETECTERS	DETHRONED	DETRUSION
DESPERADOES	DESTROY	DETECTING	DETHRONER	DETRUSIONS
DESPERADOS	DESTROYED	DETECTION	DETHRONERS	DEUCE
DESPERATE	DESTROYER	DETECTIONS	DETHRONES	DEUCED
DESPISAL	DESTROYERS	DETECTIVE	DETHRONING	DEUCEDLY
DESPISALS	DESTROYING	DETECTIVES	DETICK	DEUCES
DESPISE	DESTROYS	DETECTOR	DETICKED	DEUCING
DESPISED	DESTRUCT	DETECTORS	DETICKER	DEUTERATE
DESPISER	DESTRUCTED	DETECTS	DETICKERS	DEUTERATED
DESPISERS	DESTRUCTING	DETENT	DETICKING	DEUTERATES
DESPISES	DESTRUCTS	DETENTE	DETICKS	DEUTERATING
DESPISING	DESUETUDE	DETENTES	DETINUE	DEUTERIC
DESPITE	DESUETUDES	DETENTION	DETINUES	DEUTERIDE
DESPITED	DESUGAR	DETENTIONS	DETONABLE	DEUTERIDES
DESPITES	DESUGARED	DETENTIST	DETONATE	DEUTERIUM
DESPITING	DESUGARING	DETENTISTS	DETONATED	DEUTERIUMS
DESPOIL	DESUGARS	DETENTS	DETONATES	DEUTERON
DESPOILED	DESULFUR	DETER	DETONATING	DEUTERONS
DESPOILER	DESULFURED	DETERGE	DETONATOR	DEUTZIA
DESPOILERS	DESULFURING	DETERGED	DETONATORS	DEUTZIAS
DESPOILING	DESULFURS	DETERGENT	DETOUR	DEV
DESPOILS	DESULTORY	DETERGENTS	DETOURED	DEVA
DESPOND	DETACH	DETERGER	DETOURING	DEVALUATE
DESPONDED	DETACHED	DETERGERS	DETOURS	DEVALUATED
DESPONDING	DETACHER	DETERGES	DETOX	DEVALUATES
DESPONDS	DETACHERS	DETERGING	DETOXED	DEVALUATING
DESPOT	DETACHES	DETERMENT	DETOXES	DEVALUE
DESPOTIC	DETACHING	DETERMENTS	DETOXIFIED	DEVALUED
DESPOTISM	DETAIL	DETERMINE	DETOXIFIES	DEVALUES
DESPOTISMS	DETAILED	DETERMINED	DETOXIFY	DEVALUING

DEVAS	DEVILKIN	DEVOTING	DEWOOLS	DHOOLIES
DEVASTATE	DEVILKINS	DEVOTION	DEWORM	DHOOLY
DEVASTATED	DEVILLED	DEVOTIONS	DEWORMED	DHOORA
DEVASTATES	DEVILLING	DEVOUR	DEWORMER	DHOORAS
DEVASTATING	DEVILMENT	DEVOURED	DEWORMERS	DHOOTI
DEVEIN	DEVILMENTS	DEVOURER	DEWORMING	DHOOTIE
DEVEINED	DEVILRIES	DEVOURERS	DEWORMS	DHOOTIES
DEVEINING	DEVILRY	DEVOURING	DEWS	DHOOTIS
DEVEINS	DEVILS	DEVOURS	DEWY	DHOTI
DEVEL	DEVILTRIES	DEVOUT	DEX	DHOTIS
DEVELED	DEVILTRY	DEVOUTER	DEXES	DHOURRA
DEVELING	DEVILWOOD	DEVOUTEST	DEXIE	DHOURRAS
DEVELOP	DEVILWOODS	DEVOUTLY	DEXIES	DHOW
DEVELOPE	DEVIOUS	DEVS	DEXTER	DHOWS
DEVELOPED	DEVIOUSLY	DEW	DEXTERITIES	DHURNA
DEVELOPER	DEVISABLE	DEWAN	DEXTERITY	DHURNAS
DEVELOPERS	DEVISAL	DEWANS	DEXTEROUS	DHURRIE
DEVELOPES	DEVISALS	DEWAR	DEXTRAL	DHURRIES
DEVELOPING	DEVISE	DEWARS	DEXTRALLY	DHUTI
DEVELOPPE	DEVISED	DEWATER	DEXTRAN	DHUTIS
DEVELOPS	DEVISEE	DEWATERED	DEXTRANS	DIABASE
DEVELS	DEVISEES	DEWATERER	DEXTRIN	DIABASES
DEVERBAL	DEVISER	DEWATERERS	DEXTRINE	DIABASIC
DEVERBALS	DEVISERS	DEWATERING	DEXTRINES	DIABETES
DEVEST	DEVISES	DEWATERS	DEXTRINS	DIABETIC
DEVESTED	DEVISING	DEWAX	DEXTRO	DIABETICS
DEVESTING	DEVISOR	DEWAXED	DEXTRORSE	DIABLERIE
DEVESTS	DEVISORS	DEWAXES	DEXTROSE	DIABLERIES
DEVIANCE	DEVITRIFIED	DEWAXING	DEXTROSES	DIABLERY
DEVIANCES	DEVITRIFIES	DEWBERRIES	DEXTROUS	DIABOLIC
DEVIANCIES	DEVITRIFY	DEWBERRY	DEXY	DIABOLISM
DEVIANCY	DEVITRIFYING	DEWCLAW	DEY	DIABOLISMS
DEVIANT	DEVOICE	DEWCLAWED	DEYS	DIABOLIST
DEVIANTS	DEVOICED	DEWCLAWS	DEZINC	DIABOLISTS
DEVIATE	DEVOICES	DEWDROP	DEZINCED	DIABOLIZE
DEVIATED	DEVOICING	DEWDROPS	DEZINCING	DIABOLIZED
DEVIATES	DEVOID	DEWED	DEZINCKED	DIABOLIZES
DEVIATING	DEVOIR	DEWFALL	DEZINCKING	DIABOLIZING
DEVIATION	DEVOIRS	DEWFALLS	DEZINCS	DIABOLO
DEVIATIONS	DEVOLVE	DEWIER	DHAK	DIABOLOS
DEVIATIVE	DEVOLVED	DEWIEST	DHAKS	DIACETYL
DEVIATOR	DEVOLVES	DEWILY	DHAL	DIACETYLS
DEVIATORS	DEVOLVING	DEWINESS	DHALS	DIACHRONIES
DEVIATORY	DEVON	DEWINESSES	DHARMA	DIACHRONY
DEVICE	DEVONIAN	DEWING	DHARMAS	DIACID
DEVICES	DEVONS	DEWLAP	DHARMIC	DIACIDIC
DEVIL	DEVOTE	DEWLAPPED	DHARNA	DIACIDS
DEVILED	DEVOTED	DEWLAPS	DHARNAS	DIACONAL
DEVILFISH	DEVOTEDLY	DEWLESS	DHOBI	DIACONATE
DEVILFISHES	DEVOTEE	DEWOOL	DHOBIS	DIACONATES
DEVILING	DEVOTEES	DEWOOLED	DHOLE	DIACRITIC
DEVILISH	DEVOTES	DEWOOLING	DHOLES	DIACRITICS

DIACTINIC
DIADEM
DIADEMED
DIADEMING
DIADEMS
DIAERESES
DIAERESIS
DIAERETIC
DIAGNOSE
DIAGNOSED
DIAGNOSES
DIAGNOSING
DIAGNOSIS
DIAGONAL
DIAGONALS
DIAGRAM
DIAGRAMED
DIAGRAMING
DIAGRAMMED
DIAGRAMMING
DIAGRAMS
DIAGRAPH
DIAGRAPHS
DIAL
DIALECT
DIALECTAL
DIALECTIC
DIALECTICS
DIALECTS
DIALED
DIALER
DIALERS
DIALING
DIALINGS
DIALIST
DIALISTS
DIALLAGE
DIALLAGES
DIALLED
DIALLEL
DIALLER
DIALLERS
DIALLING
DIALLINGS
DIALLIST
DIALLISTS
DIALOG
DIALOGED
DIALOGER
DIALOGERS
DIALOGIC
DIALOGING

DIALOGIST
DIALOGISTS
DIALOGS
DIALOGUE
DIALOGUED
DIALOGUER
DIALOGUERS
DIALOGUES
DIALOGUING
DIALS
DIALYSATE
DIALYSATES
DIALYSE
DIALYSED
DIALYSER
DIALYSERS
DIALYSES
DIALYSING
DIALYSIS
DIALYTIC
DIALYZATE
DIALYZATES
DIALYZE
DIALYZED
DIALYZER
DIALYZERS
DIALYZES
DIALYZING
DIAMAGNET
DIAMAGNETS
DIAMANTE
DIAMANTES
DIAMETER
DIAMETERS
DIAMETRAL
DIAMETRIC
DIAMIDE
DIAMIDES
DIAMIN
DIAMINE
DIAMINES
DIAMINS
DIAMOND
DIAMONDED
DIAMONDING
DIAMONDS
DIANDROUS
DIANTHUS
DIANTHUSES
DIAPASON
DIAPASONS
DIAPAUSE

DIAPAUSED
DIAPAUSES
DIAPAUSING
DIAPER
DIAPERED
DIAPERING
DIAPERS
DIAPHONE
DIAPHONES
DIAPHONIES
DIAPHONY
DIAPHRAGM
DIAPHRAGMED
DIAPHRAGMING
DIAPHRAGMS
DIAPHYSES
DIAPHYSIS
DIAPIR
DIAPIRIC
DIAPIRS
DIAPSID
DIAPSIDS
DIARCHIC
DIARCHIES
DIARCHY
DIARIES
DIARIST
DIARISTIC
DIARISTS
DIARRHEA
DIARRHEAL
DIARRHEAS
DIARRHEIC
DIARRHOEA
DIARRHOEAS
DIARY
DIASPORA
DIASPORAS
DIASPORE
DIASPORES
DIASPORIC
DIASTASE
DIASTASES
DIASTASIC
DIASTATIC
DIASTEM
DIASTEMA
DIASTEMAS
DIASTEMATA
DIASTEMS
DIASTER
DIASTERS

DIASTOLE
DIASTOLES
DIASTOLIC
DIASTRAL
DIATHERMIES
DIATHERMY
DIATHESES
DIATHESIS
DIATHETIC
DIATOM
DIATOMIC
DIATOMITE
DIATOMITES
DIATOMS
DIATONIC
DIATRIBE
DIATRIBES
DIATRON
DIATRONS
DIATROPIC
DIAZEPAM
DIAZEPAMS
DIAZIN
DIAZINE
DIAZINES
DIAZINON
DIAZINONS
DIAZINS
DIAZO
DIAZOLE
DIAZOLES
DIAZONIUM
DIAZONIUMS
DIAZOTIZE
DIAZOTIZED
DIAZOTIZES
DIAZOTIZING
DIB
DIBASIC
DIBBED
DIBBER
DIBBERS
DIBBING
DIBBLE
DIBBLED
DIBBLER
DIBBLERS
DIBBLES
DIBBLING
DIBBUK
DIBBUKIM
DIBBUKS

DIBROMIDE
DIBROMIDES
DIBS
DICAMBA
DICAMBAS
DICAST
DICASTIC
DICASTS
DICE
DICED
DICENTRA
DICENTRAS
DICENTRIC
DICENTRICS
DICER
DICERS
DICES
DICEY
DICHASIA
DICHASIAL
DICHASIUM
DICHOGAMIES
DICHOGAMY
DICHONDRA
DICHONDRAS
DICHOTIC
DICHOTOMIES
DICHOTOMY
DICHROIC
DICHROISM
DICHROISMS
DICHROITE
DICHROITES
DICHROMAT
DICHROMATS
DICHROMIC
DICIER
DICIEST
DICING
DICK
DICKED
DICKENS
DICKENSES
DICKER
DICKERED
DICKERING
DICKERS
DICKEY
DICKEYS
DICKHEAD
DICKHEADS
DICKIE

DICKIER	DIDDLERS	DIESINKER	DIFFUSIONS	DIGITIZE
DICKIES	DIDDLES	DIESINKERS	DIFFUSIVE	DIGITIZED
DICKIEST	DIDDLEY	DIESIS	DIFFUSOR	DIGITIZER
DICKING	DIDDLEYS	DIESTER	DIFFUSORS	DIGITIZERS
DICKS	DIDDLIES	DIESTERS	DIFS	DIGITIZES
DICKY	DIDDLING	DIESTOCK	DIG	DIGITIZING
DICLINIES	DIDDLY	DIESTOCKS	DIGAMIES	DIGITONIN
DICLINISM	DIDIE	DIESTROUS	DIGAMIST	DIGITONINS
DICLINISMS	DIDIES	DIESTRUM	DIGAMISTS	DIGITOXIN
DICLINOUS	DIDJERIDU	DIESTRUMS	DIGAMMA	DIGITOXINS
DICLINY	DIDJERIDUS	DIESTRUS	DIGAMMAS	DIGITS
DICOT	DIDO	DIESTRUSES	DIGAMOUS	DIGLOSSIA
DICOTS	DIDOES	DIET	DIGAMY	DIGLOSSIAS
DICOTYL	DIDOS	DIETARIES	DIGASTRIC	DIGLOSSIC
DICOTYLS	DIDST	DIETARILY	DIGASTRICS	DIGLOT
DICROTAL	DIDY	DIETARY	DIGENESES	DIGLOTS
DICROTIC	DIDYMIUM	DIETED	DIGENESIS	DIGNIFIED
DICROTISM	DIDYMIUMS	DIETER	DIGENETIC	DIGNIFIES
DICROTISMS	DIDYMOUS	DIETERS	DIGERATI	DIGNIFY
DICTA	DIDYNAMIES	DIETETIC	DIGEST	DIGNIFYING
DICTATE	DIDYNAMY	DIETETICS	DIGESTED	DIGNITARIES
DICTATED	DIE	DIETHER	DIGESTER	DIGNITARY
DICTATES	DIEBACK	DIETHERS	DIGESTERS	DIGNITIES
DICTATING	DIEBACKS	DIETICIAN	DIGESTIF	DIGNITY
DICTATION	DIECIOUS	DIETICIANS	DIGESTIFS	DIGOXIN
DICTATIONS	DIED	DIETING	DIGESTING	DIGOXINS
DICTATOR	DIEHARD	DIETITIAN	DIGESTION	DIGRAPH
DICTATORS	DIEHARDS	DIETITIANS	DIGESTIONS	DIGRAPHIC
DICTIER	DIEING	DIETS	DIGESTIVE	DIGRAPHS
DICTIEST	DIEL	DIF	DIGESTIVES	DIGRESS
DICTION	DIELDRIN	DIFF	DIGESTOR	DIGRESSED
DICTIONAL	DIELDRINS	DIFFER	DIGESTORS	DIGRESSES
DICTIONS	DIEMAKER	DIFFERED	DIGESTS	DIGRESSING
DICTUM	DIEMAKERS	DIFFERENT	DIGGED	DIGS
DICTUMS	DIENE	DIFFERING	DIGGER	DIHEDRAL
DICTY	DIENES	DIFFERS	DIGGERS	DIHEDRALS
DICUMAROL	DIEOFF	DIFFICILE	DIGGING	DIHEDRON
DICUMAROLS	DIEOFFS	DIFFICULT	DIGGINGS	DIHEDRONS
DICYCLIC	DIERESES	DIFFIDENT	DIGHT	DIHYBRID
DICYCLIES	DIERESIS	DIFFRACT	DIGHTED	DIHYBRIDS
DICYCLY	DIERETIC	DIFFRACTED	DIGHTING	DIHYDRIC
DID	DIES	DIFFRACTING	DIGHTS	DIKDIK
DIDACT	DIESEL	DIFFRACTS	DIGIT	DIKDIKS
DIDACTIC	DIESELED	DIFFS	DIGITAL	DIKE
DIDACTICS	DIESELING	DIFFUSE	DIGITALIN	DIKED
DIDACTS	DIESELINGS	DIFFUSED	DIGITALINS	DIKER
DIDACTYL	DIESELIZE	DIFFUSELY	DIGITALIS	DIKERS
DIDAPPER	DIESELIZED	DIFFUSER	DIGITALISES	DIKES
DIDAPPERS	DIESELIZES	DIFFUSERS	DIGITALLY	DIKEY
DIDDLE	DIESELIZING	DIFFUSES	DIGITALS	DIKING
DIDDLED	DIESELS	DIFFUSING	DIGITATE	DIKTAT
DIDDLER	DIESES	DIFFUSION	DIGITATED	DIKTATS

DILATABLE	DILUVIAL	DIMPLE	DINGLES	DIOESTRUS
DILATABLY	DILUVIAN	DIMPLED	DINGO	DIOESTRUSES
DILATANCIES	DILUVION	DIMPLES	DINGOES	DIOICOUS
DILATANCY	DILUVIONS	DIMPLIER	DINGS	DIOL
DILATANT	DILUVIUM	DIMPLIEST	DINGUS	DIOLEFIN
DILATANTS	DILUVIUMS	DIMPLING	DINGUSES	DIOLEFINS
DILATATE	DIM	DIMPLY	DINGY	DIOLS
DILATATOR	DIME	DIMS	DINING	DIONYSIAC
DILATATORS	DIMENSION	DIMWIT	DINITRO	DIONYSIAN
DILATE	DIMENSIONED	DIMWITS	DINK	DIOPSIDE
DILATED	DIMENSIONING	DIMWITTED	DINKED	DIOPSIDES
DILATER	DIMENSIONS	DIN	DINKEY	DIOPSIDIC
DILATERS	DIMER	DINAR	DINKEYS	DIOPTASE
DILATES	DIMERIC	DINARS	DINKIER	DIOPTASES
DILATING	DIMERISM	DINDLE	DINKIES	DIOPTER
DILATION	DIMERISMS	DINDLED	DINKIEST	DIOPTERS
DILATIONS	DIMERIZE	DINDLES	DINKING	DIOPTRAL
DILATIVE	DIMERIZED	DINDLING	DINKLY	DIOPTRE
DILATOR	DIMERIZES	DINE	DINKS	DIOPTRES
DILATORS	DIMERIZING	DINED	DINKUM	DIOPTRIC
DILATORY	DIMEROUS	DINER	DINKUMS	DIOPTRICS
DILDO	DIMERS	DINERIC	DINKY	DIORAMA
DILDOE	DIMES	DINERO	DINNED	DIORAMAS
DILDOES	DIMETER	DINEROS	DINNER	DIORAMIC
DILDOS	DIMETERS	DINERS	DINNERS	DIORITE
DILEMMA	DIMETHYL	DINES	DINNING	DIORITES
DILEMMAS	DIMETHYLS	DINETTE	DINO	DIORITIC
DILEMMIC	DIMETRIC	DINETTES	DINOS	DIOSGENIN
DILIGENCE	DIMIDIATE	DING	DINOSAUR	DIOSGENINS
DILIGENCES	DIMIDIATED	DINGBAT	DINOSAURS	DIOXAN
DILIGENT	DIMIDIATES	DINGBATS	DINOTHERE	DIOXANE
DILL	DIMIDIATING	DINGDONG	DINOTHERES	DIOXANES
DILLED	DIMINISH	DINGDONGED	DINS	DIOXANS
DILLIES	DIMINISHED	DINGDONGING	DINT	DIOXID
DILLS	DIMINISHES	DINGDONGS	DINTED	DIOXIDE
DILLY	DIMINISHING	DINGE	DINTING	DIOXIDES
DILTIAZEM	DIMITIES	DINGED	DINTS	DIOXIDS
DILTIAZEMS	DIMITY	DINGER	DIOBOL	DIOXIN
DILUENT	DIMLY	DINGERS	DIOBOLON	DIOXINS
DILUENTS	DIMMABLE	DINGES	DIOBOLONS	DIP
DILUTE	DIMMED	DINGEY	DIOBOLS	DIPEPTIDE
DILUTED	DIMMER	DINGEYS	DIOCESAN	DIPEPTIDES
DILUTER	DIMMERS	DINGHIES	DIOCESANS	DIPHASE
DILUTERS	DIMMEST	DINGHY	DIOCESE	DIPHASIC
DILUTES	DIMMING	DINGIER	DIOCESES	DIPHENYL
DILUTING	DIMNESS	DINGIES	DIODE	DIPHENYLS
DILUTION	DIMNESSES	DINGIEST	DIODES	DIPHTHONG
DILUTIONS	DIMORPH	DINGILY	DIOECIES	DIPHTHONGED
DILUTIVE	DIMORPHIC	DINGINESS	DIOECIOUS	DIPHTHONGING
DILUTOR	DIMORPHS	DINGINESSES	DIOECISM	DIPHTHONGS
DILUTORS	DIMOUT	DINGING	DIOECISMS	DIPLEGIA
DILUVIA	DIMOUTS	DINGLE	DIOECY	DIPLEGIAS

DIPLEGIC	DIPPERS	DIRECTS	DISABUSE	DISBAND
DIPLEX	DIPPIER	DIREFUL	DISABUSED	DISBANDED
DIPLEXER	DIPPIEST	DIREFULLY	DISABUSES	DISBANDING
DIPLEXERS	DIPPINESS	DIRELY	DISABUSING	DISBANDS
DIPLOE	DIPPINESSES	DIRENESS	DISACCORD	DISBAR
DIPLOES	DIPPING	DIRENESSES	DISACCORDED	DISBARRED
DIPLOIC	DIPPY	DIRER	DISACCORDING	DISBARRING
DIPLOID	DIPROTIC	DIREST	DISACCORDS	DISBARS
DIPLOIDIC	DIPS	DIRGE	DISAFFECT	DISBELIEF
DIPLOIDIES	DIPSADES	DIRGEFUL	DISAFFECTED	DISBELIEFS
DIPLOIDS	DIPSAS	DIRGELIKE	DISAFFECTING	DISBOSOM
DIPLOIDY	DIPSHIT	DIRGES	DISAFFECTS	DISBOSOMED
DIPLOMA	DIPSHITS	DIRHAM	DISAFFIRM	DISBOSOMING
DIPLOMACIES	DIPSO	DIRHAMS	DISAFFIRMED	DISBOSOMS
DIPLOMACY	DIPSOS	DIRIGIBLE	DISAFFIRMING	DISBOUND
DIPLOMAED	DIPSTICK	DIRIGIBLES	DISAFFIRMS	DISBOWEL
DIPLOMAING	DIPSTICKS	DIRIGISME	DISAGREE	DISBOWELED
DIPLOMAS	DIPT	DIRIGISMES	DISAGREED	DISBOWELING
DIPLOMAT	DIPTERA	DIRIGISTE	DISAGREEING	DISBOWELLED
DIPLOMATA	DIPTERAL	DIRIMENT	DISAGREES	DISBOWELLING
DIPLOMATE	DIPTERAN	DIRK	DISALLOW	DISBOWELS
DIPLOMATES	DIPTERANS	DIRKED	DISALLOWED	DISBRANCH
DIPLOMATS	DIPTERON	DIRKING	DISALLOWING	DISBRANCHED
DIPLONT	DIPTEROUS	DIRKS	DISALLOWS	DISBRANCHES
DIPLONTIC	DIPTYCA	DIRL	DISANNUL	DISBRANCHING
DIPLONTS	DIPTYCAS	DIRLED	DISANNULLED	DISBUD
DIPLOPIA	DIPTYCH	DIRLING	DISANNULLING	DISBUDDED
DIPLOPIAS	DIPTYCHS	DIRLS	DISANNULS	DISBUDDING
DIPLOPIC	DIQUAT	DIRNDL	DISAPPEAR	DISBUDS
DIPLOPOD	DIQUATS	DIRNDLS	DISAPPEARED	DISBURDEN
DIPLOPODS	DIRAM	DIRT	DISAPPEARING	DISBURDENED
DIPLOSES	DIRAMS	DIRTBAG	DISAPPEARS	DISBURDENING
DIPLOSIS	DIRDUM	DIRTBAGS	DISARM	DISBURDENS
DIPLOTENE	DIRDUMS	DIRTIED	DISARMED	DISBURSAL
DIPLOTENES	DIRE	DIRTIER	DISARMER	DISBURSALS
DIPNET	DIRECT	DIRTIES	DISARMERS	DISBURSE
DIPNETS	DIRECTED	DIRTIEST	DISARMING	DISBURSED
DIPNETTED	DIRECTER	DIRTILY	DISARMS	DISBURSER
DIPNETTING	DIRECTEST	DIRTINESS	DISARRAY	DISBURSERS
DIPNOAN	DIRECTING	DIRTINESSES	DISARRAYED	DISBURSES
DIPNOANS	DIRECTION	DIRTS	DISARRAYING	DISBURSING
DIPODIC	DIRECTIONS	DIRTY	DISARRAYS	DISC
DIPODIES	DIRECTIVE	DIRTYING	DISASTER	DISCALCED
DIPODY	DIRECTIVES	DIS	DISASTERS	DISCANT
DIPOLAR	DIRECTLY	DISABLE	DISAVOW	DISCANTED
DIPOLE	DIRECTOR	DISABLED	DISAVOWAL	DISCANTING
DIPOLES	DIRECTORIES	DISABLER	DISAVOWALS	DISCANTS
DIPPABLE	DIRECTORS	DISABLERS	DISAVOWED	DISCARD
DIPPED	DIRECTORY	DISABLES	DISAVOWER	DISCARDED
DIPPER	DIRECTRICES	DISABLING	DISAVOWERS	DISCARDER
DIPPERFUL	DIRECTRIX	DISABUSAL	DISAVOWING	DISCARDERS
DIPPERFULS	DIRECTRIXES	DISABUSALS	DISAVOWS	DISCARDING

DISCARDS
DISCASE
DISCASED
DISCASES
DISCASING
DISCED
DISCEPT
DISCEPTED
DISCEPTING
DISCEPTS
DISCERN
DISCERNED
DISCERNER
DISCERNERS
DISCERNING
DISCERNS
DISCHARGE
DISCHARGED
DISCHARGES
DISCHARGING
DISCI
DISCIFORM
DISCING
DISCIPLE
DISCIPLED
DISCIPLES
DISCIPLING
DISCLAIM
DISCLAIMED
DISCLAIMING
DISCLAIMS
DISCLIKE
DISCLIMAX
DISCLIMAXES
DISCLOSE
DISCLOSED
DISCLOSER
DISCLOSERS
DISCLOSES
DISCLOSING
DISCO
DISCOED
DISCOID
DISCOIDAL
DISCOIDS
DISCOING
DISCOLOR
DISCOLORED
DISCOLORING
DISCOLORS
DISCOLOUR
DISCOLOURED

DISCOLOURING
DISCOLOURS
DISCOMFIT
DISCOMFITED
DISCOMFITING
DISCOMFITS
DISCORD
DISCORDED
DISCORDING
DISCORDS
DISCOS
DISCOUNT
DISCOUNTED
DISCOUNTING
DISCOUNTS
DISCOURSE
DISCOURSED
DISCOURSES
DISCOURSING
DISCOVER
DISCOVERED
DISCOVERIES
DISCOVERING
DISCOVERS
DISCOVERT
DISCOVERY
DISCREDIT
DISCREDITED
DISCREDITING
DISCREDITS
DISCREET
DISCREETER
DISCREETEST
DISCRETE
DISCROWN
DISCROWNED
DISCROWNING
DISCROWNS
DISCS
DISCUS
DISCUSES
DISCUSS
DISCUSSED
DISCUSSER
DISCUSSERS
DISCUSSES
DISCUSSING
DISDAIN
DISDAINED
DISDAINING
DISDAINS
DISEASE

DISEASED
DISEASES
DISEASING
DISEMBARK
DISEMBARKED
DISEMBARKING
DISEMBARKS
DISEMBODIED
DISEMBODIES
DISEMBODY
DISEMBODYING
DISEMPLOY
DISEMPLOYED
DISEMPLOYING
DISEMPLOYS
DISENABLE
DISENABLED
DISENABLES
DISENABLING
DISENDOW
DISENDOWED
DISENDOWING
DISENDOWS
DISENGAGE
DISENGAGED
DISENGAGES
DISENGAGING
DISENTAIL
DISENTAILED
DISENTAILING
DISENTAILS
DISESTEEM
DISESTEEMED
DISESTEEMING
DISESTEEMS
DISEUR
DISEURS
DISEUSE
DISEUSES
DISFAVOR
DISFAVORED
DISFAVORING
DISFAVORS
DISFAVOUR
DISFAVOURED
DISFAVOURING
DISFAVOURS
DISFIGURE
DISFIGURED
DISFIGURES
DISFIGURING
DISFROCK

DISFROCKED
DISFROCKING
DISFROCKS
DISGORGE
DISGORGED
DISGORGES
DISGORGING
DISGRACE
DISGRACED
DISGRACER
DISGRACERS
DISGRACES
DISGRACING
DISGUISE
DISGUISED
DISGUISER
DISGUISERS
DISGUISES
DISGUISING
DISGUST
DISGUSTED
DISGUSTING
DISGUSTS
DISH
DISHCLOTH
DISHCLOTHS
DISHCLOUT
DISHCLOUTS
DISHDASHA
DISHDASHAS
DISHED
DISHELM
DISHELMED
DISHELMING
DISHELMS
DISHERIT
DISHERITED
DISHERITING
DISHERITS
DISHES
DISHEVEL
DISHEVELED
DISHEVELING
DISHEVELLED
DISHEVELLING
DISHEVELS
DISHFUL
DISHFULS
DISHIER
DISHIEST
DISHING
DISHLIKE

DISHONEST
DISHONOR
DISHONORED
DISHONORING
DISHONORS
DISHPAN
DISHPANS
DISHRAG
DISHRAGS
DISHTOWEL
DISHTOWELS
DISHWARE
DISHWARES
DISHWATER
DISHWATERS
DISHY
DISINFECT
DISINFECTED
DISINFECTING
DISINFECTS
DISINFEST
DISINFESTED
DISINFESTING
DISINFESTS
DISINFORM
DISINFORMED
DISINFORMING
DISINFORMS
DISINTER
DISINTERRED
DISINTERRING
DISINTERS
DISINVEST
DISINVESTED
DISINVESTING
DISINVESTS
DISINVITE
DISINVITED
DISINVITES
DISINVITING
DISJECT
DISJECTED
DISJECTING
DISJECTS
DISJOIN
DISJOINED
DISJOINING
DISJOINS
DISJOINT
DISJOINTED
DISJOINTING
DISJOINTS

DISJUNCT
DISJUNCTS
DISK
DISKED
DISKETTE
DISKETTES
DISKING
DISKLIKE
DISKS
DISLIKE
DISLIKED
DISLIKER
DISLIKERS
DISLIKES
DISLIKING
DISLIMN
DISLIMNED
DISLIMNING
DISLIMNS
DISLOCATE
DISLOCATED
DISLOCATES
DISLOCATING
DISLODGE
DISLODGED
DISLODGES
DISLODGING
DISLOYAL
DISMAL
DISMALER
DISMALEST
DISMALLY
DISMALS
DISMANTLE
DISMANTLED
DISMANTLES
DISMANTLING
DISMAST
DISMASTED
DISMASTING
DISMASTS
DISMAY
DISMAYED
DISMAYING
DISMAYS
DISME
DISMEMBER
DISMEMBERED
DISMEMBERING
DISMEMBERS
DISMES
DISMISS

DISMISSAL
DISMISSALS
DISMISSED
DISMISSES
DISMISSING
DISMOUNT
DISMOUNTED
DISMOUNTING
DISMOUNTS
DISOBEY
DISOBEYED
DISOBEYER
DISOBEYERS
DISOBEYING
DISOBEYS
DISOBLIGE
DISOBLIGED
DISOBLIGES
DISOBLIGING
DISOMIC
DISORDER
DISORDERED
DISORDERING
DISORDERS
DISORIENT
DISORIENTED
DISORIENTING
DISORIENTS
DISOWN
DISOWNED
DISOWNING
DISOWNS
DISPARAGE
DISPARAGED
DISPARAGES
DISPARAGING
DISPARATE
DISPARITIES
DISPARITY
DISPART
DISPARTED
DISPARTING
DISPARTS
DISPATCH
DISPATCHED
DISPATCHES
DISPATCHING
DISPEL
DISPELLED
DISPELLER
DISPELLERS
DISPELLING

DISPELS
DISPEND
DISPENDED
DISPENDING
DISPENDS
DISPENSE
DISPENSED
DISPENSER
DISPENSERS
DISPENSES
DISPENSING
DISPEOPLE
DISPEOPLED
DISPEOPLES
DISPEOPLING
DISPERSAL
DISPERSALS
DISPERSE
DISPERSED
DISPERSER
DISPERSERS
DISPERSES
DISPERSING
DISPIRIT
DISPIRITED
DISPIRITING
DISPIRITS
DISPLACE
DISPLACED
DISPLACER
DISPLACERS
DISPLACES
DISPLACING
DISPLANT
DISPLANTED
DISPLANTING
DISPLANTS
DISPLAY
DISPLAYED
DISPLAYER
DISPLAYERS
DISPLAYING
DISPLAYS
DISPLEASE
DISPLEASED
DISPLEASES
DISPLEASING
DISPLODE
DISPLODED
DISPLODES
DISPLODING
DISPLUME

DISPLUMED
DISPLUMES
DISPLUMING
DISPORT
DISPORTED
DISPORTING
DISPORTS
DISPOSAL
DISPOSALS
DISPOSE
DISPOSED
DISPOSER
DISPOSERS
DISPOSES
DISPOSING
DISPOSURE
DISPOSURES
DISPRAISE
DISPRAISED
DISPRAISES
DISPRAISING
DISPREAD
DISPREADING
DISPREADS
DISPRIZE
DISPRIZED
DISPRIZES
DISPRIZING
DISPROOF
DISPROOFS
DISPROVAL
DISPROVALS
DISPROVE
DISPROVED
DISPROVEN
DISPROVER
DISPROVERS
DISPROVES
DISPROVING
DISPUTANT
DISPUTANTS
DISPUTE
DISPUTED
DISPUTER
DISPUTERS
DISPUTES
DISPUTING
DISQUIET
DISQUIETED
DISQUIETING
DISQUIETS
DISRATE

DISRATED
DISRATES
DISRATING
DISREGARD
DISREGARDED
DISREGARDING
DISREGARDS
DISRELISH
DISRELISHED
DISRELISHES
DISRELISHING
DISREPAIR
DISREPAIRS
DISREPUTE
DISREPUTES
DISROBE
DISROBED
DISROBER
DISROBERS
DISROBES
DISROBING
DISROOT
DISROOTED
DISROOTING
DISROOTS
DISRUPT
DISRUPTED
DISRUPTER
DISRUPTERS
DISRUPTING
DISRUPTOR
DISRUPTORS
DISRUPTS
DISS
DISSAVE
DISSAVED
DISSAVES
DISSAVING
DISSEAT
DISSEATED
DISSEATING
DISSEATS
DISSECT
DISSECTED
DISSECTING
DISSECTOR
DISSECTORS
DISSECTS
DISSED
DISSEISE
DISSEISED
DISSEISEE

DISSEISEES	DISSOLVED	DISTILS	DISUNITED	DITTIES
DISSEISES	DISSOLVER	DISTINCT	DISUNITER	DITTO
DISSEISIN	DISSOLVERS	DISTINCTER	DISUNITERS	DITTOED
DISSEISING	DISSOLVES	DISTINCTEST	DISUNITES	DITTOING
DISSEISINS	DISSOLVING	DISTINGUE	DISUNITIES	DITTOS
DISSEISOR	DISSONANT	DISTOME	DISUNITING	DITTY
DISSEISORS	DISSUADE	DISTOMES	DISUNITY	DITZ
DISSEIZE	DISSUADED	DISTORT	DISUSE	DITZES
DISSEIZED	DISSUADER	DISTORTED	DISUSED	DITZIER
DISSEIZEE	DISSUADERS	DISTORTER	DISUSES	DITZIEST
DISSEIZEES	DISSUADES	DISTORTERS	DISUSING	DITZINESS
DISSEIZES	DISSUADING	DISTORTING	DISVALUE	DITZINESSES
DISSEIZIN	DISTAFF	DISTORTS	DISVALUED	DITZY
DISSEIZING	DISTAFFS	DISTRACT	DISVALUES	DIURESES
DISSEIZINS	DISTAIN	DISTRACTED	DISVALUING	DIURESIS
DISSEIZOR	DISTAINED	DISTRACTING	DISYOKE	DIURETIC
DISSEIZORS	DISTAINING	DISTRACTS	DISYOKED	DIURETICS
DISSEMBLE	DISTAINS	DISTRAIN	DISYOKES	DIURNAL
DISSEMBLED	DISTAL	DISTRAINED	DISYOKING	DIURNALLY
DISSEMBLES	DISTALLY	DISTRAINING	DIT	DIURNALS
DISSEMBLING	DISTANCE	DISTRAINS	DITA	DIURON
DISSENSUS	DISTANCED	DISTRAINT	DITAS	DIURONS
DISSENSUSES	DISTANCES	DISTRAINTS	DITCH	DIVA
DISSENT	DISTANCING	DISTRAIT	DITCHED	DIVAGATE
DISSENTED	DISTANT	DISTRAITE	DITCHER	DIVAGATED
DISSENTER	DISTANTLY	DISTRESS	DITCHERS	DIVAGATES
DISSENTERS	DISTASTE	DISTRESSED	DITCHES	DIVAGATING
DISSENTING	DISTASTED	DISTRESSES	DITCHING	DIVALENCE
DISSENTS	DISTASTES	DISTRESSING	DITE	DIVALENCES
DISSERT	DISTASTING	DISTRICT	DITES	DIVALENT
DISSERTED	DISTAVES	DISTRICTED	DITHEISM	DIVAN
DISSERTING	DISTEMPER	DISTRICTING	DITHEISMS	DIVANS
DISSERTS	DISTEMPERED	DISTRICTS	DITHEIST	DIVAS
DISSERVE	DISTEMPERING	DISTRUST	DITHEISTS	DIVE
DISSERVED	DISTEMPERS	DISTRUSTED	DITHER	DIVEBOMB
DISSERVES	DISTEND	DISTRUSTING	DITHERED	DIVEBOMBED
DISSERVING	DISTENDED	DISTRUSTS	DITHERER	DIVEBOMBING
DISSES	DISTENDER	DISTURB	DITHERERS	DIVEBOMBS
DISSEVER	DISTENDERS	DISTURBED	DITHERING	DIVED
DISSEVERED	DISTENDING	DISTURBER	DITHERS	DIVER
DISSEVERING	DISTENDS	DISTURBERS	DITHERY	DIVERGE
DISSEVERS	DISTENT	DISTURBING	DITHIOL	DIVERGED
DISSIDENT	DISTICH	DISTURBS	DITHYRAMB	DIVERGENT
DISSIDENTS	DISTICHAL	DISULFATE	DITHYRAMBS	DIVERGES
DISSING	DISTICHS	DISULFATES	DITS	DIVERGING
DISSIPATE	DISTIL	DISULFID	DITSIER	DIVERS
DISSIPATED	DISTILL	DISULFIDE	DITSIEST	DIVERSE
DISSIPATES	DISTILLED	DISULFIDES	DITSINESS	DIVERSELY
DISSIPATING	DISTILLER	DISULFIDS	DITSINESSES	DIVERSIFIED
DISSOCIAL	DISTILLERS	DISUNION	DITSY	DIVERSIFIES
DISSOLUTE	DISTILLING	DISUNIONS	DITTANIES	DIVERSIFY
DISSOLVE	DISTILLS	DISUNITE	DITTANY	DIVERSIFYING

DIVERSION	DIVISOR	DIZZINESSES	DOCKAGE	DODGEMS
DIVERSIONS	DIVISORS	DIZZY	DOCKAGES	DODGER
DIVERSITIES	DIVORCE	DIZZYING	DOCKED	DODGERIES
DIVERSITY	DIVORCED	DJEBEL	DOCKER	DODGERS
DIVERT	DIVORCEE	DJEBELS	DOCKERS	DODGERY
DIVERTED	DIVORCEES	DJELLABA	DOCKET	DODGES
DIVERTER	DIVORCER	DJELLABAH	DOCKETED	DODGIER
DIVERTERS	DIVORCERS	DJELLABAHS	DOCKETING	DODGIEST
DIVERTING	DIVORCES	DJELLABAS	DOCKETS	DODGINESS
DIVERTS	DIVORCING	DJIN	DOCKHAND	DODGINESSES
DIVES	DIVORCIVE	DJINN	DOCKHANDS	DODGING
DIVEST	DIVOT	DJINNI	DOCKING	DODGY
DIVESTED	DIVOTS	DJINNS	DOCKLAND	DODO
DIVESTING	DIVULGATE	DJINNY	DOCKLANDS	DODOES
DIVESTS	DIVULGATED	DJINS	DOCKS	DODOISM
DIVESTURE	DIVULGATES	DO	DOCKSIDE	DODOISMS
DIVESTURES	DIVULGATING	DOABLE	DOCKSIDES	DODOS
DIVIDABLE	DIVULGE	DOAT	DOCKYARD	DOE
DIVIDE	DIVULGED	DOATED	DOCKYARDS	DOER
DIVIDED	DIVULGER	DOATING	DOCS	DOERS
DIVIDEDLY	DIVULGERS	DOATS	DOCTOR	DOES
DIVIDEND	DIVULGES	DOBBER	DOCTORAL	DOESKIN
DIVIDENDS	DIVULGING	DOBBERS	DOCTORATE	DOESKINS
DIVIDER	DIVULSE	DOBBIES	DOCTORATES	DOEST
DIVIDERS	DIVULSED	DOBBIN	DOCTORED	DOETH
DIVIDES	DIVULSES	DOBBINS	DOCTORIAL	DOFF
DIVIDING	DIVULSING	DOBBY	DOCTORING	DOFFED
DIVIDUAL	DIVULSION	DOBIE	DOCTORLY	DOFFER
DIVINE	DIVULSIONS	DOBIES	DOCTORS	DOFFERS
DIVINED	DIVULSIVE	DOBLA	DOCTRINAL	DOFFING
DIVINELY	DIVVIED	DOBLAS	DOCTRINE	DOFFS
DIVINER	DIVVIES	DOBLON	DOCTRINES	DOG
DIVINERS	DIVVY	DOBLONES	DOCUDRAMA	DOGBANE
DIVINES	DIVVYING	DOBLONS	DOCUDRAMAS	DOGBANES
DIVINEST	DIWAN	DOBRA	DOCUMENT	DOGBERRIES
DIVING	DIWANS	DOBRAS	DOCUMENTED	DOGBERRY
DIVINING	DIXIT	DOBRO	DOCUMENTING	DOGCART
DIVINISE	DIXITS	DOBROS	DOCUMENTS	DOGCARTS
DIVINISED	DIZEN	DOBSON	DODDER	DOGDOM
DIVINISES	DIZENED	DOBSONFLIES	DODDERED	DOGDOMS
DIVINISING	DIZENING	DOBSONFLY	DODDERER	DOGE
DIVINITIES	DIZENMENT	DOBSONS	DODDERERS	DOGEAR
DIVINITY	DIZENMENTS	DOBY	DODDERING	DOGEARED
DIVINIZE	DIZENS	DOC	DODDERS	DOGEARING
DIVINIZED	DIZYGOTIC	DOCENT	DODDERY	DOGEARS
DIVINIZES	DIZYGOUS	DOCENTS	DODECAGON	DOGEDOM
DIVINIZING	DIZZIED	DOCETIC	DODECAGONS	DOGEDOMS
DIVISIBLE	DIZZIER	DOCILE	DODGE	DOGES
DIVISIBLY	DIZZIES	DOCILELY	DODGEBALL	DOGESHIP
DIVISION	DIZZIEST	DOCILITIES	DODGEBALLS	DOGESHIPS
DIVISIONS	DIZZILY	DOCILITY	DODGED	DOGEY
DIVISIVE	DIZZINESS	DOCK	DODGEM	DOGEYS

DOGFACE	DOGMATIST	DOLCETTOS	DOLOROUS	DOMING
DOGFACES	DOGMATISTS	DOLCI	DOLORS	DOMINICAL
DOGFIGHT	DOGMATIZE	DOLDRUMS	DOLOUR	DOMINICK
DOGFIGHTING	DOGMATIZED	DOLE	DOLOURS	DOMINICKS
DOGFIGHTS	DOGMATIZES	DOLED	DOLPHIN	DOMINIE
DOGFISH	DOGMATIZING	DOLEFUL	DOLPHINS	DOMINIES
DOGFISHES	DOGNAP	DOLEFULLER	DOLS	DOMINION
DOGFOUGHT	DOGNAPED	DOLEFULLEST	DOLT	DOMINIONS
DOGGED	DOGNAPER	DOLEFULLY	DOLTISH	DOMINIQUE
DOGGEDLY	DOGNAPERS	DOLERITE	DOLTISHLY	DOMINIQUES
DOGGER	DOGNAPING	DOLERITES	DOLTS	DOMINIUM
DOGGEREL	DOGNAPPED	DOLERITIC	DOM	DOMINIUMS
DOGGERELS	DOGNAPPER	DOLES	DOMAIN	DOMINO
DOGGERIES	DOGNAPPERS	DOLESOME	DOMAINE	DOMINOES
DOGGERS	DOGNAPPING	DOLING	DOMAINES	DOMINOS
DOGGERY	DOGNAPS	DOLL	DOMAINS	DOMS
DOGGIE	DOGROBBER	DOLLAR	DOMAL	DON
DOGGIER	DOGROBBERS	DOLLARIZE	DOME	DONA
DOGGIES	DOGS	DOLLARIZED	DOMED	DONAS
DOGGIEST	DOGSBODIES	DOLLARIZES	DOMELIKE	DONATE
DOGGING	DOGSBODY	DOLLARIZING	DOMES	DONATED
DOGGISH	DOGSLED	DOLLARS	DOMESDAY	DONATES
DOGGISHLY	DOGSLEDDED	DOLLED	DOMESDAYS	DONATING
DOGGO	DOGSLEDDING	DOLLHOUSE	DOMESTIC	DONATION
DOGGONE	DOGSLEDS	DOLLHOUSES	DOMESTICS	DONATIONS
DOGGONED	DOGTEETH	DOLLIED	DOMIC	DONATIVE
DOGGONEDER	DOGTOOTH	DOLLIES	DOMICAL	DONATIVES
DOGGONEDEST	DOGTROT	DOLLING	DOMICALLY	DONATOR
DOGGONER	DOGTROTS	DOLLISH	DOMICIL	DONATORS
DOGGONES	DOGTROTTED	DOLLISHLY	DOMICILE	DONE
DOGGONEST	DOGTROTTING	DOLLOP	DOMICILED	DONEE
DOGGONING	DOGVANE	DOLLOPED	DOMICILES	DONEES
DOGGREL	DOGVANES	DOLLOPING	DOMICILING	DONENESS
DOGGRELS	DOGWATCH	DOLLOPS	DOMICILS	DONENESSES
DOGGY	DOGWATCHES	DOLLS	DOMINANCE	DONG
DOGHANGED	DOGWOOD	DOLLY	DOMINANCES	DONGA
DOGHOUSE	DOGWOODS	DOLLYBIRD	DOMINANCIES	DONGAS
DOGHOUSES	DOGY	DOLLYBIRDS	DOMINANCY	DONGLE
DOGIE	DOILED	DOLLYING	DOMINANT	DONGLES
DOGIES	DOILIES	DOLMA	DOMINANTS	DONGOLA
DOGLEG	DOILY	DOLMADES	DOMINATE	DONGOLAS
DOGLEGGED	DOING	DOLMAN	DOMINATED	DONGS
DOGLEGGING	DOINGS	DOLMANS	DOMINATES	DONJON
DOGLEGS	DOIT	DOLMAS	DOMINATING	DONJONS
DOGLIKE	DOITED	DOLMEN	DOMINATOR	DONKEY
DOGMA	DOITS	DOLMENIC	DOMINATORS	DONKEYS
DOGMAS	DOJO	DOLMENS	DOMINE	DONNA
DOGMATA	DOJOS	DOLOMITE	DOMINEER	DONNAS
DOGMATIC	DOL	DOLOMITES	DOMINEERED	DONNE
DOGMATICS	DOLABRATE	DOLOMITIC	DOMINEERING	DONNED
DOGMATISM	DOLCE	DOLOR	DOMINEERS	DONNEE
DOGMATISMS	DOLCETTO	DOLOROSO	DOMINES	DONNEES

DONNERD	DOOMIEST	DOPANT	DORMIENT	DOSSEL
DONNERED	DOOMILY	DOPANTS	DORMIN	DOSSELS
DONNERT	DOOMING	DOPAS	DORMINS	DOSSER
DONNICKER	DOOMS	DOPE	DORMITORIES	DOSSERET
DONNICKERS	DOOMSAYER	DOPED	DORMITORY	DOSSERETS
DONNIKER	DOOMSAYERS	DOPEHEAD	DORMOUSE	DOSSERS
DONNIKERS	DOOMSDAY	DOPEHEADS	DORMS	DOSSES
DONNING	DOOMSDAYS	DOPER	DORMY	DOSSHOUSE
DONNISH	DOOMSTER	DOPERS	DORNECK	DOSSHOUSES
DONNISHLY	DOOMSTERS	DOPES	DORNECKS	DOSSIER
DONOR	DOOMY	DOPESHEET	DORNICK	DOSSIERS
DONORS	DOOR	DOPESHEETS	DORNICKS	DOSSIL
DONORSHIP	DOORBELL	DOPESTER	DORNOCK	DOSSILS
DONORSHIPS	DOORBELLS	DOPESTERS	DORNOCKS	DOSSING
DONS	DOORJAMB	DOPEY	DORONICUM	DOST
DONSIE	DOORJAMBS	DOPEYNESS	DORONICUMS	DOT
DONSY	DOORKNOB	DOPEYNESSES	DORP	DOTAGE
DONUT	DOORKNOBS	DOPIER	DORPER	DOTAGES
DONUTS	DOORLESS	DOPIEST	DORPERS	DOTAL
DONZEL	DOORMAN	DOPILY	DORPS	DOTARD
DONZELS	DOORMAT	DOPINESS	DORR	DOTARDLY
DOOBIE	DOORMATS	DOPINESSES	DORRS	DOTARDS
DOOBIES	DOORMEN	DOPING	DORS	DOTATION
DOODAD	DOORNAIL	DOPINGS	DORSA	DOTATIONS
DOODADS	DOORNAILS	DOPY	DORSAD	DOTE
DOODIES	DOORPLATE	DOR	DORSAL	DOTED
DOODLE	DOORPLATES	DORADO	DORSALLY	DOTER
DOODLEBUG	DOORPOST	DORADOS	DORSALS	DOTERS
DOODLEBUGS	DOORPOSTS	DORBEETLE	DORSEL	DOTES
DOODLED	DOORS	DORBEETLES	DORSELS	DOTH
DOODLER	DOORSILL	DORBUG	DORSER	DOTIER
DOODLERS	DOORSILLS	DORBUGS	DORSERS	DOTIEST
DOODLES	DOORSTEP	DORE	DORSUM	DOTING
DOODLING	DOORSTEPS	DORHAWK	DORTY	DOTINGLY
DOODOO	DOORSTOP	DORHAWKS	DORY	DOTS
DOODOOS	DOORSTOPS	DORIES	DOS	DOTTED
DOODY	DOORWAY	DORK	DOSAGE	DOTTEL
DOOFUS	DOORWAYS	DORKIER	DOSAGES	DOTTELS
DOOFUSES	DOORWOMAN	DORKIEST	DOSE	DOTTER
DOOHICKEY	DOORWOMEN	DORKINESS	DOSED	DOTTEREL
DOOHICKEYS	DOORYARD	DORKINESSES	DOSER	DOTTERELS
DOOHICKIES	DOORYARDS	DORKS	DOSERS	DOTTERS
DOOLEE	DOOWOP	DORKY	DOSES	DOTTIER
DOOLEES	DOOWOPS	DORM	DOSIMETER	DOTTIEST
DOOLIE	DOOZER	DORMANCIES	DOSIMETERS	DOTTILY
DOOLIES	DOOZERS	DORMANCY	DOSIMETRIES	DOTTINESS
DOOLY	DOOZIE	DORMANT	DOSIMETRY	DOTTINESSES
DOOM	DOOZIES	DORMER	DOSING	DOTTING
DOOMED	DOOZY	DORMERED	DOSS	DOTTLE
DOOMFUL	DOPA	DORMERS	DOSSAL	DOTTLES
DOOMFULLY	DOPAMINE	DORMICE	DOSSALS	DOTTREL
DOOMIER	DOPAMINES	DORMIE	DOSSED	DOTTRELS

DOTTY
DOTY
DOUBLE
DOUBLED
DOUBLER
DOUBLERS
DOUBLES
DOUBLET
DOUBLETON
DOUBLETONS
DOUBLETS
DOUBLING
DOUBLOON
DOUBLOONS
DOUBLURE
DOUBLURES
DOUBLY
DOUBT
DOUBTABLE
DOUBTED
DOUBTER
DOUBTERS
DOUBTFUL
DOUBTING
DOUBTLESS
DOUBTS
DOUCE
DOUCELY
DOUCEUR
DOUCEURS
DOUCHE
DOUCHEBAG
DOUCHEBAGS
DOUCHED
DOUCHES
DOUCHING
DOUGH
DOUGHBOY
DOUGHBOYS
DOUGHFACE
DOUGHFACES
DOUGHIER
DOUGHIEST
DOUGHLIKE
DOUGHNUT
DOUGHNUTS
DOUGHS
DOUGHT
DOUGHTIER
DOUGHTIEST
DOUGHTILY
DOUGHTY

DOUGHY
DOULA
DOULAS
DOUM
DOUMA
DOUMAS
DOUMS
DOUPIONI
DOUPIONIS
DOUPPIONI
DOUPPIONIS
DOUR
DOURA
DOURAH
DOURAHS
DOURAS
DOURER
DOUREST
DOURINE
DOURINES
DOURLY
DOURNESS
DOURNESSES
DOUSE
DOUSED
DOUSER
DOUSERS
DOUSES
DOUSING
DOUX
DOUZEPER
DOUZEPERS
DOVE
DOVECOT
DOVECOTE
DOVECOTES
DOVECOTS
DOVEKEY
DOVEKEYS
DOVEKIE
DOVEKIES
DOVELIKE
DOVEN
DOVENED
DOVENING
DOVENS
DOVES
DOVETAIL
DOVETAILED
DOVETAILING
DOVETAILS
DOVISH

DOW
DOWABLE
DOWAGER
DOWAGERS
DOWDIER
DOWDIES
DOWDIEST
DOWDILY
DOWDINESS
DOWDINESSES
DOWDY
DOWDYISH
DOWED
DOWEL
DOWELED
DOWELING
DOWELLED
DOWELLING
DOWELS
DOWER
DOWERED
DOWERIES
DOWERING
DOWERLESS
DOWERS
DOWERY
DOWIE
DOWING
DOWITCHER
DOWITCHERS
DOWN
DOWNBEAT
DOWNBEATS
DOWNBOW
DOWNBOWS
DOWNBURST
DOWNBURSTS
DOWNCAST
DOWNCASTS
DOWNCOME
DOWNCOMES
DOWNCOURT
DOWNDRAFT
DOWNDRAFTS
DOWNED
DOWNER
DOWNERS
DOWNFALL
DOWNFALLS
DOWNFIELD
DOWNFORCE
DOWNFORCES

DOWNGRADE
DOWNGRADED
DOWNGRADES
DOWNGRADING
DOWNHAUL
DOWNHAULS
DOWNHILL
DOWNHILLS
DOWNIER
DOWNIEST
DOWNINESS
DOWNINESSES
DOWNING
DOWNLAND
DOWNLANDS
DOWNLESS
DOWNLIGHT
DOWNLIGHTS
DOWNLIKE
DOWNLINK
DOWNLINKED
DOWNLINKING
DOWNLINKS
DOWNLOAD
DOWNLOADED
DOWNLOADING
DOWNLOADS
DOWNPIPE
DOWNPIPES
DOWNPLAY
DOWNPLAYED
DOWNPLAYING
DOWNPLAYS
DOWNPOUR
DOWNPOURS
DOWNRANGE
DOWNRIGHT
DOWNRIVER
DOWNS
DOWNSCALE
DOWNSCALED
DOWNSCALES
DOWNSCALING
DOWNSHIFT
DOWNSHIFTED
DOWNSHIFTING
DOWNSHIFTS
DOWNSIDE
DOWNSIDES
DOWNSIZE
DOWNSIZED
DOWNSIZES

DOWNSIZING
DOWNSLIDE
DOWNSLIDES
DOWNSLOPE
DOWNSPIN
DOWNSPINS
DOWNSPOUT
DOWNSPOUTS
DOWNSTAGE
DOWNSTAGES
DOWNSTAIR
DOWNSTATE
DOWNSTATES
DOWNSWING
DOWNSWINGS
DOWNTHROW
DOWNTHROWS
DOWNTICK
DOWNTICKS
DOWNTIME
DOWNTIMES
DOWNTOWN
DOWNTOWNS
DOWNTREND
DOWNTRENDED
DOWNTRENDING
DOWNTRENDS
DOWNTROD
DOWNTURN
DOWNTURNS
DOWNWARD
DOWNWARDS
DOWNWASH
DOWNWASHES
DOWNWIND
DOWNY
DOWNZONE
DOWNZONED
DOWNZONES
DOWNZONING
DOWRIES
DOWRY
DOWS
DOWSABEL
DOWSABELS
DOWSE
DOWSED
DOWSER
DOWSERS
DOWSES
DOWSING
DOXIE

DOXIES	DRACHMAI	DRAGONFLY	DRAMMOCK	DRAWLED
DOXOLOGIES	DRACHMAS	DRAGONISH	DRAMMOCKS	DRAWLER
DOXOLOGY	DRACHMS	DRAGONS	DRAMS	DRAWLERS
DOXY	DRACONIAN	DRAGOON	DRAMSHOP	DRAWLIER
DOYEN	DRACONIC	DRAGOONED	DRAMSHOPS	DRAWLIEST
DOYENNE	DRAFF	DRAGOONING	DRANK	DRAWLING
DOYENNES	DRAFFIER	DRAGOONS	DRAPABLE	DRAWLS
DOYENS	DRAFFIEST	DRAGROPE	DRAPE	DRAWLY
DOYLEY	DRAFFISH	DRAGROPES	DRAPEABLE	DRAWN
DOYLEYS	DRAFFS	DRAGS	DRAPED	DRAWNWORK
DOYLIES	DRAFFY	DRAGSTER	DRAPER	DRAWNWORKS
DOYLY	DRAFT	DRAGSTERS	DRAPERIED	DRAWPLATE
DOZE	DRAFTABLE	DRAGSTRIP	DRAPERIES	DRAWPLATES
DOZED	DRAFTED	DRAGSTRIPS	DRAPERS	DRAWS
DOZEN	DRAFTEE	DRAIL	DRAPERY	DRAWSHAVE
DOZENED	DRAFTEES	DRAILS	DRAPES	DRAWSHAVES
DOZENING	DRAFTER	DRAIN	DRAPEY	DRAWTUBE
DOZENS	DRAFTERS	DRAINABLE	DRAPING	DRAWTUBES
DOZENTH	DRAFTIER	DRAINAGE	DRASTIC	DRAY
DOZENTHS	DRAFTIEST	DRAINAGES	DRAT	DRAYAGE
DOZER	DRAFTILY	DRAINED	DRATS	DRAYAGES
DOZERS	DRAFTING	DRAINER	DRATTED	DRAYED
DOZES	DRAFTINGS	DRAINERS	DRATTING	DRAYING
DOZIER	DRAFTS	DRAINING	DRAUGHT	DRAYMAN
DOZIEST	DRAFTSMAN	DRAINPIPE	DRAUGHTED	DRAYMEN
DOZILY	DRAFTSMEN	DRAINPIPES	DRAUGHTIER	DRAYS
DOZINESS	DRAFTY	DRAINS	DRAUGHTIEST	DREAD
DOZINESSES	DRAG	DRAKE	DRAUGHTING	DREADED
DOZING	DRAGEE	DRAKES	DRAUGHTS	DREADFUL
DOZY	DRAGEES	DRAM	DRAUGHTY	DREADFULS
DRAB	DRAGGED	DRAMA	DRAVE	DREADING
DRABBED	DRAGGER	DRAMADIES	DRAW	DREADLOCK
DRABBER	DRAGGERS	DRAMADY	DRAWABLE	DREADLOCKS
DRABBEST	DRAGGIER	DRAMAS	DRAWBACK	DREADS
DRABBET	DRAGGIEST	DRAMATIC	DRAWBACKS	DREAM
DRABBETS	DRAGGING	DRAMATICS	DRAWBAR	DREAMBOAT
DRABBING	DRAGGLE	DRAMATISE	DRAWBARS	DREAMBOATS
DRABBLE	DRAGGLED	DRAMATISED	DRAWBORE	DREAMED
DRABBLED	DRAGGLES	DRAMATISES	DRAWBORES	DREAMER
DRABBLES	DRAGGLING	DRAMATISING	DRAWDOWN	DREAMERS
DRABBLING	DRAGGY	DRAMATIST	DRAWDOWNS	DREAMFUL
DRABLY	DRAGLINE	DRAMATISTS	DRAWEE	DREAMIER
DRABNESS	DRAGLINES	DRAMATIZE	DRAWEES	DREAMIEST
DRABNESSES	DRAGNET	DRAMATIZED	DRAWER	DREAMILY
DRABS	DRAGNETS	DRAMATIZES	DRAWERFUL	DREAMING
DRACAENA	DRAGOMAN	DRAMATIZING	DRAWERFULS	DREAMLAND
DRACAENAS	DRAGOMANS	DRAMATURG	DRAWERS	DREAMLANDS
DRACENA	DRAGOMEN	DRAMATURGES	DRAWING	DREAMLESS
DRACENAS	DRAGON	DRAMEDIES	DRAWINGS	DREAMLIKE
DRACHM	DRAGONET	DRAMEDY	DRAWKNIFE	DREAMS
DRACHMA	DRAGONETS	DRAMMED	DRAWKNIVES	DREAMT
DRACHMAE	DRAGONFLIES	DRAMMING	DRAWL	DREAMTIME

DREAMTIMES	DRESSILY	DRINKABLE	DRIZZLING	DROPCLOTHS
DREAMY	DRESSING	DRINKABLES	DRIZZLY	DROPFORGE
DREAR	DRESSINGS	DRINKABLY	DROGUE	DROPFORGED
DREARIER	DRESSY	DRINKER	DROGUES	DROPFORGES
DREARIES	DREST	DRINKERS	DROID	DROPFORGING
DREARIEST	DREW	DRINKING	DROIDS	DROPHEAD
DREARILY	DRIB	DRINKINGS	DROIT	DROPHEADS
DREARS	DRIBBED	DRINKS	DROITS	DROPKICK
DREARY	DRIBBING	DRIP	DROLL	DROPKICKS
DRECK	DRIBBLE	DRIPLESS	DROLLED	DROPLET
DRECKS	DRIBBLED	DRIPPED	DROLLER	DROPLETS
DRECKY	DRIBBLER	DRIPPER	DROLLERIES	DROPLIGHT
DREDGE	DRIBBLERS	DRIPPERS	DROLLERY	DROPLIGHTS
DREDGED	DRIBBLES	DRIPPIER	DROLLEST	DROPOUT
DREDGER	DRIBBLET	DRIPPIEST	DROLLING	DROPOUTS
DREDGERS	DRIBBLETS	DRIPPILY	DROLLNESS	DROPPABLE
DREDGES	DRIBBLING	DRIPPING	DROLLNESSES	DROPPED
DREDGING	DRIBBLY	DRIPPINGS	DROLLS	DROPPER
DREDGINGS	DRIBLET	DRIPPY	DROLLY	DROPPERS
DREE	DRIBLETS	DRIPS	DROMEDARIES	DROPPING
DREED	DRIBS	DRIPSTONE	DROMEDARY	DROPPINGS
DREEING	DRIED	DRIPSTONES	DROMON	DROPS
DREES	DRIEGH	DRIPT	DROMOND	DROPSHOT
DREG	DRIER	DRIVABLE	DROMONDS	DROPSHOTS
DREGGIER	DRIERS	DRIVE	DROMONS	DROPSICAL
DREGGIEST	DRIES	DRIVEABLE	DRONE	DROPSIED
DREGGISH	DRIEST	DRIVEL	DRONED	DROPSIES
DREGGY	DRIFT	DRIVELED	DRONER	DROPSONDE
DREGS	DRIFTAGE	DRIVELER	DRONERS	DROPSONDES
DREICH	DRIFTAGES	DRIVELERS	DRONES	DROPSY
DREIDEL	DRIFTED	DRIVELINE	DRONGO	DROPT
DREIDELS	DRIFTER	DRIVELINES	DRONGOS	DROPWORT
DREIDL	DRIFTERS	DRIVELING	DRONING	DROPWORTS
DREIDLS	DRIFTIER	DRIVELLED	DRONINGLY	DROSERA
DREIGH	DRIFTIEST	DRIVELLER	DRONISH	DROSERAS
DREK	DRIFTING	DRIVELLERS	DROOL	DROSHKIES
DREKS	DRIFTPIN	DRIVELLING	DROOLED	DROSHKY
DRENCH	DRIFTPINS	DRIVELS	DROOLIER	DROSKIES
DRENCHED	DRIFTS	DRIVEN	DROOLIEST	DROSKY
DRENCHER	DRIFTWOOD	DRIVER	DROOLING	DROSS
DRENCHERS	DRIFTWOODS	DRIVERS	DROOLS	DROSSES
DRENCHES	DRIFTY	DRIVES	DROOLY	DROSSIER
DRENCHING	DRILL	DRIVEWAY	DROOP	DROSSIEST
DRESS	DRILLABLE	DRIVEWAYS	DROOPED	DROSSY
DRESSAGE	DRILLED	DRIVING	DROOPIER	DROUGHT
DRESSAGES	DRILLER	DRIVINGLY	DROOPIEST	DROUGHTIER
DRESSED	DRILLERS	DRIVINGS	DROOPILY	DROUGHTIEST
DRESSER	DRILLING	DRIZZLE	DROOPING	DROUGHTS
DRESSERS	DRILLINGS	DRIZZLED	DROOPS	DROUGHTY
DRESSES	DRILLS	DRIZZLES	DROOPY	DROUK
DRESSIER	DRILY	DRIZZLIER	DROP	DROUKED
DRESSIEST	DRINK	DRIZZLIEST	DROPCLOTH	DROUKING

DROUKS	DRUGGIEST	DRUNKEST	DUALIZES	DUCKPINS
DROUTH	DRUGGING	DRUNKS	DUALIZING	DUCKS
DROUTHIER	DRUGGIST	DRUPE	DUALLY	DUCKTAIL
DROUTHIEST	DRUGGISTS	DRUPELET	DUALS	DUCKTAILS
DROUTHS	DRUGGY	DRUPELETS	DUB	DUCKWALK
DROUTHY	DRUGMAKER	DRUPES	DUBBED	DUCKWALKED
DROVE	DRUGMAKERS	DRUSE	DUBBER	DUCKWALKING
DROVED	DRUGS	DRUSES	DUBBERS	DUCKWALKS
DROVER	DRUGSTORE	DRUTHERS	DUBBIN	DUCKWEED
DROVERS	DRUGSTORES	DRY	DUBBING	DUCKWEEDS
DROVES	DRUID	DRYABLE	DUBBINGS	DUCKY
DROVING	DRUIDESS	DRYAD	DUBBINS	DUCT
DROWN	DRUIDESSES	DRYADES	DUBIETIES	DUCTAL
DROWND	DRUIDIC	DRYADIC	DUBIETY	DUCTED
DROWNDED	DRUIDICAL	DRYADS	DUBIOSITIES	DUCTILE
DROWNDING	DRUIDISM	DRYASDUST	DUBIOSITY	DUCTILELY
DROWNDS	DRUIDISMS	DRYASDUSTS	DUBIOUS	DUCTILITIES
DROWNED	DRUIDS	DRYER	DUBIOUSLY	DUCTILITY
DROWNER	DRUM	DRYERS	DUBITABLE	DUCTING
DROWNERS	DRUMBEAT	DRYEST	DUBITABLY	DUCTINGS
DROWNING	DRUMBEATS	DRYING	DUBNIUM	DUCTLESS
DROWNS	DRUMBLE	DRYISH	DUBNIUMS	DUCTS
DROWSE	DRUMBLED	DRYLAND	DUBONNET	DUCTULE
DROWSED	DRUMBLES	DRYLOT	DUBONNETS	DUCTULES
DROWSES	DRUMBLING	DRYLOTS	DUBS	DUCTWORK
DROWSIER	DRUMFIRE	DRYLY	DUCAL	DUCTWORKS
DROWSIEST	DRUMFIRES	DRYNESS	DUCALLY	DUD
DROWSILY	DRUMFISH	DRYNESSES	DUCAT	DUDDIE
DROWSING	DRUMFISHES	DRYPOINT	DUCATS	DUDDY
DROWSY	DRUMHEAD	DRYPOINTS	DUCE	DUDE
DRUB	DRUMHEADS	DRYS	DUCES	DUDED
DRUBBED	DRUMLIER	DRYSALTER	DUCHESS	DUDEEN
DRUBBER	DRUMLIEST	DRYSALTERS	DUCHESSES	DUDEENS
DRUBBERS	DRUMLIKE	DRYSTONE	DUCHIES	DUDES
DRUBBING	DRUMLIN	DRYWALL	DUCHY	DUDGEON
DRUBBINGS	DRUMLINS	DRYWALLED	DUCI	DUDGEONS
DRUBS	DRUMLY	DRYWALLING	DUCK	DUDING
DRUDGE	DRUMMED	DRYWALLS	DUCKBILL	DUDISH
DRUDGED	DRUMMER	DRYWELL	DUCKBILLS	DUDISHLY
DRUDGER	DRUMMERS	DRYWELLS	DUCKBOARD	DUDS
DRUDGERIES	DRUMMING	DUAD	DUCKBOARDS	DUE
DRUDGERS	DRUMROLL	DUADS	DUCKED	DUECENTO
DRUDGERY	DRUMROLLS	DUAL	DUCKER	DUECENTOS
DRUDGES	DRUMS	DUALISM	DUCKERS	DUEL
DRUDGING	DRUMSTICK	DUALISMS	DUCKIE	DUELED
DRUG	DRUMSTICKS	DUALIST	DUCKIER	DUELER
DRUGGED	DRUNK	DUALISTIC	DUCKIES	DUELERS
DRUGGET	DRUNKARD	DUALISTS	DUCKIEST	DUELING
DRUGGETS	DRUNKARDS	DUALITIES	DUCKING	DUELIST
DRUGGIE	DRUNKEN	DUALITY	DUCKLING	DUELISTS
DRUGGIER	DRUNKENLY	DUALIZE	DUCKLINGS	DUELLED
DRUGGIES	DRUNKER	DUALIZED	DUCKPIN	DUELLER

DUELLERS	DULCETLY	DUMBNESS	DUNCISHLY	DUODENAL
DUELLI	DULCETS	DUMBNESSES	DUNE	DUODENUM
DUELLING	DULCIANA	DUMBO	DUNELAND	DUODENUMS
DUELLIST	DULCIANAS	DUMBOS	DUNELANDS	DUOLOG
DUELLISTS	DULCIFIED	DUMBS	DUNELIKE	DUOLOGS
DUELLO	DULCIFIES	DUMDUM	DUNES	DUOLOGUE
DUELLOS	DULCIFY	DUMDUMS	DUNG	DUOLOGUES
DUELS	DULCIFYING	DUMFOUND	DUNGAREE	DUOMI
DUENDE	DULCIMER	DUMFOUNDED	DUNGAREED	DUOMO
DUENDES	DULCIMERS	DUMFOUNDING	DUNGAREES	DUOMOS
DUENESS	DULCIMORE	DUMFOUNDS	DUNGED	DUOPOLIES
DUENESSES	DULCIMORES	DUMKA	DUNGEON	DUOPOLY
DUENNA	DULCINEA	DUMKY	DUNGEONED	DUOPSONIES
DUENNAS	DULCINEAS	DUMMIED	DUNGEONING	DUOPSONY
DUES	DULIA	DUMMIES	DUNGEONS	DUOS
DUET	DULIAS	DUMMKOPF	DUNGHILL	DUOTONE
DUETED	DULL	DUMMKOPFS	DUNGHILLS	DUOTONES
DUETING	DULLARD	DUMMY	DUNGIER	DUP
DUETS	DULLARDS	DUMMYING	DUNGIEST	DUPABLE
DUETTED	DULLED	DUMP	DUNGING	DUPE
DUETTING	DULLER	DUMPCART	DUNGS	DUPED
DUETTIST	DULLEST	DUMPCARTS	DUNGY	DUPER
DUETTISTS	DULLING	DUMPED	DUNITE	DUPERIES
DUFF	DULLISH	DUMPER	DUNITES	DUPERS
DUFFEL	DULLISHLY	DUMPERS	DUNITIC	DUPERY
DUFFELS	DULLNESS	DUMPIER	DUNK	DUPES
DUFFER	DULLNESSES	DUMPIEST	DUNKED	DUPING
DUFFERS	DULLS	DUMPILY	DUNKER	DUPLE
DUFFLE	DULLY	DUMPINESS	DUNKERS	DUPLEX
DUFFLES	DULNESS	DUMPINESSES	DUNKING	DUPLEXED
DUFFS	DULNESSES	DUMPING	DUNKS	DUPLEXER
DUFUS	DULSE	DUMPINGS	DUNLIN	DUPLEXERS
DUFUSES	DULSES	DUMPISH	DUNLINS	DUPLEXES
DUG	DULY	DUMPLING	DUNNAGE	DUPLEXING
DUGONG	DUMA	DUMPLINGS	DUNNAGES	DUPLEXITIES
DUGONGS	DUMAS	DUMPS	DUNNED	DUPLEXITY
DUGOUT	DUMB	DUMPSITE	DUNNER	DUPLICATE
DUGOUTS	DUMBBELL	DUMPSITES	DUNNESS	DUPLICATED
DUGS	DUMBBELLS	DUMPSTER	DUNNESSES	DUPLICATES
DUH	DUMBCANE	DUMPSTERS	DUNNEST	DUPLICATING
DUI	DUMBCANES	DUMPTRUCK	DUNNING	DUPLICITIES
DUIKER	DUMBED	DUMPTRUCKS	DUNNITE	DUPLICITY
DUIKERS	DUMBER	DUMPY	DUNNITES	DUPPED
DUIT	DUMBEST	DUN	DUNS	DUPPING
DUITS	DUMBFOUND	DUNAM	DUNT	DUPS
DUKE	DUMBFOUNDED	DUNAMS	DUNTED	DURA
DUKED	DUMBFOUNDING	DUNCE	DUNTING	DURABLE
DUKEDOM	DUMBFOUNDS	DUNCES	DUNTS	DURABLES
DUKEDOMS	DUMBHEAD	DUNCH	DUO	DURABLY
DUKES	DUMBHEADS	DUNCHES	DUODECIMO	DURAL
DUKING	DUMBING	DUNCICAL	DUODECIMOS	DURALUMIN
DULCET	DUMBLY	DUNCISH	DUODENA	DURALUMINS

DURAMEN	DUSKING	DUVETINE	DYBBUKIM	DYNEINS
DURAMENS	DUSKISH	DUVETINES	DYBBUKS	DYNEL
DURANCE	DUSKS	DUVETS	DYE	DYNELS
DURANCES	DUSKY	DUVETYN	DYEABLE	DYNES
DURAS	DUST	DUVETYNE	DYED	DYNODE
DURATION	DUSTBIN	DUVETYNES	DYEING	DYNODES
DURATIONS	DUSTBINS	DUVETYNS	DYEINGS	DYNORPHIN
DURATIVE	DUSTCOVER	DUXELLES	DYER	DYNORPHINS
DURATIVES	DUSTCOVERS	DWARF	DYERS	DYSCRASIA
DURBAR	DUSTED	DWARFED	DYES	DYSCRASIAS
DURBARS	DUSTER	DWARFER	DYESTUFF	DYSCRASIC
DURE	DUSTERS	DWARFEST	DYESTUFFS	DYSCRATIC
DURED	DUSTHEAP	DWARFING	DYEWEED	DYSENTERIES
DURES	DUSTHEAPS	DWARFISH	DYEWEEDS	DYSENTERY
DURESS	DUSTIER	DWARFISM	DYEWOOD	DYSGENIC
DURESSES	DUSTIEST	DWARFISMS	DYEWOODS	DYSGENICS
DURIAN	DUSTILY	DWARFLIKE	DYING	DYSLECTIC
DURIANS	DUSTINESS	DWARFNESS	DYINGS	DYSLECTICS
DURING	DUSTINESSES	DWARFNESSES	DYKE	DYSLEXIA
DURION	DUSTING	DWARFS	DYKED	DYSLEXIAS
DURIONS	DUSTINGS	DWARVES	DYKES	DYSLEXIC
DURMAST	DUSTLESS	DWEEB	DYKEY	DYSLEXICS
DURMASTS	DUSTLIKE	DWEEBIER	DYKING	DYSPEPSIA
DURN	DUSTMAN	DWEEBIEST	DYNAMETER	DYSPEPSIAS
DURNDEST	DUSTMEN	DWEEBISH	DYNAMETERS	DYSPEPSIES
DURNED	DUSTOFF	DWEEBS	DYNAMIC	DYSPEPSY
DURNEDER	DUSTOFFS	DWEEBY	DYNAMICAL	DYSPEPTIC
DURNEDEST	DUSTPAN	DWELL	DYNAMICS	DYSPEPTICS
DURNING	DUSTPANS	DWELLED	DYNAMISM	DYSPHAGIA
DURNS	DUSTPROOF	DWELLER	DYNAMISMS	DYSPHAGIAS
DURO	DUSTRAG	DWELLERS	DYNAMIST	DYSPHAGIC
DUROC	DUSTRAGS	DWELLING	DYNAMISTS	DYSPHASIA
DUROCS	DUSTS	DWELLINGS	DYNAMITE	DYSPHASIAS
DUROMETER	DUSTSTORM	DWELLS	DYNAMITED	DYSPHASIC
DUROMETERS	DUSTSTORMS	DWELT	DYNAMITER	DYSPHASICS
DUROS	DUSTUP	DWINDLE	DYNAMITERS	DYSPHONIA
DURR	DUSTUPS	DWINDLED	DYNAMITES	DYSPHONIAS
DURRA	DUSTY	DWINDLES	DYNAMITIC	DYSPHONIC
DURRAS	DUTCH	DWINDLING	DYNAMITING	DYSPHORIA
DURRIE	DUTCHMAN	DWINE	DYNAMO	DYSPHORIAS
DURRIES	DUTCHMEN	DWINED	DYNAMOS	DYSPHORIC
DURRS	DUTEOUS	DWINES	DYNAMOTOR	DYSPLASIA
DURST	DUTEOUSLY	DWINING	DYNAMOTORS	DYSPLASIAS
DURUM	DUTIABLE	DYABLE	DYNAST	DYSPNEA
DURUMS	DUTIES	DYAD	DYNASTIC	DYSPNEAL
DUSK	DUTIFUL	DYADIC	DYNASTIES	DYSPNEAS
DUSKED	DUTIFULLY	DYADICS	DYNASTS	DYSPNEIC
DUSKIER	DUTY	DYADS	DYNASTY	DYSPNOEA
DUSKIEST	DUUMVIR	DYARCHIC	DYNATRON	DYSPNOEAS
DUSKILY	DUUMVIRI	DYARCHIES	DYNATRONS	DYSPNOIC
DUSKINESS	DUUMVIRS	DYARCHY	DYNE	DYSTAXIA
DUSKINESSES	DUVET	DYBBUK	DYNEIN	DYSTAXIAS

DYSTHYMIA
DYSTHYMIAS
DYSTHYMIC
DYSTHYMICS
DYSTOCIA
DYSTOCIAS
DYSTONIA
DYSTONIAS
DYSTONIC
DYSTOPIA
DYSTOPIAN
DYSTOPIAS
DYSTROPHIES
DYSTROPHY
DYSURIA
DYSURIAS
DYSURIC
DYVOUR
DYVOURS

E

EACH
EAGER
EAGERER
EAGEREST
EAGERLY
EAGERNESS
EAGERNESSES
EAGERS
EAGLE
EAGLED
EAGLES
EAGLET
EAGLETS
EAGLEWOOD
EAGLEWOODS
EAGLING
EAGRE
EAGRES
EALDORMAN
EALDORMEN
EANLING
EANLINGS
EAR
EARACHE
EARACHES
EARBUD
EARBUDS
EARDROP

EARDROPS
EARDRUM
EARDRUMS
EARED
EARFLAP
EARFLAPS
EARFUL
EARFULS
EARING
EARINGS
EARL
EARLAP
EARLAPS
EARLDOM
EARLDOMS
EARLESS
EARLIER
EARLIEST
EARLINESS
EARLINESSES
EARLOBE
EARLOBES
EARLOCK
EARLOCKS
EARLS
EARLSHIP
EARLSHIPS
EARLY
EARLYWOOD
EARLYWOODS
EARMARK
EARMARKED
EARMARKING
EARMARKS
EARMUFF
EARMUFFS
EARN
EARNED
EARNER
EARNERS
EARNEST
EARNESTLY
EARNESTS
EARNING
EARNINGS
EARNS
EARPHONE
EARPHONES
EARPIECE
EARPIECES
EARPLUG
EARPLUGS

EARRING
EARRINGED
EARRINGS
EARS
EARSHOT
EARSHOTS
EARSTONE
EARSTONES
EARTH
EARTHBORN
EARTHED
EARTHEN
EARTHIER
EARTHIEST
EARTHILY
EARTHING
EARTHLIER
EARTHLIEST
EARTHLIKE
EARTHLING
EARTHLINGS
EARTHLY
EARTHMAN
EARTHMEN
EARTHNUT
EARTHNUTS
EARTHPEA
EARTHPEAS
EARTHRISE
EARTHRISES
EARTHS
EARTHSET
EARTHSETS
EARTHSTAR
EARTHSTARS
EARTHWARD
EARTHWORK
EARTHWORKS
EARTHWORM
EARTHWORMS
EARTHY
EARWAX
EARWAXES
EARWIG
EARWIGGED
EARWIGGING
EARWIGS
EARWORM
EARWORMS
EASE
EASED
EASEFUL

EASEFULLY
EASEL
EASELED
EASELS
EASEMENT
EASEMENTS
EASES
EASIER
EASIES
EASIEST
EASILY
EASINESS
EASINESSES
EASING
EAST
EASTBOUND
EASTER
EASTERLIES
EASTERLY
EASTERN
EASTERNER
EASTERNERS
EASTERS
EASTING
EASTINGS
EASTS
EASTWARD
EASTWARDS
EASY
EASYGOING
EAT
EATABLE
EATABLES
EATEN
EATER
EATERIES
EATERS
EATERY
EATH
EATING
EATINGS
EATS
EAU
EAUX
EAVE
EAVED
EAVES
EAVESDROP
EAVESDROPPED
EAVESDROPPING
EAVESDROPS
EBB

EBBED
EBBET
EBBETS
EBBING
EBBS
EBON
EBONICS
EBONIES
EBONISE
EBONISED
EBONISES
EBONISING
EBONITE
EBONITES
EBONIZE
EBONIZED
EBONIZES
EBONIZING
EBONS
EBONY
EBOOK
EBOOKS
EBULLIENT
ECARTE
ECARTES
ECAUDATE
ECBOLIC
ECBOLICS
ECCENTRIC
ECCENTRICS
ECCLESIA
ECCLESIAE
ECCLESIAL
ECCRINE
ECDYSES
ECDYSIAL
ECDYSIAST
ECDYSIASTS
ECDYSIS
ECDYSON
ECDYSONE
ECDYSONES
ECDYSONS
ECESIC
ECESIS
ECESISES
ECHARD
ECHARDS
ECHE
ECHED
ECHELLE
ECHELLES

ECHELON
ECHELONED
ECHELONING
ECHELONS
ECHES
ECHEVERIA
ECHEVERIAS
ECHIDNA
ECHIDNAE
ECHIDNAS
ECHINACEA
ECHINACEAS
ECHINATE
ECHINATED
ECHING
ECHINI
ECHINOID
ECHINOIDS
ECHINUS
ECHIUROID
ECHIUROIDS
ECHO
ECHOED
ECHOER
ECHOERS
ECHOES
ECHOEY
ECHOGRAM
ECHOGRAMS
ECHOIC
ECHOING
ECHOISM
ECHOISMS
ECHOLALIA
ECHOLALIAS
ECHOLALIC
ECHOLESS
ECHOS
ECHOVIRUS
ECHOVIRUSES
ECHT
ECLAIR
ECLAIRS
ECLAMPSIA
ECLAMPSIAS
ECLAMPTIC
ECLAT
ECLATS
ECLECTIC
ECLECTICS
ECLIPSE
ECLIPSED

ECLIPSER
ECLIPSERS
ECLIPSES
ECLIPSING
ECLIPSIS
ECLIPSISES
ECLIPTIC
ECLIPTICS
ECLOGITE
ECLOGITES
ECLOGUE
ECLOGUES
ECLOSION
ECLOSIONS
ECOCIDAL
ECOCIDE
ECOCIDES
ECOFREAK
ECOFREAKS
ECOLOGIC
ECOLOGIES
ECOLOGIST
ECOLOGISTS
ECOLOGY
ECONOBOX
ECONOBOXES
ECONOMIC
ECONOMICS
ECONOMIES
ECONOMISE
ECONOMISED
ECONOMISES
ECONOMISING
ECONOMIST
ECONOMISTS
ECONOMIZE
ECONOMIZED
ECONOMIZES
ECONOMIZING
ECONOMY
ECOSPHERE
ECOSPHERES
ECOSYSTEM
ECOSYSTEMS
ECOTAGE
ECOTAGES
ECOTONAL
ECOTONE
ECOTONES
ECOTOUR
ECOTOURS
ECOTYPE

ECOTYPES
ECOTYPIC
ECRASEUR
ECRASEURS
ECRU
ECRUS
ECSTASIES
ECSTASY
ECSTATIC
ECSTATICS
ECTASES
ECTASIS
ECTATIC
ECTHYMA
ECTHYMATA
ECTOBLAST
ECTOBLASTS
ECTODERM
ECTODERMS
ECTOGENIC
ECTOMERE
ECTOMERES
ECTOMERIC
ECTOMORPH
ECTOMORPHS
ECTOPIA
ECTOPIAS
ECTOPIC
ECTOPLASM
ECTOPLASMS
ECTOPROCT
ECTOPROCTS
ECTOSARC
ECTOSARCS
ECTOTHERM
ECTOTHERMS
ECTOZOA
ECTOZOAN
ECTOZOANS
ECTOZOON
ECTYPAL
ECTYPE
ECTYPES
ECU
ECUMENIC
ECUMENICS
ECUMENISM
ECUMENISMS
ECUMENIST
ECUMENISTS
ECUS
ECZEMA

ECZEMAS
ED
EDACIOUS
EDACITIES
EDACITY
EDAPHIC
EDDIED
EDDIES
EDDO
EDDOES
EDDY
EDDYING
EDELWEISS
EDELWEISSES
EDEMA
EDEMAS
EDEMATA
EDEMATOSE
EDEMATOUS
EDENIC
EDENTATE
EDENTATES
EDGE
EDGED
EDGELESS
EDGER
EDGERS
EDGES
EDGEWAYS
EDGEWISE
EDGIER
EDGIEST
EDGILY
EDGINESS
EDGINESSES
EDGING
EDGINGS
EDGY
EDH
EDHS
EDIBILITIES
EDIBILITY
EDIBLE
EDIBLES
EDICT
EDICTAL
EDICTALLY
EDICTS
EDIFICE
EDIFICES
EDIFICIAL
EDIFIED

EDIFIER
EDIFIERS
EDIFIES
EDIFY
EDIFYING
EDILE
EDILES
EDIT
EDITABLE
EDITED
EDITING
EDITION
EDITIONS
EDITOR
EDITORIAL
EDITORIALS
EDITORS
EDITRESS
EDITRESSES
EDITRICES
EDITRIX
EDITRIXES
EDITS
EDS
EDUCABLE
EDUCABLES
EDUCATE
EDUCATED
EDUCATES
EDUCATING
EDUCATION
EDUCATIONS
EDUCATIVE
EDUCATOR
EDUCATORS
EDUCATORY
EDUCE
EDUCED
EDUCES
EDUCIBLE
EDUCING
EDUCT
EDUCTION
EDUCTIONS
EDUCTIVE
EDUCTOR
EDUCTORS
EDUCTS
EEK
EEL
EELGRASS
EELGRASSES

EELIER	EFFLUVIA	EGGER	EH	EJECTING
EELIEST	EFFLUVIAL	EGGERS	EIDE	EJECTION
EELLIKE	EFFLUVIUM	EGGFRUIT	EIDER	EJECTIONS
EELPOUT	EFFLUVIUMS	EGGFRUITS	EIDERDOWN	EJECTIVE
EELPOUTS	EFFLUX	EGGHEAD	EIDERDOWNS	EJECTIVES
EELS	EFFLUXES	EGGHEADED	EIDERS	EJECTMENT
EELWORM	EFFLUXION	EGGHEADS	EIDETIC	EJECTMENTS
EELWORMS	EFFLUXIONS	EGGING	EIDOLA	EJECTOR
EELY	EFFORT	EGGLESS	EIDOLIC	EJECTORS
EERIE	EFFORTFUL	EGGNOG	EIDOLON	EJECTS
EERIER	EFFORTS	EGGNOGS	EIDOLONS	EKE
EERIEST	EFFS	EGGPLANT	EIDOS	EKED
EERILY	EFFULGE	EGGPLANTS	EIGENMODE	EKES
EERINESS	EFFULGED	EGGS	EIGENMODES	EKING
EERINESSES	EFFULGENT	EGGSHELL	EIGHT	EKISTIC
EERY	EFFULGES	EGGSHELLS	EIGHTBALL	EKISTICAL
EF	EFFULGING	EGGY	EIGHTBALLS	EKISTICS
EFF	EFFUSE	EGIS	EIGHTEEN	EKPWELE
EFFABLE	EFFUSED	EGISES	EIGHTEENS	EKPWELES
EFFACE	EFFUSES	EGLANTINE	EIGHTFOLD	EKTEXINE
EFFACED	EFFUSING	EGLANTINES	EIGHTH	EKTEXINES
EFFACER	EFFUSION	EGLATERE	EIGHTHLY	EKUELE
EFFACERS	EFFUSIONS	EGLATERES	EIGHTHS	EL
EFFACES	EFFUSIVE	EGLOMISE	EIGHTIES	ELABORATE
EFFACING	EFS	EGO	EIGHTIETH	ELABORATED
EFFECT	EFT	EGOISM	EIGHTIETHS	ELABORATES
EFFECTED	EFTS	EGOISMS	EIGHTS	ELABORATING
EFFECTER	EFTSOON	EGOIST	EIGHTVO	ELAIN
EFFECTERS	EFTSOONS	EGOISTIC	EIGHTVOS	ELAINS
EFFECTING	EGAD	EGOISTS	EIGHTY	ELAN
EFFECTIVE	EGADS	EGOLESS	EIKON	ELAND
EFFECTIVES	EGAL	EGOMANIA	EIKONES	ELANDS
EFFECTOR	EGALITE	EGOMANIAC	EIKONS	ELANS
EFFECTORS	EGALITES	EGOMANIACS	EINKORN	ELAPHINE
EFFECTS	EGER	EGOMANIAS	EINKORNS	ELAPID
EFFECTUAL	EGERS	EGOS	EINSTEIN	ELAPIDS
EFFENDI	EGEST	EGOTISM	EINSTEINS	ELAPINE
EFFENDIS	EGESTA	EGOTISMS	EIRENIC	ELAPSE
EFFERENT	EGESTED	EGOTIST	EIRENICAL	ELAPSED
EFFERENTS	EGESTING	EGOTISTIC	EISEGESES	ELAPSES
EFFETE	EGESTION	EGOTISTS	EISEGESIS	ELAPSING
EFFETELY	EGESTIONS	EGREGIOUS	EISWEIN	ELASTASE
EFFICACIES	EGESTIVE	EGRESS	EISWEINS	ELASTASES
EFFICACY	EGESTS	EGRESSED	EITHER	ELASTIC
EFFICIENT	EGG	EGRESSES	EJACULATE	ELASTICS
EFFIGIAL	EGGAR	EGRESSING	EJACULATED	ELASTIN
EFFIGIES	EGGARS	EGRESSION	EJACULATES	ELASTINS
EFFIGY	EGGBEATER	EGRESSIONS	EJACULATING	ELASTOMER
EFFLUENCE	EGGBEATERS	EGRET	EJECT	ELASTOMERS
EFFLUENCES	EGGCUP	EGRETS	EJECTA	ELATE
EFFLUENT	EGGCUPS	EGYPTIAN	EJECTABLE	ELATED
EFFLUENTS	EGGED	EGYPTIANS	EJECTED	ELATEDLY

ELATER
ELATERID
ELATERIDS
ELATERIN
ELATERINS
ELATERITE
ELATERITES
ELATERIUM
ELATERIUMS
ELATERS
ELATES
ELATING
ELATION
ELATIONS
ELATIVE
ELATIVES
ELBOW
ELBOWED
ELBOWING
ELBOWROOM
ELBOWROOMS
ELBOWS
ELD
ELDER
ELDERCARE
ELDERCARES
ELDERLIES
ELDERLY
ELDERS
ELDERSHIP
ELDERSHIPS
ELDEST
ELDRESS
ELDRESSES
ELDRICH
ELDRITCH
ELDS
ELECT
ELECTABLE
ELECTED
ELECTEE
ELECTEES
ELECTING
ELECTION
ELECTIONS
ELECTIVE
ELECTIVES
ELECTOR
ELECTORAL
ELECTORS
ELECTRESS
ELECTRESSES

ELECTRET
ELECTRETS
ELECTRIC
ELECTRICS
ELECTRIFIED
ELECTRIFIES
ELECTRIFY
ELECTRIFYING
ELECTRO
ELECTRODE
ELECTRODES
ELECTROED
ELECTROING
ELECTRON
ELECTRONS
ELECTROS
ELECTRUM
ELECTRUMS
ELECTS
ELECTUARIES
ELECTUARY
ELEDOISIN
ELEDOISINS
ELEGANCE
ELEGANCES
ELEGANCIES
ELEGANCY
ELEGANT
ELEGANTLY
ELEGIAC
ELEGIACAL
ELEGIACS
ELEGIES
ELEGISE
ELEGISED
ELEGISES
ELEGISING
ELEGIST
ELEGISTS
ELEGIT
ELEGITS
ELEGIZE
ELEGIZED
ELEGIZES
ELEGIZING
ELEGY
ELEMENT
ELEMENTAL
ELEMENTALS
ELEMENTS
ELEMI
ELEMIS

ELENCHI
ELENCHIC
ELENCHTIC
ELENCHUS
ELENCTIC
ELEOPTENE
ELEOPTENES
ELEPHANT
ELEPHANTS
ELEVATE
ELEVATED
ELEVATEDS
ELEVATES
ELEVATING
ELEVATION
ELEVATIONS
ELEVATOR
ELEVATORS
ELEVEN
ELEVENS
ELEVENSES
ELEVENTH
ELEVENTHS
ELEVON
ELEVONS
ELF
ELFIN
ELFINS
ELFISH
ELFISHLY
ELFLIKE
ELFLOCK
ELFLOCKS
ELHI
ELICIT
ELICITED
ELICITING
ELICITOR
ELICITORS
ELICITS
ELIDE
ELIDED
ELIDES
ELIDIBLE
ELIDING
ELIGIBLE
ELIGIBLES
ELIGIBLY
ELIMINATE
ELIMINATED
ELIMINATES
ELIMINATING

ELINT
ELINTS
ELISION
ELISIONS
ELITE
ELITES
ELITISM
ELITISMS
ELITIST
ELITISTS
ELIXIR
ELIXIRS
ELK
ELKHOUND
ELKHOUNDS
ELKS
ELL
ELLIPSE
ELLIPSES
ELLIPSIS
ELLIPSOID
ELLIPSOIDS
ELLIPTIC
ELLS
ELM
ELMIER
ELMIEST
ELMS
ELMY
ELOCUTION
ELOCUTIONS
ELODEA
ELODEAS
ELOIGN
ELOIGNED
ELOIGNER
ELOIGNERS
ELOIGNING
ELOIGNS
ELOIN
ELOINED
ELOINER
ELOINERS
ELOINING
ELOINMENT
ELOINMENTS
ELOINS
ELONGATE
ELONGATED
ELONGATES
ELONGATING
ELOPE

ELOPED
ELOPEMENT
ELOPEMENTS
ELOPER
ELOPERS
ELOPES
ELOPING
ELOQUENCE
ELOQUENCES
ELOQUENT
ELS
ELSE
ELSEWHERE
ELUANT
ELUANTS
ELUATE
ELUATES
ELUCIDATE
ELUCIDATED
ELUCIDATES
ELUCIDATING
ELUDE
ELUDED
ELUDER
ELUDERS
ELUDES
ELUDING
ELUENT
ELUENTS
ELUSION
ELUSIONS
ELUSIVE
ELUSIVELY
ELUSORY
ELUTE
ELUTED
ELUTES
ELUTING
ELUTION
ELUTIONS
ELUTRIATE
ELUTRIATED
ELUTRIATES
ELUTRIATING
ELUVIA
ELUVIAL
ELUVIATE
ELUVIATED
ELUVIATES
ELUVIATING
ELUVIUM
ELUVIUMS

ELVER
ELVERS
ELVES
ELVISH
ELVISHLY
ELYSIAN
ELYTRA
ELYTROID
ELYTRON
ELYTROUS
ELYTRUM
EM
EMACIATE
EMACIATED
EMACIATES
EMACIATING
EMAIL
EMAILED
EMAILING
EMAILS
EMALANGENI
EMANANT
EMANATE
EMANATED
EMANATES
EMANATING
EMANATION
EMANATIONS
EMANATIVE
EMANATOR
EMANATORS
EMBALM
EMBALMED
EMBALMER
EMBALMERS
EMBALMING
EMBALMS
EMBANK
EMBANKED
EMBANKING
EMBANKS
EMBAR
EMBARGO
EMBARGOED
EMBARGOES
EMBARGOING
EMBARK
EMBARKED
EMBARKING
EMBARKS
EMBARRASS
EMBARRASSED

EMBARRASSES
EMBARRASSING
EMBARRED
EMBARRING
EMBARS
EMBASSAGE
EMBASSAGES
EMBASSIES
EMBASSY
EMBATTLE
EMBATTLED
EMBATTLES
EMBATTLING
EMBAY
EMBAYED
EMBAYING
EMBAYMENT
EMBAYMENTS
EMBAYS
EMBED
EMBEDDED
EMBEDDING
EMBEDDINGS
EMBEDMENT
EMBEDMENTS
EMBEDS
EMBELLISH
EMBELLISHED
EMBELLISHES
EMBELLISHING
EMBER
EMBERS
EMBEZZLE
EMBEZZLED
EMBEZZLER
EMBEZZLERS
EMBEZZLES
EMBEZZLING
EMBITTER
EMBITTERED
EMBITTERING
EMBITTERS
EMBLAZE
EMBLAZED
EMBLAZER
EMBLAZERS
EMBLAZES
EMBLAZING
EMBLAZON
EMBLAZONED
EMBLAZONING
EMBLAZONS

EMBLEM
EMBLEMED
EMBLEMING
EMBLEMIZE
EMBLEMIZED
EMBLEMIZES
EMBLEMIZING
EMBLEMS
EMBODIED
EMBODIER
EMBODIERS
EMBODIES
EMBODY
EMBODYING
EMBOLDEN
EMBOLDENED
EMBOLDENING
EMBOLDENS
EMBOLI
EMBOLIC
EMBOLIES
EMBOLISM
EMBOLISMS
EMBOLUS
EMBOLY
EMBORDER
EMBORDERED
EMBORDERING
EMBORDERS
EMBOSK
EMBOSKED
EMBOSKING
EMBOSKS
EMBOSOM
EMBOSOMED
EMBOSOMING
EMBOSOMS
EMBOSS
EMBOSSED
EMBOSSER
EMBOSSERS
EMBOSSES
EMBOSSING
EMBOW
EMBOWED
EMBOWEL
EMBOWELED
EMBOWELING
EMBOWELLED
EMBOWELLING
EMBOWELS
EMBOWER

EMBOWERED
EMBOWERING
EMBOWERS
EMBOWING
EMBOWS
EMBRACE
EMBRACED
EMBRACEOR
EMBRACEORS
EMBRACER
EMBRACERIES
EMBRACERS
EMBRACERY
EMBRACES
EMBRACING
EMBRACIVE
EMBRANGLE
EMBRANGLED
EMBRANGLES
EMBRANGLING
EMBRASURE
EMBRASURES
EMBRITTLE
EMBRITTLED
EMBRITTLES
EMBRITTLING
EMBROCATE
EMBROCATED
EMBROCATES
EMBROCATING
EMBROGLIO
EMBROGLIOS
EMBROIDER
EMBROIDERED
EMBROIDERING
EMBROIDERS
EMBROIL
EMBROILED
EMBROILER
EMBROILERS
EMBROILING
EMBROILS
EMBROWN
EMBROWNED
EMBROWNING
EMBROWNS
EMBRUE
EMBRUED
EMBRUES
EMBRUING
EMBRUTE
EMBRUTED

EMBRUTES
EMBRUTING
EMBRYO
EMBRYOID
EMBRYOIDS
EMBRYON
EMBRYONAL
EMBRYONIC
EMBRYONS
EMBRYOS
EMBRYOTIC
EMCEE
EMCEED
EMCEEING
EMCEES
EMDASH
EMDASHES
EME
EMEER
EMEERATE
EMEERATES
EMEERS
EMEND
EMENDABLE
EMENDATE
EMENDATED
EMENDATES
EMENDATING
EMENDATOR
EMENDATORS
EMENDED
EMENDER
EMENDERS
EMENDING
EMENDS
EMERALD
EMERALDS
EMERGE
EMERGED
EMERGENCE
EMERGENCES
EMERGENCIES
EMERGENCY
EMERGENT
EMERGENTS
EMERGES
EMERGING
EMERIES
EMERITA
EMERITAE
EMERITAS
EMERITI

EMERITUS	EMITTERS	EMPATHIZED	EMPORIUMS	EMULSIFYING
EMEROD	EMITTING	EMPATHIZES	EMPOWER	EMULSION
EMERODS	EMMER	EMPATHIZING	EMPOWERED	EMULSIONS
EMEROID	EMMERS	EMPATHY	EMPOWERING	EMULSIVE
EMEROIDS	EMMET	EMPENNAGE	EMPOWERS	EMULSOID
EMERSED	EMMETROPE	EMPENNAGES	EMPRESS	EMULSOIDS
EMERSION	EMMETROPES	EMPERIES	EMPRESSES	EMUNCTORIES
EMERSIONS	EMMETS	EMPEROR	EMPRISE	EMUNCTORY
EMERY	EMMY	EMPERORS	EMPRISES	EMUS
EMES	EMMYS	EMPERY	EMPRIZE	EMYD
EMESES	EMODIN	EMPHASES	EMPRIZES	EMYDE
EMESIS	EMODINS	EMPHASIS	EMPTIABLE	EMYDES
EMETIC	EMOLLIENT	EMPHASISE	EMPTIED	EMYDS
EMETICS	EMOLLIENTS	EMPHASISED	EMPTIER	EN
EMETIN	EMOLUMENT	EMPHASISES	EMPTIERS	ENABLE
EMETINE	EMOLUMENTS	EMPHASISING	EMPTIES	ENABLED
EMETINES	EMOTE	EMPHASIZE	EMPTIEST	ENABLER
EMETINS	EMOTED	EMPHASIZED	EMPTILY	ENABLERS
EMEU	EMOTER	EMPHASIZES	EMPTINESS	ENABLES
EMEUS	EMOTERS	EMPHASIZING	EMPTINESSES	ENABLING
EMEUTE	EMOTES	EMPHATIC	EMPTINGS	ENACT
EMEUTES	EMOTICON	EMPHYSEMA	EMPTINS	ENACTABLE
EMIC	EMOTICONS	EMPHYSEMAS	EMPTY	ENACTED
EMIGRANT	EMOTING	EMPIRE	EMPTYING	ENACTING
EMIGRANTS	EMOTION	EMPIRES	EMPURPLE	ENACTIVE
EMIGRATE	EMOTIONAL	EMPIRIC	EMPURPLED	ENACTMENT
EMIGRATED	EMOTIONS	EMPIRICAL	EMPURPLES	ENACTMENTS
EMIGRATES	EMOTIVE	EMPIRICS	EMPURPLING	ENACTOR
EMIGRATING	EMOTIVELY	EMPLACE	EMPYEMA	ENACTORS
EMIGRE	EMOTIVITIES	EMPLACED	EMPYEMAS	ENACTORY
EMIGRES	EMOTIVITY	EMPLACES	EMPYEMATA	ENACTS
EMINENCE	EMPALE	EMPLACING	EMPYEMIC	ENALAPRIL
EMINENCES	EMPALED	EMPLANE	EMPYREAL	ENALAPRILS
EMINENCIES	EMPALER	EMPLANED	EMPYREAN	ENAMEL
EMINENCY	EMPALERS	EMPLANES	EMPYREANS	ENAMELED
EMINENT	EMPALES	EMPLANING	EMS	ENAMELER
EMINENTLY	EMPALING	EMPLOY	EMU	ENAMELERS
EMIR	EMPANADA	EMPLOYE	EMULATE	ENAMELING
EMIRATE	EMPANADAS	EMPLOYED	EMULATED	ENAMELIST
EMIRATES	EMPANEL	EMPLOYEE	EMULATES	ENAMELISTS
EMIRS	EMPANELED	EMPLOYEES	EMULATING	ENAMELLED
EMISSARIES	EMPANELING	EMPLOYER	EMULATION	ENAMELLER
EMISSARY	EMPANELLED	EMPLOYERS	EMULATIONS	ENAMELLERS
EMISSION	EMPANELLING	EMPLOYES	EMULATIVE	ENAMELLING
EMISSIONS	EMPANELS	EMPLOYING	EMULATOR	ENAMELS
EMISSIVE	EMPATHIC	EMPLOYS	EMULATORS	ENAMINE
EMIT	EMPATHIES	EMPOISON	EMULOUS	ENAMINES
EMITS	EMPATHISE	EMPOISONED	EMULOUSLY	ENAMOR
EMITTANCE	EMPATHISED	EMPOISONING	EMULSIBLE	ENAMORED
EMITTANCES	EMPATHISES	EMPOISONS	EMULSIFIED	ENAMORING
EMITTED	EMPATHISING	EMPORIA	EMULSIFIES	ENAMORS
EMITTER	EMPATHIZE	EMPORIUM	EMULSIFY	ENAMOUR

ENAMOURED	ENCHILADAS	ENCOUNTER	ENDARCH	ENDOCARP
ENAMOURING	ENCHORIAL	ENCOUNTERED	ENDARCHIES	ENDOCARPS
ENAMOURS	ENCHORIC	ENCOUNTERING	ENDARCHY	ENDOCAST
ENATE	ENCINA	ENCOUNTERS	ENDASH	ENDOCASTS
ENATES	ENCINAL	ENCOURAGE	ENDASHES	ENDOCRINE
ENATIC	ENCINAS	ENCOURAGED	ENDBRAIN	ENDOCRINES
ENATION	ENCIPHER	ENCOURAGES	ENDBRAINS	ENDOCYTIC
ENATIONS	ENCIPHERED	ENCOURAGING	ENDEAR	ENDODERM
ENCAENIA	ENCIPHERING	ENCRIMSON	ENDEARED	ENDODERMS
ENCAGE	ENCIPHERS	ENCRIMSONED	ENDEARING	ENDOERGIC
ENCAGED	ENCIRCLE	ENCRIMSONING	ENDEARS	ENDOGAMIC
ENCAGES	ENCIRCLED	ENCRIMSONS	ENDEAVOR	ENDOGAMIES
ENCAGING	ENCIRCLES	ENCRINITE	ENDEAVORED	ENDOGAMY
ENCAMP	ENCIRCLING	ENCRINITES	ENDEAVORING	ENDOGEN
ENCAMPED	ENCLASP	ENCROACH	ENDEAVORS	ENDOGENIC
ENCAMPING	ENCLASPED	ENCROACHED	ENDEAVOUR	ENDOGENIES
ENCAMPS	ENCLASPING	ENCROACHES	ENDEAVOURED	ENDOGENS
ENCAPSULE	ENCLASPS	ENCROACHING	ENDEAVOURING	ENDOGENY
ENCAPSULED	ENCLAVE	ENCRUST	ENDEAVOURS	ENDOLYMPH
ENCAPSULES	ENCLAVED	ENCRUSTED	ENDED	ENDOLYMPHS
ENCAPSULING	ENCLAVES	ENCRUSTING	ENDEMIAL	ENDOMIXIS
ENCASE	ENCLAVING	ENCRUSTS	ENDEMIC	ENDOMIXISES
ENCASED	ENCLITIC	ENCRYPT	ENDEMICAL	ENDOMORPH
ENCASES	ENCLITICS	ENCRYPTED	ENDEMICS	ENDOMORPHS
ENCASH	ENCLOSE	ENCRYPTING	ENDEMISM	ENDOPHYTE
ENCASHED	ENCLOSED	ENCRYPTS	ENDEMISMS	ENDOPHYTES
ENCASHES	ENCLOSER	ENCUMBER	ENDER	ENDOPLASM
ENCASHING	ENCLOSERS	ENCUMBERED	ENDERMIC	ENDOPLASMS
ENCASING	ENCLOSES	ENCUMBERING	ENDERS	ENDOPOD
ENCAUSTIC	ENCLOSING	ENCUMBERS	ENDEXINE	ENDOPODS
ENCAUSTICS	ENCLOSURE	ENCYCLIC	ENDEXINES	ENDOPROCT
ENCEINTE	ENCLOSURES	ENCYCLICS	ENDGAME	ENDOPROCTS
ENCEINTES	ENCODABLE	ENCYST	ENDGAMES	ENDORPHIN
ENCEPHALA	ENCODE	ENCYSTED	ENDING	ENDORPHINS
ENCEPHALON	ENCODED	ENCYSTING	ENDINGS	ENDORSE
ENCHAIN	ENCODER	ENCYSTS	ENDITE	ENDORSED
ENCHAINED	ENCODERS	END	ENDITED	ENDORSEE
ENCHAINING	ENCODES	ENDAMAGE	ENDITES	ENDORSEES
ENCHAINS	ENCODING	ENDAMAGED	ENDITING	ENDORSER
ENCHANT	ENCOMIA	ENDAMAGES	ENDIVE	ENDORSERS
ENCHANTED	ENCOMIAST	ENDAMAGING	ENDIVES	ENDORSES
ENCHANTER	ENCOMIASTS	ENDAMEBA	ENDLEAF	ENDORSING
ENCHANTERS	ENCOMIUM	ENDAMEBAE	ENDLEAFS	ENDORSIVE
ENCHANTING	ENCOMIUMS	ENDAMEBAS	ENDLEAVES	ENDORSOR
ENCHANTS	ENCOMPASS	ENDAMEBIC	ENDLESS	ENDORSORS
ENCHASE	ENCOMPASSED	ENDAMOEBA	ENDLESSLY	ENDOSARC
ENCHASED	ENCOMPASSES	ENDAMOEBAE	ENDLONG	ENDOSARCS
ENCHASER	ENCOMPASSING	ENDAMOEBAS	ENDMOST	ENDOSCOPE
ENCHASERS	ENCORE	ENDANGER	ENDNOTE	ENDOSCOPES
ENCHASES	ENCORED	ENDANGERED	ENDNOTES	ENDOSCOPIES
ENCHASING	ENCORES	ENDANGERING	ENDOBLAST	ENDOSCOPY
ENCHILADA	ENCORING	ENDANGERS	ENDOBLASTS	ENDOSMOS

ENDOSMOSES	ENDURING	ENFEVERED	ENGINEERS	ENGROSS
ENDOSOME	ENDURO	ENFEVERING	ENGINERIES	ENGROSSED
ENDOSOMES	ENDUROS	ENFEVERS	ENGINERY	ENGROSSER
ENDOSPERM	ENDWAYS	ENFILADE	ENGINES	ENGROSSERS
ENDOSPERMS	ENDWISE	ENFILADED	ENGINING	ENGROSSES
ENDOSPORE	ENEMA	ENFILADES	ENGINOUS	ENGROSSING
ENDOSPORES	ENEMAS	ENFILADING	ENGIRD	ENGS
ENDOSTEA	ENEMATA	ENFLAME	ENGIRDED	ENGULF
ENDOSTEAL	ENEMIES	ENFLAMED	ENGIRDING	ENGULFED
ENDOSTEUM	ENEMY	ENFLAMES	ENGIRDLE	ENGULFING
ENDOSTYLE	ENERGETIC	ENFLAMING	ENGIRDLED	ENGULFS
ENDOSTYLES	ENERGID	ENFOLD	ENGIRDLES	ENHALO
ENDOTHERM	ENERGIDS	ENFOLDED	ENGIRDLING	ENHALOED
ENDOTHERMS	ENERGIES	ENFOLDER	ENGIRDS	ENHALOES
ENDOTOXIC	ENERGISE	ENFOLDERS	ENGIRT	ENHALOING
ENDOTOXIN	ENERGISED	ENFOLDING	ENGLACIAL	ENHALOS
ENDOTOXINS	ENERGISES	ENFOLDS	ENGLISH	ENHANCE
ENDOW	ENERGISING	ENFORCE	ENGLISHED	ENHANCED
ENDOWED	ENERGIZE	ENFORCED	ENGLISHES	ENHANCER
ENDOWER	ENERGIZED	ENFORCER	ENGLISHING	ENHANCERS
ENDOWERS	ENERGIZER	ENFORCERS	ENGLUT	ENHANCES
ENDOWING	ENERGIZERS	ENFORCES	ENGLUTS	ENHANCING
ENDOWMENT	ENERGIZES	ENFORCING	ENGLUTTED	ENHANCIVE
ENDOWMENTS	ENERGIZING	ENFRAME	ENGLUTTING	ENIGMA
ENDOWS	ENERGUMEN	ENFRAMED	ENGORGE	ENIGMAS
ENDOZOIC	ENERGUMENS	ENFRAMES	ENGORGED	ENIGMATA
ENDPAPER	ENERGY	ENFRAMING	ENGORGES	ENIGMATIC
ENDPAPERS	ENERVATE	ENG	ENGORGING	ENISLE
ENDPLATE	ENERVATED	ENGAGE	ENGRAFT	ENISLED
ENDPLATES	ENERVATES	ENGAGED	ENGRAFTED	ENISLES
ENDPLAY	ENERVATING	ENGAGEDLY	ENGRAFTING	ENISLING
ENDPLAYED	ENERVATOR	ENGAGER	ENGRAFTS	ENJAMBED
ENDPLAYING	ENERVATORS	ENGAGERS	ENGRAIL	ENJOIN
ENDPLAYS	ENFACE	ENGAGES	ENGRAILED	ENJOINDER
ENDPOINT	ENFACED	ENGAGING	ENGRAILING	ENJOINDERS
ENDPOINTS	ENFACES	ENGARLAND	ENGRAILS	ENJOINED
ENDRIN	ENFACING	ENGARLANDED	ENGRAIN	ENJOINER
ENDRINS	ENFEEBLE	ENGARLANDING	ENGRAINED	ENJOINERS
ENDS	ENFEEBLED	ENGARLANDS	ENGRAINING	ENJOINING
ENDUE	ENFEEBLER	ENGENDER	ENGRAINS	ENJOINS
ENDUED	ENFEEBLERS	ENGENDERED	ENGRAM	ENJOY
ENDUES	ENFEEBLES	ENGENDERING	ENGRAMME	ENJOYABLE
ENDUING	ENFEEBLING	ENGENDERS	ENGRAMMES	ENJOYABLY
ENDURABLE	ENFEOFF	ENGILD	ENGRAMMIC	ENJOYED
ENDURABLY	ENFEOFFED	ENGILDED	ENGRAMS	ENJOYER
ENDURANCE	ENFEOFFING	ENGILDING	ENGRAVE	ENJOYERS
ENDURANCES	ENFEOFFS	ENGILDS	ENGRAVED	ENJOYING
ENDURE	ENFETTER	ENGINE	ENGRAVER	ENJOYMENT
ENDURED	ENFETTERED	ENGINED	ENGRAVERS	ENJOYMENTS
ENDURER	ENFETTERING	ENGINEER	ENGRAVES	ENJOYS
ENDURERS	ENFETTERS	ENGINEERED	ENGRAVING	ENKINDLE
ENDURES	ENFEVER	ENGINEERING	ENGRAVINGS	ENKINDLED

ENKINDLER	ENNUYEE	ENRAVISH	ENSHEATHES	ENSORCELLING
ENKINDLERS	ENOKI	ENRAVISHED	ENSHEATHING	ENSORCELLS
ENKINDLES	ENOKIDAKE	ENRAVISHES	ENSHEATHS	ENSORCELS
ENKINDLING	ENOKIDAKES	ENRAVISHING	ENSHRINE	ENSOUL
ENLACE	ENOKIS	ENRICH	ENSHRINED	ENSOULED
ENLACED	ENOKITAKE	ENRICHED	ENSHRINEE	ENSOULING
ENLACES	ENOKITAKES	ENRICHER	ENSHRINEES	ENSOULS
ENLACING	ENOL	ENRICHERS	ENSHRINES	ENSPHERE
ENLARGE	ENOLASE	ENRICHES	ENSHRINING	ENSPHERED
ENLARGED	ENOLASES	ENRICHING	ENSHROUD	ENSPHERES
ENLARGER	ENOLIC	ENROBE	ENSHROUDED	ENSPHERING
ENLARGERS	ENOLOGIES	ENROBED	ENSHROUDING	ENSTATITE
ENLARGES	ENOLOGIST	ENROBER	ENSHROUDS	ENSTATITES
ENLARGING	ENOLOGISTS	ENROBERS	ENSIFORM	ENSUE
ENLIGHTEN	ENOLOGY	ENROBES	ENSIGN	ENSUED
ENLIGHTENED	ENOLS	ENROBING	ENSIGNCIES	ENSUES
ENLIGHTENING	ENOPHILE	ENROL	ENSIGNCY	ENSUING
ENLIGHTENS	ENOPHILES	ENROLL	ENSIGNS	ENSURE
ENLIST	ENORM	ENROLLED	ENSILAGE	ENSURED
ENLISTED	ENORMITIES	ENROLLEE	ENSILAGED	ENSURER
ENLISTEE	ENORMITY	ENROLLEES	ENSILAGES	ENSURERS
ENLISTEES	ENORMOUS	ENROLLER	ENSILAGING	ENSURES
ENLISTER	ENOSIS	ENROLLERS	ENSILE	ENSURING
ENLISTERS	ENOSISES	ENROLLING	ENSILED	ENSWATHE
ENLISTING	ENOUGH	ENROLLS	ENSILES	ENSWATHED
ENLISTS	ENOUGHS	ENROLMENT	ENSILING	ENSWATHES
ENLIVEN	ENOUNCE	ENROLMENTS	ENSKIED	ENSWATHING
ENLIVENED	ENOUNCED	ENROLS	ENSKIES	ENTAIL
ENLIVENER	ENOUNCES	ENROOT	ENSKY	ENTAILED
ENLIVENERS	ENOUNCING	ENROOTED	ENSKYED	ENTAILER
ENLIVENING	ENOW	ENROOTING	ENSKYING	ENTAILERS
ENLIVENS	ENOWS	ENROOTS	ENSLAVE	ENTAILING
ENMESH	ENPLANE	ENS	ENSLAVED	ENTAILS
ENMESHED	ENPLANED	ENSAMPLE	ENSLAVER	ENTAMEBA
ENMESHES	ENPLANES	ENSAMPLES	ENSLAVERS	ENTAMEBAE
ENMESHING	ENPLANING	ENSCONCE	ENSLAVES	ENTAMEBAS
ENMITIES	ENQUIRE	ENSCONCED	ENSLAVING	ENTAMOEBA
ENMITY	ENQUIRED	ENSCONCES	ENSNARE	ENTAMOEBAE
ENNEAD	ENQUIRES	ENSCONCING	ENSNARED	ENTAMOEBAS
ENNEADIC	ENQUIRIES	ENSCROLL	ENSNARER	ENTANGLE
ENNEADS	ENQUIRING	ENSCROLLED	ENSNARERS	ENTANGLED
ENNEAGON	ENQUIRY	ENSCROLLING	ENSNARES	ENTANGLER
ENNEAGONS	ENRAGE	ENSCROLLS	ENSNARING	ENTANGLERS
ENNOBLE	ENRAGED	ENSEMBLE	ENSNARL	ENTANGLES
ENNOBLED	ENRAGEDLY	ENSEMBLES	ENSNARLED	ENTANGLING
ENNOBLER	ENRAGES	ENSERF	ENSNARLING	ENTASES
ENNOBLERS	ENRAGING	ENSERFED	ENSNARLS	ENTASIA
ENNOBLES	ENRAPT	ENSERFING	ENSORCEL	ENTASIAS
ENNOBLING	ENRAPTURE	ENSERFS	ENSORCELED	ENTASIS
ENNUI	ENRAPTURED	ENSHEATH	ENSORCELING	ENTASTIC
ENNUIS	ENRAPTURES	ENSHEATHE	ENSORCELL	ENTELECHIES
ENNUYE	ENRAPTURING	ENSHEATHED	ENSORCELLED	ENTELECHY

ENTELLUS	ENTIRELY	ENTRAPPING	ENUMERATING	ENVY
ENTELLUSES	ENTIRES	ENTRAPS	ENUNCIATE	ENVYING
ENTENTE	ENTIRETIES	ENTREAT	ENUNCIATED	ENVYINGLY
ENTENTES	ENTIRETY	ENTREATED	ENUNCIATES	ENWHEEL
ENTER	ENTITIES	ENTREATIES	ENUNCIATING	ENWHEELED
ENTERA	ENTITLE	ENTREATING	ENURE	ENWHEELING
ENTERABLE	ENTITLED	ENTREATS	ENURED	ENWHEELS
ENTERAL	ENTITLES	ENTREATY	ENURES	ENWIND
ENTERALLY	ENTITLING	ENTRECHAT	ENURESES	ENWINDING
ENTERED	ENTITY	ENTRECHATS	ENURESIS	ENWINDS
ENTERER	ENTOBLAST	ENTRECOTE	ENURESISES	ENWOMB
ENTERERS	ENTOBLASTS	ENTRECOTES	ENURETIC	ENWOMBED
ENTERIC	ENTODERM	ENTREE	ENURETICS	ENWOMBING
ENTERICS	ENTODERMS	ENTREES	ENURING	ENWOMBS
ENTERING	ENTOIL	ENTREMETS	ENVELOP	ENWOUND
ENTERITIDES	ENTOILED	ENTRENCH	ENVELOPE	ENWRAP
ENTERITIS	ENTOILING	ENTRENCHED	ENVELOPED	ENWRAPPED
ENTERITISES	ENTOILS	ENTRENCHES	ENVELOPER	ENWRAPPING
ENTERON	ENTOMB	ENTRENCHING	ENVELOPERS	ENWRAPS
ENTERONS	ENTOMBED	ENTREPOT	ENVELOPES	ENWREATHE
ENTERS	ENTOMBING	ENTREPOTS	ENVELOPING	ENWREATHED
ENTERTAIN	ENTOMBS	ENTRESOL	ENVELOPS	ENWREATHES
ENTERTAINED	ENTOPHYTE	ENTRESOLS	ENVENOM	ENWREATHING
ENTERTAINING	ENTOPHYTES	ENTRIES	ENVENOMED	ENZOOTIC
ENTERTAINS	ENTOPIC	ENTROPIC	ENVENOMING	ENZOOTICS
ENTHALPIES	ENTOPROCT	ENTROPIES	ENVENOMS	ENZYM
ENTHALPY	ENTOPROCTS	ENTROPION	ENVIABLE	ENZYMATIC
ENTHETIC	ENTOURAGE	ENTROPIONS	ENVIABLY	ENZYME
ENTHRAL	ENTOURAGES	ENTROPY	ENVIED	ENZYMES
ENTHRALL	ENTOZOA	ENTRUST	ENVIER	ENZYMIC
ENTHRALLED	ENTOZOAL	ENTRUSTED	ENVIERS	ENZYMS
ENTHRALLING	ENTOZOAN	ENTRUSTING	ENVIES	EOBIONT
ENTHRALLS	ENTOZOANS	ENTRUSTS	ENVIOUS	EOBIONTS
ENTHRALS	ENTOZOIC	ENTRY	ENVIOUSLY	EOCENE
ENTHRONE	ENTOZOON	ENTRYWAY	ENVIRO	EOHIPPUS
ENTHRONED	ENTRAILS	ENTRYWAYS	ENVIRON	EOHIPPUSES
ENTHRONES	ENTRAIN	ENTWINE	ENVIRONED	EOLIAN
ENTHRONING	ENTRAINED	ENTWINED	ENVIRONING	EOLIPILE
ENTHUSE	ENTRAINER	ENTWINES	ENVIRONS	EOLIPILES
ENTHUSED	ENTRAINERS	ENTWINING	ENVIROS	EOLITH
ENTHUSES	ENTRAINING	ENTWIST	ENVISAGE	EOLITHIC
ENTHUSING	ENTRAINS	ENTWISTED	ENVISAGED	EOLITHS
ENTHYMEME	ENTRANCE	ENTWISTING	ENVISAGES	EOLOPILE
ENTHYMEMES	ENTRANCED	ENTWISTS	ENVISAGING	EOLOPILES
ENTIA	ENTRANCES	ENUCLEATE	ENVISION	EON
ENTICE	ENTRANCING	ENUCLEATED	ENVISIONED	EONIAN
ENTICED	ENTRANT	ENUCLEATES	ENVISIONING	EONISM
ENTICER	ENTRANTS	ENUCLEATING	ENVISIONS	EONISMS
ENTICERS	ENTRAP	ENUF	ENVOI	EONS
ENTICES	ENTRAPPED	ENUMERATE	ENVOIS	EOSIN
ENTICING	ENTRAPPER	ENUMERATED	ENVOY	EOSINE
ENTIRE	ENTRAPPERS	ENUMERATES	ENVOYS	EOSINES

EOSINIC	EPHOD	EPIDEMICS	EPILATORS	EPISTASES
EOSINS	EPHODS	EPIDERM	EPILEPSIES	EPISTASIES
EPACT	EPHOR	EPIDERMAL	EPILEPSY	EPISTASIS
EPACTS	EPHORAL	EPIDERMIC	EPILEPTIC	EPISTASY
EPARCH	EPHORATE	EPIDERMIS	EPILEPTICS	EPISTATIC
EPARCHIAL	EPHORATES	EPIDERMISES	EPILIMNIA	EPISTAXES
EPARCHIES	EPHORI	EPIDERMS	EPILIMNION	EPISTAXIS
EPARCHS	EPHORS	EPIDOTE	EPILOG	EPISTEMIC
EPARCHY	EPIBLAST	EPIDOTES	EPILOGS	EPISTERNA
EPAULET	EPIBLASTS	EPIDOTIC	EPILOGUE	EPISTERNUM
EPAULETS	EPIBOLIC	EPIDURAL	EPILOGUED	EPISTLE
EPAULETTE	EPIBOLIES	EPIDURALS	EPILOGUES	EPISTLER
EPAULETTES	EPIBOLY	EPIFAUNA	EPILOGUING	EPISTLERS
EPAZOTE	EPIC	EPIFAUNAE	EPIMER	EPISTLES
EPAZOTES	EPICAL	EPIFAUNAL	EPIMERASE	EPISTOLER
EPEE	EPICALLY	EPIFAUNAS	EPIMERASES	EPISTOLERS
EPEEIST	EPICALYCES	EPIFOCAL	EPIMERE	EPISTOME
EPEEISTS	EPICALYX	EPIGEAL	EPIMERES	EPISTOMES
EPEES	EPICALYXES	EPIGEAN	EPIMERIC	EPISTYLE
EPEIRIC	EPICANTHI	EPIGEIC	EPIMERS	EPISTYLES
EPENDYMA	EPICANTHUS	EPIGENE	EPIMYSIA	EPITAPH
EPENDYMAS	EPICARDIA	EPIGENIC	EPIMYSIUM	EPITAPHIC
EPERGNE	EPICARDIUM	EPIGENIST	EPINAOI	EPITAPHS
EPERGNES	EPICARP	EPIGENISTS	EPINAOS	EPITASES
EPHA	EPICARPS	EPIGENOUS	EPINASTIC	EPITASIS
EPHAH	EPICEDIA	EPIGEOUS	EPINASTIES	EPITAXIAL
EPHAHS	EPICEDIUM	EPIGON	EPINASTY	EPITAXIC
EPHAS	EPICENE	EPIGONE	EPINEURIA	EPITAXIES
EPHEBE	EPICENES	EPIGONES	EPINEURIUM	EPITAXY
EPHEBES	EPICENISM	EPIGONI	EPIPHANIC	EPITHELIA
EPHEBI	EPICENISMS	EPIGONIC	EPIPHANIES	EPITHELIUM
EPHEBIC	EPICENTER	EPIGONISM	EPIPHANY	EPITHELIUMS
EPHEBOI	EPICENTERS	EPIGONISMS	EPIPHRAGM	EPITHET
EPHEBOS	EPICENTRA	EPIGONOUS	EPIPHRAGMS	EPITHETIC
EPHEBUS	EPICENTRUM	EPIGONS	EPIPHYSES	EPITHETS
EPHEDRA	EPICLIKE	EPIGONUS	EPIPHYSIS	EPITOME
EPHEDRAS	EPICOTYL	EPIGRAM	EPIPHYTE	EPITOMES
EPHEDRIN	EPICOTYLS	EPIGRAMS	EPIPHYTES	EPITOMIC
EPHEDRINE	EPICRANIA	EPIGRAPH	EPIPHYTIC	EPITOMISE
EPHEDRINES	EPICRANIUM	EPIGRAPHIES	EPIROGENIES	EPITOMISED
EPHEDRINS	EPICRITIC	EPIGRAPHS	EPIROGENY	EPITOMISES
EPHEMERA	EPICS	EPIGRAPHY	EPISCIA	EPITOMISING
EPHEMERAE	EPICURE	EPIGYNIES	EPISCIAS	EPITOMIZE
EPHEMERAL	EPICUREAN	EPIGYNOUS	EPISCOPAL	EPITOMIZED
EPHEMERALS	EPICUREANS	EPIGYNY	EPISCOPE	EPITOMIZES
EPHEMERAS	EPICURES	EPILATE	EPISCOPES	EPITOMIZING
EPHEMERID	EPICURISM	EPILATED	EPISODE	EPITOPE
EPHEMERIDES	EPICURISMS	EPILATES	EPISODES	EPITOPES
EPHEMERIDS	EPICYCLE	EPILATING	EPISODIC	EPIZOA
EPHEMERIS	EPICYCLES	EPILATION	EPISOMAL	EPIZOIC
EPHEMERON	EPICYCLIC	EPILATIONS	EPISOME	EPIZOISM
EPHEMERONS	EPIDEMIC	EPILATOR	EPISOMES	EPIZOISMS

EPIZOITE	EQUALIZE	EQUITANT	ERELONG	ERISTIC
EPIZOITES	EQUALIZED	EQUITES	EREMITE	ERISTICAL
EPIZOON	EQUALIZER	EQUITIES	EREMITES	ERISTICS
EPIZOOTIC	EQUALIZERS	EQUITY	EREMITIC	ERLKING
EPIZOOTICS	EQUALIZES	EQUIVOCAL	EREMITISH	ERLKINGS
EPIZOOTIES	EQUALIZING	EQUIVOKE	EREMITISM	ERMINE
EPIZOOTY	EQUALLED	EQUIVOKES	EREMITISMS	ERMINED
EPOCH	EQUALLING	EQUIVOQUE	EREMURI	ERMINES
EPOCHAL	EQUALLY	EQUIVOQUES	EREMURUS	ERN
EPOCHALLY	EQUALS	ER	EREMURUSES	ERNE
EPOCHS	EQUATABLE	ERA	ERENOW	ERNES
EPODE	EQUATE	ERADIATE	EREPSIN	ERNS
EPODES	EQUATED	ERADIATED	EREPSINS	ERODABLE
EPONYM	EQUATES	ERADIATES	ERETHIC	ERODE
EPONYMIC	EQUATING	ERADIATING	ERETHISM	ERODED
EPONYMIES	EQUATION	ERADICANT	ERETHISMS	ERODENT
EPONYMOUS	EQUATIONS	ERADICANTS	ERETHITIC	ERODES
EPONYMS	EQUATOR	ERADICATE	EREWHILE	ERODIBLE
EPONYMY	EQUATORS	ERADICATED	EREWHILES	ERODING
EPOPEE	EQUERRIES	ERADICATES	ERG	EROGENIC
EPOPEES	EQUERRY	ERADICATING	ERGASTIC	EROGENOUS
EPOPOEIA	EQUID	ERAS	ERGATE	EROS
EPOPOEIAS	EQUIDS	ERASABLE	ERGATES	EROSE
EPOS	EQUIMOLAL	ERASE	ERGATIVE	EROSELY
EPOSES	EQUIMOLAR	ERASED	ERGATIVES	EROSES
EPOXIDE	EQUINE	ERASER	ERGO	EROSIBLE
EPOXIDES	EQUINELY	ERASERS	ERGODIC	EROSION
EPOXIDIZE	EQUINES	ERASES	ERGOGENIC	EROSIONAL
EPOXIDIZED	EQUINITIES	ERASING	ERGOGRAPH	EROSIONS
EPOXIDIZES	EQUINITY	ERASION	ERGOGRAPHS	EROSIVE
EPOXIDIZING	EQUINOX	ERASIONS	ERGOMETER	EROSIVITIES
EPOXIED	EQUINOXES	ERASURE	ERGOMETERS	EROSIVITY
EPOXIES	EQUIP	ERASURES	ERGOMETRIES	EROTIC
EPOXY	EQUIPAGE	ERBIUM	ERGOMETRY	EROTICA
EPOXYED	EQUIPAGES	ERBIUMS	ERGONOMIC	EROTICAL
EPOXYING	EQUIPMENT	ERE	ERGOT	EROTICISM
EPSILON	EQUIPMENTS	ERECT	ERGOTIC	EROTICISMS
EPSILONIC	EQUIPOISE	ERECTABLE	ERGOTISM	EROTICIST
EPSILONS	EQUIPOISED	ERECTED	ERGOTISMS	EROTICISTS
EQUABLE	EQUIPOISES	ERECTER	ERGOTIZED	EROTICIZE
EQUABLY	EQUIPOISING	ERECTERS	ERGOTS	EROTICIZED
EQUAL	EQUIPPED	ERECTILE	ERGS	EROTICIZES
EQUALED	EQUIPPER	ERECTING	ERICA	EROTICIZING
EQUALING	EQUIPPERS	ERECTION	ERICAS	EROTICS
EQUALISE	EQUIPPING	ERECTIONS	ERICOID	EROTISM
EQUALISED	EQUIPS	ERECTIVE	ERIGERON	EROTISMS
EQUALISER	EQUISETA	ERECTLY	ERIGERONS	EROTIZE
EQUALISERS	EQUISETIC	ERECTNESS	ERINGO	EROTIZED
EQUALISES	EQUISETUM	ERECTNESSES	ERINGOES	EROTIZES
EQUALISING	EQUISETUMS	ERECTOR	ERINGOS	EROTIZING
EQUALITIES	EQUITABLE	ERECTORS	ERIOPHYID	ERR
EQUALITY	EQUITABLY	ERECTS	ERIOPHYIDS	ERRABLE

ERRANCIES	ERUPTIVE	ESCAPISM	ESERINE	ESQUIRES
ERRANCY	ERUPTIVES	ESCAPISMS	ESERINES	ESQUIRING
ERRAND	ERUPTS	ESCAPIST	ESES	ESS
ERRANDS	ERVIL	ESCAPISTS	ESKAR	ESSAY
ERRANT	ERVILS	ESCAR	ESKARS	ESSAYED
ERRANTLY	ERYNGO	ESCARGOT	ESKER	ESSAYER
ERRANTRIES	ERYNGOES	ESCARGOTS	ESKERS	ESSAYERS
ERRANTRY	ERYNGOS	ESCAROLE	ESNE	ESSAYING
ERRANTS	ERYTHEMA	ESCAROLES	ESNES	ESSAYIST
ERRATA	ERYTHEMAS	ESCARP	ESOPHAGI	ESSAYISTS
ERRATAS	ERYTHEMIC	ESCARPED	ESOPHAGUS	ESSAYS
ERRATIC	ERYTHRISM	ESCARPING	ESOTERIC	ESSENCE
ERRATICAL	ERYTHRISMS	ESCARPS	ESOTERICA	ESSENCES
ERRATICS	ERYTHRITE	ESCARS	ESOTROPIA	ESSENTIAL
ERRATUM	ERYTHRITES	ESCHALOT	ESOTROPIAS	ESSENTIALS
ERRED	ERYTHROID	ESCHALOTS	ESOTROPIC	ESSES
ERRHINE	ERYTHRON	ESCHAR	ESPALIER	ESSOIN
ERRHINES	ERYTHRONS	ESCHARS	ESPALIERED	ESSOINS
ERRING	ES	ESCHEAT	ESPALIERING	ESSONITE
ERRINGLY	ESCALADE	ESCHEATED	ESPALIERS	ESSONITES
ERRONEOUS	ESCALADED	ESCHEATING	ESPANOL	ESTABLISH
ERROR	ESCALADER	ESCHEATOR	ESPANOLES	ESTABLISHED
ERRORLESS	ESCALADERS	ESCHEATORS	ESPARTO	ESTABLISHES
ERRORS	ESCALADES	ESCHEATS	ESPARTOS	ESTABLISHING
ERRS	ESCALADING	ESCHEW	ESPECIAL	ESTAMINET
ERS	ESCALATE	ESCHEWAL	ESPERANCE	ESTAMINETS
ERSATZ	ESCALATED	ESCHEWALS	ESPERANCES	ESTANCIA
ERSATZES	ESCALATES	ESCHEWED	ESPIAL	ESTANCIAS
ERSES	ESCALATING	ESCHEWER	ESPIALS	ESTATE
ERST	ESCALATOR	ESCHEWERS	ESPIED	ESTATED
ERSTWHILE	ESCALATORS	ESCHEWING	ESPIEGLE	ESTATES
ERUCT	ESCALLOP	ESCHEWS	ESPIES	ESTATING
ERUCTATE	ESCALLOPED	ESCOLAR	ESPIONAGE	ESTEEM
ERUCTATED	ESCALLOPING	ESCOLARS	ESPIONAGES	ESTEEMED
ERUCTATES	ESCALLOPS	ESCORT	ESPLANADE	ESTEEMING
ERUCTATING	ESCALOP	ESCORTED	ESPLANADES	ESTEEMS
ERUCTED	ESCALOPE	ESCORTING	ESPOUSAL	ESTER
ERUCTING	ESCALOPED	ESCORTS	ESPOUSALS	ESTERASE
ERUCTS	ESCALOPES	ESCOT	ESPOUSE	ESTERASES
ERUDITE	ESCALOPING	ESCOTED	ESPOUSED	ESTERIFIED
ERUDITELY	ESCALOPS	ESCOTING	ESPOUSER	ESTERIFIES
ERUDITION	ESCAPABLE	ESCOTS	ESPOUSERS	ESTERIFY
ERUDITIONS	ESCAPADE	ESCROW	ESPOUSES	ESTERIFYING
ERUGO	ESCAPADES	ESCROWED	ESPOUSING	ESTERS
ERUGOS	ESCAPE	ESCROWING	ESPRESSO	ESTHESES
ERUMPENT	ESCAPED	ESCROWS	ESPRESSOS	ESTHESIA
ERUPT	ESCAPEE	ESCUAGE	ESPRIT	ESTHESIAS
ERUPTED	ESCAPEES	ESCUAGES	ESPRITS	ESTHESIS
ERUPTIBLE	ESCAPER	ESCUDO	ESPY	ESTHESISES
ERUPTING	ESCAPERS	ESCUDOS	ESPYING	ESTHETE
ERUPTION	ESCAPES	ESCULENT	ESQUIRE	ESTHETES
ERUPTIONS	ESCAPING	ESCULENTS	ESQUIRED	ESTHETIC

ESTHETICS	ESTROUS	ETERNIZE	ETHNARCH	ETOILE
ESTIMABLE	ESTRUAL	ETERNIZED	ETHNARCHIES	ETOILES
ESTIMABLY	ESTRUM	ETERNIZES	ETHNARCHS	ETOUFFEE
ESTIMATE	ESTRUMS	ETERNIZING	ETHNARCHY	ETOUFFEES
ESTIMATED	ESTRUS	ETESIAN	ETHNIC	ETUDE
ESTIMATES	ESTRUSES	ETESIANS	ETHNICAL	ETUDES
ESTIMATING	ESTUARIAL	ETH	ETHNICITIES	ETUI
ESTIMATOR	ESTUARIES	ETHANE	ETHNICITY	ETUIS
ESTIMATORS	ESTUARINE	ETHANES	ETHNICS	ETWEE
ESTIVAL	ESTUARY	ETHANOL	ETHNOLOGIES	ETWEES
ESTIVATE	ESURIENCE	ETHANOLS	ETHNOLOGY	ETYMA
ESTIVATED	ESURIENCES	ETHENE	ETHNONYM	ETYMOLOGIES
ESTIVATES	ESURIENCIES	ETHENES	ETHNONYMS	ETYMOLOGY
ESTIVATING	ESURIENCY	ETHEPHON	ETHNOS	ETYMON
ESTIVATOR	ESURIENT	ETHEPHONS	ETHNOSES	ETYMONS
ESTIVATORS	ET	ETHER	ETHOGRAM	EUCAINE
ESTOP	ETA	ETHEREAL	ETHOGRAMS	EUCAINES
ESTOPPAGE	ETAGERE	ETHERIC	ETHOLOGIES	EUCALYPT
ESTOPPAGES	ETAGERES	ETHERIFIED	ETHOLOGY	EUCALYPTI
ESTOPPED	ETALON	ETHERIFIES	ETHOS	EUCALYPTS
ESTOPPEL	ETALONS	ETHERIFY	ETHOSES	EUCALYPTUS
ESTOPPELS	ETAMIN	ETHERIFYING	ETHOXIES	EUCALYPTUSES
ESTOPPING	ETAMINE	ETHERISH	ETHOXY	EUCARYOTE
ESTOPS	ETAMINES	ETHERIZE	ETHOXYL	EUCARYOTES
ESTOVERS	ETAMINS	ETHERIZED	ETHOXYLS	EUCHARIS
ESTRADIOL	ETAPE	ETHERIZER	ETHS	EUCHARISES
ESTRADIOLS	ETAPES	ETHERIZERS	ETHYL	EUCHRE
ESTRAGON	ETAS	ETHERIZES	ETHYLATE	EUCHRED
ESTRAGONS	ETATISM	ETHERIZING	ETHYLATED	EUCHRES
ESTRAL	ETATISMS	ETHERS	ETHYLATES	EUCHRING
ESTRANGE	ETATIST	ETHIC	ETHYLATING	EUCLASE
ESTRANGED	ETCETERA	ETHICAL	ETHYLENE	EUCLASES
ESTRANGER	ETCETERAS	ETHICALLY	ETHYLENES	EUCLIDEAN
ESTRANGERS	ETCH	ETHICALS	ETHYLENIC	EUCLIDIAN
ESTRANGES	ETCHANT	ETHICIAN	ETHYLIC	EUCRITE
ESTRANGING	ETCHANTS	ETHICIANS	ETHYLS	EUCRITES
ESTRAY	ETCHED	ETHICIST	ETHYNE	EUCRITIC
ESTRAYED	ETCHER	ETHICISTS	ETHYNES	EUDAEMON
ESTRAYING	ETCHERS	ETHICIZE	ETHYNYL	EUDAEMONS
ESTRAYS	ETCHES	ETHICIZED	ETHYNYLS	EUDAIMON
ESTREAT	ETCHING	ETHICIZES	ETIC	EUDAIMONS
ESTREATED	ETCHINGS	ETHICIZING	ETIOLATE	EUDEMON
ESTREATING	ETERNAL	ETHICS	ETIOLATED	EUDEMONIA
ESTREATS	ETERNALLY	ETHINYL	ETIOLATES	EUDEMONIAS
ESTRIN	ETERNALS	ETHINYLS	ETIOLATING	EUDEMONS
ESTRINS	ETERNE	ETHION	ETIOLOGIC	EUGENIA
ESTRIOL	ETERNISE	ETHIONINE	ETIOLOGIES	EUGENIAS
ESTRIOLS	ETERNISED	ETHIONINES	ETIOLOGY	EUGENIC
ESTROGEN	ETERNISES	ETHIONS	ETIQUETTE	EUGENICAL
ESTROGENS	ETERNISING	ETHMOID	ETIQUETTES	EUGENICS
ESTRONE	ETERNITIES	ETHMOIDAL	ETNA	EUGENIST
ESTRONES	ETERNITY	ETHMOIDS	ETNAS	EUGENISTS

EUGENOL	EUPHEMISED	EURIPUS	EVACUATED	EVEN
EUGENOLS	EUPHEMISES	EURO	EVACUATES	EVENED
EUGLENA	EUPHEMISING	EUROKIES	EVACUATING	EVENER
EUGLENAS	EUPHEMISM	EUROKOUS	EVACUATOR	EVENERS
EUGLENID	EUPHEMISMS	EUROKY	EVACUATORS	EVENEST
EUGLENIDS	EUPHEMIST	EUROPIUM	EVACUEE	EVENFALL
EUGLENOID	EUPHEMISTS	EUROPIUMS	EVACUEES	EVENFALLS
EUGLENOIDS	EUPHEMIZE	EUROS	EVADABLE	EVENING
EUKARYOTE	EUPHEMIZED	EURYBATH	EVADE	EVENINGS
EUKARYOTES	EUPHEMIZES	EURYBATHS	EVADED	EVENLY
EULACHAN	EUPHEMIZING	EURYOKIES	EVADER	EVENNESS
EULACHANS	EUPHENIC	EURYOKOUS	EVADERS	EVENNESSES
EULACHON	EUPHENICS	EURYOKY	EVADES	EVENS
EULACHONS	EUPHONIC	EURYTHERM	EVADIBLE	EVENSONG
EULOGIA	EUPHONIES	EURYTHERMS	EVADING	EVENSONGS
EULOGIAE	EUPHONIUM	EURYTHMIC	EVADINGLY	EVENT
EULOGIAS	EUPHONIUMS	EURYTHMIES	EVAGINATE	EVENTFUL
EULOGIES	EUPHONIZE	EURYTHMY	EVAGINATED	EVENTIDE
EULOGISE	EUPHONIZED	EURYTOPIC	EVAGINATES	EVENTIDES
EULOGISED	EUPHONIZES	EUSOCIAL	EVAGINATING	EVENTLESS
EULOGISES	EUPHONIZING	EUSTACIES	EVALUABLE	EVENTS
EULOGISING	EUPHONY	EUSTACY	EVALUATE	EVENTUAL
EULOGIST	EUPHORBIA	EUSTASIES	EVALUATED	EVENTUATE
EULOGISTS	EUPHORBIAS	EUSTASY	EVALUATES	EVENTUATED
EULOGIUM	EUPHORIA	EUSTATIC	EVALUATING	EVENTUATES
EULOGIUMS	EUPHORIAS	EUSTELE	EVALUATOR	EVENTUATING
EULOGIZE	EUPHORIC	EUSTELES	EVALUATORS	EVER
EULOGIZED	EUPHOTIC	EUTAXIES	EVANESCE	EVERGLADE
EULOGIZER	EUPHRASIES	EUTAXY	EVANESCED	EVERGLADES
EULOGIZERS	EUPHRASY	EUTECTIC	EVANESCES	EVERGREEN
EULOGIZES	EUPHROE	EUTECTICS	EVANESCING	EVERGREENS
EULOGIZING	EUPHROES	EUTECTOID	EVANGEL	EVERMORE
EULOGY	EUPHUISM	EUTECTOIDS	EVANGELIC	EVERSIBLE
EUNUCH	EUPHUISMS	EUTHANIZE	EVANGELS	EVERSION
EUNUCHISM	EUPHUIST	EUTHANIZED	EVANISH	EVERSIONS
EUNUCHISMS	EUPHUISTS	EUTHANIZES	EVANISHED	EVERT
EUNUCHOID	EUPLASTIC	EUTHANIZING	EVANISHES	EVERTED
EUNUCHOIDS	EUPLASTICS	EUTHENICS	EVANISHING	EVERTING
EUNUCHS	EUPLOID	EUTHENIST	EVAPORATE	EVERTOR
EUONYMUS	EUPLOIDIES	EUTHENISTS	EVAPORATED	EVERTORS
EUONYMUSES	EUPLOIDS	EUTHERIAN	EVAPORATES	EVERTS
EUPATRID	EUPLOIDY	EUTHERIANS	EVAPORATING	EVERWHERE
EUPATRIDAE	EUPNEA	EUTHYROID	EVAPORITE	EVERWHICH
EUPATRIDS	EUPNEAS	EUTHYROIDS	EVAPORITES	EVERY
EUPEPSIA	EUPNEIC	EUTROPHIC	EVASION	EVERYBODY
EUPEPSIAS	EUPNOEA	EUTROPHIES	EVASIONAL	EVERYDAY
EUPEPSIES	EUPNOEAS	EUTROPHY	EVASIONS	EVERYDAYS
EUPEPSY	EUPNOEIC	EUXENITE	EVASIVE	EVERYMAN
EUPEPTIC	EUREKA	EUXENITES	EVASIVELY	EVERYMEN
EUPHAUSID	EURHYTHMIES	EVACUANT	EVE	EVERYONE
EUPHAUSIDS	EURHYTHMY	EVACUANTS	EVECTION	EVERYWAY
EUPHEMISE	EURIPI	EVACUATE	EVECTIONS	EVES

EVICT	EVOLUTE	EXALTING	EXCELS	EXCITANT
EVICTED	EVOLUTES	EXALTS	EXCELSIOR	EXCITANTS
EVICTEE	EVOLUTION	EXAM	EXCELSIORS	EXCITE
EVICTEES	EVOLUTIONS	EXAMEN	EXCEPT	EXCITED
EVICTING	EVOLVABLE	EXAMENS	EXCEPTED	EXCITEDLY
EVICTION	EVOLVE	EXAMINANT	EXCEPTING	EXCITER
EVICTIONS	EVOLVED	EXAMINANTS	EXCEPTION	EXCITERS
EVICTOR	EVOLVER	EXAMINE	EXCEPTIONS	EXCITES
EVICTORS	EVOLVERS	EXAMINED	EXCEPTIVE	EXCITING
EVICTS	EVOLVES	EXAMINEE	EXCEPTS	EXCITON
EVIDENCE	EVOLVING	EXAMINEES	EXCERPT	EXCITONIC
EVIDENCED	EVONYMUS	EXAMINER	EXCERPTED	EXCITONS
EVIDENCES	EVONYMUSES	EXAMINERS	EXCERPTER	EXCITOR
EVIDENCING	EVULSE	EXAMINES	EXCERPTERS	EXCITORS
EVIDENT	EVULSED	EXAMINING	EXCERPTING	EXCLAIM
EVIDENTLY	EVULSES	EXAMPLE	EXCERPTOR	EXCLAIMED
EVIL	EVULSING	EXAMPLED	EXCERPTORS	EXCLAIMER
EVILDOER	EVULSION	EXAMPLES	EXCERPTS	EXCLAIMERS
EVILDOERS	EVULSIONS	EXAMPLING	EXCESS	EXCLAIMING
EVILDOING	EVZONE	EXAMS	EXCESSED	EXCLAIMS
EVILDOINGS	EVZONES	EXANIMATE	EXCESSES	EXCLAVE
EVILER	EWE	EXANTHEM	EXCESSING	EXCLAVES
EVILEST	EWER	EXANTHEMA	EXCESSIVE	EXCLOSURE
EVILLER	EWERS	EXANTHEMAS	EXCHANGE	EXCLOSURES
EVILLEST	EWES	EXANTHEMATA	EXCHANGED	EXCLUDE
EVILLY	EX	EXANTHEMS	EXCHANGER	EXCLUDED
EVILNESS	EXABYTE	EXAPTED	EXCHANGERS	EXCLUDER
EVILNESSES	EXABYTES	EXAPTIVE	EXCHANGES	EXCLUDERS
EVILS	EXACT	EXARCH	EXCHANGING	EXCLUDES
EVINCE	EXACTA	EXARCHAL	EXCHEQUER	EXCLUDING
EVINCED	EXACTABLE	EXARCHATE	EXCHEQUERS	EXCLUSION
EVINCES	EXACTAS	EXARCHATES	EXCIDE	EXCLUSIONS
EVINCIBLE	EXACTED	EXARCHIES	EXCIDED	EXCLUSIVE
EVINCING	EXACTER	EXARCHS	EXCIDES	EXCLUSIVES
EVINCIVE	EXACTERS	EXARCHY	EXCIDING	EXCLUSORY
EVITABLE	EXACTEST	EXCAUDATE	EXCIMER	EXCORIATE
EVITE	EXACTING	EXCAVATE	EXCIMERS	EXCORIATED
EVITED	EXACTION	EXCAVATED	EXCIPIENT	EXCORIATES
EVITES	EXACTIONS	EXCAVATES	EXCIPIENTS	EXCORIATING
EVITING	EXACTLY	EXCAVATING	EXCIPLE	EXCREMENT
EVOCABLE	EXACTNESS	EXCAVATOR	EXCIPLES	EXCREMENTS
EVOCATION	EXACTNESSES	EXCAVATORS	EXCISABLE	EXCRETA
EVOCATIONS	EXACTOR	EXCEED	EXCISE	EXCRETAL
EVOCATIVE	EXACTORS	EXCEEDED	EXCISED	EXCRETE
EVOCATOR	EXACTS	EXCEEDER	EXCISEMAN	EXCRETED
EVOCATORS	EXAHERTZ	EXCEEDERS	EXCISEMEN	EXCRETER
EVOKE	EXAHERTZES	EXCEEDING	EXCISES	EXCRETERS
EVOKED	EXALT	EXCEEDS	EXCISING	EXCRETES
EVOKER	EXALTED	EXCEL	EXCISION	EXCRETING
EVOKERS	EXALTEDLY	EXCELLED	EXCISIONS	EXCRETION
EVOKES	EXALTER	EXCELLENT	EXCITABLE	EXCRETIONS
EVOKING	EXALTERS	EXCELLING	EXCITABLY	EXCRETIVE

EXCRETORIES	EXEGESIS	EXFOLIATED	EXILER	EXOGENISMS
EXCRETORY	EXEGETE	EXFOLIATES	EXILERS	EXOGENOUS
EXCULPATE	EXEGETES	EXFOLIATING	EXILES	EXOGENS
EXCULPATED	EXEGETIC	EXHALANT	EXILIAN	EXON
EXCULPATES	EXEGETICS	EXHALANTS	EXILIC	EXONERATE
EXCULPATING	EXEGETIST	EXHALE	EXILING	EXONERATED
EXCURRENT	EXEGETISTS	EXHALED	EXIMIOUS	EXONERATES
EXCURSION	EXEMPLA	EXHALENT	EXINE	EXONERATING
EXCURSIONS	EXEMPLAR	EXHALENTS	EXINES	EXONIC
EXCURSIVE	EXEMPLARS	EXHALES	EXING	EXONS
EXCURSUS	EXEMPLARY	EXHALING	EXIST	EXONUMIA
EXCURSUSES	EXEMPLIFIED	EXHAUST	EXISTED	EXONUMIST
EXCUSABLE	EXEMPLIFIES	EXHAUSTED	EXISTENCE	EXONUMISTS
EXCUSABLY	EXEMPLIFY	EXHAUSTER	EXISTENCES	EXONYM
EXCUSE	EXEMPLIFYING	EXHAUSTERS	EXISTENT	EXONYMS
EXCUSED	EXEMPLUM	EXHAUSTING	EXISTENTS	EXORABLE
EXCUSER	EXEMPT	EXHAUSTS	EXISTING	EXORCISE
EXCUSERS	EXEMPTED	EXHEDRA	EXISTS	EXORCISED
EXCUSES	EXEMPTING	EXHEDRAE	EXIT	EXORCISER
EXCUSING	EXEMPTION	EXHIBIT	EXITED	EXORCISERS
EXEC	EXEMPTIONS	EXHIBITED	EXITING	EXORCISES
EXECRABLE	EXEMPTIVE	EXHIBITER	EXITLESS	EXORCISING
EXECRABLY	EXEMPTS	EXHIBITERS	EXITS	EXORCISM
EXECRATE	EXEQUATUR	EXHIBITING	EXOCARP	EXORCISMS
EXECRATED	EXEQUATURS	EXHIBITOR	EXOCARPS	EXORCIST
EXECRATES	EXEQUIAL	EXHIBITORS	EXOCRINE	EXORCISTS
EXECRATING	EXEQUIES	EXHIBITS	EXOCRINES	EXORCIZE
EXECRATOR	EXEQUY	EXHORT	EXOCYCLIC	EXORCIZED
EXECRATORS	EXERCISE	EXHORTED	EXOCYTIC	EXORCIZES
EXECS	EXERCISED	EXHORTER	EXOCYTOSE	EXORCIZING
EXECUTANT	EXERCISER	EXHORTERS	EXOCYTOSED	EXORDIA
EXECUTANTS	EXERCISERS	EXHORTING	EXOCYTOSES	EXORDIAL
EXECUTE	EXERCISES	EXHORTS	EXOCYTOSING	EXORDIUM
EXECUTED	EXERCISING	EXHUME	EXODERM	EXORDIUMS
EXECUTER	EXERCYCLE	EXHUMED	EXODERMIS	EXOSMIC
EXECUTERS	EXERCYCLES	EXHUMER	EXODERMISES	EXOSMOSE
EXECUTES	EXERGONIC	EXHUMERS	EXODERMS	EXOSMOSES
EXECUTING	EXERGUAL	EXHUMES	EXODOI	EXOSMOSIS
EXECUTION	EXERGUE	EXHUMING	EXODONTIA	EXOSMOTIC
EXECUTIONS	EXERGUES	EXIGENCE	EXODONTIAS	EXOSPHERE
EXECUTIVE	EXERT	EXIGENCES	EXODOS	EXOSPHERES
EXECUTIVES	EXERTED	EXIGENCIES	EXODUS	EXOSPORE
EXECUTOR	EXERTING	EXIGENCY	EXODUSES	EXOSPORES
EXECUTORS	EXERTION	EXIGENT	EXOENZYME	EXOSPORIA
EXECUTORY	EXERTIONS	EXIGENTLY	EXOENZYMES	EXOSPORIUM
EXECUTRICES	EXERTIVE	EXIGIBLE	EXOERGIC	EXOSTOSES
EXECUTRIX	EXERTS	EXIGUITIES	EXOGAMIC	EXOSTOSIS
EXECUTRIXES	EXES	EXIGUITY	EXOGAMIES	EXOTERIC
EXED	EXEUNT	EXIGUOUS	EXOGAMOUS	EXOTIC
EXEDRA	EXFOLIANT	EXILABLE	EXOGAMY	EXOTICA
EXEDRAE	EXFOLIANTS	EXILE	EXOGEN	EXOTICISM
EXEGESES	EXFOLIATE	EXILED	EXOGENISM	EXOTICISMS

EXOTICIST	EXPELLED	EXPLAINED	EXPOSALS	EXSCINDS
EXOTICISTS	EXPELLEE	EXPLAINER	EXPOSE	EXSECANT
EXOTICS	EXPELLEES	EXPLAINERS	EXPOSED	EXSECANTS
EXOTISM	EXPELLENT	EXPLAINING	EXPOSER	EXSECT
EXOTISMS	EXPELLENTS	EXPLAINS	EXPOSERS	EXSECTED
EXOTOXIC	EXPELLER	EXPLANT	EXPOSES	EXSECTING
EXOTOXIN	EXPELLERS	EXPLANTED	EXPOSING	EXSECTION
EXOTOXINS	EXPELLING	EXPLANTING	EXPOSIT	EXSECTIONS
EXOTROPIA	EXPELS	EXPLANTS	EXPOSITED	EXSECTS
EXOTROPIAS	EXPEND	EXPLETIVE	EXPOSITING	EXSERT
EXOTROPIC	EXPENDED	EXPLETIVES	EXPOSITOR	EXSERTED
EXPAND	EXPENDER	EXPLETORY	EXPOSITORS	EXSERTILE
EXPANDED	EXPENDERS	EXPLICATE	EXPOSITS	EXSERTING
EXPANDER	EXPENDING	EXPLICATED	EXPOSURE	EXSERTION
EXPANDERS	EXPENDS	EXPLICATES	EXPOSURES	EXSERTIONS
EXPANDING	EXPENSE	EXPLICATING	EXPOUND	EXSERTS
EXPANDOR	EXPENSED	EXPLICIT	EXPOUNDED	EXSICCATE
EXPANDORS	EXPENSES	EXPLICITS	EXPOUNDER	EXSICCATED
EXPANDS	EXPENSING	EXPLODE	EXPOUNDERS	EXSICCATES
EXPANSE	EXPENSIVE	EXPLODED	EXPOUNDING	EXSICCATING
EXPANSES	EXPERT	EXPLODER	EXPOUNDS	EXSTROPHIES
EXPANSILE	EXPERTED	EXPLODERS	EXPRESS	EXSTROPHY
EXPANSION	EXPERTING	EXPLODES	EXPRESSED	EXTANT
EXPANSIONS	EXPERTISE	EXPLODING	EXPRESSER	EXTEMPORE
EXPANSIVE	EXPERTISES	EXPLOIT	EXPRESSERS	EXTEND
EXPAT	EXPERTISM	EXPLOITED	EXPRESSES	EXTENDED
EXPATIATE	EXPERTISMS	EXPLOITER	EXPRESSING	EXTENDER
EXPATIATED	EXPERTIZE	EXPLOITERS	EXPRESSLY	EXTENDERS
EXPATIATES	EXPERTIZED	EXPLOITING	EXPRESSO	EXTENDING
EXPATIATING	EXPERTIZES	EXPLOITS	EXPRESSOS	EXTENDS
EXPATS	EXPERTIZING	EXPLORE	EXPULSE	EXTENSILE
EXPECT	EXPERTLY	EXPLORED	EXPULSED	EXTENSION
EXPECTANT	EXPERTS	EXPLORER	EXPULSES	EXTENSIONS
EXPECTANTS	EXPIABLE	EXPLORERS	EXPULSING	EXTENSITIES
EXPECTED	EXPIATE	EXPLORES	EXPULSION	EXTENSITY
EXPECTER	EXPIATED	EXPLORING	EXPULSIONS	EXTENSIVE
EXPECTERS	EXPIATES	EXPLOSION	EXPULSIVE	EXTENSOR
EXPECTING	EXPIATING	EXPLOSIONS	EXPUNGE	EXTENSORS
EXPECTS	EXPIATION	EXPLOSIVE	EXPUNGED	EXTENT
EXPEDIENT	EXPIATIONS	EXPLOSIVES	EXPUNGER	EXTENTS
EXPEDIENTS	EXPIATOR	EXPO	EXPUNGERS	EXTENUATE
EXPEDITE	EXPIATORS	EXPONENT	EXPUNGES	EXTENUATED
EXPEDITED	EXPIATORY	EXPONENTS	EXPUNGING	EXTENUATES
EXPEDITER	EXPIRE	EXPORT	EXPURGATE	EXTENUATING
EXPEDITERS	EXPIRED	EXPORTED	EXPURGATED	EXTERIOR
EXPEDITES	EXPIRER	EXPORTER	EXPURGATES	EXTERIORS
EXPEDITING	EXPIRERS	EXPORTERS	EXPURGATING	EXTERMINE
EXPEDITOR	EXPIRES	EXPORTING	EXQUISITE	EXTERMINED
EXPEDITORS	EXPIRIES	EXPORTS	EXQUISITES	EXTERMINES
EXPEL	EXPIRING	EXPOS	EXSCIND	EXTERMINING
EXPELLANT	EXPIRY	EXPOSABLE	EXSCINDED	EXTERN
EXPELLANTS	EXPLAIN	EXPOSAL	EXSCINDING	EXTERNAL

EXTERNALS	EXTRAVERTS	EXULTANCIES	EYEFULS	EYESTRAINS
EXTERNE	EXTREMA	EXULTANCY	EYEGLASS	EYETEETH
EXTERNES	EXTREME	EXULTANT	EYEGLASSES	EYETOOTH
EXTERNS	EXTREMELY	EXULTED	EYEHOLE	EYEWASH
EXTINCT	EXTREMER	EXULTING	EYEHOLES	EYEWASHES
EXTINCTED	EXTREMES	EXULTS	EYEHOOK	EYEWATER
EXTINCTING	EXTREMEST	EXURB	EYEHOOKS	EYEWATERS
EXTINCTS	EXTREMISM	EXURBAN	EYEING	EYEWEAR
EXTIRPATE	EXTREMISMS	EXURBIA	EYELASH	EYEWINK
EXTIRPATED	EXTREMIST	EXURBIAS	EYELASHES	EYEWINKS
EXTIRPATES	EXTREMISTS	EXURBS	EYELESS	EYING
EXTIRPATING	EXTREMITIES	EXUVIA	EYELET	EYNE
EXTOL	EXTREMITY	EXUVIAE	EYELETS	EYRA
EXTOLL	EXTREMUM	EXUVIAL	EYELETTED	EYRAS
EXTOLLED	EXTRICATE	EXUVIATE	EYELETTING	EYRE
EXTOLLER	EXTRICATED	EXUVIATED	EYELID	EYRES
EXTOLLERS	EXTRICATES	EXUVIATES	EYELIDS	EYRIE
EXTOLLING	EXTRICATING	EXUVIATING	EYELIFT	EYRIES
EXTOLLS	EXTRINSIC	EXUVIUM	EYELIFTS	EYRIR
EXTOLMENT	EXTRORSE	EYAS	EYELIKE	EYRY
EXTOLMENTS	EXTROVERT	EYASES	EYELINER	
EXTOLS	EXTROVERTS	EYASS	EYELINERS	
EXTORT	EXTRUDE	EYASSES	EYEN	
EXTORTED	EXTRUDED	EYE	EYEOPENER	
EXTORTER	EXTRUDER	EYEABLE	EYEOPENERS	
EXTORTERS	EXTRUDERS	EYEBALL	EYEPIECE	FA
EXTORTING	EXTRUDES	EYEBALLED	EYEPIECES	FAB
EXTORTION	EXTRUDING	EYEBALLING	EYEPOINT	FABACEOUS
EXTORTIONS	EXTRUSION	EYEBALLS	EYEPOINTS	FABBER
EXTORTIVE	EXTRUSIONS	EYEBAR	EYEPOPPER	FABBEST
EXTORTS	EXTRUSIVE	EYEBARS	EYEPOPPERS	FABLE
EXTRA	EXTUBATE	EYEBEAM	EYER	FABLED
EXTRABOLD	EXTUBATED	EYEBEAMS	EYERS	FABLER
EXTRABOLDS	EXTUBATES	EYEBLACK	EYES	FABLERS
EXTRACT	EXTUBATING	EYEBLACKS	EYESHADE	FABLES
EXTRACTED	EXUBERANT	EYEBLINK	EYESHADES	FABLIAU
EXTRACTING	EXUBERATE	EYEBLINKS	EYESHINE	FABLIAUX
EXTRACTOR	EXUBERATED	EYEBOLT	EYESHINES	FABLING
EXTRACTORS	EXUBERATES	EYEBOLTS	EYESHOT	FABRIC
EXTRACTS	EXUBERATING	EYEBRIGHT	EYESHOTS	FABRICANT
EXTRADITE	EXUDATE	EYEBRIGHTS	EYESIGHT	FABRICANTS
EXTRADITED	EXUDATES	EYEBROW	EYESIGHTS	FABRICATE
EXTRADITES	EXUDATION	EYEBROWS	EYESOME	FABRICATED
EXTRADITING	EXUDATIONS	EYECUP	EYESORE	FABRICATES
EXTRADOS	EXUDATIVE	EYECUPS	EYESORES	FABRICATING
EXTRADOSES	EXUDE	EYED	EYESPOT	FABRICS
EXTRALITIES	EXUDED	EYEDNESS	EYESPOTS	FABS
EXTRALITY	EXUDES	EYEDNESSES	EYESTALK	FABULAR
EXTRANET	EXUDING	EYEDROPS	EYESTALKS	FABULATE
EXTRANETS	EXULT	EYEFOLD	EYESTONE	FABULATED
EXTRAS	EXULTANCE	EYEFOLDS	EYESTONES	FABULATES
EXTRAVERT	EXULTANCES	EYEFUL	EYESTRAIN	FABULATING

FABULATOR	FACSIMILE	FADDY	FAGOTERS	FAIRNESSES
FABULATORS	FACSIMILED	FADE	FAGOTING	FAIRS
FABULIST	FACSIMILEING	FADEAWAY	FAGOTINGS	FAIRWAY
FABULISTS	FACSIMILES	FADEAWAYS	FAGOTS	FAIRWAYS
FABULOUS	FACT	FADED	FAGS	FAIRY
FACADE	FACTFUL	FADEDLY	FAHLBAND	FAIRYHOOD
FACADES	FACTICITIES	FADEDNESS	FAHLBANDS	FAIRYHOODS
FACE	FACTICITY	FADEDNESSES	FAIENCE	FAIRYISM
FACEABLE	FACTION	FADEIN	FAIENCES	FAIRYISMS
FACECLOTH	FACTIONAL	FADEINS	FAIL	FAIRYLAND
FACECLOTHS	FACTIONS	FADELESS	FAILED	FAIRYLANDS
FACED	FACTIOUS	FADEOUT	FAILING	FAIRYLIKE
FACEDOWN	FACTITIVE	FADEOUTS	FAILINGLY	FAITH
FACEDOWNS	FACTOID	FADER	FAILINGS	FAITHED
FACELESS	FACTOIDAL	FADERS	FAILLE	FAITHFUL
FACELIFT	FACTOIDS	FADES	FAILLES	FAITHFULS
FACELIFTED	FACTOR	FADGE	FAILS	FAITHING
FACELIFTING	FACTORAGE	FADGED	FAILURE	FAITHLESS
FACELIFTS	FACTORAGES	FADGES	FAILURES	FAITHS
FACEMASK	FACTORED	FADGING	FAIN	FAITOUR
FACEMASKS	FACTORIAL	FADING	FAINEANCE	FAITOURS
FACEPLATE	FACTORIALS	FADINGS	FAINEANCES	FAJITA
FACEPLATES	FACTORIES	FADLIKE	FAINEANT	FAJITAS
FACER	FACTORING	FADO	FAINEANTS	FAKE
FACERS	FACTORIZE	FADOS	FAINER	FAKED
FACES	FACTORIZED	FADS	FAINEST	FAKEER
FACET	FACTORIZES	FAECAL	FAINT	FAKEERS
FACETE	FACTORIZING	FAECES	FAINTED	FAKER
FACETED	FACTORS	FAENA	FAINTER	FAKERIES
FACETELY	FACTORY	FAENAS	FAINTERS	FAKERS
FACETIAE	FACTOTUM	FAERIE	FAINTEST	FAKERY
FACETING	FACTOTUMS	FAERIES	FAINTING	FAKES
FACETIOUS	FACTS	FAERY	FAINTISH	FAKEY
FACETS	FACTUAL	FAG	FAINTLY	FAKING
FACETTED	FACTUALLY	FAGGED	FAINTNESS	FAKIR
FACETTING	FACTURE	FAGGIER	FAINTNESSES	FAKIRS
FACEUP	FACTURES	FAGGIEST	FAINTS	FALAFEL
FACIA	FACULA	FAGGING	FAIR	FALAFELS
FACIAE	FACULAE	FAGGOT	FAIRED	FALBALA
FACIAL	FACULAR	FAGGOTED	FAIRER	FALBALAS
FACIALLY	FACULTIES	FAGGOTING	FAIREST	FALCATE
FACIALS	FACULTY	FAGGOTINGS	FAIRGOER	FALCATED
FACIAS	FAD	FAGGOTRIES	FAIRGOERS	FALCES
FACIEND	FADABLE	FAGGOTRY	FAIRIES	FALCHION
FACIENDS	FADDIER	FAGGOTS	FAIRING	FALCHIONS
FACIES	FADDIEST	FAGGOTY	FAIRINGS	FALCIFORM
FACILE	FADDISH	FAGGY	FAIRISH	FALCON
FACILELY	FADDISHLY	FAGIN	FAIRISHLY	FALCONER
FACILITIES	FADDISM	FAGINS	FAIRLEAD	FALCONERS
FACILITY	FADDISMS	FAGOT	FAIRLEADS	FALCONET
FACING	FADDIST	FAGOTED	FAIRLY	FALCONETS
FACINGS	FADDISTS	FAGOTER	FAIRNESS	FALCONINE

FALCONOID	FALSEWORK	FANCIFIED	FANNY	FARADIC
FALCONRIES	FALSEWORKS	FANCIFIES	FANO	FARADISE
FALCONRY	FALSIE	FANCIFUL	FANON	FARADISED
FALCONS	FALSIES	FANCIFY	FANONS	FARADISES
FALDERAL	FALSIFIED	FANCIFYING	FANOS	FARADISING
FALDERALS	FALSIFIER	FANCILESS	FANS	FARADISM
FALDEROL	FALSIFIERS	FANCILY	FANTAIL	FARADISMS
FALDEROLS	FALSIFIES	FANCINESS	FANTAILED	FARADIZE
FALDSTOOL	FALSIFY	FANCINESSES	FANTAILS	FARADIZED
FALDSTOOLS	FALSIFYING	FANCY	FANTASIA	FARADIZER
FALL	FALSITIES	FANCYING	FANTASIAS	FARADIZERS
FALLACIES	FALSITY	FANCYWORK	FANTASIE	FARADIZES
FALLACY	FALTBOAT	FANCYWORKS	FANTASIED	FARADIZING
FALLAL	FALTBOATS	FANDANGO	FANTASIES	FARADS
FALLALERIES	FALTER	FANDANGOS	FANTASISE	FARANDOLE
FALLALERY	FALTERED	FANDOM	FANTASISED	FARANDOLES
FALLALS	FALTERER	FANDOMS	FANTASISES	FARAWAY
FALLAWAY	FALTERERS	FANE	FANTASISING	FARCE
FALLAWAYS	FALTERING	FANEGA	FANTASIST	FARCED
FALLBACK	FALTERS	FANEGADA	FANTASISTS	FARCER
FALLBACKS	FALX	FANEGADAS	FANTASIZE	FARCERS
FALLBOARD	FAME	FANEGAS	FANTASIZED	FARCES
FALLBOARDS	FAMED	FANES	FANTASIZES	FARCEUR
FALLEN	FAMELESS	FANFARE	FANTASIZING	FARCEURS
FALLER	FAMES	FANFARES	FANTASM	FARCI
FALLERS	FAMILIAL	FANFARON	FANTASMS	FARCICAL
FALLFISH	FAMILIAR	FANFARONS	FANTAST	FARCIE
FALLFISHES	FAMILIARS	FANFIC	FANTASTIC	FARCIES
FALLIBLE	FAMILIES	FANFICS	FANTASTICS	FARCING
FALLIBLY	FAMILISM	FANFOLD	FANTASTS	FARCY
FALLING	FAMILISMS	FANFOLDED	FANTASY	FARD
FALLOFF	FAMILY	FANFOLDING	FANTASYING	FARDED
FALLOFFS	FAMINE	FANFOLDS	FANTOD	FARDEL
FALLOUT	FAMINES	FANG	FANTODS	FARDELS
FALLOUTS	FAMING	FANGA	FANTOM	FARDING
FALLOW	FAMISH	FANGAS	FANTOMS	FARDS
FALLOWED	FAMISHED	FANGED	FANUM	FARE
FALLOWING	FAMISHES	FANGLESS	FANUMS	FAREBOX
FALLOWS	FAMISHING	FANGLIKE	FANWISE	FAREBOXES
FALLS	FAMOUS	FANGS	FANWORT	FARED
FALSE	FAMOUSLY	FANION	FANWORTS	FARER
FALSEFACE	FAMULI	FANIONS	FANZINE	FARERS
FALSEFACES	FAMULUS	FANJET	FANZINES	FARES
FALSEHOOD	FAN	FANJETS	FAQIR	FAREWELL
FALSEHOODS	FANATIC	FANLIGHT	FAQIRS	FAREWELLED
FALSELY	FANATICAL	FANLIGHTS	FAQUIR	FAREWELLING
FALSENESS	FANATICS	FANLIKE	FAQUIRS	FAREWELLS
FALSENESSES	FANCIED	FANNED	FAR	FARFAL
FALSER	FANCIER	FANNER	FARAD	FARFALLE
FALSEST	FANCIERS	FANNERS	FARADAIC	FARFALS
FALSETTO	FANCIES	FANNIES	FARADAY	FARFEL
FALSETTOS	FANCIEST	FANNING	FARADAYS	FARFELS

FARINA	FARSIDE	FASHIOUS	FATHOM	FATWOODS
FARINAS	FARSIDES	FAST	FATHOMED	FAUBOURG
FARING	FART	FASTBACK	FATHOMER	FAUBOURGS
FARINHA	FARTED	FASTBACKS	FATHOMERS	FAUCAL
FARINHAS	FARTHER	FASTBALL	FATHOMING	FAUCALS
FARINOSE	FARTHEST	FASTBALLS	FATHOMS	FAUCES
FARL	FARTHING	FASTED	FATIDIC	FAUCET
FARLE	FARTHINGS	FASTEN	FATIDICAL	FAUCETS
FARLES	FARTING	FASTENED	FATIGABLE	FAUCIAL
FARLS	FARTLEK	FASTENER	FATIGUE	FAUGH
FARM	FARTLEKS	FASTENERS	FATIGUED	FAULD
FARMABLE	FARTS	FASTENING	FATIGUES	FAULDS
FARMED	FAS	FASTENINGS	FATIGUING	FAULT
FARMER	FASCES	FASTENS	FATING	FAULTED
FARMERS	FASCIA	FASTER	FATLESS	FAULTIER
FARMHAND	FASCIAE	FASTEST	FATLIKE	FAULTIEST
FARMHANDS	FASCIAL	FASTIGIUM	FATLING	FAULTILY
FARMHOUSE	FASCIAS	FASTIGIUMS	FATLINGS	FAULTING
FARMHOUSES	FASCIATE	FASTING	FATLY	FAULTLESS
FARMING	FASCIATED	FASTINGS	FATNESS	FAULTS
FARMINGS	FASCICLE	FASTNESS	FATNESSES	FAULTY
FARMLAND	FASCICLED	FASTNESSES	FATS	FAUN
FARMLANDS	FASCICLES	FASTS	FATSO	FAUNA
FARMS	FASCICULE	FASTUOUS	FATSOES	FAUNAE
FARMSTEAD	FASCICULES	FAT	FATSOS	FAUNAL
FARMSTEADS	FASCICULI	FATAL	FATSTOCK	FAUNALLY
FARMWIFE	FASCICULUS	FATALISM	FATSTOCKS	FAUNAS
FARMWIVES	FASCIITIS	FATALISMS	FATTED	FAUNISTIC
FARMWORK	FASCIITISES	FATALIST	FATTEN	FAUNLIKE
FARMWORKS	FASCINATE	FATALISTS	FATTENED	FAUNS
FARMYARD	FASCINATED	FATALITIES	FATTENER	FAUTEUIL
FARMYARDS	FASCINATES	FATALITY	FATTENERS	FAUTEUILS
FARNESOL	FASCINATING	FATALLY	FATTENING	FAUVE
FARNESOLS	FASCINE	FATALNESS	FATTENS	FAUVES
FARNESS	FASCINES	FATALNESSES	FATTER	FAUVISM
FARNESSES	FASCISM	FATBACK	FATTEST	FAUVISMS
FARO	FASCISMS	FATBACKS	FATTIER	FAUVIST
FAROLITO	FASCIST	FATBIRD	FATTIES	FAUVISTS
FAROLITOS	FASCISTIC	FATBIRDS	FATTIEST	FAUX
FAROS	FASCISTS	FATE	FATTILY	FAVA
FAROUCHE	FASCITIS	FATED	FATTINESS	FAVAS
FARRAGO	FASCITISES	FATEFUL	FATTINESSES	FAVE
FARRAGOES	FASH	FATEFULLY	FATTING	FAVELA
FARRIER	FASHED	FATES	FATTISH	FAVELAS
FARRIERIES	FASHES	FATHEAD	FATTY	FAVELLA
FARRIERS	FASHING	FATHEADED	FATUITIES	FAVELLAS
FARRIERY	FASHION	FATHEADS	FATUITY	FAVEOLATE
FARROW	FASHIONED	FATHER	FATUOUS	FAVES
FARROWED	FASHIONER	FATHERED	FATUOUSLY	FAVISM
FARROWING	FASHIONERS	FATHERING	FATWA	FAVISMS
FARROWS	FASHIONING	FATHERLY	FATWAS	FAVONIAN
FARSEEING	FASHIONS	FATHERS	FATWOOD	FAVOR

FAVORABLE	FEARFUL	FEBRILITIES	FEEDABLE	FEINTED
FAVORABLY	FEARFULLER	FEBRILITY	FEEDBACK	FEINTING
FAVORED	FEARFULLEST	FECAL	FEEDBACKS	FEINTS
FAVORER	FEARFULLY	FECES	FEEDBAG	FEIRIE
FAVORERS	FEARING	FECIAL	FEEDBAGS	FEIST
FAVORING	FEARLESS	FECIALS	FEEDBOX	FEISTIER
FAVORITE	FEARS	FECK	FEEDBOXES	FEISTIEST
FAVORITES	FEARSOME	FECKLESS	FEEDER	FEISTILY
FAVORS	FEASANCE	FECKLY	FEEDERS	FEISTS
FAVOUR	FEASANCES	FECKS	FEEDGRAIN	FEISTY
FAVOURED	FEASE	FECULA	FEEDGRAINS	FELAFEL
FAVOURER	FEASED	FECULAE	FEEDHOLE	FELAFELS
FAVOURERS	FEASES	FECULENCE	FEEDHOLES	FELDSCHER
FAVOURING	FEASIBLE	FECULENCES	FEEDING	FELDSCHERS
FAVOURS	FEASIBLY	FECULENT	FEEDLOT	FELDSHER
FAVUS	FEASING	FECUND	FEEDLOTS	FELDSHERS
FAVUSES	FEAST	FECUNDATE	FEEDS	FELDSPAR
FAWN	FEASTED	FECUNDATED	FEEDSTOCK	FELDSPARS
FAWNED	FEASTER	FECUNDATES	FEEDSTOCKS	FELICIFIC
FAWNER	FEASTERS	FECUNDATING	FEEDSTUFF	FELICITIES
FAWNERS	FEASTFUL	FECUNDITIES	FEEDSTUFFS	FELICITY
FAWNIER	FEASTING	FECUNDITY	FEEDYARD	FELID
FAWNIEST	FEASTLESS	FED	FEEDYARDS	FELIDS
FAWNING	FEASTS	FEDAYEE	FEEING	FELINE
FAWNINGLY	FEAT	FEDAYEEN	FEEL	FELINELY
FAWNLIKE	FEATER	FEDERACIES	FEELER	FELINES
FAWNS	FEATEST	FEDERACY	FEELERS	FELINITIES
FAWNY	FEATHER	FEDERAL	FEELESS	FELINITY
FAX	FEATHERED	FEDERALLY	FEELING	FELL
FAXED	FEATHERIER	FEDERALS	FEELINGLY	FELLA
FAXES	FEATHERIEST	FEDERATE	FEELINGS	FELLABLE
FAXING	FEATHERING	FEDERATED	FEELS	FELLAH
FAY	FEATHERS	FEDERATES	FEES	FELLAHEEN
FAYALITE	FEATHERY	FEDERATING	FEET	FELLAHIN
FAYALITES	FEATLIER	FEDERATOR	FEETFIRST	FELLAHS
FAYED	FEATLIEST	FEDERATORS	FEETLESS	FELLAS
FAYING	FEATLY	FEDEX	FEEZE	FELLATE
FAYS	FEATS	FEDEXED	FEEZED	FELLATED
FAZE	FEATURE	FEDEXES	FEEZES	FELLATES
FAZED	FEATURED	FEDEXING	FEEZING	FELLATING
FAZENDA	FEATURES	FEDORA	FEH	FELLATIO
FAZENDAS	FEATURING	FEDORAS	FEHS	FELLATION
FAZES	FEAZE	FEDS	FEIGN	FELLATIONS
FAZING	FEAZED	FEE	FEIGNED	FELLATIOS
FE	FEAZES	FEEB	FEIGNEDLY	FELLATOR
FEAL	FEAZING	FEEBLE	FEIGNER	FELLATORS
FEALTIES	FEBRICITIES	FEEBLER	FEIGNERS	FELLATRICES
FEALTY	FEBRICITY	FEEBLEST	FEIGNING	FELLATRIX
FEAR	FEBRIFIC	FEEBLISH	FEIGNS	FELLATRIXES
FEARED	FEBRIFUGE	FEEBLY	FEIJOA	FELLED
FEARER	FEBRIFUGES	FEEBS	FEIJOAS	FELLER
FEARERS	FEBRILE	FEED	FEINT	FELLERS

FELLEST	FEMININES	FENNECS	FERMATA	FERRIES
FELLIES	FEMINISE	FENNEL	FERMATAS	FERRITE
FELLING	FEMINISED	FENNELS	FERMATE	FERRITES
FELLNESS	FEMINISES	FENNIER	FERMENT	FERRITIC
FELLNESSES	FEMINISING	FENNIEST	FERMENTED	FERRITIN
FELLOE	FEMINISM	FENNY	FERMENTER	FERRITINS
FELLOES	FEMINISMS	FENS	FERMENTERS	FERROCENE
FELLOW	FEMINIST	FENTANYL	FERMENTING	FERROCENES
FELLOWED	FEMINISTS	FENTANYLS	FERMENTOR	FERROTYPE
FELLOWING	FEMINITIES	FENTHION	FERMENTORS	FERROTYPED
FELLOWLY	FEMINITY	FENTHIONS	FERMENTS	FERROTYPES
FELLOWMAN	FEMINIZE	FENUGREEK	FERMI	FERROTYPING
FELLOWMEN	FEMINIZED	FENUGREEKS	FERMION	FERROUS
FELLOWS	FEMINIZES	FENURON	FERMIONIC	FERRULE
FELLS	FEMINIZING	FENURONS	FERMIONS	FERRULED
FELLY	FEMME	FEOD	FERMIS	FERRULES
FELON	FEMMES	FEODARIES	FERMIUM	FERRULING
FELONIES	FEMORA	FEODARY	FERMIUMS	FERRUM
FELONIOUS	FEMORAL	FEODS	FERN	FERRUMS
FELONRIES	FEMS	FEOFF	FERNERIES	FERRY
FELONRY	FEMUR	FEOFFED	FERNERY	FERRYBOAT
FELONS	FEMURS	FEOFFEE	FERNIER	FERRYBOATS
FELONY	FEN	FEOFFEES	FERNIEST	FERRYING
FELSIC	FENAGLE	FEOFFER	FERNINST	FERRYMAN
FELSITE	FENAGLED	FEOFFERS	FERNLESS	FERRYMEN
FELSITES	FENAGLES	FEOFFING	FERNLIKE	FERTILE
FELSITIC	FENAGLING	FEOFFMENT	FERNS	FERTILELY
FELSPAR	FENCE	FEOFFMENTS	FERNY	FERTILITIES
FELSPARS	FENCED	FEOFFOR	FEROCIOUS	FERTILITY
FELSTONE	FENCELESS	FEOFFORS	FEROCITIES	FERTILIZE
FELSTONES	FENCER	FEOFFS	FEROCITY	FERTILIZED
FELT	FENCEROW	FER	FERRATE	FERTILIZES
FELTED	FENCEROWS	FERACITIES	FERRATES	FERTILIZING
FELTING	FENCERS	FERACITY	FERREL	FERULA
FELTINGS	FENCES	FERAL	FERRELED	FERULAE
FELTLIKE	FENCIBLE	FERALS	FERRELING	FERULAS
FELTS	FENCIBLES	FERBAM	FERRELLED	FERULE
FELUCCA	FENCING	FERBAMS	FERRELLING	FERULED
FELUCCAS	FENCINGS	FERE	FERRELS	FERULES
FELWORT	FEND	FERES	FERREOUS	FERULING
FELWORTS	FENDED	FERETORIES	FERRET	FERVENCIES
FEM	FENDER	FERETORY	FERRETED	FERVENCY
FEMALE	FENDERED	FERIA	FERRETER	FERVENT
FEMALES	FENDERS	FERIAE	FERRETERS	FERVENTLY
FEME	FENDING	FERIAL	FERRETING	FERVID
FEMES	FENDS	FERIAS	FERRETINGS	FERVIDITIES
FEMINACIES	FENESTRA	FERINE	FERRETS	FERVIDITY
FEMINACY	FENESTRAE	FERITIES	FERRETY	FERVIDLY
FEMINAZI	FENESTRAL	FERITY	FERRIAGE	FERVOR
FEMINAZIS	FENLAND	FERLIE	FERRIAGES	FERVORS
FEMINIE	FENLANDS	FERLIES	FERRIC	FERVOUR
FEMININE	FENNEC	FERLY	FERRIED	FERVOURS

FES	FETICH	FEU	FEYNESS	FIBRINS
FESCUE	FETICHES	FEUAR	FEYNESSES	FIBROID
FESCUES	FETICHISM	FEUARS	FEZ	FIBROIDS
FESS	FETICHISMS	FEUD	FEZES	FIBROIN
FESSE	FETICIDAL	FEUDAL	FEZZED	FIBROINS
FESSED	FETICIDE	FEUDALISM	FEZZES	FIBROMA
FESSES	FETICIDES	FEUDALISMS	FEZZY	FIBROMAS
FESSING	FETID	FEUDALIST	FIACRE	FIBROMATA
FESSWISE	FETIDITIES	FEUDALISTS	FIACRES	FIBROSES
FEST	FETIDITY	FEUDALITIES	FIANCE	FIBROSIS
FESTAL	FETIDLY	FEUDALITY	FIANCEE	FIBROTIC
FESTALLY	FETIDNESS	FEUDALIZE	FIANCEES	FIBROUS
FESTER	FETIDNESSES	FEUDALIZED	FIANCES	FIBROUSLY
FESTERED	FETING	FEUDALIZES	FIAR	FIBS
FESTERING	FETISH	FEUDALIZING	FIARS	FIBSTER
FESTERS	FETISHES	FEUDALLY	FIASCHI	FIBSTERS
FESTINATE	FETISHISM	FEUDARIES	FIASCO	FIBULA
FESTINATED	FETISHISMS	FEUDARY	FIASCOES	FIBULAE
FESTINATES	FETISHIST	FEUDATORIES	FIASCOS	FIBULAR
FESTINATING	FETISHISTS	FEUDATORY	FIAT	FIBULAS
FESTIVAL	FETISHIZE	FEUDED	FIATS	FICE
FESTIVALS	FETISHIZED	FEUDING	FIB	FICES
FESTIVE	FETISHIZES	FEUDIST	FIBBED	FICHE
FESTIVELY	FETISHIZING	FEUDISTS	FIBBER	FICHES
FESTIVITIES	FETLOCK	FEUDS	FIBBERS	FICHU
FESTIVITY	FETLOCKS	FEUED	FIBBING	FICHUS
FESTOON	FETOLOGIES	FEUING	FIBER	FICIN
FESTOONED	FETOLOGY	FEUS	FIBERED	FICINS
FESTOONING	FETOR	FEVER	FIBERFILL	FICKLE
FESTOONS	FETORS	FEVERED	FIBERFILLS	FICKLER
FESTS	FETOSCOPE	FEVERFEW	FIBERIZE	FICKLEST
FET	FETOSCOPES	FEVERFEWS	FIBERIZED	FICKLY
FETA	FETOSCOPIES	FEVERING	FIBERIZES	FICO
FETAL	FETOSCOPY	FEVERISH	FIBERIZING	FICOES
FETAS	FETS	FEVEROUS	FIBERLESS	FICTILE
FETATION	FETTED	FEVERROOT	FIBERLIKE	FICTION
FETATIONS	FETTER	FEVERROOTS	FIBERS	FICTIONAL
FETCH	FETTERED	FEVERS	FIBRANNE	FICTIONS
FETCHED	FETTERER	FEVERWEED	FIBRANNES	FICTIVE
FETCHER	FETTERERS	FEVERWEEDS	FIBRE	FICTIVELY
FETCHERS	FETTERING	FEVERWORT	FIBREFILL	FICUS
FETCHES	FETTERS	FEVERWORTS	FIBREFILLS	FICUSES
FETCHING	FETTING	FEW	FIBRES	FID
FETE	FETTLE	FEWER	FIBRIL	FIDDLE
FETED	FETTLED	FEWEST	FIBRILLA	FIDDLED
FETERITA	FETTLES	FEWNESS	FIBRILLAE	FIDDLER
FETERITAS	FETTLING	FEWNESSES	FIBRILLAR	FIDDLERS
FETES	FETTLINGS	FEWTRILS	FIBRILS	FIDDLES
FETIAL	FETTUCINE	FEY	FIBRIN	FIDDLING
FETIALES	FETTUCINI	FEYER	FIBRINOID	FIDDLY
FETIALIS	FETUS	FEYEST	FIBRINOIDS	FIDEISM
FETIALS	FETUSES	FEYLY	FIBRINOUS	FIDEISMS

FIDEIST	FIERILY	FIGURES	FILIATES	FILMER
FIDEISTIC	FIERINESS	FIGURINE	FILIATING	FILMERS
FIDEISTS	FIERINESSES	FIGURINES	FILIATION	FILMGOER
FIDELISMO	FIERY	FIGURING	FILIATIONS	FILMGOERS
FIDELISMOS	FIESTA	FIGWORT	FILIBEG	FILMGOING
FIDELISTA	FIESTAS	FIGWORTS	FILIBEGS	FILMI
FIDELISTAS	FIFE	FIL	FILICIDE	FILMIC
FIDELITIES	FIFED	FILA	FILICIDES	FILMIER
FIDELITY	FIFER	FILAGREE	FILIFORM	FILMIEST
FIDGE	FIFERS	FILAGREED	FILIGREE	FILMILY
FIDGED	FIFES	FILAGREEING	FILIGREED	FILMINESS
FIDGES	FIFING	FILAGREES	FILIGREEING	FILMINESSES
FIDGET	FIFTEEN	FILAMENT	FILIGREES	FILMING
FIDGETED	FIFTEENS	FILAMENTS	FILING	FILMIS
FIDGETER	FIFTEENTH	FILAR	FILINGS	FILMLAND
FIDGETERS	FIFTEENTHS	FILAREE	FILISTER	FILMLANDS
FIDGETING	FIFTH	FILAREES	FILISTERS	FILMLESS
FIDGETS	FIFTHLY	FILARIA	FILL	FILMLIKE
FIDGETY	FIFTHS	FILARIAE	FILLABLE	FILMMAKER
FIDGING	FIFTIES	FILARIAL	FILLAGREE	FILMMAKERS
FIDO	FIFTIETH	FILARIAN	FILLAGREED	FILMS
FIDOS	FIFTIETHS	FILARIID	FILLAGREEING	FILMSET
FIDS	FIFTY	FILARIIDS	FILLAGREES	FILMSETS
FIDUCIAL	FIFTYISH	FILATURE	FILLE	FILMSETTING
FIDUCIARIES	FIG	FILATURES	FILLED	FILMSTRIP
FIDUCIARY	FIGEATER	FILBERT	FILLER	FILMSTRIPS
FIE	FIGEATERS	FILBERTS	FILLERS	FILMY
FIEF	FIGGED	FILCH	FILLES	FILO
FIEFDOM	FIGGING	FILCHED	FILLET	FILOPLUME
FIEFDOMS	FIGHT	FILCHER	FILLETED	FILOPLUMES
FIEFS	FIGHTABLE	FILCHERS	FILLETING	FILOPODIA
FIELD	FIGHTER	FILCHES	FILLETS	FILOPODIUM
FIELDED	FIGHTERS	FILCHING	FILLIES	FILOS
FIELDER	FIGHTING	FILE	FILLING	FILOSE
FIELDERS	FIGHTINGS	FILEABLE	FILLINGS	FILOVIRUS
FIELDFARE	FIGHTS	FILED	FILLIP	FILOVIRUSES
FIELDFARES	FIGMENT	FILEFISH	FILLIPED	FILS
FIELDING	FIGMENTS	FILEFISHES	FILLIPING	FILTER
FIELDS	FIGS	FILEMOT	FILLIPS	FILTERED
FIELDSMAN	FIGULINE	FILENAME	FILLISTER	FILTERER
FIELDSMEN	FIGULINES	FILENAMES	FILLISTERS	FILTERERS
FIELDWORK	FIGURABLE	FILER	FILLO	FILTERING
FIELDWORKS	FIGURAL	FILERS	FILLOS	FILTERS
FIEND	FIGURALLY	FILES	FILLS	FILTH
FIENDISH	FIGURANT	FILET	FILLY	FILTHIER
FIENDS	FIGURANTS	FILETED	FILM	FILTHIEST
FIERCE	FIGURATE	FILETING	FILMABLE	FILTHILY
FIERCELY	FIGURE	FILETS	FILMCARD	FILTHS
FIERCER	FIGURED	FILIAL	FILMCARDS	FILTHY
FIERCEST	FIGUREDLY	FILIALLY	FILMDOM	FILTRABLE
FIERIER	FIGURER	FILIATE	FILMDOMS	FILTRATE
FIERIEST	FIGURERS	FILIATED	FILMED	FILTRATED

FILTRATES	FINCAS	FININGS	FIREABLE	FIREGUARDS
FILTRATING	FINCH	FINIS	FIREARM	FIREHALL
FILUM	FINCHES	FINISES	FIREARMED	FIREHALLS
FIMBLE	FIND	FINISH	FIREARMS	FIREHOUSE
FIMBLES	FINDABLE	FINISHED	FIREBACK	FIREHOUSES
FIMBRIA	FINDER	FINISHER	FIREBACKS	FIRELESS
FIMBRIAE	FINDERS	FINISHERS	FIREBALL	FIRELIGHT
FIMBRIAL	FINDING	FINISHES	FIREBALLS	FIRELIGHTS
FIMBRIATE	FINDINGS	FINISHING	FIREBASE	FIRELIT
FIN	FINDS	FINITE	FIREBASES	FIRELOCK
FINABLE	FINE	FINITELY	FIREBIRD	FIRELOCKS
FINAGLE	FINEABLE	FINITES	FIREBIRDS	FIREMAN
FINAGLED	FINED	FINITO	FIREBOARD	FIREMANIC
FINAGLER	FINELY	FINITUDE	FIREBOARDS	FIREMEN
FINAGLERS	FINENESS	FINITUDES	FIREBOAT	FIREPAN
FINAGLES	FINENESSES	FINK	FIREBOATS	FIREPANS
FINAGLING	FINER	FINKED	FIREBOMB	FIREPINK
FINAL	FINERIES	FINKING	FIREBOMBED	FIREPINKS
FINALE	FINERY	FINKS	FIREBOMBING	FIREPLACE
FINALES	FINES	FINLESS	FIREBOMBS	FIREPLACES
FINALIS	FINESPUN	FINLIKE	FIREBOX	FIREPLUG
FINALISE	FINESSE	FINMARK	FIREBOXES	FIREPLUGS
FINALISED	FINESSED	FINMARKS	FIREBRAND	FIREPOT
FINALISES	FINESSES	FINNED	FIREBRANDS	FIREPOTS
FINALISING	FINESSING	FINNICKIER	FIREBRAT	FIREPOWER
FINALISM	FINEST	FINNICKIEST	FIREBRATS	FIREPOWERS
FINALISMS	FINFISH	FINNICKY	FIREBREAK	FIREPROOF
FINALIST	FINFISHES	FINNIER	FIREBREAKS	FIREPROOFED
FINALISTS	FINFOOT	FINNIEST	FIREBRICK	FIREPROOFING
FINALITIES	FINFOOTS	FINNING	FIREBRICKS	FIREPROOFS
FINALITY	FINGER	FINNMARK	FIREBUG	FIRER
FINALIZE	FINGERED	FINNMARKS	FIREBUGS	FIREROOM
FINALIZED	FINGERER	FINNY	FIRECLAY	FIREROOMS
FINALIZER	FINGERERS	FINO	FIRECLAYS	FIRERS
FINALIZERS	FINGERING	FINOCCHIO	FIRED	FIRES
FINALIZES	FINGERINGS	FINOCCHIOS	FIREDAMP	FIRESHIP
FINALIZING	FINGERS	FINOCHIO	FIREDAMPS	FIRESHIPS
FINALLY	FINGERTIP	FINOCHIOS	FIREDOG	FIRESIDE
FINALS	FINGERTIPS	FINOS	FIREDOGS	FIRESIDES
FINANCE	FINIAL	FINS	FIREDRAKE	FIRESTONE
FINANCED	FINIALED	FIORATURA	FIREDRAKES	FIRESTONES
FINANCES	FINIALS	FIORATURAE	FIREFANG	FIRESTORM
FINANCIAL	FINICAL	FIORD	FIREFANGED	FIRESTORMS
FINANCIER	FINICALLY	FIORDS	FIREFANGING	FIRETHORN
FINANCIERED	FINICKIER	FIORITURA	FIREFANGS	FIRETHORNS
FINANCIERING	FINICKIEST	FIORITURE	FIREFIGHT	FIRETRAP
FINANCIERS	FINICKIN	FIPPLE	FIREFIGHTS	FIRETRAPS
FINANCING	FINICKING	FIPPLES	FIREFLIES	FIRETRUCK
FINANCINGS	FINICKY	FIQUE	FIREFLOOD	FIRETRUCKS
FINBACK	FINIKIN	FIQUES	FIREFLOODS	FIREWALL
FINBACKS	FINIKING	FIR	FIREFLY	FIREWALLS
FINCA	FINING	FIRE	FIREGUARD	FIREWATER

FIREWATERS	FISCALS	FISHWAYS	FITLY	FIZZ
FIREWEED	FISCS	FISHWIFE	FITMENT	FIZZED
FIREWEEDS	FISH	FISHWIVES	FITMENTS	FIZZER
FIREWOOD	FISHABLE	FISHWORM	FITNESS	FIZZERS
FIREWOODS	FISHBOLT	FISHWORMS	FITNESSES	FIZZES
FIREWORK	FISHBOLTS	FISHY	FITS	FIZZIER
FIREWORKS	FISHBONE	FISSATE	FITTABLE	FIZZIEST
FIREWORM	FISHBONES	FISSILE	FITTED	FIZZING
FIREWORMS	FISHBOWL	FISSILITIES	FITTER	FIZZLE
FIRING	FISHBOWLS	FISSILITY	FITTERS	FIZZLED
FIRINGS	FISHED	FISSION	FITTEST	FIZZLES
FIRKIN	FISHER	FISSIONAL	FITTING	FIZZLING
FIRKINS	FISHERIES	FISSIONED	FITTINGLY	FIZZY
FIRM	FISHERMAN	FISSIONING	FITTINGS	FJELD
FIRMAMENT	FISHERMEN	FISSIONS	FIVE	FJELDS
FIRMAMENTS	FISHERS	FISSIPED	FIVEFOLD	FJORD
FIRMAN	FISHERY	FISSIPEDS	FIVEPINS	FJORDIC
FIRMANS	FISHES	FISSURAL	FIVER	FJORDS
FIRMED	FISHEYE	FISSURE	FIVERS	FLAB
FIRMER	FISHEYES	FISSURED	FIVES	FLABBIER
FIRMERS	FISHGIG	FISSURES	FIX	FLABBIEST
FIRMEST	FISHGIGS	FISSURING	FIXABLE	FLABBILY
FIRMING	FISHHOOK	FIST	FIXATE	FLABBY
FIRMLY	FISHHOOKS	FISTED	FIXATED	FLABELLA
FIRMNESS	FISHIER	FISTFIGHT	FIXATES	FLABELLUM
FIRMNESSES	FISHIEST	FISTFIGHTS	FIXATIF	FLABS
FIRMS	FISHILY	FISTFUL	FIXATIFS	FLACCID
FIRMWARE	FISHINESS	FISTFULS	FIXATING	FLACCIDLY
FIRMWARES	FISHINESSES	FISTIC	FIXATION	FLACK
FIRN	FISHING	FISTICUFF	FIXATIONS	FLACKED
FIRNS	FISHINGS	FISTICUFFS	FIXATIVE	FLACKERIES
FIRRIER	FISHKILL	FISTING	FIXATIVES	FLACKERY
FIRRIEST	FISHKILLS	FISTNOTE	FIXED	FLACKING
FIRRY	FISHLESS	FISTNOTES	FIXEDLY	FLACKS
FIRS	FISHLIKE	FISTS	FIXEDNESS	FLACON
FIRST	FISHLINE	FISTULA	FIXEDNESSES	FLACONS
FIRSTBORN	FISHLINES	FISTULAE	FIXER	FLAG
FIRSTBORNS	FISHMEAL	FISTULAR	FIXERS	FLAGELLA
FIRSTHAND	FISHMEALS	FISTULAS	FIXES	FLAGELLAR
FIRSTLING	FISHNET	FISTULATE	FIXING	FLAGELLIN
FIRSTLINGS	FISHNETS	FISTULOUS	FIXINGS	FLAGELLINS
FIRSTLY	FISHPLATE	FIT	FIXIT	FLAGELLUM
FIRSTNESS	FISHPLATES	FITCH	FIXITIES	FLAGELLUMS
FIRSTNESSES	FISHPOLE	FITCHEE	FIXITY	FLAGEOLET
FIRSTS	FISHPOLES	FITCHES	FIXT	FLAGEOLETS
FIRTH	FISHPOND	FITCHET	FIXTURE	FLAGGED
FIRTHS	FISHPONDS	FITCHETS	FIXTURES	FLAGGER
FISC	FISHTAIL	FITCHEW	FIXURE	FLAGGERS
FISCAL	FISHTAILED	FITCHEWS	FIXURES	FLAGGIER
FISCALIST	FISHTAILING	FITCHY	FIZ	FLAGGIEST
FISCALISTS	FISHTAILS	FITFUL	FIZGIG	FLAGGING
FISCALLY	FISHWAY	FITFULLY	FIZGIGS	FLAGGINGS

FLAGGY	FLAME	FLANNELING	FLASHOVER	FLATTENED
FLAGLESS	FLAMED	FLANNELLED	FLASHOVERS	FLATTENER
FLAGMAN	FLAMELESS	FLANNELLING	FLASHTUBE	FLATTENERS
FLAGMEN	FLAMELIKE	FLANNELLY	FLASHTUBES	FLATTENING
FLAGON	FLAMEN	FLANNELS	FLASHY	FLATTENS
FLAGONS	FLAMENCO	FLANS	FLASK	FLATTER
FLAGPOLE	FLAMENCOS	FLAP	FLASKET	FLATTERED
FLAGPOLES	FLAMENS	FLAPERON	FLASKETS	FLATTERER
FLAGRANCE	FLAMEOUT	FLAPERONS	FLASKS	FLATTERERS
FLAGRANCES	FLAMEOUTS	FLAPJACK	FLAT	FLATTERIES
FLAGRANCIES	FLAMER	FLAPJACKS	FLATBED	FLATTERING
FLAGRANCY	FLAMERS	FLAPLESS	FLATBEDS	FLATTERS
FLAGRANT	FLAMES	FLAPPABLE	FLATBOAT	FLATTERY
FLAGS	FLAMIER	FLAPPED	FLATBOATS	FLATTEST
FLAGSHIP	FLAMIEST	FLAPPER	FLATBREAD	FLATTING
FLAGSHIPS	FLAMINES	FLAPPERS	FLATBREADS	FLATTISH
FLAGSTAFF	FLAMING	FLAPPIER	FLATCAP	FLATTOP
FLAGSTAFFS	FLAMINGLY	FLAPPIEST	FLATCAPS	FLATTOPS
FLAGSTAVES	FLAMINGO	FLAPPING	FLATCAR	FLATULENT
FLAGSTICK	FLAMINGOES	FLAPPY	FLATCARS	FLATUS
FLAGSTICKS	FLAMINGOS	FLAPS	FLATFEET	FLATUSES
FLAGSTONE	FLAMMABLE	FLARE	FLATFISH	FLATWARE
FLAGSTONES	FLAMMABLES	FLAREBACK	FLATFISHES	FLATWARES
FLAIL	FLAMMED	FLAREBACKS	FLATFOOT	FLATWASH
FLAILED	FLAMMING	FLARED	FLATFOOTED	FLATWASHES
FLAILING	FLAMS	FLARES	FLATFOOTING	FLATWAYS
FLAILS	FLAMY	FLAREUP	FLATFOOTS	FLATWISE
FLAIR	FLAN	FLAREUPS	FLATHEAD	FLATWORK
FLAIRS	FLANCARD	FLARING	FLATHEADS	FLATWORKS
FLAK	FLANCARDS	FLARINGLY	FLATIRON	FLATWORM
FLAKE	FLANERIE	FLASH	FLATIRONS	FLATWORMS
FLAKED	FLANERIES	FLASHBACK	FLATLAND	FLAUNT
FLAKER	FLANES	FLASHBACKS	FLATLANDS	FLAUNTED
FLAKERS	FLANEUR	FLASHBULB	FLATLET	FLAUNTER
FLAKES	FLANEURS	FLASHBULBS	FLATLETS	FLAUNTERS
FLAKEY	FLANGE	FLASHCARD	FLATLINE	FLAUNTIER
FLAKIER	FLANGED	FLASHCARDS	FLATLINED	FLAUNTIEST
FLAKIEST	FLANGER	FLASHCUBE	FLATLINER	FLAUNTILY
FLAKILY	FLANGERS	FLASHCUBES	FLATLINERS	FLAUNTING
FLAKINESS	FLANGES	FLASHED	FLATLINES	FLAUNTS
FLAKINESSES	FLANGING	FLASHER	FLATLING	FLAUNTY
FLAKING	FLANK	FLASHERS	FLATLINGS	FLAUTA
FLAKY	FLANKED	FLASHES	FLATLINING	FLAUTAS
FLAM	FLANKEN	FLASHGUN	FLATLONG	FLAUTIST
FLAMBE	FLANKER	FLASHGUNS	FLATLY	FLAUTISTS
FLAMBEAU	FLANKERS	FLASHIER	FLATMATE	FLAVANOL
FLAMBEAUS	FLANKING	FLASHIEST	FLATMATES	FLAVANOLS
FLAMBEAUX	FLANKS	FLASHILY	FLATNESS	FLAVANONE
FLAMBEE	FLANNEL	FLASHING	FLATNESSES	FLAVANONES
FLAMBEED	FLANNELED	FLASHINGS	FLATS	FLAVIN
FLAMBEING	FLANNELET	FLASHLAMP	FLATTED	FLAVINE
FLAMBES	FLANNELETS	FLASHLAMPS	FLATTEN	FLAVINES

FLAVINS	FLEABITES	FLEETED	FLETCHINGS	FLIER
FLAVONE	FLEAM	FLEETER	FLEURON	FLIERS
FLAVONES	FLEAMS	FLEETEST	FLEURONS	FLIES
FLAVONOID	FLEAPIT	FLEETING	FLEURY	FLIEST
FLAVONOIDS	FLEAPITS	FLEETLY	FLEW	FLIGHT
FLAVONOL	FLEAS	FLEETNESS	FLEWS	FLIGHTED
FLAVONOLS	FLEAWORT	FLEETNESSES	FLEX	FLIGHTIER
FLAVOR	FLEAWORTS	FLEETS	FLEXAGON	FLIGHTIEST
FLAVORED	FLECHE	FLEHMEN	FLEXAGONS	FLIGHTILY
FLAVORER	FLECHES	FLEHMENED	FLEXED	FLIGHTING
FLAVORERS	FLECHETTE	FLEHMENING	FLEXES	FLIGHTS
FLAVORFUL	FLECHETTES	FLEHMENS	FLEXIBLE	FLIGHTY
FLAVORING	FLECK	FLEISHIG	FLEXIBLY	FLIMFLAM
FLAVORINGS	FLECKED	FLEMISH	FLEXILE	FLIMFLAMMED
FLAVORIST	FLECKING	FLEMISHED	FLEXING	FLIMFLAMMING
FLAVORISTS	FLECKLESS	FLEMISHES	FLEXION	FLIMFLAMS
FLAVOROUS	FLECKS	FLEMISHING	FLEXIONAL	FLIMSIER
FLAVORS	FLECKY	FLENCH	FLEXIONS	FLIMSIES
FLAVORY	FLECTION	FLENCHED	FLEXITIME	FLIMSIEST
FLAVOUR	FLECTIONS	FLENCHES	FLEXITIMES	FLIMSILY
FLAVOURED	FLED	FLENCHING	FLEXOR	FLIMSY
FLAVOURING	FLEDGE	FLENSE	FLEXORS	FLINCH
FLAVOURS	FLEDGED	FLENSED	FLEXTIME	FLINCHED
FLAVOURY	FLEDGES	FLENSER	FLEXTIMER	FLINCHER
FLAW	FLEDGIER	FLENSERS	FLEXTIMERS	FLINCHERS
FLAWED	FLEDGIEST	FLENSES	FLEXTIMES	FLINCHES
FLAWIER	FLEDGING	FLENSING	FLEXUOSE	FLINCHING
FLAWIEST	FLEDGLING	FLESH	FLEXUOUS	FLINDER
FLAWING	FLEDGLINGS	FLESHED	FLEXURAL	FLINDERS
FLAWLESS	FLEDGY	FLESHER	FLEXURE	FLING
FLAWS	FLEE	FLESHERS	FLEXURES	FLINGER
FLAWY	FLEECE	FLESHES	FLEY	FLINGERS
FLAX	FLEECED	FLESHIER	FLEYED	FLINGING
FLAXEN	FLEECER	FLESHIEST	FLEYING	FLINGS
FLAXES	FLEECERS	FLESHILY	FLEYS	FLINKITE
FLAXIER	FLEECES	FLESHING	FLIC	FLINKITES
FLAXIEST	FLEECH	FLESHINGS	FLICHTER	FLINT
FLAXSEED	FLEECHED	FLESHLESS	FLICHTERED	FLINTED
FLAXSEEDS	FLEECHES	FLESHLIER	FLICHTERING	FLINTHEAD
FLAXY	FLEECHING	FLESHLIEST	FLICHTERS	FLINTHEADS
FLAY	FLEECIER	FLESHLY	FLICK	FLINTIER
FLAYED	FLEECIEST	FLESHMENT	FLICKABLE	FLINTIEST
FLAYER	FLEECILY	FLESHMENTS	FLICKED	FLINTILY
FLAYERS	FLEECING	FLESHPOT	FLICKER	FLINTING
FLAYING	FLEECY	FLESHPOTS	FLICKERED	FLINTLIKE
FLAYS	FLEEING	FLESHY	FLICKERING	FLINTLOCK
FLEA	FLEER	FLETCH	FLICKERS	FLINTLOCKS
FLEABAG	FLEERED	FLETCHED	FLICKERY	FLINTS
FLEABAGS	FLEERING	FLETCHER	FLICKING	FLINTY
FLEABANE	FLEERS	FLETCHERS	FLICKS	FLIP
FLEABANES	FLEES	FLETCHES	FLICS	FLIPBOOK
FLEABITE	FLEET	FLETCHING	FLIED	FLIPBOOKS

FLIPFLOP	FLOATIER	FLOODS	FLORETS	FLOUNDERS
FLIPFLOPPED	FLOATIEST	FLOODTIDE	FLORIATED	FLOUR
FLIPFLOPPING	FLOATING	FLOODTIDES	FLORICANE	FLOURED
FLIPFLOPS	FLOATS	FLOODWALL	FLORICANES	FLOURING
FLIPPANCIES	FLOATY	FLOODWALLS	FLORID	FLOURISH
FLIPPANCY	FLOC	FLOODWAY	FLORIDITIES	FLOURISHED
FLIPPANT	FLOCCED	FLOODWAYS	FLORIDITY	FLOURISHES
FLIPPED	FLOCCI	FLOOEY	FLORIDLY	FLOURISHING
FLIPPER	FLOCCING	FLOOIE	FLORIGEN	FLOURLESS
FLIPPERS	FLOCCOSE	FLOOR	FLORIGENS	FLOURS
FLIPPEST	FLOCCULE	FLOORAGE	FLORIN	FLOURY
FLIPPING	FLOCCULES	FLOORAGES	FLORINS	FLOUT
FLIPPY	FLOCCULI	FLOORED	FLORIST	FLOUTED
FLIPS	FLOCCULUS	FLOORER	FLORISTIC	FLOUTER
FLIR	FLOCCUS	FLOORERS	FLORISTRIES	FLOUTERS
FLIRS	FLOCK	FLOORING	FLORISTRY	FLOUTING
FLIRT	FLOCKED	FLOORINGS	FLORISTS	FLOUTS
FLIRTED	FLOCKIER	FLOORLESS	FLORUIT	FLOW
FLIRTER	FLOCKIEST	FLOORS	FLORUITS	FLOWAGE
FLIRTERS	FLOCKING	FLOORSHOW	FLOSS	FLOWAGES
FLIRTIER	FLOCKINGS	FLOORSHOWS	FLOSSED	FLOWCHART
FLIRTIEST	FLOCKLESS	FLOOSIE	FLOSSER	FLOWCHARTS
FLIRTING	FLOCKS	FLOOSIES	FLOSSERS	FLOWED
FLIRTS	FLOCKY	FLOOSY	FLOSSES	FLOWER
FLIRTY	FLOCS	FLOOZIE	FLOSSIE	FLOWERAGE
FLIT	FLOE	FLOOZIES	FLOSSIER	FLOWERAGES
FLITCH	FLOES	FLOOZY	FLOSSIES	FLOWERED
FLITCHED	FLOG	FLOP	FLOSSIEST	FLOWERER
FLITCHES	FLOGGABLE	FLOPHOUSE	FLOSSILY	FLOWERERS
FLITCHING	FLOGGED	FLOPHOUSES	FLOSSING	FLOWERET
FLITE	FLOGGER	FLOPOVER	FLOSSY	FLOWERETS
FLITED	FLOGGERS	FLOPOVERS	FLOTA	FLOWERFUL
FLITES	FLOGGING	FLOPPED	FLOTAGE	FLOWERIER
FLITING	FLOGGINGS	FLOPPER	FLOTAGES	FLOWERIEST
FLITS	FLOGS	FLOPPERS	FLOTAS	FLOWERILY
FLITTED	FLOKATI	FLOPPIER	FLOTATION	FLOWERING
FLITTER	FLOKATIS	FLOPPIES	FLOTATIONS	FLOWERPOT
FLITTERED	FLONG	FLOPPIEST	FLOTILLA	FLOWERPOTS
FLITTERING	FLONGS	FLOPPILY	FLOTILLAS	FLOWERS
FLITTERS	FLOOD	FLOPPING	FLOTSAM	FLOWERY
FLITTING	FLOODABLE	FLOPPY	FLOTSAMS	FLOWING
FLIVVER	FLOODED	FLOPS	FLOUNCE	FLOWINGLY
FLIVVERS	FLOODER	FLORA	FLOUNCED	FLOWMETER
FLOAT	FLOODERS	FLORAE	FLOUNCES	FLOWMETERS
FLOATABLE	FLOODGATE	FLORAL	FLOUNCIER	FLOWN
FLOATAGE	FLOODGATES	FLORALLY	FLOUNCIEST	FLOWS
FLOATAGES	FLOODING	FLORALS	FLOUNCING	FLOWSTONE
FLOATED	FLOODLIGHT	FLORAS	FLOUNCINGS	FLOWSTONES
FLOATEL	FLOODLIGHTED	FLOREATED	FLOUNCY	FLU
FLOATELS	FLOODLIGHTING	FLORENCE	FLOUNDER	FLUB
FLOATER	FLOODLIGHTS	FLORENCES	FLOUNDERED	FLUBBED
FLOATERS	FLOODLIT	FLORET	FLOUNDERING	FLUBBER

FLUBBERS	FLUIDS	FLUORIDS	FLUTY	FLYSCHES
FLUBBING	FLUISH	FLUORIN	FLUVIAL	FLYSHEET
FLUBDUB	FLUKE	FLUORINE	FLUX	FLYSHEETS
FLUBDUBS	FLUKED	FLUORINES	FLUXED	FLYSPECK
FLUBS	FLUKES	FLUORINS	FLUXES	FLYSPECKED
FLUCTUANT	FLUKEY	FLUORITE	FLUXGATE	FLYSPECKING
FLUCTUATE	FLUKIER	FLUORITES	FLUXGATES	FLYSPECKS
FLUCTUATED	FLUKIEST	FLUOROSES	FLUXING	FLYTE
FLUCTUATES	FLUKILY	FLUOROSIS	FLUXION	FLYTED
FLUCTUATING	FLUKINESS	FLUOROTIC	FLUXIONAL	FLYTES
FLUE	FLUKINESSES	FLUORS	FLUXIONS	FLYTIER
FLUED	FLUKING	FLUORSPAR	FLUYT	FLYTIERS
FLUENCIES	FLUKY	FLUORSPARS	FLUYTS	FLYTING
FLUENCY	FLUME	FLURRIED	FLY	FLYTINGS
FLUENT	FLUMED	FLURRIES	FLYABLE	FLYTRAP
FLUENTLY	FLUMES	FLURRY	FLYAWAY	FLYTRAPS
FLUERIC	FLUMING	FLURRYING	FLYAWAYS	FLYWAY
FLUERICS	FLUMMERIES	FLUS	FLYBELT	FLYWAYS
FLUES	FLUMMERY	FLUSH	FLYBELTS	FLYWEIGHT
FLUFF	FLUMMOX	FLUSHABLE	FLYBLEW	FLYWEIGHTS
FLUFFED	FLUMMOXED	FLUSHED	FLYBLOW	FLYWHEEL
FLUFFER	FLUMMOXES	FLUSHER	FLYBLOWING	FLYWHEELS
FLUFFERS	FLUMMOXING	FLUSHERS	FLYBLOWN	FOAL
FLUFFIER	FLUMP	FLUSHES	FLYBLOWS	FOALED
FLUFFIEST	FLUMPED	FLUSHEST	FLYBOAT	FOALING
FLUFFILY	FLUMPING	FLUSHING	FLYBOATS	FOALS
FLUFFING	FLUMPS	FLUSHNESS	FLYBOY	FOAM
FLUFFS	FLUNG	FLUSHNESSES	FLYBOYS	FOAMABLE
FLUFFY	FLUNK	FLUSTER	FLYBRIDGE	FOAMED
FLUID	FLUNKED	FLUSTERED	FLYBRIDGES	FOAMER
FLUIDAL	FLUNKER	FLUSTERING	FLYBY	FOAMERS
FLUIDALLY	FLUNKERS	FLUSTERS	FLYBYS	FOAMIER
FLUIDIC	FLUNKEY	FLUTE	FLYER	FOAMIEST
FLUIDICS	FLUNKEYS	FLUTED	FLYERS	FOAMILY
FLUIDISE	FLUNKIE	FLUTELIKE	FLYING	FOAMINESS
FLUIDISED	FLUNKIES	FLUTER	FLYINGS	FOAMINESSES
FLUIDISES	FLUNKING	FLUTERS	FLYLEAF	FOAMING
FLUIDISING	FLUNKS	FLUTES	FLYLEAVES	FOAMLESS
FLUIDITIES	FLUNKY	FLUTEY	FLYLESS	FOAMLIKE
FLUIDITY	FLUNKYISM	FLUTIER	FLYMAN	FOAMS
FLUIDIZE	FLUNKYISMS	FLUTIEST	FLYMEN	FOAMY
FLUIDIZED	FLUOR	FLUTING	FLYOFF	FOB
FLUIDIZER	FLUORENE	FLUTINGS	FLYOFFS	FOBBED
FLUIDIZERS	FLUORENES	FLUTIST	FLYOVER	FOBBING
FLUIDIZES	FLUORESCE	FLUTISTS	FLYOVERS	FOBS
FLUIDIZING	FLUORESCED	FLUTTER	FLYPAPER	FOCACCIA
FLUIDLIKE	FLUORESCES	FLUTTERED	FLYPAPERS	FOCACCIAS
FLUIDLY	FLUORESCING	FLUTTERER	FLYPAST	FOCAL
FLUIDNESS	FLUORIC	FLUTTERERS	FLYPASTS	FOCALISE
FLUIDNESSES	FLUORID	FLUTTERING	FLYRODDER	FOCALISED
FLUIDRAM	FLUORIDE	FLUTTERS	FLYRODDERS	FOCALISES
FLUIDRAMS	FLUORIDES	FLUTTERY	FLYSCH	FOCALISING

FOCALIZE
FOCALIZED
FOCALIZES
FOCALIZING
FOCALLY
FOCI
FOCUS
FOCUSABLE
FOCUSED
FOCUSER
FOCUSERS
FOCUSES
FOCUSING
FOCUSLESS
FOCUSSED
FOCUSSES
FOCUSSING
FODDER
FODDERED
FODDERING
FODDERS
FODGEL
FOE
FOEHN
FOEHNS
FOEMAN
FOEMEN
FOES
FOETAL
FOETID
FOETOR
FOETORS
FOETUS
FOETUSES
FOG
FOGBOUND
FOGBOW
FOGBOWS
FOGDOG
FOGDOGS
FOGEY
FOGEYISH
FOGEYISM
FOGEYISMS
FOGEYS
FOGFRUIT
FOGFRUITS
FOGGAGE
FOGGAGES
FOGGED
FOGGER
FOGGERS

FOGGIER
FOGGIEST
FOGGILY
FOGGINESS
FOGGINESSES
FOGGING
FOGGY
FOGHORN
FOGHORNS
FOGIE
FOGIES
FOGLESS
FOGS
FOGY
FOGYISH
FOGYISM
FOGYISMS
FOH
FOHN
FOHNS
FOIBLE
FOIBLES
FOIL
FOILABLE
FOILED
FOILING
FOILS
FOILSMAN
FOILSMEN
FOIN
FOINED
FOINING
FOINS
FOISON
FOISONS
FOIST
FOISTED
FOISTING
FOISTS
FOLACIN
FOLACINS
FOLATE
FOLATES
FOLD
FOLDABLE
FOLDAWAY
FOLDAWAYS
FOLDBOAT
FOLDBOATS
FOLDED
FOLDER
FOLDEROL

FOLDEROLS
FOLDERS
FOLDING
FOLDOUT
FOLDOUTS
FOLDS
FOLDUP
FOLDUPS
FOLEY
FOLEYS
FOLIA
FOLIAGE
FOLIAGED
FOLIAGES
FOLIAR
FOLIATE
FOLIATED
FOLIATES
FOLIATING
FOLIATION
FOLIATIONS
FOLIC
FOLIO
FOLIOED
FOLIOING
FOLIOLATE
FOLIOS
FOLIOSE
FOLIOUS
FOLIUM
FOLIUMS
FOLK
FOLKIE
FOLKIER
FOLKIES
FOLKIEST
FOLKISH
FOLKLIFE
FOLKLIKE
FOLKLIVES
FOLKLORE
FOLKLORES
FOLKLORIC
FOLKMOOT
FOLKMOOTS
FOLKMOT
FOLKMOTE
FOLKMOTES
FOLKMOTS
FOLKS
FOLKSIER
FOLKSIEST

FOLKSILY
FOLKSONG
FOLKSONGS
FOLKSY
FOLKTALE
FOLKTALES
FOLKWAY
FOLKWAYS
FOLKY
FOLLES
FOLLICLE
FOLLICLES
FOLLIES
FOLLIS
FOLLOW
FOLLOWED
FOLLOWER
FOLLOWERS
FOLLOWING
FOLLOWINGS
FOLLOWS
FOLLOWUP
FOLLOWUPS
FOLLY
FOMENT
FOMENTED
FOMENTER
FOMENTERS
FOMENTING
FOMENTS
FOMITE
FOMITES
FON
FOND
FONDANT
FONDANTS
FONDED
FONDER
FONDEST
FONDING
FONDLE
FONDLED
FONDLER
FONDLERS
FONDLES
FONDLING
FONDLINGS
FONDLY
FONDNESS
FONDNESSES
FONDS
FONDU

FONDUE
FONDUED
FONDUEING
FONDUES
FONDUING
FONDUS
FONS
FONT
FONTAL
FONTANEL
FONTANELS
FONTINA
FONTINAS
FONTS
FOOD
FOODIE
FOODIES
FOODLESS
FOODS
FOODSTUFF
FOODSTUFFS
FOODWAYS
FOOFARAW
FOOFARAWS
FOOL
FOOLED
FOOLERIES
FOOLERY
FOOLFISH
FOOLFISHES
FOOLHARDIER
FOOLHARDIEST
FOOLHARDY
FOOLING
FOOLISH
FOOLISHER
FOOLISHEST
FOOLISHLY
FOOLPROOF
FOOLS
FOOLSCAP
FOOLSCAPS
FOOSBALL
FOOSBALLS
FOOT
FOOTAGE
FOOTAGES
FOOTBAG
FOOTBAGS
FOOTBALL
FOOTBALLS
FOOTBATH

FOOTBATHS	FOOTPATHS	FOPS	FORCEFUL	FORECHECKING
FOOTBOARD	FOOTPRINT	FOR	FORCELESS	FORECHECKS
FOOTBOARDS	FOOTPRINTS	FORA	FORCEMEAT	FORECLOSE
FOOTBOY	FOOTRACE	FORAGE	FORCEMEATS	FORECLOSED
FOOTBOYS	FOOTRACES	FORAGED	FORCEPS	FORECLOSES
FOOTCLOTH	FOOTREST	FORAGER	FORCER	FORECLOSING
FOOTCLOTHS	FOOTRESTS	FORAGERS	FORCERS	FORECOURT
FOOTED	FOOTROPE	FORAGES	FORCES	FORECOURTS
FOOTER	FOOTROPES	FORAGING	FORCIBLE	FOREDATE
FOOTERS	FOOTS	FORAM	FORCIBLY	FOREDATED
FOOTFALL	FOOTSIE	FORAMEN	FORCING	FOREDATES
FOOTFALLS	FOOTSIES	FORAMENS	FORCIPES	FOREDATING
FOOTFAULT	FOOTSLOG	FORAMINA	FORD	FOREDECK
FOOTFAULTED	FOOTSLOGGED	FORAMINAL	FORDABLE	FOREDECKS
FOOTFAULTING	FOOTSLOGGING	FORAMS	FORDED	FOREDID
FOOTFAULTS	FOOTSLOGS	FORASMUCH	FORDID	FOREDO
FOOTGEAR	FOOTSORE	FORAY	FORDING	FOREDOES
FOOTGEARS	FOOTSTALK	FORAYED	FORDLESS	FOREDOING
FOOTHILL	FOOTSTALKS	FORAYER	FORDO	FOREDONE
FOOTHILLS	FOOTSTALL	FORAYERS	FORDOES	FOREDOOM
FOOTHOLD	FOOTSTALLS	FORAYING	FORDOING	FOREDOOMED
FOOTHOLDS	FOOTSTEP	FORAYS	FORDONE	FOREDOOMING
FOOTIE	FOOTSTEPS	FORB	FORDS	FOREDOOMS
FOOTIER	FOOTSTOCK	FORBAD	FORE	FOREFACE
FOOTIES	FOOTSTOCKS	FORBADE	FOREARM	FOREFACES
FOOTIEST	FOOTSTONE	FORBARE	FOREARMED	FOREFEEL
FOOTING	FOOTSTONES	FORBEAR	FOREARMING	FOREFEELING
FOOTINGS	FOOTSTOOL	FORBEARER	FOREARMS	FOREFEELS
FOOTLE	FOOTSTOOLS	FORBEARERS	FOREBAY	FOREFEET
FOOTLED	FOOTSY	FORBEARING	FOREBAYS	FOREFELT
FOOTLER	FOOTWALL	FORBEARS	FOREBEAR	FOREFEND
FOOTLERS	FOOTWALLS	FORBID	FOREBEARS	FOREFENDED
FOOTLES	FOOTWAY	FORBIDAL	FOREBODE	FOREFENDING
FOOTLESS	FOOTWAYS	FORBIDALS	FOREBODED	FOREFENDS
FOOTLIGHT	FOOTWEAR	FORBIDDEN	FOREBODER	FOREFOOT
FOOTLIGHTS	FOOTWORK	FORBIDDER	FOREBODERS	FOREFRONT
FOOTLIKE	FOOTWORKS	FORBIDDERS	FOREBODES	FOREFRONTS
FOOTLING	FOOTWORN	FORBIDDING	FOREBODIES	FOREGO
FOOTLOOSE	FOOTY	FORBIDS	FOREBODING	FOREGOER
FOOTMAN	FOOZLE	FORBODE	FOREBODY	FOREGOERS
FOOTMARK	FOOZLED	FORBODED	FOREBOOM	FOREGOES
FOOTMARKS	FOOZLER	FORBODES	FOREBOOMS	FOREGOING
FOOTMEN	FOOZLERS	FORBODING	FOREBRAIN	FOREGONE
FOOTNOTE	FOOZLES	FORBORE	FOREBRAINS	FOREGUT
FOOTNOTED	FOOZLING	FORBORNE	FOREBY	FOREGUTS
FOOTNOTES	FOP	FORBS	FOREBYE	FOREHAND
FOOTNOTING	FOPPED	FORBY	FORECAST	FOREHANDS
FOOTPACE	FOPPERIES	FORBYE	FORECASTED	FOREHEAD
FOOTPACES	FOPPERY	FORCE	FORECASTING	FOREHEADS
FOOTPAD	FOPPING	FORCEABLE	FORECASTS	FOREHOOF
FOOTPADS	FOPPISH	FORCED	FORECHECK	FOREHOOFS
FOOTPATH	FOPPISHLY	FORCEDLY	FORECHECKED	FOREHOOVES

FOREIGN	FOREREACHES	FORESTER	FORFEND	FORKEDLY
FOREIGNER	FOREREACHING	FORESTERS	FORFENDED	FORKER
FOREIGNERS	FORERUN	FORESTIAL	FORFENDING	FORKERS
FOREJUDGE	FORERUNNING	FORESTING	FORFENDS	FORKFUL
FOREJUDGED	FORERUNS	FORESTRIES	FORFICATE	FORKFULS
FOREJUDGES	FORES	FORESTRY	FORGAT	FORKIER
FOREJUDGING	FORESAID	FORESTS	FORGATHER	FORKIEST
FOREKNEW	FORESAIL	FORESWEAR	FORGATHERED	FORKINESS
FOREKNOW	FORESAILS	FORESWEARING	FORGATHERING	FORKINESSES
FOREKNOWING	FORESAW	FORESWEARS	FORGATHERS	FORKING
FOREKNOWN	FORESEE	FORESWORE	FORGAVE	FORKLESS
FOREKNOWS	FORESEEING	FORESWORN	FORGE	FORKLIFT
FORELADIES	FORESEEN	FORETASTE	FORGEABLE	FORKLIFTED
FORELADY	FORESEER	FORETASTED	FORGED	FORKLIFTING
FORELAND	FORESEERS	FORETASTES	FORGER	FORKLIFTS
FORELANDS	FORESEES	FORETASTING	FORGERIES	FORKLIKE
FORELEG	FORESHANK	FORETEETH	FORGERS	FORKS
FORELEGS	FORESHANKS	FORETELL	FORGERY	FORKSFUL
FORELIMB	FORESHEET	FORETELLING	FORGES	FORKY
FORELIMBS	FORESHEETS	FORETELLS	FORGET	FORLORN
FORELOCK	FORESHOCK	FORETIME	FORGETFUL	FORLORNER
FORELOCKED	FORESHOCKS	FORETIMES	FORGETIVE	FORLORNEST
FORELOCKING	FORESHORE	FORETOKEN	FORGETS	FORLORNLY
FORELOCKS	FORESHORES	FORETOKENED	FORGETTER	FORM
FOREMAN	FORESHOW	FORETOKENING	FORGETTERS	FORMABLE
FOREMAST	FORESHOWED	FORETOKENS	FORGETTING	FORMABLY
FOREMASTS	FORESHOWING	FORETOLD	FORGING	FORMAL
FOREMEN	FORESHOWN	FORETOOTH	FORGINGS	FORMALIN
FOREMILK	FORESHOWS	FORETOP	FORGIVE	FORMALINS
FOREMILKS	FORESIDE	FORETOPS	FORGIVEN	FORMALISE
FOREMOST	FORESIDES	FOREVER	FORGIVER	FORMALISED
FORENAME	FORESIGHT	FOREVERS	FORGIVERS	FORMALISES
FORENAMED	FORESIGHTS	FOREWARN	FORGIVES	FORMALISING
FORENAMES	FORESKIN	FOREWARNED	FORGIVING	FORMALISM
FORENOON	FORESKINS	FOREWARNING	FORGO	FORMALISMS
FORENOONS	FORESPAKE	FOREWARNS	FORGOER	FORMALIST
FORENSIC	FORESPEAK	FOREWENT	FORGOERS	FORMALISTS
FORENSICS	FORESPEAKING	FOREWING	FORGOES	FORMALITIES
FOREPART	FORESPEAKS	FOREWINGS	FORGOING	FORMALITY
FOREPARTS	FORESPOKE	FOREWOMAN	FORGONE	FORMALIZE
FOREPAST	FORESPOKEN	FOREWOMEN	FORGOT	FORMALIZED
FOREPAW	FOREST	FOREWORD	FORGOTTEN	FORMALIZES
FOREPAWS	FORESTAGE	FOREWORDS	FORINT	FORMALIZING
FOREPEAK	FORESTAGES	FOREWORN	FORINTS	FORMALLY
FOREPEAKS	FORESTAL	FOREYARD	FORJUDGE	FORMALS
FOREPLAY	FORESTALL	FOREYARDS	FORJUDGED	FORMAMIDE
FOREPLAYS	FORESTALLED	FORFEIT	FORJUDGES	FORMAMIDES
FORERAN	FORESTALLING	FORFEITED	FORJUDGING	FORMANT
FORERANK	FORESTALLS	FORFEITER	FORK	FORMANTS
FORERANKS	FORESTAY	FORFEITERS	FORKBALL	FORMAT
FOREREACH	FORESTAYS	FORFEITING	FORKBALLS	FORMATE
FOREREACHED	FORESTED	FORFEITS	FORKED	FORMATES

FORMATION	FORNICATED	FORTUNATE	FOSTER	FOURPENCES
FORMATIONS	FORNICATES	FORTUNATES	FOSTERAGE	FOURPENNIES
FORMATIVE	FORNICATING	FORTUNE	FOSTERAGES	FOURPENNY
FORMATIVES	FORNICES	FORTUNED	FOSTERED	FOURPLEX
FORMATS	FORNIX	FORTUNES	FOSTERER	FOURPLEXES
FORMATTED	FORRADER	FORTUNING	FOSTERERS	FOURS
FORMATTER	FORRARDER	FORTY	FOSTERING	FOURSCORE
FORMATTERS	FORRIT	FORTYISH	FOSTERS	FOURSOME
FORMATTING	FORSAKE	FORUM	FOU	FOURSOMES
FORME	FORSAKEN	FORUMS	FOUETTE	FOURTEEN
FORMED	FORSAKER	FORWARD	FOUETTES	FOURTEENS
FORMEE	FORSAKERS	FORWARDED	FOUGHT	FOURTH
FORMER	FORSAKES	FORWARDER	FOUGHTEN	FOURTHLY
FORMERLY	FORSAKING	FORWARDERS	FOUL	FOURTHS
FORMERS	FORSOOK	FORWARDEST	FOULARD	FOVEA
FORMES	FORSOOTH	FORWARDING	FOULARDS	FOVEAE
FORMFUL	FORSPENT	FORWARDLY	FOULBROOD	FOVEAL
FORMIC	FORSWEAR	FORWARDS	FOULBROODS	FOVEAS
FORMICA	FORSWEARING	FORWENT	FOULED	FOVEATE
FORMICARIES	FORSWEARS	FORWHY	FOULER	FOVEATED
FORMICARY	FORSWORE	FORWORN	FOULEST	FOVEIFORM
FORMICAS	FORSWORN	FORZANDI	FOULING	FOVEOLA
FORMING	FORSYTHIA	FORZANDO	FOULINGS	FOVEOLAE
FORMLESS	FORSYTHIAS	FORZANDOS	FOULLY	FOVEOLAR
FORMOL	FORT	FOSCARNET	FOULNESS	FOVEOLAS
FORMOLS	FORTALICE	FOSCARNETS	FOULNESSES	FOVEOLATE
FORMS	FORTALICES	FOSS	FOULS	FOVEOLE
FORMULA	FORTE	FOSSA	FOUND	FOVEOLES
FORMULAE	FORTES	FOSSAE	FOUNDED	FOVEOLET
FORMULAIC	FORTH	FOSSAS	FOUNDER	FOVEOLETS
FORMULARIES	FORTHWITH	FOSSATE	FOUNDERED	FOWL
FORMULARY	FORTIES	FOSSE	FOUNDERING	FOWLED
FORMULAS	FORTIETH	FOSSES	FOUNDERS	FOWLER
FORMULATE	FORTIETHS	FOSSETTE	FOUNDING	FOWLERS
FORMULATED	FORTIFIED	FOSSETTES	FOUNDLING	FOWLING
FORMULATES	FORTIFIER	FOSSICK	FOUNDLINGS	FOWLINGS
FORMULATING	FORTIFIERS	FOSSICKED	FOUNDRIES	FOWLPOX
FORMULISM	FORTIFIES	FOSSICKER	FOUNDRY	FOWLPOXES
FORMULISMS	FORTIFY	FOSSICKERS	FOUNDS	FOWLS
FORMULIST	FORTIFYING	FOSSICKING	FOUNT	FOX
FORMULISTS	FORTIS	FOSSICKS	FOUNTAIN	FOXED
FORMULIZE	FORTITUDE	FOSSIL	FOUNTAINED	FOXES
FORMULIZED	FORTITUDES	FOSSILISE	FOUNTAINING	FOXFIRE
FORMULIZES	FORTNIGHT	FOSSILISED	FOUNTAINS	FOXFIRES
FORMULIZING	FORTNIGHTS	FOSSILISES	FOUNTS	FOXFISH
FORMWORK	FORTRESS	FOSSILISING	FOUR	FOXFISHES
FORMWORKS	FORTRESSED	FOSSILIZE	FOURCHEE	FOXGLOVE
FORMYL	FORTRESSES	FOSSILIZED	FOUREYED	FOXGLOVES
FORMYLS	FORTRESSING	FOSSILIZES	FOURFOLD	FOXHOLE
FORNENT	FORTS	FOSSILIZING	FOURGON	FOXHOLES
FORNICAL	FORTUITIES	FOSSILS	FOURGONS	FOXHOUND
FORNICATE	FORTUITY	FOSSORIAL	FOURPENCE	FOXHOUNDS

FOXHUNT	FRACTURS	FRAMINGS	FRAUDS	FREEBOOTED
FOXHUNTED	FRACTUS	FRANC	FRAUDSTER	FREEBOOTING
FOXHUNTER	FRAE	FRANCHISE	FRAUDSTERS	FREEBOOTS
FOXHUNTERS	FRAENA	FRANCHISED	FRAUGHT	FREEBORN
FOXHUNTING	FRAENUM	FRANCHISES	FRAUGHTED	FREED
FOXHUNTS	FRAENUMS	FRANCHISING	FRAUGHTING	FREEDMAN
FOXIER	FRAG	FRANCIUM	FRAUGHTS	FREEDMEN
FOXIEST	FRAGGED	FRANCIUMS	FRAULEIN	FREEDOM
FOXILY	FRAGGING	FRANCIZE	FRAULEINS	FREEDOMS
FOXINESS	FRAGGINGS	FRANCIZED	FRAY	FREEFORM
FOXINESSES	FRAGILE	FRANCIZES	FRAYED	FREEHAND
FOXING	FRAGILELY	FRANCIZING	FRAYING	FREEHOLD
FOXINGS	FRAGILITIES	FRANCOLIN	FRAYINGS	FREEHOLDS
FOXLIKE	FRAGILITY	FRANCOLINS	FRAYS	FREEING
FOXSKIN	FRAGMENT	FRANCS	FRAZIL	FREELANCE
FOXSKINS	FRAGMENTED	FRANGIBLE	FRAZILS	FREELANCED
FOXTAIL	FRAGMENTING	FRANGLAIS	FRAZZLE	FREELANCES
FOXTAILS	FRAGMENTS	FRANK	FRAZZLED	FREELANCING
FOXTROT	FRAGRANCE	FRANKABLE	FRAZZLES	FREELOAD
FOXTROTS	FRAGRANCES	FRANKED	FRAZZLING	FREELOADED
FOXTROTTED	FRAGRANCIES	FRANKER	FREAK	FREELOADING
FOXTROTTING	FRAGRANCY	FRANKERS	FREAKED	FREELOADS
FOXY	FRAGRANT	FRANKEST	FREAKIER	FREELY
FOY	FRAGS	FRANKFORT	FREAKIEST	FREEMAN
FOYER	FRAIL	FRANKFORTS	FREAKILY	FREEMASON
FOYERS	FRAILER	FRANKFURT	FREAKING	FREEMASONS
FOYS	FRAILEST	FRANKFURTS	FREAKISH	FREEMEN
FOZIER	FRAILLY	FRANKING	FREAKOUT	FREENESS
FOZIEST	FRAILNESS	FRANKLIN	FREAKOUTS	FREENESSES
FOZINESS	FRAILNESSES	FRANKLINS	FREAKS	FREER
FOZINESSES	FRAILS	FRANKLY	FREAKY	FREERS
FOZY	FRAILTIES	FRANKNESS	FRECKLE	FREES
FRABJOUS	FRAILTY	FRANKNESSES	FRECKLED	FREESIA
FRACAS	FRAISE	FRANKS	FRECKLES	FREESIAS
FRACASES	FRAISES	FRANSERIA	FRECKLIER	FREEST
FRACTAL	FRAKTUR	FRANSERIAS	FRECKLIEST	FREESTONE
FRACTALS	FRAKTURS	FRANTIC	FRECKLING	FREESTONES
FRACTED	FRAMABLE	FRANTICLY	FRECKLY	FREESTYLE
FRACTI	FRAMBESIA	FRAP	FREE	FREESTYLES
FRACTION	FRAMBESIAS	FRAPPE	FREEBASE	FREEWARE
FRACTIONED	FRAMBOISE	FRAPPED	FREEBASED	FREEWARES
FRACTIONING	FRAMBOISES	FRAPPES	FREEBASER	FREEWAY
FRACTIONS	FRAME	FRAPPING	FREEBASERS	FREEWAYS
FRACTIOUS	FRAMEABLE	FRAPS	FREEBASES	FREEWHEEL
FRACTUR	FRAMED	FRASS	FREEBASING	FREEWHEELED
FRACTURAL	FRAMELESS	FRASSES	FREEBEE	FREEWHEELING
FRACTURE	FRAMER	FRAT	FREEBEES	FREEWHEELS
FRACTURED	FRAMERS	FRATER	FREEBIE	FREEWILL
FRACTURER	FRAMES	FRATERNAL	FREEBIES	FREEWRITE
FRACTURERS	FRAMEWORK	FRATERS	FREEBOARD	FREEWRITES
FRACTURES	FRAMEWORKS	FRATS	FREEBOARDS	FREEWRITING
FRACTURING	FRAMING	FRAUD	FREEBOOT	FREEWRITTEN

FREEWROTE	FRESCOER	FRIARLY	FRIGID	FRITES
FREEZABLE	FRESCOERS	FRIARS	FRIGIDITIES	FRITH
FREEZE	FRESCOES	FRIARY	FRIGIDITY	FRITHS
FREEZER	FRESCOING	FRIBBLE	FRIGIDLY	FRITS
FREEZERS	FRESCOIST	FRIBBLED	FRIGS	FRITT
FREEZES	FRESCOISTS	FRIBBLER	FRIJOL	FRITTATA
FREEZING	FRESCOS	FRIBBLERS	FRIJOLE	FRITTATAS
FREIGHT	FRESH	FRIBBLES	FRIJOLES	FRITTED
FREIGHTED	FRESHED	FRIBBLING	FRILL	FRITTER
FREIGHTER	FRESHEN	FRICANDO	FRILLED	FRITTERED
FREIGHTERS	FRESHENED	FRICANDOES	FRILLER	FRITTERER
FREIGHTING	FRESHENER	FRICASSEE	FRILLERS	FRITTERERS
FREIGHTS	FRESHENERS	FRICASSEED	FRILLIER	FRITTERING
FREMD	FRESHENING	FRICASSEEING	FRILLIEST	FRITTERS
FREMITUS	FRESHENS	FRICASSEES	FRILLING	FRITTING
FREMITUSES	FRESHER	FRICATIVE	FRILLINGS	FRITTS
FRENA	FRESHES	FRICATIVES	FRILLS	FRITZ
FRENCH	FRESHEST	FRICTION	FRILLY	FRITZES
FRENCHED	FRESHET	FRICTIONS	FRINGE	FRIVOL
FRENCHES	FRESHETS	FRIDGE	FRINGED	FRIVOLED
FRENCHIFIED	FRESHING	FRIDGES	FRINGES	FRIVOLER
FRENCHIFIES	FRESHLY	FRIED	FRINGIER	FRIVOLERS
FRENCHIFY	FRESHMAN	FRIEDCAKE	FRINGIEST	FRIVOLING
FRENCHIFYING	FRESHMEN	FRIEDCAKES	FRINGING	FRIVOLITIES
FRENCHING	FRESHNESS	FRIEND	FRINGY	FRIVOLITY
FRENETIC	FRESHNESSES	FRIENDED	FRIPPERIES	FRIVOLLED
FRENETICS	FRESNEL	FRIENDING	FRIPPERY	FRIVOLLER
FRENULA	FRESNELS	FRIENDLIER	FRISBEE	FRIVOLLERS
FRENULAR	FRET	FRIENDLIES	FRISBEES	FRIVOLLING
FRENULUM	FRETBOARD	FRIENDLIEST	FRISE	FRIVOLOUS
FRENULUMS	FRETBOARDS	FRIENDLY	FRISEE	FRIVOLS
FRENUM	FRETFUL	FRIENDS	FRISEES	FRIZ
FRENUMS	FRETFULLY	FRIER	FRISES	FRIZED
FRENZIED	FRETLESS	FRIERS	FRISETTE	FRIZER
FRENZIES	FRETS	FRIES	FRISETTES	FRIZERS
FRENZILY	FRETSAW	FRIEZE	FRISEUR	FRIZES
FRENZY	FRETSAWS	FRIEZES	FRISEURS	FRIZETTE
FRENZYING	FRETSOME	FRIG	FRISK	FRIZETTES
FREQUENCE	FRETTED	FRIGATE	FRISKED	FRIZING
FREQUENCES	FRETTER	FRIGATES	FRISKER	FRIZZ
FREQUENCIES	FRETTERS	FRIGES	FRISKERS	FRIZZED
FREQUENCY	FRETTIER	FRIGGED	FRISKET	FRIZZER
FREQUENT	FRETTIEST	FRIGGING	FRISKETS	FRIZZERS
FREQUENTED	FRETTING	FRIGHT	FRISKIER	FRIZZES
FREQUENTER	FRETTY	FRIGHTED	FRISKIEST	FRIZZIER
FREQUENTEST	FRETWORK	FRIGHTEN	FRISKILY	FRIZZIES
FREQUENTING	FRETWORKS	FRIGHTENED	FRISKING	FRIZZIEST
FREQUENTS	FRIABLE	FRIGHTENING	FRISKS	FRIZZILY
FRERE	FRIAR	FRIGHTENS	FRISKY	FRIZZING
FRERES	FRIARBIRD	FRIGHTFUL	FRISSON	FRIZZLE
FRESCO	FRIARBIRDS	FRIGHTING	FRISSONS	FRIZZLED
FRESCOED	FRIARIES	FRIGHTS	FRIT	FRIZZLER

FRIZZLERS	FRONDOSE	FROSTLINE	FROWZIEST	FRUMP
FRIZZLES	FRONDS	FROSTLINES	FROWZILY	FRUMPIER
FRIZZLIER	FRONS	FROSTNIP	FROWZY	FRUMPIEST
FRIZZLIEST	FRONT	FROSTNIPS	FROZE	FRUMPILY
FRIZZLING	FRONTAGE	FROSTS	FROZEN	FRUMPISH
FRIZZLY	FRONTAGES	FROSTWORK	FROZENLY	FRUMPS
FRIZZY	FRONTAL	FROSTWORKS	FRUCTIFIED	FRUMPY
FRO	FRONTALLY	FROSTY	FRUCTIFIES	FRUSTA
FROCK	FRONTALS	FROTH	FRUCTIFY	FRUSTRATE
FROCKED	FRONTED	FROTHED	FRUCTIFYING	FRUSTRATED
FROCKING	FRONTENIS	FROTHER	FRUCTOSE	FRUSTRATES
FROCKLESS	FRONTENISES	FROTHERS	FRUCTOSES	FRUSTRATING
FROCKS	FRONTER	FROTHIER	FRUCTUOUS	FRUSTULE
FROE	FRONTES	FROTHIEST	FRUG	FRUSTULES
FROES	FRONTIER	FROTHILY	FRUGAL	FRUSTUM
FROG	FRONTIERS	FROTHING	FRUGALITIES	FRUSTUMS
FROGEYE	FRONTING	FROTHS	FRUGALITY	FRUTICOSE
FROGEYED	FRONTLESS	FROTHY	FRUGALLY	FRY
FROGEYES	FRONTLET	FROTTAGE	FRUGGED	FRYABLE
FROGFISH	FRONTLETS	FROTTAGES	FRUGGING	FRYBREAD
FROGFISHES	FRONTLINE	FROTTEUR	FRUGIVORE	FRYBREADS
FROGGED	FRONTLINES	FROTTEURS	FRUGIVORES	FRYER
FROGGIER	FRONTLIST	FROUFROU	FRUGS	FRYERS
FROGGIEST	FRONTLISTS	FROUFROUS	FRUIT	FRYING
FROGGING	FRONTMAN	FROUNCE	FRUITAGE	FRYPAN
FROGGY	FRONTMEN	FROUNCED	FRUITAGES	FRYPANS
FROGLET	FRONTON	FROUNCES	FRUITCAKE	FUB
FROGLETS	FRONTONS	FROUNCING	FRUITCAKES	FUBAR
FROGLIKE	FRONTPAGE	FROUZIER	FRUITED	FUBBED
FROGMAN	FRONTPAGED	FROUZIEST	FRUITER	FUBBING
FROGMARCH	FRONTPAGES	FROUZY	FRUITERER	FUBS
FROGMARCHED	FRONTPAGING	FROW	FRUITERERS	FUBSIER
FROGMARCHES	FRONTS	FROWARD	FRUITERS	FUBSIEST
FROGMARCHING	FRONTWARD	FROWARDLY	FRUITFUL	FUBSY
FROGMEN	FRORE	FROWN	FRUITFULLER	FUCHSIA
FROGS	FROSH	FROWNED	FRUITFULLEST	FUCHSIAS
FROLIC	FROST	FROWNER	FRUITIER	FUCHSIN
FROLICKED	FROSTBIT	FROWNERS	FRUITIEST	FUCHSINE
FROLICKER	FROSTBITE	FROWNING	FRUITILY	FUCHSINES
FROLICKERS	FROSTBITES	FROWNS	FRUITING	FUCHSINS
FROLICKING	FROSTBITING	FROWS	FRUITION	FUCI
FROLICKY	FROSTBITTEN	FROWSIER	FRUITIONS	FUCK
FROLICS	FROSTED	FROWSIEST	FRUITLESS	FUCKED
FROM	FROSTEDS	FROWST	FRUITLET	FUCKER
FROMAGE	FROSTFISH	FROWSTED	FRUITLETS	FUCKERS
FROMAGES	FROSTFISHES	FROWSTIER	FRUITLIKE	FUCKING
FROMENTIES	FROSTIER	FROWSTIEST	FRUITS	FUCKOFF
FROMENTY	FROSTIEST	FROWSTING	FRUITWOOD	FUCKOFFS
FROND	FROSTILY	FROWSTS	FRUITWOODS	FUCKS
FRONDED	FROSTING	FROWSTY	FRUITY	FUCKUP
FRONDEUR	FROSTINGS	FROWSY	FRUMENTIES	FUCKUPS
FRONDEURS	FROSTLESS	FROWZIER	FRUMENTY	FUCOID

FUCOIDAL	FUGLED	FULLERED	FUMER	FUNFAIRS
FUCOIDS	FUGLEMAN	FULLERENE	FUMERS	FUNFEST
FUCOSE	FUGLEMEN	FULLERENES	FUMES	FUNFESTS
FUCOSES	FUGLES	FULLERIES	FUMET	FUNGAL
FUCOUS	FUGLING	FULLERING	FUMETS	FUNGALS
FUCUS	FUGS	FULLERS	FUMETTE	FUNGI
FUCUSES	FUGU	FULLERY	FUMETTES	FUNGIBLE
FUD	FUGUE	FULLEST	FUMIER	FUNGIBLES
FUDDIES	FUGUED	FULLFACE	FUMIEST	FUNGIC
FUDDLE	FUGUELIKE	FULLFACES	FUMIGANT	FUNGICIDE
FUDDLED	FUGUES	FULLING	FUMIGANTS	FUNGICIDES
FUDDLES	FUGUING	FULLNESS	FUMIGATE	FUNGIFORM
FUDDLING	FUGUIST	FULLNESSES	FUMIGATED	FUNGISTAT
FUDDY	FUGUISTS	FULLS	FUMIGATES	FUNGISTATS
FUDGE	FUGUS	FULLY	FUMIGATING	FUNGO
FUDGED	FUHRER	FULMAR	FUMIGATOR	FUNGOES
FUDGES	FUHRERS	FULMARS	FUMIGATORS	FUNGOID
FUDGING	FUJI	FULMINANT	FUMING	FUNGOIDS
FUDS	FUJIS	FULMINATE	FUMINGLY	FUNGOUS
FUEHRER	FULCRA	FULMINATED	FUMITORIES	FUNGUS
FUEHRERS	FULCRUM	FULMINATES	FUMITORY	FUNGUSES
FUEL	FULCRUMS	FULMINATING	FUMULI	FUNHOUSE
FUELED	FULFIL	FULMINE	FUMULUS	FUNHOUSES
FUELER	FULFILL	FULMINED	FUMY	FUNICLE
FUELERS	FULFILLED	FULMINES	FUN	FUNICLES
FUELING	FULFILLER	FULMINIC	FUNCTION	FUNICULAR
FUELLED	FULFILLERS	FULMINING	FUNCTIONED	FUNICULARS
FUELLER	FULFILLING	FULNESS	FUNCTIONING	FUNICULI
FUELLERS	FULFILLS	FULNESSES	FUNCTIONS	FUNICULUS
FUELLING	FULFILS	FULSOME	FUNCTOR	FUNK
FUELS	FULGENT	FULSOMELY	FUNCTORS	FUNKED
FUELWOOD	FULGENTLY	FULVOUS	FUND	FUNKER
FUELWOODS	FULGID	FUMARASE	FUNDAMENT	FUNKERS
FUG	FULGURANT	FUMARASES	FUNDAMENTS	FUNKIA
FUGACIOUS	FULGURATE	FUMARATE	FUNDED	FUNKIAS
FUGACITIES	FULGURATED	FUMARATES	FUNDER	FUNKIER
FUGACITY	FULGURATES	FUMARIC	FUNDERS	FUNKIEST
FUGAL	FULGURATING	FUMAROLE	FUNDI	FUNKILY
FUGALLY	FULGURITE	FUMAROLES	FUNDIC	FUNKINESS
FUGATO	FULGURITES	FUMAROLIC	FUNDING	FUNKINESSES
FUGATOS	FULGUROUS	FUMATORIES	FUNDRAISE	FUNKING
FUGGED	FULHAM	FUMATORY	FUNDRAISED	FUNKS
FUGGIER	FULHAMS	FUMBLE	FUNDRAISES	FUNKY
FUGGIEST	FULL	FUMBLED	FUNDRAISING	FUNNED
FUGGILY	FULLAM	FUMBLER	FUNDS	FUNNEL
FUGGING	FULLAMS	FUMBLERS	FUNDUS	FUNNELED
FUGGY	FULLBACK	FUMBLES	FUNERAL	FUNNELING
FUGIO	FULLBACKS	FUMBLING	FUNERALS	FUNNELLED
FUGIOS	FULLBLOOD	FUME	FUNERARY	FUNNELLING
FUGITIVE	FULLBLOODS	FUMED	FUNEREAL	FUNNELS
FUGITIVES	FULLED	FUMELESS	FUNEST	FUNNER
FUGLE	FULLER	FUMELIKE	FUNFAIR	FUNNEST

FUNNIER	FURIES	FURRINGS	FUSILLADE	FUTHORK
FUNNIES	FURIOSO	FURROW	FUSILLADED	FUTHORKS
FUNNIEST	FURIOUS	FURROWED	FUSILLADES	FUTILE
FUNNILY	FURIOUSLY	FURROWER	FUSILLADING	FUTILELY
FUNNINESS	FURL	FURROWERS	FUSILLI	FUTILITIES
FUNNINESSES	FURLABLE	FURROWING	FUSILLIS	FUTILITY
FUNNING	FURLED	FURROWS	FUSILS	FUTON
FUNNY	FURLER	FURROWY	FUSING	FUTONS
FUNNYMAN	FURLERS	FURRY	FUSION	FUTTOCK
FUNNYMEN	FURLESS	FURS	FUSIONAL	FUTTOCKS
FUNPLEX	FURLING	FURTHER	FUSIONISM	FUTURAL
FUNPLEXES	FURLONG	FURTHERED	FUSIONISMS	FUTURE
FUNS	FURLONGS	FURTHERER	FUSIONIST	FUTURES
FUR	FURLOUGH	FURTHERERS	FUSIONISTS	FUTURISM
FURAN	FURLOUGHED	FURTHERING	FUSIONS	FUTURISMS
FURANE	FURLOUGHING	FURTHERS	FUSS	FUTURIST
FURANES	FURLOUGHS	FURTHEST	FUSSED	FUTURISTS
FURANOSE	FURLS	FURTIVE	FUSSER	FUTURITIES
FURANOSES	FURMENTIES	FURTIVELY	FUSSERS	FUTURITY
FURANS	FURMENTY	FURUNCLE	FUSSES	FUTZ
FURBEARER	FURMETIES	FURUNCLES	FUSSIER	FUTZED
FURBEARERS	FURMETY	FURY	FUSSIEST	FUTZES
FURBELOW	FURMITIES	FURZE	FUSSILY	FUTZING
FURBELOWED	FURMITY	FURZES	FUSSINESS	FUZE
FURBELOWING	FURNACE	FURZIER	FUSSINESSES	FUZED
FURBELOWS	FURNACED	FURZIEST	FUSSING	FUZEE
FURBISH	FURNACES	FURZY	FUSSPOT	FUZEES
FURBISHED	FURNACING	FUSAIN	FUSSPOTS	FUZES
FURBISHER	FURNISH	FUSAINS	FUSSY	FUZIL
FURBISHERS	FURNISHED	FUSARIA	FUSTIAN	FUZILS
FURBISHES	FURNISHER	FUSARIUM	FUSTIANS	FUZING
FURBISHING	FURNISHERS	FUSCOUS	FUSTIC	FUZZ
FURCATE	FURNISHES	FUSE	FUSTICS	FUZZED
FURCATED	FURNISHING	FUSED	FUSTIER	FUZZES
FURCATELY	FURNITURE	FUSEE	FUSTIEST	FUZZIER
FURCATES	FURNITURES	FUSEES	FUSTIGATE	FUZZIEST
FURCATING	FUROR	FUSEL	FUSTIGATED	FUZZILY
FURCATION	FURORE	FUSELAGE	FUSTIGATES	FUZZINESS
FURCATIONS	FURORES	FUSELAGES	FUSTIGATING	FUZZINESSES
FURCRAEA	FURORS	FUSELESS	FUSTILY	FUZZING
FURCRAEAS	FURRED	FUSELIKE	FUSTINESS	FUZZTONE
FURCULA	FURRIER	FUSELS	FUSTINESSES	FUZZTONES
FURCULAE	FURRIERIES	FUSES	FUSTY	FUZZY
FURCULAR	FURRIERS	FUSIBLE	FUSULINID	FYCE
FURCULUM	FURRIERY	FUSIBLY	FUSULINIDS	FYCES
FURFUR	FURRIEST	FUSIFORM	FUSUMA	FYKE
FURFURAL	FURRILY	FUSIL	FUTHARC	FYKES
FURFURALS	FURRINER	FUSILE	FUTHARCS	FYLFOT
FURFURAN	FURRINERS	FUSILEER	FUTHARK	FYLFOTS
FURFURANS	FURRINESS	FUSILEERS	FUTHARKS	FYNBOS
FURFURES	FURRINESSES	FUSILIER	FUTHORC	FYTTE
FURIBUND	FURRING	FUSILIERS	FUTHORCS	FYTTES

G

GAB
GABARDINE
GABARDINES
GABBARD
GABBARDS
GABBART
GABBARTS
GABBED
GABBER
GABBERS
GABBIER
GABBIEST
GABBINESS
GABBINESSES
GABBING
GABBLE
GABBLED
GABBLER
GABBLERS
GABBLES
GABBLING
GABBRO
GABBROIC
GABBROID
GABBROS
GABBY
GABELLE
GABELLED
GABELLES
GABERDINE
GABERDINES
GABFEST
GABFESTS
GABIES
GABION
GABIONS
GABLE
GABLED
GABLELIKE
GABLES
GABLING
GABOON
GABOONS
GABS
GABY
GAD
GADABOUT
GADABOUTS

GADARENE
GADDED
GADDER
GADDERS
GADDI
GADDING
GADDIS
GADFLIES
GADFLY
GADGET
GADGETEER
GADGETEERS
GADGETRIES
GADGETRY
GADGETS
GADGETY
GADI
GADID
GADIDS
GADIS
GADJE
GADJO
GADOID
GADOIDS
GADROON
GADROONED
GADROONING
GADROONS
GADS
GADWALL
GADWALLS
GADZOOKS
GAE
GAED
GAEING
GAEN
GAES
GAFF
GAFFE
GAFFED
GAFFER
GAFFERS
GAFFES
GAFFING
GAFFS
GAG
GAGA
GAGAKU
GAGAKUS
GAGE
GAGED
GAGER

GAGERS
GAGES
GAGGED
GAGGER
GAGGERS
GAGGING
GAGGLE
GAGGLED
GAGGLES
GAGGLING
GAGING
GAGMAN
GAGMEN
GAGS
GAGSTER
GAGSTERS
GAHNITE
GAHNITES
GAIETIES
GAIETY
GAIJIN
GAILY
GAIN
GAINABLE
GAINED
GAINER
GAINERS
GAINFUL
GAINFULLY
GAINING
GAINLESS
GAINLIER
GAINLIEST
GAINLY
GAINS
GAINSAID
GAINSAY
GAINSAYER
GAINSAYERS
GAINSAYING
GAINSAYS
GAINST
GAIT
GAITED
GAITER
GAITERS
GAITING
GAITS
GAL
GALA
GALABIA
GALABIAS

GALABIEH
GALABIEHS
GALABIYA
GALABIYAH
GALABIYAHS
GALABIYAS
GALACTIC
GALACTOSE
GALACTOSES
GALAGO
GALAGOS
GALAH
GALAHS
GALANGA
GALANGAL
GALANGALS
GALANGAS
GALANTINE
GALANTINES
GALAS
GALATEA
GALATEAS
GALAVANT
GALAVANTED
GALAVANTING
GALAVANTS
GALAX
GALAXES
GALAXIES
GALAXY
GALBANUM
GALBANUMS
GALE
GALEA
GALEAE
GALEAS
GALEATE
GALEATED
GALENA
GALENAS
GALENIC
GALENICAL
GALENICALS
GALENITE
GALENITES
GALERE
GALERES
GALES
GALETTE
GALETTES
GALILEE
GALILEES

GALINGALE
GALINGALES
GALIOT
GALIOTS
GALIPOT
GALIPOTS
GALIVANT
GALIVANTED
GALIVANTING
GALIVANTS
GALL
GALLAMINE
GALLAMINES
GALLANT
GALLANTED
GALLANTING
GALLANTLY
GALLANTRIES
GALLANTRY
GALLANTS
GALLATE
GALLATES
GALLEASS
GALLEASSES
GALLED
GALLEIN
GALLEINS
GALLEON
GALLEONS
GALLERIA
GALLERIAS
GALLERIED
GALLERIES
GALLERY
GALLERYING
GALLET
GALLETA
GALLETAS
GALLETED
GALLETING
GALLETS
GALLEY
GALLEYS
GALLFLIES
GALLFLY
GALLIARD
GALLIARDS
GALLIASS
GALLIASSES
GALLIC
GALLICA
GALLICAN

GALLICAS	GALLUSES	GAMBES	GAMETES	GANG
GALLICISM	GALLY	GAMBESON	GAMETIC	GANGBANG
GALLICISMS	GALLYING	GAMBESONS	GAMEY	GANGBANGED
GALLICIZE	GALOOT	GAMBIA	GAMIC	GANGBANGING
GALLICIZED	GALOOTS	GAMBIAS	GAMIER	GANGBANGS
GALLICIZES	GALOP	GAMBIER	GAMIEST	GANGED
GALLICIZING	GALOPADE	GAMBIERS	GAMILY	GANGER
GALLIED	GALOPADES	GAMBIR	GAMIN	GANGERS
GALLIES	GALOPED	GAMBIRS	GAMINE	GANGING
GALLING	GALOPING	GAMBIT	GAMINES	GANGLAND
GALLINGLY	GALOPS	GAMBITS	GAMINESS	GANGLANDS
GALLINULE	GALORE	GAMBLE	GAMINESSES	GANGLIA
GALLINULES	GALORES	GAMBLED	GAMING	GANGLIAL
GALLIOT	GALOSH	GAMBLER	GAMINGS	GANGLIAR
GALLIOTS	GALOSHE	GAMBLERS	GAMINS	GANGLIATE
GALLIPOT	GALOSHED	GAMBLES	GAMMA	GANGLIER
GALLIPOTS	GALOSHES	GAMBLING	GAMMADIA	GANGLIEST
GALLIUM	GALS	GAMBOGE	GAMMADION	GANGLING
GALLIUMS	GALUMPH	GAMBOGES	GAMMAS	GANGLION
GALLIVANT	GALUMPHED	GAMBOGIAN	GAMMED	GANGLIONS
GALLIVANTED	GALUMPHING	GAMBOL	GAMMER	GANGLY
GALLIVANTING	GALUMPHS	GAMBOLED	GAMMERS	GANGPLANK
GALLIVANTS	GALVANIC	GAMBOLING	GAMMIER	GANGPLANKS
GALLIWASP	GALVANISE	GAMBOLLED	GAMMIEST	GANGPLOW
GALLIWASPS	GALVANISED	GAMBOLLING	GAMMING	GANGPLOWS
GALLNUT	GALVANISES	GAMBOLS	GAMMON	GANGREL
GALLNUTS	GALVANISING	GAMBREL	GAMMONED	GANGRELS
GALLON	GALVANISM	GAMBRELS	GAMMONER	GANGRENE
GALLONAGE	GALVANISMS	GAMBS	GAMMONERS	GANGRENED
GALLONAGES	GALVANIZE	GAMBUSIA	GAMMONING	GANGRENES
GALLONS	GALVANIZED	GAMBUSIAS	GAMMONS	GANGRENING
GALLOON	GALVANIZES	GAME	GAMMY	GANGS
GALLOONED	GALVANIZING	GAMECOCK	GAMODEME	GANGSTA
GALLOONS	GALYAC	GAMECOCKS	GAMODEMES	GANGSTAS
GALLOOT	GALYACS	GAMED	GAMP	GANGSTER
GALLOOTS	GALYAK	GAMELAN	GAMPS	GANGSTERS
GALLOP	GALYAKS	GAMELANS	GAMS	GANGUE
GALLOPADE	GAM	GAMELIKE	GAMUT	GANGUES
GALLOPADES	GAMA	GAMELY	GAMUTS	GANGWAY
GALLOPED	GAMAS	GAMENESS	GAMY	GANGWAYS
GALLOPER	GAMASHES	GAMENESSES	GAN	GANISTER
GALLOPERS	GAMAY	GAMER	GANACHE	GANISTERS
GALLOPING	GAMAYS	GAMERS	GANACHES	GANJA
GALLOPS	GAMB	GAMES	GANDER	GANJAH
GALLOUS	GAMBA	GAMESMAN	GANDERED	GANJAHS
GALLOWS	GAMBADE	GAMESMEN	GANDERING	GANJAS
GALLOWSES	GAMBADES	GAMESOME	GANDERS	GANNET
GALLS	GAMBADO	GAMEST	GANE	GANNETS
GALLSTONE	GAMBADOES	GAMESTER	GANEF	GANNISTER
GALLSTONES	GAMBADOS	GAMESTERS	GANEFS	GANNISTERS
GALLUS	GAMBAS	GAMETAL	GANEV	GANOF
GALLUSED	GAMBE	GAMETE	GANEVS	GANOFS

GANOID	GARBAGE	GARGLERS	GAROTTER	GASELIER
GANOIDS	GARBAGES	GARGLES	GAROTTERS	GASELIERS
GANTELOPE	GARBAGEY	GARGLING	GAROTTES	GASEOUS
GANTELOPES	GARBAGY	GARGOYLE	GAROTTING	GASES
GANTLET	GARBANZO	GARGOYLED	GARPIKE	GASH
GANTLETED	GARBANZOS	GARGOYLES	GARPIKES	GASHED
GANTLETING	GARBED	GARIBALDI	GARRED	GASHER
GANTLETS	GARBING	GARIBALDIS	GARRET	GASHES
GANTLINE	GARBLE	GARIGUE	GARRETED	GASHEST
GANTLINES	GARBLED	GARIGUES	GARRETS	GASHING
GANTLOPE	GARBLER	GARISH	GARRING	GASHOLDER
GANTLOPES	GARBLERS	GARISHLY	GARRISON	GASHOLDERS
GANTRIES	GARBLES	GARLAND	GARRISONED	GASHOUSE
GANTRY	GARBLESS	GARLANDED	GARRISONING	GASHOUSES
GANYMEDE	GARBLING	GARLANDING	GARRISONS	GASIFIED
GANYMEDES	GARBOARD	GARLANDS	GARRON	GASIFIER
GAOL	GARBOARDS	GARLIC	GARRONS	GASIFIERS
GAOLED	GARBOIL	GARLICKED	GARROTE	GASIFIES
GAOLER	GARBOILS	GARLICKIER	GARROTED	GASIFORM
GAOLERS	GARBOLOGIES	GARLICKIEST	GARROTER	GASIFY
GAOLING	GARBOLOGY	GARLICKING	GARROTERS	GASIFYING
GAOLS	GARBS	GARLICKY	GARROTES	GASKET
GAP	GARCON	GARLICS	GARROTING	GASKETS
GAPE	GARCONS	GARMENT	GARROTTE	GASKIN
GAPED	GARDA	GARMENTED	GARROTTED	GASKING
GAPER	GARDAI	GARMENTING	GARROTTES	GASKINGS
GAPERS	GARDANT	GARMENTS	GARROTTING	GASKINS
GAPES	GARDEN	GARNER	GARRULITIES	GASLESS
GAPESEED	GARDENED	GARNERED	GARRULITY	GASLIGHT
GAPESEEDS	GARDENER	GARNERING	GARRULOUS	GASLIGHTS
GAPEWORM	GARDENERS	GARNERS	GARS	GASLIT
GAPEWORMS	GARDENFUL	GARNET	GARTER	GASMAN
GAPING	GARDENFULS	GARNETS	GARTERED	GASMEN
GAPINGLY	GARDENIA	GARNI	GARTERING	GASOGENE
GAPLESS	GARDENIAS	GARNISH	GARTERS	GASOGENES
GAPOSIS	GARDENING	GARNISHED	GARTH	GASOHOL
GAPOSISES	GARDENS	GARNISHEE	GARTHS	GASOHOLS
GAPPED	GARDEROBE	GARNISHEED	GARVEY	GASOLENE
GAPPIER	GARDEROBES	GARNISHEEING	GARVEYS	GASOLENES
GAPPIEST	GARDYLOO	GARNISHEES	GAS	GASOLIER
GAPPING	GARFISH	GARNISHER	GASALIER	GASOLIERS
GAPPY	GARFISHES	GARNISHERS	GASALIERS	GASOLINE
GAPS	GARGANEY	GARNISHES	GASBAG	GASOLINES
GAPY	GARGANEYS	GARNISHING	GASBAGS	GASOLINIC
GAR	GARGANTUA	GARNITURE	GASCON	GASOMETER
GARAGE	GARGANTUAS	GARNITURES	GASCONADE	GASOMETERS
GARAGED	GARGET	GAROTE	GASCONADED	GASP
GARAGEMAN	GARGETS	GAROTED	GASCONADES	GASPED
GARAGEMEN	GARGETY	GAROTES	GASCONADING	GASPER
GARAGES	GARGLE	GAROTING	GASCONS	GASPEREAU
GARAGING	GARGLED	GAROTTE	GASEITIES	GASPEREAUX
GARB	GARGLER	GAROTTED	GASEITY	GASPERS

GASPING	GATED	GAUGEABLE	GAVELS	GAZAR
GASPINGLY	GATEFOLD	GAUGED	GAVIAL	GAZARS
GASPS	GATEFOLDS	GAUGER	GAVIALOID	GAZE
GASSED	GATEHOUSE	GAUGERS	GAVIALS	GAZEBO
GASSER	GATEHOUSES	GAUGES	GAVOT	GAZEBOES
GASSERS	GATELESS	GAUGING	GAVOTS	GAZEBOS
GASSES	GATELIKE	GAULEITER	GAVOTTE	GAZED
GASSIER	GATEMAN	GAULEITERS	GAVOTTED	GAZEHOUND
GASSIEST	GATEMEN	GAULT	GAVOTTES	GAZEHOUNDS
GASSILY	GATEPOST	GAULTS	GAVOTTING	GAZELLE
GASSINESS	GATEPOSTS	GAUM	GAWK	GAZELLES
GASSINESSES	GATER	GAUMED	GAWKED	GAZER
GASSING	GATERS	GAUMING	GAWKER	GAZERS
GASSINGS	GATES	GAUMS	GAWKERS	GAZES
GASSY	GATEWAY	GAUN	GAWKIER	GAZETTE
GAST	GATEWAYS	GAUNT	GAWKIES	GAZETTED
GASTED	GATHER	GAUNTER	GAWKIEST	GAZETTEER
GASTER	GATHERED	GAUNTEST	GAWKILY	GAZETTEERS
GASTERS	GATHERER	GAUNTLET	GAWKINESS	GAZETTES
GASTIGHT	GATHERERS	GAUNTLETED	GAWKINESSES	GAZETTING
GASTING	GATHERING	GAUNTLETING	GAWKING	GAZILLION
GASTNESS	GATHERINGS	GAUNTLETS	GAWKISH	GAZILLIONS
GASTNESSES	GATHERS	GAUNTLY	GAWKISHLY	GAZING
GASTRAEA	GATING	GAUNTNESS	GAWKS	GAZOGENE
GASTRAEAS	GATINGS	GAUNTNESSES	GAWKY	GAZOGENES
GASTRAL	GATOR	GAUNTRIES	GAWP	GAZOO
GASTREA	GATORS	GAUNTRY	GAWPED	GAZOOS
GASTREAS	GATS	GAUR	GAWPER	GAZPACHO
GASTRIC	GAUCHE	GAURS	GAWPERS	GAZPACHOS
GASTRIN	GAUCHELY	GAUSS	GAWPING	GAZUMP
GASTRINS	GAUCHER	GAUSSES	GAWPS	GAZUMPED
GASTRITIC	GAUCHERIE	GAUZE	GAWSIE	GAZUMPER
GASTRITIDES	GAUCHERIES	GAUZELIKE	GAWSY	GAZUMPERS
GASTRITIS	GAUCHEST	GAUZES	GAY	GAZUMPING
GASTRITISES	GAUCHO	GAUZIER	GAYAL	GAZUMPS
GASTROPOD	GAUCHOS	GAUZIEST	GAYALS	GEAR
GASTROPODS	GAUD	GAUZILY	GAYDAR	GEARBOX
GASTRULA	GAUDERIES	GAUZINESS	GAYDARS	GEARBOXES
GASTRULAE	GAUDERY	GAUZINESSES	GAYER	GEARCASE
GASTRULAR	GAUDIER	GAUZY	GAYEST	GEARCASES
GASTRULAS	GAUDIES	GAVAGE	GAYETIES	GEARED
GASTS	GAUDIEST	GAVAGES	GAYETY	GEARHEAD
GASWORKS	GAUDILY	GAVE	GAYLY	GEARHEADS
GAT	GAUDINESS	GAVEL	GAYNESS	GEARING
GATE	GAUDINESSES	GAVELED	GAYNESSES	GEARINGS
GATEAU	GAUDS	GAVELING	GAYS	GEARLESS
GATEAUS	GAUDY	GAVELKIND	GAYWINGS	GEARS
GATEAUX	GAUFFER	GAVELKINDS	GAZABO	GEARSHIFT
GATECRASH	GAUFFERED	GAVELLED	GAZABOES	GEARSHIFTS
GATECRASHED	GAUFFERING	GAVELLING	GAZABOS	GEARWHEEL
GATECRASHES	GAUFFERS	GAVELOCK	GAZANIA	GEARWHEELS
GATECRASHING	GAUGE	GAVELOCKS	GAZANIAS	GECK

GECKED	GELATO	GEMMILY	GENERICS	GENOISE
GECKING	GELATOS	GEMMINESS	GENEROUS	GENOISES
GECKO	GELCAP	GEMMINESSES	GENES	GENOM
GECKOES	GELCAPS	GEMMING	GENESES	GENOME
GECKOS	GELD	GEMMOLOGIES	GENESIS	GENOMES
GECKS	GELDED	GEMMOLOGY	GENET	GENOMIC
GED	GELDER	GEMMULE	GENETIC	GENOMICS
GEDS	GELDERS	GEMMULES	GENETICAL	GENOMS
GEE	GELDING	GEMMY	GENETICS	GENOTYPE
GEED	GELDINGS	GEMOLOGIES	GENETS	GENOTYPES
GEEGAW	GELDS	GEMOLOGY	GENETTE	GENOTYPIC
GEEGAWS	GELEE	GEMOT	GENETTES	GENRE
GEEING	GELEES	GEMOTE	GENEVA	GENRES
GEEK	GELID	GEMOTES	GENEVAS	GENRO
GEEKDOM	GELIDITIES	GEMOTS	GENIAL	GENROS
GEEKDOMS	GELIDITY	GEMS	GENIALITIES	GENS
GEEKED	GELIDLY	GEMSBOK	GENIALITY	GENSENG
GEEKIER	GELIDNESS	GEMSBOKS	GENIALLY	GENSENGS
GEEKIEST	GELIDNESSES	GEMSBUCK	GENIC	GENT
GEEKINESS	GELIGNITE	GEMSBUCKS	GENICALLY	GENTEEL
GEEKINESSES	GELIGNITES	GEMSTONE	GENIE	GENTEELER
GEEKS	GELLANT	GEMSTONES	GENIES	GENTEELEST
GEEKY	GELLANTS	GEMUTLICH	GENII	GENTEELLY
GEEPOUND	GELLED	GEN	GENIP	GENTES
GEEPOUNDS	GELLING	GENDARME	GENIPAP	GENTIAN
GEES	GELS	GENDARMES	GENIPAPS	GENTIANS
GEESE	GELSEMIA	GENDER	GENIPS	GENTIL
GEEST	GELSEMIUM	GENDERED	GENISTEIN	GENTILE
GEESTS	GELSEMIUMS	GENDERING	GENISTEINS	GENTILES
GEEZ	GELT	GENDERIZE	GENITAL	GENTILITIES
GEEZER	GELTS	GENDERIZED	GENITALIA	GENTILITY
GEEZERS	GEM	GENDERIZES	GENITALIC	GENTLE
GEISHA	GEMATRIA	GENDERIZING	GENITALLY	GENTLED
GEISHAS	GEMATRIAS	GENDERS	GENITALS	GENTLEMAN
GEL	GEMINAL	GENE	GENITIVAL	GENTLEMEN
GELABLE	GEMINALLY	GENEALOGIES	GENITIVE	GENTLER
GELADA	GEMINATE	GENEALOGY	GENITIVES	GENTLES
GELADAS	GEMINATED	GENERA	GENITOR	GENTLEST
GELANT	GEMINATES	GENERABLE	GENITORS	GENTLING
GELANTS	GEMINATING	GENERAL	GENITURE	GENTLY
GELATE	GEMLIKE	GENERALCIES	GENITURES	GENTOO
GELATED	GEMMA	GENERALCY	GENIUS	GENTOOS
GELATES	GEMMAE	GENERALLY	GENIUSES	GENTRICE
GELATI	GEMMATE	GENERALS	GENNAKER	GENTRICES
GELATIN	GEMMATED	GENERATE	GENNAKERS	GENTRIES
GELATINE	GEMMATES	GENERATED	GENOA	GENTRIFIED
GELATINES	GEMMATING	GENERATES	GENOAS	GENTRIFIES
GELATING	GEMMATION	GENERATING	GENOCIDAL	GENTRIFY
GELATINS	GEMMATIONS	GENERATOR	GENOCIDE	GENTRIFYING
GELATION	GEMMED	GENERATORS	GENOCIDES	GENTRY
GELATIONS	GEMMIER	GENERIC	GENOGRAM	GENTS
GELATIS	GEMMIEST	GENERICAL	GENOGRAMS	GENU

GENUA	GEOMETRIC	GERM	GESTAPO	GHARRIS
GENUFLECT	GEOMETRICS	GERMAN	GESTAPOS	GHARRY
GENUFLECTED	GEOMETRID	GERMANDER	GESTATE	GHAST
GENUFLECTING	GEOMETRIDS	GERMANDERS	GESTATED	GHASTFUL
GENUFLECTS	GEOMETRIES	GERMANE	GESTATES	GHASTLIER
GENUINE	GEOMETRY	GERMANELY	GESTATING	GHASTLIEST
GENUINELY	GEOPHAGIA	GERMANIC	GESTATION	GHASTLY
GENUS	GEOPHAGIAS	GERMANIUM	GESTATIONS	GHAT
GENUSES	GEOPHAGIES	GERMANIUMS	GESTATIVE	GHATS
GEOBOTANIES	GEOPHAGY	GERMANIZE	GESTATORY	GHAUT
GEOBOTANY	GEOPHONE	GERMANIZED	GESTE	GHAUTS
GEOCORONA	GEOPHONES	GERMANIZES	GESTES	GHAZI
GEOCORONAE	GEOPHYTE	GERMANIZING	GESTIC	GHAZIES
GEOCORONAS	GEOPHYTES	GERMANS	GESTICAL	GHAZIS
GEODE	GEOPHYTIC	GERMEN	GESTS	GHEE
GEODES	GEOPONIC	GERMENS	GESTURAL	GHEES
GEODESIC	GEOPONICS	GERMFREE	GESTURE	GHERAO
GEODESICS	GEOPROBE	GERMICIDE	GESTURED	GHERAOED
GEODESIES	GEOPROBES	GERMICIDES	GESTURER	GHERAOES
GEODESIST	GEORGETTE	GERMIER	GESTURERS	GHERAOING
GEODESISTS	GEORGETTES	GERMIEST	GESTURES	GHERKIN
GEODESY	GEORGIC	GERMINA	GESTURING	GHERKINS
GEODETIC	GEORGICAL	GERMINAL	GET	GHETTO
GEODETICS	GEORGICS	GERMINANT	GETA	GHETTOED
GEODIC	GEOTACTIC	GERMINATE	GETABLE	GHETTOES
GEODUCK	GEOTAXES	GERMINATED	GETAS	GHETTOING
GEODUCKS	GEOTAXIS	GERMINATES	GETATABLE	GHETTOIZE
GEOGNOSIES	GEOTROPIC	GERMINATING	GETAWAY	GHETTOIZED
GEOGNOSY	GERAH	GERMINESS	GETAWAYS	GHETTOIZES
GEOGRAPHIES	GERAHS	GERMINESSES	GETS	GHETTOIZING
GEOGRAPHY	GERANIAL	GERMLIKE	GETTABLE	GHETTOS
GEOID	GERANIALS	GERMPLASM	GETTER	GHI
GEOIDAL	GERANIOL	GERMPLASMS	GETTERED	GHIBLI
GEOIDS	GERANIOLS	GERMPROOF	GETTERING	GHIBLIS
GEOLOGER	GERANIUM	GERMS	GETTERS	GHILLIE
GEOLOGERS	GERANIUMS	GERMY	GETTING	GHILLIES
GEOLOGIC	GERARDIA	GERONTIC	GETUP	GHIS
GEOLOGIES	GERARDIAS	GERUND	GETUPS	GHOST
GEOLOGIST	GERBERA	GERUNDIAL	GEUM	GHOSTED
GEOLOGISTS	GERBERAS	GERUNDIVE	GEUMS	GHOSTIER
GEOLOGIZE	GERBIL	GERUNDIVES	GEWGAW	GHOSTIEST
GEOLOGIZED	GERBILLE	GERUNDS	GEWGAWED	GHOSTING
GEOLOGIZES	GERBILLES	GESNERIA	GEWGAWS	GHOSTINGS
GEOLOGIZING	GERBILS	GESNERIAD	GEY	GHOSTLIER
GEOLOGY	GERENT	GESNERIADS	GEYSER	GHOSTLIEST
GEOMANCER	GERENTS	GESSO	GEYSERITE	GHOSTLIKE
GEOMANCERS	GERENUK	GESSOED	GEYSERITES	GHOSTLY
GEOMANCIES	GERENUKS	GESSOES	GEYSERS	GHOSTS
GEOMANCY	GERFALCON	GEST	GHARIAL	GHOSTY
GEOMANTIC	GERFALCONS	GESTALT	GHARIALS	GHOUL
GEOMETER	GERIATRIC	GESTALTEN	GHARRI	GHOULIE
GEOMETERS	GERIATRICS	GESTALTS	GHARRIES	GHOULIES

GHOULISH	GIDDAP	GIGATONS	GILT	GINGELY
GHOULS	GIDDIED	GIGAWATT	GILTHEAD	GINGER
GHYLL	GIDDIER	GIGAWATTS	GILTHEADS	GINGERED
GHYLLS	GIDDIES	GIGGED	GILTS	GINGERING
GIANT	GIDDIEST	GIGGING	GIMBAL	GINGERLY
GIANTESS	GIDDILY	GIGGLE	GIMBALED	GINGERS
GIANTESSES	GIDDINESS	GIGGLED	GIMBALING	GINGERY
GIANTISM	GIDDINESSES	GIGGLER	GIMBALLED	GINGHAM
GIANTISMS	GIDDY	GIGGLERS	GIMBALLING	GINGHAMS
GIANTLIKE	GIDDYAP	GIGGLES	GIMBALS	GINGILI
GIANTS	GIDDYING	GIGGLIER	GIMCRACK	GINGILIS
GIAOUR	GIDDYUP	GIGGLIEST	GIMCRACKS	GINGILLI
GIAOURS	GIDS	GIGGLING	GIMEL	GINGILLIS
GIARDIA	GIE	GIGGLY	GIMELS	GINGIVA
GIARDIAS	GIED	GIGHE	GIMLET	GINGIVAE
GIB	GIEING	GIGLET	GIMLETED	GINGIVAL
GIBBED	GIEN	GIGLETS	GIMLETING	GINGKO
GIBBER	GIES	GIGLOT	GIMLETS	GINGKOES
GIBBERED	GIFT	GIGLOTS	GIMMAL	GINGKOS
GIBBERING	GIFTABLE	GIGOLO	GIMMALS	GINK
GIBBERISH	GIFTABLES	GIGOLOS	GIMME	GINKGO
GIBBERISHES	GIFTED	GIGOT	GIMMES	GINKGOES
GIBBERS	GIFTEDLY	GIGOTS	GIMMICK	GINKGOS
GIBBET	GIFTEE	GIGS	GIMMICKED	GINKS
GIBBETED	GIFTEES	GIGUE	GIMMICKING	GINNED
GIBBETING	GIFTING	GIGUES	GIMMICKRIES	GINNER
GIBBETS	GIFTLESS	GILBERT	GIMMICKRY	GINNERS
GIBBETTED	GIFTS	GILBERTS	GIMMICKS	GINNIER
GIBBETTING	GIFTWARE	GILD	GIMMICKY	GINNIEST
GIBBING	GIFTWARES	GILDED	GIMMIE	GINNING
GIBBON	GIFTWRAP	GILDER	GIMMIES	GINNINGS
GIBBONS	GIFTWRAPPED	GILDERS	GIMP	GINNY
GIBBOSE	GIFTWRAPPING	GILDHALL	GIMPED	GINS
GIBBOSITIES	GIFTWRAPS	GILDHALLS	GIMPIER	GINSENG
GIBBOSITY	GIG	GILDING	GIMPIEST	GINSENGS
GIBBOUS	GIGA	GILDINGS	GIMPING	GINZO
GIBBOUSLY	GIGABIT	GILDS	GIMPS	GINZOES
GIBBSITE	GIGABITS	GILL	GIMPY	GIP
GIBBSITES	GIGABYTE	GILLED	GIN	GIPON
GIBE	GIGABYTES	GILLER	GINGAL	GIPONS
GIBED	GIGACYCLE	GILLERS	GINGALL	GIPPED
GIBER	GIGACYCLES	GILLIE	GINGALLS	GIPPER
GIBERS	GIGAFLOP	GILLIED	GINGALS	GIPPERS
GIBES	GIGAFLOPS	GILLIES	GINGELEY	GIPPING
GIBING	GIGAHERTZ	GILLING	GINGELEYS	GIPS
GIBINGLY	GIGAHERTZES	GILLNET	GINGELI	GIPSIED
GIBLET	GIGANTEAN	GILLNETS	GINGELIES	GIPSIES
GIBLETS	GIGANTIC	GILLNETTED	GINGELIS	GIPSY
GIBS	GIGANTISM	GILLNETTING	GINGELLI	GIPSYING
GIBSON	GIGANTISMS	GILLS	GINGELLIES	GIRAFFE
GIBSONS	GIGAS	GILLY	GINGELLIS	GIRAFFES
GID	GIGATON	GILLYING	GINGELLY	GIRAFFISH

GIRANDOLA	GIRTING	GLACIER	GLAIRY	GLASSFUL
GIRANDOLAS	GIRTS	GLACIERED	GLAIVE	GLASSFULS
GIRANDOLE	GISARME	GLACIERS	GLAIVED	GLASSIE
GIRANDOLES	GISARMES	GLACIS	GLAIVES	GLASSIER
GIRASOL	GISMO	GLACISES	GLAM	GLASSIES
GIRASOLE	GISMOS	GLAD	GLAMOR	GLASSIEST
GIRASOLES	GIST	GLADDED	GLAMORISE	GLASSILY
GIRASOLS	GISTS	GLADDEN	GLAMORISED	GLASSINE
GIRD	GIT	GLADDENED	GLAMORISES	GLASSINES
GIRDED	GITANO	GLADDENER	GLAMORISING	GLASSING
GIRDER	GITANOS	GLADDENERS	GLAMORIZE	GLASSLESS
GIRDERS	GITE	GLADDENING	GLAMORIZED	GLASSMAN
GIRDING	GITES	GLADDENS	GLAMORIZES	GLASSMEN
GIRDINGLY	GITS	GLADDER	GLAMORIZING	GLASSWARE
GIRDLE	GITTED	GLADDEST	GLAMOROUS	GLASSWARES
GIRDLED	GITTERN	GLADDING	GLAMORS	GLASSWORK
GIRDLER	GITTERNS	GLADE	GLAMOUR	GLASSWORKS
GIRDLERS	GITTIN	GLADELIKE	GLAMOURED	GLASSWORM
GIRDLES	GITTING	GLADES	GLAMOURING	GLASSWORMS
GIRDLING	GIVE	GLADIATE	GLAMOURS	GLASSWORT
GIRDS	GIVEABLE	GLADIATOR	GLAMS	GLASSWORTS
GIRL	GIVEAWAY	GLADIATORS	GLANCE	GLASSY
GIRLHOOD	GIVEAWAYS	GLADIER	GLANCED	GLAUCOMA
GIRLHOODS	GIVEBACK	GLADIEST	GLANCER	GLAUCOMAS
GIRLIE	GIVEBACKS	GLADIOLA	GLANCERS	GLAUCOUS
GIRLIER	GIVEN	GLADIOLAR	GLANCES	GLAZE
GIRLIES	GIVENS	GLADIOLAS	GLANCING	GLAZED
GIRLIEST	GIVER	GLADIOLI	GLAND	GLAZER
GIRLISH	GIVERS	GLADIOLUS	GLANDERED	GLAZERS
GIRLISHLY	GIVES	GLADIOLUSES	GLANDERS	GLAZES
GIRLS	GIVING	GLADLIER	GLANDES	GLAZIER
GIRLY	GIZMO	GLADLIEST	GLANDLESS	GLAZIERIES
GIRN	GIZMOS	GLADLY	GLANDS	GLAZIERS
GIRNED	GIZZARD	GLADNESS	GLANDULAR	GLAZIERY
GIRNING	GIZZARDS	GLADNESSES	GLANDULE	GLAZIEST
GIRNS	GJETOST	GLADS	GLANDULES	GLAZILY
GIRO	GJETOSTS	GLADSOME	GLANS	GLAZINESS
GIROLLE	GLABELLA	GLADSOMER	GLARE	GLAZINESSES
GIROLLES	GLABELLAE	GLADSOMEST	GLARED	GLAZING
GIRON	GLABELLAR	GLADSTONE	GLARES	GLAZINGS
GIRONS	GLABRATE	GLADSTONES	GLARIER	GLAZY
GIROS	GLABROUS	GLADY	GLARIEST	GLEAM
GIROSOL	GLACE	GLAIKET	GLARINESS	GLEAMED
GIROSOLS	GLACEED	GLAIKIT	GLARINESSES	GLEAMER
GIRSH	GLACEING	GLAIR	GLARING	GLEAMERS
GIRSHES	GLACES	GLAIRE	GLARINGLY	GLEAMIER
GIRT	GLACIAL	GLAIRED	GLARY	GLEAMIEST
GIRTED	GLACIALLY	GLAIRES	GLASNOST	GLEAMING
GIRTH	GLACIATE	GLAIRIER	GLASNOSTS	GLEAMS
GIRTHED	GLACIATED	GLAIRIEST	GLASS	GLEAMY
GIRTHING	GLACIATES	GLAIRING	GLASSED	GLEAN
GIRTHS	GLACIATING	GLAIRS	GLASSES	GLEANABLE

GLEANED	GLIADINE	GLISSADING	GLOBALIZING	GLONOINS
GLEANER	GLIADINES	GLISSANDI	GLOBALLY	GLOOM
GLEANERS	GLIADINS	GLISSANDO	GLOBATE	GLOOMED
GLEANING	GLIAL	GLISSANDOS	GLOBATED	GLOOMFUL
GLEANINGS	GLIAS	GLISTEN	GLOBBIER	GLOOMIER
GLEANS	GLIB	GLISTENED	GLOBBIEST	GLOOMIEST
GLEBA	GLIBBER	GLISTENING	GLOBBY	GLOOMILY
GLEBAE	GLIBBEST	GLISTENS	GLOBE	GLOOMING
GLEBE	GLIBLY	GLISTER	GLOBED	GLOOMINGS
GLEBELESS	GLIBNESS	GLISTERED	GLOBEFISH	GLOOMS
GLEBES	GLIBNESSES	GLISTERING	GLOBEFISHES	GLOOMY
GLED	GLIDE	GLISTERS	GLOBELIKE	GLOP
GLEDE	GLIDED	GLITCH	GLOBES	GLOPPED
GLEDES	GLIDEPATH	GLITCHES	GLOBETROT	GLOPPIER
GLEDS	GLIDEPATHS	GLITCHIER	GLOBETROTS	GLOPPIEST
GLEE	GLIDER	GLITCHIEST	GLOBETROTTED	GLOPPING
GLEED	GLIDERS	GLITCHY	GLOBETROTTING	GLOPPY
GLEEDS	GLIDES	GLITTER	GLOBIN	GLOPS
GLEEFUL	GLIDING	GLITTERED	GLOBING	GLORIA
GLEEFULLY	GLIFF	GLITTERING	GLOBINS	GLORIAS
GLEEK	GLIFFS	GLITTERS	GLOBOID	GLORIED
GLEEKED	GLIM	GLITTERY	GLOBOIDS	GLORIES
GLEEKING	GLIME	GLITZ	GLOBOSE	GLORIFIED
GLEEKS	GLIMED	GLITZED	GLOBOSELY	GLORIFIER
GLEEMAN	GLIMES	GLITZES	GLOBOSITIES	GLORIFIERS
GLEEMEN	GLIMING	GLITZIER	GLOBOSITY	GLORIFIES
GLEES	GLIMMER	GLITZIEST	GLOBOUS	GLORIFY
GLEESOME	GLIMMERED	GLITZING	GLOBS	GLORIFYING
GLEET	GLIMMERING	GLITZY	GLOBULAR	GLORIOLE
GLEETED	GLIMMERS	GLOAM	GLOBULARS	GLORIOLES
GLEETIER	GLIMPSE	GLOAMING	GLOBULE	GLORIOUS
GLEETIEST	GLIMPSED	GLOAMINGS	GLOBULES	GLORY
GLEETING	GLIMPSER	GLOAMS	GLOBULIN	GLORYING
GLEETS	GLIMPSERS	GLOAT	GLOBULINS	GLOSS
GLEETY	GLIMPSES	GLOATED	GLOCHID	GLOSSA
GLEG	GLIMPSING	GLOATER	GLOCHIDIA	GLOSSAE
GLEGLY	GLIMS	GLOATERS	GLOCHIDIUM	GLOSSAL
GLEGNESS	GLINT	GLOATING	GLOCHIDS	GLOSSARIES
GLEGNESSES	GLINTED	GLOATS	GLOGG	GLOSSARY
GLEN	GLINTIER	GLOB	GLOGGS	GLOSSAS
GLENGARRIES	GLINTIEST	GLOBAL	GLOM	GLOSSATOR
GLENGARRY	GLINTING	GLOBALISE	GLOMERA	GLOSSATORS
GLENLIKE	GLINTS	GLOBALISED	GLOMERATE	GLOSSED
GLENOID	GLINTY	GLOBALISES	GLOMERULE	GLOSSEME
GLENS	GLIOMA	GLOBALISING	GLOMERULES	GLOSSEMES
GLEY	GLIOMAS	GLOBALISM	GLOMERULI	GLOSSER
GLEYED	GLIOMATA	GLOBALISMS	GLOMERULUS	GLOSSERS
GLEYING	GLISSADE	GLOBALIST	GLOMMED	GLOSSES
GLEYINGS	GLISSADED	GLOBALISTS	GLOMMING	GLOSSIER
GLEYS	GLISSADER	GLOBALIZE	GLOMS	GLOSSIES
GLIA	GLISSADERS	GLOBALIZED	GLOMUS	GLOSSIEST
GLIADIN	GLISSADES	GLOBALIZES	GLONOIN	GLOSSILY

GLOSSINA	GLUCOSE	GLUTAMINES	GLYPHIC	GNOMES
GLOSSINAS	GLUCOSES	GLUTE	GLYPHS	GNOMIC
GLOSSING	GLUCOSIC	GLUTEAL	GLYPTIC	GNOMICAL
GLOSSITIC	GLUCOSIDE	GLUTEI	GLYPTICS	GNOMISH
GLOSSITIS	GLUCOSIDES	GLUTELIN	GNAR	GNOMIST
GLOSSITISES	GLUE	GLUTELINS	GNARL	GNOMISTS
GLOSSY	GLUED	GLUTEN	GNARLED	GNOMON
GLOST	GLUEING	GLUTENIN	GNARLIER	GNOMONIC
GLOSTS	GLUELIKE	GLUTENINS	GNARLIEST	GNOMONS
GLOTTAL	GLUEPOT	GLUTENOUS	GNARLING	GNOSES
GLOTTIC	GLUEPOTS	GLUTENS	GNARLS	GNOSIS
GLOTTIDES	GLUER	GLUTES	GNARLY	GNOSTIC
GLOTTIS	GLUERS	GLUTEUS	GNARR	GNOSTICAL
GLOTTISES	GLUES	GLUTINOUS	GNARRED	GNOSTICS
GLOUT	GLUEY	GLUTS	GNARRING	GNU
GLOUTED	GLUEYNESS	GLUTTED	GNARRS	GNUS
GLOUTING	GLUEYNESSES	GLUTTING	GNARS	GO
GLOUTS	GLUG	GLUTTON	GNASH	GOA
GLOVE	GLUGGED	GLUTTONIES	GNASHED	GOAD
GLOVED	GLUGGING	GLUTTONS	GNASHES	GOADED
GLOVER	GLUGS	GLUTTONY	GNASHING	GOADING
GLOVERS	GLUHWEIN	GLYCAN	GNAT	GOADLIKE
GLOVES	GLUHWEINS	GLYCANS	GNATHAL	GOADS
GLOVING	GLUIER	GLYCERIC	GNATHIC	GOAL
GLOW	GLUIEST	GLYCERIDE	GNATHION	GOALED
GLOWED	GLUILY	GLYCERIDES	GNATHIONS	GOALIE
GLOWER	GLUINESS	GLYCERIN	GNATHITE	GOALIES
GLOWERED	GLUINESSES	GLYCERINE	GNATHITES	GOALING
GLOWERING	GLUING	GLYCERINES	GNATHONIC	GOALLESS
GLOWERS	GLUM	GLYCERINS	GNATLIKE	GOALMOUTH
GLOWFLIES	GLUME	GLYCEROL	GNATS	GOALMOUTHS
GLOWFLY	GLUMES	GLYCEROLS	GNATTIER	GOALPOST
GLOWING	GLUMLY	GLYCERYL	GNATTIEST	GOALPOSTS
GLOWINGLY	GLUMMER	GLYCERYLS	GNATTY	GOALS
GLOWS	GLUMMEST	GLYCIN	GNAW	GOALWARD
GLOWWORM	GLUMNESS	GLYCINE	GNAWABLE	GOANNA
GLOWWORMS	GLUMNESSES	GLYCINES	GNAWED	GOANNAS
GLOXINIA	GLUMPIER	GLYCINS	GNAWER	GOAS
GLOXINIAS	GLUMPIEST	GLYCOGEN	GNAWERS	GOAT
GLOZE	GLUMPILY	GLYCOGENS	GNAWING	GOATEE
GLOZED	GLUMPY	GLYCOL	GNAWINGLY	GOATEED
GLOZES	GLUMS	GLYCOLIC	GNAWINGS	GOATEES
GLOZING	GLUNCH	GLYCOLS	GNAWN	GOATFISH
GLUCAGON	GLUNCHED	GLYCONIC	GNAWS	GOATFISHES
GLUCAGONS	GLUNCHES	GLYCONICS	GNEISS	GOATHERD
GLUCAN	GLUNCHING	GLYCOSIDE	GNEISSES	GOATHERDS
GLUCANS	GLUON	GLYCOSIDES	GNEISSIC	GOATISH
GLUCINIC	GLUONS	GLYCOSYL	GNEISSOID	GOATISHLY
GLUCINUM	GLUT	GLYCOSYLS	GNEISSOSE	GOATLIKE
GLUCINUMS	GLUTAMATE	GLYCYL	GNOCCHI	GOATS
GLUCONATE	GLUTAMATES	GLYCYLS	GNOME	GOATSKIN
GLUCONATES	GLUTAMINE	GLYPH	GNOMELIKE	GOATSKINS

GOB	GODFATHER	GOGGLER	GOLDSTONE	GONADIC
GOBAN	GODFATHERED	GOGGLERS	GOLDSTONES	GONADS
GOBANG	GODFATHERING	GOGGLES	GOLDTONE	GONDOLA
GOBANGS	GODFATHERS	GOGGLIER	GOLDURN	GONDOLAS
GOBANS	GODHEAD	GOGGLIEST	GOLDURNS	GONDOLIER
GOBBED	GODHEADS	GOGGLING	GOLEM	GONDOLIERS
GOBBET	GODHOOD	GOGGLY	GOLEMS	GONE
GOBBETS	GODHOODS	GOGLET	GOLF	GONEF
GOBBING	GODLESS	GOGLETS	GOLFED	GONEFS
GOBBLE	GODLESSLY	GOGO	GOLFER	GONENESS
GOBBLED	GODLIER	GOGOS	GOLFERS	GONENESSES
GOBBLER	GODLIEST	GOING	GOLFING	GONER
GOBBLERS	GODLIKE	GOINGS	GOLFINGS	GONERS
GOBBLES	GODLILY	GOITER	GOLFS	GONFALON
GOBBLING	GODLINESS	GOITERS	GOLGOTHA	GONFALONS
GOBIES	GODLINESSES	GOITRE	GOLGOTHAS	GONFANON
GOBIOID	GODLING	GOITRES	GOLIARD	GONFANONS
GOBIOIDS	GODLINGS	GOITROGEN	GOLIARDIC	GONG
GOBLET	GODLY	GOITROGENS	GOLIARDS	GONGED
GOBLETS	GODMOTHER	GOITROUS	GOLIATH	GONGING
GOBLIN	GODMOTHERED	GOLCONDA	GOLIATHS	GONGLIKE
GOBLINS	GODMOTHERING	GOLCONDAS	GOLLIWOG	GONGS
GOBO	GODMOTHERS	GOLD	GOLLIWOGG	GONIA
GOBOES	GODOWN	GOLDARN	GOLLIWOGGS	GONIDIA
GOBONEE	GODOWNS	GOLDARNS	GOLLIWOGS	GONIDIAL
GOBONY	GODPARENT	GOLDBRICK	GOLLY	GONIDIC
GOBOS	GODPARENTS	GOLDBRICKED	GOLLYWOG	GONIDIUM
GOBS	GODROON	GOLDBRICKING	GOLLYWOGS	GONIF
GOBSHITE	GODROONS	GOLDBRICKS	GOLOSH	GONIFF
GOBSHITES	GODS	GOLDBUG	GOLOSHE	GONIFFS
GOBY	GODSEND	GOLDBUGS	GOLOSHES	GONIFS
GOD	GODSENDS	GOLDEN	GOMBEEN	GONION
GODAMNDEST	GODSHIP	GOLDENER	GOMBEENS	GONIUM
GODCHILD	GODSHIPS	GOLDENEST	GOMBO	GONOCOCCI
GODCHILDREN	GODSON	GOLDENEYE	GOMBOS	GONOCOCCUS
GODDAM	GODSONS	GOLDENEYES	GOMBROON	GONOCYTE
GODDAMMED	GODWIT	GOLDENLY	GOMBROONS	GONOCYTES
GODDAMMING	GODWITS	GOLDENROD	GOMER	GONOF
GODDAMN	GOER	GOLDENRODS	GOMERAL	GONOFS
GODDAMNED	GOERS	GOLDER	GOMERALS	GONOPH
GODDAMNEDEST	GOES	GOLDEST	GOMEREL	GONOPHORE
GODDAMNING	GOETHITE	GOLDEYE	GOMERELS	GONOPHORES
GODDAMNS	GOETHITES	GOLDEYES	GOMERIL	GONOPHS
GODDAMS	GOFER	GOLDFIELD	GOMERILS	GONOPORE
GODDED	GOFERS	GOLDFIELDS	GOMERS	GONOPORES
GODDESS	GOFFER	GOLDFINCH	GOMPHOSES	GONORRHEA
GODDESSES	GOFFERED	GOLDFINCHES	GOMPHOSIS	GONORRHEAS
GODDING	GOFFERING	GOLDFISH	GOMUTI	GONZO
GODET	GOFFERINGS	GOLDFISHES	GOMUTIS	GOO
GODETIA	GOFFERS	GOLDS	GONAD	GOOBER
GODETIAS	GOGGLE	GOLDSMITH	GONADAL	GOOBERS
GODETS	GOGGLED	GOLDSMITHS	GONADIAL	GOOD

GOODBY	GOONIER	GORGERIN	GOSPELLY	GOURAMI
GOODBYE	GOONIES	GORGERINS	GOSPELS	GOURAMIES
GOODBYES	GOONIEST	GORGERS	GOSPORT	GOURAMIS
GOODBYS	GOONS	GORGES	GOSPORTS	GOURD
GOODIE	GOONY	GORGET	GOSSAMER	GOURDE
GOODIES	GOOP	GORGETED	GOSSAMERS	GOURDES
GOODISH	GOOPIER	GORGETS	GOSSAMERY	GOURDS
GOODLIER	GOOPIEST	GORGING	GOSSAN	GOURMAND
GOODLIEST	GOOPS	GORGON	GOSSANS	GOURMANDS
GOODLY	GOOPY	GORGONIAN	GOSSIP	GOURMET
GOODMAN	GOORAL	GORGONIANS	GOSSIPED	GOURMETS
GOODMEN	GOORALS	GORGONIZE	GOSSIPER	GOUT
GOODNESS	GOOS	GORGONIZED	GOSSIPERS	GOUTIER
GOODNESSES	GOOSANDER	GORGONIZES	GOSSIPING	GOUTIEST
GOODS	GOOSANDERS	GORGONIZING	GOSSIPPED	GOUTILY
GOODWIFE	GOOSE	GORGONS	GOSSIPPER	GOUTINESS
GOODWILL	GOOSED	GORHEN	GOSSIPPERS	GOUTINESSES
GOODWILLS	GOOSEFISH	GORHENS	GOSSIPPING	GOUTS
GOODWIVES	GOOSEFISHES	GORIER	GOSSIPRIES	GOUTY
GOODY	GOOSEFOOT	GORIEST	GOSSIPRY	GOVERN
GOOEY	GOOSEFOOTS	GORILLA	GOSSIPS	GOVERNED
GOOEYNESS	GOOSEHERD	GORILLAS	GOSSIPY	GOVERNESS
GOOEYNESSES	GOOSEHERDS	GORILY	GOSSOON	GOVERNESSES
GOOF	GOOSENECK	GORINESS	GOSSOONS	GOVERNING
GOOFBALL	GOOSENECKS	GORINESSES	GOSSYPOL	GOVERNOR
GOOFBALLS	GOOSES	GORING	GOSSYPOLS	GOVERNORS
GOOFED	GOOSEY	GORM	GOT	GOVERNS
GOOFIER	GOOSIER	GORMAND	GOTCHA	GOWAN
GOOFIEST	GOOSIEST	GORMANDS	GOTCHAS	GOWANED
GOOFILY	GOOSING	GORMED	GOTH	GOWANS
GOOFINESS	GOOSY	GORMING	GOTHIC	GOWANY
GOOFINESSES	GOPHER	GORMLESS	GOTHICISM	GOWD
GOOFING	GOPHERS	GORMS	GOTHICISMS	GOWDS
GOOFS	GOPIK	GORP	GOTHICIZE	GOWK
GOOFY	GOR	GORPS	GOTHICIZED	GOWKS
GOOGLIES	GORAL	GORSE	GOTHICIZES	GOWN
GOOGLY	GORALS	GORSES	GOTHICIZING	GOWNED
GOOGOL	GORBELLIES	GORSIER	GOTHICS	GOWNING
GOOGOLS	GORBELLY	GORSIEST	GOTHITE	GOWNS
GOOIER	GORBLIMY	GORSY	GOTHITES	GOWNSMAN
GOOIEST	GORCOCK	GORY	GOTHS	GOWNSMEN
GOOK	GORCOCKS	GOS	GOTTEN	GOX
GOOKS	GORDITA	GOSH	GOUACHE	GOXES
GOOKY	GORDITAS	GOSHAWK	GOUACHES	GOY
GOOMBAH	GORE	GOSHAWKS	GOUGE	GOYIM
GOOMBAHS	GORED	GOSLING	GOUGED	GOYISH
GOOMBAY	GORES	GOSLINGS	GOUGER	GOYS
GOOMBAYS	GORGE	GOSPEL	GOUGERS	GRAAL
GOON	GORGED	GOSPELER	GOUGES	GRAALS
GOONEY	GORGEDLY	GOSPELERS	GOUGING	GRAB
GOONEYS	GORGEOUS	GOSPELLER	GOULASH	GRABBABLE
GOONIE	GORGER	GOSPELLERS	GOULASHES	GRABBED

GRABBER	GRADING	GRAMARYE	GRANDMAMAS	GRANULES
GRABBERS	GRADINS	GRAMARYES	GRANDMAS	GRANULITE
GRABBIER	GRADS	GRAMAS	GRANDNESS	GRANULITES
GRABBIEST	GRADUAL	GRAMERCIES	GRANDNESSES	GRANULOMA
GRABBING	GRADUALLY	GRAMERCY	GRANDPA	GRANULOMAS
GRABBLE	GRADUALS	GRAMMA	GRANDPAPA	GRANULOMATA
GRABBLED	GRADUAND	GRAMMAR	GRANDPAPAS	GRANULOSE
GRABBLER	GRADUANDS	GRAMMARS	GRANDPAS	GRANUM
GRABBLERS	GRADUATE	GRAMMAS	GRANDS	GRAPE
GRABBLES	GRADUATED	GRAMME	GRANDSIR	GRAPELIKE
GRABBLING	GRADUATES	GRAMMES	GRANDSIRE	GRAPERIES
GRABBY	GRADUATING	GRAMP	GRANDSIRES	GRAPERY
GRABEN	GRADUATOR	GRAMPA	GRANDSIRS	GRAPES
GRABENS	GRADUATORS	GRAMPAS	GRANDSON	GRAPESHOT
GRABS	GRADUS	GRAMPS	GRANDSONS	GRAPEVINE
GRACE	GRADUSES	GRAMPUS	GRANGE	GRAPEVINES
GRACED	GRAECIZE	GRAMPUSES	GRANGER	GRAPEY
GRACEFUL	GRAECIZED	GRAMS	GRANGERS	GRAPH
GRACEFULLER	GRAECIZES	GRAN	GRANGES	GRAPHED
GRACEFULLEST	GRAECIZING	GRANA	GRANITA	GRAPHEME
GRACELESS	GRAFFITI	GRANARIES	GRANITAS	GRAPHEMES
GRACES	GRAFFITIED	GRANARY	GRANITE	GRAPHEMIC
GRACILE	GRAFFITIING	GRAND	GRANITES	GRAPHIC
GRACILES	GRAFFITING	GRANDAD	GRANITIC	GRAPHICAL
GRACILIS	GRAFFITIS	GRANDADDIES	GRANITOID	GRAPHICS
GRACILITIES	GRAFFITO	GRANDADDY	GRANNIE	GRAPHING
GRACILITY	GRAFT	GRANDADS	GRANNIES	GRAPHITE
GRACING	GRAFTAGE	GRANDAM	GRANNY	GRAPHITES
GRACIOSO	GRAFTAGES	GRANDAME	GRANOLA	GRAPHITIC
GRACIOSOS	GRAFTED	GRANDAMES	GRANOLAS	GRAPHS
GRACIOUS	GRAFTER	GRANDAMS	GRANOLITH	GRAPIER
GRACKLE	GRAFTERS	GRANDAUNT	GRANOLITHS	GRAPIEST
GRACKLES	GRAFTING	GRANDAUNTS	GRANS	GRAPINESS
GRAD	GRAFTS	GRANDBABIES	GRANT	GRAPINESSES
GRADABLE	GRAHAM	GRANDBABY	GRANTABLE	GRAPLIN
GRADATE	GRAHAMS	GRANDDAD	GRANTED	GRAPLINE
GRADATED	GRAIL	GRANDDADS	GRANTEE	GRAPLINES
GRADATES	GRAILS	GRANDDAM	GRANTEES	GRAPLINS
GRADATING	GRAIN	GRANDDAMS	GRANTER	GRAPNEL
GRADATION	GRAINED	GRANDEE	GRANTERS	GRAPNELS
GRADATIONS	GRAINER	GRANDEES	GRANTING	GRAPPA
GRADE	GRAINERS	GRANDER	GRANTOR	GRAPPAS
GRADED	GRAINIER	GRANDEST	GRANTORS	GRAPPLE
GRADELESS	GRAINIEST	GRANDEUR	GRANTS	GRAPPLED
GRADER	GRAINING	GRANDEURS	GRANTSMAN	GRAPPLER
GRADERS	GRAINLESS	GRANDIOSE	GRANTSMEN	GRAPPLERS
GRADES	GRAINS	GRANDIOSO	GRANULAR	GRAPPLES
GRADIENT	GRAINY	GRANDKID	GRANULATE	GRAPPLING
GRADIENTS	GRAM	GRANDKIDS	GRANULATED	GRAPPLINGS
GRADIN	GRAMA	GRANDLY	GRANULATES	GRAPY
GRADINE	GRAMARIES	GRANDMA	GRANULATING	GRASP
GRADINES	GRAMARY	GRANDMAMA	GRANULE	GRASPABLE

GRASPED	GRATUITY	GRAVITINO	GRAZINGS	GREENBUG
GRASPER	GRATULATE	GRAVITINOS	GRAZIOSO	GREENBUGS
GRASPERS	GRATULATED	GRAVITON	GREASE	GREENED
GRASPING	GRATULATES	GRAVITONS	GREASED	GREENER
GRASPS	GRATULATING	GRAVITY	GREASER	GREENERIES
GRASS	GRAUPEL	GRAVLAKS	GREASERS	GREENERY
GRASSED	GRAUPELS	GRAVLAX	GREASES	GREENEST
GRASSES	GRAVAMEN	GRAVURE	GREASIER	GREENFLIES
GRASSIER	GRAVAMENS	GRAVURES	GREASIEST	GREENFLY
GRASSIEST	GRAVAMINA	GRAVY	GREASILY	GREENGAGE
GRASSILY	GRAVE	GRAY	GREASING	GREENGAGES
GRASSING	GRAVED	GRAYBACK	GREASY	GREENHEAD
GRASSLAND	GRAVEL	GRAYBACKS	GREAT	GREENHEADS
GRASSLANDS	GRAVELED	GRAYBEARD	GREATCOAT	GREENHORN
GRASSLESS	GRAVELESS	GRAYBEARDS	GREATCOATS	GREENHORNS
GRASSLIKE	GRAVELIKE	GRAYED	GREATEN	GREENIE
GRASSPLOT	GRAVELING	GRAYER	GREATENED	GREENIER
GRASSPLOTS	GRAVELLED	GRAYEST	GREATENING	GREENIES
GRASSROOT	GRAVELLING	GRAYFISH	GREATENS	GREENIEST
GRASSY	GRAVELLY	GRAYFISHES	GREATER	GREENING
GRAT	GRAVELS	GRAYHOUND	GREATEST	GREENINGS
GRATE	GRAVELY	GRAYHOUNDS	GREATLY	GREENISH
GRATED	GRAVEN	GRAYING	GREATNESS	GREENLET
GRATEFUL	GRAVENESS	GRAYISH	GREATNESSES	GREENLETS
GRATEFULLER	GRAVENESSES	GRAYLAG	GREATS	GREENLIGHT
GRATEFULLEST	GRAVER	GRAYLAGS	GREAVE	GREENLIGHTED
GRATELESS	GRAVERS	GRAYLING	GREAVED	GREENLIGHTING
GRATER	GRAVES	GRAYLINGS	GREAVES	GREENLIGHTS
GRATERS	GRAVESIDE	GRAYLY	GREBE	GREENLING
GRATES	GRAVESIDES	GRAYMAIL	GREBES	GREENLINGS
GRATICULE	GRAVESITE	GRAYMAILS	GRECIZE	GREENLIT
GRATICULES	GRAVESITES	GRAYNESS	GRECIZED	GREENLY
GRATIFIED	GRAVEST	GRAYNESSES	GRECIZES	GREENMAIL
GRATIFIER	GRAVEWARD	GRAYOUT	GRECIZING	GREENMAILED
GRATIFIERS	GRAVEYARD	GRAYOUTS	GREE	GREENMAILING
GRATIFIES	GRAVEYARDS	GRAYS	GREED	GREENMAILS
GRATIFY	GRAVID	GRAYSCALE	GREEDIER	GREENNESS
GRATIFYING	GRAVIDA	GRAYWACKE	GREEDIEST	GREENNESSES
GRATIN	GRAVIDAE	GRAYWACKES	GREEDILY	GREENROOM
GRATINE	GRAVIDAS	GRAYWATER	GREEDLESS	GREENROOMS
GRATINEE	GRAVIDITIES	GRAYWATERS	GREEDS	GREENS
GRATINEED	GRAVIDITY	GRAZABLE	GREEDSOME	GREENSAND
GRATINEEING	GRAVIDLY	GRAZE	GREEDY	GREENSANDS
GRATINEES	GRAVIES	GRAZEABLE	GREEGREE	GREENSICK
GRATING	GRAVING	GRAZED	GREEGREES	GREENTH
GRATINGLY	GRAVITAS	GRAZER	GREEING	GREENTHS
GRATINGS	GRAVITASES	GRAZERS	GREEK	GREENWASH
GRATINS	GRAVITATE	GRAZES	GREEN	GREENWASHES
GRATIS	GRAVITATED	GRAZIER	GREENBACK	GREENWAY
GRATITUDE	GRAVITATES	GRAZIERS	GREENBACKS	GREENWAYS
GRATITUDES	GRAVITATING	GRAZING	GREENBELT	GREENWING
GRATUITIES	GRAVITIES	GRAZINGLY	GREENBELTS	GREENWINGS

GREENWOOD	GRIBBLE	GRIGRIS	GRINDELIAS	GRISLIER
GREENWOODS	GRIBBLES	GRIGS	GRINDER	GRISLIEST
GREENY	GRID	GRILL	GRINDERIES	GRISLY
GREES	GRIDDED	GRILLADE	GRINDERS	GRISON
GREET	GRIDDER	GRILLADES	GRINDERY	GRISONS
GREETED	GRIDDERS	GRILLAGE	GRINDING	GRIST
GREETER	GRIDDLE	GRILLAGES	GRINDS	GRISTER
GREETERS	GRIDDLED	GRILLE	GRINGA	GRISTERS
GREETING	GRIDDLES	GRILLED	GRINGAS	GRISTLE
GREETINGS	GRIDDLING	GRILLER	GRINGO	GRISTLES
GREETS	GRIDE	GRILLERIES	GRINGOS	GRISTLIER
GREGARINE	GRIDED	GRILLERS	GRINNED	GRISTLIEST
GREGARINES	GRIDES	GRILLERY	GRINNER	GRISTLY
GREGO	GRIDING	GRILLES	GRINNERS	GRISTMILL
GREGOS	GRIDIRON	GRILLING	GRINNING	GRISTMILLS
GREIGE	GRIDIRONED	GRILLROOM	GRINS	GRISTS
GREIGES	GRIDIRONING	GRILLROOMS	GRIOT	GRIT
GREISEN	GRIDIRONS	GRILLS	GRIOTS	GRITH
GREISENS	GRIDLOCK	GRILLWORK	GRIP	GRITHS
GREMIAL	GRIDLOCKED	GRILLWORKS	GRIPE	GRITS
GREMIALS	GRIDLOCKING	GRILSE	GRIPED	GRITTED
GREMLIN	GRIDLOCKS	GRILSES	GRIPER	GRITTER
GREMLINS	GRIDS	GRIM	GRIPERS	GRITTERS
GREMMIE	GRIEF	GRIMACE	GRIPES	GRITTIER
GREMMIES	GRIEFS	GRIMACED	GRIPEY	GRITTIEST
GREMMY	GRIEVANCE	GRIMACER	GRIPIER	GRITTILY
GRENADE	GRIEVANCES	GRIMACERS	GRIPIEST	GRITTING
GRENADES	GRIEVANT	GRIMACES	GRIPING	GRITTY
GRENADIER	GRIEVANTS	GRIMACING	GRIPMAN	GRIVET
GRENADIERS	GRIEVE	GRIMALKIN	GRIPMEN	GRIVETS
GRENADINE	GRIEVED	GRIMALKINS	GRIPPE	GRIZZLE
GRENADINES	GRIEVER	GRIME	GRIPPED	GRIZZLED
GREW	GRIEVERS	GRIMED	GRIPPER	GRIZZLER
GREWSOME	GRIEVES	GRIMES	GRIPPERS	GRIZZLERS
GREWSOMER	GRIEVING	GRIMIER	GRIPPES	GRIZZLES
GREWSOMEST	GRIEVOUS	GRIMIEST	GRIPPIER	GRIZZLIER
GREY	GRIFF	GRIMILY	GRIPPIEST	GRIZZLIES
GREYED	GRIFFE	GRIMINESS	GRIPPING	GRIZZLIEST
GREYER	GRIFFES	GRIMINESSES	GRIPPLE	GRIZZLING
GREYEST	GRIFFIN	GRIMING	GRIPPY	GRIZZLY
GREYHEN	GRIFFINS	GRIMLY	GRIPS	GROAN
GREYHENS	GRIFFON	GRIMMER	GRIPSACK	GROANED
GREYHOUND	GRIFFONS	GRIMMEST	GRIPSACKS	GROANER
GREYHOUNDS	GRIFFS	GRIMNESS	GRIPT	GROANERS
GREYING	GRIFT	GRIMNESSES	GRIPY	GROANING
GREYISH	GRIFTED	GRIMY	GRISAILLE	GROANS
GREYLAG	GRIFTER	GRIN	GRISAILLES	GROAT
GREYLAGS	GRIFTERS	GRINCH	GRISEOUS	GROATS
GREYLY	GRIFTING	GRINCHES	GRISETTE	GROCER
GREYNESS	GRIFTS	GRIND	GRISETTES	GROCERIES
GREYNESSES	GRIG	GRINDED	GRISKIN	GROCERS
GREYS	GRIGRI	GRINDELIA	GRISKINS	GROCERY

GRODIER	GROPINGLY	GROUNDS	GROWL	GRUELLING
GRODIEST	GROSBEAK	GROUNDSEL	GROWLED	GRUELLINGS
GRODY	GROSBEAKS	GROUNDSELS	GROWLER	GRUELS
GROG	GROSCHEN	GROUP	GROWLERS	GRUES
GROGGERIES	GROSGRAIN	GROUPABLE	GROWLIER	GRUESOME
GROGGERY	GROSGRAINS	GROUPED	GROWLIEST	GRUESOMER
GROGGIER	GROSS	GROUPER	GROWLING	GRUESOMEST
GROGGIEST	GROSSED	GROUPERS	GROWLS	GRUFF
GROGGILY	GROSSER	GROUPIE	GROWLY	GRUFFED
GROGGY	GROSSERS	GROUPIES	GROWN	GRUFFER
GROGRAM	GROSSES	GROUPING	GROWNUP	GRUFFEST
GROGRAMS	GROSSEST	GROUPINGS	GROWNUPS	GRUFFIER
GROGS	GROSSING	GROUPOID	GROWS	GRUFFIEST
GROGSHOP	GROSSLY	GROUPOIDS	GROWTH	GRUFFILY
GROGSHOPS	GROSSNESS	GROUPS	GROWTHIER	GRUFFING
GROIN	GROSSNESSES	GROUPWARE	GROWTHIEST	GRUFFISH
GROINED	GROSSULAR	GROUPWARES	GROWTHS	GRUFFLY
GROINING	GROSSULARS	GROUSE	GROWTHY	GRUFFNESS
GROINS	GROSZ	GROUSED	GROYNE	GRUFFNESSES
GROK	GROSZE	GROUSER	GROYNES	GRUFFS
GROKKED	GROSZY	GROUSERS	GRUB	GRUFFY
GROKKING	GROT	GROUSES	GRUBBED	GRUGRU
GROKS	GROTESQUE	GROUSING	GRUBBER	GRUGRUS
GROMMET	GROTESQUES	GROUT	GRUBBERS	GRUIFORM
GROMMETED	GROTS	GROUTED	GRUBBIER	GRUM
GROMMETING	GROTTIER	GROUTER	GRUBBIEST	GRUMBLE
GROMMETS	GROTTIEST	GROUTERS	GRUBBILY	GRUMBLED
GROMWELL	GROTTO	GROUTIER	GRUBBING	GRUMBLER
GROMWELLS	GROTTOED	GROUTIEST	GRUBBY	GRUMBLERS
GROOM	GROTTOES	GROUTING	GRUBS	GRUMBLES
GROOMED	GROTTOS	GROUTS	GRUBSTAKE	GRUMBLING
GROOMER	GROTTY	GROUTY	GRUBSTAKED	GRUMBLY
GROOMERS	GROUCH	GROVE	GRUBSTAKES	GRUME
GROOMING	GROUCHED	GROVED	GRUBSTAKING	GRUMES
GROOMS	GROUCHES	GROVEL	GRUBWORM	GRUMMER
GROOMSMAN	GROUCHIER	GROVELED	GRUBWORMS	GRUMMEST
GROOMSMEN	GROUCHIEST	GROVELER	GRUDGE	GRUMMET
GROOVE	GROUCHILY	GROVELERS	GRUDGED	GRUMMETED
GROOVED	GROUCHING	GROVELESS	GRUDGER	GRUMMETING
GROOVER	GROUCHY	GROVELING	GRUDGERS	GRUMMETS
GROOVERS	GROUND	GROVELLED	GRUDGES	GRUMOSE
GROOVES	GROUNDED	GROVELLER	GRUDGING	GRUMOUS
GROOVIER	GROUNDER	GROVELLERS	GRUE	GRUMP
GROOVIEST	GROUNDERS	GROVELLING	GRUEL	GRUMPED
GROOVING	GROUNDHOG	GROVELS	GRUELED	GRUMPHIE
GROOVY	GROUNDHOGS	GROVES	GRUELER	GRUMPHIES
GROPE	GROUNDING	GROW	GRUELERS	GRUMPHY
GROPED	GROUNDINGS	GROWABLE	GRUELING	GRUMPIER
GROPER	GROUNDNUT	GROWER	GRUELINGS	GRUMPIEST
GROPERS	GROUNDNUTS	GROWERS	GRUELLED	GRUMPILY
GROPES	GROUNDOUT	GROWING	GRUELLER	GRUMPING
GROPING	GROUNDOUTS	GROWINGLY	GRUELLERS	GRUMPISH

GRUMPS	GUANASES	GUAVA	GUGLETS	GUILTS
GRUMPY	GUANAY	GUAVAS	GUID	GUILTY
GRUNGE	GUANAYS	GUAYABERA	GUIDABLE	GUIMPE
GRUNGER	GUANIDIN	GUAYABERAS	GUIDANCE	GUIMPES
GRUNGERS	GUANIDINE	GUAYULE	GUIDANCES	GUINEA
GRUNGES	GUANIDINES	GUAYULES	GUIDE	GUINEAS
GRUNGIER	GUANIDINS	GUCK	GUIDEBOOK	GUIPURE
GRUNGIEST	GUANIN	GUCKS	GUIDEBOOKS	GUIPURES
GRUNGY	GUANINE	GUDE	GUIDED	GUIRO
GRUNION	GUANINES	GUDES	GUIDELESS	GUIROS
GRUNIONS	GUANINS	GUDGEON	GUIDELINE	GUISARD
GRUNT	GUANO	GUDGEONED	GUIDELINES	GUISARDS
GRUNTED	GUANOS	GUDGEONING	GUIDEPOST	GUISE
GRUNTER	GUANOSINE	GUDGEONS	GUIDEPOSTS	GUISED
GRUNTERS	GUANOSINES	GUENON	GUIDER	GUISES
GRUNTING	GUANS	GUENONS	GUIDERS	GUISING
GRUNTLE	GUAR	GUERDON	GUIDES	GUITAR
GRUNTLED	GUARANA	GUERDONED	GUIDEWAY	GUITARIST
GRUNTLES	GUARANAS	GUERDONING	GUIDEWAYS	GUITARISTS
GRUNTLING	GUARANI	GUERDONS	GUIDEWORD	GUITARS
GRUNTS	GUARANIES	GUERIDON	GUIDEWORDS	GUITGUIT
GRUSHIE	GUARANIS	GUERIDONS	GUIDING	GUITGUITS
GRUTCH	GUARANTEE	GUERILLA	GUIDON	GUL
GRUTCHED	GUARANTEED	GUERILLAS	GUIDONS	GULAG
GRUTCHES	GUARANTEEING	GUERNSEY	GUIDS	GULAGS
GRUTCHING	GUARANTEES	GUERNSEYS	GUILD	GULAR
GRUTTEN	GUARANTIED	GUERRILLA	GUILDER	GULCH
GRUYERE	GUARANTIES	GUERRILLAS	GUILDERS	GULCHES
GRUYERES	GUARANTOR	GUESS	GUILDHALL	GULDEN
GRYPHON	GUARANTORS	GUESSABLE	GUILDHALLS	GULDENS
GRYPHONS	GUARANTY	GUESSED	GUILDS	GULES
GUACAMOLE	GUARANTYING	GUESSER	GUILDSHIP	GULF
GUACAMOLES	GUARD	GUESSERS	GUILDSHIPS	GULFED
GUACHARO	GUARDANT	GUESSES	GUILDSMAN	GULFIER
GUACHAROES	GUARDANTS	GUESSING	GUILDSMEN	GULFIEST
GUACHAROS	GUARDDOG	GUESSWORK	GUILE	GULFING
GUACO	GUARDDOGS	GUESSWORKS	GUILED	GULFLIKE
GUACOS	GUARDED	GUEST	GUILEFUL	GULFS
GUAIAC	GUARDEDLY	GUESTED	GUILELESS	GULFWEED
GUAIACOL	GUARDER	GUESTING	GUILES	GULFWEEDS
GUAIACOLS	GUARDERS	GUESTS	GUILING	GULFY
GUAIACS	GUARDIAN	GUFF	GUILLEMET	GULL
GUAIACUM	GUARDIANS	GUFFAW	GUILLEMETS	GULLABLE
GUAIACUMS	GUARDING	GUFFAWED	GUILLEMOT	GULLABLY
GUAIOCUM	GUARDRAIL	GUFFAWING	GUILLEMOTS	GULLED
GUAIOCUMS	GUARDRAILS	GUFFAWS	GUILLOCHE	GULLET
GUAN	GUARDROOM	GUFFS	GUILLOCHES	GULLETS
GUANABANA	GUARDROOMS	GUGGLE	GUILT	GULLEY
GUANABANAS	GUARDS	GUGGLED	GUILTIER	GULLEYS
GUANACO	GUARDSMAN	GUGGLES	GUILTIEST	GULLIBLE
GUANACOS	GUARDSMEN	GUGGLING	GUILTILY	GULLIBLY
GUANASE	GUARS	GUGLET	GUILTLESS	GULLIED

GULLIES	GUMMOSIS	GUNNELS	GURNARDS	GUSTS
GULLING	GUMMOUS	GUNNEN	GURNET	GUSTY
GULLS	GUMMY	GUNNER	GURNETS	GUT
GULLWING	GUMPTION	GUNNERIES	GURNEY	GUTBUCKET
GULLY	GUMPTIONS	GUNNERS	GURNEYS	GUTBUCKETS
GULLYING	GUMPTIOUS	GUNNERY	GURRIES	GUTLESS
GULOSITIES	GUMS	GUNNIES	GURRY	GUTLIKE
GULOSITY	GUMSHOE	GUNNING	GURSH	GUTS
GULP	GUMSHOED	GUNNINGS	GURSHES	GUTSIER
GULPED	GUMSHOEING	GUNNY	GURU	GUTSIEST
GULPER	GUMSHOES	GUNNYBAG	GURUS	GUTSILY
GULPERS	GUMTREE	GUNNYBAGS	GURUSHIP	GUTSINESS
GULPIER	GUMTREES	GUNNYSACK	GURUSHIPS	GUTSINESSES
GULPIEST	GUMWEED	GUNNYSACKS	GUSH	GUTSY
GULPING	GUMWEEDS	GUNPAPER	GUSHED	GUTTA
GULPINGLY	GUMWOOD	GUNPAPERS	GUSHER	GUTTAE
GULPS	GUMWOODS	GUNPLAY	GUSHERS	GUTTATE
GULPY	GUN	GUNPLAYS	GUSHES	GUTTATED
GULS	GUNBOAT	GUNPOINT	GUSHIER	GUTTATION
GUM	GUNBOATS	GUNPOINTS	GUSHIEST	GUTTATIONS
GUMBALL	GUNCOTTON	GUNPOWDER	GUSHILY	GUTTED
GUMBALLS	GUNCOTTONS	GUNPOWDERS	GUSHINESS	GUTTER
GUMBO	GUNDOG	GUNROOM	GUSHINESSES	GUTTERED
GUMBOIL	GUNDOGS	GUNROOMS	GUSHING	GUTTERING
GUMBOILS	GUNFIGHT	GUNRUNNER	GUSHINGLY	GUTTERINGS
GUMBOOT	GUNFIGHTING	GUNRUNNERS	GUSHY	GUTTERS
GUMBOOTS	GUNFIGHTS	GUNS	GUSSET	GUTTERY
GUMBOS	GUNFIRE	GUNSEL	GUSSETED	GUTTIER
GUMBOTIL	GUNFIRES	GUNSELS	GUSSETING	GUTTIEST
GUMBOTILS	GUNFLINT	GUNSHIP	GUSSETS	GUTTING
GUMDROP	GUNFLINTS	GUNSHIPS	GUSSIE	GUTTLE
GUMDROPS	GUNFOUGHT	GUNSHOT	GUSSIED	GUTTLED
GUMLESS	GUNITE	GUNSHOTS	GUSSIES	GUTTLER
GUMLIKE	GUNITES	GUNSMITH	GUSSY	GUTTLERS
GUMLINE	GUNK	GUNSMITHS	GUSSYING	GUTTLES
GUMLINES	GUNKHOLE	GUNSTOCK	GUST	GUTTLING
GUMMA	GUNKHOLED	GUNSTOCKS	GUSTABLE	GUTTURAL
GUMMAS	GUNKHOLES	GUNWALE	GUSTABLES	GUTTURALS
GUMMATA	GUNKHOLING	GUNWALES	GUSTATION	GUTTY
GUMMATOUS	GUNKIER	GUPPIES	GUSTATIONS	GUV
GUMMED	GUNKIEST	GUPPY	GUSTATIVE	GUVS
GUMMER	GUNKS	GURGE	GUSTATORY	GUY
GUMMERS	GUNKY	GURGED	GUSTED	GUYED
GUMMIER	GUNLESS	GURGES	GUSTIER	GUYING
GUMMIEST	GUNLOCK	GURGING	GUSTIEST	GUYLINE
GUMMINESS	GUNLOCKS	GURGLE	GUSTILY	GUYLINES
GUMMINESSES	GUNMAN	GURGLED	GUSTINESS	GUYOT
GUMMING	GUNMEN	GURGLES	GUSTINESSES	GUYOTS
GUMMITE	GUNMETAL	GURGLET	GUSTING	GUYS
GUMMITES	GUNMETALS	GURGLETS	GUSTLESS	GUZZLE
GUMMOSE	GUNNED	GURGLING	GUSTO	GUZZLED
GUMMOSES	GUNNEL	GURNARD	GUSTOES	GUZZLER

GUZZLERS
GUZZLES
GUZZLING
GWEDUC
GWEDUCK
GWEDUCKS
GWEDUCS
GWINE
GYBE
GYBED
GYBES
GYBING
GYM
GYMKHANA
GYMKHANAS
GYMNASIA
GYMNASIAL
GYMNASIUM
GYMNASIUMS
GYMNAST
GYMNASTIC
GYMNASTICS
GYMNASTS
GYMS
GYNAECEA
GYNAECEUM
GYNAECIA
GYNAECIUM
GYNANDRIES
GYNANDRY
GYNARCHIC
GYNARCHIES
GYNARCHY
GYNECIA
GYNECIC
GYNECIUM
GYNECOID
GYNIATRIES
GYNIATRY
GYNOECIA
GYNOECIUM
GYNOPHOBE
GYNOPHOBES
GYNOPHORE
GYNOPHORES
GYOZA
GYOZAS
GYP
GYPLURE
GYPLURES
GYPPED
GYPPER

GYPPERS
GYPPING
GYPS
GYPSEIAN
GYPSEOUS
GYPSIED
GYPSIES
GYPSTER
GYPSTERS
GYPSUM
GYPSUMS
GYPSY
GYPSYDOM
GYPSYDOMS
GYPSYING
GYPSYISH
GYPSYISM
GYPSYISMS
GYRAL
GYRALLY
GYRASE
GYRASES
GYRATE
GYRATED
GYRATES
GYRATING
GYRATION
GYRATIONS
GYRATOR
GYRATORS
GYRATORY
GYRE
GYRED
GYRENE
GYRENES
GYRES
GYRFALCON
GYRFALCONS
GYRI
GYRING
GYRO
GYROIDAL
GYRON
GYRONS
GYROPILOT
GYROPILOTS
GYROPLANE
GYROPLANES
GYROS
GYROSCOPE
GYROSCOPES
GYROSE

GYROSTAT
GYROSTATS
GYRUS
GYTTJA
GYTTJAS
GYVE
GYVED
GYVES
GYVING

H

HA
HAAF
HAAFS
HAAR
HAARS
HABANERA
HABANERAS
HABANERO
HABANEROS
HABDALAH
HABDALAHS
HABERGEON
HABERGEONS
HABILE
HABIT
HABITABLE
HABITABLY
HABITAN
HABITANS
HABITANT
HABITANTS
HABITAT
HABITATS
HABITED
HABITING
HABITS
HABITUAL
HABITUATE
HABITUATED
HABITUATES
HABITUATING
HABITUDE
HABITUDES
HABITUE
HABITUES
HABITUS
HABOOB
HABOOBS

HABU
HABUS
HACEK
HACEKS
HACENDADO
HACENDADOS
HACHURE
HACHURED
HACHURES
HACHURING
HACIENDA
HACIENDAS
HACK
HACKABLE
HACKAMORE
HACKAMORES
HACKBERRIES
HACKBERRY
HACKBUT
HACKBUTS
HACKED
HACKEE
HACKEES
HACKER
HACKERS
HACKIE
HACKIES
HACKING
HACKLE
HACKLED
HACKLER
HACKLERS
HACKLES
HACKLIER
HACKLIEST
HACKLING
HACKLY
HACKMAN
HACKMEN
HACKNEY
HACKNEYED
HACKNEYING
HACKNEYS
HACKS
HACKSAW
HACKSAWED
HACKSAWING
HACKSAWN
HACKSAWS
HACKWORK
HACKWORKS
HAD

HADAL
HADARIM
HADDEST
HADDOCK
HADDOCKS
HADE
HADED
HADES
HADING
HADITH
HADITHS
HADJ
HADJEE
HADJEES
HADJES
HADJI
HADJIS
HADRON
HADRONIC
HADRONS
HADROSAUR
HADROSAURS
HADST
HAE
HAECCEITIES
HAECCEITY
HAED
HAEING
HAEM
HAEMAL
HAEMATAL
HAEMATIC
HAEMATICS
HAEMATIN
HAEMATINS
HAEMATITE
HAEMATITES
HAEMIC
HAEMIN
HAEMINS
HAEMOID
HAEMS
HAEN
HAEREDES
HAERES
HAES
HAET
HAETS
HAFFET
HAFFETS
HAFFIT
HAFFITS

HAFIZ	HAGGISH	HAIRCAPS	HALACHIC	HALFLIFE
HAFIZES	HAGGISHLY	HAIRCLOTH	HALACHIST	HALFLIVES
HAFNIUM	HAGGLE	HAIRCLOTHS	HALACHISTS	HALFNESS
HAFNIUMS	HAGGLED	HAIRCUT	HALACHOT	HALFNESSES
HAFT	HAGGLER	HAIRCUTS	HALACHOTH	HALFPENCE
HAFTARA	HAGGLERS	HAIRDO	HALAKAH	HALFPENNIES
HAFTARAH	HAGGLES	HAIRDOS	HALAKAHS	HALFPENNY
HAFTARAHS	HAGGLING	HAIRED	HALAKHA	HALFPIPE
HAFTARAS	HAGIARCHIES	HAIRIER	HALAKHAH	HALFPIPES
HAFTAROT	HAGIARCHY	HAIRIEST	HALAKHAHS	HALFTIME
HAFTAROTH	HAGIOLOGIES	HAIRINESS	HALAKHAS	HALFTIMES
HAFTED	HAGIOLOGY	HAIRINESSES	HALAKHIC	HALFTONE
HAFTER	HAGRIDDEN	HAIRLESS	HALAKHIST	HALFTONES
HAFTERS	HAGRIDE	HAIRLIKE	HALAKHISTS	HALFTRACK
HAFTING	HAGRIDER	HAIRLINE	HALAKHOT	HALFTRACKS
HAFTORAH	HAGRIDERS	HAIRLINES	HALAKHOTH	HALFWAY
HAFTORAHS	HAGRIDES	HAIRLOCK	HALAKIC	HALIBUT
HAFTOROS	HAGRIDING	HAIRLOCKS	HALAKIST	HALIBUTS
HAFTOROT	HAGRODE	HAIRNET	HALAKISTS	HALID
HAFTOROTH	HAGS	HAIRNETS	HALAKOTH	HALIDE
HAFTS	HAH	HAIRPIECE	HALAL	HALIDES
HAG	HAHA	HAIRPIECES	HALALA	HALIDOM
HAGADIC	HAHAS	HAIRPIN	HALALAH	HALIDOME
HAGADIST	HAHNIUM	HAIRPINS	HALALAHS	HALIDOMES
HAGADISTS	HAHNIUMS	HAIRS	HALALAS	HALIDOMS
HAGBERRIES	HAHS	HAIRSPRAY	HALALS	HALIDS
HAGBERRY	HAIK	HAIRSPRAYS	HALATION	HALING
HAGBORN	HAIKA	HAIRSTYLE	HALATIONS	HALITE
HAGBUSH	HAIKS	HAIRSTYLES	HALAVAH	HALITES
HAGBUSHES	HAIKU	HAIRWORK	HALAVAHS	HALITOSES
HAGBUT	HAIKUS	HAIRWORKS	HALAZONE	HALITOSIS
HAGBUTS	HAIL	HAIRWORM	HALAZONES	HALITUS
HAGDON	HAILED	HAIRWORMS	HALBERD	HALITUSES
HAGDONS	HAILER	HAIRY	HALBERDS	HALL
HAGFISH	HAILERS	HAJ	HALBERT	HALLAH
HAGFISHES	HAILING	HAJES	HALBERTS	HALLAHS
HAGGADA	HAILS	HAJI	HALCYON	HALLAL
HAGGADAH	HAILSTONE	HAJIS	HALCYONS	HALLEL
HAGGADAHS	HAILSTONES	HAJJ	HALE	HALLELS
HAGGADAS	HAILSTORM	HAJJES	HALED	HALLIARD
HAGGADIC	HAILSTORMS	HAJJI	HALENESS	HALLIARDS
HAGGADIST	HAIMISH	HAJJIS	HALENESSES	HALLMARK
HAGGADISTS	HAINT	HAKE	HALER	HALLMARKED
HAGGADOT	HAINTS	HAKEEM	HALERS	HALLMARKING
HAGGADOTH	HAIR	HAKEEMS	HALERU	HALLMARKS
HAGGARD	HAIRBALL	HAKES	HALES	HALLO
HAGGARDLY	HAIRBALLS	HAKIM	HALEST	HALLOA
HAGGARDS	HAIRBAND	HAKIMS	HALF	HALLOAED
HAGGED	HAIRBANDS	HAKU	HALFBACK	HALLOAING
HAGGING	HAIRBRUSH	HAKUS	HALFBACKS	HALLOAS
HAGGIS	HAIRBRUSHES	HALACHA	HALFBEAK	HALLOED
HAGGISES	HAIRCAP	HALACHAS	HALFBEAKS	HALLOES

HALLOING
HALLOO
HALLOOED
HALLOOING
HALLOOS
HALLOS
HALLOT
HALLOTH
HALLOW
HALLOWED
HALLOWER
HALLOWERS
HALLOWING
HALLOWS
HALLS
HALLUCAL
HALLUCES
HALLUX
HALLWAY
HALLWAYS
HALM
HALMA
HALMAS
HALMS
HALO
HALOBIONT
HALOBIONTS
HALOCLINE
HALOCLINES
HALOED
HALOES
HALOGEN
HALOGENS
HALOGETON
HALOGETONS
HALOID
HALOIDS
HALOING
HALOLIKE
HALON
HALONS
HALOPHILE
HALOPHILES
HALOPHYTE
HALOPHYTES
HALOS
HALOTHANE
HALOTHANES
HALT
HALTED
HALTER
HALTERE

HALTERED
HALTERES
HALTERING
HALTERS
HALTING
HALTINGLY
HALTLESS
HALTS
HALUTZ
HALUTZIM
HALVA
HALVAH
HALVAHS
HALVAS
HALVE
HALVED
HALVERS
HALVES
HALVING
HALYARD
HALYARDS
HAM
HAMADA
HAMADAS
HAMADRYAD
HAMADRYADES
HAMADRYADS
HAMADRYAS
HAMADRYASES
HAMAL
HAMALS
HAMARTIA
HAMARTIAS
HAMATE
HAMATES
HAMAUL
HAMAULS
HAMBONE
HAMBONED
HAMBONES
HAMBONING
HAMBURG
HAMBURGER
HAMBURGERS
HAMBURGS
HAME
HAMES
HAMLET
HAMLETS
HAMMADA
HAMMADAS
HAMMAL

HAMMALS
HAMMAM
HAMMAMS
HAMMED
HAMMER
HAMMERED
HAMMERER
HAMMERERS
HAMMERING
HAMMERKOP
HAMMERKOPS
HAMMERS
HAMMERTOE
HAMMERTOES
HAMMIER
HAMMIEST
HAMMILY
HAMMINESS
HAMMINESSES
HAMMING
HAMMOCK
HAMMOCKS
HAMMY
HAMPER
HAMPERED
HAMPERER
HAMPERERS
HAMPERING
HAMPERS
HAMS
HAMSTER
HAMSTERS
HAMSTRING
HAMSTRINGING
HAMSTRINGS
HAMSTRUNG
HAMULAR
HAMULATE
HAMULI
HAMULOSE
HAMULOUS
HAMULUS
HAMZA
HAMZAH
HAMZAHS
HAMZAS
HANAPER
HANAPERS
HANCE
HANCES
HAND
HANDAX

HANDAXES
HANDBAG
HANDBAGS
HANDBALL
HANDBALLS
HANDBELL
HANDBELLS
HANDBILL
HANDBILLS
HANDBLOWN
HANDBOOK
HANDBOOKS
HANDCAR
HANDCARS
HANDCART
HANDCARTS
HANDCLAP
HANDCLAPS
HANDCLASP
HANDCLASPS
HANDCRAFT
HANDCRAFTED
HANDCRAFTING
HANDCRAFTS
HANDCUFF
HANDCUFFED
HANDCUFFING
HANDCUFFS
HANDED
HANDER
HANDERS
HANDFAST
HANDFASTED
HANDFASTING
HANDFASTS
HANDFUL
HANDFULS
HANDGRIP
HANDGRIPS
HANDGUN
HANDGUNS
HANDHELD
HANDHELDS
HANDHOLD
HANDHOLDS
HANDICAP
HANDICAPPED
HANDICAPPING
HANDICAPS
HANDIER
HANDIEST
HANDILY

HANDINESS
HANDINESSES
HANDING
HANDIWORK
HANDIWORKS
HANDLE
HANDLEBAR
HANDLEBARS
HANDLED
HANDLER
HANDLERS
HANDLES
HANDLESS
HANDLIKE
HANDLING
HANDLINGS
HANDLIST
HANDLISTS
HANDLOOM
HANDLOOMS
HANDMADE
HANDMAID
HANDMAIDS
HANDOFF
HANDOFFS
HANDOUT
HANDOUTS
HANDOVER
HANDOVERS
HANDPICK
HANDPICKED
HANDPICKING
HANDPICKS
HANDPRESS
HANDPRESSES
HANDPRINT
HANDPRINTS
HANDRAIL
HANDRAILS
HANDS
HANDSAW
HANDSAWS
HANDSEL
HANDSELED
HANDSELING
HANDSELLED
HANDSELLING
HANDSELS
HANDSET
HANDSETS
HANDSEWN
HANDSFUL

HANDSHAKE	HANGOVER	HAPHTARA	HARANGUER	HARDENER
HANDSHAKES	HANGOVERS	HAPHTARAH	HARANGUERS	HARDENERS
HANDSOME	HANGS	HAPHTARAHS	HARANGUES	HARDENING
HANDSOMER	HANGTAG	HAPHTARAS	HARANGUING	HARDENINGS
HANDSOMEST	HANGTAGS	HAPHTAROT	HARASS	HARDENS
HANDSPIKE	HANGUL	HAPHTAROTH	HARASSED	HARDER
HANDSPIKES	HANGUP	HAPKIDO	HARASSER	HARDEST
HANDSTAMP	HANGUPS	HAPKIDOS	HARASSERS	HARDGOODS
HANDSTAMPED	HANIWA	HAPLESS	HARASSES	HARDHACK
HANDSTAMPING	HANK	HAPLESSLY	HARASSING	HARDHACKS
HANDSTAMPS	HANKED	HAPLITE	HARBINGER	HARDHAT
HANDSTAND	HANKER	HAPLITES	HARBINGERED	HARDHATS
HANDSTANDS	HANKERED	HAPLOID	HARBINGERING	HARDHEAD
HANDWHEEL	HANKERER	HAPLOIDIC	HARBINGERS	HARDHEADS
HANDWHEELS	HANKERERS	HAPLOIDIES	HARBOR	HARDIER
HANDWORK	HANKERING	HAPLOIDS	HARBORAGE	HARDIES
HANDWORKS	HANKERINGS	HAPLOIDY	HARBORAGES	HARDIEST
HANDWOVEN	HANKERS	HAPLOLOGIES	HARBORED	HARDIHOOD
HANDWRIT	HANKIE	HAPLOLOGY	HARBORER	HARDIHOODS
HANDWRITE	HANKIES	HAPLONT	HARBORERS	HARDILY
HANDWRITES	HANKING	HAPLONTIC	HARBORFUL	HARDIMENT
HANDWRITING	HANKS	HAPLONTS	HARBORFULS	HARDIMENTS
HANDWRITTEN	HANKY	HAPLOPIA	HARBORING	HARDINESS
HANDWROTE	HANSA	HAPLOPIAS	HARBOROUS	HARDINESSES
HANDY	HANSAS	HAPLOSES	HARBORS	HARDLINE
HANDYMAN	HANSE	HAPLOSIS	HARBOUR	HARDLY
HANDYMEN	HANSEATIC	HAPLOTYPE	HARBOURED	HARDNESS
HANG	HANSEL	HAPLOTYPES	HARBOURING	HARDNESSES
HANGABLE	HANSELED	HAPLY	HARBOURS	HARDNOSE
HANGAR	HANSELING	HAPPED	HARD	HARDNOSES
HANGARED	HANSELLED	HAPPEN	HARDASS	HARDPACK
HANGARING	HANSELLING	HAPPENED	HARDASSES	HARDPACKS
HANGARS	HANSELS	HAPPENING	HARDBACK	HARDPAN
HANGBIRD	HANSES	HAPPENINGS	HARDBACKS	HARDPANS
HANGBIRDS	HANSOM	HAPPENS	HARDBALL	HARDS
HANGDOG	HANSOMS	HAPPIER	HARDBALLS	HARDSET
HANGDOGS	HANT	HAPPIEST	HARDBOARD	HARDSHIP
HANGED	HANTED	HAPPILY	HARDBOARDS	HARDSHIPS
HANGER	HANTING	HAPPINESS	HARDBOOT	HARDSTAND
HANGERS	HANTLE	HAPPINESSES	HARDBOOTS	HARDSTANDS
HANGFIRE	HANTLES	HAPPING	HARDBOUND	HARDTACK
HANGFIRES	HANTS	HAPPY	HARDBOUNDS	HARDTACKS
HANGING	HANUMAN	HAPS	HARDCASE	HARDTOP
HANGINGS	HANUMANS	HAPTEN	HARDCORE	HARDTOPS
HANGMAN	HAO	HAPTENE	HARDCORES	HARDWARE
HANGMEN	HAOLE	HAPTENES	HARDCOURT	HARDWARES
HANGNAIL	HAOLES	HAPTENIC	HARDCOVER	HARDWIRE
HANGNAILS	HAP	HAPTENS	HARDCOVERS	HARDWIRED
HANGNEST	HAPAX	HAPTIC	HARDEDGE	HARDWIRES
HANGNESTS	HAPAXES	HAPTICAL	HARDEDGES	HARDWIRING
HANGOUT	HAPHAZARD	HARANGUE	HARDEN	HARDWOOD
HANGOUTS	HAPHAZARDS	HARANGUED	HARDENED	HARDWOODS

HARDY	HARMINS	HARRIES	HASHISH	HATCHELED
HARE	HARMLESS	HARROW	HASHISHES	HATCHELING
HAREBELL	HARMONIC	HARROWED	HASLET	HATCHELLED
HAREBELLS	HARMONICA	HARROWER	HASLETS	HATCHELLING
HARED	HARMONICAS	HARROWERS	HASP	HATCHELS
HAREEM	HARMONICS	HARROWING	HASPED	HATCHER
HAREEMS	HARMONIES	HARROWS	HASPING	HATCHERIES
HARELIKE	HARMONISE	HARRUMPH	HASPS	HATCHERS
HARELIP	HARMONISED	HARRUMPHED	HASSEL	HATCHERY
HARELIPS	HARMONISES	HARRUMPHING	HASSELS	HATCHES
HAREM	HARMONISING	HARRUMPHS	HASSIUM	HATCHET
HAREMS	HARMONIST	HARRY	HASSIUMS	HATCHETS
HARES	HARMONISTS	HARRYING	HASSLE	HATCHING
HARIANA	HARMONIUM	HARSH	HASSLED	HATCHINGS
HARIANAS	HARMONIUMS	HARSHEN	HASSLES	HATCHLING
HARICOT	HARMONIZE	HARSHENED	HASSLING	HATCHLINGS
HARICOTS	HARMONIZED	HARSHENING	HASSOCK	HATCHMENT
HARIJAN	HARMONIZES	HARSHENS	HASSOCKS	HATCHMENTS
HARIJANS	HARMONIZING	HARSHER	HAST	HATCHWAY
HARING	HARMONY	HARSHEST	HASTATE	HATCHWAYS
HARISSA	HARMS	HARSHLY	HASTATELY	HATE
HARISSAS	HARNESS	HARSHNESS	HASTE	HATEABLE
HARK	HARNESSED	HARSHNESSES	HASTED	HATED
HARKED	HARNESSES	HARSLET	HASTEFUL	HATEFUL
HARKEN	HARNESSING	HARSLETS	HASTEN	HATEFULLY
HARKENED	HARP	HART	HASTENED	HATER
HARKENER	HARPED	HARTAL	HASTENER	HATERS
HARKENERS	HARPER	HARTALS	HASTENERS	HATES
HARKENING	HARPERS	HARTS	HASTENING	HATFUL
HARKENS	HARPIES	HARTSHORN	HASTENS	HATFULS
HARKING	HARPIN	HARTSHORNS	HASTES	HATH
HARKS	HARPING	HARUMPH	HASTIER	HATING
HARL	HARPINGS	HARUMPHED	HASTIEST	HATLESS
HARLEQUIN	HARPINS	HARUMPHING	HASTILY	HATLIKE
HARLEQUINS	HARPIST	HARUMPHS	HASTINESS	HATMAKER
HARLOT	HARPISTS	HARUSPEX	HASTINESSES	HATMAKERS
HARLOTRIES	HARPOON	HARUSPICES	HASTING	HATPIN
HARLOTRY	HARPOONED	HARVEST	HASTY	HATPINS
HARLOTS	HARPOONER	HARVESTED	HAT	HATRACK
HARLS	HARPOONERS	HARVESTER	HATABLE	HATRACKS
HARM	HARPOONING	HARVESTERS	HATBAND	HATRED
HARMATTAN	HARPOONS	HARVESTING	HATBANDS	HATREDS
HARMATTANS	HARPS	HARVESTS	HATBOX	HATS
HARMED	HARPY	HAS	HATBOXES	HATSFUL
HARMER	HARPYLIKE	HASH	HATCH	HATTED
HARMERS	HARQUEBUS	HASHED	HATCHABLE	HATTER
HARMFUL	HARQUEBUSES	HASHEESH	HATCHBACK	HATTERIA
HARMFULLY	HARRIDAN	HASHEESHES	HATCHBACKS	HATTERIAS
HARMIN	HARRIDANS	HASHES	HATCHECK	HATTERS
HARMINE	HARRIED	HASHHEAD	HATCHECKS	HATTING
HARMINES	HARRIER	HASHHEADS	HATCHED	HAUBERK
HARMING	HARRIERS	HASHING	HATCHEL	HAUBERKS

HAUGH	HAVE	HAWKNOSE	HAYSTACKS	HEADCOUNT
HAUGHS	HAVELOCK	HAWKNOSES	HAYWARD	HEADCOUNTS
HAUGHTIER	HAVELOCKS	HAWKS	HAYWARDS	HEADDRESS
HAUGHTIEST	HAVEN	HAWKSBILL	HAYWIRE	HEADDRESSES
HAUGHTILY	HAVENED	HAWKSBILLS	HAYWIRES	HEADED
HAUGHTY	HAVENING	HAWKSHAW	HAZAN	HEADEND
HAUL	HAVENS	HAWKSHAWS	HAZANIM	HEADENDS
HAULAGE	HAVER	HAWKWEED	HAZANS	HEADER
HAULAGES	HAVERED	HAWKWEEDS	HAZARD	HEADERS
HAULED	HAVEREL	HAWS	HAZARDED	HEADFIRST
HAULER	HAVERELS	HAWSE	HAZARDER	HEADFISH
HAULERS	HAVERING	HAWSEHOLE	HAZARDERS	HEADFISHES
HAULIER	HAVERS	HAWSEHOLES	HAZARDING	HEADFUL
HAULIERS	HAVERSACK	HAWSEPIPE	HAZARDOUS	HEADFULS
HAULING	HAVERSACKS	HAWSEPIPES	HAZARDS	HEADGATE
HAULM	HAVES	HAWSER	HAZE	HEADGATES
HAULMIER	HAVING	HAWSERS	HAZED	HEADGEAR
HAULMIEST	HAVIOR	HAWSES	HAZEL	HEADGEARS
HAULMS	HAVIORS	HAWTHORN	HAZELHEN	HEADHUNT
HAULMY	HAVIOUR	HAWTHORNS	HAZELHENS	HEADHUNTED
HAULS	HAVIOURS	HAWTHORNY	HAZELLY	HEADHUNTING
HAULYARD	HAVOC	HAY	HAZELNUT	HEADHUNTS
HAULYARDS	HAVOCKED	HAYCOCK	HAZELNUTS	HEADIER
HAUNCH	HAVOCKER	HAYCOCKS	HAZELS	HEADIEST
HAUNCHED	HAVOCKERS	HAYED	HAZER	HEADILY
HAUNCHES	HAVOCKING	HAYER	HAZERS	HEADINESS
HAUNT	HAVOCS	HAYERS	HAZES	HEADINESSES
HAUNTED	HAW	HAYEY	HAZIER	HEADING
HAUNTER	HAWALA	HAYFIELD	HAZIEST	HEADINGS
HAUNTERS	HAWALAS	HAYFIELDS	HAZILY	HEADLAMP
HAUNTING	HAWED	HAYFORK	HAZINESS	HEADLAMPS
HAUNTS	HAWFINCH	HAYFORKS	HAZINESSES	HEADLAND
HAUSEN	HAWFINCHES	HAYING	HAZING	HEADLANDS
HAUSENS	HAWING	HAYINGS	HAZINGS	HEADLESS
HAUSFRAU	HAWK	HAYLAGE	HAZMAT	HEADLIGHT
HAUSFRAUEN	HAWKBILL	HAYLAGES	HAZMATS	HEADLIGHTS
HAUSFRAUS	HAWKBILLS	HAYLOFT	HAZY	HEADLINE
HAUSTELLA	HAWKED	HAYLOFTS	HAZZAN	HEADLINED
HAUSTELLUM	HAWKER	HAYMAKER	HAZZANIM	HEADLINER
HAUSTORIA	HAWKERS	HAYMAKERS	HAZZANS	HEADLINERS
HAUSTORIUM	HAWKEY	HAYMOW	HE	HEADLINES
HAUT	HAWKEYED	HAYMOWS	HEAD	HEADLINING
HAUTBOIS	HAWKEYS	HAYRACK	HEADACHE	HEADLOCK
HAUTBOY	HAWKIE	HAYRACKS	HEADACHES	HEADLOCKS
HAUTBOYS	HAWKIES	HAYRICK	HEADACHEY	HEADLONG
HAUTE	HAWKING	HAYRICKS	HEADACHIER	HEADMAN
HAUTEUR	HAWKINGS	HAYRIDE	HEADACHIEST	HEADMEN
HAUTEURS	HAWKISH	HAYRIDES	HEADACHY	HEADMOST
HAVARTI	HAWKISHLY	HAYS	HEADBAND	HEADNOTE
HAVARTIS	HAWKLIKE	HAYSEED	HEADBANDS	HEADNOTES
HAVDALAH	HAWKMOTH	HAYSEEDS	HEADBOARD	HEADPHONE
HAVDALAHS	HAWKMOTHS	HAYSTACK	HEADBOARDS	HEADPHONES

HEADPIECE	HEALTHIEST	HEARTIES	HEAVENLY	HEDER
HEADPIECES	HEALTHILY	HEARTIEST	HEAVENS	HEDERS
HEADPIN	HEALTHS	HEARTILY	HEAVER	HEDGE
HEADPINS	HEALTHY	HEARTING	HEAVERS	HEDGED
HEADRACE	HEAP	HEARTLAND	HEAVES	HEDGEHOG
HEADRACES	HEAPED	HEARTLANDS	HEAVIER	HEDGEHOGS
HEADREST	HEAPER	HEARTLESS	HEAVIES	HEDGEHOP
HEADRESTS	HEAPERS	HEARTS	HEAVIEST	HEDGEHOPPED
HEADROOM	HEAPING	HEARTSICK	HEAVILY	HEDGEHOPPING
HEADROOMS	HEAPS	HEARTSOME	HEAVINESS	HEDGEHOPS
HEADS	HEAPY	HEARTSORE	HEAVINESSES	HEDGEPIG
HEADSAIL	HEAR	HEARTWOOD	HEAVING	HEDGEPIGS
HEADSAILS	HEARABLE	HEARTWOODS	HEAVY	HEDGER
HEADSET	HEARD	HEARTWORM	HEAVYSET	HEDGEROW
HEADSETS	HEARER	HEARTWORMS	HEBDOMAD	HEDGEROWS
HEADSHIP	HEARERS	HEARTY	HEBDOMADS	HEDGERS
HEADSHIPS	HEARING	HEAT	HEBE	HEDGES
HEADSMAN	HEARINGS	HEATABLE	HEBES	HEDGIER
HEADSMEN	HEARKEN	HEATED	HEBETATE	HEDGIEST
HEADSPACE	HEARKENED	HEATEDLY	HEBETATED	HEDGING
HEADSPACES	HEARKENER	HEATER	HEBETATES	HEDGINGLY
HEADSTALL	HEARKENERS	HEATERS	HEBETATING	HEDGY
HEADSTALLS	HEARKENING	HEATH	HEBETIC	HEDONIC
HEADSTAND	HEARKENS	HEATHBIRD	HEBETUDE	HEDONICS
HEADSTANDS	HEARS	HEATHBIRDS	HEBETUDES	HEDONISM
HEADSTAY	HEARSAY	HEATHEN	HEBRAIZE	HEDONISMS
HEADSTAYS	HEARSAYS	HEATHENRIES	HEBRAIZED	HEDONIST
HEADSTOCK	HEARSE	HEATHENRY	HEBRAIZES	HEDONISTS
HEADSTOCKS	HEARSED	HEATHENS	HEBRAIZING	HEED
HEADSTONE	HEARSES	HEATHER	HECATOMB	HEEDED
HEADSTONES	HEARSING	HEATHERED	HECATOMBS	HEEDER
HEADWATER	HEART	HEATHERS	HECK	HEEDERS
HEADWATERS	HEARTACHE	HEATHERY	HECKLE	HEEDFUL
HEADWAY	HEARTACHES	HEATHIER	HECKLED	HEEDFULLY
HEADWAYS	HEARTBEAT	HEATHIEST	HECKLER	HEEDING
HEADWIND	HEARTBEATS	HEATHLAND	HECKLERS	HEEDLESS
HEADWINDS	HEARTBURN	HEATHLANDS	HECKLES	HEEDS
HEADWORD	HEARTBURNS	HEATHLESS	HECKLING	HEEHAW
HEADWORDS	HEARTED	HEATHLIKE	HECKS	HEEHAWED
HEADWORK	HEARTEN	HEATHS	HECTARE	HEEHAWING
HEADWORKS	HEARTENED	HEATHY	HECTARES	HEEHAWS
HEADY	HEARTENER	HEATING	HECTIC	HEEL
HEAL	HEARTENERS	HEATLESS	HECTICAL	HEELBALL
HEALABLE	HEARTENING	HEATPROOF	HECTICLY	HEELBALLS
HEALED	HEARTENS	HEATS	HECTOGRAM	HEELED
HEALER	HEARTFELT	HEAUME	HECTOGRAMS	HEELER
HEALERS	HEARTFREE	HEAUMES	HECTOR	HEELERS
HEALING	HEARTH	HEAVE	HECTORED	HEELING
HEALS	HEARTHRUG	HEAVED	HECTORING	HEELINGS
HEALTH	HEARTHRUGS	HEAVEN	HECTORS	HEELLESS
HEALTHFUL	HEARTHS	HEAVENLIER	HEDDLE	HEELPIECE
HEALTHIER	HEARTIER	HEAVENLIEST	HEDDLES	HEELPIECES

HEELPLATE	HEIGHTISM	HELICON	HELLENIZE	HELOTS
HEELPLATES	HEIGHTISMS	HELICONIA	HELLENIZED	HELP
HEELPOST	HEIGHTS	HELICONIAS	HELLENIZES	HELPABLE
HEELPOSTS	HEIL	HELICONS	HELLENIZING	HELPED
HEELS	HEILED	HELICOPT	HELLER	HELPER
HEELTAP	HEILING	HELICOPTED	HELLERI	HELPERS
HEELTAPS	HEILS	HELICOPTING	HELLERIES	HELPFUL
HEEZE	HEIMISH	HELICOPTS	HELLERIS	HELPFULLY
HEEZED	HEINIE	HELICTITE	HELLERS	HELPING
HEEZES	HEINIES	HELICTITES	HELLERY	HELPINGS
HEEZING	HEINOUS	HELILIFT	HELLFIRE	HELPLESS
HEFT	HEINOUSLY	HELILIFTED	HELLFIRES	HELPMATE
HEFTED	HEIR	HELILIFTING	HELLHOLE	HELPMATES
HEFTER	HEIRDOM	HELILIFTS	HELLHOLES	HELPMEET
HEFTERS	HEIRDOMS	HELIO	HELLHOUND	HELPMEETS
HEFTIER	HEIRED	HELIOGRAM	HELLHOUNDS	HELPS
HEFTIEST	HEIRESS	HELIOGRAMS	HELLING	HELVE
HEFTILY	HEIRESSES	HELIOS	HELLION	HELVED
HEFTINESS	HEIRING	HELIOSTAT	HELLIONS	HELVES
HEFTINESSES	HEIRLESS	HELIOSTATS	HELLISH	HELVING
HEFTING	HEIRLOOM	HELIOTYPE	HELLISHLY	HEM
HEFTS	HEIRLOOMS	HELIOTYPED	HELLKITE	HEMAGOG
HEFTY	HEIRS	HELIOTYPES	HELLKITES	HEMAGOGS
HEGARI	HEIRSHIP	HELIOTYPIES	HELLO	HEMAL
HEGARIS	HEIRSHIPS	HELIOTYPING	HELLOED	HEMATAL
HEGEMON	HEISHI	HELIOTYPY	HELLOES	HEMATEIN
HEGEMONIC	HEIST	HELIOZOAN	HELLOING	HEMATEINS
HEGEMONIES	HEISTED	HELIOZOANS	HELLOS	HEMATIC
HEGEMONS	HEISTER	HELIOZOIC	HELLS	HEMATICS
HEGEMONY	HEISTERS	HELIPAD	HELLUVA	HEMATIN
HEGIRA	HEISTING	HELIPADS	HELM	HEMATINE
HEGIRAS	HEISTS	HELIPORT	HELMED	HEMATINES
HEGUMEN	HEJIRA	HELIPORTS	HELMET	HEMATINIC
HEGUMENE	HEJIRAS	HELISTOP	HELMETED	HEMATINICS
HEGUMENES	HEKTARE	HELISTOPS	HELMETING	HEMATINS
HEGUMENIES	HEKTARES	HELIUM	HELMETS	HEMATITE
HEGUMENOS	HEKTOGRAM	HELIUMS	HELMING	HEMATITES
HEGUMENOSES	HEKTOGRAMS	HELIX	HELMINTH	HEMATITIC
HEGUMENS	HELD	HELIXES	HELMINTHS	HEMATOID
HEGUMENY	HELIAC	HELL	HELMLESS	HEMATOMA
HEH	HELIACAL	HELLBENT	HELMS	HEMATOMAS
HEHS	HELIAST	HELLBOX	HELMSMAN	HEMATOMATA
HEIFER	HELIASTS	HELLBOXES	HELMSMEN	HEMATOSES
HEIFERS	HELICAL	HELLBROTH	HELO	HEMATOSIS
HEIGH	HELICALLY	HELLBROTHS	HELOS	HEMATOZOA
HEIGHT	HELICES	HELLCAT	HELOT	HEMATOZOON
HEIGHTEN	HELICITIES	HELLCATS	HELOTAGE	HEMATURIA
HEIGHTENED	HELICITY	HELLDIVER	HELOTAGES	HEMATURIAS
HEIGHTENING	HELICLINE	HELLDIVERS	HELOTISM	HEMATURIC
HEIGHTENS	HELICLINES	HELLEBORE	HELOTISMS	HEME
HEIGHTH	HELICOID	HELLEBORES	HELOTRIES	HEMELYTRA
HEIGHTHS	HELICOIDS	HELLED	HELOTRY	HEMELYTRON

HEMELYTRUM	HEMPIE	HENRIES	HERB	HEREBY
HEMES	HEMPIER	HENRY	HERBAGE	HEREDES
HEMIALGIA	HEMPIEST	HENRYS	HERBAGED	HEREDITIES
HEMIALGIAS	HEMPLIKE	HENS	HERBAGES	HEREDITY
HEMIC	HEMPS	HENT	HERBAL	HEREIN
HEMICYCLE	HEMPSEED	HENTED	HERBALISM	HEREINTO
HEMICYCLES	HEMPSEEDS	HENTING	HERBALISMS	HEREOF
HEMIN	HEMPWEED	HENTS	HERBALIST	HEREON
HEMINS	HEMPWEEDS	HEP	HERBALISTS	HERES
HEMIOLA	HEMPY	HEPARIN	HERBALS	HERESIES
HEMIOLAS	HEMS	HEPARINS	HERBARIA	HERESY
HEMIOLIA	HEMSTITCH	HEPATIC	HERBARIAL	HERETIC
HEMIOLIAS	HEMSTITCHED	HEPATICA	HERBARIUM	HERETICAL
HEMIPTER	HEMSTITCHES	HEPATICAE	HERBARIUMS	HERETICS
HEMIPTERS	HEMSTITCHING	HEPATICAS	HERBED	HERETO
HEMISTICH	HEN	HEPATICS	HERBICIDE	HERETRICES
HEMISTICHS	HENBANE	HEPATITIDES	HERBICIDES	HERETRIX
HEMITROPE	HENBANES	HEPATITIS	HERBIER	HERETRIXES
HEMITROPES	HENBIT	HEPATITISES	HERBIEST	HEREUNDER
HEMLINE	HENBITS	HEPATIZE	HERBIVORE	HEREUNTO
HEMLINES	HENCE	HEPATIZED	HERBIVORES	HEREUPON
HEMLOCK	HENCHMAN	HEPATIZES	HERBIVORIES	HEREWITH
HEMLOCKS	HENCHMEN	HEPATIZING	HERBIVORY	HERIOT
HEMMED	HENCOOP	HEPATOMA	HERBLESS	HERIOTS
HEMMER	HENCOOPS	HEPATOMAS	HERBLIKE	HERITABLE
HEMMERS	HENDIADYS	HEPATOMATA	HERBOLOGIES	HERITABLY
HEMMING	HENDIADYSES	HEPCAT	HERBOLOGY	HERITAGE
HEMOCOEL	HENEQUEN	HEPCATS	HERBS	HERITAGES
HEMOCOELS	HENEQUENS	HEPPER	HERBY	HERITOR
HEMOCYTE	HENEQUIN	HEPPEST	HERCULEAN	HERITORS
HEMOCYTES	HENEQUINS	HEPTAD	HERCULES	HERITRICES
HEMOID	HENGE	HEPTADS	HERCULESES	HERITRIX
HEMOLYMPH	HENGES	HEPTAGON	HERD	HERITRIXES
HEMOLYMPHS	HENHOUSE	HEPTAGONS	HERDED	HERL
HEMOLYSES	HENHOUSES	HEPTANE	HERDER	HERLS
HEMOLYSIN	HENIQUEN	HEPTANES	HERDERS	HERM
HEMOLYSINS	HENIQUENS	HEPTARCH	HERDIC	HERMA
HEMOLYSIS	HENLEY	HEPTARCHIES	HERDICS	HERMAE
HEMOLYTIC	HENLEYS	HEPTARCHS	HERDING	HERMAEAN
HEMOLYZE	HENLIKE	HEPTARCHY	HERDLIKE	HERMAI
HEMOLYZED	HENNA	HEPTOSE	HERDMAN	HERMETIC
HEMOLYZES	HENNAED	HEPTOSES	HERDMEN	HERMETISM
HEMOLYZING	HENNAING	HER	HERDS	HERMETISMS
HEMOPHILE	HENNAS	HERALD	HERDSMAN	HERMETIST
HEMOPHILES	HENNERIES	HERALDED	HERDSMEN	HERMETISTS
HEMOSTAT	HENNERY	HERALDIC	HERE	HERMIT
HEMOSTATS	HENNISH	HERALDING	HEREABOUT	HERMITAGE
HEMOTOXIC	HENNISHLY	HERALDIST	HEREAFTER	HERMITAGES
HEMOTOXIN	HENPECK	HERALDISTS	HEREAFTERS	HERMITIC
HEMOTOXINS	HENPECKED	HERALDRIES	HEREAT	HERMITISM
HEMP	HENPECKING	HERALDRY	HEREAWAY	HERMITISMS
HEMPEN	HENPECKS	HERALDS	HEREAWAYS	HERMITRIES

HERMITRY	HERTZES	HEURISTIC	HEXONE	HIDDEN
HERMITS	HES	HEURISTICS	HEXONES	HIDDENITE
HERMS	HESITANCE	HEW	HEXOSAN	HIDDENITES
HERN	HESITANCES	HEWABLE	HEXOSANS	HIDDENLY
HERNIA	HESITANCIES	HEWED	HEXOSE	HIDE
HERNIAE	HESITANCY	HEWER	HEXOSES	HIDEAWAY
HERNIAL	HESITANT	HEWERS	HEXYL	HIDEAWAYS
HERNIAS	HESITATE	HEWING	HEXYLIC	HIDEBOUND
HERNIATE	HESITATED	HEWN	HEXYLS	HIDED
HERNIATED	HESITATER	HEWS	HEY	HIDELESS
HERNIATES	HESITATERS	HEX	HEYDAY	HIDEOSITIES
HERNIATING	HESITATES	HEXACHORD	HEYDAYS	HIDEOSITY
HERNS	HESITATING	HEXACHORDS	HEYDEY	HIDEOUS
HERO	HESITATOR	HEXAD	HEYDEYS	HIDEOUSLY
HEROES	HESITATORS	HEXADE	HI	HIDEOUT
HEROIC	HESSIAN	HEXADES	HIATAL	HIDEOUTS
HEROICAL	HESSIANS	HEXADIC	HIATUS	HIDER
HEROICIZE	HESSITE	HEXADS	HIATUSES	HIDERS
HEROICIZED	HESSITES	HEXAGON	HIBACHI	HIDES
HEROICIZES	HESSONITE	HEXAGONAL	HIBACHIS	HIDING
HEROICIZING	HESSONITES	HEXAGONS	HIBAKUSHA	HIDINGS
HEROICS	HEST	HEXAGRAM	HIBERNAL	HIDROSES
HEROIN	HESTS	HEXAGRAMS	HIBERNATE	HIDROSIS
HEROINE	HET	HEXAHEDRA	HIBERNATED	HIDROTIC
HEROINES	HETAERA	HEXAHEDRON	HIBERNATES	HIDROTICS
HEROINISM	HETAERAE	HEXAHEDRONS	HIBERNATING	HIE
HEROINISMS	HETAERAS	HEXAMETER	HIBISCUS	HIED
HEROINS	HETAERIC	HEXAMETERS	HIBISCUSES	HIEING
HEROISM	HETAERISM	HEXAMINE	HIC	HIEMAL
HEROISMS	HETAERISMS	HEXAMINES	HICCOUGH	HIERARCH
HEROIZE	HETAIRA	HEXANE	HICCOUGHED	HIERARCHIES
HEROIZED	HETAIRAI	HEXANES	HICCOUGHING	HIERARCHS
HEROIZES	HETAIRAS	HEXAPLA	HICCOUGHS	HIERARCHY
HEROIZING	HETAIRISM	HEXAPLAR	HICCUP	HIERATIC
HERON	HETAIRISMS	HEXAPLAS	HICCUPED	HIERODULE
HERONRIES	HETERO	HEXAPLOID	HICCUPING	HIERODULES
HERONRY	HETERODOX	HEXAPLOIDS	HICCUPPED	HIEROLOGIES
HERONS	HETERONYM	HEXAPOD	HICCUPPING	HIEROLOGY
HEROS	HETERONYMS	HEXAPODIES	HICCUPS	HIERURGIES
HERPES	HETEROS	HEXAPODS	HICK	HIERURGY
HERPETIC	HETEROSES	HEXAPODY	HICKEY	HIES
HERRIED	HETEROSIS	HEXARCHIES	HICKEYS	HIFALUTIN
HERRIES	HETEROTIC	HEXARCHY	HICKIE	HIGGLE
HERRING	HETH	HEXASTICH	HICKIES	HIGGLED
HERRINGS	HETHS	HEXASTICHS	HICKISH	HIGGLER
HERRY	HETMAN	HEXED	HICKORIES	HIGGLERS
HERRYING	HETMANS	HEXER	HICKORY	HIGGLES
HERS	HETS	HEXEREI	HICKS	HIGGLING
HERSELF	HEUCH	HEXEREIS	HID	HIGH
HERSTORIES	HEUCHS	HEXERS	HIDABLE	HIGHBALL
HERSTORY	HEUGH	HEXES	HIDALGO	HIGHBALLED
HERTZ	HEUGHS	HEXING	HIDALGOS	HIGHBALLING

HIGHBALLS	HIJAB	HILLOS	HINNIES	HIRED
HIGHBORN	HIJABS	HILLS	HINNY	HIREE
HIGHBOY	HIJACK	HILLSIDE	HINNYING	HIREES
HIGHBOYS	HIJACKED	HILLSIDES	HINS	HIRELING
HIGHBRED	HIJACKER	HILLSLOPE	HINT	HIRELINGS
HIGHBROW	HIJACKERS	HILLSLOPES	HINTED	HIRER
HIGHBROWS	HIJACKING	HILLTOP	HINTER	HIRERS
HIGHBUSH	HIJACKS	HILLTOPS	HINTERS	HIRES
HIGHCHAIR	HIJINKS	HILLY	HINTING	HIRING
HIGHCHAIRS	HIJRA	HILT	HINTS	HIRPLE
HIGHER	HIJRAH	HILTED	HIP	HIRPLED
HIGHEST	HIJRAHS	HILTING	HIPBONE	HIRPLES
HIGHFLIER	HIJRAS	HILTLESS	HIPBONES	HIRPLING
HIGHFLIERS	HIKE	HILTS	HIPHUGGER	HIRSEL
HIGHFLYER	HIKED	HILUM	HIPLESS	HIRSELED
HIGHFLYERS	HIKER	HILUS	HIPLIKE	HIRSELING
HIGHJACK	HIKERS	HIM	HIPLINE	HIRSELLED
HIGHJACKED	HIKES	HIMATIA	HIPLINES	HIRSELLING
HIGHJACKING	HIKING	HIMATION	HIPLY	HIRSELS
HIGHJACKS	HILA	HIMATIONS	HIPNESS	HIRSLE
HIGHLAND	HILAR	HIMS	HIPNESSES	HIRSLED
HIGHLANDS	HILARIOUS	HIMSELF	HIPPARCH	HIRSLES
HIGHLIFE	HILARITIES	HIN	HIPPARCHS	HIRSLING
HIGHLIFES	HILARITY	HIND	HIPPED	HIRSUTE
HIGHLIGHT	HILDING	HINDBRAIN	HIPPER	HIRSUTISM
HIGHLIGHTED	HILDINGS	HINDBRAINS	HIPPEST	HIRSUTISMS
HIGHLIGHTING	HILI	HINDER	HIPPIE	HIRUDIN
HIGHLIGHTS	HILL	HINDERED	HIPPIEDOM	HIRUDINS
HIGHLY	HILLBILLIES	HINDERER	HIPPIEDOMS	HIS
HIGHNESS	HILLBILLY	HINDERERS	HIPPIEISH	HISN
HIGHNESSES	HILLCREST	HINDERING	HIPPIER	HISPANISM
HIGHRISE	HILLCRESTS	HINDERS	HIPPIES	HISPANISMS
HIGHRISES	HILLED	HINDGUT	HIPPIEST	HISPID
HIGHROAD	HILLER	HINDGUTS	HIPPINESS	HISPIDITIES
HIGHROADS	HILLERS	HINDMOST	HIPPINESSES	HISPIDITY
HIGHS	HILLIER	HINDRANCE	HIPPING	HISS
HIGHSPOT	HILLIEST	HINDRANCES	HIPPISH	HISSED
HIGHSPOTS	HILLINESS	HINDS	HIPPO	HISSELF
HIGHT	HILLINESSES	HINDSHANK	HIPPOCRAS	HISSER
HIGHTAIL	HILLING	HINDSHANKS	HIPPOCRASES	HISSERS
HIGHTAILED	HILLO	HINDSIGHT	HIPPOS	HISSES
HIGHTAILING	HILLOA	HINDSIGHTS	HIPPY	HISSIER
HIGHTAILS	HILLOAED	HINGE	HIPS	HISSIES
HIGHTED	HILLOAING	HINGED	HIPSHOT	HISSIEST
HIGHTH	HILLOAS	HINGER	HIPSTER	HISSING
HIGHTHS	HILLOCK	HINGERS	HIPSTERS	HISSINGS
HIGHTING	HILLOCKED	HINGES	HIRABLE	HISSY
HIGHTOP	HILLOCKS	HINGING	HIRAGANA	HIST
HIGHTOPS	HILLOCKY	HINKIER	HIRAGANAS	HISTAMIN
HIGHTS	HILLOED	HINKIEST	HIRCINE	HISTAMINE
HIGHWAY	HILLOES	HINKY	HIRE	HISTAMINES
HIGHWAYS	HILLOING	HINNIED	HIREABLE	HISTAMINS

HISTED	HO	HOBBLERS	HODDINS	HOGWASHES
HISTIDIN	HOACTZIN	HOBBLES	HODOSCOPE	HOGWEED
HISTIDINE	HOACTZINES	HOBBLING	HODOSCOPES	HOGWEEDS
HISTIDINES	HOACTZINS	HOBBY	HODS	HOICK
HISTIDINS	HOAGIE	HOBBYIST	HOE	HOICKED
HISTING	HOAGIES	HOBBYISTS	HOECAKE	HOICKING
HISTOGEN	HOAGY	HOBGOBLIN	HOECAKES	HOICKS
HISTOGENS	HOAR	HOBGOBLINS	HOED	HOIDEN
HISTOGRAM	HOARD	HOBLIKE	HOEDOWN	HOIDENED
HISTOGRAMS	HOARDED	HOBNAIL	HOEDOWNS	HOIDENING
HISTOID	HOARDER	HOBNAILED	HOEING	HOIDENS
HISTOLOGIES	HOARDERS	HOBNAILING	HOELIKE	HOISE
HISTOLOGY	HOARDING	HOBNAILS	HOER	HOISED
HISTONE	HOARDINGS	HOBNOB	HOERS	HOISES
HISTONES	HOARDS	HOBNOBBED	HOES	HOISING
HISTORIAN	HOARFROST	HOBNOBBER	HOG	HOIST
HISTORIANS	HOARFROSTS	HOBNOBBERS	HOGAN	HOISTED
HISTORIC	HOARIER	HOBNOBBING	HOGANS	HOISTER
HISTORIED	HOARIEST	HOBNOBS	HOGBACK	HOISTERS
HISTORIES	HOARILY	HOBO	HOGBACKS	HOISTING
HISTORY	HOARINESS	HOBOED	HOGFISH	HOISTS
HISTS	HOARINESSES	HOBOES	HOGFISHES	HOKE
HIT	HOARS	HOBOING	HOGG	HOKED
HITCH	HOARSE	HOBOISM	HOGGED	HOKES
HITCHED	HOARSELY	HOBOISMS	HOGGER	HOKEY
HITCHER	HOARSEN	HOBOS	HOGGERS	HOKEYNESS
HITCHERS	HOARSENED	HOBS	HOGGET	HOKEYNESSES
HITCHES	HOARSENING	HOCK	HOGGETS	HOKIER
HITCHHIKE	HOARSENS	HOCKED	HOGGING	HOKIEST
HITCHHIKED	HOARSER	HOCKER	HOGGISH	HOKILY
HITCHHIKES	HOARSEST	HOCKERS	HOGGISHLY	HOKINESS
HITCHHIKING	HOARY	HOCKEY	HOGGS	HOKINESSES
HITCHING	HOATZIN	HOCKEYS	HOGLIKE	HOKING
HITHER	HOATZINES	HOCKING	HOGMANAY	HOKKU
HITHERTO	HOATZINS	HOCKS	HOGMANAYS	HOKUM
HITLESS	HOAX	HOCKSHOP	HOGMANE	HOKUMS
HITMAN	HOAXED	HOCKSHOPS	HOGMANES	HOKYPOKIES
HITMEN	HOAXER	HOCUS	HOGMENAY	HOKYPOKY
HITS	HOAXERS	HOCUSED	HOGMENAYS	HOLANDRIC
HITTABLE	HOAXES	HOCUSES	HOGNOSE	HOLARD
HITTER	HOAXING	HOCUSING	HOGNOSES	HOLARDS
HITTERS	HOB	HOCUSSED	HOGNUT	HOLD
HITTING	HOBBED	HOCUSSES	HOGNUTS	HOLDABLE
HIVE	HOBBER	HOCUSSING	HOGS	HOLDALL
HIVED	HOBBERS	HOD	HOGSHEAD	HOLDALLS
HIVELESS	HOBBIES	HODAD	HOGSHEADS	HOLDBACK
HIVES	HOBBING	HODADDIES	HOGTIE	HOLDBACKS
HIVING	HOBBIT	HODADDY	HOGTIED	HOLDDOWN
HIZZONER	HOBBITS	HODADS	HOGTIEING	HOLDDOWNS
HIZZONERS	HOBBLE	HODDEN	HOGTIES	HOLDEN
HM	HOBBLED	HODDENS	HOGTYING	HOLDER
HMM	HOBBLER	HODDIN	HOGWASH	HOLDERS

HOLDFAST	HOLLOA	HOLS	HOMEMADE	HOMIE
HOLDFASTS	HOLLOAED	HOLSTEIN	HOMEMAKER	HOMIER
HOLDING	HOLLOAING	HOLSTEINS	HOMEMAKERS	HOMIES
HOLDINGS	HOLLOAS	HOLSTER	HOMEOBOX	HOMIEST
HOLDOUT	HOLLOED	HOLSTERED	HOMEOBOXES	HOMILETIC
HOLDOUTS	HOLLOES	HOLSTERING	HOMEOPATH	HOMILIES
HOLDOVER	HOLLOING	HOLSTERS	HOMEOPATHS	HOMILIST
HOLDOVERS	HOLLOO	HOLT	HOMEOTIC	HOMILISTS
HOLDS	HOLLOOED	HOLTS	HOMEOWNER	HOMILY
HOLDUP	HOLLOOING	HOLY	HOMEOWNERS	HOMINES
HOLDUPS	HOLLOOS	HOLYDAY	HOMEPAGE	HOMINESS
HOLE	HOLLOS	HOLYDAYS	HOMEPAGES	HOMINESSES
HOLED	HOLLOW	HOLYSTONE	HOMEPLACE	HOMING
HOLELESS	HOLLOWARE	HOLYSTONED	HOMEPLACES	HOMINIAN
HOLES	HOLLOWARES	HOLYSTONES	HOMEPORT	HOMINIANS
HOLEY	HOLLOWED	HOLYSTONING	HOMEPORTED	HOMINID
HOLIBUT	HOLLOWER	HOLYTIDE	HOMEPORTING	HOMINIDS
HOLIBUTS	HOLLOWEST	HOLYTIDES	HOMEPORTS	HOMINIES
HOLIDAY	HOLLOWING	HOMAGE	HOMER	HOMININE
HOLIDAYED	HOLLOWLY	HOMAGED	HOMERED	HOMINIZE
HOLIDAYER	HOLLOWS	HOMAGER	HOMERIC	HOMINIZED
HOLIDAYERS	HOLLY	HOMAGERS	HOMERING	HOMINIZES
HOLIDAYING	HOLLYHOCK	HOMAGES	HOMEROOM	HOMINIZING
HOLIDAYS	HOLLYHOCKS	HOMAGING	HOMEROOMS	HOMINOID
HOLIER	HOLM	HOMBRE	HOMERS	HOMINOIDS
HOLIES	HOLMIC	HOMBRES	HOMES	HOMINY
HOLIEST	HOLMIUM	HOMBURG	HOMESICK	HOMMOCK
HOLILY	HOLMIUMS	HOMBURGS	HOMESITE	HOMMOCKS
HOLINESS	HOLMS	HOME	HOMESITES	HOMMOS
HOLINESSES	HOLOCAUST	HOMEBODIES	HOMESPUN	HOMMOSES
HOLING	HOLOCAUSTS	HOMEBODY	HOMESPUNS	HOMO
HOLISM	HOLOCENE	HOMEBOUND	HOMESTAND	HOMOCERCIES
HOLISMS	HOLOCRINE	HOMEBOY	HOMESTANDS	HOMOCERCY
HOLIST	HOLOGAMIES	HOMEBOYS	HOMESTAY	HOMOGAMIES
HOLISTIC	HOLOGAMY	HOMEBRED	HOMESTAYS	HOMOGAMY
HOLISTS	HOLOGRAM	HOMEBREDS	HOMESTEAD	HOMOGENIES
HOLK	HOLOGRAMS	HOMEBREW	HOMESTEADED	HOMOGENY
HOLKED	HOLOGRAPH	HOMEBREWS	HOMESTEADING	HOMOGONIES
HOLKING	HOLOGRAPHED	HOMEBUILT	HOMESTEADS	HOMOGONY
HOLKS	HOLOGRAPHING	HOMECOMER	HOMETOWN	HOMOGRAFT
HOLLA	HOLOGRAPHS	HOMECOMERS	HOMETOWNS	HOMOGRAFTS
HOLLAED	HOLOGYNIC	HOMED	HOMEWARD	HOMOGRAPH
HOLLAING	HOLOGYNIES	HOMEGIRL	HOMEWARDS	HOMOGRAPHS
HOLLAND	HOLOGYNY	HOMEGIRLS	HOMEWORK	HOMOLOG
HOLLANDS	HOLOPHYTE	HOMEGROWN	HOMEWORKS	HOMOLOGIC
HOLLAS	HOLOPHYTES	HOMELAND	HOMEY	HOMOLOGIES
HOLLER	HOLOTYPE	HOMELANDS	HOMEYNESS	HOMOLOGS
HOLLERED	HOLOTYPES	HOMELESS	HOMEYNESSES	HOMOLOGUE
HOLLERING	HOLOTYPIC	HOMELIER	HOMEYS	HOMOLOGUES
HOLLERS	HOLOZOIC	HOMELIEST	HOMICIDAL	HOMOLOGY
HOLLIES	HOLP	HOMELIKE	HOMICIDE	HOMOLYSES
HOLLO	HOLPEN	HOMELY	HOMICIDES	HOMOLYSIS

HOMOLYTIC	HONESTIES	HONORARIUM	HOOFBEATS	HOOPOES
HOMONYM	HONESTLY	HONORARIUMS	HOOFBOUND	HOOPOO
HOMONYMIC	HONESTY	HONORARY	HOOFED	HOOPOOS
HOMONYMIES	HONEWORT	HONORED	HOOFER	HOOPS
HOMONYMS	HONEWORTS	HONOREE	HOOFERS	HOOPSKIRT
HOMONYMY	HONEY	HONOREES	HOOFING	HOOPSKIRTS
HOMOPHILE	HONEYBEE	HONORER	HOOFLESS	HOOPSTER
HOMOPHILES	HONEYBEES	HONORERS	HOOFLIKE	HOOPSTERS
HOMOPHOBE	HONEYBUN	HONORIFIC	HOOFPRINT	HOORAH
HOMOPHOBES	HONEYBUNS	HONORIFICS	HOOFPRINTS	HOORAHED
HOMOPHONE	HONEYCOMB	HONORING	HOOFS	HOORAHING
HOMOPHONES	HONEYCOMBED	HONORS	HOOK	HOORAHS
HOMOPHONIES	HONEYCOMBING	HONOUR	HOOKA	HOORAY
HOMOPHONY	HONEYCOMBS	HONOURED	HOOKAH	HOORAYED
HOMOPHYLIES	HONEYDEW	HONOURER	HOOKAHS	HOORAYING
HOMOPHYLY	HONEYDEWS	HONOURERS	HOOKAS	HOORAYS
HOMOPLASIES	HONEYED	HONOURING	HOOKED	HOOSEGOW
HOMOPLASY	HONEYFUL	HONOURS	HOOKER	HOOSEGOWS
HOMOPOLAR	HONEYING	HONS	HOOKERS	HOOSGOW
HOMOS	HONEYMOON	HOOCH	HOOKEY	HOOSGOWS
HOMOSEX	HONEYMOONED	HOOCHES	HOOKEYS	HOOT
HOMOSEXES	HONEYMOONING	HOOCHIE	HOOKIER	HOOTCH
HOMOSPORIES	HONEYMOONS	HOOCHIES	HOOKIES	HOOTCHES
HOMOSPORY	HONEYPOT	HOOD	HOOKIEST	HOOTED
HOMOSTYLIES	HONEYPOTS	HOODED	HOOKING	HOOTER
HOMOSTYLY	HONEYS	HOODIE	HOOKLESS	HOOTERS
HOMOTAXES	HONG	HOODIER	HOOKLET	HOOTIER
HOMOTAXIS	HONGI	HOODIES	HOOKLETS	HOOTIEST
HOMUNCULI	HONGIED	HOODIEST	HOOKLIKE	HOOTING
HOMUNCULUS	HONGIES	HOODING	HOOKNOSE	HOOTS
HOMY	HONGIING	HOODLESS	HOOKNOSED	HOOTY
HON	HONGS	HOODLIKE	HOOKNOSES	HOOVED
HONAN	HONIED	HOODLUM	HOOKS	HOOVER
HONANS	HONING	HOODLUMS	HOOKUP	HOOVERED
HONCHO	HONK	HOODMOLD	HOOKUPS	HOOVERING
HONCHOED	HONKED	HOODMOLDS	HOOKWORM	HOOVERS
HONCHOING	HONKER	HOODOO	HOOKWORMS	HOOVES
HONCHOS	HONKERS	HOODOOED	HOOKY	HOP
HONDA	HONKEY	HOODOOING	HOOLIE	HOPE
HONDAS	HONKEYS	HOODOOISM	HOOLIGAN	HOPED
HONDLE	HONKIE	HOODOOISMS	HOOLIGANS	HOPEFUL
HONDLED	HONKIES	HOODOOS	HOOLY	HOPEFULLY
HONDLES	HONKING	HOODS	HOOP	HOPEFULS
HONDLING	HONKS	HOODWINK	HOOPED	HOPELESS
HONE	HONKY	HOODWINKED	HOOPER	HOPER
HONED	HONOR	HOODWINKING	HOOPERS	HOPERS
HONER	HONORABLE	HOODWINKS	HOOPING	HOPES
HONERS	HONORABLY	HOODY	HOOPLA	HOPHEAD
HONES	HONORAND	HOOEY	HOOPLAS	HOPHEADS
HONEST	HONORANDS	HOOEYS	HOOPLESS	HOPING
HONESTER	HONORARIA	HOOF	HOOPLIKE	HOPINGLY
HONESTEST	HONORARIES	HOOFBEAT	HOOPOE	HOPLITE

HOPLITES	HORNBOOKS	HORRIFIED	HORSINESS	HOSTELED
HOPLITIC	HORNED	HORRIFIES	HORSINESSES	HOSTELER
HOPPED	HORNET	HORRIFY	HORSING	HOSTELERS
HOPPER	HORNETS	HORRIFYING	HORST	HOSTELING
HOPPERS	HORNFELS	HORROR	HORSTE	HOSTELLED
HOPPIER	HORNIER	HORRORS	HORSTES	HOSTELLER
HOPPIEST	HORNIEST	HORSE	HORSTS	HOSTELLERS
HOPPING	HORNILY	HORSEBACK	HORSY	HOSTELLING
HOPPINGS	HORNINESS	HORSEBACKS	HORTATIVE	HOSTELRIES
HOPPLE	HORNINESSES	HORSEBEAN	HORTATORY	HOSTELRY
HOPPLED	HORNING	HORSEBEANS	HOS	HOSTELS
HOPPLES	HORNINGS	HORSECAR	HOSANNA	HOSTESS
HOPPLING	HORNIST	HORSECARS	HOSANNAED	HOSTESSED
HOPPY	HORNISTS	HORSED	HOSANNAH	HOSTESSES
HOPS	HORNITO	HORSEFLIES	HOSANNAHS	HOSTESSING
HOPSACK	HORNITOS	HORSEFLY	HOSANNAING	HOSTILE
HOPSACKS	HORNLESS	HORSEHAIR	HOSANNAS	HOSTILELY
HOPSCOTCH	HORNLIKE	HORSEHAIRS	HOSE	HOSTILES
HOPSCOTCHED	HORNPIPE	HORSEHIDE	HOSED	HOSTILITIES
HOPSCOTCHES	HORNPIPES	HORSEHIDES	HOSEL	HOSTILITY
HOPSCOTCHING	HORNPOUT	HORSELESS	HOSELIKE	HOSTING
HOPTOAD	HORNPOUTS	HORSELIKE	HOSELS	HOSTLER
HOPTOADS	HORNS	HORSEMAN	HOSEN	HOSTLERS
HORA	HORNSTONE	HORSEMEN	HOSEPIPE	HOSTLY
HORAH	HORNSTONES	HORSEMINT	HOSEPIPES	HOSTS
HORAHS	HORNTAIL	HORSEMINTS	HOSER	HOT
HORAL	HORNTAILS	HORSEPLAY	HOSERS	HOTBED
HORARY	HORNWORM	HORSEPLAYS	HOSES	HOTBEDS
HORAS	HORNWORMS	HORSEPOX	HOSEY	HOTBLOOD
HORDE	HORNWORT	HORSEPOXES	HOSEYED	HOTBLOODS
HORDED	HORNWORTS	HORSERACE	HOSEYING	HOTBOX
HORDEIN	HORNY	HORSERACES	HOSEYS	HOTBOXES
HORDEINS	HOROLOGE	HORSES	HOSIER	HOTCAKE
HORDEOLA	HOROLOGER	HORSESHIT	HOSIERIES	HOTCAKES
HORDEOLUM	HOROLOGERS	HORSESHITS	HOSIERS	HOTCH
HORDES	HOROLOGES	HORSESHOD	HOSIERY	HOTCHED
HORDING	HOROLOGIC	HORSESHOE	HOSING	HOTCHES
HOREHOUND	HOROLOGIES	HORSESHOED	HOSPICE	HOTCHING
HOREHOUNDS	HOROLOGY	HORSESHOEING	HOSPICES	HOTCHPOT
HORIZON	HOROSCOPE	HORSESHOES	HOSPITAL	HOTCHPOTS
HORIZONAL	HOROSCOPES	HORSETAIL	HOSPITALS	HOTDOG
HORIZONS	HOROSCOPIES	HORSETAILS	HOSPITIA	HOTDOGGED
HORMONAL	HOROSCOPY	HORSEWEED	HOSPITIUM	HOTDOGGER
HORMONE	HORRENT	HORSEWEEDS	HOSPODAR	HOTDOGGERS
HORMONES	HORRIBLE	HORSEWHIP	HOSPODARS	HOTDOGGING
HORMONIC	HORRIBLES	HORSEWHIPPED	HOST	HOTDOGS
HORN	HORRIBLY	HORSEWHIPPING	HOSTA	HOTEL
HORNBEAM	HORRID	HORSEWHIPS	HOSTAGE	HOTELDOM
HORNBEAMS	HORRIDER	HORSEY	HOSTAGES	HOTELDOMS
HORNBILL	HORRIDEST	HORSIER	HOSTAS	HOTELIER
HORNBILLS	HORRIDLY	HORSIEST	HOSTED	HOTELIERS
HORNBOOK	HORRIFIC	HORSILY	HOSTEL	HOTELMAN

HOTELMEN	HOURIS	HOUSEWIVES	HOWLS	HUELESS
HOTELS	HOURLIES	HOUSEWORK	HOWS	HUES
HOTFOOT	HOURLONG	HOUSEWORKS	HOWSOEVER	HUFF
HOTFOOTED	HOURLY	HOUSING	HOY	HUFFED
HOTFOOTING	HOURS	HOUSINGS	HOYA	HUFFIER
HOTFOOTS	HOUSE	HOUSTONIA	HOYAS	HUFFIEST
HOTHEAD	HOUSEBOAT	HOUSTONIAS	HOYDEN	HUFFILY
HOTHEADED	HOUSEBOATS	HOVE	HOYDENED	HUFFINESS
HOTHEADS	HOUSEBOY	HOVEL	HOYDENING	HUFFINESSES
HOTHOUSE	HOUSEBOYS	HOVELED	HOYDENISH	HUFFING
HOTHOUSED	HOUSECARL	HOVELING	HOYDENS	HUFFISH
HOTHOUSES	HOUSECARLS	HOVELLED	HOYLE	HUFFISHLY
HOTHOUSING	HOUSECOAT	HOVELLING	HOYLES	HUFFS
HOTLINE	HOUSECOATS	HOVELS	HOYS	HUFFY
HOTLINES	HOUSED	HOVER	HRYVNA	HUG
HOTLINK	HOUSEFLIES	HOVERED	HRYVNAS	HUGE
HOTLINKS	HOUSEFLY	HOVERER	HRYVNIA	HUGELY
HOTLY	HOUSEFUL	HOVERERS	HRYVNIAS	HUGENESS
HOTNESS	HOUSEFULS	HOVERFLIES	HUARACHE	HUGENESSES
HOTNESSES	HOUSEHOLD	HOVERFLY	HUARACHES	HUGEOUS
HOTPRESS	HOUSEHOLDS	HOVERING	HUARACHO	HUGEOUSLY
HOTPRESSED	HOUSEKEEP	HOVERS	HUARACHOS	HUGER
HOTPRESSES	HOUSEKEEPING	HOW	HUB	HUGEST
HOTPRESSING	HOUSEKEEPS	HOWBEIT	HUBBIES	HUGGABLE
HOTROD	HOUSEKEPT	HOWDAH	HUBBLY	HUGGED
HOTRODS	HOUSEL	HOWDAHS	HUBBUB	HUGGER
HOTS	HOUSELED	HOWDIE	HUBBUBS	HUGGERS
HOTSHOT	HOUSELEEK	HOWDIED	HUBBY	HUGGING
HOTSHOTS	HOUSELEEKS	HOWDIES	HUBCAP	HUGS
HOTSPOT	HOUSELESS	HOWDY	HUBCAPS	HUH
HOTSPOTS	HOUSELING	HOWDYING	HUBRIS	HUIC
HOTSPUR	HOUSELLED	HOWE	HUBRISES	HUIPIL
HOTSPURS	HOUSELLING	HOWES	HUBRISTIC	HUIPILES
HOTTED	HOUSELS	HOWEVER	HUBS	HUIPILS
HOTTER	HOUSEMAID	HOWF	HUCK	HUISACHE
HOTTEST	HOUSEMAIDS	HOWFF	HUCKABACK	HUISACHES
HOTTIE	HOUSEMAN	HOWFFS	HUCKABACKS	HULA
HOTTIES	HOUSEMATE	HOWFS	HUCKLE	HULAS
HOTTING	HOUSEMATES	HOWITZER	HUCKLES	HULK
HOTTISH	HOUSEMEN	HOWITZERS	HUCKS	HULKED
HOUDAH	HOUSER	HOWK	HUCKSTER	HULKIER
HOUDAHS	HOUSEROOM	HOWKED	HUCKSTERED	HULKIEST
HOUND	HOUSEROOMS	HOWKING	HUCKSTERING	HULKING
HOUNDED	HOUSERS	HOWKS	HUCKSTERS	HULKS
HOUNDER	HOUSES	HOWL	HUDDLE	HULKY
HOUNDERS	HOUSESAT	HOWLED	HUDDLED	HULL
HOUNDING	HOUSESIT	HOWLER	HUDDLER	HULLED
HOUNDS	HOUSESITS	HOWLERS	HUDDLERS	HULLER
HOUR	HOUSESITTING	HOWLET	HUDDLES	HULLERS
HOURGLASS	HOUSETOP	HOWLETS	HUDDLING	HULLING
HOURGLASSES	HOUSETOPS	HOWLING	HUE	HULLO
HOURI	HOUSEWIFE	HOWLINGLY	HUED	HULLOA

HULLOAED	HUMBLES	HUMMOCKS	HUNDREDTH	HURL
HULLOAING	HUMBLEST	HUMMOCKY	HUNDREDTHS	HURLED
HULLOAS	HUMBLING	HUMMUS	HUNG	HURLER
HULLOED	HUMBLY	HUMMUSES	HUNGER	HURLERS
HULLOES	HUMBUG	HUMONGOUS	HUNGERED	HURLEY
HULLOING	HUMBUGGED	HUMOR	HUNGERING	HURLEYS
HULLOO	HUMBUGGER	HUMORAL	HUNGERS	HURLIES
HULLOOED	HUMBUGGERS	HUMORED	HUNGOVER	HURLING
HULLOOING	HUMBUGGING	HUMORFUL	HUNGRIER	HURLINGS
HULLOOS	HUMBUGS	HUMORING	HUNGRIEST	HURLS
HULLOS	HUMDINGER	HUMORIST	HUNGRILY	HURLY
HULLS	HUMDINGERS	HUMORISTS	HUNGRY	HURRAH
HUM	HUMDRUM	HUMORLESS	HUNH	HURRAHED
HUMAN	HUMDRUMS	HUMOROUS	HUNK	HURRAHING
HUMANE	HUMECTANT	HUMORS	HUNKER	HURRAHS
HUMANELY	HUMECTANTS	HUMOUR	HUNKERED	HURRAY
HUMANER	HUMERAL	HUMOURED	HUNKERING	HURRAYED
HUMANEST	HUMERALS	HUMOURING	HUNKERS	HURRAYING
HUMANHOOD	HUMERI	HUMOURS	HUNKEY	HURRAYS
HUMANHOODS	HUMERUS	HUMP	HUNKEYS	HURRICANE
HUMANISE	HUMIC	HUMPBACK	HUNKIE	HURRICANES
HUMANISED	HUMID	HUMPBACKS	HUNKIER	HURRIED
HUMANISES	HUMIDEX	HUMPED	HUNKIES	HURRIEDLY
HUMANISING	HUMIDEXES	HUMPER	HUNKIEST	HURRIER
HUMANISM	HUMIDIFIED	HUMPERS	HUNKS	HURRIERS
HUMANISMS	HUMIDIFIES	HUMPH	HUNKY	HURRIES
HUMANIST	HUMIDIFY	HUMPHED	HUNNISH	HURRY
HUMANISTS	HUMIDIFYING	HUMPHING	HUNS	HURRYING
HUMANITIES	HUMIDITIES	HUMPHS	HUNT	HURST
HUMANITY	HUMIDITY	HUMPIER	HUNTABLE	HURSTS
HUMANIZE	HUMIDLY	HUMPIEST	HUNTED	HURT
HUMANIZED	HUMIDNESS	HUMPINESS	HUNTEDLY	HURTER
HUMANIZER	HUMIDNESSES	HUMPINESSES	HUNTER	HURTERS
HUMANIZERS	HUMIDOR	HUMPING	HUNTERS	HURTFUL
HUMANIZES	HUMIDORS	HUMPLESS	HUNTING	HURTFULLY
HUMANIZING	HUMIFIED	HUMPS	HUNTINGS	HURTING
HUMANKIND	HUMILIATE	HUMPY	HUNTRESS	HURTLE
HUMANLIKE	HUMILIATED	HUMS	HUNTRESSES	HURTLED
HUMANLY	HUMILIATES	HUMUNGOUS	HUNTS	HURTLES
HUMANNESS	HUMILIATING	HUMUS	HUNTSMAN	HURTLESS
HUMANNESSES	HUMILITIES	HUMUSES	HUNTSMEN	HURTLING
HUMANOID	HUMILITY	HUMVEE	HUP	HURTS
HUMANOIDS	HUMITURE	HUMVEES	HUPPAH	HUSBAND
HUMANS	HUMITURES	HUN	HUPPAHS	HUSBANDED
HUMATE	HUMMABLE	HUNCH	HURDIES	HUSBANDER
HUMATES	HUMMED	HUNCHBACK	HURDLE	HUSBANDERS
HUMBLE	HUMMER	HUNCHBACKS	HURDLED	HUSBANDING
HUMBLEBEE	HUMMERS	HUNCHED	HURDLER	HUSBANDLY
HUMBLEBEES	HUMMING	HUNCHES	HURDLERS	HUSBANDRIES
HUMBLED	HUMMOCK	HUNCHING	HURDLES	HUSBANDRY
HUMBLER	HUMMOCKED	HUNDRED	HURDLING	HUSBANDS
HUMBLERS	HUMMOCKING	HUNDREDS	HURDS	HUSH

HUSHABY	HUZZA	HYDRANGEAS	HYDROLYZED	HYLAS
HUSHED	HUZZAED	HYDRANT	HYDROLYZES	HYLOZOIC
HUSHEDLY	HUZZAH	HYDRANTH	HYDROLYZING	HYLOZOISM
HUSHES	HUZZAHED	HYDRANTHS	HYDROMEL	HYLOZOISMS
HUSHFUL	HUZZAHING	HYDRANTS	HYDROMELS	HYLOZOIST
HUSHING	HUZZAHS	HYDRAS	HYDRONIC	HYLOZOISTS
HUSHPUPPIES	HUZZAING	HYDRASE	HYDRONIUM	HYMEN
HUSHPUPPY	HUZZAS	HYDRASES	HYDRONIUMS	HYMENAL
HUSK	HWAN	HYDRASTIS	HYDROPATH	HYMENEAL
HUSKED	HYACINTH	HYDRASTISES	HYDROPATHS	HYMENEALS
HUSKER	HYACINTHS	HYDRATE	HYDROPIC	HYMENIA
HUSKERS	HYAENA	HYDRATED	HYDROPS	HYMENIAL
HUSKIER	HYAENAS	HYDRATES	HYDROPSES	HYMENIUM
HUSKIES	HYAENIC	HYDRATING	HYDROPSIES	HYMENIUMS
HUSKIEST	HYALIN	HYDRATION	HYDROPSY	HYMENS
HUSKILY	HYALINE	HYDRATIONS	HYDROS	HYMN
HUSKINESS	HYALINES	HYDRATOR	HYDROSERE	HYMNAL
HUSKINESSES	HYALINS	HYDRATORS	HYDROSERES	HYMNALS
HUSKING	HYALITE	HYDRAULIC	HYDROSKI	HYMNARIES
HUSKINGS	HYALITES	HYDRAZIDE	HYDROSKIS	HYMNARY
HUSKLIKE	HYALOGEN	HYDRAZIDES	HYDROSOL	HYMNBOOK
HUSKS	HYALOGENS	HYDRAZINE	HYDROSOLS	HYMNBOOKS
HUSKY	HYALOID	HYDRAZINES	HYDROSTAT	HYMNED
HUSSAR	HYALOIDS	HYDRIA	HYDROSTATS	HYMNING
HUSSARS	HYBRID	HYDRIAE	HYDROUS	HYMNIST
HUSSIES	HYBRIDISM	HYDRIC	HYDROXIDE	HYMNISTS
HUSSY	HYBRIDISMS	HYDRID	HYDROXIDES	HYMNLESS
HUSTINGS	HYBRIDIST	HYDRIDE	HYDROXY	HYMNLIKE
HUSTLE	HYBRIDISTS	HYDRIDES	HYDROXYL	HYMNODIES
HUSTLED	HYBRIDITIES	HYDRIDS	HYDROXYLS	HYMNODIST
HUSTLER	HYBRIDITY	HYDRILLA	HYDROZOAN	HYMNODISTS
HUSTLERS	HYBRIDIZE	HYDRILLAS	HYDROZOANS	HYMNODY
HUSTLES	HYBRIDIZED	HYDRO	HYENA	HYMNOLOGIES
HUSTLING	HYBRIDIZES	HYDROCAST	HYENAS	HYMNOLOGY
HUSWIFE	HYBRIDIZING	HYDROCASTS	HYENIC	HYMNS
HUSWIFES	HYBRIDOMA	HYDROCELE	HYENINE	HYOID
HUSWIVES	HYBRIDOMAS	HYDROCELES	HYENOID	HYOIDAL
HUT	HYBRIDS	HYDROFOIL	HYETAL	HYOIDEAN
HUTCH	HYBRIS	HYDROFOILS	HYGEIST	HYOIDS
HUTCHED	HYBRISES	HYDROGEL	HYGEISTS	HYOSCINE
HUTCHES	HYBRISTIC	HYDROGELS	HYGIEIST	HYOSCINES
HUTCHING	HYDATHODE	HYDROGEN	HYGIEISTS	HYP
HUTLIKE	HYDATHODES	HYDROGENS	HYGIENE	HYPALLAGE
HUTMENT	HYDATID	HYDROID	HYGIENES	HYPALLAGES
HUTMENTS	HYDATIDS	HYDROIDS	HYGIENIC	HYPANTHIA
HUTS	HYDRA	HYDROLASE	HYGIENICS	HYPANTHIUM
HUTTED	HYDRACID	HYDROLASES	HYGIENIST	HYPE
HUTTING	HYDRACIDS	HYDROLOGIES	HYGIENISTS	HYPED
HUTZPA	HYDRAE	HYDROLOGY	HYGROSTAT	HYPER
HUTZPAH	HYDRAGOG	HYDROLYTE	HYGROSTATS	HYPERACID
HUTZPAHS	HYDRAGOGS	HYDROLYTES	HYING	HYPERARID
HUTZPAS	HYDRANGEA	HYDROLYZE	HYLA	HYPERBOLA

HYPERBOLAE	HYPNOLOGY	HYPONYM	IAMBIC	ICHNOLITES
HYPERBOLAS	HYPNOSES	HYPONYMIES	IAMBICS	ICHNOLOGIES
HYPERBOLE	HYPNOSIS	HYPONYMS	IAMBS	ICHNOLOGY
HYPERBOLES	HYPNOTIC	HYPONYMY	IAMBUS	ICHOR
HYPERCUBE	HYPNOTICS	HYPOPLOID	IAMBUSES	ICHOROUS
HYPERCUBES	HYPNOTISM	HYPOPLOIDS	IATRIC	ICHORS
HYPEREMIA	HYPNOTISMS	HYPOPNEA	IATRICAL	ICHS
HYPEREMIAS	HYPNOTIST	HYPOPNEAS	IBEX	ICHTHYIC
HYPEREMIC	HYPNOTISTS	HYPOPNEIC	IBEXES	ICHTHYOID
HYPERFINE	HYPNOTIZE	HYPOPYON	IBICES	ICHTHYOIDS
HYPERGAMIES	HYPNOTIZED	HYPOPYONS	IBIDEM	ICICLE
HYPERGAMY	HYPNOTIZES	HYPOS	IBIS	ICICLED
HYPERGOL	HYPNOTIZING	HYPOSTOME	IBISES	ICICLES
HYPERGOLS	HYPO	HYPOSTOMES	IBOGAINE	ICIER
HYPERLINK	HYPOACID	HYPOSTYLE	IBOGAINES	ICIEST
HYPERLINKED	HYPOBARIC	HYPOSTYLES	IBUPROFEN	ICILY
HYPERLINKING	HYPOBLAST	HYPOTAXES	IBUPROFENS	ICINESS
HYPERLINKS	HYPOBLASTS	HYPOTAXIS	ICE	ICINESSES
HYPERON	HYPOCAUST	HYPOTHEC	ICEBERG	ICING
HYPERONS	HYPOCAUSTS	HYPOTHECS	ICEBERGS	ICINGS
HYPEROPE	HYPOCOTYL	HYPOTONIA	ICEBLINK	ICK
HYPEROPES	HYPOCOTYLS	HYPOTONIAS	ICEBLINKS	ICKER
HYPEROPIA	HYPOCRISIES	HYPOTONIC	ICEBOAT	ICKERS
HYPEROPIAS	HYPOCRISY	HYPOXEMIA	ICEBOATER	ICKIER
HYPEROPIC	HYPOCRITE	HYPOXEMIAS	ICEBOATERS	ICKIEST
HYPERPNEA	HYPOCRITES	HYPOXEMIC	ICEBOATS	ICKILY
HYPERPNEAS	HYPODERM	HYPOXIA	ICEBOUND	ICKINESS
HYPERPURE	HYPODERMA	HYPOXIAS	ICEBOX	ICKINESSES
HYPERS	HYPODERMAS	HYPOXIC	ICEBOXES	ICKY
HYPERTEXT	HYPODERMS	HYPS	ICECAP	ICON
HYPERTEXTS	HYPOED	HYRACES	ICECAPPED	ICONES
HYPES	HYPOGEA	HYRACOID	ICECAPS	ICONIC
HYPETHRAL	HYPOGEAL	HYRACOIDS	ICED	ICONICAL
HYPHA	HYPOGEAN	HYRAX	ICEFALL	ICONICITIES
HYPHAE	HYPOGENE	HYRAXES	ICEFALLS	ICONICITY
HYPHAL	HYPOGEOUS	HYSON	ICEHOUSE	ICONOLOGIES
HYPHEMIA	HYPOGEUM	HYSONS	ICEHOUSES	ICONOLOGY
HYPHEMIAS	HYPOGYNIES	HYSSOP	ICEKHANA	ICONS
HYPHEN	HYPOGYNY	HYSSOPS	ICEKHANAS	ICTERIC
HYPHENATE	HYPOING	HYSTERIA	ICELESS	ICTERICAL
HYPHENATED	HYPOMANIA	HYSTERIAS	ICELIKE	ICTERICS
HYPHENATES	HYPOMANIAS	HYSTERIC	ICEMAKER	ICTERUS
HYPHENATING	HYPOMANIC	HYSTERICS	ICEMAKERS	ICTERUSES
HYPHENED	HYPOMANICS	HYSTEROID	ICEMAN	ICTIC
HYPHENIC	HYPOMORPH	HYTE	ICEMEN	ICTUS
HYPHENING	HYPOMORPHS		ICES	ICTUSES
HYPHENS	HYPONASTIES		ICH	ICY
HYPING	HYPONASTY	**I**	ICHNEUMON	ID
HYPNIC	HYPONEA		ICHNEUMONS	IDEA
HYPNOID	HYPONEAS		ICHNITE	IDEAL
HYPNOIDAL	HYPONOIA	IAMB	ICHNITES	IDEALESS
HYPNOLOGIES	HYPONOIAS	IAMBI	ICHNOLITE	IDEALISE

IDEALISED	IDES	IDOLIZE	IGNITING	ILIA
IDEALISES	IDIOBLAST	IDOLIZED	IGNITION	ILIAC
IDEALISING	IDIOBLASTS	IDOLIZER	IGNITIONS	ILIAD
IDEALISM	IDIOCIES	IDOLIZERS	IGNITOR	ILIADS
IDEALISMS	IDIOCY	IDOLIZES	IGNITORS	ILIAL
IDEALIST	IDIOLECT	IDOLIZING	IGNITRON	ILIUM
IDEALISTS	IDIOLECTS	IDOLS	IGNITRONS	ILK
IDEALITIES	IDIOM	IDONEITIES	IGNOBLE	ILKA
IDEALITY	IDIOMATIC	IDONEITY	IGNOBLY	ILKS
IDEALIZE	IDIOMS	IDONEOUS	IGNOMINIES	ILL
IDEALIZED	IDIOPATHIES	IDS	IGNOMINY	ILLATION
IDEALIZER	IDIOPATHY	IDYL	IGNORABLE	ILLATIONS
IDEALIZERS	IDIOPLASM	IDYLIST	IGNORAMI	ILLATIVE
IDEALIZES	IDIOPLASMS	IDYLISTS	IGNORAMUS	ILLATIVES
IDEALIZING	IDIOT	IDYLL	IGNORAMUSES	ILLEGAL
IDEALLESS	IDIOTIC	IDYLLIC	IGNORANCE	ILLEGALLY
IDEALLY	IDIOTICAL	IDYLLIST	IGNORANCES	ILLEGALS
IDEALOGIES	IDIOTISM	IDYLLISTS	IGNORANT	ILLEGIBLE
IDEALOGUE	IDIOTISMS	IDYLLS	IGNORE	ILLEGIBLY
IDEALOGUES	IDIOTS	IDYLS	IGNORED	ILLER
IDEALOGY	IDIOTYPE	IF	IGNORER	ILLEST
IDEALS	IDIOTYPES	IFF	IGNORERS	ILLIBERAL
IDEAS	IDIOTYPIC	IFFIER	IGNORES	ILLICIT
IDEATE	IDLE	IFFIEST	IGNORING	ILLICITLY
IDEATED	IDLED	IFFINESS	IGUANA	ILLINIUM
IDEATES	IDLENESS	IFFINESSES	IGUANAS	ILLINIUMS
IDEATING	IDLENESSES	IFFY	IGUANIAN	ILLIQUID
IDEATION	IDLER	IFS	IGUANIANS	ILLITE
IDEATIONS	IDLERS	IGG	IGUANID	ILLITES
IDEATIVE	IDLES	IGGED	IGUANIDS	ILLITIC
IDEM	IDLESSE	IGGING	IGUANODON	ILLNESS
IDENTIC	IDLESSES	IGGS	IGUANODONS	ILLNESSES
IDENTICAL	IDLEST	IGLOO	IHRAM	ILLOGIC
IDENTIFIED	IDLING	IGLOOS	IHRAMS	ILLOGICAL
IDENTIFIES	IDLY	IGLU	IKAT	ILLOGICS
IDENTIFY	IDOCRASE	IGLUS	IKATS	ILLS
IDENTIFYING	IDOCRASES	IGNATIA	IKEBANA	ILLUDE
IDENTIKIT	IDOL	IGNATIAS	IKEBANAS	ILLUDED
IDENTITIES	IDOLATER	IGNEOUS	IKON	ILLUDES
IDENTITY	IDOLATERS	IGNESCENT	IKONS	ILLUDING
IDEOGRAM	IDOLATOR	IGNESCENTS	ILEA	ILLUME
IDEOGRAMS	IDOLATORS	IGNIFIED	ILEAC	ILLUMED
IDEOGRAPH	IDOLATRIES	IGNIFIES	ILEAL	ILLUMES
IDEOGRAPHS	IDOLATRY	IGNIFY	ILEITIDES	ILLUMINE
IDEOLOGIC	IDOLISE	IGNIFYING	ILEITIS	ILLUMINED
IDEOLOGIES	IDOLISED	IGNITABLE	ILEOSTOMIES	ILLUMINES
IDEOLOGUE	IDOLISER	IGNITE	ILEOSTOMY	ILLUMING
IDEOLOGUES	IDOLISERS	IGNITED	ILEUM	ILLUMINING
IDEOLOGY	IDOLISES	IGNITER	ILEUS	ILLUSION
IDEOMOTOR	IDOLISING	IGNITERS	ILEUSES	ILLUSIONS
IDEOPHONE	IDOLISM	IGNITES	ILEX	ILLUSIVE
IDEOPHONES	IDOLISMS	IGNITIBLE	ILEXES	ILLUSORY

ILLUVIA	IMBALMING	IMBROWNS	IMMENSITY	IMMOVABLE
ILLUVIAL	IMBALMS	IMBRUE	IMMERGE	IMMOVABLES
ILLUVIATE	IMBARK	IMBRUED	IMMERGED	IMMOVABLY
ILLUVIATED	IMBARKED	IMBRUES	IMMERGES	IMMUNE
ILLUVIATES	IMBARKING	IMBRUING	IMMERGING	IMMUNES
ILLUVIATING	IMBARKS	IMBRUTE	IMMERSE	IMMUNISE
ILLUVIUM	IMBECILE	IMBRUTED	IMMERSED	IMMUNISED
ILLUVIUMS	IMBECILES	IMBRUTES	IMMERSES	IMMUNISES
ILLY	IMBECILIC	IMBRUTING	IMMERSING	IMMUNISING
ILMENITE	IMBED	IMBUE	IMMERSION	IMMUNITIES
ILMENITES	IMBEDDED	IMBUED	IMMERSIONS	IMMUNITY
IMAGE	IMBEDDING	IMBUEMENT	IMMESH	IMMUNIZE
IMAGEABLE	IMBEDS	IMBUEMENTS	IMMESHED	IMMUNIZED
IMAGED	IMBIBE	IMBUES	IMMESHES	IMMUNIZER
IMAGER	IMBIBED	IMBUING	IMMESHING	IMMUNIZERS
IMAGERIES	IMBIBER	IMID	IMMIES	IMMUNIZES
IMAGERS	IMBIBERS	IMIDAZOLE	IMMIGRANT	IMMUNIZING
IMAGERY	IMBIBES	IMIDAZOLES	IMMIGRANTS	IMMUNOGEN
IMAGES	IMBIBING	IMIDE	IMMIGRATE	IMMUNOGENS
IMAGINAL	IMBITTER	IMIDES	IMMIGRATED	IMMURE
IMAGINARIES	IMBITTERED	IMIDIC	IMMIGRATES	IMMURED
IMAGINARY	IMBITTERING	IMIDO	IMMIGRATING	IMMURES
IMAGINE	IMBITTERS	IMIDS	IMMINENCE	IMMURING
IMAGINED	IMBLAZE	IMINE	IMMINENCES	IMMUTABLE
IMAGINER	IMBLAZED	IMINES	IMMINENCIES	IMMUTABLY
IMAGINERS	IMBLAZES	IMINO	IMMINENCY	IMMY
IMAGINES	IMBLAZING	IMITABLE	IMMINENT	IMP
IMAGING	IMBODIED	IMITATE	IMMINGLE	IMPACT
IMAGINGS	IMBODIES	IMITATED	IMMINGLED	IMPACTED
IMAGINING	IMBODY	IMITATES	IMMINGLES	IMPACTER
IMAGISM	IMBODYING	IMITATING	IMMINGLING	IMPACTERS
IMAGISMS	IMBOLDEN	IMITATION	IMMIX	IMPACTFUL
IMAGIST	IMBOLDENED	IMITATIONS	IMMIXED	IMPACTING
IMAGISTIC	IMBOLDENING	IMITATIVE	IMMIXES	IMPACTION
IMAGISTS	IMBOLDENS	IMITATOR	IMMIXING	IMPACTIONS
IMAGO	IMBOSOM	IMITATORS	IMMIXTURE	IMPACTIVE
IMAGOES	IMBOSOMED	IMMANE	IMMIXTURES	IMPACTOR
IMAGOS	IMBOSOMING	IMMANENCE	IMMOBILE	IMPACTORS
IMAM	IMBOSOMS	IMMANENCES	IMMODEST	IMPACTS
IMAMATE	IMBOWER	IMMANENCIES	IMMODESTIES	IMPAINT
IMAMATES	IMBOWERED	IMMANENCY	IMMODESTY	IMPAINTED
IMAMS	IMBOWERING	IMMANENT	IMMOLATE	IMPAINTING
IMARET	IMBOWERS	IMMATURE	IMMOLATED	IMPAINTS
IMARETS	IMBRICATE	IMMATURES	IMMOLATES	IMPAIR
IMAUM	IMBRICATED	IMMEDIACIES	IMMOLATING	IMPAIRED
IMAUMS	IMBRICATES	IMMEDIACY	IMMOLATOR	IMPAIRER
IMBALANCE	IMBRICATING	IMMEDIATE	IMMOLATORS	IMPAIRERS
IMBALANCES	IMBROGLIO	IMMENSE	IMMORAL	IMPAIRING
IMBALM	IMBROGLIOS	IMMENSELY	IMMORALLY	IMPAIRS
IMBALMED	IMBROWN	IMMENSER	IMMORTAL	IMPALA
IMBALMER	IMBROWNED	IMMENSEST	IMMORTALS	IMPALAS
IMBALMERS	IMBROWNING	IMMENSITIES	IMMOTILE	IMPALE

IMPALED	IMPEARLED	IMPETUSES	IMPLODING	IMPOTENCE
IMPALER	IMPEARLING	IMPHEE	IMPLORE	IMPOTENCES
IMPALERS	IMPEARLS	IMPHEES	IMPLORED	IMPOTENCIES
IMPALES	IMPECCANT	IMPI	IMPLORER	IMPOTENCY
IMPALING	IMPED	IMPIETIES	IMPLORERS	IMPOTENT
IMPANEL	IMPEDANCE	IMPIETY	IMPLORES	IMPOTENTS
IMPANELED	IMPEDANCES	IMPING	IMPLORING	IMPOUND
IMPANELING	IMPEDE	IMPINGE	IMPLOSION	IMPOUNDED
IMPANELLED	IMPEDED	IMPINGED	IMPLOSIONS	IMPOUNDER
IMPANELLING	IMPEDER	IMPINGER	IMPLOSIVE	IMPOUNDERS
IMPANELS	IMPEDERS	IMPINGERS	IMPLOSIVES	IMPOUNDING
IMPARITIES	IMPEDES	IMPINGES	IMPLY	IMPOUNDS
IMPARITY	IMPEDING	IMPINGING	IMPLYING	IMPOWER
IMPARK	IMPEL	IMPINGS	IMPOLICIES	IMPOWERED
IMPARKED	IMPELLED	IMPIOUS	IMPOLICY	IMPOWERING
IMPARKING	IMPELLENT	IMPIOUSLY	IMPOLITE	IMPOWERS
IMPARKS	IMPELLENTS	IMPIS	IMPOLITIC	IMPRECATE
IMPART	IMPELLER	IMPISH	IMPONE	IMPRECATED
IMPARTED	IMPELLERS	IMPISHLY	IMPONED	IMPRECATES
IMPARTER	IMPELLING	IMPLANT	IMPONES	IMPRECATING
IMPARTERS	IMPELLOR	IMPLANTED	IMPONING	IMPRECISE
IMPARTIAL	IMPELLORS	IMPLANTER	IMPOROUS	IMPREGN
IMPARTING	IMPELS	IMPLANTERS	IMPORT	IMPREGNED
IMPARTS	IMPEND	IMPLANTING	IMPORTANT	IMPREGNING
IMPASSE	IMPENDED	IMPLANTS	IMPORTED	IMPREGNS
IMPASSES	IMPENDENT	IMPLEAD	IMPORTER	IMPRESA
IMPASSION	IMPENDING	IMPLEADED	IMPORTERS	IMPRESAS
IMPASSIONED	IMPENDS	IMPLEADER	IMPORTING	IMPRESE
IMPASSIONING	IMPERATOR	IMPLEADERS	IMPORTS	IMPRESES
IMPASSIONS	IMPERATORS	IMPLEADING	IMPORTUNE	IMPRESS
IMPASSIVE	IMPERFECT	IMPLEADS	IMPORTUNED	IMPRESSED
IMPASTE	IMPERFECTS	IMPLED	IMPORTUNES	IMPRESSES
IMPASTED	IMPERIA	IMPLEDGE	IMPORTUNING	IMPRESSING
IMPASTES	IMPERIAL	IMPLEDGED	IMPOSABLE	IMPREST
IMPASTING	IMPERIALS	IMPLEDGES	IMPOSE	IMPRESTS
IMPASTO	IMPERIL	IMPLEDGING	IMPOSED	IMPRIMIS
IMPASTOED	IMPERILED	IMPLEMENT	IMPOSER	IMPRINT
IMPASTOS	IMPERILING	IMPLEMENTED	IMPOSERS	IMPRINTED
IMPATIENS	IMPERILLED	IMPLEMENTING	IMPOSES	IMPRINTER
IMPATIENT	IMPERILLING	IMPLEMENTS	IMPOSING	IMPRINTERS
IMPAVID	IMPERILS	IMPLETION	IMPOST	IMPRINTING
IMPAWN	IMPERIOUS	IMPLETIONS	IMPOSTED	IMPRINTS
IMPAWNED	IMPERIUM	IMPLICATE	IMPOSTER	IMPRISON
IMPAWNING	IMPERIUMS	IMPLICATED	IMPOSTERS	IMPRISONED
IMPAWNS	IMPETIGO	IMPLICATES	IMPOSTING	IMPRISONING
IMPEACH	IMPETIGOS	IMPLICATING	IMPOSTOR	IMPRISONS
IMPEACHED	IMPETRATE	IMPLICIT	IMPOSTORS	IMPROBITIES
IMPEACHER	IMPETRATED	IMPLIED	IMPOSTS	IMPROBITY
IMPEACHERS	IMPETRATES	IMPLIES	IMPOSTUME	IMPROMPTU
IMPEACHES	IMPETRATING	IMPLODE	IMPOSTUMES	IMPROMPTUS
IMPEACHING	IMPETUOUS	IMPLODED	IMPOSTURE	IMPROPER
IMPEARL	IMPETUS	IMPLODES	IMPOSTURES	IMPROV

IMPROVE	INACTIVE	INBREEDING	INCH	INCLIP
IMPROVED	INAMORATA	INBREEDS	INCHED	INCLIPPED
IMPROVER	INAMORATAS	INBUILT	INCHER	INCLIPPING
IMPROVERS	INAMORATO	INBURST	INCHERS	INCLIPS
IMPROVES	INAMORATOS	INBURSTS	INCHES	INCLOSE
IMPROVING	INANE	INBY	INCHING	INCLOSED
IMPROVISE	INANELY	INBYE	INCHMEAL	INCLOSER
IMPROVISED	INANENESS	INCAGE	INCHOATE	INCLOSERS
IMPROVISES	INANENESSES	INCAGED	INCHWORM	INCLOSES
IMPROVISING	INANER	INCAGES	INCHWORMS	INCLOSING
IMPROVS	INANES	INCAGING	INCIDENCE	INCLOSURE
IMPRUDENT	INANEST	INCANT	INCIDENCES	INCLOSURES
IMPS	INANIMATE	INCANTED	INCIDENT	INCLUDE
IMPUDENCE	INANITIES	INCANTING	INCIDENTS	INCLUDED
IMPUDENCES	INANITION	INCANTS	INCIPIENT	INCLUDES
IMPUDENCIES	INANITIONS	INCAPABLE	INCIPIT	INCLUDING
IMPUDENCY	INANITY	INCAPABLY	INCIPITS	INCLUSION
IMPUDENT	INAPT	INCARNATE	INCISAL	INCLUSIONS
IMPUGN	INAPTLY	INCARNATED	INCISE	INCLUSIVE
IMPUGNED	INAPTNESS	INCARNATES	INCISED	INCOG
IMPUGNER	INAPTNESSES	INCARNATING	INCISES	INCOGNITA
IMPUGNERS	INARABLE	INCASE	INCISING	INCOGNITAS
IMPUGNING	INARCH	INCASED	INCISION	INCOGNITO
IMPUGNS	INARCHED	INCASES	INCISIONS	INCOGNITOS
IMPULSE	INARCHES	INCASING	INCISIVE	INCOGS
IMPULSED	INARCHING	INCAUTION	INCISOR	INCOME
IMPULSES	INARM	INCAUTIONS	INCISORS	INCOMER
IMPULSING	INARMED	INCENSE	INCISORY	INCOMERS
IMPULSION	INARMING	INCENSED	INCISURE	INCOMES
IMPULSIONS	INARMS	INCENSES	INCISURES	INCOMING
IMPULSIVE	INAUDIBLE	INCENSING	INCITABLE	INCOMINGS
IMPUNITIES	INAUDIBLY	INCENT	INCITANT	INCOMMODE
IMPUNITY	INAUGURAL	INCENTED	INCITANTS	INCOMMODED
IMPURE	INAUGURALS	INCENTER	INCITE	INCOMMODES
IMPURELY	INBEING	INCENTERS	INCITED	INCOMMODING
IMPURER	INBEINGS	INCENTING	INCITER	INCOMPACT
IMPUREST	INBOARD	INCENTIVE	INCITERS	INCONDITE
IMPURITIES	INBOARDS	INCENTIVES	INCITES	INCONNU
IMPURITY	INBORN	INCENTS	INCITING	INCONNUS
IMPUTABLE	INBOUND	INCEPT	INCIVIL	INCONY
IMPUTABLY	INBOUNDED	INCEPTED	INCLASP	INCORPSE
IMPUTE	INBOUNDING	INCEPTING	INCLASPED	INCORPSED
IMPUTED	INBOUNDS	INCEPTION	INCLASPING	INCORPSES
IMPUTER	INBREATHE	INCEPTIONS	INCLASPS	INCORPSING
IMPUTERS	INBREATHED	INCEPTIVE	INCLEMENT	INCORRECT
IMPUTES	INBREATHES	INCEPTIVES	INCLINE	INCORRUPT
IMPUTING	INBREATHING	INCEPTOR	INCLINED	INCREASE
IN	INBRED	INCEPTORS	INCLINER	INCREASED
INABILITIES	INBREDS	INCEPTS	INCLINERS	INCREASER
INABILITY	INBREED	INCESSANT	INCLINES	INCREASERS
INACTION	INBREEDER	INCEST	INCLINING	INCREASES
INACTIONS	INBREEDERS	INCESTS	INCLININGS	INCREASING

INCREATE	INCURSIONS	INDENTIONS	INDIGENCY	INDORSORS
INCREMENT	INCURSIVE	INDENTOR	INDIGENE	INDOW
INCREMENTS	INCURVATE	INDENTORS	INDIGENES	INDOWED
INCRETION	INCURVATED	INDENTS	INDIGENS	INDOWING
INCRETIONS	INCURVATES	INDENTURE	INDIGENT	INDOWS
INCROSS	INCURVATING	INDENTURED	INDIGENTS	INDOXYL
INCROSSED	INCURVE	INDENTURES	INDIGN	INDOXYLS
INCROSSES	INCURVED	INDENTURING	INDIGNANT	INDRAFT
INCROSSING	INCURVES	INDEVOUT	INDIGNITIES	INDRAFTS
INCRUST	INCURVING	INDEX	INDIGNITY	INDRAUGHT
INCRUSTED	INCUS	INDEXABLE	INDIGNLY	INDRAUGHTS
INCRUSTING	INCUSE	INDEXED	INDIGO	INDRAWN
INCRUSTS	INCUSED	INDEXER	INDIGOES	INDRI
INCUBATE	INCUSES	INDEXERS	INDIGOID	INDRIS
INCUBATED	INCUSING	INDEXES	INDIGOIDS	INDUCE
INCUBATES	INDABA	INDEXICAL	INDIGOS	INDUCED
INCUBATING	INDABAS	INDEXICALS	INDIGOTIN	INDUCER
INCUBATOR	INDAGATE	INDEXING	INDIGOTINS	INDUCERS
INCUBATORS	INDAGATED	INDEXINGS	INDINAVIR	INDUCES
INCUBI	INDAGATES	INDICAN	INDINAVIRS	INDUCIBLE
INCUBUS	INDAGATING	INDICANS	INDIRECT	INDUCING
INCUBUSES	INDAGATOR	INDICANT	INDISPOSE	INDUCT
INCUDAL	INDAGATORS	INDICANTS	INDISPOSED	INDUCTED
INCUDATE	INDAMIN	INDICATE	INDISPOSES	INDUCTEE
INCUDES	INDAMINE	INDICATED	INDISPOSING	INDUCTEES
INCULCATE	INDAMINES	INDICATES	INDITE	INDUCTILE
INCULCATED	INDAMINS	INDICATING	INDITED	INDUCTING
INCULCATES	INDEBTED	INDICATOR	INDITER	INDUCTION
INCULCATING	INDECENCIES	INDICATORS	INDITERS	INDUCTIONS
INCULPATE	INDECENCY	INDICES	INDITES	INDUCTIVE
INCULPATED	INDECENT	INDICIA	INDITING	INDUCTOR
INCULPATES	INDECENTER	INDICIAS	INDIUM	INDUCTORS
INCULPATING	INDECENTEST	INDICIUM	INDIUMS	INDUCTS
INCULT	INDECORUM	INDICIUMS	INDOCILE	INDUE
INCUMBENT	INDECORUMS	INDICT	INDOL	INDUED
INCUMBENTS	INDEED	INDICTED	INDOLE	INDUES
INCUMBER	INDELIBLE	INDICTEE	INDOLENCE	INDUING
INCUMBERED	INDELIBLY	INDICTEES	INDOLENCES	INDULGE
INCUMBERING	INDEMNIFIED	INDICTER	INDOLENT	INDULGED
INCUMBERS	INDEMNIFIES	INDICTERS	INDOLES	INDULGENT
INCUNABLE	INDEMNIFY	INDICTING	INDOLS	INDULGER
INCUNABLES	INDEMNIFYING	INDICTION	INDOOR	INDULGERS
INCUR	INDEMNITIES	INDICTIONS	INDOORS	INDULGES
INCURABLE	INDEMNITY	INDICTOR	INDORSE	INDULGING
INCURABLES	INDENE	INDICTORS	INDORSED	INDULIN
INCURABLY	INDENES	INDICTS	INDORSEE	INDULINE
INCURIOUS	INDENT	INDIE	INDORSEES	INDULINES
INCURRED	INDENTED	INDIES	INDORSER	INDULINS
INCURRENT	INDENTER	INDIGEN	INDORSERS	INDULT
INCURRING	INDENTERS	INDIGENCE	INDORSES	INDULTS
INCURS	INDENTING	INDIGENCES	INDORSING	INDURATE
INCURSION	INDENTION	INDIGENCIES	INDORSOR	INDURATED

INDURATES	INERTS	INFEOFFS	INFIXED	INFOBAHN
INDURATING	INEXACT	INFER	INFIXES	INFOBAHNS
INDUSIA	INEXACTLY	INFERABLE	INFIXING	INFOLD
INDUSIAL	INEXPERT	INFERABLY	INFIXION	INFOLDED
INDUSIATE	INEXPERTS	INFERENCE	INFIXIONS	INFOLDER
INDUSIUM	INFALL	INFERENCES	INFLAME	INFOLDERS
INDUSTRIES	INFALLING	INFERIOR	INFLAMED	INFOLDING
INDUSTRY	INFALLS	INFERIORS	INFLAMER	INFOLDS
INDWELL	INFAMIES	INFERNAL	INFLAMERS	INFORM
INDWELLER	INFAMOUS	INFERNO	INFLAMES	INFORMAL
INDWELLERS	INFAMY	INFERNOS	INFLAMING	INFORMANT
INDWELLING	INFANCIES	INFERRED	INFLATE	INFORMANTS
INDWELLS	INFANCY	INFERRER	INFLATED	INFORMED
INDWELT	INFANT	INFERRERS	INFLATER	INFORMER
INEARTH	INFANTA	INFERRING	INFLATERS	INFORMERS
INEARTHED	INFANTAS	INFERS	INFLATES	INFORMING
INEARTHING	INFANTE	INFERTILE	INFLATING	INFORMS
INEARTHS	INFANTES	INFEST	INFLATION	INFOS
INEBRIANT	INFANTILE	INFESTANT	INFLATIONS	INFOUGHT
INEBRIANTS	INFANTINE	INFESTANTS	INFLATOR	INFRA
INEBRIATE	INFANTRIES	INFESTED	INFLATORS	INFRACT
INEBRIATED	INFANTRY	INFESTER	INFLECT	INFRACTED
INEBRIATES	INFANTS	INFESTERS	INFLECTED	INFRACTING
INEBRIATING	INFARCT	INFESTING	INFLECTING	INFRACTOR
INEBRIETIES	INFARCTED	INFESTS	INFLECTOR	INFRACTORS
INEBRIETY	INFARCTS	INFIDEL	INFLECTORS	INFRACTS
INEDIBLE	INFARE	INFIDELIC	INFLECTS	INFRARED
INEDIBLY	INFARES	INFIDELS	INFLEXED	INFRAREDS
INEDITA	INFATUATE	INFIELD	INFLEXION	INFRINGE
INEDITED	INFATUATED	INFIELDER	INFLEXIONS	INFRINGED
INEFFABLE	INFATUATES	INFIELDERS	INFLICT	INFRINGER
INEFFABLY	INFATUATING	INFIELDS	INFLICTED	INFRINGERS
INELASTIC	INFAUNA	INFIGHT	INFLICTER	INFRINGES
INELEGANT	INFAUNAE	INFIGHTER	INFLICTERS	INFRINGING
INEPT	INFAUNAL	INFIGHTERS	INFLICTING	INFRUGAL
INEPTLY	INFAUNAS	INFIGHTING	INFLICTOR	INFURIATE
INEPTNESS	INFECT	INFIGHTS	INFLICTORS	INFURIATED
INEPTNESSES	INFECTANT	INFILL	INFLICTS	INFURIATES
INEQUITIES	INFECTED	INFINITE	INFLIGHT	INFURIATING
INEQUITY	INFECTER	INFINITES	INFLOW	INFUSCATE
INERRABLE	INFECTERS	INFINITIES	INFLOWS	INFUSE
INERRANCIES	INFECTING	INFINITY	INFLUENCE	INFUSED
INERRANCY	INFECTION	INFIRM	INFLUENCED	INFUSER
INERRANT	INFECTIONS	INFIRMARIES	INFLUENCES	INFUSERS
INERT	INFECTIVE	INFIRMARY	INFLUENCING	INFUSES
INERTIA	INFECTOR	INFIRMED	INFLUENT	INFUSIBLE
INERTIAE	INFECTORS	INFIRMING	INFLUENTS	INFUSING
INERTIAL	INFECTS	INFIRMITIES	INFLUENZA	INFUSION
INERTIAS	INFECUND	INFIRMITY	INFLUENZAS	INFUSIONS
INERTLY	INFEOFF	INFIRMLY	INFLUX	INFUSIVE
INERTNESS	INFEOFFED	INFIRMS	INFLUXES	INGATE
INERTNESSES	INFEOFFING	INFIX	INFO	INGATES

INGATHER	INHABITED	INHUMAN	INJUSTICES	INLIER
INGATHERED	INHABITER	INHUMANE	INK	INLIERS
INGATHERING	INHABITERS	INHUMANLY	INKBERRIES	INLY
INGATHERS	INHABITING	INHUME	INKBERRY	INLYING
INGENIOUS	INHABITS	INHUMED	INKBLOT	INMATE
INGENUE	INHALANT	INHUMER	INKBLOTS	INMATES
INGENUES	INHALANTS	INHUMERS	INKED	INMESH
INGENUITIES	INHALATOR	INHUMES	INKER	INMESHED
INGENUITY	INHALATORS	INHUMING	INKERS	INMESHES
INGENUOUS	INHALE	INIA	INKHORN	INMESHING
INGEST	INHALED	INIMICAL	INKHORNS	INMOST
INGESTA	INHALER	INION	INKIER	INN
INGESTED	INHALERS	INIONS	INKIEST	INNAGE
INGESTING	INHALES	INIQUITIES	INKINESS	INNAGES
INGESTION	INHALING	INIQUITY	INKINESSES	INNARDS
INGESTIONS	INHARMONIES	INITIAL	INKING	INNATE
INGESTIVE	INHARMONY	INITIALED	INKJET	INNATELY
INGESTS	INHAUL	INITIALER	INKLE	INNED
INGLE	INHAULER	INITIALERS	INKLES	INNER
INGLENOOK	INHAULERS	INITIALING	INKLESS	INNERLY
INGLENOOKS	INHAULS	INITIALLED	INKLIKE	INNERMOST
INGLES	INHERE	INITIALLING	INKLING	INNERMOSTS
INGOING	INHERED	INITIALLY	INKLINGS	INNERNESS
INGOT	INHERENCE	INITIALS	INKPOT	INNERNESSES
INGOTED	INHERENCES	INITIATE	INKPOTS	INNERS
INGOTING	INHERENCIES	INITIATED	INKS	INNERSOLE
INGOTS	INHERENCY	INITIATES	INKSTAND	INNERSOLES
INGRAFT	INHERENT	INITIATING	INKSTANDS	INNERVATE
INGRAFTED	INHERES	INITIATOR	INKSTONE	INNERVATED
INGRAFTING	INHERING	INITIATORS	INKSTONES	INNERVATES
INGRAFTS	INHERIT	INJECT	INKWELL	INNERVATING
INGRAIN	INHERITED	INJECTANT	INKWELLS	INNERVE
INGRAINED	INHERITING	INJECTANTS	INKWOOD	INNERVED
INGRAINING	INHERITOR	INJECTED	INKWOODS	INNERVES
INGRAINS	INHERITORS	INJECTING	INKY	INNERVING
INGRATE	INHERITS	INJECTION	INLACE	INNING
INGRATES	INHESION	INJECTIONS	INLACED	INNINGS
INGRESS	INHESIONS	INJECTIVE	INLACES	INNKEEPER
INGRESSES	INHIBIN	INJECTOR	INLACING	INNKEEPERS
INGROUND	INHIBINS	INJECTORS	INLAID	INNLESS
INGROUP	INHIBIT	INJECTS	INLAND	INNOCENCE
INGROUPS	INHIBITED	INJURABLE	INLANDER	INNOCENCES
INGROWING	INHIBITER	INJURE	INLANDERS	INNOCENCIES
INGROWN	INHIBITERS	INJURED	INLANDS	INNOCENCY
INGROWTH	INHIBITING	INJURER	INLAY	INNOCENT
INGROWTHS	INHIBITOR	INJURERS	INLAYER	INNOCENTER
INGUINAL	INHIBITORS	INJURES	INLAYERS	INNOCENTEST
INGULF	INHIBITS	INJURIES	INLAYING	INNOCENTS
INGULFED	INHOLDER	INJURING	INLAYS	INNOCUOUS
INGULFING	INHOLDERS	INJURIOUS	INLET	INNOVATE
INGULFS	INHOLDING	INJURY	INLETS	INNOVATED
INHABIT	INHOLDINGS	INJUSTICE	INLETTING	INNOVATES

INNOVATING	INQUIRER	INSERT	INSNARERS	INSTABLE
INNOVATOR	INQUIRERS	INSERTED	INSNARES	INSTAL
INNOVATORS	INQUIRES	INSERTER	INSNARING	INSTALL
INNOXIOUS	INQUIRIES	INSERTERS	INSOFAR	INSTALLED
INNS	INQUIRING	INSERTING	INSOLATE	INSTALLER
INNUENDO	INQUIRY	INSERTION	INSOLATED	INSTALLERS
INNUENDOED	INRO	INSERTIONS	INSOLATES	INSTALLING
INNUENDOES	INROAD	INSERTS	INSOLATING	INSTALLS
INNUENDOING	INROADS	INSET	INSOLE	INSTALS
INNUENDOS	INRUN	INSETS	INSOLENCE	INSTANCE
INOCULA	INRUNS	INSETTED	INSOLENCES	INSTANCED
INOCULANT	INRUSH	INSETTER	INSOLENT	INSTANCES
INOCULANTS	INRUSHES	INSETTERS	INSOLENTS	INSTANCIES
INOCULATE	INRUSHING	INSETTING	INSOLES	INSTANCING
INOCULATED	INRUSHINGS	INSHEATH	INSOLUBLE	INSTANCY
INOCULATES	INS	INSHEATHE	INSOLUBLES	INSTANT
INOCULATING	INSANE	INSHEATHED	INSOLUBLY	INSTANTER
INOCULUM	INSANELY	INSHEATHES	INSOLVENT	INSTANTLY
INOCULUMS	INSANER	INSHEATHING	INSOLVENTS	INSTANTS
INODOROUS	INSANEST	INSHEATHS	INSOMNIA	INSTAR
INORGANIC	INSANITIES	INSHORE	INSOMNIAC	INSTARRED
INOSINE	INSANITY	INSHRINE	INSOMNIACS	INSTARRING
INOSINES	INSATIATE	INSHRINED	INSOMNIAS	INSTARS
INOSITE	INSCAPE	INSHRINES	INSOMUCH	INSTATE
INOSITES	INSCAPES	INSHRINING	INSOUL	INSTATED
INOSITOL	INSCRIBE	INSIDE	INSOULED	INSTATES
INOSITOLS	INSCRIBED	INSIDER	INSOULING	INSTATING
INOTROPIC	INSCRIBER	INSIDERS	INSOULS	INSTEAD
INPATIENT	INSCRIBERS	INSIDES	INSPAN	INSTEP
INPATIENTS	INSCRIBES	INSIDIOUS	INSPANNED	INSTEPS
INPHASE	INSCRIBING	INSIGHT	INSPANNING	INSTIGATE
INPOUR	INSCROLL	INSIGHTS	INSPANS	INSTIGATED
INPOURED	INSCROLLED	INSIGNE	INSPECT	INSTIGATES
INPOURING	INSCROLLING	INSIGNIA	INSPECTED	INSTIGATING
INPOURINGS	INSCROLLS	INSIGNIAS	INSPECTING	INSTIL
INPOURS	INSCULP	INSINCERE	INSPECTOR	INSTILL
INPUT	INSCULPED	INSINUATE	INSPECTORS	INSTILLED
INPUTS	INSCULPING	INSINUATED	INSPECTS	INSTILLER
INPUTTED	INSCULPS	INSINUATES	INSPHERE	INSTILLERS
INPUTTER	INSEAM	INSINUATING	INSPHERED	INSTILLING
INPUTTERS	INSEAMS	INSIPID	INSPHERES	INSTILLS
INPUTTING	INSECT	INSIPIDLY	INSPHERING	INSTILS
INQUEST	INSECTAN	INSIST	INSPIRE	INSTINCT
INQUESTS	INSECTARIES	INSISTED	INSPIRED	INSTINCTS
INQUIET	INSECTARY	INSISTENT	INSPIRER	INSTITUTE
INQUIETED	INSECTILE	INSISTER	INSPIRERS	INSTITUTED
INQUIETING	INSECTS	INSISTERS	INSPIRES	INSTITUTES
INQUIETS	INSECURE	INSISTING	INSPIRING	INSTITUTING
INQUILINE	INSELBERG	INSISTS	INSPIRIT	INSTROKE
INQUILINES	INSELBERGE	INSNARE	INSPIRITED	INSTROKES
INQUIRE	INSELBERGS	INSNARED	INSPIRITING	INSTRUCT
INQUIRED	INSENSATE	INSNARER	INSPIRITS	INSTRUCTED

INSTRUCTING	INTEGERS	INTERARCHING	INTERFLOW	INTERLENDING
INSTRUCTS	INTEGRAL	INTERBANK	INTERFLOWED	INTERLENDS
INSULANT	INTEGRALS	INTERBED	INTERFLOWING	INTERLENT
INSULANTS	INTEGRAND	INTERBEDDED	INTERFLOWS	INTERLINE
INSULAR	INTEGRANDS	INTERBEDDING	INTERFOLD	INTERLINED
INSULARLY	INTEGRANT	INTERBEDS	INTERFOLDED	INTERLINES
INSULARS	INTEGRANTS	INTERBRED	INTERFOLDING	INTERLINING
INSULATE	INTEGRATE	INTERBREED	INTERFOLDS	INTERLINK
INSULATED	INTEGRATED	INTERBREEDING	INTERFUSE	INTERLINKED
INSULATES	INTEGRATES	INTERBREEDS	INTERFUSED	INTERLINKING
INSULATING	INTEGRATING	INTERCEDE	INTERFUSES	INTERLINKS
INSULATOR	INTEGRITIES	INTERCEDED	INTERFUSING	INTERLOAN
INSULATORS	INTEGRITY	INTERCEDES	INTERGANG	INTERLOANS
INSULIN	INTELLECT	INTERCEDING	INTERIM	INTERLOCK
INSULINS	INTELLECTS	INTERCELL	INTERIMS	INTERLOCKED
INSULT	INTEND	INTERCEPT	INTERIOR	INTERLOCKING
INSULTED	INTENDANT	INTERCEPTED	INTERIORS	INTERLOCKS
INSULTER	INTENDANTS	INTERCEPTING	INTERJECT	INTERLOOP
INSULTERS	INTENDED	INTERCEPTS	INTERJECTED	INTERLOOPED
INSULTING	INTENDEDS	INTERCITY	INTERJECTING	INTERLOOPING
INSULTS	INTENDER	INTERCLAN	INTERJECTS	INTERLOOPS
INSURABLE	INTENDERS	INTERCLUB	INTERJOIN	INTERLOPE
INSURANCE	INTENDING	INTERCOM	INTERJOINED	INTERLOPED
INSURANCES	INTENDS	INTERCOMS	INTERJOINING	INTERLOPES
INSURANT	INTENSE	INTERCROP	INTERJOINS	INTERLOPING
INSURANTS	INTENSELY	INTERCROPPED	INTERKNIT	INTERLUDE
INSURE	INTENSER	INTERCROPPING	INTERKNITS	INTERLUDES
INSURED	INTENSEST	INTERCROPS	INTERKNITTED	INTERMALE
INSUREDS	INTENSIFIED	INTERCUT	INTERKNITTING	INTERMAT
INSURER	INTENSIFIES	INTERCUTS	INTERKNOT	INTERMATS
INSURERS	INTENSIFY	INTERCUTTING	INTERKNOTS	INTERMATTED
INSURES	INTENSIFYING	INTERDICT	INTERKNOTTED	INTERMATTING
INSURGENT	INTENSION	INTERDICTED	INTERKNOTTING	INTERMENT
INSURGENTS	INTENSIONS	INTERDICTING	INTERLACE	INTERMENTS
INSURING	INTENSITIES	INTERDICTS	INTERLACED	INTERMESH
INSWATHE	INTENSITY	INTEREST	INTERLACES	INTERMESHED
INSWATHED	INTENSIVE	INTERESTED	INTERLACING	INTERMESHES
INSWATHES	INTENSIVES	INTERESTING	INTERLAID	INTERMESHING
INSWATHING	INTENT	INTERESTS	INTERLAP	INTERMIT
INSWEPT	INTENTION	INTERFACE	INTERLAPPED	INTERMITS
INTACT	INTENTIONS	INTERFACED	INTERLAPPING	INTERMITTED
INTACTLY	INTENTLY	INTERFACES	INTERLAPS	INTERMITTING
INTAGLI	INTENTS	INTERFACING	INTERLARD	INTERMIX
INTAGLIO	INTER	INTERFERE	INTERLARDED	INTERMIXED
INTAGLIOED	INTERACT	INTERFERED	INTERLARDING	INTERMIXES
INTAGLIOING	INTERACTED	INTERFERES	INTERLARDS	INTERMIXING
INTAGLIOS	INTERACTING	INTERFERING	INTERLAY	INTERMONT
INTAKE	INTERACTS	INTERFILE	INTERLAYING	INTERN
INTAKES	INTERAGE	INTERFILED	INTERLAYS	INTERNAL
INTARSIA	INTERARCH	INTERFILES	INTERLEAF	INTERNALS
INTARSIAS	INTERARCHED	INTERFILING	INTERLEAVES	INTERNE
INTEGER	INTERARCHES	INTERFIRM	INTERLEND	INTERNED

INTERNEE	INTERVALE	INTIMATE	INTRENCH	INTRUSIVE
INTERNEES	INTERVALES	INTIMATED	INTRENCHED	INTRUSIVES
INTERNES	INTERVALS	INTIMATER	INTRENCHES	INTRUST
INTERNING	INTERVENE	INTIMATERS	INTRENCHING	INTRUSTED
INTERNIST	INTERVENED	INTIMATES	INTREPID	INTRUSTING
INTERNISTS	INTERVENES	INTIMATING	INTRICACIES	INTRUSTS
INTERNODE	INTERVENING	INTIME	INTRICACY	INTUBATE
INTERNODES	INTERVIEW	INTIMIST	INTRICATE	INTUBATED
INTERNS	INTERVIEWED	INTIMISTS	INTRIGANT	INTUBATES
INTERPLAY	INTERVIEWING	INTINE	INTRIGANTS	INTUBATING
INTERPLAYED	INTERVIEWS	INTINES	INTRIGUE	INTUIT
INTERPLAYING	INTERWAR	INTIS	INTRIGUED	INTUITED
INTERPLAYS	INTERWEAVE	INTITLE	INTRIGUER	INTUITING
INTERPLEAD	INTERWEAVED	INTITLED	INTRIGUERS	INTUITION
INTERPLEADED	INTERWEAVES	INTITLES	INTRIGUES	INTUITIONS
INTERPLEADING	INTERWEAVING	INTITLING	INTRIGUING	INTUITIVE
INTERPLEADS	INTERWORK	INTITULE	INTRINSIC	INTUITS
INTERPLED	INTERWORKED	INTITULED	INTRO	INTUMESCE
INTERPOSE	INTERWORKING	INTITULES	INTRODUCE	INTUMESCED
INTERPOSED	INTERWORKS	INTITULING	INTRODUCED	INTUMESCES
INTERPOSES	INTERWOVE	INTO	INTRODUCES	INTUMESCING
INTERPOSING	INTERWOVEN	INTOMB	INTRODUCING	INTURN
INTERPRET	INTERZONE	INTOMBED	INTROFIED	INTURNED
INTERPRETED	INTESTACIES	INTOMBING	INTROFIES	INTURNS
INTERPRETING	INTESTACY	INTOMBS	INTROFY	INTWINE
INTERPRETS	INTESTATE	INTONATE	INTROFYING	INTWINED
INTERRACE	INTESTATES	INTONATED	INTROIT	INTWINES
INTERRED	INTESTINE	INTONATES	INTROITS	INTWINING
INTERREGES	INTESTINES	INTONATING	INTROJECT	INTWIST
INTERREX	INTHRAL	INTONE	INTROJECTED	INTWISTED
INTERRING	INTHRALL	INTONED	INTROJECTING	INTWISTING
INTERROW	INTHRALLED	INTONER	INTROJECTS	INTWISTS
INTERRUPT	INTHRALLING	INTONERS	INTROMIT	INULASE
INTERRUPTED	INTHRALLS	INTONES	INTROMITS	INULASES
INTERRUPTING	INTHRALS	INTONING	INTROMITTED	INULIN
INTERRUPTS	INTHRONE	INTORT	INTROMITTING	INULINS
INTERS	INTHRONED	INTORTED	INTRON	INUNCTION
INTERSECT	INTHRONES	INTORTING	INTRONS	INUNCTIONS
INTERSECTED	INTHRONING	INTORTS	INTRORSE	INUNDANT
INTERSECTING	INTI	INTOWN	INTROS	INUNDATE
INTERSECTS	INTIFADA	INTRACITY	INTROVERT	INUNDATED
INTERSEX	INTIFADAH	INTRADAY	INTROVERTED	INUNDATES
INTERSEXES	INTIFADAHS	INTRADOS	INTROVERTING	INUNDATING
INTERTERM	INTIFADAS	INTRADOSES	INTROVERTS	INUNDATOR
INTERTIE	INTIFADEH	INTRANET	INTRUDE	INUNDATORS
INTERTIES	INTIFADEHS	INTRANETS	INTRUDED	INURBANE
INTERTILL	INTIMA	INTRANT	INTRUDER	INURE
INTERTILLED	INTIMACIES	INTRANTS	INTRUDERS	INURED
INTERTILLING	INTIMACY	INTREAT	INTRUDES	INUREMENT
INTERTILLS	INTIMAE	INTREATED	INTRUDING	INUREMENTS
INTERUNIT	INTIMAL	INTREATING	INTRUSION	INURES
INTERVAL	INTIMAS	INTREATS	INTRUSIONS	INURING

INURN	INVENTORIED	INVITER	INWRAPPED	IONISED
INURNED	INVENTORIES	INVITERS	INWRAPPING	IONISES
INURNING	INVENTORS	INVITES	INWRAPS	IONISING
INURNMENT	INVENTORY	INVITING	INWROUGHT	IONIUM
INURNMENTS	INVENTORYING	INVOCATE	IODATE	IONIUMS
INURNS	INVENTS	INVOCATED	IODATED	IONIZABLE
INUTILE	INVERITIES	INVOCATES	IODATES	IONIZE
INUTILELY	INVERITY	INVOCATING	IODATING	IONIZED
INUTILITIES	INVERNESS	INVOICE	IODATION	IONIZER
INUTILITY	INVERNESSES	INVOICED	IODATIONS	IONIZERS
INVADE	INVERSE	INVOICES	IODIC	IONIZES
INVADED	INVERSED	INVOICING	IODID	IONIZING
INVADER	INVERSELY	INVOKE	IODIDE	IONOGEN
INVADERS	INVERSES	INVOKED	IODIDES	IONOGENIC
INVADES	INVERSING	INVOKER	IODIDS	IONOGENS
INVADING	INVERSION	INVOKERS	IODIN	IONOMER
INVALID	INVERSIONS	INVOKES	IODINATE	IONOMERS
INVALIDED	INVERSIVE	INVOKING	IODINATED	IONONE
INVALIDING	INVERT	INVOLUCEL	IODINATES	IONONES
INVALIDLY	INVERTASE	INVOLUCELS	IODINATING	IONOPHORE
INVALIDS	INVERTASES	INVOLUCRA	IODINE	IONOPHORES
INVAR	INVERTED	INVOLUCRE	IODINES	IONOSONDE
INVARIANT	INVERTER	INVOLUCRES	IODINS	IONOSONDES
INVARIANTS	INVERTERS	INVOLUCRUM	IODISE	IONS
INVARS	INVERTIN	INVOLUTE	IODISED	IOTA
INVASION	INVERTING	INVOLUTED	IODISES	IOTACISM
INVASIONS	INVERTINS	INVOLUTES	IODISING	IOTACISMS
INVASIVE	INVERTOR	INVOLUTING	IODISM	IOTAS
INVECTED	INVERTORS	INVOLVE	IODISMS	IPECAC
INVECTIVE	INVERTS	INVOLVED	IODIZE	IPECACS
INVECTIVES	INVEST	INVOLVER	IODIZED	IPOMOEA
INVEIGH	INVESTED	INVOLVERS	IODIZER	IPOMOEAS
INVEIGHED	INVESTING	INVOLVES	IODIZERS	IRACUND
INVEIGHER	INVESTOR	INVOLVING	IODIZES	IRADE
INVEIGHERS	INVESTORS	INWALL	IODIZING	IRADES
INVEIGHING	INVESTS	INWALLED	IODOFORM	IRASCIBLE
INVEIGHS	INVIABLE	INWALLING	IODOFORMS	IRASCIBLY
INVEIGLE	INVIABLY	INWALLS	IODOMETRIES	IRATE
INVEIGLED	INVIDIOUS	INWARD	IODOMETRY	IRATELY
INVEIGLER	INVIOLACIES	INWARDLY	IODOPHOR	IRATENESS
INVEIGLERS	INVIOLACY	INWARDS	IODOPHORS	IRATENESSES
INVEIGLES	INVIOLATE	INWEAVE	IODOPSIN	IRATER
INVEIGLING	INVIRILE	INWEAVED	IODOPSINS	IRATEST
INVENT	INVISCID	INWEAVES	IODOUS	IRE
INVENTED	INVISIBLE	INWEAVING	IOLITE	IRED
INVENTER	INVISIBLES	INWIND	IOLITES	IREFUL
INVENTERS	INVISIBLY	INWINDING	ION	IREFULLY
INVENTING	INVITAL	INWINDS	IONIC	IRELESS
INVENTION	INVITE	INWOUND	IONICITIES	IRENIC
INVENTIONS	INVITED	INWOVE	IONICITY	IRENICAL
INVENTIVE	INVITEE	INWOVEN	IONICS	IRENICS
INVENTOR	INVITEES	INWRAP	IONISE	IRES

IRID	IRONSIDE	IRRUPT	ISM	ISOGENIES
IRIDES	IRONSIDES	IRRUPTED	ISMS	ISOGENOUS
IRIDIC	IRONSMITH	IRRUPTING	ISOBAR	ISOGENY
IRIDIUM	IRONSMITHS	IRRUPTION	ISOBARE	ISOGLOSS
IRIDIUMS	IRONSTONE	IRRUPTIONS	ISOBARES	ISOGLOSSES
IRIDOLOGIES	IRONSTONES	IRRUPTIVE	ISOBARIC	ISOGON
IRIDOLOGY	IRONWARE	IRRUPTS	ISOBARISM	ISOGONAL
IRIDS	IRONWARES	IS	ISOBARISMS	ISOGONALS
IRING	IRONWEED	ISAGOGE	ISOBARS	ISOGONE
IRIS	IRONWEEDS	ISAGOGES	ISOBATH	ISOGONES
IRISED	IRONWOMAN	ISAGOGIC	ISOBATHIC	ISOGONIC
IRISES	IRONWOMEN	ISAGOGICS	ISOBATHS	ISOGONICS
IRISING	IRONWOOD	ISALLOBAR	ISOBUTANE	ISOGONIES
IRITIC	IRONWOODS	ISALLOBARS	ISOBUTANES	ISOGONS
IRITIS	IRONWORK	ISARITHM	ISOBUTENE	ISOGONY
IRITISES	IRONWORKS	ISARITHMS	ISOBUTENES	ISOGRAFT
IRK	IRONY	ISATIN	ISOBUTYL	ISOGRAFTED
IRKED	IRRADIANT	ISATINE	ISOBUTYLS	ISOGRAFTING
IRKING	IRRADIATE	ISATINES	ISOCHEIM	ISOGRAFTS
IRKS	IRRADIATED	ISATINIC	ISOCHEIMS	ISOGRAM
IRKSOME	IRRADIATES	ISATINS	ISOCHIME	ISOGRAMS
IRKSOMELY	IRRADIATING	ISBA	ISOCHIMES	ISOGRAPH
IROKO	IRREAL	ISBAS	ISOCHOR	ISOGRAPHS
IROKOS	IRREALITIES	ISCHAEMIA	ISOCHORE	ISOGRIV
IRON	IRREALITY	ISCHAEMIAS	ISOCHORES	ISOGRIVS
IRONBARK	IRREDENTA	ISCHEMIA	ISOCHORIC	ISOHEL
IRONBARKS	IRREDENTAS	ISCHEMIAS	ISOCHORS	ISOHELS
IRONBOUND	IRREGULAR	ISCHEMIC	ISOCHRON	ISOHYET
IRONCLAD	IRREGULARS	ISCHIA	ISOCHRONE	ISOHYETAL
IRONCLADS	IRRIDENTA	ISCHIADIC	ISOCHRONES	ISOHYETS
IRONE	IRRIDENTAS	ISCHIAL	ISOCHRONS	ISOLABLE
IRONED	IRRIGABLE	ISCHIATIC	ISOCLINAL	ISOLATE
IRONER	IRRIGABLY	ISCHIUM	ISOCLINALS	ISOLATED
IRONERS	IRRIGATE	ISEIKONIA	ISOCLINE	ISOLATES
IRONES	IRRIGATED	ISEIKONIAS	ISOCLINES	ISOLATING
IRONIC	IRRIGATES	ISEIKONIC	ISOCLINIC	ISOLATION
IRONICAL	IRRIGATING	ISINGLASS	ISOCLINICS	ISOLATIONS
IRONIES	IRRIGATOR	ISINGLASSES	ISOCRACIES	ISOLATOR
IRONING	IRRIGATORS	ISLAND	ISOCRACY	ISOLATORS
IRONINGS	IRRIGUOUS	ISLANDED	ISOCYCLIC	ISOLEAD
IRONIST	IRRITABLE	ISLANDER	ISODOSE	ISOLEADS
IRONISTS	IRRITABLY	ISLANDERS	ISOENZYME	ISOLINE
IRONIZE	IRRITANCIES	ISLANDING	ISOENZYMES	ISOLINES
IRONIZED	IRRITANCY	ISLANDS	ISOFORM	ISOLOG
IRONIZES	IRRITANT	ISLE	ISOFORMS	ISOLOGOUS
IRONIZING	IRRITANTS	ISLED	ISOGAMETE	ISOLOGS
IRONLIKE	IRRITATE	ISLELESS	ISOGAMETES	ISOLOGUE
IRONMAN	IRRITATED	ISLES	ISOGAMIES	ISOLOGUES
IRONMEN	IRRITATES	ISLET	ISOGAMOUS	ISOMER
IRONNESS	IRRITATING	ISLETED	ISOGAMY	ISOMERASE
IRONNESSES	IRRITATOR	ISLETS	ISOGENEIC	ISOMERASES
IRONS	IRRITATORS	ISLING	ISOGENIC	ISOMERIC

ISOMERISM	ISOTHERAL	ITALICIZED	ITSELF	JACARANDAS
ISOMERISMS	ISOTHERE	ITALICIZES	IVIED	JACINTH
ISOMERIZE	ISOTHERES	ITALICIZING	IVIES	JACINTHE
ISOMERIZED	ISOTHERM	ITALICS	IVORIES	JACINTHES
ISOMERIZES	ISOTHERMS	ITCH	IVORY	JACINTHS
ISOMERIZING	ISOTONE	ITCHED	IVORYBILL	JACK
ISOMEROUS	ISOTONES	ITCHES	IVORYBILLS	JACKAL
ISOMERS	ISOTONIC	ITCHIER	IVORYLIKE	JACKALS
ISOMETRIC	ISOTOPE	ITCHIEST	IVY	JACKAROO
ISOMETRICS	ISOTOPES	ITCHILY	IVYLIKE	JACKAROOS
ISOMETRIES	ISOTOPIC	ITCHINESS	IWIS	JACKASS
ISOMETRY	ISOTOPIES	ITCHINESSES	IXIA	JACKASSES
ISOMORPH	ISOTOPY	ITCHING	IXIAS	JACKBOOT
ISOMORPHS	ISOTROPIC	ITCHINGS	IXODID	JACKBOOTS
ISONIAZID	ISOTROPIES	ITCHY	IXODIDS	JACKDAW
ISONIAZIDS	ISOTROPY	ITEM	IXORA	JACKDAWS
ISONOMIC	ISOTYPE	ITEMED	IXORAS	JACKED
ISONOMIES	ISOTYPES	ITEMING	IXTLE	JACKER
ISONOMY	ISOTYPIC	ITEMISE	IXTLES	JACKEROO
ISOOCTANE	ISOZYME	ITEMISED	IZAR	JACKEROOS
ISOOCTANES	ISOZYMES	ITEMISES	IZARS	JACKERS
ISOPACH	ISOZYMIC	ITEMISING	IZZARD	JACKET
ISOPACHS	ISSEI	ITEMIZE	IZZARDS	JACKETED
ISOPHOTAL	ISSEIS	ITEMIZED		JACKETING
ISOPHOTE	ISSUABLE	ITEMIZER	**J**	JACKETS
ISOPHOTES	ISSUABLY	ITEMIZERS		JACKFISH
ISOPLETH	ISSUANCE	ITEMIZES		JACKFISHES
ISOPLETHS	ISSUANCES	ITEMIZING		JACKFRUIT
ISOPOD	ISSUANT	ITEMS	JAB	JACKFRUITS
ISOPODAN	ISSUE	ITERANCE	JABBED	JACKIES
ISOPODANS	ISSUED	ITERANCES	JABBER	JACKING
ISOPODS	ISSUELESS	ITERANT	JABBERED	JACKKNIFE
ISOPRENE	ISSUER	ITERATE	JABBERER	JACKKNIFED
ISOPRENES	ISSUERS	ITERATED	JABBERERS	JACKKNIFES
ISOPROPYL	ISSUES	ITERATES	JABBERING	JACKKNIFING
ISOPROPYLS	ISSUING	ITERATING	JABBERS	JACKKNIVES
ISOPYCNIC	ISTHMI	ITERATION	JABBING	JACKLEG
ISOSCELES	ISTHMIAN	ITERATIONS	JABIRU	JACKLEGS
ISOSMOTIC	ISTHMIANS	ITERATIVE	JABIRUS	JACKLIGHT
ISOSPIN	ISTHMIC	ITERUM	JABORANDI	JACKLIGHTED
ISOSPINS	ISTHMOID	ITHER	JABORANDIS	JACKLIGHTING
ISOSPORIES	ISTHMUS	ITINERACIES	JABOT	JACKLIGHTS
ISOSPORY	ISTHMUSES	ITINERACY	JABOTS	JACKPLANE
ISOSTACIES	ISTLE	ITINERANT	JABS	JACKPLANES
ISOSTACY	ISTLES	ITINERANTS	JACAL	JACKPOT
ISOSTASIES	IT	ITINERARIES	JACALES	JACKPOTS
ISOSTASY	ITALIC	ITINERARY	JACALS	JACKROLL
ISOSTATIC	ITALICISE	ITINERATE	JACAMAR	JACKROLLED
ISOSTERIC	ITALICISED	ITINERATED	JACAMARS	JACKROLLING
ISOTACH	ITALICISES	ITINERATES	JACANA	JACKROLLS
ISOTACHS	ITALICISING	ITINERATING	JACANAS	JACKS
ISOTACTIC	ITALICIZE	ITS	JACARANDA	JACKSCREW

JACKSCREWS	JAGGARY	JALOPS	JAPANIZE	JAROSITES
JACKSHAFT	JAGGED	JALOPY	JAPANIZED	JAROVIZE
JACKSHAFTS	JAGGEDER	JALOUSIE	JAPANIZES	JAROVIZED
JACKSMELT	JAGGEDEST	JALOUSIED	JAPANIZING	JAROVIZES
JACKSMELTS	JAGGEDLY	JALOUSIES	JAPANNED	JAROVIZING
JACKSNIPE	JAGGER	JAM	JAPANNER	JARRAH
JACKSNIPES	JAGGERIES	JAMB	JAPANNERS	JARRAHS
JACKSTAY	JAGGERS	JAMBALAYA	JAPANNING	JARRED
JACKSTAYS	JAGGERY	JAMBALAYAS	JAPANS	JARRING
JACKSTONE	JAGGHERIES	JAMBE	JAPE	JARRINGLY
JACKSTONES	JAGGHERY	JAMBEAU	JAPED	JARS
JACKSTRAW	JAGGIER	JAMBEAUX	JAPER	JARSFUL
JACKSTRAWS	JAGGIES	JAMBED	JAPERIES	JARVEY
JACKY	JAGGIEST	JAMBES	JAPERS	JARVEYS
JACOBIN	JAGGING	JAMBING	JAPERY	JASMIN
JACOBINS	JAGGS	JAMBOREE	JAPES	JASMINE
JACOBUS	JAGGY	JAMBOREES	JAPING	JASMINES
JACOBUSES	JAGLESS	JAMBS	JAPINGLY	JASMINS
JACONET	JAGRA	JAMLIKE	JAPONICA	JASPER
JACONETS	JAGRAS	JAMMABLE	JAPONICAS	JASPERS
JACQUARD	JAGS	JAMMED	JAR	JASPERY
JACQUARDS	JAGUAR	JAMMER	JARFUL	JASPILITE
JACQUERIE	JAGUARS	JAMMERS	JARFULS	JASPILITES
JACQUERIES	JAIL	JAMMIER	JARGON	JASSID
JACTATION	JAILABLE	JAMMIES	JARGONED	JASSIDS
JACTATIONS	JAILBAIT	JAMMIEST	JARGONEER	JATO
JACULATE	JAILBIRD	JAMMING	JARGONEERS	JATOS
JACULATED	JAILBIRDS	JAMMY	JARGONEL	JAUK
JACULATES	JAILBREAK	JAMPACKED	JARGONELS	JAUKED
JACULATING	JAILBREAKS	JAMS	JARGONING	JAUKING
JACUZZI	JAILED	JANE	JARGONISH	JAUKS
JACUZZIS	JAILER	JANES	JARGONIST	JAUNCE
JADE	JAILERS	JANGLE	JARGONISTS	JAUNCED
JADED	JAILHOUSE	JANGLED	JARGONIZE	JAUNCES
JADEDLY	JAILHOUSES	JANGLER	JARGONIZED	JAUNCING
JADEDNESS	JAILING	JANGLERS	JARGONIZES	JAUNDICE
JADEDNESSES	JAILOR	JANGLES	JARGONIZING	JAUNDICED
JADEITE	JAILORS	JANGLIER	JARGONS	JAUNDICES
JADEITES	JAILS	JANGLIEST	JARGONY	JAUNDICING
JADELIKE	JAKE	JANGLING	JARGOON	JAUNT
JADES	JAKES	JANGLY	JARGOONS	JAUNTED
JADING	JALAP	JANIFORM	JARHEAD	JAUNTIER
JADISH	JALAPENO	JANISARIES	JARHEADS	JAUNTIEST
JADISHLY	JALAPENOS	JANISARY	JARINA	JAUNTILY
JADITIC	JALAPIC	JANISSARIES	JARINAS	JAUNTING
JAEGER	JALAPIN	JANISSARY	JARL	JAUNTS
JAEGERS	JALAPINS	JANITOR	JARLDOM	JAUNTY
JAG	JALAPS	JANITORS	JARLDOMS	JAUP
JAGER	JALOP	JANIZARIES	JARLS	JAUPED
JAGERS	JALOPIES	JANIZARY	JARLSBERG	JAUPING
JAGG	JALOPPIES	JANTY	JARLSBERGS	JAUPS
JAGGARIES	JALOPPY	JAPAN	JAROSITE	JAVA

JAVAS	JAZZING	JELLIFIED	JERKIER	JESUITS
JAVELIN	JAZZLIKE	JELLIFIES	JERKIES	JET
JAVELINA	JAZZMAN	JELLIFY	JERKIEST	JETBEAD
JAVELINAS	JAZZMEN	JELLIFYING	JERKILY	JETBEADS
JAVELINED	JAZZY	JELLING	JERKIN	JETE
JAVELINING	JEALOUS	JELLO	JERKINESS	JETES
JAVELINS	JEALOUSIES	JELLOS	JERKINESSES	JETFOIL
JAW	JEALOUSLY	JELLS	JERKING	JETFOILS
JAWAN	JEALOUSY	JELLY	JERKINGLY	JETLAG
JAWANS	JEAN	JELLYBEAN	JERKINS	JETLAGS
JAWBONE	JEANED	JELLYBEANS	JERKS	JETLIKE
JAWBONED	JEANS	JELLYFISH	JERKWATER	JETLINER
JAWBONER	JEBEL	JELLYFISHES	JERKWATERS	JETLINERS
JAWBONERS	JEBELS	JELLYING	JERKY	JETON
JAWBONES	JEE	JELLYLIKE	JEROBOAM	JETONS
JAWBONING	JEED	JELLYROLL	JEROBOAMS	JETPORT
JAWBONINGS	JEEING	JELLYROLLS	JERREED	JETPORTS
JAWED	JEEP	JELUTONG	JERREEDS	JETS
JAWING	JEEPED	JELUTONGS	JERRICAN	JETSAM
JAWLESS	JEEPERS	JEMADAR	JERRICANS	JETSAMS
JAWLIKE	JEEPING	JEMADARS	JERRID	JETSOM
JAWLINE	JEEPNEY	JEMIDAR	JERRIDS	JETSOMS
JAWLINES	JEEPNEYS	JEMIDARS	JERRIES	JETSTREAM
JAWS	JEEPS	JEMMIED	JERRY	JETSTREAMS
JAY	JEER	JEMMIES	JERRYCAN	JETTED
JAYBIRD	JEERED	JEMMY	JERRYCANS	JETTIED
JAYBIRDS	JEERER	JEMMYING	JERSEY	JETTIER
JAYGEE	JEERERS	JENNET	JERSEYED	JETTIES
JAYGEES	JEERING	JENNETS	JERSEYS	JETTIEST
JAYHAWKER	JEERINGLY	JENNIES	JESS	JETTINESS
JAYHAWKERS	JEERS	JENNY	JESSAMINE	JETTINESSES
JAYS	JEES	JEON	JESSAMINES	JETTING
JAYVEE	JEEZ	JEOPARD	JESSANT	JETTISON
JAYVEES	JEFE	JEOPARDED	JESSE	JETTISONED
JAYWALK	JEFES	JEOPARDIES	JESSED	JETTISONING
JAYWALKED	JEHAD	JEOPARDING	JESSES	JETTISONS
JAYWALKER	JEHADS	JEOPARDS	JESSING	JETTON
JAYWALKERS	JEHU	JEOPARDY	JEST	JETTONS
JAYWALKING	JEHUS	JEQUIRITIES	JESTED	JETTY
JAYWALKS	JEJUNA	JEQUIRITY	JESTER	JETTYING
JAZZ	JEJUNAL	JERBOA	JESTERS	JETWAY
JAZZBO	JEJUNE	JERBOAS	JESTFUL	JETWAYS
JAZZBOS	JEJUNELY	JEREED	JESTING	JEU
JAZZED	JEJUNITIES	JEREEDS	JESTINGLY	JEUX
JAZZER	JEJUNITY	JEREMIAD	JESTINGS	JEW
JAZZERS	JEJUNUM	JEREMIADS	JESTS	JEWED
JAZZES	JELL	JERID	JESUIT	JEWEL
JAZZIER	JELLABA	JERIDS	JESUITIC	JEWELED
JAZZIEST	JELLABAS	JERK	JESUITISM	JEWELER
JAZZILY	JELLED	JERKED	JESUITISMS	JEWELERS
JAZZINESS	JELLIED	JERKER	JESUITRIES	JEWELFISH
JAZZINESSES	JELLIES	JERKERS	JESUITRY	JEWELFISHES

JEWELING
JEWELLED
JEWELLER
JEWELLERIES
JEWELLERS
JEWELLERY
JEWELLIKE
JEWELLING
JEWELRIES
JEWELRY
JEWELS
JEWELWEED
JEWELWEEDS
JEWFISH
JEWFISHES
JEWING
JEWS
JEZAIL
JEZAILS
JEZEBEL
JEZEBELS
JIAO
JIB
JIBB
JIBBED
JIBBER
JIBBERS
JIBBING
JIBBOOM
JIBBOOMS
JIBBS
JIBE
JIBED
JIBER
JIBERS
JIBES
JIBING
JIBINGLY
JIBS
JICAMA
JICAMAS
JIFF
JIFFIES
JIFFS
JIFFY
JIG
JIGABOO
JIGABOOS
JIGGED
JIGGER
JIGGERED
JIGGERING

JIGGERS
JIGGIER
JIGGIEST
JIGGING
JIGGISH
JIGGLE
JIGGLED
JIGGLES
JIGGLIER
JIGGLIEST
JIGGLING
JIGGLY
JIGGY
JIGLIKE
JIGS
JIGSAW
JIGSAWED
JIGSAWING
JIGSAWN
JIGSAWS
JIHAD
JIHADS
JILL
JILLION
JILLIONS
JILLS
JILT
JILTED
JILTER
JILTERS
JILTING
JILTS
JIMINY
JIMJAMS
JIMMIE
JIMMIED
JIMMIES
JIMMINY
JIMMY
JIMMYING
JIMP
JIMPER
JIMPEST
JIMPLY
JIMPY
JIN
JINGAL
JINGALL
JINGALLS
JINGALS
JINGKO
JINGKOES

JINGLE
JINGLED
JINGLER
JINGLERS
JINGLES
JINGLIER
JINGLIEST
JINGLING
JINGLY
JINGO
JINGOES
JINGOISH
JINGOISM
JINGOISMS
JINGOIST
JINGOISTS
JINK
JINKED
JINKER
JINKERS
JINKING
JINKS
JINN
JINNEE
JINNI
JINNIS
JINNS
JINRIKSHA
JINRIKSHAS
JINS
JINX
JINXED
JINXES
JINXING
JIPIJAPA
JIPIJAPAS
JISM
JISMS
JITNEY
JITNEYS
JITTER
JITTERBUG
JITTERBUGGED
JITTERBUGGING
JITTERBUGS
JITTERED
JITTERIER
JITTERIEST
JITTERING
JITTERS
JITTERY
JIUJITSU

JIUJITSUS
JIUJUTSU
JIUJUTSUS
JIVE
JIVEASS
JIVED
JIVER
JIVERS
JIVES
JIVEY
JIVIER
JIVIEST
JIVING
JIVY
JNANA
JNANAS
JO
JOANNES
JOB
JOBBED
JOBBER
JOBBERIES
JOBBERS
JOBBERY
JOBBING
JOBHOLDER
JOBHOLDERS
JOBLESS
JOBNAME
JOBNAMES
JOBS
JOCK
JOCKETTE
JOCKETTES
JOCKEY
JOCKEYED
JOCKEYING
JOCKEYISH
JOCKEYS
JOCKO
JOCKOS
JOCKS
JOCKSTRAP
JOCKSTRAPS
JOCOSE
JOCOSELY
JOCOSITIES
JOCOSITY
JOCULAR
JOCULARLY
JOCUND
JOCUNDITIES

JOCUNDITY
JOCUNDLY
JODHPUR
JODHPURS
JOE
JOES
JOEY
JOEYS
JOG
JOGGED
JOGGER
JOGGERS
JOGGING
JOGGINGS
JOGGLE
JOGGLED
JOGGLER
JOGGLERS
JOGGLES
JOGGLING
JOGS
JOHANNES
JOHN
JOHNBOAT
JOHNBOATS
JOHNNIE
JOHNNIES
JOHNNY
JOHNS
JOHNSON
JOHNSONS
JOIN
JOINABLE
JOINDER
JOINDERS
JOINED
JOINER
JOINERIES
JOINERS
JOINERY
JOINING
JOININGS
JOINS
JOINT
JOINTED
JOINTEDLY
JOINTER
JOINTERS
JOINTING
JOINTLESS
JOINTLY
JOINTRESS

JOINTRESSES	JOLT	JOTTING	JOWLINESSES	JUBILES
JOINTS	JOLTED	JOTTINGS	JOWLS	JUCO
JOINTURE	JOLTER	JOTTY	JOWLY	JUCOS
JOINTURED	JOLTERS	JOUAL	JOWS	JUDAS
JOINTURES	JOLTIER	JOUALS	JOY	JUDASES
JOINTURING	JOLTIEST	JOUK	JOYANCE	JUDDER
JOINTWEED	JOLTILY	JOUKED	JOYANCES	JUDDERED
JOINTWEEDS	JOLTING	JOUKING	JOYED	JUDDERING
JOINTWORM	JOLTINGLY	JOUKS	JOYFUL	JUDDERS
JOINTWORMS	JOLTS	JOULE	JOYFULLER	JUDGE
JOIST	JOLTY	JOULES	JOYFULLEST	JUDGED
JOISTED	JOMON	JOUNCE	JOYFULLY	JUDGEMENT
JOISTING	JONES	JOUNCED	JOYING	JUDGEMENTS
JOISTS	JONESED	JOUNCES	JOYLESS	JUDGER
JOJOBA	JONESES	JOUNCIER	JOYLESSLY	JUDGERS
JOJOBAS	JONESING	JOUNCIEST	JOYOUS	JUDGES
JOKE	JONGLEUR	JOUNCING	JOYOUSLY	JUDGESHIP
JOKED	JONGLEURS	JOUNCY	JOYPOP	JUDGESHIPS
JOKER	JONNYCAKE	JOURNAL	JOYPOPPED	JUDGING
JOKERS	JONNYCAKES	JOURNALED	JOYPOPPER	JUDGMATIC
JOKES	JONQUIL	JOURNALING	JOYPOPPERS	JUDGMENT
JOKESTER	JONQUILS	JOURNALS	JOYPOPPING	JUDGMENTS
JOKESTERS	JORAM	JOURNEY	JOYPOPS	JUDICABLE
JOKEY	JORAMS	JOURNEYED	JOYRIDDEN	JUDICIAL
JOKIER	JORDAN	JOURNEYER	JOYRIDE	JUDICIARIES
JOKIEST	JORDANS	JOURNEYERS	JOYRIDER	JUDICIARY
JOKILY	JORUM	JOURNEYING	JOYRIDERS	JUDICIOUS
JOKINESS	JORUMS	JOURNEYS	JOYRIDES	JUDO
JOKINESSES	JOSEPH	JOURNO	JOYRIDING	JUDOIST
JOKING	JOSEPHS	JOURNOS	JOYRIDINGS	JUDOISTS
JOKINGLY	JOSH	JOUST	JOYRODE	JUDOKA
JOKY	JOSHED	JOUSTED	JOYS	JUDOKAS
JOLE	JOSHER	JOUSTER	JOYSTICK	JUDOS
JOLES	JOSHERS	JOUSTERS	JOYSTICKS	JUG
JOLLIED	JOSHES	JOUSTING	JUBA	JUGA
JOLLIER	JOSHING	JOUSTS	JUBAS	JUGAL
JOLLIERS	JOSHINGLY	JOVIAL	JUBBAH	JUGATE
JOLLIES	JOSS	JOVIALITIES	JUBBAHS	JUGFUL
JOLLIEST	JOSSES	JOVIALITY	JUBE	JUGFULS
JOLLIFIED	JOSTLE	JOVIALLY	JUBES	JUGGED
JOLLIFIES	JOSTLED	JOVIALTIES	JUBHAH	JUGGING
JOLLIFY	JOSTLER	JOVIALTY	JUBHAHS	JUGGLE
JOLLIFYING	JOSTLERS	JOW	JUBILANCE	JUGGLED
JOLLILY	JOSTLES	JOWAR	JUBILANCES	JUGGLER
JOLLINESS	JOSTLING	JOWARS	JUBILANT	JUGGLERIES
JOLLINESSES	JOT	JOWED	JUBILATE	JUGGLERS
JOLLITIES	JOTA	JOWING	JUBILATED	JUGGLERY
JOLLITY	JOTAS	JOWL	JUBILATES	JUGGLES
JOLLY	JOTS	JOWLED	JUBILATING	JUGGLING
JOLLYBOAT	JOTTED	JOWLIER	JUBILE	JUGGLINGS
JOLLYBOATS	JOTTER	JOWLIEST	JUBILEE	JUGHEAD
JOLLYING	JOTTERS	JOWLINESS	JUBILEES	JUGHEADS

JUGS	JULIENNING	JUNIORITY	JURIST	JUVENALS
JUGSFUL	JUMBAL	JUNIORS	JURISTIC	JUVENILE
JUGULA	JUMBALS	JUNIPER	JURISTS	JUVENILES
JUGULAR	JUMBLE	JUNIPERS	JUROR	JUVENILIA
JUGULARS	JUMBLED	JUNK	JURORS	JUXTAPOSE
JUGULATE	JUMBLER	JUNKED	JURY	JUXTAPOSED
JUGULATED	JUMBLERS	JUNKER	JURYING	JUXTAPOSES
JUGULATES	JUMBLES	JUNKERS	JURYLESS	JUXTAPOSING
JUGULATING	JUMBLING	JUNKET	JURYMAN	
JUGULUM	JUMBO	JUNKETED	JURYMEN	
JUGUM	JUMBOS	JUNKETEER	JURYWOMAN	K
JUGUMS	JUMBUCK	JUNKETEERED	JURYWOMEN	
JUICE	JUMBUCKS	JUNKETEERING	JUS	
JUICED	JUMP	JUNKETEERS	JUSSIVE	KA
JUICEHEAD	JUMPABLE	JUNKETER	JUSSIVES	KAAS
JUICEHEADS	JUMPED	JUNKETERS	JUST	KAB
JUICELESS	JUMPER	JUNKETING	JUSTED	KABAB
JUICER	JUMPERS	JUNKETS	JUSTER	KABABS
JUICERS	JUMPIER	JUNKIE	JUSTERS	KABAKA
JUICES	JUMPIEST	JUNKIER	JUSTEST	KABAKAS
JUICIER	JUMPILY	JUNKIES	JUSTICE	KABALA
JUICIEST	JUMPINESS	JUNKIEST	JUSTICES	KABALAS
JUICILY	JUMPINESSES	JUNKING	JUSTICIAR	KABALISM
JUICINESS	JUMPING	JUNKMAN	JUSTICIARS	KABALISMS
JUICINESSES	JUMPINGLY	JUNKMEN	JUSTIFIED	KABALIST
JUICING	JUMPOFF	JUNKS	JUSTIFIER	KABALISTS
JUICY	JUMPOFFS	JUNKY	JUSTIFIERS	KABAR
JUJITSU	JUMPS	JUNKYARD	JUSTIFIES	KABARS
JUJITSUS	JUMPSUIT	JUNKYARDS	JUSTIFY	KABAYA
JUJU	JUMPSUITS	JUNTA	JUSTIFYING	KABAYAS
JUJUBE	JUMPY	JUNTAS	JUSTING	KABBALA
JUJUBES	JUN	JUNTO	JUSTLE	KABBALAH
JUJUISM	JUNCO	JUNTOS	JUSTLED	KABBALAHS
JUJUISMS	JUNCOES	JUPE	JUSTLES	KABBALAS
JUJUIST	JUNCOS	JUPES	JUSTLING	KABBALISM
JUJUISTS	JUNCTION	JUPON	JUSTLY	KABBALISMS
JUJUS	JUNCTIONS	JUPONS	JUSTNESS	KABBALIST
JUJUTSU	JUNCTURAL	JURA	JUSTNESSES	KABBALISTS
JUJUTSUS	JUNCTURE	JURAL	JUSTS	KABELJOU
JUKE	JUNCTURES	JURALLY	JUT	KABELJOUS
JUKEBOX	JUNGLE	JURANT	JUTE	KABIKI
JUKEBOXES	JUNGLED	JURANTS	JUTELIKE	KABIKIS
JUKED	JUNGLEGYM	JURASSIC	JUTES	KABOB
JUKES	JUNGLEGYMS	JURAT	JUTS	KABOBS
JUKING	JUNGLES	JURATORY	JUTTED	KABS
JUKU	JUNGLIER	JURATS	JUTTIED	KABUKI
JUKUS	JUNGLIEST	JUREL	JUTTIES	KABUKIS
JULEP	JUNGLY	JURELS	JUTTING	KACHINA
JULEPS	JUNIOR	JURIDIC	JUTTINGLY	KACHINAS
JULIENNE	JUNIORATE	JURIDICAL	JUTTY	KADDISH
JULIENNED	JUNIORATES	JURIED	JUTTYING	KADDISHES
JULIENNES	JUNIORITIES	JURIES	JUVENAL	KADDISHIM

KADI	KAKI	KAMACITES	KAPOK	KASHAS
KADIS	KAKIEMON	KAMALA	KAPOKS	KASHER
KAE	KAKIEMONS	KAMALAS	KAPPA	KASHERED
KAES	KAKIS	KAME	KAPPAS	KASHERING
KAF	KALAM	KAMES	KAPUT	KASHERS
KAFFIR	KALAMATA	KAMI	KAPUTT	KASHMIR
KAFFIRS	KALAMATAS	KAMIK	KARABINER	KASHMIRS
KAFFIYAH	KALAMS	KAMIKAZE	KARABINERS	KASHRUT
KAFFIYAHS	KALANCHOE	KAMIKAZES	KARAKUL	KASHRUTH
KAFFIYEH	KALANCHOES	KAMIKS	KARAKULS	KASHRUTHS
KAFFIYEHS	KALE	KAMPONG	KARAOKE	KASHRUTS
KAFIR	KALENDS	KAMPONGS	KARAOKES	KAT
KAFIRS	KALES	KAMSEEN	KARAT	KATA
KAFS	KALEWIFE	KAMSEENS	KARATE	KATABATIC
KAFTAN	KALEWIVES	KAMSIN	KARATEIST	KATAKANA
KAFTANS	KALEYARD	KAMSINS	KARATEISTS	KATAKANAS
KAGU	KALEYARDS	KANA	KARATES	KATAS
KAGUS	KALIAN	KANAKA	KARATS	KATCHINA
KAHUNA	KALIANS	KANAKAS	KARMA	KATCHINAS
KAHUNAS	KALIF	KANAMYCIN	KARMAS	KATCINA
KAIAK	KALIFATE	KANAMYCINS	KARMIC	KATCINAS
KAIAKS	KALIFATES	KANAS	KARN	KATHARSES
KAIF	KALIFS	KANBAN	KARNS	KATHARSIS
KAIFS	KALIMBA	KANBANS	KAROO	KATHODAL
KAIL	KALIMBAS	KANE	KAROOS	KATHODE
KAILS	KALIPH	KANES	KAROSS	KATHODES
KAILYARD	KALIPHATE	KANGAROO	KAROSSES	KATHODIC
KAILYARDS	KALIPHATES	KANGAROOS	KARROO	KATION
KAIN	KALIPHS	KANJI	KARROOS	KATIONS
KAINIT	KALIUM	KANJIS	KARST	KATS
KAINITE	KALIUMS	KANTAR	KARSTIC	KATSURA
KAINITES	KALLIDIN	KANTARS	KARSTS	KATSURAS
KAINITS	KALLIDINS	KANTELE	KART	KATYDID
KAINS	KALMIA	KANTELES	KARTING	KATYDIDS
KAIROMONE	KALMIAS	KANZU	KARTINGS	KAURI
KAIROMONES	KALONG	KANZUS	KARTS	KAURIES
KAISER	KALONGS	KAOLIANG	KARYOGAMIES	KAURIS
KAISERDOM	KALPA	KAOLIANGS	KARYOGAMY	KAURY
KAISERDOMS	KALPAC	KAOLIN	KARYOLOGIES	KAVA
KAISERIN	KALPACS	KAOLINE	KARYOLOGY	KAVAKAVA
KAISERINS	KALPAK	KAOLINES	KARYOSOME	KAVAKAVAS
KAISERISM	KALPAKS	KAOLINIC	KARYOSOMES	KAVAS
KAISERISMS	KALPAS	KAOLINITE	KARYOTIN	KAVASS
KAISERS	KALSOMINE	KAOLINITES	KARYOTINS	KAVASSES
KAJEPUT	KALSOMINED	KAOLINS	KARYOTYPE	KAY
KAJEPUTS	KALSOMINES	KAON	KARYOTYPED	KAYAK
KAKA	KALSOMINING	KAONIC	KARYOTYPES	KAYAKED
KAKAPO	KALYPTRA	KAONS	KARYOTYPING	KAYAKER
KAKAPOS	KALYPTRAS	KAPA	KAS	KAYAKERS
KAKAS	KAMAAINA	KAPAS	KASBAH	KAYAKING
KAKEMONO	KAMAAINAS	KAPH	KASBAHS	KAYAKINGS
KAKEMONOS	KAMACITE	KAPHS	KASHA	KAYAKS

KAYLES	KEEK	KEFFIYAH	KEMPS	KERATOSE
KAYO	KEEKED	KEFFIYAHS	KEMPT	KERATOSES
KAYOED	KEEKING	KEFFIYEH	KEN	KERATOSIC
KAYOES	KEEKS	KEFFIYEHS	KENAF	KERATOSIS
KAYOING	KEEL	KEFIR	KENAFS	KERATOTIC
KAYOS	KEELAGE	KEFIRS	KENCH	KERB
KAYS	KEELAGES	KEFS	KENCHES	KERBED
KAZACHKI	KEELBOAT	KEG	KENDO	KERBING
KAZACHOK	KEELBOATS	KEGELER	KENDOS	KERBS
KAZATSKI	KEELED	KEGELERS	KENNED	KERCHIEF
KAZATSKIES	KEELHALE	KEGGED	KENNEL	KERCHIEFS
KAZATSKY	KEELHALED	KEGGER	KENNELED	KERCHIEVES
KAZILLION	KEELHALES	KEGGERS	KENNELING	KERCHOO
KAZILLIONS	KEELHALING	KEGGING	KENNELLED	KERF
KAZOO	KEELHAUL	KEGLER	KENNELLING	KERFED
KAZOOS	KEELHAULED	KEGLERS	KENNELS	KERFING
KBAR	KEELHAULING	KEGLING	KENNING	KERFLOOEY
KBARS	KEELHAULS	KEGLINGS	KENNINGS	KERFS
KEA	KEELING	KEGS	KENO	KERFUFFLE
KEAS	KEELLESS	KEIR	KENOS	KERFUFFLES
KEBAB	KEELS	KEIRETSU	KENOSIS	KERMES
KEBABS	KEELSON	KEIRETSUS	KENOSISES	KERMESS
KEBAR	KEELSONS	KEIRS	KENOTIC	KERMESSE
KEBARS	KEEN	KEISTER	KENOTRON	KERMESSES
KEBBIE	KEENED	KEISTERS	KENOTRONS	KERMIS
KEBBIES	KEENER	KEITLOA	KENS	KERMISES
KEBBOCK	KEENERS	KEITLOAS	KENT	KERN
KEBBOCKS	KEENEST	KELEP	KENTE	KERNE
KEBBUCK	KEENING	KELEPS	KENTES	KERNED
KEBBUCKS	KEENLY	KELIM	KENTLEDGE	KERNEL
KEBLAH	KEENNESS	KELIMS	KENTLEDGES	KERNELED
KEBLAHS	KEENNESSES	KELLIES	KEP	KERNELING
KEBOB	KEENS	KELLY	KEPHALIN	KERNELLED
KEBOBS	KEEP	KELOID	KEPHALINS	KERNELLING
KECK	KEEPABLE	KELOIDAL	KEPI	KERNELLY
KECKED	KEEPER	KELOIDS	KEPIS	KERNELS
KECKING	KEEPERS	KELP	KEPPED	KERNES
KECKLE	KEEPING	KELPED	KEPPEN	KERNING
KECKLED	KEEPINGS	KELPIE	KEPPING	KERNITE
KECKLES	KEEPS	KELPIES	KEPS	KERNITES
KECKLING	KEEPSAKE	KELPING	KEPT	KERNS
KECKS	KEEPSAKES	KELPS	KERAMIC	KEROGEN
KEDDAH	KEESHOND	KELPY	KERAMICS	KEROGENS
KEDDAHS	KEESHONDEN	KELSON	KERATIN	KEROSENE
KEDGE	KEESHONDS	KELSONS	KERATINS	KEROSENES
KEDGED	KEESTER	KELT	KERATITIDES	KEROSINE
KEDGEREE	KEESTERS	KELTER	KERATITIS	KEROSINES
KEDGEREES	KEET	KELTERS	KERATITISES	KERPLUNK
KEDGES	KEETS	KELTS	KERATOID	KERPLUNKED
KEDGING	KEEVE	KELVIN	KERATOMA	KERPLUNKING
KEEF	KEEVES	KELVINS	KERATOMAS	KERPLUNKS
KEEFS	KEF	KEMP	KERATOMATA	KERRIA

KERRIAS	KEYED	KHAMSINS	KIBBUTZIM	KICKY
KERRIES	KEYHOLE	KHAN	KIBE	KID
KERRY	KEYHOLES	KHANATE	KIBEI	KIDDED
KERSEY	KEYING	KHANATES	KIBEIS	KIDDER
KERSEYS	KEYLESS	KHANS	KIBES	KIDDERS
KERYGMA	KEYNOTE	KHAPH	KIBITZ	KIDDIE
KERYGMAS	KEYNOTED	KHAPHS	KIBITZED	KIDDIES
KERYGMATA	KEYNOTER	KHAT	KIBITZER	KIDDING
KESTREL	KEYNOTERS	KHATS	KIBITZERS	KIDDINGLY
KESTRELS	KEYNOTES	KHAZEN	KIBITZES	KIDDISH
KETAMINE	KEYNOTING	KHAZENIM	KIBITZING	KIDDO
KETAMINES	KEYPAD	KHAZENS	KIBLA	KIDDOES
KETCH	KEYPADS	KHEDA	KIBLAH	KIDDOS
KETCHES	KEYPAL	KHEDAH	KIBLAHS	KIDDUSH
KETCHUP	KEYPALS	KHEDAHS	KIBLAS	KIDDUSHES
KETCHUPS	KEYPUNCH	KHEDAS	KIBOSH	KIDDY
KETENE	KEYPUNCHED	KHEDIVAL	KIBOSHED	KIDLIKE
KETENES	KEYPUNCHES	KHEDIVE	KIBOSHES	KIDNAP
KETO	KEYPUNCHING	KHEDIVES	KIBOSHING	KIDNAPED
KETOGENIC	KEYS	KHEDIVIAL	KICK	KIDNAPEE
KETOL	KEYSET	KHET	KICKABLE	KIDNAPEES
KETOLS	KEYSETS	KHETH	KICKBACK	KIDNAPER
KETONE	KEYSTER	KHETHS	KICKBACKS	KIDNAPERS
KETONEMIA	KEYSTERS	KHETS	KICKBALL	KIDNAPING
KETONEMIAS	KEYSTONE	KHI	KICKBALLS	KIDNAPPED
KETONES	KEYSTONES	KHIRKAH	KICKBOARD	KIDNAPPEE
KETONIC	KEYSTROKE	KHIRKAHS	KICKBOARDS	KIDNAPPEES
KETONURIA	KEYSTROKED	KHIS	KICKBOX	KIDNAPPER
KETONURIAS	KEYSTROKES	KHOUM	KICKBOXED	KIDNAPPERS
KETOSE	KEYSTROKING	KHOUMS	KICKBOXER	KIDNAPPING
KETOSES	KEYWAY	KI	KICKBOXERS	KIDNAPS
KETOSIS	KEYWAYS	KIANG	KICKBOXES	KIDNEY
KETOTIC	KEYWORD	KIANGS	KICKBOXING	KIDNEYS
KETTLE	KEYWORDS	KIAUGH	KICKED	KIDS
KETTLES	KHADDAR	KIAUGHS	KICKER	KIDSKIN
KEVEL	KHADDARS	KIBBE	KICKERS	KIDSKINS
KEVELS	KHADI	KIBBEH	KICKIER	KIDVID
KEVIL	KHADIS	KIBBEHS	KICKIEST	KIDVIDS
KEVILS	KHAF	KIBBES	KICKING	KIEF
KEWPIE	KHAFS	KIBBI	KICKOFF	KIEFS
KEWPIES	KHAKI	KIBBIS	KICKOFFS	KIELBASA
KEX	KHAKILIKE	KIBBITZ	KICKS	KIELBASAS
KEXES	KHAKIS	KIBBITZED	KICKSHAW	KIELBASI
KEY	KHALIF	KIBBITZER	KICKSHAWS	KIELBASY
KEYBOARD	KHALIFA	KIBBITZERS	KICKSTAND	KIER
KEYBOARDED	KHALIFAS	KIBBITZES	KICKSTANDS	KIERS
KEYBOARDING	KHALIFATE	KIBBITZING	KICKSTART	KIESELGUR
KEYBOARDS	KHALIFATES	KIBBLE	KICKSTARTED	KIESELGURS
KEYBUTTON	KHALIFS	KIBBLED	KICKSTARTING	KIESERITE
KEYBUTTONS	KHAMSEEN	KIBBLES	KICKSTARTS	KIESERITES
KEYCARD	KHAMSEENS	KIBBLING	KICKUP	KIESTER
KEYCARDS	KHAMSIN	KIBBUTZ	KICKUPS	KIESTERS

KIF	KILOGRAM	KINDEST	KINGING	KIPPEN
KIFS	KILOGRAMS	KINDLE	KINGLESS	KIPPER
KIKE	KILOHERTZ	KINDLED	KINGLET	KIPPERED
KIKES	KILOHERTZES	KINDLER	KINGLETS	KIPPERER
KILDERKIN	KILOJOULE	KINDLERS	KINGLIER	KIPPERERS
KILDERKINS	KILOJOULES	KINDLES	KINGLIEST	KIPPERING
KILIM	KILOLITER	KINDLESS	KINGLIKE	KIPPERS
KILIMS	KILOLITERS	KINDLIER	KINGLY	KIPPING
KILL	KILOLITRE	KINDLIEST	KINGMAKER	KIPS
KILLABLE	KILOLITRES	KINDLING	KINGMAKERS	KIPSKIN
KILLDEE	KILOMETER	KINDLINGS	KINGPIN	KIPSKINS
KILLDEER	KILOMETERS	KINDLY	KINGPINS	KIR
KILLDEERS	KILOMETRE	KINDNESS	KINGPOST	KIRIGAMI
KILLDEES	KILOMETRES	KINDNESSES	KINGPOSTS	KIRIGAMIS
KILLED	KILOMOLE	KINDRED	KINGS	KIRK
KILLER	KILOMOLES	KINDREDS	KINGSHIP	KIRKMAN
KILLERS	KILORAD	KINDS	KINGSHIPS	KIRKMEN
KILLICK	KILORADS	KINE	KINGSIDE	KIRKS
KILLICKS	KILOS	KINEMA	KINGSIDES	KIRMESS
KILLIE	KILOTON	KINEMAS	KINGSNAKE	KIRMESSES
KILLIES	KILOTONS	KINEMATIC	KINGSNAKES	KIRN
KILLIFISH	KILOVOLT	KINES	KINGWOOD	KIRNED
KILLIFISHES	KILOVOLTS	KINESCOPE	KINGWOODS	KIRNING
KILLING	KILOWATT	KINESCOPED	KININ	KIRNS
KILLINGLY	KILOWATTS	KINESCOPES	KININS	KIRS
KILLINGS	KILT	KINESCOPING	KINK	KIRSCH
KILLJOY	KILTED	KINESES	KINKAJOU	KIRSCHES
KILLJOYS	KILTER	KINESIC	KINKAJOUS	KIRTLE
KILLOCK	KILTERS	KINESICS	KINKED	KIRTLED
KILLOCKS	KILTIE	KINESIS	KINKIER	KIRTLES
KILLS	KILTIES	KINETIC	KINKIEST	KIS
KILN	KILTING	KINETICS	KINKILY	KISHKA
KILNED	KILTINGS	KINETIN	KINKINESS	KISHKAS
KILNING	KILTLIKE	KINETINS	KINKINESSES	KISHKE
KILNS	KILTS	KINFOLK	KINKING	KISHKES
KILO	KILTY	KINFOLKS	KINKS	KISMAT
KILOBAR	KIMCHEE	KING	KINKY	KISMATS
KILOBARS	KIMCHEES	KINGBIRD	KINLESS	KISMET
KILOBASE	KIMCHI	KINGBIRDS	KINO	KISMETIC
KILOBASES	KIMCHIS	KINGBOLT	KINOS	KISMETS
KILOBAUD	KIMONO	KINGBOLTS	KINS	KISS
KILOBAUDS	KIMONOED	KINGCRAFT	KINSFOLK	KISSABLE
KILOBIT	KIMONOS	KINGCRAFTS	KINSHIP	KISSABLY
KILOBITS	KIN	KINGCUP	KINSHIPS	KISSED
KILOBYTE	KINA	KINGCUPS	KINSMAN	KISSER
KILOBYTES	KINARA	KINGDOM	KINSMEN	KISSERS
KILOCURIE	KINARAS	KINGDOMS	KINSWOMAN	KISSES
KILOCURIES	KINAS	KINGED	KINSWOMEN	KISSING
KILOCYCLE	KINASE	KINGFISH	KIOSK	KISSY
KILOCYCLES	KINASES	KINGFISHES	KIOSKS	KIST
KILOGAUSS	KIND	KINGHOOD	KIP	KISTFUL
KILOGAUSSES	KINDER	KINGHOODS	KIPPED	KISTFULS

KISTS	KIVAS	KLUTZIEST	KNEEHOLE	KNOB
KIT	KIWI	KLUTZY	KNEEHOLES	KNOBBED
KITBAG	KIWIFRUIT	KLYSTRON	KNEEING	KNOBBIER
KITBAGS	KIWIFRUITS	KLYSTRONS	KNEEL	KNOBBIEST
KITCHEN	KIWIS	KNACK	KNEELED	KNOBBLIER
KITCHENET	KLATCH	KNACKED	KNEELER	KNOBBLIEST
KITCHENETS	KLATCHES	KNACKER	KNEELERS	KNOBBLY
KITCHENS	KLATSCH	KNACKERED	KNEELING	KNOBBY
KITE	KLATSCHES	KNACKERIES	KNEELS	KNOBLIKE
KITED	KLAVERN	KNACKERS	KNEEPAD	KNOBS
KITELIKE	KLAVERNS	KNACKERY	KNEEPADS	KNOCK
KITER	KLAXON	KNACKING	KNEEPAN	KNOCKDOWN
KITERS	KLAXONS	KNACKS	KNEEPANS	KNOCKDOWNS
KITES	KLEAGLE	KNAP	KNEEPIECE	KNOCKED
KITH	KLEAGLES	KNAPPED	KNEEPIECES	KNOCKER
KITHARA	KLEENEX	KNAPPER	KNEES	KNOCKERS
KITHARAS	KLEENEXES	KNAPPERS	KNEESIES	KNOCKING
KITHE	KLEPHT	KNAPPING	KNEESOCK	KNOCKLESS
KITHED	KLEPHTIC	KNAPS	KNEESOCKS	KNOCKOFF
KITHES	KLEPHTS	KNAPSACK	KNELL	KNOCKOFFS
KITHING	KLEPTO	KNAPSACKS	KNELLED	KNOCKOUT
KITHS	KLEPTOS	KNAPWEED	KNELLING	KNOCKOUTS
KITING	KLEZMER	KNAPWEEDS	KNELLS	KNOCKS
KITLING	KLEZMERS	KNAR	KNELT	KNOLL
KITLINGS	KLEZMORIM	KNARRED	KNESSET	KNOLLED
KITS	KLICK	KNARRY	KNESSETS	KNOLLER
KITSCH	KLICKS	KNARS	KNEW	KNOLLERS
KITSCHES	KLIK	KNAUR	KNICKERS	KNOLLING
KITSCHIFIED	KLIKS	KNAURS	KNIFE	KNOLLS
KITSCHIFIES	KLISTER	KNAVE	KNIFED	KNOLLY
KITSCHIFY	KLISTERS	KNAVERIES	KNIFELIKE	KNOP
KITSCHIFYING	KLONDIKE	KNAVERY	KNIFER	KNOPPED
KITSCHY	KLONDIKES	KNAVES	KNIFERS	KNOPS
KITTED	KLONG	KNAVISH	KNIFES	KNOSP
KITTEL	KLONGS	KNAVISHLY	KNIFING	KNOSPS
KITTEN	KLOOF	KNAWE	KNIGHT	KNOT
KITTENED	KLOOFS	KNAWEL	KNIGHTED	KNOTGRASS
KITTENING	KLUDGE	KNAWELS	KNIGHTING	KNOTGRASSES
KITTENISH	KLUDGED	KNAWES	KNIGHTLY	KNOTHOLE
KITTENS	KLUDGES	KNEAD	KNIGHTS	KNOTHOLES
KITTIES	KLUDGEY	KNEADABLE	KNISH	KNOTLESS
KITTING	KLUDGIER	KNEADED	KNISHES	KNOTLIKE
KITTIWAKE	KLUDGIEST	KNEADER	KNIT	KNOTS
KITTIWAKES	KLUDGING	KNEADERS	KNITS	KNOTTED
KITTLE	KLUDGY	KNEADING	KNITTABLE	KNOTTER
KITTLED	KLUGE	KNEADS	KNITTED	KNOTTERS
KITTLER	KLUGED	KNEE	KNITTER	KNOTTIER
KITTLES	KLUGES	KNEECAP	KNITTERS	KNOTTIEST
KITTLEST	KLUGING	KNEECAPPED	KNITTING	KNOTTILY
KITTLING	KLUTZ	KNEECAPPING	KNITTINGS	KNOTTING
KITTY	KLUTZES	KNEECAPS	KNITWEAR	KNOTTINGS
KIVA	KLUTZIER	KNEED	KNIVES	KNOTTY

KNOTWEED	KOBS	KOODOOS	KOTOWS	KRISES
KNOTWEEDS	KOEL	KOOK	KOUMIS	KRONA
KNOUT	KOELS	KOOKIE	KOUMISES	KRONE
KNOUTED	KOHL	KOOKIER	KOUMISS	KRONEN
KNOUTING	KOHLRABI	KOOKIEST	KOUMISSES	KRONER
KNOUTS	KOHLRABIES	KOOKINESS	KOUMYS	KRONOR
KNOW	KOHLS	KOOKINESSES	KOUMYSES	KRONUR
KNOWABLE	KOI	KOOKS	KOUMYSS	KROON
KNOWER	KOINE	KOOKY	KOUMYSSES	KROONI
KNOWERS	KOINES	KOP	KOUPREY	KROONS
KNOWING	KOIS	KOPECK	KOUPREYS	KRUBI
KNOWINGER	KOJI	KOPECKS	KOUROI	KRUBIS
KNOWINGEST	KOJIS	KOPEK	KOUROS	KRUBUT
KNOWINGLY	KOKANEE	KOPEKS	KOUSSO	KRUBUTS
KNOWINGS	KOKANEES	KOPH	KOUSSOS	KRULLER
KNOWLEDGE	KOLA	KOPHS	KOWTOW	KRULLERS
KNOWLEDGES	KOLACKY	KOPIYKA	KOWTOWED	KRUMHORN
KNOWN	KOLAS	KOPIYKAS	KOWTOWER	KRUMHORNS
KNOWNS	KOLBASI	KOPJE	KOWTOWERS	KRUMKAKE
KNOWS	KOLBASIS	KOPJES	KOWTOWING	KRUMKAKES
KNUBBIER	KOLBASSI	KOPPA	KOWTOWS	KRUMMHOLZ
KNUBBIEST	KOLBASSIS	KOPPAS	KRAAL	KRUMMHORN
KNUBBY	KOLHOZ	KOPPIE	KRAALED	KRUMMHORNS
KNUCKLE	KOLHOZES	KOPPIES	KRAALING	KRYOLITE
KNUCKLED	KOLHOZY	KOPS	KRAALS	KRYOLITES
KNUCKLER	KOLINSKI	KOR	KRAFT	KRYOLITH
KNUCKLERS	KOLINSKIES	KORA	KRAFTS	KRYOLITHS
KNUCKLES	KOLINSKY	KORAI	KRAIT	KRYPTON
KNUCKLIER	KOLKHOS	KORAS	KRAITS	KRYPTONS
KNUCKLIEST	KOLKHOSES	KORAT	KRAKEN	KUCHEN
KNUCKLING	KOLKHOSY	KORATS	KRAKENS	KUCHENS
KNUCKLY	KOLKHOZ	KORE	KRATER	KUDO
KNUR	KOLKHOZES	KORMA	KRATERS	KUDOS
KNURL	KOLKHOZY	KORMAS	KRAUT	KUDU
KNURLED	KOLKOZ	KORS	KRAUTS	KUDUS
KNURLIER	KOLKOZES	KORUN	KREEP	KUDZU
KNURLIEST	KOLKOZY	KORUNA	KREEPS	KUDZUS
KNURLING	KOLO	KORUNAS	KREMLIN	KUE
KNURLS	KOLOS	KORUNY	KREMLINS	KUES
KNURLY	KOMATIK	KOS	KREPLACH	KUFI
KNURS	KOMATIKS	KOSHER	KREPLECH	KUFIS
KOA	KOMBU	KOSHERED	KREUTZER	KUGEL
KOALA	KOMBUS	KOSHERING	KREUTZERS	KUGELS
KOALAS	KOMONDOR	KOSHERS	KREUZER	KUKRI
KOAN	KOMONDOROCK	KOSS	KREUZERS	KUKRIS
KOANS	KOMONDOROK	KOTO	KREWE	KULAK
KOAS	KOMONDORS	KOTOS	KREWES	KULAKI
KOB	KONK	KOTOW	KRILL	KULAKS
KOBO	KONKED	KOTOWED	KRILLS	KULTUR
KOBOLD	KONKING	KOTOWER	KRIMMER	KULTURS
KOBOLDS	KONKS	KOTOWERS	KRIMMERS	KUMISS
KOBOS	KOODOO	KOTOWING	KRIS	KUMISSES

KUMMEL	KYACK	LAB	LABOURING	LACK
KUMMELS	KYACKS	LABARA	LABOURS	LACKADAY
KUMQUAT	KYAK	LABARUM	LABRA	LACKED
KUMQUATS	KYAKS	LABARUMS	LABRADOR	LACKER
KUMYS	KYANISE	LABDANUM	LABRADORS	LACKERED
KUMYSES	KYANISED	LABDANUMS	LABRET	LACKERING
KUNA	KYANISES	LABEL	LABRETS	LACKERS
KUNDALINI	KYANISING	LABELABLE	LABROID	LACKEY
KUNDALINIS	KYANITE	LABELED	LABROIDS	LACKEYED
KUNE	KYANITES	LABELER	LABRUM	LACKEYING
KUNZITE	KYANIZE	LABELERS	LABRUMS	LACKEYS
KUNZITES	KYANIZED	LABELING	LABRUSCA	LACKING
KURBASH	KYANIZES	LABELLA	LABS	LACKS
KURBASHED	KYANIZING	LABELLATE	LABURNUM	LACONIC
KURBASHES	KYAR	LABELLED	LABURNUMS	LACONISM
KURBASHING	KYARS	LABELLER	LABYRINTH	LACONISMS
KURGAN	KYAT	LABELLERS	LABYRINTHS	LACQUER
KURGANS	KYATS	LABELLING	LAC	LACQUERED
KURRAJONG	KYBOSH	LABELLOID	LACCOLITH	LACQUERER
KURRAJONGS	KYBOSHED	LABELLUM	LACCOLITHS	LACQUERERS
KURTA	KYBOSHES	LABELS	LACE	LACQUERING
KURTAS	KYBOSHING	LABIA	LACED	LACQUERS
KURTOSES	KYE	LABIAL	LACELESS	LACQUEY
KURTOSIS	KYES	LABIALITIES	LACELIKE	LACQUEYED
KURTOSISES	KYLIKES	LABIALITY	LACER	LACQUEYING
KURU	KYLIX	LABIALIZE	LACERABLE	LACQUEYS
KURUS	KYMOGRAM	LABIALIZED	LACERATE	LACRIMAL
KUSSO	KYMOGRAMS	LABIALIZES	LACERATED	LACRIMALS
KUSSOS	KYMOGRAPH	LABIALIZING	LACERATES	LACROSSE
KUVASZ	KYMOGRAPHS	LABIALLY	LACERATING	LACROSSES
KUVASZOK	KYPHOSES	LABIALS	LACERS	LACS
KVAS	KYPHOSIS	LABIATE	LACERTID	LACTAM
KVASES	KYPHOTIC	LABIATED	LACERTIDS	LACTAMS
KVASS	KYRIE	LABIATES	LACES	LACTARY
KVASSES	KYRIES	LABILE	LACEWING	LACTASE
KVELL	KYTE	LABILITIES	LACEWINGS	LACTASES
KVELLED	KYTES	LABILITY	LACEWOOD	LACTATE
KVELLING	KYTHE	LABIUM	LACEWOODS	LACTATED
KVELLS	KYTHED	LABOR	LACEWORK	LACTATES
KVETCH	KYTHES	LABORED	LACEWORKS	LACTATING
KVETCHED	KYTHING	LABOREDLY	LACEY	LACTATION
KVETCHER		LABORER	LACHES	LACTATIONS
KVETCHERS		LABORERS	LACHRYMAL	LACTEAL
KVETCHES	**L**	LABORING	LACHRYMALS	LACTEALLY
KVETCHIER		LABORIOUS	LACIER	LACTEALS
KVETCHIEST		LABORITE	LACIEST	LACTEAN
KVETCHING	LA	LABORITES	LACILY	LACTEOUS
KVETCHY	LAAGER	LABORS	LACINESS	LACTIC
KWACHA	LAAGERED	LABOUR	LACINESSES	LACTONE
KWACHAS	LAAGERING	LABOURED	LACING	LACTONES
KWANZA	LAAGERS	LABOURER	LACINGS	LACTONIC
KWANZAS	LAARI	LABOURERS	LACINIATE	LACTOSE

LACTOSES	LADS	LAGUNE	LAKESHORES	LAMBIE
LACUNA	LADY	LAGUNES	LAKESIDE	LAMBIER
LACUNAE	LADYBIRD	LAHAR	LAKESIDES	LAMBIES
LACUNAL	LADYBIRDS	LAHARS	LAKH	LAMBIEST
LACUNAR	LADYBUG	LAIC	LAKHS	LAMBING
LACUNARIA	LADYBUGS	LAICAL	LAKIER	LAMBKILL
LACUNARS	LADYFISH	LAICALLY	LAKIEST	LAMBKILLS
LACUNARY	LADYFISHES	LAICH	LAKING	LAMBKIN
LACUNAS	LADYHOOD	LAICHS	LAKINGS	LAMBKINS
LACUNATE	LADYHOODS	LAICISE	LAKY	LAMBLIKE
LACUNE	LADYISH	LAICISED	LALIQUE	LAMBRUSCO
LACUNES	LADYKIN	LAICISES	LALIQUES	LAMBRUSCOS
LACUNOSE	LADYKINS	LAICISING	LALL	LAMBS
LACY	LADYLIKE	LAICISM	LALLAN	LAMBSKIN
LAD	LADYLOVE	LAICISMS	LALLAND	LAMBSKINS
LADANUM	LADYLOVES	LAICIZE	LALLANDS	LAMBY
LADANUMS	LADYPALM	LAICIZED	LALLANS	LAME
LADDER	LADYPALMS	LAICIZES	LALLATION	LAMEBRAIN
LADDERED	LADYSHIP	LAICIZING	LALLATIONS	LAMEBRAINS
LADDERING	LADYSHIPS	LAICS	LALLED	LAMED
LADDERS	LAETRILE	LAID	LALLING	LAMEDH
LADDIE	LAETRILES	LAIGH	LALLS	LAMEDHS
LADDIES	LAEVO	LAIGHS	LALLYGAG	LAMEDS
LADDISH	LAG	LAIN	LALLYGAGGED	LAMELLA
LADE	LAGAN	LAIR	LALLYGAGGING	LAMELLAE
LADED	LAGANS	LAIRD	LALLYGAGS	LAMELLAR
LADEN	LAGEND	LAIRDLY	LAM	LAMELLAS
LADENED	LAGENDS	LAIRDS	LAMA	LAMELLATE
LADENING	LAGER	LAIRDSHIP	LAMAS	LAMELLOSE
LADENS	LAGERED	LAIRDSHIPS	LAMASERIES	LAMELY
LADER	LAGERING	LAIRED	LAMASERY	LAMENESS
LADERS	LAGERS	LAIRING	LAMB	LAMENESSES
LADES	LAGGARD	LAIRS	LAMBADA	LAMENT
LADHOOD	LAGGARDLY	LAITANCE	LAMBADAS	LAMENTED
LADHOODS	LAGGARDS	LAITANCES	LAMBAST	LAMENTER
LADIES	LAGGED	LAITH	LAMBASTE	LAMENTERS
LADING	LAGGER	LAITHLY	LAMBASTED	LAMENTING
LADINGS	LAGGERS	LAITIES	LAMBASTES	LAMENTS
LADINO	LAGGING	LAITY	LAMBASTING	LAMER
LADINOS	LAGGINGS	LAKE	LAMBASTS	LAMES
LADLE	LAGNAPPE	LAKEBED	LAMBDA	LAMEST
LADLED	LAGNAPPES	LAKEBEDS	LAMBDAS	LAMIA
LADLEFUL	LAGNIAPPE	LAKED	LAMBDOID	LAMIAE
LADLEFULS	LAGNIAPPES	LAKEFRONT	LAMBED	LAMIAS
LADLER	LAGOMORPH	LAKEFRONTS	LAMBENCIES	LAMINA
LADLERS	LAGOMORPHS	LAKELIKE	LAMBENCY	LAMINABLE
LADLES	LAGOON	LAKEPORT	LAMBENT	LAMINAE
LADLING	LAGOONAL	LAKEPORTS	LAMBENTLY	LAMINAL
LADRON	LAGOONS	LAKER	LAMBER	LAMINALS
LADRONE	LAGS	LAKERS	LAMBERS	LAMINAR
LADRONES	LAGUNA	LAKES	LAMBERT	LAMINARIA
LADRONS	LAGUNAS	LAKESHORE	LAMBERTS	LAMINARIAS

LAMINARIN	LAMPYRIDS	LANDLERS	LANGRAGES	LANOLINS
LAMINARINS	LAMS	LANDLESS	LANGREL	LANOSE
LAMINARY	LAMSTER	LANDLINE	LANGRELS	LANOSITIES
LAMINAS	LAMSTERS	LANDLINES	LANGRIDGE	LANOSITY
LAMINATE	LANAI	LANDLOPER	LANGRIDGES	LANTANA
LAMINATED	LANAIS	LANDLOPERS	LANGSHAN	LANTANAS
LAMINATES	LANATE	LANDLORD	LANGSHANS	LANTERN
LAMINATING	LANATED	LANDLORDS	LANGSYNE	LANTERNS
LAMINATOR	LANCE	LANDMAN	LANGSYNES	LANTHANON
LAMINATORS	LANCED	LANDMARK	LANGUAGE	LANTHANONS
LAMING	LANCELET	LANDMARKED	LANGUAGES	LANTHANUM
LAMININ	LANCELETS	LANDMARKING	LANGUE	LANTHANUMS
LAMININS	LANCER	LANDMARKS	LANGUES	LANTHORN
LAMINITIS	LANCERS	LANDMASS	LANGUET	LANTHORNS
LAMINITISES	LANCES	LANDMASSES	LANGUETS	LANUGO
LAMINOSE	LANCET	LANDMEN	LANGUETTE	LANUGOS
LAMINOUS	LANCETED	LANDOWNER	LANGUETTES	LANYARD
LAMISTER	LANCETS	LANDOWNERS	LANGUID	LANYARDS
LAMISTERS	LANCEWOOD	LANDS	LANGUIDLY	LAOGAI
LAMMED	LANCEWOODS	LANDSCAPE	LANGUISH	LAOGAIS
LAMMING	LANCIERS	LANDSCAPED	LANGUISHED	LAP
LAMP	LANCIFORM	LANDSCAPES	LANGUISHES	LAPBOARD
LAMPAD	LANCINATE	LANDSCAPING	LANGUISHING	LAPBOARDS
LAMPADS	LANCINATED	LANDSIDE	LANGUOR	LAPDOG
LAMPAS	LANCINATES	LANDSIDES	LANGUORS	LAPDOGS
LAMPASES	LANCINATING	LANDSKIP	LANGUR	LAPEL
LAMPBLACK	LANCING	LANDSKIPS	LANGURS	LAPELED
LAMPBLACKS	LAND	LANDSLEIT	LANIARD	LAPELLED
LAMPED	LANDAU	LANDSLID	LANIARDS	LAPELS
LAMPERS	LANDAULET	LANDSLIDDEN	LANIARIES	LAPFUL
LAMPERSES	LANDAULETS	LANDSLIDE	LANIARY	LAPFULS
LAMPING	LANDAUS	LANDSLIDES	LANITAL	LAPIDARIES
LAMPION	LANDED	LANDSLIDING	LANITALS	LAPIDARY
LAMPIONS	LANDER	LANDSLIP	LANK	LAPIDATE
LAMPLIGHT	LANDERS	LANDSLIPS	LANKER	LAPIDATED
LAMPLIGHTS	LANDFALL	LANDSMAN	LANKEST	LAPIDATES
LAMPOON	LANDFALLS	LANDSMEN	LANKIER	LAPIDATING
LAMPOONED	LANDFILL	LANDWARD	LANKIEST	LAPIDES
LAMPOONER	LANDFILLED	LANDWARDS	LANKILY	LAPIDIFIED
LAMPOONERS	LANDFILLING	LANE	LANKINESS	LAPIDIFIES
LAMPOONING	LANDFILLS	LANELY	LANKINESSES	LAPIDIFY
LAMPOONS	LANDFORM	LANES	LANKLY	LAPIDIFYING
LAMPPOST	LANDFORMS	LANEWAY	LANKNESS	LAPIDIST
LAMPPOSTS	LANDGRAB	LANEWAYS	LANKNESSES	LAPIDISTS
LAMPREY	LANDGRABS	LANG	LANKY	LAPILLI
LAMPREYS	LANDGRAVE	LANGLAUF	LANNER	LAPILLUS
LAMPS	LANDGRAVES	LANGLAUFS	LANNERET	LAPIN
LAMPSHADE	LANDING	LANGLEY	LANNERETS	LAPINS
LAMPSHADES	LANDINGS	LANGLEYS	LANNERS	LAPIS
LAMPSHELL	LANDLADIES	LANGOUSTE	LANOLIN	LAPISES
LAMPSHELLS	LANDLADY	LANGOUSTES	LANOLINE	LAPPED
LAMPYRID	LANDLER	LANGRAGE	LANOLINES	LAPPER

LAPPERED	LARES	LARVA	LASSOES	LATERALLY
LAPPERING	LARGANDO	LARVAE	LASSOING	LATERALS
LAPPERS	LARGE	LARVAL	LASSOS	LATERBORN
LAPPET	LARGELY	LARVAS	LAST	LATERBORNS
LAPPETED	LARGENESS	LARVICIDE	LASTBORN	LATERITE
LAPPETS	LARGENESSES	LARVICIDES	LASTBORNS	LATERITES
LAPPING	LARGER	LARYNGAL	LASTED	LATERITIC
LAPS	LARGES	LARYNGALS	LASTER	LATERIZE
LAPSABLE	LARGESS	LARYNGEAL	LASTERS	LATERIZED
LAPSE	LARGESSE	LARYNGEALS	LASTING	LATERIZES
LAPSED	LARGESSES	LARYNGES	LASTINGLY	LATERIZING
LAPSER	LARGEST	LARYNX	LASTINGS	LATEST
LAPSERS	LARGHETTO	LARYNXES	LASTLY	LATESTS
LAPSES	LARGHETTOS	LAS	LASTS	LATEWOOD
LAPSIBLE	LARGISH	LASAGNA	LAT	LATEWOODS
LAPSING	LARGO	LASAGNAS	LATAKIA	LATEX
LAPSTRAKE	LARGOS	LASAGNE	LATAKIAS	LATEXES
LAPSTREAK	LARI	LASAGNES	LATCH	LATH
LAPSUS	LARIAT	LASCAR	LATCHED	LATHE
LAPTOP	LARIATED	LASCARS	LATCHES	LATHED
LAPTOPS	LARIATING	LASE	LATCHET	LATHER
LAPWING	LARIATS	LASED	LATCHETS	LATHERED
LAPWINGS	LARINE	LASER	LATCHING	LATHERER
LAR	LARIS	LASERDISC	LATCHKEY	LATHERERS
LARBOARD	LARK	LASERDISCS	LATCHKEYS	LATHERING
LARBOARDS	LARKED	LASERDISK	LATE	LATHERS
LARCENER	LARKER	LASERDISKS	LATECOMER	LATHERY
LARCENERS	LARKERS	LASERS	LATECOMERS	LATHES
LARCENIES	LARKIER	LASES	LATED	LATHI
LARCENIST	LARKIEST	LASH	LATEEN	LATHIER
LARCENISTS	LARKINESS	LASHED	LATEENER	LATHIEST
LARCENOUS	LARKINESSES	LASHER	LATEENERS	LATHING
LARCENY	LARKING	LASHERS	LATEENS	LATHINGS
LARCH	LARKISH	LASHES	LATELY	LATHIS
LARCHEN	LARKS	LASHING	LATEN	LATHS
LARCHES	LARKSOME	LASHINGS	LATENCIES	LATHWORK
LARD	LARKSPUR	LASHINS	LATENCY	LATHWORKS
LARDED	LARKSPURS	LASHKAR	LATENED	LATHY
LARDER	LARKY	LASHKARS	LATENESS	LATHYRISM
LARDERS	LARRIGAN	LASING	LATENESSES	LATHYRISMS
LARDIER	LARRIGANS	LASS	LATENING	LATI
LARDIEST	LARRIKIN	LASSES	LATENS	LATICES
LARDING	LARRIKINS	LASSI	LATENT	LATICIFER
LARDLIKE	LARRUP	LASSIE	LATENTLY	LATICIFERS
LARDON	LARRUPED	LASSIES	LATENTS	LATIGO
LARDONS	LARRUPER	LASSIS	LATER	LATIGOES
LARDOON	LARRUPERS	LASSITUDE	LATERAD	LATIGOS
LARDOONS	LARRUPING	LASSITUDES	LATERAL	LATILLA
LARDS	LARRUPS	LASSO	LATERALED	LATILLAS
LARDY	LARS	LASSOED	LATERALING	LATIMERIA
LAREE	LARUM	LASSOER	LATERALLED	LATIMERIAS
LAREES	LARUMS	LASSOERS	LATERALLING	LATINA

LATINAS
LATINITIES
LATINITY
LATINIZE
LATINIZED
LATINIZES
LATINIZING
LATINO
LATINOS
LATISH
LATITUDE
LATITUDES
LATKE
LATKES
LATOSOL
LATOSOLIC
LATOSOLS
LATRIA
LATRIAS
LATRINE
LATRINES
LATS
LATTE
LATTEN
LATTENS
LATTER
LATTERLY
LATTES
LATTICE
LATTICED
LATTICES
LATTICING
LATTICINGS
LATTIN
LATTINS
LATU
LAUAN
LAUANS
LAUD
LAUDABLE
LAUDABLY
LAUDANUM
LAUDANUMS
LAUDATION
LAUDATIONS
LAUDATIVE
LAUDATOR
LAUDATORS
LAUDATORY
LAUDED
LAUDER
LAUDERS

LAUDING
LAUDS
LAUGH
LAUGHABLE
LAUGHABLY
LAUGHED
LAUGHER
LAUGHERS
LAUGHING
LAUGHINGS
LAUGHLINE
LAUGHLINES
LAUGHS
LAUGHTER
LAUGHTERS
LAUNCE
LAUNCES
LAUNCH
LAUNCHED
LAUNCHER
LAUNCHERS
LAUNCHES
LAUNCHING
LAUNCHPAD
LAUNCHPADS
LAUNDER
LAUNDERED
LAUNDERER
LAUNDERERS
LAUNDERING
LAUNDERS
LAUNDRESS
LAUNDRESSES
LAUNDRIES
LAUNDRY
LAURA
LAURAE
LAURAS
LAUREATE
LAUREATED
LAUREATES
LAUREATING
LAUREL
LAURELED
LAURELING
LAURELLED
LAURELLING
LAURELS
LAUWINE
LAUWINES
LAV
LAVA

LAVABO
LAVABOES
LAVABOS
LAVAGE
LAVAGES
LAVALAVA
LAVALAVAS
LAVALIER
LAVALIERE
LAVALIERES
LAVALIERS
LAVALIKE
LAVAS
LAVASH
LAVASHES
LAVATION
LAVATIONS
LAVATORIES
LAVATORY
LAVE
LAVED
LAVEER
LAVEERED
LAVEERING
LAVEERS
LAVENDER
LAVENDERED
LAVENDERING
LAVENDERS
LAVER
LAVEROCK
LAVEROCKS
LAVERS
LAVES
LAVING
LAVISH
LAVISHED
LAVISHER
LAVISHERS
LAVISHES
LAVISHEST
LAVISHING
LAVISHLY
LAVROCK
LAVROCKS
LAVS
LAW
LAWBOOK
LAWBOOKS
LAWED
LAWFUL
LAWFULLY

LAWGIVER
LAWGIVERS
LAWGIVING
LAWGIVINGS
LAWINE
LAWINES
LAWING
LAWINGS
LAWLESS
LAWLESSLY
LAWLIKE
LAWMAKER
LAWMAKERS
LAWMAKING
LAWMAKINGS
LAWMAN
LAWMEN
LAWN
LAWNMOWER
LAWNMOWERS
LAWNS
LAWNY
LAWS
LAWSUIT
LAWSUITS
LAWYER
LAWYERED
LAWYERING
LAWYERINGS
LAWYERLY
LAWYERS
LAX
LAXATION
LAXATIONS
LAXATIVE
LAXATIVES
LAXER
LAXES
LAXEST
LAXITIES
LAXITY
LAXLY
LAXNESS
LAXNESSES
LAY
LAYABOUT
LAYABOUTS
LAYAWAY
LAYAWAYS
LAYED
LAYER
LAYERAGE

LAYERAGES
LAYERED
LAYERING
LAYERINGS
LAYERS
LAYETTE
LAYETTES
LAYIN
LAYING
LAYINS
LAYMAN
LAYMEN
LAYOFF
LAYOFFS
LAYOUT
LAYOUTS
LAYOVER
LAYOVERS
LAYPEOPLE
LAYPERSON
LAYPERSONS
LAYS
LAYUP
LAYUPS
LAYWOMAN
LAYWOMEN
LAZAR
LAZARET
LAZARETS
LAZARETTE
LAZARETTES
LAZARETTO
LAZARETTOS
LAZARS
LAZE
LAZED
LAZES
LAZIED
LAZIER
LAZIES
LAZIEST
LAZILY
LAZINESS
LAZINESSES
LAZING
LAZULI
LAZULIS
LAZULITE
LAZULITES
LAZURITE
LAZURITES
LAZY

LAZYBONES	LEAFIER	LEANERS	LEAST	LECTORS
LAZYING	LEAFIEST	LEANEST	LEASTS	LECTOTYPE
LAZYISH	LEAFINESS	LEANING	LEASTWAYS	LECTOTYPES
LAZZARONE	LEAFINESSES	LEANINGS	LEASTWISE	LECTURE
LAZZARONI	LEAFING	LEANLY	LEATHER	LECTURED
LEA	LEAFLESS	LEANNESS	LEATHERED	LECTURER
LEACH	LEAFLET	LEANNESSES	LEATHERING	LECTURERS
LEACHABLE	LEAFLETED	LEANS	LEATHERN	LECTURES
LEACHATE	LEAFLETER	LEANT	LEATHERS	LECTURING
LEACHATES	LEAFLETERS	LEAP	LEATHERY	LECYTHI
LEACHED	LEAFLETING	LEAPED	LEAVE	LECYTHIS
LEACHER	LEAFLETS	LEAPER	LEAVED	LECYTHUS
LEACHERS	LEAFLETTED	LEAPERS	LEAVEN	LED
LEACHES	LEAFLETTING	LEAPFROG	LEAVENED	LEDGE
LEACHIER	LEAFLIKE	LEAPFROGGED	LEAVENING	LEDGER
LEACHIEST	LEAFS	LEAPFROGGING	LEAVENINGS	LEDGERS
LEACHING	LEAFSTALK	LEAPFROGS	LEAVENS	LEDGES
LEACHY	LEAFSTALKS	LEAPING	LEAVER	LEDGIER
LEAD	LEAFWORM	LEAPS	LEAVERS	LEDGIEST
LEADED	LEAFWORMS	LEAPT	LEAVES	LEDGY
LEADEN	LEAFY	LEAR	LEAVIER	LEE
LEADENED	LEAGUE	LEARIER	LEAVIEST	LEEBOARD
LEADENING	LEAGUED	LEARIEST	LEAVING	LEEBOARDS
LEADENLY	LEAGUER	LEARN	LEAVINGS	LEECH
LEADENS	LEAGUERED	LEARNABLE	LEAVY	LEECHED
LEADER	LEAGUERING	LEARNED	LEBEN	LEECHES
LEADERS	LEAGUERS	LEARNEDLY	LEBENS	LEECHING
LEADIER	LEAGUES	LEARNER	LEBKUCHEN	LEECHLIKE
LEADIEST	LEAGUING	LEARNERS	LECH	LEEK
LEADING	LEAK	LEARNING	LECHAYIM	LEEKS
LEADINGS	LEAKAGE	LEARNINGS	LECHAYIMS	LEER
LEADLESS	LEAKAGES	LEARNS	LECHED	LEERED
LEADMAN	LEAKED	LEARNT	LECHER	LEERIER
LEADMEN	LEAKER	LEARS	LECHERED	LEERIEST
LEADOFF	LEAKERS	LEARY	LECHERIES	LEERILY
LEADOFFS	LEAKIER	LEAS	LECHERING	LEERINESS
LEADPLANT	LEAKIEST	LEASABLE	LECHEROUS	LEERINESSES
LEADPLANTS	LEAKILY	LEASE	LECHERS	LEERING
LEADS	LEAKINESS	LEASEBACK	LECHERY	LEERINGLY
LEADSCREW	LEAKINESSES	LEASEBACKS	LECHES	LEERS
LEADSCREWS	LEAKING	LEASED	LECHING	LEERY
LEADSMAN	LEAKLESS	LEASEHOLD	LECHWE	LEES
LEADSMEN	LEAKPROOF	LEASEHOLDS	LECHWES	LEET
LEADWORK	LEAKS	LEASER	LECITHIN	LEETS
LEADWORKS	LEAKY	LEASERS	LECITHINS	LEEWARD
LEADWORT	LEAL	LEASES	LECTERN	LEEWARDLY
LEADWORTS	LEALLY	LEASH	LECTERNS	LEEWARDS
LEADY	LEALTIES	LEASHED	LECTIN	LEEWAY
LEAF	LEALTY	LEASHES	LECTINS	LEEWAYS
LEAFAGE	LEAN	LEASHING	LECTION	LEFT
LEAFAGES	LEANED	LEASING	LECTIONS	LEFTER
LEAFED	LEANER	LEASINGS	LECTOR	LEFTEST

LEFTIES	LEGEND	LEGUMES	LEMMINGS	LENITIVES
LEFTISH	LEGENDARIES	LEGUMIN	LEMNISCAL	LENITY
LEFTISM	LEGENDARY	LEGUMINS	LEMNISCI	LENO
LEFTISMS	LEGENDIZE	LEGWARMER	LEMNISCUS	LENOS
LEFTIST	LEGENDIZED	LEGWARMERS	LEMON	LENS
LEFTISTS	LEGENDIZES	LEGWORK	LEMONADE	LENSE
LEFTMOST	LEGENDIZING	LEGWORKS	LEMONADES	LENSED
LEFTMOSTS	LEGENDRIES	LEHAYIM	LEMONISH	LENSES
LEFTOVER	LEGENDRY	LEHAYIMS	LEMONLIKE	LENSING
LEFTOVERS	LEGENDS	LEHR	LEMONS	LENSLESS
LEFTS	LEGER	LEHRS	LEMONY	LENSMAN
LEFTWARD	LEGERITIES	LEHUA	LEMPIRA	LENSMEN
LEFTWARDS	LEGERITY	LEHUAS	LEMPIRAS	LENT
LEFTWING	LEGERS	LEI	LEMUR	LENTANDO
LEFTY	LEGES	LEIOMYOMA	LEMURES	LENTEN
LEG	LEGGED	LEIOMYOMAS	LEMURINE	LENTIC
LEGACIES	LEGGIER	LEIOMYOMATA	LEMURLIKE	LENTICEL
LEGACY	LEGGIERO	LEIS	LEMUROID	LENTICELS
LEGAL	LEGGIEST	LEISTER	LEMUROIDS	LENTICULE
LEGALESE	LEGGIN	LEISTERED	LEMURS	LENTICULES
LEGALESES	LEGGINESS	LEISTERING	LEND	LENTIGINES
LEGALISE	LEGGINESSES	LEISTERS	LENDABLE	LENTIGO
LEGALISED	LEGGING	LEISURE	LENDER	LENTIL
LEGALISES	LEGGINGS	LEISURED	LENDERS	LENTILS
LEGALISING	LEGGINS	LEISURELY	LENDING	LENTISK
LEGALISM	LEGGY	LEISURES	LENDS	LENTISKS
LEGALISMS	LEGHORN	LEITMOTIF	LENES	LENTO
LEGALIST	LEGHORNS	LEITMOTIFS	LENGTH	LENTOID
LEGALISTS	LEGIBLE	LEITMOTIV	LENGTHEN	LENTOIDS
LEGALITIES	LEGIBLY	LEITMOTIVS	LENGTHENED	LENTOS
LEGALITY	LEGION	LEK	LENGTHENING	LEONE
LEGALIZE	LEGIONARIES	LEKE	LENGTHENS	LEONES
LEGALIZED	LEGIONARY	LEKKED	LENGTHIER	LEONINE
LEGALIZER	LEGIONS	LEKKING	LENGTHIEST	LEOPARD
LEGALIZERS	LEGISLATE	LEKS	LENGTHILY	LEOPARDS
LEGALIZES	LEGISLATED	LEKU	LENGTHS	LEOTARD
LEGALIZING	LEGISLATES	LEKVAR	LENGTHY	LEOTARDED
LEGALLY	LEGISLATING	LEKVARS	LENIENCE	LEOTARDS
LEGALS	LEGIST	LEKYTHI	LENIENCES	LEPER
LEGATE	LEGISTS	LEKYTHOI	LENIENCIES	LEPERS
LEGATED	LEGIT	LEKYTHOS	LENIENCY	LEPIDOTE
LEGATEE	LEGITS	LEKYTHUS	LENIENT	LEPIDOTES
LEGATEES	LEGLESS	LEMAN	LENIENTLY	LEPORID
LEGATES	LEGLIKE	LEMANS	LENIS	LEPORIDAE
LEGATINE	LEGMAN	LEMMA	LENITE	LEPORIDS
LEGATING	LEGMEN	LEMMAS	LENITED	LEPORINE
LEGATION	LEGONG	LEMMATA	LENITES	LEPROSE
LEGATIONS	LEGONGS	LEMMATIZE	LENITIES	LEPROSIES
LEGATO	LEGROOM	LEMMATIZED	LENITING	LEPROSY
LEGATOR	LEGROOMS	LEMMATIZES	LENITION	LEPROTIC
LEGATORS	LEGS	LEMMATIZING	LENITIONS	LEPROUS
LEGATOS	LEGUME	LEMMING	LENITIVE	LEPROUSLY

LEPT	LETHARGIC	LEUKOCYTES	LEVIATHANS	LEXICALLY
LEPTA	LETHARGIES	LEUKOMA	LEVIED	LEXICON
LEPTIN	LETHARGY	LEUKOMAS	LEVIER	LEXICONS
LEPTINS	LETHE	LEUKON	LEVIERS	LEXIS
LEPTON	LETHEAN	LEUKONS	LEVIES	LEY
LEPTONIC	LETHES	LEUKOSES	LEVIGATE	LEYS
LEPTONS	LETS	LEUKOSIS	LEVIGATED	LEZ
LEPTOPHOS	LETTED	LEUKOTIC	LEVIGATES	LEZZES
LEPTOPHOSES	LETTER	LEUKOTOMIES	LEVIGATING	LEZZIE
LEPTOSOME	LETTERBOX	LEUKOTOMY	LEVIN	LEZZIES
LEPTOSOMES	LETTERBOXED	LEV	LEVINS	LEZZY
LEPTOTENE	LETTERBOXES	LEVA	LEVIRATE	LI
LEPTOTENES	LETTERBOXING	LEVANT	LEVIRATES	LIABILITIES
LES	LETTERED	LEVANTED	LEVIRATIC	LIABILITY
LESBIAN	LETTERER	LEVANTER	LEVIS	LIABLE
LESBIANS	LETTERERS	LEVANTERS	LEVITATE	LIAISE
LESBO	LETTERING	LEVANTINE	LEVITATED	LIAISED
LESBOS	LETTERINGS	LEVANTINES	LEVITATES	LIAISES
LESES	LETTERMAN	LEVANTING	LEVITATING	LIAISING
LESION	LETTERMEN	LEVANTS	LEVITATOR	LIAISON
LESIONED	LETTERS	LEVATOR	LEVITATORS	LIAISONS
LESIONING	LETTING	LEVATORES	LEVITIES	LIANA
LESIONS	LETTUCE	LEVATORS	LEVITY	LIANAS
LESPEDEZA	LETTUCES	LEVEE	LEVO	LIANE
LESPEDEZAS	LETUP	LEVEED	LEVODOPA	LIANES
LESS	LETUPS	LEVEEING	LEVODOPAS	LIANG
LESSEE	LEU	LEVEES	LEVOGYRE	LIANGS
LESSEES	LEUCEMIA	LEVEL	LEVULIN	LIANOID
LESSEN	LEUCEMIAS	LEVELED	LEVULINS	LIAR
LESSENED	LEUCEMIC	LEVELER	LEVULOSE	LIARD
LESSENING	LEUCIN	LEVELERS	LEVULOSES	LIARDS
LESSENS	LEUCINE	LEVELING	LEVY	LIARS
LESSER	LEUCINES	LEVELLED	LEVYING	LIB
LESSON	LEUCINS	LEVELLER	LEWD	LIBATION
LESSONED	LEUCITE	LEVELLERS	LEWDER	LIBATIONS
LESSONING	LEUCITES	LEVELLING	LEWDEST	LIBBER
LESSONS	LEUCITIC	LEVELLY	LEWDLY	LIBBERS
LESSOR	LEUCOCYTE	LEVELNESS	LEWDNESS	LIBECCHIO
LESSORS	LEUCOCYTES	LEVELNESSES	LEWDNESSES	LIBECCHIOS
LEST	LEUCOMA	LEVELS	LEWIS	LIBECCIO
LET	LEUCOMAS	LEVER	LEWISES	LIBECCIOS
LETCH	LEUD	LEVERAGE	LEWISITE	LIBEL
LETCHED	LEUDES	LEVERAGED	LEWISITES	LIBELANT
LETCHES	LEUDS	LEVERAGES	LEWISSON	LIBELANTS
LETCHING	LEUKAEMIA	LEVERAGING	LEWISSONS	LIBELED
LETDOWN	LEUKAEMIAS	LEVERED	LEX	LIBELEE
LETDOWNS	LEUKEMIA	LEVERET	LEXEME	LIBELEES
LETHAL	LEUKEMIAS	LEVERETS	LEXEMES	LIBELER
LETHALITIES	LEUKEMIC	LEVERING	LEXEMIC	LIBELERS
LETHALITY	LEUKEMICS	LEVERS	LEXES	LIBELING
LETHALLY	LEUKEMOID	LEVIABLE	LEXICA	LIBELIST
LETHALS	LEUKOCYTE	LEVIATHAN	LEXICAL	LIBELISTS

LIBELLANT	LICENCE	LICKSPIT	LIFEFUL	LIGATIONS
LIBELLANTS	LICENCED	LICKSPITS	LIFEGUARD	LIGATIVE
LIBELLED	LICENCEE	LICORICE	LIFEGUARDED	LIGATURE
LIBELLEE	LICENCEES	LICORICES	LIFEGUARDING	LIGATURED
LIBELLEES	LICENCER	LICTOR	LIFEGUARDS	LIGATURES
LIBELLER	LICENCERS	LICTORIAN	LIFELESS	LIGATURING
LIBELLERS	LICENCES	LICTORS	LIFELIKE	LIGER
LIBELLING	LICENCING	LID	LIFELINE	LIGERS
LIBELLOUS	LICENSE	LIDAR	LIFELINES	LIGHT
LIBELOUS	LICENSED	LIDARS	LIFELONG	LIGHTBULB
LIBELS	LICENSEE	LIDDED	LIFER	LIGHTBULBS
LIBER	LICENSEES	LIDDING	LIFERS	LIGHTED
LIBERAL	LICENSER	LIDLESS	LIFESAVER	LIGHTEN
LIBERALLY	LICENSERS	LIDO	LIFESAVERS	LIGHTENED
LIBERALS	LICENSES	LIDOCAINE	LIFESPAN	LIGHTENER
LIBERATE	LICENSING	LIDOCAINES	LIFESPANS	LIGHTENERS
LIBERATED	LICENSOR	LIDOS	LIFESTYLE	LIGHTENING
LIBERATES	LICENSORS	LIDS	LIFESTYLES	LIGHTENS
LIBERATING	LICENSURE	LIE	LIFETIME	LIGHTER
LIBERATOR	LICENSURES	LIED	LIFETIMES	LIGHTERED
LIBERATORS	LICENTE	LIEDER	LIFEWAY	LIGHTERING
LIBERS	LICH	LIEF	LIFEWAYS	LIGHTERS
LIBERTIES	LICHEE	LIEFER	LIFEWORK	LIGHTEST
LIBERTINE	LICHEES	LIEFEST	LIFEWORKS	LIGHTFACE
LIBERTINES	LICHEN	LIEFLY	LIFEWORLD	LIGHTFACES
LIBERTY	LICHENED	LIEGE	LIFEWORLDS	LIGHTFAST
LIBIDINAL	LICHENIN	LIEGEMAN	LIFT	LIGHTFUL
LIBIDO	LICHENING	LIEGEMEN	LIFTABLE	LIGHTING
LIBIDOS	LICHENINS	LIEGES	LIFTED	LIGHTINGS
LIBLAB	LICHENOSE	LIEN	LIFTER	LIGHTISH
LIBLABS	LICHENOUS	LIENABLE	LIFTERS	LIGHTLESS
LIBRA	LICHENS	LIENAL	LIFTGATE	LIGHTLY
LIBRAE	LICHES	LIENS	LIFTGATES	LIGHTNESS
LIBRARIAN	LICHI	LIENTERIES	LIFTING	LIGHTNESSES
LIBRARIANS	LICHIS	LIENTERY	LIFTMAN	LIGHTNING
LIBRARIES	LICHT	LIER	LIFTMEN	LIGHTNINGED
LIBRARY	LICHTED	LIERNE	LIFTOFF	LIGHTNINGS
LIBRAS	LICHTING	LIERNES	LIFTOFFS	LIGHTS
LIBRATE	LICHTLY	LIERS	LIFTS	LIGHTSHIP
LIBRATED	LICHTS	LIES	LIGAMENT	LIGHTSHIPS
LIBRATES	LICIT	LIEU	LIGAMENTS	LIGHTSOME
LIBRATING	LICITLY	LIEUS	LIGAN	LIGHTWAVE
LIBRATION	LICITNESS	LIEVE	LIGAND	LIGHTWOOD
LIBRATIONS	LICITNESSES	LIEVER	LIGANDS	LIGHTWOODS
LIBRATORY	LICK	LIEVEST	LIGANS	LIGNALOES
LIBRETTI	LICKED	LIFE	LIGASE	LIGNAN
LIBRETTO	LICKER	LIFEBLOOD	LIGASES	LIGNANS
LIBRETTOS	LICKERISH	LIFEBLOODS	LIGATE	LIGNEOUS
LIBRI	LICKERS	LIFEBOAT	LIGATED	LIGNIFIED
LIBRIFORM	LICKING	LIFEBOATS	LIGATES	LIGNIFIES
LIBS	LICKINGS	LIFECARE	LIGATING	LIGNIFY
LICE	LICKS	LIFECARES	LIGATION	LIGNIFYING

LIGNIN	LILTING	LIMERICKS	LIMPER	LINEAMENT
LIGNINS	LILTINGLY	LIMES	LIMPERS	LINEAMENTS
LIGNITE	LILTS	LIMESTONE	LIMPEST	LINEAR
LIGNITES	LILY	LIMESTONES	LIMPET	LINEARISE
LIGNITIC	LILYLIKE	LIMEWATER	LIMPETS	LINEARISED
LIGROIN	LIMA	LIMEWATERS	LIMPID	LINEARISES
LIGROINE	LIMACINE	LIMEY	LIMPIDITIES	LINEARISING
LIGROINES	LIMACON	LIMEYS	LIMPIDITY	LINEARITIES
LIGROINS	LIMACONS	LIMIER	LIMPIDLY	LINEARITY
LIGULA	LIMAN	LIMIEST	LIMPING	LINEARIZE
LIGULAE	LIMANS	LIMINA	LIMPINGLY	LINEARIZED
LIGULAR	LIMAS	LIMINAL	LIMPKIN	LINEARIZES
LIGULAS	LIMB	LIMINESS	LIMPKINS	LINEARIZING
LIGULATE	LIMBA	LIMINESSES	LIMPLY	LINEARLY
LIGULATED	LIMBAS	LIMING	LIMPNESS	LINEATE
LIGULE	LIMBATE	LIMIT	LIMPNESSES	LINEATED
LIGULES	LIMBECK	LIMITABLE	LIMPS	LINEATION
LIGULOID	LIMBECKS	LIMITARY	LIMPSEY	LINEATIONS
LIGURE	LIMBED	LIMITED	LIMPSIER	LINEBRED
LIGURES	LIMBER	LIMITEDLY	LIMPSIEST	LINECUT
LIKABLE	LIMBERED	LIMITEDS	LIMPSY	LINECUTS
LIKE	LIMBERER	LIMITER	LIMULI	LINED
LIKEABLE	LIMBEREST	LIMITERS	LIMULOID	LINELESS
LIKED	LIMBERING	LIMITES	LIMULOIDS	LINELIKE
LIKELIER	LIMBERLY	LIMITING	LIMULUS	LINEMAN
LIKELIEST	LIMBERS	LIMITLESS	LIMY	LINEMEN
LIKELY	LIMBI	LIMITS	LIN	LINEN
LIKEN	LIMBIC	LIMMER	LINABLE	LINENS
LIKENED	LIMBIER	LIMMERS	LINAC	LINENY
LIKENESS	LIMBIEST	LIMN	LINACS	LINEOLATE
LIKENESSES	LIMBING	LIMNED	LINAGE	LINER
LIKENING	LIMBLESS	LIMNER	LINAGES	LINERLESS
LIKENS	LIMBO	LIMNERS	LINALOL	LINERS
LIKER	LIMBOS	LIMNETIC	LINALOLS	LINES
LIKERS	LIMBS	LIMNIC	LINALOOL	LINESMAN
LIKES	LIMBUS	LIMNING	LINALOOLS	LINESMEN
LIKEST	LIMBUSES	LIMNOLOGIES	LINCHPIN	LINEUP
LIKEWISE	LIMBY	LIMNOLOGY	LINCHPINS	LINEUPS
LIKING	LIME	LIMNS	LINDANE	LINEY
LIKINGS	LIMEADE	LIMO	LINDANES	LING
LIKUTA	LIMEADES	LIMONENE	LINDEN	LINGA
LILAC	LIMED	LIMONENES	LINDENS	LINGAM
LILACS	LIMEKILN	LIMONITE	LINDIES	LINGAMS
LILANGENI	LIMEKILNS	LIMONITES	LINDY	LINGAS
LILIED	LIMELESS	LIMONITIC	LINE	LINGBERRIES
LILIES	LIMELIGHT	LIMOS	LINEABLE	LINGBERRY
LILLIPUT	LIMELIGHTED	LIMOUSINE	LINEAGE	LINGCOD
LILLIPUTS	LIMELIGHTING	LIMOUSINES	LINEAGES	LINGCODS
LILO	LIMELIGHTS	LIMP	LINEAL	LINGER
LILOS	LIMEN	LIMPA	LINEALITIES	LINGERED
LILT	LIMENS	LIMPAS	LINEALITY	LINGERER
LILTED	LIMERICK	LIMPED	LINEALLY	LINGERERS

LINGERIE	LINKSMAN	LINURON	LIPOSOMES	LIQUIDLY
LINGERIES	LINKSMEN	LINURONS	LIPOTROPIES	LIQUIDS
LINGERING	LINKUP	LINY	LIPOTROPY	LIQUIFIED
LINGERS	LINKUPS	LION	LIPPED	LIQUIFIES
LINGIER	LINKWORK	LIONESS	LIPPEN	LIQUIFY
LINGIEST	LINKWORKS	LIONESSES	LIPPENED	LIQUIFYING
LINGO	LINKY	LIONFISH	LIPPENING	LIQUOR
LINGOES	LINN	LIONFISHES	LIPPENS	LIQUORED
LINGS	LINNET	LIONISE	LIPPER	LIQUORICE
LINGUA	LINNETS	LIONISED	LIPPERED	LIQUORICES
LINGUAE	LINNS	LIONISER	LIPPERING	LIQUORING
LINGUAL	LINO	LIONISERS	LIPPERS	LIQUORISH
LINGUALLY	LINOCUT	LIONISES	LIPPIER	LIQUORS
LINGUALS	LINOCUTS	LIONISING	LIPPIEST	LIRA
LINGUICA	LINOLEATE	LIONIZE	LIPPINESS	LIRAS
LINGUICAS	LINOLEATES	LIONIZED	LIPPINESSES	LIRE
LINGUINE	LINOLEUM	LIONIZER	LIPPING	LIRI
LINGUINES	LINOLEUMS	LIONIZERS	LIPPINGS	LIRIOPE
LINGUINI	LINOS	LIONIZES	LIPPY	LIRIOPES
LINGUINIS	LINOTYPE	LIONIZING	LIPREAD	LIRIPIPE
LINGUISA	LINOTYPED	LIONLIKE	LIPREADER	LIRIPIPES
LINGUISAS	LINOTYPER	LIONS	LIPREADERS	LIROT
LINGUIST	LINOTYPERS	LIP	LIPREADING	LIROTH
LINGUISTS	LINOTYPES	LIPA	LIPREADS	LIS
LINGULA	LINOTYPING	LIPASE	LIPS	LISENTE
LINGULAE	LINS	LIPASES	LIPSTICK	LISLE
LINGULAR	LINSANG	LIPE	LIPSTICKS	LISLES
LINGULATE	LINSANGS	LIPECTOMIES	LIQUATE	LISP
LINGY	LINSEED	LIPECTOMY	LIQUATED	LISPED
LINIER	LINSEEDS	LIPID	LIQUATES	LISPER
LINIEST	LINSEY	LIPIDE	LIQUATING	LISPERS
LINIMENT	LINSEYS	LIPIDES	LIQUATION	LISPING
LINIMENTS	LINSTOCK	LIPIDIC	LIQUATIONS	LISPINGLY
LININ	LINSTOCKS	LIPIDS	LIQUEFIED	LISPS
LINING	LINT	LIPIN	LIQUEFIER	LISSOM
LININGS	LINTED	LIPINS	LIQUEFIERS	LISSOME
LININS	LINTEL	LIPLESS	LIQUEFIES	LISSOMELY
LINK	LINTELS	LIPLIKE	LIQUEFY	LISSOMLY
LINKABLE	LINTER	LIPOCYTE	LIQUEFYING	LIST
LINKAGE	LINTERS	LIPOCYTES	LIQUEUR	LISTABLE
LINKAGES	LINTIER	LIPOID	LIQUEURS	LISTED
LINKBOY	LINTIEST	LIPOIDAL	LIQUID	LISTEE
LINKBOYS	LINTING	LIPOIDS	LIQUIDATE	LISTEES
LINKED	LINTLESS	LIPOLITIC	LIQUIDATED	LISTEL
LINKER	LINTOL	LIPOLYSES	LIQUIDATES	LISTELS
LINKERS	LINTOLS	LIPOLYSIS	LIQUIDATING	LISTEN
LINKING	LINTS	LIPOLYTIC	LIQUIDITIES	LISTENED
LINKMAN	LINTWHITE	LIPOMA	LIQUIDITY	LISTENER
LINKMEN	LINTWHITES	LIPOMAS	LIQUIDIZE	LISTENERS
LINKS	LINTY	LIPOMATA	LIQUIDIZED	LISTENING
LINKSLAND	LINUM	LIPOSOMAL	LIQUIDIZES	LISTENS
LINKSLANDS	LINUMS	LIPOSOME	LIQUIDIZING	LISTER

LISTERIA	LITHIFYING	LITTLISH	LIVIDITIES	LOAMINESS
LISTERIAS	LITHIUM	LITTORAL	LIVIDITY	LOAMINESSES
LISTERS	LITHIUMS	LITTORALS	LIVIDLY	LOAMING
LISTING	LITHO	LITU	LIVIDNESS	LOAMLESS
LISTINGS	LITHOED	LITURGIC	LIVIDNESSES	LOAMS
LISTLESS	LITHOID	LITURGICS	LIVIER	LOAMY
LISTS	LITHOIDAL	LITURGIES	LIVIERS	LOAN
LIT	LITHOING	LITURGISM	LIVING	LOANABLE
LITAI	LITHOLOGIES	LITURGISMS	LIVINGLY	LOANED
LITANIES	LITHOLOGY	LITURGIST	LIVINGS	LOANER
LITANY	LITHOPONE	LITURGISTS	LIVRE	LOANERS
LITAS	LITHOPONES	LITURGY	LIVRES	LOANING
LITCHI	LITHOPS	LIVABLE	LIVYER	LOANINGS
LITCHIS	LITHOS	LIVE	LIVYERS	LOANS
LITE	LITHOSOL	LIVEABLE	LIXIVIA	LOANSHIFT
LITENESS	LITHOSOLS	LIVED	LIXIVIAL	LOANSHIFTS
LITENESSES	LITHOTOMIES	LIVELIER	LIXIVIATE	LOANWORD
LITER	LITHOTOMY	LIVELIEST	LIXIVIATED	LOANWORDS
LITERACIES	LITIGABLE	LIVELILY	LIXIVIATES	LOATH
LITERACY	LITIGANT	LIVELONG	LIXIVIATING	LOATHE
LITERAL	LITIGANTS	LIVELY	LIXIVIUM	LOATHED
LITERALLY	LITIGATE	LIVEN	LIXIVIUMS	LOATHER
LITERALS	LITIGATED	LIVENED	LIZARD	LOATHERS
LITERARY	LITIGATES	LIVENER	LIZARDS	LOATHES
LITERATE	LITIGATING	LIVENERS	LLAMA	LOATHFUL
LITERATES	LITIGATOR	LIVENESS	LLAMAS	LOATHING
LITERATI	LITIGATORS	LIVENESSES	LLANO	LOATHINGS
LITERATIM	LITIGIOUS	LIVENING	LLANOS	LOATHLY
LITERATOR	LITMUS	LIVENS	LO	LOATHNESS
LITERATORS	LITMUSES	LIVER	LOACH	LOATHNESSES
LITERATUS	LITORAL	LIVERED	LOACHES	LOATHSOME
LITERS	LITOTES	LIVERIED	LOAD	LOAVES
LITHARGE	LITOTIC	LIVERIES	LOADED	LOB
LITHARGES	LITRE	LIVERING	LOADER	LOBAR
LITHE	LITRES	LIVERISH	LOADERS	LOBATE
LITHELY	LITS	LIVERLEAF	LOADING	LOBATED
LITHEMIA	LITTEN	LIVERLEAVES	LOADINGS	LOBATELY
LITHEMIAS	LITTER	LIVERS	LOADS	LOBATION
LITHEMIC	LITTERBAG	LIVERWORT	LOADSTAR	LOBATIONS
LITHENESS	LITTERBAGS	LIVERWORTS	LOADSTARS	LOBBED
LITHENESSES	LITTERBUG	LIVERY	LOADSTONE	LOBBER
LITHER	LITTERBUGS	LIVERYMAN	LOADSTONES	LOBBERS
LITHESOME	LITTERED	LIVERYMEN	LOAF	LOBBIED
LITHEST	LITTERER	LIVES	LOAFED	LOBBIES
LITHIA	LITTERERS	LIVEST	LOAFER	LOBBING
LITHIAS	LITTERING	LIVESTOCK	LOAFERS	LOBBY
LITHIASES	LITTERS	LIVESTOCKS	LOAFING	LOBBYER
LITHIASIS	LITTERY	LIVETRAP	LOAFS	LOBBYERS
LITHIC	LITTLE	LIVETRAPPED	LOAM	LOBBYGOW
LITHIFIED	LITTLER	LIVETRAPPING	LOAMED	LOBBYGOWS
LITHIFIES	LITTLES	LIVETRAPS	LOAMIER	LOBBYING
LITHIFY	LITTLEST	LIVID	LOAMIEST	LOBBYISM

LOBBYISMS	LOCALITE	LOCKNUT	LODE	LOGGED
LOBBYIST	LOCALITES	LOCKNUTS	LODEN	LOGGER
LOBBYISTS	LOCALITIES	LOCKOUT	LODENS	LOGGERS
LOBE	LOCALITY	LOCKOUTS	LODES	LOGGETS
LOBECTOMIES	LOCALIZE	LOCKRAM	LODESTAR	LOGGIA
LOBECTOMY	LOCALIZED	LOCKRAMS	LODESTARS	LOGGIAS
LOBED	LOCALIZER	LOCKS	LODESTONE	LOGGIE
LOBEFIN	LOCALIZERS	LOCKSET	LODESTONES	LOGGIER
LOBEFINS	LOCALIZES	LOCKSETS	LODGE	LOGGIEST
LOBELIA	LOCALIZING	LOCKSMITH	LODGED	LOGGING
LOBELIAS	LOCALLY	LOCKSMITHS	LODGEMENT	LOGGINGS
LOBELINE	LOCALNESS	LOCKSTEP	LODGEMENTS	LOGGISH
LOBELINES	LOCALNESSES	LOCKSTEPS	LODGER	LOGGY
LOBES	LOCALS	LOCKUP	LODGERS	LOGIA
LOBLOLLIES	LOCATABLE	LOCKUPS	LODGES	LOGIC
LOBLOLLY	LOCATE	LOCO	LODGING	LOGICAL
LOBO	LOCATED	LOCOED	LODGINGS	LOGICALLY
LOBOS	LOCATER	LOCOES	LODGMENT	LOGICIAN
LOBOTOMIES	LOCATERS	LOCOFOCO	LODGMENTS	LOGICIANS
LOBOTOMY	LOCATES	LOCOFOCOS	LODICULE	LOGICISE
LOBS	LOCATING	LOCOING	LODICULES	LOGICISED
LOBSCOUSE	LOCATION	LOCOISM	LOESS	LOGICISES
LOBSCOUSES	LOCATIONS	LOCOISMS	LOESSAL	LOGICISING
LOBSTER	LOCATIVE	LOCOMOTE	LOESSES	LOGICIZE
LOBSTERED	LOCATIVES	LOCOMOTED	LOESSIAL	LOGICIZED
LOBSTERER	LOCATOR	LOCOMOTES	LOFT	LOGICIZES
LOBSTERERS	LOCATORS	LOCOMOTING	LOFTED	LOGICIZING
LOBSTERING	LOCH	LOCOMOTOR	LOFTER	LOGICLESS
LOBSTERS	LOCHAN	LOCOMOTORS	LOFTERS	LOGICS
LOBSTICK	LOCHANS	LOCOS	LOFTIER	LOGIER
LOBSTICKS	LOCHIA	LOCOWEED	LOFTIEST	LOGIEST
LOBULAR	LOCHIAL	LOCOWEEDS	LOFTILY	LOGILY
LOBULARLY	LOCHS	LOCULAR	LOFTINESS	LOGIN
LOBULATE	LOCI	LOCULATE	LOFTINESSES	LOGINESS
LOBULATED	LOCK	LOCULATED	LOFTING	LOGINESSES
LOBULE	LOCKABLE	LOCULE	LOFTLESS	LOGINS
LOBULES	LOCKAGE	LOCULED	LOFTLIKE	LOGION
LOBULOSE	LOCKAGES	LOCULES	LOFTS	LOGIONS
LOBWORM	LOCKBOX	LOCULI	LOFTY	LOGISTIC
LOBWORMS	LOCKBOXES	LOCULUS	LOG	LOGISTICS
LOCA	LOCKDOWN	LOCUM	LOGAN	LOGJAM
LOCAL	LOCKDOWNS	LOCUMS	LOGANIA	LOGJAMMED
LOCALE	LOCKED	LOCUS	LOGANS	LOGJAMMING
LOCALES	LOCKER	LOCUST	LOGAOEDIC	LOGJAMS
LOCALISE	LOCKERS	LOCUSTA	LOGAOEDICS	LOGNORMAL
LOCALISED	LOCKET	LOCUSTAE	LOGARITHM	LOGO
LOCALISES	LOCKETS	LOCUSTAL	LOGARITHMS	LOGOGRAM
LOCALISING	LOCKING	LOCUSTS	LOGBOOK	LOGOGRAMS
LOCALISM	LOCKJAW	LOCUTION	LOGBOOKS	LOGOGRAPH
LOCALISMS	LOCKJAWS	LOCUTIONS	LOGE	LOGOGRAPHS
LOCALIST	LOCKMAKER	LOCUTORIES	LOGES	LOGOGRIPH
LOCALISTS	LOCKMAKERS	LOCUTORY	LOGGATS	LOGOGRIPHS

LOGOI	LOLLOPED	LONGHAIRS	LOOFAHS	LOOPILY
LOGOMACH	LOLLOPING	LONGHAND	LOOFAS	LOOPINESS
LOGOMACHIES	LOLLOPS	LONGHANDS	LOOFS	LOOPINESSES
LOGOMACHS	LOLLOPY	LONGHEAD	LOOIE	LOOPING
LOGOMACHY	LOLLS	LONGHEADS	LOOIES	LOOPS
LOGON	LOLLY	LONGHORN	LOOING	LOOPY
LOGONS	LOLLYGAG	LONGHORNS	LOOK	LOOS
LOGOPHILE	LOLLYGAGGED	LONGHOUSE	LOOKALIKE	LOOSE
LOGOPHILES	LOLLYGAGGING	LONGHOUSES	LOOKALIKES	LOOSED
LOGORRHEA	LOLLYGAGS	LONGICORN	LOOKDOWN	LOOSELY
LOGORRHEAS	LOLLYPOP	LONGICORNS	LOOKDOWNS	LOOSEN
LOGOS	LOLLYPOPS	LONGIES	LOOKED	LOOSENED
LOGOTYPE	LOMEIN	LONGING	LOOKER	LOOSENER
LOGOTYPES	LOMEINS	LONGINGLY	LOOKERS	LOOSENERS
LOGOTYPIES	LOMENT	LONGINGS	LOOKING	LOOSENESS
LOGOTYPY	LOMENTA	LONGISH	LOOKISM	LOOSENESSES
LOGROLL	LOMENTS	LONGITUDE	LOOKISMS	LOOSENING
LOGROLLED	LOMENTUM	LONGITUDES	LOOKIST	LOOSENS
LOGROLLER	LOMENTUMS	LONGJUMP	LOOKISTS	LOOSER
LOGROLLERS	LONE	LONGJUMPED	LOOKOUT	LOOSES
LOGROLLING	LONELIER	LONGJUMPING	LOOKOUTS	LOOSEST
LOGROLLS	LONELIEST	LONGJUMPS	LOOKS	LOOSING
LOGS	LONELILY	LONGLEAF	LOOKSISM	LOOT
LOGWAY	LONELY	LONGLEAVES	LOOKSISMS	LOOTED
LOGWAYS	LONENESS	LONGLINE	LOOKUP	LOOTER
LOGWOOD	LONENESSES	LONGLINES	LOOKUPS	LOOTERS
LOGWOODS	LONER	LONGLY	LOOM	LOOTING
LOGY	LONERS	LONGNECK	LOOMED	LOOTS
LOID	LONESOME	LONGNECKS	LOOMING	LOP
LOIDED	LONESOMES	LONGNESS	LOOMS	LOPE
LOIDING	LONG	LONGNESSES	LOON	LOPED
LOIDS	LONGAN	LONGS	LOONEY	LOPER
LOIN	LONGANS	LONGSHIP	LOONEYS	LOPERS
LOINCLOTH	LONGBOAT	LONGSHIPS	LOONIE	LOPES
LOINCLOTHS	LONGBOATS	LONGSHORE	LOONIER	LOPING
LOINS	LONGBOW	LONGSOME	LOONIES	LOPPED
LOITER	LONGBOWS	LONGSPUR	LOONIEST	LOPPER
LOITERED	LONGCLOTH	LONGSPURS	LOONILY	LOPPERED
LOITERER	LONGCLOTHS	LONGTIME	LOONINESS	LOPPERING
LOITERERS	LONGE	LONGUEUR	LOONINESSES	LOPPERS
LOITERING	LONGED	LONGUEURS	LOONS	LOPPIER
LOITERS	LONGEING	LONGWAYS	LOONY	LOPPIEST
LOLL	LONGER	LONGWISE	LOOP	LOPPING
LOLLED	LONGERON	LOO	LOOPED	LOPPY
LOLLER	LONGERONS	LOOBIES	LOOPER	LOPS
LOLLERS	LONGERS	LOOBY	LOOPERS	LOPSIDED
LOLLIES	LONGES	LOOED	LOOPHOLE	LOPSTICK
LOLLING	LONGEST	LOOEY	LOOPHOLED	LOPSTICKS
LOLLINGLY	LONGEVITIES	LOOEYS	LOOPHOLES	LOQUACITIES
LOLLIPOP	LONGEVITY	LOOF	LOOPHOLING	LOQUACITY
LOLLIPOPS	LONGEVOUS	LOOFA	LOOPIER	LOQUAT
LOLLOP	LONGHAIR	LOOFAH	LOOPIEST	LOQUATS

LORAL	LOSE	LOUDER	LOUTISHLY	LOWBORN
LORAN	LOSEL	LOUDEST	LOUTS	LOWBOY
LORANS	LOSELS	LOUDISH	LOUVER	LOWBOYS
LORAZEPAM	LOSER	LOUDLIER	LOUVERED	LOWBRED
LORAZEPAMS	LOSERS	LOUDLIEST	LOUVERS	LOWBROW
LORD	LOSES	LOUDLY	LOUVRE	LOWBROWED
LORDED	LOSING	LOUDMOUTH	LOUVRED	LOWBROWS
LORDING	LOSINGLY	LOUDMOUTHS	LOUVRES	LOWDOWN
LORDINGS	LOSINGS	LOUDNESS	LOVABLE	LOWDOWNS
LORDLESS	LOSS	LOUDNESSES	LOVABLY	LOWE
LORDLIER	LOSSES	LOUGH	LOVAGE	LOWED
LORDLIEST	LOSSLESS	LOUGHS	LOVAGES	LOWER
LORDLIKE	LOSSY	LOUIE	LOVAT	LOWERCASE
LORDLING	LOST	LOUIES	LOVATS	LOWERCASED
LORDLINGS	LOSTNESS	LOUIS	LOVE	LOWERCASES
LORDLY	LOSTNESSES	LOUMA	LOVEABLE	LOWERCASING
LORDOMA	LOT	LOUMAS	LOVEABLY	LOWERED
LORDOMAS	LOTA	LOUNGE	LOVEBIRD	LOWERING
LORDOSES	LOTAH	LOUNGED	LOVEBIRDS	LOWERMOST
LORDOSIS	LOTAHS	LOUNGER	LOVEBUG	LOWERS
LORDOTIC	LOTAS	LOUNGERS	LOVEBUGS	LOWERY
LORDS	LOTH	LOUNGES	LOVED	LOWES
LORDSHIP	LOTHARIO	LOUNGING	LOVEFEST	LOWEST
LORDSHIPS	LOTHARIOS	LOUNGY	LOVEFESTS	LOWING
LORE	LOTHSOME	LOUP	LOVELESS	LOWINGS
LOREAL	LOTI	LOUPE	LOVELIER	LOWISH
LORES	LOTIC	LOUPED	LOVELIES	LOWLAND
LORGNETTE	LOTION	LOUPEN	LOVELIEST	LOWLANDER
LORGNETTES	LOTIONS	LOUPES	LOVELILY	LOWLANDERS
LORGNON	LOTOS	LOUPING	LOVELOCK	LOWLANDS
LORGNONS	LOTOSES	LOUPS	LOVELOCKS	LOWLIER
LORICA	LOTS	LOUR	LOVELORN	LOWLIEST
LORICAE	LOTTE	LOURED	LOVELY	LOWLIFE
LORICATE	LOTTED	LOURING	LOVEMAKER	LOWLIFER
LORICATED	LOTTER	LOURS	LOVEMAKERS	LOWLIFERS
LORICATES	LOTTERIES	LOURY	LOVER	LOWLIFES
LORIES	LOTTERS	LOUSE	LOVERLY	LOWLIGHT
LORIKEET	LOTTERY	LOUSED	LOVERS	LOWLIGHTS
LORIKEETS	LOTTES	LOUSES	LOVES	LOWLIHEAD
LORIMER	LOTTING	LOUSEWORT	LOVESEAT	LOWLIHEADS
LORIMERS	LOTTO	LOUSEWORTS	LOVESEATS	LOWLILY
LORINER	LOTTOS	LOUSIER	LOVESICK	LOWLINESS
LORINERS	LOTUS	LOUSIEST	LOVESOME	LOWLINESSES
LORIS	LOTUSES	LOUSILY	LOVEVINE	LOWLIVES
LORISES	LOTUSLAND	LOUSINESS	LOVEVINES	LOWLY
LORN	LOTUSLANDS	LOUSINESSES	LOVING	LOWN
LORNNESS	LOUCHE	LOUSING	LOVINGLY	LOWNESS
LORNNESSES	LOUD	LOUSY	LOW	LOWNESSES
LORRIES	LOUDEN	LOUT	LOWBALL	LOWRIDER
LORRY	LOUDENED	LOUTED	LOWBALLED	LOWRIDERS
LORY	LOUDENING	LOUTING	LOWBALLING	LOWS
LOSABLE	LOUDENS	LOUTISH	LOWBALLS	LOWSE

LOX	LUCID	LUGES	LUMINAIRES	LUNATION
LOXED	LUCIDITIES	LUGGAGE	LUMINAL	LUNATIONS
LOXES	LUCIDITY	LUGGAGES	LUMINANCE	LUNCH
LOXING	LUCIDLY	LUGGED	LUMINANCES	LUNCHBOX
LOXODROME	LUCIDNESS	LUGGER	LUMINARIA	LUNCHBOXES
LOXODROMES	LUCIDNESSES	LUGGERS	LUMINARIAS	LUNCHED
LOYAL	LUCIFER	LUGGIE	LUMINARIES	LUNCHEON
LOYALER	LUCIFERIN	LUGGIES	LUMINARY	LUNCHEONS
LOYALEST	LUCIFERINS	LUGGING	LUMINESCE	LUNCHER
LOYALISM	LUCIFERS	LUGING	LUMINESCED	LUNCHERS
LOYALISMS	LUCITE	LUGS	LUMINESCES	LUNCHES
LOYALIST	LUCITES	LUGSAIL	LUMINESCING	LUNCHING
LOYALISTS	LUCK	LUGSAILS	LUMINISM	LUNCHMEAT
LOYALLY	LUCKED	LUGWORM	LUMINISMS	LUNCHMEATS
LOYALTIES	LUCKIE	LUGWORMS	LUMINIST	LUNCHROOM
LOYALTY	LUCKIER	LUKEWARM	LUMINISTS	LUNCHROOMS
LOZENGE	LUCKIES	LULL	LUMINOUS	LUNCHTIME
LOZENGES	LUCKIEST	LULLABIED	LUMMOX	LUNCHTIMES
LUAU	LUCKILY	LULLABIES	LUMMOXES	LUNE
LUAUS	LUCKINESS	LULLABY	LUMP	LUNES
LUBBER	LUCKINESSES	LULLABYING	LUMPED	LUNET
LUBBERLY	LUCKING	LULLED	LUMPEN	LUNETS
LUBBERS	LUCKLESS	LULLER	LUMPENS	LUNETTE
LUBE	LUCKS	LULLERS	LUMPER	LUNETTES
LUBED	LUCKY	LULLING	LUMPERS	LUNG
LUBES	LUCRATIVE	LULLS	LUMPFISH	LUNGAN
LUBING	LUCRE	LULU	LUMPFISHES	LUNGANS
LUBRIC	LUCRES	LULUS	LUMPIER	LUNGE
LUBRICAL	LUCUBRATE	LUM	LUMPIEST	LUNGED
LUBRICANT	LUCUBRATED	LUMA	LUMPILY	LUNGEE
LUBRICANTS	LUCUBRATES	LUMAS	LUMPINESS	LUNGEES
LUBRICATE	LUCUBRATING	LUMBAGO	LUMPINESSES	LUNGER
LUBRICATED	LUCULENT	LUMBAGOS	LUMPING	LUNGERS
LUBRICATES	LUDE	LUMBAR	LUMPINGLY	LUNGES
LUBRICATING	LUDES	LUMBARS	LUMPISH	LUNGFISH
LUBRICITIES	LUDIC	LUMBER	LUMPISHLY	LUNGFISHES
LUBRICITY	LUDICROUS	LUMBERED	LUMPS	LUNGFUL
LUBRICOUS	LUES	LUMBERER	LUMPY	LUNGFULS
LUCARNE	LUETIC	LUMBERERS	LUMS	LUNGI
LUCARNES	LUETICS	LUMBERING	LUNA	LUNGING
LUCE	LUFF	LUMBERINGS	LUNACIES	LUNGIS
LUCENCE	LUFFA	LUMBERLY	LUNACY	LUNGS
LUCENCES	LUFFAS	LUMBERMAN	LUNAR	LUNGWORM
LUCENCIES	LUFFED	LUMBERMEN	LUNARIAN	LUNGWORMS
LUCENCY	LUFFING	LUMBERS	LUNARIANS	LUNGWORT
LUCENT	LUFFS	LUMBRICAL	LUNARS	LUNGWORTS
LUCENTLY	LUG	LUMBRICALS	LUNAS	LUNGYI
LUCERN	LUGE	LUMEN	LUNATE	LUNGYIS
LUCERNE	LUGED	LUMENAL	LUNATED	LUNIER
LUCERNES	LUGEING	LUMENS	LUNATELY	LUNIES
LUCERNS	LUGER	LUMINA	LUNATIC	LUNIEST
LUCES	LUGERS	LUMINAIRE	LUNATICS	LUNISOLAR

LUNITIDAL	LURINGLY	LUTANIST	LUXURIATING	LYNX
LUNK	LURK	LUTANISTS	LUXURIES	LYNXES
LUNKER	LURKED	LUTE	LUXURIOUS	LYONNAISE
LUNKERS	LURKER	LUTEA	LUXURY	LYOPHILE
LUNKHEAD	LURKERS	LUTEAL	LWEI	LYOPHILED
LUNKHEADS	LURKING	LUTECIUM	LWEIS	LYOPHILIC
LUNKS	LURKINGLY	LUTECIUMS	LYARD	LYOPHOBIC
LUNT	LURKS	LUTED	LYART	LYRATE
LUNTED	LUSCIOUS	LUTEFISK	LYASE	LYRATED
LUNTING	LUSH	LUTEFISKS	LYASES	LYRATELY
LUNTS	LUSHED	LUTEIN	LYCEA	LYRE
LUNULA	LUSHER	LUTEINIZE	LYCEE	LYREBIRD
LUNULAE	LUSHES	LUTEINIZED	LYCEES	LYREBIRDS
LUNULAR	LUSHEST	LUTEINIZES	LYCEUM	LYRES
LUNULATE	LUSHING	LUTEINIZING	LYCEUMS	LYRIC
LUNULATED	LUSHLY	LUTEINS	LYCH	LYRICAL
LUNULE	LUSHNESS	LUTENIST	LYCHEE	LYRICALLY
LUNULES	LUSHNESSES	LUTENISTS	LYCHEES	LYRICISE
LUNY	LUST	LUTEOLIN	LYCHES	LYRICISED
LUPANAR	LUSTED	LUTEOLINS	LYCHNIS	LYRICISES
LUPANARS	LUSTER	LUTEOUS	LYCHNISES	LYRICISING
LUPIN	LUSTERED	LUTES	LYCOPENE	LYRICISM
LUPINE	LUSTERING	LUTETIUM	LYCOPENES	LYRICISMS
LUPINES	LUSTERS	LUTETIUMS	LYCOPOD	LYRICIST
LUPINS	LUSTFUL	LUTEUM	LYCOPODS	LYRICISTS
LUPOUS	LUSTFULLY	LUTFISK	LYCRA	LYRICIZE
LUPULIN	LUSTIER	LUTFISKS	LYCRAS	LYRICIZED
LUPULINS	LUSTIEST	LUTHERN	LYDDITE	LYRICIZES
LUPUS	LUSTIHOOD	LUTHERNS	LYDDITES	LYRICIZING
LUPUSES	LUSTIHOODS	LUTHIER	LYE	LYRICON
LURCH	LUSTILY	LUTHIERS	LYES	LYRICONS
LURCHED	LUSTINESS	LUTING	LYING	LYRICS
LURCHER	LUSTINESSES	LUTINGS	LYINGLY	LYRIFORM
LURCHERS	LUSTING	LUTIST	LYINGS	LYRISM
LURCHES	LUSTRA	LUTISTS	LYMPH	LYRISMS
LURCHING	LUSTRAL	LUTZ	LYMPHATIC	LYRIST
LURDAN	LUSTRATE	LUTZES	LYMPHATICS	LYRISTS
LURDANE	LUSTRATED	LUV	LYMPHOID	LYSATE
LURDANES	LUSTRATES	LUVS	LYMPHOMA	LYSATES
LURDANS	LUSTRATING	LUX	LYMPHOMAS	LYSE
LURE	LUSTRE	LUXATE	LYMPHOMATA	LYSED
LURED	LUSTRED	LUXATED	LYMPHS	LYSES
LURER	LUSTRES	LUXATES	LYNCEAN	LYSIMETER
LURERS	LUSTRING	LUXATING	LYNCH	LYSIMETERS
LURES	LUSTRINGS	LUXATION	LYNCHED	LYSIN
LUREX	LUSTROUS	LUXATIONS	LYNCHER	LYSINE
LUREXES	LUSTRUM	LUXE	LYNCHERS	LYSINES
LURID	LUSTRUMS	LUXES	LYNCHES	LYSING
LURIDLY	LUSTS	LUXURIANT	LYNCHING	LYSINS
LURIDNESS	LUSTY	LUXURIATE	LYNCHINGS	LYSIS
LURIDNESSES	LUSUS	LUXURIATED	LYNCHPIN	LYSOGEN
LURING	LUSUSES	LUXURIATES	LYNCHPINS	LYSOGENIC

LYSOGENIES	MACCOBOY	MACKINAW	MADAMS	MADRONES
LYSOGENS	MACCOBOYS	MACKINAWS	MADCAP	MADRONO
LYSOGENY	MACE	MACKLE	MADCAPS	MADRONOS
LYSOSOMAL	MACED	MACKLED	MADDED	MADS
LYSOSOME	MACEDOINE	MACKLES	MADDEN	MADTOM
LYSOSOMES	MACEDOINES	MACKLING	MADDENED	MADTOMS
LYSOZYME	MACER	MACKS	MADDENING	MADURO
LYSOZYMES	MACERATE	MACLE	MADDENS	MADUROS
LYSSA	MACERATED	MACLED	MADDER	MADWOMAN
LYSSAS	MACERATER	MACLES	MADDERS	MADWOMEN
LYTIC	MACERATERS	MACON	MADDEST	MADWORT
LYTICALLY	MACERATES	MACONS	MADDING	MADWORTS
LYTTA	MACERATING	MACRAME	MADDISH	MADZOON
LYTTAE	MACERATOR	MACRAMES	MADE	MADZOONS
LYTTAS	MACERATORS	MACRO	MADEIRA	MAE
	MACERS	MACROCOSM	MADEIRAS	MAELSTROM
	MACES	MACROCOSMS	MADELEINE	MAELSTROMS
M	MACH	MACROCYST	MADELEINES	MAENAD
	MACHE	MACROCYSTS	MADERIZE	MAENADES
	MACHES	MACROCYTE	MADERIZED	MAENADIC
MA	MACHETE	MACROCYTES	MADERIZES	MAENADISM
MAAR	MACHETES	MACRODONT	MADERIZING	MAENADISMS
MAARS	MACHINATE	MACROMERE	MADHOUSE	MAENADS
MABE	MACHINATED	MACROMERES	MADHOUSES	MAES
MABES	MACHINATES	MACROMOLE	MADLY	MAESTOSO
MAC	MACHINATING	MACROMOLES	MADMAN	MAESTOSOS
MACABER	MACHINE	MACRON	MADMEN	MAESTRI
MACABRE	MACHINED	MACRONS	MADNESS	MAESTRO
MACABRELY	MACHINERIES	MACROS	MADNESSES	MAESTROS
MACACO	MACHINERY	MACRURAL	MADONNA	MAFFIA
MACACOS	MACHINES	MACRURAN	MADONNAS	MAFFIAS
MACADAM	MACHINING	MACRURANS	MADRAS	MAFFICK
MACADAMIA	MACHINIST	MACRUROUS	MADRASA	MAFFICKED
MACADAMIAS	MACHINISTS	MACS	MADRASAH	MAFFICKER
MACADAMS	MACHISMO	MACULA	MADRASAHS	MAFFICKERS
MACAQUE	MACHISMOS	MACULAE	MADRASAS	MAFFICKING
MACAQUES	MACHO	MACULAR	MADRASES	MAFFICKS
MACARONI	MACHOISM	MACULAS	MADRASSA	MAFIA
MACARONIC	MACHOISMS	MACULATE	MADRASSAH	MAFIAS
MACARONICS	MACHOS	MACULATED	MADRASSAHS	MAFIC
MACARONIES	MACHREE	MACULATES	MADRASSAS	MAFIOSI
MACARONIS	MACHREES	MACULATING	MADRE	MAFIOSO
MACAROON	MACHS	MACULE	MADREPORE	MAFIOSOS
MACAROONS	MACHZOR	MACULED	MADREPORES	MAFTIR
MACAW	MACHZORIM	MACULES	MADRES	MAFTIRS
MACAWS	MACHZORS	MACULING	MADRIGAL	MAG
MACCABAW	MACING	MACUMBA	MADRIGALS	MAGALOG
MACCABAWS	MACINTOSH	MACUMBAS	MADRILENE	MAGALOGS
MACCABOY	MACINTOSHES	MAD	MADRILENES	MAGALOGUE
MACCABOYS	MACK	MADAM	MADRONA	MAGALOGUES
MACCHIA	MACKEREL	MADAME	MADRONAS	MAGAZINE
MACCHIE	MACKERELS	MADAMES	MADRONE	MAGAZINES

MAGDALEN	MAGNETITE	MAHJONGG	MAILLOTS	MAJESTY
MAGDALENE	MAGNETITES	MAHJONGGS	MAILLS	MAJOLICA
MAGDALENES	MAGNETIZE	MAHJONGS	MAILMAN	MAJOLICAS
MAGDALENS	MAGNETIZED	MAHLSTICK	MAILMEN	MAJOR
MAGE	MAGNETIZES	MAHLSTICKS	MAILROOM	MAJORDOMO
MAGENTA	MAGNETIZING	MAHOE	MAILROOMS	MAJORDOMOS
MAGENTAS	MAGNETO	MAHOES	MAILS	MAJORED
MAGES	MAGNETON	MAHOGANIES	MAIM	MAJORETTE
MAGGOT	MAGNETONS	MAHOGANY	MAIMED	MAJORETTES
MAGGOTS	MAGNETOS	MAHONIA	MAIMER	MAJORING
MAGGOTY	MAGNETRON	MAHONIAS	MAIMERS	MAJORITIES
MAGI	MAGNETRONS	MAHOUT	MAIMING	MAJORITY
MAGIAN	MAGNETS	MAHOUTS	MAIMS	MAJORLY
MAGIANS	MAGNIFIC	MAHUANG	MAIN	MAJORS
MAGIC	MAGNIFICO	MAHUANGS	MAINFRAME	MAJUSCULE
MAGICAL	MAGNIFICOES	MAHZOR	MAINFRAMES	MAJUSCULES
MAGICALLY	MAGNIFICOS	MAHZORIM	MAINLAND	MAKABLE
MAGICIAN	MAGNIFIED	MAHZORS	MAINLANDS	MAKAR
MAGICIANS	MAGNIFIER	MAIASAUR	MAINLINE	MAKARS
MAGICKED	MAGNIFIERS	MAIASAURA	MAINLINED	MAKE
MAGICKING	MAGNIFIES	MAIASAURAS	MAINLINER	MAKEABLE
MAGICS	MAGNIFY	MAIASAURS	MAINLINERS	MAKEBATE
MAGILP	MAGNIFYING	MAID	MAINLINES	MAKEBATES
MAGILPS	MAGNITUDE	MAIDEN	MAINLINING	MAKEFAST
MAGISTER	MAGNITUDES	MAIDENLY	MAINLY	MAKEFASTS
MAGISTERS	MAGNOLIA	MAIDENS	MAINMAST	MAKEOVER
MAGISTRAL	MAGNOLIAS	MAIDHOOD	MAINMASTS	MAKEOVERS
MAGLEV	MAGNUM	MAIDHOODS	MAINS	MAKER
MAGLEVS	MAGNUMS	MAIDISH	MAINSAIL	MAKEREADIES
MAGMA	MAGOT	MAIDS	MAINSAILS	MAKEREADY
MAGMAS	MAGOTS	MAIEUTIC	MAINSHEET	MAKERS
MAGMATA	MAGPIE	MAIGRE	MAINSHEETS	MAKES
MAGMATIC	MAGPIES	MAIHEM	MAINSTAY	MAKESHIFT
MAGNATE	MAGS	MAIHEMS	MAINSTAYS	MAKESHIFTS
MAGNATES	MAGUEY	MAIL	MAINTAIN	MAKEUP
MAGNESIA	MAGUEYS	MAILABLE	MAINTAINED	MAKEUPS
MAGNESIAN	MAGUS	MAILBAG	MAINTAINING	MAKIMONO
MAGNESIAS	MAHARAJA	MAILBAGS	MAINTAINS	MAKIMONOS
MAGNESIC	MAHARAJAH	MAILBOX	MAINTOP	MAKING
MAGNESITE	MAHARAJAHS	MAILBOXES	MAINTOPS	MAKINGS
MAGNESITES	MAHARAJAS	MAILE	MAIOLICA	MAKO
MAGNESIUM	MAHARANEE	MAILED	MAIOLICAS	MAKOS
MAGNESIUMS	MAHARANEES	MAILER	MAIR	MAKUTA
MAGNET	MAHARANI	MAILERS	MAIRS	MALACCA
MAGNETIC	MAHARANIS	MAILES	MAIST	MALACCAS
MAGNETICS	MAHARISHI	MAILGRAM	MAISTS	MALACHITE
MAGNETISE	MAHARISHIS	MAILGRAMS	MAIZE	MALACHITES
MAGNETISED	MAHATMA	MAILING	MAIZES	MALADIES
MAGNETISES	MAHATMAS	MAILINGS	MAJAGUA	MALADROIT
MAGNETISING	MAHIMAHI	MAILL	MAJAGUAS	MALADROITS
MAGNETISM	MAHIMAHIS	MAILLESS	MAJESTIC	MALADY
MAGNETISMS	MAHJONG	MAILLOT	MAJESTIES	MALAGUENA

MALAGUENAS	MALIGNANT	MALOTI	MAMMAL	MANAGE
MALAISE	MALIGNED	MALPIGHIA	MAMMALIAN	MANAGED
MALAISES	MALIGNER	MALPOSED	MAMMALIANS	MANAGER
MALAMUTE	MALIGNERS	MALT	MAMMALITIES	MANAGERS
MALAMUTES	MALIGNING	MALTASE	MAMMALITY	MANAGES
MALANDERS	MALIGNITIES	MALTASES	MAMMALOGIES	MANAGING
MALANGA	MALIGNITY	MALTED	MAMMALOGY	MANAKIN
MALANGAS	MALIGNLY	MALTEDS	MAMMALS	MANAKINS
MALAPERT	MALIGNS	MALTHA	MAMMARY	MANANA
MALAPERTS	MALIHINI	MALTHAS	MAMMAS	MANANAS
MALAPROP	MALIHINIS	MALTIER	MAMMATE	MANAS
MALAPROPS	MALINE	MALTIEST	MAMMATI	MANAT
MALAR	MALINES	MALTINESS	MAMMATUS	MANATEE
MALARIA	MALINGER	MALTINESSES	MAMMEE	MANATEES
MALARIAL	MALINGERED	MALTING	MAMMEES	MANATOID
MALARIAN	MALINGERING	MALTOL	MAMMER	MANATS
MALARIAS	MALINGERS	MALTOLS	MAMMERED	MANCHE
MALARIOUS	MALISON	MALTOSE	MAMMERING	MANCHES
MALARKEY	MALISONS	MALTOSES	MAMMERS	MANCHET
MALARKEYS	MALKIN	MALTREAT	MAMMET	MANCHETS
MALARKIES	MALKINS	MALTREATED	MAMMETS	MANCIPLE
MALARKY	MALL	MALTREATING	MAMMEY	MANCIPLES
MALAROMA	MALLARD	MALTREATS	MAMMEYS	MANDALA
MALAROMAS	MALLARDS	MALTS	MAMMIE	MANDALAS
MALARS	MALLEABLE	MALTSTER	MAMMIES	MANDALIC
MALATE	MALLEABLY	MALTSTERS	MAMMILLA	MANDAMUS
MALATES	MALLED	MALTY	MAMMILLAE	MANDAMUSED
MALATHION	MALLEE	MALVASIA	MAMMITIDES	MANDAMUSES
MALATHIONS	MALLEES	MALVASIAN	MAMMITIS	MANDAMUSING
MALE	MALLEI	MALVASIAS	MAMMOCK	MANDARIN
MALEATE	MALLEMUCK	MAMA	MAMMOCKED	MANDARINS
MALEATES	MALLEMUCKS	MAMALIGA	MAMMOCKING	MANDATARIES
MALEDICT	MALLEOLAR	MAMALIGAS	MAMMOCKS	MANDATARY
MALEDICTED	MALLEOLI	MAMAS	MAMMOGRAM	MANDATE
MALEDICTING	MALLEOLUS	MAMBA	MAMMOGRAMS	MANDATED
MALEDICTS	MALLET	MAMBAS	MAMMON	MANDATES
MALEFIC	MALLETS	MAMBO	MAMMONISM	MANDATING
MALEMIUT	MALLEUS	MAMBOED	MAMMONISMS	MANDATOR
MALEMIUTS	MALLING	MAMBOES	MAMMONIST	MANDATORIES
MALEMUTE	MALLINGS	MAMBOING	MAMMONISTS	MANDATORS
MALEMUTES	MALLOW	MAMBOS	MAMMONS	MANDATORY
MALENESS	MALLOWS	MAMELUKE	MAMMOTH	MANDIBLE
MALENESSES	MALLS	MAMELUKES	MAMMOTHS	MANDIBLES
MALES	MALM	MAMEY	MAMMY	MANDIOCA
MALFED	MALMIER	MAMEYES	MAMZER	MANDIOCAS
MALFORMED	MALMIEST	MAMEYS	MAMZERS	MANDOLA
MALGRE	MALMS	MAMIE	MAN	MANDOLAS
MALIC	MALMSEY	MAMIES	MANA	MANDOLIN
MALICE	MALMSEYS	MAMLUK	MANACLE	MANDOLINE
MALICES	MALMY	MAMLUKS	MANACLED	MANDOLINES
MALICIOUS	MALODOR	MAMMA	MANACLES	MANDOLINS
MALIGN	MALODORS	MAMMAE	MANACLING	MANDRAKE

MANDRAKES	MANGLED	MANIFOLDING	MANNIKIN	MANTICORE
MANDREL	MANGLER	MANIFOLDS	MANNIKINS	MANTICORES
MANDRELS	MANGLERS	MANIHOT	MANNING	MANTID
MANDRIL	MANGLES	MANIHOTS	MANNISH	MANTIDS
MANDRILL	MANGLING	MANIKIN	MANNISHLY	MANTILLA
MANDRILLS	MANGO	MANIKINS	MANNITE	MANTILLAS
MANDRILS	MANGOES	MANILA	MANNITES	MANTIS
MANDUCATE	MANGOLD	MANILAS	MANNITIC	MANTISES
MANDUCATED	MANGOLDS	MANILLA	MANNITOL	MANTISSA
MANDUCATES	MANGONEL	MANILLAS	MANNITOLS	MANTISSAS
MANDUCATING	MANGONELS	MANILLE	MANNOSE	MANTLE
MANE	MANGOS	MANILLES	MANNOSES	MANTLED
MANED	MANGROVE	MANIOC	MANO	MANTLES
MANEGE	MANGROVES	MANIOCA	MANOEUVRE	MANTLET
MANEGES	MANGY	MANIOCAS	MANOEUVRED	MANTLETS
MANELESS	MANHANDLE	MANIOCS	MANOEUVRES	MANTLING
MANES	MANHANDLED	MANIPLE	MANOEUVRING	MANTLINGS
MANEUVER	MANHANDLES	MANIPLES	MANOMETER	MANTRA
MANEUVERED	MANHANDLING	MANIPULAR	MANOMETERS	MANTRAM
MANEUVERING	MANHATTAN	MANIPULARS	MANOMETRIES	MANTRAMS
MANEUVERS	MANHATTANS	MANITO	MANOMETRY	MANTRAP
MANFUL	MANHOLE	MANITOS	MANOR	MANTRAPS
MANFULLY	MANHOLES	MANITOU	MANORIAL	MANTRAS
MANGA	MANHOOD	MANITOUS	MANORS	MANTRIC
MANGABEY	MANHOODS	MANITU	MANOS	MANTUA
MANGABEYS	MANHUNT	MANITUS	MANPACK	MANTUAS
MANGABIES	MANHUNTS	MANKIND	MANPOWER	MANUAL
MANGABY	MANIA	MANLESS	MANPOWERS	MANUALLY
MANGANATE	MANIAC	MANLIER	MANQUE	MANUALS
MANGANATES	MANIACAL	MANLIEST	MANROPE	MANUARY
MANGANESE	MANIACS	MANLIKE	MANROPES	MANUBRIA
MANGANESES	MANIAS	MANLIKELY	MANS	MANUBRIAL
MANGANIC	MANIC	MANLILY	MANSARD	MANUBRIUM
MANGANIN	MANICALLY	MANLINESS	MANSARDED	MANUBRIUMS
MANGANINS	MANICOTTI	MANLINESSES	MANSARDS	MANUMIT
MANGANITE	MANICOTTIS	MANLY	MANSE	MANUMITS
MANGANITES	MANICS	MANMADE	MANSES	MANUMITTED
MANGANOUS	MANICURE	MANNA	MANSION	MANUMITTING
MANGAS	MANICURED	MANNAN	MANSIONS	MANURE
MANGE	MANICURES	MANNANS	MANSLAYER	MANURED
MANGEL	MANICURING	MANNAS	MANSLAYERS	MANURER
MANGELS	MANIFEST	MANNED	MANTA	MANURERS
MANGER	MANIFESTED	MANNEQUIN	MANTAS	MANURES
MANGERS	MANIFESTING	MANNEQUINS	MANTEAU	MANURIAL
MANGES	MANIFESTO	MANNER	MANTEAUS	MANURING
MANGEY	MANIFESTOED	MANNERED	MANTEAUX	MANUS
MANGIER	MANIFESTOES	MANNERISM	MANTEL	MANWARD
MANGIEST	MANIFESTOING	MANNERISMS	MANTELET	MANWARDS
MANGILY	MANIFESTOS	MANNERIST	MANTELETS	MANWISE
MANGINESS	MANIFESTS	MANNERISTS	MANTELS	MANY
MANGINESSES	MANIFOLD	MANNERLY	MANTES	MANYFOLD
MANGLE	MANIFOLDED	MANNERS	MANTIC	MANYPLIES

MANZANITA	MARAVEDIS	MAREMME	MARINAS	MARLIER
MANZANITAS	MARBELIZE	MARENGO	MARINATE	MARLIEST
MAP	MARBELIZED	MARES	MARINATED	MARLIN
MAPLE	MARBELIZES	MARGARIC	MARINATES	MARLINE
MAPLELIKE	MARBELIZING	MARGARIN	MARINATING	MARLINES
MAPLES	MARBLE	MARGARINE	MARINE	MARLING
MAPLIKE	MARBLED	MARGARINES	MARINER	MARLINGS
MAPMAKER	MARBLEISE	MARGARINS	MARINERS	MARLINS
MAPMAKERS	MARBLEISED	MARGARITA	MARINES	MARLITE
MAPMAKING	MARBLEISES	MARGARITAS	MARIPOSA	MARLITES
MAPMAKINGS	MARBLEISING	MARGARITE	MARIPOSAS	MARLITIC
MAPPABLE	MARBLEIZE	MARGARITES	MARISH	MARLS
MAPPED	MARBLEIZED	MARGAY	MARISHES	MARLSTONE
MAPPER	MARBLEIZES	MARGAYS	MARITAL	MARLSTONES
MAPPERS	MARBLEIZING	MARGE	MARITALLY	MARLY
MAPPING	MARBLER	MARGENT	MARITIME	MARMALADE
MAPPINGS	MARBLERS	MARGENTED	MARJORAM	MARMALADES
MAPS	MARBLES	MARGENTING	MARJORAMS	MARMITE
MAQUETTE	MARBLIER	MARGENTS	MARK	MARMITES
MAQUETTES	MARBLIEST	MARGES	MARKA	MARMOREAL
MAQUI	MARBLING	MARGIN	MARKAS	MARMOREAN
MAQUILA	MARBLINGS	MARGINAL	MARKDOWN	MARMOSET
MAQUILAS	MARBLY	MARGINALS	MARKDOWNS	MARMOSETS
MAQUIS	MARC	MARGINATE	MARKED	MARMOT
MAR	MARCASITE	MARGINATED	MARKEDLY	MARMOTS
MARA	MARCASITES	MARGINATES	MARKER	MAROCAIN
MARABOU	MARCATO	MARGINATING	MARKERS	MAROCAINS
MARABOUS	MARCATOS	MARGINED	MARKET	MAROON
MARABOUT	MARCEL	MARGINING	MARKETED	MAROONED
MARABOUTS	MARCELLED	MARGINS	MARKETEER	MAROONING
MARACA	MARCELLER	MARGRAVE	MARKETEERS	MAROONS
MARACAS	MARCELLERS	MARGRAVES	MARKETER	MARPLOT
MARANATHA	MARCELLING	MARIA	MARKETERS	MARPLOTS
MARANATHAS	MARCELS	MARIACHI	MARKETING	MARQUE
MARANTA	MARCH	MARIACHIS	MARKETINGS	MARQUEE
MARANTAS	MARCHED	MARIGOLD	MARKETS	MARQUEES
MARAS	MARCHEN	MARIGOLDS	MARKHOOR	MARQUES
MARASCA	MARCHER	MARIHUANA	MARKHOORS	MARQUESS
MARASCAS	MARCHERS	MARIHUANAS	MARKHOR	MARQUESSES
MARASMIC	MARCHES	MARIJUANA	MARKHORS	MARQUETRIES
MARASMOID	MARCHESA	MARIJUANAS	MARKING	MARQUETRY
MARASMUS	MARCHESE	MARIMBA	MARKINGS	MARQUIS
MARASMUSES	MARCHESI	MARIMBAS	MARKKA	MARQUISE
MARATHON	MARCHING	MARIMBIST	MARKKAA	MARQUISES
MARATHONS	MARCHLAND	MARIMBISTS	MARKKAS	MARRAM
MARAUD	MARCHLANDS	MARINA	MARKS	MARRAMS
MARAUDED	MARCHLIKE	MARINADE	MARKSMAN	MARRANO
MARAUDER	MARCHPANE	MARINADED	MARKSMEN	MARRANOS
MARAUDERS	MARCHPANES	MARINADES	MARKUP	MARRED
MARAUDING	MARCS	MARINADING	MARKUPS	MARRER
MARAUDS	MARE	MARINARA	MARL	MARRERS
MARAVEDI	MAREMMA	MARINARAS	MARLED	MARRIAGE

MARRIAGES	MARTELLOS	MASCARAS	MASS	MASTERING
MARRIED	MARTEN	MASCON	MASSA	MASTERLY
MARRIEDS	MARTENS	MASCONS	MASSACRE	MASTERS
MARRIER	MARTIAL	MASCOT	MASSACRED	MASTERY
MARRIERS	MARTIALLY	MASCOTS	MASSACRER	MASTHEAD
MARRIES	MARTIAN	MASCULINE	MASSACRERS	MASTHEADED
MARRING	MARTIANS	MASCULINES	MASSACRES	MASTHEADING
MARRON	MARTIN	MASER	MASSACRING	MASTHEADS
MARRONS	MARTINET	MASERS	MASSAGE	MASTIC
MARROW	MARTINETS	MASH	MASSAGED	MASTICATE
MARROWED	MARTING	MASHED	MASSAGER	MASTICATED
MARROWFAT	MARTINGAL	MASHER	MASSAGERS	MASTICATES
MARROWFATS	MARTINGALS	MASHERS	MASSAGES	MASTICATING
MARROWING	MARTINI	MASHES	MASSAGING	MASTICHE
MARROWS	MARTINIS	MASHGIACH	MASSAS	MASTICHES
MARROWY	MARTINS	MASHGIAH	MASSCULT	MASTICS
MARRY	MARTLET	MASHGICHIM	MASSCULTS	MASTIFF
MARRYING	MARTLETS	MASHGIHIM	MASSE	MASTIFFS
MARS	MARTS	MASHIE	MASSED	MASTING
MARSALA	MARTYR	MASHIES	MASSEDLY	MASTITIC
MARSALAS	MARTYRDOM	MASHING	MASSES	MASTITIDES
MARSE	MARTYRDOMS	MASHY	MASSETER	MASTITIS
MARSEILLE	MARTYRED	MASJID	MASSETERS	MASTIX
MARSEILLES	MARTYRIES	MASJIDS	MASSEUR	MASTIXES
MARSES	MARTYRING	MASK	MASSEURS	MASTLESS
MARSH	MARTYRIZE	MASKABLE	MASSEUSE	MASTLIKE
MARSHAL	MARTYRIZED	MASKED	MASSEUSES	MASTODON
MARSHALCIES	MARTYRIZES	MASKEG	MASSICOT	MASTODONS
MARSHALCY	MARTYRIZING	MASKEGS	MASSICOTS	MASTODONT
MARSHALED	MARTYRLY	MASKER	MASSIER	MASTODONTS
MARSHALING	MARTYRS	MASKERS	MASSIEST	MASTOID
MARSHALL	MARTYRY	MASKING	MASSIF	MASTOIDS
MARSHALLED	MARVEL	MASKINGS	MASSIFS	MASTOPEXIES
MARSHALLING	MARVELED	MASKLIKE	MASSINESS	MASTOPEXY
MARSHALLS	MARVELING	MASKS	MASSINESSES	MASTS
MARSHALS	MARVELLED	MASOCHISM	MASSING	MASURIUM
MARSHES	MARVELLING	MASOCHISMS	MASSIVE	MASURIUMS
MARSHIER	MARVELOUS	MASOCHIST	MASSIVELY	MAT
MARSHIEST	MARVELS	MASOCHISTS	MASSLESS	MATADOR
MARSHLAND	MARVY	MASON	MASSY	MATADORS
MARSHLANDS	MARYJANE	MASONED	MAST	MATAMBALA
MARSHLIKE	MARYJANES	MASONIC	MASTABA	MATCH
MARSHY	MARZIPAN	MASONING	MASTABAH	MATCHABLE
MARSUPIA	MARZIPANS	MASONITE	MASTABAHS	MATCHBOOK
MARSUPIAL	MAS	MASONITES	MASTABAS	MATCHBOOKS
MARSUPIALS	MASA	MASONRIES	MASTED	MATCHBOX
MARSUPIUM	MASALA	MASONRY	MASTER	MATCHBOXES
MART	MASALAS	MASONS	MASTERDOM	MATCHED
MARTAGON	MASAS	MASQUE	MASTERDOMS	MATCHER
MARTAGONS	MASCARA	MASQUER	MASTERED	MATCHERS
MARTED	MASCARAED	MASQUERS	MASTERFUL	MATCHES
MARTELLO	MASCARAING	MASQUES	MASTERIES	MATCHING

MATCHLESS
MATCHLOCK
MATCHLOCKS
MATCHMADE
MATCHMAKE
MATCHMAKES
MATCHMAKING
MATCHMARK
MATCHMARKED
MATCHMARKING
MATCHMARKS
MATCHUP
MATCHUPS
MATCHWOOD
MATCHWOODS
MATE
MATED
MATELASSE
MATELASSES
MATELESS
MATELOT
MATELOTE
MATELOTES
MATELOTS
MATER
MATERIAL
MATERIALS
MATERIEL
MATERIELS
MATERNAL
MATERNITIES
MATERNITY
MATERS
MATES
MATESHIP
MATESHIPS
MATEY
MATEYNESS
MATEYNESSES
MATEYS
MATH
MATHS
MATIER
MATIEST
MATILDA
MATILDAS
MATIN
MATINAL
MATINEE
MATINEES
MATINESS
MATINESSES

MATING
MATINGS
MATINS
MATLESS
MATRASS
MATRASSES
MATRES
MATRIARCH
MATRIARCHS
MATRICES
MATRICIDE
MATRICIDES
MATRIMONIES
MATRIMONY
MATRIX
MATRIXES
MATRON
MATRONAL
MATRONIZE
MATRONIZED
MATRONIZES
MATRONIZING
MATRONLY
MATRONS
MATS
MATSAH
MATSAHS
MATSUTAKE
MATSUTAKES
MATT
MATTE
MATTED
MATTEDLY
MATTER
MATTERED
MATTERFUL
MATTERING
MATTERS
MATTERY
MATTES
MATTIN
MATTING
MATTINGS
MATTINS
MATTOCK
MATTOCKS
MATTOID
MATTOIDS
MATTRASS
MATTRASSES
MATTRESS
MATTRESSES

MATTS
MATURATE
MATURATED
MATURATES
MATURATING
MATURE
MATURED
MATURELY
MATURER
MATURERS
MATURES
MATUREST
MATURING
MATURITIES
MATURITY
MATUTINAL
MATZA
MATZAH
MATZAHS
MATZAS
MATZO
MATZOH
MATZOHS
MATZOON
MATZOONS
MATZOS
MATZOT
MATZOTH
MAUD
MAUDLIN
MAUDLINLY
MAUDS
MAUGER
MAUGRE
MAUL
MAULED
MAULER
MAULERS
MAULING
MAULS
MAULSTICK
MAULSTICKS
MAUMET
MAUMETRIES
MAUMETRY
MAUMETS
MAUN
MAUND
MAUNDER
MAUNDERED
MAUNDERER
MAUNDERERS

MAUNDERING
MAUNDERS
MAUNDIES
MAUNDS
MAUNDY
MAUSOLEA
MAUSOLEAN
MAUSOLEUM
MAUSOLEUMS
MAUT
MAUTS
MAUVE
MAUVES
MAVEN
MAVENS
MAVERICK
MAVERICKS
MAVIE
MAVIES
MAVIN
MAVINS
MAVIS
MAVISES
MAVOURNIN
MAVOURNINS
MAW
MAWED
MAWING
MAWKISH
MAWKISHLY
MAWN
MAWS
MAX
MAXED
MAXES
MAXI
MAXICOAT
MAXICOATS
MAXILLA
MAXILLAE
MAXILLARIES
MAXILLARY
MAXILLAS
MAXIM
MAXIMA
MAXIMAL
MAXIMALLY
MAXIMALS
MAXIMIN
MAXIMINS
MAXIMISE
MAXIMISED

MAXIMISES
MAXIMISING
MAXIMITE
MAXIMITES
MAXIMIZE
MAXIMIZED
MAXIMIZER
MAXIMIZERS
MAXIMIZES
MAXIMIZING
MAXIMS
MAXIMUM
MAXIMUMLY
MAXIMUMS
MAXING
MAXIS
MAXIXE
MAXIXES
MAXWELL
MAXWELLS
MAY
MAYA
MAYAN
MAYAPPLE
MAYAPPLES
MAYAS
MAYBE
MAYBES
MAYBIRD
MAYBIRDS
MAYBUSH
MAYBUSHES
MAYDAY
MAYDAYS
MAYED
MAYEST
MAYFLIES
MAYFLOWER
MAYFLOWERS
MAYFLY
MAYHAP
MAYHAPPEN
MAYHEM
MAYHEMS
MAYING
MAYINGS
MAYO
MAYOR
MAYORAL
MAYORALTIES
MAYORALTY
MAYORESS

MAYORESSES	MEADOWY	MEASLIEST	MEDAKAS	MEDIATIZE
MAYORS	MEADS	MEASLY	MEDAL	MEDIATIZED
MAYORSHIP	MEAGER	MEASURE	MEDALED	MEDIATIZES
MAYORSHIPS	MEAGERLY	MEASURED	MEDALING	MEDIATIZING
MAYOS	MEAGRE	MEASURER	MEDALIST	MEDIATOR
MAYPOLE	MEAGRELY	MEASURERS	MEDALISTS	MEDIATORS
MAYPOLES	MEAL	MEASURES	MEDALLED	MEDIATORY
MAYPOP	MEALIE	MEASURING	MEDALLIC	MEDIATRICES
MAYPOPS	MEALIER	MEAT	MEDALLING	MEDIATRIX
MAYS	MEALIES	MEATAL	MEDALLION	MEDIATRIXES
MAYST	MEALIEST	MEATBALL	MEDALLIONS	MEDIC
MAYVIN	MEALINESS	MEATBALLS	MEDALLIST	MEDICABLE
MAYVINS	MEALINESSES	MEATED	MEDALLISTS	MEDICAID
MAYWEED	MEALLESS	MEATHEAD	MEDALS	MEDICAIDS
MAYWEEDS	MEALS	MEATHEADS	MEDDLE	MEDICAL
MAZAEDIA	MEALTIME	MEATIER	MEDDLED	MEDICALLY
MAZAEDIUM	MEALTIMES	MEATIEST	MEDDLER	MEDICALS
MAZARD	MEALWORM	MEATILY	MEDDLERS	MEDICANT
MAZARDS	MEALWORMS	MEATINESS	MEDDLES	MEDICANTS
MAZE	MEALY	MEATINESSES	MEDDLING	MEDICARE
MAZED	MEALYBUG	MEATLESS	MEDEVAC	MEDICARES
MAZEDLY	MEALYBUGS	MEATLOAF	MEDEVACED	MEDICATE
MAZEDNESS	MEAN	MEATLOAVES	MEDEVACING	MEDICATED
MAZEDNESSES	MEANDER	MEATMAN	MEDEVACKED	MEDICATES
MAZELIKE	MEANDERED	MEATMEN	MEDEVACKING	MEDICATING
MAZELTOV	MEANDERER	MEATS	MEDEVACS	MEDICIDE
MAZER	MEANDERERS	MEATUS	MEDFLIES	MEDICIDES
MAZERS	MEANDERING	MEATUSES	MEDFLY	MEDICINAL
MAZES	MEANDERS	MEATY	MEDIA	MEDICINALS
MAZIER	MEANDROUS	MECCA	MEDIACIES	MEDICINE
MAZIEST	MEANER	MECCAS	MEDIACY	MEDICINED
MAZILY	MEANERS	MECHANIC	MEDIAD	MEDICINES
MAZINESS	MEANEST	MECHANICS	MEDIAE	MEDICINING
MAZINESSES	MEANIE	MECHANISM	MEDIAEVAL	MEDICK
MAZING	MEANIES	MECHANISMS	MEDIAEVALS	MEDICKS
MAZOURKA	MEANING	MECHANIST	MEDIAL	MEDICO
MAZOURKAS	MEANINGLY	MECHANISTS	MEDIALLY	MEDICOS
MAZUMA	MEANINGS	MECHANIZE	MEDIALS	MEDICS
MAZUMAS	MEANLY	MECHANIZED	MEDIAN	MEDIEVAL
MAZURKA	MEANNESS	MECHANIZES	MEDIANLY	MEDIEVALS
MAZURKAS	MEANNESSES	MECHANIZING	MEDIANS	MEDIGAP
MAZY	MEANS	MECHITZA	MEDIANT	MEDIGAPS
MAZZARD	MEANT	MECHITZAS	MEDIANTS	MEDII
MAZZARDS	MEANTIME	MECHITZOT	MEDIAS	MEDINA
MBAQANGA	MEANTIMES	MECLIZINE	MEDIATE	MEDINAS
MBAQANGAS	MEANWHILE	MECLIZINES	MEDIATED	MEDIOCRE
MBIRA	MEANWHILES	MECONIUM	MEDIATELY	MEDITATE
MBIRAS	MEANY	MECONIUMS	MEDIATES	MEDITATED
ME	MEASLE	MED	MEDIATING	MEDITATES
MEAD	MEASLED	MEDAILLON	MEDIATION	MEDITATING
MEADOW	MEASLES	MEDAILLONS	MEDIATIONS	MEDITATOR
MEADOWS	MEASLIER	MEDAKA	MEDIATIVE	MEDITATORS

MEDIUM	MEGABUCK	MEGATHERES	MELANIZE	MELLOW
MEDIUMS	MEGABUCKS	MEGATON	MELANIZED	MELLOWED
MEDIUS	MEGABYTE	MEGATONS	MELANIZES	MELLOWER
MEDIVAC	MEGABYTES	MEGAVOLT	MELANIZING	MELLOWEST
MEDIVACED	MEGACITIES	MEGAVOLTS	MELANOID	MELLOWING
MEDIVACING	MEGACITY	MEGAWATT	MELANOIDS	MELLOWLY
MEDIVACKED	MEGACYCLE	MEGAWATTS	MELANOMA	MELLOWS
MEDIVACKING	MEGACYCLES	MEGILLA	MELANOMAS	MELLS
MEDIVACS	MEGADEAL	MEGILLAH	MELANOMATA	MELODEON
MEDLAR	MEGADEALS	MEGILLAHS	MELANOSES	MELODEONS
MEDLARS	MEGADEATH	MEGILLAS	MELANOSIS	MELODIA
MEDLEY	MEGADEATHS	MEGILP	MELANOTIC	MELODIAS
MEDLEYS	MEGADOSE	MEGILPH	MELANOUS	MELODIC
MEDS	MEGADOSES	MEGILPHS	MELAPHYRE	MELODICA
MEDULLA	MEGADYNE	MEGILPS	MELAPHYRES	MELODICAS
MEDULLAE	MEGADYNES	MEGOHM	MELASTOME	MELODIES
MEDULLAR	MEGAFAUNA	MEGOHMS	MELATONIN	MELODIOUS
MEDULLARY	MEGAFAUNAE	MEGRIM	MELATONINS	MELODISE
MEDULLAS	MEGAFAUNAS	MEGRIMS	MELD	MELODISED
MEDUSA	MEGAFLOP	MEGS	MELDED	MELODISES
MEDUSAE	MEGAFLOPS	MEHNDI	MELDER	MELODISING
MEDUSAL	MEGAHERTZ	MEHNDIS	MELDERS	MELODIST
MEDUSAN	MEGAHERTZES	MEIKLE	MELDING	MELODISTS
MEDUSANS	MEGAHIT	MEINIE	MELDS	MELODIZE
MEDUSAS	MEGAHITS	MEINIES	MELEE	MELODIZED
MEDUSOID	MEGALITH	MEINY	MELEES	MELODIZER
MEDUSOIDS	MEGALITHS	MEIOSES	MELENA	MELODIZERS
MEED	MEGALOPIC	MEIOSIS	MELENAS	MELODIZES
MEEDS	MEGALOPS	MEIOTIC	MELIC	MELODIZING
MEEK	MEGALOPSES	MEISTER	MELILITE	MELODRAMA
MEEKER	MEGAPHONE	MEISTERS	MELILITES	MELODRAMAS
MEEKEST	MEGAPHONED	MEL	MELILOT	MELODY
MEEKLY	MEGAPHONES	MELALEUCA	MELILOTS	MELOID
MEEKNESS	MEGAPHONING	MELALEUCAS	MELINITE	MELOIDS
MEEKNESSES	MEGAPIXEL	MELAMDIM	MELINITES	MELON
MEERKAT	MEGAPIXELS	MELAMED	MELIORATE	MELONGENE
MEERKATS	MEGAPLEX	MELAMINE	MELIORATED	MELONGENES
MEET	MEGAPLEXES	MELAMINES	MELIORATES	MELONS
MEETER	MEGAPOD	MELANGE	MELIORATING	MELPHALAN
MEETERS	MEGAPODE	MELANGES	MELIORISM	MELPHALANS
MEETING	MEGAPODES	MELANIAN	MELIORISMS	MELS
MEETINGS	MEGAPODS	MELANIC	MELIORIST	MELT
MEETLY	MEGARA	MELANICS	MELIORISTS	MELTABLE
MEETNESS	MEGARON	MELANIN	MELISMA	MELTAGE
MEETNESSES	MEGASPORE	MELANINS	MELISMAS	MELTAGES
MEETS	MEGASPORES	MELANISM	MELISMATA	MELTDOWN
MEG	MEGASS	MELANISMS	MELL	MELTDOWNS
MEGA	MEGASSE	MELANIST	MELLED	MELTED
MEGABAR	MEGASSES	MELANISTS	MELLIFIC	MELTER
MEGABARS	MEGASTAR	MELANITE	MELLING	MELTERS
MEGABIT	MEGASTARS	MELANITES	MELLOTRON	MELTING
MEGABITS	MEGATHERE	MELANITIC	MELLOTRONS	MELTINGLY

MELTON
MELTONS
MELTS
MELTWATER
MELTWATERS
MELTY
MEM
MEMBER
MEMBERED
MEMBERS
MEMBRANAL
MEMBRANE
MEMBRANED
MEMBRANES
MEME
MEMENTO
MEMENTOES
MEMENTOS
MEMES
MEMETICS
MEMO
MEMOIR
MEMOIRIST
MEMOIRISTS
MEMOIRS
MEMORABLE
MEMORABLY
MEMORANDA
MEMORANDUM
MEMORANDUMS
MEMORIAL
MEMORIALS
MEMORIES
MEMORISE
MEMORISED
MEMORISES
MEMORISING
MEMORITER
MEMORIZE
MEMORIZED
MEMORIZER
MEMORIZERS
MEMORIZES
MEMORIZING
MEMORY
MEMOS
MEMS
MEMSAHIB
MEMSAHIBS
MEN
MENACE
MENACED

MENACER
MENACERS
MENACES
MENACING
MENAD
MENADIONE
MENADIONES
MENADS
MENAGE
MENAGERIE
MENAGERIES
MENAGES
MENARCHE
MENARCHES
MENAZON
MENAZONS
MEND
MENDABLE
MENDACITIES
MENDACITY
MENDED
MENDER
MENDERS
MENDICANT
MENDICANTS
MENDICITIES
MENDICITY
MENDIGO
MENDIGOS
MENDING
MENDINGS
MENDS
MENFOLK
MENFOLKS
MENHADEN
MENHADENS
MENHIR
MENHIRS
MENIAL
MENIALLY
MENIALS
MENINGEAL
MENINGES
MENINX
MENISCAL
MENISCATE
MENISCI
MENISCOID
MENISCUS
MENISCUSES
MENO
MENOLOGIES

MENOLOGY
MENOPAUSE
MENOPAUSES
MENORAH
MENORAHS
MENORRHEA
MENORRHEAS
MENSA
MENSAE
MENSAL
MENSAS
MENSCH
MENSCHEN
MENSCHES
MENSCHY
MENSE
MENSED
MENSEFUL
MENSELESS
MENSES
MENSH
MENSHEN
MENSHES
MENSING
MENSTRUA
MENSTRUAL
MENSTRUUM
MENSTRUUMS
MENSURAL
MENSWEAR
MENTA
MENTAL
MENTALESE
MENTALESES
MENTALISM
MENTALISMS
MENTALIST
MENTALISTS
MENTALITIES
MENTALITY
MENTALLY
MENTATION
MENTATIONS
MENTEE
MENTEES
MENTHENE
MENTHENES
MENTHOL
MENTHOLS
MENTION
MENTIONED
MENTIONER

MENTIONERS
MENTIONING
MENTIONS
MENTOR
MENTORED
MENTORING
MENTORS
MENTUM
MENU
MENUDO
MENUDOS
MENUS
MEOU
MEOUED
MEOUING
MEOUS
MEOW
MEOWED
MEOWING
MEOWS
MEPHITIC
MEPHITIS
MEPHITISES
MERBROMIN
MERBROMINS
MERC
MERCAPTAN
MERCAPTANS
MERCAPTO
MERCENARIES
MERCENARY
MERCER
MERCERIES
MERCERISE
MERCERISED
MERCERISES
MERCERISING
MERCERIZE
MERCERIZED
MERCERIZES
MERCERIZING
MERCERS
MERCERY
MERCES
MERCH
MERCHANT
MERCHANTED
MERCHANTING
MERCHANTS
MERCHES
MERCIES
MERCIFUL

MERCILESS
MERCS
MERCURATE
MERCURATED
MERCURATES
MERCURATING
MERCURIAL
MERCURIALS
MERCURIC
MERCURIES
MERCUROUS
MERCURY
MERCY
MERDE
MERDES
MERE
MERELY
MERENGUE
MERENGUES
MERER
MERES
MEREST
MERGANSER
MERGANSERS
MERGE
MERGED
MERGEE
MERGEES
MERGENCE
MERGENCES
MERGER
MERGERS
MERGES
MERGING
MERIDIAN
MERIDIANS
MERINGUE
MERINGUES
MERINO
MERINOS
MERISES
MERISIS
MERISTEM
MERISTEMS
MERISTIC
MERIT
MERITED
MERITING
MERITLESS
MERITS
MERK
MERKS

MERL	MESHUGA	MESOPAUSES	MESTEES	METALMARKS
MERLE	MESHUGAAS	MESOPHYL	MESTESO	METALS
MERLES	MESHUGAH	MESOPHYLL	MESTESOES	METALWARE
MERLIN	MESHUGGA	MESOPHYLLS	MESTESOS	METALWARES
MERLINS	MESHUGGAH	MESOPHYLS	MESTINO	METALWORK
MERLON	MESHUGGE	MESOPHYTE	MESTINOES	METALWORKS
MERLONS	MESHWORK	MESOPHYTES	MESTINOS	METAMER
MERLOT	MESHWORKS	MESOSCALE	MESTIZA	METAMERE
MERLOTS	MESHY	MESOSOME	MESTIZAS	METAMERES
MERLS	MESIAL	MESOSOMES	MESTIZO	METAMERIC
MERMAID	MESIALLY	MESOTRON	MESTIZOES	METAMERS
MERMAIDS	MESIAN	MESOTRONS	MESTIZOS	METAPHASE
MERMAN	MESIC	MESOZOAN	MESTRANOL	METAPHASES
MERMEN	MESICALLY	MESOZOANS	MESTRANOLS	METAPHOR
MEROCRINE	MESMERIC	MESOZOIC	MET	METAPHORS
MEROPIA	MESMERISE	MESQUIT	META	METAPLASM
MEROPIAS	MESMERISED	MESQUITE	METABOLIC	METAPLASMS
MEROPIC	MESMERISES	MESQUITES	METACARPI	METATAG
MEROZOITE	MESMERISING	MESQUITS	METACARPUS	METATAGS
MEROZOITES	MESMERISM	MESS	METAGE	METATARSI
MERRIER	MESMERISMS	MESSAGE	METAGENIC	METATARSUS
MERRIEST	MESMERIST	MESSAGED	METAGES	METATE
MERRILY	MESMERISTS	MESSAGES	METAL	METATES
MERRIMENT	MESMERIZE	MESSAGING	METALED	METAXYLEM
MERRIMENTS	MESMERIZED	MESSALINE	METALHEAD	METAXYLEMS
MERRINESS	MESMERIZES	MESSALINES	METALHEADS	METAZOA
MERRINESSES	MESMERIZING	MESSAN	METALING	METAZOAL
MERRY	MESNALTIES	MESSANS	METALISE	METAZOAN
MESA	MESNALTY	MESSED	METALISED	METAZOANS
MESALLY	MESNE	MESSENGER	METALISES	METAZOIC
MESARCH	MESNES	MESSENGERED	METALISING	METAZOON
MESAS	MESOBLAST	MESSENGERING	METALIST	METE
MESCAL	MESOBLASTS	MESSENGERS	METALISTS	METED
MESCALINE	MESOCARP	MESSES	METALIZE	METEOR
MESCALINES	MESOCARPS	MESSIAH	METALIZED	METEORIC
MESCALS	MESOCRANIES	MESSIAHS	METALIZES	METEORITE
MESCLUN	MESOCRANY	MESSIANIC	METALIZING	METEORITES
MESCLUNS	MESODERM	MESSIER	METALLED	METEOROID
MESDAMES	MESODERMS	MESSIEST	METALLIC	METEOROIDS
MESEEMED	MESOGLEA	MESSIEURS	METALLICS	METEORS
MESEEMETH	MESOGLEAL	MESSILY	METALLIKE	METEPA
MESEEMS	MESOGLEAS	MESSINESS	METALLINE	METEPAS
MESENTERA	MESOGLOEA	MESSINESSES	METALLING	METER
MESENTERIES	MESOGLOEAS	MESSING	METALLIST	METERAGE
MESENTERON	MESOMERE	MESSMAN	METALLISTS	METERAGES
MESENTERY	MESOMERES	MESSMATE	METALLIZE	METERED
MESH	MESOMORPH	MESSMATES	METALLIZED	METERING
MESHED	MESOMORPHS	MESSMEN	METALLIZES	METERS
MESHES	MESON	MESSUAGE	METALLIZING	METES
MESHIER	MESONIC	MESSUAGES	METALLOID	METESTRUS
MESHIEST	MESONS	MESSY	METALLOIDS	METESTRUSES
MESHING	MESOPAUSE	MESTEE	METALMARK	METFORMIN

METFORMINS	METING	METROPLEXES	MIAOUS	MICROBARS
METH	METIS	METROS	MIAOW	MICROBE
METHADON	METISSE	METTLE	MIAOWED	MICROBEAM
METHADONE	METISSES	METTLED	MIAOWING	MICROBEAMS
METHADONES	METOL	METTLES	MIAOWS	MICROBES
METHADONS	METOLS	METUMP	MIASM	MICROBIAL
METHANE	METONYM	METUMPS	MIASMA	MICROBIAN
METHANES	METONYMIC	MEUNIERE	MIASMAL	MICROBIC
METHANOL	METONYMIES	MEW	MIASMAS	MICROBREW
METHANOLS	METONYMS	MEWED	MIASMATA	MICROBREWS
METHEGLIN	METONYMY	MEWING	MIASMATIC	MICROBUS
METHEGLINS	METOPAE	MEWL	MIASMIC	MICROBUSES
METHINKS	METOPE	MEWLED	MIASMS	MICROBUSSES
METHOD	METOPES	MEWLER	MIAUL	MICROCAP
METHODIC	METOPIC	MEWLERS	MIAULED	MICROCHIP
METHODISE	METOPON	MEWLING	MIAULING	MICROCHIPS
METHODISED	METOPONS	MEWLS	MIAULS	MICROCODE
METHODISES	METRALGIA	MEWS	MIB	MICROCODES
METHODISING	METRALGIAS	MEZCAL	MIBS	MICROCOPIES
METHODISM	METRAZOL	MEZCALS	MIC	MICROCOPY
METHODISMS	METRAZOLS	MEZE	MICA	MICROCOSM
METHODIST	METRE	MEZEREON	MICACEOUS	MICROCOSMS
METHODISTS	METRED	MEZEREONS	MICAS	MICROCYTE
METHODIZE	METRES	MEZEREUM	MICAWBER	MICROCYTES
METHODIZED	METRIC	MEZEREUMS	MICAWBERS	MICRODONT
METHODIZES	METRICAL	MEZES	MICE	MICRODOT
METHODIZING	METRICATE	MEZQUIT	MICELL	MICRODOTS
METHODS	METRICATED	MEZQUITE	MICELLA	MICROFILM
METHOUGHT	METRICATES	MEZQUITES	MICELLAE	MICROFILMED
METHOXIDE	METRICATING	MEZQUITS	MICELLAR	MICROFILMING
METHOXIDES	METRICISM	MEZUZA	MICELLE	MICROFILMS
METHOXY	METRICISMS	MEZUZAH	MICELLES	MICROFORM
METHOXYL	METRICIZE	MEZUZAHS	MICELLS	MICROFORMS
METHS	METRICIZED	MEZUZAS	MICHE	MICROGRAM
METHYL	METRICIZES	MEZUZOT	MICHED	MICROGRAMS
METHYLAL	METRICIZING	MEZUZOTH	MICHES	MICROHM
METHYLALS	METRICS	MEZZALUNA	MICHING	MICROHMS
METHYLASE	METRIFIED	MEZZALUNAS	MICK	MICROINCH
METHYLASES	METRIFIES	MEZZANINE	MICKEY	MICROINCHES
METHYLATE	METRIFY	MEZZANINES	MICKEYS	MICROLITH
METHYLATED	METRIFYING	MEZZO	MICKLE	MICROLITHS
METHYLATES	METRING	MEZZOS	MICKLER	MICROLOAN
METHYLATING	METRIST	MEZZOTINT	MICKLES	MICROLOANS
METHYLENE	METRISTS	MEZZOTINTED	MICKLEST	MICROLUCES
METHYLENES	METRITIS	MEZZOTINTING	MICKS	MICROLUX
METHYLIC	METRITISES	MEZZOTINTS	MICRA	MICROLUXES
METHYLS	METRO	MHO	MICRIFIED	MICROMERE
METICAIS	METROLOGIES	MHOS	MICRIFIES	MICROMERES
METICAL	METROLOGY	MI	MICRIFY	MICROMHO
METICALS	METRONOME	MIAOU	MICRIFYING	MICROMHOS
METIER	METRONOMES	MIAOUED	MICRO	MICROMINI
METIERS	METROPLEX	MIAOUING	MICROBAR	MICROMINIS

MICROMOLE	MIDDLEMAN	MIDRASHOT	MIFFIEST	MIKVOT
MICROMOLES	MIDDLEMEN	MIDRASHOTH	MIFFINESS	MIKVOTH
MICRON	MIDDLER	MIDRIB	MIFFINESSES	MIL
MICRONIZE	MIDDLERS	MIDRIBS	MIFFING	MILADI
MICRONIZED	MIDDLES	MIDRIFF	MIFFS	MILADIES
MICRONIZES	MIDDLING	MIDRIFFS	MIFFY	MILADIS
MICRONIZING	MIDDLINGS	MIDS	MIG	MILADY
MICRONS	MIDDORSAL	MIDSHIP	MIGG	MILAGE
MICROPORE	MIDDY	MIDSHIPS	MIGGLE	MILAGES
MICROPORES	MIDFIELD	MIDSIZE	MIGGLES	MILCH
MICROPYLE	MIDFIELDS	MIDSIZED	MIGGS	MILCHIG
MICROPYLES	MIDGE	MIDSOLE	MIGHT	MILD
MICROS	MIDGES	MIDSOLES	MIGHTIER	MILDED
MICROSOME	MIDGET	MIDSPACE	MIGHTIEST	MILDEN
MICROSOMES	MIDGETS	MIDSPACES	MIGHTILY	MILDENED
MICROTOME	MIDGUT	MIDST	MIGHTS	MILDENING
MICROTOMES	MIDGUTS	MIDSTORIES	MIGHTY	MILDENS
MICROTOMIES	MIDI	MIDSTORY	MIGNON	MILDER
MICROTOMY	MIDINETTE	MIDSTREAM	MIGNONNE	MILDEST
MICROTONE	MIDINETTES	MIDSTREAMS	MIGNONS	MILDEW
MICROTONES	MIDIRON	MIDSTS	MIGRAINE	MILDEWED
MICROVOLT	MIDIRONS	MIDSUMMER	MIGRAINES	MILDEWING
MICROVOLTS	MIDIS	MIDSUMMERS	MIGRANT	MILDEWS
MICROWATT	MIDISKIRT	MIDTERM	MIGRANTS	MILDEWY
MICROWATTS	MIDISKIRTS	MIDTERMS	MIGRATE	MILDING
MICROWAVE	MIDLAND	MIDTOWN	MIGRATED	MILDLY
MICROWAVED	MIDLANDS	MIDTOWNS	MIGRATES	MILDNESS
MICROWAVES	MIDLEG	MIDWATCH	MIGRATING	MILDNESSES
MICROWAVING	MIDLEGS	MIDWATCHES	MIGRATION	MILDS
MICRURGIES	MIDLIFE	MIDWAY	MIGRATIONS	MILE
MICRURGY	MIDLIFER	MIDWAYS	MIGRATOR	MILEAGE
MICS	MIDLIFERS	MIDWEEK	MIGRATORS	MILEAGES
MICTURATE	MIDLINE	MIDWEEKLY	MIGRATORY	MILEPOST
MICTURATED	MIDLINES	MIDWEEKS	MIGS	MILEPOSTS
MICTURATES	MIDLIST	MIDWIFE	MIHRAB	MILER
MICTURATING	MIDLISTS	MIDWIFED	MIHRABS	MILERS
MID	MIDLIVES	MIDWIFERIES	MIJNHEER	MILES
MIDAIR	MIDMONTH	MIDWIFERY	MIJNHEERS	MILESIAN
MIDAIRS	MIDMONTHS	MIDWIFES	MIKADO	MILESIMO
MIDBRAIN	MIDMOST	MIDWIFING	MIKADOS	MILESIMOS
MIDBRAINS	MIDMOSTS	MIDWINTER	MIKE	MILESTONE
MIDCAP	MIDNIGHT	MIDWINTERS	MIKED	MILESTONES
MIDCOURSE	MIDNIGHTS	MIDWIVED	MIKES	MILFOIL
MIDCULT	MIDNOON	MIDWIVES	MIKING	MILFOILS
MIDCULTS	MIDNOONS	MIDWIVING	MIKRA	MILIA
MIDDAY	MIDPOINT	MIDYEAR	MIKRON	MILIARIA
MIDDAYS	MIDPOINTS	MIDYEARS	MIKRONS	MILIARIAL
MIDDEN	MIDRANGE	MIEN	MIKVAH	MILIARIAS
MIDDENS	MIDRANGES	MIENS	MIKVAHS	MILIARY
MIDDIES	MIDRASH	MIFF	MIKVEH	MILIEU
MIDDLE	MIDRASHIC	MIFFED	MIKVEHS	MILIEUS
MIDDLED	MIDRASHIM	MIFFIER	MIKVOS	MILIEUX

MILITANCE	MILLBOARD	MILLIMOLES	MILTING	MINCIEST
MILITANCES	MILLBOARDS	MILLINE	MILTS	MINCING
MILITANCIES	MILLCAKE	MILLINER	MILTY	MINCINGLY
MILITANCY	MILLCAKES	MILLINERIES	MIM	MINCY
MILITANT	MILLDAM	MILLINERS	MIMBAR	MIND
MILITANTS	MILLDAMS	MILLINERY	MIMBARS	MINDED
MILITARIA	MILLE	MILLINES	MIME	MINDER
MILITARIES	MILLED	MILLING	MIMED	MINDERS
MILITARY	MILLENARIES	MILLINGS	MIMEO	MINDFUL
MILITATE	MILLENARY	MILLIOHM	MIMEOED	MINDFULLY
MILITATED	MILLENNIA	MILLIOHMS	MIMEOING	MINDING
MILITATES	MILLENNIUM	MILLION	MIMEOS	MINDLESS
MILITATING	MILLENNIUMS	MILLIONS	MIMER	MINDS
MILITIA	MILLEPED	MILLIONTH	MIMERS	MINDSET
MILITIAS	MILLEPEDE	MILLIONTHS	MIMES	MINDSETS
MILIUM	MILLEPEDES	MILLIPED	MIMESES	MINE
MILK	MILLEPEDS	MILLIPEDE	MIMESIS	MINEABLE
MILKED	MILLEPORE	MILLIPEDES	MIMESISES	MINED
MILKER	MILLEPORES	MILLIPEDS	MIMETIC	MINEFIELD
MILKERS	MILLER	MILLIREM	MIMETITE	MINEFIELDS
MILKFISH	MILLERITE	MILLIREMS	MIMETITES	MINELAYER
MILKFISHES	MILLERITES	MILLIVOLT	MIMIC	MINELAYERS
MILKIER	MILLERS	MILLIVOLTS	MIMICAL	MINER
MILKIEST	MILLES	MILLIWATT	MIMICKED	MINERAL
MILKILY	MILLET	MILLIWATTS	MIMICKER	MINERALS
MILKINESS	MILLETS	MILLPOND	MIMICKERS	MINERS
MILKINESSES	MILLHOUSE	MILLPONDS	MIMICKING	MINES
MILKING	MILLHOUSES	MILLRACE	MIMICRIES	MINESHAFT
MILKLESS	MILLIARD	MILLRACES	MIMICRY	MINESHAFTS
MILKMAID	MILLIARDS	MILLRUN	MIMICS	MINGIER
MILKMAIDS	MILLIARE	MILLRUNS	MIMING	MINGIEST
MILKMAN	MILLIARES	MILLS	MIMOSA	MINGLE
MILKMEN	MILLIARIES	MILLSTONE	MIMOSAS	MINGLED
MILKS	MILLIARY	MILLSTONES	MINA	MINGLER
MILKSHAKE	MILLIBAR	MILLWORK	MINABLE	MINGLERS
MILKSHAKES	MILLIBARS	MILLWORKS	MINACIOUS	MINGLES
MILKSHED	MILLIEME	MILNEB	MINACITIES	MINGLING
MILKSHEDS	MILLIEMES	MILNEBS	MINACITY	MINGY
MILKSOP	MILLIER	MILO	MINAE	MINI
MILKSOPPY	MILLIERS	MILORD	MINARET	MINIATURE
MILKSOPS	MILLIGAL	MILORDS	MINARETED	MINIATURES
MILKWEED	MILLIGALS	MILOS	MINARETS	MINIBAR
MILKWEEDS	MILLIGRAM	MILPA	MINAS	MINIBARS
MILKWOOD	MILLIGRAMS	MILPAS	MINATORY	MINIBIKE
MILKWOODS	MILLILUCES	MILREIS	MINCE	MINIBIKER
MILKWORT	MILLILUX	MILS	MINCED	MINIBIKERS
MILKWORTS	MILLILUXES	MILT	MINCEMEAT	MINIBIKES
MILKY	MILLIME	MILTED	MINCEMEATS	MINIBUS
MILL	MILLIMES	MILTER	MINCER	MINIBUSES
MILLABLE	MILLIMHO	MILTERS	MINCERS	MINIBUSSES
MILLAGE	MILLIMHOS	MILTIER	MINCES	MINICAB
MILLAGES	MILLIMOLE	MILTIEST	MINCIER	MINICABS

MINICAM	MINISHED	MINTERS	MIRANDIZED	MISADJUST
MINICAMP	MINISHES	MINTIER	MIRANDIZES	MISADJUSTED
MINICAMPS	MINISHING	MINTIEST	MIRANDIZING	MISADJUSTING
MINICAMS	MINISKI	MINTING	MIRE	MISADJUSTS
MINICAR	MINISKIRT	MINTS	MIRED	MISADVICE
MINICARS	MINISKIRTS	MINTY	MIREPOIX	MISADVICES
MINIDISC	MINISKIS	MINUEND	MIRES	MISADVISE
MINIDISCS	MINISTATE	MINUENDS	MIREX	MISADVISED
MINIDRESS	MINISTATES	MINUET	MIREXES	MISADVISES
MINIDRESSES	MINISTER	MINUETS	MIRI	MISADVISING
MINIFIED	MINISTERED	MINUS	MIRIER	MISAGENT
MINIFIES	MINISTERING	MINUSCULE	MIRIEST	MISAGENTS
MINIFY	MINISTERS	MINUSCULES	MIRIN	MISAIM
MINIFYING	MINISTRIES	MINUSES	MIRINESS	MISAIMED
MINIKIN	MINISTRY	MINUTE	MIRINESSES	MISAIMING
MINIKINS	MINITOWER	MINUTED	MIRING	MISAIMS
MINILAB	MINITOWERS	MINUTELY	MIRINS	MISALIGN
MINILABS	MINITRACK	MINUTEMAN	MIRK	MISALIGNED
MINIM	MINITRACKS	MINUTEMEN	MIRKER	MISALIGNING
MINIMA	MINIUM	MINUTER	MIRKEST	MISALIGNS
MINIMAL	MINIUMS	MINUTES	MIRKIER	MISALLIED
MINIMALLY	MINIVAN	MINUTEST	MIRKIEST	MISALLIES
MINIMALS	MINIVANS	MINUTIA	MIRKILY	MISALLOT
MINIMAX	MINIVER	MINUTIAE	MIRKS	MISALLOTS
MINIMAXES	MINIVERS	MINUTIAL	MIRKY	MISALLOTTED
MINIMILL	MINK	MINUTING	MIRLITON	MISALLOTTING
MINIMILLS	MINKE	MINX	MIRLITONS	MISALLY
MINIMISE	MINKES	MINXES	MIRROR	MISALLYING
MINIMISED	MINKS	MINXISH	MIRRORED	MISALTER
MINIMISES	MINNIES	MINYAN	MIRRORING	MISALTERED
MINIMISING	MINNOW	MINYANIM	MIRRORS	MISALTERING
MINIMIZE	MINNOWS	MINYANS	MIRS	MISALTERS
MINIMIZED	MINNY	MIOCENE	MIRTH	MISANDRIES
MINIMIZER	MINOR	MIOSES	MIRTHFUL	MISANDRY
MINIMIZERS	MINORCA	MIOSIS	MIRTHLESS	MISAPPLIED
MINIMIZES	MINORCAS	MIOTIC	MIRTHS	MISAPPLIES
MINIMIZING	MINORED	MIOTICS	MIRY	MISAPPLY
MINIMS	MINORING	MIPS	MIRZA	MISAPPLYING
MINIMUM	MINORITIES	MIQUELET	MIRZAS	MISASSAY
MINIMUMS	MINORITY	MIQUELETS	MIS	MISASSAYED
MINING	MINORS	MIR	MISACT	MISASSAYING
MININGS	MINOXIDIL	MIRABELLE	MISACTED	MISASSAYS
MINION	MINOXIDILS	MIRABELLES	MISACTING	MISASSIGN
MINIONS	MINSTER	MIRACIDIA	MISACTS	MISASSIGNED
MINIPARK	MINSTERS	MIRACIDIUM	MISADAPT	MISASSIGNING
MINIPARKS	MINSTREL	MIRACLE	MISADAPTED	MISASSIGNS
MINIPILL	MINSTRELS	MIRACLES	MISADAPTING	MISATE
MINIPILLS	MINT	MIRADOR	MISADAPTS	MISATONE
MINIS	MINTAGE	MIRADORS	MISADD	MISATONED
MINISCULE	MINTAGES	MIRAGE	MISADDED	MISATONES
MINISCULES	MINTED	MIRAGES	MISADDING	MISATONING
MINISH	MINTER	MIRANDIZE	MISADDS	MISAVER

MISAVERRED	MISCALLER	MISCOOKED	MISDIRECTED	MISENTERS
MISAVERRING	MISCALLERS	MISCOOKING	MISDIRECTING	MISENTRIES
MISAVERS	MISCALLING	MISCOOKS	MISDIRECTS	MISENTRY
MISAWARD	MISCALLS	MISCOPIED	MISDIVIDE	MISER
MISAWARDED	MISCARRIED	MISCOPIES	MISDIVIDED	MISERABLE
MISAWARDING	MISCARRIES	MISCOPY	MISDIVIDES	MISERABLES
MISAWARDS	MISCARRY	MISCOPYING	MISDIVIDING	MISERABLY
MISBECAME	MISCARRYING	MISCOUNT	MISDO	MISERERE
MISBECOME	MISCAST	MISCOUNTED	MISDOER	MISERERES
MISBECOMES	MISCASTING	MISCOUNTING	MISDOERS	MISERIES
MISBECOMING	MISCASTS	MISCOUNTS	MISDOES	MISERLY
MISBEGAN	MISCHANCE	MISCREANT	MISDOING	MISERS
MISBEGIN	MISCHANCES	MISCREANTS	MISDOINGS	MISERY
MISBEGINNING	MISCHARGE	MISCREATE	MISDONE	MISES
MISBEGINS	MISCHARGED	MISCREATED	MISDOUBT	MISESTEEM
MISBEGOT	MISCHARGES	MISCREATES	MISDOUBTED	MISESTEEMED
MISBEGUN	MISCHARGING	MISCREATING	MISDOUBTING	MISESTEEMING
MISBEHAVE	MISCHIEF	MISCUE	MISDOUBTS	MISESTEEMS
MISBEHAVED	MISCHIEFS	MISCUED	MISDRAW	MISEVENT
MISBEHAVES	MISCHOICE	MISCUES	MISDRAWING	MISEVENTS
MISBEHAVING	MISCHOICES	MISCUING	MISDRAWN	MISFAITH
MISBELIEF	MISCHOOSE	MISCUT	MISDRAWS	MISFAITHS
MISBELIEFS	MISCHOOSES	MISCUTS	MISDREW	MISFEASOR
MISBIAS	MISCHOOSING	MISCUTTING	MISDRIVE	MISFEASORS
MISBIASED	MISCHOSE	MISDATE	MISDRIVEN	MISFED
MISBIASES	MISCHOSEN	MISDATED	MISDRIVES	MISFEED
MISBIASING	MISCIBLE	MISDATES	MISDRIVING	MISFEEDING
MISBIASSED	MISCITE	MISDATING	MISDROVE	MISFEEDS
MISBIASSES	MISCITED	MISDEAL	MISE	MISFIELD
MISBIASSING	MISCITES	MISDEALER	MISEASE	MISFIELDED
MISBILL	MISCITING	MISDEALERS	MISEASES	MISFIELDING
MISBILLED	MISCLAIM	MISDEALING	MISEAT	MISFIELDS
MISBILLING	MISCLAIMED	MISDEALS	MISEATEN	MISFILE
MISBILLS	MISCLAIMING	MISDEALT	MISEATING	MISFILED
MISBIND	MISCLAIMS	MISDEED	MISEATS	MISFILES
MISBINDING	MISCLASS	MISDEEDS	MISEDIT	MISFILING
MISBINDS	MISCLASSED	MISDEEM	MISEDITED	MISFIRE
MISBOUND	MISCLASSES	MISDEEMED	MISEDITING	MISFIRED
MISBRAND	MISCLASSING	MISDEEMING	MISEDITS	MISFIRES
MISBRANDED	MISCODE	MISDEEMS	MISEMPLOY	MISFIRING
MISBRANDING	MISCODED	MISDEFINE	MISEMPLOYED	MISFIT
MISBRANDS	MISCODES	MISDEFINED	MISEMPLOYING	MISFITS
MISBUILD	MISCODING	MISDEFINES	MISEMPLOYS	MISFITTED
MISBUILDING	MISCOIN	MISDEFINING	MISENROL	MISFITTING
MISBUILDS	MISCOINED	MISDIAL	MISENROLL	MISFOCUS
MISBUILT	MISCOINING	MISDIALED	MISENROLLED	MISFOCUSED
MISBUTTON	MISCOINS	MISDIALING	MISENROLLING	MISFOCUSES
MISBUTTONED	MISCOLOR	MISDIALLED	MISENROLLS	MISFOCUSING
MISBUTTONING	MISCOLORED	MISDIALLING	MISENROLS	MISFOCUSSED
MISBUTTONS	MISCOLORING	MISDIALS	MISENTER	MISFOCUSSES
MISCALL	MISCOLORS	MISDID	MISENTERED	MISFOCUSSING
MISCALLED	MISCOOK	MISDIRECT	MISENTERING	MISFORM

MISFORMED	MISHEAR	MISLABELLING	MISMAKE	MISORDERING
MISFORMING	MISHEARD	MISLABELS	MISMAKES	MISORDERS
MISFORMS	MISHEARING	MISLABOR	MISMAKING	MISORIENT
MISFRAME	MISHEARS	MISLABORED	MISMANAGE	MISORIENTED
MISFRAMED	MISHEGAAS	MISLABORING	MISMANAGED	MISORIENTING
MISFRAMES	MISHEGOSS	MISLABORS	MISMANAGES	MISORIENTS
MISFRAMING	MISHIT	MISLAID	MISMANAGING	MISOS
MISGAUGE	MISHITS	MISLAIN	MISMARK	MISPAGE
MISGAUGED	MISHITTING	MISLAY	MISMARKED	MISPAGED
MISGAUGES	MISHMASH	MISLAYER	MISMARKING	MISPAGES
MISGAUGING	MISHMASHES	MISLAYERS	MISMARKS	MISPAGING
MISGAVE	MISHMOSH	MISLAYING	MISMATCH	MISPAINT
MISGIVE	MISHMOSHES	MISLAYS	MISMATCHED	MISPAINTED
MISGIVEN	MISINFER	MISLEAD	MISMATCHES	MISPAINTING
MISGIVES	MISINFERRED	MISLEADER	MISMATCHING	MISPAINTS
MISGIVING	MISINFERRING	MISLEADERS	MISMATE	MISPARSE
MISGIVINGS	MISINFERS	MISLEADING	MISMATED	MISPARSED
MISGOVERN	MISINFORM	MISLEADS	MISMATES	MISPARSES
MISGOVERNED	MISINFORMED	MISLEARED	MISMATING	MISPARSING
MISGOVERNING	MISINFORMING	MISLEARN	MISMEET	MISPART
MISGOVERNS	MISINFORMS	MISLEARNED	MISMEETING	MISPARTED
MISGRADE	MISINTER	MISLEARNING	MISMEETS	MISPARTING
MISGRADED	MISINTERRED	MISLEARNS	MISMET	MISPARTS
MISGRADES	MISINTERRING	MISLEARNT	MISMOVE	MISPATCH
MISGRADING	MISINTERS	MISLED	MISMOVED	MISPATCHED
MISGRAFT	MISJOIN	MISLIE	MISMOVES	MISPATCHES
MISGRAFTED	MISJOINED	MISLIES	MISMOVING	MISPATCHING
MISGRAFTING	MISJOINING	MISLIGHT	MISNAME	MISPEN
MISGRAFTS	MISJOINS	MISLIGHTED	MISNAMED	MISPENNED
MISGREW	MISJUDGE	MISLIGHTING	MISNAMES	MISPENNING
MISGROW	MISJUDGED	MISLIGHTS	MISNAMING	MISPENS
MISGROWING	MISJUDGES	MISLIKE	MISNOMER	MISPHRASE
MISGROWN	MISJUDGING	MISLIKED	MISNOMERS	MISPHRASED
MISGROWS	MISKAL	MISLIKER	MISNUMBER	MISPHRASES
MISGUESS	MISKALS	MISLIKERS	MISNUMBERED	MISPHRASING
MISGUESSED	MISKEEP	MISLIKES	MISNUMBERING	MISPICKEL
MISGUESSES	MISKEEPING	MISLIKING	MISNUMBERS	MISPICKELS
MISGUESSING	MISKEEPS	MISLIT	MISO	MISPLACE
MISGUIDE	MISKEPT	MISLIVE	MISOGAMIC	MISPLACED
MISGUIDED	MISKICK	MISLIVED	MISOGAMIES	MISPLACES
MISGUIDER	MISKICKED	MISLIVES	MISOGAMY	MISPLACING
MISGUIDERS	MISKICKING	MISLIVING	MISOGYNIC	MISPLAN
MISGUIDES	MISKICKS	MISLOCATE	MISOGYNIES	MISPLANNED
MISGUIDING	MISKNEW	MISLOCATED	MISOGYNY	MISPLANNING
MISHANDLE	MISKNOW	MISLOCATES	MISOLOGIES	MISPLANS
MISHANDLED	MISKNOWING	MISLOCATING	MISOLOGY	MISPLANT
MISHANDLES	MISKNOWN	MISLODGE	MISONEISM	MISPLANTED
MISHANDLING	MISKNOWS	MISLODGED	MISONEISMS	MISPLANTING
MISHANTER	MISLABEL	MISLODGES	MISONEIST	MISPLANTS
MISHANTERS	MISLABELED	MISLODGING	MISONEISTS	MISPLAY
MISHAP	MISLABELING	MISLYING	MISORDER	MISPLAYED
MISHAPS	MISLABELLED	MISMADE	MISORDERED	MISPLAYING

MISPLAYS
MISPLEAD
MISPLEADED
MISPLEADING
MISPLEADS
MISPLED
MISPOINT
MISPOINTED
MISPOINTING
MISPOINTS
MISPOISE
MISPOISED
MISPOISES
MISPOISING
MISPRICE
MISPRICED
MISPRICES
MISPRICING
MISPRINT
MISPRINTED
MISPRINTING
MISPRINTS
MISPRIZE
MISPRIZED
MISPRIZER
MISPRIZERS
MISPRIZES
MISPRIZING
MISQUOTE
MISQUOTED
MISQUOTER
MISQUOTERS
MISQUOTES
MISQUOTING
MISRAISE
MISRAISED
MISRAISES
MISRAISING
MISRATE
MISRATED
MISRATES
MISRATING
MISREAD
MISREADING
MISREADS
MISRECKON
MISRECKONED
MISRECKONING
MISRECKONS
MISRECORD
MISRECORDED
MISRECORDING

MISRECORDS
MISREFER
MISREFERRED
MISREFERRING
MISREFERS
MISRELATE
MISRELATED
MISRELATES
MISRELATING
MISRELIED
MISRELIES
MISRELY
MISRELYING
MISRENDER
MISRENDERED
MISRENDERING
MISRENDERS
MISREPORT
MISREPORTED
MISREPORTING
MISREPORTS
MISRHYMED
MISROUTE
MISROUTED
MISROUTES
MISROUTING
MISRULE
MISRULED
MISRULES
MISRULING
MISS
MISSABLE
MISSAID
MISSAL
MISSALS
MISSAY
MISSAYING
MISSAYS
MISSEAT
MISSEATED
MISSEATING
MISSEATS
MISSED
MISSEL
MISSELS
MISSEND
MISSENDING
MISSENDS
MISSENSE
MISSENSES
MISSENT
MISSES

MISSET
MISSETS
MISSETTING
MISSHAPE
MISSHAPED
MISSHAPEN
MISSHAPER
MISSHAPERS
MISSHAPES
MISSHAPING
MISSHOD
MISSIES
MISSILE
MISSILEER
MISSILEERS
MISSILERIES
MISSILERY
MISSILES
MISSILRIES
MISSILRY
MISSING
MISSION
MISSIONAL
MISSIONED
MISSIONER
MISSIONERS
MISSIONING
MISSIONS
MISSIS
MISSISES
MISSIVE
MISSIVES
MISSORT
MISSORTED
MISSORTING
MISSORTS
MISSOUND
MISSOUNDED
MISSOUNDING
MISSOUNDS
MISSOUT
MISSOUTS
MISSPACE
MISSPACED
MISSPACES
MISSPACING
MISSPEAK
MISSPEAKING
MISSPEAKS
MISSPELL
MISSPELLED
MISSPELLING

MISSPELLS
MISSPELT
MISSPEND
MISSPENDING
MISSPENDS
MISSPENT
MISSPOKE
MISSPOKEN
MISSTAMP
MISSTAMPED
MISSTAMPING
MISSTAMPS
MISSTART
MISSTARTED
MISSTARTING
MISSTARTS
MISSTATE
MISSTATED
MISSTATES
MISSTATING
MISSTEER
MISSTEERED
MISSTEERING
MISSTEERS
MISSTEP
MISSTEPPED
MISSTEPPING
MISSTEPS
MISSTOP
MISSTOPPED
MISSTOPPING
MISSTOPS
MISSTRICKEN
MISSTRIKE
MISSTRIKES
MISSTRIKING
MISSTRUCK
MISSTYLE
MISSTYLED
MISSTYLES
MISSTYLING
MISSUIT
MISSUITED
MISSUITING
MISSUITS
MISSUS
MISSUSES
MISSY
MIST
MISTAKE
MISTAKEN
MISTAKER

MISTAKERS
MISTAKES
MISTAKING
MISTAUGHT
MISTBOW
MISTBOWS
MISTEACH
MISTEACHES
MISTEACHING
MISTED
MISTEND
MISTENDED
MISTENDING
MISTENDS
MISTER
MISTERM
MISTERMED
MISTERMING
MISTERMS
MISTERS
MISTEUK
MISTHINK
MISTHINKING
MISTHINKS
MISTHOUGHT
MISTHREW
MISTHROW
MISTHROWING
MISTHROWN
MISTHROWS
MISTIER
MISTIEST
MISTILY
MISTIME
MISTIMED
MISTIMES
MISTIMING
MISTINESS
MISTINESSES
MISTING
MISTITLE
MISTITLED
MISTITLES
MISTITLING
MISTLETOE
MISTLETOES
MISTOOK
MISTOUCH
MISTOUCHED
MISTOUCHES
MISTOUCHING
MISTRACE

MISTRACED	MISVALUED	MITRE	MO	MOCHA
MISTRACES	MISVALUES	MITRED	MOA	MOCHAS
MISTRACING	MISVALUING	MITRES	MOAN	MOCHILA
MISTRAIN	MISWORD	MITREWORT	MOANED	MOCHILAS
MISTRAINED	MISWORDED	MITREWORTS	MOANER	MOCK
MISTRAINING	MISWORDING	MITRING	MOANERS	MOCKABLE
MISTRAINS	MISWORDS	MITSVAH	MOANFUL	MOCKED
MISTRAL	MISWRIT	MITSVAHS	MOANING	MOCKER
MISTRALS	MISWRITE	MITSVOTH	MOANINGLY	MOCKERIES
MISTREAT	MISWRITES	MITT	MOANS	MOCKERS
MISTREATED	MISWRITING	MITTEN	MOAS	MOCKERY
MISTREATING	MISWRITTEN	MITTENED	MOAT	MOCKING
MISTREATS	MISWROTE	MITTENS	MOATED	MOCKINGLY
MISTRESS	MISYOKE	MITTIMUS	MOATING	MOCKS
MISTRESSES	MISYOKED	MITTIMUSES	MOATLIKE	MOCKTAIL
MISTRIAL	MISYOKES	MITTS	MOATS	MOCKTAILS
MISTRIALS	MISYOKING	MITY	MOB	MOCKUP
MISTRUST	MITE	MITZVAH	MOBBED	MOCKUPS
MISTRUSTED	MITER	MITZVAHS	MOBBER	MOCS
MISTRUSTING	MITERED	MITZVOTH	MOBBERS	MOD
MISTRUSTS	MITERER	MIX	MOBBING	MODAL
MISTRUTH	MITERERS	MIXABLE	MOBBISH	MODALITIES
MISTRUTHS	MITERING	MIXED	MOBBISHLY	MODALITY
MISTRYST	MITERS	MIXEDLY	MOBBISM	MODALLY
MISTRYSTED	MITERWORT	MIXER	MOBBISMS	MODALS
MISTRYSTING	MITERWORTS	MIXERS	MOBCAP	MODE
MISTRYSTS	MITES	MIXES	MOBCAPS	MODEL
MISTS	MITHER	MIXIBLE	MOBILE	MODELED
MISTUNE	MITHERS	MIXING	MOBILES	MODELER
MISTUNED	MITICIDAL	MIXOLOGIES	MOBILISE	MODELERS
MISTUNES	MITICIDE	MIXOLOGY	MOBILISED	MODELING
MISTUNING	MITICIDES	MIXT	MOBILISES	MODELINGS
MISTUTOR	MITIER	MIXTURE	MOBILISING	MODELIST
MISTUTORED	MITIEST	MIXTURES	MOBILITIES	MODELISTS
MISTUTORING	MITIGABLE	MIXUP	MOBILITY	MODELLED
MISTUTORS	MITIGATE	MIXUPS	MOBILIZE	MODELLER
MISTY	MITIGATED	MIZEN	MOBILIZED	MODELLERS
MISTYPE	MITIGATES	MIZENMAST	MOBILIZER	MODELLING
MISTYPED	MITIGATING	MIZENMASTS	MOBILIZERS	MODELS
MISTYPES	MITIGATOR	MIZENS	MOBILIZES	MODEM
MISTYPING	MITIGATORS	MIZUNA	MOBILIZING	MODEMED
MISUNION	MITIS	MIZUNAS	MOBLED	MODEMING
MISUNIONS	MITISES	MIZZEN	MOBOCRACIES	MODEMS
MISUSAGE	MITOGEN	MIZZENS	MOBOCRACY	MODERATE
MISUSAGES	MITOGENIC	MIZZLE	MOBOCRAT	MODERATED
MISUSE	MITOGENS	MIZZLED	MOBOCRATS	MODERATES
MISUSED	MITOMYCIN	MIZZLES	MOBS	MODERATING
MISUSER	MITOMYCINS	MIZZLING	MOBSTER	MODERATO
MISUSERS	MITOSES	MIZZLY	MOBSTERS	MODERATOR
MISUSES	MITOSIS	MM	MOC	MODERATORS
MISUSING	MITOTIC	MNEMONIC	MOCCASIN	MODERATOS
MISVALUE	MITRAL	MNEMONICS	MOCCASINS	MODERN

MODERNE	MODULATING	MOISTENED	MOLECULAR	MOLTS
MODERNER	MODULATOR	MOISTENER	MOLECULE	MOLY
MODERNES	MODULATORS	MOISTENERS	MOLECULES	MOLYBDATE
MODERNEST	MODULE	MOISTENING	MOLEHILL	MOLYBDATES
MODERNISE	MODULES	MOISTENS	MOLEHILLS	MOLYBDIC
MODERNISED	MODULI	MOISTER	MOLES	MOLYBDOUS
MODERNISES	MODULO	MOISTEST	MOLESKIN	MOM
MODERNISING	MODULUS	MOISTFUL	MOLESKINS	MOME
MODERNISM	MODUS	MOISTLY	MOLEST	MOMENT
MODERNISMS	MOFETTE	MOISTNESS	MOLESTED	MOMENTA
MODERNIST	MOFETTES	MOISTNESSES	MOLESTER	MOMENTARY
MODERNISTS	MOFFETTE	MOISTURE	MOLESTERS	MOMENTLY
MODERNITIES	MOFFETTES	MOISTURES	MOLESTING	MOMENTO
MODERNITY	MOG	MOJARRA	MOLESTS	MOMENTOES
MODERNIZE	MOGGED	MOJARRAS	MOLIES	MOMENTOS
MODERNIZED	MOGGIE	MOJO	MOLINE	MOMENTOUS
MODERNIZES	MOGGIES	MOJOES	MOLL	MOMENTS
MODERNIZING	MOGGING	MOJOS	MOLLAH	MOMENTUM
MODERNLY	MOGGY	MOKE	MOLLAHS	MOMENTUMS
MODERNS	MOGHUL	MOKES	MOLLIE	MOMES
MODES	MOGHULS	MOL	MOLLIES	MOMI
MODEST	MOGS	MOLA	MOLLIFIED	MOMISM
MODESTER	MOGUL	MOLAL	MOLLIFIER	MOMISMS
MODESTEST	MOGULED	MOLALITIES	MOLLIFIERS	MOMMA
MODESTIES	MOGULS	MOLALITY	MOLLIFIES	MOMMAS
MODESTLY	MOHAIR	MOLAR	MOLLIFY	MOMMIES
MODESTY	MOHAIRS	MOLARITIES	MOLLIFYING	MOMMY
MODI	MOHALIM	MOLARITY	MOLLS	MOMS
MODICA	MOHAWK	MOLARS	MOLLUSC	MOMSER
MODICUM	MOHAWKS	MOLAS	MOLLUSCA	MOMSERS
MODICUMS	MOHEL	MOLASSES	MOLLUSCAN	MOMUS
MODIFIED	MOHELIM	MOLASSESES	MOLLUSCANS	MOMUSES
MODIFIER	MOHELS	MOLD	MOLLUSCS	MOMZER
MODIFIERS	MOHUR	MOLDABLE	MOLLUSCUM	MOMZERS
MODIFIES	MOHURS	MOLDBOARD	MOLLUSK	MON
MODIFY	MOIDORE	MOLDBOARDS	MOLLUSKAN	MONACHAL
MODIFYING	MOIDORES	MOLDED	MOLLUSKANS	MONACHISM
MODILLION	MOIETIES	MOLDER	MOLLUSKS	MONACHISMS
MODILLIONS	MOIETY	MOLDERED	MOLLY	MONACID
MODIOLI	MOIL	MOLDERING	MOLLYMAWK	MONACIDIC
MODIOLUS	MOILED	MOLDERS	MOLLYMAWKS	MONACIDS
MODISH	MOILER	MOLDIER	MOLOCH	MONAD
MODISHLY	MOILERS	MOLDIEST	MOLOCHS	MONADAL
MODISTE	MOILING	MOLDINESS	MOLS	MONADES
MODISTES	MOILINGLY	MOLDINESSES	MOLT	MONADIC
MODS	MOILS	MOLDING	MOLTED	MONADICAL
MODULAR	MOIRA	MOLDINGS	MOLTEN	MONADISM
MODULARLY	MOIRAI	MOLDS	MOLTENLY	MONADISMS
MODULARS	MOIRE	MOLDWARP	MOLTER	MONADNOCK
MODULATE	MOIRES	MOLDWARPS	MOLTERS	MONADNOCKS
MODULATED	MOIST	MOLDY	MOLTING	MONADS
MODULATES	MOISTEN	MOLE	MOLTO	MONANDRIES

MONANDRY	MONGEESE	MONKEYING	MONODISTS	MONOLOGUES
MONARCH	MONGER	MONKEYISH	MONODRAMA	MONOLOGUING
MONARCHAL	MONGERED	MONKEYPOD	MONODRAMAS	MONOLOGY
MONARCHIC	MONGERING	MONKEYPODS	MONODY	MONOMANIA
MONARCHIES	MONGERS	MONKEYPOT	MONOECIES	MONOMANIAS
MONARCHS	MONGO	MONKEYPOTS	MONOECISM	MONOMER
MONARCHY	MONGOE	MONKEYS	MONOECISMS	MONOMERIC
MONARDA	MONGOES	MONKFISH	MONOECY	MONOMERS
MONARDAS	MONGOL	MONKFISHES	MONOESTER	MONOMETER
MONAS	MONGOLIAN	MONKHOOD	MONOESTERS	MONOMETERS
MONASTERIES	MONGOLISM	MONKHOODS	MONOFIL	MONOMIAL
MONASTERY	MONGOLISMS	MONKISH	MONOFILS	MONOMIALS
MONASTIC	MONGOLOID	MONKISHLY	MONOFUEL	MONOPHAGIES
MONASTICS	MONGOLOIDS	MONKS	MONOFUELS	MONOPHAGY
MONATOMIC	MONGOLS	MONKSHOOD	MONOGAMIC	MONOPHONIES
MONAURAL	MONGOOSE	MONKSHOODS	MONOGAMIES	MONOPHONY
MONAXIAL	MONGOOSES	MONO	MONOGAMY	MONOPHYLIES
MONAXON	MONGOS	MONOACID	MONOGENIC	MONOPHYLY
MONAXONS	MONGREL	MONOACIDS	MONOGENIES	MONOPLANE
MONAZITE	MONGRELLY	MONOAMINE	MONOGENY	MONOPLANES
MONAZITES	MONGRELS	MONOAMINES	MONOGERM	MONOPLOID
MONDE	MONGST	MONOBASIC	MONOGLOT	MONOPLOIDS
MONDES	MONICKER	MONOCARP	MONOGLOTS	MONOPOD
MONDO	MONICKERS	MONOCARPS	MONOGRAM	MONOPODE
MONDOS	MONIE	MONOCHORD	MONOGRAMED	MONOPODES
MONECIAN	MONIED	MONOCHORDS	MONOGRAMING	MONOPODIA
MONECIOUS	MONIES	MONOCLE	MONOGRAMMED	MONOPODIES
MONELLIN	MONIKER	MONOCLED	MONOGRAMMING	MONOPODIUM
MONELLINS	MONIKERS	MONOCLES	MONOGRAMS	MONOPODS
MONERAN	MONISH	MONOCLINE	MONOGRAPH	MONOPODY
MONERANS	MONISHED	MONOCLINES	MONOGRAPHED	MONOPOLE
MONETARY	MONISHES	MONOCOQUE	MONOGRAPHING	MONOPOLES
MONETISE	MONISHING	MONOCOQUES	MONOGRAPHS	MONOPOLIES
MONETISED	MONISM	MONOCOT	MONOGYNIES	MONOPOLY
MONETISES	MONISMS	MONOCOTS	MONOGYNY	MONOPSONIES
MONETISING	MONIST	MONOCOTYL	MONOHULL	MONOPSONY
MONETIZE	MONISTIC	MONOCOTYLS	MONOHULLS	MONORAIL
MONETIZED	MONISTS	MONOCRACIES	MONOICOUS	MONORAILS
MONETIZES	MONITION	MONOCRACY	MONOKINE	MONORCHID
MONETIZING	MONITIONS	MONOCRAT	MONOKINES	MONORCHIDS
MONEY	MONITIVE	MONOCRATS	MONOLAYER	MONORHYME
MONEYBAG	MONITOR	MONOCULAR	MONOLAYERS	MONORHYMES
MONEYBAGS	MONITORED	MONOCULARS	MONOLITH	MONOS
MONEYED	MONITORIES	MONOCYCLE	MONOLITHS	MONOSOME
MONEYER	MONITORING	MONOCYCLES	MONOLOG	MONOSOMES
MONEYERS	MONITORS	MONOCYTE	MONOLOGGED	MONOSOMIC
MONEYLESS	MONITORY	MONOCYTES	MONOLOGGING	MONOSOMICS
MONEYMAN	MONK	MONOCYTIC	MONOLOGIC	MONOSOMIES
MONEYMEN	MONKERIES	MONODIC	MONOLOGIES	MONOSOMY
MONEYS	MONKERY	MONODICAL	MONOLOGS	MONOSTELE
MONEYWORT	MONKEY	MONODIES	MONOLOGUE	MONOSTELES
MONEYWORTS	MONKEYED	MONODIST	MONOLOGUED	MONOSTELIES

MONOSTELY	MONTICULES	MOONFISHES	MOONY	MOPING
MONOSTICH	MONUMENT	MOONIER	MOOR	MOPINGLY
MONOSTICHS	MONUMENTS	MOONIEST	MOORAGE	MOPISH
MONOSTOME	MONURON	MOONILY	MOORAGES	MOPISHLY
MONOTINT	MONURONS	MOONINESS	MOORCOCK	MOPOKE
MONOTINTS	MONY	MOONINESSES	MOORCOCKS	MOPOKES
MONOTONE	MONZONITE	MOONING	MOORED	MOPPED
MONOTONES	MONZONITES	MOONISH	MOORFOWL	MOPPER
MONOTONIC	MOO	MOONISHLY	MOORFOWLS	MOPPERS
MONOTONIES	MOOCH	MOONLESS	MOORHEN	MOPPET
MONOTONY	MOOCHED	MOONLET	MOORHENS	MOPPETS
MONOTREME	MOOCHER	MOONLETS	MOORIER	MOPPING
MONOTREMES	MOOCHERS	MOONLIGHT	MOORIEST	MOPS
MONOTYPE	MOOCHES	MOONLIGHTED	MOORING	MOPY
MONOTYPES	MOOCHING	MOONLIGHTING	MOORINGS	MOQUETTE
MONOTYPIC	MOOD	MOONLIGHTS	MOORISH	MOQUETTES
MONOVULAR	MOODIER	MOONLIKE	MOORLAND	MOR
MONOXIDE	MOODIEST	MOONLIT	MOORLANDS	MORA
MONOXIDES	MOODILY	MOONPORT	MOORS	MORAE
MONS	MOODINESS	MOONPORTS	MOORWORT	MORAINAL
MONSIEUR	MOODINESSES	MOONQUAKE	MOORWORTS	MORAINE
MONSIGNOR	MOODS	MOONQUAKES	MOORY	MORAINES
MONSIGNORI	MOODY	MOONRISE	MOOS	MORAINIC
MONSIGNORS	MOOED	MOONRISES	MOOSE	MORAL
MONSOON	MOOING	MOONROOF	MOOSEBIRD	MORALE
MONSOONAL	MOOL	MOONROOFS	MOOSEBIRDS	MORALES
MONSOONS	MOOLA	MOONS	MOOSEWOOD	MORALISE
MONSTER	MOOLAH	MOONSAIL	MOOSEWOODS	MORALISED
MONSTERA	MOOLAHS	MOONSAILS	MOOT	MORALISES
MONSTERAS	MOOLAS	MOONSCAPE	MOOTED	MORALISING
MONSTERS	MOOLEY	MOONSCAPES	MOOTER	MORALISM
MONSTROUS	MOOLEYS	MOONSEED	MOOTERS	MORALISMS
MONTADALE	MOOLS	MOONSEEDS	MOOTING	MORALIST
MONTADALES	MOON	MOONSET	MOOTNESS	MORALISTS
MONTAGE	MOONBEAM	MOONSETS	MOOTNESSES	MORALITIES
MONTAGED	MOONBEAMS	MOONSHINE	MOOTS	MORALITY
MONTAGES	MOONBLIND	MOONSHINED	MOP	MORALIZE
MONTAGING	MOONBOW	MOONSHINES	MOPBOARD	MORALIZED
MONTANE	MOONBOWS	MOONSHINING	MOPBOARDS	MORALIZER
MONTANES	MOONCALF	MOONSHINY	MOPE	MORALIZERS
MONTE	MOONCALVES	MOONSHOT	MOPED	MORALIZES
MONTEITH	MOONCHILD	MOONSHOTS	MOPEDS	MORALIZING
MONTEITHS	MOONCHILDREN	MOONSTONE	MOPER	MORALLY
MONTERO	MOONDUST	MOONSTONES	MOPERIES	MORALS
MONTEROS	MOONDUSTS	MOONWALK	MOPERS	MORAS
MONTES	MOONED	MOONWALKED	MOPERY	MORASS
MONTH	MOONER	MOONWALKING	MOPES	MORASSES
MONTHLIES	MOONERS	MOONWALKS	MOPEY	MORASSY
MONTHLONG	MOONEYE	MOONWARD	MOPIER	MORATORIA
MONTHLY	MOONEYES	MOONWARDS	MOPIEST	MORATORIUM
MONTHS	MOONFACED	MOONWORT	MOPINESS	MORATORIUMS
MONTICULE	MOONFISH	MOONWORTS	MOPINESSES	MORATORY

MORAY	MOROCCOS	MORTALITIES	MOSAICIST	MOT
MORAYS	MORON	MORTALITY	MOSAICISTS	MOTE
MORBID	MORONIC	MORTALLY	MOSAICKED	MOTEL
MORBIDITIES	MORONISM	MORTALS	MOSAICKING	MOTELS
MORBIDITY	MORONISMS	MORTAR	MOSAICS	MOTES
MORBIDLY	MORONITIES	MORTARED	MOSASAUR	MOTET
MORBIFIC	MORONITY	MORTARING	MOSASAURS	MOTETS
MORBILLI	MORONS	MORTARMAN	MOSCHATE	MOTEY
MORCEAU	MOROSE	MORTARMEN	MOSCHATEL	MOTH
MORCEAUX	MOROSELY	MORTARS	MOSCHATELS	MOTHBALL
MORDACITIES	MOROSITIES	MORTARY	MOSEY	MOTHBALLED
MORDACITY	MOROSITY	MORTGAGE	MOSEYED	MOTHBALLING
MORDANCIES	MORPH	MORTGAGED	MOSEYING	MOTHBALLS
MORDANCY	MORPHED	MORTGAGEE	MOSEYS	MOTHER
MORDANT	MORPHEME	MORTGAGEES	MOSH	MOTHERED
MORDANTED	MORPHEMES	MORTGAGER	MOSHAV	MOTHERING
MORDANTING	MORPHEMIC	MORTGAGERS	MOSHAVIM	MOTHERINGS
MORDANTLY	MORPHIA	MORTGAGES	MOSHED	MOTHERLY
MORDANTS	MORPHIAS	MORTGAGING	MOSHER	MOTHERS
MORDENT	MORPHIC	MORTGAGOR	MOSHERS	MOTHERY
MORDENTS	MORPHIN	MORTGAGORS	MOSHES	MOTHIER
MORE	MORPHINE	MORTICE	MOSHING	MOTHIEST
MOREEN	MORPHINES	MORTICED	MOSHINGS	MOTHLIKE
MOREENS	MORPHING	MORTICES	MOSK	MOTHPROOF
MOREL	MORPHINGS	MORTICIAN	MOSKS	MOTHPROOFED
MORELLE	MORPHINIC	MORTICIANS	MOSQUE	MOTHPROOFING
MORELLES	MORPHINS	MORTICING	MOSQUES	MOTHPROOFS
MORELLO	MORPHO	MORTIFIED	MOSQUITO	MOTHS
MORELLOS	MORPHOGEN	MORTIFIER	MOSQUITOES	MOTHY
MORELS	MORPHOGENS	MORTIFIERS	MOSQUITOS	MOTIF
MORENESS	MORPHOS	MORTIFIES	MOSS	MOTIFIC
MORENESSES	MORPHOSES	MORTIFY	MOSSBACK	MOTIFS
MOREOVER	MORPHOSIS	MORTIFYING	MOSSBACKS	MOTILE
MORES	MORPHS	MORTISE	MOSSED	MOTILES
MORESQUE	MORRION	MORTISED	MOSSER	MOTILITIES
MORESQUES	MORRIONS	MORTISER	MOSSERS	MOTILITY
MORGAN	MORRIS	MORTISERS	MOSSES	MOTION
MORGANITE	MORRISES	MORTISES	MOSSGROWN	MOTIONAL
MORGANITES	MORRO	MORTISING	MOSSIER	MOTIONED
MORGANS	MORROS	MORTMAIN	MOSSIEST	MOTIONER
MORGEN	MORROW	MORTMAINS	MOSSINESS	MOTIONERS
MORGENS	MORROWS	MORTS	MOSSINESSES	MOTIONING
MORGUE	MORS	MORTUARIES	MOSSING	MOTIONS
MORGUES	MORSE	MORTUARY	MOSSLIKE	MOTIVATE
MORIBUND	MORSEL	MORULA	MOSSO	MOTIVATED
MORION	MORSELED	MORULAE	MOSSY	MOTIVATES
MORIONS	MORSELING	MORULAR	MOST	MOTIVATING
MORN	MORSELLED	MORULAS	MOSTE	MOTIVATOR
MORNING	MORSELLING	MOS	MOSTEST	MOTIVATORS
MORNINGS	MORSELS	MOSAIC	MOSTESTS	MOTIVE
MORNS	MORT	MOSAICISM	MOSTLY	MOTIVED
MOROCCO	MORTAL	MOSAICISMS	MOSTS	MOTIVES

MOTIVIC	MOTORSHIP	MOULTERS	MOUSINESS	MOVIEDOMS
MOTIVING	MOTORSHIPS	MOULTING	MOUSINESSES	MOVIEGOER
MOTIVITIES	MOTORWAY	MOULTS	MOUSING	MOVIEGOERS
MOTIVITY	MOTORWAYS	MOUND	MOUSINGS	MOVIEOLA
MOTLEY	MOTS	MOUNDBIRD	MOUSSAKA	MOVIEOLAS
MOTLEYER	MOTT	MOUNDBIRDS	MOUSSAKAS	MOVIES
MOTLEYEST	MOTTE	MOUNDED	MOUSSE	MOVING
MOTLEYS	MOTTES	MOUNDING	MOUSSED	MOVINGLY
MOTLIER	MOTTLE	MOUNDS	MOUSSES	MOVIOLA
MOTLIEST	MOTTLED	MOUNT	MOUSSING	MOVIOLAS
MOTMOT	MOTTLER	MOUNTABLE	MOUSTACHE	MOW
MOTMOTS	MOTTLERS	MOUNTAIN	MOUSTACHES	MOWED
MOTOCROSS	MOTTLES	MOUNTAINS	MOUSY	MOWER
MOTOCROSSES	MOTTLING	MOUNTAINY	MOUTH	MOWERS
MOTOR	MOTTO	MOUNTED	MOUTHED	MOWING
MOTORBIKE	MOTTOES	MOUNTER	MOUTHER	MOWINGS
MOTORBIKED	MOTTOS	MOUNTERS	MOUTHERS	MOWN
MOTORBIKES	MOTTS	MOUNTING	MOUTHFEEL	MOWS
MOTORBIKING	MOUCH	MOUNTINGS	MOUTHFEELS	MOXA
MOTORBOAT	MOUCHED	MOUNTS	MOUTHFUL	MOXAS
MOTORBOATED	MOUCHES	MOURN	MOUTHFULS	MOXIE
MOTORBOATING	MOUCHING	MOURNED	MOUTHIER	MOXIES
MOTORBOATS	MOUCHOIR	MOURNER	MOUTHIEST	MOZETTA
MOTORBUS	MOUCHOIRS	MOURNERS	MOUTHILY	MOZETTAS
MOTORBUSES	MOUE	MOURNFUL	MOUTHING	MOZETTE
MOTORBUSSES	MOUES	MOURNFULLER	MOUTHLESS	MOZO
MOTORCADE	MOUFFLON	MOURNFULLEST	MOUTHLIKE	MOZOS
MOTORCADED	MOUFFLONS	MOURNING	MOUTHPART	MOZZETTA
MOTORCADES	MOUFLON	MOURNINGS	MOUTHPARTS	MOZZETTAS
MOTORCADING	MOUFLONS	MOURNS	MOUTHS	MOZZETTE
MOTORCAR	MOUILLE	MOUSAKA	MOUTHWASH	MRIDANGA
MOTORCARS	MOUJIK	MOUSAKAS	MOUTHWASHES	MRIDANGAM
MOTORDOM	MOUJIKS	MOUSE	MOUTHY	MRIDANGAMS
MOTORDOMS	MOULAGE	MOUSEBIRD	MOUTON	MRIDANGAS
MOTORED	MOULAGES	MOUSEBIRDS	MOUTONNEE	MU
MOTORIC	MOULD	MOUSED	MOUTONS	MUCH
MOTORING	MOULDED	MOUSELIKE	MOVABLE	MUCHACHO
MOTORINGS	MOULDER	MOUSEPAD	MOVABLES	MUCHACHOS
MOTORISE	MOULDERED	MOUSEPADS	MOVABLY	MUCHES
MOTORISED	MOULDERING	MOUSER	MOVE	MUCHLY
MOTORISES	MOULDERS	MOUSERS	MOVEABLE	MUCHNESS
MOTORISING	MOULDIER	MOUSES	MOVEABLES	MUCHNESSES
MOTORIST	MOULDIEST	MOUSETAIL	MOVEABLY	MUCHO
MOTORISTS	MOULDING	MOUSETAILS	MOVED	MUCID
MOTORIZE	MOULDINGS	MOUSETRAP	MOVELESS	MUCIDITIES
MOTORIZED	MOULDS	MOUSETRAPPED	MOVEMENT	MUCIDITY
MOTORIZES	MOULDY	MOUSETRAPPING	MOVEMENTS	MUCILAGE
MOTORIZING	MOULIN	MOUSETRAPS	MOVER	MUCILAGES
MOTORLESS	MOULINS	MOUSEY	MOVERS	MUCIN
MOTORMAN	MOULT	MOUSIER	MOVES	MUCINOGEN
MOTORMEN	MOULTED	MOUSIEST	MOVIE	MUCINOGENS
MOTORS	MOULTER	MOUSILY	MOVIEDOM	MUCINOID

MUCINOUS	MUDCAPPING	MUDSILLS	MUGGY	MULLEINS
MUCINS	MUDCAPS	MUDSLIDE	MUGHAL	MULLEN
MUCK	MUDCAT	MUDSLIDES	MUGHALS	MULLENS
MUCKAMUCK	MUDCATS	MUDSTONE	MUGS	MULLER
MUCKAMUCKS	MUDDED	MUDSTONES	MUGWORT	MULLERS
MUCKED	MUDDER	MUEDDIN	MUGWORTS	MULLET
MUCKER	MUDDERS	MUEDDINS	MUGWUMP	MULLETS
MUCKERS	MUDDIED	MUENSTER	MUGWUMPS	MULLEY
MUCKIER	MUDDIER	MUENSTERS	MUHLIES	MULLEYS
MUCKIEST	MUDDIES	MUESLI	MUHLY	MULLIGAN
MUCKILY	MUDDIEST	MUESLIS	MUJAHEDIN	MULLIGANS
MUCKING	MUDDILY	MUEZZIN	MUJAHIDIN	MULLING
MUCKLE	MUDDINESS	MUEZZINS	MUJIK	MULLION
MUCKLES	MUDDINESSES	MUFF	MUJIKS	MULLIONED
MUCKLUCK	MUDDING	MUFFED	MUKLUK	MULLIONING
MUCKLUCKS	MUDDLE	MUFFIN	MUKLUKS	MULLIONS
MUCKRAKE	MUDDLED	MUFFINEER	MUKTUK	MULLITE
MUCKRAKED	MUDDLER	MUFFINEERS	MUKTUKS	MULLITES
MUCKRAKER	MUDDLERS	MUFFING	MULATTO	MULLOCK
MUCKRAKERS	MUDDLES	MUFFINS	MULATTOES	MULLOCKS
MUCKRAKES	MUDDLING	MUFFLE	MULATTOS	MULLOCKY
MUCKRAKING	MUDDLY	MUFFLED	MULBERRIES	MULLS
MUCKS	MUDDY	MUFFLER	MULBERRY	MULTIAGE
MUCKWORM	MUDDYING	MUFFLERED	MULCH	MULTIATOM
MUCKWORMS	MUDFISH	MUFFLERS	MULCHED	MULTIBAND
MUCKY	MUDFISHES	MUFFLES	MULCHES	MULTIBANK
MUCLUC	MUDFLAP	MUFFLING	MULCHING	MULTICAR
MUCLUCS	MUDFLAPS	MUFFS	MULCT	MULTICELL
MUCOID	MUDFLAT	MUFTI	MULCTED	MULTICITY
MUCOIDAL	MUDFLATS	MUFTIS	MULCTING	MULTICOPY
MUCOIDS	MUDFLOW	MUG	MULCTS	MULTIDAY
MUCOLYTIC	MUDFLOWS	MUGFUL	MULE	MULTIDISC
MUCOR	MUDGUARD	MUGFULS	MULED	MULTIDRUG
MUCORS	MUDGUARDS	MUGG	MULES	MULTIFID
MUCOSA	MUDHEN	MUGGAR	MULETA	MULTIFOIL
MUCOSAE	MUDHENS	MUGGARS	MULETAS	MULTIFOILS
MUCOSAL	MUDHOLE	MUGGED	MULETEER	MULTIFOLD
MUCOSAS	MUDHOLES	MUGGEE	MULETEERS	MULTIFORM
MUCOSE	MUDLARK	MUGGEES	MULEY	MULTIGERM
MUCOSITIES	MUDLARKS	MUGGER	MULEYS	MULTIGRID
MUCOSITY	MUDPACK	MUGGERS	MULING	MULTIHUED
MUCOUS	MUDPACKS	MUGGIER	MULISH	MULTIHULL
MUCRO	MUDPUPPIES	MUGGIEST	MULISHLY	MULTIHULLS
MUCRONATE	MUDPUPPY	MUGGILY	MULL	MULTIJET
MUCRONES	MUDRA	MUGGINESS	MULLA	MULTILANE
MUCUS	MUDRAS	MUGGINESSES	MULLAH	MULTILANES
MUCUSES	MUDROCK	MUGGING	MULLAHISM	MULTILINE
MUD	MUDROCKS	MUGGINGS	MULLAHISMS	MULTILOBE
MUDBUG	MUDROOM	MUGGINS	MULLAHS	MULTILOBES
MUDBUGS	MUDROOMS	MUGGS	MULLAS	MULTIMODE
MUDCAP	MUDS	MUGGUR	MULLED	MULTIPACK
MUDCAPPED	MUDSILL	MUGGURS	MULLEIN	MULTIPACKS

MULTIPAGE	MUMBLING	MUNGOS	MUREIN	MURRS
MULTIPARA	MUMBLY	MUNI	MUREINS	MURRY
MULTIPARAE	MUMM	MUNICIPAL	MURES	MURTHER
MULTIPARAS	MUMMED	MUNICIPALS	MUREX	MURTHERED
MULTIPART	MUMMER	MUNIMENT	MUREXES	MURTHERING
MULTIPATH	MUMMERIES	MUNIMENTS	MURIATE	MURTHERS
MULTIPED	MUMMERS	MUNIS	MURIATED	MUS
MULTIPEDE	MUMMERY	MUNITION	MURIATES	MUSCA
MULTIPEDES	MUMMICHOG	MUNITIONED	MURICATE	MUSCADEL
MULTIPEDS	MUMMICHOGS	MUNITIONING	MURICATED	MUSCADELS
MULTIPION	MUMMIED	MUNITIONS	MURICES	MUSCADET
MULTIPLE	MUMMIES	MUNNION	MURID	MUSCADETS
MULTIPLES	MUMMIFIED	MUNNIONS	MURIDS	MUSCADINE
MULTIPLET	MUMMIFIES	MUNS	MURINE	MUSCADINES
MULTIPLETS	MUMMIFY	MUNSTER	MURINES	MUSCAE
MULTIPLEX	MUMMIFYING	MUNSTERS	MURING	MUSCARINE
MULTIPLEXED	MUMMING	MUNTIN	MURK	MUSCARINES
MULTIPLEXES	MUMMS	MUNTING	MURKER	MUSCAT
MULTIPLEXING	MUMMY	MUNTINGS	MURKEST	MUSCATEL
MULTIPLIED	MUMMYING	MUNTINS	MURKIER	MUSCATELS
MULTIPLIES	MUMP	MUNTJAC	MURKIEST	MUSCATS
MULTIPLY	MUMPED	MUNTJACS	MURKILY	MUSCID
MULTIPLYING	MUMPER	MUNTJAK	MURKINESS	MUSCIDS
MULTIPOLE	MUMPERS	MUNTJAKS	MURKINESSES	MUSCLE
MULTIPOLES	MUMPING	MUON	MURKLY	MUSCLED
MULTIPORT	MUMPS	MUONIC	MURKS	MUSCLEMAN
MULTIROOM	MUMS	MUONIUM	MURKY	MUSCLEMEN
MULTISITE	MUMU	MUONIUMS	MURMUR	MUSCLES
MULTISIZE	MUMUS	MUONS	MURMURED	MUSCLING
MULTISTEP	MUN	MURA	MURMURER	MUSCLY
MULTITASK	MUNCH	MURAENID	MURMURERS	MUSCOVADO
MULTITASKED	MUNCHABLE	MURAENIDS	MURMURING	MUSCOVADOS
MULTITASKING	MUNCHED	MURAL	MURMUROUS	MUSCOVITE
MULTITASKS	MUNCHER	MURALED	MURMURS	MUSCOVITES
MULTITON	MUNCHERS	MURALIST	MURPHIES	MUSCULAR
MULTITONE	MUNCHES	MURALISTS	MURPHY	MUSE
MULTITONES	MUNCHIES	MURALLED	MURR	MUSED
MULTITUDE	MUNCHING	MURALS	MURRA	MUSEFUL
MULTITUDES	MUNCHKIN	MURAS	MURRAIN	MUSEOLOGIES
MULTIUNIT	MUNCHKINS	MURDER	MURRAINS	MUSEOLOGY
MULTIUSE	MUNDANE	MURDERED	MURRAS	MUSER
MULTIUSER	MUNDANELY	MURDEREE	MURRE	MUSERS
MULTIWALL	MUNDANITIES	MURDEREES	MURRELET	MUSES
MULTIYEAR	MUNDANITY	MURDERER	MURRELETS	MUSETTE
MULTURE	MUNDUNGO	MURDERERS	MURRES	MUSETTES
MULTURES	MUNDUNGOS	MURDERESS	MURREY	MUSEUM
MUM	MUNDUNGUS	MURDERESSES	MURREYS	MUSEUMS
MUMBLE	MUNDUNGUSES	MURDERING	MURRHA	MUSH
MUMBLED	MUNGO	MURDEROUS	MURRHAS	MUSHED
MUMBLER	MUNGOES	MURDERS	MURRHINE	MUSHER
MUMBLERS	MUNGOOSE	MURE	MURRIES	MUSHERS
MUMBLES	MUNGOOSES	MURED	MURRINE	MUSHES

MUSHIER
MUSHIEST
MUSHILY
MUSHINESS
MUSHINESSES
MUSHING
MUSHROOM
MUSHROOMED
MUSHROOMING
MUSHROOMS
MUSHY
MUSIC
MUSICAL
MUSICALE
MUSICALES
MUSICALLY
MUSICALS
MUSICIAN
MUSICIANS
MUSICK
MUSICKED
MUSICKING
MUSICKS
MUSICLESS
MUSICS
MUSING
MUSINGLY
MUSINGS
MUSJID
MUSJIDS
MUSK
MUSKEG
MUSKEGS
MUSKET
MUSKETEER
MUSKETEERS
MUSKETRIES
MUSKETRY
MUSKETS
MUSKIE
MUSKIER
MUSKIES
MUSKIEST
MUSKILY
MUSKINESS
MUSKINESSES
MUSKIT
MUSKITS
MUSKMELON
MUSKMELONS
MUSKOX

MUSKOXEN
MUSKRAT
MUSKRATS
MUSKROOT
MUSKROOTS
MUSKS
MUSKY
MUSLIN
MUSLINS
MUSPIKE
MUSPIKES
MUSQUASH
MUSQUASHES
MUSS
MUSSED
MUSSEL
MUSSELS
MUSSES
MUSSIER
MUSSIEST
MUSSILY
MUSSINESS
MUSSINESSES
MUSSING
MUSSY
MUST
MUSTACHE
MUSTACHED
MUSTACHES
MUSTACHIO
MUSTACHIOS
MUSTANG
MUSTANGS
MUSTARD
MUSTARDS
MUSTARDY
MUSTED
MUSTEE
MUSTEES
MUSTELID
MUSTELIDS
MUSTELINE
MUSTER
MUSTERED
MUSTERING
MUSTERS
MUSTH
MUSTHS
MUSTIER
MUSTIEST
MUSTILY

MUSTINESS
MUSTINESSES
MUSTING
MUSTS
MUSTY
MUT
MUTABLE
MUTABLY
MUTAGEN
MUTAGENIC
MUTAGENS
MUTANT
MUTANTS
MUTASE
MUTASES
MUTATE
MUTATED
MUTATES
MUTATING
MUTATION
MUTATIONS
MUTATIVE
MUTCH
MUTCHES
MUTCHKIN
MUTCHKINS
MUTE
MUTED
MUTEDLY
MUTELY
MUTENESS
MUTENESSES
MUTER
MUTES
MUTEST
MUTICOUS
MUTILATE
MUTILATED
MUTILATES
MUTILATING
MUTILATOR
MUTILATORS
MUTINE
MUTINED
MUTINEER
MUTINEERED
MUTINEERING
MUTINEERS
MUTINES
MUTING
MUTINIED

MUTINIES
MUTINING
MUTINOUS
MUTINY
MUTINYING
MUTISM
MUTISMS
MUTON
MUTONS
MUTS
MUTT
MUTTER
MUTTERED
MUTTERER
MUTTERERS
MUTTERING
MUTTERS
MUTTON
MUTTONS
MUTTONY
MUTTS
MUTUAL
MUTUALISM
MUTUALISMS
MUTUALIST
MUTUALISTS
MUTUALITIES
MUTUALITY
MUTUALIZE
MUTUALIZED
MUTUALIZES
MUTUALIZING
MUTUALLY
MUTUALS
MUTUEL
MUTUELS
MUTULAR
MUTULE
MUTULES
MUUMUU
MUUMUUS
MUZHIK
MUZHIKS
MUZJIK
MUZJIKS
MUZZIER
MUZZIEST
MUZZILY
MUZZINESS
MUZZINESSES
MUZZLE

MUZZLED
MUZZLER
MUZZLERS
MUZZLES
MUZZLING
MUZZY
MY
MYALGIA
MYALGIAS
MYALGIC
MYASES
MYASIS
MYC
MYCELE
MYCELES
MYCELIA
MYCELIAL
MYCELIAN
MYCELIUM
MYCELOID
MYCETOMA
MYCETOMAS
MYCETOMATA
MYCOFLORA
MYCOFLORAE
MYCOFLORAS
MYCOLOGIC
MYCOLOGIES
MYCOLOGY
MYCOPHAGIES
MYCOPHAGY
MYCOPHILE
MYCOPHILES
MYCORHIZA
MYCORHIZAE
MYCORHIZAS
MYCOSES
MYCOSIS
MYCOTIC
MYCOTOXIN
MYCOTOXINS
MYCOVIRUS
MYCOVIRUSES
MYCS
MYDRIASES
MYDRIASIS
MYDRIATIC
MYDRIATICS
MYELIN
MYELINE
MYELINES

MYELINIC
MYELINS
MYELITIDES
MYELITIS
MYELOCYTE
MYELOCYTES
MYELOGRAM
MYELOGRAMS
MYELOID
MYELOMA
MYELOMAS
MYELOMATA
MYIASES
MYIASIS
MYLAR
MYLARS
MYLONITE
MYLONITES
MYNA
MYNAH
MYNAHS
MYNAS
MYNHEER
MYNHEERS
MYOBLAST
MYOBLASTS
MYOCARDIA
MYOCARDIUM
MYOCLONIC
MYOCLONUS
MYOCLONUSES
MYOFIBRIL
MYOFIBRILS
MYOGENIC
MYOGLOBIN
MYOGLOBINS
MYOGRAPH
MYOGRAPHS
MYOID
MYOLOGIC
MYOLOGIES
MYOLOGIST
MYOLOGISTS
MYOLOGY
MYOMA
MYOMAS
MYOMATA
MYOMATOUS
MYONEURAL
MYOPATHIC
MYOPATHIES

MYOPATHY
MYOPE
MYOPES
MYOPIA
MYOPIAS
MYOPIC
MYOPIES
MYOPY
MYOSCOPE
MYOSCOPES
MYOSES
MYOSIN
MYOSINS
MYOSIS
MYOSITIS
MYOSITISES
MYOSOTE
MYOSOTES
MYOSOTIS
MYOSOTISES
MYOTIC
MYOTICS
MYOTOME
MYOTOMES
MYOTONIA
MYOTONIAS
MYOTONIC
MYRIAD
MYRIADS
MYRIAPOD
MYRIAPODS
MYRICA
MYRICAS
MYRIOPOD
MYRIOPODS
MYRMIDON
MYRMIDONES
MYRMIDONS
MYROBALAN
MYROBALANS
MYRRH
MYRRHIC
MYRRHS
MYRTLE
MYRTLES
MYSELF
MYSID
MYSIDS
MYSOST
MYSOSTS
MYSTAGOG

MYSTAGOGIES
MYSTAGOGS
MYSTAGOGY
MYSTERIES
MYSTERY
MYSTIC
MYSTICAL
MYSTICETE
MYSTICETES
MYSTICISM
MYSTICISMS
MYSTICLY
MYSTICS
MYSTIFIED
MYSTIFIER
MYSTIFIERS
MYSTIFIES
MYSTIFY
MYSTIFYING
MYSTIQUE
MYSTIQUES
MYTH
MYTHIC
MYTHICAL
MYTHICIZE
MYTHICIZED
MYTHICIZES
MYTHICIZING
MYTHIER
MYTHIEST
MYTHMAKER
MYTHMAKERS
MYTHOI
MYTHOLOGIES
MYTHOLOGY
MYTHOPEIC
MYTHOS
MYTHS
MYTHY
MYXAMEBA
MYXAMEBAE
MYXAMEBAS
MYXAMOEBA
MYXAMOEBAE
MYXAMOEBAS
MYXEDEMA
MYXEDEMAS
MYXEDEMIC
MYXOCYTE
MYXOCYTES
MYXOEDEMA

MYXOEDEMAS
MYXOID
MYXOMA
MYXOMAS
MYXOMATA
MYXOVIRAL
MYXOVIRUS
MYXOVIRUSES

N

NA
NAAN
NAANS
NAB
NABBED
NABBER
NABBERS
NABBING
NABE
NABES
NABIS
NABOB
NABOBERIES
NABOBERY
NABOBESS
NABOBESSES
NABOBISH
NABOBISM
NABOBISMS
NABOBS
NABS
NACELLE
NACELLES
NACHAS
NACHES
NACHO
NACHOS
NACRE
NACRED
NACREOUS
NACRES
NADA
NADAS
NADIR
NADIRAL
NADIRS
NAE
NAETHING

NAETHINGS
NAEVI
NAEVOID
NAEVUS
NAFF
NAFFED
NAFFING
NAFFS
NAG
NAGANA
NAGANAS
NAGGED
NAGGER
NAGGERS
NAGGIER
NAGGIEST
NAGGING
NAGGINGLY
NAGGY
NAGS
NAH
NAIAD
NAIADES
NAIADS
NAIF
NAIFS
NAIL
NAILBITER
NAILBITERS
NAILBRUSH
NAILBRUSHES
NAILED
NAILER
NAILERS
NAILFOLD
NAILFOLDS
NAILHEAD
NAILHEADS
NAILING
NAILS
NAILSET
NAILSETS
NAINSOOK
NAINSOOKS
NAIRA
NAIRAS
NAIRU
NAIRUS
NAISSANCE
NAISSANCES
NAIVE

NAIVELY	NANDINA	NAPHTOLS	NARCOTIZES	NASALISE
NAIVENESS	NANDINAS	NAPIFORM	NARCOTIZING	NASALISED
NAIVENESSES	NANDINS	NAPKIN	NARCS	NASALISES
NAIVER	NANISM	NAPKINS	NARD	NASALISING
NAIVES	NANISMS	NAPLESS	NARDINE	NASALISM
NAIVEST	NANKEEN	NAPOLEON	NARDS	NASALISMS
NAIVETE	NANKEENS	NAPOLEONS	NARES	NASALITIES
NAIVETES	NANKIN	NAPPA	NARGHILE	NASALITY
NAIVETIES	NANKINS	NAPPAS	NARGHILES	NASALIZE
NAIVETY	NANNIE	NAPPE	NARGILE	NASALIZED
NAKED	NANNIES	NAPPED	NARGILEH	NASALIZES
NAKEDER	NANNY	NAPPER	NARGILEHS	NASALIZING
NAKEDEST	NANNYISH	NAPPERS	NARGILES	NASALLY
NAKEDLY	NANOGRAM	NAPPES	NARIAL	NASALS
NAKEDNESS	NANOGRAMS	NAPPIE	NARIC	NASCENCE
NAKEDNESSES	NANOMETER	NAPPIER	NARINE	NASCENCES
NAKFA	NANOMETERS	NAPPIES	NARIS	NASCENCIES
NAKFAS	NANOMETRE	NAPPIEST	NARK	NASCENCY
NALA	NANOMETRES	NAPPINESS	NARKED	NASCENT
NALAS	NANOSCALE	NAPPINESSES	NARKING	NASEBERRIES
NALED	NANOTECH	NAPPING	NARKS	NASEBERRY
NALEDS	NANOTECHS	NAPPY	NARKY	NASIAL
NALOXONE	NANOTESLA	NAPROXEN	NARRATE	NASION
NALOXONES	NANOTESLAS	NAPROXENS	NARRATED	NASIONS
NAM	NANOTUBE	NAPS	NARRATER	NASTIC
NAMABLE	NANOTUBES	NARC	NARRATERS	NASTIER
NAMAYCUSH	NANOWATT	NARCEIN	NARRATES	NASTIES
NAMAYCUSHES	NANOWATTS	NARCEINE	NARRATING	NASTIEST
NAME	NANS	NARCEINES	NARRATION	NASTILY
NAMEABLE	NAOI	NARCEINS	NARRATIONS	NASTINESS
NAMED	NAOS	NARCISM	NARRATIVE	NASTINESSES
NAMELESS	NAP	NARCISMS	NARRATIVES	NASTY
NAMELY	NAPA	NARCISSI	NARRATOR	NATAL
NAMEPLATE	NAPALM	NARCISSUS	NARRATORS	NATALITIES
NAMEPLATES	NAPALMED	NARCISSUSES	NARROW	NATALITY
NAMER	NAPALMING	NARCIST	NARROWED	NATANT
NAMERS	NAPALMS	NARCISTIC	NARROWER	NATANTLY
NAMES	NAPAS	NARCISTS	NARROWEST	NATATION
NAMESAKE	NAPE	NARCO	NARROWING	NATATIONS
NAMESAKES	NAPERIES	NARCOMA	NARROWISH	NATATORIA
NAMETAG	NAPERY	NARCOMAS	NARROWLY	NATATORIUM
NAMETAGS	NAPES	NARCOMATA	NARROWS	NATATORIUMS
NAMING	NAPHTHA	NARCOS	NARTHEX	NATATORY
NAN	NAPHTHAS	NARCOSE	NARTHEXES	NATCH
NANA	NAPHTHENE	NARCOSES	NARWAL	NATES
NANAS	NAPHTHENES	NARCOSIS	NARWALS	NATHELESS
NANCE	NAPHTHOL	NARCOTIC	NARWHAL	NATHLESS
NANCES	NAPHTHOLS	NARCOTICS	NARWHALE	NATION
NANCIES	NAPHTHOUS	NARCOTISM	NARWHALES	NATIONAL
NANCIFIED	NAPHTHYL	NARCOTISMS	NARWHALS	NATIONALS
NANCY	NAPHTHYLS	NARCOTIZE	NARY	NATIONS
NANDIN	NAPHTOL	NARCOTIZED	NASAL	NATIVE

NATIVELY	NAUSEANT	NAYSAY	NEBS	NECROPOLIS
NATIVES	NAUSEANTS	NAYSAYER	NEBULA	NECROPOLISES
NATIVISM	NAUSEAS	NAYSAYERS	NEBULAE	NECROPSIED
NATIVISMS	NAUSEATE	NAYSAYING	NEBULAR	NECROPSIES
NATIVIST	NAUSEATED	NAYSAYINGS	NEBULAS	NECROPSY
NATIVISTS	NAUSEATES	NAYSAYS	NEBULE	NECROPSYING
NATIVITIES	NAUSEATING	NAZI	NEBULISE	NECROSE
NATIVITY	NAUSEOUS	NAZIFIED	NEBULISED	NECROSED
NATRIUM	NAUTCH	NAZIFIES	NEBULISES	NECROSES
NATRIUMS	NAUTCHES	NAZIFY	NEBULISING	NECROSING
NATROLITE	NAUTICAL	NAZIFYING	NEBULIZE	NECROSIS
NATROLITES	NAUTILI	NAZIS	NEBULIZED	NECROTIC
NATRON	NAUTILOID	NE	NEBULIZER	NECROTIZE
NATRONS	NAUTILOIDS	NEAP	NEBULIZERS	NECROTIZED
NATTER	NAUTILUS	NEAPS	NEBULIZES	NECROTIZES
NATTERED	NAUTILUSES	NEAR	NEBULIZING	NECROTIZING
NATTERING	NAVAID	NEARBY	NEBULOSE	NECROTOMIES
NATTERS	NAVAIDS	NEARED	NEBULOUS	NECROTOMY
NATTIER	NAVAL	NEARER	NEBULY	NECTAR
NATTIEST	NAVALLY	NEAREST	NECESSARIES	NECTAREAN
NATTILY	NAVAR	NEARING	NECESSARY	NECTARIAL
NATTINESS	NAVARS	NEARLIER	NECESSITIES	NECTARIED
NATTINESSES	NAVE	NEARLIEST	NECESSITY	NECTARIES
NATTY	NAVEL	NEARLY	NECK	NECTARINE
NATURAL	NAVELS	NEARNESS	NECKBAND	NECTARINES
NATURALLY	NAVELWORT	NEARNESSES	NECKBANDS	NECTAROUS
NATURALS	NAVELWORTS	NEARS	NECKCLOTH	NECTARS
NATURE	NAVES	NEARSHORE	NECKCLOTHS	NECTARY
NATURED	NAVETTE	NEARSIDE	NECKED	NEDDIES
NATURES	NAVETTES	NEARSIDES	NECKER	NEDDY
NATURISM	NAVICERT	NEAT	NECKERS	NEE
NATURISMS	NAVICERTS	NEATEN	NECKING	NEED
NATURIST	NAVICULAR	NEATENED	NECKINGS	NEEDED
NATURISTS	NAVICULARS	NEATENING	NECKLACE	NEEDER
NAUGAHYDE	NAVIES	NEATENS	NECKLACED	NEEDERS
NAUGAHYDES	NAVIGABLE	NEATER	NECKLACES	NEEDFUL
NAUGHT	NAVIGABLY	NEATEST	NECKLACING	NEEDFULLY
NAUGHTIER	NAVIGATE	NEATH	NECKLESS	NEEDFULS
NAUGHTIES	NAVIGATED	NEATHERD	NECKLIKE	NEEDIER
NAUGHTIEST	NAVIGATES	NEATHERDS	NECKLINE	NEEDIEST
NAUGHTILY	NAVIGATING	NEATLY	NECKLINES	NEEDILY
NAUGHTS	NAVIGATOR	NEATNESS	NECKPIECE	NEEDINESS
NAUGHTY	NAVIGATORS	NEATNESSES	NECKPIECES	NEEDINESSES
NAUMACHIA	NAVVIES	NEATNIK	NECKS	NEEDING
NAUMACHIAE	NAVVY	NEATNIKS	NECKTIE	NEEDLE
NAUMACHIAS	NAVY	NEATS	NECKTIES	NEEDLED
NAUMACHIES	NAW	NEB	NECKWEAR	NEEDLER
NAUMACHY	NAWAB	NEBBISH	NECROLOGIES	NEEDLERS
NAUPLIAL	NAWABS	NEBBISHES	NECROLOGY	NEEDLES
NAUPLII	NAY	NEBBISHY	NECROPOLEIS	NEEDLESS
NAUPLIUS	NAYS	NEBENKERN	NECROPOLES	NEEDLING
NAUSEA	NAYSAID	NEBENKERNS	NECROPOLI	NEEDLINGS

NEEDS	NEGROPHILS	NEODYMIUM	NEPETAS	NERTS
NEEDY	NEGS	NEODYMIUMS	NEPHELINE	NERTZ
NEEM	NEGUS	NEOGENE	NEPHELINES	NERVATE
NEEMS	NEGUSES	NEOLITH	NEPHELITE	NERVATION
NEEP	NEIF	NEOLITHIC	NEPHELITES	NERVATIONS
NEEPS	NEIFS	NEOLITHS	NEPHEW	NERVATURE
NEFARIOUS	NEIGH	NEOLOGIC	NEPHEWS	NERVATURES
NEG	NEIGHBOR	NEOLOGIES	NEPHOGRAM	NERVE
NEGATE	NEIGHBORED	NEOLOGISM	NEPHOGRAMS	NERVED
NEGATED	NEIGHBORING	NEOLOGISMS	NEPHOLOGIES	NERVELESS
NEGATER	NEIGHBORS	NEOLOGIST	NEPHOLOGY	NERVES
NEGATERS	NEIGHBOUR	NEOLOGISTS	NEPHRIC	NERVIER
NEGATES	NEIGHBOURED	NEOLOGIZE	NEPHRIDIA	NERVIEST
NEGATING	NEIGHBOURING	NEOLOGIZED	NEPHRIDIUM	NERVILY
NEGATION	NEIGHBOURS	NEOLOGIZES	NEPHRISM	NERVINE
NEGATIONS	NEIGHED	NEOLOGIZING	NEPHRISMS	NERVINES
NEGATIVE	NEIGHING	NEOLOGY	NEPHRITE	NERVINESS
NEGATIVED	NEIGHS	NEOMORPH	NEPHRITES	NERVINESSES
NEGATIVES	NEIST	NEOMORPHS	NEPHRITIC	NERVING
NEGATIVING	NEITHER	NEOMYCIN	NEPHRITIDES	NERVINGS
NEGATON	NEKTON	NEOMYCINS	NEPHRITIS	NERVOSITIES
NEGATONS	NEKTONIC	NEON	NEPHRITISES	NERVOSITY
NEGATOR	NEKTONS	NEONATAL	NEPHRON	NERVOUS
NEGATORS	NELLIE	NEONATE	NEPHRONS	NERVOUSLY
NEGATRON	NELLIES	NEONATES	NEPHROSES	NERVULE
NEGATRONS	NELLY	NEONED	NEPHROSIS	NERVULES
NEGLECT	NELSON	NEONS	NEPHROTIC	NERVURE
NEGLECTED	NELSONS	NEOPHILIA	NEPHROTICS	NERVURES
NEGLECTER	NELUMBIUM	NEOPHILIAS	NEPOTIC	NERVY
NEGLECTERS	NELUMBIUMS	NEOPHYTE	NEPOTISM	NESCIENCE
NEGLECTING	NELUMBO	NEOPHYTES	NEPOTISMS	NESCIENCES
NEGLECTOR	NELUMBOS	NEOPHYTIC	NEPOTIST	NESCIENT
NEGLECTORS	NEMA	NEOPLASIA	NEPOTISTS	NESCIENTS
NEGLECTS	NEMAS	NEOPLASIAS	NEPTUNIUM	NESS
NEGLIGE	NEMATIC	NEOPLASM	NEPTUNIUMS	NESSES
NEGLIGEE	NEMATODE	NEOPLASMS	NERD	NEST
NEGLIGEES	NEMATODES	NEOPLASTIES	NERDIER	NESTABLE
NEGLIGENT	NEMERTEAN	NEOPLASTY	NERDIEST	NESTED
NEGLIGES	NEMERTEANS	NEOPRENE	NERDINESS	NESTER
NEGOTIANT	NEMERTINE	NEOPRENES	NERDINESSES	NESTERS
NEGOTIANTS	NEMERTINES	NEOTENIC	NERDISH	NESTING
NEGOTIATE	NEMESES	NEOTENIES	NERDS	NESTLE
NEGOTIATED	NEMESIS	NEOTENOUS	NERDY	NESTLED
NEGOTIATES	NEMOPHILA	NEOTENY	NEREID	NESTLER
NEGOTIATING	NEMOPHILAS	NEOTERIC	NEREIDES	NESTLERS
NEGRITUDE	NENE	NEOTERICS	NEREIDS	NESTLES
NEGRITUDES	NENES	NEOTROPIC	NEREIS	NESTLIKE
NEGROID	NEOCON	NEOTYPE	NERITIC	NESTLING
NEGROIDS	NEOCONS	NEOTYPES	NEROL	NESTLINGS
NEGRONI	NEOCORTEX	NEPENTHE	NEROLI	NESTOR
NEGRONIS	NEOCORTEXES	NEPENTHES	NEROLIS	NESTORS
NEGROPHIL	NEOCORTICES	NEPETA	NEROLS	NESTS

NET	NEURAXON	NEUTRINOS	NEWSGROUPS	NIB
NETHER	NEURAXONS	NEUTRON	NEWSHAWK	NIBBED
NETIZEN	NEURINE	NEUTRONIC	NEWSHAWKS	NIBBING
NETIZENS	NEURINES	NEUTRONS	NEWSHOUND	NIBBLE
NETLESS	NEURITIC	NEVE	NEWSHOUNDS	NIBBLED
NETLIKE	NEURITICS	NEVER	NEWSIE	NIBBLER
NETMINDER	NEURITIDES	NEVERMIND	NEWSIER	NIBBLERS
NETMINDERS	NEURITIS	NEVERMINDS	NEWSIES	NIBBLES
NETOP	NEURITISES	NEVERMORE	NEWSIEST	NIBBLING
NETOPS	NEUROCOEL	NEVES	NEWSINESS	NIBLICK
NETS	NEUROCOELS	NEVI	NEWSINESSES	NIBLICKS
NETSUKE	NEUROGLIA	NEVOID	NEWSLESS	NIBLIKE
NETSUKES	NEUROGLIAS	NEVUS	NEWSMAKER	NIBS
NETT	NEUROID	NEW	NEWSMAKERS	NICAD
NETTABLE	NEUROLOGIES	NEWBIE	NEWSMAN	NICADS
NETTED	NEUROLOGY	NEWBIES	NEWSMEN	NICCOLITE
NETTER	NEUROMA	NEWBORN	NEWSPAPER	NICCOLITES
NETTERS	NEUROMAS	NEWBORNS	NEWSPAPERED	NICE
NETTIER	NEUROMAST	NEWCOMER	NEWSPAPERING	NICELY
NETTIEST	NEUROMASTS	NEWCOMERS	NEWSPAPERS	NICENESS
NETTING	NEUROMATA	NEWEL	NEWSPEAK	NICENESSES
NETTINGS	NEURON	NEWELS	NEWSPEAKS	NICER
NETTLE	NEURONAL	NEWER	NEWSPRINT	NICEST
NETTLED	NEURONE	NEWEST	NEWSPRINTS	NICETIES
NETTLER	NEURONES	NEWFOUND	NEWSREEL	NICETY
NETTLERS	NEURONIC	NEWIE	NEWSREELS	NICHE
NETTLES	NEURONS	NEWIES	NEWSROOM	NICHED
NETTLIER	NEUROPATH	NEWISH	NEWSROOMS	NICHES
NETTLIEST	NEUROPATHS	NEWLY	NEWSSTAND	NICHING
NETTLING	NEUROSAL	NEWLYWED	NEWSSTANDS	NICK
NETTLY	NEUROSES	NEWLYWEDS	NEWSWIRE	NICKED
NETTS	NEUROSIS	NEWMARKET	NEWSWIRES	NICKEL
NETTY	NEUROTIC	NEWMARKETS	NEWSWOMAN	NICKELED
NETWORK	NEUROTICS	NEWMOWN	NEWSWOMEN	NICKELIC
NETWORKED	NEUROTOMIES	NEWNESS	NEWSY	NICKELING
NETWORKER	NEUROTOMY	NEWNESSES	NEWT	NICKELLED
NETWORKERS	NEURULA	NEWS	NEWTON	NICKELLING
NETWORKING	NEURULAE	NEWSAGENT	NEWTONS	NICKELOUS
NETWORKS	NEURULAR	NEWSAGENTS	NEWTS	NICKELS
NEUK	NEURULAS	NEWSBEAT	NEWWAVER	NICKER
NEUKS	NEUSTIC	NEWSBEATS	NEWWAVERS	NICKERED
NEUM	NEUSTON	NEWSBOY	NEXT	NICKERING
NEUMATIC	NEUSTONIC	NEWSBOYS	NEXTDOOR	NICKERS
NEUME	NEUSTONS	NEWSBREAK	NEXUS	NICKING
NEUMES	NEUTER	NEWSBREAKS	NEXUSES	NICKLE
NEUMIC	NEUTERED	NEWSCAST	NGULTRUM	NICKLED
NEUMS	NEUTERING	NEWSCASTS	NGULTRUMS	NICKLES
NEURAL	NEUTERS	NEWSDESK	NGWEE	NICKLING
NEURALGIA	NEUTRAL	NEWSDESKS	NIACIN	NICKNACK
NEURALGIAS	NEUTRALLY	NEWSGIRL	NIACINS	NICKNACKS
NEURALGIC	NEUTRALS	NEWSGIRLS	NIALAMIDE	NICKNAME
NEURALLY	NEUTRINO	NEWSGROUP	NIALAMIDES	NICKNAMED

NICKNAMER	NIELLI	NIGHTCLUBBING	NILGAI	NINNY
NICKNAMERS	NIELLIST	NIGHTCLUBS	NILGAIS	NINNYISH
NICKNAMES	NIELLISTS	NIGHTFALL	NILGAU	NINON
NICKNAMING	NIELLO	NIGHTFALLS	NILGAUS	NINONS
NICKS	NIELLOED	NIGHTGLOW	NILGHAI	NINTH
NICOISE	NIELLOING	NIGHTGLOWS	NILGHAIS	NINTHLY
NICOL	NIELLOS	NIGHTGOWN	NILGHAU	NINTHS
NICOLS	NIEVE	NIGHTGOWNS	NILGHAUS	NIOBATE
NICOTIANA	NIEVES	NIGHTHAWK	NILL	NIOBATES
NICOTIANAS	NIFFER	NIGHTHAWKS	NILLED	NIOBIC
NICOTIN	NIFFERED	NIGHTIE	NILLING	NIOBITE
NICOTINE	NIFFERING	NIGHTIES	NILLS	NIOBITES
NICOTINES	NIFFERS	NIGHTJAR	NILPOTENT	NIOBIUM
NICOTINIC	NIFTIER	NIGHTJARS	NILPOTENTS	NIOBIUMS
NICOTINS	NIFTIES	NIGHTLESS	NILS	NIOBOUS
NICTATE	NIFTIEST	NIGHTLIFE	NIM	NIP
NICTATED	NIFTILY	NIGHTLIFES	NIMBI	NIPA
NICTATES	NIFTINESS	NIGHTLIVES	NIMBLE	NIPAS
NICTATING	NIFTINESSES	NIGHTLONG	NIMBLER	NIPPED
NICTATION	NIFTY	NIGHTLY	NIMBLEST	NIPPER
NICTATIONS	NIGELLA	NIGHTMARE	NIMBLY	NIPPERS
NICTITANT	NIGELLAS	NIGHTMARES	NIMBUS	NIPPIER
NICTITATE	NIGGARD	NIGHTS	NIMBUSED	NIPPIEST
NICTITATED	NIGGARDED	NIGHTSIDE	NIMBUSES	NIPPILY
NICTITATES	NIGGARDING	NIGHTSIDES	NIMBYNESS	NIPPINESS
NICTITATING	NIGGARDLY	NIGHTSPOT	NIMBYNESSES	NIPPINESSES
NIDAL	NIGGARDS	NIGHTSPOTS	NIMIETIES	NIPPING
NIDATE	NIGGER	NIGHTTIDE	NIMIETY	NIPPINGLY
NIDATED	NIGGERS	NIGHTTIDES	NIMIOUS	NIPPLE
NIDATES	NIGGLE	NIGHTTIME	NIMMED	NIPPLED
NIDATING	NIGGLED	NIGHTTIMES	NIMMING	NIPPLES
NIDATION	NIGGLER	NIGHTWEAR	NIMROD	NIPPY
NIDATIONS	NIGGLERS	NIGHTY	NIMRODS	NIPS
NIDDERING	NIGGLES	NIGRIFIED	NIMS	NIRVANA
NIDDERINGS	NIGGLIER	NIGRIFIES	NINE	NIRVANAS
NIDE	NIGGLIEST	NIGRIFY	NINEBARK	NIRVANIC
NIDED	NIGGLING	NIGRIFYING	NINEBARKS	NISEI
NIDERING	NIGGLINGS	NIGRITUDE	NINEFOLD	NISEIS
NIDERINGS	NIGGLY	NIGRITUDES	NINEPIN	NISI
NIDES	NIGH	NIGROSIN	NINEPINS	NISUS
NIDGET	NIGHED	NIGROSINE	NINES	NIT
NIDGETS	NIGHER	NIGROSINES	NINETEEN	NITCHIE
NIDI	NIGHEST	NIGROSINS	NINETEENS	NITCHIES
NIDIFIED	NIGHING	NIHIL	NINETIES	NITE
NIDIFIES	NIGHNESS	NIHILISM	NINETIETH	NITER
NIDIFY	NIGHNESSES	NIHILISMS	NINETIETHS	NITERIE
NIDIFYING	NIGHS	NIHILIST	NINETY	NITERIES
NIDING	NIGHT	NIHILISTS	NINHYDRIN	NITERS
NIDUS	NIGHTCAP	NIHILITIES	NINHYDRINS	NITERY
NIDUSES	NIGHTCAPS	NIHILITY	NINJA	NITES
NIECE	NIGHTCLUB	NIHILS	NINJAS	NITID
NIECES	NIGHTCLUBBED	NIL	NINNIES	NITINOL

NITINOLS
NITON
NITONS
NITPICK
NITPICKED
NITPICKER
NITPICKERS
NITPICKIER
NITPICKIEST
NITPICKING
NITPICKS
NITPICKY
NITRATE
NITRATED
NITRATES
NITRATING
NITRATION
NITRATIONS
NITRATOR
NITRATORS
NITRE
NITRES
NITRIC
NITRID
NITRIDE
NITRIDED
NITRIDES
NITRIDING
NITRIDS
NITRIFIED
NITRIFIER
NITRIFIERS
NITRIFIES
NITRIFY
NITRIFYING
NITRIL
NITRILE
NITRILES
NITRILS
NITRITE
NITRITES
NITRO
NITROGEN
NITROGENS
NITROLIC
NITROS
NITROSO
NITROSYL
NITROSYLS
NITROUS
NITS
NITTIER

NITTIEST
NITTY
NITWIT
NITWITS
NIVAL
NIVEOUS
NIX
NIXE
NIXED
NIXES
NIXIE
NIXIES
NIXING
NIXY
NIZAM
NIZAMATE
NIZAMATES
NIZAMS
NO
NOB
NOBBIER
NOBBIEST
NOBBILY
NOBBLE
NOBBLED
NOBBLER
NOBBLERS
NOBBLES
NOBBLING
NOBBY
NOBELIUM
NOBELIUMS
NOBILIARY
NOBILITIES
NOBILITY
NOBLE
NOBLEMAN
NOBLEMEN
NOBLENESS
NOBLENESSES
NOBLER
NOBLES
NOBLESSE
NOBLESSES
NOBLEST
NOBLY
NOBODIES
NOBODY
NOBS
NOCENT
NOCK
NOCKED

NOCKING
NOCKS
NOCTILUCA
NOCTILUCAS
NOCTUID
NOCTUIDS
NOCTULE
NOCTULES
NOCTUOID
NOCTURN
NOCTURNAL
NOCTURNE
NOCTURNES
NOCTURNS
NOCUOUS
NOCUOUSLY
NOD
NODAL
NODALITIES
NODALITY
NODALLY
NODDED
NODDER
NODDERS
NODDIES
NODDING
NODDINGLY
NODDLE
NODDLED
NODDLES
NODDLING
NODDY
NODE
NODES
NODI
NODICAL
NODOSE
NODOSITIES
NODOSITY
NODOUS
NODS
NODULAR
NODULE
NODULES
NODULOSE
NODULOUS
NODUS
NOEL
NOELS
NOES
NOESIS
NOESISES

NOETIC
NOG
NOGG
NOGGED
NOGGIN
NOGGING
NOGGINGS
NOGGINS
NOGGS
NOGS
NOH
NOHOW
NOIL
NOILS
NOILY
NOIR
NOIRISH
NOIRS
NOISE
NOISED
NOISELESS
NOISES
NOISETTE
NOISETTES
NOISIER
NOISIEST
NOISILY
NOISINESS
NOISINESSES
NOISING
NOISOME
NOISOMELY
NOISY
NOLO
NOLOS
NOM
NOMA
NOMAD
NOMADIC
NOMADISM
NOMADISMS
NOMADS
NOMARCH
NOMARCHIES
NOMARCHS
NOMARCHY
NOMAS
NOMBLES
NOMBRIL
NOMBRILS
NOME
NOMEN

NOMES
NOMINA
NOMINAL
NOMINALLY
NOMINALS
NOMINATE
NOMINATED
NOMINATES
NOMINATING
NOMINATOR
NOMINATORS
NOMINEE
NOMINEES
NOMISM
NOMISMS
NOMISTIC
NOMOGRAM
NOMOGRAMS
NOMOGRAPH
NOMOGRAPHS
NOMOI
NOMOLOGIC
NOMOLOGIES
NOMOLOGY
NOMOS
NOMS
NONA
NONACID
NONACIDIC
NONACIDS
NONACTING
NONACTION
NONACTIONS
NONACTIVE
NONACTOR
NONACTORS
NONADDICT
NONADDICTS
NONADULT
NONADULTS
NONAGE
NONAGES
NONAGON
NONAGONAL
NONAGONS
NONANIMAL
NONANSWER
NONANSWERS
NONARABLE
NONART
NONARTIST
NONARTISTS

NONARTS
NONAS
NONATOMIC
NONAUTHOR
NONAUTHORS
NONBANK
NONBANKS
NONBASIC
NONBEING
NONBEINGS
NONBELIEF
NONBELIEFS
NONBINARY
NONBITING
NONBLACK
NONBLACKS
NONBODIES
NONBODY
NONBONDED
NONBOOK
NONBOOKS
NONBRAND
NONBUYING
NONCAKING
NONCAMPUS
NONCAREER
NONCASH
NONCASUAL
NONCAUSAL
NONCE
NONCEREAL
NONCES
NONCHURCH
NONCLASS
NONCLASSES
NONCLING
NONCODING
NONCOITAL
NONCOKING
NONCOLA
NONCOLAS
NONCOLOR
NONCOLORS
NONCOM
NONCOMBAT
NONCOMS
NONCONCUR
NONCONCURRED
NONCONCURRING
NONCONCURS
NONCORE
NONCOUNTY

NONCREDIT
NONCRIME
NONCRIMES
NONCRISES
NONCRISIS
NONCYCLIC
NONDAIRY
NONDANCE
NONDANCER
NONDANCERS
NONDANCES
NONDEGREE
NONDEMAND
NONDEMANDS
NONDESERT
NONDOCTOR
NONDOCTORS
NONDOLLAR
NONDRIP
NONDRIVER
NONDRIVERS
NONDRUG
NONDRYING
NONE
NONEDIBLE
NONEDIBLES
NONEGO
NONEGOS
NONELECT
NONELITE
NONEMPTY
NONENDING
NONENERGY
NONENTITIES
NONENTITY
NONENTRIES
NONENTRY
NONEQUAL
NONEQUALS
NONEROTIC
NONES
NONESUCH
NONESUCHES
NONET
NONETHNIC
NONETHNICS
NONETS
NONEVENT
NONEVENTS
NONEXEMPT
NONEXEMPTS
NONEXOTIC

NONEXPERT
NONEXPERTS
NONEXTANT
NONFACT
NONFACTOR
NONFACTORS
NONFACTS
NONFADING
NONFAMILIES
NONFAMILY
NONFAN
NONFANS
NONFARM
NONFARMER
NONFARMERS
NONFAT
NONFATAL
NONFATTY
NONFEUDAL
NONFILIAL
NONFINAL
NONFINITE
NONFISCAL
NONFLUID
NONFLUIDS
NONFLYING
NONFOCAL
NONFOOD
NONFORMAL
NONFOSSIL
NONFROZEN
NONFUEL
NONFUNDED
NONGAME
NONGAY
NONGAYS
NONGHETTO
NONGLARE
NONGLARES
NONGLAZED
NONGLOSSY
NONGOLFER
NONGOLFERS
NONGRADED
NONGREASY
NONGREEN
NONGROWTH
NONGUEST
NONGUESTS
NONGUILT
NONGUILTS
NONHARDY

NONHEME
NONHERO
NONHEROES
NONHEROIC
NONHOME
NONHUMAN
NONHUMANS
NONHUNTER
NONHUNTERS
NONIDEAL
NONILLION
NONILLIONS
NONIMAGE
NONIMAGES
NONIMMUNE
NONIMPACT
NONINERT
NONINJURY
NONINSECT
NONINSECTS
NONIONIC
NONIRON
NONISSUE
NONISSUES
NONJOINER
NONJOINERS
NONJURIES
NONJURING
NONJUROR
NONJURORS
NONJURY
NONKOSHER
NONKOSHERS
NONLABOR
NONLAWYER
NONLAWYERS
NONLEADED
NONLEAFY
NONLEAGUE
NONLEGAL
NONLEGUME
NONLEGUMES
NONLETHAL
NONLEVEL
NONLIABLE
NONLIFE
NONLINEAL
NONLINEAR
NONLIQUID
NONLIQUIDS
NONLIVES
NONLIVING

NONLIVINGS
NONLOCAL
NONLOCALS
NONLOVING
NONLOYAL
NONLYRIC
NONMAJOR
NONMAJORS
NONMAN
NONMANUAL
NONMARKET
NONMARKETS
NONMATURE
NONMEAT
NONMEMBER
NONMEMBERS
NONMEN
NONMENTAL
NONMETAL
NONMETALS
NONMETRIC
NONMETRO
NONMOBILE
NONMODAL
NONMODERN
NONMODERNS
NONMONEY
NONMORAL
NONMORTAL
NONMORTALS
NONMOTILE
NONMOVING
NONMUSIC
NONMUSICS
NONMUTANT
NONMUTANTS
NONMUTUAL
NONNASAL
NONNATIVE
NONNATIVES
NONNAVAL
NONNEURAL
NONNEWS
NONNOBLE
NONNORMAL
NONNOVEL
NONNOVELS
NONOBESE
NONOHMIC
NONOILY
NONORAL
NONORALLY

NONOWNER	NONQUOTA	NONSTICK	NONVECTORS	NOOKLIKE
NONOWNERS	NONRACIAL	NONSTICKY	NONVENOUS	NOOKS
NONPAGAN	NONRANDOM	NONSTOP	NONVERBAL	NOOKY
NONPAGANS	NONRATED	NONSTOPS	NONVESTED	NOON
NONPAID	NONREADER	NONSTORIES	NONVIABLE	NOONDAY
NONPAPAL	NONREADERS	NONSTORY	NONVIEWER	NOONDAYS
NONPAPIST	NONRHOTIC	NONSTYLE	NONVIEWERS	NOONING
NONPAPISTS	NONRIGID	NONSTYLES	NONVIRAL	NOONINGS
NONPAR	NONRIOTER	NONSUCH	NONVIRGIN	NOONS
NONPAREIL	NONRIOTERS	NONSUCHES	NONVIRGINS	NOONTIDE
NONPAREILS	NONRIVAL	NONSUGAR	NONVIRILE	NOONTIDES
NONPARENT	NONRIVALS	NONSUGARS	NONVISUAL	NOONTIME
NONPARENTS	NONROYAL	NONSUIT	NONVITAL	NOONTIMES
NONPARITIES	NONRUBBER	NONSUITED	NONVOCAL	NOOSE
NONPARITY	NONRULING	NONSUITING	NONVOCALS	NOOSED
NONPARTIES	NONRURAL	NONSUITS	NONVOTER	NOOSER
NONPARTY	NONSACRED	NONSYSTEM	NONVOTERS	NOOSERS
NONPAST	NONSALINE	NONSYSTEMS	NONVOTING	NOOSES
NONPASTS	NONSCHOOL	NONTALKER	NONWAGE	NOOSING
NONPAYING	NONSECRET	NONTALKERS	NONWAR	NOOSPHERE
NONPEAK	NONSECRETS	NONTARGET	NONWARS	NOOSPHERES
NONPERSON	NONSECURE	NONTARIFF	NONWHITE	NOOTROPIC
NONPERSONS	NONSELF	NONTAX	NONWHITES	NOOTROPICS
NONPLANAR	NONSELVES	NONTAXES	NONWINGED	NOPAL
NONPLAY	NONSENSE	NONTHEIST	NONWOODY	NOPALES
NONPLAYER	NONSENSES	NONTHEISTS	NONWOOL	NOPALITO
NONPLAYERS	NONSERIAL	NONTIDAL	NONWORD	NOPALITOS
NONPLAYS	NONSERIALS	NONTITLE	NONWORDS	NOPALS
NONPLIANT	NONSEXIST	NONTONAL	NONWORK	NOPE
NONPLUS	NONSEXUAL	NONTONIC	NONWORKER	NOPLACE
NONPLUSED	NONSHRINK	NONTOXIC	NONWORKERS	NOR
NONPLUSES	NONSIGNER	NONTRAGIC	NONWOVEN	NORDIC
NONPLUSING	NONSIGNERS	NONTRIBAL	NONWOVENS	NORI
NONPLUSSED	NONSKATER	NONTRUMP	NONWRITER	NORIA
NONPLUSSES	NONSKATERS	NONTRUTH	NONWRITERS	NORIAS
NONPLUSSING	NONSKED	NONTRUTHS	NONYL	NORIS
NONPOETIC	NONSKEDS	NONUNION	NONYLS	NORITE
NONPOINT	NONSKID	NONUNIONS	NONZERO	NORITES
NONPOLAR	NONSKIER	NONUNIQUE	NOO	NORITIC
NONPOLICE	NONSKIERS	NONUPLE	NOODGE	NORLAND
NONPOOR	NONSLIP	NONUPLES	NOODGED	NORLANDS
NONPOROUS	NONSMOKER	NONURBAN	NOODGES	NORM
NONPOSTAL	NONSMOKERS	NONURGENT	NOODGING	NORMAL
NONPRINT	NONSOCIAL	NONUSABLE	NOODLE	NORMALCIES
NONPROFIT	NONSOLAR	NONUSE	NOODLED	NORMALCY
NONPROFITS	NONSOLID	NONUSER	NOODLES	NORMALISE
NONPROS	NONSOLIDS	NONUSERS	NOODLING	NORMALISED
NONPROSSED	NONSPEECH	NONUSES	NOOGIE	NORMALISES
NONPROSSES	NONSTAPLE	NONUSING	NOOGIES	NORMALISING
NONPROSSING	NONSTAPLES	NONVACANT	NOOK	NORMALITIES
NONPROVEN	NONSTATIC	NONVALID	NOOKIE	NORMALITY
NONPUBLIC	NONSTEADY	NONVECTOR	NOOKIES	NORMALIZE

NORMALIZED	NOSEWHEEL	NOTCH	NOTTURNI	NOVELTIES
NORMALIZES	NOSEWHEELS	NOTCHBACK	NOTTURNO	NOVELTY
NORMALIZING	NOSEY	NOTCHBACKS	NOTUM	NOVENA
NORMALLY	NOSH	NOTCHED	NOUGAT	NOVENAE
NORMALS	NOSHED	NOTCHER	NOUGATS	NOVENAS
NORMANDE	NOSHER	NOTCHERS	NOUGHT	NOVERCAL
NORMATIVE	NOSHERS	NOTCHES	NOUGHTS	NOVICE
NORMED	NOSHES	NOTCHING	NOUMENA	NOVICES
NORMLESS	NOSHING	NOTE	NOUMENAL	NOVICIATE
NORMS	NOSIER	NOTEBOOK	NOUMENON	NOVICIATES
NORTH	NOSIEST	NOTEBOOKS	NOUN	NOVITIATE
NORTHEAST	NOSILY	NOTECARD	NOUNAL	NOVITIATES
NORTHEASTS	NOSINESS	NOTECARDS	NOUNALLY	NOVOCAINE
NORTHER	NOSINESSES	NOTECASE	NOUNLESS	NOVOCAINES
NORTHERLIES	NOSING	NOTECASES	NOUNS	NOW
NORTHERLY	NOSINGS	NOTED	NOURISH	NOWADAYS
NORTHERN	NOSOLOGIC	NOTEDLY	NOURISHED	NOWAY
NORTHERNS	NOSOLOGIES	NOTEDNESS	NOURISHER	NOWAYS
NORTHERS	NOSOLOGY	NOTEDNESSES	NOURISHERS	NOWHERE
NORTHING	NOSTALGIA	NOTELESS	NOURISHES	NOWHERES
NORTHINGS	NOSTALGIAS	NOTEPAD	NOURISHING	NOWHITHER
NORTHLAND	NOSTALGIC	NOTEPADS	NOUS	NOWISE
NORTHLANDS	NOSTALGICS	NOTEPAPER	NOUSES	NOWNESS
NORTHMOST	NOSTOC	NOTEPAPERS	NOUVEAU	NOWNESSES
NORTHS	NOSTOCS	NOTER	NOUVELLE	NOWS
NORTHWARD	NOSTOLOGIES	NOTERS	NOUVELLES	NOWT
NORTHWARDS	NOSTOLOGY	NOTES	NOVA	NOWTS
NORTHWEST	NOSTRIL	NOTHER	NOVAE	NOXIOUS
NORTHWESTS	NOSTRILS	NOTHING	NOVALIKE	NOXIOUSLY
NOS	NOSTRUM	NOTHINGS	NOVAS	NOYADE
NOSE	NOSTRUMS	NOTICE	NOVATION	NOYADES
NOSEBAG	NOSY	NOTICED	NOVATIONS	NOZZLE
NOSEBAGS	NOT	NOTICER	NOVEL	NOZZLES
NOSEBAND	NOTA	NOTICERS	NOVELETTE	NTH
NOSEBANDS	NOTABILIA	NOTICES	NOVELETTES	NU
NOSEBLEED	NOTABLE	NOTICING	NOVELISE	NUANCE
NOSEBLEEDS	NOTABLES	NOTIFIED	NOVELISED	NUANCED
NOSED	NOTABLY	NOTIFIER	NOVELISES	NUANCES
NOSEDIVE	NOTAL	NOTIFIERS	NOVELISING	NUB
NOSEDIVED	NOTARIAL	NOTIFIES	NOVELIST	NUBBIER
NOSEDIVES	NOTARIES	NOTIFY	NOVELISTS	NUBBIEST
NOSEDIVING	NOTARIZE	NOTIFYING	NOVELIZE	NUBBIN
NOSEDOVE	NOTARIZED	NOTING	NOVELIZED	NUBBINESS
NOSEGAY	NOTARIZES	NOTION	NOVELIZER	NUBBINESSES
NOSEGAYS	NOTARIZING	NOTIONAL	NOVELIZERS	NUBBINS
NOSEGUARD	NOTARY	NOTIONS	NOVELIZES	NUBBLE
NOSEGUARDS	NOTATE	NOTOCHORD	NOVELIZING	NUBBLES
NOSELESS	NOTATED	NOTOCHORDS	NOVELLA	NUBBLIER
NOSELIKE	NOTATES	NOTORIETIES	NOVELLAS	NUBBLIEST
NOSEPIECE	NOTATING	NOTORIETY	NOVELLE	NUBBLY
NOSEPIECES	NOTATION	NOTORIOUS	NOVELLY	NUBBY
NOSES	NOTATIONS	NOTORNIS	NOVELS	NUBIA

NUBIAS	NUDGE	NUMB	NUNATAK	NUTATION
NUBILE	NUDGED	NUMBAT	NUNATAKS	NUTATIONS
NUBILITIES	NUDGER	NUMBATS	NUNCHAKU	NUTBROWN
NUBILITY	NUDGERS	NUMBED	NUNCHAKUS	NUTCASE
NUBILOSE	NUDGES	NUMBER	NUNCIO	NUTCASES
NUBILOUS	NUDGING	NUMBERED	NUNCIOS	NUTGALL
NUBS	NUDICAUL	NUMBERER	NUNCLE	NUTGALLS
NUBUCK	NUDIE	NUMBERERS	NUNCLES	NUTGRASS
NUBUCKS	NUDIES	NUMBERING	NUNLIKE	NUTGRASSES
NUCELLAR	NUDISM	NUMBERS	NUNNATION	NUTHATCH
NUCELLI	NUDISMS	NUMBEST	NUNNATIONS	NUTHATCHES
NUCELLUS	NUDIST	NUMBFISH	NUNNERIES	NUTHOUSE
NUCHA	NUDISTS	NUMBFISHES	NUNNERY	NUTHOUSES
NUCHAE	NUDITIES	NUMBING	NUNNISH	NUTLET
NUCHAL	NUDITY	NUMBINGLY	NUNS	NUTLETS
NUCHALS	NUDNICK	NUMBLES	NUPTIAL	NUTLIKE
NUCLEAL	NUDNICKS	NUMBLY	NUPTIALLY	NUTMEAT
NUCLEAR	NUDNIK	NUMBNESS	NUPTIALS	NUTMEATS
NUCLEASE	NUDNIKS	NUMBNESSES	NURD	NUTMEG
NUCLEASES	NUDZH	NUMBS	NURDS	NUTMEGS
NUCLEATE	NUDZHED	NUMBSKULL	NURL	NUTPICK
NUCLEATED	NUDZHES	NUMBSKULLS	NURLED	NUTPICKS
NUCLEATES	NUDZHING	NUMCHUCK	NURLING	NUTRIA
NUCLEATING	NUGATORY	NUMCHUCKS	NURLS	NUTRIAS
NUCLEATOR	NUGGET	NUMEN	NURSE	NUTRIENT
NUCLEATORS	NUGGETS	NUMERABLE	NURSED	NUTRIENTS
NUCLEI	NUGGETY	NUMERABLY	NURSEMAID	NUTRIMENT
NUCLEIN	NUISANCE	NUMERACIES	NURSEMAIDS	NUTRIMENTS
NUCLEINIC	NUISANCES	NUMERACY	NURSER	NUTRITION
NUCLEINS	NUKE	NUMERAL	NURSERIES	NUTRITIONS
NUCLEOID	NUKED	NUMERALLY	NURSERS	NUTRITIVE
NUCLEOIDS	NUKES	NUMERALS	NURSERY	NUTRITIVES
NUCLEOLAR	NUKING	NUMERARY	NURSES	NUTS
NUCLEOLE	NULL	NUMERATE	NURSING	NUTSEDGE
NUCLEOLES	NULLAH	NUMERATED	NURSINGS	NUTSEDGES
NUCLEOLI	NULLAHS	NUMERATES	NURSLING	NUTSHELL
NUCLEOLUS	NULLED	NUMERATING	NURSLINGS	NUTSHELLS
NUCLEON	NULLIFIED	NUMERATOR	NURTURAL	NUTSIER
NUCLEONIC	NULLIFIER	NUMERATORS	NURTURANT	NUTSIEST
NUCLEONS	NULLIFIERS	NUMERIC	NURTURE	NUTSY
NUCLEUS	NULLIFIES	NUMERICAL	NURTURED	NUTTED
NUCLEUSES	NULLIFY	NUMERICS	NURTURER	NUTTER
NUCLIDE	NULLIFYING	NUMEROUS	NURTURERS	NUTTERS
NUCLIDES	NULLING	NUMINA	NURTURES	NUTTIER
NUCLIDIC	NULLIPARA	NUMINOUS	NURTURING	NUTTIEST
NUDE	NULLIPARAE	NUMMARY	NUS	NUTTILY
NUDELY	NULLIPARAS	NUMMULAR	NUT	NUTTINESS
NUDENESS	NULLIPORE	NUMMULITE	NUTANT	NUTTINESSES
NUDENESSES	NULLIPORES	NUMMULITES	NUTATE	NUTTING
NUDER	NULLITIES	NUMSKULL	NUTATED	NUTTINGS
NUDES	NULLITY	NUMSKULLS	NUTATES	NUTTY
NUDEST	NULLS	NUN	NUTATING	NUTWOOD

NUTWOODS	OAKUM	OBEDIENCE	OBITUARY	OBLIQUELY
NUZZLE	OAKUMS	OBEDIENCES	OBJECT	OBLIQUES
NUZZLED	OAKY	OBEDIENT	OBJECTED	OBLIQUING
NUZZLER	OAR	OBEISANCE	OBJECTIFIED	OBLIQUITIES
NUZZLERS	OARED	OBEISANCES	OBJECTIFIES	OBLIQUITY
NUZZLES	OARFISH	OBEISANT	OBJECTIFY	OBLIVION
NUZZLING	OARFISHES	OBELI	OBJECTIFYING	OBLIVIONS
NYALA	OARING	OBELIA	OBJECTING	OBLIVIOUS
NYALAS	OARLESS	OBELIAS	OBJECTION	OBLONG
NYLGHAI	OARLIKE	OBELISCAL	OBJECTIONS	OBLONGLY
NYLGHAIS	OARLOCK	OBELISE	OBJECTIVE	OBLONGS
NYLGHAU	OARLOCKS	OBELISED	OBJECTIVES	OBLOQUIAL
NYLGHAUS	OARS	OBELISES	OBJECTOR	OBLOQUIES
NYLON	OARSMAN	OBELISING	OBJECTORS	OBLOQUY
NYLONS	OARSMEN	OBELISK	OBJECTS	OBNOXIOUS
NYMPH	OARSWOMAN	OBELISKS	OBJET	OBOE
NYMPHA	OARSWOMEN	OBELISM	OBJETS	OBOES
NYMPHAE	OASES	OBELISMS	OBJURGATE	OBOIST
NYMPHAL	OASIS	OBELIZE	OBJURGATED	OBOISTS
NYMPHALID	OAST	OBELIZED	OBJURGATES	OBOL
NYMPHALIDS	OASTHOUSE	OBELIZES	OBJURGATING	OBOLE
NYMPHEAN	OASTHOUSES	OBELIZING	OBLAST	OBOLES
NYMPHET	OASTS	OBELUS	OBLASTI	OBOLI
NYMPHETIC	OAT	OBENTO	OBLASTS	OBOLS
NYMPHETS	OATCAKE	OBENTOS	OBLATE	OBOLUS
NYMPHETTE	OATCAKES	OBES	OBLATELY	OBOVATE
NYMPHETTES	OATEN	OBESE	OBLATES	OBOVOID
NYMPHO	OATER	OBESELY	OBLATION	OBSCENE
NYMPHOS	OATERS	OBESENESS	OBLATIONS	OBSCENELY
NYMPHS	OATH	OBESENESSES	OBLATORY	OBSCENER
NYSTAGMIC	OATHS	OBESITIES	OBLIGABLE	OBSCENEST
NYSTAGMUS	OATLIKE	OBESITY	OBLIGATE	OBSCENITIES
NYSTAGMUSES	OATMEAL	OBEY	OBLIGATED	OBSCENITY
NYSTATIN	OATMEALS	OBEYABLE	OBLIGATES	OBSCURANT
NYSTATINS	OATS	OBEYED	OBLIGATI	OBSCURANTS
	OAVES	OBEYER	OBLIGATING	OBSCURE
	OBA	OBEYERS	OBLIGATO	OBSCURED
O	OBAS	OBEYING	OBLIGATOR	OBSCURELY
	OBBLIGATI	OBEYS	OBLIGATORS	OBSCURER
	OBBLIGATO	OBFUSCATE	OBLIGATOS	OBSCURES
OAF	OBBLIGATOS	OBFUSCATED	OBLIGE	OBSCUREST
OAFISH	OBCONIC	OBFUSCATES	OBLIGED	OBSCURING
OAFISHLY	OBCONICAL	OBFUSCATING	OBLIGEE	OBSCURITIES
OAFS	OBCORDATE	OBI	OBLIGEES	OBSCURITY
OAK	OBDURACIES	OBIA	OBLIGER	OBSECRATE
OAKEN	OBDURACY	OBIAS	OBLIGERS	OBSECRATED
OAKIER	OBDURATE	OBIISM	OBLIGES	OBSECRATES
OAKIEST	OBE	OBIISMS	OBLIGING	OBSECRATING
OAKLIKE	OBEAH	OBIS	OBLIGOR	OBSEQUIES
OAKMOSS	OBEAHISM	OBIT	OBLIGORS	OBSEQUY
OAKMOSSES	OBEAHISMS	OBITS	OBLIQUE	OBSERVANT
OAKS	OBEAHS	OBITUARIES	OBLIQUED	OBSERVANTS

OBSERVE	OBTRUDER	OCCASION	OCEANAUT	OCTAMETER
OBSERVED	OBTRUDERS	OCCASIONED	OCEANAUTS	OCTAMETERS
OBSERVER	OBTRUDES	OCCASIONING	OCEANIC	OCTAN
OBSERVERS	OBTRUDING	OCCASIONS	OCEANS	OCTANE
OBSERVES	OBTRUSION	OCCIDENT	OCELLAR	OCTANES
OBSERVING	OBTRUSIONS	OCCIDENTS	OCELLATE	OCTANGLE
OBSESS	OBTRUSIVE	OCCIPITA	OCELLATED	OCTANGLES
OBSESSED	OBTUND	OCCIPITAL	OCELLI	OCTANOL
OBSESSES	OBTUNDED	OCCIPITALS	OCELLUS	OCTANOLS
OBSESSING	OBTUNDENT	OCCIPUT	OCELOID	OCTANS
OBSESSION	OBTUNDENTS	OCCIPUTS	OCELOT	OCTANT
OBSESSIONS	OBTUNDING	OCCLUDE	OCELOTS	OCTANTAL
OBSESSIVE	OBTUNDITIES	OCCLUDED	OCHER	OCTANTS
OBSESSIVES	OBTUNDITY	OCCLUDENT	OCHERED	OCTARCHIES
OBSESSOR	OBTUNDS	OCCLUDES	OCHERING	OCTARCHY
OBSESSORS	OBTURATE	OCCLUDING	OCHEROUS	OCTAVAL
OBSIDIAN	OBTURATED	OCCLUSAL	OCHERS	OCTAVE
OBSIDIANS	OBTURATES	OCCLUSION	OCHERY	OCTAVES
OBSOLESCE	OBTURATING	OCCLUSIONS	OCHLOCRAT	OCTAVO
OBSOLESCED	OBTURATOR	OCCLUSIVE	OCHLOCRATS	OCTAVOS
OBSOLESCES	OBTURATORS	OCCLUSIVES	OCHONE	OCTENNIAL
OBSOLESCING	OBTUSE	OCCULT	OCHRE	OCTET
OBSOLETE	OBTUSELY	OCCULTED	OCHREA	OCTETS
OBSOLETED	OBTUSER	OCCULTER	OCHREAE	OCTETTE
OBSOLETES	OBTUSEST	OCCULTERS	OCHRED	OCTETTES
OBSOLETING	OBTUSITIES	OCCULTING	OCHREOUS	OCTILLION
OBSTACLE	OBTUSITY	OCCULTISM	OCHRES	OCTILLIONS
OBSTACLES	OBVERSE	OCCULTISMS	OCHRING	OCTONARIES
OBSTETRIC	OBVERSELY	OCCULTIST	OCHROID	OCTONARY
OBSTINACIES	OBVERSES	OCCULTISTS	OCHROUS	OCTOPI
OBSTINACY	OBVERSION	OCCULTLY	OCHRY	OCTOPLOID
OBSTINATE	OBVERSIONS	OCCULTS	OCICAT	OCTOPLOIDS
OBSTRUCT	OBVERT	OCCUPANCIES	OCICATS	OCTOPOD
OBSTRUCTED	OBVERTED	OCCUPANCY	OCKER	OCTOPODAN
OBSTRUCTING	OBVERTING	OCCUPANT	OCKERS	OCTOPODANS
OBSTRUCTS	OBVERTS	OCCUPANTS	OCOTILLO	OCTOPODES
OBSTRUENT	OBVIABLE	OCCUPIED	OCOTILLOS	OCTOPODS
OBSTRUENTS	OBVIATE	OCCUPIER	OCREA	OCTOPUS
OBTAIN	OBVIATED	OCCUPIERS	OCREAE	OCTOPUSES
OBTAINED	OBVIATES	OCCUPIES	OCREATE	OCTOROON
OBTAINER	OBVIATING	OCCUPY	OCTACHORD	OCTOROONS
OBTAINERS	OBVIATION	OCCUPYING	OCTACHORDS	OCTOTHORP
OBTAINING	OBVIATIONS	OCCUR	OCTAD	OCTOTHORPS
OBTAINS	OBVIATOR	OCCURRED	OCTADIC	OCTROI
OBTECT	OBVIATORS	OCCURRENT	OCTADS	OCTROIS
OBTECTED	OBVIOUS	OCCURRENTS	OCTAGON	OCTUPLE
OBTEST	OBVIOUSLY	OCCURRING	OCTAGONAL	OCTUPLED
OBTESTED	OBVOLUTE	OCCURS	OCTAGONS	OCTUPLES
OBTESTING	OCA	OCEAN	OCTAHEDRA	OCTUPLET
OBTESTS	OCARINA	OCEANARIA	OCTAHEDRON	OCTUPLETS
OBTRUDE	OCARINAS	OCEANARIUM	OCTAHEDRONS	OCTUPLEX
OBTRUDED	OCAS	OCEANARIUMS	OCTAL	OCTUPLING

OCTUPLY	ODOGRAPH	OES	OFFERTORIES	OFFSTAGE
OCTYL	ODOGRAPHS	OESOPHAGI	OFFERTORY	OFFSTAGES
OCTYLS	ODOMETER	OESOPHAGUS	OFFHAND	OFFTRACK
OCULAR	ODOMETERS	OESTRIN	OFFHANDED	OFT
OCULARIST	ODOMETRIES	OESTRINS	OFFICE	OFTEN
OCULARISTS	ODOMETRY	OESTRIOL	OFFICER	OFTENER
OCULARLY	ODONATE	OESTRIOLS	OFFICERED	OFTENEST
OCULARS	ODONATES	OESTROGEN	OFFICERING	OFTER
OCULI	ODONTOID	OESTROGENS	OFFICERS	OFTEST
OCULIST	ODONTOIDS	OESTRONE	OFFICES	OFTTIMES
OCULISTS	ODOR	OESTRONES	OFFICIAL	OGAM
OCULUS	ODORANT	OESTROUS	OFFICIALS	OGAMS
OD	ODORANTS	OESTRUM	OFFICIANT	OGDOAD
ODA	ODORED	OESTRUMS	OFFICIANTS	OGDOADS
ODAH	ODORFUL	OESTRUS	OFFICIARIES	OGEE
ODAHS	ODORIZE	OESTRUSES	OFFICIARY	OGEES
ODALISK	ODORIZED	OEUVRE	OFFICIATE	OGHAM
ODALISKS	ODORIZES	OEUVRES	OFFICIATED	OGHAMIC
ODALISQUE	ODORIZING	OF	OFFICIATES	OGHAMIST
ODALISQUES	ODORLESS	OFAY	OFFICIATING	OGHAMISTS
ODAS	ODOROUS	OFAYS	OFFICINAL	OGHAMS
ODD	ODOROUSLY	OFF	OFFICINALS	OGIVAL
ODDBALL	ODORS	OFFAL	OFFICIOUS	OGIVE
ODDBALLS	ODOUR	OFFALS	OFFING	OGIVES
ODDER	ODOURFUL	OFFBEAT	OFFINGS	OGLE
ODDEST	ODOURS	OFFBEATS	OFFISH	OGLED
ODDISH	ODS	OFFCAST	OFFISHLY	OGLER
ODDITIES	ODYL	OFFCASTS	OFFKEY	OGLERS
ODDITY	ODYLE	OFFCUT	OFFLINE	OGLES
ODDLY	ODYLES	OFFCUTS	OFFLOAD	OGLING
ODDMENT	ODYLS	OFFED	OFFLOADED	OGRE
ODDMENTS	ODYSSEY	OFFENCE	OFFLOADING	OGREISH
ODDNESS	ODYSSEYS	OFFENCES	OFFLOADS	OGREISHLY
ODDNESSES	OE	OFFEND	OFFPRINT	OGREISM
ODDS	OECOLOGIES	OFFENDED	OFFPRINTED	OGREISMS
ODDSMAKER	OECOLOGY	OFFENDER	OFFPRINTING	OGRES
ODDSMAKERS	OEDEMA	OFFENDERS	OFFPRINTS	OGRESS
ODE	OEDEMAS	OFFENDING	OFFRAMP	OGRESSES
ODEA	OEDEMATA	OFFENDS	OFFRAMPS	OGRISH
ODEON	OEDIPAL	OFFENSE	OFFS	OGRISHLY
ODEONS	OEDIPALLY	OFFENSES	OFFSCREEN	OGRISM
ODES	OEDIPEAN	OFFENSIVE	OFFSET	OGRISMS
ODEUM	OEILLADE	OFFENSIVES	OFFSETS	OH
ODEUMS	OEILLADES	OFFER	OFFSETTING	OHED
ODIC	OENOLOGIES	OFFERED	OFFSHOOT	OHIA
ODIFEROUS	OENOLOGY	OFFERER	OFFSHOOTS	OHIAS
ODIOUS	OENOMEL	OFFERERS	OFFSHORE	OHING
ODIOUSLY	OENOMELS	OFFERING	OFFSHORES	OHM
ODIST	OENOPHILE	OFFERINGS	OFFSIDE	OHMAGE
ODISTS	OENOPHILES	OFFEROR	OFFSIDES	OHMAGES
ODIUM	OERSTED	OFFERORS	OFFSPRING	OHMIC
ODIUMS	OERSTEDS	OFFERS	OFFSPRINGS	OHMICALLY

OHMMETER	OINOLOGY	OLECRANONS	OLIVES	OMITS
OHMMETERS	OINOMEL	OLEFIN	OLIVINE	OMITTED
OHMS	OINOMELS	OLEFINE	OLIVINES	OMITTER
OHO	OINTMENT	OLEFINES	OLIVINIC	OMITTERS
OHS	OINTMENTS	OLEFINIC	OLLA	OMITTING
OI	OITICICA	OLEFINS	OLLAS	OMMATIDIA
OIDIA	OITICICAS	OLEIC	OLOGIES	OMMATIDIUM
OIDIOID	OKA	OLEIN	OLOGIST	OMNIARCH
OIDIUM	OKAPI	OLEINE	OLOGISTS	OMNIARCHS
OIL	OKAPIS	OLEINES	OLOGY	OMNIBUS
OILBIRD	OKAS	OLEINS	OLOLIUQUI	OMNIBUSES
OILBIRDS	OKAY	OLEO	OLOLIUQUIS	OMNIBUSSES
OILCAMP	OKAYED	OLEOGRAPH	OLOROSO	OMNIFIC
OILCAMPS	OKAYING	OLEOGRAPHS	OLOROSOS	OMNIFORM
OILCAN	OKAYS	OLEORESIN	OLYMPIAD	OMNIMODE
OILCANS	OKE	OLEORESINS	OLYMPIADS	OMNIRANGE
OILCLOTH	OKEH	OLEOS	OM	OMNIRANGES
OILCLOTHS	OKEHS	OLES	OMASA	OMNIVORA
OILCUP	OKES	OLESTRA	OMASUM	OMNIVORE
OILCUPS	OKEYDOKE	OLESTRAS	OMBER	OMNIVORES
OILED	OKEYDOKEY	OLEUM	OMBERS	OMOPHAGIA
OILER	OKRA	OLEUMS	OMBRE	OMOPHAGIAS
OILERS	OKRAS	OLFACTION	OMBRES	OMOPHAGIC
OILHOLE	OLD	OLFACTIONS	OMBUDSMAN	OMOPHAGIES
OILHOLES	OLDEN	OLFACTIVE	OMBUDSMEN	OMOPHAGY
OILIER	OLDER	OLFACTORIES	OMEGA	OMPHALI
OILIEST	OLDEST	OLFACTORY	OMEGAS	OMPHALOS
OILILY	OLDIE	OLIBANUM	OMELET	OMS
OILINESS	OLDIES	OLIBANUMS	OMELETS	ON
OILINESSES	OLDISH	OLICOOK	OMELETTE	ONAGER
OILING	OLDNESS	OLICOOKS	OMELETTES	ONAGERS
OILMAN	OLDNESSES	OLIGARCH	OMEN	ONAGRI
OILMEN	OLDS	OLIGARCHIES	OMENED	ONANISM
OILPAPER	OLDSQUAW	OLIGARCHS	OMENING	ONANISMS
OILPAPERS	OLDSQUAWS	OLIGARCHY	OMENS	ONANIST
OILPROOF	OLDSTER	OLIGOCENE	OMENTA	ONANISTIC
OILS	OLDSTERS	OLIGOGENE	OMENTAL	ONANISTS
OILSEED	OLDSTYLE	OLIGOGENES	OMENTUM	ONBOARD
OILSEEDS	OLDSTYLES	OLIGOMER	OMENTUMS	ONCE
OILSKIN	OLDWIFE	OLIGOMERS	OMER	ONCET
OILSKINS	OLDWIVES	OLIGOPOLIES	OMERS	ONCIDIUM
OILSTONE	OLDY	OLIGOPOLY	OMICRON	ONCIDIUMS
OILSTONES	OLE	OLIGURIA	OMICRONS	ONCOGENE
OILTIGHT	OLEA	OLIGURIAS	OMIKRON	ONCOGENES
OILWAY	OLEANDER	OLINGO	OMIKRONS	ONCOGENIC
OILWAYS	OLEANDERS	OLINGOS	OMINOUS	ONCOLOGIC
OILY	OLEASTER	OLIO	OMINOUSLY	ONCOLOGIES
OINK	OLEASTERS	OLIOS	OMISSIBLE	ONCOLOGY
OINKED	OLEATE	OLIVARY	OMISSION	ONCOMING
OINKING	OLEATES	OLIVE	OMISSIONS	ONCOMINGS
OINKS	OLECRANAL	OLIVENITE	OMISSIVE	ONCOVIRUS
OINOLOGIES	OLECRANON	OLIVENITES	OMIT	ONCOVIRUSES

ONDOGRAM	ONTOGENIC	OOMIACK	OPAHS	OPERATIVE
ONDOGRAMS	ONTOGENIES	OOMIACKS	OPAL	OPERATIVES
ONE	ONTOGENY	OOMIACS	OPALESCE	OPERATOR
ONEFOLD	ONTOLOGIC	OOMIAK	OPALESCED	OPERATORS
ONEIRIC	ONTOLOGIES	OOMIAKS	OPALESCES	OPERCELE
ONENESS	ONTOLOGY	OOMPAH	OPALESCING	OPERCELES
ONENESSES	ONUS	OOMPAHED	OPALINE	OPERCULA
ONERIER	ONUSES	OOMPAHING	OPALINES	OPERCULAR
ONERIEST	ONWARD	OOMPAHS	OPALS	OPERCULARS
ONEROUS	ONWARDS	OOMPH	OPAQUE	OPERCULE
ONEROUSLY	ONYX	OOMPHS	OPAQUED	OPERCULES
ONERY	ONYXES	OOPHYTE	OPAQUELY	OPERCULUM
ONES	OOCYST	OOPHYTES	OPAQUER	OPERCULUMS
ONESELF	OOCYSTS	OOPHYTIC	OPAQUES	OPERETTA
ONETIME	OOCYTE	OOPS	OPAQUEST	OPERETTAS
ONGOING	OOCYTES	OORALI	OPAQUING	OPERON
ONION	OODLES	OORALIS	OPE	OPERONS
ONIONS	OODLINS	OORIE	OPED	OPEROSE
ONIONSKIN	OOGAMETE	OOSPERM	OPEN	OPEROSELY
ONIONSKINS	OOGAMETES	OOSPERMS	OPENABLE	OPES
ONIONY	OOGAMIES	OOSPHERE	OPENCAST	OPHIDIAN
ONIUM	OOGAMOUS	OOSPHERES	OPENED	OPHIDIANS
ONLAY	OOGAMY	OOSPORE	OPENER	OPHIOLITE
ONLAYS	OOGENESES	OOSPORES	OPENERS	OPHIOLITES
ONLINE	OOGENESIS	OOSPORIC	OPENEST	OPHIOLOGIES
ONLOAD	OOGENETIC	OOT	OPENING	OPHIOLOGY
ONLOADED	OOGENIES	OOTHECA	OPENINGS	OPHITE
ONLOADING	OOGENY	OOTHECAE	OPENLY	OPHITES
ONLOADS	OOGONIA	OOTHECAL	OPENNESS	OPHITIC
ONLOOKER	OOGONIAL	OOTID	OPENNESSES	OPHIUROID
ONLOOKERS	OOGONIUM	OOTIDS	OPENS	OPHIUROIDS
ONLOOKING	OOGONIUMS	OOTS	OPENWORK	OPIATE
ONLY	OOH	OOZE	OPENWORKS	OPIATED
ONO	OOHED	OOZED	OPERA	OPIATES
ONOMASTIC	OOHING	OOZES	OPERABLE	OPIATING
ONOS	OOHS	OOZIER	OPERABLY	OPINE
ONRUSH	OOLACHAN	OOZIEST	OPERAGOER	OPINED
ONRUSHES	OOLACHANS	OOZILY	OPERAGOERS	OPINES
ONRUSHING	OOLITE	OOZINESS	OPERAND	OPING
ONS	OOLITES	OOZINESSES	OPERANDS	OPINING
ONSCREEN	OOLITH	OOZING	OPERANT	OPINION
ONSET	OOLITHS	OOZY	OPERANTLY	OPINIONED
ONSETS	OOLITIC	OP	OPERANTS	OPINIONS
ONSHORE	OOLOGIC	OPACIFIED	OPERAS	OPIOID
ONSIDE	OOLOGICAL	OPACIFIER	OPERATE	OPIOIDS
ONSLAUGHT	OOLOGIES	OPACIFIERS	OPERATED	OPIUM
ONSLAUGHTS	OOLOGIST	OPACIFIES	OPERATES	OPIUMISM
ONSTAGE	OOLOGISTS	OPACIFY	OPERATIC	OPIUMISMS
ONSTREAM	OOLOGY	OPACIFYING	OPERATICS	OPIUMS
ONTIC	OOLONG	OPACITIES	OPERATING	OPOSSUM
ONTICALLY	OOLONGS	OPACITY	OPERATION	OPOSSUMS
ONTO	OOMIAC	OPAH	OPERATIONS	OPPIDAN

OPPIDANS
OPPILANT
OPPILATE
OPPILATED
OPPILATES
OPPILATING
OPPONENCIES
OPPONENCY
OPPONENT
OPPONENTS
OPPORTUNE
OPPOSABLE
OPPOSE
OPPOSED
OPPOSER
OPPOSERS
OPPOSES
OPPOSING
OPPOSITE
OPPOSITES
OPPRESS
OPPRESSED
OPPRESSES
OPPRESSING
OPPRESSOR
OPPRESSORS
OPPUGN
OPPUGNANT
OPPUGNED
OPPUGNER
OPPUGNERS
OPPUGNING
OPPUGNS
OPS
OPSIN
OPSINS
OPSONIC
OPSONIFIED
OPSONIFIES
OPSONIFY
OPSONIFYING
OPSONIN
OPSONINS
OPSONIZE
OPSONIZED
OPSONIZES
OPSONIZING
OPT
OPTATIVE
OPTATIVES
OPTED
OPTIC

OPTICAL
OPTICALLY
OPTICIAN
OPTICIANS
OPTICIST
OPTICISTS
OPTICS
OPTIMA
OPTIMAL
OPTIMALLY
OPTIME
OPTIMES
OPTIMISE
OPTIMISED
OPTIMISES
OPTIMISING
OPTIMISM
OPTIMISMS
OPTIMIST
OPTIMISTS
OPTIMIZE
OPTIMIZED
OPTIMIZER
OPTIMIZERS
OPTIMIZES
OPTIMIZING
OPTIMUM
OPTIMUMS
OPTING
OPTION
OPTIONAL
OPTIONALS
OPTIONED
OPTIONEE
OPTIONEES
OPTIONING
OPTIONS
OPTOMETER
OPTOMETERS
OPTOMETRIES
OPTOMETRY
OPTS
OPULENCE
OPULENCES
OPULENCIES
OPULENCY
OPULENT
OPULENTLY
OPUNTIA
OPUNTIAS
OPUS
OPUSCULA

OPUSCULAR
OPUSCULE
OPUSCULES
OPUSCULUM
OPUSES
OQUASSA
OQUASSAS
OR
ORA
ORACH
ORACHE
ORACHES
ORACLE
ORACLES
ORACULAR
ORAD
ORAL
ORALISM
ORALISMS
ORALIST
ORALISTS
ORALITIES
ORALITY
ORALLY
ORALS
ORANG
ORANGE
ORANGEADE
ORANGEADES
ORANGERIE
ORANGERIES
ORANGERY
ORANGES
ORANGEY
ORANGIER
ORANGIEST
ORANGISH
ORANGS
ORANGUTAN
ORANGUTANS
ORANGY
ORATE
ORATED
ORATES
ORATING
ORATION
ORATIONS
ORATOR
ORATORIES
ORATORIO
ORATORIOS
ORATORS

ORATORY
ORATRESS
ORATRESSES
ORATRICES
ORATRIX
ORB
ORBED
ORBICULAR
ORBIER
ORBIEST
ORBING
ORBIT
ORBITAL
ORBITALS
ORBITED
ORBITER
ORBITERS
ORBITING
ORBITS
ORBLESS
ORBS
ORBY
ORC
ORCA
ORCAS
ORCEIN
ORCEINS
ORCHARD
ORCHARDS
ORCHESTRA
ORCHESTRAS
ORCHID
ORCHIDS
ORCHIL
ORCHILS
ORCHIS
ORCHISES
ORCHITIC
ORCHITIS
ORCHITISES
ORCIN
ORCINOL
ORCINOLS
ORCINS
ORCS
ORDAIN
ORDAINED
ORDAINER
ORDAINERS
ORDAINING
ORDAINS
ORDEAL

ORDEALS
ORDER
ORDERABLE
ORDERED
ORDERER
ORDERERS
ORDERING
ORDERLESS
ORDERLIES
ORDERLY
ORDERS
ORDINAL
ORDINALLY
ORDINALS
ORDINANCE
ORDINANCES
ORDINAND
ORDINANDS
ORDINARIER
ORDINARIES
ORDINARIEST
ORDINARY
ORDINATE
ORDINATES
ORDINES
ORDNANCE
ORDNANCES
ORDO
ORDOS
ORDURE
ORDURES
ORDUROUS
ORE
OREAD
OREADS
ORECTIC
ORECTIVE
OREGANO
OREGANOS
OREIDE
OREIDES
OREODONT
OREODONTS
ORES
ORFRAY
ORFRAYS
ORGAN
ORGANA
ORGANDIE
ORGANDIES
ORGANDY
ORGANELLE

ORGANELLES	ORIEL	ORMOLUS	ORRICE	OSCULATED
ORGANIC	ORIELS	ORNAMENT	ORRICES	OSCULATES
ORGANICS	ORIENT	ORNAMENTED	ORRIS	OSCULATING
ORGANISE	ORIENTAL	ORNAMENTING	ORRISES	OSCULE
ORGANISED	ORIENTALS	ORNAMENTS	ORRISROOT	OSCULES
ORGANISER	ORIENTATE	ORNATE	ORRISROOTS	OSCULUM
ORGANISERS	ORIENTATED	ORNATELY	ORS	OSE
ORGANISES	ORIENTATES	ORNERIER	ORT	OSES
ORGANISING	ORIENTATING	ORNERIEST	ORTHICON	OSETRA
ORGANISM	ORIENTED	ORNERY	ORTHICONS	OSETRAS
ORGANISMS	ORIENTEER	ORNIS	ORTHO	OSIER
ORGANIST	ORIENTEERS	ORNITHES	ORTHODOX	OSIERED
ORGANISTS	ORIENTER	ORNITHIC	ORTHODOXES	OSIERS
ORGANIZE	ORIENTERS	ORNITHINE	ORTHODOXIES	OSMATIC
ORGANIZED	ORIENTING	ORNITHINES	ORTHODOXY	OSMETERIA
ORGANIZER	ORIENTS	ORNITHOID	ORTHOEPIC	OSMETERIUM
ORGANIZERS	ORIFICE	OROGENIC	ORTHOEPIES	OSMIC
ORGANIZES	ORIFICES	OROGENIES	ORTHOEPY	OSMICALLY
ORGANIZING	ORIFICIAL	OROGENY	ORTHOPTER	OSMICS
ORGANON	ORIFLAMME	OROGRAPHIES	ORTHOPTERS	OSMIOUS
ORGANONS	ORIFLAMMES	OROGRAPHY	ORTHOPTIC	OSMIUM
ORGANOSOL	ORIGAMI	OROIDE	ORTHOSES	OSMIUMS
ORGANOSOLS	ORIGAMIS	OROIDES	ORTHOSIS	OSMOL
ORGANS	ORIGAN	OROLOGIES	ORTHOTIC	OSMOLAL
ORGANUM	ORIGANS	OROLOGIST	ORTHOTICS	OSMOLAR
ORGANUMS	ORIGANUM	OROLOGISTS	ORTHOTIST	OSMOLE
ORGANZA	ORIGANUMS	OROLOGY	ORTHOTISTS	OSMOLES
ORGANZAS	ORIGIN	OROMETER	ORTOLAN	OSMOLS
ORGANZINE	ORIGINAL	OROMETERS	ORTOLANS	OSMOMETER
ORGANZINES	ORIGINALS	OROTUND	ORTS	OSMOMETERS
ORGASM	ORIGINATE	ORPHAN	ORYX	OSMOMETRIES
ORGASMED	ORIGINATED	ORPHANAGE	ORYXES	OSMOMETRY
ORGASMIC	ORIGINATES	ORPHANAGES	ORZO	OSMOSE
ORGASMING	ORIGINATING	ORPHANED	ORZOS	OSMOSED
ORGASMS	ORIGINS	ORPHANING	OS	OSMOSES
ORGASTIC	ORINASAL	ORPHANS	OSAR	OSMOSING
ORGEAT	ORINASALS	ORPHIC	OSCILLATE	OSMOSIS
ORGEATS	ORIOLE	ORPHICAL	OSCILLATED	OSMOTIC
ORGIAC	ORIOLES	ORPHISM	OSCILLATES	OSMOUS
ORGIAST	ORISHA	ORPHISMS	OSCILLATING	OSMUND
ORGIASTIC	ORISHAS	ORPHREY	OSCINE	OSMUNDA
ORGIASTS	ORISON	ORPHREYED	OSCINES	OSMUNDAS
ORGIC	ORISONS	ORPHREYS	OSCININE	OSMUNDINE
ORGIES	ORLE	ORPIMENT	OSCITANCE	OSMUNDINES
ORGONE	ORLES	ORPIMENTS	OSCITANCES	OSMUNDS
ORGONES	ORLON	ORPIN	OSCITANCIES	OSNABURG
ORGULOUS	ORLONS	ORPINE	OSCITANCY	OSNABURGS
ORGY	ORLOP	ORPINES	OSCITANT	OSPREY
ORIBATID	ORLOPS	ORPINS	OSCULA	OSPREYS
ORIBATIDS	ORMER	ORRA	OSCULANT	OSSA
ORIBI	ORMERS	ORRERIES	OSCULAR	OSSATURE
ORIBIS	ORMOLU	ORRERY	OSCULATE	OSSATURES

OSSEIN	OSTIOLAR	OTITIS	OUPHS	OUTBAWL
OSSEINS	OSTIOLE	OTITISES	OUR	OUTBAWLED
OSSEOUS	OSTIOLES	OTOCYST	OURANG	OUTBAWLING
OSSEOUSLY	OSTIUM	OTOCYSTIC	OURANGS	OUTBAWLS
OSSETRA	OSTLER	OTOCYSTS	OURARI	OUTBEAM
OSSETRAS	OSTLERS	OTOLITH	OURARIS	OUTBEAMED
OSSIA	OSTMARK	OTOLITHIC	OUREBI	OUTBEAMING
OSSICLE	OSTMARKS	OTOLITHS	OUREBIS	OUTBEAMS
OSSICLES	OSTOMATE	OTOLOGIES	OURIE	OUTBEG
OSSICULAR	OSTOMATES	OTOLOGIST	OURS	OUTBEGGED
OSSIFIC	OSTOMIES	OTOLOGISTS	OURSELF	OUTBEGGING
OSSIFIED	OSTOMY	OTOLOGY	OURSELVES	OUTBEGS
OSSIFIER	OSTOSES	OTOPLASTIES	OUSEL	OUTBID
OSSIFIERS	OSTOSIS	OTOPLASTY	OUSELS	OUTBIDDEN
OSSIFIES	OSTOSISES	OTOSCOPE	OUST	OUTBIDDER
OSSIFRAGE	OSTRACA	OTOSCOPES	OUSTED	OUTBIDDERS
OSSIFRAGES	OSTRACISE	OTOSCOPIES	OUSTER	OUTBIDDING
OSSIFY	OSTRACISED	OTOSCOPY	OUSTERS	OUTBIDS
OSSIFYING	OSTRACISES	OTOTOXIC	OUSTING	OUTBITCH
OSSUARIES	OSTRACISING	OTTAR	OUSTS	OUTBITCHED
OSSUARY	OSTRACISM	OTTARS	OUT	OUTBITCHES
OSTEAL	OSTRACISMS	OTTAVA	OUTACT	OUTBITCHING
OSTEITIC	OSTRACIZE	OTTAVAS	OUTACTED	OUTBLAZE
OSTEITIDES	OSTRACIZED	OTTER	OUTACTING	OUTBLAZED
OSTEITIS	OSTRACIZES	OTTERS	OUTACTS	OUTBLAZES
OSTENSIVE	OSTRACIZING	OTTO	OUTADD	OUTBLAZING
OSTENSORIES	OSTRACOD	OTTOMAN	OUTADDED	OUTBLEAT
OSTENSORY	OSTRACODE	OTTOMANS	OUTADDING	OUTBLEATED
OSTEOCYTE	OSTRACODES	OTTOS	OUTADDS	OUTBLEATING
OSTEOCYTES	OSTRACODS	OUABAIN	OUTAGE	OUTBLEATS
OSTEOID	OSTRACON	OUABAINS	OUTAGES	OUTBLESS
OSTEOIDS	OSTRAKA	OUBLIETTE	OUTARGUE	OUTBLESSED
OSTEOLOGIES	OSTRAKON	OUBLIETTES	OUTARGUED	OUTBLESSES
OSTEOLOGY	OSTRICH	OUCH	OUTARGUES	OUTBLESSING
OSTEOMA	OSTRICHES	OUCHED	OUTARGUING	OUTBLOOM
OSTEOMAS	OTALGIA	OUCHES	OUTASK	OUTBLOOMED
OSTEOMATA	OTALGIAS	OUCHING	OUTASKED	OUTBLOOMING
OSTEOPATH	OTALGIC	OUD	OUTASKING	OUTBLOOMS
OSTEOPATHS	OTALGIES	OUDS	OUTASKS	OUTBLUFF
OSTEOSES	OTALGY	OUGHT	OUTATE	OUTBLUFFED
OSTEOSIS	OTHER	OUGHTED	OUTBACK	OUTBLUFFING
OSTEOSISES	OTHERNESS	OUGHTING	OUTBACKER	OUTBLUFFS
OSTEOTOME	OTHERNESSES	OUGHTS	OUTBACKERS	OUTBLUSH
OSTEOTOMES	OTHERS	OUGUIYA	OUTBACKS	OUTBLUSHED
OSTEOTOMIES	OTHERWISE	OUGUIYAS	OUTBAKE	OUTBLUSHES
OSTEOTOMY	OTIC	OUISTITI	OUTBAKED	OUTBLUSHING
OSTIA	OTIOSE	OUISTITIS	OUTBAKES	OUTBOARD
OSTIARIES	OTIOSELY	OUNCE	OUTBAKING	OUTBOARDS
OSTIARY	OTIOSITIES	OUNCES	OUTBARK	OUTBOAST
OSTINATI	OTIOSITY	OUPH	OUTBARKED	OUTBOASTED
OSTINATO	OTITIC	OUPHE	OUTBARKING	OUTBOASTING
OSTINATOS	OTITIDES	OUPHES	OUTBARKS	OUTBOASTS

OUTBOUGHT	OUTBURNT	OUTCLIMB	OUTDANCING	OUTDRESSING
OUTBOUND	OUTBURST	OUTCLIMBED	OUTDARE	OUTDREW
OUTBOX	OUTBURSTS	OUTCLIMBING	OUTDARED	OUTDRINK
OUTBOXED	OUTBUY	OUTCLIMBS	OUTDARES	OUTDRINKING
OUTBOXES	OUTBUYING	OUTCLOMB	OUTDARING	OUTDRINKS
OUTBOXING	OUTBUYS	OUTCOACH	OUTDATE	OUTDRIVE
OUTBRAG	OUTBY	OUTCOACHED	OUTDATED	OUTDRIVEN
OUTBRAGGED	OUTBYE	OUTCOACHES	OUTDATES	OUTDRIVES
OUTBRAGGING	OUTCALL	OUTCOACHING	OUTDATING	OUTDRIVING
OUTBRAGS	OUTCALLS	OUTCOME	OUTDAZZLE	OUTDROP
OUTBRAVE	OUTCAPER	OUTCOMES	OUTDAZZLED	OUTDROPPED
OUTBRAVED	OUTCAPERED	OUTCOOK	OUTDAZZLES	OUTDROPPING
OUTBRAVES	OUTCAPERING	OUTCOOKED	OUTDAZZLING	OUTDROPS
OUTBRAVING	OUTCAPERS	OUTCOOKING	OUTDEBATE	OUTDROVE
OUTBRAWL	OUTCAST	OUTCOOKS	OUTDEBATED	OUTDRUNK
OUTBRAWLED	OUTCASTE	OUTCOUNT	OUTDEBATES	OUTDUEL
OUTBRAWLING	OUTCASTES	OUTCOUNTED	OUTDEBATING	OUTDUELED
OUTBRAWLS	OUTCASTS	OUTCOUNTING	OUTDESIGN	OUTDUELING
OUTBRAZEN	OUTCATCH	OUTCOUNTS	OUTDESIGNED	OUTDUELLED
OUTBRAZENED	OUTCATCHES	OUTCRAWL	OUTDESIGNING	OUTDUELLING
OUTBRAZENING	OUTCATCHING	OUTCRAWLED	OUTDESIGNS	OUTDUELS
OUTBRAZENS	OUTCAUGHT	OUTCRAWLING	OUTDID	OUTEARN
OUTBREAK	OUTCAVIL	OUTCRAWLS	OUTDO	OUTEARNED
OUTBREAKS	OUTCAVILED	OUTCRIED	OUTDODGE	OUTEARNING
OUTBRED	OUTCAVILING	OUTCRIES	OUTDODGED	OUTEARNS
OUTBREED	OUTCAVILLED	OUTCROP	OUTDODGES	OUTEAT
OUTBREEDING	OUTCAVILLING	OUTCROPPED	OUTDODGING	OUTEATEN
OUTBREEDS	OUTCAVILS	OUTCROPPING	OUTDOER	OUTEATING
OUTBRIBE	OUTCHARGE	OUTCROPS	OUTDOERS	OUTEATS
OUTBRIBED	OUTCHARGED	OUTCROSS	OUTDOES	OUTECHO
OUTBRIBES	OUTCHARGES	OUTCROSSED	OUTDOING	OUTECHOED
OUTBRIBING	OUTCHARGING	OUTCROSSES	OUTDONE	OUTECHOES
OUTBUILD	OUTCHARM	OUTCROSSING	OUTDOOR	OUTECHOING
OUTBUILDING	OUTCHARMED	OUTCROW	OUTDOORS	OUTED
OUTBUILDS	OUTCHARMING	OUTCROWD	OUTDOORSY	OUTER
OUTBUILT	OUTCHARMS	OUTCROWDED	OUTDRAG	OUTERCOAT
OUTBULGE	OUTCHEAT	OUTCROWDING	OUTDRAGGED	OUTERCOATS
OUTBULGED	OUTCHEATED	OUTCROWDS	OUTDRAGGING	OUTERMOST
OUTBULGES	OUTCHEATING	OUTCROWED	OUTDRAGS	OUTERS
OUTBULGING	OUTCHEATS	OUTCROWING	OUTDRANK	OUTERWEAR
OUTBULK	OUTCHID	OUTCROWS	OUTDRAW	OUTFABLE
OUTBULKED	OUTCHIDDEN	OUTCRY	OUTDRAWING	OUTFABLED
OUTBULKING	OUTCHIDE	OUTCRYING	OUTDRAWN	OUTFABLES
OUTBULKS	OUTCHIDED	OUTCURSE	OUTDRAWS	OUTFABLING
OUTBULLIED	OUTCHIDES	OUTCURSED	OUTDREAM	OUTFACE
OUTBULLIES	OUTCHIDING	OUTCURSES	OUTDREAMED	OUTFACED
OUTBULLY	OUTCITIES	OUTCURSING	OUTDREAMING	OUTFACES
OUTBULLYING	OUTCITY	OUTCURVE	OUTDREAMS	OUTFACING
OUTBURN	OUTCLASS	OUTCURVES	OUTDREAMT	OUTFALL
OUTBURNED	OUTCLASSED	OUTDANCE	OUTDRESS	OUTFALLS
OUTBURNING	OUTCLASSES	OUTDANCED	OUTDRESSED	OUTFAST
OUTBURNS	OUTCLASSING	OUTDANCES	OUTDRESSES	OUTFASTED

OUTFASTING	OUTFLOATING	OUTGIVE	OUTGUN	OUTJOCKEYS
OUTFASTS	OUTFLOATS	OUTGIVEN	OUTGUNNED	OUTJUGGLE
OUTFAWN	OUTFLOW	OUTGIVES	OUTGUNNING	OUTJUGGLED
OUTFAWNED	OUTFLOWED	OUTGIVING	OUTGUNS	OUTJUGGLES
OUTFAWNING	OUTFLOWING	OUTGIVINGS	OUTGUSH	OUTJUGGLING
OUTFAWNS	OUTFLOWN	OUTGLARE	OUTGUSHED	OUTJUMP
OUTFEAST	OUTFLOWS	OUTGLARED	OUTGUSHES	OUTJUMPED
OUTFEASTED	OUTFLY	OUTGLARES	OUTGUSHING	OUTJUMPING
OUTFEASTING	OUTFLYING	OUTGLARING	OUTHANDLE	OUTJUMPS
OUTFEASTS	OUTFOOL	OUTGLEAM	OUTHANDLED	OUTJUT
OUTFEEL	OUTFOOLED	OUTGLEAMED	OUTHANDLES	OUTJUTS
OUTFEELING	OUTFOOLING	OUTGLEAMING	OUTHANDLING	OUTJUTTED
OUTFEELS	OUTFOOLS	OUTGLEAMS	OUTHAUL	OUTJUTTING
OUTFELT	OUTFOOT	OUTGLOW	OUTHAULS	OUTKEEP
OUTFENCE	OUTFOOTED	OUTGLOWED	OUTHEAR	OUTKEEPING
OUTFENCED	OUTFOOTING	OUTGLOWING	OUTHEARD	OUTKEEPS
OUTFENCES	OUTFOOTS	OUTGLOWS	OUTHEARING	OUTKEPT
OUTFENCING	OUTFOUGHT	OUTGNAW	OUTHEARS	OUTKICK
OUTFIELD	OUTFOUND	OUTGNAWED	OUTHIT	OUTKICKED
OUTFIELDS	OUTFOX	OUTGNAWING	OUTHITS	OUTKICKING
OUTFIGHT	OUTFOXED	OUTGNAWN	OUTHITTING	OUTKICKS
OUTFIGHTING	OUTFOXES	OUTGNAWS	OUTHOMER	OUTKILL
OUTFIGHTS	OUTFOXING	OUTGO	OUTHOMERED	OUTKILLED
OUTFIGURE	OUTFROWN	OUTGOES	OUTHOMERING	OUTKILLING
OUTFIGURED	OUTFROWNED	OUTGOING	OUTHOMERS	OUTKILLS
OUTFIGURES	OUTFROWNING	OUTGOINGS	OUTHOUSE	OUTKISS
OUTFIGURING	OUTFROWNS	OUTGONE	OUTHOUSES	OUTKISSED
OUTFIND	OUTFUMBLE	OUTGREW	OUTHOWL	OUTKISSES
OUTFINDING	OUTFUMBLED	OUTGRIN	OUTHOWLED	OUTKISSING
OUTFINDS	OUTFUMBLES	OUTGRINNED	OUTHOWLING	OUTLAID
OUTFIRE	OUTFUMBLING	OUTGRINNING	OUTHOWLS	OUTLAIN
OUTFIRED	OUTGAIN	OUTGRINS	OUTHUMOR	OUTLAND
OUTFIRES	OUTGAINED	OUTGROSS	OUTHUMORED	OUTLANDER
OUTFIRING	OUTGAINING	OUTGROSSED	OUTHUMORING	OUTLANDERS
OUTFISH	OUTGAINS	OUTGROSSES	OUTHUMORS	OUTLANDS
OUTFISHED	OUTGALLOP	OUTGROSSING	OUTHUNT	OUTLAST
OUTFISHES	OUTGALLOPED	OUTGROUP	OUTHUNTED	OUTLASTED
OUTFISHING	OUTGALLOPING	OUTGROUPS	OUTHUNTING	OUTLASTING
OUTFIT	OUTGALLOPS	OUTGROW	OUTHUNTS	OUTLASTS
OUTFITS	OUTGAMBLE	OUTGROWING	OUTHUSTLE	OUTLAUGH
OUTFITTED	OUTGAMBLED	OUTGROWN	OUTHUSTLED	OUTLAUGHED
OUTFITTER	OUTGAMBLES	OUTGROWS	OUTHUSTLES	OUTLAUGHING
OUTFITTERS	OUTGAMBLING	OUTGROWTH	OUTHUSTLING	OUTLAUGHS
OUTFITTING	OUTGAS	OUTGROWTHS	OUTING	OUTLAW
OUTFLANK	OUTGASSED	OUTGUESS	OUTINGS	OUTLAWED
OUTFLANKED	OUTGASSES	OUTGUESSED	OUTJINX	OUTLAWING
OUTFLANKING	OUTGASSING	OUTGUESSES	OUTJINXED	OUTLAWRIES
OUTFLANKS	OUTGAVE	OUTGUESSING	OUTJINXES	OUTLAWRY
OUTFLEW	OUTGAZE	OUTGUIDE	OUTJINXING	OUTLAWS
OUTFLIES	OUTGAZED	OUTGUIDED	OUTJOCKEY	OUTLAY
OUTFLOAT	OUTGAZES	OUTGUIDES	OUTJOCKEYED	OUTLAYING
OUTFLOATED	OUTGAZING	OUTGUIDING	OUTJOCKEYING	OUTLAYS

OUTLEAD	OUTMATCHED	OUTPLANNING	OUTPRICE	OUTRANKING
OUTLEADING	OUTMATCHES	OUTPLANS	OUTPRICED	OUTRANKS
OUTLEADS	OUTMATCHING	OUTPLAY	OUTPRICES	OUTRATE
OUTLEAP	OUTMODE	OUTPLAYED	OUTPRICING	OUTRATED
OUTLEAPED	OUTMODED	OUTPLAYING	OUTPULL	OUTRATES
OUTLEAPING	OUTMODES	OUTPLAYS	OUTPULLED	OUTRATING
OUTLEAPS	OUTMODING	OUTPLOD	OUTPULLING	OUTRAVE
OUTLEAPT	OUTMOST	OUTPLODDED	OUTPULLS	OUTRAVED
OUTLEARN	OUTMOVE	OUTPLODDING	OUTPUNCH	OUTRAVES
OUTLEARNED	OUTMOVED	OUTPLODS	OUTPUNCHED	OUTRAVING
OUTLEARNING	OUTMOVES	OUTPLOT	OUTPUNCHES	OUTRE
OUTLEARNS	OUTMOVING	OUTPLOTS	OUTPUNCHING	OUTREACH
OUTLEARNT	OUTMUSCLE	OUTPLOTTED	OUTPUPIL	OUTREACHED
OUTLED	OUTMUSCLED	OUTPLOTTING	OUTPUPILS	OUTREACHES
OUTLET	OUTMUSCLES	OUTPOINT	OUTPURSUE	OUTREACHING
OUTLETS	OUTMUSCLING	OUTPOINTED	OUTPURSUED	OUTREAD
OUTLIE	OUTNUMBER	OUTPOINTING	OUTPURSUES	OUTREADING
OUTLIER	OUTNUMBERED	OUTPOINTS	OUTPURSUING	OUTREADS
OUTLIERS	OUTNUMBERING	OUTPOLL	OUTPUSH	OUTREASON
OUTLIES	OUTNUMBERS	OUTPOLLED	OUTPUSHED	OUTREASONED
OUTLINE	OUTOFFICE	OUTPOLLING	OUTPUSHES	OUTREASONING
OUTLINED	OUTOFFICES	OUTPOLLS	OUTPUSHING	OUTREASONS
OUTLINER	OUTPACE	OUTPORT	OUTPUT	OUTRECKON
OUTLINERS	OUTPACED	OUTPORTS	OUTPUTS	OUTRECKONED
OUTLINES	OUTPACES	OUTPOST	OUTPUTTED	OUTRECKONING
OUTLINING	OUTPACING	OUTPOSTS	OUTPUTTING	OUTRECKONS
OUTLIVE	OUTPAINT	OUTPOUR	OUTQUOTE	OUTRIDDEN
OUTLIVED	OUTPAINTED	OUTPOURED	OUTQUOTED	OUTRIDE
OUTLIVER	OUTPAINTING	OUTPOURER	OUTQUOTES	OUTRIDER
OUTLIVERS	OUTPAINTS	OUTPOURERS	OUTQUOTING	OUTRIDERS
OUTLIVES	OUTPASS	OUTPOURING	OUTRACE	OUTRIDES
OUTLIVING	OUTPASSED	OUTPOURS	OUTRACED	OUTRIDING
OUTLOOK	OUTPASSES	OUTPOWER	OUTRACES	OUTRIG
OUTLOOKS	OUTPASSING	OUTPOWERED	OUTRACING	OUTRIGGED
OUTLOVE	OUTPEOPLE	OUTPOWERING	OUTRAGE	OUTRIGGER
OUTLOVED	OUTPEOPLED	OUTPOWERS	OUTRAGED	OUTRIGGERS
OUTLOVES	OUTPEOPLES	OUTPRAY	OUTRAGES	OUTRIGGING
OUTLOVING	OUTPEOPLING	OUTPRAYED	OUTRAGING	OUTRIGHT
OUTLYING	OUTPITCH	OUTPRAYING	OUTRAISE	OUTRIGS
OUTMAN	OUTPITCHED	OUTPRAYS	OUTRAISED	OUTRING
OUTMANNED	OUTPITCHES	OUTPREACH	OUTRAISES	OUTRINGING
OUTMANNING	OUTPITCHING	OUTPREACHED	OUTRAISING	OUTRINGS
OUTMANS	OUTPITIED	OUTPREACHES	OUTRAN	OUTRIVAL
OUTMARCH	OUTPITIES	OUTPREACHING	OUTRANCE	OUTRIVALED
OUTMARCHED	OUTPITY	OUTPREEN	OUTRANCES	OUTRIVALING
OUTMARCHES	OUTPITYING	OUTPREENED	OUTRANG	OUTRIVALLED
OUTMARCHING	OUTPLACE	OUTPREENING	OUTRANGE	OUTRIVALLING
OUTMASTER	OUTPLACED	OUTPREENS	OUTRANGED	OUTRIVALS
OUTMASTERED	OUTPLACES	OUTPRESS	OUTRANGES	OUTROAR
OUTMASTERING	OUTPLACING	OUTPRESSED	OUTRANGING	OUTROARED
OUTMASTERS	OUTPLAN	OUTPRESSES	OUTRANK	OUTROARING
OUTMATCH	OUTPLANNED	OUTPRESSING	OUTRANKED	OUTROARS

OUTROCK	OUTSCOOPED	OUTSIGHTS	OUTSOARS	OUTSTARTING
OUTROCKED	OUTSCOOPING	OUTSIN	OUTSOLD	OUTSTARTS
OUTROCKING	OUTSCOOPS	OUTSING	OUTSOLE	OUTSTATE
OUTROCKS	OUTSCORE	OUTSINGING	OUTSOLES	OUTSTATED
OUTRODE	OUTSCORED	OUTSINGS	OUTSOURCE	OUTSTATES
OUTROLL	OUTSCORES	OUTSINNED	OUTSOURCED	OUTSTATING
OUTROLLED	OUTSCORING	OUTSINNING	OUTSOURCES	OUTSTAY
OUTROLLING	OUTSCORN	OUTSINS	OUTSOURCING	OUTSTAYED
OUTROLLS	OUTSCORNED	OUTSIT	OUTSPAN	OUTSTAYING
OUTROOT	OUTSCORNING	OUTSITS	OUTSPANNED	OUTSTAYS
OUTROOTED	OUTSCORNS	OUTSITTING	OUTSPANNING	OUTSTEER
OUTROOTING	OUTSCREAM	OUTSIZE	OUTSPANS	OUTSTEERED
OUTROOTS	OUTSCREAMED	OUTSIZED	OUTSPEAK	OUTSTEERING
OUTROW	OUTSCREAMING	OUTSIZES	OUTSPEAKING	OUTSTEERS
OUTROWED	OUTSCREAMS	OUTSKATE	OUTSPEAKS	OUTSTOOD
OUTROWING	OUTSEE	OUTSKATED	OUTSPED	OUTSTRIDDEN
OUTROWS	OUTSEEING	OUTSKATES	OUTSPEED	OUTSTRIDE
OUTRUN	OUTSEEN	OUTSKATING	OUTSPEEDED	OUTSTRIDES
OUTRUNG	OUTSEES	OUTSKIRT	OUTSPEEDING	OUTSTRIDING
OUTRUNNER	OUTSELL	OUTSKIRTS	OUTSPEEDS	OUTSTRIP
OUTRUNNERS	OUTSELLING	OUTSLEEP	OUTSPELL	OUTSTRIPPED
OUTRUNNING	OUTSELLS	OUTSLEEPING	OUTSPELLED	OUTSTRIPPING
OUTRUNS	OUTSERT	OUTSLEEPS	OUTSPELLING	OUTSTRIPS
OUTRUSH	OUTSERTS	OUTSLEPT	OUTSPELLS	OUTSTRIVE
OUTRUSHED	OUTSERVE	OUTSLICK	OUTSPELT	OUTSTRIVEN
OUTRUSHES	OUTSERVED	OUTSLICKED	OUTSPEND	OUTSTRIVES
OUTRUSHING	OUTSERVES	OUTSLICKING	OUTSPENDING	OUTSTRIVING
OUTS	OUTSERVING	OUTSLICKS	OUTSPENDS	OUTSTRODE
OUTSAID	OUTSET	OUTSMART	OUTSPENT	OUTSTROKE
OUTSAIL	OUTSETS	OUTSMARTED	OUTSPOKE	OUTSTROKES
OUTSAILED	OUTSHAME	OUTSMARTING	OUTSPOKEN	OUTSTROVE
OUTSAILING	OUTSHAMED	OUTSMARTS	OUTSPRANG	OUTSTUDIED
OUTSAILS	OUTSHAMES	OUTSMELL	OUTSPREAD	OUTSTUDIES
OUTSANG	OUTSHAMING	OUTSMELLED	OUTSPREADING	OUTSTUDY
OUTSAT	OUTSHINE	OUTSMELLING	OUTSPREADS	OUTSTUDYING
OUTSAVOR	OUTSHINED	OUTSMELLS	OUTSPRING	OUTSTUNT
OUTSAVORED	OUTSHINES	OUTSMELT	OUTSPRINGING	OUTSTUNTED
OUTSAVORING	OUTSHINING	OUTSMILE	OUTSPRINGS	OUTSTUNTING
OUTSAVORS	OUTSHONE	OUTSMILED	OUTSPRINT	OUTSTUNTS
OUTSAW	OUTSHOOT	OUTSMILES	OUTSPRINTED	OUTSULK
OUTSAY	OUTSHOOTING	OUTSMILING	OUTSPRINTING	OUTSULKED
OUTSAYING	OUTSHOOTS	OUTSMOKE	OUTSPRINTS	OUTSULKING
OUTSAYS	OUTSHOT	OUTSMOKED	OUTSPRUNG	OUTSULKS
OUTSCHEME	OUTSHOUT	OUTSMOKES	OUTSTAND	OUTSUNG
OUTSCHEMED	OUTSHOUTED	OUTSMOKING	OUTSTANDING	OUTSWAM
OUTSCHEMES	OUTSHOUTING	OUTSNORE	OUTSTANDS	OUTSWARE
OUTSCHEMING	OUTSHOUTS	OUTSNORED	OUTSTARE	OUTSWEAR
OUTSCOLD	OUTSIDE	OUTSNORES	OUTSTARED	OUTSWEARING
OUTSCOLDED	OUTSIDER	OUTSNORING	OUTSTARES	OUTSWEARS
OUTSCOLDING	OUTSIDERS	OUTSOAR	OUTSTARING	OUTSWEEP
OUTSCOLDS	OUTSIDES	OUTSOARED	OUTSTART	OUTSWEEPING
OUTSCOOP	OUTSIGHT	OUTSOARING	OUTSTARTED	OUTSWEEPS

OUTSWEPT	OUTTOWERING	OUTWALKING	OUTWISHED	OVARIOLE
OUTSWIM	OUTTOWERS	OUTWALKS	OUTWISHES	OVARIOLES
OUTSWIMMING	OUTTRADE	OUTWAR	OUTWISHING	OVARITIDES
OUTSWIMS	OUTTRADED	OUTWARD	OUTWIT	OVARITIS
OUTSWING	OUTTRADES	OUTWARDLY	OUTWITH	OVARY
OUTSWINGING	OUTTRADING	OUTWARDS	OUTWITS	OVATE
OUTSWINGS	OUTTRAVEL	OUTWARRED	OUTWITTED	OVATELY
OUTSWORE	OUTTRAVELED	OUTWARRING	OUTWITTING	OVATION
OUTSWORN	OUTTRAVELING	OUTWARS	OUTWORE	OVATIONAL
OUTSWUM	OUTTRAVELLED	OUTWASH	OUTWORK	OVATIONS
OUTSWUNG	OUTTRAVELLING	OUTWASHES	OUTWORKED	OVEN
OUTTAKE	OUTTRAVELS	OUTWASTE	OUTWORKER	OVENBIRD
OUTTAKES	OUTTRICK	OUTWASTED	OUTWORKERS	OVENBIRDS
OUTTALK	OUTTRICKED	OUTWASTES	OUTWORKING	OVENLIKE
OUTTALKED	OUTTRICKING	OUTWASTING	OUTWORKS	OVENPROOF
OUTTALKING	OUTTRICKS	OUTWATCH	OUTWORN	OVENS
OUTTALKS	OUTTROT	OUTWATCHED	OUTWRIT	OVENWARE
OUTTASK	OUTTROTS	OUTWATCHES	OUTWRITE	OVENWARES
OUTTASKED	OUTTROTTED	OUTWATCHING	OUTWRITES	OVER
OUTTASKING	OUTTROTTING	OUTWEAR	OUTWRITING	OVERABLE
OUTTASKS	OUTTRUMP	OUTWEARIED	OUTWRITTEN	OVERACT
OUTTELL	OUTTRUMPED	OUTWEARIES	OUTWROTE	OVERACTED
OUTTELLING	OUTTRUMPING	OUTWEARING	OUTWROUGHT	OVERACTING
OUTTELLS	OUTTRUMPS	OUTWEARS	OUTYELL	OVERACTS
OUTTHANK	OUTTURN	OUTWEARY	OUTYELLED	OVERACUTE
OUTTHANKED	OUTTURNS	OUTWEARYING	OUTYELLING	OVERAGE
OUTTHANKING	OUTVALUE	OUTWEEP	OUTYELLS	OVERAGED
OUTTHANKS	OUTVALUED	OUTWEEPING	OUTYELP	OVERAGES
OUTTHIEVE	OUTVALUES	OUTWEEPS	OUTYELPED	OVERALERT
OUTTHIEVED	OUTVALUING	OUTWEIGH	OUTYELPING	OVERALL
OUTTHIEVES	OUTVAUNT	OUTWEIGHED	OUTYELPS	OVERALLED
OUTTHIEVING	OUTVAUNTED	OUTWEIGHING	OUTYIELD	OVERALLS
OUTTHINK	OUTVAUNTING	OUTWEIGHS	OUTYIELDED	OVERAPT
OUTTHINKING	OUTVAUNTS	OUTWENT	OUTYIELDING	OVERARCH
OUTTHINKS	OUTVIE	OUTWEPT	OUTYIELDS	OVERARCHED
OUTTHOUGHT	OUTVIED	OUTWHIRL	OUZEL	OVERARCHES
OUTTHREW	OUTVIES	OUTWHIRLED	OUZELS	OVERARCHING
OUTTHROB	OUTVOICE	OUTWHIRLING	OUZO	OVERARM
OUTTHROBBED	OUTVOICED	OUTWHIRLS	OUZOS	OVERARMED
OUTTHROBBING	OUTVOICES	OUTWILE	OVA	OVERARMING
OUTTHROBS	OUTVOICING	OUTWILED	OVAL	OVERARMS
OUTTHROW	OUTVOTE	OUTWILES	OVALBUMIN	OVERATE
OUTTHROWING	OUTVOTED	OUTWILING	OVALBUMINS	OVERAWE
OUTTHROWN	OUTVOTES	OUTWILL	OVALITIES	OVERAWED
OUTTHROWS	OUTVOTING	OUTWILLED	OVALITY	OVERAWES
OUTTHRUST	OUTVYING	OUTWILLING	OVALLY	OVERAWING
OUTTHRUSTED	OUTWAIT	OUTWILLS	OVALNESS	OVERBAKE
OUTTHRUSTING	OUTWAITED	OUTWIND	OVALNESSES	OVERBAKED
OUTTHRUSTS	OUTWAITING	OUTWINDED	OVALS	OVERBAKES
OUTTOLD	OUTWAITS	OUTWINDING	OVARIAL	OVERBAKING
OUTTOWER	OUTWALK	OUTWINDS	OVARIAN	OVERBEAR
OUTTOWERED	OUTWALKED	OUTWISH	OVARIES	OVERBEARING

OVERBEARS	OVERBROAD	OVERCOAT	OVERDECKS	OVEREAT
OVERBEAT	OVERBUILD	OVERCOATS	OVERDID	OVEREATEN
OVERBEATEN	OVERBUILDING	OVERCOLD	OVERDO	OVEREATER
OVERBEATING	OVERBUILDS	OVERCOLOR	OVERDOER	OVEREATERS
OVERBEATS	OVERBUILT	OVERCOLORED	OVERDOERS	OVEREATING
OVERBED	OVERBURN	OVERCOLORING	OVERDOES	OVEREATS
OVERBET	OVERBURNED	OVERCOLORS	OVERDOG	OVERED
OVERBETS	OVERBURNING	OVERCOME	OVERDOGS	OVEREDIT
OVERBETTED	OVERBURNS	OVERCOMER	OVERDOING	OVEREDITED
OVERBETTING	OVERBURNT	OVERCOMERS	OVERDONE	OVEREDITING
OVERBID	OVERBUSY	OVERCOMES	OVERDOSE	OVEREDITS
OVERBIDDEN	OVERBUY	OVERCOMING	OVERDOSED	OVEREMOTE
OVERBIDDING	OVERBUYING	OVERCOOK	OVERDOSES	OVEREMOTED
OVERBIDS	OVERBUYS	OVERCOOKED	OVERDOSING	OVEREMOTES
OVERBIG	OVERCALL	OVERCOOKING	OVERDRAFT	OVEREMOTING
OVERBILL	OVERCALLED	OVERCOOKS	OVERDRAFTS	OVEREXERT
OVERBILLED	OVERCALLING	OVERCOOL	OVERDRANK	OVEREXERTED
OVERBILLING	OVERCALLS	OVERCOOLED	OVERDRAW	OVEREXERTING
OVERBILLS	OVERCAME	OVERCOOLING	OVERDRAWING	OVEREXERTS
OVERBITE	OVERCAST	OVERCOOLS	OVERDRAWN	OVERFAR
OVERBITES	OVERCASTED	OVERCOUNT	OVERDRAWS	OVERFAST
OVERBLEW	OVERCASTING	OVERCOUNTED	OVERDRESS	OVERFAT
OVERBLOW	OVERCASTS	OVERCOUNTING	OVERDRESSED	OVERFAVOR
OVERBLOWING	OVERCHEAP	OVERCOUNTS	OVERDRESSES	OVERFAVORED
OVERBLOWN	OVERCHILL	OVERCOY	OVERDRESSING	OVERFAVORING
OVERBLOWS	OVERCHILLED	OVERCRAM	OVERDREW	OVERFAVORS
OVERBOARD	OVERCHILLING	OVERCRAMMED	OVERDRIED	OVERFEAR
OVERBOIL	OVERCHILLS	OVERCRAMMING	OVERDRIES	OVERFEARED
OVERBOILED	OVERCIVIL	OVERCRAMS	OVERDRINK	OVERFEARING
OVERBOILING	OVERCLAIM	OVERCROP	OVERDRINKING	OVERFEARS
OVERBOILS	OVERCLAIMED	OVERCROPPED	OVERDRINKS	OVERFED
OVERBOLD	OVERCLAIMING	OVERCROPPING	OVERDRIVE	OVERFEED
OVERBOOK	OVERCLAIMS	OVERCROPS	OVERDRIVEN	OVERFEEDING
OVERBOOKED	OVERCLASS	OVERCROWD	OVERDRIVES	OVERFEEDS
OVERBOOKING	OVERCLASSES	OVERCROWDED	OVERDRIVING	OVERFILL
OVERBOOKS	OVERCLEAN	OVERCROWDING	OVERDROVE	OVERFILLED
OVERBORE	OVERCLEANED	OVERCROWDS	OVERDRUNK	OVERFILLING
OVERBORN	OVERCLEANING	OVERCURE	OVERDRY	OVERFILLS
OVERBORNE	OVERCLEANS	OVERCURED	OVERDRYING	OVERFISH
OVERBOUGHT	OVERCLEAR	OVERCURES	OVERDUB	OVERFISHED
OVERBRAKE	OVERCLEARED	OVERCURING	OVERDUBBED	OVERFISHES
OVERBRAKED	OVERCLEARING	OVERCUT	OVERDUBBING	OVERFISHING
OVERBRAKES	OVERCLEARS	OVERCUTS	OVERDUBS	OVERFIT
OVERBRAKING	OVERCLOSE	OVERCUTTING	OVERDUE	OVERFLEW
OVERBRED	OVERCLOUD	OVERDARE	OVERDYE	OVERFLIES
OVERBREED	OVERCLOUDED	OVERDARED	OVERDYED	OVERFLOOD
OVERBREEDING	OVERCLOUDING	OVERDARES	OVERDYEING	OVERFLOODED
OVERBREEDS	OVERCLOUDS	OVERDARING	OVERDYER	OVERFLOODING
OVERBRIEF	OVERCOACH	OVERDEAR	OVERDYERS	OVERFLOODS
OVERBRIEFED	OVERCOACHED	OVERDECK	OVERDYES	OVERFLOW
OVERBRIEFING	OVERCOACHES	OVERDECKED	OVEREAGER	OVERFLOWED
OVERBRIEFS	OVERCOACHING	OVERDECKING	OVEREASY	OVERFLOWING

OVERFLOWN	OVERGROWN	OVERHUNTS	OVERLEARNED	OVERMATCHING
OVERFLOWS	OVERGROWS	OVERHYPE	OVERLEARNING	OVERMEEK
OVERFLY	OVERHAND	OVERHYPED	OVERLEARNS	OVERMELT
OVERFLYING	OVERHANDED	OVERHYPES	OVERLEARNT	OVERMELTED
OVERFOCUS	OVERHANDING	OVERHYPING	OVERLEND	OVERMELTING
OVERFOCUSED	OVERHANDS	OVERIDLE	OVERLENDING	OVERMELTS
OVERFOCUSES	OVERHANG	OVERING	OVERLENDS	OVERMEN
OVERFOCUSING	OVERHANGING	OVERISSUE	OVERLENT	OVERMILD
OVERFOCUSSED	OVERHANGS	OVERISSUED	OVERLET	OVERMILK
OVERFOCUSSES	OVERHARD	OVERISSUES	OVERLETS	OVERMILKED
OVERFOCUSSING	OVERHASTY	OVERISSUING	OVERLETTING	OVERMILKING
OVERFOND	OVERHATE	OVERJOY	OVERLEWD	OVERMILKS
OVERFOUL	OVERHATED	OVERJOYED	OVERLIE	OVERMINE
OVERFRANK	OVERHATES	OVERJOYING	OVERLIES	OVERMINED
OVERFREE	OVERHATING	OVERJOYS	OVERLIGHT	OVERMINES
OVERFULL	OVERHAUL	OVERJUST	OVERLIGHTED	OVERMINING
OVERFUND	OVERHAULED	OVERKEEN	OVERLIGHTING	OVERMIX
OVERFUNDED	OVERHAULING	OVERKILL	OVERLIGHTS	OVERMIXED
OVERFUNDING	OVERHAULS	OVERKILLED	OVERLIT	OVERMIXES
OVERFUNDS	OVERHEAD	OVERKILLING	OVERLIVE	OVERMIXING
OVERFUSSY	OVERHEADS	OVERKILLS	OVERLIVED	OVERMUCH
OVERGILD	OVERHEAP	OVERKIND	OVERLIVES	OVERMUCHES
OVERGILDED	OVERHEAPED	OVERLABOR	OVERLIVING	OVERNEAR
OVERGILDING	OVERHEAPING	OVERLABORED	OVERLOAD	OVERNEAT
OVERGILDS	OVERHEAPS	OVERLABORING	OVERLOADED	OVERNEW
OVERGILT	OVERHEAR	OVERLABORS	OVERLOADING	OVERNICE
OVERGIRD	OVERHEARD	OVERLADE	OVERLOADS	OVERNIGHT
OVERGIRDED	OVERHEARING	OVERLADED	OVERLONG	OVERNIGHTED
OVERGIRDING	OVERHEARS	OVERLADEN	OVERLOOK	OVERNIGHTING
OVERGIRDS	OVERHEAT	OVERLADES	OVERLOOKED	OVERNIGHTS
OVERGIRT	OVERHEATED	OVERLADING	OVERLOOKING	OVERPACK
OVERGLAD	OVERHEATING	OVERLAID	OVERLOOKS	OVERPACKED
OVERGLAZE	OVERHEATS	OVERLAIN	OVERLORD	OVERPACKING
OVERGLAZED	OVERHELD	OVERLAND	OVERLORDED	OVERPACKS
OVERGLAZES	OVERHIGH	OVERLANDS	OVERLORDING	OVERPAID
OVERGLAZING	OVERHOLD	OVERLAP	OVERLORDS	OVERPASS
OVERGOAD	OVERHOLDING	OVERLAPPED	OVERLOUD	OVERPASSED
OVERGOADED	OVERHOLDS	OVERLAPPING	OVERLOVE	OVERPASSES
OVERGOADING	OVERHOLY	OVERLAPS	OVERLOVED	OVERPASSING
OVERGOADS	OVERHONOR	OVERLARGE	OVERLOVES	OVERPAST
OVERGRADE	OVERHONORED	OVERLATE	OVERLOVING	OVERPAY
OVERGRADED	OVERHONORING	OVERLAX	OVERLUSH	OVERPAYING
OVERGRADES	OVERHONORS	OVERLAY	OVERLY	OVERPAYS
OVERGRADING	OVERHOPE	OVERLAYING	OVERLYING	OVERPEDAL
OVERGRAZE	OVERHOPED	OVERLAYS	OVERMAN	OVERPEDALED
OVERGRAZED	OVERHOPES	OVERLEAF	OVERMANNED	OVERPEDALING
OVERGRAZES	OVERHOPING	OVERLEAP	OVERMANNING	OVERPEDALLED
OVERGRAZING	OVERHOT	OVERLEAPED	OVERMANS	OVERPEDALLING
OVERGREAT	OVERHUNG	OVERLEAPING	OVERMANY	OVERPEDALS
OVERGREW	OVERHUNT	OVERLEAPS	OVERMATCH	OVERPERT
OVERGROW	OVERHUNTED	OVERLEAPT	OVERMATCHED	OVERPLAID
OVERGROWING	OVERHUNTING	OVERLEARN	OVERMATCHES	OVERPLAIDS

OVERPLAN	OVERREACH	OVERSCORED	OVERSLEEPING	OVERSTEERS
OVERPLANNED	OVERREACHED	OVERSCORES	OVERSLEEPS	OVERSTEP
OVERPLANNING	OVERREACHES	OVERSCORING	OVERSLEPT	OVERSTEPPED
OVERPLANS	OVERREACHING	OVERSEA	OVERSLIP	OVERSTEPPING
OVERPLANT	OVERREACT	OVERSEAS	OVERSLIPPED	OVERSTEPS
OVERPLANTED	OVERREACTED	OVERSEE	OVERSLIPPING	OVERSTIR
OVERPLANTING	OVERREACTING	OVERSEED	OVERSLIPS	OVERSTIRRED
OVERPLANTS	OVERREACTS	OVERSEEDED	OVERSLIPT	OVERSTIRRING
OVERPLAY	OVERRICH	OVERSEEDING	OVERSLOW	OVERSTIRS
OVERPLAYED	OVERRIDDEN	OVERSEEDS	OVERSMOKE	OVERSTOCK
OVERPLAYING	OVERRIDE	OVERSEEING	OVERSMOKED	OVERSTOCKED
OVERPLAYS	OVERRIDES	OVERSEEN	OVERSMOKES	OVERSTOCKING
OVERPLIED	OVERRIDING	OVERSEER	OVERSMOKING	OVERSTOCKS
OVERPLIES	OVERRIFE	OVERSEERS	OVERSOAK	OVERSTORIES
OVERPLOT	OVERRIGID	OVERSEES	OVERSOAKED	OVERSTORY
OVERPLOTS	OVERRIPE	OVERSELL	OVERSOAKING	OVERSTREW
OVERPLOTTED	OVERROAST	OVERSELLING	OVERSOAKS	OVERSTREWED
OVERPLOTTING	OVERROASTED	OVERSELLS	OVERSOFT	OVERSTREWING
OVERPLUS	OVERROASTING	OVERSET	OVERSOLD	OVERSTREWN
OVERPLUSES	OVERROASTS	OVERSETS	OVERSOON	OVERSTREWS
OVERPLY	OVERRODE	OVERSETTING	OVERSOUL	OVERSTUDIED
OVERPLYING	OVERRUDE	OVERSEW	OVERSOULS	OVERSTUDIES
OVERPOWER	OVERRUFF	OVERSEWED	OVERSPEND	OVERSTUDY
OVERPOWERED	OVERRUFFED	OVERSEWING	OVERSPENDING	OVERSTUDYING
OVERPOWERING	OVERRUFFING	OVERSEWN	OVERSPENDS	OVERSTUFF
OVERPOWERS	OVERRUFFS	OVERSEWS	OVERSPENT	OVERSTUFFED
OVERPRICE	OVERRULE	OVERSEXED	OVERSPICE	OVERSTUFFING
OVERPRICED	OVERRULED	OVERSHADE	OVERSPICED	OVERSTUFFS
OVERPRICES	OVERRULES	OVERSHADED	OVERSPICES	OVERSUDS
OVERPRICING	OVERRULING	OVERSHADES	OVERSPICING	OVERSUDSED
OVERPRINT	OVERRUN	OVERSHADING	OVERSPILL	OVERSUDSES
OVERPRINTED	OVERRUNNING	OVERSHARP	OVERSPILLED	OVERSUDSING
OVERPRINTING	OVERRUNS	OVERSHIRT	OVERSPILLING	OVERSUP
OVERPRINTS	OVERS	OVERSHIRTS	OVERSPILLS	OVERSUPPED
OVERPRIZE	OVERSAD	OVERSHOE	OVERSPILT	OVERSUPPING
OVERPRIZED	OVERSALE	OVERSHOES	OVERSPIN	OVERSUPS
OVERPRIZES	OVERSALES	OVERSHOOT	OVERSPINS	OVERSURE
OVERPRIZING	OVERSALT	OVERSHOOTING	OVERSTAFF	OVERSWEET
OVERPROOF	OVERSALTED	OVERSHOOTS	OVERSTAFFED	OVERSWING
OVERPROUD	OVERSALTING	OVERSHOT	OVERSTAFFING	OVERSWINGING
OVERPUMP	OVERSALTS	OVERSHOTS	OVERSTAFFS	OVERSWINGS
OVERPUMPED	OVERSAUCE	OVERSICK	OVERSTATE	OVERSWUNG
OVERPUMPING	OVERSAUCED	OVERSIDE	OVERSTATED	OVERT
OVERPUMPS	OVERSAUCES	OVERSIDES	OVERSTATES	OVERTAKE
OVERQUICK	OVERSAUCING	OVERSIGHT	OVERSTATING	OVERTAKEN
OVERRAN	OVERSAVE	OVERSIGHTS	OVERSTAY	OVERTAKES
OVERRANK	OVERSAVED	OVERSIZE	OVERSTAYED	OVERTAKING
OVERRASH	OVERSAVES	OVERSIZED	OVERSTAYING	OVERTALK
OVERRATE	OVERSAVING	OVERSIZES	OVERSTAYS	OVERTALKED
OVERRATED	OVERSAW	OVERSKIRT	OVERSTEER	OVERTALKING
OVERRATES	OVERSCALE	OVERSKIRTS	OVERSTEERED	OVERTALKS
OVERRATING	OVERSCORE	OVERSLEEP	OVERSTEERING	OVERTAME

OVERTART	OVERTRADE	OVERWARMS	OVERWRITTEN	OW
OVERTASK	OVERTRADED	OVERWARY	OVERWROTE	OWE
OVERTASKED	OVERTRADES	OVERWATCH	OVERWROUGHT	OWED
OVERTASKING	OVERTRADING	OVERWATCHED	OVERZEAL	OWES
OVERTASKS	OVERTRAIN	OVERWATCHES	OVERZEALS	OWING
OVERTAUGHT	OVERTRAINED	OVERWATCHING	OVIBOS	OWL
OVERTAX	OVERTRAINING	OVERWATER	OVICIDAL	OWLET
OVERTAXED	OVERTRAINS	OVERWATERED	OVICIDE	OWLETS
OVERTAXES	OVERTREAT	OVERWATERING	OVICIDES	OWLISH
OVERTAXING	OVERTREATED	OVERWATERS	OVIDUCAL	OWLISHLY
OVERTEACH	OVERTREATING	OVERWEAK	OVIDUCT	OWLLIKE
OVERTEACHES	OVERTREATS	OVERWEAR	OVIDUCTAL	OWLS
OVERTEACHING	OVERTRICK	OVERWEARIED	OVIDUCTS	OWN
OVERTHICK	OVERTRICKS	OVERWEARIES	OVIFEROUS	OWNABLE
OVERTHIN	OVERTRIM	OVERWEARING	OVIFORM	OWNED
OVERTHINK	OVERTRIMMED	OVERWEARS	OVINE	OWNER
OVERTHINKING	OVERTRIMMING	OVERWEARY	OVINES	OWNERS
OVERTHINKS	OVERTRIMS	OVERWEARYING	OVIPARA	OWNERSHIP
OVERTHOUGHT	OVERTRUMP	OVERWEEN	OVIPARITIES	OWNERSHIPS
OVERTHREW	OVERTRUMPED	OVERWEENED	OVIPARITY	OWNING
OVERTHROW	OVERTRUMPING	OVERWEENING	OVIPAROUS	OWNS
OVERTHROWING	OVERTRUMPS	OVERWEENS	OVIPOSIT	OWSE
OVERTHROWN	OVERTURE	OVERWEIGH	OVIPOSITED	OWSEN
OVERTHROWS	OVERTURED	OVERWEIGHED	OVIPOSITING	OX
OVERTIGHT	OVERTURES	OVERWEIGHING	OVIPOSITS	OXACILLIN
OVERTIME	OVERTURING	OVERWEIGHS	OVIRAPTOR	OXACILLINS
OVERTIMED	OVERTURN	OVERWET	OVIRAPTORS	OXALATE
OVERTIMES	OVERTURNED	OVERWETS	OVISAC	OXALATED
OVERTIMID	OVERTURNING	OVERWETTED	OVISACS	OXALATES
OVERTIMING	OVERTURNS	OVERWETTING	OVOID	OXALATING
OVERTIP	OVERURGE	OVERWHELM	OVOIDAL	OXALIC
OVERTIPPED	OVERURGED	OVERWHELMED	OVOIDALS	OXALIS
OVERTIPPING	OVERURGES	OVERWHELMING	OVOIDS	OXALISES
OVERTIPS	OVERURGING	OVERWHELMS	OVOLI	OXAZEPAM
OVERTIRE	OVERUSE	OVERWIDE	OVOLO	OXAZEPAMS
OVERTIRED	OVERUSED	OVERWILY	OVOLOS	OXAZINE
OVERTIRES	OVERUSES	OVERWIND	OVONIC	OXAZINES
OVERTIRING	OVERUSING	OVERWINDING	OVONICS	OXBLOOD
OVERTLY	OVERVALUE	OVERWINDS	OVOTESTES	OXBLOODS
OVERTNESS	OVERVALUED	OVERWISE	OVOTESTIS	OXBOW
OVERTNESSES	OVERVALUES	OVERWORD	OVULAR	OXBOWS
OVERTOIL	OVERVALUING	OVERWORDS	OVULARY	OXCART
OVERTOILED	OVERVIEW	OVERWORE	OVULATE	OXCARTS
OVERTOILING	OVERVIEWS	OVERWORK	OVULATED	OXEN
OVERTOILS	OVERVIVID	OVERWORKED	OVULATES	OXES
OVERTONE	OVERVOTE	OVERWORKING	OVULATING	OXEYE
OVERTONES	OVERVOTED	OVERWORKS	OVULATION	OXEYES
OVERTOOK	OVERVOTES	OVERWORN	OVULATIONS	OXFORD
OVERTOP	OVERVOTING	OVERWOUND	OVULATORY	OXFORDS
OVERTOPPED	OVERWARM	OVERWRITE	OVULE	OXHEART
OVERTOPPING	OVERWARMED	OVERWRITES	OVULES	OXHEARTS
OVERTOPS	OVERWARMING	OVERWRITING	OVUM	OXID

OXIDABLE	OXYCODONE	OZOCERITE	PACHALIC	PACKLY
OXIDANT	OXYCODONES	OZOCERITES	PACHALICS	PACKMAN
OXIDANTS	OXYGEN	OZOKERITE	PACHAS	PACKMEN
OXIDASE	OXYGENASE	OZOKERITES	PACHINKO	PACKNESS
OXIDASES	OXYGENASES	OZONATE	PACHINKOS	PACKNESSES
OXIDASIC	OXYGENATE	OZONATED	PACHISI	PACKS
OXIDATE	OXYGENATED	OZONATES	PACHISIS	PACKSACK
OXIDATED	OXYGENATES	OZONATING	PACHOULI	PACKSACKS
OXIDATES	OXYGENATING	OZONATION	PACHOULIS	PACKWAX
OXIDATING	OXYGENIC	OZONATIONS	PACHUCO	PACKWAXES
OXIDATION	OXYGENIZE	OZONE	PACHUCOS	PACS
OXIDATIONS	OXYGENIZED	OZONES	PACHYDERM	PACT
OXIDATIVE	OXYGENIZES	OZONIC	PACHYDERMS	PACTION
OXIDE	OXYGENIZING	OZONIDE	PACHYTENE	PACTIONS
OXIDES	OXYGENOUS	OZONIDES	PACHYTENES	PACTS
OXIDIC	OXYGENS	OZONISE	PACIER	PACY
OXIDISE	OXYMORA	OZONISED	PACIEST	PAD
OXIDISED	OXYMORON	OZONISES	PACIFIC	PADAUK
OXIDISER	OXYMORONS	OZONISING	PACIFICAL	PADAUKS
OXIDISERS	OXYPHIL	OZONIZE	PACIFIED	PADDED
OXIDISES	OXYPHILE	OZONIZED	PACIFIER	PADDER
OXIDISING	OXYPHILES	OZONIZER	PACIFIERS	PADDERS
OXIDIZE	OXYPHILIC	OZONIZERS	PACIFIES	PADDIES
OXIDIZED	OXYPHILS	OZONIZES	PACIFISM	PADDING
OXIDIZER	OXYSALT	OZONIZING	PACIFISMS	PADDINGS
OXIDIZERS	OXYSALTS	OZONOUS	PACIFIST	PADDLE
OXIDIZES	OXYSOME		PACIFISTS	PADDLED
OXIDIZING	OXYSOMES		PACIFY	PADDLER
OXIDS	OXYTOCIC	**P**	PACIFYING	PADDLERS
OXIM	OXYTOCICS		PACING	PADDLES
OXIME	OXYTOCIN		PACK	PADDLING
OXIMES	OXYTOCINS		PACKABLE	PADDLINGS
OXIMETER	OXYTONE	PA	PACKAGE	PADDOCK
OXIMETERS	OXYTONES	PABLUM	PACKAGED	PADDOCKED
OXIMETRIES	OY	PABLUMS	PACKAGER	PADDOCKING
OXIMETRY	OYER	PABULAR	PACKAGERS	PADDOCKS
OXIMS	OYERS	PABULUM	PACKAGES	PADDY
OXLIKE	OYES	PABULUMS	PACKAGING	PADDYWACK
OXLIP	OYESSES	PAC	PACKAGINGS	PADDYWACKED
OXLIPS	OYEZ	PACA	PACKBOARD	PADDYWACKING
OXO	OYEZES	PACAS	PACKBOARDS	PADDYWACKS
OXPECKER	OYSTER	PACE	PACKED	PADI
OXPECKERS	OYSTERED	PACED	PACKER	PADIS
OXTAIL	OYSTERER	PACEMAKER	PACKERS	PADISHAH
OXTAILS	OYSTERERS	PACEMAKERS	PACKET	PADISHAHS
OXTER	OYSTERING	PACER	PACKETED	PADLE
OXTERS	OYSTERINGS	PACERS	PACKETING	PADLES
OXTONGUE	OYSTERMAN	PACES	PACKETS	PADLOCK
OXTONGUES	OYSTERMEN	PACEY	PACKHORSE	PADLOCKED
OXY	OYSTERS	PACHA	PACKHORSES	PADLOCKING
OXYACID	OZALID	PACHADOM	PACKING	PADLOCKS
OXYACIDS	OZALIDS	PACHADOMS	PACKINGS	PADNAG

PADNAGS	PAGEANTS	PAINFULLY	PALAESTRAE	PALESTRAE
PADOUK	PAGEBOY	PAINING	PALAESTRAS	PALESTRAL
PADOUKS	PAGEBOYS	PAINLESS	PALAIS	PALESTRAS
PADRE	PAGED	PAINS	PALANKEEN	PALET
PADRES	PAGEFUL	PAINT	PALANKEENS	PALETOT
PADRI	PAGEFULS	PAINTABLE	PALANQUIN	PALETOTS
PADRONE	PAGER	PAINTBALL	PALANQUINS	PALETS
PADRONES	PAGERS	PAINTBALLS	PALAPA	PALETTE
PADRONI	PAGES	PAINTED	PALAPAS	PALETTES
PADRONISM	PAGINAL	PAINTER	PALATABLE	PALEWAYS
PADRONISMS	PAGINATE	PAINTERLY	PALATABLY	PALEWISE
PADS	PAGINATED	PAINTERS	PALATAL	PALFREY
PADSHAH	PAGINATES	PAINTIER	PALATALLY	PALFREYS
PADSHAHS	PAGINATING	PAINTIEST	PALATALS	PALIER
PADUASOY	PAGING	PAINTING	PALATE	PALIEST
PADUASOYS	PAGINGS	PAINTINGS	PALATES	PALIKAR
PAEAN	PAGOD	PAINTS	PALATIAL	PALIKARS
PAEANISM	PAGODA	PAINTWORK	PALATINE	PALIMONIES
PAEANISMS	PAGODAS	PAINTWORKS	PALATINES	PALIMONY
PAEANS	PAGODS	PAINTY	PALAVER	PALING
PAELLA	PAGURIAN	PAIR	PALAVERED	PALINGS
PAELLAS	PAGURIANS	PAIRED	PALAVERER	PALINODE
PAEON	PAGURID	PAIRING	PALAVERERS	PALINODES
PAEONS	PAGURIDS	PAIRINGS	PALAVERING	PALISADE
PAESAN	PAH	PAIRS	PALAVERS	PALISADED
PAESANI	PAHLAVI	PAISA	PALAZZI	PALISADES
PAESANO	PAHLAVIS	PAISAN	PALAZZO	PALISADING
PAESANOS	PAHOEHOE	PAISANA	PALAZZOS	PALISH
PAESANS	PAHOEHOES	PAISANAS	PALE	PALL
PAGAN	PAID	PAISANO	PALEA	PALLADIA
PAGANDOM	PAIK	PAISANOS	PALEAE	PALLADIC
PAGANDOMS	PAIKED	PAISANS	PALEAL	PALLADIUM
PAGANISE	PAIKING	PAISAS	PALEATE	PALLADIUMS
PAGANISED	PAIKS	PAISE	PALED	PALLADOUS
PAGANISES	PAIL	PAISLEY	PALEFACE	PALLED
PAGANISH	PAILFUL	PAISLEYS	PALEFACES	PALLET
PAGANISING	PAILFULS	PAJAMA	PALELY	PALLETED
PAGANISM	PAILLARD	PAJAMAED	PALENESS	PALLETING
PAGANISMS	PAILLARDS	PAJAMAS	PALENESSES	PALLETISE
PAGANIST	PAILLASSE	PAKEHA	PALEOCENE	PALLETISED
PAGANISTS	PAILLASSES	PAKEHAS	PALEOGENE	PALLETISES
PAGANIZE	PAILLETTE	PAKORA	PALEOLITH	PALLETISING
PAGANIZED	PAILLETTES	PAKORAS	PALEOLITHS	PALLETIZE
PAGANIZER	PAILS	PAL	PALEOLOGIES	PALLETIZED
PAGANIZERS	PAILSFUL	PALABRA	PALEOLOGY	PALLETIZES
PAGANIZES	PAIN	PALABRAS	PALEOSOL	PALLETIZING
PAGANIZING	PAINCH	PALACE	PALEOSOLS	PALLETS
PAGANS	PAINCHES	PALACED	PALEOZOIC	PALLETTE
PAGE	PAINED	PALACES	PALER	PALLETTES
PAGEANT	PAINFUL	PALADIN	PALES	PALLIA
PAGEANTRIES	PAINFULLER	PALADINS	PALEST	PALLIAL
PAGEANTRY	PAINFULLEST	PALAESTRA	PALESTRA	PALLIASSE

PALLIASSES	PALMTOPS	PALTERS	PANCRATIC	PANELLINGS
PALLIATE	PALMY	PALTRIER	PANCRATIUM	PANELS
PALLIATED	PALMYRA	PALTRIEST	PANCREAS	PANES
PALLIATES	PALMYRAS	PALTRILY	PANCREASES	PANETELA
PALLIATING	PALOMINO	PALTRY	PANDA	PANETELAS
PALLIATOR	PALOMINOS	PALUDAL	PANDANI	PANETELLA
PALLIATORS	PALOOKA	PALUDISM	PANDANUS	PANETELLAS
PALLID	PALOOKAS	PALUDISMS	PANDANUSES	PANETTONE
PALLIDLY	PALOVERDE	PALY	PANDAS	PANETTONES
PALLIER	PALOVERDES	PAM	PANDECT	PANETTONI
PALLIEST	PALP	PAMPA	PANDECTS	PANFISH
PALLING	PALPABLE	PAMPAS	PANDEMIC	PANFISHES
PALLIUM	PALPABLY	PAMPEAN	PANDEMICS	PANFRIED
PALLIUMS	PALPAL	PAMPEANS	PANDER	PANFRIES
PALLOR	PALPATE	PAMPER	PANDERED	PANFRY
PALLORS	PALPATED	PAMPERED	PANDERER	PANFRYING
PALLS	PALPATES	PAMPERER	PANDERERS	PANFUL
PALLY	PALPATING	PAMPERERS	PANDERING	PANFULS
PALM	PALPATION	PAMPERING	PANDERS	PANG
PALMAR	PALPATIONS	PAMPERO	PANDIED	PANGA
PALMARY	PALPATOR	PAMPEROS	PANDIES	PANGAS
PALMATE	PALPATORS	PAMPERS	PANDIT	PANGED
PALMATED	PALPATORY	PAMPHLET	PANDITS	PANGEN
PALMATELY	PALPEBRA	PAMPHLETS	PANDOOR	PANGENE
PALMATION	PALPEBRAE	PAMS	PANDOORS	PANGENES
PALMATIONS	PALPEBRAL	PAN	PANDORA	PANGENS
PALMED	PALPEBRAS	PANACEA	PANDORAS	PANGING
PALMER	PALPED	PANACEAN	PANDORE	PANGOLIN
PALMERS	PALPI	PANACEAS	PANDORES	PANGOLINS
PALMETTE	PALPING	PANACHE	PANDOUR	PANGRAM
PALMETTES	PALPITANT	PANACHES	PANDOURS	PANGRAMS
PALMETTO	PALPITATE	PANADA	PANDOWDIES	PANGS
PALMETTOES	PALPITATED	PANADAS	PANDOWDY	PANHANDLE
PALMETTOS	PALPITATES	PANAMA	PANDURA	PANHANDLED
PALMFUL	PALPITATING	PANAMAS	PANDURAS	PANHANDLES
PALMFULS	PALPS	PANATELA	PANDURATE	PANHANDLING
PALMIER	PALPUS	PANATELAS	PANDY	PANHUMAN
PALMIEST	PALS	PANATELLA	PANDYING	PANIC
PALMING	PALSGRAVE	PANATELLAS	PANE	PANICALLY
PALMIST	PALSGRAVES	PANBROIL	PANED	PANICKED
PALMISTER	PALSHIP	PANBROILED	PANEGYRIC	PANICKIER
PALMISTERS	PALSHIPS	PANBROILING	PANEGYRICS	PANICKIEST
PALMISTRIES	PALSIED	PANBROILS	PANEL	PANICKING
PALMISTRY	PALSIES	PANCAKE	PANELED	PANICKY
PALMISTS	PALSY	PANCAKED	PANELESS	PANICLE
PALMITATE	PALSYING	PANCAKES	PANELING	PANICLED
PALMITATES	PALSYLIKE	PANCAKING	PANELINGS	PANICLES
PALMITIN	PALTER	PANCETTA	PANELIST	PANICS
PALMITINS	PALTERED	PANCETTAS	PANELISTS	PANICUM
PALMLIKE	PALTERER	PANCHAX	PANELIZED	PANICUMS
PALMS	PALTERERS	PANCHAXES	PANELLED	PANIER
PALMTOP	PALTERING	PANCRATIA	PANELLING	PANIERS

PANINI	PANTHEISM	PAPAL	PAPISTRY	PARADED
PANINO	PANTHEISMS	PAPALLY	PAPISTS	PARADER
PANJANDRA	PANTHEIST	PAPARAZZI	PAPOOSE	PARADERS
PANJANDRUM	PANTHEISTS	PAPARAZZO	PAPOOSES	PARADES
PANJANDRUMS	PANTHEON	PAPAS	PAPPADAM	PARADIGM
PANMICTIC	PANTHEONS	PAPAW	PAPPADAMS	PARADIGMS
PANMIXES	PANTHER	PAPAWS	PAPPI	PARADING
PANMIXIA	PANTHERS	PAPAYA	PAPPIER	PARADISAL
PANMIXIAS	PANTIE	PAPAYAN	PAPPIES	PARADISE
PANMIXIS	PANTIES	PAPAYAS	PAPPIEST	PARADISES
PANNE	PANTIHOSE	PAPER	PAPPOOSE	PARADOR
PANNED	PANTILE	PAPERBACK	PAPPOOSES	PARADORES
PANNER	PANTILED	PAPERBACKS	PAPPOSE	PARADORS
PANNERS	PANTILES	PAPERBARK	PAPPOUS	PARADOS
PANNES	PANTING	PAPERBARKS	PAPPUS	PARADOSES
PANNIER	PANTINGLY	PAPERBOY	PAPPY	PARADOX
PANNIERED	PANTO	PAPERBOYS	PAPRICA	PARADOXES
PANNIERS	PANTOFFLE	PAPERCLIP	PAPRICAS	PARADROP
PANNIKIN	PANTOFFLES	PAPERCLIPS	PAPRIKA	PARADROPPED
PANNIKINS	PANTOFLE	PAPERED	PAPRIKAS	PARADROPPING
PANNING	PANTOFLES	PAPERER	PAPS	PARADROPS
PANOCHA	PANTOMIME	PAPERERS	PAPULA	PARAE
PANOCHAS	PANTOMIMED	PAPERGIRL	PAPULAE	PARAFFIN
PANOCHE	PANTOMIMES	PAPERGIRLS	PAPULAR	PARAFFINE
PANOCHES	PANTOMIMING	PAPERING	PAPULE	PARAFFINED
PANOPLIED	PANTOS	PAPERLESS	PAPULES	PARAFFINES
PANOPLIES	PANTOUM	PAPERS	PAPULOSE	PARAFFINING
PANOPLY	PANTOUMS	PAPERWORK	PAPYRAL	PARAFFINS
PANOPTIC	PANTRIES	PAPERWORKS	PAPYRI	PARAFOIL
PANORAMA	PANTROPIC	PAPERY	PAPYRIAN	PARAFOILS
PANORAMAS	PANTRY	PAPETERIE	PAPYRINE	PARAFORM
PANORAMIC	PANTRYMAN	PAPETERIES	PAPYRUS	PARAFORMS
PANPIPE	PANTRYMEN	PAPHIAN	PAPYRUSES	PARAGLIDE
PANPIPES	PANTS	PAPHIANS	PAR	PARAGLIDED
PANS	PANTSUIT	PAPILLA	PARA	PARAGLIDES
PANSEXUAL	PANTSUITS	PAPILLAE	PARABLAST	PARAGLIDING
PANSEXUALS	PANTY	PAPILLAR	PARABLASTS	PARAGOGE
PANSIES	PANTYHOSE	PAPILLARY	PARABLE	PARAGOGES
PANSOPHIC	PANZER	PAPILLATE	PARABLES	PARAGON
PANSOPHIES	PANZERS	PAPILLOMA	PARABOLA	PARAGONED
PANSOPHY	PAP	PAPILLOMAS	PARABOLAS	PARAGONING
PANSY	PAPA	PAPILLOMATA	PARABOLIC	PARAGONS
PANT	PAPACIES	PAPILLON	PARACHOR	PARAGRAPH
PANTALET	PAPACY	PAPILLONS	PARACHORS	PARAGRAPHED
PANTALETS	PAPADAM	PAPILLOSE	PARACHUTE	PARAGRAPHING
PANTALONE	PAPADAMS	PAPILLOTE	PARACHUTED	PARAGRAPHS
PANTALONES	PAPADOM	PAPILLOTES	PARACHUTES	PARAKEET
PANTALOON	PAPADOMS	PAPISM	PARACHUTING	PARAKEETS
PANTALOONS	PAPADUM	PAPISMS	PARACLETE	PARAKITE
PANTDRESS	PAPADUMS	PAPIST	PARACLETES	PARAKITES
PANTDRESSES	PAPAIN	PAPISTIC	PARACRINE	PARALEGAL
PANTED	PAPAINS	PAPISTRIES	PARADE	PARALEGALS

PARALLAX	PARANOICS	PARBOILS	PAREIRA	PARIAN
PARALLAXES	PARANOID	PARBUCKLE	PAREIRAS	PARIANS
PARALLEL	PARANOIDS	PARBUCKLED	PARENT	PARIES
PARALLELED	PARANYMPH	PARBUCKLES	PARENTAGE	PARIETAL
PARALLELING	PARANYMPHS	PARBUCKLING	PARENTAGES	PARIETALS
PARALLELLED	PARAPET	PARCEL	PARENTAL	PARIETES
PARALLELLING	PARAPETED	PARCELED	PARENTED	PARING
PARALLELS	PARAPETS	PARCELING	PARENTING	PARINGS
PARALYSE	PARAPH	PARCELLED	PARENTINGS	PARIS
PARALYSED	PARAPHS	PARCELLING	PARENTS	PARISES
PARALYSES	PARAPODIA	PARCELS	PAREO	PARISH
PARALYSING	PARAPODIUM	PARCENARIES	PAREOS	PARISHES
PARALYSIS	PARAQUAT	PARCENARY	PARER	PARITIES
PARALYTIC	PARAQUATS	PARCENER	PARERGA	PARITY
PARALYTICS	PARAQUET	PARCENERS	PARERGON	PARK
PARALYZE	PARAQUETS	PARCH	PARERS	PARKA
PARALYZED	PARAS	PARCHED	PARES	PARKADE
PARALYZER	PARASAIL	PARCHEESI	PARESES	PARKADES
PARALYZERS	PARASAILED	PARCHEESIS	PARESIS	PARKAS
PARALYZES	PARASAILING	PARCHES	PARETIC	PARKED
PARALYZING	PARASAILS	PARCHESI	PARETICS	PARKER
PARAMATTA	PARASANG	PARCHESIS	PAREU	PARKERS
PARAMATTAS	PARASANGS	PARCHING	PAREUS	PARKETTE
PARAMECIA	PARASHAH	PARCHISI	PAREVE	PARKETTES
PARAMECIUM	PARASHAHS	PARCHISIS	PARFAIT	PARKING
PARAMECIUMS	PARASHIOTH	PARCHMENT	PARFAITS	PARKINGS
PARAMEDIC	PARASHOT	PARCHMENTS	PARFLECHE	PARKLAND
PARAMEDICS	PARASHOTH	PARCLOSE	PARFLECHES	PARKLANDS
PARAMENT	PARASITE	PARCLOSES	PARFLESH	PARKLIKE
PARAMENTA	PARASITES	PARD	PARFLESHES	PARKS
PARAMENTS	PARASITIC	PARDAH	PARFOCAL	PARKWAY
PARAMETER	PARASOL	PARDAHS	PARGE	PARKWAYS
PARAMETERS	PARASOLED	PARDEE	PARGED	PARLANCE
PARAMO	PARASOLS	PARDI	PARGES	PARLANCES
PARAMORPH	PARATAXES	PARDIE	PARGET	PARLANDO
PARAMORPHS	PARATAXIS	PARDINE	PARGETED	PARLANTE
PARAMOS	PARATHION	PARDNER	PARGETING	PARLAY
PARAMOUNT	PARATHIONS	PARDNERS	PARGETINGS	PARLAYED
PARAMOUNTS	PARATROOP	PARDON	PARGETS	PARLAYING
PARAMOUR	PARAVANE	PARDONED	PARGETTED	PARLAYS
PARAMOURS	PARAVANES	PARDONER	PARGETTING	PARLE
PARAMYLUM	PARAWING	PARDONERS	PARGING	PARLED
PARAMYLUMS	PARAWINGS	PARDONING	PARGINGS	PARLES
PARANG	PARAZOAN	PARDONS	PARGO	PARLEY
PARANGS	PARAZOANS	PARDS	PARGOS	PARLEYED
PARANOEA	PARBAKE	PARDY	PARGYLINE	PARLEYER
PARANOEAS	PARBAKED	PARE	PARGYLINES	PARLEYERS
PARANOIA	PARBAKES	PARECISM	PARHELIA	PARLEYING
PARANOIAC	PARBAKING	PARECISMS	PARHELIC	PARLEYS
PARANOIACS	PARBOIL	PARED	PARHELION	PARLING
PARANOIAS	PARBOILED	PAREGORIC	PARIAH	PARLOR
PARANOIC	PARBOILING	PAREGORICS	PARIAHS	PARLORS

PARLOUR	PARRAKEETS	PARSONS	PARTY	PASSABLE
PARLOURS	PARRAL	PART	PARTYER	PASSABLY
PARLOUS	PARRALS	PARTAKE	PARTYERS	PASSADE
PARLOUSLY	PARRED	PARTAKEN	PARTYGOER	PASSADES
PARMESAN	PARREL	PARTAKER	PARTYGOERS	PASSADO
PARMESANS	PARRELS	PARTAKERS	PARTYING	PASSADOES
PAROCHIAL	PARRICIDE	PARTAKES	PARURA	PASSADOS
PARODIC	PARRICIDES	PARTAKING	PARURAS	PASSAGE
PARODICAL	PARRIDGE	PARTAN	PARURE	PASSAGED
PARODIED	PARRIDGES	PARTANS	PARURES	PASSAGES
PARODIES	PARRIED	PARTED	PARVE	PASSAGING
PARODIST	PARRIER	PARTERRE	PARVENU	PASSALONG
PARODISTS	PARRIERS	PARTERRES	PARVENUE	PASSALONGS
PARODOI	PARRIES	PARTIAL	PARVENUES	PASSANT
PARODOS	PARRING	PARTIALLY	PARVENUS	PASSBAND
PARODY	PARRITCH	PARTIALS	PARVIS	PASSBANDS
PARODYING	PARRITCHES	PARTIBLE	PARVISE	PASSBOOK
PAROL	PARROKET	PARTICLE	PARVISES	PASSBOOKS
PAROLABLE	PARROKETS	PARTICLES	PARVO	PASSE
PAROLE	PARROT	PARTIED	PARVOLIN	PASSED
PAROLED	PARROTED	PARTIER	PARVOLINE	PASSEE
PAROLEE	PARROTER	PARTIERS	PARVOLINES	PASSEL
PAROLEES	PARROTERS	PARTIES	PARVOLINS	PASSELS
PAROLES	PARROTING	PARTING	PARVOS	PASSENGER
PAROLING	PARROTS	PARTINGS	PAS	PASSENGERS
PAROLS	PARROTY	PARTISAN	PASCAL	PASSEPIED
PARONYM	PARRS	PARTISANS	PASCALS	PASSEPIEDS
PARONYMIC	PARRY	PARTITA	PASCHAL	PASSER
PARONYMS	PARRYING	PARTITAS	PASCHALS	PASSERBY
PAROQUET	PARS	PARTITE	PASE	PASSERINE
PAROQUETS	PARSABLE	PARTITION	PASEO	PASSERINES
PAROSMIA	PARSE	PARTITIONED	PASEOS	PASSERS
PAROSMIAS	PARSEC	PARTITIONING	PASES	PASSERSBY
PAROTIC	PARSECS	PARTITIONS	PASH	PASSES
PAROTID	PARSED	PARTITIVE	PASHA	PASSIBLE
PAROTIDS	PARSER	PARTITIVES	PASHADOM	PASSIM
PAROTITIC	PARSERS	PARTIZAN	PASHADOMS	PASSING
PAROTITIS	PARSES	PARTIZANS	PASHALIC	PASSINGLY
PAROTITISES	PARSIMONIES	PARTLET	PASHALICS	PASSINGS
PAROTOID	PARSIMONY	PARTLETS	PASHALIK	PASSION
PAROTOIDS	PARSING	PARTLY	PASHALIKS	PASSIONAL
PAROUS	PARSLEY	PARTNER	PASHAS	PASSIONALS
PAROXYSM	PARSLEYED	PARTNERED	PASHED	PASSIONS
PAROXYSMS	PARSLEYS	PARTNERING	PASHES	PASSIVATE
PARQUET	PARSLIED	PARTNERS	PASHING	PASSIVATED
PARQUETED	PARSNIP	PARTON	PASHMINA	PASSIVATES
PARQUETING	PARSNIPS	PARTONS	PASHMINAS	PASSIVATING
PARQUETRIES	PARSON	PARTOOK	PASODOBLE	PASSIVE
PARQUETRY	PARSONAGE	PARTRIDGE	PASODOBLES	PASSIVELY
PARQUETS	PARSONAGES	PARTRIDGES	PASQUIL	PASSIVES
PARR	PARSONIC	PARTS	PASQUILS	PASSIVISM
PARRAKEET	PARSONISH	PARTWAY	PASS	PASSIVISMS

PASSIVIST	PASTINESSES	PATCHED	PATHOLOGIES	PATRILINIES
PASSIVISTS	PASTING	PATCHER	PATHOLOGY	PATRILINY
PASSIVITIES	PASTIS	PATCHERS	PATHOS	PATRIMONIES
PASSIVITY	PASTISES	PATCHES	PATHOSES	PATRIMONY
PASSKEY	PASTITSIO	PATCHIER	PATHS	PATRIOT
PASSKEYS	PASTITSIOS	PATCHIEST	PATHWAY	PATRIOTIC
PASSLESS	PASTITSO	PATCHILY	PATHWAYS	PATRIOTS
PASSOVER	PASTITSOS	PATCHING	PATIENCE	PATRISTIC
PASSOVERS	PASTLESS	PATCHOULI	PATIENCES	PATROL
PASSPORT	PASTNESS	PATCHOULIES	PATIENT	PATROLLED
PASSPORTS	PASTNESSES	PATCHOULIS	PATIENTER	PATROLLER
PASSUS	PASTOR	PATCHOULY	PATIENTEST	PATROLLERS
PASSUSES	PASTORAL	PATCHWORK	PATIENTLY	PATROLLING
PASSWORD	PASTORALE	PATCHWORKED	PATIENTS	PATROLMAN
PASSWORDS	PASTORALES	PATCHWORKING	PATIN	PATROLMEN
PAST	PASTORALI	PATCHWORKS	PATINA	PATROLS
PASTA	PASTORALS	PATCHY	PATINAE	PATRON
PASTALIKE	PASTORATE	PATE	PATINAED	PATRONAGE
PASTAS	PASTORATES	PATED	PATINAS	PATRONAGES
PASTE	PASTORED	PATELLA	PATINATE	PATRONAL
PASTED	PASTORING	PATELLAE	PATINATED	PATRONESS
PASTEDOWN	PASTORIUM	PATELLAR	PATINATES	PATRONESSES
PASTEDOWNS	PASTORIUMS	PATELLAS	PATINATING	PATRONISE
PASTEL	PASTORLY	PATELLATE	PATINE	PATRONISED
PASTELIST	PASTORS	PATEN	PATINED	PATRONISES
PASTELISTS	PASTRAMI	PATENCIES	PATINES	PATRONISING
PASTELS	PASTRAMIS	PATENCY	PATINING	PATRONIZE
PASTER	PASTRIES	PATENS	PATINIZE	PATRONIZED
PASTERN	PASTROMI	PATENT	PATINIZED	PATRONIZES
PASTERNS	PASTROMIS	PATENTED	PATINIZES	PATRONIZING
PASTERS	PASTRY	PATENTEE	PATINIZING	PATRONLY
PASTES	PASTS	PATENTEES	PATINS	PATRONS
PASTEUP	PASTURAGE	PATENTING	PATIO	PATROON
PASTEUPS	PASTURAGES	PATENTLY	PATIOS	PATROONS
PASTICCI	PASTURAL	PATENTOR	PATISSIER	PATS
PASTICCIO	PASTURE	PATENTORS	PATISSIERS	PATSIES
PASTICCIOS	PASTURED	PATENTS	PATLY	PATSY
PASTICHE	PASTURER	PATER	PATNESS	PATTAMAR
PASTICHES	PASTURERS	PATERNAL	PATNESSES	PATTAMARS
PASTIE	PASTURES	PATERNITIES	PATOIS	PATTED
PASTIER	PASTURING	PATERNITY	PATOOTIE	PATTEE
PASTIES	PASTY	PATERS	PATOOTIES	PATTEN
PASTIEST	PAT	PATES	PATRIARCH	PATTENED
PASTIL	PATACA	PATH	PATRIARCHS	PATTENS
PASTILLE	PATACAS	PATHETIC	PATRIATE	PATTER
PASTILLES	PATAGIA	PATHLESS	PATRIATED	PATTERED
PASTILS	PATAGIAL	PATHOGEN	PATRIATES	PATTERER
PASTIME	PATAGIUM	PATHOGENE	PATRIATING	PATTERERS
PASTIMES	PATAMAR	PATHOGENES	PATRICIAN	PATTERING
PASTINA	PATAMARS	PATHOGENIES	PATRICIANS	PATTERN
PASTINAS	PATCH	PATHOGENS	PATRICIDE	PATTERNED
PASTINESS	PATCHABLE	PATHOGENY	PATRICIDES	PATTERNING

PATTERNS	PAVED	PAWNER	PAZAZZ	PEAKLIKE
PATTERS	PAVEED	PAWNERS	PAZAZZES	PEAKS
PATTIE	PAVEMENT	PAWNING	PE	PEAKY
PATTIES	PAVEMENTS	PAWNOR	PEA	PEAL
PATTING	PAVER	PAWNORS	PEACE	PEALED
PATTY	PAVERS	PAWNS	PEACEABLE	PEALIKE
PATTYPAN	PAVES	PAWNSHOP	PEACEABLY	PEALING
PATTYPANS	PAVID	PAWNSHOPS	PEACED	PEALS
PATULENT	PAVILION	PAWPAW	PEACEFUL	PEAN
PATULOUS	PAVILIONED	PAWPAWS	PEACEFULLER	PEANS
PATY	PAVILIONING	PAWS	PEACEFULLEST	PEANUT
PATZER	PAVILIONS	PAX	PEACENIK	PEANUTS
PATZERS	PAVILLON	PAXES	PEACENIKS	PEAR
PAUCITIES	PAVILLONS	PAXWAX	PEACES	PEARL
PAUCITY	PAVIN	PAXWAXES	PEACETIME	PEARLASH
PAUGHTY	PAVING	PAY	PEACETIMES	PEARLASHES
PAULDRON	PAVINGS	PAYABLE	PEACH	PEARLED
PAULDRONS	PAVINS	PAYABLES	PEACHBLOW	PEARLER
PAULIN	PAVIOR	PAYABLY	PEACHBLOWS	PEARLERS
PAULINS	PAVIORS	PAYBACK	PEACHED	PEARLIER
PAULOWNIA	PAVIOUR	PAYBACKS	PEACHER	PEARLIEST
PAULOWNIAS	PAVIOURS	PAYCHECK	PEACHERS	PEARLING
PAUNCH	PAVIS	PAYCHECKS	PEACHES	PEARLITE
PAUNCHED	PAVISE	PAYDAY	PEACHIER	PEARLITES
PAUNCHES	PAVISER	PAYDAYS	PEACHIEST	PEARLITIC
PAUNCHIER	PAVISERS	PAYED	PEACHING	PEARLIZED
PAUNCHIEST	PAVISES	PAYEE	PEACHY	PEARLS
PAUNCHY	PAVISSE	PAYEES	PEACING	PEARLY
PAUPER	PAVISSES	PAYER	PEACOAT	PEARMAIN
PAUPERED	PAVLOVA	PAYERS	PEACOATS	PEARMAINS
PAUPERING	PAVLOVAS	PAYGRADE	PEACOCK	PEARS
PAUPERISM	PAVONINE	PAYGRADES	PEACOCKED	PEART
PAUPERISMS	PAW	PAYING	PEACOCKIER	PEARTER
PAUPERIZE	PAWED	PAYLOAD	PEACOCKIEST	PEARTEST
PAUPERIZED	PAWER	PAYLOADS	PEACOCKING	PEARTLY
PAUPERIZES	PAWERS	PAYMASTER	PEACOCKS	PEARTNESS
PAUPERIZING	PAWING	PAYMASTERS	PEACOCKY	PEARTNESSES
PAUPERS	PAWKIER	PAYMENT	PEAFOWL	PEARWOOD
PAUPIETTE	PAWKIEST	PAYMENTS	PEAFOWLS	PEARWOODS
PAUPIETTES	PAWKILY	PAYNIM	PEAG	PEAS
PAUSAL	PAWKINESS	PAYNIMS	PEAGE	PEASANT
PAUSE	PAWKINESSES	PAYOFF	PEAGES	PEASANTRIES
PAUSED	PAWKY	PAYOFFS	PEAGS	PEASANTRY
PAUSER	PAWL	PAYOLA	PEAHEN	PEASANTS
PAUSERS	PAWLS	PAYOLAS	PEAHENS	PEASCOD
PAUSES	PAWN	PAYOR	PEAK	PEASCODS
PAUSING	PAWNABLE	PAYORS	PEAKED	PEASE
PAVAN	PAWNAGE	PAYOUT	PEAKIER	PEASECOD
PAVANE	PAWNAGES	PAYOUTS	PEAKIEST	PEASECODS
PAVANES	PAWNED	PAYROLL	PEAKING	PEASEN
PAVANS	PAWNEE	PAYROLLS	PEAKISH	PEASES
PAVE	PAWNEES	PAYS	PEAKLESS	PEASOUPER

PEASOUPERS	PECTATE	PEDANTIC	PEDLERS	PEEPS
PEAT	PECTATES	PEDANTRIES	PEDLERY	PEEPSHOW
PEATIER	PECTEN	PEDANTRY	PEDOCAL	PEEPSHOWS
PEATIEST	PECTENS	PEDANTS	PEDOCALIC	PEEPUL
PEATS	PECTIC	PEDATE	PEDOCALS	PEEPULS
PEATY	PECTIN	PEDATELY	PEDOGENIC	PEER
PEAVEY	PECTINATE	PEDDLE	PEDOLOGIC	PEERAGE
PEAVEYS	PECTINES	PEDDLED	PEDOLOGIES	PEERAGES
PEAVIES	PECTINOUS	PEDDLER	PEDOLOGY	PEERED
PEAVY	PECTINS	PEDDLERIES	PEDOMETER	PEERESS
PEBBLE	PECTIZE	PEDDLERS	PEDOMETERS	PEERESSES
PEBBLED	PECTIZED	PEDDLERY	PEDOPHILE	PEERIE
PEBBLES	PECTIZES	PEDDLES	PEDOPHILES	PEERIES
PEBBLIER	PECTIZING	PEDDLING	PEDORTHIC	PEERING
PEBBLIEST	PECTORAL	PEDERAST	PEDRO	PEERLESS
PEBBLING	PECTORALS	PEDERASTIES	PEDROS	PEERS
PEBBLY	PECULATE	PEDERASTS	PEDS	PEERY
PEC	PECULATED	PEDERASTY	PEDUNCLE	PEES
PECAN	PECULATES	PEDES	PEDUNCLED	PEESWEEP
PECANS	PECULATING	PEDESTAL	PEDUNCLES	PEESWEEPS
PECCABLE	PECULATOR	PEDESTALED	PEE	PEETWEET
PECCANCIES	PECULATORS	PEDESTALING	PEEBEEN	PEETWEETS
PECCANCY	PECULIA	PEDESTALLED	PEEBEENS	PEEVE
PECCANT	PECULIAR	PEDESTALLING	PEED	PEEVED
PECCANTLY	PECULIARS	PEDESTALS	PEEING	PEEVES
PECCARIES	PECULIUM	PEDIATRIC	PEEK	PEEVING
PECCARY	PECUNIARY	PEDICAB	PEEKABOO	PEEVISH
PECCAVI	PED	PEDICABS	PEEKABOOS	PEEVISHLY
PECCAVIS	PEDAGOG	PEDICEL	PEEKAPOO	PEEWEE
PECH	PEDAGOGIC	PEDICELS	PEEKAPOOS	PEEWEES
PECHAN	PEDAGOGIES	PEDICLE	PEEKED	PEEWIT
PECHANS	PEDAGOGS	PEDICLED	PEEKING	PEEWITS
PECHED	PEDAGOGUE	PEDICLES	PEEKS	PEG
PECHING	PEDAGOGUES	PEDICULAR	PEEL	PEGBOARD
PECHS	PEDAGOGY	PEDICURE	PEELABLE	PEGBOARDS
PECK	PEDAL	PEDICURED	PEELED	PEGBOX
PECKED	PEDALED	PEDICURES	PEELER	PEGBOXES
PECKER	PEDALER	PEDICURING	PEELERS	PEGGED
PECKERS	PEDALERS	PEDIFORM	PEELING	PEGGING
PECKIER	PEDALFER	PEDIGREE	PEELINGS	PEGLEGGED
PECKIEST	PEDALFERS	PEDIGREED	PEELS	PEGLESS
PECKING	PEDALIER	PEDIGREES	PEEN	PEGLIKE
PECKISH	PEDALIERS	PEDIMENT	PEENED	PEGMATITE
PECKISHLY	PEDALING	PEDIMENTS	PEENING	PEGMATITES
PECKS	PEDALLED	PEDIPALP	PEENS	PEGS
PECKY	PEDALLER	PEDIPALPS	PEEP	PEH
PECORINI	PEDALLERS	PEDLAR	PEEPED	PEHS
PECORINO	PEDALLING	PEDLARIES	PEEPER	PEIGNOIR
PECORINOS	PEDALO	PEDLARS	PEEPERS	PEIGNOIRS
PECS	PEDALOS	PEDLARY	PEEPHOLE	PEIN
PECTASE	PEDALS	PEDLER	PEEPHOLES	PEINED
PECTASES	PEDANT	PEDLERIES	PEEPING	PEINING

PEINS	PELLICLE	PEMPHIX	PENDRAGONS	PENNED
PEISE	PELLICLES	PEMPHIXES	PENDS	PENNER
PEISED	PELLITORIES	PEN	PENDULAR	PENNERS
PEISES	PELLITORY	PENAL	PENDULOUS	PENNI
PEISING	PELLMELL	PENALISE	PENDULUM	PENNIA
PEKAN	PELLMELLS	PENALISED	PENDULUMS	PENNIES
PEKANS	PELLUCID	PENALISES	PENEPLAIN	PENNILESS
PEKE	PELMET	PENALISING	PENEPLAINS	PENNINE
PEKEPOO	PELMETS	PENALITIES	PENEPLANE	PENNINES
PEKEPOOS	PELON	PENALITY	PENEPLANES	PENNING
PEKES	PELORIA	PENALIZE	PENES	PENNIS
PEKIN	PELORIAN	PENALIZED	PENETRANT	PENNON
PEKINS	PELORIAS	PENALIZES	PENETRANTS	PENNONCEL
PEKOE	PELORIC	PENALIZING	PENETRATE	PENNONCELS
PEKOES	PELORUS	PENALLY	PENETRATED	PENNONED
PELAGE	PELORUSES	PENALTIES	PENETRATES	PENNONS
PELAGES	PELOTA	PENALTY	PENETRATING	PENNY
PELAGIAL	PELOTAS	PENANCE	PENGO	PENNYWISE
PELAGIC	PELOTON	PENANCED	PENGOS	PENNYWORT
PELAGICS	PELOTONS	PENANCES	PENGUIN	PENNYWORTS
PELE	PELT	PENANCING	PENGUINS	PENOCHE
PELECYPOD	PELTAST	PENANG	PENHOLDER	PENOCHES
PELECYPODS	PELTASTS	PENANGS	PENHOLDERS	PENOLOGIES
PELERINE	PELTATE	PENATES	PENIAL	PENOLOGY
PELERINES	PELTATELY	PENCE	PENICIL	PENONCEL
PELES	PELTATION	PENCEL	PENICILS	PENONCELS
PELF	PELTATIONS	PENCELS	PENILE	PENPOINT
PELFS	PELTED	PENCHANT	PENINSULA	PENPOINTS
PELICAN	PELTER	PENCHANTS	PENINSULAS	PENS
PELICANS	PELTERED	PENCIL	PENIS	PENSEE
PELISSE	PELTERING	PENCILED	PENISES	PENSEES
PELISSES	PELTERS	PENCILER	PENITENCE	PENSIL
PELITE	PELTING	PENCILERS	PENITENCES	PENSILE
PELITES	PELTLESS	PENCILING	PENITENT	PENSILS
PELITIC	PELTRIES	PENCILINGS	PENITENTS	PENSION
PELLAGRA	PELTRY	PENCILLED	PENKNIFE	PENSIONE
PELLAGRAS	PELTS	PENCILLER	PENKNIVES	PENSIONED
PELLAGRIN	PELVES	PENCILLERS	PENLIGHT	PENSIONER
PELLAGRINS	PELVIC	PENCILLING	PENLIGHTS	PENSIONERS
PELLET	PELVICS	PENCILS	PENLITE	PENSIONES
PELLETAL	PELVIS	PEND	PENLITES	PENSIONING
PELLETED	PELVISES	PENDANT	PENMAN	PENSIONS
PELLETING	PEMBINA	PENDANTLY	PENMEN	PENSIVE
PELLETISE	PEMBINAS	PENDANTS	PENNA	PENSIVELY
PELLETISED	PEMICAN	PENDED	PENNAE	PENSTEMON
PELLETISES	PEMICANS	PENDENCIES	PENNAME	PENSTEMONS
PELLETISING	PEMMICAN	PENDENCY	PENNAMES	PENSTER
PELLETIZE	PEMMICANS	PENDENT	PENNANT	PENSTERS
PELLETIZED	PEMOLINE	PENDENTLY	PENNANTS	PENSTOCK
PELLETIZES	PEMOLINES	PENDENTS	PENNATE	PENSTOCKS
PELLETIZING	PEMPHIGUS	PENDING	PENNATED	PENT
PELLETS	PEMPHIGUSES	PENDRAGON	PENNE	PENTACLE

PENTACLES	PENURIES	PEPPIEST	PERCEIVER	PERENNATED
PENTAD	PENURIOUS	PEPPILY	PERCEIVERS	PERENNATES
PENTADS	PENURY	PEPPINESS	PERCEIVES	PERENNATING
PENTAGON	PEON	PEPPINESSES	PERCEIVING	PERENNIAL
PENTAGONS	PEONAGE	PEPPING	PERCENT	PERENNIALS
PENTAGRAM	PEONAGES	PEPPY	PERCENTAL	PEREON
PENTAGRAMS	PEONES	PEPS	PERCENTS	PEREONS
PENTAMERIES	PEONIES	PEPSIN	PERCEPT	PEREOPOD
PENTAMERY	PEONISM	PEPSINATE	PERCEPTS	PEREOPODS
PENTANE	PEONISMS	PEPSINATED	PERCH	PERES
PENTANES	PEONS	PEPSINATES	PERCHANCE	PERFECT
PENTANGLE	PEONY	PEPSINATING	PERCHED	PERFECTA
PENTANGLES	PEOPLE	PEPSINE	PERCHER	PERFECTAS
PENTANOL	PEOPLED	PEPSINES	PERCHERS	PERFECTED
PENTANOLS	PEOPLER	PEPSINS	PERCHES	PERFECTER
PENTARCH	PEOPLERS	PEPTALK	PERCHING	PERFECTERS
PENTARCHIES	PEOPLES	PEPTALKED	PERCOID	PERFECTEST
PENTARCHS	PEOPLING	PEPTALKING	PERCOIDS	PERFECTING
PENTARCHY	PEP	PEPTALKS	PERCOLATE	PERFECTLY
PENTENE	PEPEROMIA	PEPTIC	PERCOLATED	PERFECTO
PENTENES	PEPEROMIAS	PEPTICS	PERCOLATES	PERFECTOS
PENTHOUSE	PEPERONI	PEPTID	PERCOLATING	PERFECTS
PENTHOUSES	PEPERONIS	PEPTIDASE	PERCUSS	PERFERVID
PENTODE	PEPINO	PEPTIDASES	PERCUSSED	PERFIDIES
PENTODES	PEPINOS	PEPTIDE	PERCUSSES	PERFIDY
PENTOMIC	PEPLA	PEPTIDES	PERCUSSING	PERFORATE
PENTOSAN	PEPLOS	PEPTIDIC	PERCUSSOR	PERFORATED
PENTOSANS	PEPLOSES	PEPTIDS	PERCUSSORS	PERFORATES
PENTOSE	PEPLUM	PEPTIZE	PERDIE	PERFORATING
PENTOSES	PEPLUMED	PEPTIZED	PERDITION	PERFORCE
PENTOSIDE	PEPLUMS	PEPTIZER	PERDITIONS	PERFORM
PENTOSIDES	PEPLUS	PEPTIZERS	PERDU	PERFORMED
PENTOXIDE	PEPLUSES	PEPTIZES	PERDUE	PERFORMER
PENTOXIDES	PEPO	PEPTIZING	PERDUES	PERFORMERS
PENTYL	PEPONIDA	PEPTONE	PERDURE	PERFORMING
PENTYLS	PEPONIDAS	PEPTONES	PERDURED	PERFORMS
PENUCHE	PEPONIUM	PEPTONIC	PERDURES	PERFUME
PENUCHES	PEPONIUMS	PEPTONIZE	PERDURING	PERFUMED
PENUCHI	PEPOS	PEPTONIZED	PERDUS	PERFUMER
PENUCHIS	PEPPED	PEPTONIZES	PERDY	PERFUMERIES
PENUCHLE	PEPPER	PEPTONIZING	PERE	PERFUMERS
PENUCHLES	PEPPERBOX	PER	PEREA	PERFUMERY
PENUCKLE	PEPPERBOXES	PERACID	PEREGRIN	PERFUMES
PENUCKLES	PEPPERED	PERACIDS	PEREGRINE	PERFUMING
PENULT	PEPPERER	PERBORATE	PEREGRINES	PERFUMY
PENULTIMA	PEPPERERS	PERBORATES	PEREGRINS	PERFUSATE
PENULTIMAS	PEPPERING	PERCALE	PEREIA	PERFUSATES
PENULTS	PEPPERONI	PERCALES	PEREION	PERFUSE
PENUMBRA	PEPPERONIS	PERCALINE	PEREIONS	PERFUSED
PENUMBRAE	PEPPERS	PERCALINES	PEREIOPOD	PERFUSES
PENUMBRAL	PEPPERY	PERCEIVE	PEREIOPODS	PERFUSING
PENUMBRAS	PEPPIER	PERCEIVED	PERENNATE	PERFUSION

PERFUSIONS	PERILS	PERISTOME	PERMEATOR	PERPLEXES
PERFUSIVE	PERILUNE	PERISTOMES	PERMEATORS	PERPLEXING
PERGOLA	PERILUNES	PERISTYLE	PERMED	PERPS
PERGOLAS	PERILYMPH	PERISTYLES	PERMIAN	PERRIES
PERHAPS	PERILYMPHS	PERITI	PERMING	PERRON
PERHAPSES	PERIMETER	PERITONEA	PERMIT	PERRONS
PERI	PERIMETERS	PERITONEUM	PERMITS	PERRY
PERIANTH	PERIMETRIES	PERITONEUMS	PERMITTED	PERSALT
PERIANTHS	PERIMETRY	PERITRICH	PERMITTEE	PERSALTS
PERIAPSES	PERIMORPH	PERITRICHA	PERMITTEES	PERSE
PERIAPSIS	PERIMORPHS	PERITRICHS	PERMITTER	PERSECUTE
PERIAPT	PERIMYSIA	PERITUS	PERMITTERS	PERSECUTED
PERIAPTS	PERIMYSIUM	PERIWIG	PERMITTING	PERSECUTES
PERIBLEM	PERINATAL	PERIWIGS	PERMS	PERSECUTING
PERIBLEMS	PERINEA	PERJURE	PERMUTE	PERSES
PERICARP	PERINEAL	PERJURED	PERMUTED	PERSEVERE
PERICARPS	PERINEUM	PERJURER	PERMUTES	PERSEVERED
PERICOPAE	PERIOD	PERJURERS	PERMUTING	PERSEVERES
PERICOPAL	PERIODATE	PERJURES	PERNIO	PERSEVERING
PERICOPE	PERIODATES	PERJURIES	PERNIONES	PERSIMMON
PERICOPES	PERIODIC	PERJURING	PERNOD	PERSIMMONS
PERICOPIC	PERIODID	PERJURY	PERNODS	PERSIST
PERICYCLE	PERIODIDS	PERK	PERONEAL	PERSISTED
PERICYCLES	PERIODS	PERKED	PERORAL	PERSISTER
PERIDERM	PERIOSTEA	PERKIER	PERORALLY	PERSISTERS
PERIDERMS	PERIOSTEUM	PERKIEST	PERORATE	PERSISTING
PERIDIA	PERIOTIC	PERKILY	PERORATED	PERSISTS
PERIDIAL	PERIPATUS	PERKINESS	PERORATES	PERSON
PERIDIUM	PERIPATUSES	PERKINESSES	PERORATING	PERSONA
PERIDOT	PERIPETIA	PERKING	PERORATOR	PERSONAE
PERIDOTIC	PERIPETIAS	PERKISH	PERORATORS	PERSONAGE
PERIDOTS	PERIPETIES	PERKS	PEROXID	PERSONAGES
PERIGEAL	PERIPETY	PERKY	PEROXIDE	PERSONAL
PERIGEAN	PERIPHERIES	PERLITE	PEROXIDED	PERSONALS
PERIGEE	PERIPHERY	PERLITES	PEROXIDES	PERSONAS
PERIGEES	PERIPLASM	PERLITIC	PEROXIDIC	PERSONATE
PERIGON	PERIPLASMS	PERM	PEROXIDING	PERSONATED
PERIGONS	PERIPLAST	PERMALLOY	PEROXIDS	PERSONATES
PERIGYNIES	PERIPLASTS	PERMALLOYS	PEROXY	PERSONATING
PERIGYNY	PERIPTER	PERMANENT	PERP	PERSONIFIED
PERIHELIA	PERIPTERS	PERMANENTS	PERPEND	PERSONIFIES
PERIHELION	PERIQUE	PERMEABLE	PERPENDED	PERSONIFY
PERIKARYA	PERIQUES	PERMEABLY	PERPENDING	PERSONIFYING
PERIKARYON	PERIS	PERMEANCE	PERPENDS	PERSONNEL
PERIL	PERISARC	PERMEANCES	PERPENT	PERSONNELS
PERILED	PERISARCS	PERMEANT	PERPENTS	PERSONS
PERILING	PERISCOPE	PERMEASE	PERPETUAL	PERSPEX
PERILLA	PERISCOPES	PERMEASES	PERPETUALS	PERSPEXES
PERILLAS	PERISH	PERMEATE	PERPLEX	PERSPIRE
PERILLED	PERISHED	PERMEATED	PERPLEXED	PERSPIRED
PERILLING	PERISHES	PERMEATES	PERPLEXER	PERSPIRES
PERILOUS	PERISHING	PERMEATING	PERPLEXERS	PERSPIRING

PERSPIRY	PERVERTED	PET	PETNAPPING	PETTLES
PERSUADE	PERVERTER	PETABYTE	PETNAPS	PETTLING
PERSUADED	PERVERTERS	PETABYTES	PETRALE	PETTO
PERSUADER	PERVERTING	PETAHERTZ	PETRALES	PETTY
PERSUADERS	PERVERTS	PETAHERTZES	PETREL	PETULANCE
PERSUADES	PERVIOUS	PETAL	PETRELS	PETULANCES
PERSUADING	PERVS	PETALED	PETRIFIED	PETULANCIES
PERT	PES	PETALINE	PETRIFIER	PETULANCY
PERTAIN	PESADE	PETALLED	PETRIFIERS	PETULANT
PERTAINED	PESADES	PETALLIKE	PETRIFIES	PETUNIA
PERTAINING	PESETA	PETALODIES	PETRIFY	PETUNIAS
PERTAINS	PESETAS	PETALODY	PETRIFYING	PETUNTSE
PERTER	PESEWA	PETALOID	PETROGENIES	PETUNTSES
PERTEST	PESEWAS	PETALOUS	PETROGENY	PETUNTZE
PERTINENT	PESKIER	PETALS	PETROL	PETUNTZES
PERTLY	PESKIEST	PETARD	PETROLEUM	PEW
PERTNESS	PESKILY	PETARDS	PETROLEUMS	PEWEE
PERTNESSES	PESKINESS	PETASOS	PETROLIC	PEWEES
PERTURB	PESKINESSES	PETASOSES	PETROLOGIES	PEWHOLDER
PERTURBED	PESKY	PETASUS	PETROLOGY	PEWHOLDERS
PERTURBER	PESO	PETASUSES	PETROLS	PEWIT
PERTURBERS	PESOS	PETCOCK	PETRONEL	PEWITS
PERTURBING	PESSARIES	PETCOCKS	PETRONELS	PEWS
PERTURBS	PESSARY	PETECHIA	PETROSAL	PEWTER
PERTUSSAL	PESSIMISM	PETECHIAE	PETROUS	PEWTERER
PERTUSSES	PESSIMISMS	PETECHIAL	PETS	PEWTERERS
PERTUSSIS	PESSIMIST	PETER	PETSAI	PEWTERS
PERTUSSISES	PESSIMISTS	PETERED	PETSAIS	PEYOTE
PERUKE	PEST	PETERING	PETTABLE	PEYOTES
PERUKED	PESTER	PETERS	PETTED	PEYOTL
PERUKES	PESTERED	PETIOLAR	PETTEDLY	PEYOTLS
PERUSABLE	PESTERER	PETIOLATE	PETTER	PEYTRAL
PERUSAL	PESTERERS	PETIOLE	PETTERS	PEYTRALS
PERUSALS	PESTERING	PETIOLED	PETTI	PEYTREL
PERUSE	PESTERS	PETIOLES	PETTICOAT	PEYTRELS
PERUSED	PESTHOLE	PETIOLULE	PETTICOATS	PFENNIG
PERUSER	PESTHOLES	PETIOLULES	PETTIER	PFENNIGE
PERUSERS	PESTHOUSE	PETIT	PETTIEST	PFENNIGS
PERUSES	PESTHOUSES	PETITE	PETTIFOG	PFFT
PERUSING	PESTICIDE	PETITES	PETTIFOGGED	PFUI
PERV	PESTICIDES	PETITION	PETTIFOGGING	PHAETON
PERVADE	PESTIER	PETITIONED	PETTIFOGS	PHAETONS
PERVADED	PESTIEST	PETITIONING	PETTILY	PHAGE
PERVADER	PESTILENT	PETITIONS	PETTINESS	PHAGEDENA
PERVADERS	PESTLE	PETNAP	PETTINESSES	PHAGEDENAS
PERVADES	PESTLED	PETNAPER	PETTING	PHAGES
PERVADING	PESTLES	PETNAPERS	PETTINGS	PHAGOCYTE
PERVASION	PESTLING	PETNAPING	PETTISH	PHAGOCYTES
PERVASIONS	PESTO	PETNAPINGS	PETTISHLY	PHAGOSOME
PERVASIVE	PESTOS	PETNAPPED	PETTITOES	PHAGOSOMES
PERVERSE	PESTS	PETNAPPER	PETTLE	PHALANGAL
PERVERT	PESTY	PETNAPPERS	PETTLED	PHALANGE

PHALANGER	PHASIC	PHENOMENONS	PHILTRING	PHONES
PHALANGERS	PHASING	PHENOMS	PHILTRUM	PHONETIC
PHALANGES	PHASIS	PHENOTYPE	PHIMOSES	PHONETICS
PHALANX	PHASMID	PHENOTYPES	PHIMOSIS	PHONETIST
PHALANXES	PHASMIDS	PHENOXIDE	PHIMOTIC	PHONETISTS
PHALAROPE	PHAT	PHENOXIDES	PHIS	PHONEY
PHALAROPES	PHATIC	PHENOXY	PHIZ	PHONEYED
PHALLI	PHATTER	PHENYL	PHIZES	PHONEYING
PHALLIC	PHATTEST	PHENYLENE	PHLEBITIC	PHONEYS
PHALLISM	PHEASANT	PHENYLENES	PHLEBITIDES	PHONIC
PHALLISMS	PHEASANTS	PHENYLIC	PHLEBITIS	PHONICS
PHALLIST	PHELLEM	PHENYLS	PHLEBITISES	PHONIED
PHALLISTS	PHELLEMS	PHENYTOIN	PHLEGM	PHONIER
PHALLUS	PHELLOGEN	PHENYTOINS	PHLEGMIER	PHONIES
PHALLUSES	PHELLOGENS	PHERESES	PHLEGMIEST	PHONIEST
PHANTASIED	PHELONIA	PHERESIS	PHLEGMS	PHONILY
PHANTASIES	PHELONION	PHEROMONE	PHLEGMY	PHONINESS
PHANTASM	PHELONIONS	PHEROMONES	PHLOEM	PHONINESSES
PHANTASMA	PHENACITE	PHEW	PHLOEMS	PHONING
PHANTASMATA	PHENACITES	PHI	PHLORIZIN	PHONO
PHANTASMS	PHENAKITE	PHIAL	PHLORIZINS	PHONOGRAM
PHANTAST	PHENAKITES	PHIALS	PHLOX	PHONOGRAMS
PHANTASTS	PHENATE	PHILABEG	PHLOXES	PHONOLITE
PHANTASY	PHENATES	PHILABEGS	PHLYCTENA	PHONOLITES
PHANTASYING	PHENAZIN	PHILANDER	PHLYCTENAE	PHONOLOGIES
PHANTOM	PHENAZINE	PHILANDERED	PHOBIA	PHONOLOGY
PHANTOMS	PHENAZINES	PHILANDERING	PHOBIAS	PHONON
PHARAOH	PHENAZINS	PHILANDERS	PHOBIC	PHONONS
PHARAOHS	PHENETIC	PHILATELIES	PHOBICS	PHONOS
PHARAONIC	PHENETICS	PHILATELY	PHOCINE	PHONOTYPE
PHARISAIC	PHENETOL	PHILIBEG	PHOEBE	PHONOTYPES
PHARISEE	PHENETOLE	PHILIBEGS	PHOEBES	PHONOTYPIES
PHARISEES	PHENETOLES	PHILIPPIC	PHOEBUS	PHONOTYPY
PHARMACIES	PHENETOLS	PHILIPPICS	PHOEBUSES	PHONS
PHARMACY	PHENIX	PHILISTIA	PHOENIX	PHONY
PHARMING	PHENIXES	PHILISTIAS	PHOENIXES	PHONYING
PHARMINGS	PHENOCOPIES	PHILOGYNIES	PHON	PHOOEY
PHAROS	PHENOCOPY	PHILOGYNY	PHONAL	PHORATE
PHAROSES	PHENOL	PHILOLOGIES	PHONATE	PHORATES
PHARYNGAL	PHENOLATE	PHILOLOGY	PHONATED	PHORESIES
PHARYNGALS	PHENOLATED	PHILOMEL	PHONATES	PHORESY
PHARYNGES	PHENOLATES	PHILOMELA	PHONATHON	PHORONID
PHARYNX	PHENOLATING	PHILOMELAS	PHONATHONS	PHORONIDS
PHARYNXES	PHENOLIC	PHILOMELS	PHONATING	PHOSGENE
PHASE	PHENOLICS	PHILTER	PHONATION	PHOSGENES
PHASEAL	PHENOLOGIES	PHILTERED	PHONATIONS	PHOSPHATE
PHASED	PHENOLOGY	PHILTERING	PHONE	PHOSPHATES
PHASEDOWN	PHENOLS	PHILTERS	PHONED	PHOSPHENE
PHASEDOWNS	PHENOM	PHILTRA	PHONEME	PHOSPHENES
PHASEOUT	PHENOMENA	PHILTRE	PHONEMES	PHOSPHID
PHASEOUTS	PHENOMENAS	PHILTRED	PHONEMIC	PHOSPHIDE
PHASES	PHENOMENON	PHILTRES	PHONEMICS	PHOSPHIDES

PHOSPHIDS	PHOTOSCANNED	PHTHALEINS	PHYSICAL	PIASABA
PHOSPHIN	PHOTOSCANNING	PHTHALIC	PHYSICALS	PIASABAS
PHOSPHINE	PHOTOSCANS	PHTHALIN	PHYSICIAN	PIASAVA
PHOSPHINES	PHOTOSET	PHTHALINS	PHYSICIANS	PIASAVAS
PHOSPHINS	PHOTOSETS	PHTHISES	PHYSICIST	PIASSABA
PHOSPHITE	PHOTOSETTING	PHTHISIC	PHYSICISTS	PIASSABAS
PHOSPHITES	PHOTOSTAT	PHTHISICS	PHYSICKED	PIASSAVA
PHOSPHOR	PHOTOSTATED	PHTHISIS	PHYSICKING	PIASSAVAS
PHOSPHORE	PHOTOSTATING	PHUT	PHYSICS	PIASTER
PHOSPHORES	PHOTOSTATS	PHUTS	PHYSIQUE	PIASTERS
PHOSPHORI	PHOTOSTATTED	PHYCOLOGIES	PHYSIQUED	PIASTRE
PHOSPHORS	PHOTOSTATTING	PHYCOLOGY	PHYSIQUES	PIASTRES
PHOSPHORUS	PHOTOTAXIES	PHYLA	PHYSIS	PIAZZA
PHOT	PHOTOTAXY	PHYLAE	PHYTANE	PIAZZAS
PHOTIC	PHOTOTUBE	PHYLAR	PHYTANES	PIAZZE
PHOTICS	PHOTOTUBES	PHYLAXIS	PHYTIN	PIBAL
PHOTO	PHOTOTYPE	PHYLAXISES	PHYTINS	PIBALS
PHOTOCELL	PHOTOTYPES	PHYLE	PHYTOGENIES	PIBROCH
PHOTOCELLS	PHOTS	PHYLESES	PHYTOGENY	PIBROCHS
PHOTOCOPIED	PHPHT	PHYLESIS	PHYTOID	PIC
PHOTOCOPIES	PHRASAL	PHYLESISES	PHYTOL	PICA
PHOTOCOPY	PHRASALLY	PHYLETIC	PHYTOLITH	PICACHO
PHOTOCOPYING	PHRASE	PHYLETICS	PHYTOLITHS	PICACHOS
PHOTOED	PHRASED	PHYLIC	PHYTOLOGIES	PICADILLO
PHOTOG	PHRASES	PHYLLARIES	PHYTOLOGY	PICADILLOS
PHOTOGENE	PHRASING	PHYLLARY	PHYTOLS	PICADOR
PHOTOGENES	PHRASINGS	PHYLLITE	PHYTON	PICADORES
PHOTOGRAM	PHRATRAL	PHYLLITES	PHYTONIC	PICADORS
PHOTOGRAMS	PHRATRIC	PHYLLITIC	PHYTONS	PICAL
PHOTOGS	PHRATRIES	PHYLLO	PHYTOTRON	PICANINNIES
PHOTOING	PHRATRY	PHYLLODE	PHYTOTRONS	PICANINNY
PHOTOLYZE	PHREAK	PHYLLODES	PI	PICANTE
PHOTOLYZED	PHREAKED	PHYLLODIA	PIA	PICARA
PHOTOLYZES	PHREAKER	PHYLLODIUM	PIACULAR	PICARAS
PHOTOLYZING	PHREAKERS	PHYLLOID	PIAFFE	PICARO
PHOTOMAP	PHREAKING	PHYLLOIDS	PIAFFED	PICAROON
PHOTOMAPPED	PHREAKINGS	PHYLLOME	PIAFFER	PICAROONED
PHOTOMAPPING	PHREAKS	PHYLLOMES	PIAFFERS	PICAROONING
PHOTOMAPS	PHREATIC	PHYLLOMIC	PIAFFES	PICAROONS
PHOTOMASK	PHRENETIC	PHYLLOPOD	PIAFFING	PICAROS
PHOTOMASKS	PHRENIC	PHYLLOPODS	PIAL	PICAS
PHOTON	PHRENITIDES	PHYLLOS	PIAN	PICAYUNE
PHOTONIC	PHRENITIS	PHYLOGENIES	PIANIC	PICAYUNES
PHOTONICS	PHRENITISES	PHYLOGENY	PIANISM	PICCATA
PHOTONS	PHRENSIED	PHYLON	PIANISMS	PICCOLO
PHOTOPIA	PHRENSIES	PHYLUM	PIANIST	PICCOLOS
PHOTOPIAS	PHRENSY	PHYSED	PIANISTIC	PICE
PHOTOPIC	PHRENSYING	PHYSEDS	PIANISTS	PICEOUS
PHOTOPLAY	PHT	PHYSES	PIANO	PICHOLINE
PHOTOPLAYS	PHTHALATE	PHYSIATRIES	PIANOS	PICHOLINES
PHOTOS	PHTHALATES	PHYSIATRY	PIANS	PICIFORM
PHOTOSCAN	PHTHALEIN	PHYSIC	PIAS	PICK

PICKABACK	PICLORAMS	PICTURIZES	PIERCES	PIGLET
PICKABACKED	PICNIC	PICTURIZING	PIERCING	PIGLETS
PICKABACKING	PICNICKED	PICUL	PIERCINGS	PIGLIKE
PICKABACKS	PICNICKER	PICULS	PIERIDINE	PIGMENT
PICKADIL	PICNICKERS	PIDDLE	PIEROGI	PIGMENTED
PICKADILS	PICNICKING	PIDDLED	PIEROGIES	PIGMENTING
PICKAROON	PICNICKY	PIDDLER	PIERROT	PIGMENTS
PICKAROONS	PICNICS	PIDDLERS	PIERROTS	PIGMIES
PICKAX	PICOFARAD	PIDDLES	PIERS	PIGMY
PICKAXE	PICOFARADS	PIDDLING	PIES	PIGNOLI
PICKAXED	PICOGRAM	PIDDLY	PIETA	PIGNOLIA
PICKAXES	PICOGRAMS	PIDDOCK	PIETAS	PIGNOLIAS
PICKAXING	PICOLIN	PIDDOCKS	PIETIES	PIGNOLIS
PICKED	PICOLINE	PIDGIN	PIETISM	PIGNORA
PICKEER	PICOLINES	PIDGINIZE	PIETISMS	PIGNUS
PICKEERED	PICOLINS	PIDGINIZED	PIETIST	PIGNUT
PICKEERING	PICOMETER	PIDGINIZES	PIETISTIC	PIGNUTS
PICKEERS	PICOMETERS	PIDGINIZING	PIETISTS	PIGOUT
PICKER	PICOMETRE	PIDGINS	PIETY	PIGOUTS
PICKEREL	PICOMETRES	PIE	PIFFLE	PIGPEN
PICKERELS	PICOMOLE	PIEBALD	PIFFLED	PIGPENS
PICKERS	PICOMOLES	PIEBALDS	PIFFLES	PIGS
PICKET	PICOT	PIECE	PIFFLING	PIGSKIN
PICKETED	PICOTED	PIECED	PIG	PIGSKINS
PICKETER	PICOTEE	PIECEMEAL	PIGBOAT	PIGSNEY
PICKETERS	PICOTEES	PIECER	PIGBOATS	PIGSNEYS
PICKETING	PICOTING	PIECERS	PIGEON	PIGSTICK
PICKETS	PICOTS	PIECES	PIGEONITE	PIGSTICKED
PICKIER	PICOWAVE	PIECEWISE	PIGEONITES	PIGSTICKING
PICKIEST	PICOWAVED	PIECEWORK	PIGEONS	PIGSTICKS
PICKINESS	PICOWAVES	PIECEWORKS	PIGFISH	PIGSTIES
PICKINESSES	PICOWAVING	PIECING	PIGFISHES	PIGSTY
PICKING	PICQUET	PIECINGS	PIGGED	PIGTAIL
PICKINGS	PICQUETS	PIECRUST	PIGGERIES	PIGTAILED
PICKLE	PICRATE	PIECRUSTS	PIGGERY	PIGTAILS
PICKLED	PICRATED	PIED	PIGGIE	PIGWEED
PICKLES	PICRATES	PIEDFORT	PIGGIER	PIGWEEDS
PICKLING	PICRIC	PIEDFORTS	PIGGIES	PIING
PICKLOCK	PICRITE	PIEDMONT	PIGGIEST	PIKA
PICKLOCKS	PICRITES	PIEDMONTS	PIGGIN	PIKAKE
PICKOFF	PICRITIC	PIEFORT	PIGGINESS	PIKAKES
PICKOFFS	PICS	PIEFORTS	PIGGINESSES	PIKAS
PICKPROOF	PICTOGRAM	PIEHOLE	PIGGING	PIKE
PICKS	PICTOGRAMS	PIEHOLES	PIGGINS	PIKED
PICKTHANK	PICTORIAL	PIEING	PIGGISH	PIKEMAN
PICKTHANKS	PICTORIALS	PIEPLANT	PIGGISHLY	PIKEMEN
PICKUP	PICTURE	PIEPLANTS	PIGGY	PIKEPERCH
PICKUPS	PICTURED	PIER	PIGGYBACK	PIKEPERCHES
PICKWICK	PICTURES	PIERCE	PIGGYBACKED	PIKER
PICKWICKS	PICTURING	PIERCED	PIGGYBACKING	PIKERS
PICKY	PICTURIZE	PIERCER	PIGGYBACKS	PIKES
PICLORAM	PICTURIZED	PIERCERS	PIGHEADED	PIKESTAFF

PIKESTAFFS	PILLAGED	PIMENTOS	PINDLING	PINIONED
PIKESTAVES	PILLAGER	PIMIENTO	PINE	PINIONING
PIKI	PILLAGERS	PIMIENTOS	PINEAL	PINIONS
PIKING	PILLAGES	PIMP	PINEALS	PINITE
PIKIS	PILLAGING	PIMPED	PINEAPPLE	PINITES
PILAF	PILLAR	PIMPERNEL	PINEAPPLES	PINITOL
PILAFF	PILLARED	PIMPERNELS	PINECONE	PINITOLS
PILAFFS	PILLARING	PIMPING	PINECONES	PINK
PILAFS	PILLARS	PIMPLE	PINED	PINKED
PILAR	PILLBOX	PIMPLED	PINEDROPS	PINKEN
PILASTER	PILLBOXES	PIMPLES	PINELAND	PINKENED
PILASTERS	PILLED	PIMPLIER	PINELANDS	PINKENING
PILAU	PILLING	PIMPLIEST	PINELIKE	PINKENS
PILAUS	PILLION	PIMPLY	PINENE	PINKER
PILAW	PILLIONS	PIMPS	PINENES	PINKERS
PILAWS	PILLORIED	PIN	PINERIES	PINKEST
PILCHARD	PILLORIES	PINA	PINERY	PINKEY
PILCHARDS	PILLORY	PINACEOUS	PINES	PINKEYE
PILE	PILLORYING	PINAFORE	PINESAP	PINKEYES
PILEA	PILLOW	PINAFORED	PINESAPS	PINKEYS
PILEATE	PILLOWED	PINAFORES	PINETA	PINKIE
PILEATED	PILLOWING	PINANG	PINETUM	PINKIES
PILED	PILLOWS	PINANGS	PINEWOOD	PINKING
PILEI	PILLOWY	PINAS	PINEWOODS	PINKINGS
PILELESS	PILLS	PINASTER	PINEY	PINKISH
PILEOUS	PILONIDAL	PINASTERS	PINFISH	PINKLY
PILES	PILOSE	PINATA	PINFISHES	PINKNESS
PILEUM	PILOSITIES	PINATAS	PINFOLD	PINKNESSES
PILEUP	PILOSITY	PINBALL	PINFOLDED	PINKO
PILEUPS	PILOT	PINBALLED	PINFOLDING	PINKOES
PILEUS	PILOTAGE	PINBALLING	PINFOLDS	PINKOS
PILEWORT	PILOTAGES	PINBALLS	PING	PINKROOT
PILEWORTS	PILOTED	PINBONE	PINGED	PINKROOTS
PILFER	PILOTFISH	PINBONES	PINGER	PINKS
PILFERAGE	PILOTFISHES	PINCER	PINGERS	PINKY
PILFERAGES	PILOTING	PINCERS	PINGING	PINNA
PILFERED	PILOTINGS	PINCH	PINGO	PINNACE
PILFERER	PILOTLESS	PINCHBECK	PINGOES	PINNACES
PILFERERS	PILOTS	PINCHBECKS	PINGOS	PINNACLE
PILFERING	PILOUS	PINCHBUG	PINGRASS	PINNACLED
PILFERS	PILSENER	PINCHBUGS	PINGRASSES	PINNACLES
PILGARLIC	PILSENERS	PINCHCOCK	PINGS	PINNACLING
PILGARLICS	PILSNER	PINCHCOCKS	PINGUID	PINNAE
PILGRIM	PILSNERS	PINCHECK	PINHEAD	PINNAL
PILGRIMS	PILULAR	PINCHECKS	PINHEADED	PINNAS
PILI	PILULE	PINCHED	PINHEADS	PINNATE
PILIFORM	PILULES	PINCHER	PINHOLE	PINNATED
PILING	PILUS	PINCHERS	PINHOLES	PINNATELY
PILINGS	PILY	PINCHES	PINIER	PINNATION
PILIS	PIMA	PINCHING	PINIEST	PINNATIONS
PILL	PIMAS	PINDER	PINING	PINNED
PILLAGE	PIMENTO	PINDERS	PINION	PINNER

PINNERS	PINTLE	PIPEFISH	PIQUANT	PISCARY
PINNIES	PINTLES	PIPEFISHES	PIQUANTLY	PISCATOR
PINNING	PINTO	PIPEFUL	PIQUE	PISCATORS
PINNIPED	PINTOES	PIPEFULS	PIQUED	PISCATORY
PINNIPEDS	PINTOS	PIPELESS	PIQUES	PISCIFORM
PINNULA	PINTS	PIPELIKE	PIQUET	PISCINA
PINNULAE	PINTSIZE	PIPELINE	PIQUETS	PISCINAE
PINNULAR	PINTSIZED	PIPELINED	PIQUING	PISCINAL
PINNULATE	PINUP	PIPELINES	PIRACETAM	PISCINAS
PINNULE	PINUPS	PIPELINING	PIRACETAMS	PISCINE
PINNULES	PINWALE	PIPER	PIRACIES	PISCIVORE
PINNY	PINWALES	PIPERINE	PIRACY	PISCIVORES
PINOCHLE	PINWEED	PIPERINES	PIRAGUA	PISCO
PINOCHLES	PINWEEDS	PIPERONAL	PIRAGUAS	PISCOS
PINOCLE	PINWHEEL	PIPERONALS	PIRANA	PISH
PINOCLES	PINWHEELED	PIPERS	PIRANAS	PISHED
PINOCYTIC	PINWHEELING	PIPES	PIRANHA	PISHER
PINOLE	PINWHEELS	PIPESTEM	PIRANHAS	PISHERS
PINOLES	PINWORK	PIPESTEMS	PIRARUCU	PISHES
PINON	PINWORKS	PIPESTONE	PIRARUCUS	PISHING
PINONES	PINWORM	PIPESTONES	PIRATE	PISHOGE
PINONS	PINWORMS	PIPET	PIRATED	PISHOGES
PINOT	PINWRENCH	PIPETS	PIRATES	PISHOGUE
PINOTS	PINWRENCHES	PIPETTE	PIRATIC	PISHOGUES
PINPOINT	PINY	PIPETTED	PIRATICAL	PISIFORM
PINPOINTED	PINYIN	PIPETTES	PIRATING	PISIFORMS
PINPOINTING	PINYON	PIPETTING	PIRAYA	PISMIRE
PINPOINTS	PINYONS	PIPIER	PIRAYAS	PISMIRES
PINPRICK	PIOLET	PIPIEST	PIRIFORM	PISO
PINPRICKED	PIOLETS	PIPINESS	PIRN	PISOLITE
PINPRICKING	PION	PIPINESSES	PIRNS	PISOLITES
PINPRICKS	PIONEER	PIPING	PIROG	PISOLITH
PINS	PIONEERED	PIPINGLY	PIROGEN	PISOLITHS
PINSCHER	PIONEERING	PIPINGS	PIROGHI	PISOLITIC
PINSCHERS	PIONEERS	PIPISTREL	PIROGI	PISOS
PINSETTER	PIONIC	PIPISTRELS	PIROGIES	PISS
PINSETTERS	PIONS	PIPIT	PIROGUE	PISSANT
PINSTRIPE	PIOSITIES	PIPITS	PIROGUES	PISSANTS
PINSTRIPES	PIOSITY	PIPKIN	PIROJKI	PISSED
PINT	PIOUS	PIPKINS	PIROPLASM	PISSER
PINTA	PIOUSLY	PIPPED	PIROPLASMS	PISSERS
PINTADA	PIOUSNESS	PIPPIN	PIROQUE	PISSES
PINTADAS	PIOUSNESSES	PIPPING	PIROQUES	PISSING
PINTADO	PIP	PIPPINS	PIROSHKI	PISSOIR
PINTADOES	PIPAGE	PIPS	PIROUETTE	PISSOIRS
PINTADOS	PIPAGES	PIPSQUEAK	PIROUETTED	PISTACHE
PINTAIL	PIPAL	PIPSQUEAKS	PIROUETTES	PISTACHES
PINTAILED	PIPALS	PIPY	PIROUETTING	PISTACHIO
PINTAILS	PIPE	PIQUANCE	PIROZHKI	PISTACHIOS
PINTANO	PIPEAGE	PIQUANCES	PIROZHOK	PISTAREEN
PINTANOS	PIPEAGES	PIQUANCIES	PIS	PISTAREENS
PINTAS	PIPED	PIQUANCY	PISCARIES	PISTE

PISTES	PITCHPOLING	PIVOT	PLACATION	PLAGUERS
PISTIL	PITCHY	PIVOTABLE	PLACATIONS	PLAGUES
PISTILS	PITEOUS	PIVOTAL	PLACATIVE	PLAGUEY
PISTOL	PITEOUSLY	PIVOTALLY	PLACATORY	PLAGUILY
PISTOLE	PITFALL	PIVOTED	PLACE	PLAGUING
PISTOLED	PITFALLS	PIVOTING	PLACEABLE	PLAGUY
PISTOLEER	PITH	PIVOTMAN	PLACEBO	PLAICE
PISTOLEERS	PITHEAD	PIVOTMEN	PLACEBOES	PLAICES
PISTOLERO	PITHEADS	PIVOTS	PLACEBOS	PLAID
PISTOLEROS	PITHECOID	PIX	PLACED	PLAIDED
PISTOLES	PITHED	PIXEL	PLACEKICK	PLAIDS
PISTOLIER	PITHIER	PIXELS	PLACEKICKED	PLAIN
PISTOLIERS	PITHIEST	PIXES	PLACEKICKING	PLAINED
PISTOLING	PITHILY	PIXIE	PLACEKICKS	PLAINER
PISTOLLED	PITHINESS	PIXIEISH	PLACELESS	PLAINEST
PISTOLLING	PITHINESSES	PIXIES	PLACEMAN	PLAINING
PISTOLS	PITHING	PIXILATED	PLACEMEN	PLAINLY
PISTON	PITHLESS	PIXINESS	PLACEMENT	PLAINNESS
PISTONS	PITHS	PIXINESSES	PLACEMENTS	PLAINNESSES
PISTOU	PITHY	PIXY	PLACENTA	PLAINS
PISTOUS	PITIABLE	PIXYISH	PLACENTAE	PLAINSMAN
PIT	PITIABLY	PIZAZZ	PLACENTAL	PLAINSMEN
PITA	PITIED	PIZAZZES	PLACENTALS	PLAINSONG
PITAHAYA	PITIER	PIZAZZY	PLACENTAS	PLAINSONGS
PITAHAYAS	PITIERS	PIZZA	PLACER	PLAINT
PITAPAT	PITIES	PIZZALIKE	PLACERS	PLAINTEXT
PITAPATS	PITIFUL	PIZZAS	PLACES	PLAINTEXTS
PITAPATTED	PITIFULLER	PIZZAZ	PLACET	PLAINTFUL
PITAPATTING	PITIFULLEST	PIZZAZES	PLACETS	PLAINTIFF
PITAS	PITIFULLY	PIZZAZZ	PLACID	PLAINTIFFS
PITAYA	PITILESS	PIZZAZZES	PLACIDITIES	PLAINTIVE
PITAYAS	PITMAN	PIZZAZZY	PLACIDITY	PLAINTS
PITCH	PITMANS	PIZZELLE	PLACIDLY	PLAISTER
PITCHED	PITMEN	PIZZELLES	PLACING	PLAISTERED
PITCHER	PITON	PIZZERIA	PLACK	PLAISTERING
PITCHERS	PITONS	PIZZERIAS	PLACKET	PLAISTERS
PITCHES	PITS	PIZZICATI	PLACKETS	PLAIT
PITCHFORK	PITSAW	PIZZICATO	PLACKS	PLAITED
PITCHFORKED	PITSAWS	PIZZLE	PLACODERM	PLAITER
PITCHFORKING	PITTA	PIZZLES	PLACODERMS	PLAITERS
PITCHFORKS	PITTANCE	PLACABLE	PLACOID	PLAITING
PITCHIER	PITTANCES	PLACABLY	PLACOIDS	PLAITINGS
PITCHIEST	PITTAS	PLACARD	PLAFOND	PLAITS
PITCHILY	PITTED	PLACARDED	PLAFONDS	PLAN
PITCHING	PITTING	PLACARDING	PLAGAL	PLANAR
PITCHMAN	PITTINGS	PLACARDS	PLAGE	PLANARIA
PITCHMEN	PITUITARIES	PLACATE	PLAGES	PLANARIAN
PITCHOUT	PITUITARY	PLACATED	PLAGIARIES	PLANARIANS
PITCHOUTS	PITY	PLACATER	PLAGIARY	PLANARIAS
PITCHPOLE	PITYING	PLACATERS	PLAGUE	PLANARITIES
PITCHPOLED	PITYINGLY	PLACATES	PLAGUED	PLANARITY
PITCHPOLES	PIU	PLACATING	PLAGUER	PLANATE

PLANATION	PLANOSOLS	PLASMONS	PLATINA	PLAYBILL
PLANATIONS	PLANS	PLASMS	PLATINAS	PLAYBILLS
PLANCH	PLANT	PLASTER	PLATING	PLAYBOOK
PLANCHE	PLANTABLE	PLASTERED	PLATINGS	PLAYBOOKS
PLANCHES	PLANTAIN	PLASTERER	PLATINIC	PLAYBOY
PLANCHET	PLANTAINS	PLASTERERS	PLATINIZE	PLAYBOYS
PLANCHETS	PLANTAR	PLASTERING	PLATINIZED	PLAYDATE
PLANE	PLANTED	PLASTERS	PLATINIZES	PLAYDATES
PLANED	PLANTER	PLASTERY	PLATINIZING	PLAYDAY
PLANELOAD	PLANTERS	PLASTIC	PLATINOID	PLAYDAYS
PLANELOADS	PLANTING	PLASTICKY	PLATINOIDS	PLAYDOWN
PLANENESS	PLANTINGS	PLASTICLY	PLATINOUS	PLAYDOWNS
PLANENESSES	PLANTLET	PLASTICS	PLATINUM	PLAYED
PLANER	PLANTLETS	PLASTID	PLATINUMS	PLAYER
PLANERS	PLANTLIKE	PLASTIDS	PLATITUDE	PLAYERS
PLANES	PLANTS	PLASTIQUE	PLATITUDES	PLAYFIELD
PLANESIDE	PLANTSMAN	PLASTIQUES	PLATONIC	PLAYFIELDS
PLANESIDES	PLANTSMEN	PLASTISOL	PLATONISM	PLAYFUL
PLANET	PLANULA	PLASTISOLS	PLATONISMS	PLAYFULLY
PLANETARIES	PLANULAE	PLASTRAL	PLATOON	PLAYGIRL
PLANETARY	PLANULAR	PLASTRON	PLATOONED	PLAYGIRLS
PLANETOID	PLANULATE	PLASTRONS	PLATOONING	PLAYGOER
PLANETOIDS	PLANULOID	PLASTRUM	PLATOONS	PLAYGOERS
PLANETS	PLAQUE	PLASTRUMS	PLATS	PLAYGOING
PLANFORM	PLAQUES	PLAT	PLATTED	PLAYGOINGS
PLANFORMS	PLASH	PLATAN	PLATTER	PLAYGROUP
PLANGENCIES	PLASHED	PLATANE	PLATTERS	PLAYGROUPS
PLANGENCY	PLASHER	PLATANES	PLATTING	PLAYHOUSE
PLANGENT	PLASHERS	PLATANS	PLATY	PLAYHOUSES
PLANING	PLASHES	PLATE	PLATYFISH	PLAYING
PLANISH	PLASHIER	PLATEAU	PLATYFISHES	PLAYLAND
PLANISHED	PLASHIEST	PLATEAUED	PLATYPI	PLAYLANDS
PLANISHER	PLASHING	PLATEAUING	PLATYPUS	PLAYLESS
PLANISHERS	PLASHY	PLATEAUS	PLATYPUSES	PLAYLET
PLANISHES	PLASM	PLATEAUX	PLATYS	PLAYLETS
PLANISHING	PLASMA	PLATED	PLAUDIT	PLAYLIKE
PLANK	PLASMAGEL	PLATEFUL	PLAUDITS	PLAYLIST
PLANKED	PLASMAGELS	PLATEFULS	PLAUSIBLE	PLAYLISTS
PLANKING	PLASMAS	PLATELET	PLAUSIBLY	PLAYMAKER
PLANKINGS	PLASMASOL	PLATELETS	PLAUSIVE	PLAYMAKERS
PLANKS	PLASMASOLS	PLATELIKE	PLAY	PLAYMATE
PLANKTER	PLASMATIC	PLATEN	PLAYA	PLAYMATES
PLANKTERS	PLASMIC	PLATENS	PLAYABLE	PLAYOFF
PLANKTON	PLASMID	PLATER	PLAYACT	PLAYOFFS
PLANKTONS	PLASMIDS	PLATERS	PLAYACTED	PLAYPEN
PLANLESS	PLASMIN	PLATES	PLAYACTING	PLAYPENS
PLANNED	PLASMINS	PLATESFUL	PLAYACTOR	PLAYROOM
PLANNER	PLASMODIA	PLATFORM	PLAYACTORS	PLAYROOMS
PLANNERS	PLASMODIUM	PLATFORMS	PLAYACTS	PLAYS
PLANNING	PLASMOID	PLATIER	PLAYAS	PLAYSUIT
PLANNINGS	PLASMOIDS	PLATIES	PLAYBACK	PLAYSUITS
PLANOSOL	PLASMON	PLATIEST	PLAYBACKS	PLAYTHING

PLAYTHINGS	PLECTRONS	PLEOPOD	PLIGHTING	PLOTTAGES
PLAYTIME	PLECTRUM	PLEOPODS	PLIGHTS	PLOTTED
PLAYTIMES	PLECTRUMS	PLESSOR	PLIMSOL	PLOTTER
PLAYWEAR	PLED	PLESSORS	PLIMSOLE	PLOTTERS
PLAZA	PLEDGE	PLETHORA	PLIMSOLES	PLOTTIER
PLAZAS	PLEDGED	PLETHORAS	PLIMSOLL	PLOTTIES
PLEA	PLEDGEE	PLETHORIC	PLIMSOLLS	PLOTTIEST
PLEACH	PLEDGEES	PLEURA	PLIMSOLS	PLOTTING
PLEACHED	PLEDGEOR	PLEURAE	PLINK	PLOTTY
PLEACHES	PLEDGEORS	PLEURAL	PLINKED	PLOTZ
PLEACHING	PLEDGER	PLEURAS	PLINKER	PLOTZED
PLEAD	PLEDGERS	PLEURISIES	PLINKERS	PLOTZES
PLEADABLE	PLEDGES	PLEURISY	PLINKING	PLOTZING
PLEADED	PLEDGET	PLEURITIC	PLINKS	PLOUGH
PLEADER	PLEDGETS	PLEURON	PLINTH	PLOUGHED
PLEADERS	PLEDGING	PLEUSTON	PLINTHS	PLOUGHER
PLEADING	PLEDGOR	PLEUSTONS	PLIOCENE	PLOUGHERS
PLEADINGS	PLEDGORS	PLEW	PLIOFILM	PLOUGHING
PLEADS	PLEIAD	PLEWS	PLIOFILMS	PLOUGHS
PLEAS	PLEIADES	PLEX	PLIOTRON	PLOVER
PLEASANCE	PLEIADS	PLEXAL	PLIOTRONS	PLOVERS
PLEASANCES	PLEIOCENE	PLEXES	PLISKIE	PLOW
PLEASANT	PLEIOTAXIES	PLEXIFORM	PLISKIES	PLOWABLE
PLEASANTER	PLEIOTAXY	PLEXOR	PLISKY	PLOWBACK
PLEASANTEST	PLENA	PLEXORS	PLISSE	PLOWBACKS
PLEASE	PLENARIES	PLEXUS	PLISSES	PLOWBOY
PLEASED	PLENARILY	PLEXUSES	PLOD	PLOWBOYS
PLEASER	PLENARY	PLIABLE	PLODDED	PLOWED
PLEASERS	PLENCH	PLIABLY	PLODDER	PLOWER
PLEASES	PLENCHES	PLIANCIES	PLODDERS	PLOWERS
PLEASING	PLENISH	PLIANCY	PLODDING	PLOWHEAD
PLEASURE	PLENISHED	PLIANT	PLODS	PLOWHEADS
PLEASURED	PLENISHES	PLIANTLY	PLOIDIES	PLOWING
PLEASURES	PLENISHING	PLICA	PLOIDY	PLOWLAND
PLEASURING	PLENISM	PLICAE	PLONK	PLOWLANDS
PLEAT	PLENISMS	PLICAL	PLONKED	PLOWMAN
PLEATED	PLENIST	PLICATE	PLONKING	PLOWMEN
PLEATER	PLENISTS	PLICATED	PLONKS	PLOWS
PLEATERS	PLENITUDE	PLICATELY	PLOP	PLOWSHARE
PLEATHER	PLENITUDES	PLICATION	PLOPPED	PLOWSHARES
PLEATHERS	PLENTEOUS	PLICATIONS	PLOPPING	PLOY
PLEATING	PLENTIES	PLICATURE	PLOPS	PLOYED
PLEATLESS	PLENTIFUL	PLICATURES	PLOSION	PLOYING
PLEATS	PLENTY	PLIE	PLOSIONS	PLOYS
PLEB	PLENUM	PLIED	PLOSIVE	PLUCK
PLEBE	PLENUMS	PLIER	PLOSIVES	PLUCKED
PLEBEIAN	PLEON	PLIERS	PLOT	PLUCKER
PLEBEIANS	PLEONAL	PLIES	PLOTLESS	PLUCKERS
PLEBES	PLEONASM	PLIGHT	PLOTLINE	PLUCKIER
PLEBS	PLEONASMS	PLIGHTED	PLOTLINES	PLUCKIEST
PLECTRA	PLEONIC	PLIGHTER	PLOTS	PLUCKILY
PLECTRON	PLEONS	PLIGHTERS	PLOTTAGE	PLUCKING

PLUCKS	PLUMMER	PLUNKING	PLYING	POCOSIN
PLUCKY	PLUMMEST	PLUNKS	PLYINGLY	POCOSINS
PLUG	PLUMMET	PLUNKY	PLYWOOD	POCOSON
PLUGGED	PLUMMETED	PLURAL	PLYWOODS	POCOSONS
PLUGGER	PLUMMETING	PLURALISM	PNEUMA	POD
PLUGGERS	PLUMMETS	PLURALISMS	PNEUMAS	PODAGRA
PLUGGING	PLUMMIER	PLURALIST	PNEUMATIC	PODAGRAL
PLUGLESS	PLUMMIEST	PLURALISTS	PNEUMATICS	PODAGRAS
PLUGOLA	PLUMMY	PLURALITIES	PNEUMONIA	PODAGRIC
PLUGOLAS	PLUMOSE	PLURALITY	PNEUMONIAS	PODAGROUS
PLUGS	PLUMOSELY	PLURALIZE	PNEUMONIC	PODDED
PLUGUGLIES	PLUMOSITIES	PLURALIZED	POACEOUS	PODDING
PLUGUGLY	PLUMOSITY	PLURALIZES	POACH	PODESTA
PLUM	PLUMP	PLURALIZING	POACHABLE	PODESTAS
PLUMAGE	PLUMPED	PLURALLY	POACHED	PODGIER
PLUMAGED	PLUMPEN	PLURALS	POACHER	PODGIEST
PLUMAGES	PLUMPENED	PLUS	POACHERS	PODGILY
PLUMATE	PLUMPENING	PLUSES	POACHES	PODGY
PLUMB	PLUMPENS	PLUSH	POACHIER	PODIA
PLUMBABLE	PLUMPER	PLUSHER	POACHIEST	PODIATRIC
PLUMBAGO	PLUMPERS	PLUSHES	POACHING	PODIATRIES
PLUMBAGOS	PLUMPEST	PLUSHEST	POACHY	PODIATRY
PLUMBED	PLUMPING	PLUSHIER	POBLANO	PODITE
PLUMBEOUS	PLUMPISH	PLUSHIEST	POBLANOS	PODITES
PLUMBER	PLUMPLY	PLUSHILY	POBOY	PODITIC
PLUMBERIES	PLUMPNESS	PLUSHLY	POBOYS	PODIUM
PLUMBERS	PLUMPNESSES	PLUSHNESS	POCHARD	PODIUMS
PLUMBERY	PLUMPS	PLUSHNESSES	POCHARDS	PODLIKE
PLUMBIC	PLUMS	PLUSHY	POCK	PODOCARP
PLUMBING	PLUMULAR	PLUSSAGE	POCKED	PODOMERE
PLUMBINGS	PLUMULE	PLUSSAGES	POCKET	PODOMERES
PLUMBISM	PLUMULES	PLUSSES	POCKETED	PODS
PLUMBISMS	PLUMULOSE	PLUTEI	POCKETER	PODSOL
PLUMBNESS	PLUMY	PLUTEUS	POCKETERS	PODSOLIC
PLUMBNESSES	PLUNDER	PLUTOCRAT	POCKETFUL	PODSOLS
PLUMBOUS	PLUNDERED	PLUTOCRATS	POCKETFULS	PODZOL
PLUMBS	PLUNDERER	PLUTON	POCKETING	PODZOLIC
PLUMBUM	PLUNDERERS	PLUTONIAN	POCKETS	PODZOLIZE
PLUMBUMS	PLUNDERING	PLUTONIC	POCKETSFUL	PODZOLIZED
PLUME	PLUNDERS	PLUTONISM	POCKIER	PODZOLIZES
PLUMED	PLUNGE	PLUTONISMS	POCKIEST	PODZOLIZING
PLUMELET	PLUNGED	PLUTONIUM	POCKILY	PODZOLS
PLUMELETS	PLUNGER	PLUTONIUMS	POCKING	POECHORE
PLUMERIA	PLUNGERS	PLUTONS	POCKMARK	POECHORES
PLUMERIAS	PLUNGES	PLUVIAL	POCKMARKED	POEM
PLUMES	PLUNGING	PLUVIALS	POCKMARKING	POEMS
PLUMIER	PLUNK	PLUVIAN	POCKMARKS	POENOLOGIES
PLUMIEST	PLUNKED	PLUVIOSE	POCKS	POENOLOGY
PLUMING	PLUNKER	PLUVIOUS	POCKY	POESIES
PLUMIPED	PLUNKERS	PLY	POCO	POESY
PLUMIPEDS	PLUNKIER	PLYER	POCOSEN	POET
PLUMLIKE	PLUNKIEST	PLYERS	POCOSENS	POETASTER

POETASTERS
POETESS
POETESSES
POETIC
POETICAL
POETICISM
POETICISMS
POETICIZE
POETICIZED
POETICIZES
POETICIZING
POETICS
POETISE
POETISED
POETISER
POETISERS
POETISES
POETISING
POETIZE
POETIZED
POETIZER
POETIZERS
POETIZES
POETIZING
POETLESS
POETLIKE
POETRIES
POETRY
POETS
POGEY
POGEYS
POGIES
POGONIA
POGONIAS
POGONIP
POGONIPS
POGROM
POGROMED
POGROMING
POGROMIST
POGROMISTS
POGROMS
POGY
POH
POI
POIGNANCE
POIGNANCES
POIGNANCIES
POIGNANCY
POIGNANT
POILU
POILUS

POINCIANA
POINCIANAS
POIND
POINDED
POINDING
POINDS
POINT
POINTABLE
POINTE
POINTED
POINTEDLY
POINTELLE
POINTELLES
POINTER
POINTERS
POINTES
POINTIER
POINTIEST
POINTING
POINTLESS
POINTMAN
POINTMEN
POINTS
POINTY
POIS
POISE
POISED
POISER
POISERS
POISES
POISHA
POISING
POISON
POISONED
POISONER
POISONERS
POISONING
POISONOUS
POISONS
POITREL
POITRELS
POKABLE
POKE
POKEBERRIES
POKEBERRY
POKED
POKER
POKEROOT
POKEROOTS
POKERS
POKES
POKEWEED

POKEWEEDS
POKEY
POKEYS
POKIER
POKIES
POKIEST
POKILY
POKINESS
POKINESSES
POKING
POKY
POL
POLAR
POLARISE
POLARISED
POLARISES
POLARISING
POLARITIES
POLARITY
POLARIZE
POLARIZED
POLARIZER
POLARIZERS
POLARIZES
POLARIZING
POLARON
POLARONS
POLARS
POLDER
POLDERS
POLE
POLEAX
POLEAXE
POLEAXED
POLEAXES
POLEAXING
POLECAT
POLECATS
POLED
POLEIS
POLELESS
POLEMIC
POLEMICAL
POLEMICS
POLEMIST
POLEMISTS
POLEMIZE
POLEMIZED
POLEMIZES
POLEMIZING
POLENTA
POLENTAS

POLER
POLERS
POLES
POLESTAR
POLESTARS
POLEWARD
POLEYN
POLEYNS
POLICE
POLICED
POLICEMAN
POLICEMEN
POLICER
POLICERS
POLICES
POLICIES
POLICING
POLICY
POLIES
POLING
POLIO
POLIOS
POLIS
POLISH
POLISHED
POLISHER
POLISHERS
POLISHES
POLISHING
POLITBURO
POLITBUROS
POLITE
POLITELY
POLITER
POLITESSE
POLITESSES
POLITEST
POLITIC
POLITICAL
POLITICK
POLITICKED
POLITICKING
POLITICKS
POLITICLY
POLITICO
POLITICOES
POLITICOS
POLITICS
POLITIES
POLITY
POLKA
POLKAED

POLKAING
POLKAS
POLL
POLLACK
POLLACKS
POLLARD
POLLARDED
POLLARDING
POLLARDS
POLLED
POLLEE
POLLEES
POLLEN
POLLENATE
POLLENATED
POLLENATES
POLLENATING
POLLENED
POLLENING
POLLENS
POLLER
POLLERS
POLLEX
POLLICAL
POLLICES
POLLINATE
POLLINATED
POLLINATES
POLLINATING
POLLING
POLLINIA
POLLINIC
POLLINIUM
POLLINIZE
POLLINIZED
POLLINIZES
POLLINIZING
POLLIST
POLLISTS
POLLIWOG
POLLIWOGS
POLLOCK
POLLOCKS
POLLS
POLLSTER
POLLSTERS
POLLTAKER
POLLTAKERS
POLLUTANT
POLLUTANTS
POLLUTE
POLLUTED

POLLUTER	POLYGENES	POLYPHONE	POLYZOIC	PONCHOED
POLLUTERS	POLYGENIC	POLYPHONES	POM	PONCHOS
POLLUTES	POLYGLOT	POLYPHONIES	POMACE	PONCING
POLLUTING	POLYGLOTS	POLYPHONY	POMACEOUS	POND
POLLUTION	POLYGON	POLYPI	POMACES	PONDED
POLLUTIONS	POLYGONAL	POLYPIDE	POMADE	PONDER
POLLUTIVE	POLYGONIES	POLYPIDES	POMADED	PONDERED
POLLYWOG	POLYGONS	POLYPLOID	POMADES	PONDERER
POLLYWOGS	POLYGONUM	POLYPLOIDS	POMADING	PONDERERS
POLO	POLYGONUMS	POLYPNEA	POMANDER	PONDERING
POLOIST	POLYGONY	POLYPNEAS	POMANDERS	PONDEROSA
POLOISTS	POLYGRAPH	POLYPNEIC	POMATUM	PONDEROSAS
POLONAISE	POLYGRAPHED	POLYPOD	POMATUMS	PONDEROUS
POLONAISES	POLYGRAPHING	POLYPODIES	POME	PONDERS
POLONIUM	POLYGRAPHS	POLYPODS	POMELO	PONDING
POLONIUMS	POLYGYNIES	POLYPODY	POMELOS	PONDS
POLOS	POLYGYNY	POLYPOID	POMES	PONDWEED
POLS	POLYHEDRA	POLYPORE	POMFRET	PONDWEEDS
POLTROON	POLYHEDRON	POLYPORES	POMFRETS	PONE
POLTROONS	POLYHEDRONS	POLYPOUS	POMMEE	PONENT
POLY	POLYIMIDE	POLYPS	POMMEL	PONES
POLYAMIDE	POLYIMIDES	POLYPTYCH	POMMELED	PONG
POLYAMIDES	POLYMATH	POLYPTYCHS	POMMELING	PONGED
POLYAMINE	POLYMATHIES	POLYPUS	POMMELLED	PONGEE
POLYAMINES	POLYMATHS	POLYPUSES	POMMELLING	PONGEES
POLYANDRIES	POLYMATHY	POLYS	POMMELS	PONGID
POLYANDRY	POLYMER	POLYSEMIC	POMMIE	PONGIDS
POLYANTHA	POLYMERIC	POLYSEMIES	POMMIES	PONGING
POLYANTHAS	POLYMERS	POLYSEMY	POMMY	PONGS
POLYANTHI	POLYMORPH	POLYSOME	POMO	PONIARD
POLYANTHUS	POLYMORPHS	POLYSOMES	POMOLOGIES	PONIARDED
POLYANTHUSES	POLYMYXIN	POLYSOMIC	POMOLOGY	PONIARDING
POLYBASIC	POLYMYXINS	POLYSOMICS	POMOS	PONIARDS
POLYBRID	POLYNYA	POLYTENE	POMP	PONIED
POLYBRIDS	POLYNYAS	POLYTENIES	POMPADOUR	PONIES
POLYCARPIES	POLYNYI	POLYTENY	POMPADOURS	PONS
POLYCARPY	POLYOL	POLYTHENE	POMPANO	PONTES
POLYCHETE	POLYOLS	POLYTHENES	POMPANOS	PONTIFEX
POLYCHETES	POLYOMA	POLYTONAL	POMPOM	PONTIFF
POLYCOT	POLYOMAS	POLYTYPE	POMPOMS	PONTIFFS
POLYCOTS	POLYONYMIES	POLYTYPES	POMPON	PONTIFIC
POLYENE	POLYONYMY	POLYTYPIC	POMPONS	PONTIFICES
POLYENES	POLYP	POLYURIA	POMPOSITIES	PONTIL
POLYENIC	POLYPARIA	POLYURIAS	POMPOSITY	PONTILS
POLYESTER	POLYPARIES	POLYURIC	POMPOUS	PONTINE
POLYESTERS	POLYPARIUM	POLYVINYL	POMPOUSLY	PONTON
POLYGALA	POLYPARY	POLYWATER	POMPS	PONTONIER
POLYGALAS	POLYPED	POLYWATERS	POMS	PONTONIERS
POLYGAMIC	POLYPEDS	POLYZOAN	PONCE	PONTONS
POLYGAMIES	POLYPHAGIES	POLYZOANS	PONCED	PONTOON
POLYGAMY	POLYPHAGY	POLYZOARIES	PONCES	PONTOONS
POLYGENE	POLYPHASE	POLYZOARY	PONCHO	PONY

PONYING	POORISH	POPPIED	PORISM	PORTABLY
PONYTAIL	POORLY	POPPIES	PORISMS	PORTAGE
PONYTAILS	POORMOUTH	POPPING	PORK	PORTAGED
POO	POORMOUTHED	POPPLE	PORKED	PORTAGES
POOCH	POORMOUTHING	POPPLED	PORKER	PORTAGING
POOCHED	POORMOUTHS	POPPLES	PORKERS	PORTAL
POOCHES	POORNESS	POPPLING	PORKIER	PORTALED
POOCHING	POORNESSES	POPPY	PORKIES	PORTALS
POOD	POORTITH	POPPYCOCK	PORKIEST	PORTANCE
POODLE	POORTITHS	POPPYCOCKS	PORKINESS	PORTANCES
POODLES	POOS	POPPYHEAD	PORKINESSES	PORTAPACK
POODS	POOVE	POPPYHEADS	PORKING	PORTAPACKS
POOED	POOVES	POPS	PORKPIE	PORTAPAK
POOF	POP	POPSICLE	PORKPIES	PORTAPAKS
POOFS	POPCORN	POPSICLES	PORKS	PORTATIVE
POOFTAH	POPCORNS	POPSIE	PORKWOOD	PORTED
POOFTAHS	POPE	POPSIES	PORKWOODS	PORTEND
POOFTER	POPEDOM	POPSY	PORKY	PORTENDED
POOFTERS	POPEDOMS	POPULACE	PORN	PORTENDING
POOFY	POPELESS	POPULACES	PORNIER	PORTENDS
POOH	POPELIKE	POPULAR	PORNIEST	PORTENT
POOHED	POPERIES	POPULARLY	PORNO	PORTENTS
POOHING	POPERY	POPULATE	PORNOS	PORTER
POOHS	POPES	POPULATED	PORNS	PORTERAGE
POOING	POPEYED	POPULATES	PORNY	PORTERAGES
POOL	POPGUN	POPULATING	POROMERIC	PORTERED
POOLED	POPGUNS	POPULISM	POROMERICS	PORTERESS
POOLER	POPINJAY	POPULISMS	POROSE	PORTERESSES
POOLERS	POPINJAYS	POPULIST	POROSITIES	PORTERING
POOLHALL	POPISH	POPULISTS	POROSITY	PORTERS
POOLHALLS	POPISHLY	POPULOUS	POROUS	PORTFOLIO
POOLING	POPLAR	PORBEAGLE	POROUSLY	PORTFOLIOS
POOLROOM	POPLARS	PORBEAGLES	PORPHYRIA	PORTHOLE
POOLROOMS	POPLIN	PORCELAIN	PORPHYRIAS	PORTHOLES
POOLS	POPLINS	PORCELAINS	PORPHYRIC	PORTICO
POOLSIDE	POPLITEAL	PORCH	PORPHYRIES	PORTICOED
POOLSIDES	POPLITEI	PORCHES	PORPHYRIN	PORTICOES
POON	POPLITEUS	PORCINE	PORPHYRINS	PORTICOS
POONS	POPLITIC	PORCINI	PORPHYRY	PORTIERE
POONTANG	POPOVER	PORCINIS	PORPOISE	PORTIERES
POONTANGS	POPOVERS	PORCINO	PORPOISED	PORTING
POOP	POPPA	PORCUPINE	PORPOISES	PORTION
POOPED	POPPADOM	PORCUPINES	PORPOISING	PORTIONED
POOPING	POPPADOMS	PORE	PORRECT	PORTIONER
POOPS	POPPADUM	PORED	PORRIDGE	PORTIONERS
POOR	POPPADUMS	PORES	PORRIDGES	PORTIONING
POORER	POPPAS	PORGIES	PORRIDGY	PORTIONS
POOREST	POPPED	PORGY	PORRINGER	PORTLESS
POORHOUSE	POPPER	PORIFERAL	PORRINGERS	PORTLIER
POORHOUSES	POPPERS	PORIFERAN	PORT	PORTLIEST
POORI	POPPET	PORIFERANS	PORTABLE	PORTLY
POORIS	POPPETS	PORING	PORTABLES	PORTRAIT

PORTRAITS	POSOLOGY	POSTEEN	POSTNASAL	POTABLES
PORTRAY	POSSE	POSTEENS	POSTNATAL	POTAGE
PORTRAYAL	POSSES	POSTER	POSTOP	POTAGES
PORTRAYALS	POSSESS	POSTERIOR	POSTOPS	POTAMIC
PORTRAYED	POSSESSED	POSTERIORS	POSTORAL	POTASH
PORTRAYER	POSSESSES	POSTERITIES	POSTPAID	POTASHES
PORTRAYERS	POSSESSING	POSTERITY	POSTPONE	POTASSIC
PORTRAYING	POSSESSOR	POSTERN	POSTPONED	POTASSIUM
PORTRAYS	POSSESSORS	POSTERNS	POSTPONER	POTASSIUMS
PORTRESS	POSSET	POSTERS	POSTPONERS	POTATION
PORTRESSES	POSSETS	POSTFACE	POSTPONES	POTATIONS
PORTS	POSSIBLE	POSTFACES	POSTPONING	POTATO
PORTSIDE	POSSIBLER	POSTFAULT	POSTPOSE	POTATOBUG
PORTULACA	POSSIBLEST	POSTFIRE	POSTPOSED	POTATOBUGS
PORTULACAS	POSSIBLY	POSTFIX	POSTPOSES	POTATOES
POSABLE	POSSUM	POSTFIXAL	POSTPOSING	POTATORY
POSADA	POSSUMS	POSTFIXED	POSTPUNK	POTBELLIES
POSADAS	POST	POSTFIXES	POSTRACE	POTBELLY
POSE	POSTAGE	POSTFIXING	POSTRIDER	POTBOIL
POSED	POSTAGES	POSTFORM	POSTRIDERS	POTBOILED
POSER	POSTAL	POSTFORMED	POSTRIOT	POTBOILER
POSERS	POSTALLY	POSTFORMING	POSTS	POTBOILERS
POSES	POSTALS	POSTFORMS	POSTSHOW	POTBOILING
POSEUR	POSTANAL	POSTGAME	POSTSYNC	POTBOILS
POSEURS	POSTAXIAL	POSTGRAD	POSTSYNCED	POTBOUND
POSH	POSTBAG	POSTGRADS	POSTSYNCING	POTBOY
POSHER	POSTBAGS	POSTHASTE	POSTSYNCS	POTBOYS
POSHEST	POSTBASE	POSTHASTES	POSTTAX	POTEEN
POSHLY	POSTBOX	POSTHEAT	POSTTEEN	POTEENS
POSHNESS	POSTBOXES	POSTHEATS	POSTTEENS	POTENCE
POSHNESSES	POSTBOY	POSTHOLE	POSTTEST	POTENCES
POSIES	POSTBOYS	POSTHOLES	POSTTESTS	POTENCIES
POSING	POSTBURN	POSTICHE	POSTTRIAL	POTENCY
POSINGLY	POSTCARD	POSTICHES	POSTULANT	POTENT
POSIT	POSTCARDS	POSTIE	POSTULANTS	POTENTATE
POSITED	POSTCAVA	POSTIES	POSTULATE	POTENTATES
POSITING	POSTCAVAE	POSTILION	POSTULATED	POTENTIAL
POSITION	POSTCAVAL	POSTILIONS	POSTULATES	POTENTIALS
POSITIONED	POSTCAVAS	POSTIN	POSTULATING	POTENTLY
POSITIONING	POSTCODE	POSTING	POSTURAL	POTFUL
POSITIONS	POSTCODES	POSTINGS	POSTURE	POTFULS
POSITIVE	POSTCOUP	POSTINS	POSTURED	POTHEAD
POSITIVER	POSTCRASH	POSTIQUE	POSTURER	POTHEADS
POSITIVES	POSTDATE	POSTIQUES	POSTURERS	POTHEEN
POSITIVEST	POSTDATED	POSTLUDE	POSTURES	POTHEENS
POSITRON	POSTDATES	POSTLUDES	POSTURING	POTHER
POSITRONS	POSTDATING	POSTMAN	POSTURIST	POTHERB
POSITS	POSTDIVE	POSTMARK	POSTURISTS	POTHERBS
POSOLE	POSTDOC	POSTMARKED	POSTWAR	POTHERED
POSOLES	POSTDOCS	POSTMARKING	POSY	POTHERING
POSOLOGIC	POSTDRUG	POSTMARKS	POT	POTHERS
POSOLOGIES	POSTED	POSTMEN	POTABLE	POTHOLDER

POTHOLDERS
POTHOLE
POTHOLED
POTHOLES
POTHOOK
POTHOOKS
POTHOS
POTHOUSE
POTHOUSES
POTHUNTER
POTHUNTERS
POTICHE
POTICHES
POTION
POTIONS
POTLACH
POTLACHE
POTLACHES
POTLATCH
POTLATCHED
POTLATCHES
POTLATCHING
POTLIKE
POTLINE
POTLINES
POTLUCK
POTLUCKS
POTMAN
POTMEN
POTOMETER
POTOMETERS
POTPIE
POTPIES
POTPOURRI
POTPOURRIS
POTS
POTSHARD
POTSHARDS
POTSHERD
POTSHERDS
POTSHOT
POTSHOTS
POTSHOTTING
POTSIE
POTSIES
POTSTONE
POTSTONES
POTSY
POTTAGE
POTTAGES
POTTED
POTTEEN

POTTEENS
POTTER
POTTERED
POTTERER
POTTERERS
POTTERIES
POTTERING
POTTERS
POTTERY
POTTIER
POTTIES
POTTIEST
POTTINESS
POTTINESSES
POTTING
POTTLE
POTTLES
POTTO
POTTOS
POTTY
POTZER
POTZERS
POUCH
POUCHED
POUCHES
POUCHIER
POUCHIEST
POUCHING
POUCHY
POUF
POUFED
POUFF
POUFFE
POUFFED
POUFFES
POUFFS
POUFFY
POUFS
POULARD
POULARDE
POULARDES
POULARDS
POULT
POULTER
POULTERER
POULTERERS
POULTERS
POULTICE
POULTICED
POULTICES
POULTICING
POULTRIES

POULTRY
POULTS
POUNCE
POUNCED
POUNCER
POUNCERS
POUNCES
POUNCING
POUND
POUNDAGE
POUNDAGES
POUNDAL
POUNDALS
POUNDCAKE
POUNDCAKES
POUNDED
POUNDER
POUNDERS
POUNDING
POUNDS
POUR
POURABLE
POURBOIRE
POURBOIRES
POURED
POURER
POURERS
POURING
POURINGLY
POURPOINT
POURPOINTS
POURS
POUSSETTE
POUSSETTED
POUSSETTES
POUSSETTING
POUSSIE
POUSSIES
POUT
POUTED
POUTER
POUTERS
POUTFUL
POUTIER
POUTIEST
POUTINE
POUTINES
POUTING
POUTINGLY
POUTS
POUTY
POVERTIES

POVERTY
POW
POWDER
POWDERED
POWDERER
POWDERERS
POWDERING
POWDERS
POWDERY
POWER
POWERBOAT
POWERBOATS
POWERED
POWERFUL
POWERING
POWERLESS
POWERS
POWS
POWTER
POWTERS
POWWOW
POWWOWED
POWWOWING
POWWOWS
POX
POXED
POXES
POXIER
POXIEST
POXING
POXVIRUS
POXVIRUSES
POXY
POYOU
POYOUS
POZOLE
POZOLES
POZZOLAN
POZZOLANA
POZZOLANAS
POZZOLANS
PRAAM
PRAAMS
PRACTIC
PRACTICAL
PRACTICALS
PRACTICE
PRACTICED
PRACTICER
PRACTICERS
PRACTICES
PRACTICING

PRACTICUM
PRACTICUMS
PRACTISE
PRACTISED
PRACTISES
PRACTISING
PRAECIPE
PRAECIPES
PRAEDIAL
PRAEFECT
PRAEFECTS
PRAELECT
PRAELECTED
PRAELECTING
PRAELECTS
PRAENOMEN
PRAENOMENS
PRAENOMINA
PRAESIDIA
PRAESIDIUM
PRAESIDIUMS
PRAETOR
PRAETORS
PRAGMATIC
PRAGMATICS
PRAHU
PRAHUS
PRAIRIE
PRAIRIES
PRAISE
PRAISED
PRAISER
PRAISERS
PRAISES
PRAISING
PRAJNA
PRAJNAS
PRALINE
PRALINES
PRAM
PRAMS
PRANCE
PRANCED
PRANCER
PRANCERS
PRANCES
PRANCING
PRANDIAL
PRANG
PRANGED
PRANGING
PRANGS

PRANK	PREACCUSE	PREAMP	PREBIOTIC	PRECEDES
PRANKED	PREACCUSED	PREAMPS	PREBIRTH	PRECEDING
PRANKING	PREACCUSES	PREANAL	PREBIRTHS	PRECENSOR
PRANKISH	PREACCUSING	PREAPPLIED	PREBLESS	PRECENSORED
PRANKS	PREACH	PREAPPLIES	PREBLESSED	PRECENSORING
PRANKSTER	PREACHED	PREAPPLY	PREBLESSES	PRECENSORS
PRANKSTERS	PREACHER	PREAPPLYING	PREBLESSING	PRECENT
PRAO	PREACHERS	PREARM	PREBOARD	PRECENTED
PRAOS	PREACHES	PREARMED	PREBOARDED	PRECENTING
PRASE	PREACHIER	PREARMING	PREBOARDING	PRECENTOR
PRASES	PREACHIEST	PREARMS	PREBOARDS	PRECENTORS
PRAT	PREACHIFIED	PREASSIGN	PREBOIL	PRECENTS
PRATE	PREACHIFIES	PREASSIGNED	PREBOILED	PRECEPT
PRATED	PREACHIFY	PREASSIGNING	PREBOILING	PRECEPTOR
PRATER	PREACHIFYING	PREASSIGNS	PREBOILS	PRECEPTORS
PRATERS	PREACHILY	PREASSURE	PREBOOK	PRECEPTS
PRATES	PREACHING	PREASSURED	PREBOOKED	PRECESS
PRATFALL	PREACHY	PREASSURES	PREBOOKING	PRECESSED
PRATFALLS	PREACT	PREASSURING	PREBOOKS	PRECESSES
PRATING	PREACTED	PREATOMIC	PREBOOM	PRECESSING
PRATINGLY	PREACTING	PREATTUNE	PREBOUGHT	PRECHARGE
PRATIQUE	PREACTS	PREATTUNED	PREBOUND	PRECHARGED
PRATIQUES	PREADAPT	PREATTUNES	PREBUDGET	PRECHARGES
PRATS	PREADAPTED	PREATTUNING	PREBUDGETS	PRECHARGING
PRATTLE	PREADAPTING	PREAUDIT	PREBUILD	PRECHECK
PRATTLED	PREADAPTS	PREAUDITS	PREBUILDING	PRECHECKED
PRATTLER	PREADJUST	PREAVER	PREBUILDS	PRECHECKING
PRATTLERS	PREADJUSTED	PREAVERRED	PREBUILT	PRECHECKS
PRATTLES	PREADJUSTING	PREAVERRING	PREBUY	PRECHILL
PRATTLING	PREADJUSTS	PREAVERS	PREBUYING	PRECHILLED
PRAU	PREADMIT	PREAXIAL	PREBUYS	PRECHILLING
PRAUS	PREADMITS	PREBADE	PRECANCEL	PRECHILLS
PRAWN	PREADMITTED	PREBAKE	PRECANCELED	PRECHOOSE
PRAWNED	PREADMITTING	PREBAKED	PRECANCELING	PRECHOOSES
PRAWNER	PREADOPT	PREBAKES	PRECANCELLED	PRECHOOSING
PRAWNERS	PREADOPTED	PREBAKING	PRECANCELLING	PRECHOSE
PRAWNING	PREADOPTING	PREBASAL	PRECANCELS	PRECHOSEN
PRAWNS	PREADOPTS	PREBATTLE	PRECANCER	PRECIEUSE
PRAXES	PREADULT	PREBEND	PRECANCERS	PRECIEUX
PRAXIS	PREADULTS	PREBENDAL	PRECAST	PRECINCT
PRAXISES	PREAGED	PREBENDS	PRECASTING	PRECINCTS
PRAY	PREALLOT	PREBID	PRECASTS	PRECIOUS
PRAYED	PREALLOTS	PREBIDDEN	PRECATIVE	PRECIOUSES
PRAYER	PREALLOTTED	PREBIDDING	PRECATORY	PRECIPE
PRAYERFUL	PREALLOTTING	PREBIDS	PRECAUDAL	PRECIPES
PRAYERS	PREALTER	PREBILL	PRECAVA	PRECIPICE
PRAYING	PREALTERED	PREBILLED	PRECAVAE	PRECIPICES
PRAYS	PREALTERING	PREBILLING	PRECAVAL	PRECIS
PREABSORB	PREALTERS	PREBILLS	PRECEDE	PRECISE
PREABSORBED	PREAMBLE	PREBIND	PRECEDED	PRECISED
PREABSORBING	PREAMBLED	PREBINDING	PRECEDENT	PRECISELY
PREABSORBS	PREAMBLES	PREBINDS	PRECEDENTS	PRECISER

PRECISES	PRECURING	PREDINNERS	PREEXEMPTED	PREFIXED
PRECISEST	PRECURSOR	PREDIVE	PREEXEMPTING	PREFIXES
PRECISIAN	PRECURSORS	PREDRAFT	PREEXEMPTS	PREFIXING
PRECISIANS	PRECUT	PREDRIED	PREEXILIC	PREFIXION
PRECISING	PRECUTS	PREDRIES	PREEXIST	PREFIXIONS
PRECISION	PRECUTTING	PREDRILL	PREEXISTED	PREFLAME
PRECISIONS	PREDACITIES	PREDRILLED	PREEXISTING	PREFLIGHT
PRECITED	PREDACITY	PREDRILLING	PREEXISTS	PREFLIGHTED
PRECLEAN	PREDATE	PREDRILLS	PREEXPOSE	PREFLIGHTING
PRECLEANED	PREDATED	PREDRY	PREEXPOSED	PREFLIGHTS
PRECLEANING	PREDATES	PREDRYING	PREEXPOSES	PREFOCUS
PRECLEANS	PREDATING	PREDUSK	PREEXPOSING	PREFOCUSED
PRECLEAR	PREDATION	PREDUSKS	PREFAB	PREFOCUSES
PRECLEARED	PREDATIONS	PREE	PREFABBED	PREFOCUSING
PRECLEARING	PREDATISM	PREED	PREFABBING	PREFOCUSSED
PRECLEARS	PREDATISMS	PREEDIT	PREFABS	PREFOCUSSES
PRECLUDE	PREDATOR	PREEDITED	PREFACE	PREFOCUSSING
PRECLUDED	PREDATORS	PREEDITING	PREFACED	PREFORM
PRECLUDES	PREDATORY	PREEDITS	PREFACER	PREFORMAT
PRECLUDING	PREDAWN	PREEING	PREFACERS	PREFORMATS
PRECOCIAL	PREDAWNS	PREELECT	PREFACES	PREFORMATTED
PRECOCITIES	PREDEATH	PREELECTED	PREFACING	PREFORMATTING
PRECOCITY	PREDEATHS	PREELECTING	PREFADE	PREFORMED
PRECODE	PREDEBATE	PREELECTS	PREFADED	PREFORMING
PRECODED	PREDEDUCT	PREEMIE	PREFADES	PREFORMS
PRECODES	PREDEDUCTED	PREEMIES	PREFADING	PREFRANK
PRECODING	PREDEDUCTING	PREEMPT	PREFATORY	PREFRANKED
PRECOITAL	PREDEDUCTS	PREEMPTED	PREFECT	PREFRANKING
PRECONIZE	PREDEFINE	PREEMPTING	PREFECTS	PREFRANKS
PRECONIZED	PREDEFINED	PREEMPTOR	PREFER	PREFREEZE
PRECONIZES	PREDEFINES	PREEMPTORS	PREFERRED	PREFREEZES
PRECONIZING	PREDEFINING	PREEMPTS	PREFERRER	PREFREEZING
PRECOOK	PREDELLA	PREEN	PREFERRERS	PREFROZE
PRECOOKED	PREDELLAS	PREENACT	PREFERRING	PREFROZEN
PRECOOKER	PREDIAL	PREENACTED	PREFERS	PREFUND
PRECOOKERS	PREDICANT	PREENACTING	PREFEUDAL	PREFUNDED
PRECOOKING	PREDICANTS	PREENACTS	PREFIGHT	PREFUNDING
PRECOOKS	PREDICATE	PREENED	PREFIGURE	PREFUNDS
PRECOOL	PREDICATED	PREENER	PREFIGURED	PREGAME
PRECOOLED	PREDICATES	PREENERS	PREFIGURES	PREGAMES
PRECOOLING	PREDICATING	PREENING	PREFIGURING	PREGGERS
PRECOOLS	PREDICT	PREENS	PREFILE	PREGNABLE
PRECOUP	PREDICTED	PREERECT	PREFILED	PREGNANCIES
PRECRASH	PREDICTING	PREERECTED	PREFILES	PREGNANCY
PRECREASE	PREDICTOR	PREERECTING	PREFILING	PREGNANT
PRECREASED	PREDICTORS	PREERECTS	PREFILLED	PREGROWTH
PRECREASES	PREDICTS	PREES	PREFIRE	PREGROWTHS
PRECREASING	PREDIGEST	PREEXCITE	PREFIRED	PREGUIDE
PRECRISIS	PREDIGESTED	PREEXCITED	PREFIRES	PREGUIDED
PRECURE	PREDIGESTING	PREEXCITES	PREFIRING	PREGUIDES
PRECURED	PREDIGESTS	PREEXCITING	PREFIX	PREGUIDING
PRECURES	PREDINNER	PREEXEMPT	PREFIXAL	PREHANDLE

PREHANDLED
PREHANDLES
PREHANDLING
PREHARDEN
PREHARDENED
PREHARDENING
PREHARDENS
PREHEAT
PREHEATED
PREHEATER
PREHEATERS
PREHEATING
PREHEATS
PREHIRING
PREHUMAN
PREHUMANS
PREIMPOSE
PREIMPOSED
PREIMPOSES
PREIMPOSING
PREINFORM
PREINFORMED
PREINFORMING
PREINFORMS
PREINSERT
PREINSERTED
PREINSERTING
PREINSERTS
PREINVITE
PREINVITED
PREINVITES
PREINVITING
PREJUDGE
PREJUDGED
PREJUDGER
PREJUDGERS
PREJUDGES
PREJUDGING
PREJUDICE
PREJUDICED
PREJUDICES
PREJUDICING
PRELACIES
PRELACY
PRELATE
PRELATES
PRELATIC
PRELATISM
PRELATISMS
PRELATURE
PRELATURES
PRELAUNCH

PRELAUNCHED
PRELAUNCHES
PRELAUNCHING
PRELAW
PRELECT
PRELECTED
PRELECTING
PRELECTOR
PRELECTORS
PRELECTS
PRELEGAL
PRELIFE
PRELIM
PRELIMIT
PRELIMITED
PRELIMITING
PRELIMITS
PRELIMS
PRELIVES
PRELOAD
PRELOADED
PRELOADING
PRELOADS
PRELOCATE
PRELOCATED
PRELOCATES
PRELOCATING
PRELUDE
PRELUDED
PRELUDER
PRELUDERS
PRELUDES
PRELUDIAL
PRELUDING
PRELUNCH
PRELUSION
PRELUSIONS
PRELUSIVE
PRELUSORY
PREMADE
PREMAN
PREMARKET
PREMARKETED
PREMARKETING
PREMARKETS
PREMATURE
PREMATURES
PREMEAL
PREMED
PREMEDIC
PREMEDICS
PREMEDS

PREMEET
PREMEN
PREMERGER
PREMIE
PREMIER
PREMIERE
PREMIERED
PREMIERES
PREMIERING
PREMIERS
PREMIES
PREMISE
PREMISED
PREMISES
PREMISING
PREMISS
PREMISSES
PREMIUM
PREMIUMS
PREMIX
PREMIXED
PREMIXES
PREMIXING
PREMIXT
PREMODERN
PREMODIFIED
PREMODIFIES
PREMODIFY
PREMODIFYING
PREMOLAR
PREMOLARS
PREMOLD
PREMOLDED
PREMOLDING
PREMOLDS
PREMOLT
PREMONISH
PREMONISHED
PREMONISHES
PREMONISHING
PREMORAL
PREMORSE
PREMUNE
PRENAME
PRENAMES
PRENATAL
PRENOMEN
PRENOMENS
PRENOMINA
PRENOON
PRENOTIFIED
PRENOTIFIES

PRENOTIFY
PRENOTIFYING
PRENOTION
PRENOTIONS
PRENTICE
PRENTICED
PRENTICES
PRENTICING
PRENUMBER
PRENUMBERED
PRENUMBERING
PRENUMBERS
PREOBTAIN
PREOBTAINED
PREOBTAINING
PREOBTAINS
PREOCCUPIED
PREOCCUPIES
PREOCCUPY
PREOCCUPYING
PREOP
PREOPS
PREOPTION
PREOPTIONS
PREORAL
PREORDAIN
PREORDAINED
PREORDAINING
PREORDAINS
PREORDER
PREORDERED
PREORDERING
PREORDERS
PREOWNED
PREP
PREPACK
PREPACKED
PREPACKING
PREPACKS
PREPAID
PREPARE
PREPARED
PREPARER
PREPARERS
PREPARES
PREPARING
PREPASTE
PREPASTED
PREPASTES
PREPASTING
PREPAVE
PREPAVED

PREPAVES
PREPAVING
PREPAY
PREPAYING
PREPAYS
PREPENSE
PREPILL
PREPLACE
PREPLACED
PREPLACES
PREPLACING
PREPLAN
PREPLANNED
PREPLANNING
PREPLANS
PREPLANT
PREPOTENT
PREPPED
PREPPIE
PREPPIER
PREPPIES
PREPPIEST
PREPPILY
PREPPING
PREPPY
PREPREG
PREPREGS
PREPRESS
PREPRICE
PREPRICED
PREPRICES
PREPRICING
PREPRINT
PREPRINTED
PREPRINTING
PREPRINTS
PREPS
PREPUBES
PREPUBIS
PREPUCE
PREPUCES
PREPUEBLO
PREPUNCH
PREPUNCHED
PREPUNCHES
PREPUNCHING
PREPUPA
PREPUPAE
PREPUPAL
PREPUPAS
PREPUTIAL
PREQUEL

PREQUELS	PRESE	PRESHRUNKEN	PRESSING	PRESURVEYS
PRERACE	PRESEASON	PRESIDE	PRESSINGS	PRETAPE
PRERADIO	PRESEASONS	PRESIDED	PRESSMAN	PRETAPED
PRERECORD	PRESELECT	PRESIDENT	PRESSMARK	PRETAPES
PRERECORDED	PRESELECTED	PRESIDENTS	PRESSMARKS	PRETAPING
PRERECORDING	PRESELECTING	PRESIDER	PRESSMEN	PRETASTE
PRERECORDS	PRESELECTS	PRESIDERS	PRESSOR	PRETASTED
PRERECTAL	PRESELL	PRESIDES	PRESSORS	PRETASTES
PREREFORM	PRESELLING	PRESIDIA	PRESSROOM	PRETASTING
PRERENAL	PRESELLS	PRESIDIAL	PRESSROOMS	PRETAX
PRERETURN	PRESENCE	PRESIDING	PRESSRUN	PRETEEN
PREREVIEW	PRESENCES	PRESIDIO	PRESSRUNS	PRETEENS
PRERINSE	PRESENT	PRESIDIOS	PRESSURE	PRETELL
PRERINSED	PRESENTED	PRESIDIUM	PRESSURED	PRETELLING
PRERINSES	PRESENTEE	PRESIDIUMS	PRESSURES	PRETELLS
PRERINSING	PRESENTEES	PRESIFT	PRESSURING	PRETENCE
PRERIOT	PRESENTER	PRESIFTED	PRESSWORK	PRETENCES
PREROCK	PRESENTERS	PRESIFTING	PRESSWORKS	PRETEND
PRESA	PRESENTING	PRESIFTS	PREST	PRETENDED
PRESAGE	PRESENTLY	PRESIGNAL	PRESTAMP	PRETENDER
PRESAGED	PRESENTS	PRESIGNALED	PRESTAMPED	PRETENDERS
PRESAGER	PRESERVE	PRESIGNALING	PRESTAMPING	PRETENDING
PRESAGERS	PRESERVED	PRESIGNALLED	PRESTAMPS	PRETENDS
PRESAGES	PRESERVER	PRESIGNALLING	PRESTER	PRETENSE
PRESAGING	PRESERVERS	PRESIGNALS	PRESTERNA	PRETENSES
PRESALE	PRESERVES	PRESLEEP	PRESTERNUM	PRETERIT
PRESALES	PRESERVING	PRESLICE	PRESTERS	PRETERITE
PRESBYOPE	PRESET	PRESLICED	PRESTIGE	PRETERITES
PRESBYOPES	PRESETS	PRESLICES	PRESTIGES	PRETERITS
PRESBYTER	PRESETTING	PRESLICING	PRESTO	PRETERM
PRESBYTERS	PRESETTLE	PRESOAK	PRESTORE	PRETERMIT
PRESCHOOL	PRESETTLED	PRESOAKED	PRESTORED	PRETERMITS
PRESCHOOLS	PRESETTLES	PRESOAKING	PRESTORES	PRETERMITTED
PRESCIENT	PRESETTLING	PRESOAKS	PRESTORING	PRETERMITTING
PRESCIND	PRESHAPE	PRESOLD	PRESTOS	PRETERMS
PRESCINDED	PRESHAPED	PRESOLVE	PRESTRESS	PRETEST
PRESCINDING	PRESHAPES	PRESOLVED	PRESTRESSED	PRETESTED
PRESCINDS	PRESHAPING	PRESOLVES	PRESTRESSES	PRETESTING
PRESCORE	PRESHIP	PRESOLVING	PRESTRESSING	PRETESTS
PRESCORED	PRESHIPPED	PRESONG	PRESTRIKE	PRETEXT
PRESCORES	PRESHIPPING	PRESORT	PRESTRIKES	PRETEXTED
PRESCORING	PRESHIPS	PRESORTED	PRESTS	PRETEXTING
PRESCREEN	PRESHOW	PRESORTING	PRESUME	PRETEXTS
PRESCREENED	PRESHOWED	PRESORTS	PRESUMED	PRETOLD
PRESCREENING	PRESHOWING	PRESPLIT	PRESUMER	PRETOR
PRESCREENS	PRESHOWN	PRESS	PRESUMERS	PRETORIAL
PRESCRIBE	PRESHOWS	PRESSED	PRESUMES	PRETORIAN
PRESCRIBED	PRESHRANK	PRESSER	PRESUMING	PRETORIANS
PRESCRIBES	PRESHRINK	PRESSERS	PRESUMMIT	PRETORS
PRESCRIBING	PRESHRINKING	PRESSES	PRESUMMITS	PRETRAIN
PRESCRIPT	PRESHRINKS	PRESSGANG	PRESURVEY	PRETRAINED
PRESCRIPTS	PRESHRUNK	PRESSGANGS	PRESURVEYED	PRETRAINING
			PRESURVEYING	

PRETRAINS	PREVENTING	PREWORK	PRICKLES	PRIMARILY
PRETRAVEL	PREVENTS	PREWORKED	PRICKLIER	PRIMARY
PRETREAT	PREVERB	PREWORKING	PRICKLIEST	PRIMAS
PRETREATED	PREVERBAL	PREWORKS	PRICKLING	PRIMATAL
PRETREATING	PREVERBS	PREWORN	PRICKLY	PRIMATALS
PRETREATS	PREVIABLE	PREWRAP	PRICKS	PRIMATE
PRETRIAL	PREVIEW	PREWRAPPED	PRICKY	PRIMATES
PRETRIALS	PREVIEWED	PREWRAPPING	PRICY	PRIMATIAL
PRETRIM	PREVIEWER	PREWRAPS	PRIDE	PRIMATIALS
PRETRIMMED	PREVIEWERS	PREX	PRIDED	PRIMAVERA
PRETRIMMING	PREVIEWING	PREXES	PRIDEFUL	PRIMAVERAS
PRETRIMS	PREVIEWS	PREXIES	PRIDES	PRIME
PRETTIED	PREVIOUS	PREXY	PRIDING	PRIMED
PRETTIER	PREVISE	PREY	PRIED	PRIMELY
PRETTIES	PREVISED	PREYED	PRIEDIEU	PRIMENESS
PRETTIEST	PREVISES	PREYER	PRIEDIEUS	PRIMENESSES
PRETTIFIED	PREVISING	PREYERS	PRIEDIEUX	PRIMER
PRETTIFIES	PREVISION	PREYING	PRIER	PRIMERO
PRETTIFY	PREVISIONED	PREYS	PRIERS	PRIMEROS
PRETTIFYING	PREVISIONING	PREZ	PRIES	PRIMERS
PRETTILY	PREVISIONS	PREZES	PRIEST	PRIMES
PRETTY	PREVISIT	PRIAPEAN	PRIESTED	PRIMEVAL
PRETTYING	PREVISITED	PRIAPI	PRIESTESS	PRIMI
PRETTYISH	PREVISITING	PRIAPIC	PRIESTESSES	PRIMINE
PRETYPE	PREVISITS	PRIAPISM	PRIESTING	PRIMINES
PRETYPED	PREVISOR	PRIAPISMS	PRIESTLIER	PRIMING
PRETYPES	PREVISORS	PRIAPUS	PRIESTLIEST	PRIMINGS
PRETYPING	PREVUE	PRIAPUSES	PRIESTLY	PRIMIPARA
PRETZEL	PREVUED	PRICE	PRIESTS	PRIMIPARAE
PRETZELS	PREVUES	PRICEABLE	PRIG	PRIMIPARAS
PREUNION	PREVUING	PRICED	PRIGGED	PRIMITIVE
PREUNIONS	PREWAR	PRICELESS	PRIGGERIES	PRIMITIVES
PREUNITE	PREWARM	PRICER	PRIGGERY	PRIMLY
PREUNITED	PREWARMED	PRICERS	PRIGGING	PRIMMED
PREUNITES	PREWARMING	PRICES	PRIGGISH	PRIMMER
PREUNITING	PREWARMS	PRICEY	PRIGGISM	PRIMMEST
PREVAIL	PREWARN	PRICIER	PRIGGISMS	PRIMMING
PREVAILED	PREWARNED	PRICIEST	PRIGS	PRIMNESS
PREVAILER	PREWARNING	PRICILY	PRILL	PRIMNESSES
PREVAILERS	PREWARNS	PRICING	PRILLED	PRIMO
PREVAILING	PREWASH	PRICK	PRILLING	PRIMORDIA
PREVAILS	PREWASHED	PRICKED	PRILLS	PRIMORDIUM
PREVALENT	PREWASHES	PRICKER	PRIM	PRIMOS
PREVALENTS	PREWASHING	PRICKERS	PRIMA	PRIMP
PREVALUE	PREWEIGH	PRICKET	PRIMACIES	PRIMPED
PREVALUED	PREWEIGHED	PRICKETS	PRIMACY	PRIMPING
PREVALUES	PREWEIGHING	PRICKIER	PRIMAGE	PRIMPS
PREVALUING	PREWEIGHS	PRICKIEST	PRIMAGES	PRIMROSE
PREVENT	PREWIRE	PRICKING	PRIMAL	PRIMROSES
PREVENTED	PREWIRED	PRICKINGS	PRIMALITIES	PRIMS
PREVENTER	PREWIRES	PRICKLE	PRIMALITY	PRIMSIE
PREVENTERS	PREWIRING	PRICKLED	PRIMARIES	PRIMULA

PRIMULAS
PRIMUS
PRIMUSES
PRINCE
PRINCEDOM
PRINCEDOMS
PRINCEKIN
PRINCEKINS
PRINCELET
PRINCELETS
PRINCELIER
PRINCELIEST
PRINCELY
PRINCES
PRINCESS
PRINCESSE
PRINCESSES
PRINCIPAL
PRINCIPALS
PRINCIPE
PRINCIPI
PRINCIPIA
PRINCIPIUM
PRINCIPLE
PRINCIPLES
PRINCOCK
PRINCOCKS
PRINCOX
PRINCOXES
PRINK
PRINKED
PRINKER
PRINKERS
PRINKING
PRINKS
PRINT
PRINTABLE
PRINTED
PRINTER
PRINTERIES
PRINTERS
PRINTERY
PRINTHEAD
PRINTHEADS
PRINTING
PRINTINGS
PRINTLESS
PRINTOUT
PRINTOUTS
PRINTS
PRION
PRIONS

PRIOR
PRIORATE
PRIORATES
PRIORESS
PRIORESSES
PRIORIES
PRIORITIES
PRIORITY
PRIORLY
PRIORS
PRIORSHIP
PRIORSHIPS
PRIORY
PRISE
PRISED
PRISERE
PRISERES
PRISES
PRISING
PRISM
PRISMATIC
PRISMOID
PRISMOIDS
PRISMS
PRISON
PRISONED
PRISONER
PRISONERS
PRISONING
PRISONS
PRISS
PRISSED
PRISSES
PRISSIER
PRISSIES
PRISSIEST
PRISSILY
PRISSING
PRISSY
PRISTANE
PRISTANES
PRISTINE
PRITHEE
PRIVACIES
PRIVACY
PRIVATE
PRIVATEER
PRIVATEERED
PRIVATEERING
PRIVATEERS
PRIVATELY
PRIVATER

PRIVATES
PRIVATEST
PRIVATION
PRIVATIONS
PRIVATISE
PRIVATISED
PRIVATISES
PRIVATISING
PRIVATISM
PRIVATISMS
PRIVATIST
PRIVATISTS
PRIVATIVE
PRIVATIVES
PRIVATIZE
PRIVATIZED
PRIVATIZES
PRIVATIZING
PRIVET
PRIVETS
PRIVIER
PRIVIES
PRIVIEST
PRIVILEGE
PRIVILEGED
PRIVILEGES
PRIVILEGING
PRIVILY
PRIVITIES
PRIVITY
PRIVY
PRIZE
PRIZED
PRIZER
PRIZERS
PRIZES
PRIZING
PRO
PROA
PROACTION
PROACTIONS
PROACTIVE
PROAS
PROBABLE
PROBABLES
PROBABLY
PROBAND
PROBANDS
PROBANG
PROBANGS
PROBATE
PROBATED

PROBATES
PROBATING
PROBATION
PROBATIONS
PROBATIVE
PROBATORY
PROBE
PROBED
PROBER
PROBERS
PROBES
PROBING
PROBINGLY
PROBIOTIC
PROBIOTICS
PROBIT
PROBITIES
PROBITS
PROBITY
PROBLEM
PROBLEMS
PROBOSCIDES
PROBOSCIS
PROBOSCISES
PROCAINE
PROCAINES
PROCAMBIA
PROCAMBIUM
PROCAMBIUMS
PROCARP
PROCARPS
PROCEDURE
PROCEDURES
PROCEED
PROCEEDED
PROCEEDER
PROCEEDERS
PROCEEDING
PROCEEDS
PROCESS
PROCESSED
PROCESSER
PROCESSERS
PROCESSES
PROCESSING
PROCESSOR
PROCESSORS
PROCHAIN
PROCHEIN
PROCHOICE
PROCHURCH
PROCLAIM

PROCLAIMED
PROCLAIMING
PROCLAIMS
PROCLISES
PROCLISIS
PROCLITIC
PROCLITICS
PROCONSUL
PROCONSULS
PROCREANT
PROCREATE
PROCREATED
PROCREATES
PROCREATING
PROCTITIDES
PROCTITIS
PROCTITISES
PROCTODEA
PROCTODEUM
PROCTODEUMS
PROCTOR
PROCTORED
PROCTORING
PROCTORS
PROCURAL
PROCURALS
PROCURE
PROCURED
PROCURER
PROCURERS
PROCURES
PROCURESS
PROCURESSES
PROCURING
PROD
PRODDED
PRODDER
PRODDERS
PRODDING
PRODIGAL
PRODIGALS
PRODIGIES
PRODIGY
PRODROMAL
PRODROMATA
PRODROME
PRODROMES
PRODROMIC
PRODRUG
PRODRUGS
PRODS
PRODUCE

PRODUCED	PROFITER	PROHIBITS	PROLOGUED	PROMPTING
PRODUCER	PROFITERS	PROJECT	PROLOGUES	PROMPTLY
PRODUCERS	PROFITING	PROJECTED	PROLOGUING	PROMPTS
PRODUCES	PROFITS	PROJECTING	PROLONG	PROMS
PRODUCING	PROFLUENT	PROJECTOR	PROLONGE	PROMULGE
PRODUCT	PROFORMA	PROJECTORS	PROLONGED	PROMULGED
PRODUCTS	PROFOUND	PROJECTS	PROLONGER	PROMULGES
PROEM	PROFOUNDER	PROJET	PROLONGERS	PROMULGING
PROEMIAL	PROFOUNDEST	PROJETS	PROLONGES	PRONATE
PROEMS	PROFOUNDS	PROLABOR	PROLONGING	PRONATED
PROENZYME	PROFS	PROLACTIN	PROLONGS	PRONATES
PROENZYMES	PROFUSE	PROLACTINS	PROLUSION	PRONATING
PROESTRUS	PROFUSELY	PROLAMIN	PROLUSIONS	PRONATION
PROESTRUSES	PROFUSION	PROLAMINE	PROLUSORY	PRONATIONS
PROETTE	PROFUSIONS	PROLAMINES	PROM	PRONATOR
PROETTES	PROFUSIVE	PROLAMINS	PROMENADE	PRONATORES
PROF	PROG	PROLAN	PROMENADED	PRONATORS
PROFAMILY	PROGENIES	PROLANS	PROMENADES	PRONE
PROFANE	PROGENY	PROLAPSE	PROMENADING	PRONELY
PROFANED	PROGERIA	PROLAPSED	PROMETRIC	PRONENESS
PROFANELY	PROGERIAS	PROLAPSES	PROMINE	PRONENESSES
PROFANER	PROGESTIN	PROLAPSING	PROMINENT	PRONEPHRA
PROFANERS	PROGESTINS	PROLAPSUS	PROMINES	PRONEPHROI
PROFANES	PROGGED	PROLATE	PROMISE	PRONEPHROS
PROFANING	PROGGER	PROLATELY	PROMISED	PRONG
PROFANITIES	PROGGERS	PROLE	PROMISEE	PRONGED
PROFANITY	PROGGING	PROLEG	PROMISEES	PRONGHORN
PROFESS	PROGNOSE	PROLEGS	PROMISER	PRONGHORNS
PROFESSED	PROGNOSED	PROLEPSES	PROMISERS	PRONGING
PROFESSES	PROGNOSES	PROLEPSIS	PROMISES	PRONGS
PROFESSING	PROGNOSING	PROLEPTIC	PROMISING	PRONOTA
PROFESSOR	PROGNOSIS	PROLES	PROMISOR	PRONOTUM
PROFESSORS	PROGRADE	PROLETARIES	PROMISORS	PRONOUN
PROFFER	PROGRAM	PROLETARY	PROMO	PRONOUNCE
PROFFERED	PROGRAMED	PROLIFIC	PROMODERN	PRONOUNCED
PROFFERER	PROGRAMER	PROLINE	PROMOED	PRONOUNCES
PROFFERERS	PROGRAMERS	PROLINES	PROMOING	PRONOUNCING
PROFFERING	PROGRAMING	PROLIX	PROMOS	PRONOUNS
PROFFERS	PROGRAMME	PROLIXITIES	PROMOTE	PRONTO
PROFILE	PROGRAMMED	PROLIXITY	PROMOTED	PRONUCLEI
PROFILED	PROGRAMMES	PROLIXLY	PROMOTER	PRONUCLEUS
PROFILER	PROGRAMMING	PROLOG	PROMOTERS	PRONUCLEUSES
PROFILERS	PROGRAMS	PROLOGED	PROMOTES	PROOF
PROFILES	PROGRESS	PROLOGING	PROMOTING	PROOFED
PROFILING	PROGRESSED	PROLOGIST	PROMOTION	PROOFER
PROFILINGS	PROGRESSES	PROLOGISTS	PROMOTIONS	PROOFERS
PROFIT	PROGRESSING	PROLOGIZE	PROMOTIVE	PROOFING
PROFITED	PROGS	PROLOGIZED	PROMPT	PROOFREAD
PROFITEER	PROGUN	PROLOGIZES	PROMPTED	PROOFREADING
PROFITEERED	PROHIBIT	PROLOGIZING	PROMPTER	PROOFREADS
PROFITEERING	PROHIBITED	PROLOGS	PROMPTERS	PROOFROOM
PROFITEERS	PROHIBITING	PROLOGUE	PROMPTEST	PROOFROOMS

PROOFS	PROPINED	PRORATED	PROSIMIAN	PROTEAN
PROP	PROPINES	PRORATES	PROSIMIANS	PROTEANS
PROPAGATE	PROPINING	PRORATING	PROSINESS	PROTEAS
PROPAGATED	PROPJET	PRORATION	PROSINESSES	PROTEASE
PROPAGATES	PROPJETS	PRORATIONS	PROSING	PROTEASES
PROPAGATING	PROPMAN	PROREFORM	PROSIT	PROTECT
PROPAGULE	PROPMEN	PROROGATE	PROSO	PROTECTED
PROPAGULES	PROPOLIS	PROROGATED	PROSODIC	PROTECTER
PROPANE	PROPOLISES	PROROGATES	PROSODIES	PROTECTERS
PROPANES	PROPONE	PROROGATING	PROSODIST	PROTECTING
PROPEL	PROPONED	PROROGUE	PROSODISTS	PROTECTOR
PROPELLED	PROPONENT	PROROGUED	PROSODY	PROTECTORS
PROPELLER	PROPONENTS	PROROGUES	PROSOMA	PROTECTS
PROPELLERS	PROPONES	PROROGUING	PROSOMAL	PROTEGE
PROPELLING	PROPONING	PROS	PROSOMAS	PROTEGEE
PROPELLOR	PROPOSAL	PROSAIC	PROSOMATA	PROTEGEES
PROPELLORS	PROPOSALS	PROSAICAL	PROSOS	PROTEGES
PROPELS	PROPOSE	PROSAISM	PROSPECT	PROTEI
PROPEND	PROPOSED	PROSAISMS	PROSPECTED	PROTEID
PROPENDED	PROPOSER	PROSAIST	PROSPECTING	PROTEIDE
PROPENDING	PROPOSERS	PROSAISTS	PROSPECTS	PROTEIDES
PROPENDS	PROPOSES	PROSATEUR	PROSPER	PROTEIDS
PROPENE	PROPOSING	PROSATEURS	PROSPERED	PROTEIN
PROPENES	PROPOSITI	PROSCENIA	PROSPERING	PROTEINIC
PROPENOL	PROPOSITUS	PROSCENIUM	PROSPERS	PROTEINS
PROPENOLS	PROPOUND	PROSCENIUMS	PROSS	PROTEND
PROPENSE	PROPOUNDED	PROSCRIBE	PROSSES	PROTENDED
PROPENYL	PROPOUNDING	PROSCRIBED	PROSSIE	PROTENDING
PROPER	PROPOUNDS	PROSCRIBES	PROSSIES	PROTENDS
PROPERDIN	PROPPED	PROSCRIBING	PROST	PROTEOME
PROPERDINS	PROPPING	PROSE	PROSTATE	PROTEOMES
PROPERER	PROPRETOR	PROSECT	PROSTATES	PROTEOMIC
PROPEREST	PROPRETORS	PROSECTED	PROSTATIC	PROTEOSE
PROPERLY	PROPRIA	PROSECTING	PROSTIE	PROTEOSES
PROPERS	PROPRIETIES	PROSECTOR	PROSTIES	PROTEST
PROPERTIES	PROPRIETY	PROSECTORS	PROSTOMIA	PROTESTED
PROPERTY	PROPRIUM	PROSECTS	PROSTOMIUM	PROTESTER
PROPHAGE	PROPS	PROSECUTE	PROSTRATE	PROTESTERS
PROPHAGES	PROPTOSES	PROSECUTED	PROSTRATED	PROTESTING
PROPHASE	PROPTOSIS	PROSECUTES	PROSTRATES	PROTESTOR
PROPHASES	PROPYL	PROSECUTING	PROSTRATING	PROTESTORS
PROPHASIC	PROPYLA	PROSED	PROSTYLE	PROTESTS
PROPHECIES	PROPYLAEA	PROSELYTE	PROSTYLES	PROTEUS
PROPHECY	PROPYLAEUM	PROSELYTED	PROSY	PROTEUSES
PROPHESIED	PROPYLENE	PROSELYTES	PROTAMIN	PROTHALLI
PROPHESIES	PROPYLENES	PROSELYTING	PROTAMINE	PROTHALLUS
PROPHESY	PROPYLIC	PROSER	PROTAMINES	PROTHALLUSES
PROPHESYING	PROPYLITE	PROSERS	PROTAMINS	PROTHESES
PROPHET	PROPYLITES	PROSES	PROTASES	PROTHESIS
PROPHETIC	PROPYLON	PROSIER	PROTASIS	PROTHETIC
PROPHETS	PROPYLS	PROSIEST	PROTATIC	PROTHORACES
PROPINE	PRORATE	PROSILY	PROTEA	PROTHORAX

PROTHORAXES	PROTRUDING	PROVOKED	PRUNERS	PSAMMONS
PROTIST	PROTYL	PROVOKER	PRUNES	PSCHENT
PROTISTAN	PROTYLE	PROVOKERS	PRUNING	PSCHENTS
PROTISTANS	PROTYLES	PROVOKES	PRUNUS	PSEPHITE
PROTISTIC	PROTYLS	PROVOKING	PRUNUSES	PSEPHITES
PROTISTS	PROUD	PROVOLONE	PRURIENCE	PSEPHITIC
PROTIUM	PROUDER	PROVOLONES	PRURIENCES	PSEUD
PROTIUMS	PROUDEST	PROVOST	PRURIENCIES	PSEUDO
PROTOCOL	PROUDFUL	PROVOSTS	PRURIENCY	PSEUDONYM
PROTOCOLED	PROUDLY	PROW	PRURIENT	PSEUDONYMS
PROTOCOLING	PROUDNESS	PROWAR	PRURIGO	PSEUDOPOD
PROTOCOLLED	PROUDNESSES	PROWER	PRURIGOS	PSEUDOPODS
PROTOCOLLING	PROUNION	PROWESS	PRURITIC	PSEUDOS
PROTOCOLS	PROUSTITE	PROWESSES	PRURITUS	PSEUDS
PROTODERM	PROUSTITES	PROWEST	PRURITUSES	PSHAW
PROTODERMS	PROVABLE	PROWL	PRUSSIATE	PSHAWED
PROTON	PROVABLY	PROWLED	PRUSSIATES	PSHAWING
PROTONATE	PROVE	PROWLER	PRUSSIC	PSHAWS
PROTONATED	PROVED	PROWLERS	PRUTA	PSI
PROTONATES	PROVEN	PROWLING	PRUTAH	PSILOCIN
PROTONATING	PROVENDER	PROWLS	PRUTOT	PSILOCINS
PROTONEMA	PROVENDERS	PROWS	PRUTOTH	PSILOSES
PROTONEMATA	PROVENLY	PROXEMIC	PRY	PSILOSIS
PROTONIC	PROVER	PROXEMICS	PRYER	PSILOTIC
PROTONS	PROVERB	PROXIES	PRYERS	PSIS
PROTOPOD	PROVERBED	PROXIMAL	PRYING	PSOAE
PROTOPODS	PROVERBING	PROXIMATE	PRYINGLY	PSOAI
PROTOSTAR	PROVERBS	PROXIMITIES	PRYTHEE	PSOAS
PROTOSTARS	PROVERS	PROXIMITY	PSALM	PSOATIC
PROTOTYPE	PROVES	PROXIMO	PSALMBOOK	PSOCID
PROTOTYPED	PROVIDE	PROXY	PSALMBOOKS	PSOCIDS
PROTOTYPES	PROVIDED	PRUDE	PSALMED	PSORALEA
PROTOTYPING	PROVIDENT	PRUDENCE	PSALMIC	PSORALEAS
PROTOXID	PROVIDER	PRUDENCES	PSALMING	PSORALEN
PROTOXIDE	PROVIDERS	PRUDENT	PSALMIST	PSORALENS
PROTOXIDES	PROVIDES	PRUDENTLY	PSALMISTS	PSORIASES
PROTOXIDS	PROVIDING	PRUDERIES	PSALMODIC	PSORIASIS
PROTOZOA	PROVINCE	PRUDERY	PSALMODIES	PSORIATIC
PROTOZOAL	PROVINCES	PRUDES	PSALMODY	PSORIATICS
PROTOZOAN	PROVING	PRUDISH	PSALMS	PSST
PROTOZOANS	PROVIRAL	PRUDISHLY	PSALTER	PST
PROTOZOIC	PROVIRUS	PRUINOSE	PSALTERIA	PSYCH
PROTOZOON	PROVIRUSES	PRUNABLE	PSALTERIES	PSYCHE
PROTOZOONS	PROVISION	PRUNE	PSALTERIUM	PSYCHED
PROTRACT	PROVISIONED	PRUNED	PSALTERS	PSYCHES
PROTRACTED	PROVISIONING	PRUNELLA	PSALTERY	PSYCHIC
PROTRACTING	PROVISIONS	PRUNELLAS	PSALTRIES	PSYCHICAL
PROTRACTS	PROVISO	PRUNELLE	PSALTRY	PSYCHICS
PROTRADE	PROVISOES	PRUNELLES	PSAMMITE	PSYCHING
PROTRUDE	PROVISORY	PRUNELLO	PSAMMITES	PSYCHO
PROTRUDED	PROVISOS	PRUNELLOS	PSAMMITIC	PSYCHOS
PROTRUDES	PROVOKE	PRUNER	PSAMMON	PSYCHOSES

PSYCHOSIS	PUBES	PUDDLERS	PUG	PULICIDE
PSYCHOTIC	PUBESCENT	PUDDLES	PUGAREE	PULICIDES
PSYCHOTICS	PUBIC	PUDDLIER	PUGAREES	PULIK
PSYCHS	PUBIS	PUDDLIEST	PUGGAREE	PULING
PSYLLA	PUBLIC	PUDDLING	PUGGAREES	PULINGLY
PSYLLAS	PUBLICAN	PUDDLINGS	PUGGED	PULINGS
PSYLLID	PUBLICANS	PUDDLY	PUGGIER	PULIS
PSYLLIDS	PUBLICISE	PUDENCIES	PUGGIEST	PULL
PSYLLIUM	PUBLICISED	PUDENCY	PUGGINESS	PULLBACK
PSYLLIUMS	PUBLICISES	PUDENDA	PUGGINESSES	PULLBACKS
PSYOPS	PUBLICISING	PUDENDAL	PUGGING	PULLED
PSYWAR	PUBLICIST	PUDENDUM	PUGGISH	PULLER
PSYWARS	PUBLICISTS	PUDGIER	PUGGREE	PULLERS
PTARMIGAN	PUBLICITIES	PUDGIEST	PUGGREES	PULLET
PTARMIGANS	PUBLICITY	PUDGILY	PUGGRIES	PULLETS
PTERIDINE	PUBLICIZE	PUDGINESS	PUGGRY	PULLEY
PTERIDINES	PUBLICIZED	PUDGINESSES	PUGGY	PULLEYS
PTERIN	PUBLICIZES	PUDGY	PUGH	PULLING
PTERINS	PUBLICIZING	PUDIBUND	PUGILISM	PULLMAN
PTEROPOD	PUBLICLY	PUDIC	PUGILISMS	PULLMANS
PTEROPODS	PUBLICS	PUDS	PUGILIST	PULLOUT
PTEROSAUR	PUBLISH	PUEBLO	PUGILISTS	PULLOUTS
PTEROSAURS	PUBLISHED	PUEBLOS	PUGMARK	PULLOVER
PTERYGIA	PUBLISHER	PUERILE	PUGMARKS	PULLOVERS
PTERYGIAL	PUBLISHERS	PUERILELY	PUGNACITIES	PULLS
PTERYGIUM	PUBLISHES	PUERILISM	PUGNACITY	PULLULATE
PTERYGIUMS	PUBLISHING	PUERILISMS	PUGREE	PULLULATED
PTERYGOID	PUBS	PUERILITIES	PUGREES	PULLULATES
PTERYGOIDS	PUCCOON	PUERILITY	PUGS	PULLULATING
PTERYLA	PUCCOONS	PUERPERA	PUISNE	PULLUP
PTERYLAE	PUCE	PUERPERAE	PUISNES	PULLUPS
PTISAN	PUCES	PUERPERAL	PUISSANCE	PULMONARY
PTISANS	PUCK	PUERPERIA	PUISSANCES	PULMONATE
PTOMAIN	PUCKA	PUERPERIUM	PUISSANT	PULMONATES
PTOMAINE	PUCKER	PUFF	PUJA	PULMONIC
PTOMAINES	PUCKERED	PUFFBALL	PUJAH	PULMOTOR
PTOMAINIC	PUCKERER	PUFFBALLS	PUJAHS	PULMOTORS
PTOMAINS	PUCKERERS	PUFFED	PUJAS	PULP
PTOOEY	PUCKERIER	PUFFER	PUKE	PULPAL
PTOSES	PUCKERIEST	PUFFERIES	PUKED	PULPALLY
PTOSIS	PUCKERING	PUFFERS	PUKES	PULPED
PTOTIC	PUCKERS	PUFFERY	PUKING	PULPER
PTUI	PUCKERY	PUFFIER	PUKKA	PULPERS
PTYALIN	PUCKISH	PUFFIEST	PUL	PULPIER
PTYALINS	PUCKISHLY	PUFFILY	PULA	PULPIEST
PTYALISM	PUCKS	PUFFIN	PULE	PULPILY
PTYALISMS	PUD	PUFFINESS	PULED	PULPINESS
PUB	PUDDING	PUFFINESSES	PULER	PULPINESSES
PUBERAL	PUDDINGS	PUFFING	PULERS	PULPING
PUBERTAL	PUDDLE	PUFFINS	PULES	PULPIT
PUBERTIES	PUDDLED	PUFFS	PULI	PULPITAL
PUBERTY	PUDDLER	PUFFY	PULICENE	PULPITS

PULPLESS	PUMELO	PUNCTUATE	PUNKIES	PUPILAR
PULPOUS	PUMELOS	PUNCTUATED	PUNKIEST	PUPILARY
PULPS	PUMICE	PUNCTUATES	PUNKIN	PUPILLAGE
PULPWOOD	PUMICED	PUNCTUATING	PUNKINESS	PUPILLAGES
PULPWOODS	PUMICEOUS	PUNCTURE	PUNKINESSES	PUPILLARY
PULPY	PUMICER	PUNCTURED	PUNKINS	PUPILS
PULQUE	PUMICERS	PUNCTURES	PUNKISH	PUPPED
PULQUES	PUMICES	PUNCTURING	PUNKS	PUPPET
PULS	PUMICING	PUNDIT	PUNKY	PUPPETEER
PULSANT	PUMICITE	PUNDITIC	PUNNED	PUPPETEERED
PULSAR	PUMICITES	PUNDITRIES	PUNNER	PUPPETEERING
PULSARS	PUMMEL	PUNDITRY	PUNNERS	PUPPETEERS
PULSATE	PUMMELED	PUNDITS	PUNNET	PUPPETRIES
PULSATED	PUMMELING	PUNG	PUNNETS	PUPPETRY
PULSATES	PUMMELLED	PUNGENCIES	PUNNIER	PUPPETS
PULSATILE	PUMMELLING	PUNGENCY	PUNNIEST	PUPPIES
PULSATING	PUMMELO	PUNGENT	PUNNING	PUPPING
PULSATION	PUMMELOS	PUNGENTLY	PUNNINGLY	PUPPY
PULSATIONS	PUMMELS	PUNGLE	PUNNY	PUPPYDOM
PULSATIVE	PUMP	PUNGLED	PUNS	PUPPYDOMS
PULSATOR	PUMPED	PUNGLES	PUNSTER	PUPPYHOOD
PULSATORS	PUMPER	PUNGLING	PUNSTERS	PUPPYHOODS
PULSATORY	PUMPERS	PUNGS	PUNT	PUPPYISH
PULSE	PUMPING	PUNIER	PUNTED	PUPPYLIKE
PULSED	PUMPKIN	PUNIEST	PUNTER	PUPS
PULSEJET	PUMPKINS	PUNILY	PUNTERS	PUPU
PULSEJETS	PUMPLESS	PUNINESS	PUNTIES	PUPUS
PULSER	PUMPLIKE	PUNINESSES	PUNTING	PUR
PULSERS	PUMPS	PUNISH	PUNTO	PURANA
PULSES	PUN	PUNISHED	PUNTOS	PURANAS
PULSING	PUNA	PUNISHER	PUNTS	PURANIC
PULSION	PUNAS	PUNISHERS	PUNTY	PURBLIND
PULSIONS	PUNCH	PUNISHES	PUNY	PURCHASE
PULSOJET	PUNCHBALL	PUNISHING	PUP	PURCHASED
PULSOJETS	PUNCHBALLS	PUNITION	PUPA	PURCHASER
PULVERISE	PUNCHED	PUNITIONS	PUPAE	PURCHASERS
PULVERISED	PUNCHEON	PUNITIVE	PUPAL	PURCHASES
PULVERISES	PUNCHEONS	PUNITORY	PUPARIA	PURCHASING
PULVERISING	PUNCHER	PUNJI	PUPARIAL	PURDA
PULVERIZE	PUNCHERS	PUNJIS	PUPARIUM	PURDAH
PULVERIZED	PUNCHES	PUNK	PUPAS	PURDAHS
PULVERIZES	PUNCHIER	PUNKA	PUPATE	PURDAS
PULVERIZING	PUNCHIEST	PUNKAH	PUPATED	PURE
PULVILLAR	PUNCHILY	PUNKAHS	PUPATES	PUREBLOOD
PULVILLI	PUNCHING	PUNKAS	PUPATING	PUREBLOODS
PULVILLUS	PUNCHLESS	PUNKER	PUPATION	PUREBRED
PULVINAR	PUNCHY	PUNKERS	PUPATIONS	PUREBREDS
PULVINATE	PUNCTATE	PUNKEST	PUPFISH	PUREE
PULVINI	PUNCTATED	PUNKEY	PUPFISHES	PUREED
PULVINUS	PUNCTILIO	PUNKEYS	PUPIL	PUREEING
PUMA	PUNCTILIOS	PUNKIE	PUPILAGE	PUREES
PUMAS	PUNCTUAL	PUNKIER	PUPILAGES	PURELY

PURENESS	PURLINE	PURSIEST	PUSHIER	PUTDOWN
PURENESSES	PURLINES	PURSILY	PUSHIEST	PUTDOWNS
PURER	PURLING	PURSINESS	PUSHILY	PUTLOG
PUREST	PURLINGS	PURSINESSES	PUSHINESS	PUTLOGS
PURFLE	PURLINS	PURSING	PUSHINESSES	PUTOFF
PURFLED	PURLOIN	PURSLANE	PUSHING	PUTOFFS
PURFLER	PURLOINED	PURSLANES	PUSHINGLY	PUTON
PURFLERS	PURLOINER	PURSUABLE	PUSHOVER	PUTONGHUA
PURFLES	PURLOINERS	PURSUANCE	PUSHOVERS	PUTONGHUAS
PURFLING	PURLOINING	PURSUANCES	PUSHPIN	PUTONS
PURFLINGS	PURLOINS	PURSUANT	PUSHPINS	PUTOUT
PURGATION	PURLS	PURSUE	PUSHROD	PUTOUTS
PURGATIONS	PUROMYCIN	PURSUED	PUSHRODS	PUTREFIED
PURGATIVE	PUROMYCINS	PURSUER	PUSHUP	PUTREFIER
PURGATIVES	PURPLE	PURSUERS	PUSHUPS	PUTREFIERS
PURGATORIES	PURPLED	PURSUES	PUSHY	PUTREFIES
PURGATORY	PURPLER	PURSUING	PUSLEY	PUTREFY
PURGE	PURPLES	PURSUIT	PUSLEYS	PUTREFYING
PURGEABLE	PURPLEST	PURSUITS	PUSLIKE	PUTRID
PURGED	PURPLING	PURSY	PUSS	PUTRIDITIES
PURGER	PURPLISH	PURTIER	PUSSES	PUTRIDITY
PURGERS	PURPLY	PURTIEST	PUSSIER	PUTRIDLY
PURGES	PURPORT	PURTY	PUSSIES	PUTS
PURGING	PURPORTED	PURULENCE	PUSSIEST	PUTSCH
PURGINGS	PURPORTING	PURULENCES	PUSSLEY	PUTSCHES
PURI	PURPORTS	PURULENCIES	PUSSLEYS	PUTSCHIST
PURIFIED	PURPOSE	PURULENCY	PUSSLIES	PUTSCHISTS
PURIFIER	PURPOSED	PURULENT	PUSSLIKE	PUTT
PURIFIERS	PURPOSELY	PURVEY	PUSSLY	PUTTED
PURIFIES	PURPOSES	PURVEYED	PUSSY	PUTTEE
PURIFY	PURPOSING	PURVEYING	PUSSYCAT	PUTTEES
PURIFYING	PURPOSIVE	PURVEYOR	PUSSYCATS	PUTTER
PURIN	PURPURA	PURVEYORS	PUSSYFOOT	PUTTERED
PURINE	PURPURAS	PURVEYS	PUSSYFOOTED	PUTTERER
PURINES	PURPURE	PURVIEW	PUSSYFOOTING	PUTTERERS
PURINS	PURPURES	PURVIEWS	PUSSYFOOTS	PUTTERING
PURIS	PURPURIC	PUS	PUSSYTOES	PUTTERS
PURISM	PURPURIN	PUSES	PUSTULANT	PUTTI
PURISMS	PURPURINS	PUSH	PUSTULANTS	PUTTIE
PURIST	PURR	PUSHBALL	PUSTULAR	PUTTIED
PURISTIC	PURRED	PUSHBALLS	PUSTULATE	PUTTIER
PURISTS	PURRING	PUSHCART	PUSTULATED	PUTTIERS
PURITAN	PURRINGLY	PUSHCARTS	PUSTULATES	PUTTIES
PURITANIC	PURRS	PUSHCHAIR	PUSTULATING	PUTTING
PURITANS	PURS	PUSHCHAIRS	PUSTULE	PUTTO
PURITIES	PURSE	PUSHDOWN	PUSTULED	PUTTS
PURITY	PURSED	PUSHDOWNS	PUSTULES	PUTTY
PURL	PURSELIKE	PUSHED	PUSTULOUS	PUTTYING
PURLED	PURSER	PUSHER	PUT	PUTTYLESS
PURLIEU	PURSERS	PUSHERS	PUTAMEN	PUTTYLIKE
PURLIEUS	PURSES	PUSHES	PUTAMINA	PUTTYROOT
PURLIN	PURSIER	PUSHFUL	PUTATIVE	PUTTYROOTS

PUTZ	PYKNOTIC	PYRIDIC	PYROSISES	QINDARS
PUTZED	PYLON	PYRIDINE	PYROSTAT	QINTAR
PUTZES	PYLONS	PYRIDINES	PYROSTATS	QINTARS
PUTZING	PYLORI	PYRIDOXAL	PYROXENE	QIS
PUZZLE	PYLORIC	PYRIDOXALS	PYROXENES	QIVIUT
PUZZLED	PYLORUS	PYRIDOXIN	PYROXENIC	QIVIUTS
PUZZLEDLY	PYLORUSES	PYRIDOXINS	PYROXYLIN	QOPH
PUZZLER	PYODERMA	PYRIFORM	PYROXYLINS	QOPHS
PUZZLERS	PYODERMAS	PYRITE	PYRRHIC	QUA
PUZZLES	PYODERMIC	PYRITES	PYRRHICS	QUAALUDE
PUZZLING	PYOGENIC	PYRITIC	PYRROL	QUAALUDES
PYA	PYOID	PYRITICAL	PYRROLE	QUACK
PYAEMIA	PYORRHEA	PYRITOUS	PYRROLES	QUACKED
PYAEMIAS	PYORRHEAL	PYRO	PYRROLIC	QUACKERIES
PYAEMIC	PYORRHEAS	PYROCERAM	PYRROLS	QUACKERY
PYAS	PYORRHOEA	PYROCERAMS	PYRUVATE	QUACKIER
PYCNIDIA	PYORRHOEAS	PYROGEN	PYRUVATES	QUACKIEST
PYCNIDIAL	PYOSES	PYROGENIC	PYTHON	QUACKING
PYCNIDIUM	PYOSIS	PYROGENS	PYTHONESS	QUACKISH
PYCNOSES	PYRALID	PYROLA	PYTHONESSES	QUACKISM
PYCNOSIS	PYRALIDID	PYROLAS	PYTHONIC	QUACKISMS
PYCNOTIC	PYRALIDIDS	PYROLIZE	PYTHONS	QUACKS
PYE	PYRALIDS	PYROLIZED	PYURIA	QUACKY
PYELITIC	PYRAMID	PYROLIZES	PYURIAS	QUAD
PYELITIS	PYRAMIDAL	PYROLIZING	PYX	QUADDED
PYELITISES	PYRAMIDED	PYROLOGIES	PYXES	QUADDING
PYELOGRAM	PYRAMIDIC	PYROLOGY	PYXIDES	QUADPLEX
PYELOGRAMS	PYRAMIDING	PYROLYSES	PYXIDIA	QUADPLEXES
PYEMIA	PYRAMIDS	PYROLYSIS	PYXIDIUM	QUADRANS
PYEMIAS	PYRAN	PYROLYTIC	PYXIE	QUADRANT
PYEMIC	PYRANOID	PYROLYZE	PYXIES	QUADRANTES
PYES	PYRANOSE	PYROLYZED	PYXIS	QUADRANTS
PYGIDIA	PYRANOSES	PYROLYZER		QUADRAT
PYGIDIAL	PYRANS	PYROLYZERS		QUADRATE
PYGIDIUM	PYRE	PYROLYZES		QUADRATED
PYGMAEAN	PYRENE	PYROLYZING		QUADRATES
PYGMEAN	PYRENES	PYROMANCIES		QUADRATIC
PYGMIES	PYRENOID	PYROMANCY	QABALA	QUADRATICS
PYGMOID	PYRENOIDS	PYROMANIA	QABALAH	QUADRATING
PYGMY	PYRES	PYROMANIAS	QABALAHS	QUADRATS
PYGMYISH	PYRETHRIN	PYROMETER	QABALAS	QUADRIC
PYGMYISM	PYRETHRINS	PYROMETERS	QADI	QUADRICEP
PYGMYISMS	PYRETHRUM	PYROMETRIES	QADIS	QUADRICEPS
PYIC	PYRETHRUMS	PYROMETRY	QAID	QUADRICS
PYIN	PYRETIC	PYRONE	QAIDS	QUADRIFID
PYINS	PYREX	PYRONES	QANAT	QUADRIGA
PYJAMA	PYREXES	PYRONINE	QANATS	QUADRIGAE
PYJAMAS	PYREXIA	PYRONINES	QAT	QUADRILLE
PYKNIC	PYREXIAL	PYROPE	QATS	QUADRILLES
PYKNICS	PYREXIAS	PYROPES	QI	QUADRIVIA
PYKNOSES	PYREXIC	PYROS	QINDAR	QUADRIVIUM
PYKNOSIS	PYRIC	PYROSIS	QINDARKA	QUADROON

QUADROONS	QUAKER	QUANTITY	QUARTIER	QUBYTES
QUADRUPED	QUAKERS	QUANTIZE	QUARTIERS	QUEAN
QUADRUPEDS	QUAKES	QUANTIZED	QUARTILE	QUEANS
QUADRUPLE	QUAKIER	QUANTIZER	QUARTILES	QUEASIER
QUADRUPLED	QUAKIEST	QUANTIZERS	QUARTO	QUEASIEST
QUADRUPLES	QUAKILY	QUANTIZES	QUARTOS	QUEASILY
QUADRUPLING	QUAKINESS	QUANTIZING	QUARTS	QUEASY
QUADRUPLY	QUAKINESSES	QUANTONG	QUARTZ	QUEAZIER
QUADS	QUAKING	QUANTONGS	QUARTZES	QUEAZIEST
QUAERE	QUAKINGLY	QUANTS	QUARTZITE	QUEAZY
QUAERES	QUAKY	QUANTUM	QUARTZITES	QUEBRACHO
QUAESTOR	QUALE	QUARE	QUARTZOSE	QUEBRACHOS
QUAESTORS	QUALIA	QUARK	QUARTZOUS	QUEEN
QUAFF	QUALIFIED	QUARKS	QUASAR	QUEENDOM
QUAFFED	QUALIFIER	QUARREL	QUASARS	QUEENDOMS
QUAFFER	QUALIFIERS	QUARRELED	QUASH	QUEENED
QUAFFERS	QUALIFIES	QUARRELER	QUASHED	QUEENING
QUAFFING	QUALIFY	QUARRELERS	QUASHER	QUEENLIER
QUAFFS	QUALIFYING	QUARRELING	QUASHERS	QUEENLIEST
QUAG	QUALITIES	QUARRELLED	QUASHES	QUEENLY
QUAGGA	QUALITY	QUARRELLING	QUASHING	QUEENS
QUAGGAS	QUALM	QUARRELS	QUASI	QUEENSHIP
QUAGGIER	QUALMIER	QUARRIED	QUASS	QUEENSHIPS
QUAGGIEST	QUALMIEST	QUARRIER	QUASSES	QUEENSIDE
QUAGGY	QUALMISH	QUARRIERS	QUASSIA	QUEENSIDES
QUAGMIRE	QUALMS	QUARRIES	QUASSIAS	QUEER
QUAGMIRES	QUALMY	QUARRY	QUASSIN	QUEERED
QUAGMIRIER	QUAMASH	QUARRYING	QUASSINS	QUEERER
QUAGMIRIEST	QUAMASHES	QUARRYINGS	QUATE	QUEEREST
QUAGMIRY	QUANDANG	QUARRYMAN	QUATORZE	QUEERING
QUAGS	QUANDANGS	QUARRYMEN	QUATORZES	QUEERISH
QUAHAUG	QUANDARIES	QUART	QUATRAIN	QUEERLY
QUAHAUGS	QUANDARY	QUARTAN	QUATRAINS	QUEERNESS
QUAHOG	QUANDONG	QUARTANS	QUATRE	QUEERNESSES
QUAHOGS	QUANDONGS	QUARTE	QUATRES	QUEERS
QUAI	QUANGO	QUARTER	QUAVER	QUELEA
QUAICH	QUANGOS	QUARTERED	QUAVERED	QUELEAS
QUAICHES	QUANT	QUARTERER	QUAVERER	QUELL
QUAICHS	QUANTA	QUARTERERS	QUAVERERS	QUELLABLE
QUAIGH	QUANTAL	QUARTERING	QUAVERING	QUELLED
QUAIGHS	QUANTALLY	QUARTERLIES	QUAVERS	QUELLER
QUAIL	QUANTED	QUARTERLY	QUAVERY	QUELLERS
QUAILED	QUANTIC	QUARTERN	QUAY	QUELLING
QUAILING	QUANTICS	QUARTERNS	QUAYAGE	QUELLS
QUAILS	QUANTIFIED	QUARTERS	QUAYAGES	QUENCH
QUAINT	QUANTIFIES	QUARTES	QUAYLIKE	QUENCHED
QUAINTER	QUANTIFY	QUARTET	QUAYS	QUENCHER
QUAINTEST	QUANTIFYING	QUARTETS	QUAYSIDE	QUENCHERS
QUAINTLY	QUANTILE	QUARTETTE	QUAYSIDES	QUENCHES
QUAIS	QUANTILES	QUARTETTES	QUBIT	QUENCHING
QUAKE	QUANTING	QUARTIC	QUBITS	QUENELLE
QUAKED	QUANTITIES	QUARTICS	QUBYTE	QUENELLES

QUERCETIC	QUICK	QUIETUS	QUININS	QUIP
QUERCETIN	QUICKEN	QUIETUSES	QUINNAT	QUIPPED
QUERCETINS	QUICKENED	QUIFF	QUINNATS	QUIPPER
QUERCINE	QUICKENER	QUIFFS	QUINOA	QUIPPERS
QUERIDA	QUICKENERS	QUILL	QUINOAS	QUIPPIER
QUERIDAS	QUICKENING	QUILLAI	QUINOID	QUIPPIEST
QUERIED	QUICKENS	QUILLAIA	QUINOIDAL	QUIPPING
QUERIER	QUICKER	QUILLAIAS	QUINOIDS	QUIPPISH
QUERIERS	QUICKEST	QUILLAIS	QUINOL	QUIPPU
QUERIES	QUICKIE	QUILLAJA	QUINOLIN	QUIPPUS
QUERIST	QUICKIES	QUILLAJAS	QUINOLINE	QUIPPY
QUERISTS	QUICKLIME	QUILLBACK	QUINOLINES	QUIPS
QUERN	QUICKLIMES	QUILLBACKS	QUINOLINS	QUIPSTER
QUERNS	QUICKLY	QUILLED	QUINOLONE	QUIPSTERS
QUERULOUS	QUICKNESS	QUILLET	QUINOLONES	QUIPU
QUERY	QUICKNESSES	QUILLETS	QUINOLS	QUIPUS
QUERYING	QUICKS	QUILLING	QUINONE	QUIRE
QUEST	QUICKSAND	QUILLINGS	QUINONES	QUIRED
QUESTED	QUICKSANDS	QUILLS	QUINONOID	QUIRES
QUESTER	QUICKSET	QUILLWORK	QUINS	QUIRING
QUESTERS	QUICKSETS	QUILLWORKS	QUINSIED	QUIRK
QUESTING	QUICKSTEP	QUILLWORT	QUINSIES	QUIRKED
QUESTION	QUICKSTEPS	QUILLWORTS	QUINSY	QUIRKIER
QUESTIONED	QUID	QUILT	QUINT	QUIRKIEST
QUESTIONING	QUIDDITIES	QUILTED	QUINTA	QUIRKILY
QUESTIONS	QUIDDITY	QUILTER	QUINTAIN	QUIRKING
QUESTOR	QUIDNUNC	QUILTERS	QUINTAINS	QUIRKISH
QUESTORS	QUIDNUNCS	QUILTING	QUINTAL	QUIRKS
QUESTS	QUIDS	QUILTINGS	QUINTALS	QUIRKY
QUETZAL	QUIESCENT	QUILTS	QUINTAN	QUIRT
QUETZALES	QUIET	QUIN	QUINTANS	QUIRTED
QUETZALS	QUIETED	QUINARIES	QUINTAR	QUIRTING
QUEUE	QUIETEN	QUINARY	QUINTARS	QUIRTS
QUEUED	QUIETENED	QUINATE	QUINTAS	QUISLING
QUEUEING	QUIETENER	QUINCE	QUINTE	QUISLINGS
QUEUER	QUIETENERS	QUINCES	QUINTES	QUIT
QUEUERS	QUIETENING	QUINCUNX	QUINTET	QUITCH
QUEUES	QUIETENS	QUINCUNXES	QUINTETS	QUITCHES
QUEUING	QUIETER	QUINELA	QUINTETTE	QUITCLAIM
QUEY	QUIETERS	QUINELAS	QUINTETTES	QUITCLAIMED
QUEYS	QUIETEST	QUINELLA	QUINTIC	QUITCLAIMING
QUEZAL	QUIETING	QUINELLAS	QUINTICS	QUITCLAIMS
QUEZALES	QUIETISM	QUINIC	QUINTILE	QUITE
QUEZALS	QUIETISMS	QUINIDINE	QUINTILES	QUITRENT
QUIBBLE	QUIETIST	QUINIDINES	QUINTIN	QUITRENTS
QUIBBLED	QUIETISTS	QUINIELA	QUINTINS	QUITS
QUIBBLER	QUIETLY	QUINIELAS	QUINTS	QUITTANCE
QUIBBLERS	QUIETNESS	QUININ	QUINTUPLE	QUITTANCES
QUIBBLES	QUIETNESSES	QUININA	QUINTUPLED	QUITTED
QUIBBLING	QUIETS	QUININAS	QUINTUPLES	QUITTER
QUICHE	QUIETUDE	QUININE	QUINTUPLING	QUITTERS
QUICHES	QUIETUDES	QUININES	QUINTUPLY	QUITTING

QUITTOR	QUOTE	RABBLER	RACHIDES	RACLETTE
QUITTORS	QUOTED	RABBLERS	RACHILLA	RACLETTES
QUIVER	QUOTER	RABBLES	RACHILLAE	RACON
QUIVERED	QUOTERS	RABBLING	RACHIS	RACONS
QUIVERER	QUOTES	RABBONI	RACHISES	RACONTEUR
QUIVERERS	QUOTH	RABBONIS	RACHITIC	RACONTEURS
QUIVERING	QUOTHA	RABIC	RACHITIDES	RACOON
QUIVERS	QUOTIDIAN	RABID	RACHITIS	RACOONS
QUIVERY	QUOTIDIANS	RABIDITIES	RACIAL	RACQUET
QUIXOTE	QUOTIENT	RABIDITY	RACIALISM	RACQUETS
QUIXOTES	QUOTIENTS	RABIDLY	RACIALISMS	RACY
QUIXOTIC	QUOTING	RABIDNESS	RACIALIST	RAD
QUIXOTISM	QURSH	RABIDNESSES	RACIALISTS	RADAR
QUIXOTISMS	QURSHES	RABIES	RACIALIZE	RADARS
QUIXOTRIES	QURUSH	RABIETIC	RACIALIZED	RADDED
QUIXOTRY	QURUSHES	RACCOON	RACIALIZES	RADDING
QUIZ	QWERTY	RACCOONS	RACIALIZING	RADDLE
QUIZZED	QWERTYS	RACE	RACIALLY	RADDLED
QUIZZER		RACED	RACIER	RADDLES
QUIZZERS		RACEHORSE	RACIEST	RADDLING
QUIZZES	**R**	RACEHORSES	RACILY	RADIABLE
QUIZZICAL		RACEMATE	RACINESS	RADIAL
QUIZZING		RACEMATES	RACINESSES	RADIALE
QUOD		RACEME	RACING	RADIALIA
QUODLIBET	RABAT	RACEMED	RACINGS	RADIALLY
QUODLIBETS	RABATO	RACEMES	RACISM	RADIALS
QUODS	RABATOS	RACEMIC	RACISMS	RADIAN
QUOHOG	RABATS	RACEMISM	RACIST	RADIANCE
QUOHOGS	RABBET	RACEMISMS	RACISTS	RADIANCES
QUOIN	RABBETED	RACEMIZE	RACK	RADIANCIES
QUOINED	RABBETING	RACEMIZED	RACKED	RADIANCY
QUOINING	RABBETS	RACEMIZES	RACKER	RADIANS
QUOINS	RABBI	RACEMIZING	RACKERS	RADIANT
QUOIT	RABBIES	RACEMOID	RACKET	RADIANTLY
QUOITED	RABBIN	RACEMOSE	RACKETED	RADIANTS
QUOITING	RABBINATE	RACEMOUS	RACKETEER	RADIATE
QUOITS	RABBINATES	RACER	RACKETEERED	RADIATED
QUOKKA	RABBINIC	RACERS	RACKETEERING	RADIATELY
QUOKKAS	RABBINISM	RACES	RACKETEERS	RADIATES
QUOLL	RABBINISMS	RACETRACK	RACKETIER	RADIATING
QUOLLS	RABBINS	RACETRACKS	RACKETIEST	RADIATION
QUOMODO	RABBIS	RACEWALK	RACKETING	RADIATIONS
QUOMODOS	RABBIT	RACEWALKED	RACKETS	RADIATIVE
QUONDAM	RABBITED	RACEWALKING	RACKETY	RADIATOR
QUORUM	RABBITER	RACEWALKS	RACKFUL	RADIATORS
QUORUMS	RABBITERS	RACEWAY	RACKFULS	RADICAL
QUOTA	RABBITING	RACEWAYS	RACKING	RADICALLY
QUOTABLE	RABBITRIES	RACHET	RACKINGLY	RADICALS
QUOTABLY	RABBITRY	RACHETED	RACKLE	RADICAND
QUOTAS	RABBITS	RACHETING	RACKS	RADICANDS
QUOTATION	RABBITY	RACHETS	RACKWORK	RADICATE
QUOTATIONS	RABBLE	RACHIAL	RACKWORKS	RADICATED
	RABBLED			

RADICATES	RAFFLER	RAGOUTING	RAINBAND	RAISING
RADICATING	RAFFLERS	RAGOUTS	RAINBANDS	RAISINGS
RADICCHIO	RAFFLES	RAGPICKER	RAINBIRD	RAISINS
RADICCHIOS	RAFFLESIA	RAGPICKERS	RAINBIRDS	RAISINY
RADICEL	RAFFLESIAS	RAGS	RAINBOW	RAISONNE
RADICELS	RAFFLING	RAGTAG	RAINBOWS	RAITA
RADICES	RAFFS	RAGTAGS	RAINCHECK	RAITAS
RADICLE	RAFT	RAGTIME	RAINCHECKS	RAJ
RADICLES	RAFTED	RAGTIMES	RAINCOAT	RAJA
RADICULAR	RAFTER	RAGTOP	RAINCOATS	RAJAH
RADII	RAFTERED	RAGTOPS	RAINDROP	RAJAHS
RADIO	RAFTERS	RAGWEED	RAINDROPS	RAJAS
RADIOED	RAFTING	RAGWEEDS	RAINED	RAJES
RADIOGRAM	RAFTS	RAGWORT	RAINFALL	RAKE
RADIOGRAMS	RAFTSMAN	RAGWORTS	RAINFALLS	RAKED
RADIOING	RAFTSMEN	RAH	RAINIER	RAKEE
RADIOLOGIES	RAG	RAI	RAINIEST	RAKEES
RADIOLOGY	RAGA	RAIA	RAINILY	RAKEHELL
RADIOMAN	RAGAS	RAIAS	RAININESS	RAKEHELLS
RADIOMEN	RAGBAG	RAID	RAININESSES	RAKEHELLY
RADIONICS	RAGBAGS	RAIDED	RAINING	RAKEOFF
RADIOS	RAGE	RAIDER	RAINLESS	RAKEOFFS
RADISH	RAGED	RAIDERS	RAINMAKER	RAKER
RADISHES	RAGEE	RAIDING	RAINMAKERS	RAKERS
RADIUM	RAGEES	RAIDS	RAINOUT	RAKES
RADIUMS	RAGES	RAIL	RAINOUTS	RAKI
RADIUS	RAGG	RAILBIRD	RAINPROOF	RAKING
RADIUSES	RAGGED	RAILBIRDS	RAINPROOFED	RAKIS
RADIX	RAGGEDER	RAILBUS	RAINPROOFING	RAKISH
RADIXES	RAGGEDEST	RAILBUSES	RAINPROOFS	RAKISHLY
RADOME	RAGGEDIER	RAILBUSSES	RAINS	RAKU
RADOMES	RAGGEDIEST	RAILCAR	RAINSPOUT	RAKUS
RADON	RAGGEDLY	RAILCARS	RAINSPOUTS	RALE
RADONS	RAGGEDY	RAILED	RAINSTORM	RALES
RADS	RAGGEE	RAILER	RAINSTORMS	RALLIED
RADULA	RAGGEES	RAILERS	RAINWASH	RALLIER
RADULAE	RAGGIES	RAILHEAD	RAINWASHED	RALLIERS
RADULAR	RAGGING	RAILHEADS	RAINWASHES	RALLIES
RADULAS	RAGGLE	RAILING	RAINWASHING	RALLIFORM
RADWASTE	RAGGLES	RAILINGS	RAINWATER	RALLINE
RADWASTES	RAGGS	RAILLERIES	RAINWATERS	RALLY
RAFF	RAGGY	RAILLERY	RAINWEAR	RALLYE
RAFFIA	RAGI	RAILROAD	RAINY	RALLYES
RAFFIAS	RAGING	RAILROADED	RAIS	RALLYING
RAFFINATE	RAGINGLY	RAILROADING	RAISABLE	RALLYINGS
RAFFINATES	RAGIS	RAILROADS	RAISE	RALLYIST
RAFFINOSE	RAGLAN	RAILS	RAISEABLE	RALLYISTS
RAFFINOSES	RAGLANS	RAILWAY	RAISED	RALPH
RAFFISH	RAGMAN	RAILWAYS	RAISER	RALPHED
RAFFISHLY	RAGMEN	RAIMENT	RAISERS	RALPHING
RAFFLE	RAGOUT	RAIMENTS	RAISES	RALPHS
RAFFLED	RAGOUTED	RAIN	RAISIN	RAM

RAMADA	RAMOSITY	RANCHERS	RANGY	RAPACITY
RAMADAS	RAMOUS	RANCHES	RANI	RAPE
RAMAL	RAMP	RANCHING	RANID	RAPED
RAMATE	RAMPAGE	RANCHLESS	RANIDS	RAPER
RAMBLA	RAMPAGED	RANCHLIKE	RANIS	RAPERS
RAMBLAS	RAMPAGER	RANCHMAN	RANK	RAPES
RAMBLE	RAMPAGERS	RANCHMEN	RANKED	RAPESEED
RAMBLED	RAMPAGES	RANCHO	RANKER	RAPESEEDS
RAMBLER	RAMPAGING	RANCHOS	RANKERS	RAPHAE
RAMBLERS	RAMPANCIES	RANCID	RANKEST	RAPHE
RAMBLES	RAMPANCY	RANCIDITIES	RANKING	RAPHES
RAMBLING	RAMPANT	RANCIDITY	RANKINGS	RAPHIA
RAMBUTAN	RAMPANTLY	RANCIDLY	RANKISH	RAPHIAS
RAMBUTANS	RAMPART	RANCOR	RANKLE	RAPHIDE
RAMEE	RAMPARTED	RANCORED	RANKLED	RAPHIDES
RAMEES	RAMPARTING	RANCOROUS	RANKLES	RAPHIS
RAMEKIN	RAMPARTS	RANCORS	RANKLESS	RAPID
RAMEKINS	RAMPED	RANCOUR	RANKLING	RAPIDER
RAMEN	RAMPIKE	RANCOURED	RANKLY	RAPIDEST
RAMENTA	RAMPIKES	RANCOURS	RANKNESS	RAPIDITIES
RAMENTUM	RAMPING	RAND	RANKNESSES	RAPIDITY
RAMEQUIN	RAMPION	RANDAN	RANKS	RAPIDLY
RAMEQUINS	RAMPIONS	RANDANS	RANPIKE	RAPIDNESS
RAMET	RAMPOLE	RANDIER	RANPIKES	RAPIDNESSES
RAMETS	RAMPOLES	RANDIES	RANSACK	RAPIDS
RAMI	RAMPS	RANDIEST	RANSACKED	RAPIER
RAMIE	RAMROD	RANDINESS	RANSACKER	RAPIERED
RAMIES	RAMRODDED	RANDINESSES	RANSACKERS	RAPIERS
RAMIFIED	RAMRODDING	RANDOM	RANSACKING	RAPINE
RAMIFIES	RAMRODS	RANDOMIZE	RANSACKS	RAPINES
RAMIFORM	RAMS	RANDOMIZED	RANSOM	RAPING
RAMIFY	RAMSHORN	RANDOMIZES	RANSOMED	RAPINI
RAMIFYING	RAMSHORNS	RANDOMIZING	RANSOMER	RAPIST
RAMILIE	RAMSON	RANDOMLY	RANSOMERS	RAPISTS
RAMILIES	RAMSONS	RANDOMS	RANSOMING	RAPPAREE
RAMILLIE	RAMTIL	RANDS	RANSOMS	RAPPAREES
RAMILLIES	RAMTILLA	RANDY	RANT	RAPPED
RAMJET	RAMTILLAS	RANEE	RANTED	RAPPEE
RAMJETS	RAMTILS	RANEES	RANTER	RAPPEES
RAMMED	RAMULOSE	RANG	RANTERS	RAPPEL
RAMMER	RAMULOUS	RANGE	RANTING	RAPPELED
RAMMERS	RAMUS	RANGED	RANTINGLY	RAPPELING
RAMMIER	RAN	RANGELAND	RANTS	RAPPELLED
RAMMIEST	RANCE	RANGELANDS	RANULA	RAPPELLING
RAMMING	RANCES	RANGER	RANULAR	RAPPELS
RAMMISH	RANCH	RANGERS	RANULAS	RAPPEN
RAMMY	RANCHED	RANGES	RANUNCULI	RAPPER
RAMONA	RANCHER	RANGIER	RANUNCULUS	RAPPERS
RAMONAS	RANCHERIA	RANGIEST	RANUNCULUSES	RAPPING
RAMOSE	RANCHERIAS	RANGINESS	RAP	RAPPINI
RAMOSELY	RANCHERO	RANGINESSES	RAPACIOUS	RAPPORT
RAMOSITIES	RANCHEROS	RANGING	RAPACITIES	RAPPORTS

RAPS
RAPT
RAPTLY
RAPTNESS
RAPTNESSES
RAPTOR
RAPTORIAL
RAPTORS
RAPTURE
RAPTURED
RAPTURES
RAPTURING
RAPTUROUS
RARE
RAREBIT
RAREBITS
RARED
RAREFIED
RAREFIER
RAREFIERS
RAREFIES
RAREFY
RAREFYING
RARELY
RARENESS
RARENESSES
RARER
RARERIPE
RARERIPES
RARES
RAREST
RARIFIED
RARIFIES
RARIFY
RARIFYING
RARING
RARITIES
RARITY
RAS
RASBORA
RASBORAS
RASCAL
RASCALITIES
RASCALITY
RASCALLY
RASCALS
RASE
RASED
RASER
RASERS
RASES
RASH

RASHER
RASHERS
RASHES
RASHEST
RASHLIKE
RASHLY
RASHNESS
RASHNESSES
RASING
RASORIAL
RASP
RASPBERRIES
RASPBERRY
RASPED
RASPER
RASPERS
RASPIER
RASPIEST
RASPINESS
RASPINESSES
RASPING
RASPINGLY
RASPINGS
RASPISH
RASPS
RASPY
RASSLE
RASSLED
RASSLES
RASSLING
RASTER
RASTERS
RASURE
RASURES
RAT
RATABLE
RATABLES
RATABLY
RATAFEE
RATAFEES
RATAFIA
RATAFIAS
RATAL
RATALS
RATAN
RATANIES
RATANS
RATANY
RATAPLAN
RATAPLANNED
RATAPLANNING
RATAPLANS

RATATAT
RATATATS
RATBAG
RATBAGS
RATCH
RATCHES
RATCHET
RATCHETED
RATCHETING
RATCHETS
RATE
RATEABLE
RATEABLY
RATED
RATEL
RATELS
RATEMETER
RATEMETERS
RATEPAYER
RATEPAYERS
RATER
RATERS
RATES
RATFINK
RATFINKS
RATFISH
RATFISHES
RATH
RATHE
RATHER
RATHOLE
RATHOLES
RATICIDE
RATICIDES
RATIFIED
RATIFIER
RATIFIERS
RATIFIES
RATIFY
RATIFYING
RATINE
RATINES
RATING
RATINGS
RATIO
RATION
RATIONAL
RATIONALE
RATIONALES
RATIONALS
RATIONED
RATIONING

RATIONS
RATIOS
RATITE
RATITES
RATLIKE
RATLIN
RATLINE
RATLINES
RATLINS
RATO
RATOON
RATOONED
RATOONER
RATOONERS
RATOONING
RATOONS
RATOS
RATS
RATSBANE
RATSBANES
RATTAIL
RATTAILED
RATTAILS
RATTAN
RATTANS
RATTED
RATTEEN
RATTEENS
RATTEN
RATTENED
RATTENER
RATTENERS
RATTENING
RATTENS
RATTER
RATTERS
RATTIER
RATTIEST
RATTING
RATTISH
RATTLE
RATTLEBOX
RATTLEBOXES
RATTLED
RATTLER
RATTLERS
RATTLES
RATTLING
RATTLINGS
RATTLY
RATTON
RATTONS

RATTOON
RATTOONED
RATTOONING
RATTOONS
RATTRAP
RATTRAPS
RATTY
RAUCITIES
RAUCITY
RAUCOUS
RAUCOUSLY
RAUNCH
RAUNCHES
RAUNCHIER
RAUNCHIEST
RAUNCHILY
RAUNCHY
RAUWOLFIA
RAUWOLFIAS
RAVAGE
RAVAGED
RAVAGER
RAVAGERS
RAVAGES
RAVAGING
RAVE
RAVED
RAVEL
RAVELED
RAVELER
RAVELERS
RAVELIN
RAVELING
RAVELINGS
RAVELINS
RAVELLED
RAVELLER
RAVELLERS
RAVELLING
RAVELLINGS
RAVELLY
RAVELMENT
RAVELMENTS
RAVELS
RAVEN
RAVENED
RAVENER
RAVENERS
RAVENING
RAVENINGS
RAVENLIKE
RAVENOUS

RAVENS	RAYING	REACCUSED	READIEST	REALIGNS
RAVER	RAYLESS	REACCUSES	READILY	REALISE
RAVERS	RAYLIKE	REACCUSING	READINESS	REALISED
RAVES	RAYON	REACH	READINESSES	REALISER
RAVIGOTE	RAYONS	REACHABLE	READING	REALISERS
RAVIGOTES	RAYS	REACHED	READINGS	REALISES
RAVIGOTTE	RAZE	REACHER	READJUST	REALISING
RAVIGOTTES	RAZED	REACHERS	READJUSTED	REALISM
RAVIN	RAZEE	REACHES	READJUSTING	REALISMS
RAVINE	RAZEED	REACHING	READJUSTS	REALIST
RAVINED	RAZEEING	REACQUIRE	READMIT	REALISTIC
RAVINES	RAZEES	REACQUIRED	READMITS	REALISTS
RAVING	RAZER	REACQUIRES	READMITTED	REALITIES
RAVINGLY	RAZERS	REACQUIRING	READMITTING	REALITY
RAVINGS	RAZES	REACT	READOPT	REALIZE
RAVINING	RAZING	REACTANCE	READOPTED	REALIZED
RAVINS	RAZOR	REACTANCES	READOPTING	REALIZER
RAVIOLI	RAZORBACK	REACTANT	READOPTS	REALIZERS
RAVIOLIS	RAZORBACKS	REACTANTS	READORN	REALIZES
RAVISH	RAZORBILL	REACTED	READORNED	REALIZING
RAVISHED	RAZORBILLS	REACTING	READORNING	REALLOT
RAVISHER	RAZORED	REACTION	READORNS	REALLOTS
RAVISHERS	RAZORING	REACTIONS	READOUT	REALLOTTED
RAVISHES	RAZORS	REACTIVE	READOUTS	REALLOTTING
RAVISHING	RAZZ	REACTOR	READS	REALLY
RAW	RAZZBERRIES	REACTORS	READY	REALM
RAWBONED	RAZZBERRY	REACTS	READYING	REALMS
RAWER	RAZZED	READ	READYMADE	REALNESS
RAWEST	RAZZES	READABLE	READYMADES	REALNESSES
RAWHIDE	RAZZING	READABLY	REAFFIRM	REALS
RAWHIDED	RE	READAPT	REAFFIRMED	REALTER
RAWHIDES	REABSORB	READAPTED	REAFFIRMING	REALTERED
RAWHIDING	REABSORBED	READAPTING	REAFFIRMS	REALTERING
RAWIN	REABSORBING	READAPTS	REAFFIX	REALTERS
RAWINS	REABSORBS	READD	REAFFIXED	REALTIES
RAWISH	REACCEDE	READDED	REAFFIXES	REALTOR
RAWLY	REACCEDED	READDICT	REAFFIXING	REALTORS
RAWNESS	REACCEDES	READDICTED	REAGENT	REALTY
RAWNESSES	REACCEDING	READDICTING	REAGENTS	REAM
RAWS	REACCENT	READDICTS	REAGIN	REAMED
RAX	REACCENTED	READDING	REAGINIC	REAMER
RAXED	REACCENTING	READDRESS	REAGINS	REAMERS
RAXES	REACCENTS	READDRESSED	REAL	REAMING
RAXING	REACCEPT	READDRESSES	REALER	REAMS
RAY	REACCEPTED	READDRESSING	REALES	REANALYZE
RAYA	REACCEPTING	READDS	REALEST	REANALYZED
RAYAH	REACCEPTS	READER	REALGAR	REANALYZES
RAYAHS	REACCLAIM	READERLY	REALGARS	REANALYZING
RAYAS	REACCLAIMED	READERS	REALIA	REANIMATE
RAYED	REACCLAIMING	READIED	REALIGN	REANIMATED
RAYGRASS	REACCLAIMS	READIER	REALIGNED	REANIMATES
RAYGRASSES	REACCUSE	READIES	REALIGNING	REANIMATING

REANNEX	REAROUSE	REASSURE	REBALANCED	REBIRTHS
REANNEXED	REAROUSED	REASSURED	REBALANCES	REBLEND
REANNEXES	REAROUSES	REASSURES	REBALANCING	REBLENDED
REANNEXING	REAROUSING	REASSURING	REBAPTISM	REBLENDING
REANOINT	REARRANGE	REATA	REBAPTISMS	REBLENDS
REANOINTED	REARRANGED	REATAS	REBAPTIZE	REBLENT
REANOINTING	REARRANGES	REATTACH	REBAPTIZED	REBLOOM
REANOINTS	REARRANGING	REATTACHED	REBAPTIZES	REBLOOMED
REAP	REARREST	REATTACHES	REBAPTIZING	REBLOOMING
REAPABLE	REARRESTED	REATTACHING	REBAR	REBLOOMS
REAPED	REARRESTING	REATTACK	REBARS	REBOANT
REAPER	REARRESTS	REATTACKED	REBATE	REBOARD
REAPERS	REARS	REATTACKING	REBATED	REBOARDED
REAPHOOK	REARWARD	REATTACKS	REBATER	REBOARDING
REAPHOOKS	REARWARDS	REATTAIN	REBATERS	REBOARDS
REAPING	REASCEND	REATTAINED	REBATES	REBODIED
REAPPEAR	REASCENDED	REATTAINING	REBATING	REBODIES
REAPPEARED	REASCENDING	REATTAINS	REBATO	REBODY
REAPPEARING	REASCENDS	REATTEMPT	REBATOS	REBODYING
REAPPEARS	REASCENT	REATTEMPTED	REBBE	REBOIL
REAPPLIED	REASCENTS	REATTEMPTING	REBBES	REBOILED
REAPPLIES	REASON	REATTEMPTS	REBBETZIN	REBOILING
REAPPLY	REASONED	REAVAIL	REBBETZINS	REBOILS
REAPPLYING	REASONER	REAVAILED	REBEC	REBOOK
REAPPOINT	REASONERS	REAVAILING	REBECK	REBOOKED
REAPPOINTED	REASONING	REAVAILS	REBECKS	REBOOKING
REAPPOINTING	REASONINGS	REAVE	REBECS	REBOOKS
REAPPOINTS	REASONS	REAVED	REBEGAN	REBOOT
REAPPROVE	REASSAIL	REAVER	REBEGIN	REBOOTED
REAPPROVED	REASSAILED	REAVERS	REBEGINNING	REBOOTING
REAPPROVES	REASSAILING	REAVES	REBEGINS	REBOOTS
REAPPROVING	REASSAILS	REAVING	REBEGUN	REBOP
REAPS	REASSERT	REAVOW	REBEL	REBOPS
REAR	REASSERTED	REAVOWED	REBELDOM	REBORE
REARED	REASSERTING	REAVOWING	REBELDOMS	REBORED
REARER	REASSERTS	REAVOWS	REBELLED	REBORES
REARERS	REASSESS	REAWAKE	REBELLING	REBORING
REARGUARD	REASSESSED	REAWAKED	REBELLION	REBORN
REARGUE	REASSESSES	REAWAKEN	REBELLIONS	REBOTTLE
REARGUED	REASSESSING	REAWAKENED	REBELS	REBOTTLED
REARGUES	REASSIGN	REAWAKENING	REBID	REBOTTLES
REARGUING	REASSIGNED	REAWAKENS	REBIDDEN	REBOTTLING
REARING	REASSIGNING	REAWAKES	REBIDDING	REBOUGHT
REARM	REASSIGNS	REAWAKING	REBIDS	REBOUND
REARMED	REASSORT	REAWOKE	REBILL	REBOUNDED
REARMICE	REASSORTED	REAWOKEN	REBILLED	REBOUNDER
REARMING	REASSORTING	REB	REBILLING	REBOUNDERS
REARMOST	REASSORTS	REBAIT	REBILLS	REBOUNDING
REARMOUSE	REASSUME	REBAITED	REBIND	REBOUNDS
REARMS	REASSUMED	REBAITING	REBINDING	REBOZO
REAROUSAL	REASSUMES	REBAITS	REBINDS	REBOZOS
REAROUSALS	REASSUMING	REBALANCE	REBIRTH	REBRANCH

REBRANCHED	RECALLS	RECEIVE	RECHARGED	RECKED
REBRANCHES	RECAMIER	RECEIVED	RECHARGER	RECKING
REBRANCHING	RECAMIERS	RECEIVER	RECHARGERS	RECKLESS
REBRED	RECANE	RECEIVERS	RECHARGES	RECKON
REBREED	RECANED	RECEIVES	RECHARGING	RECKONED
REBREEDING	RECANES	RECEIVING	RECHART	RECKONER
REBREEDS	RECANING	RECEMENT	RECHARTED	RECKONERS
REBS	RECANT	RECEMENTED	RECHARTER	RECKONING
REBUFF	RECANTED	RECEMENTING	RECHARTERED	RECKONINGS
REBUFFED	RECANTER	RECEMENTS	RECHARTERING	RECKONS
REBUFFING	RECANTERS	RECENCIES	RECHARTERS	RECKS
REBUFFS	RECANTING	RECENCY	RECHARTING	RECLAD
REBUILD	RECANTS	RECENSION	RECHARTS	RECLADDED
REBUILDED	RECAP	RECENSIONS	RECHAUFFE	RECLADDING
REBUILDING	RECAPPED	RECENSOR	RECHAUFFES	RECLADS
REBUILDS	RECAPPING	RECENSORED	RECHEAT	RECLAIM
REBUILT	RECAPS	RECENSORING	RECHEATS	RECLAIMED
REBUKE	RECAPTURE	RECENSORS	RECHECK	RECLAIMER
REBUKED	RECAPTURED	RECENT	RECHECKED	RECLAIMERS
REBUKER	RECAPTURES	RECENTER	RECHECKING	RECLAIMING
REBUKERS	RECAPTURING	RECENTEST	RECHECKS	RECLAIMS
REBUKES	RECARPET	RECENTLY	RECHERCHE	RECLAME
REBUKING	RECARPETED	RECEPT	RECHEW	RECLAMES
REBURIAL	RECARPETING	RECEPTION	RECHEWED	RECLASP
REBURIALS	RECARPETS	RECEPTIONS	RECHEWING	RECLASPED
REBURIED	RECARRIED	RECEPTIVE	RECHEWS	RECLASPING
REBURIES	RECARRIES	RECEPTOR	RECHOOSE	RECLASPS
REBURY	RECARRY	RECEPTORS	RECHOOSES	RECLEAN
REBURYING	RECARRYING	RECEPTS	RECHOOSING	RECLEANED
REBUS	RECAST	RECERTIFIED	RECHOSE	RECLEANING
REBUSES	RECASTING	RECERTIFIES	RECHOSEN	RECLEANS
REBUT	RECASTS	RECERTIFY	RECIPE	RECLINATE
REBUTS	RECATALOG	RECERTIFYING	RECIPES	RECLINE
REBUTTAL	RECATALOGED	RECESS	RECIPIENT	RECLINED
REBUTTALS	RECATALOGING	RECESSED	RECIPIENTS	RECLINER
REBUTTED	RECATALOGS	RECESSES	RECIRCLE	RECLINERS
REBUTTER	RECAUTION	RECESSING	RECIRCLED	RECLINES
REBUTTERS	RECAUTIONED	RECESSION	RECIRCLES	RECLINING
REBUTTING	RECAUTIONING	RECESSIONS	RECIRCLING	RECLOTHE
REBUTTON	RECAUTIONS	RECESSIVE	RECISION	RECLOTHED
REBUTTONED	RECCE	RECESSIVES	RECISIONS	RECLOTHES
REBUTTONING	RECCES	RECHANGE	RECIT	RECLOTHING
REBUTTONS	RECEDE	RECHANGED	RECITAL	RECLUSE
REBUY	RECEDED	RECHANGES	RECITALS	RECLUSES
REBUYING	RECEDES	RECHANGING	RECITE	RECLUSION
REBUYS	RECEDING	RECHANNEL	RECITED	RECLUSIONS
REC	RECEIPT	RECHANNELED	RECITER	RECLUSIVE
RECALL	RECEIPTED	RECHANNELING	RECITERS	RECOAL
RECALLED	RECEIPTING	RECHANNELLED	RECITES	RECOALED
RECALLER	RECEIPTOR	RECHANNELLING	RECITING	RECOALING
RECALLERS	RECEIPTORS	RECHANNELS	RECITS	RECOALS
RECALLING	RECEIPTS	RECHARGE	RECK	RECOAT

RECOATED	RECOMMENDED	RECONSIGN	RECORDS	RECROWN
RECOATING	RECOMMENDING	RECONSIGNED	RECORK	RECROWNED
RECOATS	RECOMMENDS	RECONSIGNING	RECORKED	RECROWNING
RECOCK	RECOMMIT	RECONSIGNS	RECORKING	RECROWNS
RECOCKED	RECOMMITS	RECONSOLE	RECORKS	RECRUIT
RECOCKING	RECOMMITTED	RECONSOLED	RECOUNT	RECRUITED
RECOCKS	RECOMMITTING	RECONSOLES	RECOUNTAL	RECRUITER
RECODE	RECOMPILE	RECONSOLING	RECOUNTALS	RECRUITERS
RECODED	RECOMPILED	RECONSULT	RECOUNTED	RECRUITING
RECODES	RECOMPILES	RECONSULTED	RECOUNTER	RECRUITS
RECODIFIED	RECOMPILING	RECONSULTING	RECOUNTERS	RECS
RECODIFIES	RECOMPOSE	RECONSULTS	RECOUNTING	RECTA
RECODIFY	RECOMPOSED	RECONTACT	RECOUNTS	RECTAL
RECODIFYING	RECOMPOSES	RECONTACTED	RECOUP	RECTALLY
RECODING	RECOMPOSING	RECONTACTING	RECOUPE	RECTANGLE
RECOGNISE	RECOMPUTE	RECONTACTS	RECOUPED	RECTANGLES
RECOGNISED	RECOMPUTED	RECONTOUR	RECOUPING	RECTI
RECOGNISES	RECOMPUTES	RECONTOURED	RECOUPLE	RECTIFIED
RECOGNISING	RECOMPUTING	RECONTOURING	RECOUPLED	RECTIFIER
RECOGNIZE	RECON	RECONTOURS	RECOUPLES	RECTIFIERS
RECOGNIZED	RECONCILE	RECONVENE	RECOUPLING	RECTIFIES
RECOGNIZES	RECONCILED	RECONVENED	RECOUPS	RECTIFY
RECOGNIZING	RECONCILES	RECONVENES	RECOURSE	RECTIFYING
RECOIL	RECONCILING	RECONVENING	RECOURSES	RECTITUDE
RECOILED	RECONDITE	RECONVERT	RECOVER	RECTITUDES
RECOILER	RECONDUCT	RECONVERTED	RECOVERED	RECTO
RECOILERS	RECONDUCTED	RECONVERTING	RECOVERER	RECTOCELE
RECOILING	RECONDUCTING	RECONVERTS	RECOVERERS	RECTOCELES
RECOILS	RECONDUCTS	RECONVEY	RECOVERIES	RECTOR
RECOIN	RECONFER	RECONVEYED	RECOVERING	RECTORATE
RECOINAGE	RECONFERRED	RECONVEYING	RECOVERS	RECTORATES
RECOINAGES	RECONFERRING	RECONVEYS	RECOVERY	RECTORIAL
RECOINED	RECONFERS	RECONVICT	RECRATE	RECTORIES
RECOINING	RECONFINE	RECONVICTED	RECRATED	RECTORS
RECOINS	RECONFINED	RECONVICTING	RECRATES	RECTORY
RECOLLECT	RECONFINES	RECONVICTS	RECRATING	RECTOS
RECOLLECTED	RECONFINING	RECOOK	RECREANCE	RECTRICES
RECOLLECTING	RECONFIRM	RECOOKED	RECREANCES	RECTRIX
RECOLLECTS	RECONFIRMED	RECOOKING	RECREANCIES	RECTUM
RECOLOR	RECONFIRMING	RECOOKS	RECREANCY	RECTUMS
RECOLORED	RECONFIRMS	RECOPIED	RECREANT	RECTUS
RECOLORING	RECONNECT	RECOPIES	RECREANTS	RECUMBENT
RECOLORS	RECONNECTED	RECOPY	RECREATE	RECUR
RECOMB	RECONNECTING	RECOPYING	RECREATED	RECURRED
RECOMBED	RECONNECTS	RECORD	RECREATES	RECURRENT
RECOMBINE	RECONNED	RECORDED	RECREATING	RECURRING
RECOMBINED	RECONNING	RECORDER	RECREMENT	RECURS
RECOMBINES	RECONQUER	RECORDERS	RECREMENTS	RECURSION
RECOMBING	RECONQUERED	RECORDING	RECROSS	RECURSIONS
RECOMBINING	RECONQUERING	RECORDINGS	RECROSSED	RECURSIVE
RECOMBS	RECONQUERS	RECORDIST	RECROSSES	RECURVATE
RECOMMEND	RECONS	RECORDISTS	RECROSSING	RECURVE

RECURVED
RECURVES
RECURVING
RECUSAL
RECUSALS
RECUSANCIES
RECUSANCY
RECUSANT
RECUSANTS
RECUSE
RECUSED
RECUSES
RECUSING
RECUT
RECUTS
RECUTTING
RECYCLE
RECYCLED
RECYCLER
RECYCLERS
RECYCLES
RECYCLING
RED
REDACT
REDACTED
REDACTING
REDACTION
REDACTIONS
REDACTOR
REDACTORS
REDACTS
REDAMAGE
REDAMAGED
REDAMAGES
REDAMAGING
REDAN
REDANS
REDARGUE
REDARGUED
REDARGUES
REDARGUING
REDATE
REDATED
REDATES
REDATING
REDBAIT
REDBAITED
REDBAITER
REDBAITERS
REDBAITING
REDBAITS
REDBAY

REDBAYS
REDBIRD
REDBIRDS
REDBONE
REDBONES
REDBREAST
REDBREASTS
REDBRICK
REDBRICKS
REDBUD
REDBUDS
REDBUG
REDBUGS
REDCAP
REDCAPS
REDCOAT
REDCOATS
REDD
REDDED
REDDEN
REDDENED
REDDENING
REDDENS
REDDER
REDDERS
REDDEST
REDDING
REDDISH
REDDLE
REDDLED
REDDLES
REDDLING
REDDS
REDE
REDEAR
REDEARS
REDECIDE
REDECIDED
REDECIDES
REDECIDING
REDED
REDEEM
REDEEMED
REDEEMER
REDEEMERS
REDEEMING
REDEEMS
REDEFEAT
REDEFEATED
REDEFEATING
REDEFEATS
REDEFECT

REDEFECTED
REDEFECTING
REDEFECTS
REDEFIED
REDEFIES
REDEFINE
REDEFINED
REDEFINES
REDEFINING
REDEFY
REDEFYING
REDELIVER
REDELIVERED
REDELIVERING
REDELIVERS
REDEMAND
REDEMANDED
REDEMANDING
REDEMANDS
REDENIED
REDENIES
REDENY
REDENYING
REDEPLOY
REDEPLOYED
REDEPLOYING
REDEPLOYS
REDEPOSIT
REDEPOSITED
REDEPOSITING
REDEPOSITS
REDES
REDESCEND
REDESCENDED
REDESCENDING
REDESCENDS
REDESIGN
REDESIGNED
REDESIGNING
REDESIGNS
REDEVELOP
REDEVELOPED
REDEVELOPING
REDEVELOPS
REDEYE
REDEYES
REDFIN
REDFINS
REDFISH
REDFISHES
REDHEAD
REDHEADED

REDHEADS
REDHORSE
REDHORSES
REDIA
REDIAE
REDIAL
REDIALED
REDIALING
REDIALLED
REDIALLING
REDIALS
REDIAS
REDICTATE
REDICTATED
REDICTATES
REDICTATING
REDID
REDIGEST
REDIGESTED
REDIGESTING
REDIGESTS
REDIGRESS
REDIGRESSED
REDIGRESSES
REDIGRESSING
REDING
REDINGOTE
REDINGOTES
REDIP
REDIPPED
REDIPPING
REDIPS
REDIPT
REDIRECT
REDIRECTED
REDIRECTING
REDIRECTS
REDISCUSS
REDISCUSSED
REDISCUSSES
REDISCUSSING
REDISPLAY
REDISPLAYED
REDISPLAYING
REDISPLAYS
REDISPOSE
REDISPOSED
REDISPOSES
REDISPOSING
REDISTILL
REDISTILLED
REDISTILLING

REDISTILLS
REDIVIDE
REDIVIDED
REDIVIDES
REDIVIDING
REDIVIVUS
REDIVORCE
REDIVORCED
REDIVORCES
REDIVORCING
REDLEG
REDLEGS
REDLINE
REDLINED
REDLINER
REDLINERS
REDLINES
REDLINING
REDLININGS
REDLY
REDNECK
REDNECKED
REDNECKS
REDNESS
REDNESSES
REDO
REDOCK
REDOCKED
REDOCKING
REDOCKS
REDOES
REDOING
REDOLENCE
REDOLENCES
REDOLENCIES
REDOLENCY
REDOLENT
REDON
REDONE
REDONNED
REDONNING
REDONS
REDOS
REDOUBLE
REDOUBLED
REDOUBLER
REDOUBLERS
REDOUBLES
REDOUBLING
REDOUBT
REDOUBTS
REDOUND

REDOUNDED
REDOUNDING
REDOUNDS
REDOUT
REDOUTS
REDOWA
REDOWAS
REDOX
REDOXES
REDPOLL
REDPOLLS
REDRAFT
REDRAFTED
REDRAFTING
REDRAFTS
REDRAW
REDRAWER
REDRAWERS
REDRAWING
REDRAWN
REDRAWS
REDREAM
REDREAMED
REDREAMING
REDREAMS
REDREAMT
REDRESS
REDRESSED
REDRESSER
REDRESSERS
REDRESSES
REDRESSING
REDRESSOR
REDRESSORS
REDREW
REDRIED
REDRIES
REDRILL
REDRILLED
REDRILLING
REDRILLS
REDRIVE
REDRIVEN
REDRIVES
REDRIVING
REDROOT
REDROOTS
REDROVE
REDRY
REDRYING
REDS
REDSHANK

REDSHANKS
REDSHIFT
REDSHIFTS
REDSHIRT
REDSHIRTED
REDSHIRTING
REDSHIRTS
REDSKIN
REDSKINS
REDSTART
REDSTARTS
REDTAIL
REDTAILS
REDTOP
REDTOPS
REDUB
REDUBBED
REDUBBING
REDUBS
REDUCE
REDUCED
REDUCER
REDUCERS
REDUCES
REDUCIBLE
REDUCIBLY
REDUCING
REDUCTANT
REDUCTANTS
REDUCTASE
REDUCTASES
REDUCTION
REDUCTIONS
REDUCTIVE
REDUCTOR
REDUCTORS
REDUNDANT
REDUVIID
REDUVIIDS
REDUX
REDWARE
REDWARES
REDWING
REDWINGS
REDWOOD
REDWOODS
REDYE
REDYED
REDYEING
REDYES
REE
REEARN

REEARNED
REEARNING
REEARNS
REECHIER
REECHIEST
REECHO
REECHOED
REECHOES
REECHOING
REECHY
REED
REEDBIRD
REEDBIRDS
REEDBUCK
REEDBUCKS
REEDED
REEDIER
REEDIEST
REEDIFIED
REEDIFIES
REEDIFY
REEDIFYING
REEDILY
REEDINESS
REEDINESSES
REEDING
REEDINGS
REEDIT
REEDITED
REEDITING
REEDITION
REEDITIONS
REEDITS
REEDLIKE
REEDLING
REEDLINGS
REEDMAN
REEDMEN
REEDS
REEDUCATE
REEDUCATED
REEDUCATES
REEDUCATING
REEDY
REEF
REEFABLE
REEFED
REEFER
REEFERS
REEFIER
REEFIEST
REEFING

REEFS
REEFY
REEJECT
REEJECTED
REEJECTING
REEJECTS
REEK
REEKED
REEKER
REEKERS
REEKIER
REEKIEST
REEKING
REEKS
REEKY
REEL
REELABLE
REELECT
REELECTED
REELECTING
REELECTS
REELED
REELER
REELERS
REELEVATE
REELEVATED
REELEVATES
REELEVATING
REELING
REELINGS
REELS
REEMBARK
REEMBARKED
REEMBARKING
REEMBARKS
REEMBODIED
REEMBODIES
REEMBODY
REEMBODYING
REEMBRACE
REEMBRACED
REEMBRACES
REEMBRACING
REEMERGE
REEMERGED
REEMERGES
REEMERGING
REEMIT
REEMITS
REEMITTED
REEMITTING
REEMPLOY

REEMPLOYED
REEMPLOYING
REEMPLOYS
REENACT
REENACTED
REENACTING
REENACTOR
REENACTORS
REENACTS
REENDOW
REENDOWED
REENDOWING
REENDOWS
REENFORCE
REENFORCED
REENFORCES
REENFORCING
REENGAGE
REENGAGED
REENGAGES
REENGAGING
REENGRAVE
REENGRAVED
REENGRAVES
REENGRAVING
REENJOY
REENJOYED
REENJOYING
REENJOYS
REENLARGE
REENLARGED
REENLARGES
REENLARGING
REENLIST
REENLISTED
REENLISTING
REENLISTS
REENROLL
REENROLLED
REENROLLING
REENROLLS
REENSLAVE
REENSLAVED
REENSLAVES
REENSLAVING
REENTER
REENTERED
REENTERING
REENTERS
REENTRANT
REENTRANTS
REENTRIES

REENTRY	REEXPOSES	REFEREED	REFINE	REFLIES
REEQUIP	REEXPOSING	REFEREEING	REFINED	REFLOAT
REEQUIPPED	REEXPRESS	REFEREES	REFINER	REFLOATED
REEQUIPPING	REEXPRESSED	REFERENCE	REFINERIES	REFLOATING
REEQUIPS	REEXPRESSES	REFERENCED	REFINERS	REFLOATS
REERECT	REEXPRESSING	REFERENCES	REFINERY	REFLOOD
REERECTED	REF	REFERENCING	REFINES	REFLOODED
REERECTING	REFACE	REFERENDA	REFINING	REFLOODING
REERECTS	REFACED	REFERENDUM	REFINISH	REFLOODS
REES	REFACES	REFERENDUMS	REFINISHED	REFLOW
REEST	REFACING	REFERENT	REFINISHES	REFLOWED
REESTED	REFALL	REFERENTS	REFINISHING	REFLOWER
REESTING	REFALLEN	REFERRAL	REFIRE	REFLOWERED
REESTS	REFALLING	REFERRALS	REFIRED	REFLOWERING
REEVE	REFALLS	REFERRED	REFIRES	REFLOWERS
REEVED	REFASHION	REFERRER	REFIRING	REFLOWING
REEVES	REFASHIONED	REFERRERS	REFIT	REFLOWN
REEVING	REFASHIONING	REFERRING	REFITS	REFLOWS
REEVOKE	REFASHIONS	REFERS	REFITTED	REFLUENCE
REEVOKED	REFASTEN	REFFED	REFITTING	REFLUENCES
REEVOKES	REFASTENED	REFFING	REFIX	REFLUENT
REEVOKING	REFASTENING	REFIGHT	REFIXED	REFLUX
REEXAMINE	REFASTENS	REFIGHTING	REFIXES	REFLUXED
REEXAMINED	REFECT	REFIGHTS	REFIXING	REFLUXES
REEXAMINES	REFECTED	REFIGURE	REFLAG	REFLUXING
REEXAMINING	REFECTING	REFIGURED	REFLAGGED	REFLY
REEXECUTE	REFECTION	REFIGURES	REFLAGGING	REFLYING
REEXECUTED	REFECTIONS	REFIGURING	REFLAGS	REFOCUS
REEXECUTES	REFECTIVE	REFILE	REFLATE	REFOCUSED
REEXECUTING	REFECTORIES	REFILED	REFLATED	REFOCUSES
REEXHIBIT	REFECTORY	REFILES	REFLATES	REFOCUSING
REEXHIBITED	REFECTS	REFILING	REFLATING	REFOCUSSED
REEXHIBITING	REFED	REFILL	REFLATION	REFOCUSSES
REEXHIBITS	REFEED	REFILLED	REFLATIONS	REFOCUSSING
REEXPEL	REFEEDING	REFILLING	REFLECT	REFOLD
REEXPELLED	REFEEDS	REFILLS	REFLECTED	REFOLDED
REEXPELLING	REFEEL	REFILM	REFLECTING	REFOLDING
REEXPELS	REFEELING	REFILMED	REFLECTOR	REFOLDS
REEXPLAIN	REFEELS	REFILMING	REFLECTORS	REFOREST
REEXPLAINED	REFEL	REFILMS	REFLECTS	REFORESTED
REEXPLAINING	REFELL	REFILTER	REFLET	REFORESTING
REEXPLAINS	REFELLED	REFILTERED	REFLETS	REFORESTS
REEXPLORE	REFELLING	REFILTERING	REFLEW	REFORGE
REEXPLORED	REFELS	REFILTERS	REFLEX	REFORGED
REEXPLORES	REFELT	REFINABLE	REFLEXED	REFORGES
REEXPLORING	REFENCE	REFINANCE	REFLEXES	REFORGING
REEXPORT	REFENCED	REFINANCED	REFLEXING	REFORM
REEXPORTED	REFENCES	REFINANCES	REFLEXION	REFORMAT
REEXPORTING	REFENCING	REFINANCING	REFLEXIONS	REFORMATE
REEXPORTS	REFER	REFIND	REFLEXIVE	REFORMATES
REEXPOSE	REFERABLE	REFINDING	REFLEXIVES	REFORMATS
REEXPOSED	REFEREE	REFINDS	REFLEXLY	REFORMATTED

REFORMATTING	REFRONTING	REFUTAL	REGELATING	REGLET
REFORMED	REFRONTS	REFUTALS	REGENCIES	REGLETS
REFORMER	REFROZE	REFUTE	REGENCY	REGLORIFIED
REFORMERS	REFROZEN	REFUTED	REGENT	REGLORIFIES
REFORMING	REFRY	REFUTER	REGENTAL	REGLORIFY
REFORMISM	REFRYING	REFUTERS	REGENTS	REGLORIFYING
REFORMISMS	REFS	REFUTES	REGES	REGLOSS
REFORMIST	REFT	REFUTING	REGGAE	REGLOSSED
REFORMISTS	REFUEL	REG	REGGAES	REGLOSSES
REFORMS	REFUELED	REGAIN	REGICIDAL	REGLOSSING
REFORTIFIED	REFUELING	REGAINED	REGICIDE	REGLOW
REFORTIFIES	REFUELLED	REGAINER	REGICIDES	REGLOWED
REFORTIFY	REFUELLING	REGAINERS	REGILD	REGLOWING
REFORTIFYING	REFUELS	REGAINING	REGILDED	REGLOWS
REFOUGHT	REFUGE	REGAINS	REGILDING	REGLUE
REFOUND	REFUGED	REGAL	REGILDS	REGLUED
REFOUNDED	REFUGEE	REGALE	REGILT	REGLUES
REFOUNDING	REFUGEES	REGALED	REGIME	REGLUING
REFOUNDS	REFUGES	REGALER	REGIMEN	REGMA
REFRACT	REFUGIA	REGALERS	REGIMENS	REGMATA
REFRACTED	REFUGING	REGALES	REGIMENT	REGNA
REFRACTING	REFUGIUM	REGALIA	REGIMENTED	REGNAL
REFRACTOR	REFULGENT	REGALING	REGIMENTING	REGNANCIES
REFRACTORS	REFUND	REGALITIES	REGIMENTS	REGNANCY
REFRACTS	REFUNDED	REGALITY	REGIMES	REGNANT
REFRAIN	REFUNDER	REGALLY	REGINA	REGNUM
REFRAINED	REFUNDERS	REGALNESS	REGINAE	REGOLITH
REFRAINER	REFUNDING	REGALNESSES	REGINAL	REGOLITHS
REFRAINERS	REFUNDS	REGARD	REGINAS	REGORGE
REFRAINING	REFURBISH	REGARDANT	REGION	REGORGED
REFRAINS	REFURBISHED	REGARDED	REGIONAL	REGORGES
REFRAME	REFURBISHES	REGARDFUL	REGIONALS	REGORGING
REFRAMED	REFURBISHING	REGARDING	REGIONS	REGOSOL
REFRAMES	REFURNISH	REGARDS	REGISSEUR	REGOSOLS
REFRAMING	REFURNISHED	REGATHER	REGISSEURS	REGRADE
REFREEZE	REFURNISHES	REGATHERED	REGISTER	REGRADED
REFREEZES	REFURNISHING	REGATHERING	REGISTERED	REGRADES
REFREEZING	REFUSABLE	REGATHERS	REGISTERING	REGRADING
REFRESH	REFUSAL	REGATTA	REGISTERS	REGRAFT
REFRESHED	REFUSALS	REGATTAS	REGISTRAR	REGRAFTED
REFRESHEN	REFUSE	REGAUGE	REGISTRARS	REGRAFTING
REFRESHENED	REFUSED	REGAUGED	REGISTRIES	REGRAFTS
REFRESHENING	REFUSENIK	REGAUGES	REGISTRY	REGRANT
REFRESHENS	REFUSENIKS	REGAUGING	REGIUS	REGRANTED
REFRESHER	REFUSER	REGAVE	REGIVE	REGRANTING
REFRESHERS	REFUSERS	REGEAR	REGIVEN	REGRANTS
REFRESHES	REFUSES	REGEARED	REGIVES	REGRATE
REFRESHING	REFUSING	REGEARING	REGIVING	REGRATED
REFRIED	REFUSNIK	REGEARS	REGLAZE	REGRATES
REFRIES	REFUSNIKS	REGELATE	REGLAZED	REGRATING
REFRONT	REFUTABLE	REGELATED	REGLAZES	REGREEN
REFRONTED	REFUTABLY	REGELATES	REGLAZING	REGREENED

REGREENING	REGULATORS	REHEELING	REIMBURSES	REINFLAMES
REGREENS	REGULI	REHEELS	REIMBURSING	REINFLAMING
REGREET	REGULINE	REHEM	REIMMERSE	REINFLATE
REGREETED	REGULUS	REHEMMED	REIMMERSED	REINFLATED
REGREETING	REGULUSES	REHEMMING	REIMMERSES	REINFLATES
REGREETS	REHAB	REHEMS	REIMMERSING	REINFLATING
REGRESS	REHABBED	REHINGE	REIMPLANT	REINFORCE
REGRESSED	REHABBER	REHINGED	REIMPLANTED	REINFORCED
REGRESSES	REHABBERS	REHINGES	REIMPLANTING	REINFORCES
REGRESSING	REHABBING	REHINGING	REIMPLANTS	REINFORCING
REGRESSOR	REHABS	REHIRE	REIMPORT	REINFORM
REGRESSORS	REHAMMER	REHIRED	REIMPORTED	REINFORMED
REGRET	REHAMMERED	REHIRES	REIMPORTING	REINFORMING
REGRETFUL	REHAMMERING	REHIRING	REIMPORTS	REINFORMS
REGRETS	REHAMMERS	REHOBOAM	REIMPOSE	REINFUSE
REGRETTED	REHANDLE	REHOBOAMS	REIMPOSED	REINFUSED
REGRETTER	REHANDLED	REHOUSE	REIMPOSES	REINFUSES
REGRETTERS	REHANDLES	REHOUSED	REIMPOSING	REINFUSING
REGRETTING	REHANDLING	REHOUSES	REIN	REINHABIT
REGREW	REHANG	REHOUSING	REINCITE	REINHABITED
REGRIND	REHANGED	REHUNG	REINCITED	REINHABITING
REGRINDING	REHANGING	REHYDRATE	REINCITES	REINHABITS
REGRINDS	REHANGS	REHYDRATED	REINCITING	REINING
REGROOM	REHARDEN	REHYDRATES	REINCUR	REINJECT
REGROOMED	REHARDENED	REHYDRATING	REINCURRED	REINJECTED
REGROOMING	REHARDENING	REI	REINCURRING	REINJECTING
REGROOMS	REHARDENS	REIF	REINCURS	REINJECTS
REGROOVE	REHASH	REIFIED	REINDEER	REINJURE
REGROOVED	REHASHED	REIFIER	REINDEERS	REINJURED
REGROOVES	REHASHES	REIFIERS	REINDEX	REINJURES
REGROOVING	REHASHING	REIFIES	REINDEXED	REINJURIES
REGROUND	REHEAR	REIFS	REINDEXES	REINJURING
REGROUP	REHEARD	REIFY	REINDEXING	REINJURY
REGROUPED	REHEARING	REIFYING	REINDICT	REINK
REGROUPING	REHEARINGS	REIGN	REINDICTED	REINKED
REGROUPS	REHEARS	REIGNED	REINDICTING	REINKING
REGROW	REHEARSAL	REIGNING	REINDICTS	REINKS
REGROWING	REHEARSALS	REIGNITE	REINDUCE	REINLESS
REGROWN	REHEARSE	REIGNITED	REINDUCED	REINS
REGROWS	REHEARSED	REIGNITES	REINDUCES	REINSERT
REGROWTH	REHEARSER	REIGNITING	REINDUCING	REINSERTED
REGROWTHS	REHEARSERS	REIGNS	REINDUCT	REINSERTING
REGS	REHEARSES	REIMAGE	REINDUCTED	REINSERTS
REGULABLE	REHEARSING	REIMAGED	REINDUCTING	REINSMAN
REGULAR	REHEAT	REIMAGES	REINDUCTS	REINSMEN
REGULARLY	REHEATED	REIMAGINE	REINED	REINSPECT
REGULARS	REHEATER	REIMAGINED	REINFECT	REINSPECTED
REGULATE	REHEATERS	REIMAGINES	REINFECTED	REINSPECTING
REGULATED	REHEATING	REIMAGING	REINFECTING	REINSPECTS
REGULATES	REHEATS	REIMAGINING	REINFECTS	REINSPIRE
REGULATING	REHEEL	REIMBURSE	REINFLAME	REINSPIRED
REGULATOR	REHEELED	REIMBURSED	REINFLAMED	REINSPIRES

REINSPIRING	REITERATE	REJUGGLE	RELATEDLY	RELENDING
REINSTALL	REITERATED	REJUGGLED	RELATER	RELENDS
REINSTALLED	REITERATES	REJUGGLES	RELATERS	RELENT
REINSTALLING	REITERATING	REJUGGLING	RELATES	RELENTED
REINSTALLS	REIVE	REJUSTIFIED	RELATING	RELENTING
REINSTATE	REIVED	REJUSTIFIES	RELATION	RELENTS
REINSTATED	REIVER	REJUSTIFY	RELATIONS	RELET
REINSTATES	REIVERS	REJUSTIFYING	RELATIVE	RELETS
REINSTATING	REIVES	REKEY	RELATIVES	RELETTER
REINSURE	REIVING	REKEYED	RELATOR	RELETTERED
REINSURED	REJACKET	REKEYING	RELATORS	RELETTERING
REINSURER	REJACKETED	REKEYS	RELAUNCH	RELETTERS
REINSURERS	REJACKETING	REKINDLE	RELAUNCHED	RELETTING
REINSURES	REJACKETS	REKINDLED	RELAUNCHES	RELEVANCE
REINSURING	REJECT	REKINDLES	RELAUNCHING	RELEVANCES
REINTER	REJECTED	REKINDLING	RELAUNDER	RELEVANCIES
REINTERRED	REJECTEE	REKNIT	RELAUNDERED	RELEVANCY
REINTERRING	REJECTEES	REKNITS	RELAUNDERING	RELEVANT
REINTERS	REJECTER	REKNITTED	RELAUNDERS	RELEVE
REINVADE	REJECTERS	REKNITTING	RELAX	RELEVES
REINVADED	REJECTING	REKNOT	RELAXABLE	RELIABLE
REINVADES	REJECTION	REKNOTS	RELAXANT	RELIABLES
REINVADING	REJECTIONS	REKNOTTED	RELAXANTS	RELIABLY
REINVENT	REJECTIVE	REKNOTTING	RELAXED	RELIANCE
REINVENTED	REJECTOR	RELABEL	RELAXEDLY	RELIANCES
REINVENTING	REJECTORS	RELABELED	RELAXER	RELIANT
REINVENTS	REJECTS	RELABELING	RELAXERS	RELIANTLY
REINVEST	REJIG	RELABELLED	RELAXES	RELIC
REINVESTED	REJIGGED	RELABELLING	RELAXIN	RELICENSE
REINVESTING	REJIGGER	RELABELS	RELAXING	RELICENSED
REINVESTS	REJIGGERED	RELACE	RELAXINS	RELICENSES
REINVITE	REJIGGERING	RELACED	RELAY	RELICENSING
REINVITED	REJIGGERS	RELACES	RELAYED	RELICS
REINVITES	REJIGGING	RELACING	RELAYING	RELICT
REINVITING	REJIGS	RELACQUER	RELAYS	RELICTION
REINVOKE	REJOICE	RELACQUERED	RELEARN	RELICTIONS
REINVOKED	REJOICED	RELACQUERING	RELEARNED	RELICTS
REINVOKES	REJOICER	RELACQUERS	RELEARNING	RELIED
REINVOKING	REJOICERS	RELAID	RELEARNS	RELIEF
REINVOLVE	REJOICES	RELAND	RELEARNT	RELIEFS
REINVOLVED	REJOICING	RELANDED	RELEASE	RELIER
REINVOLVES	REJOICINGS	RELANDING	RELEASED	RELIERS
REINVOLVING	REJOIN	RELANDS	RELEASER	RELIES
REIS	REJOINDER	RELAPSE	RELEASERS	RELIEVE
REISSUE	REJOINDERS	RELAPSED	RELEASES	RELIEVED
REISSUED	REJOINED	RELAPSER	RELEASING	RELIEVER
REISSUER	REJOINING	RELAPSERS	RELEGABLE	RELIEVERS
REISSUERS	REJOINS	RELAPSES	RELEGATE	RELIEVES
REISSUES	REJUDGE	RELAPSING	RELEGATED	RELIEVING
REISSUING	REJUDGED	RELATABLE	RELEGATES	RELIEVO
REITBOK	REJUDGES	RELATE	RELEGATING	RELIEVOS
REITBOKS	REJUDGING	RELATED	RELEND	RELIGHT

RELIGHTED	RELOCATEE	REMAND	REMEDIES	REMISSIVE
RELIGHTING	RELOCATEES	REMANDED	REMEDY	REMISSLY
RELIGHTS	RELOCATES	REMANDING	REMEDYING	REMIT
RELIGION	RELOCATING	REMANDS	REMEET	REMITMENT
RELIGIONS	RELOCK	REMANENCE	REMEETING	REMITMENTS
RELIGIOSE	RELOCKED	REMANENCES	REMEETS	REMITS
RELIGIOUS	RELOCKING	REMANENT	REMELT	REMITTAL
RELINE	RELOCKS	REMANNED	REMELTED	REMITTALS
RELINED	RELOOK	REMANNING	REMELTING	REMITTED
RELINES	RELOOKED	REMANS	REMELTS	REMITTENT
RELINING	RELOOKING	REMAP	REMEMBER	REMITTER
RELINK	RELOOKS	REMAPPED	REMEMBERED	REMITTERS
RELINKED	RELUCENT	REMAPPING	REMEMBERING	REMITTING
RELINKING	RELUCT	REMAPS	REMEMBERS	REMITTOR
RELINKS	RELUCTANT	REMARK	REMEND	REMITTORS
RELIQUARIES	RELUCTATE	REMARKED	REMENDED	REMIX
RELIQUARY	RELUCTATED	REMARKER	REMENDING	REMIXED
RELIQUE	RELUCTATES	REMARKERS	REMENDS	REMIXES
RELIQUEFIED	RELUCTATING	REMARKET	REMERGE	REMIXING
RELIQUEFIES	RELUCTED	REMARKETED	REMERGED	REMIXT
RELIQUEFY	RELUCTING	REMARKETING	REMERGES	REMIXTURE
RELIQUEFYING	RELUCTS	REMARKETS	REMERGING	REMIXTURES
RELIQUES	RELUME	REMARKING	REMET	REMNANT
RELIQUIAE	RELUMED	REMARKS	REMEX	REMNANTAL
RELISH	RELUMES	REMARQUE	REMIGES	REMNANTS
RELISHED	RELUMINE	REMARQUES	REMIGIAL	REMODEL
RELISHES	RELUMINED	REMARRIED	REMIGRATE	REMODELED
RELISHING	RELUMINES	REMARRIES	REMIGRATED	REMODELER
RELIST	RELUMING	REMARRY	REMIGRATES	REMODELERS
RELISTED	RELUMINING	REMARRYING	REMIGRATING	REMODELING
RELISTING	RELY	REMASTER	REMIND	REMODELLED
RELISTS	RELYING	REMASTERED	REMINDED	REMODELLING
RELIT	REM	REMASTERING	REMINDER	REMODELS
RELIVABLE	REMADE	REMASTERS	REMINDERS	REMODIFIED
RELIVE	REMAIL	REMATCH	REMINDFUL	REMODIFIES
RELIVED	REMAILED	REMATCHED	REMINDING	REMODIFY
RELIVES	REMAILING	REMATCHES	REMINDS	REMODIFYING
RELIVING	REMAILS	REMATCHING	REMINISCE	REMOISTEN
RELLENO	REMAIN	REMATE	REMINISCED	REMOISTENED
RELLENOS	REMAINDER	REMATED	REMINISCES	REMOISTENING
RELOAD	REMAINDERED	REMATES	REMINISCING	REMOISTENS
RELOADED	REMAINDERING	REMATING	REMINT	REMOLADE
RELOADER	REMAINDERS	REMEASURE	REMINTED	REMOLADES
RELOADERS	REMAINED	REMEASURED	REMINTING	REMOLD
RELOADING	REMAINING	REMEASURES	REMINTS	REMOLDED
RELOADS	REMAINS	REMEASURING	REMISE	REMOLDING
RELOAN	REMAKE	REMEDIAL	REMISED	REMOLDS
RELOANED	REMAKER	REMEDIATE	REMISES	REMONTANT
RELOANING	REMAKERS	REMEDIATED	REMISING	REMONTANTS
RELOANS	REMAKES	REMEDIATES	REMISS	REMORA
RELOCATE	REMAKING	REMEDIATING	REMISSION	REMORAS
RELOCATED	REMAN	REMEDIED	REMISSIONS	REMORID

REMORSE
REMORSES
REMOTE
REMOTELY
REMOTER
REMOTES
REMOTEST
REMOTION
REMOTIONS
REMOULADE
REMOULADES
REMOUNT
REMOUNTED
REMOUNTING
REMOUNTS
REMOVABLE
REMOVABLY
REMOVAL
REMOVALS
REMOVE
REMOVED
REMOVEDLY
REMOVER
REMOVERS
REMOVES
REMOVING
REMS
REMUDA
REMUDAS
RENAIL
RENAILED
RENAILING
RENAILS
RENAL
RENAME
RENAMED
RENAMES
RENAMING
RENASCENT
RENATURE
RENATURED
RENATURES
RENATURING
RENCONTRE
RENCONTRES
REND
RENDED
RENDER
RENDERED
RENDERER
RENDERERS
RENDERING

RENDERINGS
RENDERS
RENDIBLE
RENDING
RENDITION
RENDITIONS
RENDS
RENDZINA
RENDZINAS
RENEGADE
RENEGADED
RENEGADES
RENEGADING
RENEGADO
RENEGADOES
RENEGADOS
RENEGE
RENEGED
RENEGER
RENEGERS
RENEGES
RENEGING
RENEST
RENESTED
RENESTING
RENESTS
RENEW
RENEWABLE
RENEWABLES
RENEWABLY
RENEWAL
RENEWALS
RENEWED
RENEWEDLY
RENEWER
RENEWERS
RENEWING
RENEWS
RENIFORM
RENIG
RENIGGED
RENIGGING
RENIGS
RENIN
RENINS
RENITENCE
RENITENCES
RENITENCIES
RENITENCY
RENITENT
RENMINBI
RENNASE

RENNASES
RENNET
RENNETS
RENNIN
RENNINS
RENOGRAM
RENOGRAMS
RENOTIFIED
RENOTIFIES
RENOTIFY
RENOTIFYING
RENOUNCE
RENOUNCED
RENOUNCER
RENOUNCERS
RENOUNCES
RENOUNCING
RENOVATE
RENOVATED
RENOVATES
RENOVATING
RENOVATOR
RENOVATORS
RENOWN
RENOWNED
RENOWNING
RENOWNS
RENT
RENTABLE
RENTAL
RENTALS
RENTE
RENTED
RENTER
RENTERS
RENTES
RENTIER
RENTIERS
RENTING
RENTS
RENUMBER
RENUMBERED
RENUMBERING
RENUMBERS
RENVOI
RENVOIS
REOBJECT
REOBJECTED
REOBJECTING
REOBJECTS
REOBSERVE
REOBSERVED

REOBSERVES
REOBSERVING
REOBTAIN
REOBTAINED
REOBTAINING
REOBTAINS
REOCCUPIED
REOCCUPIES
REOCCUPY
REOCCUPYING
REOCCUR
REOCCURRED
REOCCURRING
REOCCURS
REOFFER
REOFFERED
REOFFERING
REOFFERS
REOIL
REOILED
REOILING
REOILS
REOPEN
REOPENED
REOPENING
REOPENS
REOPERATE
REOPERATED
REOPERATES
REOPERATING
REOPPOSE
REOPPOSED
REOPPOSES
REOPPOSING
REORDAIN
REORDAINED
REORDAINING
REORDAINS
REORDER
REORDERED
REORDERING
REORDERS
REORIENT
REORIENTED
REORIENTING
REORIENTS
REOUTFIT
REOUTFITS
REOUTFITTED
REOUTFITTING
REOVIRUS
REOVIRUSES

REOXIDIZE
REOXIDIZED
REOXIDIZES
REOXIDIZING
REP
REPACIFIED
REPACIFIES
REPACIFY
REPACIFYING
REPACK
REPACKAGE
REPACKAGED
REPACKAGES
REPACKAGING
REPACKED
REPACKING
REPACKS
REPAID
REPAINT
REPAINTED
REPAINTING
REPAINTS
REPAIR
REPAIRED
REPAIRER
REPAIRERS
REPAIRING
REPAIRMAN
REPAIRMEN
REPAIRS
REPAND
REPANDLY
REPANEL
REPANELED
REPANELING
REPANELLED
REPANELLING
REPANELS
REPAPER
REPAPERED
REPAPERING
REPAPERS
REPARABLE
REPARABLY
REPARK
REPARKED
REPARKING
REPARKS
REPARTEE
REPARTEES
REPASS
REPASSAGE

REPASSAGES	REPELLING	REPLANTS	REPLIER	REPOSITS
REPASSED	REPELS	REPLASTER	REPLIERS	REPOSSESS
REPASSES	REPENT	REPLASTERED	REPLIES	REPOSSESSED
REPASSING	REPENTANT	REPLASTERING	REPLOT	REPOSSESSES
REPAST	REPENTED	REPLASTERS	REPLOTS	REPOSSESSING
REPASTED	REPENTER	REPLATE	REPLOTTED	REPOT
REPASTING	REPENTERS	REPLATED	REPLOTTING	REPOTS
REPASTS	REPENTING	REPLATES	REPLOW	REPOTTED
REPATCH	REPENTS	REPLATING	REPLOWED	REPOTTING
REPATCHED	REPEOPLE	REPLAY	REPLOWING	REPOUR
REPATCHES	REPEOPLED	REPLAYED	REPLOWS	REPOURED
REPATCHING	REPEOPLES	REPLAYING	REPLUMB	REPOURING
REPATTERN	REPEOPLING	REPLAYS	REPLUMBED	REPOURS
REPATTERNED	REPERK	REPLEAD	REPLUMBING	REPOUSSE
REPATTERNING	REPERKED	REPLEADED	REPLUMBS	REPOUSSES
REPATTERNS	REPERKING	REPLEADER	REPLUNGE	REPOWER
REPAVE	REPERKS	REPLEADERS	REPLUNGED	REPOWERED
REPAVED	REPERTORIES	REPLEADING	REPLUNGES	REPOWERING
REPAVES	REPERTORY	REPLEADS	REPLUNGING	REPOWERS
REPAVING	REPETEND	REPLED	REPLY	REPP
REPAY	REPETENDS	REPLEDGE	REPLYING	REPPED
REPAYABLE	REPHRASE	REPLEDGED	REPO	REPPING
REPAYING	REPHRASED	REPLEDGES	REPOLISH	REPPS
REPAYMENT	REPHRASES	REPLEDGING	REPOLISHED	REPREHEND
REPAYMENTS	REPHRASING	REPLENISH	REPOLISHES	REPREHENDED
REPAYS	REPIGMENT	REPLENISHED	REPOLISHING	REPREHENDING
REPEAL	REPIGMENTED	REPLENISHES	REPOLL	REPREHENDS
REPEALED	REPIGMENTING	REPLENISHING	REPOLLED	REPRESENT
REPEALER	REPIGMENTS	REPLETE	REPOLLING	REPRESENTED
REPEALERS	REPIN	REPLETELY	REPOLLS	REPRESENTING
REPEALING	REPINE	REPLETES	REPORT	REPRESENTS
REPEALS	REPINED	REPLETION	REPORTAGE	REPRESS
REPEAT	REPINER	REPLETIONS	REPORTAGES	REPRESSED
REPEATED	REPINERS	REPLEVIED	REPORTED	REPRESSER
REPEATER	REPINES	REPLEVIES	REPORTER	REPRESSERS
REPEATERS	REPINING	REPLEVIN	REPORTERS	REPRESSES
REPEATING	REPINNED	REPLEVINED	REPORTING	REPRESSING
REPEATS	REPINNING	REPLEVINING	REPORTS	REPRESSOR
REPECHAGE	REPINS	REPLEVINS	REPOS	REPRESSORS
REPECHAGES	REPLACE	REPLEVY	REPOSAL	REPRICE
REPEG	REPLACED	REPLEVYING	REPOSALS	REPRICED
REPEGGED	REPLACER	REPLICA	REPOSE	REPRICES
REPEGGING	REPLACERS	REPLICAS	REPOSED	REPRICING
REPEGS	REPLACES	REPLICASE	REPOSEDLY	REPRIEVAL
REPEL	REPLACING	REPLICASES	REPOSEFUL	REPRIEVALS
REPELLANT	REPLAN	REPLICATE	REPOSER	REPRIEVE
REPELLANTS	REPLANNED	REPLICATED	REPOSERS	REPRIEVED
REPELLED	REPLANNING	REPLICATES	REPOSES	REPRIEVES
REPELLENT	REPLANS	REPLICATING	REPOSING	REPRIEVING
REPELLENTS	REPLANT	REPLICON	REPOSIT	REPRIMAND
REPELLER	REPLANTED	REPLICONS	REPOSITED	REPRIMANDED
REPELLERS	REPLANTING	REPLIED	REPOSITING	REPRIMANDING

REPRIMANDS	REPTANT	REPUTES	REREBRACES	REROUTES
REPRINT	REPTILE	REPUTING	RERECORD	REROUTING
REPRINTED	REPTILES	REQUALIFIED	RERECORDED	RERUN
REPRINTER	REPTILIA	REQUALIFIES	RERECORDING	RERUNNING
REPRINTERS	REPTILIAN	REQUALIFY	RERECORDS	RERUNS
REPRINTING	REPTILIANS	REQUALIFYING	REREDOS	RES
REPRINTS	REPTILIUM	REQUEST	REREDOSES	RESADDLE
REPRISAL	REPUBLIC	REQUESTED	RERELEASE	RESADDLED
REPRISALS	REPUBLICS	REQUESTER	RERELEASED	RESADDLES
REPRISE	REPUBLISH	REQUESTERS	RERELEASES	RESADDLING
REPRISED	REPUBLISHED	REQUESTING	RERELEASING	RESAID
REPRISES	REPUBLISHES	REQUESTOR	REREMICE	RESAIL
REPRISING	REPUBLISHING	REQUESTORS	REREMIND	RESAILED
REPRO	REPUDIATE	REQUESTS	REREMINDED	RESAILING
REPROACH	REPUDIATED	REQUIEM	REREMINDING	RESAILS
REPROACHED	REPUDIATES	REQUIEMS	REREMINDS	RESALABLE
REPROACHES	REPUDIATING	REQUIN	REREMOUSE	RESALE
REPROACHING	REPUGN	REQUINS	RERENT	RESALES
REPROBATE	REPUGNANT	REQUIRE	RERENTED	RESALUTE
REPROBATED	REPUGNED	REQUIRED	RERENTING	RESALUTED
REPROBATES	REPUGNING	REQUIRER	RERENTS	RESALUTES
REPROBATING	REPUGNS	REQUIRERS	REREPEAT	RESALUTING
REPROBE	REPULSE	REQUIRES	REREPEATED	RESAMPLE
REPROBED	REPULSED	REQUIRING	REREPEATING	RESAMPLED
REPROBES	REPULSER	REQUISITE	REREPEATS	RESAMPLES
REPROBING	REPULSERS	REQUISITES	REREVIEW	RESAMPLING
REPROCESS	REPULSES	REQUITAL	REREVIEWED	RESAT
REPROCESSED	REPULSING	REQUITALS	REREVIEWING	RESAW
REPROCESSES	REPULSION	REQUITE	REREVIEWS	RESAWED
REPROCESSING	REPULSIONS	REQUITED	REREWARD	RESAWING
REPRODUCE	REPULSIVE	REQUITER	REREWARDS	RESAWN
REPRODUCED	REPUMP	REQUITERS	RERIG	RESAWS
REPRODUCES	REPUMPED	REQUITES	RERIGGED	RESAY
REPRODUCING	REPUMPING	REQUITING	RERIGGING	RESAYING
REPROGRAM	REPUMPS	RERACK	RERIGS	RESAYS
REPROGRAMED	REPURIFIED	RERACKED	RERISE	RESCALE
REPROGRAMING	REPURIFIES	RERACKING	RERISEN	RESCALED
REPROGRAMMED	REPURIFY	RERACKS	RERISES	RESCALES
REPROGRAMMING	REPURIFYING	RERADIATE	RERISING	RESCALING
REPROGRAMS	REPURPOSE	RERADIATED	REROLL	RESCHOOL
REPROOF	REPURPOSED	RERADIATES	REROLLED	RESCHOOLED
REPROOFS	REPURPOSES	RERADIATING	REROLLER	RESCHOOLING
REPROS	REPURPOSING	RERAISE	REROLLERS	RESCHOOLS
REPROVAL	REPURSUE	RERAISED	REROLLING	RESCIND
REPROVALS	REPURSUED	RERAISES	REROLLS	RESCINDED
REPROVE	REPURSUES	RERAISING	REROOF	RESCINDER
REPROVED	REPURSUING	RERAN	REROOFED	RESCINDERS
REPROVER	REPUTABLE	REREAD	REROOFING	RESCINDING
REPROVERS	REPUTABLY	REREADING	REROOFS	RESCINDS
REPROVES	REPUTE	REREADINGS	REROSE	RESCORE
REPROVING	REPUTED	REREADS	REROUTE	RESCORED
REPS	REPUTEDLY	REREBRACE	REROUTED	RESCORES

RESCORING	RESEEDING	RESERVOIR	RESHONE	RESIGNING
RESCREEN	RESEEDS	RESERVOIRS	RESHOOT	RESIGNS
RESCREENED	RESEEING	RESET	RESHOOTING	RESILE
RESCREENING	RESEEK	RESETS	RESHOOTS	RESILED
RESCREENS	RESEEKING	RESETTER	RESHOT	RESILES
RESCRIPT	RESEEKS	RESETTERS	RESHOW	RESILIENT
RESCRIPTS	RESEEN	RESETTING	RESHOWED	RESILIN
RESCUABLE	RESEES	RESETTLE	RESHOWER	RESILING
RESCUE	RESEIZE	RESETTLED	RESHOWERED	RESILINS
RESCUED	RESEIZED	RESETTLES	RESHOWERING	RESILVER
RESCUER	RESEIZES	RESETTLING	RESHOWERS	RESILVERED
RESCUERS	RESEIZING	RESEW	RESHOWING	RESILVERING
RESCUES	RESEIZURE	RESEWED	RESHOWN	RESILVERS
RESCUING	RESEIZURES	RESEWING	RESHOWS	RESIN
RESCULPT	RESELECT	RESEWN	RESHUFFLE	RESINATE
RESCULPTED	RESELECTED	RESEWS	RESHUFFLED	RESINATED
RESCULPTING	RESELECTING	RESH	RESHUFFLES	RESINATES
RESCULPTS	RESELECTS	RESHAPE	RESHUFFLING	RESINATING
RESEAL	RESELL	RESHAPED	RESID	RESINED
RESEALED	RESELLER	RESHAPER	RESIDE	RESINIFIED
RESEALING	RESELLERS	RESHAPERS	RESIDED	RESINIFIES
RESEALS	RESELLING	RESHAPES	RESIDENCE	RESINIFY
RESEARCH	RESELLS	RESHAPING	RESIDENCES	RESINIFYING
RESEARCHED	RESEMBLE	RESHARPEN	RESIDENCIES	RESINING
RESEARCHES	RESEMBLED	RESHARPENED	RESIDENCY	RESINLIKE
RESEARCHING	RESEMBLER	RESHARPENING	RESIDENT	RESINOID
RESEASON	RESEMBLERS	RESHARPENS	RESIDENTS	RESINOIDS
RESEASONED	RESEMBLES	RESHAVE	RESIDER	RESINOUS
RESEASONING	RESEMBLING	RESHAVED	RESIDERS	RESINS
RESEASONS	RESEND	RESHAVEN	RESIDES	RESINY
RESEAT	RESENDING	RESHAVES	RESIDING	RESIST
RESEATED	RESENDS	RESHAVING	RESIDS	RESISTANT
RESEATING	RESENT	RESHES	RESIDUA	RESISTANTS
RESEATS	RESENTED	RESHINE	RESIDUAL	RESISTED
RESEAU	RESENTFUL	RESHINED	RESIDUALS	RESISTER
RESEAUS	RESENTING	RESHINES	RESIDUARY	RESISTERS
RESEAUX	RESENTIVE	RESHINGLE	RESIDUE	RESISTING
RESECT	RESENTS	RESHINGLED	RESIDUES	RESISTIVE
RESECTED	RESERPINE	RESHINGLES	RESIDUUM	RESISTOR
RESECTING	RESERPINES	RESHINGLING	RESIDUUMS	RESISTORS
RESECTION	RESERVE	RESHINING	RESIFT	RESISTS
RESECTIONS	RESERVED	RESHIP	RESIFTED	RESIT
RESECTS	RESERVER	RESHIPPED	RESIFTING	RESITE
RESECURE	RESERVERS	RESHIPPER	RESIFTS	RESITED
RESECURED	RESERVES	RESHIPPERS	RESIGHT	RESITES
RESECURES	RESERVICE	RESHIPPING	RESIGHTED	RESITING
RESECURING	RESERVICED	RESHIPS	RESIGHTING	RESITS
RESEDA	RESERVICES	RESHOD	RESIGHTS	RESITTING
RESEDAS	RESERVICING	RESHOE	RESIGN	RESITTINGS
RESEE	RESERVING	RESHOED	RESIGNED	RESITUATE
RESEED	RESERVIST	RESHOEING	RESIGNER	RESITUATED
RESEEDED	RESERVISTS	RESHOES	RESIGNERS	RESITUATES

RESITUATING	RESOLVENTS	RESPECIFY	RESPRAYS	RESTIFORM
RESIZE	RESOLVER	RESPECIFYING	RESPREAD	RESTING
RESIZED	RESOLVERS	RESPECT	RESPREADING	RESTITCH
RESIZES	RESOLVES	RESPECTED	RESPREADS	RESTITCHED
RESIZING	RESOLVING	RESPECTER	RESPRING	RESTITCHES
RESKETCH	RESONANCE	RESPECTERS	RESPRINGING	RESTITCHING
RESKETCHED	RESONANCES	RESPECTING	RESPRINGS	RESTITUTE
RESKETCHES	RESONANT	RESPECTS	RESPROUT	RESTITUTED
RESKETCHING	RESONANTS	RESPELL	RESPROUTED	RESTITUTES
RESLATE	RESONATE	RESPELLED	RESPROUTING	RESTITUTING
RESLATED	RESONATED	RESPELLING	RESPROUTS	RESTIVE
RESLATES	RESONATES	RESPELLS	RESPRUNG	RESTIVELY
RESLATING	RESONATING	RESPELT	REST	RESTLESS
RESMELT	RESONATOR	RESPIRE	RESTABLE	RESTOCK
RESMELTED	RESONATORS	RESPIRED	RESTABLED	RESTOCKED
RESMELTING	RESORB	RESPIRES	RESTABLES	RESTOCKING
RESMELTS	RESORBED	RESPIRING	RESTABLING	RESTOCKS
RESMOOTH	RESORBING	RESPITE	RESTACK	RESTOKE
RESMOOTHED	RESORBS	RESPITED	RESTACKED	RESTOKED
RESMOOTHING	RESORCIN	RESPITES	RESTACKING	RESTOKES
RESMOOTHS	RESORCINS	RESPITING	RESTACKS	RESTOKING
RESOAK	RESORT	RESPLICE	RESTAFF	RESTORAL
RESOAKED	RESORTED	RESPLICED	RESTAFFED	RESTORALS
RESOAKING	RESORTER	RESPLICES	RESTAFFING	RESTORE
RESOAKS	RESORTERS	RESPLICING	RESTAFFS	RESTORED
RESOD	RESORTING	RESPLIT	RESTAGE	RESTORER
RESODDED	RESORTS	RESPLITS	RESTAGED	RESTORERS
RESODDING	RESOUGHT	RESPLITTING	RESTAGES	RESTORES
RESODS	RESOUND	RESPOKE	RESTAGING	RESTORING
RESOFTEN	RESOUNDED	RESPOKEN	RESTAMP	RESTRAIN
RESOFTENED	RESOUNDING	RESPOND	RESTAMPED	RESTRAINED
RESOFTENING	RESOUNDS	RESPONDED	RESTAMPING	RESTRAINING
RESOFTENS	RESOURCE	RESPONDER	RESTAMPS	RESTRAINS
RESOJET	RESOURCES	RESPONDERS	RESTART	RESTRAINT
RESOJETS	RESOW	RESPONDING	RESTARTED	RESTRAINTS
RESOLD	RESOWED	RESPONDS	RESTARTING	RESTRESS
RESOLDER	RESOWING	RESPONSA	RESTARTS	RESTRESSED
RESOLDERED	RESOWN	RESPONSE	RESTATE	RESTRESSES
RESOLDERING	RESOWS	RESPONSES	RESTATED	RESTRESSING
RESOLDERS	RESPACE	RESPONSUM	RESTATES	RESTRETCH
RESOLE	RESPACED	RESPOOL	RESTATING	RESTRETCHED
RESOLED	RESPACES	RESPOOLED	RESTATION	RESTRETCHES
RESOLES	RESPACING	RESPOOLING	RESTATIONED	RESTRETCHING
RESOLING	RESPADE	RESPOOLS	RESTATIONING	RESTRICKEN
RESOLUBLE	RESPADED	RESPOT	RESTATIONS	RESTRICT
RESOLUTE	RESPADES	RESPOTS	RESTED	RESTRICTED
RESOLUTER	RESPADING	RESPOTTED	RESTER	RESTRICTING
RESOLUTES	RESPEAK	RESPOTTING	RESTERS	RESTRICTS
RESOLUTEST	RESPEAKING	RESPRANG	RESTFUL	RESTRIKE
RESOLVE	RESPEAKS	RESPRAY	RESTFULLER	RESTRIKES
RESOLVED	RESPECIFIED	RESPRAYED	RESTFULLEST	RESTRIKING
RESOLVENT	RESPECIFIES	RESPRAYING	RESTFULLY	RESTRING

RESTRINGING	RESUPPLIES	RETAILORS	RETCHING	RETIARIUS
RESTRINGS	RESUPPLY	RETAILS	RETE	RETIARY
RESTRIVE	RESUPPLYING	RETAIN	RETEACH	RETICENCE
RESTRIVEN	RESURFACE	RETAINED	RETEACHES	RETICENCES
RESTRIVES	RESURFACED	RETAINER	RETEACHING	RETICENCIES
RESTRIVING	RESURFACES	RETAINERS	RETEAM	RETICENCY
RESTROOM	RESURFACING	RETAINING	RETEAMED	RETICENT
RESTROOMS	RESURGE	RETAINS	RETEAMING	RETICLE
RESTROVE	RESURGED	RETAKE	RETEAMS	RETICLES
RESTRUCK	RESURGENT	RETAKEN	RETEAR	RETICULA
RESTRUNG	RESURGES	RETAKER	RETEARING	RETICULAR
RESTS	RESURGING	RETAKERS	RETEARS	RETICULE
RESTUDIED	RESURRECT	RETAKES	RETELL	RETICULES
RESTUDIES	RESURRECTED	RETAKING	RETELLING	RETICULUM
RESTUDY	RESURRECTING	RETALIATE	RETELLINGS	RETICULUMS
RESTUDYING	RESURRECTS	RETALIATED	RETELLS	RETIE
RESTUFF	RESURVEY	RETALIATES	RETEM	RETIED
RESTUFFED	RESURVEYED	RETALIATING	RETEMPER	RETIEING
RESTUFFING	RESURVEYING	RETALLIED	RETEMPERED	RETIES
RESTUFFS	RESURVEYS	RETALLIES	RETEMPERING	RETIFORM
RESTYLE	RESUSPEND	RETALLY	RETEMPERS	RETIGHTEN
RESTYLED	RESUSPENDED	RETALLYING	RETEMS	RETIGHTENED
RESTYLES	RESUSPENDING	RETAPE	RETENE	RETIGHTENING
RESTYLING	RESUSPENDS	RETAPED	RETENES	RETIGHTENS
RESUBJECT	RESWALLOW	RETAPES	RETENTION	RETILE
RESUBJECTED	RESWALLOWED	RETAPING	RETENTIONS	RETILED
RESUBJECTING	RESWALLOWING	RETARD	RETENTIVE	RETILES
RESUBJECTS	RESWALLOWS	RETARDANT	RETEST	RETILING
RESUBMIT	RET	RETARDANTS	RETESTED	RETIME
RESUBMITS	RETABLE	RETARDATE	RETESTIFIED	RETIMED
RESUBMITTED	RETABLES	RETARDATES	RETESTIFIES	RETIMES
RESUBMITTING	RETACK	RETARDED	RETESTIFY	RETIMING
RESULT	RETACKED	RETARDER	RETESTIFYING	RETINA
RESULTANT	RETACKING	RETARDERS	RETESTING	RETINAE
RESULTANTS	RETACKLE	RETARDING	RETESTS	RETINAL
RESULTED	RETACKLED	RETARDS	RETEXTURE	RETINALS
RESULTFUL	RETACKLES	RETARGET	RETEXTURED	RETINAS
RESULTING	RETACKLING	RETARGETED	RETEXTURES	RETINE
RESULTS	RETACKS	RETARGETING	RETEXTURING	RETINENE
RESUMABLE	RETAG	RETARGETS	RETHINK	RETINENES
RESUME	RETAGGED	RETASTE	RETHINKER	RETINES
RESUMED	RETAGGING	RETASTED	RETHINKERS	RETINITE
RESUMER	RETAGS	RETASTES	RETHINKING	RETINITES
RESUMERS	RETAIL	RETASTING	RETHINKS	RETINITIDES
RESUMES	RETAILED	RETAUGHT	RETHOUGHT	RETINITIS
RESUMING	RETAILER	RETAX	RETHREAD	RETINITISES
RESUMMON	RETAILERS	RETAXED	RETHREADED	RETINOID
RESUMMONED	RETAILING	RETAXES	RETHREADING	RETINOIDS
RESUMMONING	RETAILINGS	RETAXING	RETHREADS	RETINOL
RESUMMONS	RETAILOR	RETCH	RETIA	RETINOLS
RESUPINE	RETAILORED	RETCHED	RETIAL	RETINT
RESUPPLIED	RETAILORING	RETCHES	RETIARII	RETINTED

RETINTING
RETINTS
RETINUE
RETINUED
RETINUES
RETINULA
RETINULAE
RETINULAR
RETINULAS
RETIRANT
RETIRANTS
RETIRE
RETIRED
RETIREDLY
RETIREE
RETIREES
RETIRER
RETIRERS
RETIRES
RETIRING
RETITLE
RETITLED
RETITLES
RETITLING
RETOLD
RETOOK
RETOOL
RETOOLED
RETOOLING
RETOOLS
RETORE
RETORN
RETORSION
RETORSIONS
RETORT
RETORTED
RETORTER
RETORTERS
RETORTING
RETORTION
RETORTIONS
RETORTS
RETOTAL
RETOTALED
RETOTALING
RETOTALLED
RETOTALLING
RETOTALS
RETOUCH
RETOUCHED
RETOUCHER
RETOUCHERS

RETOUCHES
RETOUCHING
RETRACE
RETRACED
RETRACER
RETRACERS
RETRACES
RETRACING
RETRACK
RETRACKED
RETRACKING
RETRACKS
RETRACT
RETRACTED
RETRACTING
RETRACTOR
RETRACTORS
RETRACTS
RETRAIN
RETRAINED
RETRAINEE
RETRAINEES
RETRAINING
RETRAINS
RETRAL
RETRALLY
RETREAD
RETREADED
RETREADING
RETREADS
RETREAT
RETREATED
RETREATER
RETREATERS
RETREATING
RETREATS
RETRENCH
RETRENCHED
RETRENCHES
RETRENCHING
RETRIAL
RETRIALS
RETRIED
RETRIES
RETRIEVAL
RETRIEVALS
RETRIEVE
RETRIEVED
RETRIEVER
RETRIEVERS
RETRIEVES
RETRIEVING

RETRIM
RETRIMMED
RETRIMMING
RETRIMS
RETRO
RETROACT
RETROACTED
RETROACTING
RETROACTS
RETROCEDE
RETROCEDED
RETROCEDES
RETROCEDING
RETRODICT
RETRODICTED
RETRODICTING
RETRODICTS
RETROFIRE
RETROFIRED
RETROFIRES
RETROFIRING
RETROFIT
RETROFITS
RETROFITTED
RETROFITTING
RETROFLEX
RETROFLEXES
RETRONYM
RETRONYMS
RETROPACK
RETROPACKS
RETRORSE
RETROS
RETROUSSE
RETRY
RETRYING
RETS
RETSINA
RETSINAS
RETTED
RETTING
RETUNE
RETUNED
RETUNES
RETUNING
RETURN
RETURNED
RETURNEE
RETURNEES
RETURNER
RETURNERS
RETURNING

RETURNS
RETUSE
RETWIST
RETWISTED
RETWISTING
RETWISTS
RETYING
RETYPE
RETYPED
RETYPES
RETYPING
REUNIFIED
REUNIFIES
REUNIFY
REUNIFYING
REUNION
REUNIONS
REUNITE
REUNITED
REUNITER
REUNITERS
REUNITES
REUNITING
REUPTAKE
REUPTAKES
REUSABLE
REUSABLES
REUSE
REUSED
REUSES
REUSING
REUTILIZE
REUTILIZED
REUTILIZES
REUTILIZING
REUTTER
REUTTERED
REUTTERING
REUTTERS
REV
REVALUATE
REVALUATED
REVALUATES
REVALUATING
REVALUE
REVALUED
REVALUES
REVALUING
REVAMP
REVAMPED
REVAMPER
REVAMPERS

REVAMPING
REVAMPS
REVANCHE
REVANCHES
REVARNISH
REVARNISHED
REVARNISHES
REVARNISHING
REVEAL
REVEALED
REVEALER
REVEALERS
REVEALING
REVEALS
REVEHENT
REVEILLE
REVEILLES
REVEL
REVELATOR
REVELATORS
REVELED
REVELER
REVELERS
REVELING
REVELLED
REVELLER
REVELLERS
REVELLING
REVELMENT
REVELMENTS
REVELRIES
REVELROUS
REVELRY
REVELS
REVENANT
REVENANTS
REVENGE
REVENGED
REVENGER
REVENGERS
REVENGES
REVENGING
REVENUAL
REVENUE
REVENUED
REVENUER
REVENUERS
REVENUES
REVERABLE
REVERB
REVERBED
REVERBING

REVERBS	REVETTED	REVIVED	REWAKEN	REWIN
REVERE	REVETTING	REVIVER	REWAKENED	REWIND
REVERED	REVIBRATE	REVIVERS	REWAKENING	REWINDED
REVERENCE	REVIBRATED	REVIVES	REWAKENS	REWINDER
REVERENCED	REVIBRATES	REVIVIFIED	REWAKES	REWINDERS
REVERENCES	REVIBRATING	REVIVIFIES	REWAKING	REWINDING
REVERENCING	REVICTUAL	REVIVIFY	REWAN	REWINDS
REVEREND	REVICTUALED	REVIVIFYING	REWARD	REWINNING
REVERENDS	REVICTUALING	REVIVING	REWARDED	REWINS
REVERENT	REVICTUALLED	REVOCABLE	REWARDER	REWIRE
REVERER	REVICTUALLING	REVOCABLY	REWARDERS	REWIRED
REVERERS	REVICTUALS	REVOICE	REWARDING	REWIRES
REVERES	REVIEW	REVOICED	REWARDS	REWIRING
REVERIE	REVIEWAL	REVOICES	REWARM	REWOKE
REVERIES	REVIEWALS	REVOICING	REWARMED	REWOKEN
REVERIFIED	REVIEWED	REVOKABLE	REWARMING	REWON
REVERIFIES	REVIEWER	REVOKE	REWARMS	REWORD
REVERIFY	REVIEWERS	REVOKED	REWASH	REWORDED
REVERIFYING	REVIEWING	REVOKER	REWASHED	REWORDING
REVERING	REVIEWS	REVOKERS	REWASHES	REWORDS
REVERS	REVILE	REVOKES	REWASHING	REWORE
REVERSAL	REVILED	REVOKING	REWAX	REWORK
REVERSALS	REVILER	REVOLT	REWAXED	REWORKED
REVERSE	REVILERS	REVOLTED	REWAXES	REWORKING
REVERSED	REVILES	REVOLTER	REWAXING	REWORKS
REVERSELY	REVILING	REVOLTERS	REWEAR	REWORN
REVERSER	REVIOLATE	REVOLTING	REWEARING	REWOUND
REVERSERS	REVIOLATED	REVOLTS	REWEARS	REWOVE
REVERSES	REVIOLATES	REVOLUTE	REWEAVE	REWOVEN
REVERSING	REVIOLATING	REVOLVE	REWEAVED	REWRAP
REVERSION	REVISABLE	REVOLVED	REWEAVES	REWRAPPED
REVERSIONS	REVISAL	REVOLVER	REWEAVING	REWRAPPING
REVERSO	REVISALS	REVOLVERS	REWED	REWRAPS
REVERSOS	REVISE	REVOLVES	REWEDDED	REWRAPT
REVERT	REVISED	REVOLVING	REWEDDING	REWRITE
REVERTANT	REVISER	REVOTE	REWEDS	REWRITER
REVERTANTS	REVISERS	REVOTED	REWEIGH	REWRITERS
REVERTED	REVISES	REVOTES	REWEIGHED	REWRITES
REVERTER	REVISING	REVOTING	REWEIGHING	REWRITING
REVERTERS	REVISION	REVS	REWEIGHS	REWRITTEN
REVERTING	REVISIONS	REVUE	REWELD	REWROTE
REVERTIVE	REVISIT	REVUES	REWELDED	REWROUGHT
REVERTS	REVISITED	REVUIST	REWELDING	REX
REVERY	REVISITING	REVUISTS	REWELDS	REXES
REVEST	REVISITS	REVULSED	REWET	REXINE
REVESTED	REVISOR	REVULSION	REWETS	REXINES
REVESTING	REVISORS	REVULSIONS	REWETTED	REYNARD
REVESTS	REVISORY	REVULSIVE	REWETTING	REYNARDS
REVET	REVIVABLE	REVVED	REWIDEN	REZERO
REVETMENT	REVIVAL	REVVING	REWIDENED	REZEROED
REVETMENTS	REVIVALS	REWAKE	REWIDENING	REZEROES
REVETS	REVIVE	REWAKED	REWIDENS	REZEROING

REZEROS	RHESUSES	RHODIUMS	RHYTHMIST	RIBLET
REZONE	RHETOR	RHODOLITE	RHYTHMISTS	RIBLETS
REZONED	RHETORIC	RHODOLITES	RHYTHMIZE	RIBLIKE
REZONES	RHETORICS	RHODONITE	RHYTHMIZED	RIBOSE
REZONING	RHETORS	RHODONITES	RHYTHMIZES	RIBOSES
RHABDOM	RHEUM	RHODOPSIN	RHYTHMIZING	RIBOSOMAL
RHABDOMAL	RHEUMATIC	RHODOPSINS	RHYTHMS	RIBOSOME
RHABDOME	RHEUMATICS	RHODORA	RHYTIDOME	RIBOSOMES
RHABDOMES	RHEUMATIZ	RHODORAS	RHYTIDOMES	RIBOZYMAL
RHABDOMS	RHEUMATIZES	RHOMB	RHYTON	RIBOZYME
RHACHIDES	RHEUMIC	RHOMBI	RHYTONS	RIBOZYMES
RHACHIS	RHEUMIER	RHOMBIC	RIA	RIBS
RHACHISES	RHEUMIEST	RHOMBICAL	RIAL	RIBWORT
RHAMNOSE	RHEUMS	RHOMBOID	RIALS	RIBWORTS
RHAMNOSES	RHEUMY	RHOMBOIDS	RIALTO	RICE
RHAMNUS	RHIGOLENE	RHOMBS	RIALTOS	RICEBIRD
RHAMNUSES	RHIGOLENES	RHOMBUS	RIANT	RICEBIRDS
RHAPHAE	RHINAL	RHOMBUSES	RIANTLY	RICED
RHAPHE	RHINITIDES	RHONCHAL	RIAS	RICER
RHAPHES	RHINITIS	RHONCHI	RIATA	RICERCAR
RHAPSODE	RHINO	RHONCHIAL	RIATAS	RICERCARE
RHAPSODES	RHINOCERI	RHONCHUS	RIB	RICERCARI
RHAPSODIC	RHINOCEROS	RHOS	RIBALD	RICERCARS
RHAPSODIES	RHINOCEROSES	RHOTACISM	RIBALDLY	RICERS
RHAPSODY	RHINOLOGIES	RHOTACISMS	RIBALDRIES	RICES
RHATANIES	RHINOLOGY	RHOTIC	RIBALDRY	RICH
RHATANY	RHINOS	RHUBARB	RIBALDS	RICHEN
RHEA	RHIZOBIA	RHUBARBS	RIBAND	RICHENED
RHEAS	RHIZOBIAL	RHUMB	RIBANDS	RICHENING
RHEBOK	RHIZOBIUM	RHUMBA	RIBAVIRIN	RICHENS
RHEBOKS	RHIZOID	RHUMBAED	RIBAVIRINS	RICHER
RHEMATIC	RHIZOIDAL	RHUMBAING	RIBBAND	RICHES
RHEME	RHIZOIDS	RHUMBAS	RIBBANDS	RICHEST
RHEMES	RHIZOMA	RHUMBS	RIBBED	RICHLY
RHENIUM	RHIZOMATA	RHUS	RIBBER	RICHNESS
RHENIUMS	RHIZOME	RHUSES	RIBBERS	RICHNESSES
RHEOBASE	RHIZOMES	RHYME	RIBBIER	RICHWEED
RHEOBASES	RHIZOMIC	RHYMED	RIBBIEST	RICHWEEDS
RHEOBASIC	RHIZOPI	RHYMELESS	RIBBING	RICIN
RHEOLOGIC	RHIZOPOD	RHYMER	RIBBINGS	RICING
RHEOLOGIES	RHIZOPODS	RHYMERS	RIBBON	RICINS
RHEOLOGY	RHIZOPUS	RHYMES	RIBBONED	RICINUS
RHEOMETER	RHIZOPUSES	RHYMESTER	RIBBONING	RICINUSES
RHEOMETERS	RHIZOTOMIES	RHYMESTERS	RIBBONS	RICK
RHEOPHIL	RHIZOTOMY	RHYMING	RIBBONY	RICKED
RHEOPHILE	RHO	RHYOLITE	RIBBY	RICKETIER
RHEOPHILES	RHODAMIN	RHYOLITES	RIBES	RICKETIEST
RHEOSTAT	RHODAMINE	RHYOLITIC	RIBGRASS	RICKETS
RHEOSTATS	RHODAMINES	RHYTA	RIBGRASSES	RICKETY
RHEOTAXES	RHODAMINS	RHYTHM	RIBIER	RICKEY
RHEOTAXIS	RHODIC	RHYTHMIC	RIBIERS	RICKEYS
RHESUS	RHODIUM	RHYTHMICS	RIBLESS	RICKING

RICKRACK	RIDGELINGS	RIFFLES	RIGHTMOST	RILLETTES
RICKRACKS	RIDGELS	RIFFLING	RIGHTNESS	RILLING
RICKS	RIDGEPOLE	RIFFRAFF	RIGHTNESSES	RILLS
RICKSHA	RIDGEPOLES	RIFFRAFFS	RIGHTO	RIM
RICKSHAS	RIDGES	RIFFS	RIGHTS	RIME
RICKSHAW	RIDGETOP	RIFLE	RIGHTSIZE	RIMED
RICKSHAWS	RIDGETOPS	RIFLEBIRD	RIGHTSIZED	RIMER
RICOCHET	RIDGIER	RIFLEBIRDS	RIGHTSIZES	RIMERS
RICOCHETED	RIDGIEST	RIFLED	RIGHTSIZING	RIMES
RICOCHETING	RIDGIL	RIFLEMAN	RIGHTWARD	RIMESTER
RICOCHETS	RIDGILS	RIFLEMEN	RIGHTY	RIMESTERS
RICOCHETTED	RIDGING	RIFLER	RIGID	RIMFIRE
RICOCHETTING	RIDGLING	RIFLERIES	RIGIDIFIED	RIMFIRES
RICOTTA	RIDGLINGS	RIFLERS	RIGIDIFIES	RIMIER
RICOTTAS	RIDGY	RIFLERY	RIGIDIFY	RIMIEST
RICRAC	RIDICULE	RIFLES	RIGIDIFYING	RIMINESS
RICRACS	RIDICULED	RIFLING	RIGIDITIES	RIMINESSES
RICTAL	RIDICULER	RIFLINGS	RIGIDITY	RIMING
RICTUS	RIDICULERS	RIFLIP	RIGIDLY	RIMLAND
RICTUSES	RIDICULES	RIFLIPS	RIGIDNESS	RIMLANDS
RID	RIDICULING	RIFS	RIGIDNESSES	RIMLESS
RIDABLE	RIDING	RIFT	RIGMAROLE	RIMMED
RIDDANCE	RIDINGS	RIFTED	RIGMAROLES	RIMMER
RIDDANCES	RIDLEY	RIFTING	RIGOR	RIMMERS
RIDDED	RIDLEYS	RIFTLESS	RIGORISM	RIMMING
RIDDEN	RIDOTTO	RIFTS	RIGORISMS	RIMOSE
RIDDER	RIDOTTOS	RIG	RIGORIST	RIMOSELY
RIDDERS	RIDS	RIGADOON	RIGORISTS	RIMOSITIES
RIDDING	RIEL	RIGADOONS	RIGOROUS	RIMOSITY
RIDDLE	RIELS	RIGATONI	RIGORS	RIMOUS
RIDDLED	RIESLING	RIGATONIS	RIGOUR	RIMPLE
RIDDLER	RIESLINGS	RIGAUDON	RIGOURS	RIMPLED
RIDDLERS	RIEVER	RIGAUDONS	RIGS	RIMPLES
RIDDLES	RIEVERS	RIGGED	RIJSTAFEL	RIMPLING
RIDDLING	RIF	RIGGER	RIJSTAFELS	RIMROCK
RIDE	RIFAMPIN	RIGGERS	RIKISHA	RIMROCKS
RIDEABLE	RIFAMPINS	RIGGING	RIKISHAS	RIMS
RIDENT	RIFAMYCIN	RIGGINGS	RIKSHAW	RIMSHOT
RIDER	RIFAMYCINS	RIGHT	RIKSHAWS	RIMSHOTS
RIDERLESS	RIFE	RIGHTED	RILE	RIMY
RIDERS	RIFELY	RIGHTEOUS	RILED	RIN
RIDERSHIP	RIFENESS	RIGHTER	RILES	RIND
RIDERSHIPS	RIFENESSES	RIGHTERS	RILEY	RINDED
RIDES	RIFER	RIGHTEST	RILIEVI	RINDLESS
RIDGE	RIFEST	RIGHTFUL	RILIEVO	RINDS
RIDGEBACK	RIFF	RIGHTIES	RILING	RINDY
RIDGEBACKS	RIFFED	RIGHTING	RILL	RING
RIDGED	RIFFING	RIGHTISM	RILLE	RINGBARK
RIDGEL	RIFFLE	RIGHTISMS	RILLED	RINGBARKED
RIDGELINE	RIFFLED	RIGHTIST	RILLES	RINGBARKING
RIDGELINES	RIFFLER	RIGHTISTS	RILLET	RINGBARKS
RIDGELING	RIFFLERS	RIGHTLY	RILLETS	RINGBOLT

RINGBOLTS	RIOTOUS	RIPRAPPING	RITTER	RIVERWEEDS
RINGBONE	RIOTOUSLY	RIPRAPS	RITTERS	RIVES
RINGBONES	RIOTS	RIPS	RITUAL	RIVET
RINGDOVE	RIP	RIPSAW	RITUALISM	RIVETED
RINGDOVES	RIPARIAN	RIPSAWED	RITUALISMS	RIVETER
RINGED	RIPCORD	RIPSAWING	RITUALIST	RIVETERS
RINGENT	RIPCORDS	RIPSAWN	RITUALISTS	RIVETING
RINGER	RIPE	RIPSAWS	RITUALIZE	RIVETS
RINGERS	RIPED	RIPSTOP	RITUALIZED	RIVETTED
RINGGIT	RIPELY	RIPSTOPS	RITUALIZES	RIVETTING
RINGGITS	RIPEN	RIPTIDE	RITUALIZING	RIVIERA
RINGHALS	RIPENED	RIPTIDES	RITUALLY	RIVIERAS
RINGHALSES	RIPENER	RISE	RITUALS	RIVIERE
RINGING	RIPENERS	RISEN	RITZ	RIVIERES
RINGINGLY	RIPENESS	RISER	RITZES	RIVING
RINGLET	RIPENESSES	RISERS	RITZIER	RIVULET
RINGLETED	RIPENING	RISES	RITZIEST	RIVULETS
RINGLETS	RIPENS	RISHI	RITZILY	RIVULOSE
RINGLIKE	RIPER	RISHIS	RITZINESS	RIYAL
RINGNECK	RIPES	RISIBLE	RITZINESSES	RIYALS
RINGNECKS	RIPEST	RISIBLES	RITZY	ROACH
RINGS	RIPIENI	RISIBLY	RIVAGE	ROACHED
RINGSIDE	RIPIENO	RISING	RIVAGES	ROACHES
RINGSIDES	RIPIENOS	RISINGS	RIVAL	ROACHING
RINGTAIL	RIPING	RISK	RIVALED	ROAD
RINGTAILS	RIPOFF	RISKED	RIVALING	ROADBED
RINGTAW	RIPOFFS	RISKER	RIVALLED	ROADBEDS
RINGTAWS	RIPOST	RISKERS	RIVALLING	ROADBLOCK
RINGTOSS	RIPOSTE	RISKIER	RIVALRIES	ROADBLOCKED
RINGTOSSES	RIPOSTED	RISKIEST	RIVALROUS	ROADBLOCKING
RINGWORM	RIPOSTES	RISKILY	RIVALRY	ROADBLOCKS
RINGWORMS	RIPOSTING	RISKINESS	RIVALS	ROADEO
RINK	RIPOSTS	RISKINESSES	RIVE	ROADEOS
RINKS	RIPPABLE	RISKING	RIVED	ROADHOUSE
RINNING	RIPPED	RISKLESS	RIVEN	ROADHOUSES
RINS	RIPPER	RISKS	RIVER	ROADIE
RINSABLE	RIPPERS	RISKY	RIVERBANK	ROADIES
RINSE	RIPPING	RISOTTO	RIVERBANKS	ROADKILL
RINSED	RIPPINGLY	RISOTTOS	RIVERBED	ROADKILLS
RINSER	RIPPLE	RISQUE	RIVERBEDS	ROADLESS
RINSERS	RIPPLED	RISSOLE	RIVERBOAT	ROADS
RINSES	RIPPLER	RISSOLES	RIVERBOATS	ROADSHOW
RINSIBLE	RIPPLERS	RISTRA	RIVERHEAD	ROADSHOWS
RINSING	RIPPLES	RISTRAS	RIVERHEADS	ROADSIDE
RINSINGS	RIPPLET	RISUS	RIVERINE	ROADSIDES
RIOJA	RIPPLETS	RISUSES	RIVERLESS	ROADSTEAD
RIOJAS	RIPPLIER	RITARD	RIVERLIKE	ROADSTEADS
RIOT	RIPPLIEST	RITARDS	RIVERS	ROADSTER
RIOTED	RIPPLING	RITE	RIVERSIDE	ROADSTERS
RIOTER	RIPPLY	RITES	RIVERSIDES	ROADWAY
RIOTERS	RIPRAP	RITONAVIR	RIVERWARD	ROADWAYS
RIOTING	RIPRAPPED	RITONAVIRS	RIVERWEED	ROADWORK

ROADWORKS	ROBOTIZED	ROCKINESS	ROGER	ROLLMOPS
ROAM	ROBOTIZES	ROCKINESSES	ROGERED	ROLLOUT
ROAMED	ROBOTIZING	ROCKING	ROGERING	ROLLOUTS
ROAMER	ROBOTRIES	ROCKINGLY	ROGERS	ROLLOVER
ROAMERS	ROBOTRY	ROCKLESS	ROGUE	ROLLOVERS
ROAMING	ROBOTS	ROCKLIKE	ROGUED	ROLLS
ROAMS	ROBS	ROCKLING	ROGUEING	ROLLTOP
ROAN	ROBUST	ROCKLINGS	ROGUERIES	ROLLWAY
ROANS	ROBUSTA	ROCKOON	ROGUERY	ROLLWAYS
ROAR	ROBUSTAS	ROCKOONS	ROGUES	ROM
ROARED	ROBUSTER	ROCKROSE	ROGUING	ROMAINE
ROARER	ROBUSTEST	ROCKROSES	ROGUISH	ROMAINES
ROARERS	ROBUSTLY	ROCKS	ROGUISHLY	ROMAJI
ROARING	ROC	ROCKSHAFT	ROIL	ROMAJIS
ROARINGLY	ROCAILLE	ROCKSHAFTS	ROILED	ROMAN
ROARINGS	ROCAILLES	ROCKSLIDE	ROILIER	ROMANCE
ROARS	ROCAMBOLE	ROCKSLIDES	ROILIEST	ROMANCED
ROAST	ROCAMBOLES	ROCKWEED	ROILING	ROMANCER
ROASTED	ROCHET	ROCKWEEDS	ROILS	ROMANCERS
ROASTER	ROCHETS	ROCKWORK	ROILY	ROMANCES
ROASTERS	ROCK	ROCKWORKS	ROISTER	ROMANCING
ROASTING	ROCKABIES	ROCKY	ROISTERED	ROMANISE
ROASTS	ROCKABLE	ROCOCO	ROISTERER	ROMANISED
ROB	ROCKABY	ROCOCOS	ROISTERERS	ROMANISES
ROBALO	ROCKABYE	ROCS	ROISTERING	ROMANISING
ROBALOS	ROCKABYES	ROD	ROISTERS	ROMANIZE
ROBAND	ROCKAWAY	RODDED	ROLAMITE	ROMANIZED
ROBANDS	ROCKAWAYS	RODDING	ROLAMITES	ROMANIZES
ROBBED	ROCKBOUND	RODE	ROLE	ROMANIZING
ROBBER	ROCKED	RODENT	ROLES	ROMANO
ROBBERIES	ROCKER	RODENTS	ROLF	ROMANOS
ROBBERS	ROCKERIES	RODEO	ROLFED	ROMANS
ROBBERY	ROCKERS	RODEOED	ROLFER	ROMANTIC
ROBBIN	ROCKERY	RODEOING	ROLFERS	ROMANTICS
ROBBING	ROCKET	RODEOS	ROLFING	ROMAUNT
ROBBINS	ROCKETED	RODES	ROLFS	ROMAUNTS
ROBE	ROCKETEER	RODLESS	ROLL	ROMELDALE
ROBED	ROCKETEERS	RODLIKE	ROLLAWAY	ROMELDALES
ROBES	ROCKETER	RODMAN	ROLLAWAYS	ROMEO
ROBIN	ROCKETERS	RODMEN	ROLLBACK	ROMEOS
ROBING	ROCKETING	RODS	ROLLBACKS	ROMP
ROBINS	ROCKETRIES	RODSMAN	ROLLED	ROMPED
ROBLE	ROCKETRY	RODSMEN	ROLLER	ROMPER
ROBLES	ROCKETS	ROE	ROLLERS	ROMPERS
ROBORANT	ROCKFALL	ROEBUCK	ROLLICK	ROMPING
ROBORANTS	ROCKFALLS	ROEBUCKS	ROLLICKED	ROMPINGLY
ROBOT	ROCKFISH	ROENTGEN	ROLLICKING	ROMPISH
ROBOTIC	ROCKFISHES	ROENTGENS	ROLLICKS	ROMPS
ROBOTICS	ROCKHOUND	ROES	ROLLICKY	ROMS
ROBOTISM	ROCKHOUNDS	ROGATION	ROLLING	RONDEAU
ROBOTISMS	ROCKIER	ROGATIONS	ROLLINGS	RONDEAUX
ROBOTIZE	ROCKIEST	ROGATORY	ROLLMOP	RONDEL

RONDELET	ROOMETTES	ROOTLIKE	ROSARY	ROSINOUS
RONDELETS	ROOMFUL	ROOTLING	ROSCOE	ROSINS
RONDELLE	ROOMFULS	ROOTS	ROSCOES	ROSINWEED
RONDELLES	ROOMIE	ROOTSTALK	ROSE	ROSINWEEDS
RONDELS	ROOMIER	ROOTSTALKS	ROSEATE	ROSINY
RONDO	ROOMIES	ROOTSTOCK	ROSEATELY	ROSOLIO
RONDOS	ROOMIEST	ROOTSTOCKS	ROSEBAY	ROSOLIOS
RONDURE	ROOMILY	ROOTWORM	ROSEBAYS	ROSTELLA
RONDURES	ROOMINESS	ROOTWORMS	ROSEBUD	ROSTELLAR
RONION	ROOMINESSES	ROOTY	ROSEBUDS	ROSTELLUM
RONIONS	ROOMING	ROPABLE	ROSEBUSH	ROSTELLUMS
RONNEL	ROOMMATE	ROPE	ROSEBUSHES	ROSTER
RONNELS	ROOMMATES	ROPED	ROSED	ROSTERS
RONTGEN	ROOMS	ROPELIKE	ROSEFISH	ROSTRA
RONTGENS	ROOMY	ROPER	ROSEFISHES	ROSTRAL
RONYON	ROORBACH	ROPERIES	ROSEHIP	ROSTRALLY
RONYONS	ROORBACHS	ROPERS	ROSEHIPS	ROSTRATE
ROOD	ROORBACK	ROPERY	ROSELIKE	ROSTRUM
ROODS	ROORBACKS	ROPES	ROSELLE	ROSTRUMS
ROOF	ROOSE	ROPEWALK	ROSELLES	ROSULATE
ROOFED	ROOSED	ROPEWALKS	ROSEMARIES	ROSY
ROOFER	ROOSER	ROPEWAY	ROSEMARY	ROT
ROOFERS	ROOSERS	ROPEWAYS	ROSEOLA	ROTA
ROOFIE	ROOSES	ROPEY	ROSEOLAR	ROTAMETER
ROOFIES	ROOSING	ROPIER	ROSEOLAS	ROTAMETERS
ROOFING	ROOST	ROPIEST	ROSERIES	ROTARIES
ROOFINGS	ROOSTED	ROPILY	ROSEROOT	ROTARY
ROOFLESS	ROOSTER	ROPINESS	ROSEROOTS	ROTAS
ROOFLIKE	ROOSTERS	ROPINESSES	ROSERY	ROTATABLE
ROOFLINE	ROOSTING	ROPING	ROSES	ROTATE
ROOFLINES	ROOSTS	ROPY	ROSESLUG	ROTATED
ROOFS	ROOT	ROQUE	ROSESLUGS	ROTATES
ROOFTOP	ROOTAGE	ROQUES	ROSET	ROTATING
ROOFTOPS	ROOTAGES	ROQUET	ROSETS	ROTATION
ROOFTREE	ROOTCAP	ROQUETED	ROSETTE	ROTATIONS
ROOFTREES	ROOTCAPS	ROQUETING	ROSETTES	ROTATIVE
ROOK	ROOTED	ROQUETS	ROSEWATER	ROTATOR
ROOKED	ROOTER	ROQUETTE	ROSEWOOD	ROTATORES
ROOKERIES	ROOTERS	ROQUETTES	ROSEWOODS	ROTATORS
ROOKERY	ROOTHOLD	RORQUAL	ROSHI	ROTATORY
ROOKIE	ROOTHOLDS	RORQUALS	ROSHIS	ROTAVIRUS
ROOKIER	ROOTIER	ROSACEA	ROSIER	ROTAVIRUSES
ROOKIES	ROOTIEST	ROSACEAS	ROSIEST	ROTCH
ROOKIEST	ROOTINESS	ROSACEOUS	ROSILY	ROTCHE
ROOKING	ROOTINESSES	ROSANILIN	ROSIN	ROTCHES
ROOKS	ROOTING	ROSANILINS	ROSINED	ROTE
ROOKY	ROOTLE	ROSARIA	ROSINESS	ROTENONE
ROOM	ROOTLED	ROSARIAN	ROSINESSES	ROTENONES
ROOMED	ROOTLES	ROSARIANS	ROSING	ROTES
ROOMER	ROOTLESS	ROSARIES	ROSINING	ROTGUT
ROOMERS	ROOTLET	ROSARIUM	ROSINOL	ROTGUTS
ROOMETTE	ROOTLETS	ROSARIUMS	ROSINOLS	ROTI

ROTIFER	ROUGHCAST	ROUNDELAY	ROUT	ROWEL
ROTIFERAL	ROUGHCASTING	ROUNDELAYS	ROUTE	ROWELED
ROTIFERAN	ROUGHCASTS	ROUNDELS	ROUTED	ROWELING
ROTIFERANS	ROUGHDRIED	ROUNDER	ROUTEMAN	ROWELLED
ROTIFERS	ROUGHDRIES	ROUNDERS	ROUTEMEN	ROWELLING
ROTIFORM	ROUGHDRY	ROUNDEST	ROUTER	ROWELS
ROTIS	ROUGHDRYING	ROUNDHEEL	ROUTERS	ROWEN
ROTL	ROUGHED	ROUNDHEELS	ROUTES	ROWENS
ROTLS	ROUGHEN	ROUNDING	ROUTEWAY	ROWER
ROTO	ROUGHENED	ROUNDISH	ROUTEWAYS	ROWERS
ROTOR	ROUGHENING	ROUNDLET	ROUTH	ROWING
ROTORS	ROUGHENS	ROUNDLETS	ROUTHS	ROWINGS
ROTOS	ROUGHER	ROUNDLY	ROUTINE	ROWLOCK
ROTOTILL	ROUGHERS	ROUNDNESS	ROUTINELY	ROWLOCKS
ROTOTILLED	ROUGHEST	ROUNDNESSES	ROUTINES	ROWS
ROTOTILLING	ROUGHHEW	ROUNDS	ROUTING	ROWTH
ROTOTILLS	ROUGHHEWED	ROUNDSMAN	ROUTINISM	ROWTHS
ROTS	ROUGHHEWING	ROUNDSMEN	ROUTINISMS	ROYAL
ROTTE	ROUGHHEWN	ROUNDTRIP	ROUTINIST	ROYALISM
ROTTED	ROUGHHEWS	ROUNDTRIPS	ROUTINISTS	ROYALISMS
ROTTEN	ROUGHIES	ROUNDUP	ROUTINIZE	ROYALIST
ROTTENER	ROUGHING	ROUNDUPS	ROUTINIZED	ROYALISTS
ROTTENEST	ROUGHISH	ROUNDWOOD	ROUTINIZES	ROYALLY
ROTTENLY	ROUGHLEG	ROUNDWOODS	ROUTINIZING	ROYALMAST
ROTTER	ROUGHLEGS	ROUNDWORM	ROUTS	ROYALMASTS
ROTTERS	ROUGHLY	ROUNDWORMS	ROUX	ROYALS
ROTTES	ROUGHNECK	ROUP	ROVE	ROYALTIES
ROTTING	ROUGHNECKED	ROUPED	ROVED	ROYALTY
ROTUND	ROUGHNECKING	ROUPET	ROVEN	ROYSTER
ROTUNDA	ROUGHNECKS	ROUPIER	ROVER	ROYSTERED
ROTUNDAS	ROUGHNESS	ROUPIEST	ROVERS	ROYSTERING
ROTUNDITIES	ROUGHNESSES	ROUPILY	ROVES	ROYSTERS
ROTUNDITY	ROUGHS	ROUPING	ROVING	ROZZER
ROTUNDLY	ROUGHSHOD	ROUPS	ROVINGLY	ROZZERS
ROTURIER	ROUGHY	ROUPY	ROVINGS	RUANA
ROTURIERS	ROUGING	ROUSE	ROW	RUANAS
ROUBLE	ROUILLE	ROUSED	ROWABLE	RUB
ROUBLES	ROUILLES	ROUSEMENT	ROWAN	RUBABOO
ROUCHE	ROULADE	ROUSEMENTS	ROWANS	RUBABOOS
ROUCHES	ROULADES	ROUSER	ROWBOAT	RUBACE
ROUE	ROULEAU	ROUSERS	ROWBOATS	RUBACES
ROUEN	ROULEAUS	ROUSES	ROWDIER	RUBAIYAT
ROUENS	ROULEAUX	ROUSING	ROWDIES	RUBASSE
ROUES	ROULETTE	ROUSINGLY	ROWDIEST	RUBASSES
ROUGE	ROULETTED	ROUSSEAU	ROWDILY	RUBATI
ROUGED	ROULETTES	ROUSSEAUS	ROWDINESS	RUBATO
ROUGES	ROULETTING	ROUST	ROWDINESSES	RUBATOS
ROUGH	ROUND	ROUSTED	ROWDY	RUBBABOO
ROUGHAGE	ROUNDBALL	ROUSTER	ROWDYISH	RUBBABOOS
ROUGHAGES	ROUNDBALLS	ROUSTERS	ROWDYISM	RUBBED
ROUGHBACK	ROUNDED	ROUSTING	ROWDYISMS	RUBBER
ROUGHBACKS	ROUNDEL	ROUSTS	ROWED	RUBBERED

RUBBERIER	RUBOFF	RUDDLES	RUGAL	RULERSHIPS
RUBBERIEST	RUBOFFS	RUDDLING	RUGALACH	RULES
RUBBERING	RUBOUT	RUDDOCK	RUGATE	RULIER
RUBBERIZE	RUBOUTS	RUDDOCKS	RUGBIES	RULIEST
RUBBERIZED	RUBRIC	RUDDS	RUGBY	RULING
RUBBERIZES	RUBRICAL	RUDDY	RUGELACH	RULINGS
RUBBERIZING	RUBRICATE	RUDE	RUGGED	RULY
RUBBERS	RUBRICATED	RUDELY	RUGGEDER	RUM
RUBBERY	RUBRICATES	RUDENESS	RUGGEDEST	RUMAKI
RUBBIES	RUBRICATING	RUDENESSES	RUGGEDIZE	RUMAKIS
RUBBING	RUBRICIAN	RUDER	RUGGEDIZED	RUMBA
RUBBINGS	RUBRICIANS	RUDERAL	RUGGEDIZES	RUMBAED
RUBBISH	RUBRICS	RUDERALS	RUGGEDIZING	RUMBAING
RUBBISHES	RUBS	RUDERIES	RUGGEDLY	RUMBAS
RUBBISHY	RUBUS	RUDERY	RUGGER	RUMBLE
RUBBLE	RUBY	RUDESBIES	RUGGERS	RUMBLED
RUBBLED	RUBYING	RUDESBY	RUGGING	RUMBLER
RUBBLES	RUBYLIKE	RUDEST	RUGLIKE	RUMBLERS
RUBBLIER	RUCHE	RUDIMENT	RUGOLA	RUMBLES
RUBBLIEST	RUCHED	RUDIMENTS	RUGOLAS	RUMBLING
RUBBLING	RUCHES	RUE	RUGOSA	RUMBLINGS
RUBBLY	RUCHING	RUED	RUGOSAS	RUMBLY
RUBBOARD	RUCHINGS	RUEFUL	RUGOSE	RUMEN
RUBBOARDS	RUCK	RUEFULLY	RUGOSELY	RUMENS
RUBBY	RUCKED	RUER	RUGOSITIES	RUMINA
RUBDOWN	RUCKING	RUERS	RUGOSITY	RUMINAL
RUBDOWNS	RUCKLE	RUES	RUGOUS	RUMINANT
RUBE	RUCKLED	RUFESCENT	RUGS	RUMINANTS
RUBEL	RUCKLES	RUFF	RUGULOSE	RUMINATE
RUBELLA	RUCKLING	RUFFE	RUIN	RUMINATED
RUBELLAS	RUCKS	RUFFED	RUINABLE	RUMINATES
RUBELLITE	RUCKSACK	RUFFES	RUINATE	RUMINATING
RUBELLITES	RUCKSACKS	RUFFIAN	RUINATED	RUMINATOR
RUBELS	RUCKUS	RUFFIANLY	RUINATES	RUMINATORS
RUBEOLA	RUCKUSES	RUFFIANS	RUINATING	RUMMAGE
RUBEOLAR	RUCTION	RUFFING	RUINATION	RUMMAGED
RUBEOLAS	RUCTIONS	RUFFLE	RUINATIONS	RUMMAGER
RUBES	RUCTIOUS	RUFFLED	RUINED	RUMMAGERS
RUBESCENT	RUDBECKIA	RUFFLER	RUINER	RUMMAGES
RUBICUND	RUDBECKIAS	RUFFLERS	RUINERS	RUMMAGING
RUBIDIC	RUDD	RUFFLES	RUING	RUMMER
RUBIDIUM	RUDDER	RUFFLIER	RUINING	RUMMERS
RUBIDIUMS	RUDDERS	RUFFLIEST	RUINOUS	RUMMEST
RUBIED	RUDDIER	RUFFLIKE	RUINOUSLY	RUMMIER
RUBIER	RUDDIEST	RUFFLING	RUINS	RUMMIES
RUBIES	RUDDILY	RUFFLY	RULABLE	RUMMIEST
RUBIEST	RUDDINESS	RUFFS	RULE	RUMMY
RUBIGO	RUDDINESSES	RUFIYAA	RULED	RUMOR
RUBIGOS	RUDDLE	RUFOUS	RULELESS	RUMORED
RUBIOUS	RUDDLED	RUG	RULER	RUMORING
RUBLE	RUDDLEMAN	RUGA	RULERS	RUMORS
RUBLES	RUDDLEMEN	RUGAE	RULERSHIP	RUMOUR

RUMOURED	RUNNER	RURALIZES	RUSTING	RYNDS
RUMOURING	RUNNERS	RURALIZING	RUSTLE	RYOKAN
RUMOURS	RUNNIER	RURALLY	RUSTLED	RYOKANS
RUMP	RUNNIEST	RURBAN	RUSTLER	RYOT
RUMPLE	RUNNINESS	RUSE	RUSTLERS	RYOTS
RUMPLED	RUNNINESSES	RUSES	RUSTLES	
RUMPLES	RUNNING	RUSH	RUSTLESS	
RUMPLESS	RUNNINGS	RUSHED	RUSTLING	**S**
RUMPLIER	RUNNY	RUSHEE	RUSTPROOF	
RUMPLIEST	RUNOFF	RUSHEES	RUSTPROOFED	
RUMPLING	RUNOFFS	RUSHER	RUSTPROOFING	SAB
RUMPLY	RUNOUT	RUSHERS	RUSTPROOFS	SABADILLA
RUMPS	RUNOUTS	RUSHES	RUSTS	SABADILLAS
RUMPUS	RUNOVER	RUSHIER	RUSTY	SABAL
RUMPUSES	RUNOVERS	RUSHIEST	RUT	SABALS
RUMRUNNER	RUNROUND	RUSHING	RUTABAGA	SABATON
RUMRUNNERS	RUNROUNDS	RUSHINGS	RUTABAGAS	SABATONS
RUMS	RUNS	RUSHLIGHT	RUTH	SABAYON
RUN	RUNT	RUSHLIGHTS	RUTHENIC	SABAYONS
RUNABOUT	RUNTIER	RUSHLIKE	RUTHENIUM	SABBAT
RUNABOUTS	RUNTIEST	RUSHY	RUTHENIUMS	SABBATH
RUNAGATE	RUNTINESS	RUSINE	RUTHFUL	SABBATHS
RUNAGATES	RUNTINESSES	RUSK	RUTHFULLY	SABBATIC
RUNAROUND	RUNTISH	RUSKS	RUTHLESS	SABBATICS
RUNAROUNDS	RUNTISHLY	RUSSET	RUTHS	SABBATS
RUNAWAY	RUNTS	RUSSETING	RUTILANT	SABBED
RUNAWAYS	RUNTY	RUSSETINGS	RUTILE	SABBING
RUNBACK	RUNWAY	RUSSETS	RUTILES	SABE
RUNBACKS	RUNWAYS	RUSSETY	RUTIN	SABED
RUNCINATE	RUPEE	RUSSIFIED	RUTINS	SABEING
RUNDLE	RUPEES	RUSSIFIES	RUTS	SABER
RUNDLES	RUPIAH	RUSSIFY	RUTTED	SABERED
RUNDLET	RUPIAHS	RUSSIFYING	RUTTIER	SABERING
RUNDLETS	RUPTURE	RUST	RUTTIEST	SABERLIKE
RUNDOWN	RUPTURED	RUSTABLE	RUTTILY	SABERS
RUNDOWNS	RUPTURES	RUSTED	RUTTINESS	SABES
RUNE	RUPTURING	RUSTIC	RUTTINESSES	SABIN
RUNELIKE	RURAL	RUSTICAL	RUTTING	SABINE
RUNES	RURALISE	RUSTICALS	RUTTISH	SABINES
RUNG	RURALISED	RUSTICATE	RUTTISHLY	SABINS
RUNGLESS	RURALISES	RUSTICATED	RUTTY	SABIR
RUNGS	RURALISING	RUSTICATES	RYA	SABIRS
RUNIC	RURALISM	RUSTICATING	RYAS	SABLE
RUNKLE	RURALISMS	RUSTICITIES	RYE	SABLEFISH
RUNKLED	RURALIST	RUSTICITY	RYEGRASS	SABLEFISHES
RUNKLES	RURALISTS	RUSTICLY	RYEGRASSES	SABLES
RUNKLING	RURALITE	RUSTICS	RYES	SABOT
RUNLESS	RURALITES	RUSTIER	RYKE	SABOTAGE
RUNLET	RURALITIES	RUSTIEST	RYKED	SABOTAGED
RUNLETS	RURALITY	RUSTILY	RYKES	SABOTAGES
RUNNEL	RURALIZE	RUSTINESS	RYKING	SABOTAGING
RUNNELS	RURALIZED	RUSTINESSES	RYND	SABOTEUR

SABOTEURS	SACQUES	SADDLING	SAFROLE	SAGUM
SABOTS	SACRA	SADE	SAFROLES	SAGY
SABRA	SACRAL	SADES	SAFROLS	SAHIB
SABRAS	SACRALIZE	SADHE	SAG	SAHIBS
SABRE	SACRALIZED	SADHES	SAGA	SAHIWAL
SABRED	SACRALIZES	SADHU	SAGACIOUS	SAHIWALS
SABRES	SACRALIZING	SADHUS	SAGACITIES	SAHUARO
SABRING	SACRALS	SADI	SAGACITY	SAHUAROS
SABS	SACRAMENT	SADIRON	SAGAMAN	SAICE
SABULOSE	SACRAMENTS	SADIRONS	SAGAMEN	SAICES
SABULOUS	SACRARIA	SADIS	SAGAMORE	SAID
SAC	SACRARIAL	SADISM	SAGAMORES	SAIDS
SACATON	SACRARIUM	SADISMS	SAGANASH	SAIGA
SACATONS	SACRED	SADIST	SAGANASHES	SAIGAS
SACBUT	SACREDLY	SADISTIC	SAGAS	SAIL
SACBUTS	SACRIFICE	SADISTS	SAGBUT	SAILABLE
SACCADE	SACRIFICED	SADLY	SAGBUTS	SAILBOARD
SACCADES	SACRIFICES	SADNESS	SAGE	SAILBOARDED
SACCADIC	SACRIFICING	SADNESSES	SAGEBRUSH	SAILBOARDING
SACCATE	SACRILEGE	SAE	SAGEBRUSHES	SAILBOARDS
SACCHARIC	SACRILEGES	SAFARI	SAGELY	SAILBOAT
SACCHARIN	SACRING	SAFARIED	SAGENESS	SAILBOATS
SACCHARINS	SACRINGS	SAFARIING	SAGENESSES	SAILCLOTH
SACCULAR	SACRIST	SAFARIS	SAGER	SAILCLOTHS
SACCULATE	SACRISTAN	SAFE	SAGES	SAILED
SACCULE	SACRISTANS	SAFEGUARD	SAGEST	SAILER
SACCULES	SACRISTIES	SAFEGUARDED	SAGGAR	SAILERS
SACCULI	SACRISTS	SAFEGUARDING	SAGGARD	SAILFISH
SACCULUS	SACRISTY	SAFEGUARDS	SAGGARDS	SAILFISHES
SACHEM	SACRUM	SAFELIGHT	SAGGARED	SAILING
SACHEMIC	SACRUMS	SAFELIGHTS	SAGGARING	SAILINGS
SACHEMS	SACS	SAFELY	SAGGARS	SAILLESS
SACHET	SAD	SAFENESS	SAGGED	SAILMAKER
SACHETED	SADDEN	SAFENESSES	SAGGER	SAILMAKERS
SACHETS	SADDENED	SAFER	SAGGERED	SAILOR
SACK	SADDENING	SAFES	SAGGERING	SAILORLY
SACKBUT	SADDENS	SAFEST	SAGGERS	SAILORS
SACKBUTS	SADDER	SAFETIED	SAGGIER	SAILPLANE
SACKCLOTH	SADDEST	SAFETIES	SAGGIEST	SAILPLANED
SACKCLOTHS	SADDHU	SAFETY	SAGGING	SAILPLANES
SACKED	SADDHUS	SAFETYING	SAGGY	SAILPLANING
SACKER	SADDLE	SAFETYMAN	SAGIER	SAILS
SACKERS	SADDLEBAG	SAFETYMEN	SAGIEST	SAIMIN
SACKFUL	SADDLEBAGS	SAFFLOWER	SAGITTAL	SAIMINS
SACKFULS	SADDLEBOW	SAFFLOWERS	SAGITTARIES	SAIN
SACKING	SADDLEBOWS	SAFFRON	SAGITTARY	SAINED
SACKINGS	SADDLED	SAFFRONS	SAGITTATE	SAINFOIN
SACKLIKE	SADDLER	SAFRANIN	SAGO	SAINFOINS
SACKS	SADDLERIES	SAFRANINE	SAGOS	SAINING
SACKSFUL	SADDLERS	SAFRANINES	SAGS	SAINS
SACLIKE	SADDLERY	SAFRANINS	SAGUARO	SAINT
SACQUE	SADDLES	SAFROL	SAGUAROS	SAINTDOM

SAINTDOMS	SALE	SALIVATED	SALPS	SALTWORK
SAINTED	SALEABLE	SALIVATES	SALS	SALTWORKS
SAINTHOOD	SALEABLY	SALIVATING	SALSA	SALTWORT
SAINTHOODS	SALEP	SALIVATOR	SALSAS	SALTWORTS
SAINTING	SALEPS	SALIVATORS	SALSIFIES	SALTY
SAINTLIER	SALERATUS	SALL	SALSIFY	SALUBRITIES
SAINTLIEST	SALERATUSES	SALLET	SALSILLA	SALUBRITY
SAINTLIKE	SALEROOM	SALLETS	SALSILLAS	SALUKI
SAINTLY	SALEROOMS	SALLIED	SALT	SALUKIS
SAINTS	SALES	SALLIER	SALTANT	SALURETIC
SAINTSHIP	SALESGIRL	SALLIERS	SALTATION	SALURETICS
SAINTSHIPS	SALESGIRLS	SALLIES	SALTATIONS	SALUTARY
SAITH	SALESLADIES	SALLOW	SALTATORY	SALUTE
SAITHE	SALESLADY	SALLOWED	SALTBOX	SALUTED
SAIYID	SALESMAN	SALLOWER	SALTBOXES	SALUTER
SAIYIDS	SALESMEN	SALLOWEST	SALTBUSH	SALUTERS
SAJOU	SALESROOM	SALLOWING	SALTBUSHES	SALUTES
SAJOUS	SALESROOMS	SALLOWISH	SALTCHUCK	SALUTING
SAKE	SALIC	SALLOWLY	SALTCHUCKS	SALVABLE
SAKER	SALICIN	SALLOWS	SALTED	SALVABLY
SAKERS	SALICINE	SALLOWY	SALTER	SALVAGE
SAKES	SALICINES	SALLY	SALTERN	SALVAGED
SAKI	SALICINS	SALLYING	SALTERNS	SALVAGEE
SAKIS	SALIENCE	SALMI	SALTERS	SALVAGEES
SAL	SALIENCES	SALMIS	SALTEST	SALVAGER
SALAAM	SALIENCIES	SALMON	SALTIE	SALVAGERS
SALAAMED	SALIENCY	SALMONID	SALTIER	SALVAGES
SALAAMING	SALIENT	SALMONIDS	SALTIERS	SALVAGING
SALAAMS	SALIENTLY	SALMONOID	SALTIES	SALVARSAN
SALABLE	SALIENTS	SALMONOIDS	SALTIEST	SALVARSANS
SALABLY	SALIFIED	SALMONS	SALTILY	SALVATION
SALACIOUS	SALIFIES	SALOL	SALTINE	SALVATIONS
SALACITIES	SALIFY	SALOLS	SALTINES	SALVE
SALACITY	SALIFYING	SALOMETER	SALTINESS	SALVED
SALAD	SALIMETER	SALOMETERS	SALTINESSES	SALVER
SALADANG	SALIMETERS	SALON	SALTING	SALVERS
SALADANGS	SALIMETRIES	SALONS	SALTINGS	SALVES
SALADS	SALIMETRY	SALOON	SALTIRE	SALVIA
SALAL	SALINA	SALOONS	SALTIRES	SALVIAS
SALALS	SALINAS	SALOOP	SALTISH	SALVIFIC
SALAMI	SALINE	SALOOPS	SALTLESS	SALVING
SALAMIS	SALINES	SALP	SALTLIKE	SALVO
SALARIAT	SALINITIES	SALPA	SALTNESS	SALVOED
SALARIATS	SALINITY	SALPAE	SALTNESSES	SALVOES
SALARIED	SALINIZE	SALPAS	SALTPAN	SALVOING
SALARIES	SALINIZED	SALPIAN	SALTPANS	SALVOR
SALARY	SALINIZES	SALPIANS	SALTPETER	SALVORS
SALARYING	SALINIZING	SALPID	SALTPETERS	SALVOS
SALARYMAN	SALIVA	SALPIDS	SALTPETRE	SAMADHI
SALARYMEN	SALIVARY	SALPIFORM	SALTPETRES	SAMADHIS
SALCHOW	SALIVAS	SALPINGES	SALTS	SAMARA
SALCHOWS	SALIVATE	SALPINX	SALTWATER	SAMARAS

SAMARITAN	SAMPHIRE	SANDBANKS	SANDPIPERS	SANIES
SAMARITANS	SAMPHIRES	SANDBAR	SANDPIT	SANING
SAMARIUM	SAMPLE	SANDBARS	SANDPITS	SANIOUS
SAMARIUMS	SAMPLED	SANDBLAST	SANDS	SANITARIA
SAMBA	SAMPLER	SANDBLASTED	SANDSHOE	SANITARIES
SAMBAED	SAMPLERS	SANDBLASTING	SANDSHOES	SANITARIUM
SAMBAING	SAMPLES	SANDBLASTS	SANDSOAP	SANITARIUMS
SAMBAL	SAMPLING	SANDBOX	SANDSOAPS	SANITARY
SAMBALS	SAMPLINGS	SANDBOXES	SANDSPUR	SANITATE
SAMBAR	SAMPS	SANDBUR	SANDSPURS	SANITATED
SAMBARS	SAMSARA	SANDBURR	SANDSTONE	SANITATES
SAMBAS	SAMSARAS	SANDBURRS	SANDSTONES	SANITATING
SAMBHAR	SAMSHU	SANDBURS	SANDSTORM	SANITIES
SAMBHARS	SAMSHUS	SANDCRACK	SANDSTORMS	SANITISE
SAMBHUR	SAMURAI	SANDCRACKS	SANDWICH	SANITISED
SAMBHURS	SAMURAIS	SANDDAB	SANDWICHED	SANITISES
SAMBO	SANATIVE	SANDDABS	SANDWICHES	SANITISING
SAMBOS	SANATORIA	SANDED	SANDWICHING	SANITIZE
SAMBUCA	SANATORIUM	SANDER	SANDWORM	SANITIZED
SAMBUCAS	SANATORIUMS	SANDERS	SANDWORMS	SANITIZER
SAMBUKE	SANBENITO	SANDFISH	SANDWORT	SANITIZERS
SAMBUKES	SANBENITOS	SANDFISHES	SANDWORTS	SANITIZES
SAMBUR	SANCTA	SANDFLIES	SANDY	SANITIZING
SAMBURS	SANCTIFIED	SANDFLY	SANE	SANITORIA
SAME	SANCTIFIES	SANDGLASS	SANED	SANITORIUM
SAMECH	SANCTIFY	SANDGLASSES	SANELY	SANITORIUMS
SAMECHS	SANCTIFYING	SANDHI	SANENESS	SANITY
SAMEK	SANCTION	SANDHIS	SANENESSES	SANJAK
SAMEKH	SANCTIONED	SANDHOG	SANER	SANJAKS
SAMEKHS	SANCTIONING	SANDHOGS	SANES	SANK
SAMEKS	SANCTIONS	SANDIER	SANEST	SANNOP
SAMENESS	SANCTITIES	SANDIEST	SANG	SANNOPS
SAMENESSES	SANCTITY	SANDINESS	SANGA	SANNUP
SAMIEL	SANCTUARIES	SANDINESSES	SANGAR	SANNUPS
SAMIELS	SANCTUARY	SANDING	SANGAREE	SANNYASI
SAMISEN	SANCTUM	SANDLESS	SANGAREES	SANNYASIN
SAMISENS	SANCTUMS	SANDLIKE	SANGARS	SANNYASINS
SAMITE	SAND	SANDLING	SANGAS	SANNYASIS
SAMITES	SANDABLE	SANDLINGS	SANGER	SANS
SAMIZDAT	SANDAL	SANDLOT	SANGERS	SANSAR
SAMIZDATS	SANDALED	SANDLOTS	SANGFROID	SANSARS
SAMLET	SANDALING	SANDMAN	SANGFROIDS	SANSEI
SAMLETS	SANDALLED	SANDMEN	SANGH	SANSEIS
SAMOSA	SANDALLING	SANDPAPER	SANGHS	SANSERIF
SAMOSAS	SANDALS	SANDPAPERED	SANGRIA	SANSERIFS
SAMOVAR	SANDARAC	SANDPAPERING	SANGRIAS	SANTALIC
SAMOVARS	SANDARACS	SANDPAPERS	SANGUINE	SANTALOL
SAMOYED	SANDBAG	SANDPEEP	SANGUINES	SANTALOLS
SAMOYEDS	SANDBAGGED	SANDPEEPS	SANICLE	SANTERA
SAMP	SANDBAGGING	SANDPILE	SANICLES	SANTERAS
SAMPAN	SANDBAGS	SANDPILES	SANIDINE	SANTERIA
SAMPANS	SANDBANK	SANDPIPER	SANIDINES	SANTERIAS

SANTERO	SAPOGENINS	SAPROPELS	SARDONYXES	SASHAYS
SANTEROS	SAPONATED	SAPROZOIC	SARDS	SASHED
SANTIMI	SAPONIFIED	SAPS	SAREE	SASHES
SANTIMS	SAPONIFIES	SAPSAGO	SAREES	SASHIMI
SANTIMU	SAPONIFY	SAPSAGOS	SARGASSO	SASHIMIS
SANTIR	SAPONIFYING	SAPSUCKER	SARGASSOS	SASHING
SANTIRS	SAPONIN	SAPSUCKERS	SARGASSUM	SASHLESS
SANTO	SAPONINE	SAPWOOD	SARGASSUMS	SASIN
SANTOL	SAPONINES	SAPWOODS	SARGE	SASINS
SANTOLINA	SAPONINS	SARABAND	SARGES	SASKATOON
SANTOLINAS	SAPONITE	SARABANDE	SARGO	SASKATOONS
SANTOLS	SAPONITES	SARABANDES	SARGOS	SASQUATCH
SANTONICA	SAPOR	SARABANDS	SARI	SASQUATCHES
SANTONICAS	SAPORIFIC	SARAN	SARIN	SASS
SANTONIN	SAPOROUS	SARANS	SARINS	SASSABIES
SANTONINS	SAPORS	SARAPE	SARIS	SASSABY
SANTOOR	SAPOTA	SARAPES	SARK	SASSAFRAS
SANTOORS	SAPOTAS	SARCASM	SARKIER	SASSAFRASES
SANTOS	SAPOTE	SARCASMS	SARKIEST	SASSED
SANTOUR	SAPOTES	SARCASTIC	SARKS	SASSES
SANTOURS	SAPOUR	SARCENET	SARKY	SASSIER
SANTUR	SAPOURS	SARCENETS	SARMENT	SASSIES
SANTURS	SAPPED	SARCINA	SARMENTA	SASSIEST
SAP	SAPPER	SARCINAE	SARMENTS	SASSILY
SAPAJOU	SAPPERS	SARCINAS	SARMENTUM	SASSINESS
SAPAJOUS	SAPPHIC	SARCOCARP	SAROD	SASSINESSES
SAPANWOOD	SAPPHICS	SARCOCARPS	SARODE	SASSING
SAPANWOODS	SAPPHIRE	SARCOID	SARODES	SASSWOOD
SAPHEAD	SAPPHIRES	SARCOIDS	SARODIST	SASSWOODS
SAPHEADED	SAPPHISM	SARCOLOGIES	SARODISTS	SASSY
SAPHEADS	SAPPHISMS	SARCOLOGY	SARODS	SASSYWOOD
SAPHENA	SAPPHIST	SARCOMA	SARONG	SASSYWOODS
SAPHENAE	SAPPHISTS	SARCOMAS	SARONGS	SASTRUGA
SAPHENAS	SAPPIER	SARCOMATA	SAROS	SASTRUGI
SAPHENOUS	SAPPIEST	SARCOMERE	SAROSES	SAT
SAPID	SAPPILY	SARCOMERES	SARSAR	SATANG
SAPIDITIES	SAPPINESS	SARCOSOME	SARSARS	SATANGS
SAPIDITY	SAPPINESSES	SARCOSOMES	SARSEN	SATANIC
SAPIENCE	SAPPING	SARCOUS	SARSENET	SATANICAL
SAPIENCES	SAPPY	SARD	SARSENETS	SATANISM
SAPIENCIES	SAPRAEMIA	SARDANA	SARSENS	SATANISMS
SAPIENCY	SAPRAEMIAS	SARDANAS	SARSNET	SATANIST
SAPIENS	SAPREMIA	SARDAR	SARSNETS	SATANISTS
SAPIENT	SAPREMIAS	SARDARS	SARTOR	SATARA
SAPIENTLY	SAPREMIC	SARDINE	SARTORIAL	SATARAS
SAPIENTS	SAPROBE	SARDINED	SARTORII	SATAY
SAPLESS	SAPROBES	SARDINES	SARTORIUS	SATAYS
SAPLING	SAPROBIAL	SARDINING	SARTORS	SATCHEL
SAPLINGS	SAPROBIC	SARDIUS	SASH	SATCHELED
SAPODILLA	SAPROLITE	SARDIUSES	SASHAY	SATCHELS
SAPODILLAS	SAPROLITES	SARDONIC	SASHAYED	SATE
SAPOGENIN	SAPROPEL	SARDONYX	SASHAYING	SATED

SATEEN	SATISFIERS	SAUCIERS	SAVAGERIES	SAVOURERS
SATEENS	SATISFIES	SAUCIEST	SAVAGERY	SAVOURIER
SATELLITE	SATISFY	SAUCILY	SAVAGES	SAVOURIES
SATELLITES	SATISFYING	SAUCINESS	SAVAGEST	SAVOURIEST
SATEM	SATORI	SAUCINESSES	SAVAGING	SAVOURING
SATES	SATORIS	SAUCING	SAVAGISM	SAVOURS
SATI	SATRAP	SAUCY	SAVAGISMS	SAVOURY
SATIABLE	SATRAPIES	SAUGER	SAVANNA	SAVOY
SATIABLY	SATRAPS	SAUGERS	SAVANNAH	SAVOYS
SATIATE	SATRAPY	SAUGH	SAVANNAHS	SAVVIED
SATIATED	SATSUMA	SAUGHS	SAVANNAS	SAVVIER
SATIATES	SATSUMAS	SAUGHY	SAVANT	SAVVIES
SATIATING	SATURABLE	SAUL	SAVANTS	SAVVIEST
SATIATION	SATURANT	SAULS	SAVARIN	SAVVILY
SATIATIONS	SATURANTS	SAULT	SAVARINS	SAVVINESS
SATIETIES	SATURATE	SAULTS	SAVATE	SAVVINESSES
SATIETY	SATURATED	SAUNA	SAVATES	SAVVY
SATIN	SATURATER	SAUNAED	SAVE	SAVVYING
SATINET	SATURATERS	SAUNAING	SAVEABLE	SAW
SATINETS	SATURATES	SAUNAS	SAVED	SAWBILL
SATINETTE	SATURATING	SAUNTER	SAVELOY	SAWBILLS
SATINETTES	SATURATOR	SAUNTERED	SAVELOYS	SAWBONES
SATING	SATURATORS	SAUNTERER	SAVER	SAWBONESES
SATINPOD	SATURNIID	SAUNTERERS	SAVERS	SAWBUCK
SATINPODS	SATURNIIDS	SAUNTERING	SAVES	SAWBUCKS
SATINS	SATURNINE	SAUNTERS	SAVIN	SAWDUST
SATINWOOD	SATURNISM	SAUREL	SAVINE	SAWDUSTS
SATINWOODS	SATURNISMS	SAURELS	SAVINES	SAWDUSTY
SATINY	SATYR	SAURIAN	SAVING	SAWED
SATIRE	SATYRIC	SAURIANS	SAVINGLY	SAWER
SATIRES	SATYRICAL	SAURIES	SAVINGS	SAWERS
SATIRIC	SATYRID	SAUROPOD	SAVINS	SAWFISH
SATIRICAL	SATYRIDS	SAUROPODS	SAVIOR	SAWFISHES
SATIRISE	SATYRLIKE	SAURY	SAVIORS	SAWFLIES
SATIRISED	SATYRS	SAUSAGE	SAVIOUR	SAWFLY
SATIRISES	SAU	SAUSAGES	SAVIOURS	SAWHORSE
SATIRISING	SAUCE	SAUTE	SAVOR	SAWHORSES
SATIRIST	SAUCEBOAT	SAUTED	SAVORED	SAWING
SATIRISTS	SAUCEBOATS	SAUTEED	SAVORER	SAWLIKE
SATIRIZE	SAUCEBOX	SAUTEING	SAVORERS	SAWLOG
SATIRIZED	SAUCEBOXES	SAUTERNE	SAVORIER	SAWLOGS
SATIRIZER	SAUCED	SAUTERNES	SAVORIES	SAWMILL
SATIRIZERS	SAUCEPAN	SAUTES	SAVORIEST	SAWMILLS
SATIRIZES	SAUCEPANS	SAUTOIR	SAVORILY	SAWN
SATIRIZING	SAUCEPOT	SAUTOIRE	SAVORING	SAWNEY
SATIS	SAUCEPOTS	SAUTOIRES	SAVORLESS	SAWNEYS
SATISFICE	SAUCER	SAUTOIRS	SAVOROUS	SAWS
SATISFICED	SAUCERS	SAVABLE	SAVORS	SAWTEETH
SATISFICES	SAUCES	SAVAGE	SAVORY	SAWTIMBER
SATISFICING	SAUCH	SAVAGED	SAVOUR	SAWTIMBERS
SATISFIED	SAUCHS	SAVAGELY	SAVOURED	SAWTOOTH
SATISFIER	SAUCIER	SAVAGER	SAVOURER	SAWYER

SAWYERS
SAX
SAXATILE
SAXES
SAXHORN
SAXHORNS
SAXIFRAGE
SAXIFRAGES
SAXITOXIN
SAXITOXINS
SAXONIES
SAXONY
SAXOPHONE
SAXOPHONES
SAXTUBA
SAXTUBAS
SAY
SAYABLE
SAYED
SAYEDS
SAYER
SAYERS
SAYEST
SAYID
SAYIDS
SAYING
SAYINGS
SAYONARA
SAYONARAS
SAYS
SAYST
SAYYID
SAYYIDS
SCAB
SCABBARD
SCABBARDED
SCABBARDING
SCABBARDS
SCABBED
SCABBIER
SCABBIEST
SCABBILY
SCABBING
SCABBLE
SCABBLED
SCABBLES
SCABBLING
SCABBY
SCABIES
SCABIETIC
SCABIOSA
SCABIOSAS

SCABIOUS
SCABIOUSES
SCABLAND
SCABLANDS
SCABLIKE
SCABROUS
SCABS
SCAD
SCADS
SCAFFOLD
SCAFFOLDED
SCAFFOLDING
SCAFFOLDS
SCAG
SCAGLIOLA
SCAGLIOLAS
SCAGS
SCALABLE
SCALABLY
SCALADE
SCALADES
SCALADO
SCALADOS
SCALAGE
SCALAGES
SCALAR
SCALARE
SCALARES
SCALARS
SCALATION
SCALATIONS
SCALAWAG
SCALAWAGS
SCALD
SCALDED
SCALDIC
SCALDING
SCALDS
SCALE
SCALED
SCALELESS
SCALELIKE
SCALENE
SCALENI
SCALENUS
SCALEPAN
SCALEPANS
SCALER
SCALERS
SCALES
SCALETAIL
SCALETAILS

SCALEUP
SCALEUPS
SCALIER
SCALIEST
SCALINESS
SCALINESSES
SCALING
SCALL
SCALLAWAG
SCALLAWAGS
SCALLION
SCALLIONS
SCALLOP
SCALLOPED
SCALLOPER
SCALLOPERS
SCALLOPING
SCALLOPS
SCALLS
SCALLYWAG
SCALLYWAGS
SCALOGRAM
SCALOGRAMS
SCALP
SCALPED
SCALPEL
SCALPELS
SCALPER
SCALPERS
SCALPING
SCALPS
SCALY
SCAM
SCAMMED
SCAMMER
SCAMMERS
SCAMMING
SCAMMONIES
SCAMMONY
SCAMP
SCAMPED
SCAMPER
SCAMPERED
SCAMPERER
SCAMPERERS
SCAMPERING
SCAMPERS
SCAMPI
SCAMPIES
SCAMPING
SCAMPISH
SCAMPS

SCAMS
SCAMSTER
SCAMSTERS
SCAN
SCANDAL
SCANDALED
SCANDALING
SCANDALLED
SCANDALLING
SCANDALS
SCANDENT
SCANDIA
SCANDIAS
SCANDIC
SCANDIUM
SCANDIUMS
SCANNABLE
SCANNED
SCANNER
SCANNERS
SCANNING
SCANNINGS
SCANS
SCANSION
SCANSIONS
SCANT
SCANTED
SCANTER
SCANTEST
SCANTIER
SCANTIES
SCANTIEST
SCANTILY
SCANTING
SCANTLING
SCANTLINGS
SCANTLY
SCANTNESS
SCANTNESSES
SCANTS
SCANTY
SCAPE
SCAPED
SCAPEGOAT
SCAPEGOATED
SCAPEGOATING
SCAPEGOATS
SCAPES
SCAPHOID
SCAPHOIDS
SCAPHOPOD
SCAPHOPODS

SCAPING
SCAPOLITE
SCAPOLITES
SCAPOSE
SCAPULA
SCAPULAE
SCAPULAR
SCAPULARS
SCAPULARY
SCAPULAS
SCAR
SCARAB
SCARABAEI
SCARABAEUS
SCARABAEUSES
SCARABOID
SCARABS
SCARCE
SCARCELY
SCARCER
SCARCEST
SCARCITIES
SCARCITY
SCARE
SCARECROW
SCARECROWS
SCARED
SCAREDER
SCAREDEST
SCAREHEAD
SCAREHEADS
SCARER
SCARERS
SCARES
SCAREY
SCARF
SCARFED
SCARFER
SCARFERS
SCARFING
SCARFPIN
SCARFPINS
SCARFS
SCARFSKIN
SCARFSKINS
SCARIER
SCARIEST
SCARIFIED
SCARIFIER
SCARIFIERS
SCARIFIES
SCARIFY

SCARIFYING	SCATTIER	SCHAPPES	SCHLEMIEL	SCHMOOS
SCARILY	SCATTIEST	SCHATCHEN	SCHLEMIELS	SCHMOOSE
SCARINESS	SCATTING	SCHATCHENS	SCHLEMIHL	SCHMOOSED
SCARINESSES	SCATTS	SCHAV	SCHLEMIHLS	SCHMOOSES
SCARING	SCATTY	SCHAVS	SCHLEP	SCHMOOSING
SCARIOSE	SCAUP	SCHEDULAR	SCHLEPP	SCHMOOZE
SCARIOUS	SCAUPER	SCHEDULE	SCHLEPPED	SCHMOOZED
SCARLESS	SCAUPERS	SCHEDULED	SCHLEPPING	SCHMOOZER
SCARLET	SCAUPS	SCHEDULER	SCHLEPPS	SCHMOOZERS
SCARLETS	SCAUR	SCHEDULERS	SCHLEPS	SCHMOOZES
SCARP	SCAURS	SCHEDULES	SCHLIERE	SCHMOOZIER
SCARPED	SCAVENGE	SCHEDULING	SCHLIEREN	SCHMOOZIEST
SCARPER	SCAVENGED	SCHEELITE	SCHLIERIC	SCHMOOZING
SCARPERED	SCAVENGER	SCHEELITES	SCHLOCK	SCHMOOZY
SCARPERING	SCAVENGERS	SCHEMA	SCHLOCKIER	SCHMOS
SCARPERS	SCAVENGES	SCHEMAS	SCHLOCKIEST	SCHMUCK
SCARPH	SCAVENGING	SCHEMATA	SCHLOCKS	SCHMUCKS
SCARPHED	SCENA	SCHEMATIC	SCHLOCKY	SCHNAPPER
SCARPHING	SCENARIO	SCHEMATICS	SCHLUB	SCHNAPPERS
SCARPHS	SCENARIOS	SCHEME	SCHLUBS	SCHNAPPS
SCARPING	SCENARIST	SCHEMED	SCHLUMP	SCHNAPS
SCARPS	SCENARISTS	SCHEMER	SCHLUMPED	SCHNAUZER
SCARRED	SCENAS	SCHEMERS	SCHLUMPIER	SCHNAUZERS
SCARRIER	SCEND	SCHEMES	SCHLUMPIEST	SCHNECKE
SCARRIEST	SCENDED	SCHEMING	SCHLUMPING	SCHNECKEN
SCARRING	SCENDING	SCHERZI	SCHLUMPS	SCHNITZEL
SCARRY	SCENDS	SCHERZO	SCHLUMPY	SCHNITZELS
SCARS	SCENE	SCHERZOS	SCHMALTZ	SCHNOOK
SCART	SCENERIES	SCHILLER	SCHMALTZES	SCHNOOKS
SCARTED	SCENERY	SCHILLERS	SCHMALTZIER	SCHNORKEL
SCARTING	SCENES	SCHILLING	SCHMALTZIEST	SCHNORKELED
SCARTS	SCENIC	SCHILLINGS	SCHMALTZY	SCHNORKELING
SCARVES	SCENICAL	SCHISM	SCHMALZ	SCHNORKELS
SCARY	SCENICS	SCHISMS	SCHMALZES	SCHNORRER
SCAT	SCENT	SCHIST	SCHMALZIER	SCHNORRERS
SCATBACK	SCENTED	SCHISTOSE	SCHMALZIEST	SCHNOZ
SCATBACKS	SCENTING	SCHISTOUS	SCHMALZY	SCHNOZES
SCATHE	SCENTLESS	SCHISTS	SCHMATTE	SCHNOZZ
SCATHED	SCENTS	SCHIZIER	SCHMATTES	SCHNOZZES
SCATHES	SCEPTER	SCHIZIEST	SCHMEAR	SCHNOZZLE
SCATHING	SCEPTERED	SCHIZO	SCHMEARED	SCHNOZZLES
SCATOLOGIES	SCEPTERING	SCHIZOID	SCHMEARING	SCHOLAR
SCATOLOGY	SCEPTERS	SCHIZOIDS	SCHMEARS	SCHOLARLY
SCATS	SCEPTIC	SCHIZONT	SCHMEER	SCHOLARS
SCATT	SCEPTICAL	SCHIZONTS	SCHMEERED	SCHOLIA
SCATTED	SCEPTICS	SCHIZOPOD	SCHMEERING	SCHOLIAST
SCATTER	SCEPTRAL	SCHIZOPODS	SCHMEERS	SCHOLIASTS
SCATTERED	SCEPTRE	SCHIZOS	SCHMELZE	SCHOLIUM
SCATTERER	SCEPTRED	SCHIZY	SCHMELZES	SCHOLIUMS
SCATTERERS	SCEPTRES	SCHIZZIER	SCHMO	SCHOOL
SCATTERING	SCEPTRING	SCHIZZIEST	SCHMOE	SCHOOLBAG
SCATTERS	SCHAPPE	SCHIZZY	SCHMOES	SCHOOLBAGS

SCHOOLBOY	SCIENTISM	SCLAFFERS	SCOLIOMAS	SCOPULAS
SCHOOLBOYS	SCIENTISMS	SCLAFFING	SCOLIOSES	SCOPULATE
SCHOOLED	SCIENTIST	SCLAFFS	SCOLIOSIS	SCORBUTIC
SCHOOLING	SCIENTISTS	SCLERA	SCOLIOTIC	SCORCH
SCHOOLINGS	SCIENTIZE	SCLERAE	SCOLLOP	SCORCHED
SCHOOLKID	SCIENTIZED	SCLERAL	SCOLLOPED	SCORCHER
SCHOOLKIDS	SCIENTIZES	SCLERAS	SCOLLOPING	SCORCHERS
SCHOOLMAN	SCIENTIZING	SCLEREID	SCOLLOPS	SCORCHES
SCHOOLMEN	SCILICET	SCLEREIDS	SCOMBRID	SCORCHING
SCHOOLS	SCILLA	SCLERITE	SCOMBRIDS	SCORE
SCHOONER	SCILLAS	SCLERITES	SCOMBROID	SCORECARD
SCHOONERS	SCIMETAR	SCLERITIC	SCOMBROIDS	SCORECARDS
SCHORL	SCIMETARS	SCLERITIS	SCONCE	SCORED
SCHORLS	SCIMITAR	SCLERITISES	SCONCED	SCORELESS
SCHRIK	SCIMITARS	SCLEROID	SCONCES	SCOREPAD
SCHRIKS	SCIMITER	SCLEROMA	SCONCHEON	SCOREPADS
SCHROD	SCIMITERS	SCLEROMAS	SCONCHEONS	SCORER
SCHRODS	SCINCOID	SCLEROMATA	SCONCING	SCORERS
SCHTICK	SCINCOIDS	SCLEROSAL	SCONE	SCORES
SCHTICKS	SCINTILLA	SCLEROSE	SCONES	SCORIA
SCHTIK	SCINTILLAE	SCLEROSED	SCOOCH	SCORIAE
SCHTIKS	SCINTILLAS	SCLEROSES	SCOOCHED	SCORIFIED
SCHUIT	SCIOLISM	SCLEROSING	SCOOCHES	SCORIFIER
SCHUITS	SCIOLISMS	SCLEROSIS	SCOOCHING	SCORIFIERS
SCHUL	SCIOLIST	SCLEROTIA	SCOOP	SCORIFIES
SCHULN	SCIOLISTS	SCLEROTIC	SCOOPABLE	SCORIFY
SCHULS	SCION	SCLEROTICS	SCOOPED	SCORIFYING
SCHUSS	SCIONS	SCLEROTIN	SCOOPER	SCORING
SCHUSSED	SCIROCCO	SCLEROTINS	SCOOPERS	SCORN
SCHUSSER	SCIROCCOS	SCLEROTIUM	SCOOPFUL	SCORNED
SCHUSSERS	SCIRRHI	SCLEROUS	SCOOPFULS	SCORNER
SCHUSSES	SCIRRHOID	SCOFF	SCOOPING	SCORNERS
SCHUSSING	SCIRRHOUS	SCOFFED	SCOOPS	SCORNFUL
SCHVARTZE	SCIRRHUS	SCOFFER	SCOOPSFUL	SCORNING
SCHVARTZES	SCIRRHUSES	SCOFFERS	SCOOT	SCORNS
SCHWA	SCISSILE	SCOFFING	SCOOTCH	SCORPIOID
SCHWARTZE	SCISSION	SCOFFLAW	SCOOTCHED	SCORPION
SCHWARTZES	SCISSIONS	SCOFFLAWS	SCOOTCHES	SCORPIONS
SCHWAS	SCISSOR	SCOFFS	SCOOTCHING	SCOT
SCIAENID	SCISSORED	SCOLD	SCOOTED	SCOTCH
SCIAENIDS	SCISSORING	SCOLDED	SCOOTER	SCOTCHED
SCIAENOID	SCISSORS	SCOLDER	SCOOTERS	SCOTCHES
SCIAENOIDS	SCISSURE	SCOLDERS	SCOOTING	SCOTCHING
SCIAMACHIES	SCISSURES	SCOLDING	SCOOTS	SCOTER
SCIAMACHY	SCIURID	SCOLDINGS	SCOP	SCOTERS
SCIATIC	SCIURIDS	SCOLDS	SCOPE	SCOTIA
SCIATICA	SCIURINE	SCOLECES	SCOPED	SCOTIAS
SCIATICAS	SCIURINES	SCOLECITE	SCOPES	SCOTOMA
SCIATICS	SCIUROID	SCOLECITES	SCOPING	SCOTOMAS
SCIENCE	SCLAFF	SCOLEX	SCOPS	SCOTOMATA
SCIENCES	SCLAFFED	SCOLICES	SCOPULA	SCOTOPHIL
SCIENTIAL	SCLAFFER	SCOLIOMA	SCOPULAE	SCOTOPIA

SCOTOPIAS	SCRABBLERS	SCRAPINGS	SCREECHIER	SCRIES
SCOTOPIC	SCRABBLES	SCRAPPAGE	SCREECHIEST	SCRIEVE
SCOTS	SCRABBLIER	SCRAPPAGES	SCREECHING	SCRIEVED
SCOTTIE	SCRABBLIEST	SCRAPPED	SCREECHY	SCRIEVES
SCOTTIES	SCRABBLING	SCRAPPER	SCREED	SCRIEVING
SCOUNDREL	SCRABBLY	SCRAPPERS	SCREEDED	SCRIM
SCOUNDRELS	SCRAG	SCRAPPIER	SCREEDING	SCRIMMAGE
SCOUR	SCRAGGED	SCRAPPIEST	SCREEDS	SCRIMMAGED
SCOURED	SCRAGGIER	SCRAPPILY	SCREEN	SCRIMMAGES
SCOURER	SCRAGGIEST	SCRAPPING	SCREENED	SCRIMMAGING
SCOURERS	SCRAGGILY	SCRAPPLE	SCREENER	SCRIMP
SCOURGE	SCRAGGING	SCRAPPLES	SCREENERS	SCRIMPED
SCOURGED	SCRAGGLIER	SCRAPPY	SCREENFUL	SCRIMPER
SCOURGER	SCRAGGLIEST	SCRAPS	SCREENFULS	SCRIMPERS
SCOURGERS	SCRAGGLY	SCRATCH	SCREENING	SCRIMPIER
SCOURGES	SCRAGS	SCRATCHED	SCREENINGS	SCRIMPIEST
SCOURGING	SCRAICH	SCRATCHER	SCREENS	SCRIMPILY
SCOURING	SCRAICHED	SCRATCHERS	SCREES	SCRIMPING
SCOURINGS	SCRAICHING	SCRATCHES	SCREW	SCRIMPIT
SCOURS	SCRAICHS	SCRATCHIER	SCREWABLE	SCRIMPS
SCOUSE	SCRAIGH	SCRATCHIEST	SCREWBALL	SCRIMPY
SCOUSES	SCRAIGHED	SCRATCHING	SCREWBALLS	SCRIMS
SCOUT	SCRAIGHING	SCRATCHY	SCREWBEAN	SCRIMSHAW
SCOUTED	SCRAIGHS	SCRAWL	SCREWBEANS	SCRIMSHAWED
SCOUTER	SCRAM	SCRAWLED	SCREWED	SCRIMSHAWING
SCOUTERS	SCRAMBLE	SCRAWLER	SCREWER	SCRIMSHAWS
SCOUTH	SCRAMBLED	SCRAWLERS	SCREWERS	SCRIP
SCOUTHER	SCRAMBLER	SCRAWLIER	SCREWIER	SCRIPS
SCOUTHERED	SCRAMBLERS	SCRAWLIEST	SCREWIEST	SCRIPT
SCOUTHERING	SCRAMBLES	SCRAWLING	SCREWING	SCRIPTED
SCOUTHERS	SCRAMBLING	SCRAWLS	SCREWLIKE	SCRIPTER
SCOUTHS	SCRAMJET	SCRAWLY	SCREWS	SCRIPTERS
SCOUTING	SCRAMJETS	SCRAWNIER	SCREWUP	SCRIPTING
SCOUTINGS	SCRAMMED	SCRAWNIEST	SCREWUPS	SCRIPTS
SCOUTS	SCRAMMING	SCRAWNY	SCREWWORM	SCRIPTURE
SCOW	SCRAMS	SCREAK	SCREWWORMS	SCRIPTURES
SCOWDER	SCRANNEL	SCREAKED	SCREWY	SCRIVE
SCOWDERED	SCRANNELS	SCREAKING	SCRIBAL	SCRIVED
SCOWDERING	SCRAP	SCREAKS	SCRIBBLE	SCRIVENER
SCOWDERS	SCRAPBOOK	SCREAKY	SCRIBBLED	SCRIVENERS
SCOWED	SCRAPBOOKS	SCREAM	SCRIBBLER	SCRIVES
SCOWING	SCRAPE	SCREAMED	SCRIBBLERS	SCRIVING
SCOWL	SCRAPED	SCREAMER	SCRIBBLES	SCROD
SCOWLED	SCRAPER	SCREAMERS	SCRIBBLING	SCRODS
SCOWLER	SCRAPERS	SCREAMING	SCRIBBLY	SCROFULA
SCOWLERS	SCRAPES	SCREAMS	SCRIBE	SCROFULAS
SCOWLING	SCRAPHEAP	SCREE	SCRIBED	SCROGGIER
SCOWLS	SCRAPHEAPS	SCREECH	SCRIBER	SCROGGIEST
SCOWS	SCRAPIE	SCREECHED	SCRIBERS	SCROGGY
SCRABBLE	SCRAPIES	SCREECHER	SCRIBES	SCROLL
SCRABBLED	SCRAPING	SCREECHERS	SCRIBING	SCROLLED
SCRABBLER		SCREECHES	SCRIED	SCROLLING

SCROLLS	SCRUMMAGED	SCULL	SCUNNERING	SCUTTLES
SCROOCH	SCRUMMAGES	SCULLED	SCUNNERS	SCUTTLING
SCROOCHED	SCRUMMAGING	SCULLER	SCUP	SCUTUM
SCROOCHES	SCRUMMED	SCULLERIES	SCUPPAUG	SCUTWORK
SCROOCHING	SCRUMMING	SCULLERS	SCUPPAUGS	SCUTWORKS
SCROOGE	SCRUMS	SCULLERY	SCUPPER	SCUZZ
SCROOGES	SCRUNCH	SCULLING	SCUPPERED	SCUZZBALL
SCROOP	SCRUNCHED	SCULLION	SCUPPERING	SCUZZBALLS
SCROOPED	SCRUNCHES	SCULLIONS	SCUPPERS	SCUZZES
SCROOPING	SCRUNCHIE	SCULLS	SCUPS	SCUZZIER
SCROOPS	SCRUNCHIES	SCULP	SCURF	SCUZZIEST
SCROOTCH	SCRUNCHING	SCULPED	SCURFIER	SCUZZY
SCROOTCHED	SCRUNCHY	SCULPIN	SCURFIEST	SCYPHATE
SCROOTCHES	SCRUPLE	SCULPING	SCURFS	SCYPHI
SCROOTCHING	SCRUPLED	SCULPINS	SCURFY	SCYPHUS
SCROTA	SCRUPLES	SCULPS	SCURRIED	SCYTHE
SCROTAL	SCRUPLING	SCULPT	SCURRIES	SCYTHED
SCROTUM	SCRUTABLE	SCULPTED	SCURRIL	SCYTHES
SCROTUMS	SCRUTINIES	SCULPTING	SCURRILE	SCYTHING
SCROUGE	SCRUTINY	SCULPTOR	SCURRY	SEA
SCROUGED	SCRY	SCULPTORS	SCURRYING	SEABAG
SCROUGES	SCRYING	SCULPTS	SCURVIER	SEABAGS
SCROUGING	SCUBA	SCULPTURE	SCURVIES	SEABEACH
SCROUNGE	SCUBAED	SCULPTURED	SCURVIEST	SEABEACHES
SCROUNGED	SCUBAING	SCULPTURES	SCURVILY	SEABED
SCROUNGER	SCUBAS	SCULPTURING	SCURVY	SEABEDS
SCROUNGERS	SCUD	SCULTCH	SCUT	SEABIRD
SCROUNGES	SCUDDED	SCULTCHES	SCUTA	SEABIRDS
SCROUNGIER	SCUDDING	SCUM	SCUTAGE	SEABOARD
SCROUNGIEST	SCUDI	SCUMBAG	SCUTAGES	SEABOARDS
SCROUNGING	SCUDO	SCUMBAGS	SCUTATE	SEABOOT
SCROUNGY	SCUDS	SCUMBLE	SCUTCH	SEABOOTS
SCRUB	SCUFF	SCUMBLED	SCUTCHED	SEABORNE
SCRUBBED	SCUFFED	SCUMBLES	SCUTCHEON	SEACOAST
SCRUBBER	SCUFFER	SCUMBLING	SCUTCHEONS	SEACOASTS
SCRUBBERS	SCUFFERS	SCUMLESS	SCUTCHER	SEACOCK
SCRUBBIER	SCUFFING	SCUMLIKE	SCUTCHERS	SEACOCKS
SCRUBBIEST	SCUFFLE	SCUMMED	SCUTCHES	SEACRAFT
SCRUBBILY	SCUFFLED	SCUMMER	SCUTCHING	SEACRAFTS
SCRUBBING	SCUFFLER	SCUMMERS	SCUTE	SEADOG
SCRUBBY	SCUFFLERS	SCUMMIER	SCUTELLA	SEADOGS
SCRUBLAND	SCUFFLES	SCUMMIEST	SCUTELLAR	SEADROME
SCRUBLANDS	SCUFFLING	SCUMMILY	SCUTELLUM	SEADROMES
SCRUBS	SCUFFS	SCUMMING	SCUTES	SEAFARER
SCRUFF	SCULCH	SCUMMY	SCUTIFORM	SEAFARERS
SCRUFFIER	SCULCHES	SCUMS	SCUTS	SEAFARING
SCRUFFIEST	SCULK	SCUNCHEON	SCUTTER	SEAFARINGS
SCRUFFILY	SCULKED	SCUNCHEONS	SCUTTERED	SEAFLOOR
SCRUFFS	SCULKER	SCUNGILLI	SCUTTERING	SEAFLOORS
SCRUFFY	SCULKERS	SCUNGILLIS	SCUTTERS	SEAFOOD
SCRUM	SCULKING	SCUNNER	SCUTTLE	SEAFOODS
SCRUMMAGE	SCULKS	SCUNNERED	SCUTTLED	SEAFOWL

SEAFOWLS	SEAPIECES	SEATERS	SECEDERS	SECRETORS
SEAFRONT	SEAPLANE	SEATING	SECEDES	SECRETORY
SEAFRONTS	SEAPLANES	SEATINGS	SECEDING	SECRETS
SEAGIRT	SEAPORT	SEATLESS	SECERN	SECS
SEAGOING	SEAPORTS	SEATMATE	SECERNED	SECT
SEAGULL	SEAQUAKE	SEATMATES	SECERNING	SECTARIAN
SEAGULLS	SEAQUAKES	SEATRAIN	SECERNS	SECTARIANS
SEAHORSE	SEAR	SEATRAINS	SECESSION	SECTARIES
SEAHORSES	SEARCH	SEATROUT	SECESSIONS	SECTARY
SEAL	SEARCHED	SEATROUTS	SECLUDE	SECTILE
SEALABLE	SEARCHER	SEATS	SECLUDED	SECTILITIES
SEALANT	SEARCHERS	SEATWORK	SECLUDES	SECTILITY
SEALANTS	SEARCHES	SEATWORKS	SECLUDING	SECTION
SEALED	SEARCHING	SEAWALL	SECLUSION	SECTIONAL
SEALER	SEARED	SEAWALLS	SECLUSIONS	SECTIONALS
SEALERIES	SEARER	SEAWAN	SECLUSIVE	SECTIONED
SEALERS	SEAREST	SEAWANS	SECONAL	SECTIONING
SEALERY	SEARING	SEAWANT	SECONALS	SECTIONS
SEALIFT	SEARINGLY	SEAWANTS	SECOND	SECTOR
SEALIFTED	SEAROBIN	SEAWARD	SECONDARIES	SECTORAL
SEALIFTING	SEAROBINS	SEAWARDS	SECONDARY	SECTORED
SEALIFTS	SEARS	SEAWARE	SECONDE	SECTORIAL
SEALING	SEAS	SEAWARES	SECONDED	SECTORIALS
SEALLIKE	SEASCAPE	SEAWATER	SECONDER	SECTORING
SEALS	SEASCAPES	SEAWATERS	SECONDERS	SECTORS
SEALSKIN	SEASCOUT	SEAWAY	SECONDES	SECTS
SEALSKINS	SEASCOUTS	SEAWAYS	SECONDI	SECULAR
SEAM	SEASHELL	SEAWEED	SECONDING	SECULARLY
SEAMAN	SEASHELLS	SEAWEEDS	SECONDLY	SECULARS
SEAMANLY	SEASHORE	SEAWORTHIER	SECONDO	SECUND
SEAMARK	SEASHORES	SEAWORTHIEST	SECONDS	SECUNDLY
SEAMARKS	SEASICK	SEAWORTHY	SECPAR	SECUNDUM
SEAMED	SEASIDE	SEBACEOUS	SECPARS	SECURABLE
SEAMEN	SEASIDES	SEBACIC	SECRECIES	SECURANCE
SEAMER	SEASON	SEBASIC	SECRECY	SECURANCES
SEAMERS	SEASONAL	SEBORRHEA	SECRET	SECURE
SEAMIER	SEASONALS	SEBORRHEAS	SECRETARIES	SECURED
SEAMIEST	SEASONED	SEBUM	SECRETARY	SECURELY
SEAMINESS	SEASONER	SEBUMS	SECRETE	SECURER
SEAMINESSES	SEASONERS	SEC	SECRETED	SECURERS
SEAMING	SEASONING	SECALOSE	SECRETER	SECURES
SEAMLESS	SEASONINGS	SECALOSES	SECRETES	SECUREST
SEAMLIKE	SEASONS	SECANT	SECRETEST	SECURING
SEAMOUNT	SEASTRAND	SECANTLY	SECRETIN	SECURITIES
SEAMOUNTS	SEASTRANDS	SECANTS	SECRETING	SECURITY
SEAMS	SEAT	SECATEUR	SECRETINS	SEDAN
SEAMSTER	SEATBACK	SECATEURS	SECRETION	SEDANS
SEAMSTERS	SEATBACKS	SECCO	SECRETIONS	SEDARIM
SEAMY	SEATBELT	SECCOS	SECRETIVE	SEDATE
SEANCE	SEATBELTS	SECEDE	SECRETLY	SEDATED
SEANCES	SEATED	SECEDED	SECRETOR	SEDATELY
SEAPIECE	SEATER	SECEDER	SECRETORIES	SEDATER

SEDATES	SEEDCASE	SEEN	SEICHES	SEIZING
SEDATEST	SEEDCASES	SEEP	SEIDEL	SEIZINGS
SEDATING	SEEDEATER	SEEPAGE	SEIDELS	SEIZINS
SEDATION	SEEDEATERS	SEEPAGES	SEIF	SEIZOR
SEDATIONS	SEEDED	SEEPED	SEIFS	SEIZORS
SEDATIVE	SEEDER	SEEPIER	SEIGNEUR	SEIZURE
SEDATIVES	SEEDERS	SEEPIEST	SEIGNEURIES	SEIZURES
SEDENTARY	SEEDIER	SEEPING	SEIGNEURS	SEJANT
SEDER	SEEDIEST	SEEPS	SEIGNEURY	SEJEANT
SEDERS	SEEDILY	SEEPY	SEIGNIOR	SEL
SEDERUNT	SEEDINESS	SEER	SEIGNIORIES	SELACHIAN
SEDERUNTS	SEEDINESSES	SEERESS	SEIGNIORS	SELACHIANS
SEDGE	SEEDING	SEERESSES	SEIGNIORY	SELADANG
SEDGES	SEEDLESS	SEERS	SEIGNORIES	SELADANGS
SEDGIER	SEEDLIKE	SEES	SEIGNORY	SELAH
SEDGIEST	SEEDLING	SEESAW	SEINE	SELAHS
SEDGY	SEEDLINGS	SEESAWED	SEINED	SELAMLIK
SEDILE	SEEDMAN	SEESAWING	SEINER	SELAMLIKS
SEDILIA	SEEDMEN	SEESAWS	SEINERS	SELCOUTH
SEDILIUM	SEEDPOD	SEETHE	SEINES	SELDOM
SEDIMENT	SEEDPODS	SEETHED	SEINING	SELDOMLY
SEDIMENTED	SEEDS	SEETHES	SEIS	SELECT
SEDIMENTING	SEEDSMAN	SEETHING	SEISABLE	SELECTED
SEDIMENTS	SEEDSMEN	SEG	SEISE	SELECTEE
SEDITION	SEEDSTOCK	SEGETAL	SEISED	SELECTEES
SEDITIONS	SEEDSTOCKS	SEGGAR	SEISER	SELECTING
SEDITIOUS	SEEDTIME	SEGGARS	SEISERS	SELECTION
SEDUCE	SEEDTIMES	SEGMENT	SEISES	SELECTIONS
SEDUCED	SEEDY	SEGMENTAL	SEISIN	SELECTIVE
SEDUCER	SEEING	SEGMENTED	SEISING	SELECTLY
SEDUCERS	SEEINGS	SEGMENTING	SEISINGS	SELECTMAN
SEDUCES	SEEK	SEGMENTS	SEISINS	SELECTMEN
SEDUCIBLE	SEEKER	SEGNI	SEISM	SELECTOR
SEDUCING	SEEKERS	SEGNO	SEISMAL	SELECTORS
SEDUCIVE	SEEKING	SEGNOS	SEISMIC	SELECTS
SEDUCTION	SEEKS	SEGO	SEISMICAL	SELENATE
SEDUCTIONS	SEEL	SEGOS	SEISMISM	SELENATES
SEDUCTIVE	SEELED	SEGREGANT	SEISMISMS	SELENIC
SEDULITIES	SEELING	SEGREGANTS	SEISMS	SELENIDE
SEDULITY	SEELS	SEGREGATE	SEISOR	SELENIDES
SEDULOUS	SEELY	SEGREGATED	SEISORS	SELENIOUS
SEDUM	SEEM	SEGREGATES	SEISURE	SELENITE
SEDUMS	SEEMED	SEGREGATING	SEISURES	SELENITES
SEE	SEEMER	SEGS	SEITAN	SELENITIC
SEEABLE	SEEMERS	SEGUE	SEITANS	SELENIUM
SEECATCH	SEEMING	SEGUED	SEIZABLE	SELENIUMS
SEECATCHIE	SEEMINGLY	SEGUEING	SEIZE	SELENOSES
SEED	SEEMINGS	SEGUES	SEIZED	SELENOSIS
SEEDBED	SEEMLIER	SEI	SEIZER	SELENOUS
SEEDBEDS	SEEMLIEST	SEICENTO	SEIZERS	SELF
SEEDCAKE	SEEMLY	SEICENTOS	SEIZES	SELFDOM
SEEDCAKES	SEEMS	SEICHE	SEIZIN	SELFDOMS

SELFED	SEMANTICS	SEMIFLUIDS	SEMIRURAL	SENEGA
SELFHEAL	SEMAPHORE	SEMIGALA	SEMIS	SENEGAS
SELFHEALS	SEMAPHORED	SEMIGLOSS	SEMISES	SENESCENT
SELFHOOD	SEMAPHORES	SEMIGLOSSES	SEMISOFT	SENESCHAL
SELFHOODS	SEMAPHORING	SEMIGROUP	SEMISOLID	SENESCHALS
SELFING	SEMATIC	SEMIGROUPS	SEMISOLIDS	SENGI
SELFISH	SEMBLABLE	SEMIHARD	SEMISTIFF	SENHOR
SELFISHLY	SEMBLABLES	SEMIHIGH	SEMISWEET	SENHORA
SELFLESS	SEMBLABLY	SEMIHOBO	SEMITIST	SENHORAS
SELFNESS	SEMBLANCE	SEMIHOBOES	SEMITISTS	SENHORES
SELFNESSES	SEMBLANCES	SEMIHOBOS	SEMITONAL	SENHORITA
SELFS	SEME	SEMILLON	SEMITONE	SENHORITAS
SELFSAME	SEMEIOTIC	SEMILLONS	SEMITONES	SENHORS
SELFWARD	SEMEIOTICS	SEMILOG	SEMITONIC	SENILE
SELFWARDS	SEMEME	SEMILUNAR	SEMITRUCK	SENILELY
SELKIE	SEMEMES	SEMIMAT	SEMITRUCKS	SENILES
SELKIES	SEMEMIC	SEMIMATT	SEMIURBAN	SENILITIES
SELL	SEMEN	SEMIMATTE	SEMIVOWEL	SENILITY
SELLABLE	SEMENS	SEMIMETAL	SEMIVOWELS	SENIOR
SELLE	SEMES	SEMIMETALS	SEMIWILD	SENIORITIES
SELLER	SEMESTER	SEMIMICRO	SEMIWORKS	SENIORITY
SELLERS	SEMESTERS	SEMIMILD	SEMOLINA	SENIORS
SELLES	SEMESTRAL	SEMIMOIST	SEMOLINAS	SENITI
SELLING	SEMI	SEMIMUTE	SEMPLE	SENNA
SELLOFF	SEMIANGLE	SEMINA	SEMPLICE	SENNACHIE
SELLOFFS	SEMIANGLES	SEMINAL	SEMPRE	SENNACHIES
SELLOTAPE	SEMIARID	SEMINALLY	SEN	SENNAS
SELLOTAPED	SEMIBALD	SEMINAR	SENARII	SENNET
SELLOTAPES	SEMIBREVE	SEMINARIES	SENARIUS	SENNETS
SELLOTAPING	SEMIBREVES	SEMINARS	SENARY	SENNIGHT
SELLOUT	SEMICOLON	SEMINARY	SENATE	SENNIGHTS
SELLOUTS	SEMICOLONS	SEMINOMA	SENATES	SENNIT
SELLS	SEMICOMA	SEMINOMAD	SENATOR	SENNITS
SELS	SEMICOMAS	SEMINOMADS	SENATORS	SENOPIA
SELSYN	SEMICURED	SEMINOMAS	SEND	SENOPIAS
SELSYNS	SEMIDEAF	SEMINOMATA	SENDABLE	SENOR
SELTZER	SEMIDEIFIED	SEMINUDE	SENDAL	SENORA
SELTZERS	SEMIDEIFIES	SEMIOLOGIES	SENDALS	SENORAS
SELVA	SEMIDEIFY	SEMIOLOGY	SENDED	SENORES
SELVAGE	SEMIDEIFYING	SEMIOPEN	SENDER	SENORITA
SELVAGED	SEMIDOME	SEMIOSES	SENDERS	SENORITAS
SELVAGES	SEMIDOMED	SEMIOSIS	SENDING	SENORS
SELVAS	SEMIDOMES	SEMIOTIC	SENDOFF	SENRYU
SELVEDGE	SEMIDRY	SEMIOTICS	SENDOFFS	SENSA
SELVEDGED	SEMIDWARF	SEMIOVAL	SENDS	SENSATE
SELVEDGES	SEMIDWARFS	SEMIPIOUS	SENDUP	SENSATED
SELVES	SEMIDWARVES	SEMIPRO	SENDUPS	SENSATELY
SEMAINIER	SEMIERECT	SEMIPROS	SENE	SENSATES
SEMAINIERS	SEMIFINAL	SEMIRAW	SENECA	SENSATING
SEMANTEME	SEMIFINALS	SEMIRIGID	SENECAS	SENSATION
SEMANTEMES	SEMIFIT	SEMIROUND	SENECIO	SENSATIONS
SEMANTIC	SEMIFLUID	SEMIROUNDS	SENECIOS	SENSE

SENSED	SENTIENTS	SEPTETTE	SEQUESTRA	SERENITY
SENSEFUL	SENTIMENT	SEPTETTES	SEQUESTRUM	SERER
SENSEI	SENTIMENTS	SEPTIC	SEQUESTRUMS	SERES
SENSEIS	SENTIMO	SEPTICAL	SEQUIN	SEREST
SENSELESS	SENTIMOS	SEPTICITIES	SEQUINED	SERF
SENSES	SENTINEL	SEPTICITY	SEQUINING	SERFAGE
SENSIBLE	SENTINELED	SEPTICS	SEQUINNED	SERFAGES
SENSIBLER	SENTINELING	SEPTIME	SEQUINS	SERFDOM
SENSIBLES	SENTINELLED	SEPTIMES	SEQUITUR	SERFDOMS
SENSIBLEST	SENTINELLING	SEPTS	SEQUITURS	SERFHOOD
SENSIBLY	SENTINELS	SEPTUM	SEQUOIA	SERFHOODS
SENSILLA	SENTRIES	SEPTUMS	SEQUOIAS	SERFISH
SENSILLAE	SENTRY	SEPTUPLE	SER	SERFLIKE
SENSILLUM	SEPAL	SEPTUPLED	SERA	SERFS
SENSING	SEPALED	SEPTUPLES	SERAC	SERGE
SENSITISE	SEPALINE	SEPTUPLET	SERACS	SERGEANCIES
SENSITISED	SEPALLED	SEPTUPLETS	SERAGLIO	SERGEANCY
SENSITISES	SEPALOID	SEPTUPLING	SERAGLIOS	SERGEANT
SENSITISING	SEPALOUS	SEPULCHER	SERAI	SERGEANTIES
SENSITIVE	SEPALS	SEPULCHERED	SERAIL	SERGEANTS
SENSITIVES	SEPARABLE	SEPULCHERING	SERAILS	SERGEANTY
SENSITIZE	SEPARABLY	SEPULCHERS	SERAIS	SERGED
SENSITIZED	SEPARATE	SEPULCHRE	SERAL	SERGER
SENSITIZES	SEPARATED	SEPULCHRED	SERAPE	SERGERS
SENSITIZING	SEPARATES	SEPULCHRES	SERAPES	SERGES
SENSOR	SEPARATING	SEPULCHRING	SERAPH	SERGING
SENSORIA	SEPARATOR	SEPULTURE	SERAPHIC	SERGINGS
SENSORIAL	SEPARATORS	SEPULTURES	SERAPHIM	SERIAL
SENSORIUM	SEPIA	SEQUACITIES	SERAPHIMS	SERIALISE
SENSORIUMS	SEPIAS	SEQUACITY	SERAPHIN	SERIALISED
SENSORS	SEPIC	SEQUEL	SERAPHINS	SERIALISES
SENSORY	SEPIOLITE	SEQUELA	SERAPHS	SERIALISING
SENSUAL	SEPIOLITES	SEQUELAE	SERDAB	SERIALISM
SENSUALLY	SEPOY	SEQUELIZE	SERDABS	SERIALISMS
SENSUM	SEPOYS	SEQUELIZED	SERE	SERIALIST
SENSUOUS	SEPPUKU	SEQUELIZES	SERED	SERIALISTS
SENT	SEPPUKUS	SEQUELIZING	SEREIN	SERIALIZE
SENTE	SEPSES	SEQUELS	SEREINS	SERIALIZED
SENTENCE	SEPSIS	SEQUENCE	SERENADE	SERIALIZES
SENTENCED	SEPT	SEQUENCED	SERENADED	SERIALIZING
SENTENCER	SEPTA	SEQUENCER	SERENADER	SERIALLY
SENTENCERS	SEPTAGE	SEQUENCERS	SERENADERS	SERIALS
SENTENCES	SEPTAGES	SEQUENCES	SERENADES	SERIATE
SENTENCING	SEPTAL	SEQUENCIES	SERENADING	SERIATED
SENTENTIA	SEPTARIA	SEQUENCING	SERENATA	SERIATELY
SENTENTIAE	SEPTARIAN	SEQUENCY	SERENATAS	SERIATES
SENTI	SEPTARIUM	SEQUENT	SERENATE	SERIATIM
SENTIENCE	SEPTATE	SEQUENTS	SERENE	SERIATING
SENTIENCES	SEPTENARIES	SEQUESTER	SERENELY	SERIATION
SENTIENCIES	SEPTENARY	SEQUESTERED	SERENER	SERIATIONS
SENTIENCY	SEPTET	SEQUESTERING	SERENES	SERICEOUS
SENTIENT	SEPTETS	SEQUESTERS	SERENEST	SERICIN

SERICINS	SEROVARS	SERVILITIES	SETS	SEVICHE
SERIEMA	SEROW	SERVILITY	SETSCREW	SEVICHES
SERIEMAS	SEROWS	SERVING	SETSCREWS	SEVRUGA
SERIES	SERPENT	SERVINGS	SETT	SEVRUGAS
SERIF	SERPENTS	SERVITOR	SETTEE	SEW
SERIFED	SERPIGINES	SERVITORS	SETTEES	SEWABLE
SERIFFED	SERPIGO	SERVITUDE	SETTER	SEWAGE
SERIFS	SERPIGOES	SERVITUDES	SETTERS	SEWAGES
SERIGRAPH	SERPIGOS	SERVO	SETTING	SEWAN
SERIGRAPHS	SERRANID	SERVOS	SETTINGS	SEWANS
SERIN	SERRANIDS	SESAME	SETTLE	SEWAR
SERINE	SERRANO	SESAMES	SETTLED	SEWARS
SERINES	SERRANOID	SESAMOID	SETTLER	SEWED
SERING	SERRANOS	SESAMOIDS	SETTLERS	SEWER
SERINGA	SERRATE	SESSILE	SETTLES	SEWERAGE
SERINGAS	SERRATED	SESSILITIES	SETTLING	SEWERAGES
SERINS	SERRATES	SESSILITY	SETTLINGS	SEWERED
SERIOUS	SERRATING	SESSION	SETTLOR	SEWERING
SERIOUSLY	SERRATION	SESSIONAL	SETTLORS	SEWERLESS
SERJEANT	SERRATIONS	SESSIONS	SETTS	SEWERLIKE
SERJEANTIES	SERRATURE	SESSPOOL	SETULOSE	SEWERS
SERJEANTS	SERRATURES	SESSPOOLS	SETULOUS	SEWING
SERJEANTY	SERRIED	SESTERCE	SETUP	SEWINGS
SERMON	SERRIEDLY	SESTERCES	SETUPS	SEWN
SERMONIC	SERRIES	SESTERTIA	SEVEN	SEWS
SERMONIZE	SERRULATE	SESTERTIUM	SEVENFOLD	SEX
SERMONIZED	SERRY	SESTET	SEVENS	SEXED
SERMONIZES	SERRYING	SESTETS	SEVENTEEN	SEXENNIAL
SERMONIZING	SERS	SESTINA	SEVENTEENS	SEXENNIALS
SERMONS	SERUM	SESTINAS	SEVENTH	SEXES
SEROLOGIC	SERUMAL	SESTINE	SEVENTHLY	SEXIER
SEROLOGIES	SERUMS	SESTINES	SEVENTHS	SEXIEST
SEROLOGY	SERVABLE	SET	SEVENTIES	SEXILY
SEROSA	SERVAL	SETA	SEVENTY	SEXINESS
SEROSAE	SERVALS	SETACEOUS	SEVER	SEXINESSES
SEROSAL	SERVANT	SETAE	SEVERABLE	SEXING
SEROSAS	SERVANTS	SETAL	SEVERAL	SEXISM
SEROSITIES	SERVE	SETBACK	SEVERALLY	SEXISMS
SEROSITY	SERVED	SETBACKS	SEVERALS	SEXIST
SEROTINAL	SERVER	SETENANT	SEVERALTIES	SEXISTS
SEROTINE	SERVERS	SETENANTS	SEVERALTY	SEXLESS
SEROTINES	SERVES	SETIFORM	SEVERANCE	SEXLESSLY
SEROTINIES	SERVICE	SETLINE	SEVERANCES	SEXOLOGIC
SEROTINY	SERVICED	SETLINES	SEVERE	SEXOLOGIES
SEROTONIN	SERVICER	SETOFF	SEVERED	SEXOLOGY
SEROTONINS	SERVICERS	SETOFFS	SEVERELY	SEXPOT
SEROTYPE	SERVICES	SETON	SEVERER	SEXPOTS
SEROTYPED	SERVICING	SETONS	SEVEREST	SEXT
SEROTYPES	SERVIETTE	SETOSE	SEVERING	SEXTAIN
SEROTYPING	SERVIETTES	SETOUS	SEVERITIES	SEXTAINS
SEROUS	SERVILE	SETOUT	SEVERITY	SEXTAN
SEROVAR	SERVILELY	SETOUTS	SEVERS	SEXTANS

SEXTANT	SHACKLED	SHADOWING	SHAKINESS	SHAMEFAST
SEXTANTS	SHACKLER	SHADOWS	SHAKINESSES	SHAMEFUL
SEXTARII	SHACKLERS	SHADOWY	SHAKING	SHAMELESS
SEXTARIUS	SHACKLES	SHADRACH	SHAKO	SHAMES
SEXTET	SHACKLING	SHADRACHS	SHAKOES	SHAMING
SEXTETS	SHACKO	SHADS	SHAKOS	SHAMISEN
SEXTETTE	SHACKOES	SHADUF	SHAKY	SHAMISENS
SEXTETTES	SHACKOS	SHADUFS	SHALE	SHAMMAS
SEXTILE	SHACKS	SHADY	SHALED	SHAMMASH
SEXTILES	SHAD	SHAFT	SHALELIKE	SHAMMASHIM
SEXTO	SHADBERRIES	SHAFTED	SHALES	SHAMMASIM
SEXTON	SHADBERRY	SHAFTING	SHALEY	SHAMMED
SEXTONS	SHADBLOW	SHAFTINGS	SHALIER	SHAMMER
SEXTOS	SHADBLOWS	SHAFTS	SHALIEST	SHAMMERS
SEXTS	SHADBUSH	SHAG	SHALL	SHAMMES
SEXTUPLE	SHADBUSHES	SHAGBARK	SHALLOON	SHAMMIED
SEXTUPLED	SHADCHAN	SHAGBARKS	SHALLOONS	SHAMMIES
SEXTUPLES	SHADCHANIM	SHAGGED	SHALLOP	SHAMMING
SEXTUPLET	SHADCHANS	SHAGGIER	SHALLOPS	SHAMMOS
SEXTUPLETS	SHADDOCK	SHAGGIEST	SHALLOT	SHAMMOSIM
SEXTUPLING	SHADDOCKS	SHAGGILY	SHALLOTS	SHAMMY
SEXTUPLY	SHADE	SHAGGING	SHALLOW	SHAMMYING
SEXUAL	SHADED	SHAGGY	SHALLOWED	SHAMOIS
SEXUALITIES	SHADELESS	SHAGREEN	SHALLOWER	SHAMOS
SEXUALITY	SHADER	SHAGREENS	SHALLOWEST	SHAMOSIM
SEXUALIZE	SHADERS	SHAGS	SHALLOWING	SHAMOY
SEXUALIZED	SHADES	SHAH	SHALLOWLY	SHAMOYED
SEXUALIZES	SHADFLIES	SHAHDOM	SHALLOWS	SHAMOYING
SEXUALIZING	SHADFLY	SHAHDOMS	SHALOM	SHAMOYS
SEXUALLY	SHADIER	SHAHS	SHALOMS	SHAMPOO
SEXY	SHADIEST	SHAIRD	SHALT	SHAMPOOED
SFERICS	SHADILY	SHAIRDS	SHALY	SHAMPOOER
SFORZANDI	SHADINESS	SHAIRN	SHAM	SHAMPOOERS
SFORZANDO	SHADINESSES	SHAIRNS	SHAMABLE	SHAMPOOING
SFORZANDOS	SHADING	SHAITAN	SHAMABLY	SHAMPOOS
SFORZATO	SHADINGS	SHAITANS	SHAMAN	SHAMROCK
SFORZATOS	SHADKHAN	SHAKABLE	SHAMANIC	SHAMROCKS
SFUMATO	SHADKHANIM	SHAKE	SHAMANISM	SHAMS
SFUMATOS	SHADKHANS	SHAKEABLE	SHAMANISMS	SHAMUS
SGRAFFITI	SHADOOF	SHAKEDOWN	SHAMANIST	SHAMUSES
SGRAFFITO	SHADOOFS	SHAKEDOWNS	SHAMANISTS	SHANACHIE
SH	SHADOW	SHAKEN	SHAMANS	SHANACHIES
SHA	SHADOWBOX	SHAKEOUT	SHAMAS	SHANDIES
SHABBATOT	SHADOWBOXED	SHAKEOUTS	SHAMBLE	SHANDY
SHABBIER	SHADOWBOXES	SHAKER	SHAMBLED	SHANGHAI
SHABBIEST	SHADOWBOXING	SHAKERS	SHAMBLES	SHANGHAIED
SHABBILY	SHADOWED	SHAKES	SHAMBLING	SHANGHAIING
SHABBY	SHADOWER	SHAKEUP	SHAMBOLIC	SHANGHAIS
SHACK	SHADOWERS	SHAKEUPS	SHAME	SHANK
SHACKED	SHADOWIER	SHAKIER	SHAMEABLE	SHANKED
SHACKING	SHADOWIEST	SHAKIEST	SHAMEABLY	SHANKING
SHACKLE	SHADOWILY	SHAKILY	SHAMED	SHANKS

SHANNIES	SHARING	SHAVE	SHEATH	SHEEPMAN
SHANNY	SHARK	SHAVED	SHEATHE	SHEEPMEN
SHANTEY	SHARKED	SHAVELING	SHEATHED	SHEEPSKIN
SHANTEYS	SHARKER	SHAVELINGS	SHEATHER	SHEEPSKINS
SHANTI	SHARKERS	SHAVEN	SHEATHERS	SHEEPWALK
SHANTIES	SHARKING	SHAVER	SHEATHES	SHEEPWALKS
SHANTIH	SHARKLIKE	SHAVERS	SHEATHING	SHEER
SHANTIHS	SHARKS	SHAVES	SHEATHINGS	SHEERED
SHANTIS	SHARKSKIN	SHAVETAIL	SHEATHS	SHEERER
SHANTUNG	SHARKSKINS	SHAVETAILS	SHEAVE	SHEEREST
SHANTUNGS	SHARN	SHAVIE	SHEAVED	SHEERING
SHANTY	SHARNS	SHAVIES	SHEAVES	SHEERLEGS
SHANTYMAN	SHARNY	SHAVING	SHEAVING	SHEERLY
SHANTYMEN	SHARP	SHAVINGS	SHEBANG	SHEERNESS
SHAPABLE	SHARPED	SHAW	SHEBANGS	SHEERNESSES
SHAPE	SHARPEN	SHAWED	SHEBEAN	SHEERS
SHAPEABLE	SHARPENED	SHAWING	SHEBEANS	SHEESH
SHAPED	SHARPENER	SHAWL	SHEBEEN	SHEET
SHAPELESS	SHARPENERS	SHAWLED	SHEBEENS	SHEETED
SHAPELIER	SHARPENING	SHAWLING	SHED	SHEETER
SHAPELIEST	SHARPENS	SHAWLS	SHEDABLE	SHEETERS
SHAPELY	SHARPER	SHAWM	SHEDDABLE	SHEETFED
SHAPEN	SHARPERS	SHAWMS	SHEDDED	SHEETING
SHAPER	SHARPEST	SHAWN	SHEDDER	SHEETINGS
SHAPERS	SHARPIE	SHAWS	SHEDDERS	SHEETLESS
SHAPES	SHARPIES	SHAY	SHEDDING	SHEETLIKE
SHAPEUP	SHARPING	SHAYS	SHEDLIKE	SHEETROCK
SHAPEUPS	SHARPLY	SHAZAM	SHEDS	SHEETROCKED
SHAPEWEAR	SHARPNESS	SHE	SHEEN	SHEETROCKING
SHAPING	SHARPNESSES	SHEA	SHEENED	SHEETROCKS
SHARABLE	SHARPS	SHEAF	SHEENEY	SHEETS
SHARD	SHARPY	SHEAFED	SHEENEYS	SHEEVE
SHARDS	SHASHLICK	SHEAFING	SHEENFUL	SHEEVES
SHARE	SHASHLICKS	SHEAFLIKE	SHEENIE	SHEGETZ
SHAREABLE	SHASHLIK	SHEAFS	SHEENIER	SHEIK
SHARECROP	SHASHLIKS	SHEAL	SHEENIES	SHEIKDOM
SHARECROPPED	SHASLIK	SHEALING	SHEENIEST	SHEIKDOMS
SHARECROPPING	SHASLIKS	SHEALINGS	SHEENING	SHEIKH
SHARECROPS	SHAT	SHEALS	SHEENS	SHEIKHDOM
SHARED	SHATTER	SHEAR	SHEENY	SHEIKHDOMS
SHARER	SHATTERED	SHEARED	SHEEP	SHEIKHS
SHARERS	SHATTERER	SHEARER	SHEEPCOT	SHEIKS
SHARES	SHATTERERS	SHEARERS	SHEEPCOTE	SHEILA
SHAREWARE	SHATTERING	SHEARING	SHEEPCOTES	SHEILAS
SHAREWARES	SHATTERS	SHEARINGS	SHEEPCOTS	SHEITAN
SHARIA	SHAUGH	SHEARLEGS	SHEEPDOG	SHEITANS
SHARIAH	SHAUGHS	SHEARLING	SHEEPDOGS	SHEKALIM
SHARIAHS	SHAUL	SHEARLINGS	SHEEPFOLD	SHEKEL
SHARIAS	SHAULED	SHEARS	SHEEPFOLDS	SHEKELIM
SHARIF	SHAULING	SHEAS	SHEEPHEAD	SHEKELS
SHARIFIAN	SHAULS	SHEATFISH	SHEEPHEADS	SHELDRAKE
SHARIFS	SHAVABLE	SHEATFISHES	SHEEPISH	SHELDRAKES

SHELDUCK	SHEND	SHIATSU	SHIKKERS	SHINGLING
SHELDUCKS	SHENDING	SHIATSUS	SHIKSA	SHINGLY
SHELF	SHENDS	SHIATZU	SHIKSAS	SHINGUARD
SHELFFUL	SHENT	SHIATZUS	SHIKSE	SHINGUARDS
SHELFFULS	SHEOL	SHIBAH	SHIKSEH	SHINIER
SHELFLIKE	SHEOLS	SHIBAHS	SHIKSEHS	SHINIEST
SHELL	SHEPHERD	SHICKER	SHIKSES	SHINILY
SHELLAC	SHEPHERDED	SHICKERED	SHILINGI	SHININESS
SHELLACK	SHEPHERDING	SHICKERS	SHILL	SHININESSES
SHELLACKED	SHEPHERDS	SHICKSA	SHILLALA	SHINING
SHELLACKING	SHEQALIM	SHICKSAS	SHILLALAH	SHININGLY
SHELLACKS	SHEQEL	SHIED	SHILLALAHS	SHINLEAF
SHELLACS	SHEQELS	SHIEL	SHILLALAS	SHINLEAFS
SHELLBACK	SHERBERT	SHIELD	SHILLED	SHINLEAVES
SHELLBACKS	SHERBERTS	SHIELDED	SHILLELAH	SHINNED
SHELLBARK	SHERBET	SHIELDER	SHILLELAHS	SHINNERIES
SHELLBARKS	SHERBETS	SHIELDERS	SHILLING	SHINNERY
SHELLED	SHERD	SHIELDING	SHILLINGS	SHINNEY
SHELLER	SHERDS	SHIELDS	SHILLS	SHINNEYED
SHELLERS	SHEREEF	SHIELING	SHILPIT	SHINNEYING
SHELLFIRE	SHEREEFS	SHIELINGS	SHILY	SHINNEYS
SHELLFIRES	SHERIF	SHIELS	SHIM	SHINNIED
SHELLFISH	SHERIFF	SHIER	SHIMMED	SHINNIES
SHELLFISHES	SHERIFFS	SHIERS	SHIMMER	SHINNING
SHELLIER	SHERIFS	SHIES	SHIMMERED	SHINNY
SHELLIEST	SHERLOCK	SHIEST	SHIMMERING	SHINNYING
SHELLING	SHERLOCKS	SHIFT	SHIMMERS	SHINS
SHELLS	SHEROOT	SHIFTABLE	SHIMMERY	SHINY
SHELLWORK	SHEROOTS	SHIFTED	SHIMMIED	SHIP
SHELLWORKS	SHERPA	SHIFTER	SHIMMIES	SHIPBOARD
SHELLY	SHERPAS	SHIFTERS	SHIMMING	SHIPBOARDS
SHELTA	SHERRIES	SHIFTIER	SHIMMY	SHIPBORNE
SHELTAS	SHERRIS	SHIFTIEST	SHIMMYING	SHIPLAP
SHELTER	SHERRISES	SHIFTILY	SHIMS	SHIPLAPS
SHELTERED	SHERRY	SHIFTING	SHIN	SHIPLESS
SHELTERER	SHES	SHIFTLESS	SHINBONE	SHIPLOAD
SHELTERERS	SHETLAND	SHIFTS	SHINBONES	SHIPLOADS
SHELTERING	SHETLANDS	SHIFTY	SHINDIES	SHIPMAN
SHELTERS	SHEUCH	SHIGELLA	SHINDIG	SHIPMATE
SHELTIE	SHEUCHS	SHIGELLAE	SHINDIGS	SHIPMATES
SHELTIES	SHEUGH	SHIGELLAS	SHINDY	SHIPMEN
SHELTY	SHEUGHS	SHIITAKE	SHINDYS	SHIPMENT
SHELVE	SHEW	SHIITAKES	SHINE	SHIPMENTS
SHELVED	SHEWBREAD	SHIKAR	SHINED	SHIPOWNER
SHELVER	SHEWBREADS	SHIKAREE	SHINER	SHIPOWNERS
SHELVERS	SHEWED	SHIKAREES	SHINERS	SHIPPABLE
SHELVES	SHEWER	SHIKARI	SHINES	SHIPPED
SHELVIER	SHEWERS	SHIKARIS	SHINGLE	SHIPPEN
SHELVIEST	SHEWING	SHIKARRED	SHINGLED	SHIPPENS
SHELVING	SHEWN	SHIKARRING	SHINGLER	SHIPPER
SHELVINGS	SHEWS	SHIKARS	SHINGLERS	SHIPPERS
SHELVY	SHH	SHIKKER	SHINGLES	SHIPPING

SHIPPINGS	SHITLISTS	SHLUB	SHODDY	SHOOFLY
SHIPPON	SHITLOAD	SHLUBS	SHOE	SHOOING
SHIPPONS	SHITLOADS	SHLUMP	SHOEBILL	SHOOK
SHIPS	SHITS	SHLUMPED	SHOEBILLS	SHOOKS
SHIPSHAPE	SHITTAH	SHLUMPING	SHOEBLACK	SHOOL
SHIPSIDE	SHITTAHS	SHLUMPS	SHOEBLACKS	SHOOLED
SHIPSIDES	SHITTED	SHLUMPY	SHOEBOX	SHOOLING
SHIPWAY	SHITTIER	SHMALTZ	SHOEBOXES	SHOOLS
SHIPWAYS	SHITTIEST	SHMALTZES	SHOED	SHOON
SHIPWORM	SHITTIM	SHMALTZIER	SHOEHORN	SHOOS
SHIPWORMS	SHITTIMS	SHMALTZIEST	SHOEHORNED	SHOOT
SHIPWRECK	SHITTING	SHMALTZY	SHOEHORNING	SHOOTDOWN
SHIPWRECKED	SHITTY	SHMEAR	SHOEHORNS	SHOOTDOWNS
SHIPWRECKING	SHIV	SHMEARS	SHOEING	SHOOTER
SHIPWRECKS	SHIVA	SHMO	SHOELACE	SHOOTERS
SHIPYARD	SHIVAH	SHMOES	SHOELACES	SHOOTING
SHIPYARDS	SHIVAHS	SHMOOZE	SHOELESS	SHOOTINGS
SHIRE	SHIVAREE	SHMOOZED	SHOEMAKER	SHOOTOUT
SHIRES	SHIVAREED	SHMOOZES	SHOEMAKERS	SHOOTOUTS
SHIRK	SHIVAREEING	SHMOOZING	SHOEPAC	SHOOTS
SHIRKED	SHIVAREES	SHMUCK	SHOEPACK	SHOP
SHIRKER	SHIVAS	SHMUCKS	SHOEPACKS	SHOPBOY
SHIRKERS	SHIVE	SHNAPPS	SHOEPACS	SHOPBOYS
SHIRKING	SHIVER	SHNAPS	SHOER	SHOPGIRL
SHIRKS	SHIVERED	SHNOOK	SHOERS	SHOPGIRLS
SHIRR	SHIVERER	SHNOOKS	SHOES	SHOPHAR
SHIRRED	SHIVERERS	SHNORRER	SHOESHINE	SHOPHARS
SHIRRING	SHIVERING	SHNORRERS	SHOESHINES	SHOPHROTH
SHIRRINGS	SHIVERS	SHOAL	SHOETREE	SHOPLIFT
SHIRRS	SHIVERY	SHOALED	SHOETREES	SHOPLIFTED
SHIRT	SHIVES	SHOALER	SHOFAR	SHOPLIFTING
SHIRTIER	SHIVITI	SHOALEST	SHOFARS	SHOPLIFTS
SHIRTIEST	SHIVITIS	SHOALIER	SHOFROTH	SHOPMAN
SHIRTING	SHIVS	SHOALIEST	SHOG	SHOPMEN
SHIRTINGS	SHKOTZIM	SHOALING	SHOGGED	SHOPPE
SHIRTLESS	SHLEMIEHL	SHOALS	SHOGGING	SHOPPED
SHIRTS	SHLEMIEHLS	SHOALY	SHOGI	SHOPPER
SHIRTTAIL	SHLEMIEL	SHOAT	SHOGIS	SHOPPERS
SHIRTTAILED	SHLEMIELS	SHOATS	SHOGS	SHOPPES
SHIRTTAILING	SHLEP	SHOCK	SHOGUN	SHOPPING
SHIRTTAILS	SHLEPP	SHOCKABLE	SHOGUNAL	SHOPPINGS
SHIRTY	SHLEPPED	SHOCKED	SHOGUNATE	SHOPS
SHIST	SHLEPPING	SHOCKER	SHOGUNATES	SHOPTALK
SHISTS	SHLEPPS	SHOCKERS	SHOGUNS	SHOPTALKS
SHIT	SHLEPS	SHOCKING	SHOJI	SHOPWORN
SHITAKE	SHLIMAZEL	SHOCKS	SHOJIS	SHORAN
SHITAKES	SHLIMAZELS	SHOD	SHOLOM	SHORANS
SHITFACED	SHLOCK	SHODDEN	SHOLOMS	SHORE
SHITHEAD	SHLOCKIER	SHODDIER	SHONE	SHOREBIRD
SHITHEADS	SHLOCKIEST	SHODDIES	SHOO	SHOREBIRDS
SHITLESS	SHLOCKS	SHODDIEST	SHOOED	SHORED
SHITLIST	SHLOCKY	SHODDILY	SHOOFLIES	SHORELESS

SHORELINE	SHORTSTOPS	SHOVING	SHOWY	SHRIMPED
SHORELINES	SHORTWAVE	SHOW	SHOYU	SHRIMPER
SHORES	SHORTWAVED	SHOWABLE	SHOYUS	SHRIMPERS
SHORESIDE	SHORTWAVES	SHOWBIZ	SHRANK	SHRIMPIER
SHOREWARD	SHORTWAVING	SHOWBIZZES	SHRAPNEL	SHRIMPIEST
SHORING	SHORTY	SHOWBIZZY	SHRED	SHRIMPING
SHORINGS	SHOT	SHOWBOAT	SHREDDED	SHRIMPS
SHORL	SHOTE	SHOWBOATED	SHREDDER	SHRIMPY
SHORLS	SHOTES	SHOWBOATING	SHREDDERS	SHRINE
SHORN	SHOTGUN	SHOWBOATS	SHREDDING	SHRINED
SHORT	SHOTGUNNED	SHOWBREAD	SHREDS	SHRINES
SHORTAGE	SHOTGUNNING	SHOWBREADS	SHREW	SHRINING
SHORTAGES	SHOTGUNS	SHOWCASE	SHREWD	SHRINK
SHORTCAKE	SHOTHOLE	SHOWCASED	SHREWDER	SHRINKAGE
SHORTCAKES	SHOTHOLES	SHOWCASES	SHREWDEST	SHRINKAGES
SHORTCUT	SHOTS	SHOWCASING	SHREWDIE	SHRINKER
SHORTCUTS	SHOTT	SHOWDOWN	SHREWDIES	SHRINKERS
SHORTCUTTING	SHOTTED	SHOWDOWNS	SHREWDLY	SHRINKING
SHORTED	SHOTTEN	SHOWED	SHREWED	SHRINKS
SHORTEN	SHOTTING	SHOWER	SHREWING	SHRIS
SHORTENED	SHOTTS	SHOWERED	SHREWISH	SHRIVE
SHORTENER	SHOULD	SHOWERER	SHREWLIKE	SHRIVED
SHORTENERS	SHOULDER	SHOWERERS	SHREWMICE	SHRIVEL
SHORTENING	SHOULDERED	SHOWERING	SHREWMOUSE	SHRIVELED
SHORTENS	SHOULDERING	SHOWERS	SHREWS	SHRIVELING
SHORTER	SHOULDERS	SHOWERY	SHRI	SHRIVELLED
SHORTEST	SHOULDEST	SHOWGIRL	SHRIEK	SHRIVELLING
SHORTFALL	SHOULDST	SHOWGIRLS	SHRIEKED	SHRIVELS
SHORTFALLS	SHOUT	SHOWIER	SHRIEKER	SHRIVEN
SHORTHAIR	SHOUTED	SHOWIEST	SHRIEKERS	SHRIVER
SHORTHAIRS	SHOUTER	SHOWILY	SHRIEKIER	SHRIVERS
SHORTHAND	SHOUTERS	SHOWINESS	SHRIEKIEST	SHRIVES
SHORTHANDS	SHOUTING	SHOWINESSES	SHRIEKING	SHRIVING
SHORTHEAD	SHOUTS	SHOWING	SHRIEKS	SHROFF
SHORTHEADS	SHOVE	SHOWINGS	SHRIEKY	SHROFFED
SHORTHORN	SHOVED	SHOWMAN	SHRIEVAL	SHROFFING
SHORTHORNS	SHOVEL	SHOWMANLY	SHRIEVE	SHROFFS
SHORTIA	SHOVELED	SHOWMEN	SHRIEVED	SHROUD
SHORTIAS	SHOVELER	SHOWN	SHRIEVES	SHROUDED
SHORTIE	SHOVELERS	SHOWOFF	SHRIEVING	SHROUDING
SHORTIES	SHOVELFUL	SHOWOFFS	SHRIFT	SHROUDS
SHORTING	SHOVELFULS	SHOWPIECE	SHRIFTS	SHROVE
SHORTISH	SHOVELING	SHOWPIECES	SHRIKE	SHRUB
SHORTLIST	SHOVELLED	SHOWPLACE	SHRIKES	SHRUBBERIES
SHORTLISTED	SHOVELLER	SHOWPLACES	SHRILL	SHRUBBERY
SHORTLISTING	SHOVELLERS	SHOWRING	SHRILLED	SHRUBBIER
SHORTLISTS	SHOVELLING	SHOWRINGS	SHRILLER	SHRUBBIEST
SHORTLY	SHOVELS	SHOWROOM	SHRILLEST	SHRUBBY
SHORTNESS	SHOVELSFUL	SHOWROOMS	SHRILLING	SHRUBLAND
SHORTNESSES	SHOVER	SHOWS	SHRILLS	SHRUBLANDS
SHORTS	SHOVERS	SHOWTIME	SHRILLY	SHRUBLIKE
SHORTSTOP	SHOVES	SHOWTIMES	SHRIMP	SHRUBS

SHRUG	SHUNT	SHYLY	SICKBED	SIDEBARS
SHRUGGED	SHUNTED	SHYNESS	SICKBEDS	SIDEBOARD
SHRUGGING	SHUNTER	SHYNESSES	SICKED	SIDEBOARDS
SHRUGS	SHUNTERS	SHYSTER	SICKEE	SIDEBURNS
SHRUNK	SHUNTING	SHYSTERS	SICKEES	SIDECAR
SHRUNKEN	SHUNTS	SI	SICKEN	SIDECARS
SHTETEL	SHUSH	SIAL	SICKENED	SIDECHECK
SHTETELS	SHUSHED	SIALIC	SICKENER	SIDECHECKS
SHTETL	SHUSHER	SIALID	SICKENERS	SIDED
SHTETLACH	SHUSHERS	SIALIDAN	SICKENING	SIDEDNESS
SHTETLS	SHUSHES	SIALIDANS	SICKENS	SIDEDNESSES
SHTICK	SHUSHING	SIALIDS	SICKER	SIDEDRESS
SHTICKIER	SHUT	SIALOID	SICKERLY	SIDEDRESSES
SHTICKIEST	SHUTDOWN	SIALS	SICKEST	SIDEHILL
SHTICKS	SHUTDOWNS	SIAMANG	SICKIE	SIDEHILLS
SHTICKY	SHUTE	SIAMANGS	SICKIES	SIDEKICK
SHTIK	SHUTED	SIAMESE	SICKING	SIDEKICKS
SHTIKS	SHUTES	SIAMESES	SICKISH	SIDELIGHT
SHUCK	SHUTEYE	SIB	SICKISHLY	SIDELIGHTS
SHUCKED	SHUTEYES	SIBB	SICKLE	SIDELINE
SHUCKER	SHUTING	SIBBS	SICKLED	SIDELINED
SHUCKERS	SHUTOFF	SIBILANCE	SICKLEMIA	SIDELINER
SHUCKING	SHUTOFFS	SIBILANCES	SICKLEMIAS	SIDELINERS
SHUCKINGS	SHUTOUT	SIBILANCIES	SICKLEMIC	SIDELINES
SHUCKS	SHUTOUTS	SIBILANCY	SICKLES	SIDELING
SHUDDER	SHUTS	SIBILANT	SICKLIED	SIDELINING
SHUDDERED	SHUTTER	SIBILANTS	SICKLIER	SIDELONG
SHUDDERING	SHUTTERED	SIBILATE	SICKLIES	SIDEMAN
SHUDDERS	SHUTTERING	SIBILATED	SICKLIEST	SIDEMEN
SHUDDERY	SHUTTERS	SIBILATES	SICKLILY	SIDEPIECE
SHUFFLE	SHUTTING	SIBILATING	SICKLING	SIDEPIECES
SHUFFLED	SHUTTLE	SIBILATOR	SICKLY	SIDEREAL
SHUFFLER	SHUTTLED	SIBILATORS	SICKLYING	SIDERITE
SHUFFLERS	SHUTTLER	SIBLING	SICKNESS	SIDERITES
SHUFFLES	SHUTTLERS	SIBLINGS	SICKNESSES	SIDERITIC
SHUFFLING	SHUTTLES	SIBS	SICKO	SIDEROSES
SHUL	SHUTTLING	SIBYL	SICKOS	SIDEROSIS
SHULN	SHVARTZE	SIBYLIC	SICKOUT	SIDEROTIC
SHULS	SHVARTZES	SIBYLLIC	SICKOUTS	SIDES
SHUN	SHWA	SIBYLLINE	SICKROOM	SIDESHOW
SHUNNABLE	SHWANPAN	SIBYLS	SICKROOMS	SIDESHOWS
SHUNNED	SHWANPANS	SIC	SICKS	SIDESLIP
SHUNNER	SHWAS	SICCAN	SICS	SIDESLIPPED
SHUNNERS	SHY	SICCATIVE	SIDDUR	SIDESLIPPING
SHUNNING	SHYER	SICCATIVES	SIDDURIM	SIDESLIPS
SHUNPIKE	SHYERS	SICCED	SIDDURS	SIDESPIN
SHUNPIKED	SHYEST	SICCING	SIDE	SIDESPINS
SHUNPIKER	SHYING	SICE	SIDEARM	SIDESTEP
SHUNPIKERS	SHYLOCK	SICES	SIDEARMS	SIDESTEPPED
SHUNPIKES	SHYLOCKED	SICK	SIDEBAND	SIDESTEPPING
SHUNPIKING	SHYLOCKING	SICKBAY	SIDEBANDS	SIDESTEPS
SHUNS	SHYLOCKS	SICKBAYS	SIDEBAR	SIDESWIPE

SIDESWIPED	SIFAKAS	SIGN	SIGNIORS	SILICIDE
SIDESWIPES	SIFFLEUR	SIGNA	SIGNIORY	SILICIDES
SIDESWIPING	SIFFLEURS	SIGNAGE	SIGNOR	SILICIFIED
SIDETRACK	SIFT	SIGNAGES	SIGNORA	SILICIFIES
SIDETRACKED	SIFTED	SIGNAL	SIGNORAS	SILICIFY
SIDETRACKING	SIFTER	SIGNALED	SIGNORE	SILICIFYING
SIDETRACKS	SIFTERS	SIGNALER	SIGNORI	SILICIOUS
SIDEWALK	SIFTING	SIGNALERS	SIGNORIES	SILICIUM
SIDEWALKS	SIFTINGS	SIGNALING	SIGNORINA	SILICIUMS
SIDEWALL	SIFTS	SIGNALISE	SIGNORINAS	SILICLE
SIDEWALLS	SIGANID	SIGNALISED	SIGNORINE	SILICLES
SIDEWARD	SIGANIDS	SIGNALISES	SIGNORS	SILICON
SIDEWARDS	SIGH	SIGNALISING	SIGNORY	SILICONE
SIDEWAY	SIGHED	SIGNALIZE	SIGNPOST	SILICONES
SIDEWAYS	SIGHER	SIGNALIZED	SIGNPOSTED	SILICONS
SIDEWISE	SIGHERS	SIGNALIZES	SIGNPOSTING	SILICOSES
SIDH	SIGHING	SIGNALIZING	SIGNPOSTS	SILICOSIS
SIDHE	SIGHLESS	SIGNALLED	SIGNS	SILICOTIC
SIDING	SIGHLIKE	SIGNALLER	SIKA	SILICOTICS
SIDINGS	SIGHS	SIGNALLERS	SIKAS	SILICULA
SIDLE	SIGHT	SIGNALLING	SIKE	SILICULAE
SIDLED	SIGHTED	SIGNALLY	SIKER	SILIQUA
SIDLER	SIGHTER	SIGNALMAN	SIKES	SILIQUAE
SIDLERS	SIGHTERS	SIGNALMEN	SILAGE	SILIQUE
SIDLES	SIGHTING	SIGNALS	SILAGES	SILIQUES
SIDLING	SIGHTINGS	SIGNATORIES	SILANE	SILIQUOSE
SIDLINGLY	SIGHTLESS	SIGNATORY	SILANES	SILIQUOUS
SIEGE	SIGHTLIER	SIGNATURE	SILD	SILK
SIEGED	SIGHTLIEST	SIGNATURES	SILDS	SILKALINE
SIEGES	SIGHTLINE	SIGNBOARD	SILENCE	SILKALINES
SIEGING	SIGHTLINES	SIGNBOARDS	SILENCED	SILKED
SIEMENS	SIGHTLY	SIGNED	SILENCER	SILKEN
SIENITE	SIGHTS	SIGNEE	SILENCERS	SILKIE
SIENITES	SIGHTSAW	SIGNEES	SILENCES	SILKIER
SIENNA	SIGHTSEE	SIGNER	SILENCING	SILKIES
SIENNAS	SIGHTSEEING	SIGNERS	SILENI	SILKIEST
SIEROZEM	SIGHTSEEN	SIGNET	SILENT	SILKILY
SIEROZEMS	SIGHTSEER	SIGNETED	SILENTER	SILKINESS
SIERRA	SIGHTSEERS	SIGNETING	SILENTEST	SILKINESSES
SIERRAN	SIGHTSEES	SIGNETS	SILENTLY	SILKING
SIERRAS	SIGIL	SIGNIFICS	SILENTS	SILKLIKE
SIESTA	SIGILS	SIGNIFIED	SILENUS	SILKOLINE
SIESTAS	SIGLA	SIGNIFIEDS	SILESIA	SILKOLINES
SIEUR	SIGLOI	SIGNIFIER	SILESIAS	SILKS
SIEURS	SIGLOS	SIGNIFIERS	SILEX	SILKWEED
SIEVE	SIGLUM	SIGNIFIES	SILEXES	SILKWEEDS
SIEVED	SIGMA	SIGNIFY	SILICA	SILKWORM
SIEVERT	SIGMAS	SIGNIFYING	SILICAS	SILKWORMS
SIEVERTS	SIGMATE	SIGNING	SILICATE	SILKY
SIEVES	SIGMOID	SIGNIOR	SILICATES	SILL
SIEVING	SIGMOIDAL	SIGNIORI	SILICEOUS	SILLABUB
SIFAKA	SIGMOIDS	SIGNIORIES	SILICIC	SILLABUBS

SILLER	SILVICS	SIMPLE	SINCIPUTS	SINK
SILLERS	SIM	SIMPLER	SINE	SINKABLE
SILLIBUB	SIMA	SIMPLES	SINECURE	SINKAGE
SILLIBUBS	SIMAR	SIMPLEST	SINECURES	SINKAGES
SILLIER	SIMARS	SIMPLETON	SINES	SINKER
SILLIES	SIMARUBA	SIMPLETONS	SINEW	SINKERS
SILLIEST	SIMARUBAS	SIMPLEX	SINEWED	SINKHOLE
SILLILY	SIMAS	SIMPLEXES	SINEWING	SINKHOLES
SILLINESS	SIMAZINE	SIMPLICES	SINEWLESS	SINKING
SILLINESSES	SIMAZINES	SIMPLICIA	SINEWS	SINKS
SILLS	SIMIAN	SIMPLIFIED	SINEWY	SINLESS
SILLY	SIMIANS	SIMPLIFIES	SINFONIA	SINLESSLY
SILO	SIMILAR	SIMPLIFY	SINFONIAS	SINNED
SILOED	SIMILARLY	SIMPLIFYING	SINFONIE	SINNER
SILOING	SIMILE	SIMPLISM	SINFUL	SINNERS
SILOS	SIMILES	SIMPLISMS	SINFULLY	SINNING
SILOXANE	SIMIOID	SIMPLIST	SING	SINOLOGIES
SILOXANES	SIMIOUS	SIMPLISTS	SINGABLE	SINOLOGUE
SILT	SIMITAR	SIMPLY	SINGALONG	SINOLOGUES
SILTATION	SIMITARS	SIMPS	SINGALONGS	SINOLOGY
SILTATIONS	SIMLIN	SIMS	SINGE	SINOPIA
SILTED	SIMLINS	SIMULACRA	SINGED	SINOPIAS
SILTIER	SIMMER	SIMULACRE	SINGEING	SINOPIE
SILTIEST	SIMMERED	SIMULACRES	SINGER	SINS
SILTING	SIMMERING	SIMULACRUM	SINGERS	SINSYNE
SILTS	SIMMERS	SIMULACRUMS	SINGES	SINTER
SILTSTONE	SIMNEL	SIMULANT	SINGING	SINTERED
SILTSTONES	SIMNELS	SIMULANTS	SINGLE	SINTERING
SILTY	SIMOLEON	SIMULAR	SINGLED	SINTERS
SILURIAN	SIMOLEONS	SIMULARS	SINGLES	SINUATE
SILURID	SIMONIAC	SIMULATE	SINGLET	SINUATED
SILURIDS	SIMONIACS	SIMULATED	SINGLETON	SINUATELY
SILUROID	SIMONIES	SIMULATES	SINGLETONS	SINUATES
SILUROIDS	SIMONIST	SIMULATING	SINGLETS	SINUATING
SILVA	SIMONISTS	SIMULATOR	SINGLING	SINUATION
SILVAE	SIMONIZE	SIMULATORS	SINGLY	SINUATIONS
SILVAN	SIMONIZED	SIMULCAST	SINGS	SINUOSITIES
SILVANS	SIMONIZES	SIMULCASTED	SINGSONG	SINUOSITY
SILVAS	SIMONIZING	SIMULCASTING	SINGSONGS	SINUOUS
SILVER	SIMONY	SIMULCASTS	SINGSONGY	SINUOUSLY
SILVERED	SIMOOM	SIN	SINGSPIEL	SINUS
SILVERER	SIMOOMS	SINAPISM	SINGSPIELS	SINUSES
SILVERERS	SIMOON	SINAPISMS	SINGULAR	SINUSITIS
SILVERING	SIMOONS	SINCE	SINGULARS	SINUSITISES
SILVERINGS	SIMP	SINCERE	SINH	SINUSLIKE
SILVERLY	SIMPATICO	SINCERELY	SINHS	SINUSOID
SILVERN	SIMPER	SINCERER	SINICIZE	SINUSOIDS
SILVERS	SIMPERED	SINCEREST	SINICIZED	SIP
SILVERY	SIMPERER	SINCERITIES	SINICIZES	SIPE
SILVEX	SIMPERERS	SINCERITY	SINICIZING	SIPED
SILVEXES	SIMPERING	SINCIPITA	SINISTER	SIPES
SILVICAL	SIMPERS	SINCIPUT	SINISTRAL	SIPHON

SIPHONAGE	SISKIN	SITUS	SIZZLER	SKEES
SIPHONAGES	SISKINS	SITUSES	SIZZLERS	SKEET
SIPHONAL	SISSES	SITZMARK	SIZZLES	SKEETER
SIPHONED	SISSIER	SITZMARKS	SIZZLING	SKEETERS
SIPHONIC	SISSIES	SIVER	SJAMBOK	SKEETS
SIPHONING	SISSIEST	SIVERS	SJAMBOKED	SKEG
SIPHONS	SISSIFIED	SIX	SJAMBOKING	SKEGS
SIPING	SISSINESS	SIXES	SJAMBOKS	SKEIGH
SIPPED	SISSINESSES	SIXFOLD	SKA	SKEIN
SIPPER	SISSY	SIXMO	SKAG	SKEINED
SIPPERS	SISSYISH	SIXMOS	SKAGS	SKEINING
SIPPET	SISSYNESS	SIXPENCE	SKALD	SKEINS
SIPPETS	SISSYNESSES	SIXPENCES	SKALDIC	SKELETAL
SIPPING	SISTER	SIXPENNY	SKALDS	SKELETON
SIPS	SISTERED	SIXTE	SKALDSHIP	SKELETONS
SIR	SISTERING	SIXTEEN	SKALDSHIPS	SKELL
SIRDAR	SISTERLY	SIXTEENMO	SKANK	SKELLS
SIRDARS	SISTERS	SIXTEENMOS	SKANKED	SKELLUM
SIRE	SISTRA	SIXTEENS	SKANKER	SKELLUMS
SIRED	SISTROID	SIXTEENTH	SKANKERS	SKELM
SIREE	SISTRUM	SIXTEENTHS	SKANKIER	SKELMS
SIREES	SISTRUMS	SIXTES	SKANKIEST	SKELP
SIREN	SIT	SIXTH	SKANKING	SKELPED
SIRENIAN	SITAR	SIXTHLY	SKANKS	SKELPING
SIRENIANS	SITARIST	SIXTHS	SKANKY	SKELPIT
SIRENS	SITARISTS	SIXTIES	SKAS	SKELPS
SIRES	SITARS	SIXTIETH	SKAT	SKELTER
SIRING	SITCOM	SIXTIETHS	SKATE	SKELTERED
SIRLOIN	SITCOMS	SIXTY	SKATED	SKELTERING
SIRLOINS	SITE	SIXTYISH	SKATER	SKELTERS
SIROCCO	SITED	SIZABLE	SKATERS	SKENE
SIROCCOS	SITES	SIZABLY	SKATES	SKENES
SIRRA	SITH	SIZAR	SKATING	SKEP
SIRRAH	SITHENCE	SIZARS	SKATINGS	SKEPS
SIRRAHS	SITHENS	SIZARSHIP	SKATOL	SKEPSIS
SIRRAS	SITING	SIZARSHIPS	SKATOLE	SKEPSISES
SIRREE	SITOLOGIES	SIZE	SKATOLES	SKEPTIC
SIRREES	SITOLOGY	SIZEABLE	SKATOLS	SKEPTICAL
SIRS	SITS	SIZEABLY	SKATS	SKEPTICS
SIRUP	SITTEN	SIZED	SKEAN	SKERRIES
SIRUPED	SITTER	SIZER	SKEANE	SKERRY
SIRUPIER	SITTERS	SIZERS	SKEANES	SKETCH
SIRUPIEST	SITTING	SIZES	SKEANS	SKETCHED
SIRUPING	SITTINGS	SIZIER	SKEDADDLE	SKETCHER
SIRUPS	SITUATE	SIZIEST	SKEDADDLED	SKETCHERS
SIRUPY	SITUATED	SIZINESS	SKEDADDLES	SKETCHES
SIRVENTE	SITUATES	SIZINESSES	SKEDADDLING	SKETCHIER
SIRVENTES	SITUATING	SIZING	SKEE	SKETCHIEST
SIS	SITUATION	SIZINGS	SKEED	SKETCHILY
SISAL	SITUATIONS	SIZY	SKEEING	SKETCHING
SISALS	SITUP	SIZZLE	SKEEN	SKETCHPAD
SISES	SITUPS	SIZZLED	SKEENS	SKETCHPADS

SKETCHY	SKIES	SKINFLINT	SKIRRETS	SKOSHES
SKEW	SKIEY	SKINFLINTS	SKIRRING	SKREEGH
SKEWBACK	SKIFF	SKINFUL	SKIRRS	SKREEGHED
SKEWBACKS	SKIFFLE	SKINFULS	SKIRT	SKREEGHING
SKEWBALD	SKIFFLED	SKINHEAD	SKIRTED	SKREEGHS
SKEWBALDS	SKIFFLES	SKINHEADS	SKIRTER	SKREIGH
SKEWED	SKIFFLESS	SKINK	SKIRTERS	SKREIGHED
SKEWER	SKIFFLING	SKINKED	SKIRTING	SKREIGHING
SKEWERED	SKIFFS	SKINKER	SKIRTINGS	SKREIGHS
SKEWERING	SKIING	SKINKERS	SKIRTLESS	SKUA
SKEWERS	SKIINGS	SKINKING	SKIRTLIKE	SKUAS
SKEWING	SKIJORER	SKINKS	SKIRTS	SKULK
SKEWNESS	SKIJORERS	SKINLESS	SKIS	SKULKED
SKEWNESSES	SKIJORING	SKINLIKE	SKIT	SKULKER
SKEWS	SKIJORINGS	SKINNED	SKITE	SKULKERS
SKI	SKILFUL	SKINNER	SKITED	SKULKING
SKIABLE	SKILFULLY	SKINNERS	SKITES	SKULKS
SKIAGRAM	SKILL	SKINNIER	SKITING	SKULL
SKIAGRAMS	SKILLED	SKINNIEST	SKITS	SKULLCAP
SKIAGRAPH	SKILLESS	SKINNING	SKITTER	SKULLCAPS
SKIAGRAPHS	SKILLET	SKINNY	SKITTERED	SKULLED
SKIASCOPE	SKILLETS	SKINS	SKITTERIER	SKULLING
SKIASCOPES	SKILLFUL	SKINT	SKITTERIEST	SKULLS
SKIASCOPIES	SKILLING	SKINTIGHT	SKITTERING	SKUNK
SKIASCOPY	SKILLINGS	SKIORING	SKITTERS	SKUNKED
SKIBOB	SKILLS	SKIORINGS	SKITTERY	SKUNKIER
SKIBOBBER	SKIM	SKIP	SKITTISH	SKUNKIEST
SKIBOBBERS	SKIMBOARD	SKIPJACK	SKITTLE	SKUNKING
SKIBOBS	SKIMBOARDS	SKIPJACKS	SKITTLES	SKUNKS
SKID	SKIMMED	SKIPLANE	SKIVE	SKUNKWEED
SKIDDED	SKIMMER	SKIPLANES	SKIVED	SKUNKWEEDS
SKIDDER	SKIMMERS	SKIPPABLE	SKIVER	SKUNKY
SKIDDERS	SKIMMING	SKIPPED	SKIVERS	SKY
SKIDDIER	SKIMMINGS	SKIPPER	SKIVES	SKYBOARD
SKIDDIEST	SKIMO	SKIPPERED	SKIVING	SKYBOARDS
SKIDDING	SKIMOBILE	SKIPPERING	SKIVVIED	SKYBORNE
SKIDDOO	SKIMOBILED	SKIPPERS	SKIVVIES	SKYBOX
SKIDDOOED	SKIMOBILES	SKIPPET	SKIVVY	SKYBOXES
SKIDDOOING	SKIMOBILING	SKIPPETS	SKIVVYING	SKYBRIDGE
SKIDDOOS	SKIMOS	SKIPPING	SKIWEAR	SKYBRIDGES
SKIDDY	SKIMP	SKIPS	SKLENT	SKYCAP
SKIDOO	SKIMPED	SKIRL	SKLENTED	SKYCAPS
SKIDOOED	SKIMPIER	SKIRLED	SKLENTING	SKYDIVE
SKIDOOING	SKIMPIEST	SKIRLING	SKLENTS	SKYDIVED
SKIDOOS	SKIMPILY	SKIRLS	SKOAL	SKYDIVER
SKIDPROOF	SKIMPING	SKIRMISH	SKOALED	SKYDIVERS
SKIDS	SKIMPS	SKIRMISHED	SKOALING	SKYDIVES
SKIDWAY	SKIMPY	SKIRMISHES	SKOALS	SKYDIVING
SKIDWAYS	SKIMS	SKIRMISHING	SKOOKUM	SKYDIVINGS
SKIED	SKIN	SKIRR	SKORT	SKYDOVE
SKIER	SKINFLICK	SKIRRED	SKORTS	SKYED
SKIERS	SKINFLICKS	SKIRRET	SKOSH	SKYEY

SKYHOOK	SLABBER	SLAMDANCING	SLASHING	SLAWS
SKYHOOKS	SLABBERED	SLAMMED	SLASHINGS	SLAY
SKYING	SLABBERING	SLAMMER	SLAT	SLAYABLE
SKYJACK	SLABBERS	SLAMMERS	SLATCH	SLAYED
SKYJACKED	SLABBERY	SLAMMING	SLATCHES	SLAYER
SKYJACKER	SLABBING	SLAMMINGS	SLATE	SLAYERS
SKYJACKERS	SLABLIKE	SLAMS	SLATED	SLAYING
SKYJACKING	SLABS	SLANDER	SLATELIKE	SLAYS
SKYJACKS	SLACK	SLANDERED	SLATER	SLEAVE
SKYLARK	SLACKED	SLANDERER	SLATERS	SLEAVED
SKYLARKED	SLACKEN	SLANDERERS	SLATES	SLEAVES
SKYLARKER	SLACKENED	SLANDERING	SLATEY	SLEAVING
SKYLARKERS	SLACKENER	SLANDERS	SLATHER	SLEAZE
SKYLARKING	SLACKENERS	SLANG	SLATHERED	SLEAZEBAG
SKYLARKS	SLACKENING	SLANGED	SLATHERING	SLEAZEBAGS
SKYLIGHT	SLACKENS	SLANGIER	SLATHERS	SLEAZES
SKYLIGHTS	SLACKER	SLANGIEST	SLATIER	SLEAZIER
SKYLIKE	SLACKERS	SLANGILY	SLATIEST	SLEAZIEST
SKYLINE	SLACKEST	SLANGING	SLATINESS	SLEAZILY
SKYLINES	SLACKING	SLANGS	SLATINESSES	SLEAZO
SKYLIT	SLACKLY	SLANGUAGE	SLATING	SLEAZOID
SKYMAN	SLACKNESS	SLANGUAGES	SLATINGS	SLEAZOIDS
SKYMEN	SLACKNESSES	SLANGY	SLATS	SLEAZY
SKYPHOI	SLACKS	SLANK	SLATTED	SLED
SKYPHOS	SLAG	SLANT	SLATTERN	SLEDDED
SKYROCKET	SLAGGED	SLANTED	SLATTERNS	SLEDDER
SKYROCKETED	SLAGGIER	SLANTING	SLATTING	SLEDDERS
SKYROCKETING	SLAGGIEST	SLANTLY	SLATTINGS	SLEDDING
SKYROCKETS	SLAGGING	SLANTS	SLATY	SLEDDINGS
SKYSAIL	SLAGGY	SLANTWAYS	SLAUGHTER	SLEDGE
SKYSAILS	SLAGS	SLANTWISE	SLAUGHTERED	SLEDGED
SKYSURF	SLAIN	SLANTY	SLAUGHTERING	SLEDGES
SKYSURFED	SLAINTE	SLAP	SLAUGHTERS	SLEDGING
SKYSURFER	SLAKABLE	SLAPDASH	SLAVE	SLEDS
SKYSURFERS	SLAKE	SLAPDASHES	SLAVED	SLEEK
SKYSURFING	SLAKED	SLAPHAPPIER	SLAVER	SLEEKED
SKYSURFS	SLAKER	SLAPHAPPIEST	SLAVERED	SLEEKEN
SKYWALK	SLAKERS	SLAPHAPPY	SLAVERER	SLEEKENED
SKYWALKS	SLAKES	SLAPJACK	SLAVERERS	SLEEKENING
SKYWARD	SLAKING	SLAPJACKS	SLAVERIES	SLEEKENS
SKYWARDS	SLALOM	SLAPPED	SLAVERING	SLEEKER
SKYWAY	SLALOMED	SLAPPER	SLAVERS	SLEEKERS
SKYWAYS	SLALOMER	SLAPPERS	SLAVERY	SLEEKEST
SKYWRITE	SLALOMERS	SLAPPING	SLAVES	SLEEKIER
SKYWRITER	SLALOMING	SLAPS	SLAVEY	SLEEKIEST
SKYWRITERS	SLALOMIST	SLAPSTICK	SLAVEYS	SLEEKING
SKYWRITES	SLALOMISTS	SLAPSTICKS	SLAVING	SLEEKIT
SKYWRITING	SLALOMS	SLASH	SLAVISH	SLEEKLY
SKYWRITTEN	SLAM	SLASHED	SLAVISHLY	SLEEKNESS
SKYWROTE	SLAMDANCE	SLASHER	SLAVOCRAT	SLEEKNESSES
SLAB	SLAMDANCED	SLASHERS	SLAVOCRATS	SLEEKS
SLABBED	SLAMDANCES	SLASHES	SLAW	SLEEKY

SLEEP	SLEWING	SLIM	SLIPCOVERS	SLITHERING
SLEEPAWAY	SLEWS	SLIME	SLIPDRESS	SLITHERS
SLEEPER	SLICE	SLIMEBALL	SLIPDRESSES	SLITHERY
SLEEPERS	SLICEABLE	SLIMEBALLS	SLIPE	SLITLESS
SLEEPIER	SLICED	SLIMED	SLIPED	SLITLIKE
SLEEPIEST	SLICER	SLIMES	SLIPES	SLITS
SLEEPILY	SLICERS	SLIMIER	SLIPFORM	SLITTED
SLEEPING	SLICES	SLIMIEST	SLIPFORMED	SLITTER
SLEEPINGS	SLICING	SLIMILY	SLIPFORMING	SLITTERS
SLEEPLESS	SLICK	SLIMINESS	SLIPFORMS	SLITTIER
SLEEPLIKE	SLICKED	SLIMINESSES	SLIPING	SLITTIEST
SLEEPOVER	SLICKEN	SLIMING	SLIPKNOT	SLITTING
SLEEPOVERS	SLICKENED	SLIMLY	SLIPKNOTS	SLITTY
SLEEPS	SLICKENER	SLIMMED	SLIPLESS	SLIVER
SLEEPWALK	SLICKENERS	SLIMMER	SLIPOUT	SLIVERED
SLEEPWALKED	SLICKENING	SLIMMERS	SLIPOUTS	SLIVERER
SLEEPWALKING	SLICKENS	SLIMMEST	SLIPOVER	SLIVERERS
SLEEPWALKS	SLICKER	SLIMMING	SLIPOVERS	SLIVERING
SLEEPWEAR	SLICKERS	SLIMNESS	SLIPPAGE	SLIVERS
SLEEPY	SLICKEST	SLIMNESSES	SLIPPAGES	SLIVOVIC
SLEET	SLICKING	SLIMPSIER	SLIPPED	SLIVOVICES
SLEETED	SLICKLY	SLIMPSIEST	SLIPPER	SLIVOVITZ
SLEETIER	SLICKNESS	SLIMPSY	SLIPPERED	SLIVOVITZES
SLEETIEST	SLICKNESSES	SLIMS	SLIPPERIER	SLOB
SLEETING	SLICKROCK	SLIMSIER	SLIPPERIEST	SLOBBER
SLEETS	SLICKROCKS	SLIMSIEST	SLIPPERS	SLOBBERED
SLEETY	SLICKS	SLIMSY	SLIPPERY	SLOBBERER
SLEEVE	SLICKSTER	SLIMY	SLIPPIER	SLOBBERERS
SLEEVED	SLICKSTERS	SLING	SLIPPIEST	SLOBBERING
SLEEVELET	SLID	SLINGBACK	SLIPPILY	SLOBBERS
SLEEVELETS	SLIDABLE	SLINGBACKS	SLIPPING	SLOBBERY
SLEEVES	SLIDDEN	SLINGER	SLIPPY	SLOBBIER
SLEEVING	SLIDE	SLINGERS	SLIPS	SLOBBIEST
SLEIGH	SLIDER	SLINGING	SLIPSHEET	SLOBBISH
SLEIGHED	SLIDERS	SLINGS	SLIPSHEETED	SLOBBY
SLEIGHER	SLIDES	SLINGSHOT	SLIPSHEETING	SLOBS
SLEIGHERS	SLIDEWAY	SLINGSHOTS	SLIPSHEETS	SLOE
SLEIGHING	SLIDEWAYS	SLINK	SLIPSHOD	SLOES
SLEIGHS	SLIDING	SLINKED	SLIPSLOP	SLOG
SLEIGHT	SLIER	SLINKIER	SLIPSLOPS	SLOGAN
SLEIGHTS	SLIEST	SLINKIEST	SLIPSOLE	SLOGANEER
SLENDER	SLIEVE	SLINKILY	SLIPSOLES	SLOGANEERED
SLENDERER	SLIEVES	SLINKING	SLIPT	SLOGANEERING
SLENDEREST	SLIGHT	SLINKS	SLIPUP	SLOGANEERS
SLENDERLY	SLIGHTED	SLINKY	SLIPUPS	SLOGANIZE
SLEPT	SLIGHTER	SLIP	SLIPWARE	SLOGANIZED
SLEUTH	SLIGHTERS	SLIPCASE	SLIPWARES	SLOGANIZES
SLEUTHED	SLIGHTEST	SLIPCASED	SLIPWAY	SLOGANIZING
SLEUTHING	SLIGHTING	SLIPCASES	SLIPWAYS	SLOGANS
SLEUTHS	SLIGHTLY	SLIPCOVER	SLIT	SLOGGED
SLEW	SLIGHTS	SLIPCOVERED	SLITHER	SLOGGER
SLEWED	SLILY	SLIPCOVERING	SLITHERED	SLOGGERS

SLOGGING
SLOGS
SLOID
SLOIDS
SLOJD
SLOJDS
SLOOP
SLOOPS
SLOP
SLOPE
SLOPED
SLOPER
SLOPERS
SLOPES
SLOPING
SLOPINGLY
SLOPPED
SLOPPIER
SLOPPIEST
SLOPPILY
SLOPPING
SLOPPY
SLOPS
SLOPWORK
SLOPWORKS
SLOSH
SLOSHED
SLOSHES
SLOSHIER
SLOSHIEST
SLOSHING
SLOSHY
SLOT
SLOTBACK
SLOTBACKS
SLOTH
SLOTHFUL
SLOTHS
SLOTS
SLOTTED
SLOTTER
SLOTTERS
SLOTTING
SLOUCH
SLOUCHED
SLOUCHER
SLOUCHERS
SLOUCHES
SLOUCHIER
SLOUCHIEST
SLOUCHILY
SLOUCHING

SLOUCHY
SLOUGH
SLOUGHED
SLOUGHIER
SLOUGHIEST
SLOUGHING
SLOUGHS
SLOUGHY
SLOVEN
SLOVENLIER
SLOVENLIEST
SLOVENLY
SLOVENS
SLOW
SLOWDOWN
SLOWDOWNS
SLOWED
SLOWER
SLOWEST
SLOWING
SLOWISH
SLOWLY
SLOWNESS
SLOWNESSES
SLOWPOKE
SLOWPOKES
SLOWS
SLOWWORM
SLOWWORMS
SLOYD
SLOYDS
SLUB
SLUBBED
SLUBBER
SLUBBERED
SLUBBERING
SLUBBERS
SLUBBING
SLUBBINGS
SLUBS
SLUDGE
SLUDGED
SLUDGES
SLUDGIER
SLUDGIEST
SLUDGING
SLUDGY
SLUE
SLUED
SLUES
SLUFF
SLUFFED

SLUFFING
SLUFFS
SLUG
SLUGABED
SLUGABEDS
SLUGFEST
SLUGFESTS
SLUGGARD
SLUGGARDS
SLUGGED
SLUGGER
SLUGGERS
SLUGGING
SLUGGISH
SLUGS
SLUICE
SLUICED
SLUICES
SLUICEWAY
SLUICEWAYS
SLUICING
SLUICY
SLUING
SLUM
SLUMBER
SLUMBERED
SLUMBERER
SLUMBERERS
SLUMBERING
SLUMBERS
SLUMBERY
SLUMBROUS
SLUMGUM
SLUMGUMS
SLUMISM
SLUMISMS
SLUMLORD
SLUMLORDS
SLUMMED
SLUMMER
SLUMMERS
SLUMMIER
SLUMMIEST
SLUMMING
SLUMMY
SLUMP
SLUMPED
SLUMPING
SLUMPS
SLUMS
SLUNG
SLUNGSHOT

SLUNGSHOTS
SLUNK
SLUR
SLURB
SLURBAN
SLURBS
SLURP
SLURPED
SLURPING
SLURPS
SLURRED
SLURRIED
SLURRIES
SLURRING
SLURRY
SLURRYING
SLURS
SLUSH
SLUSHED
SLUSHES
SLUSHIER
SLUSHIEST
SLUSHILY
SLUSHING
SLUSHY
SLUT
SLUTS
SLUTTIER
SLUTTIEST
SLUTTISH
SLUTTY
SLY
SLYBOOTS
SLYER
SLYEST
SLYLY
SLYNESS
SLYNESSES
SLYPE
SLYPES
SMACK
SMACKED
SMACKER
SMACKERS
SMACKING
SMACKS
SMALL
SMALLAGE
SMALLAGES
SMALLER
SMALLEST
SMALLISH

SMALLNESS
SMALLNESSES
SMALLPOX
SMALLPOXES
SMALLS
SMALLTIME
SMALT
SMALTI
SMALTINE
SMALTINES
SMALTITE
SMALTITES
SMALTO
SMALTOS
SMALTS
SMARAGD
SMARAGDE
SMARAGDES
SMARAGDS
SMARM
SMARMIER
SMARMIEST
SMARMILY
SMARMS
SMARMY
SMART
SMARTASS
SMARTASSES
SMARTED
SMARTEN
SMARTENED
SMARTENING
SMARTENS
SMARTER
SMARTEST
SMARTIE
SMARTIES
SMARTING
SMARTLY
SMARTNESS
SMARTNESSES
SMARTS
SMARTWEED
SMARTWEEDS
SMARTY
SMASH
SMASHED
SMASHER
SMASHERS
SMASHES
SMASHING
SMASHUP

SMASHUPS	SMERKS	SMITTEN	SMOOTHEN	SMUTCHED
SMATTER	SMEW	SMOCK	SMOOTHENED	SMUTCHES
SMATTERED	SMEWS	SMOCKED	SMOOTHENING	SMUTCHIER
SMATTERER	SMIDGE	SMOCKING	SMOOTHENS	SMUTCHIEST
SMATTERERS	SMIDGEN	SMOCKINGS	SMOOTHER	SMUTCHING
SMATTERING	SMIDGENS	SMOCKS	SMOOTHERS	SMUTCHY
SMATTERS	SMIDGEON	SMOG	SMOOTHES	SMUTS
SMAZE	SMIDGEONS	SMOGGIER	SMOOTHEST	SMUTTED
SMAZES	SMIDGES	SMOGGIEST	SMOOTHIE	SMUTTIER
SMEAR	SMIDGIN	SMOGGY	SMOOTHIES	SMUTTIEST
SMEARCASE	SMIDGINS	SMOGLESS	SMOOTHING	SMUTTILY
SMEARCASES	SMIERCASE	SMOGS	SMOOTHLY	SMUTTING
SMEARED	SMIERCASES	SMOKABLE	SMOOTHS	SMUTTY
SMEARER	SMILAX	SMOKE	SMOOTHY	SNACK
SMEARERS	SMILAXES	SMOKEABLE	SMOTE	SNACKED
SMEARIER	SMILE	SMOKED	SMOTHER	SNACKER
SMEARIEST	SMILED	SMOKEJACK	SMOTHERED	SNACKERS
SMEARING	SMILELESS	SMOKEJACKS	SMOTHERER	SNACKING
SMEARS	SMILER	SMOKELESS	SMOTHERERS	SNACKS
SMEARY	SMILERS	SMOKELIKE	SMOTHERING	SNAFFLE
SMECTIC	SMILES	SMOKEPOT	SMOTHERS	SNAFFLED
SMECTITE	SMILEY	SMOKEPOTS	SMOTHERY	SNAFFLES
SMECTITES	SMILEYS	SMOKER	SMOULDER	SNAFFLING
SMECTITIC	SMILING	SMOKERS	SMOULDERED	SNAFU
SMEDDUM	SMILINGLY	SMOKES	SMOULDERING	SNAFUED
SMEDDUMS	SMIRCH	SMOKEY	SMOULDERS	SNAFUING
SMEEK	SMIRCHED	SMOKIER	SMUDGE	SNAFUS
SMEEKED	SMIRCHES	SMOKIEST	SMUDGED	SNAG
SMEEKING	SMIRCHING	SMOKILY	SMUDGES	SNAGGED
SMEEKS	SMIRK	SMOKINESS	SMUDGIER	SNAGGIER
SMEGMA	SMIRKED	SMOKINESSES	SMUDGIEST	SNAGGIEST
SMEGMAS	SMIRKER	SMOKING	SMUDGILY	SNAGGING
SMELL	SMIRKERS	SMOKY	SMUDGING	SNAGGY
SMELLED	SMIRKIER	SMOLDER	SMUDGY	SNAGLIKE
SMELLER	SMIRKIEST	SMOLDERED	SMUG	SNAGS
SMELLERS	SMIRKILY	SMOLDERING	SMUGGER	SNAIL
SMELLIER	SMIRKING	SMOLDERS	SMUGGEST	SNAILED
SMELLIEST	SMIRKS	SMOLT	SMUGGLE	SNAILING
SMELLING	SMIRKY	SMOLTS	SMUGGLED	SNAILLIKE
SMELLS	SMIT	SMOOCH	SMUGGLER	SNAILS
SMELLY	SMITE	SMOOCHED	SMUGGLERS	SNAKE
SMELT	SMITER	SMOOCHER	SMUGGLES	SNAKEBIRD
SMELTED	SMITERS	SMOOCHERS	SMUGGLING	SNAKEBIRDS
SMELTER	SMITES	SMOOCHES	SMUGLY	SNAKEBIT
SMELTERIES	SMITH	SMOOCHING	SMUGNESS	SNAKEBITE
SMELTERS	SMITHERIES	SMOOCHY	SMUGNESSES	SNAKEBITES
SMELTERY	SMITHERS	SMOOSH	SMUSH	SNAKED
SMELTING	SMITHERY	SMOOSHED	SMUSHED	SNAKEFISH
SMELTS	SMITHIES	SMOOSHES	SMUSHES	SNAKEFISHES
SMERK	SMITHS	SMOOSHING	SMUSHING	SNAKEHEAD
SMERKED	SMITHY	SMOOTH	SMUT	SNAKEHEADS
SMERKING	SMITING	SMOOTHED	SMUTCH	SNAKELIKE

SNAKEPIT	SNARKY	SNEDS	SNIFFER	SNIPS
SNAKEPITS	SNARL	SNEER	SNIFFERS	SNIT
SNAKEROOT	SNARLED	SNEERED	SNIFFIER	SNITCH
SNAKEROOTS	SNARLER	SNEERER	SNIFFIEST	SNITCHED
SNAKES	SNARLERS	SNEERERS	SNIFFILY	SNITCHER
SNAKESKIN	SNARLIER	SNEERFUL	SNIFFING	SNITCHERS
SNAKESKINS	SNARLIEST	SNEERIER	SNIFFISH	SNITCHES
SNAKEWEED	SNARLING	SNEERIEST	SNIFFLE	SNITCHING
SNAKEWEEDS	SNARLS	SNEERING	SNIFFLED	SNITS
SNAKEY	SNARLY	SNEERS	SNIFFLER	SNIVEL
SNAKIER	SNASH	SNEERY	SNIFFLERS	SNIVELED
SNAKIEST	SNASHES	SNEESH	SNIFFLES	SNIVELER
SNAKILY	SNATCH	SNEESHES	SNIFFLING	SNIVELERS
SNAKINESS	SNATCHED	SNEEZE	SNIFFLY	SNIVELING
SNAKINESSES	SNATCHER	SNEEZED	SNIFFS	SNIVELLED
SNAKING	SNATCHERS	SNEEZER	SNIFFY	SNIVELLER
SNAKY	SNATCHES	SNEEZERS	SNIFTER	SNIVELLERS
SNAP	SNATCHIER	SNEEZES	SNIFTERS	SNIVELLING
SNAPBACK	SNATCHIEST	SNEEZIER	SNIGGER	SNIVELS
SNAPBACKS	SNATCHING	SNEEZIEST	SNIGGERED	SNOB
SNAPLESS	SNATCHY	SNEEZING	SNIGGERER	SNOBBERIES
SNAPPED	SNATH	SNEEZY	SNIGGERERS	SNOBBERY
SNAPPER	SNATHE	SNELL	SNIGGERING	SNOBBIER
SNAPPERS	SNATHES	SNELLED	SNIGGERS	SNOBBIEST
SNAPPIER	SNATHS	SNELLER	SNIGGLE	SNOBBILY
SNAPPIEST	SNAW	SNELLEST	SNIGGLED	SNOBBISH
SNAPPILY	SNAWED	SNELLING	SNIGGLER	SNOBBISM
SNAPPING	SNAWING	SNELLS	SNIGGLERS	SNOBBISMS
SNAPPISH	SNAWS	SNIB	SNIGGLES	SNOBBY
SNAPPY	SNAZZIER	SNIBBED	SNIGGLING	SNOBS
SNAPS	SNAZZIEST	SNIBBING	SNIGLET	SNOG
SNAPSHOT	SNAZZY	SNIBS	SNIGLETS	SNOGGED
SNAPSHOTS	SNEAK	SNICK	SNIP	SNOGGING
SNAPSHOTTED	SNEAKED	SNICKED	SNIPE	SNOGS
SNAPSHOTTING	SNEAKER	SNICKER	SNIPED	SNOOD
SNAPWEED	SNEAKERED	SNICKERED	SNIPER	SNOODED
SNAPWEEDS	SNEAKERS	SNICKERER	SNIPERS	SNOODING
SNARE	SNEAKIER	SNICKERERS	SNIPES	SNOODS
SNARED	SNEAKIEST	SNICKERING	SNIPING	SNOOK
SNARER	SNEAKILY	SNICKERS	SNIPPED	SNOOKED
SNARERS	SNEAKING	SNICKERY	SNIPPER	SNOOKER
SNARES	SNEAKS	SNICKING	SNIPPERS	SNOOKERED
SNARF	SNEAKY	SNICKS	SNIPPET	SNOOKERING
SNARFED	SNEAP	SNIDE	SNIPPETIER	SNOOKERS
SNARFING	SNEAPED	SNIDELY	SNIPPETIEST	SNOOKING
SNARFS	SNEAPING	SNIDENESS	SNIPPETS	SNOOKS
SNARING	SNEAPS	SNIDENESSES	SNIPPETY	SNOOL
SNARK	SNECK	SNIDER	SNIPPIER	SNOOLED
SNARKIER	SNECKS	SNIDEST	SNIPPIEST	SNOOLING
SNARKIEST	SNED	SNIFF	SNIPPILY	SNOOLS
SNARKILY	SNEDDED	SNIFFABLE	SNIPPING	SNOOP
SNARKS	SNEDDING	SNIFFED	SNIPPY	SNOOPED

SNOOPER	SNOTTY	SNOWILY	SNUFF	SOAPBERRIES
SNOOPERS	SNOUT	SNOWINESS	SNUFFBOX	SOAPBERRY
SNOOPIER	SNOUTED	SNOWINESSES	SNUFFBOXES	SOAPBOX
SNOOPIEST	SNOUTIER	SNOWING	SNUFFED	SOAPBOXED
SNOOPILY	SNOUTIEST	SNOWLAND	SNUFFER	SOAPBOXES
SNOOPING	SNOUTING	SNOWLANDS	SNUFFERS	SOAPBOXING
SNOOPS	SNOUTISH	SNOWLESS	SNUFFIER	SOAPED
SNOOPY	SNOUTS	SNOWLIKE	SNUFFIEST	SOAPER
SNOOT	SNOUTY	SNOWMAKER	SNUFFILY	SOAPERS
SNOOTED	SNOW	SNOWMAKERS	SNUFFING	SOAPIER
SNOOTIER	SNOWBALL	SNOWMAN	SNUFFLE	SOAPIEST
SNOOTIEST	SNOWBALLED	SNOWMELT	SNUFFLED	SOAPILY
SNOOTILY	SNOWBALLING	SNOWMELTS	SNUFFLER	SOAPINESS
SNOOTING	SNOWBALLS	SNOWMEN	SNUFFLERS	SOAPINESSES
SNOOTS	SNOWBANK	SNOWMOLD	SNUFFLES	SOAPING
SNOOTY	SNOWBANKS	SNOWMOLDS	SNUFFLIER	SOAPLESS
SNOOZE	SNOWBELL	SNOWPACK	SNUFFLIEST	SOAPLIKE
SNOOZED	SNOWBELLS	SNOWPACKS	SNUFFLING	SOAPS
SNOOZER	SNOWBELT	SNOWPLOW	SNUFFLY	SOAPSTONE
SNOOZERS	SNOWBELTS	SNOWPLOWED	SNUFFS	SOAPSTONES
SNOOZES	SNOWBERRIES	SNOWPLOWING	SNUFFY	SOAPSUDS
SNOOZIER	SNOWBERRY	SNOWPLOWS	SNUG	SOAPSUDSY
SNOOZIEST	SNOWBIRD	SNOWS	SNUGGED	SOAPWORT
SNOOZING	SNOWBIRDS	SNOWSCAPE	SNUGGER	SOAPWORTS
SNOOZLE	SNOWBLINK	SNOWSCAPES	SNUGGERIE	SOAPY
SNOOZLED	SNOWBLINKS	SNOWSHED	SNUGGERIES	SOAR
SNOOZLES	SNOWBOARD	SNOWSHEDS	SNUGGERY	SOARED
SNOOZLING	SNOWBOARDED	SNOWSHOE	SNUGGEST	SOARER
SNOOZY	SNOWBOARDING	SNOWSHOED	SNUGGIES	SOARERS
SNORE	SNOWBOARDS	SNOWSHOEING	SNUGGING	SOARING
SNORED	SNOWBOUND	SNOWSHOER	SNUGGLE	SOARINGLY
SNORER	SNOWBRUSH	SNOWSHOERS	SNUGGLED	SOARINGS
SNORERS	SNOWBRUSHES	SNOWSHOES	SNUGGLES	SOARS
SNORES	SNOWBUSH	SNOWSLIDE	SNUGGLING	SOAVE
SNORING	SNOWBUSHES	SNOWSLIDES	SNUGLY	SOAVES
SNORKEL	SNOWCAP	SNOWSTORM	SNUGNESS	SOB
SNORKELED	SNOWCAPS	SNOWSTORMS	SNUGNESSES	SOBA
SNORKELER	SNOWCAT	SNOWSUIT	SNUGS	SOBAS
SNORKELERS	SNOWCATS	SNOWSUITS	SNYE	SOBBED
SNORKELING	SNOWDRIFT	SNOWY	SNYES	SOBBER
SNORKELS	SNOWDRIFTS	SNUB	SO	SOBBERS
SNORT	SNOWDROP	SNUBBED	SOAK	SOBBING
SNORTED	SNOWDROPS	SNUBBER	SOAKAGE	SOBBINGLY
SNORTER	SNOWED	SNUBBERS	SOAKAGES	SOBEIT
SNORTERS	SNOWFALL	SNUBBIER	SOAKED	SOBER
SNORTING	SNOWFALLS	SNUBBIEST	SOAKER	SOBERED
SNORTS	SNOWFIELD	SNUBBING	SOAKERS	SOBERER
SNOT	SNOWFIELDS	SNUBBY	SOAKING	SOBEREST
SNOTS	SNOWFLAKE	SNUBNESS	SOAKS	SOBERING
SNOTTIER	SNOWFLAKES	SNUBNESSES	SOAP	SOBERIZE
SNOTTIEST	SNOWIER	SNUBS	SOAPBARK	SOBERIZED
SNOTTILY	SNOWIEST	SNUCK	SOAPBARKS	SOBERIZES

SOBERIZING	SOCIOPATH	SODOMITIC	SOFTWOODS	SOLANINES
SOBERLY	SOCIOPATHS	SODOMIZE	SOFTY	SOLANINS
SOBERNESS	SOCK	SODOMIZED	SOGGED	SOLANO
SOBERNESSES	SOCKED	SODOMIZES	SOGGIER	SOLANOS
SOBERS	SOCKET	SODOMIZING	SOGGIEST	SOLANS
SOBFUL	SOCKETED	SODOMS	SOGGILY	SOLANUM
SOBRIETIES	SOCKETING	SODOMY	SOGGINESS	SOLANUMS
SOBRIETY	SOCKETS	SODS	SOGGINESSES	SOLAR
SOBRIQUET	SOCKEYE	SOEVER	SOGGY	SOLARIA
SOBRIQUETS	SOCKEYES	SOFA	SOIGNE	SOLARISE
SOBS	SOCKING	SOFABED	SOIGNEE	SOLARISED
SOCA	SOCKLESS	SOFABEDS	SOIL	SOLARISES
SOCAGE	SOCKMAN	SOFAR	SOILAGE	SOLARISING
SOCAGER	SOCKMEN	SOFARS	SOILAGES	SOLARISM
SOCAGERS	SOCKO	SOFAS	SOILBORNE	SOLARISMS
SOCAGES	SOCKS	SOFFIT	SOILED	SOLARIUM
SOCAS	SOCLE	SOFFITS	SOILING	SOLARIUMS
SOCCAGE	SOCLES	SOFT	SOILLESS	SOLARIZE
SOCCAGES	SOCMAN	SOFTA	SOILS	SOLARIZED
SOCCER	SOCMEN	SOFTAS	SOILURE	SOLARIZES
SOCCERS	SOD	SOFTBACK	SOILURES	SOLARIZING
SOCIABLE	SODA	SOFTBACKS	SOIREE	SOLATE
SOCIABLES	SODALESS	SOFTBALL	SOIREES	SOLATED
SOCIABLY	SODALIST	SOFTBALLS	SOJA	SOLATES
SOCIAL	SODALISTS	SOFTBOUND	SOJAS	SOLATIA
SOCIALISE	SODALITE	SOFTBOUNDS	SOJOURN	SOLATING
SOCIALISED	SODALITES	SOFTCORE	SOJOURNED	SOLATION
SOCIALISES	SODALITIES	SOFTCOVER	SOJOURNER	SOLATIONS
SOCIALISING	SODALITY	SOFTCOVERS	SOJOURNERS	SOLATIUM
SOCIALISM	SODAMIDE	SOFTEN	SOJOURNING	SOLD
SOCIALISMS	SODAMIDES	SOFTENED	SOJOURNS	SOLDAN
SOCIALIST	SODAS	SOFTENER	SOKE	SOLDANS
SOCIALISTS	SODBUSTER	SOFTENERS	SOKEMAN	SOLDER
SOCIALITE	SODBUSTERS	SOFTENING	SOKEMEN	SOLDERED
SOCIALITES	SODDED	SOFTENS	SOKES	SOLDERER
SOCIALITIES	SODDEN	SOFTER	SOKOL	SOLDERERS
SOCIALITY	SODDENED	SOFTEST	SOKOLS	SOLDERING
SOCIALIZE	SODDENING	SOFTGOODS	SOL	SOLDERS
SOCIALIZED	SODDENLY	SOFTHEAD	SOLA	SOLDI
SOCIALIZES	SODDENS	SOFTHEADS	SOLACE	SOLDIER
SOCIALIZING	SODDIES	SOFTIE	SOLACED	SOLDIERED
SOCIALLY	SODDING	SOFTIES	SOLACER	SOLDIERIES
SOCIALS	SODDY	SOFTISH	SOLACERS	SOLDIERING
SOCIETAL	SODIC	SOFTLY	SOLACES	SOLDIERLY
SOCIETIES	SODIUM	SOFTNESS	SOLACING	SOLDIERS
SOCIETY	SODIUMS	SOFTNESSES	SOLAN	SOLDIERY
SOCIOGRAM	SODOM	SOFTS	SOLAND	SOLDO
SOCIOGRAMS	SODOMIES	SOFTSHELL	SOLANDER	SOLE
SOCIOLECT	SODOMIST	SOFTSHELLS	SOLANDERS	SOLECISE
SOCIOLECTS	SODOMISTS	SOFTWARE	SOLANDS	SOLECISED
SOCIOLOGIES	SODOMITE	SOFTWARES	SOLANIN	SOLECISES
SOCIOLOGY	SODOMITES	SOFTWOOD	SOLANINE	SOLECISING

SOLECISM	SOLICIT	SOLONCHAK	SOMBREROS	SONATINA
SOLECISMS	SOLICITED	SOLONCHAKS	SOMBROUS	SONATINAS
SOLECIST	SOLICITING	SOLONETS	SOME	SONATINE
SOLECISTS	SOLICITOR	SOLONETSES	SOMEBODIES	SONDE
SOLECIZE	SOLICITORS	SOLONETZ	SOMEBODY	SONDER
SOLECIZED	SOLICITS	SOLONETZES	SOMEDAY	SONDERS
SOLECIZES	SOLID	SOLONS	SOMEDEAL	SONDES
SOLECIZING	SOLIDAGO	SOLOS	SOMEHOW	SONE
SOLED	SOLIDAGOS	SOLS	SOMEONE	SONES
SOLEI	SOLIDARY	SOLSTICE	SOMEONES	SONG
SOLELESS	SOLIDER	SOLSTICES	SOMEPLACE	SONGBIRD
SOLELY	SOLIDEST	SOLUBLE	SOMEPLACES	SONGBIRDS
SOLEMN	SOLIDI	SOLUBLES	SOMERSET	SONGBOOK
SOLEMNER	SOLIDIFIED	SOLUBLY	SOMERSETED	SONGBOOKS
SOLEMNEST	SOLIDIFIES	SOLUM	SOMERSETING	SONGFEST
SOLEMNIFIED	SOLIDIFY	SOLUMS	SOMERSETS	SONGFESTS
SOLEMNIFIES	SOLIDIFYING	SOLUNAR	SOMERSETTED	SONGFUL
SOLEMNIFY	SOLIDITIES	SOLUS	SOMERSETTING	SONGFULLY
SOLEMNIFYING	SOLIDITY	SOLUTE	SOMETHING	SONGLESS
SOLEMNITIES	SOLIDLY	SOLUTES	SOMETHINGS	SONGLIKE
SOLEMNITY	SOLIDNESS	SOLUTION	SOMETIME	SONGS
SOLEMNIZE	SOLIDNESSES	SOLUTIONS	SOMETIMES	SONGSMITH
SOLEMNIZED	SOLIDS	SOLVABLE	SOMEWAY	SONGSMITHS
SOLEMNIZES	SOLIDUS	SOLVATE	SOMEWAYS	SONGSTER
SOLEMNIZING	SOLILOQUIES	SOLVATED	SOMEWHAT	SONGSTERS
SOLEMNLY	SOLILOQUY	SOLVATES	SOMEWHATS	SONHOOD
SOLENESS	SOLING	SOLVATING	SOMEWHEN	SONHOODS
SOLENESSES	SOLION	SOLVATION	SOMEWHERE	SONIC
SOLENODON	SOLIONS	SOLVATIONS	SOMEWHERES	SONICALLY
SOLENODONS	SOLIPSISM	SOLVE	SOMEWISE	SONICATE
SOLENOID	SOLIPSISMS	SOLVED	SOMITAL	SONICATED
SOLENOIDS	SOLIPSIST	SOLVENCIES	SOMITE	SONICATES
SOLEPLATE	SOLIPSISTS	SOLVENCY	SOMITES	SONICATING
SOLEPLATES	SOLIQUID	SOLVENT	SOMITIC	SONICATOR
SOLEPRINT	SOLIQUIDS	SOLVENTLY	SOMMELIER	SONICATORS
SOLEPRINTS	SOLITAIRE	SOLVENTS	SOMMELIERS	SONICS
SOLERET	SOLITAIRES	SOLVER	SOMNOLENT	SONLESS
SOLERETS	SOLITARIES	SOLVERS	SOMONI	SONLIKE
SOLES	SOLITARY	SOLVES	SOMS	SONLY
SOLEUS	SOLITON	SOLVING	SON	SONNET
SOLEUSES	SOLITONS	SOM	SONANCE	SONNETED
SOLFATARA	SOLITUDE	SOMA	SONANCES	SONNETEER
SOLFATARAS	SOLITUDES	SOMAN	SONANT	SONNETEERS
SOLFEGE	SOLLERET	SOMANS	SONANTAL	SONNETING
SOLFEGES	SOLLERETS	SOMAS	SONANTIC	SONNETIZE
SOLFEGGI	SOLO	SOMATA	SONANTS	SONNETIZED
SOLFEGGIO	SOLOED	SOMATIC	SONAR	SONNETIZES
SOLFEGGIOS	SOLOING	SOMBER	SONARMAN	SONNETIZING
SOLFERINO	SOLOIST	SOMBERLY	SONARMEN	SONNETS
SOLFERINOS	SOLOISTIC	SOMBRE	SONARS	SONNETTED
SOLGEL	SOLOISTS	SOMBRELY	SONATA	SONNETTING
SOLI	SOLON	SOMBRERO	SONATAS	SONNIES

SONNY
SONOBUOY
SONOBUOYS
SONOGRAM
SONOGRAMS
SONORANT
SONORANTS
SONORITIES
SONORITY
SONOROUS
SONOVOX
SONOVOXES
SONS
SONSHIP
SONSHIPS
SONSIE
SONSIER
SONSIEST
SONSY
SOOCHONG
SOOCHONGS
SOOEY
SOOK
SOOKS
SOON
SOONER
SOONERS
SOONEST
SOOT
SOOTED
SOOTH
SOOTHE
SOOTHED
SOOTHER
SOOTHERS
SOOTHES
SOOTHEST
SOOTHFAST
SOOTHING
SOOTHLY
SOOTHS
SOOTHSAID
SOOTHSAY
SOOTHSAYING
SOOTHSAYS
SOOTIER
SOOTIEST
SOOTILY
SOOTINESS
SOOTINESSES
SOOTING
SOOTS

SOOTY
SOP
SOPAPILLA
SOPAPILLAS
SOPH
SOPHIES
SOPHISM
SOPHISMS
SOPHIST
SOPHISTIC
SOPHISTRIES
SOPHISTRY
SOPHISTS
SOPHOMORE
SOPHOMORES
SOPHS
SOPHY
SOPITE
SOPITED
SOPITES
SOPITING
SOPOR
SOPORIFIC
SOPORIFICS
SOPORS
SOPPED
SOPPIER
SOPPIEST
SOPPINESS
SOPPINESSES
SOPPING
SOPPY
SOPRANI
SOPRANINO
SOPRANINOS
SOPRANO
SOPRANOS
SOPS
SORA
SORAS
SORB
SORBABLE
SORBATE
SORBATES
SORBED
SORBENT
SORBENTS
SORBET
SORBETS
SORBIC
SORBING
SORBITOL

SORBITOLS
SORBOSE
SORBOSES
SORBS
SORCERER
SORCERERS
SORCERESS
SORCERESSES
SORCERIES
SORCEROUS
SORCERY
SORD
SORDID
SORDIDLY
SORDINE
SORDINES
SORDINI
SORDINO
SORDOR
SORDORS
SORDS
SORE
SORED
SOREHEAD
SOREHEADS
SOREL
SORELS
SORELY
SORENESS
SORENESSES
SORER
SORES
SOREST
SORGHO
SORGHOS
SORGHUM
SORGHUMS
SORGO
SORGOS
SORI
SORICINE
SORING
SORINGS
SORITES
SORITIC
SORN
SORNED
SORNER
SORNERS
SORNING
SORNS
SOROCHE

SOROCHES
SORORAL
SORORALLY
SORORATE
SORORATES
SORORITIES
SORORITY
SOROSES
SOROSIS
SOROSISES
SORPTION
SORPTIONS
SORPTIVE
SORREL
SORRELS
SORRIER
SORRIEST
SORRILY
SORRINESS
SORRINESSES
SORROW
SORROWED
SORROWER
SORROWERS
SORROWFUL
SORROWING
SORROWS
SORRY
SORT
SORTA
SORTABLE
SORTABLY
SORTED
SORTER
SORTERS
SORTIE
SORTIED
SORTIEING
SORTIES
SORTILEGE
SORTILEGES
SORTING
SORTITION
SORTITIONS
SORTS
SORUS
SOS
SOSTENUTI
SOSTENUTO
SOSTENUTOS
SOT
SOTH

SOTHS
SOTOL
SOTOLS
SOTS
SOTTED
SOTTEDLY
SOTTISH
SOTTISHLY
SOU
SOUARI
SOUARIS
SOUBISE
SOUBISES
SOUBRETTE
SOUBRETTES
SOUCAR
SOUCARS
SOUCHONG
SOUCHONGS
SOUDAN
SOUDANS
SOUFFLE
SOUFFLED
SOUFFLEED
SOUFFLES
SOUGH
SOUGHED
SOUGHING
SOUGHS
SOUGHT
SOUK
SOUKOUS
SOUKOUSES
SOUKS
SOUL
SOULED
SOULFUL
SOULFULLY
SOULLESS
SOULLIKE
SOULMATE
SOULMATES
SOULS
SOUND
SOUNDABLE
SOUNDBOX
SOUNDBOXES
SOUNDED
SOUNDER
SOUNDERS
SOUNDEST
SOUNDING

SOUNDINGS	SOUSING	SOVRANLY	SPACESHIPS	SPAGYRICS
SOUNDLESS	SOUSLIK	SOVRANS	SPACESUIT	SPAHEE
SOUNDLY	SOUSLIKS	SOVRANTIES	SPACESUITS	SPAHEES
SOUNDMAN	SOUTACHE	SOVRANTY	SPACEWALK	SPAHI
SOUNDMEN	SOUTACHES	SOW	SPACEWALKED	SPAHIS
SOUNDNESS	SOUTANE	SOWABLE	SPACEWALKING	SPAIL
SOUNDNESSES	SOUTANES	SOWANS	SPACEWALKS	SPAILS
SOUNDS	SOUTER	SOWAR	SPACEWARD	SPAIT
SOUP	SOUTERS	SOWARS	SPACEY	SPAITS
SOUPCON	SOUTH	SOWBELLIES	SPACIAL	SPAKE
SOUPCONS	SOUTHEAST	SOWBELLY	SPACIALLY	SPALDEEN
SOUPED	SOUTHEASTS	SOWBREAD	SPACIER	SPALDEENS
SOUPIER	SOUTHED	SOWBREADS	SPACIEST	SPALE
SOUPIEST	SOUTHER	SOWCAR	SPACINESS	SPALES
SOUPING	SOUTHERLIES	SOWCARS	SPACINESSES	SPALL
SOUPLESS	SOUTHERLY	SOWED	SPACING	SPALLABLE
SOUPLIKE	SOUTHERN	SOWENS	SPACINGS	SPALLED
SOUPS	SOUTHERNS	SOWER	SPACIOUS	SPALLER
SOUPSPOON	SOUTHERS	SOWERS	SPACKLE	SPALLERS
SOUPSPOONS	SOUTHING	SOWING	SPACKLED	SPALLING
SOUPY	SOUTHINGS	SOWN	SPACKLES	SPALLS
SOUR	SOUTHLAND	SOWS	SPACKLING	SPALPEEN
SOURBALL	SOUTHLANDS	SOX	SPACY	SPALPEENS
SOURBALLS	SOUTHPAW	SOY	SPADE	SPAM
SOURCE	SOUTHPAWS	SOYA	SPADED	SPAMBOT
SOURCED	SOUTHRON	SOYAS	SPADEFISH	SPAMBOTS
SOURCEFUL	SOUTHRONS	SOYBEAN	SPADEFISHES	SPAMMED
SOURCES	SOUTHS	SOYBEANS	SPADEFUL	SPAMMER
SOURCING	SOUTHWARD	SOYMILK	SPADEFULS	SPAMMERS
SOURDINE	SOUTHWARDS	SOYMILKS	SPADER	SPAMMING
SOURDINES	SOUTHWEST	SOYS	SPADERS	SPAMS
SOURDOUGH	SOUTHWESTS	SOYUZ	SPADES	SPAN
SOURDOUGHS	SOUVENIR	SOYUZES	SPADEWORK	SPANCEL
SOURED	SOUVENIRS	SOYUZ	SPADEWORKS	SPANCELED
SOURER	SOUVLAKI	SOZIN	SPADICES	SPANCELING
SOUREST	SOUVLAKIA	SOZINE	SPADILLE	SPANCELLED
SOURING	SOUVLAKIAS	SOZINES	SPADILLES	SPANCELLING
SOURISH	SOUVLAKIS	SOZINS	SPADING	SPANCELS
SOURLY	SOVEREIGN	SOZZLED	SPADIX	SPANDEX
SOURNESS	SOVEREIGNS	SPA	SPADIXES	SPANDEXES
SOURNESSES	SOVIET	SPACE	SPADO	SPANDREL
SOURPUSS	SOVIETISM	SPACEBAND	SPADONES	SPANDRELS
SOURPUSSES	SOVIETISMS	SPACEBANDS	SPAE	SPANDRIL
SOURS	SOVIETIZE	SPACED	SPAED	SPANDRILS
SOURSOP	SOVIETIZED	SPACELESS	SPAEING	SPANG
SOURSOPS	SOVIETIZES	SPACEMAN	SPAEINGS	SPANGLE
SOURWOOD	SOVIETIZING	SPACEMEN	SPAES	SPANGLED
SOURWOODS	SOVIETS	SPACEPORT	SPAETZLE	SPANGLES
SOUS	SOVKHOZ	SPACEPORTS	SPAETZLES	SPANGLIER
SOUSE	SOVKHOZES	SPACER	SPAGHETTI	SPANGLIEST
SOUSED	SOVKHOZY	SPACERS	SPAGHETTIS	SPANGLING
SOUSES	SOVRAN	SPACES	SPAGYRIC	SPANGLY
		SPACESHIP		

SPANIEL	SPARKISH	SPATES	SPEANING	SPECK
SPANIELS	SPARKLE	SPATHAL	SPEANS	SPECKED
SPANK	SPARKLED	SPATHE	SPEAR	SPECKING
SPANKED	SPARKLER	SPATHED	SPEARED	SPECKLE
SPANKER	SPARKLERS	SPATHES	SPEARER	SPECKLED
SPANKERS	SPARKLES	SPATHIC	SPEARERS	SPECKLES
SPANKING	SPARKLET	SPATHOSE	SPEARFISH	SPECKLING
SPANKINGS	SPARKLETS	SPATIAL	SPEARFISHED	SPECKS
SPANKS	SPARKLIER	SPATIALLY	SPEARFISHES	SPECS
SPANLESS	SPARKLIEST	SPATS	SPEARFISHING	SPECTACLE
SPANNED	SPARKLING	SPATTED	SPEARGUN	SPECTACLES
SPANNER	SPARKLY	SPATTER	SPEARGUNS	SPECTATE
SPANNERS	SPARKPLUG	SPATTERED	SPEARHEAD	SPECTATED
SPANNING	SPARKPLUGGED	SPATTERING	SPEARHEADED	SPECTATES
SPANS	SPARKPLUGGING	SPATTERS	SPEARHEADING	SPECTATING
SPANSULE	SPARKPLUGS	SPATTING	SPEARHEADS	SPECTATOR
SPANSULES	SPARKS	SPATULA	SPEARING	SPECTATORS
SPANWORM	SPARKY	SPATULAR	SPEARLIKE	SPECTER
SPANWORMS	SPARLIKE	SPATULAS	SPEARMAN	SPECTERS
SPAR	SPARLING	SPATULATE	SPEARMEN	SPECTRA
SPARABLE	SPARLINGS	SPATZLE	SPEARMINT	SPECTRAL
SPARABLES	SPAROID	SPATZLES	SPEARMINTS	SPECTRE
SPARE	SPAROIDS	SPAVIE	SPEARS	SPECTRES
SPAREABLE	SPARRED	SPAVIES	SPEARWORT	SPECTRUM
SPARED	SPARRIER	SPAVIET	SPEARWORTS	SPECTRUMS
SPARELY	SPARRIEST	SPAVIN	SPEC	SPECULA
SPARENESS	SPARRING	SPAVINED	SPECCED	SPECULAR
SPARENESSES	SPARROW	SPAVINS	SPECCING	SPECULATE
SPARER	SPARROWS	SPAWN	SPECIAL	SPECULATED
SPARERIB	SPARRY	SPAWNED	SPECIALER	SPECULATES
SPARERIBS	SPARS	SPAWNER	SPECIALEST	SPECULATING
SPARERS	SPARSE	SPAWNERS	SPECIALLY	SPECULUM
SPARES	SPARSELY	SPAWNING	SPECIALS	SPECULUMS
SPAREST	SPARSER	SPAWNS	SPECIALTIES	SPED
SPARGE	SPARSEST	SPAY	SPECIALTY	SPEECH
SPARGED	SPARSITIES	SPAYED	SPECIATE	SPEECHES
SPARGER	SPARSITY	SPAYING	SPECIATED	SPEECHIFIED
SPARGERS	SPARTAN	SPAYS	SPECIATES	SPEECHIFIES
SPARGES	SPARTEINE	SPAZ	SPECIATING	SPEECHIFY
SPARGING	SPARTEINES	SPAZZ	SPECIE	SPEECHIFYING
SPARID	SPARTINA	SPAZZES	SPECIES	SPEED
SPARIDS	SPARTINAS	SPEAK	SPECIFIC	SPEEDBALL
SPARING	SPAS	SPEAKABLE	SPECIFICS	SPEEDBALLED
SPARINGLY	SPASM	SPEAKEASIES	SPECIFIED	SPEEDBALLING
SPARK	SPASMED	SPEAKEASY	SPECIFIER	SPEEDBALLS
SPARKED	SPASMING	SPEAKER	SPECIFIERS	SPEEDBOAT
SPARKER	SPASMODIC	SPEAKERS	SPECIFIES	SPEEDBOATS
SPARKERS	SPASMS	SPEAKING	SPECIFY	SPEEDED
SPARKIER	SPASTIC	SPEAKINGS	SPECIFYING	SPEEDER
SPARKIEST	SPASTICS	SPEAKS	SPECIMEN	SPEEDERS
SPARKILY	SPAT	SPEAN	SPECIMENS	SPEEDIER
SPARKING	SPATE	SPEANED	SPECIOUS	SPEEDIEST

SPEEDILY	SPELLINGS	SPHENE	SPICES	SPIGOT
SPEEDING	SPELLS	SPHENES	SPICEY	SPIGOTS
SPEEDINGS	SPELT	SPHENIC	SPICIER	SPIK
SPEEDO	SPELTER	SPHENODON	SPICIEST	SPIKE
SPEEDOS	SPELTERS	SPHENODONS	SPICILY	SPIKED
SPEEDREAD	SPELTS	SPHENOID	SPICINESS	SPIKELET
SPEEDREADING	SPELTZ	SPHENOIDS	SPICINESSES	SPIKELETS
SPEEDREADS	SPELTZES	SPHERAL	SPICING	SPIKELIKE
SPEEDS	SPELUNK	SPHERE	SPICK	SPIKENARD
SPEEDSTER	SPELUNKED	SPHERED	SPICKS	SPIKENARDS
SPEEDSTERS	SPELUNKER	SPHERES	SPICS	SPIKER
SPEEDUP	SPELUNKERS	SPHERIC	SPICULA	SPIKERS
SPEEDUPS	SPELUNKING	SPHERICAL	SPICULAE	SPIKES
SPEEDWAY	SPELUNKS	SPHERICS	SPICULAR	SPIKEY
SPEEDWAYS	SPENCE	SPHERIER	SPICULATE	SPIKIER
SPEEDWELL	SPENCER	SPHERIEST	SPICULE	SPIKIEST
SPEEDWELLS	SPENCERS	SPHERING	SPICULES	SPIKILY
SPEEDY	SPENCES	SPHEROID	SPICULUM	SPIKINESS
SPEEL	SPEND	SPHEROIDS	SPICY	SPIKINESSES
SPEELED	SPENDABLE	SPHERULAR	SPIDER	SPIKING
SPEELING	SPENDER	SPHERULE	SPIDERIER	SPIKS
SPEELS	SPENDERS	SPHERULES	SPIDERIEST	SPIKY
SPEER	SPENDIER	SPHERY	SPIDERISH	SPILE
SPEERED	SPENDIEST	SPHINCTER	SPIDERS	SPILED
SPEERING	SPENDING	SPHINCTERS	SPIDERWEB	SPILES
SPEERINGS	SPENDS	SPHINGES	SPIDERWEBS	SPILIKIN
SPEERS	SPENDY	SPHINGID	SPIDERY	SPILIKINS
SPEIL	SPENSE	SPHINGIDS	SPIED	SPILING
SPEILED	SPENSES	SPHINX	SPIEGEL	SPILINGS
SPEILING	SPENT	SPHINXES	SPIEGELS	SPILL
SPEILS	SPERM	SPHYGMIC	SPIEL	SPILLABLE
SPEIR	SPERMARIES	SPHYGMUS	SPIELED	SPILLAGE
SPEIRED	SPERMARY	SPHYGMUSES	SPIELER	SPILLAGES
SPEIRING	SPERMATIA	SPHYNX	SPIELERS	SPILLED
SPEIRS	SPERMATIC	SPHYNXES	SPIELING	SPILLER
SPEISE	SPERMATID	SPIC	SPIELS	SPILLERS
SPEISES	SPERMATIDS	SPICA	SPIER	SPILLIKIN
SPEISS	SPERMATIUM	SPICAE	SPIERED	SPILLIKINS
SPEISSES	SPERMIC	SPICAS	SPIERING	SPILLING
SPELAEAN	SPERMINE	SPICATE	SPIERS	SPILLOVER
SPELEAN	SPERMINES	SPICATED	SPIES	SPILLOVERS
SPELL	SPERMOUS	SPICCATO	SPIFF	SPILLS
SPELLBIND	SPERMS	SPICCATOS	SPIFFED	SPILLWAY
SPELLBINDING	SPEW	SPICE	SPIFFIED	SPILLWAYS
SPELLBINDS	SPEWED	SPICEBUSH	SPIFFIER	SPILT
SPELLBOUND	SPEWER	SPICEBUSHES	SPIFFIES	SPILTH
SPELLDOWN	SPEWERS	SPICED	SPIFFIEST	SPILTHS
SPELLDOWNS	SPEWING	SPICELESS	SPIFFILY	SPIN
SPELLED	SPEWS	SPICER	SPIFFING	SPINACH
SPELLER	SPHAGNOUS	SPICERIES	SPIFFS	SPINACHES
SPELLERS	SPHAGNUM	SPICERS	SPIFFY	SPINACHY
SPELLING	SPHAGNUMS	SPICERY	SPIFFYING	SPINAGE

SPINAGES	SPINOSE	SPIRITIST	SPLASHED	SPLICER
SPINAL	SPINOSELY	SPIRITISTS	SPLASHER	SPLICERS
SPINALLY	SPINOSITIES	SPIRITOSO	SPLASHERS	SPLICES
SPINALS	SPINOSITY	SPIRITOUS	SPLASHES	SPLICING
SPINATE	SPINOUS	SPIRITS	SPLASHIER	SPLIFF
SPINDLE	SPINOUT	SPIRITUAL	SPLASHIEST	SPLIFFS
SPINDLED	SPINOUTS	SPIRITUALS	SPLASHILY	SPLINE
SPINDLER	SPINS	SPIRITUEL	SPLASHING	SPLINED
SPINDLERS	SPINSTER	SPIROGYRA	SPLASHY	SPLINES
SPINDLES	SPINSTERS	SPIROGYRAS	SPLAT	SPLINING
SPINDLIER	SPINTO	SPIROID	SPLATS	SPLINT
SPINDLIEST	SPINTOS	SPIRT	SPLATTED	SPLINTED
SPINDLING	SPINULA	SPIRTED	SPLATTER	SPLINTER
SPINDLY	SPINULAE	SPIRTING	SPLATTERED	SPLINTERED
SPINDRIFT	SPINULE	SPIRTS	SPLATTERING	SPLINTERING
SPINDRIFTS	SPINULES	SPIRULA	SPLATTERS	SPLINTERS
SPINE	SPINULOSE	SPIRULAE	SPLATTING	SPLINTERY
SPINED	SPINY	SPIRULAS	SPLAY	SPLINTING
SPINEL	SPIRACLE	SPIRULINA	SPLAYED	SPLINTS
SPINELESS	SPIRACLES	SPIRULINAS	SPLAYFEET	SPLIT
SPINELIKE	SPIRAEA	SPIRY	SPLAYFOOT	SPLITS
SPINELLE	SPIRAEAS	SPIT	SPLAYING	SPLITTER
SPINELLES	SPIRAL	SPITAL	SPLAYS	SPLITTERS
SPINELS	SPIRALED	SPITALS	SPLEEN	SPLITTING
SPINES	SPIRALING	SPITBALL	SPLEENFUL	SPLODGE
SPINET	SPIRALITIES	SPITBALLS	SPLEENIER	SPLODGED
SPINETS	SPIRALITY	SPITE	SPLEENIEST	SPLODGES
SPINIER	SPIRALLED	SPITED	SPLEENISH	SPLODGING
SPINIEST	SPIRALLING	SPITEFUL	SPLEENS	SPLORE
SPINIFEX	SPIRALLY	SPITEFULLER	SPLEENY	SPLORES
SPINIFEXES	SPIRALS	SPITEFULLEST	SPLENDENT	SPLOSH
SPININESS	SPIRANT	SPITES	SPLENDID	SPLOSHED
SPININESSES	SPIRANTS	SPITFIRE	SPLENDIDER	SPLOSHES
SPINLESS	SPIRE	SPITFIRES	SPLENDIDEST	SPLOSHING
SPINNAKER	SPIREA	SPITING	SPLENDOR	SPLOTCH
SPINNAKERS	SPIREAS	SPITS	SPLENDORS	SPLOTCHED
SPINNER	SPIRED	SPITTED	SPLENDOUR	SPLOTCHES
SPINNERET	SPIREM	SPITTER	SPLENDOURS	SPLOTCHIER
SPINNERETS	SPIREME	SPITTERS	SPLENETIC	SPLOTCHIEST
SPINNERIES	SPIREMES	SPITTING	SPLENETICS	SPLOTCHING
SPINNERS	SPIREMS	SPITTLE	SPLENIA	SPLOTCHY
SPINNERY	SPIRES	SPITTLES	SPLENIAL	SPLURGE
SPINNEY	SPIRIER	SPITTOON	SPLENIC	SPLURGED
SPINNEYS	SPIRIEST	SPITTOONS	SPLENII	SPLURGER
SPINNIES	SPIRILLA	SPITZ	SPLENIUM	SPLURGERS
SPINNING	SPIRILLUM	SPITZES	SPLENIUS	SPLURGES
SPINNINGS	SPIRING	SPIV	SPLENT	SPLURGIER
SPINNY	SPIRIT	SPIVS	SPLENTS	SPLURGIEST
SPINOFF	SPIRITED	SPIVVY	SPLEUCHAN	SPLURGING
SPINOFFS	SPIRITING	SPLAKE	SPLEUCHANS	SPLURGY
SPINOR	SPIRITISM	SPLAKES	SPLICE	SPLUTTER
SPINORS	SPIRITISMS	SPLASH	SPLICED	SPLUTTERED

SPLUTTERING	SPONSIONS	SPOOR	SPORULES	SPRAWLED
SPLUTTERS	SPONSON	SPOORED	SPOT	SPRAWLER
SPLUTTERY	SPONSONS	SPOORING	SPOTLESS	SPRAWLERS
SPODE	SPONSOR	SPOORS	SPOTLIGHT	SPRAWLIER
SPODES	SPONSORED	SPORADIC	SPOTLIGHTED	SPRAWLIEST
SPODOSOL	SPONSORING	SPORAL	SPOTLIGHTING	SPRAWLING
SPODOSOLS	SPONSORS	SPORANGIA	SPOTLIGHTS	SPRAWLS
SPODUMENE	SPONTOON	SPORANGIUM	SPOTLIT	SPRAWLY
SPODUMENES	SPONTOONS	SPORE	SPOTS	SPRAY
SPOIL	SPOOF	SPORED	SPOTTABLE	SPRAYED
SPOILABLE	SPOOFED	SPORES	SPOTTED	SPRAYER
SPOILAGE	SPOOFER	SPORICIDE	SPOTTER	SPRAYERS
SPOILAGES	SPOOFERIES	SPORICIDES	SPOTTERS	SPRAYING
SPOILED	SPOOFERS	SPORING	SPOTTIER	SPRAYS
SPOILER	SPOOFERY	SPOROCARP	SPOTTIEST	SPREAD
SPOILERS	SPOOFING	SPOROCARPS	SPOTTILY	SPREADER
SPOILING	SPOOFS	SPOROCYST	SPOTTING	SPREADERS
SPOILS	SPOOFY	SPOROCYSTS	SPOTTY	SPREADING
SPOILSMAN	SPOOK	SPOROGONIES	SPOUSAL	SPREADS
SPOILSMEN	SPOOKED	SPOROGONY	SPOUSALLY	SPREE
SPOILT	SPOOKERIES	SPOROID	SPOUSALS	SPREES
SPOKE	SPOOKERY	SPOROPHYL	SPOUSE	SPRENT
SPOKED	SPOOKIER	SPOROPHYLS	SPOUSED	SPRIER
SPOKEN	SPOOKIEST	SPOROZOA	SPOUSES	SPRIEST
SPOKES	SPOOKILY	SPOROZOAL	SPOUSING	SPRIG
SPOKESMAN	SPOOKING	SPOROZOAN	SPOUT	SPRIGGED
SPOKESMEN	SPOOKISH	SPOROZOANS	SPOUTED	SPRIGGER
SPOKING	SPOOKS	SPOROZOIC	SPOUTER	SPRIGGERS
SPOLIATE	SPOOKY	SPOROZOON	SPOUTERS	SPRIGGIER
SPOLIATED	SPOOL	SPORRAN	SPOUTING	SPRIGGIEST
SPOLIATES	SPOOLED	SPORRANS	SPOUTINGS	SPRIGGING
SPOLIATING	SPOOLER	SPORT	SPOUTLESS	SPRIGGY
SPOLIATOR	SPOOLERS	SPORTED	SPOUTS	SPRIGHT
SPOLIATORS	SPOOLING	SPORTER	SPRADDLE	SPRIGHTLIER
SPONDAIC	SPOOLINGS	SPORTERS	SPRADDLED	SPRIGHTLIEST
SPONDAICS	SPOOLS	SPORTFUL	SPRADDLES	SPRIGHTLY
SPONDEE	SPOON	SPORTIER	SPRADDLING	SPRIGHTS
SPONDEES	SPOONBILL	SPORTIEST	SPRAG	SPRIGS
SPONGE	SPOONBILLS	SPORTIF	SPRAGS	SPRIGTAIL
SPONGED	SPOONED	SPORTILY	SPRAIN	SPRIGTAILS
SPONGER	SPOONEY	SPORTING	SPRAINED	SPRING
SPONGERS	SPOONEYS	SPORTIVE	SPRAINING	SPRINGAL
SPONGES	SPOONFUL	SPORTS	SPRAINS	SPRINGALD
SPONGIER	SPOONFULS	SPORTSMAN	SPRANG	SPRINGALDS
SPONGIEST	SPOONIER	SPORTSMEN	SPRANGS	SPRINGALS
SPONGILY	SPOONIES	SPORTY	SPRAT	SPRINGBOK
SPONGIN	SPOONIEST	SPORULAR	SPRATS	SPRINGBOKS
SPONGING	SPOONILY	SPORULATE	SPRATTLE	SPRINGE
SPONGINS	SPOONING	SPORULATED	SPRATTLED	SPRINGED
SPONGY	SPOONS	SPORULATES	SPRATTLES	SPRINGEING
SPONSAL	SPOONSFUL	SPORULATING	SPRATTLING	SPRINGER
SPONSION	SPOONY	SPORULE	SPRAWL	SPRINGERS

SPRINGES	SPRUE	SPURN	SQUABS	SQUASHED
SPRINGIER	SPRUES	SPURNED	SQUAD	SQUASHER
SPRINGIEST	SPRUG	SPURNER	SQUADDED	SQUASHERS
SPRINGILY	SPRUGS	SPURNERS	SQUADDING	SQUASHES
SPRINGING	SPRUNG	SPURNING	SQUADRON	SQUASHIER
SPRINGINGS	SPRY	SPURNS	SQUADRONED	SQUASHIEST
SPRINGLET	SPRYER	SPURRED	SQUADRONING	SQUASHILY
SPRINGLETS	SPRYEST	SPURRER	SQUADRONS	SQUASHING
SPRINGS	SPRYLY	SPURRERS	SQUADS	SQUASHY
SPRINGY	SPRYNESS	SPURREY	SQUALENE	SQUAT
SPRINKLE	SPRYNESSES	SPURREYS	SQUALENES	SQUATLY
SPRINKLED	SPUD	SPURRIER	SQUALID	SQUATNESS
SPRINKLER	SPUDDED	SPURRIERS	SQUALIDER	SQUATNESSES
SPRINKLERED	SPUDDER	SPURRIES	SQUALIDEST	SQUATS
SPRINKLERING	SPUDDERS	SPURRING	SQUALIDLY	SQUATTED
SPRINKLERS	SPUDDING	SPURRY	SQUALL	SQUATTER
SPRINKLES	SPUDS	SPURS	SQUALLED	SQUATTERED
SPRINKLING	SPUE	SPURT	SQUALLER	SQUATTERING
SPRINT	SPUED	SPURTED	SQUALLERS	SQUATTERS
SPRINTED	SPUES	SPURTER	SQUALLIER	SQUATTEST
SPRINTER	SPUING	SPURTERS	SQUALLIEST	SQUATTIER
SPRINTERS	SPUME	SPURTING	SQUALLING	SQUATTIEST
SPRINTING	SPUMED	SPURTLE	SQUALLISH	SQUATTILY
SPRINTS	SPUMES	SPURTLES	SQUALLS	SQUATTING
SPRIT	SPUMIER	SPURTS	SQUALLY	SQUATTY
SPRITE	SPUMIEST	SPUTA	SQUALOR	SQUAW
SPRITES	SPUMING	SPUTNIK	SQUALORS	SQUAWBUSH
SPRITS	SPUMONE	SPUTNIKS	SQUAMA	SQUAWBUSHES
SPRITSAIL	SPUMONES	SPUTTER	SQUAMAE	SQUAWFISH
SPRITSAILS	SPUMONI	SPUTTERED	SQUAMATE	SQUAWFISHES
SPRITZ	SPUMONIS	SPUTTERER	SQUAMATES	SQUAWK
SPRITZED	SPUMOUS	SPUTTERERS	SQUAMOSAL	SQUAWKED
SPRITZER	SPUMY	SPUTTERING	SQUAMOSALS	SQUAWKER
SPRITZERS	SPUN	SPUTTERS	SQUAMOSE	SQUAWKERS
SPRITZES	SPUNK	SPUTTERY	SQUAMOUS	SQUAWKING
SPRITZING	SPUNKED	SPUTUM	SQUANDER	SQUAWKS
SPROCKET	SPUNKIE	SPY	SQUANDERED	SQUAWROOT
SPROCKETS	SPUNKIER	SPYGLASS	SQUANDERING	SQUAWROOTS
SPROUT	SPUNKIES	SPYGLASSES	SQUANDERS	SQUAWS
SPROUTED	SPUNKIEST	SPYING	SQUARE	SQUEAK
SPROUTING	SPUNKILY	SPYMASTER	SQUARED	SQUEAKED
SPROUTS	SPUNKING	SPYMASTERS	SQUARELY	SQUEAKER
SPRUCE	SPUNKS	SQUAB	SQUARER	SQUEAKERS
SPRUCED	SPUNKY	SQUABBIER	SQUARERS	SQUEAKIER
SPRUCELY	SPUR	SQUABBIEST	SQUARES	SQUEAKIEST
SPRUCER	SPURGALL	SQUABBLE	SQUAREST	SQUEAKILY
SPRUCES	SPURGALLED	SQUABBLED	SQUARING	SQUEAKING
SPRUCEST	SPURGALLING	SQUABBLER	SQUARISH	SQUEAKS
SPRUCIER	SPURGALLS	SQUABBLERS	SQUARK	SQUEAKY
SPRUCIEST	SPURGE	SQUABBLES	SQUARKS	SQUEAL
SPRUCING	SPURGES	SQUABBLING	SQUARROSE	SQUEALED
SPRUCY	SPURIOUS	SQUABBY	SQUASH	SQUEALER

SQUEALERS	SQUILLAE	SQUISH	STABLINGS	STAGGARTS
SQUEALING	SQUILLAS	SQUISHED	STABLISH	STAGGED
SQUEALS	SQUILLS	SQUISHES	STABLISHED	STAGGER
SQUEAMISH	SQUINCH	SQUISHIER	STABLISHES	STAGGERED
SQUEEGEE	SQUINCHED	SQUISHIEST	STABLISHING	STAGGERER
SQUEEGEED	SQUINCHES	SQUISHING	STABLY	STAGGERERS
SQUEEGEEING	SQUINCHING	SQUISHY	STABS	STAGGERING
SQUEEGEES	SQUINNIED	SQUOOSH	STACCATI	STAGGERS
SQUEEZE	SQUINNIER	SQUOOSHED	STACCATO	STAGGERY
SQUEEZED	SQUINNIES	SQUOOSHES	STACCATOS	STAGGIE
SQUEEZER	SQUINNIEST	SQUOOSHIER	STACK	STAGGIER
SQUEEZERS	SQUINNY	SQUOOSHIEST	STACKABLE	STAGGIES
SQUEEZES	SQUINNYING	SQUOOSHING	STACKED	STAGGIEST
SQUEEZING	SQUINT	SQUOOSHY	STACKER	STAGGING
SQUEG	SQUINTED	SQUUSH	STACKERS	STAGGY
SQUEGGED	SQUINTER	SQUUSHED	STACKING	STAGHOUND
SQUEGGING	SQUINTERS	SQUUSHES	STACKLESS	STAGHOUNDS
SQUEGS	SQUINTEST	SQUUSHING	STACKS	STAGIER
SQUELCH	SQUINTIER	SRADDHA	STACKUP	STAGIEST
SQUELCHED	SQUINTIEST	SRADDHAS	STACKUPS	STAGILY
SQUELCHER	SQUINTING	SRADHA	STACTE	STAGINESS
SQUELCHERS	SQUINTS	SRADHAS	STACTES	STAGINESSES
SQUELCHES	SQUINTY	SRI	STADDLE	STAGING
SQUELCHIER	SQUIRE	SRIS	STADDLES	STAGINGS
SQUELCHIEST	SQUIRED	STAB	STADE	STAGNANCE
SQUELCHING	SQUIREEN	STABBED	STADES	STAGNANCES
SQUELCHY	SQUIREENS	STABBER	STADIA	STAGNANCIES
SQUIB	SQUIRES	STABBERS	STADIAS	STAGNANCY
SQUIBBED	SQUIRING	STABBING	STADIUM	STAGNANT
SQUIBBING	SQUIRISH	STABILE	STADIUMS	STAGNATE
SQUIBS	SQUIRM	STABILES	STAFF	STAGNATED
SQUID	SQUIRMED	STABILISE	STAFFED	STAGNATES
SQUIDDED	SQUIRMER	STABILISED	STAFFER	STAGNATING
SQUIDDING	SQUIRMERS	STABILISES	STAFFERS	STAGS
SQUIDS	SQUIRMIER	STABILISING	STAFFING	STAGY
SQUIFFED	SQUIRMIEST	STABILITIES	STAFFS	STAID
SQUIFFIER	SQUIRMING	STABILITY	STAG	STAIDER
SQUIFFIEST	SQUIRMS	STABILIZE	STAGE	STAIDEST
SQUIFFY	SQUIRMY	STABILIZED	STAGEABLE	STAIDLY
SQUIGGLE	SQUIRREL	STABILIZES	STAGED	STAIDNESS
SQUIGGLED	SQUIRRELED	STABILIZING	STAGEFUL	STAIDNESSES
SQUIGGLES	SQUIRRELING	STABLE	STAGEFULS	STAIG
SQUIGGLIER	SQUIRRELLED	STABLEBOY	STAGEHAND	STAIGS
SQUIGGLIEST	SQUIRRELLING	STABLEBOYS	STAGEHANDS	STAIN
SQUIGGLING	SQUIRRELS	STABLED	STAGELIKE	STAINABLE
SQUIGGLY	SQUIRRELY	STABLEMAN	STAGER	STAINED
SQUILGEE	SQUIRT	STABLEMEN	STAGERS	STAINER
SQUILGEED	SQUIRTED	STABLER	STAGES	STAINERS
SQUILGEEING	SQUIRTER	STABLERS	STAGEY	STAINING
SQUILGEES	SQUIRTERS	STABLES	STAGGARD	STAINLESS
SQUILL	SQUIRTING	STABLEST	STAGGARDS	STAINLESSES
SQUILLA	SQUIRTS	STABLING	STAGGART	STAINS

STAIR	STALL	STANCHION	STANNOUS	STARGAZED
STAIRCASE	STALLED	STANCHIONED	STANNUM	STARGAZER
STAIRCASES	STALLING	STANCHIONING	STANNUMS	STARGAZERS
STAIRHEAD	STALLION	STANCHIONS	STANOL	STARGAZES
STAIRHEADS	STALLIONS	STANCHLY	STANOLS	STARGAZING
STAIRLESS	STALLS	STAND	STANZA	STARING
STAIRLIKE	STALWART	STANDARD	STANZAED	STARINGLY
STAIRS	STALWARTS	STANDARDS	STANZAIC	STARK
STAIRSTEP	STALWORTH	STANDAWAY	STANZAS	STARKER
STAIRSTEPPED	STALWORTHS	STANDBY	STAPEDES	STARKERS
STAIRSTEPPING	STAMEN	STANDBYS	STAPEDIAL	STARKEST
STAIRSTEPS	STAMENED	STANDDOWN	STAPELIA	STARKLY
STAIRWAY	STAMENS	STANDDOWNS	STAPELIAS	STARKNESS
STAIRWAYS	STAMINA	STANDEE	STAPES	STARKNESSES
STAIRWELL	STAMINAL	STANDEES	STAPH	STARLESS
STAIRWELLS	STAMINAS	STANDER	STAPHS	STARLET
STAITHE	STAMINATE	STANDERS	STAPLE	STARLETS
STAITHES	STAMINEAL	STANDFAST	STAPLED	STARLIGHT
STAKE	STAMINODE	STANDFASTS	STAPLER	STARLIGHTS
STAKED	STAMINODES	STANDING	STAPLERS	STARLIKE
STAKEOUT	STAMINODIES	STANDINGS	STAPLES	STARLING
STAKEOUTS	STAMINODY	STANDISH	STAPLING	STARLINGS
STAKES	STAMMEL	STANDISHES	STAR	STARLIT
STAKING	STAMMELS	STANDOFF	STARBOARD	STARNOSE
STALAG	STAMMER	STANDOFFS	STARBOARDED	STARNOSES
STALAGS	STAMMERED	STANDOUT	STARBOARDING	STARRED
STALE	STAMMERER	STANDOUTS	STARBOARDS	STARRIER
STALED	STAMMERERS	STANDPAT	STARBURST	STARRIEST
STALELY	STAMMERING	STANDPIPE	STARBURSTS	STARRING
STALEMATE	STAMMERS	STANDPIPES	STARCH	STARRY
STALEMATED	STAMP	STANDS	STARCHED	STARS
STALEMATES	STAMPED	STANDUP	STARCHES	STARSHIP
STALEMATING	STAMPEDE	STANDUPS	STARCHIER	STARSHIPS
STALENESS	STAMPEDED	STANE	STARCHIEST	START
STALENESSES	STAMPEDER	STANED	STARCHILY	STARTED
STALER	STAMPEDERS	STANES	STARCHING	STARTER
STALES	STAMPEDES	STANG	STARCHY	STARTERS
STALEST	STAMPEDING	STANGED	STARDOM	STARTING
STALING	STAMPER	STANGING	STARDOMS	STARTLE
STALK	STAMPERS	STANGS	STARDUST	STARTLED
STALKED	STAMPING	STANHOPE	STARDUSTS	STARTLER
STALKER	STAMPLESS	STANHOPES	STARE	STARTLERS
STALKERS	STAMPS	STANINE	STARED	STARTLES
STALKIER	STANCE	STANINES	STARER	STARTLING
STALKIEST	STANCES	STANING	STARERS	STARTS
STALKILY	STANCH	STANK	STARES	STARTSY
STALKING	STANCHED	STANKS	STARETS	STARTUP
STALKINGS	STANCHER	STANNARIES	STARFISH	STARTUPS
STALKLESS	STANCHERS	STANNARY	STARFISHES	STARVE
STALKLIKE	STANCHES	STANNIC	STARFRUIT	STARVED
STALKS	STANCHEST	STANNITE	STARFRUITS	STARVER
STALKY	STANCHING	STANNITES	STARGAZE	STARVERS

STARVES	STATIONS	STAYS	STEAMY	STEEPLED
STARVING	STATISM	STAYSAIL	STEAPSIN	STEEPLES
STARWORT	STATISMS	STAYSAILS	STEAPSINS	STEEPLY
STARWORTS	STATIST	STEAD	STEARATE	STEEPNESS
STASES	STATISTIC	STEADED	STEARATES	STEEPNESSES
STASH	STATISTICS	STEADFAST	STEARIC	STEEPS
STASHED	STATISTS	STEADIED	STEARIN	STEER
STASHES	STATIVE	STEADIER	STEARINE	STEERABLE
STASHING	STATIVES	STEADIERS	STEARINES	STEERAGE
STASIMA	STATOCYST	STEADIES	STEARINS	STEERAGES
STASIMON	STATOCYSTS	STEADIEST	STEATITE	STEERED
STASIS	STATOLITH	STEADILY	STEATITES	STEERER
STAT	STATOLITHS	STEADING	STEATITIC	STEERERS
STATABLE	STATOR	STEADINGS	STEDFAST	STEERING
STATAL	STATORS	STEADS	STEED	STEERS
STATANT	STATS	STEADY	STEEDLIKE	STEERSMAN
STATE	STATUARIES	STEADYING	STEEDS	STEERSMEN
STATEABLE	STATUARY	STEAK	STEEK	STEEVE
STATED	STATUE	STEAKS	STEEKED	STEEVED
STATEDLY	STATUED	STEAL	STEEKING	STEEVES
STATEHOOD	STATUES	STEALABLE	STEEKS	STEEVING
STATEHOODS	STATUETTE	STEALAGE	STEEL	STEEVINGS
STATELESS	STATUETTES	STEALAGES	STEELED	STEGODON
STATELIER	STATURE	STEALER	STEELHEAD	STEGODONS
STATELIEST	STATURES	STEALERS	STEELHEADS	STEGOSAUR
STATELY	STATUS	STEALING	STEELIE	STEGOSAURS
STATEMENT	STATUSES	STEALINGS	STEELIER	STEIN
STATEMENTS	STATUSY	STEALS	STEELIES	STEINBOK
STATER	STATUTE	STEALTH	STEELIEST	STEINBOKS
STATEROOM	STATUTES	STEALTHIER	STEELING	STEINS
STATEROOMS	STATUTORY	STEALTHIEST	STEELS	STELA
STATERS	STAUMREL	STEALTHS	STEELWORK	STELAE
STATES	STAUMRELS	STEALTHY	STEELWORKS	STELAI
STATESIDE	STAUNCH	STEAM	STEELY	STELAR
STATESMAN	STAUNCHED	STEAMBOAT	STEELYARD	STELE
STATESMEN	STAUNCHER	STEAMBOATS	STEELYARDS	STELENE
STATEWIDE	STAUNCHES	STEAMED	STEENBOK	STELES
STATIC	STAUNCHEST	STEAMER	STEENBOKS	STELIC
STATICAL	STAUNCHING	STEAMERED	STEENBUCK	STELLA
STATICE	STAUNCHLY	STEAMERING	STEENBUCKS	STELLAR
STATICES	STAVE	STEAMERS	STEEP	STELLAS
STATICKY	STAVED	STEAMIER	STEEPED	STELLATE
STATICS	STAVES	STEAMIEST	STEEPEN	STELLATED
STATIN	STAVING	STEAMILY	STEEPENED	STELLIFIED
STATING	STAVUDINE	STEAMING	STEEPENING	STELLIFIES
STATINS	STAVUDINES	STEAMROLL	STEEPENS	STELLIFY
STATION	STAW	STEAMROLLED	STEEPER	STELLIFYING
STATIONAL	STAY	STEAMROLLING	STEEPERS	STELLITE
STATIONED	STAYED	STEAMROLLS	STEEPEST	STELLITES
STATIONER	STAYER	STEAMS	STEEPING	STELLULAR
STATIONERS	STAYERS	STEAMSHIP	STEEPISH	STEM
STATIONING	STAYING	STEAMSHIPS	STEEPLE	STEMLESS

STEMLIKE	STENT	STERLING	STEWS	STICKWEEDS
STEMMA	STENTOR	STERLINGS	STEWY	STICKWORK
STEMMAS	STENTORS	STERN	STEY	STICKWORKS
STEMMATA	STENTS	STERNA	STHENIA	STICKY
STEMMATIC	STEP	STERNAL	STHENIAS	STICTION
STEMMED	STEPCHILD	STERNER	STHENIC	STICTIONS
STEMMER	STEPCHILDREN	STERNEST	STIBIAL	STIED
STEMMERIES	STEPDAME	STERNITE	STIBINE	STIES
STEMMERS	STEPDAMES	STERNITES	STIBINES	STIFF
STEMMERY	STEPLIKE	STERNLY	STIBIUM	STIFFED
STEMMIER	STEPPE	STERNMOST	STIBIUMS	STIFFEN
STEMMIEST	STEPPED	STERNNESS	STIBNITE	STIFFENED
STEMMING	STEPPER	STERNNESSES	STIBNITES	STIFFENER
STEMMY	STEPPERS	STERNPOST	STICH	STIFFENERS
STEMS	STEPPES	STERNPOSTS	STICHIC	STIFFENING
STEMSON	STEPPING	STERNS	STICHS	STIFFENS
STEMSONS	STEPS	STERNSON	STICK	STIFFER
STEMWARE	STEPSON	STERNSONS	STICKABLE	STIFFEST
STEMWARES	STEPSONS	STERNUM	STICKBALL	STIFFIE
STENCH	STEPSTOOL	STERNUMS	STICKBALLS	STIFFIES
STENCHES	STEPSTOOLS	STERNWARD	STICKED	STIFFING
STENCHFUL	STEPWISE	STERNWAY	STICKER	STIFFISH
STENCHIER	STERADIAN	STERNWAYS	STICKERS	STIFFLY
STENCHIEST	STERADIANS	STEROID	STICKFUL	STIFFNESS
STENCHY	STERCULIA	STEROIDAL	STICKFULS	STIFFNESSES
STENCIL	STERE	STEROIDS	STICKIER	STIFFS
STENCILED	STEREO	STEROL	STICKIES	STIFLE
STENCILER	STEREOED	STEROLS	STICKIEST	STIFLED
STENCILERS	STEREOING	STERTOR	STICKILY	STIFLER
STENCILING	STEREOS	STERTORS	STICKING	STIFLERS
STENCILLED	STERES	STET	STICKIT	STIFLES
STENCILLING	STERIC	STETS	STICKLE	STIFLING
STENCILS	STERICAL	STETSON	STICKLED	STIGMA
STENGAH	STERIGMA	STETSONS	STICKLER	STIGMAL
STENGAHS	STERIGMAS	STETTED	STICKLERS	STIGMAS
STENO	STERIGMATA	STETTING	STICKLES	STIGMATA
STENOBATH	STERILANT	STEVEDORE	STICKLIKE	STIGMATIC
STENOBATHS	STERILANTS	STEVEDORED	STICKLING	STIGMATICS
STENOKIES	STERILE	STEVEDORES	STICKMAN	STILBENE
STENOKOUS	STERILELY	STEVEDORING	STICKMEN	STILBENES
STENOKY	STERILISE	STEW	STICKOUT	STILBITE
STENOS	STERILISED	STEWABLE	STICKOUTS	STILBITES
STENOSED	STERILISES	STEWARD	STICKPIN	STILE
STENOSES	STERILISING	STEWARDED	STICKPINS	STILES
STENOSIS	STERILITIES	STEWARDING	STICKS	STILETTO
STENOTIC	STERILITY	STEWARDS	STICKSEED	STILETTOED
STENOTYPE	STERILIZE	STEWBUM	STICKSEEDS	STILETTOES
STENOTYPED	STERILIZED	STEWBUMS	STICKUM	STILETTOING
STENOTYPES	STERILIZES	STEWED	STICKUMS	STILETTOS
STENOTYPIES	STERILIZING	STEWING	STICKUP	STILL
STENOTYPING	STERLET	STEWPAN	STICKUPS	STILLBORN
STENOTYPY	STERLETS	STEWPANS	STICKWEED	STILLBORNS

STILLED	STINKBUG	STIRABOUT	STOCKED	STOKEHOLE
STILLER	STINKBUGS	STIRABOUTS	STOCKER	STOKEHOLES
STILLEST	STINKER	STIRK	STOCKERS	STOKER
STILLIER	STINKEROO	STIRKS	STOCKFISH	STOKERS
STILLIEST	STINKEROOS	STIRP	STOCKFISHES	STOKES
STILLING	STINKERS	STIRPES	STOCKIER	STOKESIA
STILLMAN	STINKHORN	STIRPS	STOCKIEST	STOKESIAS
STILLMEN	STINKHORNS	STIRRED	STOCKILY	STOKING
STILLNESS	STINKIER	STIRRER	STOCKINET	STOLE
STILLNESSES	STINKIEST	STIRRERS	STOCKINETS	STOLED
STILLROOM	STINKING	STIRRING	STOCKING	STOLEN
STILLROOMS	STINKO	STIRRINGS	STOCKINGS	STOLES
STILLS	STINKPOT	STIRRUP	STOCKISH	STOLID
STILLY	STINKPOTS	STIRRUPS	STOCKIST	STOLIDER
STILT	STINKS	STIRS	STOCKISTS	STOLIDEST
STILTED	STINKWEED	STITCH	STOCKMAN	STOLIDITIES
STILTEDLY	STINKWEEDS	STITCHED	STOCKMEN	STOLIDITY
STILTING	STINKWOOD	STITCHER	STOCKPILE	STOLIDLY
STILTS	STINKWOODS	STITCHERIES	STOCKPILED	STOLLEN
STIME	STINKY	STITCHERS	STOCKPILES	STOLLENS
STIMES	STINT	STITCHERY	STOCKPILING	STOLON
STIMIED	STINTED	STITCHES	STOCKPOT	STOLONATE
STIMIES	STINTER	STITCHING	STOCKPOTS	STOLONIC
STIMULANT	STINTERS	STITHIED	STOCKROOM	STOLONS
STIMULANTS	STINTING	STITHIES	STOCKROOMS	STOLPORT
STIMULATE	STINTS	STITHY	STOCKS	STOLPORTS
STIMULATED	STIPE	STITHYING	STOCKY	STOMA
STIMULATES	STIPED	STIVER	STOCKYARD	STOMACH
STIMULATING	STIPEL	STIVERS	STOCKYARDS	STOMACHED
STIMULI	STIPELS	STOA	STODGE	STOMACHER
STIMULUS	STIPEND	STOAE	STODGED	STOMACHERS
STIMY	STIPENDS	STOAI	STODGES	STOMACHIC
STIMYING	STIPES	STOAS	STODGIER	STOMACHICS
STING	STIPIFORM	STOAT	STODGIEST	STOMACHING
STINGAREE	STIPITATE	STOATS	STODGILY	STOMACHS
STINGAREES	STIPITES	STOB	STODGING	STOMACHY
STINGER	STIPPLE	STOBBED	STODGY	STOMAL
STINGERS	STIPPLED	STOBBING	STOGEY	STOMAS
STINGIER	STIPPLER	STOBS	STOGEYS	STOMATA
STINGIEST	STIPPLERS	STOCCADO	STOGIE	STOMATAL
STINGILY	STIPPLES	STOCCADOS	STOGIES	STOMATE
STINGING	STIPPLING	STOCCATA	STOGY	STOMATES
STINGLESS	STIPPLINGS	STOCCATAS	STOIC	STOMATIC
STINGO	STIPULAR	STOCK	STOICAL	STOMATOUS
STINGOS	STIPULATE	STOCKADE	STOICALLY	STOMODAEA
STINGRAY	STIPULATED	STOCKADED	STOICISM	STOMODAEUM
STINGRAYS	STIPULATES	STOCKADES	STOICISMS	STOMODAEUMS
STINGS	STIPULATING	STOCKADING	STOICS	STOMODEA
STINGY	STIPULE	STOCKAGE	STOKE	STOMODEAL
STINK	STIPULED	STOCKAGES	STOKED	STOMODEUM
STINKARD	STIPULES	STOCKCAR	STOKEHOLD	STOMODEUMS
STINKARDS	STIR	STOCKCARS	STOKEHOLDS	STOMP

STOMPED	STOOK	STOPS	STOTTING	STRAFERS
STOMPER	STOOKED	STOPT	STOTTS	STRAFES
STOMPERS	STOOKER	STOPWATCH	STOUND	STRAFING
STOMPING	STOOKERS	STOPWATCHES	STOUNDED	STRAGGLE
STOMPS	STOOKING	STOPWORD	STOUNDING	STRAGGLED
STONABLE	STOOKS	STOPWORDS	STOUNDS	STRAGGLER
STONE	STOOL	STORABLE	STOUP	STRAGGLERS
STONEBOAT	STOOLED	STORABLES	STOUPS	STRAGGLES
STONEBOATS	STOOLIE	STORAGE	STOUR	STRAGGLIER
STONECHAT	STOOLIES	STORAGES	STOURE	STRAGGLIEST
STONECHATS	STOOLING	STORAX	STOURES	STRAGGLING
STONECROP	STOOLS	STORAXES	STOURIE	STRAGGLY
STONECROPS	STOOP	STORE	STOURS	STRAIGHT
STONED	STOOPBALL	STORED	STOURY	STRAIGHTED
STONEFISH	STOOPBALLS	STORER	STOUT	STRAIGHTER
STONEFISHES	STOOPED	STOREROOM	STOUTEN	STRAIGHTEST
STONEFLIES	STOOPER	STOREROOMS	STOUTENED	STRAIGHTING
STONEFLY	STOOPERS	STORERS	STOUTENING	STRAIGHTS
STONER	STOOPING	STORES	STOUTENS	STRAIN
STONERS	STOOPS	STORESHIP	STOUTER	STRAINED
STONES	STOP	STORESHIPS	STOUTEST	STRAINER
STONEWALL	STOPBANK	STOREWIDE	STOUTISH	STRAINERS
STONEWALLED	STOPBANKS	STOREY	STOUTLY	STRAINING
STONEWALLING	STOPCOCK	STOREYED	STOUTNESS	STRAINS
STONEWALLS	STOPCOCKS	STOREYS	STOUTNESSES	STRAIT
STONEWARE	STOPE	STORIED	STOUTS	STRAITEN
STONEWARES	STOPED	STORIES	STOVE	STRAITENED
STONEWASH	STOPER	STORING	STOVEPIPE	STRAITENING
STONEWASHED	STOPERS	STORK	STOVEPIPES	STRAITENS
STONEWASHES	STOPES	STORKS	STOVER	STRAITER
STONEWASHING	STOPGAP	STORM	STOVERS	STRAITEST
STONEWORK	STOPGAPS	STORMED	STOVES	STRAITLY
STONEWORKS	STOPING	STORMIER	STOW	STRAITS
STONEWORT	STOPLIGHT	STORMIEST	STOWABLE	STRAKE
STONEWORTS	STOPLIGHTS	STORMILY	STOWAGE	STRAKED
STONEY	STOPOFF	STORMING	STOWAGES	STRAKES
STONIER	STOPOFFS	STORMS	STOWAWAY	STRAMASH
STONIEST	STOPOVER	STORMY	STOWAWAYS	STRAMASHES
STONILY	STOPOVERS	STORY	STOWED	STRAMONIES
STONINESS	STOPPABLE	STORYBOOK	STOWING	STRAMONY
STONINESSES	STOPPAGE	STORYBOOKS	STOWP	STRAND
STONING	STOPPAGES	STORYING	STOWPS	STRANDED
STONISH	STOPPED	STOSS	STOWS	STRANDER
STONISHED	STOPPER	STOT	STRADDLE	STRANDERS
STONISHES	STOPPERED	STOTIN	STRADDLED	STRANDING
STONISHING	STOPPERING	STOTINKA	STRADDLER	STRANDS
STONY	STOPPERS	STOTINKI	STRADDLERS	STRANG
STOOD	STOPPING	STOTINOV	STRADDLES	STRANGE
STOOGE	STOPPLE	STOTINS	STRADDLING	STRANGELY
STOOGED	STOPPLED	STOTS	STRAFE	STRANGER
STOOGES	STOPPLES	STOTT	STRAFED	STRANGERED
STOOGING	STOPPLING	STOTTED	STRAFER	STRANGERING

STRANGERS	STRAVAGE	STREEKERS	STRIAE	STRINGENT
STRANGES	STRAVAGED	STREEKING	STRIATA	STRINGER
STRANGEST	STRAVAGES	STREEKS	STRIATE	STRINGERS
STRANGLE	STRAVAGING	STREEL	STRIATED	STRINGIER
STRANGLED	STRAVAIG	STREELED	STRIATES	STRINGIEST
STRANGLER	STRAVAIGED	STREELING	STRIATING	STRINGILY
STRANGLERS	STRAVAIGING	STREELS	STRIATION	STRINGING
STRANGLES	STRAVAIGS	STREET	STRIATIONS	STRINGINGS
STRANGLING	STRAW	STREETCAR	STRIATUM	STRINGS
STRANGURIES	STRAWED	STREETCARS	STRICK	STRINGY
STRANGURY	STRAWHAT	STREETS	STRICKEN	STRIP
STRAP	STRAWIER	STRENGTH	STRICKLE	STRIPE
STRAPHANG	STRAWIEST	STRENGTHS	STRICKLED	STRIPED
STRAPHANGED	STRAWING	STRENUOUS	STRICKLES	STRIPER
STRAPHANGING	STRAWS	STREP	STRICKLING	STRIPERS
STRAPHANGS	STRAWWORM	STREPS	STRICKS	STRIPES
STRAPHUNG	STRAWWORMS	STRESS	STRICT	STRIPIER
STRAPLESS	STRAWY	STRESSED	STRICTER	STRIPIEST
STRAPLESSES	STRAY	STRESSES	STRICTEST	STRIPING
STRAPPADO	STRAYED	STRESSFUL	STRICTION	STRIPINGS
STRAPPADOES	STRAYER	STRESSING	STRICTIONS	STRIPLING
STRAPPADOS	STRAYERS	STRESSOR	STRICTLY	STRIPLINGS
STRAPPED	STRAYING	STRESSORS	STRICTURE	STRIPPED
STRAPPER	STRAYS	STRETCH	STRICTURES	STRIPPER
STRAPPERS	STREAK	STRETCHED	STRIDDEN	STRIPPERS
STRAPPIER	STREAKED	STRETCHER	STRIDE	STRIPPING
STRAPPIEST	STREAKER	STRETCHERED	STRIDENCE	STRIPS
STRAPPING	STREAKERS	STRETCHERING	STRIDENCES	STRIPT
STRAPPINGS	STREAKIER	STRETCHERS	STRIDENCIES	STRIPY
STRAPPY	STREAKIEST	STRETCHES	STRIDENCY	STRIVE
STRAPS	STREAKILY	STRETCHIER	STRIDENT	STRIVED
STRASS	STREAKING	STRETCHIEST	STRIDER	STRIVEN
STRASSES	STREAKINGS	STRETCHING	STRIDERS	STRIVER
STRATA	STREAKS	STRETCHY	STRIDES	STRIVERS
STRATAGEM	STREAKY	STRETTA	STRIDING	STRIVES
STRATAGEMS	STREAM	STRETTAS	STRIDOR	STRIVING
STRATAL	STREAMBED	STRETTE	STRIDORS	STROBE
STRATAS	STREAMBEDS	STRETTI	STRIFE	STROBES
STRATEGIC	STREAMED	STRETTO	STRIFEFUL	STROBIC
STRATEGIES	STREAMER	STRETTOS	STRIFES	STROBIL
STRATEGY	STREAMERS	STREUSEL	STRIGIL	STROBILA
STRATH	STREAMIER	STREUSELS	STRIGILS	STROBILAE
STRATHS	STREAMIEST	STREW	STRIGOSE	STROBILAR
STRATI	STREAMING	STREWED	STRIKE	STROBILE
STRATIFIED	STREAMINGS	STREWER	STRIKEOUT	STROBILES
STRATIFIES	STREAMLET	STREWERS	STRIKEOUTS	STROBILI
STRATIFY	STREAMLETS	STREWING	STRIKER	STROBILS
STRATIFYING	STREAMS	STREWMENT	STRIKERS	STROBILUS
STRATOUS	STREAMY	STREWMENTS	STRIKES	STRODE
STRATUM	STREEK	STREWN	STRIKING	STROKE
STRATUMS	STREEKED	STREWS	STRING	STROKED
STRATUS	STREEKER	STRIA	STRINGED	STROKER

STROKERS	STROUDINGS	STRUTTING	STUDS	STUNNING
STROKES	STROUDS	STRYCHNIC	STUDWORK	STUNS
STROKING	STROVE	STUB	STUDWORKS	STUNSAIL
STROLL	STROW	STUBBED	STUDY	STUNSAILS
STROLLED	STROWED	STUBBIER	STUDYING	STUNT
STROLLER	STROWING	STUBBIEST	STUFF	STUNTED
STROLLERS	STROWN	STUBBILY	STUFFED	STUNTING
STROLLING	STROWS	STUBBING	STUFFER	STUNTMAN
STROLLS	STROY	STUBBLE	STUFFERS	STUNTMEN
STROMA	STROYED	STUBBLED	STUFFIER	STUNTS
STROMAL	STROYER	STUBBLES	STUFFIEST	STUPA
STROMATA	STROYERS	STUBBLIER	STUFFILY	STUPAS
STROMATIC	STROYING	STUBBLIEST	STUFFING	STUPE
STRONG	STROYS	STUBBLY	STUFFINGS	STUPEFIED
STRONGBOX	STRUCK	STUBBORN	STUFFLESS	STUPEFIER
STRONGBOXES	STRUCKEN	STUBBORNER	STUFFS	STUPEFIERS
STRONGER	STRUCTURE	STUBBORNEST	STUFFY	STUPEFIES
STRONGEST	STRUCTURED	STUBBY	STUIVER	STUPEFY
STRONGISH	STRUCTURES	STUBS	STUIVERS	STUPEFYING
STRONGLY	STRUCTURING	STUCCO	STULL	STUPES
STRONGMAN	STRUDEL	STUCCOED	STULLS	STUPID
STRONGMEN	STRUDELS	STUCCOER	STULTIFIED	STUPIDER
STRONGYL	STRUGGLE	STUCCOERS	STULTIFIES	STUPIDEST
STRONGYLE	STRUGGLED	STUCCOES	STULTIFY	STUPIDITIES
STRONGYLES	STRUGGLER	STUCCOING	STULTIFYING	STUPIDITY
STRONGYLS	STRUGGLERS	STUCCOS	STUM	STUPIDLY
STRONTIA	STRUGGLES	STUCK	STUMBLE	STUPIDS
STRONTIAN	STRUGGLING	STUD	STUMBLED	STUPOR
STRONTIANS	STRUM	STUDBOOK	STUMBLER	STUPOROUS
STRONTIAS	STRUMA	STUDBOOKS	STUMBLERS	STUPORS
STRONTIC	STRUMAE	STUDDED	STUMBLES	STURDIED
STRONTIUM	STRUMAS	STUDDIE	STUMBLING	STURDIER
STRONTIUMS	STRUMATIC	STUDDIES	STUMMED	STURDIES
STROOK	STRUMMED	STUDDING	STUMMING	STURDIEST
STROP	STRUMMER	STUDDINGS	STUMP	STURDILY
STROPHE	STRUMMERS	STUDENT	STUMPAGE	STURDY
STROPHES	STRUMMING	STUDENTS	STUMPAGES	STURGEON
STROPHIC	STRUMOSE	STUDFISH	STUMPED	STURGEONS
STROPHOID	STRUMOUS	STUDFISHES	STUMPER	STURT
STROPHOIDS	STRUMPET	STUDHORSE	STUMPERS	STURTS
STROPHULI	STRUMPETS	STUDHORSES	STUMPIER	STUTTER
STROPHULUS	STRUMS	STUDIED	STUMPIEST	STUTTERED
STROPPED	STRUNG	STUDIEDLY	STUMPING	STUTTERER
STROPPER	STRUNT	STUDIER	STUMPS	STUTTERERS
STROPPERS	STRUNTED	STUDIERS	STUMPY	STUTTERING
STROPPIER	STRUNTING	STUDIES	STUMS	STUTTERS
STROPPIEST	STRUNTS	STUDIO	STUN	STY
STROPPING	STRUT	STUDIOS	STUNG	STYE
STROPPY	STRUTS	STUDIOUS	STUNK	STYED
STROPS	STRUTTED	STUDLIER	STUNNED	STYES
STROUD	STRUTTER	STUDLIEST	STUNNER	STYGIAN
STROUDING	STRUTTERS	STUDLY	STUNNERS	STYING

STYLAR	STYPSISES	SUBAPICAL	SUBCLASSED	SUBDUCE
STYLATE	STYPTIC	SUBARCTIC	SUBCLASSES	SUBDUCED
STYLE	STYPTICAL	SUBARCTICS	SUBCLASSING	SUBDUCES
STYLEBOOK	STYPTICS	SUBAREA	SUBCLAUSE	SUBDUCING
STYLEBOOKS	STYRAX	SUBAREAS	SUBCLAUSES	SUBDUCT
STYLED	STYRAXES	SUBARID	SUBCLERK	SUBDUCTED
STYLELESS	STYRENE	SUBAS	SUBCLERKS	SUBDUCTING
STYLER	STYRENES	SUBASTRAL	SUBCLIMAX	SUBDUCTS
STYLERS	STYROFOAM	SUBATOM	SUBCLIMAXES	SUBDUE
STYLES	STYROFOAMS	SUBATOMIC	SUBCODE	SUBDUED
STYLET	SUABILITIES	SUBATOMS	SUBCODES	SUBDUEDLY
STYLETS	SUABILITY	SUBAURAL	SUBCOLONIES	SUBDUER
STYLI	SUABLE	SUBAXIAL	SUBCOLONY	SUBDUERS
STYLIFORM	SUABLY	SUBBASE	SUBCONSUL	SUBDUES
STYLING	SUASION	SUBBASES	SUBCONSULS	SUBDUING
STYLINGS	SUASIONS	SUBBASIN	SUBCOOL	SUBDURAL
STYLISE	SUASIVE	SUBBASINS	SUBCOOLED	SUBDWARF
STYLISED	SUASIVELY	SUBBASS	SUBCOOLING	SUBDWARFS
STYLISER	SUASORY	SUBBASSES	SUBCOOLS	SUBECHO
STYLISERS	SUAVE	SUBBED	SUBCORTEX	SUBECHOES
STYLISES	SUAVELY	SUBBING	SUBCORTEXES	SUBEDIT
STYLISH	SUAVENESS	SUBBINGS	SUBCORTICES	SUBEDITED
STYLISHLY	SUAVENESSES	SUBBLOCK	SUBCOSTAL	SUBEDITING
STYLISING	SUAVER	SUBBLOCKS	SUBCOSTALS	SUBEDITOR
STYLIST	SUAVEST	SUBBRANCH	SUBCOUNTIES	SUBEDITORS
STYLISTIC	SUAVITIES	SUBBRANCHES	SUBCOUNTY	SUBEDITS
STYLISTS	SUAVITY	SUBBREED	SUBCULT	SUBENTRIES
STYLITE	SUB	SUBBREEDS	SUBCULTS	SUBENTRY
STYLITES	SUBA	SUBBUREAU	SUBCUTES	SUBEPOCH
STYLITIC	SUBABBOT	SUBBUREAUS	SUBCUTIS	SUBEPOCHS
STYLITISM	SUBABBOTS	SUBBUREAUX	SUBCUTISES	SUBER
STYLITISMS	SUBACID	SUBCASTE	SUBDEACON	SUBERECT
STYLIZE	SUBACIDLY	SUBCASTES	SUBDEACONS	SUBERIC
STYLIZED	SUBACRID	SUBCAUSE	SUBDEALER	SUBERIN
STYLIZER	SUBACUTE	SUBCAUSES	SUBDEALERS	SUBERINS
STYLIZERS	SUBADAR	SUBCAVITIES	SUBDEAN	SUBERISE
STYLIZES	SUBADARS	SUBCAVITY	SUBDEANS	SUBERISED
STYLIZING	SUBADULT	SUBCELL	SUBDEB	SUBERISES
STYLOBATE	SUBADULTS	SUBCELLAR	SUBDEBS	SUBERISING
STYLOBATES	SUBAERIAL	SUBCELLARS	SUBDEPOT	SUBERIZE
STYLOID	SUBAGENCIES	SUBCELLS	SUBDEPOTS	SUBERIZED
STYLOLITE	SUBAGENCY	SUBCENTER	SUBDEPUTIES	SUBERIZES
STYLOLITES	SUBAGENT	SUBCENTERS	SUBDEPUTY	SUBERIZING
STYLUS	SUBAGENTS	SUBCHASER	SUBDERMAL	SUBEROSE
STYLUSES	SUBAH	SUBCHASERS	SUBDIVIDE	SUBEROUS
STYMIE	SUBAHDAR	SUBCHIEF	SUBDIVIDED	SUBERS
STYMIED	SUBAHDARS	SUBCHIEFS	SUBDIVIDES	SUBFAMILIES
STYMIEING	SUBAHS	SUBCLAIM	SUBDIVIDING	SUBFAMILY
STYMIES	SUBALAR	SUBCLAIMS	SUBDUABLE	SUBFIELD
STYMY	SUBALPINE	SUBCLAN	SUBDUABLY	SUBFIELDS
STYMYING	SUBALTERN	SUBCLANS	SUBDUAL	SUBFILE
STYPSIS	SUBALTERNS	SUBCLASS	SUBDUALS	SUBFILES

SUBFIX	SUBJOINING	SUBMARKET	SUBOXIDES	SUBSCRIBING
SUBFIXES	SUBJOINS	SUBMARKETS	SUBPANEL	SUBSCRIPT
SUBFLOOR	SUBJUGATE	SUBMENU	SUBPANELS	SUBSCRIPTS
SUBFLOORS	SUBJUGATED	SUBMENUS	SUBPAR	SUBSEA
SUBFLUID	SUBJUGATES	SUBMERGE	SUBPART	SUBSECT
SUBFOSSIL	SUBJUGATING	SUBMERGED	SUBPARTS	SUBSECTOR
SUBFOSSILS	SUBLATE	SUBMERGES	SUBPENA	SUBSECTORS
SUBFRAME	SUBLATED	SUBMERGING	SUBPENAED	SUBSECTS
SUBFRAMES	SUBLATES	SUBMERSE	SUBPENAING	SUBSENSE
SUBFUSC	SUBLATING	SUBMERSED	SUBPENAS	SUBSENSES
SUBFUSCS	SUBLATION	SUBMERSES	SUBPERIOD	SUBSERE
SUBGENERA	SUBLATIONS	SUBMERSING	SUBPERIODS	SUBSERES
SUBGENRE	SUBLEASE	SUBMICRON	SUBPHASE	SUBSERIES
SUBGENRES	SUBLEASED	SUBMISS	SUBPHASES	SUBSERVE
SUBGENUS	SUBLEASES	SUBMIT	SUBPHYLA	SUBSERVED
SUBGENUSES	SUBLEASING	SUBMITS	SUBPHYLAR	SUBSERVES
SUBGOAL	SUBLESSEE	SUBMITTAL	SUBPHYLUM	SUBSERVING
SUBGOALS	SUBLESSEES	SUBMITTALS	SUBPLOT	SUBSET
SUBGRADE	SUBLESSOR	SUBMITTED	SUBPLOTS	SUBSETS
SUBGRADES	SUBLESSORS	SUBMITTER	SUBPOENA	SUBSHAFT
SUBGRAPH	SUBLET	SUBMITTERS	SUBPOENAED	SUBSHAFTS
SUBGRAPHS	SUBLETHAL	SUBMITTING	SUBPOENAING	SUBSHELL
SUBGROUP	SUBLETS	SUBMUCOSA	SUBPOENAS	SUBSHELLS
SUBGROUPED	SUBLETTING	SUBMUCOSAE	SUBPOLAR	SUBSHRUB
SUBGROUPING	SUBLEVEL	SUBMUCOSAS	SUBPOTENT	SUBSHRUBS
SUBGROUPS	SUBLEVELS	SUBNASAL	SUBPUBIC	SUBSIDE
SUBGUM	SUBLIMATE	SUBNET	SUBRACE	SUBSIDED
SUBGUMS	SUBLIMATED	SUBNETS	SUBRACES	SUBSIDER
SUBHEAD	SUBLIMATES	SUBNICHE	SUBREGION	SUBSIDERS
SUBHEADS	SUBLIMATING	SUBNICHES	SUBREGIONS	SUBSIDES
SUBHUMAN	SUBLIME	SUBNODAL	SUBRENT	SUBSIDIES
SUBHUMANS	SUBLIMED	SUBNORMAL	SUBRENTS	SUBSIDING
SUBHUMID	SUBLIMELY	SUBNORMALS	SUBRING	SUBSIDISE
SUBIDEA	SUBLIMER	SUBNUCLEI	SUBRINGS	SUBSIDISED
SUBIDEAS	SUBLIMERS	SUBNUCLEUS	SUBROGATE	SUBSIDISES
SUBINDEX	SUBLIMES	SUBNUCLEUSES	SUBROGATED	SUBSIDISING
SUBINDEXES	SUBLIMEST	SUBOCEAN	SUBROGATES	SUBSIDIZE
SUBINDICES	SUBLIMING	SUBOPTIC	SUBROGATING	SUBSIDIZED
SUBINFEUD	SUBLIMIT	SUBORAL	SUBRULE	SUBSIDIZES
SUBINFEUDED	SUBLIMITIES	SUBORDER	SUBRULES	SUBSIDIZING
SUBINFEUDING	SUBLIMITS	SUBORDERS	SUBS	SUBSIDY
SUBINFEUDS	SUBLIMITY	SUBORN	SUBSALE	SUBSIST
SUBITEM	SUBLINE	SUBORNED	SUBSALES	SUBSISTED
SUBITEMS	SUBLINES	SUBORNER	SUBSAMPLE	SUBSISTER
SUBITO	SUBLOT	SUBORNERS	SUBSAMPLED	SUBSISTERS
SUBJACENT	SUBLOTS	SUBORNING	SUBSAMPLES	SUBSISTING
SUBJECT	SUBLUNAR	SUBORNS	SUBSAMPLING	SUBSISTS
SUBJECTED	SUBLUNARY	SUBOSCINE	SUBSCALE	SUBSITE
SUBJECTING	SUBMARINE	SUBOSCINES	SUBSCALES	SUBSITES
SUBJECTS	SUBMARINED	SUBOVAL	SUBSCRIBE	SUBSKILL
SUBJOIN	SUBMARINES	SUBOVATE	SUBSCRIBED	SUBSKILLS
SUBJOINED	SUBMARINING	SUBOXIDE	SUBSCRIBES	SUBSOCIAL

SUBSOIL	SUBTILITIES	SUBURBED	SUCCINCTER	SUCKLED
SUBSOILED	SUBTILITY	SUBURBIA	SUCCINCTEST	SUCKLER
SUBSOILER	SUBTILIZE	SUBURBIAS	SUCCINIC	SUCKLERS
SUBSOILERS	SUBTILIZED	SUBURBS	SUCCINYL	SUCKLES
SUBSOILING	SUBTILIZES	SUBVASSAL	SUCCINYLS	SUCKLESS
SUBSOILS	SUBTILIZING	SUBVASSALS	SUCCOR	SUCKLING
SUBSOLAR	SUBTILTIES	SUBVENE	SUCCORED	SUCKLINGS
SUBSONIC	SUBTILTY	SUBVENED	SUCCORER	SUCKS
SUBSPACE	SUBTITLE	SUBVENES	SUCCORERS	SUCKY
SUBSPACES	SUBTITLED	SUBVENING	SUCCORIES	SUCRALOSE
SUBSTAGE	SUBTITLES	SUBVERT	SUCCORING	SUCRALOSES
SUBSTAGES	SUBTITLING	SUBVERTED	SUCCORS	SUCRASE
SUBSTANCE	SUBTLE	SUBVERTER	SUCCORY	SUCRASES
SUBSTANCES	SUBTLER	SUBVERTERS	SUCCOTASH	SUCRE
SUBSTATE	SUBTLEST	SUBVERTING	SUCCOTASHES	SUCRES
SUBSTATES	SUBTLETIES	SUBVERTS	SUCCOTH	SUCROSE
SUBSTRATA	SUBTLETY	SUBVICAR	SUCCOUR	SUCROSES
SUBSTRATE	SUBTLY	SUBVICARS	SUCCOURED	SUCTION
SUBSTRATES	SUBTONE	SUBVIRAL	SUCCOURING	SUCTIONAL
SUBSTRATUM	SUBTONES	SUBVIRUS	SUCCOURS	SUCTIONED
SUBSTRATUMS	SUBTONIC	SUBVIRUSES	SUCCUBA	SUCTIONING
SUBSUME	SUBTONICS	SUBVISUAL	SUCCUBAE	SUCTIONS
SUBSUMED	SUBTOPIA	SUBVOCAL	SUCCUBAS	SUCTORIAL
SUBSUMES	SUBTOPIAS	SUBWAY	SUCCUBI	SUCTORIAN
SUBSUMING	SUBTOPIC	SUBWAYED	SUCCUBUS	SUCTORIANS
SUBSYSTEM	SUBTOPICS	SUBWAYING	SUCCUBUSES	SUDARIA
SUBSYSTEMS	SUBTORRID	SUBWAYS	SUCCULENT	SUDARIES
SUBTASK	SUBTOTAL	SUBWOOFER	SUCCULENTS	SUDARIUM
SUBTASKS	SUBTOTALED	SUBWOOFERS	SUCCUMB	SUDARY
SUBTAXA	SUBTOTALING	SUBWORLD	SUCCUMBED	SUDATION
SUBTAXON	SUBTOTALLED	SUBWORLDS	SUCCUMBING	SUDATIONS
SUBTAXONS	SUBTOTALLING	SUBWRITER	SUCCUMBS	SUDATORIA
SUBTEEN	SUBTOTALS	SUBWRITERS	SUCCUSS	SUDATORIES
SUBTEENS	SUBTRACT	SUBZERO	SUCCUSSED	SUDATORIUM
SUBTENANT	SUBTRACTED	SUBZONE	SUCCUSSES	SUDATORIUMS
SUBTENANTS	SUBTRACTING	SUBZONES	SUCCUSSING	SUDATORY
SUBTEND	SUBTRACTS	SUCCAH	SUCH	SUDD
SUBTENDED	SUBTREND	SUCCAHS	SUCHLIKE	SUDDEN
SUBTENDING	SUBTRENDS	SUCCEDENT	SUCHNESS	SUDDENLY
SUBTENDS	SUBTRIBE	SUCCEED	SUCHNESSES	SUDDENS
SUBTEST	SUBTRIBES	SUCCEEDED	SUCK	SUDDS
SUBTESTS	SUBTROPIC	SUCCEEDER	SUCKED	SUDOR
SUBTEXT	SUBTUNIC	SUCCEEDERS	SUCKER	SUDORAL
SUBTEXTS	SUBTUNICS	SUCCEEDING	SUCKERED	SUDORIFIC
SUBTHEME	SUBTYPE	SUCCEEDS	SUCKERING	SUDORIFICS
SUBTHEMES	SUBTYPES	SUCCESS	SUCKERS	SUDORS
SUBTILE	SUBULATE	SUCCESSES	SUCKFISH	SUDS
SUBTILELY	SUBUNIT	SUCCESSOR	SUCKFISHES	SUDSED
SUBTILER	SUBUNITS	SUCCESSORS	SUCKIER	SUDSER
SUBTILEST	SUBURB	SUCCINATE	SUCKIEST	SUDSERS
SUBTILIN	SUBURBAN	SUCCINATES	SUCKING	SUDSES
SUBTILINS	SUBURBANS	SUCCINCT	SUCKLE	SUDSIER

SUDSIEST	SUFFUSES	SUITED	SULFONES	SULLIES
SUDSING	SUFFUSING	SUITER	SULFONIC	SULLY
SUDSLESS	SUFFUSION	SUITERS	SULFONIUM	SULLYING
SUDSY	SUFFUSIONS	SUITES	SULFONIUMS	SULPHA
SUE	SUFFUSIVE	SUITING	SULFONYL	SULPHAS
SUED	SUGAR	SUITINGS	SULFONYLS	SULPHATE
SUEDE	SUGARBUSH	SUITLIKE	SULFOXIDE	SULPHATED
SUEDED	SUGARBUSHES	SUITOR	SULFOXIDES	SULPHATES
SUEDES	SUGARCANE	SUITORS	SULFUR	SULPHATING
SUEDING	SUGARCANES	SUITS	SULFURATE	SULPHID
SUER	SUGARCOAT	SUK	SULFURATED	SULPHIDE
SUERS	SUGARCOATED	SUKIYAKI	SULFURATES	SULPHIDES
SUES	SUGARCOATING	SUKIYAKIS	SULFURATING	SULPHIDS
SUET	SUGARCOATS	SUKKAH	SULFURED	SULPHITE
SUETS	SUGARED	SUKKAHS	SULFURET	SULPHITES
SUETY	SUGARER	SUKKOT	SULFURETED	SULPHONE
SUFFARI	SUGARERS	SUKKOTH	SULFURETING	SULPHONES
SUFFARIS	SUGARIER	SUKS	SULFURETS	SULPHUR
SUFFER	SUGARIEST	SULCAL	SULFURETTED	SULPHURED
SUFFERED	SUGARING	SULCATE	SULFURETTING	SULPHURING
SUFFERER	SUGARLESS	SULCATED	SULFURIC	SULPHURS
SUFFERERS	SUGARLIKE	SULCATION	SULFURING	SULPHURY
SUFFERING	SUGARLOAF	SULCATIONS	SULFURIZE	SULTAN
SUFFERINGS	SUGARLOAVES	SULCI	SULFURIZED	SULTANA
SUFFERS	SUGARPLUM	SULCUS	SULFURIZES	SULTANAS
SUFFICE	SUGARPLUMS	SULDAN	SULFURIZING	SULTANATE
SUFFICED	SUGARS	SULDANS	SULFUROUS	SULTANATES
SUFFICER	SUGARY	SULFA	SULFURS	SULTANESS
SUFFICERS	SUGGEST	SULFAS	SULFURY	SULTANESSES
SUFFICES	SUGGESTED	SULFATASE	SULFURYL	SULTANIC
SUFFICING	SUGGESTER	SULFATASES	SULFURYLS	SULTANS
SUFFIX	SUGGESTERS	SULFATE	SULK	SULTRIER
SUFFIXAL	SUGGESTING	SULFATED	SULKED	SULTRIEST
SUFFIXED	SUGGESTS	SULFATES	SULKER	SULTRILY
SUFFIXES	SUGH	SULFATING	SULKERS	SULTRY
SUFFIXING	SUGHED	SULFATION	SULKIER	SULU
SUFFIXION	SUGHING	SULFATIONS	SULKIES	SULUS
SUFFIXIONS	SUGHS	SULFID	SULKIEST	SUM
SUFFLATE	SUICIDAL	SULFIDE	SULKILY	SUMAC
SUFFLATED	SUICIDE	SULFIDES	SULKINESS	SUMACH
SUFFLATES	SUICIDED	SULFIDS	SULKINESSES	SUMACHS
SUFFLATING	SUICIDES	SULFINYL	SULKING	SUMACS
SUFFOCATE	SUICIDING	SULFINYLS	SULKS	SUMLESS
SUFFOCATED	SUING	SULFITE	SULKY	SUMMA
SUFFOCATES	SUINT	SULFITES	SULLAGE	SUMMABLE
SUFFOCATING	SUINTS	SULFITIC	SULLAGES	SUMMAE
SUFFRAGAN	SUIT	SULFO	SULLEN	SUMMAND
SUFFRAGANS	SUITABLE	SULFONATE	SULLENER	SUMMANDS
SUFFRAGE	SUITABLY	SULFONATED	SULLENEST	SUMMARIES
SUFFRAGES	SUITCASE	SULFONATES	SULLENLY	SUMMARILY
SUFFUSE	SUITCASES	SULFONATING	SULLIABLE	SUMMARISE
SUFFUSED	SUITE	SULFONE	SULLIED	SUMMARISED

SUMMARISES	SUMOS	SUNDERS	SUNNINESSES	SUPERADD
SUMMARISING	SUMP	SUNDEW	SUNNING	SUPERADDED
SUMMARIST	SUMPS	SUNDEWS	SUNNS	SUPERADDING
SUMMARISTS	SUMPTER	SUNDIAL	SUNNY	SUPERADDS
SUMMARIZE	SUMPTERS	SUNDIALS	SUNPORCH	SUPERATOM
SUMMARIZED	SUMPTUARY	SUNDOG	SUNPORCHES	SUPERATOMS
SUMMARIZES	SUMPTUOUS	SUNDOGS	SUNPROOF	SUPERB
SUMMARIZING	SUMPWEED	SUNDOWN	SUNRAY	SUPERBAD
SUMMARY	SUMPWEEDS	SUNDOWNED	SUNRAYS	SUPERBANK
SUMMAS	SUMS	SUNDOWNER	SUNRISE	SUPERBANKS
SUMMATE	SUN	SUNDOWNERS	SUNRISES	SUPERBER
SUMMATED	SUNBACK	SUNDOWNING	SUNROOF	SUPERBEST
SUMMATES	SUNBAKED	SUNDOWNS	SUNROOFS	SUPERBLY
SUMMATING	SUNBATH	SUNDRESS	SUNROOM	SUPERBOMB
SUMMATION	SUNBATHE	SUNDRESSES	SUNROOMS	SUPERBOMBS
SUMMATIONS	SUNBATHED	SUNDRIES	SUNS	SUPERBUG
SUMMATIVE	SUNBATHER	SUNDRILY	SUNSCALD	SUPERBUGS
SUMMED	SUNBATHERS	SUNDROPS	SUNSCALDS	SUPERCAR
SUMMER	SUNBATHES	SUNDRY	SUNSCREEN	SUPERCARS
SUMMERED	SUNBATHING	SUNFAST	SUNSCREENS	SUPERCEDE
SUMMERIER	SUNBATHS	SUNFISH	SUNSEEKER	SUPERCEDED
SUMMERIEST	SUNBEAM	SUNFISHES	SUNSEEKERS	SUPERCEDES
SUMMERING	SUNBEAMS	SUNFLOWER	SUNSET	SUPERCEDING
SUMMERLY	SUNBEAMY	SUNFLOWERS	SUNSETS	SUPERCHIC
SUMMERS	SUNBELT	SUNG	SUNSHADE	SUPERCITIES
SUMMERSET	SUNBELTS	SUNGLASS	SUNSHADES	SUPERCITY
SUMMERSETS	SUNBIRD	SUNGLASSES	SUNSHINE	SUPERCLUB
SUMMERSETTED	SUNBIRDS	SUNGLOW	SUNSHINES	SUPERCLUBS
SUMMERSETTING	SUNBLOCK	SUNGLOWS	SUNSHINY	SUPERCOIL
SUMMERY	SUNBLOCKS	SUNK	SUNSPOT	SUPERCOILED
SUMMING	SUNBONNET	SUNKEN	SUNSPOTS	SUPERCOILING
SUMMIT	SUNBONNETS	SUNKET	SUNSTONE	SUPERCOILS
SUMMITAL	SUNBOW	SUNKETS	SUNSTONES	SUPERCOOL
SUMMITED	SUNBOWS	SUNLAMP	SUNSTROKE	SUPERCOOLED
SUMMITEER	SUNBURN	SUNLAMPS	SUNSTROKES	SUPERCOOLING
SUMMITEERS	SUNBURNED	SUNLAND	SUNSTRUCK	SUPERCOOLS
SUMMITING	SUNBURNING	SUNLANDS	SUNSUIT	SUPERCOP
SUMMITRIES	SUNBURNS	SUNLESS	SUNSUITS	SUPERCOPS
SUMMITRY	SUNBURNT	SUNLIGHT	SUNTAN	SUPERCUTE
SUMMITS	SUNBURST	SUNLIGHTS	SUNTANNED	SUPERED
SUMMON	SUNBURSTS	SUNLIKE	SUNTANNING	SUPEREGO
SUMMONED	SUNCHOKE	SUNLIT	SUNTANS	SUPEREGOS
SUMMONER	SUNCHOKES	SUNN	SUNUP	SUPERETTE
SUMMONERS	SUNDAE	SUNNA	SUNUPS	SUPERETTES
SUMMONING	SUNDAES	SUNNAH	SUNWARD	SUPERFAN
SUMMONS	SUNDECK	SUNNAHS	SUNWARDS	SUPERFANS
SUMMONSED	SUNDECKS	SUNNAS	SUNWISE	SUPERFARM
SUMMONSES	SUNDER	SUNNED	SUP	SUPERFARMS
SUMMONSING	SUNDERED	SUNNIER	SUPE	SUPERFAST
SUMO	SUNDERER	SUNNIEST	SUPER	SUPERFINE
SUMOIST	SUNDERERS	SUNNILY	SUPERABLE	SUPERFIRM
SUMOISTS	SUNDERING	SUNNINESS	SUPERABLY	SUPERFIRMS

SUPERFIX	SUPERNOVAS	SUPERVENING	SUPPOSE	SURE
SUPERFIXES	SUPERPIMP	SUPERVISE	SUPPOSED	SUREFIRE
SUPERFUND	SUPERPIMPS	SUPERVISED	SUPPOSER	SURELY
SUPERFUNDS	SUPERPORT	SUPERVISES	SUPPOSERS	SURENESS
SUPERGENE	SUPERPORTS	SUPERVISING	SUPPOSES	SURENESSES
SUPERGENES	SUPERPOSE	SUPERWAVE	SUPPOSING	SURER
SUPERGLUE	SUPERPOSED	SUPERWAVES	SUPPRESS	SUREST
SUPERGLUED	SUPERPOSES	SUPERWIDE	SUPPRESSED	SURETIES
SUPERGLUES	SUPERPOSING	SUPERWIDES	SUPPRESSES	SURETY
SUPERGLUING	SUPERPRO	SUPERWIFE	SUPPRESSING	SURF
SUPERGOOD	SUPERPROS	SUPERWIVES	SUPPURATE	SURFABLE
SUPERHEAT	SUPERRACE	SUPES	SUPPURATED	SURFACE
SUPERHEATED	SUPERRACES	SUPINATE	SUPPURATES	SURFACED
SUPERHEATING	SUPERREAL	SUPINATED	SUPPURATING	SURFACER
SUPERHEATS	SUPERRICH	SUPINATES	SUPRA	SURFACERS
SUPERHERO	SUPERROAD	SUPINATING	SUPREMACIES	SURFACES
SUPERHEROES	SUPERROADS	SUPINATOR	SUPREMACY	SURFACING
SUPERHIT	SUPERS	SUPINATORS	SUPREME	SURFACINGS
SUPERHITS	SUPERSAFE	SUPINE	SUPREMELY	SURFBIRD
SUPERHOT	SUPERSALE	SUPINELY	SUPREMER	SURFBIRDS
SUPERHYPE	SUPERSALES	SUPINES	SUPREMES	SURFBOARD
SUPERHYPED	SUPERSAUR	SUPPED	SUPREMEST	SURFBOARDED
SUPERHYPES	SUPERSAURS	SUPPER	SUPREMO	SURFBOARDING
SUPERHYPING	SUPERSEDE	SUPPERS	SUPREMOS	SURFBOARDS
SUPERING	SUPERSEDED	SUPPING	SUPS	SURFBOAT
SUPERIOR	SUPERSEDES	SUPPLANT	SUQ	SURFBOATS
SUPERIORS	SUPERSEDING	SUPPLANTED	SUQS	SURFED
SUPERJET	SUPERSELL	SUPPLANTING	SURA	SURFEIT
SUPERJETS	SUPERSELLING	SUPPLANTS	SURAH	SURFEITED
SUPERJOCK	SUPERSELLS	SUPPLE	SURAHS	SURFEITER
SUPERJOCKS	SUPERSEX	SUPPLED	SURAL	SURFEITERS
SUPERLAIN	SUPERSEXES	SUPPLELY	SURAS	SURFEITING
SUPERLAY	SUPERSHOW	SUPPLER	SURBASE	SURFEITS
SUPERLIE	SUPERSHOWS	SUPPLES	SURBASED	SURFER
SUPERLIES	SUPERSIZE	SUPPLEST	SURBASES	SURFERS
SUPERLONG	SUPERSIZED	SUPPLIANT	SURCEASE	SURFFISH
SUPERLYING	SUPERSIZES	SUPPLIANTS	SURCEASED	SURFFISHES
SUPERMALE	SUPERSIZING	SUPPLIED	SURCEASES	SURFICIAL
SUPERMALES	SUPERSOFT	SUPPLIER	SURCEASING	SURFIER
SUPERMAN	SUPERSOLD	SUPPLIERS	SURCHARGE	SURFIEST
SUPERMEN	SUPERSPIES	SUPPLIES	SURCHARGED	SURFING
SUPERMIND	SUPERSPY	SUPPLING	SURCHARGES	SURFINGS
SUPERMINDS	SUPERSTAR	SUPPLY	SURCHARGING	SURFLIKE
SUPERMINI	SUPERSTARS	SUPPLYING	SURCINGLE	SURFMAN
SUPERMINIS	SUPERSTUD	SUPPORT	SURCINGLED	SURFMEN
SUPERMOM	SUPERSTUDS	SUPPORTED	SURCINGLES	SURFPERCH
SUPERMOMS	SUPERTAX	SUPPORTER	SURCINGLING	SURFPERCHES
SUPERNAL	SUPERTAXES	SUPPORTERS	SURCOAT	SURFS
SUPERNATE	SUPERTHIN	SUPPORTING	SURCOATS	SURFSIDE
SUPERNATES	SUPERVENE	SUPPORTS	SURCULOSE	SURFY
SUPERNOVA	SUPERVENED	SUPPOSAL	SURD	SURGE
SUPERNOVAE	SUPERVENES	SUPPOSALS	SURDS	SURGED

SURGEON	SURPLUSSES	SURVEY	SUSTAINERS	SWAGER
SURGEONS	SURPLUSSING	SURVEYED	SUSTAINING	SWAGERS
SURGER	SURPRINT	SURVEYING	SUSTAINS	SWAGES
SURGERIES	SURPRINTED	SURVEYINGS	SUSURRANT	SWAGGED
SURGERS	SURPRINTING	SURVEYOR	SUSURRATE	SWAGGER
SURGERY	SURPRINTS	SURVEYORS	SUSURRATED	SWAGGERED
SURGES	SURPRISAL	SURVEYS	SUSURRATES	SWAGGERER
SURGICAL	SURPRISALS	SURVIVAL	SUSURRATING	SWAGGERERS
SURGING	SURPRISE	SURVIVALS	SUSURROUS	SWAGGERING
SURGY	SURPRISED	SURVIVE	SUSURRUS	SWAGGERS
SURICATE	SURPRISER	SURVIVED	SUSURRUSES	SWAGGIE
SURICATES	SURPRISERS	SURVIVER	SUTLER	SWAGGIES
SURIMI	SURPRISES	SURVIVERS	SUTLERS	SWAGGING
SURIMIS	SURPRISING	SURVIVES	SUTRA	SWAGING
SURLIER	SURPRIZE	SURVIVING	SUTRAS	SWAGMAN
SURLIEST	SURPRIZED	SURVIVOR	SUTTA	SWAGMEN
SURLILY	SURPRIZES	SURVIVORS	SUTTAS	SWAGS
SURLINESS	SURPRIZING	SUSHI	SUTTEE	SWAIL
SURLINESSES	SURRA	SUSHIS	SUTTEES	SWAILS
SURLY	SURRAS	SUSLIK	SUTURAL	SWAIN
SURMISE	SURREAL	SUSLIKS	SUTURALLY	SWAINISH
SURMISED	SURREALLY	SUSPECT	SUTURE	SWAINS
SURMISER	SURRENDER	SUSPECTED	SUTURED	SWALE
SURMISERS	SURRENDERED	SUSPECTING	SUTURES	SWALES
SURMISES	SURRENDERING	SUSPECTS	SUTURING	SWALLOW
SURMISING	SURRENDERS	SUSPEND	SUZERAIN	SWALLOWED
SURMOUNT	SURREY	SUSPENDED	SUZERAINS	SWALLOWER
SURMOUNTED	SURREYS	SUSPENDER	SVARAJ	SWALLOWERS
SURMOUNTING	SURROGACIES	SUSPENDERS	SVARAJES	SWALLOWING
SURMOUNTS	SURROGACY	SUSPENDING	SVEDBERG	SWALLOWS
SURMULLET	SURROGATE	SUSPENDS	SVEDBERGS	SWAM
SURMULLETS	SURROGATED	SUSPENSE	SVELTE	SWAMI
SURNAME	SURROGATES	SUSPENSER	SVELTELY	SWAMIES
SURNAMED	SURROGATING	SUSPENSERS	SVELTER	SWAMIS
SURNAMER	SURROUND	SUSPENSES	SVELTEST	SWAMP
SURNAMERS	SURROUNDED	SUSPENSOR	SWAB	SWAMPED
SURNAMES	SURROUNDING	SUSPENSORS	SWABBED	SWAMPER
SURNAMING	SURROUNDS	SUSPICION	SWABBER	SWAMPERS
SURPASS	SURROYAL	SUSPICIONED	SWABBERS	SWAMPIER
SURPASSED	SURROYALS	SUSPICIONING	SWABBIE	SWAMPIEST
SURPASSER	SURTAX	SUSPICIONS	SWABBIES	SWAMPING
SURPASSERS	SURTAXED	SUSPIRE	SWABBING	SWAMPISH
SURPASSES	SURTAXES	SUSPIRED	SWABBY	SWAMPLAND
SURPASSING	SURTAXING	SUSPIRES	SWABS	SWAMPLANDS
SURPLICE	SURTITLE	SUSPIRING	SWACKED	SWAMPS
SURPLICED	SURTITLES	SUSS	SWADDLE	SWAMPY
SURPLICES	SURTOUT	SUSSED	SWADDLED	SWAMY
SURPLUS	SURTOUTS	SUSSES	SWADDLES	SWAN
SURPLUSED	SURVEIL	SUSSING	SWADDLING	SWANG
SURPLUSES	SURVEILLED	SUSTAIN	SWAG	SWANHERD
SURPLUSING	SURVEILLING	SUSTAINED	SWAGE	SWANHERDS
SURPLUSSED	SURVEILS	SUSTAINER	SWAGED	SWANK

SWANKED	SWARTHS	SWEATBOXES	SWEETSHOP	SWILL
SWANKER	SWARTHY	SWEATED	SWEETSHOPS	SWILLED
SWANKEST	SWARTNESS	SWEATER	SWEETSOP	SWILLER
SWANKIER	SWARTNESSES	SWEATERS	SWEETSOPS	SWILLERS
SWANKIEST	SWARTY	SWEATIER	SWELL	SWILLING
SWANKILY	SWASH	SWEATIEST	SWELLED	SWILLS
SWANKING	SWASHED	SWEATILY	SWELLER	SWIM
SWANKS	SWASHER	SWEATING	SWELLEST	SWIMMABLE
SWANKY	SWASHERS	SWEATS	SWELLFISH	SWIMMER
SWANLIKE	SWASHES	SWEATSHOP	SWELLFISHES	SWIMMERET
SWANNED	SWASHING	SWEATSHOPS	SWELLHEAD	SWIMMERETS
SWANNERIES	SWASTICA	SWEATSUIT	SWELLHEADS	SWIMMERS
SWANNERY	SWASTICAS	SWEATSUITS	SWELLING	SWIMMIER
SWANNING	SWASTIKA	SWEATY	SWELLINGS	SWIMMIEST
SWANNY	SWASTIKAS	SWEDE	SWELLS	SWIMMILY
SWANPAN	SWAT	SWEDES	SWELTER	SWIMMING
SWANPANS	SWATCH	SWEENEY	SWELTERED	SWIMMINGS
SWANS	SWATCHES	SWEENEYS	SWELTERING	SWIMMY
SWANSDOWN	SWATH	SWEENIES	SWELTERS	SWIMS
SWANSDOWNS	SWATHE	SWEENY	SWELTRIER	SWIMSUIT
SWANSKIN	SWATHED	SWEEP	SWELTRIEST	SWIMSUITS
SWANSKINS	SWATHER	SWEEPBACK	SWELTRY	SWIMWEAR
SWAP	SWATHERS	SWEEPBACKS	SWEPT	SWINDLE
SWAPPED	SWATHES	SWEEPER	SWEPTBACK	SWINDLED
SWAPPER	SWATHING	SWEEPERS	SWEPTWING	SWINDLER
SWAPPERS	SWATHS	SWEEPIER	SWEPTWINGS	SWINDLERS
SWAPPING	SWATS	SWEEPIEST	SWERVE	SWINDLES
SWAPS	SWATTED	SWEEPING	SWERVED	SWINDLING
SWARAJ	SWATTER	SWEEPINGS	SWERVER	SWINE
SWARAJES	SWATTERS	SWEEPS	SWERVERS	SWINEHERD
SWARAJISM	SWATTING	SWEEPY	SWERVES	SWINEHERDS
SWARAJISMS	SWAY	SWEER	SWERVING	SWINEPOX
SWARAJIST	SWAYABLE	SWEET	SWEVEN	SWINEPOXES
SWARAJISTS	SWAYBACK	SWEETEN	SWEVENS	SWING
SWARD	SWAYBACKS	SWEETENED	SWIDDEN	SWINGBY
SWARDED	SWAYED	SWEETENER	SWIDDENS	SWINGBYS
SWARDING	SWAYER	SWEETENERS	SWIFT	SWINGE
SWARDS	SWAYERS	SWEETENING	SWIFTER	SWINGED
SWARE	SWAYFUL	SWEETENS	SWIFTERS	SWINGEING
SWARF	SWAYING	SWEETER	SWIFTEST	SWINGER
SWARFS	SWAYS	SWEETEST	SWIFTLET	SWINGERS
SWARM	SWEAR	SWEETIE	SWIFTLETS	SWINGES
SWARMED	SWEARER	SWEETIES	SWIFTLY	SWINGIER
SWARMER	SWEARERS	SWEETING	SWIFTNESS	SWINGIEST
SWARMERS	SWEARING	SWEETINGS	SWIFTNESSES	SWINGING
SWARMING	SWEARS	SWEETISH	SWIFTS	SWINGINGEST
SWARMS	SWEARWORD	SWEETLY	SWIG	SWINGINGS
SWART	SWEARWORDS	SWEETMEAT	SWIGGED	SWINGLE
SWARTH	SWEAT	SWEETMEATS	SWIGGER	SWINGLED
SWARTHIER	SWEATBAND	SWEETNESS	SWIGGERS	SWINGLES
SWARTHIEST	SWEATBANDS	SWEETNESSES	SWIGGING	SWINGLING
SWARTHILY	SWEATBOX	SWEETS	SWIGS	SWINGMAN

SWINGMEN	SWIVE	SWORDFISH	SYENITES	SYLVANITES
SWINGS	SWIVED	SWORDFISHES	SYENITIC	SYLVANS
SWINGY	SWIVEL	SWORDLIKE	SYKE	SYLVAS
SWINISH	SWIVELED	SWORDMAN	SYKES	SYLVATIC
SWINISHLY	SWIVELING	SWORDMEN	SYLI	SYLVIN
SWINK	SWIVELLED	SWORDPLAY	SYLIS	SYLVINE
SWINKED	SWIVELLING	SWORDPLAYS	SYLLABARIES	SYLVINES
SWINKING	SWIVELS	SWORDS	SYLLABARY	SYLVINITE
SWINKS	SWIVES	SWORDSMAN	SYLLABI	SYLVINITES
SWINNEY	SWIVET	SWORDSMEN	SYLLABIC	SYLVINS
SWINNEYS	SWIVETS	SWORDTAIL	SYLLABICS	SYLVITE
SWIPE	SWIVING	SWORDTAILS	SYLLABIFIED	SYLVITES
SWIPED	SWIZZLE	SWORE	SYLLABIFIES	SYMBION
SWIPES	SWIZZLED	SWORN	SYLLABIFY	SYMBIONS
SWIPING	SWIZZLER	SWOT	SYLLABIFYING	SYMBIONT
SWIPLE	SWIZZLERS	SWOTS	SYLLABISM	SYMBIONTS
SWIPLES	SWIZZLES	SWOTTED	SYLLABISMS	SYMBIOSES
SWIPPLE	SWIZZLING	SWOTTER	SYLLABIZE	SYMBIOSIS
SWIPPLES	SWOB	SWOTTERS	SYLLABIZED	SYMBIOT
SWIRL	SWOBBED	SWOTTING	SYLLABIZES	SYMBIOTE
SWIRLED	SWOBBER	SWOUN	SYLLABIZING	SYMBIOTES
SWIRLIER	SWOBBERS	SWOUND	SYLLABLE	SYMBIOTIC
SWIRLIEST	SWOBBING	SWOUNDED	SYLLABLED	SYMBIOTS
SWIRLING	SWOBS	SWOUNDING	SYLLABLES	SYMBOL
SWIRLS	SWOLLEN	SWOUNDS	SYLLABLING	SYMBOLED
SWIRLY	SWOON	SWOUNED	SYLLABUB	SYMBOLIC
SWISH	SWOONED	SWOUNING	SYLLABUBS	SYMBOLING
SWISHED	SWOONER	SWOUNS	SYLLABUS	SYMBOLISE
SWISHER	SWOONERS	SWUM	SYLLABUSES	SYMBOLISED
SWISHERS	SWOONIER	SWUNG	SYLLEPSES	SYMBOLISES
SWISHES	SWOONIEST	SYBARITE	SYLLEPSIS	SYMBOLISING
SWISHIER	SWOONING	SYBARITES	SYLLEPTIC	SYMBOLISM
SWISHIEST	SWOONS	SYBARITIC	SYLLOGISM	SYMBOLISMS
SWISHING	SWOONY	SYBO	SYLLOGISMS	SYMBOLIST
SWISHY	SWOOP	SYBOES	SYLLOGIST	SYMBOLISTS
SWISS	SWOOPED	SYCAMINE	SYLLOGISTS	SYMBOLIZE
SWISSES	SWOOPER	SYCAMINES	SYLLOGIZE	SYMBOLIZED
SWITCH	SWOOPERS	SYCAMORE	SYLLOGIZED	SYMBOLIZES
SWITCHED	SWOOPIER	SYCAMORES	SYLLOGIZES	SYMBOLIZING
SWITCHER	SWOOPIEST	SYCE	SYLLOGIZING	SYMBOLLED
SWITCHERS	SWOOPING	SYCEE	SYLPH	SYMBOLLING
SWITCHES	SWOOPS	SYCEES	SYLPHIC	SYMBOLOGIES
SWITCHING	SWOOPY	SYCES	SYLPHID	SYMBOLOGY
SWITCHMAN	SWOOSH	SYCOMORE	SYLPHIDS	SYMBOLS
SWITCHMEN	SWOOSHED	SYCOMORES	SYLPHISH	SYMMETRIC
SWITH	SWOOSHES	SYCONIA	SYLPHLIKE	SYMMETRIES
SWITHE	SWOOSHING	SYCONIUM	SYLPHS	SYMMETRY
SWITHER	SWOP	SYCOPHANT	SYLPHY	SYMPATHIES
SWITHERED	SWOPPED	SYCOPHANTS	SYLVA	SYMPATHIN
SWITHERING	SWOPPING	SYCOSES	SYLVAE	SYMPATHINS
SWITHERS	SWOPS	SYCOSIS	SYLVAN	SYMPATHY
SWITHLY	SWORD	SYENITE	SYLVANITE	SYMPATICO

SYMPATRIC	SYNCING	SYNESIS	SYNTHESES	SYSOP
SYMPATRIES	SYNCLINAL	SYNESISES	SYNTHESIS	SYSOPS
SYMPATRY	SYNCLINE	SYNFUEL	SYNTHETIC	SYSTALTIC
SYMPETALIES	SYNCLINES	SYNFUELS	SYNTHETICS	SYSTEM
SYMPETALY	SYNCOM	SYNGAMIC	SYNTHPOP	SYSTEMIC
SYMPHONIC	SYNCOMS	SYNGAMIES	SYNTHPOPS	SYSTEMICS
SYMPHONIES	SYNCOPAL	SYNGAMOUS	SYNTHS	SYSTEMIZE
SYMPHONY	SYNCOPATE	SYNGAMY	SYNTONIC	SYSTEMIZED
SYMPHYSES	SYNCOPATED	SYNGAS	SYNTONIES	SYSTEMIZES
SYMPHYSIS	SYNCOPATES	SYNGASES	SYNTONY	SYSTEMIZING
SYMPODIA	SYNCOPATING	SYNGASSES	SYNURA	SYSTEMS
SYMPODIAL	SYNCOPE	SYNGENEIC	SYNURAE	SYSTOLE
SYMPODIUM	SYNCOPES	SYNGENIC	SYPH	SYSTOLES
SYMPOSIA	SYNCOPIC	SYNIZESES	SYPHER	SYSTOLIC
SYMPOSIAC	SYNCRETIC	SYNIZESIS	SYPHERED	SYZYGAL
SYMPOSIACS	SYNCS	SYNKARYA	SYPHERING	SYZYGETIC
SYMPOSIUM	SYNCYTIA	SYNKARYON	SYPHERS	SYZYGIAL
SYMPOSIUMS	SYNCYTIAL	SYNKARYONS	SYPHILIS	SYZYGIES
SYMPTOM	SYNCYTIUM	SYNOD	SYPHILISES	SYZYGY
SYMPTOMS	SYNDACTYL	SYNODAL	SYPHILOID	
SYN	SYNDACTYLS	SYNODIC	SYPHON	
SYNAGOG	SYNDESES	SYNODICAL	SYPHONED	T
SYNAGOGAL	SYNDESIS	SYNODS	SYPHONING	
SYNAGOGS	SYNDESISES	SYNOICOUS	SYPHONS	
SYNAGOGUE	SYNDET	SYNONYM	SYPHS	TA
SYNAGOGUES	SYNDETIC	SYNONYME	SYREN	TAB
SYNALEPHA	SYNDETS	SYNONYMES	SYRENS	TABANID
SYNALEPHAS	SYNDIC	SYNONYMIC	SYRETTE	TABANIDS
SYNANON	SYNDICAL	SYNONYMIES	SYRETTES	TABARD
SYNANONS	SYNDICATE	SYNONYMS	SYRINGA	TABARDED
SYNAPSE	SYNDICATED	SYNONYMY	SYRINGAS	TABARDS
SYNAPSED	SYNDICATES	SYNOPSES	SYRINGE	TABARET
SYNAPSES	SYNDICATING	SYNOPSIS	SYRINGEAL	TABARETS
SYNAPSID	SYNDICS	SYNOPSIZE	SYRINGED	TABBED
SYNAPSIDS	SYNDROME	SYNOPSIZED	SYRINGES	TABBIED
SYNAPSING	SYNDROMES	SYNOPSIZES	SYRINGING	TABBIES
SYNAPSIS	SYNDROMIC	SYNOPSIZING	SYRINX	TABBING
SYNAPTIC	SYNE	SYNOPTIC	SYRINXES	TABBIS
SYNC	SYNECTIC	SYNOVIA	SYRPHIAN	TABBISES
SYNCARP	SYNERESES	SYNOVIAL	SYRPHIANS	TABBOULEH
SYNCARPIES	SYNERESIS	SYNOVIAS	SYRPHID	TABBOULEHS
SYNCARPS	SYNERGIA	SYNOVITIS	SYRPHIDS	TABBY
SYNCARPY	SYNERGIAS	SYNOVITISES	SYRUP	TABBYING
SYNCED	SYNERGIC	SYNTACTIC	SYRUPED	TABER
SYNCH	SYNERGID	SYNTAGM	SYRUPIER	TABERED
SYNCHED	SYNERGIDS	SYNTAGMA	SYRUPIEST	TABERING
SYNCHING	SYNERGIES	SYNTAGMAS	SYRUPING	TABERS
SYNCHRO	SYNERGISM	SYNTAGMATA	SYRUPLIKE	TABES
SYNCHRONIES	SYNERGISMS	SYNTAGMS	SYRUPS	TABETIC
SYNCHRONY	SYNERGIST	SYNTAX	SYRUPY	TABETICS
SYNCHROS	SYNERGISTS	SYNTAXES	SYSADMIN	TABID
SYNCHS	SYNERGY	SYNTH	SYSADMINS	TABLA

TABLAS	TABOUR	TACIT	TACTILE	TAGMEME
TABLATURE	TABOURED	TACITLY	TACTILELY	TAGMEMES
TABLATURES	TABOURER	TACITNESS	TACTILITIES	TAGMEMIC
TABLE	TABOURERS	TACITNESSES	TACTILITY	TAGMEMICS
TABLEAU	TABOURET	TACITURN	TACTION	TAGRAG
TABLEAUS	TABOURETS	TACK	TACTIONS	TAGRAGS
TABLEAUX	TABOURING	TACKBOARD	TACTLESS	TAGS
TABLED	TABOURS	TACKBOARDS	TACTS	TAHINI
TABLEFUL	TABS	TACKED	TACTUAL	TAHINIS
TABLEFULS	TABU	TACKER	TACTUALLY	TAHR
TABLELAND	TABUED	TACKERS	TAD	TAHRS
TABLELANDS	TABUING	TACKET	TADPOLE	TAHSIL
TABLELESS	TABULABLE	TACKETS	TADPOLES	TAHSILDAR
TABLEMATE	TABULAR	TACKEY	TADS	TAHSILDARS
TABLEMATES	TABULARLY	TACKIER	TAE	TAHSILS
TABLES	TABULATE	TACKIEST	TAEKWONDO	TAIGA
TABLESFUL	TABULATED	TACKIFIED	TAEKWONDOS	TAIGAS
TABLET	TABULATES	TACKIFIER	TAEL	TAIGLACH
TABLETED	TABULATING	TACKIFIERS	TAELS	TAIL
TABLETING	TABULATOR	TACKIFIES	TAENIA	TAILBACK
TABLETOP	TABULATORS	TACKIFY	TAENIAE	TAILBACKS
TABLETOPS	TABULI	TACKIFYING	TAENIAS	TAILBOARD
TABLETS	TABULIS	TACKILY	TAENIASES	TAILBOARDS
TABLETTED	TABUN	TACKINESS	TAENIASIS	TAILBONE
TABLETTING	TABUNS	TACKINESSES	TAFFAREL	TAILBONES
TABLEWARE	TABUS	TACKING	TAFFARELS	TAILCOAT
TABLEWARES	TACAMAHAC	TACKLE	TAFFEREL	TAILCOATS
TABLING	TACAMAHACS	TACKLED	TAFFERELS	TAILED
TABLOID	TACE	TACKLER	TAFFETA	TAILENDER
TABLOIDS	TACES	TACKLERS	TAFFETAS	TAILENDERS
TABOO	TACET	TACKLES	TAFFIA	TAILER
TABOOED	TACH	TACKLESS	TAFFIAS	TAILERS
TABOOING	TACHE	TACKLING	TAFFIES	TAILFAN
TABOOLEY	TACHES	TACKLINGS	TAFFRAIL	TAILFANS
TABOOLEYS	TACHINID	TACKS	TAFFRAILS	TAILFIN
TABOOS	TACHINIDS	TACKY	TAFFY	TAILFINS
TABOR	TACHISM	TACNODE	TAFIA	TAILGATE
TABORED	TACHISME	TACNODES	TAFIAS	TAILGATED
TABORER	TACHISMES	TACO	TAG	TAILGATER
TABORERS	TACHISMS	TACONITE	TAGALONG	TAILGATERS
TABORET	TACHIST	TACONITES	TAGALONGS	TAILGATES
TABORETS	TACHISTE	TACOS	TAGBOARD	TAILGATING
TABORIN	TACHISTES	TACRINE	TAGBOARDS	TAILING
TABORINE	TACHISTS	TACRINES	TAGGANT	TAILINGS
TABORINES	TACHS	TACT	TAGGANTS	TAILLAMP
TABORING	TACHYLITE	TACTFUL	TAGGED	TAILLAMPS
TABORINS	TACHYLITES	TACTFULLY	TAGGER	TAILLE
TABORS	TACHYLYTE	TACTIC	TAGGERS	TAILLES
TABOULEH	TACHYLYTES	TACTICAL	TAGGING	TAILLESS
TABOULEHS	TACHYON	TACTICIAN	TAGLIKE	TAILLEUR
TABOULI	TACHYONIC	TACTICIANS	TAGLINE	TAILLEURS
TABOULIS	TACHYONS	TACTICS	TAGLINES	TAILLIGHT

TAILLIGHTS	TAKEN	TALIPES	TALLITS	TAMARIN
TAILLIKE	TAKEOFF	TALIPOT	TALLNESS	TAMARIND
TAILOR	TAKEOFFS	TALIPOTS	TALLNESSES	TAMARINDS
TAILORED	TAKEOUT	TALISMAN	TALLOL	TAMARINS
TAILORING	TAKEOUTS	TALISMANS	TALLOLS	TAMARIS
TAILORINGS	TAKEOVER	TALK	TALLOW	TAMARISK
TAILORS	TAKEOVERS	TALKABLE	TALLOWED	TAMARISKS
TAILPIECE	TAKER	TALKATHON	TALLOWING	TAMASHA
TAILPIECES	TAKERS	TALKATHONS	TALLOWS	TAMASHAS
TAILPIPE	TAKES	TALKATIVE	TALLOWY	TAMBAC
TAILPIPES	TAKEUP	TALKBACK	TALLS	TAMBACS
TAILPLANE	TAKEUPS	TALKBACKS	TALLY	TAMBAK
TAILPLANES	TAKIN	TALKED	TALLYHO	TAMBAKS
TAILRACE	TAKING	TALKER	TALLYHOED	TAMBALA
TAILRACES	TAKINGLY	TALKERS	TALLYHOING	TAMBALAS
TAILS	TAKINGS	TALKIE	TALLYHOS	TAMBOUR
TAILSKID	TAKINS	TALKIER	TALLYING	TAMBOURA
TAILSKIDS	TALA	TALKIES	TALLYMAN	TAMBOURAS
TAILSLIDE	TALAPOIN	TALKIEST	TALLYMEN	TAMBOURED
TAILSLIDES	TALAPOINS	TALKINESS	TALMUDIC	TAMBOURER
TAILSPIN	TALAR	TALKINESSES	TALMUDISM	TAMBOURERS
TAILSPINNED	TALARIA	TALKING	TALMUDISMS	TAMBOURIN
TAILSPINNING	TALARS	TALKINGS	TALON	TAMBOURING
TAILSPINS	TALAS	TALKS	TALONED	TAMBOURINS
TAILSTOCK	TALC	TALKY	TALONS	TAMBOURS
TAILSTOCKS	TALCED	TALL	TALOOKA	TAMBUR
TAILWATER	TALCING	TALLAGE	TALOOKAS	TAMBURA
TAILWATERS	TALCKED	TALLAGED	TALUK	TAMBURAS
TAILWIND	TALCKING	TALLAGES	TALUKA	TAMBURS
TAILWINDS	TALCKY	TALLAGING	TALUKAS	TAME
TAIN	TALCOSE	TALLAISIM	TALUKS	TAMEABLE
TAINS	TALCOUS	TALLBOY	TALUS	TAMED
TAINT	TALCS	TALLBOYS	TALUSES	TAMEIN
TAINTED	TALCUM	TALLER	TAM	TAMEINS
TAINTING	TALCUMS	TALLEST	TAMABLE	TAMELESS
TAINTLESS	TALE	TALLGRASS	TAMAL	TAMELY
TAINTS	TALEGGIO	TALLGRASSES	TAMALE	TAMENESS
TAIPAN	TALEGGIOS	TALLIED	TAMALES	TAMENESSES
TAIPANS	TALENT	TALLIER	TAMALS	TAMER
TAJ	TALENTED	TALLIERS	TAMANDU	TAMERS
TAJES	TALENTS	TALLIES	TAMANDUA	TAMES
TAKA	TALER	TALLIS	TAMANDUAS	TAMEST
TAKABLE	TALERS	TALLISES	TAMANDUS	TAMING
TAKAHE	TALES	TALLISH	TAMARACK	TAMIS
TAKAHES	TALESMAN	TALLISIM	TAMARACKS	TAMISES
TAKAS	TALESMEN	TALLIT	TAMARAO	TAMMIE
TAKE	TALEYSIM	TALLITH	TAMARAOS	TAMMIES
TAKEABLE	TALI	TALLITHES	TAMARAU	TAMMY
TAKEAWAY	TALION	TALLITHIM	TAMARAUS	TAMOXIFEN
TAKEAWAYS	TALIONS	TALLITHS	TAMARI	TAMOXIFENS
TAKEDOWN	TALIPED	TALLITIM	TAMARILLO	TAMP
TAKEDOWNS	TALIPEDS	TALLITOTH	TAMARILLOS	TAMPALA

TAMPALAS	TANGLE	TANNEST	TAP	TAPPETS
TAMPAN	TANGLED	TANNIC	TAPA	TAPPING
TAMPANS	TANGLER	TANNIN	TAPADERA	TAPPINGS
TAMPED	TANGLERS	TANNING	TAPADERAS	TAPROOM
TAMPER	TANGLES	TANNINGS	TAPADERO	TAPROOMS
TAMPERED	TANGLIER	TANNINS	TAPADEROS	TAPROOT
TAMPERER	TANGLIEST	TANNISH	TAPALO	TAPROOTS
TAMPERERS	TANGLING	TANNOY	TAPALOS	TAPS
TAMPERING	TANGLY	TANNOYS	TAPAS	TAPSTER
TAMPERS	TANGO	TANREC	TAPE	TAPSTERS
TAMPING	TANGOED	TANRECS	TAPEABLE	TAQUERIA
TAMPION	TANGOING	TANS	TAPED	TAQUERIAS
TAMPIONS	TANGOLIKE	TANSIES	TAPELESS	TAR
TAMPON	TANGOS	TANSY	TAPELIKE	TARAMA
TAMPONED	TANGRAM	TANTALATE	TAPELINE	TARAMAS
TAMPONING	TANGRAMS	TANTALATES	TAPELINES	TARANTAS
TAMPONS	TANGS	TANTALIC	TAPENADE	TARANTASES
TAMPS	TANGY	TANTALISE	TAPENADES	TARANTISM
TAMS	TANIST	TANTALISED	TAPER	TARANTISMS
TAN	TANISTRIES	TANTALISES	TAPERED	TARANTIST
TANAGER	TANISTRY	TANTALISING	TAPERER	TARANTISTS
TANAGERS	TANISTS	TANTALITE	TAPERERS	TARANTULA
TANBARK	TANK	TANTALITES	TAPERING	TARANTULAE
TANBARKS	TANKA	TANTALIZE	TAPERS	TARANTULAS
TANDEM	TANKAGE	TANTALIZED	TAPES	TARBOOSH
TANDEMS	TANKAGES	TANTALIZES	TAPESTRIED	TARBOOSHES
TANDOOR	TANKARD	TANTALIZING	TAPESTRIES	TARBUSH
TANDOORI	TANKARDS	TANTALOUS	TAPESTRY	TARBUSHES
TANDOORIS	TANKAS	TANTALUM	TAPESTRYING	TARDIER
TANDOORS	TANKED	TANTALUMS	TAPETA	TARDIES
TANG	TANKER	TANTALUS	TAPETAL	TARDIEST
TANGA	TANKERS	TANTALUSES	TAPETUM	TARDILY
TANGED	TANKFUL	TANTARA	TAPEWORM	TARDINESS
TANGELO	TANKFULS	TANTARAS	TAPEWORMS	TARDINESSES
TANGELOS	TANKING	TANTIVIES	TAPHOLE	TARDIVE
TANGENCE	TANKINI	TANTIVY	TAPHOLES	TARDO
TANGENCES	TANKINIS	TANTO	TAPHONOMIES	TARDY
TANGENCIES	TANKLESS	TANTRA	TAPHONOMY	TARDYON
TANGENCY	TANKLIKE	TANTRAS	TAPHOUSE	TARDYONS
TANGENT	TANKS	TANTRIC	TAPHOUSES	TARE
TANGENTAL	TANKSHIP	TANTRISM	TAPING	TARED
TANGENTS	TANKSHIPS	TANTRISMS	TAPIOCA	TARES
TANGERINE	TANNABLE	TANTRUM	TAPIOCAS	TARGE
TANGERINES	TANNAGE	TANTRUMS	TAPIR	TARGES
TANGIBLE	TANNAGES	TANUKI	TAPIRS	TARGET
TANGIBLES	TANNATE	TANUKIS	TAPIS	TARGETED
TANGIBLY	TANNATES	TANYARD	TAPISES	TARGETING
TANGIER	TANNED	TANYARDS	TAPPABLE	TARGETS
TANGIEST	TANNER	TANZANITE	TAPPED	TARIFF
TANGINESS	TANNERIES	TANZANITES	TAPPER	TARIFFED
TANGINESSES	TANNERS	TAO	TAPPERS	TARIFFING
TANGING	TANNERY	TAOS	TAPPET	TARIFFS

TARING	TARRY	TASKBARS	TATTERING	TAUTLY
TARLATAN	TARRYING	TASKED	TATTERS	TAUTNESS
TARLATANS	TARS	TASKING	TATTIE	TAUTNESSES
TARLETAN	TARSAL	TASKS	TATTIER	TAUTOG
TARLETANS	TARSALS	TASKWORK	TATTIES	TAUTOGS
TARMAC	TARSI	TASKWORKS	TATTIEST	TAUTOLOGIES
TARMACKED	TARSIA	TASS	TATTILY	TAUTOLOGY
TARMACKING	TARSIAS	TASSE	TATTINESS	TAUTOMER
TARMACS	TARSIER	TASSEL	TATTINESSES	TAUTOMERS
TARN	TARSIERS	TASSELED	TATTING	TAUTONYM
TARNAL	TARSUS	TASSELING	TATTINGS	TAUTONYMIES
TARNALLY	TART	TASSELLED	TATTLE	TAUTONYMS
TARNATION	TARTAN	TASSELLING	TATTLED	TAUTONYMY
TARNATIONS	TARTANA	TASSELS	TATTLER	TAUTS
TARNISH	TARTANAS	TASSES	TATTLERS	TAV
TARNISHED	TARTANS	TASSET	TATTLES	TAVERN
TARNISHES	TARTAR	TASSETS	TATTLING	TAVERNA
TARNISHING	TARTARE	TASSIE	TATTOO	TAVERNAS
TARNS	TARTARIC	TASSIES	TATTOOED	TAVERNER
TARO	TARTAROUS	TASTABLE	TATTOOER	TAVERNERS
TAROC	TARTARS	TASTE	TATTOOERS	TAVERNS
TAROCS	TARTED	TASTEABLE	TATTOOING	TAVS
TAROK	TARTER	TASTED	TATTOOIST	TAW
TAROKS	TARTEST	TASTEFUL	TATTOOISTS	TAWDRIER
TAROS	TARTIER	TASTELESS	TATTOOS	TAWDRIES
TAROT	TARTIEST	TASTER	TATTY	TAWDRIEST
TAROTS	TARTILY	TASTERS	TAU	TAWDRILY
TARP	TARTINESS	TASTES	TAUGHT	TAWDRY
TARPAN	TARTINESSES	TASTIER	TAUNT	TAWED
TARPANS	TARTING	TASTIEST	TAUNTED	TAWER
TARPAPER	TARTISH	TASTILY	TAUNTER	TAWERS
TARPAPERS	TARTLET	TASTINESS	TAUNTERS	TAWIE
TARPAULIN	TARTLETS	TASTINESSES	TAUNTING	TAWING
TARPAULINS	TARTLY	TASTING	TAUNTS	TAWNEY
TARPON	TARTNESS	TASTY	TAUON	TAWNEYS
TARPONS	TARTNESSES	TAT	TAUONS	TAWNIER
TARPS	TARTRATE	TATAMI	TAUPE	TAWNIES
TARRAGON	TARTRATED	TATAMIS	TAUPES	TAWNIEST
TARRAGONS	TARTRATES	TATAR	TAURINE	TAWNILY
TARRE	TARTS	TATARS	TAURINES	TAWNINESS
TARRED	TARTUFE	TATE	TAUS	TAWNINESSES
TARRES	TARTUFES	TATER	TAUT	TAWNY
TARRIANCE	TARTUFFE	TATERS	TAUTAUG	TAWPIE
TARRIANCES	TARTUFFES	TATES	TAUTAUGS	TAWPIES
TARRIED	TARTY	TATOUAY	TAUTED	TAWS
TARRIER	TARWEED	TATOUAYS	TAUTEN	TAWSE
TARRIERS	TARWEEDS	TATS	TAUTENED	TAWSED
TARRIES	TARZAN	TATSOI	TAUTENING	TAWSES
TARRIEST	TARZANS	TATSOIS	TAUTENS	TAWSING
TARRINESS	TAS	TATTED	TAUTER	TAX
TARRINESSES	TASK	TATTER	TAUTEST	TAXA
TARRING	TASKBAR	TATTERED	TAUTING	TAXABLE

TAXABLES	TCHOTCHKE	TEAPOT	TEASERS	TECTONISM
TAXABLY	TCHOTCHKES	TEAPOTS	TEASES	TECTONISMS
TAXATION	TEA	TEAPOY	TEASHOP	TECTORIAL
TAXATIONS	TEABERRIES	TEAPOYS	TEASHOPS	TECTRICES
TAXED	TEABERRY	TEAR	TEASING	TECTRIX
TAXEME	TEABOARD	TEARABLE	TEASINGLY	TECTUM
TAXEMES	TEABOARDS	TEARAWAY	TEASPOON	TECTUMS
TAXEMIC	TEABOWL	TEARAWAYS	TEASPOONS	TED
TAXER	TEABOWLS	TEARDOWN	TEAT	TEDDED
TAXERS	TEABOX	TEARDOWNS	TEATASTER	TEDDER
TAXES	TEABOXES	TEARDROP	TEATASTERS	TEDDERED
TAXI	TEACAKE	TEARDROPS	TEATED	TEDDERING
TAXICAB	TEACAKES	TEARED	TEATIME	TEDDERS
TAXICABS	TEACART	TEARER	TEATIMES	TEDDIES
TAXIDERMIES	TEACARTS	TEARERS	TEATS	TEDDING
TAXIDERMY	TEACH	TEARFUL	TEAWARE	TEDDY
TAXIED	TEACHABLE	TEARFULLY	TEAWARES	TEDIOUS
TAXIES	TEACHABLY	TEARGAS	TEAZEL	TEDIOUSLY
TAXIING	TEACHER	TEARGASES	TEAZELED	TEDIUM
TAXIMAN	TEACHERLY	TEARGASSED	TEAZELING	TEDIUMS
TAXIMEN	TEACHERS	TEARGASSES	TEAZELLED	TEDS
TAXIMETER	TEACHES	TEARGASSING	TEAZELLING	TEE
TAXIMETERS	TEACHING	TEARIER	TEAZELS	TEED
TAXING	TEACHINGS	TEARIEST	TEAZLE	TEEING
TAXINGLY	TEACUP	TEARILY	TEAZLED	TEEL
TAXIS	TEACUPFUL	TEARINESS	TEAZLES	TEELS
TAXITE	TEACUPFULS	TEARINESSES	TEAZLING	TEEM
TAXITES	TEACUPS	TEARING	TECH	TEEMED
TAXITIC	TEACUPSFUL	TEARLESS	TECHED	TEEMER
TAXIWAY	TEAHOUSE	TEAROOM	TECHIE	TEEMERS
TAXIWAYS	TEAHOUSES	TEAROOMS	TECHIER	TEEMING
TAXLESS	TEAK	TEARS	TECHIES	TEEMINGLY
TAXMAN	TEAKETTLE	TEARSTAIN	TECHIEST	TEEMS
TAXMEN	TEAKETTLES	TEARSTAINS	TECHILY	TEEN
TAXOL	TEAKS	TEARSTRIP	TECHNIC	TEENAGE
TAXOLS	TEAKWOOD	TEARSTRIPS	TECHNICAL	TEENAGED
TAXON	TEAKWOODS	TEARY	TECHNICALS	TEENAGER
TAXONOMIC	TEAL	TEAS	TECHNICS	TEENAGERS
TAXONOMIES	TEALIKE	TEASABLE	TECHNIQUE	TEENER
TAXONOMY	TEALS	TEASE	TECHNIQUES	TEENERS
TAXONS	TEAM	TEASED	TECHNO	TEENFUL
TAXPAID	TEAMAKER	TEASEL	TECHNOPOP	TEENIER
TAXPAYER	TEAMAKERS	TEASELED	TECHNOPOPS	TEENIEST
TAXPAYERS	TEAMED	TEASELER	TECHNOS	TEENS
TAXPAYING	TEAMING	TEASELERS	TECHS	TEENSIER
TAXPAYINGS	TEAMMATE	TEASELING	TECHY	TEENSIEST
TAXUS	TEAMMATES	TEASELLED	TECTA	TEENSY
TAXWISE	TEAMS	TEASELLER	TECTAL	TEENTSIER
TAXYING	TEAMSTER	TEASELLERS	TECTITE	TEENTSIEST
TAZZA	TEAMSTERS	TEASELLING	TECTITES	TEENTSY
TAZZAS	TEAMWORK	TEASELS	TECTONIC	TEENY
TAZZE	TEAMWORKS	TEASER	TECTONICS	TEENYBOP

TEEPEE	TEINDS	TELEONOMIES	TELEVIEWS	TELNETING
TEEPEES	TEKKIE	TELEONOMY	TELEVISE	TELNETS
TEES	TEKKIES	TELEOST	TELEVISED	TELNETTED
TEETER	TEKTITE	TELEOSTS	TELEVISES	TELNETTING
TEETERED	TEKTITES	TELEPATH	TELEVISING	TELOI
TEETERING	TEKTITIC	TELEPATHIES	TELEVISOR	TELOME
TEETERS	TEL	TELEPATHS	TELEVISORS	TELOMERE
TEETH	TELA	TELEPATHY	TELEX	TELOMERES
TEETHE	TELAE	TELEPHONE	TELEXED	TELOMES
TEETHED	TELAMON	TELEPHONED	TELEXES	TELOMIC
TEETHER	TELAMONES	TELEPHONES	TELEXING	TELOPHASE
TEETHERS	TELCO	TELEPHONIES	TELFER	TELOPHASES
TEETHES	TELCOS	TELEPHONING	TELFERED	TELOS
TEETHING	TELE	TELEPHONY	TELFERING	TELOTAXES
TEETHINGS	TELECAST	TELEPHOTO	TELFERS	TELOTAXIS
TEETHLESS	TELECASTED	TELEPHOTOS	TELFORD	TELPHER
TEETOTAL	TELECASTING	TELEPLAY	TELFORDS	TELPHERED
TEETOTALED	TELECASTS	TELEPLAYS	TELIA	TELPHERING
TEETOTALING	TELECOM	TELEPORT	TELIAL	TELPHERS
TEETOTALLED	TELECOMS	TELEPORTED	TELIC	TELS
TEETOTALLING	TELEDU	TELEPORTING	TELICALLY	TELSON
TEETOTALS	TELEDUS	TELEPORTS	TELIUM	TELSONIC
TEETOTUM	TELEFAX	TELERAN	TELL	TELSONS
TEETOTUMS	TELEFAXES	TELERANS	TELLABLE	TEMBLOR
TEFF	TELEFILM	TELES	TELLER	TEMBLORES
TEFFS	TELEFILMS	TELESCOPE	TELLERS	TEMBLORS
TEFILLIN	TELEGA	TELESCOPED	TELLIES	TEMERITIES
TEFLON	TELEGAS	TELESCOPES	TELLING	TEMERITY
TEFLONS	TELEGENIC	TELESCOPIES	TELLINGLY	TEMP
TEG	TELEGONIC	TELESCOPING	TELLS	TEMPED
TEGG	TELEGONIES	TELESCOPY	TELLTALE	TEMPEH
TEGGS	TELEGONY	TELESES	TELLTALES	TEMPEHS
TEGMEN	TELEGRAM	TELESHOP	TELLURIAN	TEMPER
TEGMENTA	TELEGRAMMED	TELESHOPPED	TELLURIANS	TEMPERA
TEGMENTAL	TELEGRAMMING	TELESHOPPING	TELLURIC	TEMPERAS
TEGMENTUM	TELEGRAMS	TELESHOPS	TELLURIDE	TEMPERATE
TEGMINA	TELEGRAPH	TELESIS	TELLURIDES	TEMPERED
TEGMINAL	TELEGRAPHED	TELESTIC	TELLURION	TEMPERER
TEGS	TELEGRAPHING	TELESTICH	TELLURIONS	TEMPERERS
TEGUA	TELEGRAPHS	TELESTICHS	TELLURITE	TEMPERING
TEGUAS	TELEMAN	TELESTICS	TELLURITES	TEMPERS
TEGULAR	TELEMARK	TELETEXT	TELLURIUM	TEMPEST
TEGULARLY	TELEMARKS	TELETEXTS	TELLURIUMS	TEMPESTED
TEGULATED	TELEMEN	TELETHON	TELLURIZE	TEMPESTING
TEGUMEN	TELEMETER	TELETHONS	TELLURIZED	TEMPESTS
TEGUMENT	TELEMETERED	TELETYPE	TELLURIZES	TEMPI
TEGUMENTS	TELEMETERING	TELETYPED	TELLURIZING	TEMPING
TEGUMINA	TELEMETERS	TELETYPES	TELLUROUS	TEMPLAR
TEIGLACH	TELEMETRIES	TELETYPING	TELLY	TEMPLARS
TEIID	TELEMETRY	TELEVIEW	TELLYS	TEMPLATE
TEIIDS	TELEOLOGIES	TELEVIEWED	TELNET	TEMPLATES
TEIND	TELEOLOGY	TELEVIEWING	TELNETED	TEMPLE

TEMPLED	TENANTS	TENIAE	TENSIONED	TENUTI
TEMPLES	TENCH	TENIAS	TENSIONER	TENUTO
TEMPLET	TENCHES	TENIASES	TENSIONERS	TENUTOS
TEMPLETS	TEND	TENIASIS	TENSIONING	TEOCALLI
TEMPO	TENDANCE	TENNER	TENSIONS	TEOCALLIS
TEMPORAL	TENDANCES	TENNERS	TENSITIES	TEOPAN
TEMPORALS	TENDED	TENNIES	TENSITY	TEOPANS
TEMPORARIES	TENDENCE	TENNIS	TENSIVE	TEOSINTE
TEMPORARY	TENDENCES	TENNISES	TENSOR	TEOSINTES
TEMPORISE	TENDENCIES	TENNIST	TENSORIAL	TEPA
TEMPORISED	TENDENCY	TENNISTS	TENSORS	TEPAL
TEMPORISES	TENDER	TENON	TENT	TEPALS
TEMPORISING	TENDERED	TENONED	TENTACLE	TEPAS
TEMPORIZE	TENDERER	TENONER	TENTACLED	TEPEE
TEMPORIZED	TENDERERS	TENONERS	TENTACLES	TEPEES
TEMPORIZES	TENDEREST	TENONING	TENTAGE	TEPEFIED
TEMPORIZING	TENDERING	TENONS	TENTAGES	TEPEFIES
TEMPOS	TENDERIZE	TENOR	TENTATIVE	TEPEFY
TEMPS	TENDERIZED	TENORIST	TENTATIVES	TEPEFYING
TEMPT	TENDERIZES	TENORISTS	TENTED	TEPHRA
TEMPTABLE	TENDERIZING	TENORITE	TENTER	TEPHRAS
TEMPTED	TENDERLY	TENORITES	TENTERED	TEPHRITE
TEMPTER	TENDERS	TENORS	TENTERING	TEPHRITES
TEMPTERS	TENDING	TENOTOMIES	TENTERS	TEPHRITIC
TEMPTING	TENDINOUS	TENOTOMY	TENTH	TEPID
TEMPTRESS	TENDON	TENOUR	TENTHLY	TEPIDITIES
TEMPTRESSES	TENDONS	TENOURS	TENTHS	TEPIDITY
TEMPTS	TENDRESSE	TENPENCE	TENTIE	TEPIDLY
TEMPURA	TENDRESSES	TENPENCES	TENTIER	TEPIDNESS
TEMPURAS	TENDRIL	TENPENNY	TENTIEST	TEPIDNESSES
TEN	TENDRILED	TENPIN	TENTING	TEPOY
TENABLE	TENDRILS	TENPINS	TENTLESS	TEPOYS
TENABLY	TENDS	TENREC	TENTLIKE	TEQUILA
TENACE	TENDU	TENRECS	TENTMAKER	TEQUILAS
TENACES	TENDUS	TENS	TENTMAKERS	TERABYTE
TENACIOUS	TENEBRAE	TENSE	TENTORIA	TERABYTES
TENACITIES	TENEBRISM	TENSED	TENTORIAL	TERAFLOP
TENACITY	TENEBRISMS	TENSELY	TENTORIUM	TERAFLOPS
TENACULA	TENEBRIST	TENSENESS	TENTS	TERAHERTZ
TENACULUM	TENEBRISTS	TENSENESSES	TENTY	TERAHERTZES
TENACULUMS	TENEBROUS	TENSER	TENUES	TERAI
TENAIL	TENEMENT	TENSES	TENUIS	TERAIS
TENAILLE	TENEMENTS	TENSEST	TENUITIES	TERAOHM
TENAILLES	TENESMIC	TENSIBLE	TENUITY	TERAOHMS
TENAILS	TENESMUS	TENSIBLY	TENUOUS	TERAPH
TENANCIES	TENESMUSES	TENSILE	TENUOUSLY	TERAPHIM
TENANCY	TENET	TENSILELY	TENURABLE	TERATISM
TENANT	TENETS	TENSILITIES	TENURE	TERATISMS
TENANTED	TENFOLD	TENSILITY	TENURED	TERATOGEN
TENANTING	TENFOLDS	TENSING	TENURES	TERATOGENS
TENANTRIES	TENGE	TENSION	TENURIAL	TERATOID
TENANTRY	TENIA	TENSIONAL	TENURING	TERATOMA

TERATOMAS	TERMITE	TERREEN	TERTIARIES	TESTIFIES
TERATOMATA	TERMITES	TERREENS	TERTIARY	TESTIFY
TERAWATT	TERMITIC	TERRELLA	TERVALENT	TESTIFYING
TERAWATTS	TERMLESS	TERRELLAS	TERYLENE	TESTILY
TERBIA	TERMLY	TERRENE	TERYLENES	TESTIMONIES
TERBIAS	TERMOR	TERRENELY	TESLA	TESTIMONY
TERBIC	TERMORS	TERRENES	TESLAS	TESTINESS
TERBIUM	TERMS	TERRET	TESSELATE	TESTINESSES
TERBIUMS	TERMTIME	TERRETS	TESSELATED	TESTING
TERCE	TERMTIMES	TERRIBLE	TESSELATES	TESTIS
TERCEL	TERN	TERRIBLY	TESSELATING	TESTON
TERCELET	TERNARIES	TERRIER	TESSERA	TESTONS
TERCELETS	TERNARY	TERRIERS	TESSERACT	TESTOON
TERCELS	TERNATE	TERRIES	TESSERACTS	TESTOONS
TERCES	TERNATELY	TERRIFIC	TESSERAE	TESTS
TERCET	TERNE	TERRIFIED	TESSITURA	TESTUDINES
TERCETS	TERNES	TERRIFIER	TESSITURAS	TESTUDO
TEREBENE	TERNION	TERRIFIERS	TESSITURE	TESTUDOS
TEREBENES	TERNIONS	TERRIFIES	TEST	TESTY
TEREBIC	TERNS	TERRIFY	TESTA	TET
TEREBINTH	TERPENE	TERRIFYING	TESTABLE	TETANAL
TEREBINTHS	TERPENES	TERRINE	TESTACEAN	TETANIC
TEREDINES	TERPENIC	TERRINES	TESTACEANS	TETANICAL
TEREDO	TERPENOID	TERRIT	TESTACIES	TETANICS
TEREDOS	TERPENOIDS	TERRITORIES	TESTACY	TETANIES
TEREFAH	TERPINEOL	TERRITORY	TESTAE	TETANISE
TERETE	TERPINEOLS	TERRITS	TESTAMENT	TETANISED
TERGA	TERPINOL	TERROR	TESTAMENTS	TETANISES
TERGAL	TERPINOLS	TERRORISE	TESTATE	TETANISING
TERGITE	TERRA	TERRORISED	TESTATES	TETANIZE
TERGITES	TERRACE	TERRORISES	TESTATOR	TETANIZED
TERGUM	TERRACED	TERRORISING	TESTATORS	TETANIZES
TERIYAKI	TERRACES	TERRORISM	TESTATRICES	TETANIZING
TERIYAKIS	TERRACING	TERRORISMS	TESTATRIX	TETANOID
TERM	TERRAE	TERRORIST	TESTATRIXES	TETANUS
TERMAGANT	TERRAFORM	TERRORISTS	TESTCROSS	TETANUSES
TERMAGANTS	TERRAFORMED	TERRORIZE	TESTCROSSED	TETANY
TERMED	TERRAFORMING	TERRORIZED	TESTCROSSES	TETCHED
TERMER	TERRAFORMS	TERRORIZES	TESTCROSSING	TETCHIER
TERMERS	TERRAIN	TERRORIZING	TESTED	TETCHIEST
TERMINAL	TERRAINS	TERRORS	TESTEE	TETCHILY
TERMINALS	TERRANE	TERRY	TESTEES	TETCHY
TERMINATE	TERRANES	TERSE	TESTER	TETH
TERMINATED	TERRAPIN	TERSELY	TESTERS	TETHER
TERMINATES	TERRAPINS	TERSENESS	TESTES	TETHERED
TERMINATING	TERRARIA	TERSENESSES	TESTICLE	TETHERING
TERMING	TERRARIUM	TERSER	TESTICLES	TETHERS
TERMINI	TERRARIUMS	TERSEST	TESTIER	TETHS
TERMINUS	TERRAS	TERTIAL	TESTIEST	TETOTUM
TERMINUSES	TERRASES	TERTIALS	TESTIFIED	TETOTUMS
TERMITARIES	TERRAZZO	TERTIAN	TESTIFIER	TETRA
TERMITARY	TERRAZZOS	TERTIANS	TESTIFIERS	TETRACID

TETRACIDS	TEXTLESS	THANKFUL	THEFTS	THEONOMY
TETRAD	TEXTS	THANKFULLER	THEGN	THEOPHANIES
TETRADIC	TEXTUAL	THANKFULLEST	THEGNLY	THEOPHANY
TETRADS	TEXTUALLY	THANKING	THEGNS	THEORBO
TETRAGON	TEXTUARIES	THANKLESS	THEIN	THEORBOS
TETRAGONS	TEXTUARY	THANKS	THEINE	THEOREM
TETRAGRAM	TEXTURAL	THARM	THEINES	THEOREMS
TETRAGRAMS	TEXTURE	THARMS	THEINS	THEORETIC
TETRALOGIES	TEXTURED	THAT	THEIR	THEORIES
TETRALOGY	TEXTURES	THATAWAY	THEIRS	THEORISE
TETRAMER	TEXTURING	THATCH	THEIRSELF	THEORISED
TETRAMERS	TEXTURIZE	THATCHED	THEISM	THEORISES
TETRAPOD	TEXTURIZED	THATCHER	THEISMS	THEORISING
TETRAPODS	TEXTURIZES	THATCHERS	THEIST	THEORIST
TETRARCH	TEXTURIZING	THATCHES	THEISTIC	THEORISTS
TETRARCHIES	THACK	THATCHIER	THEISTS	THEORIZE
TETRARCHS	THACKED	THATCHIEST	THELITIS	THEORIZED
TETRARCHY	THACKING	THATCHING	THELITISES	THEORIZER
TETRAS	THACKS	THATCHINGS	THEM	THEORIZERS
TETRI	THAE	THATCHY	THEMATIC	THEORIZES
TETRIS	THAIRM	THAW	THEMATICS	THEORIZING
TETRODE	THAIRMS	THAWED	THEME	THEORY
TETRODES	THALAMI	THAWER	THEMED	THEOSOPHIES
TETROXID	THALAMIC	THAWERS	THEMES	THEOSOPHY
TETROXIDE	THALAMUS	THAWING	THEMING	THERAPIES
TETROXIDES	THALASSIC	THAWLESS	THEN	THERAPIST
TETROXIDS	THALER	THAWS	THENAGE	THERAPISTS
TETRYL	THALERS	THE	THENAGES	THERAPSID
TETRYLS	THALLI	THEARCHIES	THENAL	THERAPSIDS
TETS	THALLIC	THEARCHY	THENAR	THERAPY
TETTER	THALLIOUS	THEATER	THENARS	THERE
TETTERS	THALLIUM	THEATERS	THENCE	THEREAT
TEUCH	THALLIUMS	THEATRE	THENS	THEREBY
TEUGH	THALLOID	THEATRES	THEOCRACIES	THEREFOR
TEUGHLY	THALLOUS	THEATRIC	THEOCRACY	THEREFORE
TEUTONIZE	THALLUS	THEATRICS	THEOCRAT	THEREFROM
TEUTONIZED	THALLUSES	THEBAINE	THEOCRATS	THEREIN
TEUTONIZES	THALWEG	THEBAINES	THEODICIES	THEREINTO
TEUTONIZING	THALWEGS	THEBE	THEODICY	THEREMIN
TEVATRON	THAN	THEBES	THEOGONIC	THEREMINS
TEVATRONS	THANAGE	THECA	THEOGONIES	THEREOF
TEW	THANAGES	THECAE	THEOGONY	THEREON
TEWED	THANATOS	THECAL	THEOLOG	THERES
TEWING	THANATOSES	THECATE	THEOLOGIC	THERETO
TEWS	THANE	THECODONT	THEOLOGIES	THEREUNTO
TEXAS	THANES	THECODONTS	THEOLOGS	THEREUPON
TEXASES	THANESHIP	THEE	THEOLOGUE	THEREWITH
TEXT	THANESHIPS	THEELIN	THEOLOGUES	THERIAC
TEXTBOOK	THANK	THEELINS	THEOLOGY	THERIACA
TEXTBOOKS	THANKED	THEELOL	THEOMACHIES	THERIACAL
TEXTILE	THANKER	THEELOLS	THEOMACHY	THERIACAS
TEXTILES	THANKERS	THEFT	THEONOMIES	THERIACS

THERIAN	THEWS	THILL	THIOTEPAS	THOLOS
THERIANS	THEWY	THILLS	THIOUREA	THONG
THERM	THEY	THIMBLE	THIOUREAS	THONGED
THERMAE	THIAMIN	THIMBLES	THIR	THONGS
THERMAL	THIAMINE	THIN	THIRAM	THORACAL
THERMALLY	THIAMINES	THINCLAD	THIRAMS	THORACES
THERMALS	THIAMINS	THINCLADS	THIRD	THORACIC
THERME	THIAZIDE	THINDOWN	THIRDHAND	THORAX
THERMEL	THIAZIDES	THINDOWNS	THIRDLY	THORAXES
THERMELS	THIAZIN	THINE	THIRDS	THORIA
THERMES	THIAZINE	THING	THIRL	THORIAS
THERMIC	THIAZINES	THINGNESS	THIRLAGE	THORIC
THERMIDOR	THIAZINS	THINGNESSES	THIRLAGES	THORITE
THERMIDORS	THIAZOL	THINGS	THIRLED	THORITES
THERMION	THIAZOLE	THINGUMMIES	THIRLING	THORIUM
THERMIONS	THIAZOLES	THINGUMMY	THIRLS	THORIUMS
THERMIT	THIAZOLS	THINK	THIRST	THORN
THERMITE	THICK	THINKABLE	THIRSTED	THORNBACK
THERMITES	THICKEN	THINKABLY	THIRSTER	THORNBACKS
THERMITS	THICKENED	THINKER	THIRSTERS	THORNBUSH
THERMOS	THICKENER	THINKERS	THIRSTIER	THORNBUSHES
THERMOSES	THICKENERS	THINKING	THIRSTIEST	THORNED
THERMOSET	THICKENING	THINKINGS	THIRSTILY	THORNIER
THERMOSETS	THICKENS	THINKS	THIRSTING	THORNIEST
THERMS	THICKER	THINLY	THIRSTS	THORNILY
THEROID	THICKEST	THINNED	THIRSTY	THORNING
THEROPOD	THICKET	THINNER	THIRTEEN	THORNLESS
THEROPODS	THICKETED	THINNERS	THIRTEENS	THORNLIKE
THESAURAL	THICKETS	THINNESS	THIRTIES	THORNS
THESAURI	THICKETY	THINNESSES	THIRTIETH	THORNY
THESAURUS	THICKHEAD	THINNEST	THIRTIETHS	THORO
THESAURUSES	THICKHEADS	THINNING	THIRTY	THORON
THESE	THICKISH	THINNISH	THIRTYISH	THORONS
THESES	THICKLY	THINS	THIS	THOROUGH
THESIS	THICKNESS	THIO	THISAWAY	THOROUGHER
THESP	THICKNESSES	THIOL	THISTLE	THOROUGHEST
THESPIAN	THICKS	THIOLIC	THISTLES	THORP
THESPIANS	THICKSET	THIOLS	THISTLIER	THORPE
THESPS	THICKSETS	THIONATE	THISTLIEST	THORPES
THETA	THIEF	THIONATES	THISTLY	THORPS
THETAS	THIEVE	THIONIC	THITHER	THOSE
THETIC	THIEVED	THIONIN	THITHERTO	THOU
THETICAL	THIEVERIES	THIONINE	THO	THOUED
THEURGIC	THIEVERY	THIONINES	THOLE	THOUGH
THEURGIES	THIEVES	THIONINS	THOLED	THOUGHT
THEURGIST	THIEVING	THIONYL	THOLEIITE	THOUGHTS
THEURGISTS	THIEVISH	THIONYLS	THOLEIITES	THOUING
THEURGY	THIGH	THIOPHEN	THOLEPIN	THOUS
THEW	THIGHBONE	THIOPHENE	THOLEPINS	THOUSAND
THEWIER	THIGHBONES	THIOPHENES	THOLES	THOUSANDS
THEWIEST	THIGHED	THIOPHENS	THOLING	THOWLESS
THEWLESS	THIGHS	THIOTEPA	THOLOI	THRALDOM

THRALDOMS	THREEPING	THROB	THRUMMIER	THUMBTACKING
THRALL	THREEPS	THROBBED	THRUMMIEST	THUMBTACKS
THRALLDOM	THREES	THROBBER	THRUMMING	THUMP
THRALLDOMS	THREESOME	THROBBERS	THRUMMY	THUMPED
THRALLED	THREESOMES	THROBBING	THRUMS	THUMPER
THRALLING	THRENODE	THROBS	THRUPUT	THUMPERS
THRALLS	THRENODES	THROE	THRUPUTS	THUMPING
THRASH	THRENODIC	THROES	THRUSH	THUMPS
THRASHED	THRENODIES	THROMBI	THRUSHES	THUNDER
THRASHER	THRENODY	THROMBIN	THRUST	THUNDERED
THRASHERS	THREONINE	THROMBINS	THRUSTED	THUNDERER
THRASHES	THREONINES	THROMBOSE	THRUSTER	THUNDERERS
THRASHING	THRESH	THROMBOSED	THRUSTERS	THUNDERING
THRASHINGS	THRESHED	THROMBOSES	THRUSTFUL	THUNDERS
THRAVE	THRESHER	THROMBOSING	THRUSTING	THUNDERY
THRAVES	THRESHERS	THROMBUS	THRUSTOR	THUNK
THRAW	THRESHES	THRONE	THRUSTORS	THUNKED
THRAWART	THRESHING	THRONED	THRUSTS	THUNKING
THRAWED	THRESHOLD	THRONES	THRUWAY	THUNKS
THRAWING	THRESHOLDS	THRONG	THRUWAYS	THURIBLE
THRAWN	THREW	THRONGED	THUD	THURIBLES
THRAWNLY	THRICE	THRONGING	THUDDED	THURIFER
THRAWS	THRIFT	THRONGS	THUDDING	THURIFERS
THREAD	THRIFTIER	THRONING	THUDS	THURL
THREADED	THRIFTIEST	THROSTLE	THUG	THURLS
THREADER	THRIFTILY	THROSTLES	THUGGEE	THUS
THREADERS	THRIFTS	THROTTLE	THUGGEES	THUSLY
THREADFIN	THRIFTY	THROTTLED	THUGGERIES	THUYA
THREADFINS	THRILL	THROTTLER	THUGGERY	THUYAS
THREADIER	THRILLED	THROTTLERS	THUGGISH	THWACK
THREADIEST	THRILLER	THROTTLES	THUGS	THWACKED
THREADING	THRILLERS	THROTTLING	THUJA	THWACKER
THREADS	THRILLING	THROUGH	THUJAS	THWACKERS
THREADY	THRILLS	THROUGHLY	THULIA	THWACKING
THREAP	THRIP	THROVE	THULIAS	THWACKS
THREAPED	THRIPS	THROW	THULIUM	THWART
THREAPER	THRIVE	THROWAWAY	THULIUMS	THWARTED
THREAPERS	THRIVED	THROWAWAYS	THUMB	THWARTER
THREAPING	THRIVEN	THROWBACK	THUMBED	THWARTERS
THREAPS	THRIVER	THROWBACKS	THUMBHOLE	THWARTING
THREAT	THRIVERS	THROWER	THUMBHOLES	THWARTLY
THREATED	THRIVES	THROWERS	THUMBING	THWARTS
THREATEN	THRIVING	THROWING	THUMBKIN	THY
THREATENED	THRO	THROWN	THUMBKINS	THYLACINE
THREATENING	THROAT	THROWS	THUMBLESS	THYLACINES
THREATENS	THROATED	THROWSTER	THUMBNAIL	THYLAKOID
THREATING	THROATIER	THROWSTERS	THUMBNAILS	THYLAKOIDS
THREATS	THROATIEST	THRU	THUMBNUT	THYME
THREE	THROATILY	THRUM	THUMBNUTS	THYMES
THREEFOLD	THROATING	THRUMMED	THUMBS	THYMEY
THREEP	THROATS	THRUMMER	THUMBTACK	THYMI
THREEPED	THROATY	THRUMMERS	THUMBTACKED	THYMIC

THYMIDINE	TICKETING	TIDEWAYS	TIGERLIKE	TILING
THYMIDINES	TICKETS	TIDIED	TIGERS	TILINGS
THYMIER	TICKING	TIDIER	TIGHT	TILL
THYMIEST	TICKINGS	TIDIERS	TIGHTEN	TILLABLE
THYMINE	TICKLE	TIDIES	TIGHTENED	TILLAGE
THYMINES	TICKLED	TIDIEST	TIGHTENER	TILLAGES
THYMOCYTE	TICKLER	TIDILY	TIGHTENERS	TILLED
THYMOCYTES	TICKLERS	TIDINESS	TIGHTENING	TILLER
THYMOL	TICKLES	TIDINESSES	TIGHTENS	TILLERED
THYMOLS	TICKLING	TIDING	TIGHTER	TILLERING
THYMOSIN	TICKLISH	TIDINGS	TIGHTEST	TILLERMAN
THYMOSINS	TICKS	TIDY	TIGHTKNIT	TILLERMEN
THYMUS	TICKSEED	TIDYING	TIGHTLY	TILLERS
THYMUSES	TICKSEEDS	TIDYTIPS	TIGHTNESS	TILLING
THYMY	TICKTACK	TIE	TIGHTNESSES	TILLITE
THYRATRON	TICKTACKED	TIEBACK	TIGHTROPE	TILLITES
THYRATRONS	TICKTACKING	TIEBACKS	TIGHTROPES	TILLS
THYREOID	TICKTACKS	TIEBREAK	TIGHTS	TILS
THYRISTOR	TICKTOCK	TIEBREAKS	TIGHTWAD	TILT
THYRISTORS	TICKTOCKED	TIECLASP	TIGHTWADS	TILTABLE
THYROID	TICKTOCKING	TIECLASPS	TIGHTWIRE	TILTED
THYROIDAL	TICKTOCKS	TIED	TIGHTWIRES	TILTER
THYROIDS	TICS	TIEING	TIGLON	TILTERS
THYROXIN	TICTAC	TIELESS	TIGLONS	TILTH
THYROXINE	TICTACKED	TIEPIN	TIGON	TILTHS
THYROXINES	TICTACKING	TIEPINS	TIGONS	TILTING
THYROXINS	TICTACS	TIER	TIGRESS	TILTMETER
THYRSE	TICTOC	TIERCE	TIGRESSES	TILTMETERS
THYRSES	TICTOCKED	TIERCED	TIGRISH	TILTROTOR
THYRSI	TICTOCKING	TIERCEL	TIKE	TILTROTORS
THYRSOID	TICTOCS	TIERCELS	TIKES	TILTS
THYRSUS	TIDAL	TIERCERON	TIKI	TILTYARD
THYSELF	TIDALLY	TIERCERONS	TIKIS	TILTYARDS
TI	TIDBIT	TIERCES	TIKKA	TIMARAU
TIARA	TIDBITS	TIERED	TIKKAS	TIMARAUS
TIARAED	TIDDLER	TIERING	TIL	TIMBAL
TIARAS	TIDDLERS	TIERS	TILAK	TIMBALE
TIBIA	TIDDLY	TIES	TILAKS	TIMBALES
TIBIAE	TIDE	TIFF	TILAPIA	TIMBALS
TIBIAL	TIDED	TIFFANIES	TILAPIAS	TIMBER
TIBIAS	TIDELAND	TIFFANY	TILBURIES	TIMBERED
TIC	TIDELANDS	TIFFED	TILBURY	TIMBERING
TICAL	TIDELESS	TIFFIN	TILDE	TIMBERINGS
TICALS	TIDELIKE	TIFFINED	TILDES	TIMBERMAN
TICCED	TIDEMARK	TIFFING	TILE	TIMBERMEN
TICCING	TIDEMARKS	TIFFINING	TILED	TIMBERS
TICK	TIDERIP	TIFFINS	TILEFISH	TIMBERY
TICKED	TIDERIPS	TIFFS	TILEFISHES	TIMBRAL
TICKER	TIDES	TIGER	TILELIKE	TIMBRE
TICKERS	TIDEWATER	TIGEREYE	TILER	TIMBREL
TICKET	TIDEWATERS	TIGEREYES	TILERS	TIMBRELS
TICKETED	TIDEWAY	TIGERISH	TILES	TIMBRES

TIME	TIN	TININESSES	TINTED	TIPSTAFF
TIMECARD	TINAMOU	TINING	TINTER	TIPSTAFFS
TIMECARDS	TINAMOUS	TINKER	TINTERS	TIPSTAVES
TIMED	TINCAL	TINKERED	TINTING	TIPSTER
TIMELESS	TINCALS	TINKERER	TINTINGS	TIPSTERS
TIMELIER	TINCT	TINKERERS	TINTLESS	TIPSTOCK
TIMELIEST	TINCTED	TINKERING	TINTS	TIPSTOCKS
TIMELINE	TINCTING	TINKERS	TINTYPE	TIPSY
TIMELINES	TINCTS	TINKERTOY	TINTYPES	TIPTOE
TIMELY	TINCTURE	TINKERTOYS	TINWARE	TIPTOED
TIMEOUS	TINCTURED	TINKLE	TINWARES	TIPTOEING
TIMEOUSLY	TINCTURES	TINKLED	TINWORK	TIPTOES
TIMEOUT	TINCTURING	TINKLER	TINWORKS	TIPTOP
TIMEOUTS	TINDER	TINKLERS	TINY	TIPTOPS
TIMEPIECE	TINDERBOX	TINKLES	TIP	TIRADE
TIMEPIECES	TINDERBOXES	TINKLIER	TIPCART	TIRADES
TIMER	TINDERS	TINKLIEST	TIPCARTS	TIRAMISU
TIMERS	TINDERY	TINKLING	TIPCAT	TIRAMISUS
TIMES	TINE	TINKLINGS	TIPCATS	TIRE
TIMESAVER	TINEA	TINKLY	TIPI	TIRED
TIMESAVERS	TINEAL	TINLIKE	TIPIS	TIREDER
TIMESCALE	TINEAS	TINMAN	TIPLESS	TIREDEST
TIMESCALES	TINED	TINMEN	TIPOFF	TIREDLY
TIMETABLE	TINEID	TINNED	TIPOFFS	TIREDNESS
TIMETABLES	TINEIDS	TINNER	TIPPABLE	TIREDNESSES
TIMEWORK	TINES	TINNERS	TIPPED	TIRELESS
TIMEWORKS	TINFOIL	TINNIER	TIPPER	TIRES
TIMEWORN	TINFOILS	TINNIEST	TIPPERS	TIRESOME
TIMID	TINFUL	TINNILY	TIPPET	TIREWOMAN
TIMIDER	TINFULS	TINNINESS	TIPPETS	TIREWOMEN
TIMIDEST	TING	TINNINESSES	TIPPIER	TIRING
TIMIDITIES	TINGE	TINNING	TIPPIEST	TIRL
TIMIDITY	TINGED	TINNITUS	TIPPING	TIRLED
TIMIDLY	TINGEING	TINNITUSES	TIPPLE	TIRLING
TIMIDNESS	TINGES	TINNY	TIPPLED	TIRLS
TIMIDNESSES	TINGING	TINPLATE	TIPPLER	TIRO
TIMING	TINGLE	TINPLATES	TIPPLERS	TIROS
TIMINGS	TINGLED	TINPOT	TIPPLES	TIRRIVEE
TIMOCRACIES	TINGLER	TINS	TIPPLING	TIRRIVEES
TIMOCRACY	TINGLERS	TINSEL	TIPPY	TIS
TIMOLOL	TINGLES	TINSELED	TIPPYTOE	TISANE
TIMOLOLS	TINGLIER	TINSELING	TIPPYTOED	TISANES
TIMOROUS	TINGLIEST	TINSELLED	TIPPYTOEING	TISSUAL
TIMOTHIES	TINGLING	TINSELLING	TIPPYTOES	TISSUE
TIMOTHY	TINGLY	TINSELLY	TIPS	TISSUED
TIMPANA	TINGS	TINSELS	TIPSHEET	TISSUES
TIMPANI	TINHORN	TINSMITH	TIPSHEETS	TISSUEY
TIMPANIST	TINHORNS	TINSMITHS	TIPSIER	TISSUING
TIMPANISTS	TINIER	TINSNIPS	TIPSIEST	TISSULAR
TIMPANO	TINIEST	TINSTONE	TIPSILY	TIT
TIMPANUM	TINILY	TINSTONES	TIPSINESS	TITAN
TIMPANUMS	TININESS	TINT	TIPSINESSES	TITANATE

TITANATES	TITMICE	TOADEATERS	TODDIES	TOGAVIRUS
TITANESS	TITMOUSE	TOADFISH	TODDLE	TOGAVIRUSES
TITANESSES	TITRABLE	TOADFISHES	TODDLED	TOGETHER
TITANIA	TITRANT	TOADFLAX	TODDLER	TOGGED
TITANIAS	TITRANTS	TOADFLAXES	TODDLERS	TOGGERIES
TITANIC	TITRATE	TOADIED	TODDLES	TOGGERY
TITANISM	TITRATED	TOADIES	TODDLING	TOGGING
TITANISMS	TITRATES	TOADISH	TODDY	TOGGLE
TITANITE	TITRATING	TOADLESS	TODIES	TOGGLED
TITANITES	TITRATION	TOADLIKE	TODS	TOGGLER
TITANIUM	TITRATIONS	TOADS	TODY	TOGGLERS
TITANIUMS	TITRATOR	TOADSTONE	TOE	TOGGLES
TITANOUS	TITRATORS	TOADSTONES	TOEA	TOGGLING
TITANS	TITRE	TOADSTOOL	TOEAS	TOGS
TITBIT	TITRES	TOADSTOOLS	TOECAP	TOGUE
TITBITS	TITS	TOADY	TOECAPS	TOGUES
TITER	TITTER	TOADYING	TOED	TOIL
TITERS	TITTERED	TOADYISH	TOEHOLD	TOILE
TITFER	TITTERER	TOADYISM	TOEHOLDS	TOILED
TITFERS	TITTERERS	TOADYISMS	TOEING	TOILER
TITHABLE	TITTERING	TOAST	TOELESS	TOILERS
TITHE	TITTERS	TOASTED	TOELIKE	TOILES
TITHED	TITTIE	TOASTER	TOENAIL	TOILET
TITHER	TITTIES	TOASTERS	TOENAILED	TOILETED
TITHERS	TITTIVATE	TOASTIER	TOENAILING	TOILETING
TITHES	TITTIVATED	TOASTIEST	TOENAILS	TOILETRIES
TITHING	TITTIVATES	TOASTING	TOEPIECE	TOILETRY
TITHINGS	TITTIVATING	TOASTS	TOEPIECES	TOILETS
TITHONIA	TITTLE	TOASTY	TOEPLATE	TOILETTE
TITHONIAS	TITTLES	TOBACCO	TOEPLATES	TOILETTES
TITI	TITTUP	TOBACCOES	TOES	TOILFUL
TITIAN	TITTUPED	TOBACCOS	TOESHOE	TOILFULLY
TITIANS	TITTUPING	TOBIES	TOESHOES	TOILING
TITILLATE	TITTUPPED	TOBOGGAN	TOFF	TOILS
TITILLATED	TITTUPPING	TOBOGGANED	TOFFEE	TOILSOME
TITILLATES	TITTUPPY	TOBOGGANING	TOFFEES	TOILWORN
TITILLATING	TITTUPS	TOBOGGANS	TOFFIES	TOIT
TITIS	TITTY	TOBY	TOFFS	TOITED
TITIVATE	TITUBANT	TOCCATA	TOFFY	TOITING
TITIVATED	TITULAR	TOCCATAS	TOFT	TOITS
TITIVATES	TITULARIES	TOCCATE	TOFTS	TOKAMAK
TITIVATING	TITULARLY	TOCHER	TOFU	TOKAMAKS
TITLARK	TITULARS	TOCHERED	TOFUS	TOKAY
TITLARKS	TITULARY	TOCHERING	TOFUTTI	TOKAYS
TITLE	TIVY	TOCHERS	TOFUTTIS	TOKE
TITLED	TIZZIES	TOCOLOGIES	TOG	TOKED
TITLES	TIZZY	TOCOLOGY	TOGA	TOKEN
TITLING	TMESES	TOCSIN	TOGAE	TOKENED
TITLIST	TMESIS	TOCSINS	TOGAED	TOKENING
TITLISTS	TO	TOD	TOGAS	TOKENISM
TITMAN	TOAD	TODAY	TOGATE	TOKENISMS
TITMEN	TOADEATER	TODAYS	TOGATED	TOKENS

TOKER	TOLLERS	TOMBAC	TONAL	TONNAGE
TOKERS	TOLLGATE	TOMBACK	TONALITIES	TONNAGES
TOKES	TOLLGATES	TOMBACKS	TONALITY	TONNE
TOKING	TOLLHOUSE	TOMBACS	TONALLY	TONNEAU
TOKOLOGIES	TOLLHOUSES	TOMBAK	TONDI	TONNEAUS
TOKOLOGY	TOLLING	TOMBAKS	TONDO	TONNEAUX
TOKOMAK	TOLLMAN	TOMBAL	TONDOS	TONNER
TOKOMAKS	TOLLMEN	TOMBED	TONE	TONNERS
TOKONOMA	TOLLS	TOMBING	TONEARM	TONNES
TOKONOMAS	TOLLWAY	TOMBLESS	TONEARMS	TONNISH
TOLA	TOLLWAYS	TOMBLIKE	TONED	TONOMETER
TOLAN	TOLU	TOMBOLA	TONELESS	TONOMETERS
TOLANE	TOLUATE	TOMBOLAS	TONEME	TONOMETRIES
TOLANES	TOLUATES	TOMBOLO	TONEMES	TONOMETRY
TOLANS	TOLUENE	TOMBOLOS	TONEMIC	TONOPLAST
TOLAR	TOLUENES	TOMBOY	TONER	TONOPLASTS
TOLARJEV	TOLUIC	TOMBOYISH	TONERS	TONS
TOLARS	TOLUID	TOMBOYS	TONES	TONSIL
TOLAS	TOLUIDE	TOMBS	TONETIC	TONSILAR
TOLBOOTH	TOLUIDES	TOMBSTONE	TONETICS	TONSILLAR
TOLBOOTHS	TOLUIDIDE	TOMBSTONES	TONETTE	TONSILS
TOLD	TOLUIDIDES	TOMCAT	TONETTES	TONSORIAL
TOLE	TOLUIDIN	TOMCATS	TONEY	TONSURE
TOLED	TOLUIDINE	TOMCATTED	TONG	TONSURED
TOLEDO	TOLUIDINES	TOMCATTING	TONGA	TONSURES
TOLEDOS	TOLUIDINS	TOMCOD	TONGAS	TONSURING
TOLERABLE	TOLUIDS	TOMCODS	TONGED	TONTINE
TOLERABLY	TOLUOL	TOME	TONGER	TONTINES
TOLERANCE	TOLUOLE	TOMENTA	TONGERS	TONUS
TOLERANCES	TOLUOLES	TOMENTOSE	TONGING	TONUSES
TOLERANT	TOLUOLS	TOMENTUM	TONGMAN	TONY
TOLERATE	TOLUS	TOMES	TONGMEN	TOO
TOLERATED	TOLUYL	TOMFOOL	TONGS	TOOK
TOLERATES	TOLUYLS	TOMFOOLS	TONGUE	TOOL
TOLERATING	TOLYL	TOMMED	TONGUED	TOOLBAR
TOLERATOR	TOLYLS	TOMMIES	TONGUES	TOOLBARS
TOLERATORS	TOM	TOMMING	TONGUING	TOOLBOX
TOLES	TOMAHAWK	TOMMY	TONGUINGS	TOOLBOXES
TOLIDIN	TOMAHAWKED	TOMMYROT	TONIC	TOOLED
TOLIDINE	TOMAHAWKING	TOMMYROTS	TONICALLY	TOOLER
TOLIDINES	TOMAHAWKS	TOMOGRAM	TONICITIES	TOOLERS
TOLIDINS	TOMALLEY	TOMOGRAMS	TONICITY	TOOLHEAD
TOLING	TOMALLEYS	TOMOGRAPH	TONICS	TOOLHEADS
TOLL	TOMAN	TOMOGRAPHS	TONIER	TOOLHOUSE
TOLLAGE	TOMANS	TOMORROW	TONIEST	TOOLHOUSES
TOLLAGES	TOMATILLO	TOMORROWS	TONIGHT	TOOLING
TOLLBAR	TOMATILLOES	TOMPION	TONIGHTS	TOOLINGS
TOLLBARS	TOMATILLOS	TOMPIONS	TONING	TOOLLESS
TOLLBOOTH	TOMATO	TOMS	TONISH	TOOLMAKER
TOLLBOOTHS	TOMATOES	TOMTIT	TONISHLY	TOOLMAKERS
TOLLED	TOMATOEY	TOMTITS	TONLET	TOOLROOM
TOLLER	TOMB	TON	TONLETS	TOOLROOMS

TOOLS	TOPEES	TOPOTYPES	TORCHIERS	TORPEDOED
TOOLSHED	TOPER	TOPPED	TORCHIEST	TORPEDOES
TOOLSHEDS	TOPERS	TOPPER	TORCHING	TORPEDOING
TOOM	TOPES	TOPPERS	TORCHLIKE	TORPEDOS
TOON	TOPFLIGHT	TOPPING	TORCHON	TORPID
TOONIE	TOPFUL	TOPPINGS	TORCHONS	TORPIDITIES
TOONIES	TOPFULL	TOPPLE	TORCHWOOD	TORPIDITY
TOONS	TOPH	TOPPLED	TORCHWOODS	TORPIDLY
TOOT	TOPHE	TOPPLES	TORCHY	TORPIDS
TOOTED	TOPHES	TOPPLING	TORCS	TORPOR
TOOTER	TOPHI	TOPS	TORE	TORPORS
TOOTERS	TOPHS	TOPSAIL	TOREADOR	TORQUATE
TOOTH	TOPHUS	TOPSAILS	TOREADORS	TORQUE
TOOTHACHE	TOPI	TOPSIDE	TORERO	TORQUED
TOOTHACHES	TOPIARIES	TOPSIDER	TOREROS	TORQUER
TOOTHED	TOPIARY	TOPSIDERS	TORES	TORQUERS
TOOTHIER	TOPIC	TOPSIDES	TOREUTIC	TORQUES
TOOTHIEST	TOPICAL	TOPSOIL	TOREUTICS	TORQUESES
TOOTHILY	TOPICALLY	TOPSOILED	TORI	TORQUING
TOOTHING	TOPICS	TOPSOILING	TORIC	TORR
TOOTHLESS	TOPING	TOPSOILS	TORICS	TORREFIED
TOOTHLIKE	TOPIS	TOPSPIN	TORIES	TORREFIES
TOOTHPICK	TOPKICK	TOPSPINS	TORII	TORREFY
TOOTHPICKS	TOPKICKS	TOPSTITCH	TORMENT	TORREFYING
TOOTHS	TOPKNOT	TOPSTITCHED	TORMENTED	TORRENT
TOOTHSOME	TOPKNOTS	TOPSTITCHES	TORMENTER	TORRENTS
TOOTHWORT	TOPLESS	TOPSTITCHING	TORMENTERS	TORRID
TOOTHWORTS	TOPLINE	TOPSTONE	TORMENTIL	TORRIDER
TOOTHY	TOPLINES	TOPSTONES	TORMENTILS	TORRIDEST
TOOTING	TOPLOFTIER	TOPWORK	TORMENTING	TORRIDITIES
TOOTLE	TOPLOFTIEST	TOPWORKED	TORMENTOR	TORRIDITY
TOOTLED	TOPLOFTY	TOPWORKING	TORMENTORS	TORRIDLY
TOOTLER	TOPMAST	TOPWORKS	TORMENTS	TORRIFIED
TOOTLERS	TOPMASTS	TOQUE	TORN	TORRIFIES
TOOTLES	TOPMINNOW	TOQUES	TORNADIC	TORRIFY
TOOTLING	TOPMINNOWS	TOQUET	TORNADO	TORRIFYING
TOOTS	TOPMOST	TOQUETS	TORNADOES	TORRS
TOOTSES	TOPNOTCH	TOR	TORNADOS	TORS
TOOTSIE	TOPO	TORA	TORNILLO	TORSADE
TOOTSIES	TOPOGRAPH	TORAH	TORNILLOS	TORSADES
TOOTSY	TOPOGRAPHS	TORAHS	TORO	TORSE
TOP	TOPOI	TORAS	TOROID	TORSES
TOPAZ	TOPOLOGIC	TORC	TOROIDAL	TORSI
TOPAZES	TOPOLOGIES	TORCH	TOROIDS	TORSION
TOPAZINE	TOPOLOGY	TORCHABLE	TOROS	TORSIONAL
TOPCOAT	TOPONYM	TORCHED	TOROSE	TORSIONS
TOPCOATS	TOPONYMIC	TORCHERE	TOROSITIES	TORSK
TOPCROSS	TOPONYMIES	TORCHERES	TOROSITY	TORSKS
TOPCROSSES	TOPONYMS	TORCHES	TOROT	TORSO
TOPE	TOPONYMY	TORCHIER	TOROTH	TORSOS
TOPED	TOPOS	TORCHIERE	TOROUS	TORT
TOPEE	TOPOTYPE	TORCHIERES	TORPEDO	TORTA

TORTAS	TOTALISE	TOUCHABLE	TOURACOS	TOWBOAT
TORTE	TOTALISED	TOUCHBACK	TOURED	TOWBOATS
TORTEN	TOTALISES	TOUCHBACKS	TOURER	TOWED
TORTES	TOTALISING	TOUCHDOWN	TOURERS	TOWEL
TORTILE	TOTALISM	TOUCHDOWNS	TOURING	TOWELED
TORTILLA	TOTALISMS	TOUCHE	TOURINGS	TOWELETTE
TORTILLAS	TOTALIST	TOUCHED	TOURISM	TOWELETTES
TORTIOUS	TOTALISTS	TOUCHER	TOURISMS	TOWELING
TORTOISE	TOTALITIES	TOUCHERS	TOURIST	TOWELINGS
TORTOISES	TOTALITY	TOUCHES	TOURISTA	TOWELLED
TORTONI	TOTALIZE	TOUCHHOLE	TOURISTAS	TOWELLING
TORTONIS	TOTALIZED	TOUCHHOLES	TOURISTED	TOWELLINGS
TORTRICID	TOTALIZER	TOUCHIER	TOURISTIC	TOWELS
TORTRICIDS	TOTALIZERS	TOUCHIEST	TOURISTS	TOWER
TORTRIX	TOTALIZES	TOUCHILY	TOURISTY	TOWERED
TORTRIXES	TOTALIZING	TOUCHING	TOURNEDOS	TOWERIER
TORTS	TOTALLED	TOUCHLINE	TOURNEY	TOWERIEST
TORTUOUS	TOTALLING	TOUCHLINES	TOURNEYED	TOWERING
TORTURE	TOTALLY	TOUCHMARK	TOURNEYING	TOWERLIKE
TORTURED	TOTALS	TOUCHMARKS	TOURNEYS	TOWERS
TORTURER	TOTAQUINE	TOUCHPAD	TOURS	TOWERY
TORTURERS	TOTAQUINES	TOUCHPADS	TOUSE	TOWHEAD
TORTURES	TOTE	TOUCHTONE	TOUSED	TOWHEADED
TORTURING	TOTEABLE	TOUCHTONES	TOUSES	TOWHEADS
TORTUROUS	TOTED	TOUCHUP	TOUSING	TOWHEE
TORULA	TOTEM	TOUCHUPS	TOUSLE	TOWHEES
TORULAE	TOTEMIC	TOUCHWOOD	TOUSLED	TOWIE
TORULAS	TOTEMISM	TOUCHWOODS	TOUSLES	TOWIES
TORUS	TOTEMISMS	TOUCHY	TOUSLING	TOWING
TORY	TOTEMIST	TOUGH	TOUT	TOWLINE
TOSH	TOTEMISTS	TOUGHED	TOUTED	TOWLINES
TOSHES	TOTEMITE	TOUGHEN	TOUTER	TOWMOND
TOSS	TOTEMITES	TOUGHENED	TOUTERS	TOWMONDS
TOSSED	TOTEMS	TOUGHENER	TOUTING	TOWMONT
TOSSER	TOTER	TOUGHENERS	TOUTS	TOWMONTS
TOSSERS	TOTERS	TOUGHENING	TOUZLE	TOWN
TOSSES	TOTES	TOUGHENS	TOUZLED	TOWNEE
TOSSING	TOTHER	TOUGHER	TOUZLES	TOWNEES
TOSSPOT	TOTING	TOUGHEST	TOUZLING	TOWNFOLK
TOSSPOTS	TOTS	TOUGHIE	TOVARICH	TOWNHOME
TOSSUP	TOTTED	TOUGHIES	TOVARICHES	TOWNHOMES
TOSSUPS	TOTTER	TOUGHING	TOVARISH	TOWNHOUSE
TOST	TOTTERED	TOUGHISH	TOVARISHES	TOWNHOUSES
TOSTADA	TOTTERER	TOUGHLY	TOW	TOWNIE
TOSTADAS	TOTTERERS	TOUGHNESS	TOWABLE	TOWNIES
TOSTADO	TOTTERING	TOUGHNESSES	TOWAGE	TOWNISH
TOSTADOS	TOTTERS	TOUGHS	TOWAGES	TOWNLESS
TOT	TOTTERY	TOUGHY	TOWARD	TOWNLET
TOTABLE	TOTTING	TOUPEE	TOWARDLY	TOWNLETS
TOTAL	TOUCAN	TOUPEES	TOWARDS	TOWNS
TOTALED	TOUCANS	TOUR	TOWAWAY	TOWNSCAPE
TOTALING	TOUCH	TOURACO	TOWAWAYS	TOWNSCAPES

TOWNSFOLK	TOYO	TRACKER	TRADUCER	TRAINS
TOWNSHIP	TOYON	TRACKERS	TRADUCERS	TRAINWAY
TOWNSHIPS	TOYONS	TRACKING	TRADUCES	TRAINWAYS
TOWNSMAN	TOYOS	TRACKINGS	TRADUCING	TRAIPSE
TOWNSMEN	TOYS	TRACKLESS	TRAFFIC	TRAIPSED
TOWNWEAR	TOYSHOP	TRACKMAN	TRAFFICKED	TRAIPSES
TOWNY	TOYSHOPS	TRACKMEN	TRAFFICKING	TRAIPSING
TOWPATH	TRABEATE	TRACKPAD	TRAFFICS	TRAIT
TOWPATHS	TRABEATED	TRACKPADS	TRAGEDIAN	TRAITOR
TOWPLANE	TRABECULA	TRACKS	TRAGEDIANS	TRAITORS
TOWPLANES	TRABECULAE	TRACKSIDE	TRAGEDIES	TRAITRESS
TOWROPE	TRABECULAS	TRACKSIDES	TRAGEDY	TRAITRESSES
TOWROPES	TRACE	TRACKSUIT	TRAGI	TRAITS
TOWS	TRACEABLE	TRACKSUITS	TRAGIC	TRAJECT
TOWSACK	TRACEABLY	TRACKWAY	TRAGICAL	TRAJECTED
TOWSACKS	TRACED	TRACKWAYS	TRAGICS	TRAJECTING
TOWY	TRACELESS	TRACT	TRAGOPAN	TRAJECTS
TOXAEMIA	TRACER	TRACTABLE	TRAGOPANS	TRAM
TOXAEMIAS	TRACERIED	TRACTABLY	TRAGUS	TRAMCAR
TOXAEMIC	TRACERIES	TRACTATE	TRAIK	TRAMCARS
TOXAPHENE	TRACERS	TRACTATES	TRAIKED	TRAMEL
TOXAPHENES	TRACERY	TRACTILE	TRAIKING	TRAMELED
TOXEMIA	TRACES	TRACTION	TRAIKS	TRAMELING
TOXEMIAS	TRACHEA	TRACTIONS	TRAIL	TRAMELL
TOXEMIC	TRACHEAE	TRACTIVE	TRAILED	TRAMELLED
TOXIC	TRACHEAL	TRACTOR	TRAILER	TRAMELLING
TOXICAL	TRACHEARY	TRACTORS	TRAILERED	TRAMELLS
TOXICALLY	TRACHEAS	TRACTS	TRAILERING	TRAMELS
TOXICANT	TRACHEATE	TRAD	TRAILERS	TRAMLESS
TOXICANTS	TRACHEATES	TRADABLE	TRAILHEAD	TRAMLINE
TOXICITIES	TRACHEID	TRADE	TRAILHEADS	TRAMLINES
TOXICITY	TRACHEIDS	TRADEABLE	TRAILING	TRAMMED
TOXICOSES	TRACHEOLE	TRADED	TRAILLESS	TRAMMEL
TOXICOSIS	TRACHEOLES	TRADEMARK	TRAILS	TRAMMELED
TOXICS	TRACHLE	TRADEMARKED	TRAILSIDE	TRAMMELER
TOXIGENIC	TRACHLED	TRADEMARKING	TRAIN	TRAMMELERS
TOXIN	TRACHLES	TRADEMARKS	TRAINABLE	TRAMMELING
TOXINE	TRACHLING	TRADEOFF	TRAINBAND	TRAMMELLED
TOXINES	TRACHOMA	TRADEOFFS	TRAINBANDS	TRAMMELLING
TOXINS	TRACHOMAS	TRADER	TRAINED	TRAMMELS
TOXOID	TRACHYTE	TRADERS	TRAINEE	TRAMMING
TOXOIDS	TRACHYTES	TRADES	TRAINEES	TRAMP
TOXOPHILIES	TRACHYTIC	TRADESMAN	TRAINER	TRAMPED
TOXOPHILY	TRACING	TRADESMEN	TRAINERS	TRAMPER
TOY	TRACINGS	TRADING	TRAINFUL	TRAMPERS
TOYED	TRACK	TRADITION	TRAINFULS	TRAMPIER
TOYER	TRACKABLE	TRADITIONS	TRAINING	TRAMPIEST
TOYERS	TRACKAGE	TRADITIVE	TRAININGS	TRAMPING
TOYING	TRACKAGES	TRADITOR	TRAINLOAD	TRAMPISH
TOYISH	TRACKBALL	TRADITORES	TRAINLOADS	TRAMPLE
TOYLESS	TRACKBALLS	TRADUCE	TRAINMAN	TRAMPLED
TOYLIKE	TRACKED	TRADUCED	TRAINMEN	TRAMPLER

TRAMPLERS	TRANSFECTED	TRANSPORTED	TRAPPING	TRAVERSAL
TRAMPLES	TRANSFECTING	TRANSPORTING	TRAPPINGS	TRAVERSALS
TRAMPLING	TRANSFECTS	TRANSPORTS	TRAPPOSE	TRAVERSE
TRAMPS	TRANSFER	TRANSPOSE	TRAPPOUS	TRAVERSED
TRAMPY	TRANSFERRED	TRANSPOSED	TRAPROCK	TRAVERSER
TRAMROAD	TRANSFERRING	TRANSPOSES	TRAPROCKS	TRAVERSERS
TRAMROADS	TRANSFERS	TRANSPOSING	TRAPS	TRAVERSES
TRAMS	TRANSFIX	TRANSSHIP	TRAPT	TRAVERSING
TRAMWAY	TRANSFIXED	TRANSSHIPPED	TRAPUNTO	TRAVES
TRAMWAYS	TRANSFIXES	TRANSSHIPPING	TRAPUNTOS	TRAVESTIED
TRANCE	TRANSFIXING	TRANSSHIPS	TRASH	TRAVESTIES
TRANCED	TRANSFIXT	TRANSUDE	TRASHED	TRAVESTY
TRANCES	TRANSFORM	TRANSUDED	TRASHER	TRAVESTYING
TRANCHE	TRANSFORMED	TRANSUDES	TRASHERS	TRAVOIS
TRANCHES	TRANSFORMING	TRANSUDING	TRASHES	TRAVOISE
TRANCING	TRANSFORMS	TRAP	TRASHIER	TRAVOISES
TRANGAM	TRANSFUSE	TRAPAN	TRASHIEST	TRAWL
TRANGAMS	TRANSFUSED	TRAPANNED	TRASHILY	TRAWLED
TRANK	TRANSFUSES	TRAPANNING	TRASHING	TRAWLER
TRANKS	TRANSFUSING	TRAPANS	TRASHMAN	TRAWLERS
TRANNIES	TRANSGENE	TRAPBALL	TRASHMEN	TRAWLEY
TRANNY	TRANSGENES	TRAPBALLS	TRASHY	TRAWLEYS
TRANQ	TRANSHIP	TRAPDOOR	TRASS	TRAWLING
TRANQS	TRANSHIPPED	TRAPDOORS	TRASSES	TRAWLNET
TRANQUIL	TRANSHIPPING	TRAPES	TRATTORIA	TRAWLNETS
TRANQUILER	TRANSHIPS	TRAPESED	TRATTORIAS	TRAWLS
TRANQUILEST	TRANSIENT	TRAPESES	TRATTORIE	TRAY
TRANQUILLER	TRANSIENTS	TRAPESING	TRAUCHLE	TRAYFUL
TRANQUILLEST	TRANSIT	TRAPEZE	TRAUCHLED	TRAYFULS
TRANS	TRANSITED	TRAPEZES	TRAUCHLES	TRAYS
TRANSACT	TRANSITING	TRAPEZIA	TRAUCHLING	TRAZODONE
TRANSACTED	TRANSITS	TRAPEZIAL	TRAUMA	TRAZODONES
TRANSACTING	TRANSLATE	TRAPEZII	TRAUMAS	TREACHERIES
TRANSACTS	TRANSLATED	TRAPEZIST	TRAUMATA	TREACHERY
TRANSAXLE	TRANSLATES	TRAPEZISTS	TRAUMATIC	TREACLE
TRANSAXLES	TRANSLATING	TRAPEZIUM	TRAVAIL	TREACLES
TRANSCEND	TRANSMIT	TRAPEZIUMS	TRAVAILED	TREACLIER
TRANSCENDED	TRANSMITS	TRAPEZIUS	TRAVAILING	TREACLIEST
TRANSCENDING	TRANSMITTED	TRAPEZIUSES	TRAVAILS	TREACLY
TRANSCENDS	TRANSMITTING	TRAPEZOID	TRAVE	TREAD
TRANSDUCE	TRANSMUTE	TRAPEZOIDS	TRAVEL	TREADED
TRANSDUCED	TRANSMUTED	TRAPLIKE	TRAVELED	TREADER
TRANSDUCES	TRANSMUTES	TRAPLINE	TRAVELER	TREADERS
TRANSDUCING	TRANSMUTING	TRAPLINES	TRAVELERS	TREADING
TRANSECT	TRANSOM	TRAPNEST	TRAVELING	TREADLE
TRANSECTED	TRANSOMS	TRAPNESTED	TRAVELLED	TREADLED
TRANSECTING	TRANSONIC	TRAPNESTING	TRAVELLER	TREADLER
TRANSECTS	TRANSPIRE	TRAPNESTS	TRAVELLERS	TREADLERS
TRANSEPT	TRANSPIRED	TRAPPEAN	TRAVELLING	TREADLES
TRANSEPTS	TRANSPIRES	TRAPPED	TRAVELOG	TREADLESS
TRANSEUNT	TRANSPIRING	TRAPPER	TRAVELOGS	TREADLING
TRANSFECT	TRANSPORT	TRAPPERS	TRAVELS	TREADMILL

TREADMILLS	TREENAIL	TRENCHED	TRESTLE	TRIBADISM
TREADS	TREENAILS	TRENCHER	TRESTLES	TRIBADISMS
TREASON	TREENS	TRENCHERS	TRET	TRIBAL
TREASONS	TREENWARE	TRENCHES	TRETINOIN	TRIBALISM
TREASURE	TREENWARES	TRENCHING	TRETINOINS	TRIBALISMS
TREASURED	TREES	TREND	TRETS	TRIBALIST
TREASURER	TREETOP	TRENDED	TREVALLIES	TRIBALISTS
TREASURERS	TREETOPS	TRENDIER	TREVALLY	TRIBALLY
TREASURES	TREF	TRENDIES	TREVALLYS	TRIBALS
TREASURIES	TREFAH	TRENDIEST	TREVET	TRIBASIC
TREASURING	TREFOIL	TRENDILY	TREVETS	TRIBE
TREASURY	TREFOILS	TRENDING	TREWS	TRIBES
TREAT	TREHALA	TRENDOID	TREY	TRIBESMAN
TREATABLE	TREHALAS	TRENDOIDS	TREYS	TRIBESMEN
TREATED	TREHALOSE	TRENDS	TRIABLE	TRIBOLOGIES
TREATER	TREHALOSES	TRENDY	TRIAC	TRIBOLOGY
TREATERS	TREILLAGE	TREPAN	TRIACID	TRIBRACH
TREATIES	TREILLAGES	TREPANG	TRIACIDS	TRIBRACHS
TREATING	TREK	TREPANGS	TRIACS	TRIBULATE
TREATISE	TREKKED	TREPANNED	TRIAD	TRIBULATED
TREATISES	TREKKER	TREPANNER	TRIADIC	TRIBULATES
TREATMENT	TREKKERS	TREPANNERS	TRIADICS	TRIBULATING
TREATMENTS	TREKKING	TREPANNING	TRIADISM	TRIBUNAL
TREATS	TREKS	TREPANS	TRIADISMS	TRIBUNALS
TREATY	TRELLIS	TREPHINE	TRIADS	TRIBUNARY
TREBBIANO	TRELLISED	TREPHINED	TRIAGE	TRIBUNATE
TREBBIANOS	TRELLISES	TREPHINES	TRIAGED	TRIBUNATES
TREBLE	TRELLISING	TREPHINING	TRIAGES	TRIBUNE
TREBLED	TREMATODE	TREPID	TRIAGING	TRIBUNES
TREBLES	TREMATODES	TREPIDANT	TRIAL	TRIBUTARIES
TREBLING	TREMBLE	TREPONEMA	TRIALOGUE	TRIBUTARY
TREBLY	TREMBLED	TREPONEMAS	TRIALOGUES	TRIBUTE
TREBUCHET	TREMBLER	TREPONEMATA	TRIALS	TRIBUTES
TREBUCHETS	TREMBLERS	TREPONEME	TRIANGLE	TRICE
TREBUCKET	TREMBLES	TREPONEMES	TRIANGLED	TRICED
TREBUCKETS	TREMBLIER	TRES	TRIANGLES	TRICEP
TRECENTO	TREMBLIEST	TRESPASS	TRIARCHIES	TRICEPS
TRECENTOS	TREMBLING	TRESPASSED	TRIARCHY	TRICEPSES
TREDDLE	TREMBLY	TRESPASSES	TRIASSIC	TRICES
TREDDLED	TREMOLITE	TRESPASSING	TRIATHLON	TRICHINA
TREDDLES	TREMOLITES	TRESS	TRIATHLONS	TRICHINAE
TREDDLING	TREMOLO	TRESSED	TRIATOMIC	TRICHINAL
TREE	TREMOLOS	TRESSEL	TRIAXIAL	TRICHINAS
TREED	TREMOR	TRESSELS	TRIAZIN	TRICHITE
TREEHOUSE	TREMOROUS	TRESSES	TRIAZINE	TRICHITES
TREEHOUSES	TREMORS	TRESSIER	TRIAZINES	TRICHOID
TREEING	TREMULANT	TRESSIEST	TRIAZINS	TRICHOME
TREELAWN	TREMULOUS	TRESSOUR	TRIAZOLE	TRICHOMES
TREELAWNS	TRENAIL	TRESSOURS	TRIAZOLES	TRICHOMIC
TREELESS	TRENAILS	TRESSURE	TRIBADE	TRICHOSES
TREELIKE	TRENCH	TRESSURES	TRIBADES	TRICHOSIS
TREEN	TRENCHANT	TRESSY	TRIBADIC	TRICHROIC

TRICHROME	TRICYCLE	TRIGGERS	TRILOBITE	TRINKUMS
TRICING	TRICYCLES	TRIGGEST	TRILOBITES	TRINODAL
TRICK	TRICYCLIC	TRIGGING	TRILOGIES	TRINOMIAL
TRICKED	TRICYCLICS	TRIGLY	TRILOGY	TRINOMIALS
TRICKER	TRIDACTYL	TRIGLYPH	TRIM	TRIO
TRICKERIES	TRIDENT	TRIGLYPHS	TRIMARAN	TRIODE
TRICKERS	TRIDENTAL	TRIGNESS	TRIMARANS	TRIODES
TRICKERY	TRIDENTS	TRIGNESSES	TRIMER	TRIOL
TRICKIE	TRIDUUM	TRIGO	TRIMERIC	TRIOLET
TRICKIER	TRIDUUMS	TRIGON	TRIMERISM	TRIOLETS
TRICKIEST	TRIED	TRIGONAL	TRIMERISMS	TRIOLS
TRICKILY	TRIENE	TRIGONOUS	TRIMEROUS	TRIOS
TRICKING	TRIENES	TRIGONS	TRIMERS	TRIOSE
TRICKISH	TRIENNIA	TRIGOS	TRIMESTER	TRIOSES
TRICKLE	TRIENNIAL	TRIGRAM	TRIMESTERS	TRIOXID
TRICKLED	TRIENNIALS	TRIGRAMS	TRIMETER	TRIOXIDE
TRICKLES	TRIENNIUM	TRIGRAPH	TRIMETERS	TRIOXIDES
TRICKLIER	TRIENNIUMS	TRIGRAPHS	TRIMETRIC	TRIOXIDS
TRICKLIEST	TRIENS	TRIGS	TRIMLY	TRIP
TRICKLING	TRIENTES	TRIHEDRA	TRIMMED	TRIPACK
TRICKLY	TRIER	TRIHEDRAL	TRIMMER	TRIPACKS
TRICKS	TRIERARCH	TRIHEDRALS	TRIMMERS	TRIPART
TRICKSIER	TRIERARCHS	TRIHEDRON	TRIMMEST	TRIPE
TRICKSIEST	TRIERS	TRIHEDRONS	TRIMMING	TRIPEDAL
TRICKSTER	TRIES	TRIHYBRID	TRIMMINGS	TRIPES
TRICKSTERS	TRIETHYL	TRIHYBRIDS	TRIMNESS	TRIPHASE
TRICKSY	TRIFACIAL	TRIJET	TRIMNESSES	TRIPLANE
TRICKY	TRIFACIALS	TRIJETS	TRIMORPH	TRIPLANES
TRICLAD	TRIFECTA	TRIJUGATE	TRIMORPHS	TRIPLE
TRICLADS	TRIFECTAS	TRIJUGOUS	TRIMOTOR	TRIPLED
TRICLINIA	TRIFID	TRIKE	TRIMOTORS	TRIPLES
TRICLINIC	TRIFLE	TRIKES	TRIMS	TRIPLET
TRICLINIUM	TRIFLED	TRILBIES	TRINAL	TRIPLETS
TRICLOSAN	TRIFLER	TRILBY	TRINARY	TRIPLEX
TRICLOSANS	TRIFLERS	TRILINEAR	TRINDLE	TRIPLEXES
TRICOLOR	TRIFLES	TRILITH	TRINDLED	TRIPLING
TRICOLORS	TRIFLING	TRILITHON	TRINDLES	TRIPLITE
TRICOLOUR	TRIFLINGS	TRILITHONS	TRINDLING	TRIPLITES
TRICOLOURS	TRIFOCAL	TRILITHS	TRINE	TRIPLOID
TRICORN	TRIFOCALS	TRILL	TRINED	TRIPLOIDIES
TRICORNE	TRIFOLD	TRILLED	TRINES	TRIPLOIDS
TRICORNES	TRIFOLIUM	TRILLER	TRINING	TRIPLOIDY
TRICORNS	TRIFOLIUMS	TRILLERS	TRINITIES	TRIPLY
TRICOT	TRIFORIA	TRILLING	TRINITY	TRIPOD
TRICOTINE	TRIFORIUM	TRILLION	TRINKET	TRIPODAL
TRICOTINES	TRIFORM	TRILLIONS	TRINKETED	TRIPODIC
TRICOTS	TRIFORMED	TRILLIUM	TRINKETER	TRIPODIES
TRICROTIC	TRIG	TRILLIUMS	TRINKETERS	TRIPODS
TRICTRAC	TRIGGED	TRILLS	TRINKETING	TRIPODY
TRICTRACS	TRIGGER	TRILOBAL	TRINKETRIES	TRIPOLI
TRICUSPID	TRIGGERED	TRILOBATE	TRINKETRY	TRIPOLIS
TRICUSPIDS	TRIGGERING	TRILOBED	TRINKETS	TRIPOS

TRIPOSES	TRISTE	TRIVIA	TROILUSES	TROOZ
TRIPPED	TRISTEZA	TRIVIAL	TROIS	TROP
TRIPPER	TRISTEZAS	TRIVIALLY	TROKE	TROPAEOLA
TRIPPERS	TRISTFUL	TRIVIUM	TROKED	TROPAEOLUM
TRIPPET	TRISTICH	TRIWEEKLIES	TROKES	TROPAEOLUMS
TRIPPETS	TRISTICHS	TRIWEEKLY	TROKING	TROPE
TRIPPIER	TRITE	TROAK	TROLAND	TROPEOLIN
TRIPPIEST	TRITELY	TROAKED	TROLANDS	TROPEOLINS
TRIPPING	TRITENESS	TROAKING	TROLL	TROPES
TRIPPINGS	TRITENESSES	TROAKS	TROLLED	TROPHIC
TRIPPY	TRITER	TROCAR	TROLLER	TROPHIED
TRIPS	TRITEST	TROCARS	TROLLERS	TROPHIES
TRIPTAN	TRITHEISM	TROCHAIC	TROLLEY	TROPHY
TRIPTANE	TRITHEISMS	TROCHAICS	TROLLEYED	TROPHYING
TRIPTANES	TRITHEIST	TROCHAL	TROLLEYING	TROPIC
TRIPTANS	TRITHEISTS	TROCHAR	TROLLEYS	TROPICAL
TRIPTYCA	TRITHING	TROCHARS	TROLLIED	TROPICALS
TRIPTYCAS	TRITHINGS	TROCHE	TROLLIES	TROPICS
TRIPTYCH	TRITIATED	TROCHEE	TROLLING	TROPIN
TRIPTYCHS	TRITICALE	TROCHEES	TROLLINGS	TROPINE
TRIPWIRE	TRITICALES	TROCHES	TROLLOP	TROPINES
TRIPWIRES	TRITICUM	TROCHIL	TROLLOPS	TROPINS
TRIREME	TRITICUMS	TROCHILI	TROLLOPY	TROPISM
TRIREMES	TRITIUM	TROCHILS	TROLLS	TROPISMS
TRISCELE	TRITIUMS	TROCHILUS	TROLLY	TROPISTIC
TRISCELES	TRITOMA	TROCHLEA	TROLLYING	TROPOLOGIES
TRISECT	TRITOMAS	TROCHLEAE	TROMBONE	TROPOLOGY
TRISECTED	TRITON	TROCHLEAR	TROMBONES	TROPONIN
TRISECTING	TRITONE	TROCHLEARS	TROMMEL	TROPONINS
TRISECTOR	TRITONES	TROCHLEAS	TROMMELS	TROT
TRISECTORS	TRITONS	TROCHOID	TROMP	TROTH
TRISECTS	TRITURATE	TROCHOIDS	TROMPE	TROTHED
TRISEME	TRITURATED	TROCK	TROMPED	TROTHING
TRISEMES	TRITURATES	TROCKED	TROMPES	TROTHS
TRISEMIC	TRITURATING	TROCKING	TROMPING	TROTLINE
TRISHAW	TRIUMPH	TROCKS	TROMPS	TROTLINES
TRISHAWS	TRIUMPHAL	TROD	TRONA	TROTS
TRISKELE	TRIUMPHED	TRODDEN	TRONAS	TROTTED
TRISKELES	TRIUMPHING	TRODE	TRONE	TROTTER
TRISKELIA	TRIUMPHS	TROFFER	TRONES	TROTTERS
TRISKELION	TRIUMVIR	TROFFERS	TROOP	TROTTING
TRISMIC	TRIUMVIRI	TROG	TROOPED	TROTYL
TRISMUS	TRIUMVIRS	TROGON	TROOPER	TROTYLS
TRISMUSES	TRIUNE	TROGONS	TROOPERS	TROUBLE
TRISODIUM	TRIUNES	TROGS	TROOPIAL	TROUBLED
TRISOME	TRIUNITIES	TROIKA	TROOPIALS	TROUBLER
TRISOMES	TRIUNITY	TROIKAS	TROOPING	TROUBLERS
TRISOMIC	TRIVALENT	TROILISM	TROOPS	TROUBLES
TRISOMICS	TRIVALVE	TROILISMS	TROOPSHIP	TROUBLING
TRISOMIES	TRIVALVES	TROILITE	TROOPSHIPS	TROUBLOUS
TRISOMY	TRIVET	TROILITES	TROOSTITE	TROUGH
TRISTATE	TRIVETS	TROILUS	TROOSTITES	TROUGHS

TROUNCE	TRUANCY	TRUEBRED	TRUNDLES	TRYPSINS
TROUNCED	TRUANT	TRUED	TRUNDLING	TRYPTIC
TROUNCER	TRUANTED	TRUEING	TRUNK	TRYSAIL
TROUNCERS	TRUANTING	TRUELOVE	TRUNKED	TRYSAILS
TROUNCES	TRUANTLY	TRUELOVES	TRUNKFISH	TRYST
TROUNCING	TRUANTRIES	TRUENESS	TRUNKFISHES	TRYSTE
TROUPE	TRUANTRY	TRUENESSES	TRUNKFUL	TRYSTED
TROUPED	TRUANTS	TRUEPENNIES	TRUNKFULS	TRYSTER
TROUPER	TRUCE	TRUEPENNY	TRUNKS	TRYSTERS
TROUPERS	TRUCED	TRUER	TRUNNEL	TRYSTES
TROUPES	TRUCELESS	TRUES	TRUNNELS	TRYSTING
TROUPIAL	TRUCES	TRUEST	TRUNNION	TRYSTS
TROUPIALS	TRUCING	TRUFFE	TRUNNIONS	TRYWORKS
TROUPING	TRUCK	TRUFFES	TRUSS	TSADDIK
TROUSER	TRUCKABLE	TRUFFLE	TRUSSED	TSADDIKIM
TROUSERS	TRUCKAGE	TRUFFLED	TRUSSER	TSADE
TROUSSEAU	TRUCKAGES	TRUFFLES	TRUSSERS	TSADES
TROUSSEAUS	TRUCKED	TRUG	TRUSSES	TSADI
TROUSSEAUX	TRUCKER	TRUGS	TRUSSING	TSADIS
TROUT	TRUCKERS	TRUING	TRUSSINGS	TSAR
TROUTIER	TRUCKFUL	TRUISM	TRUST	TSARDOM
TROUTIEST	TRUCKFULS	TRUISMS	TRUSTABLE	TSARDOMS
TROUTS	TRUCKING	TRUISTIC	TRUSTED	TSAREVNA
TROUTY	TRUCKINGS	TRULL	TRUSTEE	TSAREVNAS
TROUVERE	TRUCKLE	TRULLS	TRUSTEED	TSARINA
TROUVERES	TRUCKLED	TRULY	TRUSTEEING	TSARINAS
TROUVEUR	TRUCKLER	TRUMEAU	TRUSTEES	TSARISM
TROUVEURS	TRUCKLERS	TRUMEAUX	TRUSTER	TSARISMS
TROVE	TRUCKLES	TRUMP	TRUSTERS	TSARIST
TROVER	TRUCKLINE	TRUMPED	TRUSTFUL	TSARISTS
TROVERS	TRUCKLINES	TRUMPERIES	TRUSTIER	TSARITZA
TROVES	TRUCKLING	TRUMPERY	TRUSTIES	TSARITZAS
TROW	TRUCKLOAD	TRUMPET	TRUSTIEST	TSARS
TROWED	TRUCKLOADS	TRUMPETED	TRUSTILY	TSATSKE
TROWEL	TRUCKMAN	TRUMPETER	TRUSTING	TSATSKES
TROWELED	TRUCKMEN	TRUMPETERS	TRUSTLESS	TSETSE
TROWELER	TRUCKS	TRUMPETING	TRUSTOR	TSETSES
TROWELERS	TRUCULENT	TRUMPETS	TRUSTORS	TSIMMES
TROWELING	TRUDGE	TRUMPING	TRUSTS	TSK
TROWELLED	TRUDGED	TRUMPS	TRUSTY	TSKED
TROWELLER	TRUDGEN	TRUNCATE	TRUTH	TSKING
TROWELLERS	TRUDGENS	TRUNCATED	TRUTHFUL	TSKS
TROWELLING	TRUDGEON	TRUNCATES	TRUTHLESS	TSKTSK
TROWELS	TRUDGEONS	TRUNCATING	TRUTHS	TSKTSKED
TROWING	TRUDGER	TRUNCHEON	TRY	TSKTSKING
TROWS	TRUDGERS	TRUNCHEONED	TRYING	TSKTSKS
TROWSERS	TRUDGES	TRUNCHEONING	TRYINGLY	TSOORIS
TROWTH	TRUDGING	TRUNCHEONS	TRYMA	TSORES
TROWTHS	TRUE	TRUNDLE	TRYMATA	TSORIS
TROY	TRUEBLUE	TRUNDLED	TRYOUT	TSORRISS
TROYS	TRUEBLUES	TRUNDLER	TRYOUTS	TSOURIS
TRUANCIES	TRUEBORN	TRUNDLERS	TRYPSIN	TSUBA

TSUNAMI	TUBING	TUFTILY	TUMBREL	TUNDRAS
TSUNAMIC	TUBINGS	TUFTING	TUMBRELS	TUNE
TSUNAMIS	TUBIST	TUFTINGS	TUMBRIL	TUNEABLE
TSURIS	TUBISTS	TUFTS	TUMBRILS	TUNEABLY
TUATARA	TUBLIKE	TUFTY	TUMEFIED	TUNED
TUATARAS	TUBS	TUG	TUMEFIES	TUNEFUL
TUATERA	TUBULAR	TUGBOAT	TUMEFY	TUNEFULLY
TUATERAS	TUBULARLY	TUGBOATS	TUMEFYING	TUNELESS
TUB	TUBULATE	TUGGED	TUMESCE	TUNER
TUBA	TUBULATED	TUGGER	TUMESCED	TUNERS
TUBAE	TUBULATES	TUGGERS	TUMESCENT	TUNES
TUBAIST	TUBULATING	TUGGING	TUMESCES	TUNESMITH
TUBAISTS	TUBULATOR	TUGHRIK	TUMESCING	TUNESMITHS
TUBAL	TUBULATORS	TUGHRIKS	TUMID	TUNEUP
TUBAS	TUBULE	TUGLESS	TUMIDITIES	TUNEUPS
TUBATE	TUBULES	TUGRIK	TUMIDITY	TUNG
TUBBABLE	TUBULIN	TUGRIKS	TUMIDLY	TUNGS
TUBBED	TUBULINS	TUGS	TUMIDNESS	TUNGSTATE
TUBBER	TUBULOSE	TUI	TUMIDNESSES	TUNGSTATES
TUBBERS	TUBULOUS	TUILLE	TUMMIES	TUNGSTEN
TUBBIER	TUBULURE	TUILLES	TUMMLER	TUNGSTENS
TUBBIEST	TUBULURES	TUIS	TUMMLERS	TUNGSTIC
TUBBINESS	TUCHUN	TUITION	TUMMY	TUNGSTITE
TUBBINESSES	TUCHUNS	TUITIONAL	TUMOR	TUNGSTITES
TUBBING	TUCK	TUITIONS	TUMORAL	TUNIC
TUBBY	TUCKAHOE	TULADI	TUMORLIKE	TUNICA
TUBE	TUCKAHOES	TULADIS	TUMOROUS	TUNICAE
TUBED	TUCKED	TULAREMIA	TUMORS	TUNICATE
TUBELESS	TUCKER	TULAREMIAS	TUMOUR	TUNICATED
TUBELIKE	TUCKERED	TULAREMIC	TUMOURS	TUNICATES
TUBENOSE	TUCKERING	TULE	TUMP	TUNICLE
TUBENOSES	TUCKERS	TULES	TUMPED	TUNICLES
TUBER	TUCKET	TULIP	TUMPING	TUNICS
TUBERCLE	TUCKETS	TULIPLIKE	TUMPLINE	TUNING
TUBERCLES	TUCKING	TULIPS	TUMPLINES	TUNNAGE
TUBEROID	TUCKS	TULIPWOOD	TUMPS	TUNNAGES
TUBEROSE	TUCKSHOP	TULIPWOODS	TUMULAR	TUNNED
TUBEROSES	TUCKSHOPS	TULLE	TUMULI	TUNNEL
TUBEROUS	TUFA	TULLES	TUMULOSE	TUNNELED
TUBERS	TUFACEOUS	TULLIBEE	TUMULOUS	TUNNELER
TUBES	TUFAS	TULLIBEES	TUMULT	TUNNELERS
TUBEWORK	TUFF	TUMBLE	TUMULTS	TUNNELING
TUBEWORKS	TUFFET	TUMBLEBUG	TUMULUS	TUNNELINGS
TUBEWORM	TUFFETS	TUMBLEBUGS	TUMULUSES	TUNNELLED
TUBEWORMS	TUFFS	TUMBLED	TUN	TUNNELLER
TUBFUL	TUFOLI	TUMBLER	TUNA	TUNNELLERS
TUBFULS	TUFT	TUMBLERS	TUNABLE	TUNNELLING
TUBIFEX	TUFTED	TUMBLES	TUNABLY	TUNNELS
TUBIFEXES	TUFTER	TUMBLESET	TUNAS	TUNNIES
TUBIFICID	TUFTERS	TUMBLESETS	TUNDISH	TUNNING
TUBIFICIDS	TUFTIER	TUMBLING	TUNDISHES	TUNNY
TUBIFORM	TUFTIEST	TUMBLINGS	TUNDRA	TUNS

TUP	TURBOTS	TURNABOUTS	TURRETED	TUSSORE
TUPELO	TURBULENT	TURNCOAT	TURRETS	TUSSORES
TUPELOS	TURD	TURNCOATS	TURRICAL	TUSSORS
TUPIK	TURDINE	TURNDOWN	TURTLE	TUSSUCK
TUPIKS	TURDS	TURNDOWNS	TURTLED	TUSSUCKS
TUPPED	TUREEN	TURNED	TURTLER	TUSSUR
TUPPENCE	TUREENS	TURNER	TURTLERS	TUSSURS
TUPPENCES	TURF	TURNERIES	TURTLES	TUT
TUPPENNY	TURFED	TURNERS	TURTLING	TUTEE
TUPPING	TURFGRASS	TURNERY	TURTLINGS	TUTEES
TUPS	TURFGRASSES	TURNHALL	TURVES	TUTELAGE
TUQUE	TURFIER	TURNHALLS	TUSCHE	TUTELAGES
TUQUES	TURFIEST	TURNING	TUSCHES	TUTELAR
TURACO	TURFING	TURNINGS	TUSH	TUTELARIES
TURACOS	TURFLESS	TURNIP	TUSHED	TUTELARS
TURACOU	TURFLIKE	TURNIPS	TUSHERIES	TUTELARY
TURACOUS	TURFMAN	TURNKEY	TUSHERY	TUTOR
TURBAN	TURFMEN	TURNKEYS	TUSHES	TUTORAGE
TURBANED	TURFS	TURNOFF	TUSHIE	TUTORAGES
TURBANNED	TURFSKI	TURNOFFS	TUSHIES	TUTORED
TURBANS	TURFSKIS	TURNON	TUSHING	TUTORESS
TURBARIES	TURFY	TURNONS	TUSHY	TUTORESSES
TURBARY	TURGENCIES	TURNOUT	TUSK	TUTORIAL
TURBETH	TURGENCY	TURNOUTS	TUSKED	TUTORIALS
TURBETHS	TURGENT	TURNOVER	TUSKER	TUTORING
TURBID	TURGID	TURNOVERS	TUSKERS	TUTORS
TURBIDITE	TURGIDITIES	TURNPIKE	TUSKING	TUTORSHIP
TURBIDITES	TURGIDITY	TURNPIKES	TUSKLESS	TUTORSHIPS
TURBIDITIES	TURGIDLY	TURNS	TUSKLIKE	TUTOYED
TURBIDITY	TURGITE	TURNSOLE	TUSKS	TUTOYER
TURBIDLY	TURGITES	TURNSOLES	TUSSAH	TUTOYERED
TURBINAL	TURGOR	TURNSPIT	TUSSAHS	TUTOYERING
TURBINALS	TURGORS	TURNSPITS	TUSSAL	TUTOYERS
TURBINATE	TURION	TURNSTILE	TUSSAR	TUTS
TURBINATES	TURIONS	TURNSTILES	TUSSARS	TUTTED
TURBINE	TURISTA	TURNSTONE	TUSSEH	TUTTI
TURBINES	TURISTAS	TURNSTONES	TUSSEHS	TUTTIES
TURBIT	TURK	TURNTABLE	TUSSER	TUTTING
TURBITH	TURKEY	TURNTABLES	TUSSERS	TUTTIS
TURBITHS	TURKEYS	TURNUP	TUSSES	TUTTY
TURBITS	TURKOIS	TURNUPS	TUSSIS	TUTU
TURBO	TURKOISES	TUROPHILE	TUSSISES	TUTUED
TURBOCAR	TURKS	TUROPHILES	TUSSIVE	TUTUS
TURBOCARS	TURMERIC	TURPETH	TUSSLE	TUX
TURBOFAN	TURMERICS	TURPETHS	TUSSLED	TUXEDO
TURBOFANS	TURMOIL	TURPITUDE	TUSSLES	TUXEDOED
TURBOJET	TURMOILED	TURPITUDES	TUSSLING	TUXEDOES
TURBOJETS	TURMOILING	TURPS	TUSSOCK	TUXEDOS
TURBOPROP	TURMOILS	TURQUOIS	TUSSOCKED	TUXES
TURBOPROPS	TURN	TURQUOISE	TUSSOCKS	TUYER
TURBOS	TURNABLE	TURQUOISES	TUSSOCKY	TUYERE
TURBOT	TURNABOUT	TURRET	TUSSOR	TUYERES

TUYERS	TWEEDLED	TWIERS	TWINS	TWOFERS
TWA	TWEEDLES	TWIG	TWINSET	TWOFOLD
TWADDLE	TWEEDLING	TWIGGED	TWINSETS	TWOFOLDS
TWADDLED	TWEEDS	TWIGGEN	TWINSHIP	TWOONIE
TWADDLER	TWEEDY	TWIGGIER	TWINSHIPS	TWOONIES
TWADDLERS	TWEEN	TWIGGIEST	TWINY	TWOPENCE
TWADDLES	TWEENER	TWIGGING	TWIRL	TWOPENCES
TWADDLING	TWEENERS	TWIGGY	TWIRLED	TWOPENNY
TWAE	TWEENESS	TWIGLESS	TWIRLER	TWOS
TWAES	TWEENESSES	TWIGLIKE	TWIRLERS	TWOSOME
TWAIN	TWEENIES	TWIGS	TWIRLIER	TWOSOMES
TWAINS	TWEENS	TWILIGHT	TWIRLIEST	TWYER
TWANG	TWEENY	TWILIGHTS	TWIRLING	TWYERS
TWANGED	TWEET	TWILIT	TWIRLS	TYCOON
TWANGER	TWEETED	TWILL	TWIRLY	TYCOONS
TWANGERS	TWEETER	TWILLED	TWIRP	TYE
TWANGIER	TWEETERS	TWILLING	TWIRPS	TYEE
TWANGIEST	TWEETING	TWILLINGS	TWIST	TYEES
TWANGING	TWEETS	TWILLS	TWISTABLE	TYER
TWANGLE	TWEEZE	TWIN	TWISTED	TYERS
TWANGLED	TWEEZED	TWINBERRIES	TWISTER	TYES
TWANGLER	TWEEZER	TWINBERRY	TWISTERS	TYIN
TWANGLERS	TWEEZERS	TWINBORN	TWISTIER	TYING
TWANGLES	TWEEZES	TWINE	TWISTIEST	TYIYN
TWANGLING	TWEEZING	TWINED	TWISTING	TYKE
TWANGS	TWELFTH	TWINER	TWISTINGS	TYKES
TWANGY	TWELFTHS	TWINERS	TWISTS	TYLOSIN
TWANKIES	TWELVE	TWINES	TWISTY	TYLOSINS
TWANKY	TWELVEMO	TWINGE	TWIT	TYMBAL
TWAS	TWELVEMOS	TWINGED	TWITCH	TYMBALS
TWASOME	TWELVES	TWINGEING	TWITCHED	TYMPAN
TWASOMES	TWENTIES	TWINGES	TWITCHER	TYMPANA
TWAT	TWENTIETH	TWINGING	TWITCHERS	TYMPANAL
TWATS	TWENTIETHS	TWINIER	TWITCHES	TYMPANI
TWATTLE	TWENTY	TWINIEST	TWITCHIER	TYMPANIC
TWATTLED	TWERP	TWINIGHT	TWITCHIEST	TYMPANIES
TWATTLES	TWERPS	TWINING	TWITCHILY	TYMPANIST
TWATTLING	TWIBIL	TWINJET	TWITCHING	TYMPANISTS
TWAYBLADE	TWIBILL	TWINJETS	TWITCHY	TYMPANO
TWAYBLADES	TWIBILLS	TWINKIE	TWITS	TYMPANS
TWEAK	TWIBILS	TWINKIES	TWITTED	TYMPANUM
TWEAKED	TWICE	TWINKLE	TWITTER	TYMPANUMS
TWEAKIER	TWIDDLE	TWINKLED	TWITTERED	TYMPANY
TWEAKIEST	TWIDDLED	TWINKLER	TWITTERER	TYNE
TWEAKING	TWIDDLER	TWINKLERS	TWITTERERS	TYNED
TWEAKS	TWIDDLERS	TWINKLES	TWITTERING	TYNES
TWEAKY	TWIDDLES	TWINKLING	TWITTERS	TYNING
TWEE	TWIDDLIER	TWINKLINGS	TWITTERY	TYPABLE
TWEED	TWIDDLIEST	TWINKLY	TWITTING	TYPAL
TWEEDIER	TWIDDLING	TWINNED	TWIXT	TYPE
TWEEDIEST	TWIDDLY	TWINNING	TWO	TYPEABLE
TWEEDLE	TWIER	TWINNINGS	TWOFER	TYPEBAR

TYPEBARS	TYPOGRAPHED	TZARIST	UGLINESS	ULTIMACIES
TYPECASE	TYPOGRAPHING	TZARISTS	UGLINESSES	ULTIMACY
TYPECASES	TYPOGRAPHS	TZARITZA	UGLY	ULTIMAS
TYPECAST	TYPOLOGIC	TZARITZAS	UGSOME	ULTIMATA
TYPECASTING	TYPOLOGIES	TZARS	UH	ULTIMATE
TYPECASTS	TYPOLOGY	TZETZE	UHLAN	ULTIMATED
TYPED	TYPOS	TZETZES	UHLANS	ULTIMATES
TYPEFACE	TYPP	TZIGANE	UINTAHITE	ULTIMATING
TYPEFACES	TYPPS	TZIGANES	UINTAHITES	ULTIMATUM
TYPES	TYPY	TZIMMES	UINTAITE	ULTIMATUMS
TYPESET	TYRAMINE	TZITZIS	UINTAITES	ULTIMO
TYPESETS	TYRAMINES	TZITZIT	UITLANDER	ULTRA
TYPESETTING	TYRANNIC	TZITZITH	UITLANDERS	ULTRACHIC
TYPESTYLE	TYRANNIES	TZURIS	UKASE	ULTRACOLD
TYPESTYLES	TYRANNISE		UKASES	ULTRACOOL
TYPEWRITE	TYRANNISED		UKE	ULTRADRY
TYPEWRITES	TYRANNISES	**U**	UKELELE	ULTRAFAST
TYPEWRITING	TYRANNISING		UKELELES	ULTRAFINE
TYPEWRITTEN	TYRANNIZE		UKES	ULTRAHEAT
TYPEWROTE	TYRANNIZED	UAKARI	UKULELE	ULTRAHEATED
TYPEY	TYRANNIZES	UAKARIS	UKULELES	ULTRAHEATING
TYPHLITIC	TYRANNIZING	UBIETIES	ULAMA	ULTRAHEATS
TYPHLITIS	TYRANNOUS	UBIETY	ULAMAS	ULTRAHIGH
TYPHLITISES	TYRANNY	UBIQUE	ULAN	ULTRAHIP
TYPHOID	TYRANT	UBIQUITIES	ULANS	ULTRAHOT
TYPHOIDAL	TYRANTS	UBIQUITY	ULCER	ULTRAISM
TYPHOIDS	TYRE	UDDER	ULCERATE	ULTRAISMS
TYPHON	TYRED	UDDERS	ULCERATED	ULTRAIST
TYPHONIC	TYRES	UDO	ULCERATES	ULTRAISTS
TYPHONS	TYRING	UDOMETER	ULCERATING	ULTRALEFT
TYPHOON	TYRO	UDOMETERS	ULCERED	ULTRALOW
TYPHOONS	TYROCIDIN	UDOMETRIES	ULCERING	ULTRAPOSH
TYPHOSE	TYROCIDINS	UDOMETRY	ULCEROUS	ULTRAPURE
TYPHOUS	TYRONIC	UDON	ULCERS	ULTRARARE
TYPHUS	TYROS	UDONS	ULEMA	ULTRARED
TYPHUSES	TYROSINE	UDOS	ULEMAS	ULTRAREDS
TYPIC	TYROSINES	UFOLOGIES	ULEXITE	ULTRARICH
TYPICAL	TYTHE	UFOLOGIST	ULEXITES	ULTRAS
TYPICALLY	TYTHED	UFOLOGISTS	ULLAGE	ULTRASAFE
TYPIER	TYTHES	UFOLOGY	ULLAGED	ULTRASLOW
TYPIEST	TYTHING	UGH	ULLAGES	ULTRASOFT
TYPIFIED	TZADDIK	UGHS	ULNA	ULTRATHIN
TYPIFIER	TZADDIKIM	UGLIER	ULNAD	ULTRATINY
TYPIFIERS	TZAR	UGLIES	ULNAE	ULTRAWIDE
TYPIFIES	TZARDOM	UGLIEST	ULNAR	ULU
TYPIFY	TZARDOMS	UGLIFIED	ULNAS	ULULANT
TYPIFYING	TZAREVNA	UGLIFIER	ULPAN	ULULATE
TYPING	TZAREVNAS	UGLIFIERS	ULPANIM	ULULATED
TYPIST	TZARINA	UGLIFIES	ULSTER	ULULATES
TYPISTS	TZARINAS	UGLIFY	ULSTERS	ULULATING
TYPO	TZARISM	UGLIFYING	ULTERIOR	ULULATION
TYPOGRAPH	TZARISMS	UGLILY	ULTIMA	ULULATIONS

ULUS	UMIAQ	UNAI	UNASKED	UNBEARDED
ULVA	UMIAQS	UNAIDED	UNASSAYED	UNBEARED
ULVAS	UMLAUT	UNAIDEDLY	UNASSURED	UNBEARING
UM	UMLAUTED	UNAIMED	UNATONED	UNBEARS
UMAMI	UMLAUTING	UNAIRED	UNATTIRED	UNBEATEN
UMAMIS	UMLAUTS	UNAIS	UNATTUNED	UNBEING
UMANGITE	UMM	UNAKIN	UNAU	UNBEKNOWN
UMANGITES	UMP	UNAKITE	UNAUDITED	UNBELIEF
UMBEL	UMPED	UNAKITES	UNAUS	UNBELIEFS
UMBELED	UMPING	UNALARMED	UNAVENGED	UNBELOVED
UMBELLAR	UMPIRAGE	UNALERTED	UNAVERAGE	UNBELT
UMBELLATE	UMPIRAGES	UNALIGNED	UNAVERTED	UNBELTED
UMBELLED	UMPIRE	UNALIKE	UNAVOWED	UNBELTING
UMBELLET	UMPIRED	UNALLAYED	UNAWAKE	UNBELTS
UMBELLETS	UMPIRES	UNALLEGED	UNAWAKED	UNBEMUSED
UMBELLULE	UMPIRING	UNALLIED	UNAWARDED	UNBEND
UMBELLULES	UMPS	UNALLOWED	UNAWARE	UNBENDED
UMBELS	UMPTEEN	UNALLOYED	UNAWARELY	UNBENDING
UMBER	UMPTEENTH	UNALTERED	UNAWARES	UNBENDINGS
UMBERED	UMTEENTH	UNAMASSED	UNAWED	UNBENDS
UMBERING	UN	UNAMAZED	UNAWESOME	UNBENIGN
UMBERS	UNABASHED	UNAMENDED	UNAXED	UNBENT
UMBILICAL	UNABATED	UNAMIABLE	UNBACKED	UNBIASED
UMBILICALS	UNABATING	UNAMUSED	UNBAKED	UNBIASSED
UMBILICI	UNABETTED	UNAMUSING	UNBALANCE	UNBID
UMBILICUS	UNABIDING	UNANCHOR	UNBALANCED	UNBIDDEN
UMBILICUSES	UNABJURED	UNANCHORED	UNBALANCES	UNBIGOTED
UMBLES	UNABLE	UNANCHORING	UNBALANCING	UNBILLED
UMBO	UNABORTED	UNANCHORS	UNBALE	UNBIND
UMBONAL	UNABRADED	UNANELED	UNBALED	UNBINDING
UMBONATE	UNABUSED	UNANIMITIES	UNBALES	UNBINDS
UMBONES	UNABUSIVE	UNANIMITY	UNBALING	UNBITTED
UMBONIC	UNACCRUED	UNANIMOUS	UNBAN	UNBITTEN
UMBOS	UNACERBIC	UNANNEXED	UNBANDAGE	UNBITTER
UMBRA	UNACIDIC	UNANNOYED	UNBANDAGED	UNBLAMED
UMBRAE	UNACTABLE	UNAPPLIED	UNBANDAGES	UNBLENDED
UMBRAGE	UNACTED	UNAPT	UNBANDAGING	UNBLESSED
UMBRAGES	UNADAPTED	UNAPTLY	UNBANDED	UNBLEST
UMBRAL	UNADDED	UNAPTNESS	UNBANNED	UNBLINDED
UMBRAS	UNADEPT	UNAPTNESSES	UNBANNING	UNBLOCK
UMBRELLA	UNADEPTLY	UNARCHED	UNBANS	UNBLOCKED
UMBRELLAED	UNADMIRED	UNARGUED	UNBAR	UNBLOCKING
UMBRELLAING	UNADOPTED	UNARM	UNBARBED	UNBLOCKS
UMBRELLAS	UNADORNED	UNARMED	UNBARRED	UNBLOODED
UMBRETTE	UNADULT	UNARMING	UNBARRING	UNBLOODY
UMBRETTES	UNADVISED	UNARMORED	UNBARS	UNBLURRED
UMIAC	UNAFRAID	UNARMS	UNBASED	UNBOARDED
UMIACK	UNAGED	UNAROUSED	UNBASTED	UNBOBBED
UMIACKS	UNAGEING	UNARRAYED	UNBATED	UNBODIED
UMIACS	UNAGILE	UNARTFUL	UNBATHED	UNBOILED
UMIAK	UNAGING	UNARY	UNBE	UNBOLT
UMIAKS	UNAGREED	UNASHAMED	UNBEAR	UNBOLTED

UNBOLTING	UNBRIDLES	UNCANNY	UNCHOKING	UNCLENCHES
UNBOLTS	UNBRIDLING	UNCAP	UNCHOSEN	UNCLENCHING
UNBONDED	UNBRIEFED	UNCAPABLE	UNCHURCH	UNCLES
UNBONED	UNBRIGHT	UNCAPPED	UNCHURCHED	UNCLICHED
UNBONNET	UNBROILED	UNCAPPING	UNCHURCHES	UNCLINCH
UNBONNETED	UNBROKE	UNCAPS	UNCHURCHING	UNCLINCHED
UNBONNETING	UNBROKEN	UNCARDED	UNCI	UNCLINCHES
UNBONNETS	UNBROWNED	UNCARING	UNCIA	UNCLINCHING
UNBOOKISH	UNBRUISED	UNCARTED	UNCIAE	UNCLIP
UNBOOTED	UNBRUSHED	UNCARVED	UNCIAL	UNCLIPPED
UNBORN	UNBUCKLE	UNCASE	UNCIALLY	UNCLIPPING
UNBOSOM	UNBUCKLED	UNCASED	UNCIALS	UNCLIPS
UNBOSOMED	UNBUCKLES	UNCASES	UNCIFORM	UNCLOAK
UNBOSOMER	UNBUCKLING	UNCASHED	UNCIFORMS	UNCLOAKED
UNBOSOMERS	UNBUDGING	UNCASING	UNCINAL	UNCLOAKING
UNBOSOMING	UNBUILD	UNCASKED	UNCINARIA	UNCLOAKS
UNBOSOMS	UNBUILDING	UNCAST	UNCINARIAS	UNCLOG
UNBOTTLE	UNBUILDS	UNCATCHY	UNCINATE	UNCLOGGED
UNBOTTLED	UNBUILT	UNCATERED	UNCINI	UNCLOGGING
UNBOTTLES	UNBULKY	UNCAUGHT	UNCINUS	UNCLOGS
UNBOTTLING	UNBUNDLE	UNCAUSED	UNCIVIL	UNCLOSE
UNBOUGHT	UNBUNDLED	UNCEASING	UNCIVILLY	UNCLOSED
UNBOUNCY	UNBUNDLES	UNCEDED	UNCLAD	UNCLOSES
UNBOUND	UNBUNDLING	UNCERTAIN	UNCLAIMED	UNCLOSING
UNBOUNDED	UNBURDEN	UNCHAIN	UNCLAMP	UNCLOTHE
UNBOWED	UNBURDENED	UNCHAINED	UNCLAMPED	UNCLOTHED
UNBOWING	UNBURDENING	UNCHAINING	UNCLAMPING	UNCLOTHES
UNBOX	UNBURDENS	UNCHAINS	UNCLAMPS	UNCLOTHING
UNBOXED	UNBURIED	UNCHAIR	UNCLARITIES	UNCLOUD
UNBOXES	UNBURNED	UNCHAIRED	UNCLARITY	UNCLOUDED
UNBOXING	UNBURNT	UNCHAIRING	UNCLASP	UNCLOUDING
UNBRACE	UNBUSTED	UNCHAIRS	UNCLASPED	UNCLOUDS
UNBRACED	UNBUSY	UNCHANCY	UNCLASPING	UNCLOUDY
UNBRACES	UNBUTTON	UNCHANGED	UNCLASPS	UNCLOYED
UNBRACING	UNBUTTONED	UNCHARGE	UNCLASSY	UNCLOYING
UNBRAID	UNBUTTONING	UNCHARGED	UNCLAWED	UNCLUTTER
UNBRAIDED	UNBUTTONS	UNCHARGES	UNCLE	UNCLUTTERED
UNBRAIDING	UNCAGE	UNCHARGING	UNCLEAN	UNCLUTTERING
UNBRAIDS	UNCAGED	UNCHARRED	UNCLEANED	UNCLUTTERS
UNBRAKE	UNCAGES	UNCHARTED	UNCLEANER	UNCO
UNBRAKED	UNCAGING	UNCHARY	UNCLEANEST	UNCOATED
UNBRAKES	UNCAKE	UNCHASTE	UNCLEANLIER	UNCOATING
UNBRAKING	UNCAKED	UNCHASTER	UNCLEANLIEST	UNCOATINGS
UNBRANDED	UNCAKES	UNCHASTEST	UNCLEANLY	UNCOBBLED
UNBRED	UNCAKING	UNCHECKED	UNCLEAR	UNCOCK
UNBREECH	UNCALLED	UNCHEWED	UNCLEARED	UNCOCKED
UNBREECHED	UNCANDID	UNCHIC	UNCLEARER	UNCOCKING
UNBREECHES	UNCANDLED	UNCHICLY	UNCLEAREST	UNCOCKS
UNBREECHING	UNCANNED	UNCHILLED	UNCLEARLY	UNCODED
UNBRIDGED	UNCANNIER	UNCHOKE	UNCLEFT	UNCOERCED
UNBRIDLE	UNCANNIEST	UNCHOKED	UNCLENCH	UNCOFFIN
UNBRIDLED	UNCANNILY	UNCHOKES	UNCLENCHED	UNCOFFINED

UNCOFFINING	UNCREATING	UNDECEIVE	UNDERCLAD	UNDERGOD
UNCOFFINS	UNCREWED	UNDECEIVED	UNDERCLAY	UNDERGODS
UNCOIL	UNCROPPED	UNDECEIVES	UNDERCLAYS	UNDERGOER
UNCOILED	UNCROSS	UNDECEIVING	UNDERCOAT	UNDERGOERS
UNCOILING	UNCROSSED	UNDECIDED	UNDERCOATED	UNDERGOES
UNCOILS	UNCROSSES	UNDECIDEDS	UNDERCOATING	UNDERGOING
UNCOINED	UNCROSSING	UNDECKED	UNDERCOATS	UNDERGONE
UNCOLORED	UNCROWDED	UNDEE	UNDERCOOK	UNDERGRAD
UNCOMBED	UNCROWN	UNDEFACED	UNDERCOOKED	UNDERGRADS
UNCOMELY	UNCROWNED	UNDEFILED	UNDERCOOKING	UNDERHAIR
UNCOMIC	UNCROWNING	UNDEFINED	UNDERCOOKS	UNDERHAIRS
UNCOMMON	UNCROWNS	UNDELETED	UNDERCOOL	UNDERHAND
UNCOMMONER	UNCRUMPLE	UNDELUDED	UNDERCOOLED	UNDERHANDS
UNCOMMONEST	UNCRUMPLED	UNDENIED	UNDERCOOLING	UNDERHEAT
UNCONCERN	UNCRUMPLES	UNDENTED	UNDERCOOLS	UNDERHEATED
UNCONCERNS	UNCRUMPLING	UNDER	UNDERCUT	UNDERHEATING
UNCONFUSE	UNCRUSHED	UNDERACT	UNDERCUTS	UNDERHEATS
UNCONFUSED	UNCTION	UNDERACTED	UNDERCUTTING	UNDERHUNG
UNCONFUSES	UNCTIONS	UNDERACTING	UNDERDID	UNDERIVED
UNCONFUSING	UNCTUOUS	UNDERACTS	UNDERDO	UNDERJAW
UNCOOKED	UNCUFF	UNDERAGE	UNDERDOES	UNDERJAWS
UNCOOL	UNCUFFED	UNDERAGED	UNDERDOG	UNDERKILL
UNCOOLED	UNCUFFING	UNDERAGES	UNDERDOGS	UNDERKILLS
UNCORK	UNCUFFS	UNDERARM	UNDERDOING	UNDERLAID
UNCORKED	UNCURABLE	UNDERARMS	UNDERDONE	UNDERLAIN
UNCORKING	UNCURABLY	UNDERATE	UNDERDOSE	UNDERLAP
UNCORKS	UNCURB	UNDERBAKE	UNDERDOSED	UNDERLAPPED
UNCORRUPT	UNCURBED	UNDERBAKED	UNDERDOSES	UNDERLAPPING
UNCOS	UNCURBING	UNDERBAKES	UNDERDOSING	UNDERLAPS
UNCOUNTED	UNCURBS	UNDERBAKING	UNDEREAT	UNDERLAY
UNCOUPLE	UNCURED	UNDERBID	UNDEREATEN	UNDERLAYING
UNCOUPLED	UNCURIOUS	UNDERBIDDING	UNDEREATING	UNDERLAYS
UNCOUPLER	UNCURL	UNDERBIDS	UNDEREATS	UNDERLET
UNCOUPLERS	UNCURLED	UNDERBITE	UNDERFED	UNDERLETS
UNCOUPLES	UNCURLING	UNDERBITES	UNDERFEED	UNDERLETTING
UNCOUPLING	UNCURLS	UNDERBODIES	UNDERFEEDING	UNDERLIE
UNCOUTH	UNCURRENT	UNDERBODY	UNDERFEEDS	UNDERLIES
UNCOUTHLY	UNCURSED	UNDERBOSS	UNDERFLOW	UNDERLINE
UNCOVER	UNCUS	UNDERBOSSES	UNDERFLOWS	UNDERLINED
UNCOVERED	UNCUT	UNDERBOUGHT	UNDERFOOT	UNDERLINES
UNCOVERING	UNCUTE	UNDERBRED	UNDERFUND	UNDERLING
UNCOVERS	UNCYNICAL	UNDERBRIM	UNDERFUNDED	UNDERLINGS
UNCOY	UNDAMAGED	UNDERBRIMS	UNDERFUNDING	UNDERLINING
UNCRACKED	UNDAMPED	UNDERBUD	UNDERFUNDS	UNDERLIP
UNCRATE	UNDARING	UNDERBUDDED	UNDERFUR	UNDERLIPS
UNCRATED	UNDATABLE	UNDERBUDDING	UNDERFURS	UNDERLIT
UNCRATES	UNDATED	UNDERBUDS	UNDERGIRD	UNDERLOAD
UNCRATING	UNDAUNTED	UNDERBUY	UNDERGIRDED	UNDERLOADED
UNCRAZY	UNDE	UNDERBUYING	UNDERGIRDING	UNDERLOADING
UNCREATE	UNDEAD	UNDERBUYS	UNDERGIRDS	UNDERLOADS
UNCREATED	UNDEBATED	UNDERCARD	UNDERGIRT	UNDERLYING
UNCREATES	UNDECAYED	UNDERCARDS	UNDERGO	UNDERMINE

UNDERMINED	UNDERSIZE	UNDINE	UNDULATOR	UNEVENER
UNDERMINES	UNDERSOIL	UNDINES	UNDULATORS	UNEVENEST
UNDERMINING	UNDERSOILS	UNDIVIDED	UNDULLED	UNEVENLY
UNDERMOST	UNDERSOLD	UNDO	UNDULY	UNEVOLVED
UNDERPAID	UNDERSONG	UNDOABLE	UNDUTIFUL	UNEXALTED
UNDERPART	UNDERSONGS	UNDOCILE	UNDY	UNEXCITED
UNDERPARTS	UNDERSPIN	UNDOCK	UNDYED	UNEXCUSED
UNDERPASS	UNDERSPINS	UNDOCKED	UNDYING	UNEXOTIC
UNDERPASSES	UNDERTAKE	UNDOCKING	UNDYINGLY	UNEXPERT
UNDERPAY	UNDERTAKEN	UNDOCKS	UNDYNAMIC	UNEXPIRED
UNDERPAYING	UNDERTAKES	UNDOER	UNEAGER	UNEXPOSED
UNDERPAYS	UNDERTAKING	UNDOERS	UNEAGERLY	UNFADED
UNDERPIN	UNDERTAX	UNDOES	UNEARNED	UNFADING
UNDERPINNED	UNDERTAXED	UNDOING	UNEARTH	UNFAILING
UNDERPINNING	UNDERTAXES	UNDOINGS	UNEARTHED	UNFAIR
UNDERPINS	UNDERTAXING	UNDONE	UNEARTHING	UNFAIRER
UNDERPLAY	UNDERTINT	UNDOTTED	UNEARTHLIER	UNFAIREST
UNDERPLAYED	UNDERTINTS	UNDOUBLE	UNEARTHLIEST	UNFAIRLY
UNDERPLAYING	UNDERTONE	UNDOUBLED	UNEARTHLY	UNFAITH
UNDERPLAYS	UNDERTONES	UNDOUBLES	UNEARTHS	UNFAITHS
UNDERPLOT	UNDERTOOK	UNDOUBLING	UNEASE	UNFAKED
UNDERPLOTS	UNDERTOW	UNDOUBTED	UNEASES	UNFALLEN
UNDERPROP	UNDERTOWS	UNDRAINED	UNEASIER	UNFAMOUS
UNDERPROPPED	UNDERUSE	UNDRAPE	UNEASIEST	UNFANCY
UNDERPROPPING	UNDERUSED	UNDRAPED	UNEASILY	UNFASTEN
UNDERPROPS	UNDERUSES	UNDRAPES	UNEASY	UNFASTENED
UNDERRAN	UNDERUSING	UNDRAPING	UNEATABLE	UNFASTENING
UNDERRATE	UNDERVEST	UNDRAW	UNEATEN	UNFASTENS
UNDERRATED	UNDERVESTS	UNDRAWING	UNEDIBLE	UNFAVORED
UNDERRATES	UNDERVOTE	UNDRAWN	UNEDITED	UNFAZED
UNDERRATING	UNDERVOTES	UNDRAWS	UNEFFACED	UNFEARED
UNDERRIPE	UNDERWAY	UNDREAMED	UNELECTED	UNFEARFUL
UNDERRUN	UNDERWEAR	UNDREAMT	UNENDED	UNFEARING
UNDERRUNNING	UNDERWENT	UNDRESS	UNENDING	UNFED
UNDERRUNS	UNDERWING	UNDRESSED	UNENDOWED	UNFEELING
UNDERSEA	UNDERWINGS	UNDRESSES	UNENGAGED	UNFEIGNED
UNDERSEAS	UNDERWIRE	UNDRESSING	UNENJOYED	UNFELT
UNDERSELL	UNDERWIRES	UNDREST	UNENSURED	UNFELTED
UNDERSELLING	UNDERWOOD	UNDREW	UNENTERED	UNFENCE
UNDERSELLS	UNDERWOODS	UNDRIED	UNENVIED	UNFENCED
UNDERSET	UNDERWOOL	UNDRILLED	UNENVIOUS	UNFENCES
UNDERSETS	UNDERWOOLS	UNDRUNK	UNEQUAL	UNFENCING
UNDERSHOOT	UNDERWORK	UNDUBBED	UNEQUALED	UNFERTILE
UNDERSHOOTING	UNDERWORKED	UNDUE	UNEQUALLY	UNFETTER
UNDERSHOOTS	UNDERWORKING	UNDULANCE	UNEQUALS	UNFETTERED
UNDERSHOT	UNDERWORKS	UNDULANCES	UNERASED	UNFETTERING
UNDERSIDE	UNDESIRED	UNDULANT	UNEROTIC	UNFETTERS
UNDERSIDES	UNDEVOUT	UNDULAR	UNERRING	UNFILIAL
UNDERSIGN	UNDID	UNDULATE	UNESSAYED	UNFILLED
UNDERSIGNED	UNDIES	UNDULATED	UNETHICAL	UNFILMED
UNDERSIGNING	UNDILUTED	UNDULATES	UNEVADED	UNFIRED
UNDERSIGNS	UNDIMMED	UNDULATING	UNEVEN	UNFISHED

UNFIT	UNFUNDED	UNGROUPED	UNHARNESSES	UNHOPEFUL
UNFITLY	UNFUNNY	UNGUAL	UNHARNESSING	UNHORSE
UNFITNESS	UNFURL	UNGUARD	UNHARRIED	UNHORSED
UNFITNESSES	UNFURLED	UNGUARDED	UNHASTY	UNHORSES
UNFITS	UNFURLING	UNGUARDING	UNHAT	UNHORSING
UNFITTED	UNFURLS	UNGUARDS	UNHATCHED	UNHOSTILE
UNFITTING	UNFUSED	UNGUENT	UNHATS	UNHOUSE
UNFIX	UNFUSSILY	UNGUENTA	UNHATTED	UNHOUSED
UNFIXED	UNFUSSY	UNGUENTS	UNHATTING	UNHOUSES
UNFIXES	UNGAINLIER	UNGUENTUM	UNHEALED	UNHOUSING
UNFIXING	UNGAINLIEST	UNGUES	UNHEALTHIER	UNHUMAN
UNFIXT	UNGAINLY	UNGUIDED	UNHEALTHIEST	UNHUMANLY
UNFLAPPED	UNGALLANT	UNGUINOUS	UNHEALTHY	UNHUMBLED
UNFLASHY	UNGALLED	UNGUIS	UNHEARD	UNHUNG
UNFLAWED	UNGARBED	UNGULA	UNHEATED	UNHURRIED
UNFLEDGED	UNGATED	UNGULAE	UNHEDGED	UNHURT
UNFLEXED	UNGAZING	UNGULAR	UNHEEDED	UNHUSK
UNFLUTED	UNGELDED	UNGULATE	UNHEEDFUL	UNHUSKED
UNFLYABLE	UNGENIAL	UNGULATES	UNHEEDING	UNHUSKING
UNFOCUSED	UNGENTEEL	UNHAILED	UNHELM	UNHUSKS
UNFOILED	UNGENTLE	UNHAIR	UNHELMED	UNIALGAL
UNFOLD	UNGENTLY	UNHAIRED	UNHELMING	UNIAXIAL
UNFOLDED	UNGENUINE	UNHAIRER	UNHELMS	UNIBODY
UNFOLDER	UNGIFTED	UNHAIRERS	UNHELPED	UNICOLOR
UNFOLDERS	UNGIRD	UNHAIRING	UNHELPFUL	UNICORN
UNFOLDING	UNGIRDED	UNHAIRS	UNHEROIC	UNICORNS
UNFOLDS	UNGIRDING	UNHALLOW	UNHEWN	UNICYCLE
UNFOND	UNGIRDS	UNHALLOWED	UNHINGE	UNICYCLED
UNFORCED	UNGIRT	UNHALLOWING	UNHINGED	UNICYCLES
UNFORGED	UNGIVING	UNHALLOWS	UNHINGES	UNICYCLING
UNFORGOT	UNGLAZED	UNHALVED	UNHINGING	UNIDEAED
UNFORKED	UNGLOSSED	UNHAND	UNHIP	UNIDEAL
UNFORMED	UNGLOVE	UNHANDED	UNHIRABLE	UNIFACE
UNFOUGHT	UNGLOVED	UNHANDIER	UNHIRED	UNIFACES
UNFOUND	UNGLOVES	UNHANDIEST	UNHITCH	UNIFIABLE
UNFOUNDED	UNGLOVING	UNHANDILY	UNHITCHED	UNIFIC
UNFRAMED	UNGLUE	UNHANDING	UNHITCHES	UNIFIED
UNFREE	UNGLUED	UNHANDLED	UNHITCHING	UNIFIER
UNFREED	UNGLUES	UNHANDS	UNHOLIER	UNIFIERS
UNFREEDOM	UNGLUING	UNHANDY	UNHOLIEST	UNIFIES
UNFREEDOMS	UNGODLIER	UNHANG	UNHOLILY	UNIFILAR
UNFREEING	UNGODLIEST	UNHANGED	UNHOLY	UNIFORM
UNFREES	UNGODLY	UNHANGING	UNHONORED	UNIFORMED
UNFREEZE	UNGOT	UNHANGS	UNHOOD	UNIFORMER
UNFREEZES	UNGOTTEN	UNHAPPIER	UNHOODED	UNIFORMEST
UNFREEZING	UNGOWNED	UNHAPPIEST	UNHOODING	UNIFORMING
UNFROCK	UNGRACED	UNHAPPILY	UNHOODS	UNIFORMLY
UNFROCKED	UNGRADED	UNHAPPY	UNHOOK	UNIFORMS
UNFROCKING	UNGREASED	UNHARMED	UNHOOKED	UNIFY
UNFROCKS	UNGREEDY	UNHARMFUL	UNHOOKING	UNIFYING
UNFROZE	UNGROOMED	UNHARNESS	UNHOOKS	UNIJUGATE
UNFROZEN	UNGROUND	UNHARNESSED	UNHOPED	UNILINEAL

UNILINEAR	UNISONS	UNJOYFUL	UNLADING	UNLIMBERS
UNILOBED	UNISSUED	UNJUDGED	UNLAID	UNLIMITED
UNIMBUED	UNIT	UNJUST	UNLASH	UNLINED
UNIMPEDED	UNITAGE	UNJUSTLY	UNLASHED	UNLINK
UNINDEXED	UNITAGES	UNKEELED	UNLASHES	UNLINKED
UNINJURED	UNITARD	UNKEMPT	UNLASHING	UNLINKING
UNINSTALL	UNITARDS	UNKEND	UNLATCH	UNLINKS
UNINSTALLED	UNITARIAN	UNKENNED	UNLATCHED	UNLISTED
UNINSTALLING	UNITARIANS	UNKENNEL	UNLATCHES	UNLIT
UNINSTALLS	UNITARILY	UNKENNELED	UNLATCHING	UNLIVABLE
UNINSURED	UNITARY	UNKENNELING	UNLAWFUL	UNLIVE
UNINSUREDS	UNITE	UNKENNELLED	UNLAY	UNLIVED
UNINVITED	UNITED	UNKENNELLING	UNLAYING	UNLIVELY
UNINVOKED	UNITEDLY	UNKENNELS	UNLAYS	UNLIVES
UNION	UNITER	UNKENT	UNLEAD	UNLIVING
UNIONISE	UNITERS	UNKEPT	UNLEADED	UNLOAD
UNIONISED	UNITES	UNKIND	UNLEADEDS	UNLOADED
UNIONISES	UNITIES	UNKINDER	UNLEADING	UNLOADER
UNIONISING	UNITING	UNKINDEST	UNLEADS	UNLOADERS
UNIONISM	UNITIVE	UNKINDLED	UNLEARN	UNLOADING
UNIONISMS	UNITIVELY	UNKINDLIER	UNLEARNED	UNLOADS
UNIONIST	UNITIZE	UNKINDLIEST	UNLEARNING	UNLOBED
UNIONISTS	UNITIZED	UNKINDLY	UNLEARNS	UNLOCATED
UNIONIZE	UNITIZER	UNKINGLY	UNLEARNT	UNLOCK
UNIONIZED	UNITIZERS	UNKINK	UNLEASED	UNLOCKED
UNIONIZER	UNITIZES	UNKINKED	UNLEASH	UNLOCKING
UNIONIZERS	UNITIZING	UNKINKING	UNLEASHED	UNLOCKS
UNIONIZES	UNITRUST	UNKINKS	UNLEASHES	UNLOOSE
UNIONIZING	UNITRUSTS	UNKISSED	UNLEASHING	UNLOOSED
UNIONS	UNITS	UNKNIT	UNLED	UNLOOSEN
UNIPAROUS	UNITY	UNKNITS	UNLESS	UNLOOSENED
UNIPLANAR	UNIVALENT	UNKNITTED	UNLET	UNLOOSENING
UNIPOD	UNIVALENTS	UNKNITTING	UNLETHAL	UNLOOSENS
UNIPODS	UNIVALVE	UNKNOT	UNLETTED	UNLOOSES
UNIPOLAR	UNIVALVED	UNKNOTS	UNLEVEL	UNLOOSING
UNIPOTENT	UNIVALVES	UNKNOTTED	UNLEVELED	UNLOVABLE
UNIQUE	UNIVERSAL	UNKNOTTING	UNLEVELING	UNLOVED
UNIQUELY	UNIVERSALS	UNKNOWING	UNLEVELLED	UNLOVELIER
UNIQUER	UNIVERSE	UNKNOWINGS	UNLEVELLING	UNLOVELIEST
UNIQUES	UNIVERSES	UNKNOWN	UNLEVELS	UNLOVELY
UNIQUEST	UNIVOCAL	UNKNOWNS	UNLEVIED	UNLOVING
UNIRAMOUS	UNIVOCALS	UNKOSHER	UNLICKED	UNLUCKIER
UNIRONED	UNJADED	UNLABELED	UNLIGHTED	UNLUCKIEST
UNIRONIC	UNJAM	UNLABORED	UNLIKABLE	UNLUCKILY
UNISEX	UNJAMMED	UNLACE	UNLIKE	UNLUCKY
UNISEXES	UNJAMMING	UNLACED	UNLIKED	UNLYRICAL
UNISEXUAL	UNJAMS	UNLACES	UNLIKELIER	UNMACHO
UNISIZE	UNJOINED	UNLACING	UNLIKELIEST	UNMADE
UNISON	UNJOINT	UNLADE	UNLIKELY	UNMAILED
UNISONAL	UNJOINTED	UNLADED	UNLIMBER	UNMAKE
UNISONANT	UNJOINTING	UNLADEN	UNLIMBERED	UNMAKER
UNISONOUS	UNJOINTS	UNLADES	UNLIMBERING	UNMAKERS

UNMAKES	UNMITER	UNNATURAL	UNPERSONS	UNPRIZED
UNMAKING	UNMITERED	UNNEEDED	UNPICK	UNPROBED
UNMAN	UNMITERING	UNNEEDFUL	UNPICKED	UNPROVED
UNMANAGED	UNMITERS	UNNERVE	UNPICKING	UNPROVEN
UNMANFUL	UNMITRE	UNNERVED	UNPICKS	UNPRUNED
UNMANLIER	UNMITRED	UNNERVES	UNPIERCED	UNPUCKER
UNMANLIEST	UNMITRES	UNNERVING	UNPILE	UNPUCKERED
UNMANLY	UNMITRING	UNNOISY	UNPILED	UNPUCKERING
UNMANNED	UNMIX	UNNOTED	UNPILES	UNPUCKERS
UNMANNING	UNMIXABLE	UNNOTICED	UNPILING	UNPURE
UNMANNISH	UNMIXED	UNNUANCED	UNPIN	UNPURELY
UNMANS	UNMIXEDLY	UNOFFERED	UNPINNED	UNPURGED
UNMAPPED	UNMIXES	UNOILED	UNPINNING	UNPUZZLE
UNMARKED	UNMIXING	UNOPEN	UNPINS	UNPUZZLED
UNMARRED	UNMIXT	UNOPENED	UNPITIED	UNPUZZLES
UNMARRIED	UNMODISH	UNOPPOSED	UNPITTED	UNPUZZLING
UNMARRIEDS	UNMOLD	UNORDERED	UNPITYING	UNQUAKING
UNMASK	UNMOLDED	UNORDERLY	UNPLACED	UNQUELLED
UNMASKED	UNMOLDING	UNORNATE	UNPLAIT	UNQUIET
UNMASKER	UNMOLDS	UNOWNED	UNPLAITED	UNQUIETER
UNMASKERS	UNMOLTEN	UNPACK	UNPLAITING	UNQUIETEST
UNMASKING	UNMOOR	UNPACKED	UNPLAITS	UNQUIETLY
UNMASKS	UNMOORED	UNPACKER	UNPLANNED	UNQUIETS
UNMATCHED	UNMOORING	UNPACKERS	UNPLANTED	UNQUOTE
UNMATED	UNMOORS	UNPACKING	UNPLAYED	UNQUOTED
UNMATTED	UNMORAL	UNPACKS	UNPLEASED	UNQUOTES
UNMATURED	UNMORALLY	UNPADDED	UNPLEDGED	UNQUOTING
UNMEANING	UNMORTISE	UNPAGED	UNPLIABLE	UNRAISED
UNMEANT	UNMORTISED	UNPAID	UNPLIANT	UNRAKED
UNMEET	UNMORTISES	UNPAINFUL	UNPLOWED	UNRANKED
UNMEETLY	UNMORTISING	UNPAINTED	UNPLUCKED	UNRATED
UNMELLOW	UNMOUNTED	UNPAIRED	UNPLUG	UNRAVAGED
UNMELTED	UNMOURNED	UNPARTED	UNPLUGGED	UNRAVEL
UNMENDED	UNMOVABLE	UNPATCHED	UNPLUGGING	UNRAVELED
UNMERITED	UNMOVED	UNPAVED	UNPLUGS	UNRAVELING
UNMERRY	UNMOVING	UNPAYING	UNPLUMBED	UNRAVELLED
UNMESH	UNMOWN	UNPEELED	UNPOETIC	UNRAVELLING
UNMESHED	UNMUFFLE	UNPEG	UNPOINTED	UNRAVELS
UNMESHES	UNMUFFLED	UNPEGGED	UNPOISED	UNRAZED
UNMESHING	UNMUFFLES	UNPEGGING	UNPOLICED	UNREACHED
UNMET	UNMUFFLING	UNPEGS	UNPOLITE	UNREAD
UNMEW	UNMUSICAL	UNPEN	UNPOLITIC	UNREADIER
UNMEWED	UNMUZZLE	UNPENNED	UNPOLLED	UNREADIEST
UNMEWING	UNMUZZLED	UNPENNING	UNPOPULAR	UNREADILY
UNMEWS	UNMUZZLES	UNPENS	UNPOSED	UNREADY
UNMILLED	UNMUZZLING	UNPENT	UNPOSTED	UNREAL
UNMINDFUL	UNNAIL	UNPEOPLE	UNPOTTED	UNREALITIES
UNMINED	UNNAILED	UNPEOPLED	UNPRESSED	UNREALITY
UNMINGLE	UNNAILING	UNPEOPLES	UNPRETTY	UNREALLY
UNMINGLED	UNNAILS	UNPEOPLING	UNPRICED	UNREASON
UNMINGLES	UNNAMABLE	UNPERFECT	UNPRIMED	UNREASONED
UNMINGLING	UNNAMED	UNPERSON	UNPRINTED	UNREASONING

UNREASONS	UNRIPELY	UNSAINTLY	UNSERIOUS	UNSHOD
UNREBUKED	UNRIPENED	UNSALABLE	UNSERVED	UNSHORN
UNREEL	UNRIPER	UNSALABLY	UNSET	UNSHOWY
UNREELED	UNRIPEST	UNSALTED	UNSETS	UNSHRUNK
UNREELER	UNRIPPED	UNSAMPLED	UNSETTING	UNSHUT
UNREELERS	UNRIPPING	UNSATED	UNSETTLE	UNSICKER
UNREELING	UNRIPS	UNSAVED	UNSETTLED	UNSIFTED
UNREELS	UNRISEN	UNSAVORY	UNSETTLES	UNSIGHT
UNREEVE	UNRIVALED	UNSAVOURY	UNSETTLING	UNSIGHTED
UNREEVED	UNROASTED	UNSAWED	UNSEW	UNSIGHTING
UNREEVES	UNROBE	UNSAWN	UNSEWED	UNSIGHTLIER
UNREEVING	UNROBED	UNSAY	UNSEWING	UNSIGHTLIEST
UNREFINED	UNROBES	UNSAYABLE	UNSEWN	UNSIGHTLY
UNRELATED	UNROBING	UNSAYABLES	UNSEWS	UNSIGHTS
UNRELAXED	UNROLL	UNSAYING	UNSEX	UNSIGNED
UNRENEWED	UNROLLED	UNSAYS	UNSEXED	UNSILENT
UNRENT	UNROLLING	UNSCALED	UNSEXES	UNSIMILAR
UNRENTED	UNROLLS	UNSCANNED	UNSEXING	UNSINFUL
UNREPAID	UNROOF	UNSCARRED	UNSEXUAL	UNSIZED
UNREPAIR	UNROOFED	UNSCATHED	UNSEXY	UNSKILFUL
UNREPAIRS	UNROOFING	UNSCENTED	UNSHACKLE	UNSKILLED
UNRESERVE	UNROOFS	UNSCREW	UNSHACKLED	UNSLAKED
UNRESERVES	UNROOT	UNSCREWED	UNSHACKLES	UNSLICED
UNREST	UNROOTED	UNSCREWING	UNSHACKLING	UNSLICK
UNRESTED	UNROOTING	UNSCREWS	UNSHADED	UNSLING
UNRESTFUL	UNROOTS	UNSEAL	UNSHAKEN	UNSLINGING
UNRESTING	UNROPED	UNSEALED	UNSHAMED	UNSLINGS
UNRESTS	UNROUGH	UNSEALING	UNSHAPED	UNSLUNG
UNRETIRE	UNROUND	UNSEALS	UNSHAPELY	UNSMART
UNRETIRED	UNROUNDED	UNSEAM	UNSHAPEN	UNSMILING
UNRETIRES	UNROUNDING	UNSEAMED	UNSHARED	UNSMOKED
UNRETIRING	UNROUNDS	UNSEAMING	UNSHARP	UNSNAG
UNREVISED	UNROVE	UNSEAMS	UNSHAVED	UNSNAGGED
UNREVOKED	UNROVEN	UNSEARED	UNSHAVEN	UNSNAGGING
UNRHYMED	UNRUFFLED	UNSEAT	UNSHEATHE	UNSNAGS
UNRIBBED	UNRULED	UNSEATED	UNSHEATHED	UNSNAP
UNRIDABLE	UNRULIER	UNSEATING	UNSHEATHES	UNSNAPPED
UNRIDDLE	UNRULIEST	UNSEATS	UNSHEATHING	UNSNAPPING
UNRIDDLED	UNRULY	UNSECURED	UNSHED	UNSNAPS
UNRIDDLER	UNRUMPLED	UNSEEABLE	UNSHELL	UNSNARL
UNRIDDLERS	UNRUSHED	UNSEEDED	UNSHELLED	UNSNARLED
UNRIDDLES	UNRUSTED	UNSEEING	UNSHELLING	UNSNARLING
UNRIDDLING	UNS	UNSEEMLIER	UNSHELLS	UNSNARLS
UNRIFLED	UNSADDLE	UNSEEMLIEST	UNSHIFT	UNSOAKED
UNRIG	UNSADDLED	UNSEEMLY	UNSHIFTED	UNSOBER
UNRIGGED	UNSADDLES	UNSEEN	UNSHIFTING	UNSOBERLY
UNRIGGING	UNSADDLING	UNSEIZED	UNSHIFTS	UNSOCIAL
UNRIGS	UNSAFE	UNSELFISH	UNSHIP	UNSOILED
UNRIMED	UNSAFELY	UNSELL	UNSHIPPED	UNSOLD
UNRINSED	UNSAFETIES	UNSELLING	UNSHIPPING	UNSOLDER
UNRIP	UNSAFETY	UNSELLS	UNSHIPS	UNSOLDERED
UNRIPE	UNSAID	UNSENT	UNSHIRTED	UNSOLDERING

UNSOLDERS	UNSTALKED	UNSTRUNG	UNTEACHING	UNTORN
UNSOLID	UNSTAMPED	UNSTUCK	UNTENABLE	UNTOUCHED
UNSOLVED	UNSTARRED	UNSTUDIED	UNTENABLY	UNTOWARD
UNSONCY	UNSTATE	UNSTUFFED	UNTENDED	UNTRACED
UNSONSIE	UNSTATED	UNSTUFFY	UNTENTED	UNTRACK
UNSONSY	UNSTATES	UNSTUNG	UNTENURED	UNTRACKED
UNSOOTHED	UNSTATING	UNSTYLISH	UNTESTED	UNTRACKING
UNSORTED	UNSTAYED	UNSUBDUED	UNTETHER	UNTRACKS
UNSOUGHT	UNSTEADIED	UNSUBTLE	UNTETHERED	UNTRAINED
UNSOUND	UNSTEADIER	UNSUBTLY	UNTETHERING	UNTRAPPED
UNSOUNDED	UNSTEADIES	UNSUCCESS	UNTETHERS	UNTREAD
UNSOUNDER	UNSTEADIEST	UNSUCCESSES	UNTHANKED	UNTREADED
UNSOUNDEST	UNSTEADY	UNSUITED	UNTHAWED	UNTREADING
UNSOUNDLY	UNSTEADYING	UNSULLIED	UNTHINK	UNTREADS
UNSOURCED	UNSTEEL	UNSUNG	UNTHINKING	UNTREATED
UNSOURED	UNSTEELED	UNSUNK	UNTHINKS	UNTRENDY
UNSOWED	UNSTEELING	UNSURE	UNTHOUGHT	UNTRIED
UNSOWN	UNSTEELS	UNSURELY	UNTHREAD	UNTRIM
UNSPARING	UNSTEMMED	UNSWATHE	UNTHREADED	UNTRIMMED
UNSPEAK	UNSTEP	UNSWATHED	UNTHREADING	UNTRIMMING
UNSPEAKING	UNSTEPPED	UNSWATHES	UNTHREADS	UNTRIMS
UNSPEAKS	UNSTEPPING	UNSWATHING	UNTHRIFTY	UNTROD
UNSPENT	UNSTEPS	UNSWAYED	UNTHRONE	UNTRODDEN
UNSPHERE	UNSTERILE	UNSWEAR	UNTHRONED	UNTRUE
UNSPHERED	UNSTICK	UNSWEARING	UNTHRONES	UNTRUER
UNSPHERES	UNSTICKING	UNSWEARS	UNTHRONING	UNTRUEST
UNSPHERING	UNSTICKS	UNSWEPT	UNTIDIED	UNTRULY
UNSPILLED	UNSTINTED	UNSWOLLEN	UNTIDIER	UNTRUSS
UNSPILT	UNSTITCH	UNSWORE	UNTIDIES	UNTRUSSED
UNSPLIT	UNSTITCHED	UNSWORN	UNTIDIEST	UNTRUSSES
UNSPOILED	UNSTITCHES	UNTACK	UNTIDILY	UNTRUSSING
UNSPOILT	UNSTITCHING	UNTACKED	UNTIDY	UNTRUSTY
UNSPOKE	UNSTOCKED	UNTACKING	UNTIDYING	UNTRUTH
UNSPOKEN	UNSTONED	UNTACKS	UNTIE	UNTRUTHS
UNSPOOL	UNSTOP	UNTACTFUL	UNTIED	UNTUCK
UNSPOOLED	UNSTOPPED	UNTAGGED	UNTIEING	UNTUCKED
UNSPOOLING	UNSTOPPER	UNTAINTED	UNTIES	UNTUCKING
UNSPOOLS	UNSTOPPERED	UNTAKEN	UNTIL	UNTUCKS
UNSPOTTED	UNSTOPPERING	UNTAMABLE	UNTILLED	UNTUFTED
UNSPRAYED	UNSTOPPERS	UNTAME	UNTILTED	UNTUNABLE
UNSPRUNG	UNSTOPPING	UNTAMED	UNTIMED	UNTUNE
UNSPUN	UNSTOPS	UNTANGLE	UNTIMELIER	UNTUNED
UNSQUARED	UNSTRAP	UNTANGLED	UNTIMELIEST	UNTUNEFUL
UNSTABLE	UNSTRAPPED	UNTANGLES	UNTIMELY	UNTUNES
UNSTABLER	UNSTRAPPING	UNTANGLING	UNTIMEOUS	UNTUNING
UNSTABLEST	UNSTRAPS	UNTANNED	UNTINGED	UNTURNED
UNSTABLY	UNSTRESS	UNTAPPED	UNTIPPED	UNTUTORED
UNSTACK	UNSTRESSES	UNTASTED	UNTIRED	UNTWILLED
UNSTACKED	UNSTRING	UNTAUGHT	UNTIRING	UNTWINE
UNSTACKING	UNSTRINGING	UNTAXED	UNTITLED	UNTWINED
UNSTACKS	UNSTRINGS	UNTEACH	UNTO	UNTWINES
UNSTAINED	UNSTRIPED	UNTEACHES	UNTOLD	UNTWINING

UNTWIST	UNWATCHED	UNWOMANLY	UPBEARING	UPCURLING
UNTWISTED	UNWATERED	UNWON	UPBEARS	UPCURLS
UNTWISTING	UNWAXED	UNWONTED	UPBEAT	UPCURVE
UNTWISTS	UNWEANED	UNWOODED	UPBEATS	UPCURVED
UNTYING	UNWEARIED	UNWOOED	UPBIND	UPCURVES
UNTYPICAL	UNWEARY	UNWORKED	UPBINDING	UPCURVING
UNUNBIUM	UNWEAVE	UNWORLDLIER	UPBINDS	UPDART
UNUNBIUMS	UNWEAVES	UNWORLDLIEST	UPBOIL	UPDARTED
UNUNITED	UNWEAVING	UNWORLDLY	UPBOILED	UPDARTING
UNUNUNIUM	UNWED	UNWORN	UPBOILING	UPDARTS
UNUNUNIUMS	UNWEDDED	UNWORRIED	UPBOILS	UPDATE
UNURGED	UNWEEDED	UNWORTHIER	UPBORE	UPDATED
UNUSABLE	UNWEETING	UNWORTHIES	UPBORNE	UPDATER
UNUSED	UNWEIGHED	UNWORTHIEST	UPBOUND	UPDATERS
UNUSUAL	UNWEIGHT	UNWORTHY	UPBOW	UPDATES
UNUSUALLY	UNWEIGHTED	UNWOUND	UPBOWS	UPDATING
UNUTTERED	UNWEIGHTING	UNWOUNDED	UPBRAID	UPDIVE
UNVALUED	UNWEIGHTS	UNWOVE	UPBRAIDED	UPDIVED
UNVARIED	UNWELCOME	UNWOVEN	UPBRAIDER	UPDIVES
UNVARYING	UNWELDED	UNWRAP	UPBRAIDERS	UPDIVING
UNVEIL	UNWELL	UNWRAPPED	UPBRAIDING	UPDO
UNVEILED	UNWEPT	UNWRAPPING	UPBRAIDS	UPDOS
UNVEILING	UNWET	UNWRAPS	UPBUILD	UPDOVE
UNVEILINGS	UNWETTED	UNWREATHE	UPBUILDER	UPDRAFT
UNVEILS	UNWHIPPED	UNWREATHED	UPBUILDERS	UPDRAFTS
UNVEINED	UNWHITE	UNWREATHES	UPBUILDING	UPDRIED
UNVERSED	UNWIELDIER	UNWREATHING	UPBUILDS	UPDRIES
UNVESTED	UNWIELDIEST	UNWRINKLE	UPBUILT	UPDRY
UNVEXED	UNWIELDY	UNWRINKLED	UPBY	UPDRYING
UNVEXT	UNWIFELY	UNWRINKLES	UPBYE	UPEND
UNVIABLE	UNWILLED	UNWRINKLING	UPCAST	UPENDED
UNVISITED	UNWILLING	UNWRITTEN	UPCASTING	UPENDING
UNVOCAL	UNWIND	UNWROUGHT	UPCASTS	UPENDS
UNVOICE	UNWINDER	UNWRUNG	UPCHUCK	UPFIELD
UNVOICED	UNWINDERS	UNYEANED	UPCHUCKED	UPFLING
UNVOICES	UNWINDING	UNYOKE	UPCHUCKING	UPFLINGING
UNVOICING	UNWINDS	UNYOKED	UPCHUCKS	UPFLINGS
UNWAKENED	UNWINKING	UNYOKES	UPCLIMB	UPFLOW
UNWALLED	UNWISDOM	UNYOKING	UPCLIMBED	UPFLOWED
UNWANING	UNWISDOMS	UNYOUNG	UPCLIMBING	UPFLOWING
UNWANTED	UNWISE	UNZEALOUS	UPCLIMBS	UPFLOWS
UNWARIER	UNWISELY	UNZIP	UPCOAST	UPFLUNG
UNWARIEST	UNWISER	UNZIPPED	UPCOIL	UPFOLD
UNWARILY	UNWISEST	UNZIPPING	UPCOILED	UPFOLDED
UNWARLIKE	UNWISH	UNZIPS	UPCOILING	UPFOLDING
UNWARMED	UNWISHED	UNZONED	UPCOILS	UPFOLDS
UNWARNED	UNWISHES	UP	UPCOMING	UPFRONT
UNWARPED	UNWISHING	UPAS	UPCOUNTRIES	UPGATHER
UNWARY	UNWIT	UPASES	UPCOUNTRY	UPGATHERED
UNWASHED	UNWITS	UPBEAR	UPCOURT	UPGATHERING
UNWASHEDS	UNWITTED	UPBEARER	UPCURL	UPGATHERS
UNWASTED	UNWITTING	UPBEARERS	UPCURLED	UPGAZE

UPGAZED	UPKEEPS	UPPING	UPROUSE	UPSTAGER
UPGAZES	UPLAND	UPPINGS	UPROUSED	UPSTAGERS
UPGAZING	UPLANDER	UPPISH	UPROUSES	UPSTAGES
UPGIRD	UPLANDERS	UPPISHLY	UPROUSING	UPSTAGING
UPGIRDED	UPLANDS	UPPITY	UPRUSH	UPSTAIR
UPGIRDING	UPLEAP	UPPROP	UPRUSHED	UPSTAIRS
UPGIRDS	UPLEAPED	UPPROPPED	UPRUSHES	UPSTAND
UPGIRT	UPLEAPING	UPPROPPING	UPRUSHING	UPSTANDING
UPGOING	UPLEAPS	UPPROPS	UPS	UPSTANDS
UPGRADE	UPLEAPT	UPRAISE	UPSADAISY	UPSTARE
UPGRADED	UPLIFT	UPRAISED	UPSCALE	UPSTARED
UPGRADES	UPLIFTED	UPRAISER	UPSCALED	UPSTARES
UPGRADING	UPLIFTER	UPRAISERS	UPSCALES	UPSTARING
UPGREW	UPLIFTERS	UPRAISES	UPSCALING	UPSTART
UPGROW	UPLIFTING	UPRAISING	UPSEND	UPSTARTED
UPGROWING	UPLIFTS	UPRATE	UPSENDING	UPSTARTING
UPGROWN	UPLIGHT	UPRATED	UPSENDS	UPSTARTS
UPGROWS	UPLIGHTED	UPRATES	UPSENT	UPSTATE
UPGROWTH	UPLIGHTING	UPRATING	UPSET	UPSTATER
UPGROWTHS	UPLIGHTS	UPREACH	UPSETS	UPSTATERS
UPHEAP	UPLINK	UPREACHED	UPSETTER	UPSTATES
UPHEAPED	UPLINKED	UPREACHES	UPSETTERS	UPSTEP
UPHEAPING	UPLINKING	UPREACHING	UPSETTING	UPSTEPPED
UPHEAPS	UPLINKS	UPREAR	UPSHIFT	UPSTEPPING
UPHEAVAL	UPLIT	UPREARED	UPSHIFTED	UPSTEPS
UPHEAVALS	UPLOAD	UPREARING	UPSHIFTING	UPSTIR
UPHEAVE	UPLOADED	UPREARS	UPSHIFTS	UPSTIRRED
UPHEAVED	UPLOADING	UPRIGHT	UPSHOOT	UPSTIRRING
UPHEAVER	UPLOADS	UPRIGHTED	UPSHOOTING	UPSTIRS
UPHEAVERS	UPMANSHIP	UPRIGHTING	UPSHOOTS	UPSTOOD
UPHEAVES	UPMANSHIPS	UPRIGHTLY	UPSHOT	UPSTREAM
UPHEAVING	UPMARKET	UPRIGHTS	UPSHOTS	UPSTROKE
UPHELD	UPMOST	UPRISE	UPSIDE	UPSTROKES
UPHILL	UPO	UPRISEN	UPSIDES	UPSURGE
UPHILLS	UPON	UPRISER	UPSILON	UPSURGED
UPHOARD	UPPED	UPRISERS	UPSILONS	UPSURGES
UPHOARDED	UPPER	UPRISES	UPSIZE	UPSURGING
UPHOARDING	UPPERCASE	UPRISING	UPSIZED	UPSWEEP
UPHOARDS	UPPERCASED	UPRISINGS	UPSIZES	UPSWEEPING
UPHOLD	UPPERCASES	UPRIVER	UPSIZING	UPSWEEPS
UPHOLDER	UPPERCASING	UPRIVERS	UPSLOPE	UPSWELL
UPHOLDERS	UPPERCUT	UPROAR	UPSOAR	UPSWELLED
UPHOLDING	UPPERCUTS	UPROARS	UPSOARED	UPSWELLING
UPHOLDS	UPPERCUTTING	UPROOT	UPSOARING	UPSWELLS
UPHOLSTER	UPPERMOST	UPROOTAL	UPSOARS	UPSWEPT
UPHOLSTERED	UPPERPART	UPROOTALS	UPSPRANG	UPSWING
UPHOLSTERING	UPPERPARTS	UPROOTED	UPSPRING	UPSWINGING
UPHOLSTERS	UPPERS	UPROOTER	UPSPRINGING	UPSWINGS
UPHOVE	UPPILE	UPROOTERS	UPSPRINGS	UPSWOLLEN
UPHROE	UPPILED	UPROOTING	UPSPRUNG	UPSWUNG
UPHROES	UPPILES	UPROOTS	UPSTAGE	UPTAKE
UPKEEP	UPPILING	UPROSE	UPSTAGED	UPTAKES

UPTALK	UPWELLING	URBANISED	URETHRAE	UROLITH
UPTALKED	UPWELLINGS	URBANISES	URETHRAL	UROLITHIC
UPTALKING	UPWELLS	URBANISING	URETHRAS	UROLITHS
UPTALKS	UPWIND	URBANISM	URETIC	UROLOGIC
UPTEAR	UPWINDS	URBANISMS	URGE	UROLOGIES
UPTEARING	URACIL	URBANIST	URGED	UROLOGIST
UPTEARS	URACILS	URBANISTS	URGENCIES	UROLOGISTS
UPTEMPO	URAEI	URBANITE	URGENCY	UROLOGY
UPTEMPOS	URAEMIA	URBANITES	URGENT	UROPOD
UPTHREW	URAEMIAS	URBANITIES	URGENTLY	UROPODAL
UPTHROW	URAEMIC	URBANITY	URGER	UROPODOUS
UPTHROWING	URAEUS	URBANIZE	URGERS	UROPODS
UPTHROWN	URAEUSES	URBANIZED	URGES	UROPYGIA
UPTHROWS	URALITE	URBANIZES	URGING	UROPYGIAL
UPTHRUST	URALITES	URBANIZING	URGINGLY	UROPYGIUM
UPTHRUSTED	URALITIC	URBIA	URIAL	UROPYGIUMS
UPTHRUSTING	URANIA	URBIAS	URIALS	UROSCOPIC
UPTHRUSTS	URANIAS	URBS	URIC	UROSCOPIES
UPTICK	URANIC	URCEOLATE	URIDINE	UROSCOPY
UPTICKS	URANIDE	URCHIN	URIDINES	UROSTYLE
UPTIGHT	URANIDES	URCHINS	URINAL	UROSTYLES
UPTILT	URANINITE	URD	URINALS	URP
UPTILTED	URANISM	URDS	URINARIES	URPED
UPTILTING	URANISMS	UREA	URINARY	URPING
UPTILTS	URANITE	UREAL	URINATE	URPS
UPTIME	URANITES	UREAS	URINATED	URSA
UPTIMES	URANITIC	UREASE	URINATES	URSAE
UPTORE	URANIUM	UREASES	URINATING	URSID
UPTORN	URANIUMS	UREDIA	URINATION	URSIDS
UPTOSS	URANOLOGIES	UREDIAL	URINATIONS	URSIFORM
UPTOSSED	URANOLOGY	UREDINIA	URINATIVE	URSINE
UPTOSSES	URANOUS	UREDINIAL	URINATOR	URTEXT
UPTOSSING	URANYL	UREDINIUM	URINATORS	URTEXTS
UPTOWN	URANYLIC	UREDIUM	URINE	URTICANT
UPTOWNER	URANYLS	UREDO	URINEMIA	URTICANTS
UPTOWNERS	URARE	UREDOS	URINEMIAS	URTICARIA
UPTOWNS	URARES	UREIC	URINEMIC	URTICARIAS
UPTREND	URARI	UREIDE	URINES	URTICATE
UPTRENDS	URARIS	UREIDES	URINOSE	URTICATED
UPTURN	URASE	UREMIA	URINOUS	URTICATES
UPTURNED	URASES	UREMIAS	URN	URTICATING
UPTURNING	URATE	UREMIC	URNLIKE	URUS
UPTURNS	URATES	UREOTELIC	URNS	URUSES
UPWAFT	URATIC	URETER	UROCHORD	URUSHIOL
UPWAFTED	URB	URETERAL	UROCHORDS	URUSHIOLS
UPWAFTING	URBAN	URETERIC	UROCHROME	US
UPWAFTS	URBANE	URETERS	UROCHROMES	USABILITIES
UPWARD	URBANELY	URETHAN	URODELE	USABILITY
UPWARDLY	URBANER	URETHANE	URODELES	USABLE
UPWARDS	URBANEST	URETHANES	UROGENOUS	USABLY
UPWELL	URBANISE	URETHANS	UROKINASE	USAGE
UPWELLED		URETHRA	UROKINASES	USAGES

USANCE	UTA	UTTERLY	VACCINATES	VAGINOSIS
USANCES	UTAS	UTTERMOST	VACCINATING	VAGOTOMIES
USAUNCE	UTE	UTTERMOSTS	VACCINE	VAGOTOMY
USAUNCES	UTENSIL	UTTERNESS	VACCINEE	VAGOTONIA
USE	UTENSILS	UTTERNESSES	VACCINEES	VAGOTONIAS
USEABLE	UTERI	UTTERS	VACCINES	VAGOTONIC
USEABLY	UTERINE	UVAROVITE	VACCINIA	VAGRANCIES
USED	UTERUS	UVAROVITES	VACCINIAL	VAGRANCY
USEFUL	UTERUSES	UVEA	VACCINIAS	VAGRANT
USEFULLY	UTES	UVEAL	VACILLANT	VAGRANTLY
USELESS	UTILE	UVEAS	VACILLATE	VAGRANTS
USELESSLY	UTILIDOR	UVEITIC	VACILLATED	VAGROM
USER	UTILIDORS	UVEITIS	VACILLATES	VAGUE
USERNAME	UTILISE	UVEITISES	VACILLATING	VAGUELY
USERNAMES	UTILISED	UVEOUS	VACS	VAGUENESS
USERS	UTILISER	UVULA	VACUA	VAGUENESSES
USES	UTILISERS	UVULAE	VACUITIES	VAGUER
USHER	UTILISES	UVULAR	VACUITY	VAGUEST
USHERED	UTILISING	UVULARLY	VACUOLAR	VAGUS
USHERETTE	UTILITIES	UVULARS	VACUOLATE	VAHINE
USHERETTES	UTILITY	UVULAS	VACUOLE	VAHINES
USHERING	UTILIZE	UVULITIS	VACUOLES	VAIL
USHERS	UTILIZED	UVULITISES	VACUOUS	VAILED
USING	UTILIZER	UXORIAL	VACUOUSLY	VAILING
USNEA	UTILIZERS	UXORIALLY	VACUUM	VAILS
USNEAS	UTILIZES	UXORICIDE	VACUUMED	VAIN
USQUABAE	UTILIZING	UXORICIDES	VACUUMING	VAINER
USQUABAES	UTMOST	UXORIOUS	VACUUMS	VAINEST
USQUE	UTMOSTS		VADOSE	VAINGLORIES
USQUEBAE	UTOPIA	**V**	VAGABOND	VAINGLORY
USQUEBAES	UTOPIAN		VAGABONDED	VAINLY
USQUES	UTOPIANS		VAGABONDING	VAINNESS
USTULATE	UTOPIAS		VAGABONDS	VAINNESSES
USUAL	UTOPISM	VAC	VAGAL	VAIR
USUALLY	UTOPISMS	VACANCIES	VAGALLY	VAIRS
USUALNESS	UTOPIST	VACANCY	VAGARIES	VAKEEL
USUALNESSES	UTOPISTIC	VACANT	VAGARIOUS	VAKEELS
USUALS	UTOPISTS	VACANTLY	VAGARY	VAKIL
USUFRUCT	UTRICLE	VACATABLE	VAGI	VAKILS
USUFRUCTS	UTRICLES	VACATE	VAGILE	VALANCE
USURER	UTRICULAR	VACATED	VAGILITIES	VALANCED
USURERS	UTRICULI	VACATES	VAGILITY	VALANCES
USURIES	UTRICULUS	VACATING	VAGINA	VALANCING
USURIOUS	UTS	VACATION	VAGINAE	VALE
USURP	UTTER	VACATIONED	VAGINAL	VALENCE
USURPED	UTTERABLE	VACATIONING	VAGINALLY	VALENCES
USURPER	UTTERANCE	VACATIONS	VAGINAS	VALENCIA
USURPERS	UTTERANCES	VACCINA	VAGINATE	VALENCIAS
USURPING	UTTERED	VACCINAL	VAGINATED	VALENCIES
USURPS	UTTERER	VACCINAS	VAGINITIS	VALENCY
USURY	UTTERERS	VACCINATE	VAGINITISES	VALENTINE
UT	UTTERING	VACCINATED	VAGINOSES	VALENTINES

VALERATE	VALORISING	VAMOOSES	VANDYKES	VAPORERS
VALERATES	VALORIZE	VAMOOSING	VANE	VAPORETTI
VALERIAN	VALORIZED	VAMOSE	VANED	VAPORETTO
VALERIANS	VALORIZES	VAMOSED	VANES	VAPORETTOS
VALERIC	VALORIZING	VAMOSES	VANG	VAPORIFIC
VALES	VALOROUS	VAMOSING	VANGS	VAPORING
VALET	VALORS	VAMP	VANGUARD	VAPORINGS
VALETED	VALOUR	VAMPED	VANGUARDS	VAPORISE
VALETING	VALOURS	VAMPER	VANILLA	VAPORISED
VALETS	VALSE	VAMPERS	VANILLAS	VAPORISES
VALGOID	VALSES	VAMPIER	VANILLIC	VAPORISH
VALGUS	VALUABLE	VAMPIEST	VANILLIN	VAPORISING
VALGUSES	VALUABLES	VAMPING	VANILLINS	VAPORIZE
VALIANCE	VALUABLY	VAMPIRE	VANISH	VAPORIZED
VALIANCES	VALUATE	VAMPIRES	VANISHED	VAPORIZER
VALIANCIES	VALUATED	VAMPIRIC	VANISHER	VAPORIZERS
VALIANCY	VALUATES	VAMPIRISH	VANISHERS	VAPORIZES
VALIANT	VALUATING	VAMPIRISM	VANISHES	VAPORIZING
VALIANTLY	VALUATION	VAMPIRISMS	VANISHING	VAPORLESS
VALIANTS	VALUATIONS	VAMPISH	VANITIED	VAPORLIKE
VALID	VALUATOR	VAMPISHLY	VANITIES	VAPOROUS
VALIDATE	VALUATORS	VAMPS	VANITORIES	VAPORS
VALIDATED	VALUE	VAMPY	VANITORY	VAPORWARE
VALIDATES	VALUED	VAN	VANITY	VAPORWARES
VALIDATING	VALUELESS	VANADATE	VANLOAD	VAPORY
VALIDITIES	VALUER	VANADATES	VANLOADS	VAPOUR
VALIDITY	VALUERS	VANADIATE	VANMAN	VAPOURED
VALIDLY	VALUES	VANADIATES	VANMEN	VAPOURER
VALIDNESS	VALUING	VANADIC	VANNED	VAPOURERS
VALIDNESSES	VALUTA	VANADIUM	VANNER	VAPOURING
VALINE	VALUTAS	VANADIUMS	VANNERS	VAPOURS
VALINES	VALVAL	VANADOUS	VANNING	VAPOURY
VALISE	VALVAR	VANASPATI	VANPOOL	VAQUERO
VALISES	VALVATE	VANASPATIS	VANPOOLS	VAQUEROS
VALKYR	VALVE	VANDA	VANQUISH	VAR
VALKYRIE	VALVED	VANDAL	VANQUISHED	VARA
VALKYRIES	VALVELESS	VANDALIC	VANQUISHES	VARACTOR
VALKYRS	VALVELET	VANDALISE	VANQUISHING	VARACTORS
VALLATE	VALVELETS	VANDALISED	VANS	VARAS
VALLATION	VALVELIKE	VANDALISES	VANTAGE	VARIA
VALLATIONS	VALVES	VANDALISH	VANTAGES	VARIABLE
VALLECULA	VALVING	VANDALISING	VANWARD	VARIABLES
VALLECULAE	VALVULA	VANDALISM	VAPID	VARIABLY
VALLEY	VALVULAE	VANDALISMS	VAPIDITIES	VARIANCE
VALLEYED	VALVULAR	VANDALIZE	VAPIDITY	VARIANCES
VALLEYS	VALVULE	VANDALIZED	VAPIDLY	VARIANT
VALONIA	VALVULES	VANDALIZES	VAPIDNESS	VARIANTS
VALONIAS	VAMBRACE	VANDALIZING	VAPIDNESSES	VARIAS
VALOR	VAMBRACED	VANDALS	VAPOR	VARIATE
VALORISE	VAMBRACES	VANDAS	VAPORABLE	VARIATED
VALORISED	VAMOOSE	VANDYKE	VAPORED	VARIATES
VALORISES	VAMOOSED	VANDYKED	VAPORER	VARIATING

VARIATION	VARMINTS	VAST	VAVASOURS	VEGETABLY
VARIATIONS	VARNA	VASTER	VAVASSOR	VEGETAL
VARICELLA	VARNAS	VASTEST	VAVASSORS	VEGETALLY
VARICELLAS	VARNISH	VASTIER	VAVS	VEGETANT
VARICES	VARNISHED	VASTIEST	VAW	VEGETATE
VARICOSE	VARNISHER	VASTITIES	VAWARD	VEGETATED
VARICOSED	VARNISHERS	VASTITUDE	VAWARDS	VEGETATES
VARICOSES	VARNISHES	VASTITUDES	VAWNTIE	VEGETATING
VARICOSIS	VARNISHING	VASTITY	VAWS	VEGETE
VARIED	VARNISHY	VASTLY	VEAL	VEGETIST
VARIEDLY	VAROOM	VASTNESS	VEALED	VEGETISTS
VARIEGATE	VAROOMED	VASTNESSES	VEALER	VEGETIVE
VARIEGATED	VAROOMING	VASTS	VEALERS	VEGGED
VARIEGATES	VAROOMS	VASTY	VEALIER	VEGGIE
VARIEGATING	VARS	VAT	VEALIEST	VEGGIES
VARIER	VARSITIES	VATFUL	VEALING	VEGGING
VARIERS	VARSITY	VATFULS	VEALS	VEGIE
VARIES	VARUS	VATIC	VEALY	VEGIES
VARIETAL	VARUSES	VATICAL	VECTOR	VEHEMENCE
VARIETALS	VARVE	VATICIDE	VECTORED	VEHEMENCES
VARIETIES	VARVED	VATICIDES	VECTORIAL	VEHEMENCIES
VARIETY	VARVES	VATICINAL	VECTORING	VEHEMENCY
VARIFORM	VARY	VATS	VECTORS	VEHEMENT
VARIOLA	VARYING	VATTED	VEDALIA	VEHICLE
VARIOLAR	VARYINGLY	VATTING	VEDALIAS	VEHICLES
VARIOLAS	VAS	VATU	VEDETTE	VEHICULAR
VARIOLATE	VASA	VATUS	VEDETTES	VEIL
VARIOLATED	VASAL	VAU	VEE	VEILED
VARIOLATES	VASCULA	VAULT	VEEJAY	VEILEDLY
VARIOLATING	VASCULAR	VAULTED	VEEJAYS	VEILER
VARIOLE	VASCULUM	VAULTER	VEENA	VEILERS
VARIOLES	VASCULUMS	VAULTERS	VEENAS	VEILING
VARIOLITE	VASE	VAULTIER	VEEP	VEILINGS
VARIOLITES	VASECTOMIES	VAULTIEST	VEEPEE	VEILLIKE
VARIOLOID	VASECTOMY	VAULTING	VEEPEES	VEILS
VARIOLOIDS	VASELIKE	VAULTINGS	VEEPS	VEIN
VARIOLOUS	VASELINE	VAULTS	VEER	VEINAL
VARIORUM	VASELINES	VAULTY	VEERED	VEINED
VARIORUMS	VASES	VAUNT	VEERIES	VEINER
VARIOUS	VASIFORM	VAUNTED	VEERING	VEINERS
VARIOUSLY	VASOMOTOR	VAUNTER	VEERINGLY	VEINIER
VARISIZED	VASOSPASM	VAUNTERS	VEERS	VEINIEST
VARISTOR	VASOSPASMS	VAUNTFUL	VEERY	VEINING
VARISTORS	VASOTOCIN	VAUNTIE	VEES	VEININGS
VARIX	VASOTOCINS	VAUNTING	VEG	VEINLESS
VARLET	VASOTOMIES	VAUNTS	VEGAN	VEINLET
VARLETRIES	VASOTOMY	VAUNTY	VEGANISM	VEINLETS
VARLETRY	VASOVAGAL	VAUS	VEGANISMS	VEINLIKE
VARLETS	VASSAL	VAV	VEGANS	VEINS
VARMENT	VASSALAGE	VAVASOR	VEGES	VEINSTONE
VARMENTS	VASSALAGES	VAVASORS	VEGETABLE	VEINSTONES
VARMINT	VASSALS	VAVASOUR	VEGETABLES	VEINULE

VEINULES	VELVETEENS	VENENES	VENOUSLY	VERATRIA
VEINULET	VELVETIER	VENENOSE	VENT	VERATRIAS
VEINULETS	VELVETIEST	VENERABLE	VENTAGE	VERATRIN
VEINY	VELVETS	VENERABLES	VENTAGES	VERATRINE
VELA	VELVETY	VENERABLY	VENTAIL	VERATRINES
VELAMEN	VENA	VENERATE	VENTAILS	VERATRINS
VELAMINA	VENAE	VENERATED	VENTED	VERATRUM
VELAR	VENAL	VENERATES	VENTER	VERATRUMS
VELARIA	VENALITIES	VENERATING	VENTERS	VERB
VELARIUM	VENALITY	VENERATOR	VENTIFACT	VERBAL
VELARIZE	VENALLY	VENERATORS	VENTIFACTS	VERBALISM
VELARIZED	VENATIC	VENEREAL	VENTILATE	VERBALISMS
VELARIZES	VENATICAL	VENERIES	VENTILATED	VERBALIST
VELARIZING	VENATION	VENERY	VENTILATES	VERBALISTS
VELARS	VENATIONS	VENETIAN	VENTILATING	VERBALIZE
VELATE	VEND	VENETIANS	VENTING	VERBALIZED
VELCRO	VENDABLE	VENGE	VENTLESS	VERBALIZES
VELCROS	VENDABLES	VENGEANCE	VENTRAL	VERBALIZING
VELD	VENDACE	VENGEANCES	VENTRALLY	VERBALLY
VELDS	VENDACES	VENGED	VENTRALS	VERBALS
VELDT	VENDED	VENGEFUL	VENTRICLE	VERBATIM
VELDTS	VENDEE	VENGES	VENTRICLES	VERBENA
VELIGER	VENDEES	VENGING	VENTS	VERBENAS
VELIGERS	VENDER	VENIAL	VENTURE	VERBIAGE
VELITES	VENDERS	VENIALITIES	VENTURED	VERBIAGES
VELLEITIES	VENDETTA	VENIALITY	VENTURER	VERBICIDE
VELLEITY	VENDETTAS	VENIALLY	VENTURERS	VERBICIDES
VELLICATE	VENDEUSE	VENIN	VENTURES	VERBID
VELLICATED	VENDEUSES	VENINE	VENTURI	VERBIDS
VELLICATES	VENDIBLE	VENINES	VENTURING	VERBIFIED
VELLICATING	VENDIBLES	VENINS	VENTURIS	VERBIFIES
VELLUM	VENDIBLY	VENIRE	VENTUROUS	VERBIFY
VELLUMS	VENDING	VENIREMAN	VENUE	VERBIFYING
VELOCE	VENDITION	VENIREMEN	VENUES	VERBILE
VELOCITIES	VENDITIONS	VENIRES	VENULAR	VERBILES
VELOCITY	VENDOR	VENISON	VENULE	VERBLESS
VELODROME	VENDORS	VENISONS	VENULES	VERBOSE
VELODROMES	VENDS	VENOGRAM	VENULOSE	VERBOSELY
VELOUR	VENDUE	VENOGRAMS	VENULOUS	VERBOSITIES
VELOURS	VENDUES	VENOLOGIES	VENUS	VERBOSITY
VELOUTE	VENEER	VENOLOGY	VENUSES	VERBOTEN
VELOUTES	VENEERED	VENOM	VERA	VERBS
VELUM	VENEERER	VENOMED	VERACIOUS	VERDANCIES
VELURE	VENEERERS	VENOMER	VERACITIES	VERDANCY
VELURED	VENEERING	VENOMERS	VERACITY	VERDANT
VELURES	VENEERINGS	VENOMING	VERANDA	VERDANTLY
VELURING	VENEERS	VENOMOUS	VERANDAED	VERDERER
VELVERET	VENENATE	VENOMS	VERANDAH	VERDERERS
VELVERETS	VENENATED	VENOSE	VERANDAHS	VERDEROR
VELVET	VENENATES	VENOSITIES	VERANDAS	VERDERORS
VELVETED	VENENATING	VENOSITY	VERAPAMIL	VERDICT
VELVETEEN	VENENE	VENOUS	VERAPAMILS	VERDICTS

VERDIGRIS	VERMIAN	VERSET	VESICANT	VESTRYMAN
VERDIGRISES	VERMICIDE	VERSETS	VESICANTS	VESTRYMEN
VERDIN	VERMICIDES	VERSICLE	VESICATE	VESTS
VERDINS	VERMIFORM	VERSICLES	VESICATED	VESTURAL
VERDITER	VERMIFUGE	VERSIFIED	VESICATES	VESTURE
VERDITERS	VERMIFUGES	VERSIFIER	VESICATING	VESTURED
VERDURE	VERMILION	VERSIFIERS	VESICLE	VESTURES
VERDURED	VERMILIONED	VERSIFIES	VESICLES	VESTURING
VERDURES	VERMILIONING	VERSIFY	VESICULA	VESUVIAN
VERDUROUS	VERMILIONS	VERSIFYING	VESICULAE	VESUVIANS
VERECUND	VERMIN	VERSINE	VESICULAR	VET
VERGE	VERMINOUS	VERSINES	VESPER	VETCH
VERGED	VERMIS	VERSING	VESPERAL	VETCHES
VERGENCE	VERMOULU	VERSION	VESPERALS	VETCHLING
VERGENCES	VERMOUTH	VERSIONAL	VESPERS	VETCHLINGS
VERGER	VERMOUTHS	VERSIONS	VESPIARIES	VETERAN
VERGERS	VERMUTH	VERSO	VESPIARY	VETERANS
VERGES	VERMUTHS	VERSOS	VESPID	VETIVER
VERGING	VERNACLE	VERST	VESPIDS	VETIVERS
VERGLAS	VERNACLES	VERSTE	VESPINE	VETIVERT
VERGLASES	VERNAL	VERSTES	VESSEL	VETIVERTS
VERIDIC	VERNALIZE	VERSTS	VESSELED	VETO
VERIDICAL	VERNALIZED	VERSUS	VESSELS	VETOED
VERIER	VERNALIZES	VERT	VEST	VETOER
VERIEST	VERNALIZING	VERTEBRA	VESTA	VETOERS
VERIFIED	VERNALLY	VERTEBRAE	VESTAL	VETOES
VERIFIER	VERNATION	VERTEBRAL	VESTALLY	VETOING
VERIFIERS	VERNATIONS	VERTEBRAS	VESTALS	VETS
VERIFIES	VERNICLE	VERTEX	VESTAS	VETTED
VERIFY	VERNICLES	VERTEXES	VESTED	VETTER
VERIFYING	VERNIER	VERTICAL	VESTEE	VETTERS
VERILY	VERNIERS	VERTICALS	VESTEES	VETTING
VERISM	VERNIX	VERTICES	VESTIARIES	VEX
VERISMO	VERNIXES	VERTICIL	VESTIARY	VEXATION
VERISMOS	VERONICA	VERTICILS	VESTIBULE	VEXATIONS
VERISMS	VERONICAS	VERTIGINES	VESTIBULED	VEXATIOUS
VERIST	VERRUCA	VERTIGO	VESTIBULES	VEXED
VERISTIC	VERRUCAE	VERTIGOES	VESTIBULING	VEXEDLY
VERISTS	VERRUCAS	VERTIGOS	VESTIGE	VEXEDNESS
VERITABLE	VERRUCOSE	VERTS	VESTIGES	VEXEDNESSES
VERITABLY	VERRUCOUS	VERTU	VESTIGIA	VEXER
VERITAS	VERSAL	VERTUS	VESTIGIAL	VEXERS
VERITATES	VERSANT	VERVAIN	VESTIGIUM	VEXES
VERITE	VERSANTS	VERVAINS	VESTING	VEXIL
VERITES	VERSATILE	VERVE	VESTINGS	VEXILLA
VERITIES	VERSE	VERVES	VESTLESS	VEXILLAR
VERITY	VERSED	VERVET	VESTLIKE	VEXILLARIES
VERJUICE	VERSEMAN	VERVETS	VESTMENT	VEXILLARY
VERJUICES	VERSEMEN	VERY	VESTMENTS	VEXILLATE
VERMEIL	VERSER	VESICA	VESTRAL	VEXILLUM
VERMEILS	VERSERS	VESICAE	VESTRIES	VEXILS
VERMES	VERSES	VESICAL	VESTRY	VEXING

VEXINGLY	VIBRATORY	VICIOUSLY	VIDETTE	VIGOROUS
VEXT	VIBRATOS	VICOMTE	VIDETTES	VIGORS
VIA	VIBRIO	VICOMTES	VIDICON	VIGOUR
VIABILITIES	VIBRIOID	VICTIM	VIDICONS	VIGOURS
VIABILITY	VIBRION	VICTIMISE	VIDS	VIGS
VIABLE	VIBRIONIC	VICTIMISED	VIDUITIES	VIKING
VIABLY	VIBRIONS	VICTIMISES	VIDUITY	VIKINGS
VIADUCT	VIBRIOS	VICTIMISING	VIE	VILAYET
VIADUCTS	VIBRIOSES	VICTIMIZE	VIED	VILAYETS
VIAL	VIBRIOSIS	VICTIMIZED	VIER	VILE
VIALED	VIBRISSA	VICTIMIZES	VIERS	VILELY
VIALING	VIBRISSAE	VICTIMIZING	VIES	VILENESS
VIALLED	VIBRISSAL	VICTIMS	VIEW	VILENESSES
VIALLING	VIBRONIC	VICTOR	VIEWABLE	VILER
VIALS	VIBURNUM	VICTORIA	VIEWDATA	VILEST
VIAND	VIBURNUMS	VICTORIAS	VIEWED	VILIFIED
VIANDS	VICAR	VICTORIES	VIEWER	VILIFIER
VIATIC	VICARAGE	VICTORS	VIEWERS	VILIFIERS
VIATICA	VICARAGES	VICTORY	VIEWIER	VILIFIES
VIATICAL	VICARATE	VICTRESS	VIEWIEST	VILIFY
VIATICALS	VICARATES	VICTRESSES	VIEWING	VILIFYING
VIATICUM	VICARIAL	VICTUAL	VIEWINGS	VILIPEND
VIATICUMS	VICARIANT	VICTUALED	VIEWLESS	VILIPENDED
VIATOR	VICARIANTS	VICTUALER	VIEWPOINT	VILIPENDING
VIATORES	VICARIATE	VICTUALERS	VIEWPOINTS	VILIPENDS
VIATORS	VICARIATES	VICTUALING	VIEWS	VILL
VIBE	VICARIOUS	VICTUALLED	VIEWY	VILLA
VIBES	VICARLY	VICTUALLING	VIG	VILLADOM
VIBIST	VICARS	VICTUALS	VIGA	VILLADOMS
VIBISTS	VICARSHIP	VICUGNA	VIGAS	VILLAE
VIBRACULA	VICARSHIPS	VICUGNAS	VIGESIMAL	VILLAGE
VIBRACULUM	VICE	VICUNA	VIGIA	VILLAGER
VIBRAHARP	VICED	VICUNAS	VIGIAS	VILLAGERIES
VIBRAHARPS	VICEGERAL	VID	VIGIL	VILLAGERS
VIBRANCE	VICELESS	VIDE	VIGILANCE	VILLAGERY
VIBRANCES	VICENARY	VIDELICET	VIGILANCES	VILLAGES
VIBRANCIES	VICENNIAL	VIDEO	VIGILANT	VILLAIN
VIBRANCY	VICEREGAL	VIDEODISC	VIGILANTE	VILLAINIES
VIBRANT	VICEREINE	VIDEODISCS	VIGILANTES	VILLAINS
VIBRANTLY	VICEREINES	VIDEODISK	VIGILS	VILLAINY
VIBRANTS	VICEROY	VIDEODISKS	VIGNERON	VILLAS
VIBRATE	VICES	VIDEOLAND	VIGNERONS	VILLATIC
VIBRATED	VICHIES	VIDEOLANDS	VIGNETTE	VILLEIN
VIBRATES	VICHY	VIDEOS	VIGNETTED	VILLEINS
VIBRATILE	VICINAGE	VIDEOTAPE	VIGNETTER	VILLENAGE
VIBRATING	VICINAGES	VIDEOTAPED	VIGNETTERS	VILLENAGES
VIBRATION	VICINAL	VIDEOTAPES	VIGNETTES	VILLI
VIBRATIONS	VICING	VIDEOTAPING	VIGNETTING	VILLIFORM
VIBRATIVE	VICINITIES	VIDEOTEX	VIGOR	VILLOSE
VIBRATO	VICINITY	VIDEOTEXES	VIGORISH	VILLOSITIES
VIBRATOR	VICIOUS	VIDEOTEXT	VIGORISHES	VILLOSITY
VIBRATORS		VIDEOTEXTS	VIGOROSO	VILLOUS

VILLOUSLY	VINOS	VIPERFISHES	VIRILIZING	VISCERA
VILLS	VINOSITIES	VIPERINE	VIRILOCAL	VISCERAL
VILLUS	VINOSITY	VIPERISH	VIRION	VISCID
VIM	VINOUS	VIPEROUS	VIRIONS	VISCIDITIES
VIMEN	VINOUSLY	VIPERS	VIRL	VISCIDITY
VIMINA	VINTAGE	VIRAGO	VIRLS	VISCIDLY
VIMINAL	VINTAGER	VIRAGOES	VIROID	VISCOID
VIMINEOUS	VINTAGERS	VIRAGOS	VIROIDS	VISCOIDAL
VIMS	VINTAGES	VIRAL	VIROLOGIC	VISCOSE
VINA	VINTNER	VIRALLY	VIROLOGIES	VISCOSES
VINACEOUS	VINTNERS	VIRELAI	VIROLOGY	VISCOSITIES
VINAL	VINY	VIRELAIS	VIROSES	VISCOSITY
VINALS	VINYL	VIRELAY	VIROSIS	VISCOUNT
VINAS	VINYLIC	VIRELAYS	VIRTU	VISCOUNTIES
VINASSE	VINYLS	VIREMIA	VIRTUAL	VISCOUNTS
VINASSES	VIOL	VIREMIAS	VIRTUALLY	VISCOUNTY
VINCA	VIOLA	VIREMIC	VIRTUE	VISCOUS
VINCAS	VIOLABLE	VIREO	VIRTUES	VISCOUSLY
VINCIBLE	VIOLABLY	VIREONINE	VIRTUOSA	VISCUS
VINCIBLY	VIOLAS	VIREOS	VIRTUOSAS	VISE
VINCULA	VIOLATE	VIRES	VIRTUOSE	VISED
VINCULUM	VIOLATED	VIRESCENT	VIRTUOSI	VISEED
VINCULUMS	VIOLATER	VIRGA	VIRTUOSIC	VISEING
VINDALOO	VIOLATERS	VIRGAS	VIRTUOSO	VISELIKE
VINDALOOS	VIOLATES	VIRGATE	VIRTUOSOS	VISES
VINDICATE	VIOLATING	VIRGATES	VIRTUOUS	VISIBLE
VINDICATED	VIOLATION	VIRGIN	VIRTUS	VISIBLY
VINDICATES	VIOLATIONS	VIRGINAL	VIRUCIDAL	VISING
VINDICATING	VIOLATIVE	VIRGINALS	VIRUCIDE	VISION
VINE	VIOLATOR	VIRGINITIES	VIRUCIDES	VISIONAL
VINEAL	VIOLATORS	VIRGINITY	VIRULENCE	VISIONARIES
VINED	VIOLENCE	VIRGINS	VIRULENCES	VISIONARY
VINEGAR	VIOLENCES	VIRGULATE	VIRULENCIES	VISIONED
VINEGARED	VIOLENT	VIRGULE	VIRULENCY	VISIONING
VINEGARS	VIOLENTLY	VIRGULES	VIRULENT	VISIONS
VINEGARY	VIOLET	VIRICIDAL	VIRUS	VISIT
VINERIES	VIOLETS	VIRICIDE	VIRUSES	VISITABLE
VINERY	VIOLIN	VIRICIDES	VIRUSLIKE	VISITANT
VINES	VIOLINIST	VIRID	VIRUSOID	VISITANTS
VINEYARD	VIOLINISTS	VIRIDIAN	VIRUSOIDS	VISITED
VINEYARDS	VIOLINS	VIRIDIANS	VIS	VISITER
VINIC	VIOLIST	VIRIDITIES	VISA	VISITERS
VINIER	VIOLISTS	VIRIDITY	VISAED	VISITING
VINIEST	VIOLONE	VIRILE	VISAGE	VISITOR
VINIFERA	VIOLONES	VIRILELY	VISAGED	VISITORS
VINIFERAS	VIOLS	VIRILISM	VISAGES	VISITS
VINIFIED	VIOMYCIN	VIRILISMS	VISAING	VISIVE
VINIFIES	VIOMYCINS	VIRILITIES	VISARD	VISOR
VINIFY	VIOSTEROL	VIRILITY	VISARDS	VISORED
VINIFYING	VIOSTEROLS	VIRILIZE	VISAS	VISORING
VINING	VIPER	VIRILIZED	VISCACHA	VISORLESS
VINO	VIPERFISH	VIRILIZES	VISCACHAS	VISORS

VISTA	VITELLINS	VIVARIUM	VIZSLAS	VOGUEING
VISTAED	VITELLUS	VIVARIUMS	VOCAB	VOGUEINGS
VISTALESS	VITELLUSES	VIVARY	VOCABLE	VOGUER
VISTAS	VITESSE	VIVAS	VOCABLES	VOGUERS
VISUAL	VITESSES	VIVE	VOCABLY	VOGUES
VISUALISE	VITIABLE	VIVERRID	VOCABS	VOGUING
VISUALISED	VITIATE	VIVERRIDS	VOCABULAR	VOGUINGS
VISUALISES	VITIATED	VIVERRINE	VOCAL	VOGUISH
VISUALISING	VITIATES	VIVERRINES	VOCALESE	VOGUISHLY
VISUALIST	VITIATING	VIVERS	VOCALESES	VOICE
VISUALISTS	VITIATION	VIVID	VOCALIC	VOICED
VISUALITIES	VITIATIONS	VIVIDER	VOCALICS	VOICEFUL
VISUALITY	VITIATOR	VIVIDEST	VOCALISE	VOICELESS
VISUALIZE	VITIATORS	VIVIDLY	VOCALISED	VOICEMAIL
VISUALIZED	VITILIGO	VIVIDNESS	VOCALISES	VOICEMAILS
VISUALIZES	VITILIGOS	VIVIDNESSES	VOCALISING	VOICEOVER
VISUALIZING	VITRAIN	VIVIFIC	VOCALISM	VOICEOVERS
VISUALLY	VITRAINS	VIVIFIED	VOCALISMS	VOICER
VISUALS	VITREOUS	VIVIFIER	VOCALIST	VOICERS
VITA	VITREOUSES	VIVIFIERS	VOCALISTS	VOICES
VITAE	VITRIC	VIVIFIES	VOCALITIES	VOICING
VITAL	VITRICS	VIVIFY	VOCALITY	VOICINGS
VITALISE	VITRIFIED	VIVIFYING	VOCALIZE	VOID
VITALISED	VITRIFIES	VIVIPARA	VOCALIZED	VOIDABLE
VITALISES	VITRIFORM	VIVISECT	VOCALIZER	VOIDANCE
VITALISING	VITRIFY	VIVISECTED	VOCALIZERS	VOIDANCES
VITALISM	VITRIFYING	VIVISECTING	VOCALIZES	VOIDED
VITALISMS	VITRINE	VIVISECTS	VOCALIZING	VOIDER
VITALIST	VITRINES	VIXEN	VOCALLY	VOIDERS
VITALISTS	VITRIOL	VIXENISH	VOCALNESS	VOIDING
VITALITIES	VITRIOLED	VIXENLY	VOCALNESSES	VOIDNESS
VITALITY	VITRIOLIC	VIXENS	VOCALS	VOIDNESSES
VITALIZE	VITRIOLING	VIZARD	VOCATION	VOIDS
VITALIZED	VITRIOLLED	VIZARDED	VOCATIONS	VOILA
VITALIZER	VITRIOLLING	VIZARDS	VOCATIVE	VOILE
VITALIZERS	VITRIOLS	VIZCACHA	VOCATIVES	VOILES
VITALIZES	VITTA	VIZCACHAS	VOCES	VOLANT
VITALIZING	VITTAE	VIZIER	VOCODER	VOLANTE
VITALLY	VITTATE	VIZIERATE	VOCODERS	VOLAR
VITALNESS	VITTLE	VIZIERATES	VODKA	VOLATILE
VITALNESSES	VITTLED	VIZIERIAL	VODKAS	VOLATILES
VITALS	VITTLES	VIZIERS	VODOU	VOLCANIC
VITAMER	VITTLING	VIZIR	VODOUN	VOLCANICS
VITAMERS	VITULINE	VIZIRATE	VODOUNS	VOLCANISM
VITAMIN	VIVA	VIZIRATES	VODOUS	VOLCANISMS
VITAMINE	VIVACE	VIZIRIAL	VODUN	VOLCANIZE
VITAMINES	VIVACES	VIZIRS	VODUNS	VOLCANIZED
VITAMINIC	VIVACIOUS	VIZOR	VOE	VOLCANIZES
VITAMINS	VIVACITIES	VIZORED	VOES	VOLCANIZING
VITELLIN	VIVACITY	VIZORING	VOGIE	VOLCANO
VITELLINE	VIVARIA	VIZORS	VOGUE	VOLCANOES
VITELLINES	VIVARIES	VIZSLA	VOGUED	VOLCANOS

VOLE	VOLUTED	VORTICISMS	VOWELIZED	VULCANIZING
VOLED	VOLUTES	VORTICIST	VOWELIZES	VULGAR
VOLERIES	VOLUTIN	VORTICISTS	VOWELIZING	VULGARER
VOLERY	VOLUTINS	VORTICITIES	VOWELS	VULGAREST
VOLES	VOLUTION	VORTICITY	VOWER	VULGARIAN
VOLING	VOLUTIONS	VORTICOSE	VOWERS	VULGARIANS
VOLITANT	VOLVA	VOTABLE	VOWING	VULGARISE
VOLITION	VOLVAS	VOTARESS	VOWLESS	VULGARISED
VOLITIONS	VOLVATE	VOTARESSES	VOWS	VULGARISES
VOLITIVE	VOLVOX	VOTARIES	VOX	VULGARISING
VOLKSLIED	VOLVOXES	VOTARIST	VOYAGE	VULGARISM
VOLKSLIEDER	VOLVULI	VOTARISTS	VOYAGED	VULGARISMS
VOLLEY	VOLVULUS	VOTARY	VOYAGER	VULGARITIES
VOLLEYED	VOLVULUSES	VOTE	VOYAGERS	VULGARITY
VOLLEYER	VOMER	VOTEABLE	VOYAGES	VULGARIZE
VOLLEYERS	VOMERINE	VOTED	VOYAGEUR	VULGARIZED
VOLLEYING	VOMERS	VOTELESS	VOYAGEURS	VULGARIZES
VOLLEYS	VOMICA	VOTER	VOYAGING	VULGARIZING
VOLOST	VOMICAE	VOTERS	VOYEUR	VULGARLY
VOLOSTS	VOMIT	VOTES	VOYEURISM	VULGARS
VOLPLANE	VOMITED	VOTING	VOYEURISMS	VULGATE
VOLPLANED	VOMITER	VOTIVE	VOYEURS	VULGATES
VOLPLANES	VOMITERS	VOTIVELY	VROOM	VULGO
VOLPLANING	VOMITING	VOTIVES	VROOMED	VULGUS
VOLT	VOMITIVE	VOTRESS	VROOMING	VULGUSES
VOLTA	VOMITIVES	VOTRESSES	VROOMS	VULNERARIES
VOLTAGE	VOMITO	VOUCH	VROUW	VULNERARY
VOLTAGES	VOMITORIES	VOUCHED	VROUWS	VULPINE
VOLTAIC	VOMITORY	VOUCHEE	VROW	VULTURE
VOLTAISM	VOMITOS	VOUCHEES	VROWS	VULTURES
VOLTAISMS	VOMITOUS	VOUCHER	VUG	VULTURINE
VOLTE	VOMITS	VOUCHERED	VUGG	VULTURISH
VOLTES	VOMITUS	VOUCHERING	VUGGIER	VULTUROUS
VOLTI	VOMITUSES	VOUCHERS	VUGGIEST	VULVA
VOLTMETER	VOODOO	VOUCHES	VUGGS	VULVAE
VOLTMETERS	VOODOOED	VOUCHING	VUGGY	VULVAL
VOLTS	VOODOOING	VOUCHSAFE	VUGH	VULVAR
VOLUBLE	VOODOOISM	VOUCHSAFED	VUGHS	VULVAS
VOLUBLY	VOODOOISMS	VOUCHSAFES	VUGS	VULVATE
VOLUME	VOODOOIST	VOUCHSAFING	VULCANIAN	VULVIFORM
VOLUMED	VOODOOISTS	VOUDON	VULCANIC	VULVITIS
VOLUMES	VOODOOS	VOUDONS	VULCANISE	VULVITISES
VOLUMETER	VORACIOUS	VOUDOUN	VULCANISED	VUM
VOLUMETERS	VORACITIES	VOUDOUNS	VULCANISES	VYING
VOLUMING	VORACITY	VOUSSOIR	VULCANISING	VYINGLY
VOLUNTARIES	VORLAGE	VOUSSOIRS	VULCANISM	
VOLUNTARY	VORLAGES	VOUVRAY	VULCANISMS	
VOLUNTEER	VORTEX	VOUVRAYS	VULCANITE	
VOLUNTEERED	VORTEXES	VOW	VULCANITES	
VOLUNTEERING	VORTICAL	VOWED	VULCANIZE	
VOLUNTEERS	VORTICES	VOWEL	VULCANIZED	WAB
VOLUTE	VORTICISM	VOWELIZE	VULCANIZES	WABBLE

WABBLED	WADMAAL	WAFTURE	WAHCONDAS	WAITERS
WABBLER	WADMAALS	WAFTURES	WAHINE	WAITING
WABBLERS	WADMAL	WAG	WAHINES	WAITINGS
WABBLES	WADMALS	WAGE	WAHOO	WAITLIST
WABBLIER	WADMEL	WAGED	WAHOOS	WAITLISTED
WABBLIEST	WADMELS	WAGELESS	WAIF	WAITLISTING
WABBLING	WADMOL	WAGER	WAIFED	WAITLISTS
WABBLY	WADMOLL	WAGERED	WAIFING	WAITRESS
WABS	WADMOLLS	WAGERER	WAIFISH	WAITRESSED
WACK	WADMOLS	WAGERERS	WAIFLIKE	WAITRESSES
WACKE	WADS	WAGERING	WAIFS	WAITRESSING
WACKER	WADSET	WAGERS	WAIL	WAITRON
WACKES	WADSETS	WAGES	WAILED	WAITRONS
WACKEST	WADSETTED	WAGGED	WAILER	WAITS
WACKIER	WADSETTING	WAGGER	WAILERS	WAITSTAFF
WACKIEST	WADY	WAGGERIES	WAILFUL	WAITSTAFFS
WACKILY	WAE	WAGGERS	WAILFULLY	WAIVE
WACKINESS	WAEFUL	WAGGERY	WAILING	WAIVED
WACKINESSES	WAENESS	WAGGING	WAILINGLY	WAIVER
WACKO	WAENESSES	WAGGISH	WAILS	WAIVERS
WACKOS	WAES	WAGGISHLY	WAILSOME	WAIVES
WACKS	WAESUCK	WAGGLE	WAIN	WAIVING
WACKY	WAESUCKS	WAGGLED	WAINS	WAKAME
WAD	WAFER	WAGGLES	WAINSCOT	WAKAMES
WADABLE	WAFERED	WAGGLIER	WAINSCOTED	WAKANDA
WADDED	WAFERING	WAGGLIEST	WAINSCOTING	WAKANDAS
WADDER	WAFERS	WAGGLING	WAINSCOTS	WAKE
WADDERS	WAFERY	WAGGLY	WAINSCOTTED	WAKEBOARD
WADDIE	WAFF	WAGGON	WAINSCOTTING	WAKEBOARDS
WADDIED	WAFFED	WAGGONED	WAIR	WAKED
WADDIES	WAFFIE	WAGGONER	WAIRED	WAKEFUL
WADDING	WAFFIES	WAGGONERS	WAIRING	WAKEFULLY
WADDINGS	WAFFING	WAGGONING	WAIRS	WAKELESS
WADDLE	WAFFLE	WAGGONS	WAIST	WAKEN
WADDLED	WAFFLED	WAGING	WAISTBAND	WAKENED
WADDLER	WAFFLER	WAGON	WAISTBANDS	WAKENER
WADDLERS	WAFFLERS	WAGONAGE	WAISTCOAT	WAKENERS
WADDLES	WAFFLES	WAGONAGES	WAISTCOATS	WAKENING
WADDLING	WAFFLIER	WAGONED	WAISTED	WAKENINGS
WADDLY	WAFFLIEST	WAGONER	WAISTER	WAKENS
WADDY	WAFFLING	WAGONERS	WAISTERS	WAKER
WADDYING	WAFFLINGS	WAGONETTE	WAISTING	WAKERIFE
WADE	WAFFLY	WAGONETTES	WAISTINGS	WAKERS
WADEABLE	WAFFS	WAGONING	WAISTLESS	WAKES
WADED	WAFT	WAGONLOAD	WAISTLINE	WAKIKI
WADER	WAFTAGE	WAGONLOADS	WAISTLINES	WAKIKIS
WADERS	WAFTAGES	WAGONS	WAISTS	WAKING
WADES	WAFTED	WAGS	WAIT	WALE
WADI	WAFTER	WAGSOME	WAITED	WALED
WADIES	WAFTERS	WAGTAIL	WAITER	WALER
WADING	WAFTING	WAGTAILS	WAITERED	WALERS
WADIS	WAFTS	WAHCONDA	WAITERING	WALES

WALIES	WALLOPS	WAMUSES	WANNIGANS	WARDROBES
WALING	WALLOW	WAN	WANNING	WARDROBING
WALK	WALLOWED	WAND	WANS	WARDROOM
WALKABLE	WALLOWER	WANDER	WANT	WARDROOMS
WALKABOUT	WALLOWERS	WANDERED	WANTAGE	WARDS
WALKABOUTS	WALLOWING	WANDERER	WANTAGES	WARDSHIP
WALKATHON	WALLOWS	WANDERERS	WANTED	WARDSHIPS
WALKATHONS	WALLPAPER	WANDERING	WANTER	WARE
WALKAWAY	WALLPAPERED	WANDERINGS	WANTERS	WARED
WALKAWAYS	WALLPAPERING	WANDEROO	WANTING	WAREHOUSE
WALKED	WALLPAPERS	WANDEROOS	WANTON	WAREHOUSED
WALKER	WALLS	WANDERS	WANTONED	WAREHOUSES
WALKERS	WALLY	WANDLE	WANTONER	WAREHOUSING
WALKING	WALLYBALL	WANDS	WANTONERS	WAREROOM
WALKINGS	WALLYBALLS	WANE	WANTONING	WAREROOMS
WALKOUT	WALLYDRAG	WANED	WANTONLY	WARES
WALKOUTS	WALLYDRAGS	WANES	WANTONS	WARFARE
WALKOVER	WALNUT	WANEY	WANTS	WARFARES
WALKOVERS	WALNUTS	WANGAN	WANY	WARFARIN
WALKS	WALRUS	WANGANS	WAP	WARFARINS
WALKUP	WALRUSES	WANGLE	WAPENTAKE	WARHEAD
WALKUPS	WALTZ	WANGLED	WAPENTAKES	WARHEADS
WALKWAY	WALTZED	WANGLER	WAPITI	WARHORSE
WALKWAYS	WALTZER	WANGLERS	WAPITIS	WARHORSES
WALKYRIE	WALTZERS	WANGLES	WAPPED	WARIER
WALKYRIES	WALTZES	WANGLING	WAPPING	WARIEST
WALL	WALTZING	WANGUN	WAPS	WARILY
WALLA	WALY	WANGUNS	WAR	WARINESS
WALLABIES	WAMBLE	WANIER	WARBLE	WARINESSES
WALLABY	WAMBLED	WANIEST	WARBLED	WARING
WALLAH	WAMBLES	WANIGAN	WARBLER	WARISON
WALLAHS	WAMBLIER	WANIGANS	WARBLERS	WARISONS
WALLAROO	WAMBLIEST	WANING	WARBLES	WARK
WALLAROOS	WAMBLING	WANION	WARBLING	WARKED
WALLAS	WAMBLY	WANIONS	WARBONNET	WARKING
WALLBOARD	WAME	WANK	WARBONNETS	WARKS
WALLBOARDS	WAMEFOU	WANKED	WARCRAFT	WARLESS
WALLED	WAMEFOUS	WANKER	WARCRAFTS	WARLIKE
WALLET	WAMEFUL	WANKERS	WARD	WARLOCK
WALLETS	WAMEFULS	WANKING	WARDED	WARLOCKS
WALLEYE	WAMES	WANKS	WARDEN	WARLORD
WALLEYED	WAMMUS	WANLY	WARDENRIES	WARLORDS
WALLEYES	WAMMUSES	WANNABE	WARDENRY	WARM
WALLIE	WAMPISH	WANNABEE	WARDENS	WARMAKER
WALLIES	WAMPISHED	WANNABEES	WARDER	WARMAKERS
WALLING	WAMPISHES	WANNABES	WARDERS	WARMED
WALLOP	WAMPISHING	WANNED	WARDING	WARMER
WALLOPED	WAMPUM	WANNER	WARDLESS	WARMERS
WALLOPER	WAMPUMS	WANNESS	WARDRESS	WARMEST
WALLOPERS	WAMPUS	WANNESSES	WARDRESSES	WARMING
WALLOPING	WAMPUSES	WANNEST	WARDROBE	WARMISH
WALLOPINGS	WAMUS	WANNIGAN	WARDROBED	WARMLY

WARMNESS	WARRENER	WASHBOWLS	WASTABLE	WATCHMAN
WARMNESSES	WARRENERS	WASHCLOTH	WASTAGE	WATCHMEN
WARMONGER	WARRENS	WASHCLOTHS	WASTAGES	WATCHOUT
WARMONGERS	WARRIGAL	WASHDAY	WASTE	WATCHOUTS
WARMOUTH	WARRIGALS	WASHDAYS	WASTED	WATCHWORD
WARMOUTHS	WARRING	WASHED	WASTEFUL	WATCHWORDS
WARMS	WARRIOR	WASHER	WASTELAND	WATER
WARMTH	WARRIORS	WASHERMAN	WASTELANDS	WATERAGE
WARMTHS	WARS	WASHERMEN	WASTELOT	WATERAGES
WARMUP	WARSAW	WASHERS	WASTELOTS	WATERBED
WARMUPS	WARSAWS	WASHES	WASTER	WATERBEDS
WARN	WARSHIP	WASHHOUSE	WASTERIE	WATERBIRD
WARNED	WARSHIPS	WASHHOUSES	WASTERIES	WATERBIRDS
WARNER	WARSLE	WASHIER	WASTERS	WATERBUCK
WARNERS	WARSLED	WASHIEST	WASTERY	WATERBUCKS
WARNING	WARSLER	WASHINESS	WASTES	WATERBUS
WARNINGLY	WARSLERS	WASHINESSES	WASTEWAY	WATERBUSES
WARNINGS	WARSLES	WASHING	WASTEWAYS	WATERBUSSES
WARNS	WARSLING	WASHINGS	WASTING	WATERDOG
WARP	WARSTLE	WASHOUT	WASTINGLY	WATERDOGS
WARPAGE	WARSTLED	WASHOUTS	WASTREL	WATERED
WARPAGES	WARSTLER	WASHRAG	WASTRELS	WATERER
WARPATH	WARSTLERS	WASHRAGS	WASTRIE	WATERERS
WARPATHS	WARSTLES	WASHROOM	WASTRIES	WATERFALL
WARPED	WARSTLING	WASHROOMS	WASTRY	WATERFALLS
WARPER	WART	WASHSTAND	WASTS	WATERFOWL
WARPERS	WARTED	WASHSTANDS	WAT	WATERFOWLS
WARPING	WARTHOG	WASHTUB	WATAP	WATERHEAD
WARPLANE	WARTHOGS	WASHTUBS	WATAPE	WATERHEADS
WARPLANES	WARTIER	WASHUP	WATAPES	WATERHEN
WARPOWER	WARTIEST	WASHUPS	WATAPS	WATERHENS
WARPOWERS	WARTIME	WASHWOMAN	WATCH	WATERIER
WARPS	WARTIMES	WASHWOMEN	WATCHABLE	WATERIEST
WARPWISE	WARTLESS	WASHY	WATCHABLES	WATERILY
WARRAGAL	WARTLIKE	WASP	WATCHBAND	WATERING
WARRAGALS	WARTS	WASPIER	WATCHBANDS	WATERINGS
WARRANT	WARTY	WASPIEST	WATCHCASE	WATERISH
WARRANTED	WARWORK	WASPILY	WATCHCASES	WATERJET
WARRANTEE	WARWORKS	WASPINESS	WATCHCRIES	WATERJETS
WARRANTEES	WARWORN	WASPINESSES	WATCHCRY	WATERLEAF
WARRANTER	WARY	WASPISH	WATCHDOG	WATERLEAFS
WARRANTERS	WAS	WASPISHLY	WATCHDOGGED	WATERLESS
WARRANTIED	WASABI	WASPLIKE	WATCHDOGGING	WATERLILIES
WARRANTIES	WASABIS	WASPS	WATCHDOGS	WATERLILY
WARRANTING	WASH	WASPY	WATCHED	WATERLINE
WARRANTOR	WASHABLE	WASSAIL	WATCHER	WATERLINES
WARRANTORS	WASHABLES	WASSAILED	WATCHERS	WATERLOG
WARRANTS	WASHBASIN	WASSAILER	WATCHES	WATERLOGGED
WARRANTY	WASHBASINS	WASSAILERS	WATCHEYE	WATERLOGGING
WARRANTYING	WASHBOARD	WASSAILING	WATCHEYES	WATERLOGS
WARRED	WASHBOARDS	WASSAILS	WATCHFUL	WATERLOO
WARREN	WASHBOWL	WAST	WATCHING	WATERLOOS

WATERMAN
WATERMARK
WATERMARKED
WATERMARKING
WATERMARKS
WATERMEN
WATERS
WATERSHED
WATERSHEDS
WATERSIDE
WATERSIDES
WATERSKI
WATERSKIS
WATERWAY
WATERWAYS
WATERWEED
WATERWEEDS
WATERWORK
WATERWORKS
WATERWORN
WATERY
WATERZOOI
WATERZOOIS
WATS
WATT
WATTAGE
WATTAGES
WATTAPE
WATTAPES
WATTER
WATTEST
WATTHOUR
WATTHOURS
WATTLE
WATTLED
WATTLES
WATTLESS
WATTLING
WATTMETER
WATTMETERS
WATTS
WAUCHT
WAUCHTED
WAUCHTING
WAUCHTS
WAUGH
WAUGHT
WAUGHTED
WAUGHTING
WAUGHTS
WAUK
WAUKED

WAUKING
WAUKS
WAUL
WAULED
WAULING
WAULS
WAUR
WAVE
WAVEBAND
WAVEBANDS
WAVED
WAVEFORM
WAVEFORMS
WAVEGUIDE
WAVEGUIDES
WAVELESS
WAVELET
WAVELETS
WAVELIKE
WAVELLITE
WAVELLITES
WAVEOFF
WAVEOFFS
WAVER
WAVERED
WAVERER
WAVERERS
WAVERING
WAVERS
WAVERY
WAVES
WAVESHAPE
WAVESHAPES
WAVEY
WAVEYS
WAVICLE
WAVICLES
WAVIER
WAVIES
WAVIEST
WAVILY
WAVINESS
WAVINESSES
WAVING
WAVY
WAW
WAWL
WAWLED
WAWLING
WAWLS
WAWS
WAX

WAXABLE
WAXBERRIES
WAXBERRY
WAXBILL
WAXBILLS
WAXED
WAXEN
WAXER
WAXERS
WAXES
WAXIER
WAXIEST
WAXILY
WAXINESS
WAXINESSES
WAXING
WAXINGS
WAXLIKE
WAXPLANT
WAXPLANTS
WAXWEED
WAXWEEDS
WAXWING
WAXWINGS
WAXWORK
WAXWORKER
WAXWORKERS
WAXWORKS
WAXWORM
WAXWORMS
WAXY
WAY
WAYBILL
WAYBILLS
WAYFARER
WAYFARERS
WAYFARING
WAYFARINGS
WAYGOING
WAYGOINGS
WAYLAID
WAYLAY
WAYLAYER
WAYLAYERS
WAYLAYING
WAYLAYS
WAYLESS
WAYPOINT
WAYPOINTS
WAYS
WAYSIDE
WAYSIDES

WAYWARD
WAYWARDLY
WAYWORN
WAZOO
WAZOOS
WE
WEAK
WEAKEN
WEAKENED
WEAKENER
WEAKENERS
WEAKENING
WEAKENS
WEAKER
WEAKEST
WEAKFISH
WEAKFISHES
WEAKISH
WEAKISHLY
WEAKLIER
WEAKLIEST
WEAKLING
WEAKLINGS
WEAKLY
WEAKNESS
WEAKNESSES
WEAKON
WEAKONS
WEAKSIDE
WEAKSIDES
WEAL
WEALD
WEALDS
WEALS
WEALTH
WEALTHIER
WEALTHIEST
WEALTHILY
WEALTHS
WEALTHY
WEAN
WEANED
WEANER
WEANERS
WEANING
WEANLING
WEANLINGS
WEANS
WEAPON
WEAPONED
WEAPONEER
WEAPONEERED

WEAPONEERING
WEAPONEERS
WEAPONING
WEAPONIZE
WEAPONIZED
WEAPONIZES
WEAPONIZING
WEAPONRIES
WEAPONRY
WEAPONS
WEAR
WEARABLE
WEARABLES
WEARER
WEARERS
WEARIED
WEARIER
WEARIES
WEARIEST
WEARIFUL
WEARILESS
WEARILY
WEARINESS
WEARINESSES
WEARING
WEARINGLY
WEARISH
WEARISOME
WEARPROOF
WEARS
WEARY
WEARYING
WEASAND
WEASANDS
WEASEL
WEASELED
WEASELING
WEASELLED
WEASELLING
WEASELLY
WEASELS
WEASELY
WEASON
WEASONS
WEATHER
WEATHERED
WEATHERING
WEATHERLY
WEATHERS
WEAVE
WEAVED
WEAVER

WEAVERS	WEDELING	WEENIES	WEIGHING	WELDERS
WEAVES	WEDELN	WEENIEST	WEIGHMAN	WELDING
WEAVING	WEDELNS	WEENING	WEIGHMEN	WELDLESS
WEAZAND	WEDELS	WEENS	WEIGHS	WELDMENT
WEAZANDS	WEDGE	WEENSIER	WEIGHT	WELDMENTS
WEB	WEDGED	WEENSIEST	WEIGHTED	WELDOR
WEBBED	WEDGELIKE	WEENSY	WEIGHTER	WELDORS
WEBBIER	WEDGES	WEENY	WEIGHTERS	WELDS
WEBBIEST	WEDGIE	WEEP	WEIGHTIER	WELFARE
WEBBING	WEDGIER	WEEPER	WEIGHTIEST	WELFARES
WEBBINGS	WEDGIES	WEEPERS	WEIGHTILY	WELFARISM
WEBBY	WEDGIEST	WEEPIE	WEIGHTING	WELFARISMS
WEBCAM	WEDGING	WEEPIER	WEIGHTS	WELFARIST
WEBCAMS	WEDGY	WEEPIES	WEIGHTY	WELFARISTS
WEBCAST	WEDLOCK	WEEPIEST	WEINER	WELKIN
WEBCASTED	WEDLOCKS	WEEPINESS	WEINERS	WELKINS
WEBCASTER	WEDS	WEEPINESSES	WEIR	WELL
WEBCASTERS	WEE	WEEPING	WEIRD	WELLADAY
WEBCASTING	WEED	WEEPINGLY	WEIRDED	WELLADAYS
WEBCASTS	WEEDED	WEEPINGS	WEIRDER	WELLAWAY
WEBER	WEEDER	WEEPS	WEIRDEST	WELLAWAYS
WEBERS	WEEDERS	WEEPY	WEIRDIE	WELLBORN
WEBFED	WEEDIER	WEER	WEIRDIES	WELLCURB
WEBFEET	WEEDIEST	WEES	WEIRDING	WELLCURBS
WEBFOOT	WEEDILY	WEEST	WEIRDLY	WELLDOER
WEBLESS	WEEDINESS	WEET	WEIRDNESS	WELLDOERS
WEBLIKE	WEEDINESSES	WEETED	WEIRDNESSES	WELLED
WEBLOG	WEEDING	WEETING	WEIRDO	WELLHEAD
WEBLOGS	WEEDLESS	WEETS	WEIRDOES	WELLHEADS
WEBMASTER	WEEDLIKE	WEEVER	WEIRDOS	WELLHOLE
WEBMASTERS	WEEDS	WEEVERS	WEIRDS	WELLHOLES
WEBPAGE	WEEDY	WEEVIL	WEIRDY	WELLHOUSE
WEBPAGES	WEEK	WEEVILED	WEIRS	WELLHOUSES
WEBS	WEEKDAY	WEEVILLY	WEKA	WELLIE
WEBSITE	WEEKDAYS	WEEVILS	WEKAS	WELLIES
WEBSITES	WEEKEND	WEEVILY	WELCH	WELLING
WEBSTER	WEEKENDED	WEEWEE	WELCHED	WELLNESS
WEBSTERS	WEEKENDER	WEEWEED	WELCHER	WELLNESSES
WEBWORK	WEEKENDERS	WEEWEEING	WELCHERS	WELLS
WEBWORKS	WEEKENDING	WEEWEES	WELCHES	WELLSITE
WEBWORM	WEEKENDS	WEFT	WELCHING	WELLSITES
WEBWORMS	WEEKLIES	WEFTS	WELCOME	WELLY
WECHT	WEEKLONG	WEFTWISE	WELCOMED	WELSH
WECHTS	WEEKLY	WEIGELA	WELCOMELY	WELSHED
WED	WEEKNIGHT	WEIGELAS	WELCOMER	WELSHER
WEDDED	WEEKNIGHTS	WEIGELIA	WELCOMERS	WELSHERS
WEDDER	WEEKS	WEIGELIAS	WELCOMES	WELSHES
WEDDERS	WEEL	WEIGH	WELCOMING	WELSHING
WEDDING	WEEN	WEIGHABLE	WELD	WELT
WEDDINGS	WEENED	WEIGHED	WELDABLE	WELTED
WEDEL	WEENIE	WEIGHER	WELDED	WELTER
WEDELED	WEENIER	WEIGHERS	WELDER	WELTERED

WELTERING	WESTERN	WHALEBONE	WHEAL	WHEEZES
WELTERS	WESTERNER	WHALEBONES	WHEALS	WHEEZIER
WELTING	WESTERNERS	WHALED	WHEAT	WHEEZIEST
WELTINGS	WESTERNS	WHALELIKE	WHEATEAR	WHEEZILY
WELTS	WESTERS	WHALEMAN	WHEATEARS	WHEEZING
WEN	WESTING	WHALEMEN	WHEATEN	WHEEZY
WENCH	WESTINGS	WHALER	WHEATENS	WHELK
WENCHED	WESTMOST	WHALERS	WHEATLAND	WHELKIER
WENCHER	WESTS	WHALES	WHEATLANDS	WHELKIEST
WENCHERS	WESTWARD	WHALING	WHEATLESS	WHELKS
WENCHES	WESTWARDS	WHALINGS	WHEATS	WHELKY
WENCHING	WET	WHAM	WHEATWORM	WHELM
WEND	WETBACK	WHAMMED	WHEATWORMS	WHELMED
WENDED	WETBACKS	WHAMMIES	WHEE	WHELMING
WENDIGO	WETHER	WHAMMING	WHEEDLE	WHELMS
WENDIGOS	WETHERS	WHAMMO	WHEEDLED	WHELP
WENDING	WETLAND	WHAMMY	WHEEDLER	WHELPED
WENDS	WETLANDS	WHAMO	WHEEDLERS	WHELPING
WENNIER	WETLY	WHAMS	WHEEDLES	WHELPLESS
WENNIEST	WETNESS	WHANG	WHEEDLING	WHELPS
WENNISH	WETNESSES	WHANGED	WHEEL	WHEN
WENNY	WETPROOF	WHANGEE	WHEELBASE	WHENAS
WENS	WETS	WHANGEES	WHEELBASES	WHENCE
WENT	WETSUIT	WHANGING	WHEELED	WHENEVER
WEPT	WETSUITS	WHANGS	WHEELER	WHENS
WERE	WETTABLE	WHAP	WHEELERS	WHERE
WEREGILD	WETTED	WHAPPED	WHEELIE	WHEREAS
WEREGILDS	WETTER	WHAPPER	WHEELIES	WHEREASES
WEREWOLF	WETTERS	WHAPPERS	WHEELING	WHEREAT
WEREWOLVES	WETTEST	WHAPPING	WHEELINGS	WHEREBY
WERGELD	WETTING	WHAPS	WHEELLESS	WHEREFORE
WERGELDS	WETTINGS	WHARF	WHEELMAN	WHEREFORES
WERGELT	WETTISH	WHARFAGE	WHEELMEN	WHEREFROM
WERGELTS	WETWARE	WHARFAGES	WHEELS	WHEREIN
WERGILD	WETWARES	WHARFED	WHEELSMAN	WHEREINTO
WERGILDS	WHA	WHARFING	WHEELSMEN	WHEREOF
WERNERITE	WHACK	WHARFS	WHEELWORK	WHEREON
WERNERITES	WHACKED	WHARVE	WHEELWORKS	WHERES
WERT	WHACKER	WHARVES	WHEEN	WHERETO
WERWOLF	WHACKERS	WHAT	WHEENS	WHEREUNTO
WERWOLVES	WHACKIER	WHATEVER	WHEEP	WHEREUPON
WESKIT	WHACKIEST	WHATNESS	WHEEPED	WHEREVER
WESKITS	WHACKING	WHATNESSES	WHEEPING	WHEREWITH
WESSAND	WHACKO	WHATNOT	WHEEPLE	WHEREWITHS
WESSANDS	WHACKOS	WHATNOTS	WHEEPLED	WHERRIED
WEST	WHACKS	WHATS	WHEEPLES	WHERRIES
WESTBOUND	WHACKY	WHATSIS	WHEEPLING	WHERRY
WESTER	WHALE	WHATSISES	WHEEPS	WHERRYING
WESTERED	WHALEBACK	WHATSIT	WHEEZE	WHERVE
WESTERING	WHALEBACKS	WHATSITS	WHEEZED	WHERVES
WESTERLIES	WHALEBOAT	WHAUP	WHEEZER	WHET
WESTERLY	WHALEBOATS	WHAUPS	WHEEZERS	WHETHER

WHETS	WHIMBREL	WHIPLASH	WHIRRIES	WHITED
WHETSTONE	WHIMBRELS	WHIPLASHES	WHIRRING	WHITEFACE
WHETSTONES	WHIMPER	WHIPLIKE	WHIRRS	WHITEFACES
WHETTED	WHIMPERED	WHIPPED	WHIRRY	WHITEFISH
WHETTER	WHIMPERER	WHIPPER	WHIRRYING	WHITEFISHES
WHETTERS	WHIMPERERS	WHIPPERS	WHIRS	WHITEFLIES
WHETTING	WHIMPERING	WHIPPET	WHISH	WHITEFLY
WHEW	WHIMPERS	WHIPPETS	WHISHED	WHITEHEAD
WHEWS	WHIMS	WHIPPIER	WHISHES	WHITEHEADS
WHEY	WHIMSEY	WHIPPIEST	WHISHING	WHITELY
WHEYEY	WHIMSEYS	WHIPPING	WHISHT	WHITEN
WHEYFACE	WHIMSICAL	WHIPPINGS	WHISHTED	WHITENED
WHEYFACED	WHIMSIED	WHIPPY	WHISHTING	WHITENER
WHEYFACES	WHIMSIES	WHIPRAY	WHISHTS	WHITENERS
WHEYISH	WHIMSY	WHIPRAYS	WHISK	WHITENESS
WHEYLIKE	WHIN	WHIPS	WHISKED	WHITENESSES
WHEYS	WHINCHAT	WHIPSAW	WHISKER	WHITENING
WHICH	WHINCHATS	WHIPSAWED	WHISKERED	WHITENINGS
WHICHEVER	WHINE	WHIPSAWING	WHISKERS	WHITENS
WHICKER	WHINED	WHIPSAWN	WHISKERY	WHITEOUT
WHICKERED	WHINER	WHIPSAWS	WHISKEY	WHITEOUTS
WHICKERING	WHINERS	WHIPSNAKE	WHISKEYS	WHITER
WHICKERS	WHINES	WHIPSNAKES	WHISKIES	WHITES
WHID	WHINEY	WHIPSTALL	WHISKING	WHITEST
WHIDAH	WHINGDING	WHIPSTALLS	WHISKS	WHITETAIL
WHIDAHS	WHINGDINGS	WHIPSTOCK	WHISKY	WHITETAILS
WHIDDED	WHINGE	WHIPSTOCKS	WHISPER	WHITEWALL
WHIDDING	WHINGED	WHIPT	WHISPERED	WHITEWALLS
WHIDS	WHINGEING	WHIPTAIL	WHISPERER	WHITEWASH
WHIFF	WHINGER	WHIPTAILS	WHISPERERS	WHITEWASHED
WHIFFED	WHINGERS	WHIPWORM	WHISPERING	WHITEWASHES
WHIFFER	WHINGES	WHIPWORMS	WHISPERS	WHITEWASHING
WHIFFERS	WHINGING	WHIR	WHISPERY	WHITEWING
WHIFFET	WHINIER	WHIRL	WHIST	WHITEWINGS
WHIFFETS	WHINIEST	WHIRLED	WHISTED	WHITEWOOD
WHIFFING	WHININESS	WHIRLER	WHISTING	WHITEWOODS
WHIFFLE	WHININESSES	WHIRLERS	WHISTLE	WHITEY
WHIFFLED	WHINING	WHIRLIER	WHISTLED	WHITEYS
WHIFFLER	WHININGLY	WHIRLIES	WHISTLER	WHITHER
WHIFFLERS	WHINNIED	WHIRLIEST	WHISTLERS	WHITIER
WHIFFLES	WHINNIER	WHIRLIGIG	WHISTLES	WHITIES
WHIFFLING	WHINNIES	WHIRLIGIGS	WHISTLING	WHITIEST
WHIFFS	WHINNIEST	WHIRLING	WHISTLINGS	WHITING
WHIG	WHINNY	WHIRLPOOL	WHISTS	WHITINGS
WHIGS	WHINNYING	WHIRLPOOLS	WHIT	WHITISH
WHILE	WHINS	WHIRLS	WHITE	WHITLOW
WHILED	WHINSTONE	WHIRLWIND	WHITEBAIT	WHITLOWS
WHILES	WHINSTONES	WHIRLWINDS	WHITEBAITS	WHITRACK
WHILING	WHINY	WHIRLY	WHITECAP	WHITRACKS
WHILOM	WHIP	WHIRR	WHITECAPS	WHITS
WHILST	WHIPCORD	WHIRRED	WHITECOMB	WHITTER
WHIM	WHIPCORDS	WHIRRIED	WHITECOMBS	WHITTERS

WHITTLE	WHOMPS	WHOSOEVER	WIDEBAND	WIFE
WHITTLED	WHOMSO	WHUMP	WIDEBODIES	WIFED
WHITTLER	WHOOF	WHUMPED	WIDEBODY	WIFEDOM
WHITTLERS	WHOOFED	WHUMPING	WIDELY	WIFEDOMS
WHITTLES	WHOOFING	WHUMPS	WIDEN	WIFEHOOD
WHITTLING	WHOOFS	WHUP	WIDENED	WIFEHOODS
WHITTLINGS	WHOOP	WHUPPED	WIDENER	WIFELESS
WHITTRET	WHOOPED	WHUPPING	WIDENERS	WIFELIER
WHITTRETS	WHOOPEE	WHUPS	WIDENESS	WIFELIEST
WHITY	WHOOPEES	WHY	WIDENESSES	WIFELIKE
WHIZ	WHOOPER	WHYDAH	WIDENING	WIFELY
WHIZBANG	WHOOPERS	WHYDAHS	WIDENS	WIFES
WHIZBANGS	WHOOPIE	WHYS	WIDEOUT	WIFEY
WHIZZ	WHOOPIES	WICCA	WIDEOUTS	WIFEYS
WHIZZBANG	WHOOPING	WICCAN	WIDER	WIFING
WHIZZBANGS	WHOOPLA	WICCANS	WIDES	WIFTIER
WHIZZED	WHOOPLAS	WICCAS	WIDEST	WIFTIEST
WHIZZER	WHOOPS	WICH	WIDGEON	WIFTY
WHIZZERS	WHOOSH	WICHES	WIDGEONS	WIG
WHIZZES	WHOOSHED	WICK	WIDGET	WIGAN
WHIZZIER	WHOOSHES	WICKAPE	WIDGETS	WIGANS
WHIZZIEST	WHOOSHING	WICKAPES	WIDISH	WIGEON
WHIZZING	WHOOSIS	WICKED	WIDOW	WIGEONS
WHIZZY	WHOOSISES	WICKEDER	WIDOWBIRD	WIGGED
WHO	WHOP	WICKEDEST	WIDOWBIRDS	WIGGERIES
WHOA	WHOPPED	WICKEDLY	WIDOWED	WIGGERY
WHODUNIT	WHOPPER	WICKER	WIDOWER	WIGGIER
WHODUNITS	WHOPPERS	WICKERS	WIDOWERED	WIGGIEST
WHODUNNIT	WHOPPING	WICKET	WIDOWERS	WIGGING
WHODUNNITS	WHOPS	WICKETS	WIDOWHOOD	WIGGINGS
WHOEVER	WHORE	WICKING	WIDOWHOODS	WIGGLE
WHOLE	WHORED	WICKINGS	WIDOWING	WIGGLED
WHOLEMEAL	WHOREDOM	WICKIUP	WIDOWS	WIGGLER
WHOLENESS	WHOREDOMS	WICKIUPS	WIDTH	WIGGLERS
WHOLENESSES	WHORES	WICKLESS	WIDTHS	WIGGLES
WHOLES	WHORESON	WICKS	WIDTHWAY	WIGGLIER
WHOLESALE	WHORESONS	WICKYUP	WIDTHWAYS	WIGGLIEST
WHOLESALED	WHORING	WICKYUPS	WIDTHWISE	WIGGLING
WHOLESALES	WHORISH	WICOPIES	WIELD	WIGGLY
WHOLESALING	WHORISHLY	WICOPY	WIELDABLE	WIGGY
WHOLESOME	WHORL	WIDDER	WIELDED	WIGHT
WHOLESOMER	WHORLED	WIDDERS	WIELDER	WIGHTS
WHOLESOMEST	WHORLS	WIDDIE	WIELDERS	WIGLESS
WHOLISM	WHORT	WIDDIES	WIELDIER	WIGLET
WHOLISMS	WHORTLE	WIDDLE	WIELDIEST	WIGLETS
WHOLISTIC	WHORTLES	WIDDLED	WIELDING	WIGLIKE
WHOLLY	WHORTS	WIDDLES	WIELDS	WIGMAKER
WHOM	WHOSE	WIDDLING	WIELDY	WIGMAKERS
WHOMEVER	WHOSEVER	WIDDY	WIENER	WIGS
WHOMP	WHOSIS	WIDE	WIENERS	WIGWAG
WHOMPED	WHOSISES	WIDEAWAKE	WIENIE	WIGWAGGED
WHOMPING	WHOSO	WIDEAWAKES	WIENIES	WIGWAGGER

WIGWAGGERS	WILLED	WIMPINESS	WINDGALL	WINDTHROW
WIGWAGGING	WILLEMITE	WIMPINESSES	WINDGALLS	WINDTHROWS
WIGWAGS	WILLEMITES	WIMPING	WINDHOVER	WINDUP
WIGWAM	WILLER	WIMPISH	WINDHOVERS	WINDUPS
WIGWAMS	WILLERS	WIMPLE	WINDIER	WINDWARD
WIKIUP	WILLET	WIMPLED	WINDIEST	WINDWARDS
WIKIUPS	WILLETS	WIMPLES	WINDIGO	WINDWAY
WILCO	WILLFUL	WIMPLING	WINDIGOS	WINDWAYS
WILD	WILLFULLY	WIMPS	WINDILY	WINDY
WILDCARD	WILLIE	WIMPY	WINDINESS	WINE
WILDCARDS	WILLIED	WIN	WINDINESSES	WINED
WILDCAT	WILLIES	WINCE	WINDING	WINEGLASS
WILDCATS	WILLING	WINCED	WINDINGLY	WINEGLASSES
WILDCATTED	WILLINGER	WINCER	WINDINGS	WINELESS
WILDCATTING	WILLINGEST	WINCERS	WINDLASS	WINEMAKER
WILDED	WILLINGLY	WINCES	WINDLASSED	WINEMAKERS
WILDER	WILLIWAU	WINCEY	WINDLASSES	WINEPRESS
WILDERED	WILLIWAUS	WINCEYS	WINDLASSING	WINEPRESSES
WILDERING	WILLIWAW	WINCH	WINDLE	WINERIES
WILDERS	WILLIWAWS	WINCHED	WINDLED	WINERY
WILDEST	WILLOW	WINCHER	WINDLES	WINES
WILDFIRE	WILLOWED	WINCHERS	WINDLESS	WINESAP
WILDFIRES	WILLOWER	WINCHES	WINDLING	WINESAPS
WILDFOWL	WILLOWERS	WINCHING	WINDLINGS	WINESHOP
WILDFOWLS	WILLOWIER	WINCING	WINDMILL	WINESHOPS
WILDING	WILLOWIEST	WIND	WINDMILLED	WINESKIN
WILDINGS	WILLOWING	WINDABLE	WINDMILLING	WINESKINS
WILDISH	WILLOWS	WINDAGE	WINDMILLS	WINESOP
WILDLAND	WILLOWY	WINDAGES	WINDOW	WINESOPS
WILDLANDS	WILLPOWER	WINDBAG	WINDOWED	WINEY
WILDLIFE	WILLPOWERS	WINDBAGS	WINDOWING	WING
WILDLING	WILLS	WINDBELL	WINDOWS	WINGBACK
WILDLINGS	WILLY	WINDBELLS	WINDOWY	WINGBACKS
WILDLY	WILLYARD	WINDBLAST	WINDPIPE	WINGBOW
WILDNESS	WILLYART	WINDBLASTS	WINDPIPES	WINGBOWS
WILDNESSES	WILLYING	WINDBLOWN	WINDPROOF	WINGCHAIR
WILDS	WILLYWAW	WINDBREAK	WINDROW	WINGCHAIRS
WILDWOOD	WILLYWAWS	WINDBREAKS	WINDROWED	WINGDING
WILDWOODS	WILT	WINDBURN	WINDROWER	WINGDINGS
WILE	WILTED	WINDBURNED	WINDROWERS	WINGED
WILED	WILTING	WINDBURNING	WINDROWING	WINGEDLY
WILES	WILTS	WINDBURNS	WINDROWS	WINGER
WILFUL	WILY	WINDBURNT	WINDS	WINGERS
WILFULLY	WIMBLE	WINDCHILL	WINDSOCK	WINGIER
WILIER	WIMBLED	WINDCHILLS	WINDSOCKS	WINGIEST
WILIEST	WIMBLES	WINDED	WINDSTORM	WINGING
WILILY	WIMBLING	WINDER	WINDSTORMS	WINGLESS
WILINESS	WIMMIN	WINDERS	WINDSURF	WINGLET
WILINESSES	WIMP	WINDFALL	WINDSURFED	WINGLETS
WILING	WIMPED	WINDFALLS	WINDSURFING	WINGLIKE
WILL	WIMPIER	WINDFLAW	WINDSURFS	WINGMAN
WILLABLE	WIMPIEST	WINDFLAWS	WINDSWEPT	WINGMEN

WINGOVER	WINTERFEED	WIREPHOTO	WISHA	WITCHLIKE
WINGOVERS	WINTERFEEDING	WIREPHOTOS	WISHBONE	WITCHWEED
WINGS	WINTERFEEDS	WIRER	WISHBONES	WITCHWEEDS
WINGSPAN	WINTERIER	WIRERS	WISHED	WITCHY
WINGSPANS	WINTERIEST	WIRES	WISHER	WITE
WINGTIP	WINTERING	WIRETAP	WISHERS	WITED
WINGTIPS	WINTERISH	WIRETAPPED	WISHES	WITES
WINGY	WINTERIZE	WIRETAPPING	WISHFUL	WITH
WINIER	WINTERIZED	WIRETAPS	WISHFULLY	WITHAL
WINIEST	WINTERIZES	WIREWAY	WISHING	WITHDRAW
WINING	WINTERIZING	WIREWAYS	WISHLESS	WITHDRAWING
WINISH	WINTERLY	WIREWORK	WISING	WITHDRAWN
WINK	WINTERS	WIREWORKS	WISP	WITHDRAWS
WINKED	WINTERY	WIREWORM	WISPED	WITHDREW
WINKER	WINTLE	WIREWORMS	WISPIER	WITHE
WINKERS	WINTLED	WIRIER	WISPIEST	WITHED
WINKING	WINTLES	WIRIEST	WISPILY	WITHER
WINKINGLY	WINTLING	WIRILY	WISPINESS	WITHERED
WINKLE	WINTRIER	WIRINESS	WISPINESSES	WITHERER
WINKLED	WINTRIEST	WIRINESSES	WISPING	WITHERERS
WINKLES	WINTRILY	WIRING	WISPISH	WITHERING
WINKLING	WINTRY	WIRINGS	WISPLIKE	WITHERITE
WINKS	WINY	WIRRA	WISPS	WITHERITES
WINLESS	WINZE	WIRY	WISPY	WITHEROD
WINNABLE	WINZES	WIS	WISS	WITHERODS
WINNED	WIPE	WISDOM	WISSED	WITHERS
WINNER	WIPED	WISDOMS	WISSES	WITHES
WINNERS	WIPEOUT	WISE	WISSING	WITHHELD
WINNING	WIPEOUTS	WISEACRE	WIST	WITHHOLD
WINNINGLY	WIPER	WISEACRES	WISTARIA	WITHHOLDING
WINNINGS	WIPERS	WISEASS	WISTARIAS	WITHHOLDS
WINNOCK	WIPES	WISEASSES	WISTED	WITHIER
WINNOCKS	WIPING	WISECRACK	WISTERIA	WITHIES
WINNOW	WIRABLE	WISECRACKED	WISTERIAS	WITHIEST
WINNOWED	WIRE	WISECRACKING	WISTFUL	WITHIN
WINNOWER	WIRED	WISECRACKS	WISTFULLY	WITHING
WINNOWERS	WIREDRAW	WISED	WISTING	WITHINS
WINNOWING	WIREDRAWING	WISEGUY	WISTS	WITHOUT
WINNOWS	WIREDRAWN	WISEGUYS	WIT	WITHOUTS
WINO	WIREDRAWS	WISELIER	WITAN	WITHSTAND
WINOES	WIREDREW	WISELIEST	WITANS	WITHSTANDING
WINOS	WIREGRASS	WISELY	WITCH	WITHSTANDS
WINS	WIREGRASSES	WISENESS	WITCHED	WITHSTOOD
WINSOME	WIREHAIR	WISENESSES	WITCHERIES	WITHY
WINSOMELY	WIREHAIRS	WISENT	WITCHERY	WITING
WINSOMER	WIRELESS	WISENTS	WITCHES	WITLESS
WINSOMEST	WIRELESSED	WISER	WITCHHOOD	WITLESSLY
WINTER	WIRELESSES	WISES	WITCHHOODS	WITLING
WINTERED	WIRELESSING	WISEST	WITCHIER	WITLINGS
WINTERER	WIRELIKE	WISEWOMAN	WITCHIEST	WITLOOF
WINTERERS	WIREMAN	WISEWOMEN	WITCHING	WITLOOFS
WINTERFED	WIREMEN	WISH	WITCHINGS	WITNESS

WITNESSED	WOALD	WOLFRAM	WOMMERA	WOODCUTS
WITNESSER	WOALDS	WOLFRAMS	WOMMERAS	WOODED
WITNESSERS	WOBBLE	WOLFS	WOMYN	WOODEN
WITNESSES	WOBBLED	WOLFSBANE	WON	WOODENER
WITNESSING	WOBBLER	WOLFSBANES	WONDER	WOODENEST
WITNEY	WOBBLERS	WOLVER	WONDERED	WOODENLY
WITNEYS	WOBBLES	WOLVERINE	WONDERER	WOODGRAIN
WITS	WOBBLIER	WOLVERINES	WONDERERS	WOODGRAINS
WITTED	WOBBLIES	WOLVERS	WONDERFUL	WOODHEN
WITTICISM	WOBBLIEST	WOLVES	WONDERING	WOODHENS
WITTICISMS	WOBBLING	WOMAN	WONDERS	WOODIE
WITTIER	WOBBLY	WOMANED	WONDROUS	WOODIER
WITTIEST	WOBEGONE	WOMANHOOD	WONK	WOODIES
WITTILY	WODGE	WOMANHOODS	WONKIER	WOODIEST
WITTINESS	WODGES	WOMANING	WONKIEST	WOODINESS
WITTINESSES	WOE	WOMANISE	WONKS	WOODINESSES
WITTING	WOEBEGONE	WOMANISED	WONKY	WOODING
WITTINGLY	WOEFUL	WOMANISES	WONNED	WOODLAND
WITTINGS	WOEFULLER	WOMANISH	WONNER	WOODLANDS
WITTOL	WOEFULLEST	WOMANISING	WONNERS	WOODLARK
WITTOLS	WOEFULLY	WOMANISM	WONNING	WOODLARKS
WITTY	WOENESS	WOMANISMS	WONS	WOODLESS
WIVE	WOENESSES	WOMANIST	WONT	WOODLORE
WIVED	WOES	WOMANISTS	WONTED	WOODLORES
WIVER	WOESOME	WOMANIZE	WONTEDLY	WOODLOT
WIVERN	WOFUL	WOMANIZED	WONTING	WOODLOTS
WIVERNS	WOFULLER	WOMANIZER	WONTON	WOODMAN
WIVERS	WOFULLEST	WOMANIZERS	WONTONS	WOODMEN
WIVES	WOFULLY	WOMANIZES	WONTS	WOODNOTE
WIVING	WOG	WOMANIZING	WOO	WOODNOTES
WIZ	WOGGISH	WOMANKIND	WOOD	WOODPILE
WIZARD	WOGS	WOMANLESS	WOODBIN	WOODPILES
WIZARDLY	WOK	WOMANLIER	WOODBIND	WOODRUFF
WIZARDRIES	WOKE	WOMANLIEST	WOODBINDS	WOODRUFFS
WIZARDRY	WOKEN	WOMANLIKE	WOODBINE	WOODS
WIZARDS	WOKS	WOMANLY	WOODBINES	WOODSHED
WIZEN	WOLD	WOMANNESS	WOODBINS	WOODSHEDDED
WIZENED	WOLDS	WOMANNESSES	WOODBLOCK	WOODSHEDDING
WIZENING	WOLF	WOMANS	WOODBLOCKS	WOODSHEDS
WIZENS	WOLFBERRIES	WOMB	WOODBORER	WOODSIA
WIZES	WOLFBERRY	WOMBAT	WOODBORERS	WOODSIAS
WIZZEN	WOLFED	WOMBATS	WOODBOX	WOODSIER
WIZZENS	WOLFER	WOMBED	WOODBOXES	WOODSIEST
WIZZES	WOLFERS	WOMBIER	WOODCHAT	WOODSMAN
WO	WOLFFISH	WOMBIEST	WOODCHATS	WOODSMEN
WOAD	WOLFFISHES	WOMBS	WOODCHUCK	WOODSTOVE
WOADED	WOLFHOUND	WOMBY	WOODCHUCKS	WOODSTOVES
WOADS	WOLFHOUNDS	WOMEN	WOODCOCK	WOODSY
WOADWAX	WOLFING	WOMENFOLK	WOODCOCKS	WOODTONE
WOADWAXEN	WOLFISH	WOMENKIND	WOODCRAFT	WOODTONES
WOADWAXENS	WOLFISHLY	WOMERA	WOODCRAFTS	WOODWAX
WOADWAXES	WOLFLIKE	WOMERAS	WOODCUT	WOODWAXEN

WOODWAXENS	WOOLSHED	WORKABLE	WORKS	WORN
WOODWAXES	WOOLSHEDS	WORKABLY	WORKSHEET	WORNNESS
WOODWIND	WOOLSKIN	WORKADAY	WORKSHEETS	WORNNESSES
WOODWINDS	WOOLSKINS	WORKBAG	WORKSHOP	WORRIED
WOODWORK	WOOLWORK	WORKBAGS	WORKSHOPS	WORRIEDLY
WOODWORKS	WOOLWORKS	WORKBENCH	WORKSPACE	WORRIER
WOODWORM	WOOLY	WORKBENCHES	WORKSPACES	WORRIERS
WOODWORMS	WOOMERA	WORKBOAT	WORKTABLE	WORRIES
WOODY	WOOMERAS	WORKBOATS	WORKTABLES	WORRIMENT
WOOED	WOOPS	WORKBOOK	WORKUP	WORRIMENTS
WOOER	WOOPSED	WORKBOOKS	WORKUPS	WORRISOME
WOOERS	WOOPSES	WORKBOX	WORKWEEK	WORRIT
WOOF	WOOPSING	WORKBOXES	WORKWEEKS	WORRITED
WOOFED	WOORALI	WORKDAY	WORKWOMAN	WORRITING
WOOFER	WOORALIS	WORKDAYS	WORKWOMEN	WORRITS
WOOFERS	WOORARI	WORKED	WORLD	WORRY
WOOFING	WOORARIS	WORKER	WORLDBEAT	WORRYING
WOOFS	WOOS	WORKERS	WORLDBEATS	WORRYWART
WOOING	WOOSH	WORKFARE	WORLDLIER	WORRYWARTS
WOOINGLY	WOOSHED	WORKFARES	WORLDLIEST	WORSE
WOOL	WOOSHES	WORKFLOW	WORLDLING	WORSEN
WOOLED	WOOSHING	WORKFLOWS	WORLDLINGS	WORSENED
WOOLEN	WOOZIER	WORKFOLK	WORLDLY	WORSENING
WOOLENS	WOOZIEST	WORKFOLKS	WORLDS	WORSENS
WOOLER	WOOZILY	WORKFORCE	WORLDVIEW	WORSER
WOOLERS	WOOZINESS	WORKFORCES	WORLDVIEWS	WORSES
WOOLFELL	WOOZINESSES	WORKHORSE	WORLDWIDE	WORSET
WOOLFELLS	WOOZY	WORKHORSES	WORM	WORSETS
WOOLHAT	WOP	WORKHOUR	WORMED	WORSHIP
WOOLHATS	WOPS	WORKHOURS	WORMER	WORSHIPED
WOOLIE	WORD	WORKHOUSE	WORMERS	WORSHIPER
WOOLIER	WORDAGE	WORKHOUSES	WORMGEAR	WORSHIPERS
WOOLIES	WORDAGES	WORKING	WORMGEARS	WORSHIPING
WOOLIEST	WORDBOOK	WORKINGS	WORMHOLE	WORSHIPPED
WOOLINESS	WORDBOOKS	WORKLESS	WORMHOLES	WORSHIPPING
WOOLINESSES	WORDED	WORKLOAD	WORMIER	WORSHIPS
WOOLLED	WORDIER	WORKLOADS	WORMIEST	WORST
WOOLLEN	WORDIEST	WORKMAN	WORMIL	WORSTED
WOOLLENS	WORDILY	WORKMANLY	WORMILS	WORSTEDS
WOOLLIER	WORDINESS	WORKMATE	WORMINESS	WORSTING
WOOLLIES	WORDINESSES	WORKMATES	WORMINESSES	WORSTS
WOOLLIEST	WORDING	WORKMEN	WORMING	WORT
WOOLLIKE	WORDINGS	WORKOUT	WORMISH	WORTH
WOOLLILY	WORDLESS	WORKOUTS	WORMLIKE	WORTHED
WOOLLY	WORDPLAY	WORKPIECE	WORMROOT	WORTHFUL
WOOLMAN	WORDPLAYS	WORKPIECES	WORMROOTS	WORTHIER
WOOLMEN	WORDS	WORKPLACE	WORMS	WORTHIES
WOOLPACK	WORDSMITH	WORKPLACES	WORMSEED	WORTHIEST
WOOLPACKS	WORDSMITHS	WORKPRINT	WORMSEEDS	WORTHILY
WOOLS	WORDY	WORKPRINTS	WORMWOOD	WORTHING
WOOLSACK	WORE	WORKROOM	WORMWOODS	WORTHLESS
WOOLSACKS	WORK	WORKROOMS	WORMY	WORTHS

WORTHY	WRASSE	WRENCHING	WRINKLY	WRYEST
WORTS	WRASSES	WRENS	WRIST	WRYING
WOS	WRASSLE	WREST	WRISTBAND	WRYLY
WOST	WRASSLED	WRESTED	WRISTBANDS	WRYNECK
WOT	WRASSLES	WRESTER	WRISTIER	WRYNECKS
WOTS	WRASSLING	WRESTERS	WRISTIEST	WRYNESS
WOTTED	WRASTLE	WRESTING	WRISTLET	WRYNESSES
WOTTING	WRASTLED	WRESTLE	WRISTLETS	WUD
WOULD	WRASTLES	WRESTLED	WRISTLOCK	WULFENITE
WOULDEST	WRASTLING	WRESTLER	WRISTLOCKS	WULFENITES
WOULDST	WRATH	WRESTLERS	WRISTS	WURST
WOUND	WRATHED	WRESTLES	WRISTY	WURSTS
WOUNDED	WRATHFUL	WRESTLING	WRIT	WURTZITE
WOUNDEDLY	WRATHIER	WRESTLINGS	WRITABLE	WURTZITES
WOUNDING	WRATHIEST	WRESTS	WRITE	WURZEL
WOUNDLESS	WRATHILY	WRETCH	WRITEABLE	WURZELS
WOUNDS	WRATHING	WRETCHED	WRITER	WUSHU
WOUNDWORT	WRATHS	WRETCHEDER	WRITERLY	WUSS
WOUNDWORTS	WRATHY	WRETCHEDEST	WRITERS	WUSSES
WOVE	WREAK	WRETCHES	WRITES	WUSSIER
WOVEN	WREAKED	WRICK	WRITHE	WUSSIES
WOVENS	WREAKER	WRICKED	WRITHED	WUSSIEST
WOW	WREAKERS	WRICKING	WRITHEN	WUSSY
WOWED	WREAKING	WRICKS	WRITHER	WUTHER
WOWING	WREAKS	WRIED	WRITHERS	WUTHERED
WOWS	WREATH	WRIER	WRITHES	WUTHERING
WOWSER	WREATHE	WRIES	WRITHING	WUTHERS
WOWSERS	WREATHED	WRIEST	WRITING	WYANDOTTE
WRACK	WREATHEN	WRIGGLE	WRITINGS	WYANDOTTES
WRACKED	WREATHER	WRIGGLED	WRITS	WYCH
WRACKFUL	WREATHERS	WRIGGLER	WRITTEN	WYCHES
WRACKING	WREATHES	WRIGGLERS	WRONG	WYE
WRACKS	WREATHING	WRIGGLES	WRONGDOER	WYES
WRAITH	WREATHS	WRIGGLIER	WRONGDOERS	WYLE
WRAITHS	WREATHY	WRIGGLIEST	WRONGED	WYLED
WRANG	WRECK	WRIGGLING	WRONGER	WYLES
WRANGLE	WRECKAGE	WRIGGLY	WRONGERS	WYLIECOAT
WRANGLED	WRECKAGES	WRIGHT	WRONGEST	WYLIECOATS
WRANGLER	WRECKED	WRIGHTS	WRONGFUL	WYLING
WRANGLERS	WRECKER	WRING	WRONGING	WYN
WRANGLES	WRECKERS	WRINGED	WRONGLY	WYND
WRANGLING	WRECKFUL	WRINGER	WRONGNESS	WYNDS
WRANGS	WRECKING	WRINGERS	WRONGNESSES	WYNN
WRAP	WRECKINGS	WRINGING	WRONGS	WYNNS
WRAPPED	WRECKS	WRINGS	WROTE	WYNS
WRAPPER	WREN	WRINKLE	WROTH	WYTE
WRAPPERS	WRENCH	WRINKLED	WROTHFUL	WYTED
WRAPPING	WRENCHED	WRINKLES	WROUGHT	WYTES
WRAPPINGS	WRENCHER	WRINKLIER	WRUNG	WYTING
WRAPS	WRENCHERS	WRINKLIEST	WRY	WYVERN
WRAPT	WRENCHES	WRINKLING	WRYER	WYVERNS

X

XANTHAN
XANTHANS
XANTHATE
XANTHATES
XANTHEIN
XANTHEINS
XANTHENE
XANTHENES
XANTHIC
XANTHIN
XANTHINE
XANTHINES
XANTHINS
XANTHOMA
XANTHOMAS
XANTHOMATA
XANTHONE
XANTHONES
XANTHOUS
XEBEC
XEBECS
XENIA
XENIAL
XENIAS
XENIC
XENOBLAST
XENOBLASTS
XENOCRYST
XENOCRYSTS
XENOGAMIES
XENOGAMY
XENOGENIC
XENOGENIES
XENOGENY
XENOGRAFT
XENOGRAFTS
XENOLITH
XENOLITHS
XENON
XENONS
XENOPHILE
XENOPHILES
XENOPHOBE
XENOPHOBES
XENOPUS
XENOPUSES
XERARCH

XERIC
XERICALLY
XERISCAPE
XERISCAPES
XERODERMA
XERODERMAE
XERODERMAS
XEROPHILE
XEROPHILIES
XEROPHILY
XEROPHYTE
XEROPHYTES
XEROSERE
XEROSERES
XEROSES
XEROSIS
XEROTIC
XEROX
XEROXED
XEROXES
XEROXING
XERUS
XERUSES
XI
XIPHOID
XIPHOIDS
XIS
XU
XYLAN
XYLANS
XYLEM
XYLEMS
XYLENE
XYLENES
XYLIDIN
XYLIDINE
XYLIDINES
XYLIDINS
XYLITOL
XYLITOLS
XYLOCARP
XYLOCARPS
XYLOGRAPH
XYLOGRAPHED
XYLOGRAPHING
XYLOGRAPHS
XYLOID
XYLOL
XYLOLS
XYLOPHAGE
XYLOPHAGES

XYLOPHONE
XYLOPHONES
XYLOSE
XYLOSES
XYLOTOMIES
XYLOTOMY
XYLYL
XYLYLS
XYST
XYSTER
XYSTERS
XYSTI
XYSTOI
XYSTOS
XYSTS
XYSTUS

Y

YA
YABBER
YABBERED
YABBERING
YABBERS
YABBIE
YABBIES
YABBY
YACHT
YACHTED
YACHTER
YACHTERS
YACHTING
YACHTINGS
YACHTMAN
YACHTMEN
YACHTS
YACHTSMAN
YACHTSMEN
YACK
YACKED
YACKING
YACKS
YAFF
YAFFED
YAFFING
YAFFS
YAG
YAGER
YAGERS

YAGI
YAGIS
YAGS
YAH
YAHOO
YAHOOISM
YAHOOISMS
YAHOOS
YAHRZEIT
YAHRZEITS
YAIRD
YAIRDS
YAK
YAKITORI
YAKITORIS
YAKKED
YAKKER
YAKKERS
YAKKING
YAKS
YAKUZA
YALD
YAM
YAMALKA
YAMALKAS
YAMEN
YAMENS
YAMMER
YAMMERED
YAMMERER
YAMMERERS
YAMMERING
YAMMERS
YAMS
YAMULKA
YAMULKAS
YAMUN
YAMUNS
YANG
YANGS
YANK
YANKED
YANKING
YANKS
YANQUI
YANQUIS
YANTRA
YANTRAS
YAP
YAPOCK
YAPOCKS

YAPOK
YAPOKS
YAPON
YAPONS
YAPPED
YAPPER
YAPPERS
YAPPING
YAPPINGLY
YAPS
YAR
YARD
YARDAGE
YARDAGES
YARDARM
YARDARMS
YARDBIRD
YARDBIRDS
YARDED
YARDER
YARDERS
YARDING
YARDLAND
YARDLANDS
YARDMAN
YARDMEN
YARDS
YARDSTICK
YARDSTICKS
YARDWAND
YARDWANDS
YARDWORK
YARDWORKS
YARE
YARELY
YARER
YAREST
YARMELKE
YARMELKES
YARMULKE
YARMULKES
YARN
YARNED
YARNER
YARNERS
YARNING
YARNS
YARROW
YARROWS
YASHMAC
YASHMACS

YASHMAK	YCLAD	YEELINS	YERKS	YIPPIE
YASHMAKS	YCLEPED	YEGG	YES	YIPPIES
YASMAK	YCLEPT	YEGGMAN	YESES	YIPPING
YASMAKS	YE	YEGGMEN	YESHIVA	YIPS
YATAGAN	YEA	YEGGS	YESHIVAH	YIRD
YATAGANS	YEAH	YEH	YESHIVAHS	YIRDS
YATAGHAN	YEAHS	YELD	YESHIVAS	YIRR
YATAGHANS	YEALING	YELK	YESHIVOT	YIRRED
YATTER	YEALINGS	YELKS	YESHIVOTH	YIRRING
YATTERED	YEAN	YELL	YESSED	YIRRS
YATTERING	YEANED	YELLED	YESSES	YIRTH
YATTERS	YEANING	YELLER	YESSING	YIRTHS
YAUD	YEANLING	YELLERS	YESTER	YLEM
YAUDS	YEANLINGS	YELLING	YESTERDAY	YLEMS
YAULD	YEANS	YELLOW	YESTERDAYS	YO
YAUP	YEAR	YELLOWED	YESTEREVE	YOB
YAUPED	YEARBOOK	YELLOWER	YESTEREVES	YOBBO
YAUPER	YEARBOOKS	YELLOWEST	YESTERN	YOBBOES
YAUPERS	YEAREND	YELLOWFIN	YESTREEN	YOBBOS
YAUPING	YEARENDS	YELLOWFINS	YESTREENS	YOBS
YAUPON	YEARLIES	YELLOWING	YET	YOCK
YAUPONS	YEARLING	YELLOWISH	YETI	YOCKED
YAUPS	YEARLINGS	YELLOWLY	YETIS	YOCKING
YAUTIA	YEARLONG	YELLOWS	YETT	YOCKS
YAUTIAS	YEARLY	YELLOWY	YETTS	YOD
YAW	YEARN	YELLS	YEUK	YODEL
YAWED	YEARNED	YELP	YEUKED	YODELED
YAWEY	YEARNER	YELPED	YEUKING	YODELER
YAWING	YEARNERS	YELPER	YEUKS	YODELERS
YAWL	YEARNING	YELPERS	YEUKY	YODELING
YAWLED	YEARNINGS	YELPING	YEW	YODELLED
YAWLING	YEARNS	YELPS	YEWS	YODELLER
YAWLS	YEARS	YEN	YID	YODELLERS
YAWMETER	YEAS	YENNED	YIDS	YODELLING
YAWMETERS	YEASAYER	YENNING	YIELD	YODELS
YAWN	YEASAYERS	YENS	YIELDABLE	YODH
YAWNED	YEAST	YENTA	YIELDED	YODHS
YAWNER	YEASTED	YENTAS	YIELDER	YODLE
YAWNERS	YEASTIER	YENTE	YIELDERS	YODLED
YAWNING	YEASTIEST	YENTES	YIELDING	YODLER
YAWNINGLY	YEASTILY	YEOMAN	YIELDS	YODLERS
YAWNS	YEASTING	YEOMANLY	YIKES	YODLES
YAWP	YEASTLESS	YEOMANRIES	YILL	YODLING
YAWPED	YEASTLIKE	YEOMANRY	YILLS	YODS
YAWPER	YEASTS	YEOMEN	YIN	YOGA
YAWPERS	YEASTY	YEP	YINCE	YOGAS
YAWPING	YECCH	YEPS	YINS	YOGEE
YAWPINGS	YECCHS	YERBA	YIP	YOGEES
YAWPS	YECH	YERBAS	YIPE	YOGH
YAWS	YECHS	YERK	YIPES	YOGHOURT
YAY	YECHY	YERKED	YIPPED	YOGHOURTS
YAYS	YEELIN	YERKING	YIPPEE	YOGHS

YOGHURT
YOGHURTS
YOGI
YOGIC
YOGIN
YOGINI
YOGINIS
YOGINS
YOGIS
YOGURT
YOGURTS
YOHIMBE
YOHIMBES
YOHIMBINE
YOHIMBINES
YOICKS
YOK
YOKE
YOKED
YOKEL
YOKELESS
YOKELISH
YOKELS
YOKEMATE
YOKEMATES
YOKES
YOKING
YOKOZUNA
YOKOZUNAS
YOKS
YOLK
YOLKED
YOLKIER
YOLKIEST
YOLKS
YOLKY
YOM
YOMIM
YON
YOND
YONDER
YONI
YONIC
YONIS
YONKER
YONKERS
YORE
YORES
YOTTABYTE
YOTTABYTES
YOU
YOUNG

YOUNGER
YOUNGERS
YOUNGEST
YOUNGISH
YOUNGLING
YOUNGLINGS
YOUNGNESS
YOUNGNESSES
YOUNGS
YOUNGSTER
YOUNGSTERS
YOUNKER
YOUNKERS
YOUPON
YOUPONS
YOUR
YOURN
YOURS
YOURSELF
YOURSELVES
YOUS
YOUSE
YOUTH
YOUTHEN
YOUTHENED
YOUTHENING
YOUTHENS
YOUTHFUL
YOUTHS
YOW
YOWE
YOWED
YOWES
YOWIE
YOWIES
YOWING
YOWL
YOWLED
YOWLER
YOWLERS
YOWLING
YOWLS
YOWS
YPERITE
YPERITES
YTTERBIA
YTTERBIAS
YTTERBIC
YTTERBIUM
YTTERBIUMS
YTTERBOUS
YTTRIA

YTTRIAS
YTTRIC
YTTRIUM
YTTRIUMS
YUAN
YUANS
YUCA
YUCAS
YUCCA
YUCCAS
YUCCH
YUCH
YUCK
YUCKED
YUCKIER
YUCKIEST
YUCKINESS
YUCKINESSES
YUCKING
YUCKS
YUCKY
YUGA
YUGAS
YUK
YUKKED
YUKKIER
YUKKIEST
YUKKING
YUKKY
YUKS
YULAN
YULANS
YULE
YULES
YULETIDE
YULETIDES
YUM
YUMMIER
YUMMIES
YUMMIEST
YUMMINESS
YUMMINESSES
YUMMY
YUP
YUPON
YUPONS
YUPPIE
YUPPIEDOM
YUPPIEDOMS
YUPPIEISH
YUPPIES
YUPPIFIED

YUPPIFIES
YUPPIFY
YUPPIFYING
YUPPY
YUPS
YURT
YURTA
YURTS
YUTZ
YUTZES
YWIS

Z

ZA
ZABAIONE
ZABAIONES
ZABAJONE
ZABAJONES
ZACATON
ZACATONS
ZADDICK
ZADDIK
ZADDIKIM
ZAFFAR
ZAFFARS
ZAFFER
ZAFFERS
ZAFFIR
ZAFFIRS
ZAFFRE
ZAFFRES
ZAFTIG
ZAG
ZAGGED
ZAGGING
ZAGS
ZAIBATSU
ZAIKAI
ZAIKAIS
ZAIRE
ZAIRES
ZAMARRA
ZAMARRAS
ZAMARRO
ZAMARROS
ZAMIA
ZAMIAS
ZAMINDAR
ZAMINDARI

ZAMINDARIS
ZAMINDARS
ZANANA
ZANANAS
ZANDER
ZANDERS
ZANIER
ZANIES
ZANIEST
ZANILY
ZANINESS
ZANINESSES
ZANY
ZANYISH
ZANZA
ZANZAS
ZAP
ZAPATEADO
ZAPATEADOS
ZAPATEO
ZAPATEOS
ZAPPED
ZAPPER
ZAPPERS
ZAPPIER
ZAPPIEST
ZAPPING
ZAPPY
ZAPS
ZAPTIAH
ZAPTIAHS
ZAPTIEH
ZAPTIEHS
ZARATITE
ZARATITES
ZAREBA
ZAREBAS
ZAREEBA
ZAREEBAS
ZARF
ZARFS
ZARIBA
ZARIBAS
ZARZUELA
ZARZUELAS
ZAS
ZASTRUGA
ZASTRUGI
ZAX
ZAXES
ZAYIN
ZAYINS

ZAZEN	ZEKS	ZETTABYTE	ZINCKED	ZIRAMS
ZAZENS	ZELKOVA	ZETTABYTES	ZINCKING	ZIRCALOY
ZEAL	ZELKOVAS	ZEUGMA	ZINCKY	ZIRCALOYS
ZEALOT	ZEMINDAR	ZEUGMAS	ZINCOID	ZIRCON
ZEALOTRIES	ZEMINDARIES	ZEUGMATIC	ZINCOUS	ZIRCONIA
ZEALOTRY	ZEMINDARS	ZIBELINE	ZINCS	ZIRCONIAS
ZEALOTS	ZEMINDARY	ZIBELINES	ZINCY	ZIRCONIC
ZEALOUS	ZEMSTVA	ZIBELLINE	ZINE	ZIRCONIUM
ZEALOUSLY	ZEMSTVO	ZIBELLINES	ZINEB	ZIRCONIUMS
ZEALS	ZEMSTVOS	ZIBET	ZINEBS	ZIRCONS
ZEATIN	ZENAIDA	ZIBETH	ZINES	ZIT
ZEATINS	ZENAIDAS	ZIBETHS	ZINFANDEL	ZITHER
ZEBEC	ZENANA	ZIBETS	ZINFANDELS	ZITHERIST
ZEBECK	ZENANAS	ZIG	ZING	ZITHERISTS
ZEBECKS	ZENITH	ZIGGED	ZINGANI	ZITHERN
ZEBECS	ZENITHAL	ZIGGING	ZINGANO	ZITHERNS
ZEBRA	ZENITHS	ZIGGURAT	ZINGARA	ZITHERS
ZEBRAFISH	ZEOLITE	ZIGGURATS	ZINGARE	ZITI
ZEBRAFISHES	ZEOLITES	ZIGS	ZINGARI	ZITIS
ZEBRAIC	ZEOLITIC	ZIGZAG	ZINGARO	ZITS
ZEBRANO	ZEP	ZIGZAGGED	ZINGED	ZIZIT
ZEBRANOS	ZEPHYR	ZIGZAGGER	ZINGER	ZIZITH
ZEBRAS	ZEPHYRS	ZIGZAGGERS	ZINGERS	ZIZZLE
ZEBRASS	ZEPPELIN	ZIGZAGGING	ZINGIER	ZIZZLED
ZEBRASSES	ZEPPELINS	ZIGZAGGY	ZINGIEST	ZIZZLES
ZEBRAWOOD	ZEPPOLE	ZIGZAGS	ZINGING	ZIZZLING
ZEBRAWOODS	ZEPPOLES	ZIKKURAT	ZINGS	ZLOTE
ZEBRINE	ZEPPOLI	ZIKKURATS	ZINGY	ZLOTIES
ZEBRINES	ZEPS	ZIKURAT	ZINKENITE	ZLOTY
ZEBROID	ZERK	ZIKURATS	ZINKENITES	ZLOTYCH
ZEBU	ZERKS	ZILCH	ZINKIFIED	ZLOTYS
ZEBUS	ZERO	ZILCHES	ZINKIFIES	ZOA
ZECCHIN	ZEROED	ZILL	ZINKIFY	ZOARIA
ZECCHINI	ZEROES	ZILLAH	ZINKIFYING	ZOARIAL
ZECCHINO	ZEROING	ZILLAHS	ZINKY	ZOARIUM
ZECCHINOS	ZEROS	ZILLION	ZINNIA	ZOCALO
ZECCHINS	ZEROTH	ZILLIONS	ZINNIAS	ZOCALOS
ZECHIN	ZEST	ZILLIONTH	ZINS	ZODIAC
ZECHINS	ZESTED	ZILLS	ZIP	ZODIACAL
ZED	ZESTER	ZIN	ZIPLESS	ZODIACS
ZEDOARIES	ZESTERS	ZINC	ZIPLOCK	ZOEA
ZEDOARY	ZESTFUL	ZINCATE	ZIPPED	ZOEAE
ZEDS	ZESTFULLY	ZINCATES	ZIPPER	ZOEAL
ZEE	ZESTIER	ZINCED	ZIPPERED	ZOEAS
ZEES	ZESTIEST	ZINCIC	ZIPPERING	ZOECIA
ZEIN	ZESTILY	ZINCIFIED	ZIPPERS	ZOECIUM
ZEINS	ZESTING	ZINCIFIES	ZIPPIER	ZOFTIG
ZEITGEBER	ZESTLESS	ZINCIFY	ZIPPIEST	ZOIC
ZEITGEBERS	ZESTS	ZINCIFYING	ZIPPING	ZOISITE
ZEITGEIST	ZESTY	ZINCING	ZIPPY	ZOISITES
ZEITGEISTS	ZETA	ZINCITE	ZIPS	ZOMBI
ZEK	ZETAS	ZINCITES	ZIRAM	ZOMBIE

ZOMBIES	ZOOEY	ZOOMETRY	ZOOTOMY	ZYGOSE
ZOMBIFIED	ZOOGAMETE	ZOOMING	ZOOTY	ZYGOSES
ZOMBIFIES	ZOOGAMETES	ZOOMORPH	ZORI	ZYGOSIS
ZOMBIFY	ZOOGENIC	ZOOMORPHS	ZORIL	ZYGOSITIES
ZOMBIFYING	ZOOGENIES	ZOOMS	ZORILLA	ZYGOSITY
ZOMBIISM	ZOOGENOUS	ZOON	ZORILLAS	ZYGOSPORE
ZOMBIISMS	ZOOGENY	ZOONAL	ZORILLE	ZYGOSPORES
ZOMBIS	ZOOGLEA	ZOONED	ZORILLES	ZYGOTE
ZONA	ZOOGLEAE	ZOONING	ZORILLO	ZYGOTENE
ZONAE	ZOOGLEAL	ZOONOSES	ZORILLOS	ZYGOTENES
ZONAL	ZOOGLEAS	ZOONOSIS	ZORILS	ZYGOTES
ZONALLY	ZOOGLOEA	ZOONOTIC	ZORIS	ZYGOTIC
ZONARY	ZOOGLOEAE	ZOONS	ZOSTER	ZYMASE
ZONATE	ZOOGLOEAL	ZOOPHILE	ZOSTERS	ZYMASES
ZONATED	ZOOGLOEAS	ZOOPHILES	ZOUAVE	ZYME
ZONATION	ZOOGLOEIC	ZOOPHILIA	ZOUAVES	ZYMES
ZONATIONS	ZOOGRAPHIES	ZOOPHILIAS	ZOUK	ZYMOGEN
ZONE	ZOOGRAPHY	ZOOPHILIC	ZOUKS	ZYMOGENE
ZONED	ZOOID	ZOOPHILIES	ZOUNDS	ZYMOGENES
ZONELESS	ZOOIDAL	ZOOPHILY	ZOWIE	ZYMOGENIC
ZONER	ZOOIDS	ZOOPHOBE	ZOYSIA	ZYMOGENS
ZONERS	ZOOIER	ZOOPHOBES	ZOYSIAS	ZYMOGRAM
ZONES	ZOOIEST	ZOOPHOBIA	ZUCCHETTI	ZYMOGRAMS
ZONETIME	ZOOKEEPER	ZOOPHOBIAS	ZUCCHETTO	ZYMOLOGIC
ZONETIMES	ZOOKEEPERS	ZOOPHYTE	ZUCCHETTOS	ZYMOLOGIES
ZONING	ZOOKS	ZOOPHYTES	ZUCCHINI	ZYMOLOGY
ZONK	ZOOLATER	ZOOPHYTIC	ZUCCHINIS	ZYMOLYSES
ZONKED	ZOOLATERS	ZOOS	ZUGZWANG	ZYMOLYSIS
ZONKING	ZOOLATRIES	ZOOSPERM	ZUGZWANGS	ZYMOLYTIC
ZONKS	ZOOLATRY	ZOOSPERMS	ZUZ	ZYMOMETER
ZONULA	ZOOLOGIC	ZOOSPORE	ZUZIM	ZYMOMETERS
ZONULAE	ZOOLOGIES	ZOOSPORES	ZWIEBACK	ZYMOSAN
ZONULAR	ZOOLOGIST	ZOOSPORIC	ZWIEBACKS	ZYMOSANS
ZONULAS	ZOOLOGISTS	ZOOSTEROL	ZYDECO	ZYMOSES
ZONULE	ZOOLOGY	ZOOSTEROLS	ZYDECOS	ZYMOSIS
ZONULES	ZOOM	ZOOTIER	ZYGOID	ZYMOTIC
ZOO	ZOOMANIA	ZOOTIEST	ZYGOMA	ZYMURGIES
ZOOCHORE	ZOOMANIAS	ZOOTOMIC	ZYGOMAS	ZYMURGY
ZOOCHORES	ZOOMED	ZOOTOMIES	ZYGOMATA	ZYZZYVA
ZOOECIA	ZOOMETRIC	ZOOTOMIST	ZYGOMATIC	ZYZZYVAS
ZOOECIUM	ZOOMETRIES	ZOOTOMISTS	ZYGOMATICS	ZZZ